Books For Occupational Education Programs

Books For Occupational Education Programs

A LIST FOR COMMUNITY COLLEGES
TECHNICAL INSTITUTES AND
VOCATIONAL SCHOOLS

by EDWARD MAPP, Chief Librarian
New York City Community College

R.R. BOWKER COMPANY, New York & London 1971

Published by R.R. Bowker Co. (a Xerox company)
1180 Avenue of the Americas, New York, N.Y. 10036

Copyright © 1971 by Xerox Corporation

All rights reserved.

International Standard Book Number: 0-8352-0410-3
Library of Congress Catalog Card Number: 70-126013

Printed and bound in the United States of America

CONTENTS

FOREWORD vii
PREFACE ix

COMMERCIAL PROGRAMS

ACCOUNTING 1
Auditing 5/Cost Accounting 5

ADVERTISING 5

BEAUTY CULTURE 7
Hairdressing 8

COMMERCIAL ART 8
Color 13/Design 13/Lettering 14/Lithography 14

DATA PROCESSING AND COMPUTER SCIENCE 15
Computers 17/Languages and Programming 19

FASHION ARTS 21
Costume 26/ Jewelry 27/ Textiles 28

FOOD SCIENCE 30
Baking and Decorating 37/ Beverages 37/ Ethnic and
Geographic Cooking 38/Nutrition 40/Processing and
Preservation 41

GRAPHIC ARTS 42
Binding 47/Ink 47/Paper 48/Photography 48

HOTEL TECHNOLOGY 50
Restaurants 52

INSURANCE 53
Health Insurance 54/Life Insurance 54

INTERIOR DECORATION 54
Furniture 55

MARKETING 56
Franchising 62/International Marketing 62/Packaging 63/
Retailing 63/Supermarkets 64

REAL ESTATE 64

SECRETARIAL SCIENCE 66
Executive Secretary 70/Legal Secretary 70/Medical
Secretary 71/School Secretary 72/Technical Secretary 72

v

COMMUNITY SERVICE PROGRAMS

AGRICULTURE 73
Equipment 77/Livestock 78

CHILD CARE 79

FIRE PROTECTION 83

FORESTRY 86

LIBRARY TECHNOLOGY 88

MORTUARY SCIENCE 92

POLICE SCIENCE 95

RECREATIONAL LEADERSHIP 102

SOCIAL SERVICE 103

TEACHER AIDE 108

ENGINEERING PROGRAMS

AERONAUTICAL TECHNOLOGY 115

AIR CONDITIONING, HEATING AND
REFRIGERATION 120

AUTOMOTIVE TECHNOLOGY 121

CHEMICAL TECHNOLOGY 125
Analytical 131/Qualitative 132/Quantitative 132/
Bio-Chemistry 132/Instrumentation 133/Inorganic 133/
Organic 134/Physical 135

CONSTRUCTION TECHNOLOGY 136
Carpentry 140/Concrete 140/Plumbing 141/Surveying 141

DRAFTING 142
Architectural 143/Automotive 144/Electrical 144/
Mechanical 144/Sheet Metal 144/Structural 145

ELECTRICAL AND ELECTRONIC TECHNOLOGY 145
Electro-Mechanical 155/Lasers and Masers 155/Motors 156/
Radar 156/Radio 156/Television 157/Transistors 158

INDUSTRIAL ARTS 160

MECHANICAL TECHNOLOGY 163
Design 166/Materials 167/Metals and Metallurgy 168/
Automatic and Numerical Control 169/
Strength of Materials 170/Welding 170

HEALTH SERVICE PROGRAMS

DENTAL CAREERS 173

ENVIRONMENTAL SCIENCE 176

INHALATION THERAPY 180

MEDICAL LABORATORY TECHNOLOGY 181
Anatomy and Physiology 183/Bio-Electronics 184/
Biology 184/Cytology 185/Hematology 186/Histology 186/
Laboratory Animals 186/Microbiology 187/Parasitology 187

NURSING 187
Geriatric 194/Gynecologic 194/Neurological and Neuro-
surgical 194/ Nurses' Aids 194/Obstetrical and Maternity 194/
Orthopedic 195/Pediatric 195/Practical 195/Psychiatric 196/
Public Health 196/Surgical 197/Urologic 197

OPTICAL CAREERS 197

PHARMACY 200

X RAY TECHNOLOGY 203

RELATED MATHEMATICS 205

RELATED PARAMEDICAL FIELDS 207
Medical Emergency 208/Mental Health 208/Occupational
Therapy 209/Operating Room 209/Physical Therapy 209

INDEX 211

FOREWORD

Community colleges represent the most rapidly growing segment of higher education in the United States. The proportion of students in higher education who attend such institutions is enlarging as the numerical enrollment at community colleges increases.

Accompanying this growth—perhaps even causing it—is a broadening range of curricular offerings, including not only transfer programs (the first two years of a baccalaureate program), but also remedial and development courses, continuing education, community services and, particularly, an array of occupational programs.

Occupational programs aim to prepare people directly to enter the job market. At the community college the typical occupational program concerns semi-professional or technical-level jobs. These range from agricultural to health service occupations and from business and industrial careers to newly emerging jobs in the public service field. An appropriate library collection is an absolute prerequisite.

For those concerned with establishing new occupational curricula in community colleges, a selected guide list of library books is of great value.

LEWIS R. FIBEL
EXECUTIVE DIRECTOR, MARYLAND STATE
BOARD FOR COMMUNITY COLLEGES

PREFACE

Books for Occupational Education Programs: A List for Community Colleges, Technical Institutes and Vocational Schools fills a long recognized need for a retrospective guide to developing library collections at career-oriented educational institutions. This first edition can be a selection tool for newly emerging schools as well as an aid to updating existing collections. The list in no way conflicts with publications dealing with general education and liberal arts subject matter.

The list includes trade books, reference works, handbooks, texts, curriculum guides, continuations and other relevant titles of twenty-five pages or more with 1960 or later imprints currently used in career training. Periodicals and non-book media represent another genre and are not included. Only English language works are considered (except foreign language/English bilingual or multilingual reference works or English translations of foreign books). No titles prior to 1960 (except serials starting earlier) are listed because of the high obsolescence rate of technical literature. Out-of-print titles included in the list are not distinguished as such because constant changes diminish such information's significance. However, the 1960 cut-off date assures a higher percentage of in-print titles than is customary with published lists. Because the literature for many of the technical subjects subsumed is sparse and elusive, users will wish to conduct out-of-print searches for particularly desirable titles.

Subjects covered represent standard curricula in community colleges and other career-technical-vocational institutions. An examination of educational directories and institutional catalogs revealed those programs currently predominant. Obviously, coverage varies from subject to subject depending on the field and the extent of its literature. Rarely is a particular program presented in an identical manner at different institutions. Consequently, library support of such programs varies as well. Titles selected for this list, then, reflect the compiler's subjective comprehension of the curricula and subjects covered.

The diversity of reading levels of students at specialized career-vocational schools is recognized by the inclusion of programmed books, tutor texts and a broad range of readability levels within most fields. No attempt was made to grade individual titles since all levels are required in most institutions. Some scholarly monographs for use by faculty and exceptional students are included. Titles listed are not the only ones which might have warranted inclusion. The distinctive requirements of individual institutions will dictate'the materials they acquire.

Arrangement of the main body of the list is by curriculum field with appropriate sub-field breakdowns. Within fields and sub-fields, entries are arranged alphabetically by author. There is an author index which locates all titles by an author found in the list. The author index includes joint authors, corporate authors, editors and compilers. There is no title index since many titles are not discrete, commencing with "Handbook of..." or "Introduction to...". Each entry is listed only once. Arrangement by library classification number was avoided because institutions have not accepted any uniform classification scheme.

Each entry includes author, title, sub-title, edition (if other than first), publisher, place for little known publishers, main pagination or number of volumes, and illustration or series note. Joint authors, editors or compilers are specified when there are three or less. When there are more, only the first is listed. The list's value will be maximized by exercising sensitivity to the interrelationships between curricula. The overlapping interest and tenuous distinctions between *Commercial Art* and *Graphic Arts,* or *Child Care* and *Teacher Aide* are prime examples.

Books for Occupational Education Programs aims to offer a continuing source of relevant materials for career-oriented institutions through this and subsequent editions. This list can provide more collections for new libraries in community colleges, technical institutes and vocational schools. It can also assist the possible production by commercial book jobbers of packaged library programs ready for shelving. Established libraries can use the list as a check for gaps in their collection.

Use of the guide need not be limited to career-minded institutions, since public libraries and senior colleges are also called upon to provide these materials. Users should maintain a current awareness of titles as this guide's timeliness becomes vulnerable almost immediately upon publication. The list is not a substitute for the ingenuity of the professional librarian who will draw upon it and add to it. Suggestions and comments for improvement and expansion are welcome and will be reflected in subsequent editions.

The compiler is grateful for the assistance of individual library staff members at the following institutions:

Brooklyn College of Pharmacy, Brooklyn. New York

Central State College, Edmond, Oklahoma

Fashion Institute of Technology, New York, New York

George Westinghouse Vocational and Technical School, Brooklyn, New York

New York City Community College, The City University of New York, Brooklyn, New York

San Antonio College, San Antonio, Texas

State University of New York, Agricultural and Technical College, Farmingdale, New York.

Typists responsible for the production of the entries on cards are Helen Wittner, Nancy Booker, Carolyn Lippmann, Mildred Berk, Helen Fitzpatrick, Rose Katz and Yvonne Coaxum. Thanks are due to William Betsch for his thorough and meticulous work in editing and preparing the printer's copy and to Kenneth Kaplan for his generous assistance. Special thanks go to Miss Carole Collins at Bowker, for her advice and encouragement throughout the project.   E.M.

COMMERCIAL PROGRAMS

ACCOUNTING

AMERICAN ACCOUNTING ASSOCIATION
    A Statement of Basic Accounting Theory. American Accounting Association, 1966, 100, illus.

AMERICAN INSTITUTE OF CERTIFIED PUBLIC ACCOUNTANTS
    Accounting Principles. Commerce Clearing House, 1969, 2 vols.

ANDERSON, JOHN W., and LENTILHON, ROBERT W.
    Principles of Accounting. Simmons-Boardman, 1965, 614, illus.

ANDERSON, WILTON T., MOYER, CECIL A., and WYATT, A. R.
    Accounting: Basic Financial, Cost and Control Concepts. Wiley, 1965, 808, illus.

ANKERS, RAYMOND G.
    Opportunities in an Accounting Career. Rev. ed. Universal Publishing & Distributing, Educational Books Division, 1967, 144. (Vocational Guidance Manuals.)

ANTHONY, ROBERT N.
    Essentials of Accounting. Addison-Wesley, 1964, 158. (Addison-Wesley Programmed Text.)

―――.
    Management Accounting Principles. Rev. ed. Irwin, 1970, 506, illus. (Irwin Series in Accounting.)

ARCO PUBLISHING COMPANY, INC.
    Accountant-Auditor. 6th ed. Arco, 1968, 272.

―――.
    Assistant Accountant-Junior Accountant-Account Clerk. 2nd ed. Arco, 1969, 320.

ASHWORTH, JOHN
    Careers in Accounting. Walck, 1963, 109, illus. (Careers for Tomorrow Series.)

BACKER, MORTON, ED.
    Modern Accounting Theory. Prentice-Hall, 1966, 560, illus. (Revision of Handbook of Modern Accounting Theory.)

BECKER, E. L.
    Your Career in Accounting. Southern Publishing, Nashville, 1970, 32.

BEDFORD, NORTON M.
    Introduction to Modern Accounting. Ronald, 1968, 744, illus.

BEDFORD, NORTON M., PERRY, KENNETH W., and WYATT, ARTHUR R.
    Advanced Accounting: An Organizational Approach. 2nd ed. Wiley, 1967, 822, illus. (Wiley Publication in Accounting.)

BERG, KENNETH B., et al., eds.
    Readings in International Accounting. Houghton Mifflin, 1969, 305.

BIERMAN, HAROLD, and DREBIN, ALLAN R.
    Financial Accounting: An Introduction. Macmillan, 1968, 420, illus.

―――.
    Managerial Accounting: An Introduction. Macmillan, 1967, 414, illus.

BLACK, HOMER A., and CHAMPION, JOHN E.
    Accounting in Business Decisions: Theory, Method, and Use. 2nd ed. Prentice-Hall, 1967, 964, illus.

BOYNTON, LEWIS D., et al.
    20th Century Bookkeeping and Accounting. 23rd ed. South-Western, 1967, 690, illus.

BRILOFF, ABRAHAM J.
    The Effectiveness of Accounting Communication. Praeger, 1967, 338, illus.

BROCK, HORACE R., PALMER, CHARLES E., and ARCHER, FRED C.
    College Accounting: Intermediate/Advanced. McGraw-Hill, Gregg Division, 1966, 726.

―――.
    College Accounting: Theory/Practice, Complete. 2nd ed. McGraw-Hill, 1969, 884, illus.

BRUNS, WILLIAM J.
    Accounting for Decisions: A Business Game. Macmillan, 1966, 1 vol.

BRUNS, WILLIAM J., JR., and DeCOSTER, DON T.
    Accounting and Its Behavioral Implications. McGraw-Hill, 1969, 441, illus. (McGraw-Hill Accounting Series.)

BUCKLEY, JOHN W., COMP.
    Contemporary Accounting and Its Environment. Dickenson, Belmont, Calif., 1969, 445, illus. (Dickenson Series on Contemporary Thought in Accounting.)

BURNS, THOMAS J., and HENDRICKSON, HARVEY S.
    The Accounting Sampler: An Introduction. McGraw-Hill, 1967, 326. (McGraw-Hill Accounting Series.)

COMMERCIAL PROGRAMS

CAREY, JOHN L.
 The CPA Plans for the Future. American Institute of Certified Public Accountants, 1965, 541.
———.
 The Rise of the Accounting Profession, from Technician to Professional. American Institute of Certified Public Accountants, 1969- , vol. 1- , illus.

CAREY, JOHN L., and DOHERTY, WILLIAM O.
 Ethical Standards of the Accounting Profession. American Institute of Certified Public Accountants, 1966, 330.

CARRITHERS, WALLACE M., and WEINWURM, ERNEST H.
 Business Information and Accounting Systems. Merrill, 1967, 734, illus.

CARSON, ALBERT B., CARLSON, ARTHUR E., and BOLING, CLEM
 College Accounting. 8th ed. South-Western, 1967, 752, illus.

CASEY, WILLIAM J.
 Accounting Desk Book. Institute for Business Planning, 1965, 409.

CASHIN, JAMES A.
 Careers and Opportunities in Accounting. Dutton, 1965, 224, illus.

CATLETT, GEORGE R., and OLSON, NORMAN O.
 Accounting for Goodwill. American Institute of Certified Public Accountants, 1968, 180.

CEREPAK, JOHN R., and GEIER, GEORGE J.
 Accounting for Business. Merrill, 1968, 678, illus.

CHAMBERS, RAYMOND J.
 Accounting, Evaluation, and Economic Behavior. Prentice-Hall, 1966, 388, illus. (Prentice-Hall International Series in Management.)

COLEMAN, ALMAND R.
 Financial Accounting: A General Management Approach. Wiley, 1970, 720.

CORCORAN, A. WAYNE
 Mathematical Applications in Accounting. Harcourt, Brace & World, 1968, 249, illus. (Harbrace Series in Business and Economics.)

COUGHLAN, JOHN W.
 Guide to Contemporary Theory of Accounts. Prentice-Hall, 1965, 563, illus.

CURTIS, ARTHUR B., and COOPER, JOHN H.
 Mathematics of Accounting. 4th ed. Prentice-Hall, 1961, 566, illus. (Prentice-Hall Accounting Series.)

DALE, JOHN D.
 Managerial Accounting in the Small Company. Reinhold, 1961, 181, illus. (Reinhold Management Science Series.)

DAVIDSON, SIDNEY
 Handbook of Modern Accounting. McGraw-Hill, 1970, 1500.
———, ED.
 Principles of Accounting. Educational Methods, Chicago, 1966, 201.

DEINZER, HARVEY T.
 Development of Accounting Thought. Holt, Rinehart & Winston, 1965, 184.

DEMAREST, ROSEMARY, ED.
 Accounting Information Sources. Gale, 1969, 1 vol.

DICKEY, ROBERT I., ED.
 Accountants' Cost Handbook. 2nd ed. Ronald, 1960, 1 vol., illus.

DIXON, ROBERT L., HEPWORTH, SAMUEL R., and PATON, WILLIAM A.
 Essentials of Accounting. Macmillan, 1966, 757.

EDWARDS, JAMES D., HERMANSON, ROGER H., and SALMONSON, R. F.
 Accounting: A Programmed Text. Irwin, 1967, 2 vols., illus.

FERTIG, PAUL E., et al.
 Using Accounting Information: An Introduction. Harcourt, Brace & World, 1965, 591, illus.

FINNEY, HARRY A., and MILLER, HERBERT E.
 The Accounting Process: A Programmed Adaptation from Principles of Accounting, Introductory. 6th ed. Prentice-Hall, 1963, 164, illus.
———.
 Principles of Accounting, Advanced. 5th ed. Prentice-Hall, 1960, 834.
———.
 Principles of Accounting, Intermediate. 6th ed. Prentice-Hall, 1965, 856.
———.
 Principles of Accounting, Introductory. 6th ed. Prentice-Hall, 1963, 688, illus.
———.
 Principles of Financial Accounting: A Conceptual Approach. Prentice-Hall, 1968, 449, illus.

FOULKE, ROY A.
 Practical Financial Statement Analysis. 6th ed. McGraw-Hill, 1968, 714, illus. (McGraw-Hill Accounting Series.)

FREEMAN, MAX H., HANNA, J. MARSHALL, and KAHN, GILBERT
 Accounting 10/12. McGraw-Hill, 1968, 1 vol., illus.
———.
 Gregg Bookkeeping & Accounting. 3rd ed. McGraw-Hill, Gregg Division, 1963, 498, illus.

GELLER, LOUIS, ED.
 Accounting. D. C. Heath, 1966, 152. (New Perspectives in Business Economics Series.)

GIBBS, GEORGE
 Accounting for Management Decisions. International Textbook, 1969, 110.

GILLESPIE, CECIL M.
 Accounting Systems: Procedures and Methods. 2nd ed. Prentice-Hall, 1961, 641, illus.

GOETZ, BILLY E., and KLEIN, FREDERICK R.
 Accounting in Action: Its Meaning for Management. Houghton Mifflin, 1960, 713, illus.

GOLDBERG, LOUIS, and HILL, VIVIAN R.
 The Elements of Accounting. Cambridge University Press, 1966, 312.

GORDON, MYRON J., and SHILLINGLAW, GORDON
 Accounting: A Management Approach. 4th ed. Irwin, 1969, 855.

GRADY, PAUL
 Inventory of Generally Accepted Principles for Business Enterprises. American Institute of Certified Public Accountants, 1965, 469. (Accounting Research Study No. 7.)

HAMBURGER, EDWARD
 A Business Dictionary of Representative Terms Used in Accounting, Advertising, Banking.... Prentice-Hall, 1967, 198.

HASEMAN, WILBER C.
 Management Uses of Accounting. Allyn & Bacon, 1963, 785, illus.

HECKERT, JOSIAH B., and KERRIGAN, HARRY D.
 Accounting Systems: Design and Installation. 3rd ed. Ronald, 1967, 665, illus.

HECKERT, JOSIAH B., and WILLSON, JAMES D.
 Controllership. 2nd ed. Ronald, 1963, 808, illus.

HEIN, LEONARD W., COMP.
Contemporary Accounting and the Computer. Dickenson, Belmont, Calif., 1969, 356, illus. (Dickenson Series on Contemporary Thought in Accounting.)

HENDRIKSEN, ELDON S.
Accounting Theory. Irwin, 1965, 510. (Irwin Series in Accounting.)

HOLMES, ARTHUR W., et al.
Elementary Accounting. 3rd ed. Irwin, 1962, 799, illus. (Irwin Series in Accounting.)

HORNGREN, CHARLES T.
Accounting for Management Control: An Introduction. 2nd ed. Prentice-Hall, 1970, 589, illus.

HORWATH & HORWATH, NEW YORK
Expense and Payroll Dictionary for Clubs: For Use With the Second Revised Edition (1967) of the Uniform System of Accounts for Clubs. Club Managers Association of America, Washington, 1967, 61.

HYLTON, DELMER P.
Principles and Procedures of Modern Accounting Practice. Prentice-Hall, 1965, 261.

JAEDICKE, ROBERT K., and SPROUSE, ROBERT T.
Accounting Flows: Income, Funds, and Cash. Prentice-Hall, 1965, 167, illus. (Prentice-Hall Foundations of Finance Series.)

JANIS, ARTHUR, and MILLER, MORRIS
Fundamentals of Modern Bookkeeping. Pitman, 1965, 611.

JOHNSON, GLENN L., GENTRY, JAMES A., JR., and MILLER, HERBERT E.
Finney and Miller's Principles of Accounting, Introductory. 7th ed. Prentice-Hall, 1970, 704.

JOPLIN, BRUCE, and PATTILLO, JAMES W.
Effective Accounting Reports. Prentice-Hall, 1969, 251, illus.

KARRENBROCK, WILBERT E., and SIMONS, HARRY
Advanced Accounting: Comprehensive Volume. 4th ed. South-Western, 1968, 1046, illus.

———.
Intermediate Accounting: Comprehensive Volume. 4th ed. South-Western, 1964, 980.

KELLER, I. WAYNE, and FERRARA, W. L.
Management Accounting for Profit Control. McGraw-Hill, 1966, 744.

KEMP, PATRICK S.
Accounting for the Manager. Dow Jones-Irwin, 1970, 229, illus.

KENNEDY, RALPH D., and KURTZ, FREDERICK C.
Introduction to Financial and Managerial Accounting. 2nd ed. International Textbook, 1967, 686.

KERRIGAN, HARRY D.
Fund Accounting. McGraw-Hill, 1969, 533. (McGraw-Hill Accounting Series.)

KIESO, DONALD E., MAUTZ, ROBERT K., and MOYER, CECIL A.
Intermediate Principles of Accounting. Wiley, 1969, 825.

KOHLER, ERIC L.
Accounting for Management. Prentice-Hall, 1965, 275.

———.
A Dictionary for Accountants. 4th ed. Prentice-Hall, 1970, 456, illus.

KORN, S. WINTON, and BOYD, THOMAS
Accounting for Management Planning and Decision Making. Wiley, 1969, 745.

LASSER, JACOB K.
Handbook of Accounting Methods. 3rd ed. Van Nostrand, 1964, 970, illus. (Van Nostrand Accounting and Business Books.)

LI, DAVID H.
Accounting, Computers: Management Information Systems. McGraw-Hill, 1968, 370, illus. (McGraw-Hill Accounting Series.)

LINTON, ANDREW F.
Introduction to Mechanized Accounts and Computers. 5th ed. Pitman, London, (Sportshelf, New Rochelle, N.Y., dist.), 1966, 150, illus.

LITTLETON, ANANIAS C.
Essays on Accountancy: A Collection of Readings. University of Illinois Press, 1961, 637.

LOCKLEAR, EDMOND, JR.
Your Future in Accounting. Rev. ed. R. Rosen Press, 1963, 159. (Careers in Depth.)

MacNEILL, JAMES H., ED.
Accounting Practice Management Handbook. American Institute of Certified Public Accountants, 1962, 952, illus.

MARPLE, RAYMOND P.
Toward a Basic Accounting Philosophy. National Association of Accountants, 1964, 117.

MASHEB, CLIFFORD M., and LEBOWITZ, R. B.
Accounting Simplified: Keynotes. Barnes & Noble, 1968, 116.

McFARLAND, WALTER B.
Concepts for Management Accounting. National Association of Accountants, 1966, 166.

McRAE, THOMAS W.
The Impact of Computers on Accounting. Wiley, 1964, 304.

MEIGS, WALTER B., and JOHNSON, CHARLES E.
Accounting: the Basis for Business Decisions. 2nd ed. McGraw-Hill, 1967, 917.

MEIGS, WALTER B., JOHNSON, CHARLES E., and MOSICH, A. N.
Financial Accounting. McGraw-Hill, 1970, 600.

MEIGS, WALTER B., et al.
Intermediate Accounting. 2nd ed. McGraw-Hill, 1968, 846, illus.

MICALLEF, BENJAMIN A.
Electric Accounting Machine Fundamentals. Addison-Wesley, 1968, 216, illus.

MIDGETT, ELWIN W.
An Accounting Primer. World, 1969, 175, illus.

MIKESELL, RUFUS M., and HAY, LEON E.
Governmental Accounting. 4th ed. Irwin, 1969, 758, illus. (Willard J. Graham Series in Accounting.)

MILROY, ROBERT R., and WALDEN, ROBERT E.
Accounting Theory and Practice, Intermediate. Houghton Mifflin, 1960, 681, illus.

———.
Accounting Theory and Practice, Introductory. Houghton Mifflin, 1960, 877, illus.

MILROY, ROBERT R., WALDEN, ROBERT E., and SEAWELL, L. VANN
Accounting Theory and Practice, Advanced. Houghton Mifflin, 1961, 673, illus.

MITCHELL, HERBERT S.
Manual for School Accounting. Interstate, 1961, 93, illus.

COMMERCIAL PROGRAMS

MITCHELL, HERBERT S.
    School Accounting for Financial Management. Interstate, 1964, 128.

MOONITZ, MAURICE
    The Basic Postulates of Accounting. American Institute of Certified Public Accountants, 1961, 61. (American Institute of Certified Public Accountants Accounting Research Study No. 1.)

MOORE, CARL L., and JAEDICKE, ROBERT K.
    Managerial Accounting. 2nd ed. South-Western, 1967, 722, illus.

MOORE, FRANCIS E., and STETTLER, HOWARD F.
    Accounting Systems for Management Control. Irwin, 1963, 708, illus. (Irwin Series in Accounting.)

MUELLER, GERHARD G.
    International Accounting. Macmillan, 1967, 255. (Topics in Accounting and Finance.)

MUSSELMAN, VERNON A., and HANNA, J. MARSHALL
    Teaching Bookkeeping and Accounting. McGraw-Hill, Gregg Division, 1960, 376, illus.

MYER, JOHN N.
    Accounting for Non-Accountants. Hawthorn (for American Research Council, Rye, N.Y.), 1967, 232.

NELSON, OSCAR S., and WOODS, RICHARD S.
    Accounting Systems and Data Processing. South-Western, 1961, 643, illus.

NEWMAN, BENJAMIN, and MELLMAN, MARTIN
    Accounting Theory: A CPA Review. Wiley, 1967, 203.

NISWONGER, CLIFFORD R., and FESS, PHILIP E.
    Accounting Principles. 10th ed. South-Western, 1969, 853.

NIVEN, WILLIAM, and OHMAN, ANKA
    Basic Accounting Procedures. Prentice-Hall, 1964, 369. (Prentice-Hall Professional Business Series.)

PATILLO, JAMES W.
    The Foundation of Financial Accounting. Louisiana State University Press, 1965, 173, illus.

PHILIPS, G. EDWARD, and COPELAND, RONALD M.
    Financial Statements: Problems from Current Practice. Prentice-Hall, 1969, 158.

PRENTICE-HALL, INC.
    Accountant's Encyclopedia. Prentice-Hall, 1962, 4 vols., illus.

———.
    Encyclopedia of Accounting Forms and Reports. Prentice-Hall, 1964, 3 vols., illus.

———.
    Handbook of Forms for Profitable Accounting Practice. Prentice-Hall, 1964, 411.

PYLE, WILLIAM W., and WHITE, JOHN A.
    Fundamental Accounting Principles. 5th ed. Irwin, 1969, 813, illus. (Irwin Series in Accounting.)

RANDALL, CLARENCE B., WEIMER, SALLY W., and GREENFIELD, MAYNARD S.
    Systems and Procedures for Automated Accounting. South-Western, 1962, 616, illus.

RAY, DELMAS D.
    Accounting and Business Fluctuations. University of Florida Press, 1960, 184.

ROHN, FRED H.
    So You Want to Be an Accountant. Harper & Row, 1965, 173.

ROSSELL, JAMES H., and FRASURE, WILLIAM W.
    Financial Accounting Concepts. Merrill, 1967, 532.

———.
    Managerial Accounting. Merrill, 1964, 640.

SALMONSON, ROLAND F.
    Basic Financial Accounting Theory. Wadsworth, 1969, 152. (Wadsworth Accounting Series.)

SCHATTKE, RUDOLPH W., JENSEN, HOWARD G., and BEAN, VIRGINIA L.
    Accounting: Concepts and Uses. Allyn, 1969, 799, illus.

SEILER, ROBERT E.
    Elementary Accounting: Theory, Technique, and Applications. 2nd ed. Merrill, 1969, 846, illus.

———.
    Principles of Accounting: A Managerial Approach. Merrill, 1967, 893, illus.

SIDEBOTHAM, ROY
    Introduction to the Theory and Context of Accounting. Pergamon, 1965, 181.

SIZER, JOHN
    An Insight Into Management Accounting. Penguin, 1969, 340, illus. (Pelican Library of Business and Management.)

SLAVIN, ALBERT, REYNOLDS, ISAAC N., and MALCHMAN, LAWRENCE H.
    Basic Accounting for Managerial and Financial Control. Holt, Rinehart & Winston, 1968, 848.

SMITH, CHARLES A., and ASHBURNE, JIM G.
    Financial and Administrative Accounting. 2nd ed. McGraw-Hill, 1960, 640.

SMITH, RICHARD L.
    Management Through Accounting. Prentice-Hall, 1962, 457, illus.

STANLEY, CURTIS H.
    Objectivity in Accounting. University of Michigan Press, 1965, 126. (Michigan Business Studies Vol. 16, No. 5.)

STOREY, REED K.
    The Search for Accounting Principles: Today's Problems in Perspective. American Institute of Certified Public Accountants, 1964, 65.

TUNICK, STANLEY B., and SAXE, EMANUEL
    Fundamental Accounting: Theory and Practice. 3rd ed. Prentice-Hall, 1963, 870, illus.

VAN VOORHIS, ROBERT H., PALMER, CHARLES E., and ARCHER, FRED C.
    College Accounting: Theory and Practice. McGraw-Hill, 1963, 759, illus.

VANCE, LAWRENCE L., and TAUSSIG, RUSSELL
    Accounting Principles and Control. Rev. ed. Holt, Rinehart & Winston, 1966, 783, illus.

WALDEN, ROBERT E., and SEAWELL, L. VANN
    Introductory Accounting: A Management Approach. Houghton Mifflin, 1968, 630, illus.

WENTWORTH, GERALD O., et al.
    The Accounting Process: A Program for Self-Instruction. McGraw-Hill, 1963, 264, illus.

WHITESIDE, CONON D.
    Accountant's Guide to Profitable Management Advisory Services. Prentice-Hall, 1969, 430, illus.

———.
    Accounting Systems for the Small and Medium-Sized Business. Prentice-Hall, 1961, 264, illus.

WIXON, RUFUS, and COX, ROBERT G.
    Principles of Accounting. 2nd ed. Ronald, 1969, 827, illus.

WOHL, GERALD, and JAUCH, HEINZ
    The Computer: An Accounting Tool. Irwin, 1965, 113, illus.

WOLPERT, SAUL
    Bookkeeping and Accounting: Introductory Course. 7th ed. Prentice-Hall, 1960, 492, illus.

ZEFF, STEPHEN A.
Uses of Accounting for Small Business. University of Michigan Press, 1962, 67, illus. (Michigan Business Reports No. 39.)

ZEFF, STEPHEN A., and KELLER, THOMAS F.
Financial Accounting Theory: Issues and Controversies. McGraw-Hill, 1964-69, 2 vols., illus. (McGraw-Hill Accounting Series.)

ZWEIG, JEANNE
Accountant's Office Manual and Practice Guide. Prentice-Hall, 1969, 252.

AUDITING

ARKIN, HERBERT
Handbook of Sampling for Auditing and Accounting. McGraw-Hill, 1963- , 1 vol., illus. (McGraw-Hill Accounting Series.)

BOUTELL, WAYNE S.
Contemporary Auditing. Wadsworth, 1970, 402. (Dickenson Series on Contemporary Thought in Accounting.)

HOLMES, ARTHUR W.
Auditing: Principles and Procedures. 6th ed. Irwin, 1964, 891, illus.

JOHNSON, JAMES T., and BRASSEAUX, J. HERMAN, EDS.
Readings in Auditing. 2nd ed. South-Western, 1965, 710.

MEIGS, WALTER B., and LARSEN, E. J.
Principles of Auditing. 4th ed. Irwin, 1969, 857, illus. (Willard J. Graham Series in Accounting.)

RAY, J. C., ED.
Independent Auditing Standards: A Book of Readings. Holt, Rinehart & Winston, 1964, 510.

SILVOSO, JOSEPH A., and BAUER, ROYAL D. M.
Auditing. 2nd ed. South-Western, 1965, 2 vols.

STETTLER, HOWARD F.
Auditing Principles: Objectives, Procedures, Working Papers. 3rd ed. Prentice-Hall, 1970, 716, illus. (Prentice-Hall Accounting Series.)

———.
Systems-Based Independent Audits. Prentice-Hall, 1967, 744, illus. (Prentice-Hall Accounting Series.)

COST ACCOUNTING

BACKER, MORTON, and JACOBSEN, LYLE E.
Cost Accounting: A Managerial Approach. McGraw-Hill, 1964, 678, illus. (McGraw-Hill Accounting Series.)

BIERMAN, HAROLD, JR.
Topics in Cost Accounting and Decisions. McGraw-Hill, 1963, 210, illus.

CHACE, FRANKLIN T., SCHMIEDICKE, ROBERT E., and SHERWOOD, JOHN F.
Principles of Cost Accounting. 4th ed. South-Western, 1964, 312, illus.

CROWNINGSHIELD, GERALD R.
Cost Accounting: Principles and Managerial Applications. 2nd ed. Houghton Mifflin, 1969, 812, illus.

DEARDEN, JOHN
Cost and Budget Analysis. Prentice-Hall, 1962, 205, illus.

———.
Essentials of Cost Accounting. Addison-Wesley, 1969, 137.

DOPUCH, NICHOLAS, and BIRNBERG, JACOB G.
Cost Accounting: Accounting Data for Management's Decisions. Harcourt, Brace & World, 1969, 527, illus. (Harbrace Series in Business and Economics.)

GRANT, EUGENE L., and BELL, LAWRANCE F.
Basic Accounting and Cost Accounting. 2nd ed. McGraw-Hill, 1964, 520. (McGraw-Hill Accounting Series.)

HORNGREN, CHARLES T.
Cost Accounting: A Managerial Emphasis. Prentice-Hall, 1962, 801, illus.

HOWE, WARREN A.
Cost Accounting. International Textbook, 1969, 439, illus. (ITC Publication in Accounting.)

LI, DAVID H.
Cost Accounting for Management Applications. Merrill, 1966, 653, illus.

MATZ, ADOLPH, CURRY, OTHEL J., and FRANK, GEORGE W.
Cost Accounting: Management's Operational Tool for Planning, Control and Analysis. 4th ed. South-Western, 1967, 963, illus.

NEUNER, JOHN J. W.
Cost Accounting: Principles and Practice—The First Phase of Managerial Control for Attaining the Profit Objective of Business Operations. 7th ed. Irwin, 1967, 844, illus. (Irwin Series in Accounting.)

PRENTICE-HALL, INC.
Encyclopedia of Cost Accounting Systems. Prentice-Hall, 1965, 3 vols.

SCHMIEDICKE, ROBERT E., and GERHARDT, RODGERS
Principles of Cost Accounting. South-Western, 1970, 1 vol.

SPECTHRIE, SAMUEL W.
Basic Cost Accounting. 2nd ed. Prentice-Hall, 1963, 434.

TERRILL, WILLIAM A., and PATRICK, A. W.
Cost Accounting for Management. Holt, Rinehart & Winston, 1965, 694, illus.

THOMAS, WILLIAM E., ED.
Readings in Cost Accounting, Budgeting, and Control. 3rd ed. South-Western, 1968, 879, illus.

ADVERTISING

AD: THE INTERNATIONAL SURVEY OF ADVERTISEMENTS
Praeger, 1966- , illus., annual.

ANNUAL OF ADVERTISING, EDITORIAL, TELEVISION ART AND DESIGN
Art Directors' Club, 1921- , Vol. 1- , illus.

ARNOLD, EDMUND C.
Profitable Newspaper Advertising: Layout, Copy, and Planning for Retailers. Harper, 1960, 136, illus.

ASSOCIATION OF NATIONAL ADVERTISERS
Perspectives in Advertising Management: Advanced Concepts, Strategies and Practices Geared to the Rapidly Changing Conditions in the Present Marketing Environment. Association of National Advertisers, 1969, 245.

ANTEBI, MICHAEL
The Art of Creative Advertising: A Visual/Verbal Problem-Solving Approach. Reinhold, 1968, 1 vol., illus.

BAHR, LEONARD F.
ATA Advertising Production Handbook. 4th ed. Advertising Typographers Association of America, 1969, 158, illus.

COMMERCIAL PROGRAMS

BARBAN, ARNOLD M., and SANDAGE, C. H.
    Readings in Advertising and Promotion Strategy. Irwin, 1968, 301, illus.

BARTON, ROGER, ED.
    Handbook of Advertising Management. McGraw-Hill, 1970, 1090, illus.

———.
    Media in Advertising. McGraw-Hill, 1964, 559.

BAUER, RAYMOND A., and GREYSER, STEPHEN A.
    Advertising in America: The Consumer View. Harvard University, School of Business Administration (Research Division), 1968, 473.

BOCKUS, H. WILLIAM
    Advertising Graphics: A Workbook and Reference for the Advertising Artist. Macmillan, 1969, 1 vol., illus.

BOGART, LEO
    Strategy in Advertising. Harcourt, Brace & World, 1967, 336, illus.

BOLAND, CHARLES M.
    Careers and Opportunities in Advertising. Dutton, 1964, 215, illus.

BURTON, PHILIP W., and KREER, G. BOWMAN
    Advertising Copywriting. 2nd ed. Prentice-Hall, 1962, 484, illus.

CAPLES, JOHN
    Tested Advertising Methods. Rev. ed. Harper, 1961, 308.

CARDAMONE, TOM
    Advertising Agency and Studio Skills: A Guide to the Preparation of Art and Mechanicals for Reproduction. Watson-Guptill, 1970, 160, illus.

CLARKE, GEORGE T.
    Opportunities in Advertising Careers. Universal Publishing & Distributing, 1968, 95, illus. (Vocational Guidance Manuals.)

COMMITTEE ON ADVERTISING
    Principles of Advertising. Pitman, 1963, 560, illus.

CRAWFORD, JOHN W.
    Advertising. 2nd ed. Allyn & Bacon, 1965, 466, illus.

DIRKSEN, CHARLES J., and KROEGER, ARTHUR
    Advertising Principles and Problems. 3rd ed. Irwin, 1968, 804, illus.

DUNN, SAMUEL W.
    Advertising: Its Role in Modern Marketing. 2nd ed. Holt, Rinehart & Winston, 1969, 621, illus.

FREY, ALBERT W., and HALTERMAN, JEAN C.
    Advertising. 4th ed. Ronald, 1970, 594, illus.

GLIM, AESOP
    How Advertising is Written and Why. Dover, 1961, 150.

GRAHAM, IRVIN
    Encyclopedia of Advertising. 2nd ed. Fairchild, 1968, 494, illus.

HALPERN, GEORGE M.
    Bibliography for Advertising Production Management. Rev. ed. Nonpareil Associates, New Hyde Park, N.Y., 1969, 1 vol.

———.
    Principles of Advertising. Pitman, 1961, 1 vol.

HAUGHNEY, JOHN D.
    Effective Catalogs. Wiley, 1968, 128, illus.

HEPNER, HARRY W.
    Advertising: Creative Communication with Consumers. 4th ed. McGraw-Hill, 1964, 692, illus.

HERDEG, WALTER, ED.
    Graphis Annual...International Yearbook of Advertising Art. Hastings House, 1952-53- , vols., illus., annual.

HOPKINS, CLAUDE C.
    Scientific Advertising. Crown, 1966, 95.

HOUCK, JOHN W.
    Outdoor Advertising: History and Regulation. University of Notre Dame Press, 1969, 250, illus.

JOHNSON, GEORGE
    Your Career in Advertising. Messner, 1966, 189, illus.

KELLY, RICHARD J.
    The Advertising Budget: Preparation, Administration and Control. Association of National Advertisers, 1967, 290.

KIRKPATRICK, CHARLES A., and LITTLEFIELD, JAMES E.
    Advertising: Mass Communication in Marketing. 3rd ed. Houghton, 1970, 575, illus.

KLEPPNER, OTTO
    Advertising Procedure. 5th ed. Prentice-Hall, 1966, 619, illus.

KLEPPNER, OTTO, and SETTEL, IRVING, COMPS.
    Exploring Advertising. Prentice-Hall, 1970, 328, illus.

LATIMER, HENRY C.
    Advertising Production Planning and Copy Preparation for Offset Printing. 2nd ed. Art Directions Book Co., New York, 1969, 136, illus.

LONGYEAR, WILLIAM L.
    Advertising Layout. 4th ed. Ronald, 1966, 108, illus.

LUCAS, DARRELL B., and BRITT, STEUART H.
    Measuring Advertising Effectiveness. McGraw-Hill, 1963, 399, illus. (McGraw-Hill Series in Marketing and Advertising.)

McCLURE, LESLIE W., and FULTON, PAUL C.
    Advertising in the Printed Media. Macmillan, 1964, 338, illus.

MILTON, SHIRLEY F.
    What You Should Know about Advertising Copywriting. Oceana, 1969, 89. (Business Almanac Series No. 16.)

NATIONAL RETAIL MERCHANTS ASSOCIATION
    Directory of Art, Mat, Photographic and Other Advertising Services. National Retail Merchants Association, 1965, 1 vol.

NELSON, ROY P.
    The Design of Advertising: An Exploration of Current Practices and Techniques. W. C. Brown, 1967, 213, illus.

OBERMEYER, ERNEST
    The Myth of Trade Advertising. Fairchild, 1966, 100.

OLIVER, ROBERT E.
    Advertising. McGraw-Hill (Canada), 1969, 166.

PETERSEN, ELDRIDGE, ED.
    Who's Who in Advertising. Haire, New York, 1963, 1275.

PLEUTHNER, WILLARD A., ED.
    460 Secrets of Advertising Experts: Key Ideas on Copy, Creative Thinking, Layout, Media, Marketing, Merchandising, Outdoor, Packaging, Production, Retailing, Research and Sales Promotion.... Nelson, 1961, 288.

PRINTERS' INK
    Advertising Today, Yesterday, Tomorrow: An Omnibus of Advertising, Prepared by Printers' Ink in Its 75th Year of Publication. McGraw-Hill, 1963, 472, illus.

SAMSON, HARLAND E.
    Advertising and Displaying Merchandise. South-Western, 1967, 218, illus. (Distributive Education Series.)

SANDAGE, CHARLES H.
The Role of Advertising: A Book of Readings. McGraw-Hill, 1960, 499, illus.

SANDAGE, CHARLES H., and FRYBURGER, VERNON
Advertising Theory and Practice. 7th ed. Irwin, 1967, 710, illus.

SCHLEMMER, RICHARD M.
Handbook of Advertising Art Production. Prentice-Hall, 1966, 285, illus.

SEIL, MANNING D., and SENGER, FRANK B.
Advertising Copy and Layout. 4th ed. Interstate, 1966, 183.

SINGER, JULES B.
Your Future in Advertising. R. Rosen Press, 1960, 157. (Careers in Depth No. 1.)

STANDARD DIRECTORY OF ADVERTISING AGENCIES
The Agency Red Book No. 159. National Register, Skokie, Ill., 1970, 1 vol.

STANSFIELD, RICHARD H.
Advertising Manager's Handbook. Dartnell, 1969, 1503, illus.

WEIR, WALTER
Truth In Advertising and Other Heresies. McGraw-Hill, 1963, 224.

WILLS, FRANZ H.
Complete Introduction to Fundamentals of Layout for Newspaper and Magazine Advertising, for Page Design of Publications and for Brochures. Kenneth T. Dutfield, tr. Sterling, 1965, 124, illus.

WRIGHT, JOHN S., and WARNER, DANIEL S.
Advertising. 2nd ed. McGraw-Hill, 1966, 651, illus.

BEAUTY CULTURE

AMERICAN PERFUMER AND COSMETICS
...Cosmetic Formulary. 1970 ed. American Perfumer, 1 vol.

ANGELOGLOU, MAGGIE
A History of Make-Up. Macmillan, 1970, 143, illus.

BERGEN, POLLY
The Polly Bergen Book of Beauty, Fashion, and Charm. Prentice-Hall, 1962, 239, illus.

CARRITT, EDGAR F.
The Theory of Beauty. Barnes & Noble, 1962, 244.

CHURCHILL, REBA, and CHURCHILL, BONNIE
Reba and Bonnie's Guide to Glamour and Personality. Prentice-Hall, 1962, 224, illus.

CONOVER, JESSIE A. W.
Finishing Touches. Harper, 1961, 280, illus.

———.
Let's Make Faces [by] Candy Jones. Harper & Row, 1965, 212, illus.

ELLIS, AYTOUN
The Essence of Beauty: A History of Perfume and Cosmetics. Macmillan, 1960, 200, illus.

———.
The Essence of Beauty: A History of Scent. Rev. ed. Collier Books, 1962, 192.

FASHION GROUP
Your Future in the Beauty Business. R. Rosen Press, 1969, 159. (Careers in Depth.)

GELB, RICHARD L.
Your Future in Beauty Culture. R. Rosen Press, 1964, 160. (Careers in Depth.)

GRANT, FLORENCE
The Beautician. McGraw-Hill (Canada), 1965, 83, illus.

HARRY, RALPH G.
The Principles and Practice of Modern Cosmetics. Vol. 1: Modern Cosmeticology. J. B. Wilkinson et al., eds. Chemical, 1962, 683, illus.

———.
The Principles and Practice of Modern Cosmetics. Vol 2: Cosmetic Materials—Their Origin, Characteristics, Uses and Dermatological Action. William W. Myddleton, ed. Chemical, 1963, 803, illus.

HAUSER, GAYLORD
Mirror, Mirror on the Wall: Invitation to Beauty. Farrar, Straus & Cudahy, 1961, 364, illus.

HENSLEY, MILLIE B.
The Art of Make-Up, Skin and Hair Care. Hearthside Press, 1960, 125, illus.

HIBBOTT, H. W., ED.
Handbook of Cosmetic Science: An Introduction to Principles and Applications. Pergamon, 1963, 556, illus.

JELLINEK, JOSEPH STEPHAN
Formulation and Function of Cosmetics. 2nd ed. Wiley-Interscience, 1970, 576.

MILADY PUBLISHING CORPORATION
Standard Textbook of Cosmetology: A Practical Course on the Scientific Fundamentals of Beauty Culture for Students and Practicing Cosmetologists. Rev. ed. Milady, 1967, 494, illus.

MILO, MARY
Guide to Beauty: Your Hair, Your Face, Your Figure. Family Circle, New York, 1964, 192, illus.

MOLER, ARTHUR B.
The Moler Manual of Cosmetology. Rev. ed. Moler System of Colleges, 1962, 316, illus.

NOYES DEVELOPMENT CORPORATION
Cosmetics Industry of Europe. Noyes, 1968, 1 vol.

PERUTZ, KATHRIN
Beyond the Looking Glass: America's Beauty Culture. Morrow, 1970, 331.

ROSS, MILTON S.
Skin Health and Beauty. Funk & Wagnalls, 1969, 260.

RUTGERS UNIVERSITY, GRADUATE SCHOOL OF EDUCATION
Beauty Culture & Related Theory. Rutgers University, Curriculum Laboratory, 1962, 310, illus.

STABILE, TONI
Cosmetics: Trick or Treat. Arco, 1966, 223.

STERNBERG, THOMAS H.
More Than Skin Deep. Doubleday, 1970, 330.

THOMAS, J. R.
Cosmetology. Alabama University, Department of Trade and Industrial Education, 1969, 105.

TOLMAN, RUTH
Guide to Beauty, Charm, Poise. Milady, 1962, 356, illus.

TOULMIN, HARRY A.
A Treatise on the Law of Foods, Drugs, and Cosmetics. 2nd ed. W. H. Anderson Co., Cincinnati, 1963, 4 vols.

COMMERCIAL PROGRAMS

VAN DEAN COMPANY, INC.
    Van Dean Manual: Professional Training for Beauticians. Rev. ed. Milady, 1962, 361, illus.

VOEGE, RAY
    Beauty Secrets for the Black Woman. Cornerstone, New York, 1970, 96.

WALL, FLORENCE E.
    The Principles and Practice of Beauty Culture. 4th ed. Keystone Publications, New York, 1961, 587, illus.

WELLS, FREDERICK V., and LUBOWE, IRWIN I.
    Cosmetics and the Skin. Reinhold, 1964, 690.

WHITCOMB, HELEN, and LANG, ROSALIND
    Charm: The Career Girl's Guide to Business and Personal Success. McGraw-Hill, 1964, 472, illus.

WYKES-JOYCE, MAX
    Cosmetics and Adornment: Ancient and Contemporary Usage. Philosophical Library, 1961, 190, illus.

HAIRDRESSING

BOWERS, FRANK, ED.
    Hair Styles and Beauty Guide, Arco, 1967, 112, illus.

CORDWELL, MIRIAM, and RUDOY, MARION
    Hair Design and Fashion. Crown, 1962, 257, illus.

CORSON, RICHARD
    Fashions in Hair: The First Five Thousand Years. Hillary House, New York, 1970, 701, illus.

DEMPSEY, PATRICIA, ED.
    Best New Hairdos. Arco, 1967, 112, illus.

———.
    New Hair Style Ideas. Arco, 1964, 112, illus.

FORBES, EVELYN
    Hairdressing and Beauty as a Career. Batsford, London, 1961, 127, illus. (Batsford Career Books.)

FRANK, ELINOR, ED.
    Best Hairdos. Arco, 1962, 144, illus.

HYMAN, REBECCA
    The Complete Guide to Wigs & Hairpieces. Workman, New York, 1968, 96, illus.

LONG, TED
    Hair Styles for the Black Woman. Cornerstone Library, 1970, 1 vol.

LUBOWE, IRWIN I.
    New Hope for Your Hair: A Scientific Guide to Healthy Hair for Men, Women, and Children. Rev. ed. Dutton, 1962, 255, illus.

MORO, MICHAEL D.
    ...Air Jet Hair Styling for Men. Associated Master Barbers & Beauticians of America, 1970, 1 vol.

NEGRI, ANNA L.
    Contour Fan Cutting for Professional Hairstyling. Exposition Press, 1967, 53, illus.

POWITT, A. H.
    Lectures In Hair Structure and Chemistry for Cosmetology Teachers. Milady, 1967, 154, illus.

STEVENS, PATRICIA
    How to Set and Style Your Own Wigs. Arco, 1970, 128, illus.

TASHO, ERNEST
    Hair Styling for Women. Pergamon, 1969, 198, illus. (Library of Industrial and Commercial Education and Training—Beauty Culture and Hair Dressing.)

THOMSON, JAMES C., and THOMSON, LESLIE C.
    Healthy Hair. Arco, 1969, 1 vol., illus.

TRUSTY, L. SHERMAN
    Advanced Men's Hair Styling. Western Lithograph Co., Los Angeles, 1966, 132, illus.

———.
    Art and Science of Barbering. Trusty, Long Beach, Calif., 1968, 503, illus.

COMMERCIAL ART

ABDY, JANE
    The French Poster: Cheret to Cappiello. Potter, 1969, 176, illus.

ADELINE, JULES
    The Adeline Art Dictionary: Including Terms in Architecture, Heraldry, and Archaeology. F. Ungar, New York, 1966, 459, illus.

AHLBERG, GUDRUN, and JARNERYD, O.
    Block and Silk Screen Printing. Sterling, 1961, 88, illus.

ALBENDA, PAULINE
    Creative Painting with Tempera: A Guide to Developmental Learning in Painting. Van Nostrand-Reinhold, 1970, 95, illus.

ARNHEIM, RUDOLF
    Visual Thinking. University of California Press, 1969, 345, illus.

AUVIL, KENNETH W.
    Serigraphy: Silk Screen Techniques for the Artist. Prentice-Hall, 1965, 165, illus.

BALLINGER, RAYMOND A.
    Direct Mail Design. Reinhold, 1963, 224, illus.

———.
    Layout and Graphic Design. Van Nostrand-Reinhold, 1970, 96, illus.

BANISTER, MANLY M.
    Etching and Other Intaglio Techniques. Sterling, 1969, 128, illus.

———.
    Prints from Linoblocks and Woodcuts. Sterling, 1967, 76, illus.

BANN, STEPHEN
    Experimental Painting: Construction, Abstraction, Destruction, Reduction. Universe, 1970, 144, illus.

BETHERS, RAY
    Composition in Pictures. 2nd ed. Pitman, 1962, 255.

BETTMANN, OTTO L., ED.
    Bettmann Portable Archive: A Graphic History of Almost Everything...Presented by Way of 3669 Illustrations Culled from the Files of The Bettmann Archive... Topically arranged and Cross-Referenced to Serve as an Idea Stimulator and Image Finder. Picture House Press, 1966, 229, illus.

BIEGELEISEN, JACOB I.
    Art Directors' Book of Type Faces for Artists, Typographers, Letterers, Teachers & Students. 3rd ed. Arco, 1970, 1 vol., illus.

BIGELOW, MARYBELLE S.
    Alphabets and Design: A Text for Beginning Students in Graphic Design. Burgess, 1967, 252, illus.

BIGGS, JOHN
    Craft of Woodcuts. Sterling, 1963, 63, illus.

BING, SAMUEL
　　Artistic America, Tiffany Glass, and Art Nouveau. MIT Press, 1970, 260, illus.

BOWMAN, WILLIAM J.
　　Graphic Communication. Wiley, 1968, 210, illus. (Wiley Series on Human Communications.)

BRANDT, REXFORD E.
　　Watercolor Technique in 15 Lessons. 6th ed. Reinhold, 1963, 102, illus.

BRIGADIER, ANNE
　　Collage: A Complete Guide for Artists. Watson-Guptill, 1970, 192, illus.

BRION, MARCEL, et al.
　　Art Since 1945. Simon & Schuster, 1968, 1 vol., illus.

BRODATZ, PHIL
　　Textures: A Photographic Album for Artists and Designers. Dover, 1966, 112, illus.

BRODATZ, PHIL, and WATSON, DORI
　　The Elements of Landscape: A Photographic Handbook for Artists. Reinhold, 1968, 137, illus.

BROOKS, LEONARD
　　Course in Casein Painting. Reinhold, 1961, 60, illus.

———.
　　Course in Wash Drawing. Reinhold, 1961, 61, illus.

CARLIS, JOHN
　　How to Make Your Own Greeting Cards. Watson-Guptill, 1968, 142, illus.

CATALDO, JOHN W.
　　Graphic Design & Visual Communication. International Textbook, 1966, 293, illus. (International Textbooks in Art and Art Education.)

CHAMBERLAIN, BETTY
　　The Artist's Guide to His Market. Watson-Guptill, 1970, 128.

CHENEY, SHELDON
　　A New World History of Art. Viking, 1965, 676.

———.
　　Primer of Modern Art. Tudor, 1966, 329.

CHIEFFO, CLIFFORD T.
　　Silk-Screen as a Fine Art: A Handbook of Contemporary Silk-Screen Printing. Reinhold, 1967, 120, illus.

CIANCIOLO, PATRICIA J.
　　Illustrations in Children's Books. W. C. Brown, 1970, 130, illus. (Literature for Children.)

CLEAVER, DALE G.
　　Art: An Introduction. Harcourt, Brace & World, 1966, 293.

CUTLER, MERRITT D.
　　How to Cut Drawings on Scratchboard. Watson-Guptill, 1960, 88, illus.

DANIELS, ALFRED
　　Painting and Drawing. Arco, 1961, 176, illus.

D'ARBELOFF, NATALIE
　　Creating in Collage. Watson-Guptill, 1967, 104, illus.

DAVIS, ALEC
　　Package and Print: The Development of Container and Label Design. Potter, 1968, 112, illus.

DIRINGER, DAVID
　　The Alphabet: A Key to the History of Mankind. 3rd ed., rev. Funk & Wagnalls, 1968, 2 vols., illus.

DOBLIN, JAY
　　One Hundred Great Product Designs. Van Nostrand-Reinhold, 1970, 128, illus.

ELAM, JANE
　　Introducing Linocuts. Watson-Guptill, 1969, 95, illus.

ELLENDER, RAPHAEL
　　Basic Drawing: New Ways to See and Draw. Doubleday, 1964, 128, illus. (Doubleday Artcraft Book.)

ELLINGER, RICHARD G.
　　Color Structure and Design. International Textbook, 1963, 144.

ELLIS, JESSIE C.
　　Index to Illustrations. F. W. Faxon, 1967, 682. (Useful Reference Series No. 95.)

ELSEN, ALBERT E.
　　Purposes of Art. Holt, Rinehart, & Winston, 1967, 455.

ERICKSON, JANET D., and SPROUL, ADELAIDE
　　Print Making Without a Press. Reinhold, 1966, 123, illus.

FAMOUS ARTISTS ANNUAL 1: A TREASURY OF CONTEMPORARY ART
　　Hastings House, 1969, vol. 1- , illus.

FAULKNER, RAY N., and ZIEGFELD, EDWIN
　　Art Today: An Introduction to the Fine and Functional Arts. 5th ed. Holt, Rinehart & Winston, 1969, 542, illus.

FELDMAN, EDMUND B.
　　Art as Image and Idea. Prentice-Hall, 1967, 511.

FLANAGAN, GEORGE A.
　　Understand and Enjoy Modern Art. Crowell, 1962, 344.

FLEMING, WILLIAM
　　Arts and Ideas. Holt, Rinehart & Winston, 1963, 580.

FLETCHER, ALAN, FORBES, COLIN, and GILL, BOB
　　Graphic Design: Visual Comparisons. Reinhold, 1964, 94, illus.

FRASNAY, DANIEL
　　The Artist's World. Viking, 1969, 369, illus.

FREEMAN, LARRY, COMP.
　　Victorian Posters. Century House, Watkins Glen, N.Y., 1969, 304, illus.

FRY, EDMUND
　　Pantographia: Containing Accurate Copies of All the Known Alphabets in the World. Sherwin & Freutel, 1970, 320, illus.

FUJITA, S. NEIL
　　Aim for a Job in Graphic Design/Art. R. Rosen Press, 1968, 146, illus. (Aim High Vocational Guidance Series.)

GARDNER, HELEN
　　Gardner's Art Through the Ages. 5th ed. Horst de la Croix and Richard G. Tansey, eds. Harcourt, Brace & World, 1970, 301, illus.

GARVEY, ELEANOR M., and WICK, PETER A.
　　The Arts of the French Book, 1900-1965: Illustrated Books of the School of Paris. Southern Methodist University, 1967, 119, illus.

GASSNER, JOHN, and THOMAS, SIDNEY
　　The Nature of Art. Crown, 1964, 619.

GERSTNER, KARL
　　Designing Programmes: Four Essays and an Introduction. Rev. ed. Hastings House, 1968, 1 vol., illus. (Visual Communication Books.)

GETTENS, RUTHERFORD J., and STOUT, GEORGE L.
　　Painting Materials: A Short Encyclopaedia. Peter Smith, 1966, 333.

GETTINGS, FRED
　　Techniques of Drawing. Viking, 1969, 112, illus. (Studio Book.)

COMMERCIAL PROGRAMS

GLUCK, FELIX, ED.
    Modern Publicity 1969-70. Viking, 1969, 176, illus.
———, COMP.
    World Graphic Design: 50 Years of Advertising Art. Watson-Guptill, 1968, 175, illus.

GOMBRICH, ERNST H.
    Art and Illusion. 2nd ed. Pantheon, 1961, 466, illus.
———.
    The Story of Art. 11th ed. Oxford University Press, 1966, 488, illus.

GORDON, STEPHEN F.
    Making Picture-Books: A Method of Learning Graphic Sequence. Van Nostrand-Reinhold, 1970, 96, illus. (Art Horizons Book.)

GORE, FREDERICK
    Painting: Some Basic Principles. Van Nostrand-Reinhold, 1965, 95, illus.

GRAHAM, DONALD W.
    Composing Pictures. Van Nostrand-Reinhold, 1970, 416, illus.

GREEN, PETER
    Introducing Surface Printing. Watson-Guptill, 1967, 96, illus.
———.
    New Creative Print Making. Watson-Guptill, 1965, 120, illus.

GUTENBERG, ARTHUR W., and ALBRECHT, VAL K.
    Profitable Studio Management. Chilton, 1965, 208, illus.

HALE, ROBERT B.
    Drawing Lessons from the Great Masters. Watson-Guptill, 1964, 271.

HARLAN, CALVIN
    Vision and Invention: A Course in Art Fundamentals. Prentice-Hall, 1970, 203, illus.

HATTERER, LAWRENCE J.
    The Artist in Society: Problems and Treatment of the Creative Personality. Grove Press, 1965, 188.

HERDEG, WALTER, ED.
    Window Display: An International Survey of the Art of Window Display. Praeger, 1961, 282.

HILER, HILAIRE
    Notes on the Technique of Painting. Watson-Guptill, 1969, 347, illus.

HILLIER, BEVIS
    Posters. Stein & Day, 1969, 296, illus.

HIND, ARTHUR M.
    An Introduction to a History of Woodcut with a Detailed Survey of Work Done in the Fifteenth Century. Dover, 1963, 2 vols. in 1, illus.

HOGARTH, BURNE
    Drawing the Human Head. Watson-Guptill, 1965, 156, illus.

HOGARTH, PAUL
    Creative Ink Drawing. Watson-Guptill, 1968, 159, illus.
———.
    Creative Pencil Drawing. Watson-Guptill, 1964, 159, illus.
———.
    Drawing People. Watson-Guptill, 1970, 160, illus.

HOLDEN, DONALD
    Art Career Guide: A Guidance Handbook For Art Students, Teachers, Vocational Counselors, and Job Hunters. 2nd ed. Watson-Guptill, 1967, 258.

HORN, GEORGE F.
    Posters: Designing, Making, Reproducing. Davis Publications, Worcester, Mass., 1964, 96, illus.

HUTTER, HERIBERT
    Drawing: History and Technique. McGraw-Hill, 1968, 152, illus.

HUTTON, HELEN
    The Technique of Collage. Watson-Guptill, 1968, 144, illus.

INTERNATIONAL POSTER ANNUAL
    Pitman, 1948-49- , illus.

IVINS, WILLIAM M., JR.
    Notes on Prints. MIT Press, 1969, 194, illus.
———.
    Prints and Visual Communication. Dacapo Press, 1969, 190, illus. (Dacapo Press Series in Graphic Art Vol. 10.)

JANIS, HARRIET, and BLESH, RUDI
    Collage: Personalities, Concepts, Techniques. Rev. ed. Chilton, 1967, 342, illus.

JENSEN, LAWRENCE N.
    Synthetic Painting Media. Prentice-Hall, 1964, 138.

KAMEKURA, YUSAKU
    Trademarks and Symbols of the World. Studio Vista, London, 1966, 291, illus.

KAMPMANN, LOTHAR
    Creating with Colored Ink. Van Nostrand-Reinhold, 1969, 70, illus. (Art Media Series.)
———.
    Creating with Printing Material. Van Nostrand-Reinhold, 1969, 72, illus. (Art Media Series.)

KAUTSKY, THEODORE
    Ways with Watercolor. 2nd ed. Reinhold, 1963, 136, illus.

KELLOGG, RHODA, and O'DELL, SCOTT
    The Psychology of Children's Art. Random House, 1967, 109, illus.

KELLY, ROB ROY
    American Wood Type, 1828-1900: Notes on the Evolution of Decorated and Large Types and Comments on Related Trades of the Period. Van Nostrand-Reinhold, 1969, 350, illus.

KENT, CYRIL
    Starting with Relief Printmaking. Watson-Guptill, 1970, 1 vol., illus.

KENT, NORMAN
    100 Watercolor Techniques. Susan E. Meyer, ed. Watson-Guptill, 1968, 215, illus.

KING, ROY, and DAVIS, BURKE
    The World of Currier & Ives. Random House, 1968, 140, illus.

KINGMAN, LEE, FOSTER, JOANNA, and LONTOFT, RUTH G., COMPS.
    Illustrators of Children's Books 1957-1966. Horn Book, 1968, 295, illus.

KLEMIN, DIANA
    The Illustrated Book: Its Art and Craft. Potter (Crown, dist.), 1970, 159, illus.

LAKE, CARLTON, and MAILLARD, ROBERT, EDS.
    Dictionary of Modern Painting. Tudor, 1964, 420.

LALIBERTE, NORMAN, and MOGELON, ALEX
    Drawing with Ink: History and Modern Techniques. Van Nostrand-Reinhold, 1970, 104, illus. (Art Horizons Book.)

LAMB, LYNTON
    Drawing for Illustration. Oxford University Press, 1962, 211, illus.

COMMERCIAL ART

LAMBERT, FREDERICK
 Graphic Design Britain. Peter Owen, London, 1967, 1 vol., illus.

LAUGHTON, ROY
 TV Graphics. Studio Vista, London, (Reinhold), 1966, 95, illus. (Introductory Handbooks to Art and Design.)

LEHNER, ERNST
 Alphabets and Ornaments. Dover, 1968, 256, illus.

LEVITAN, ELI L.
 Animation Art in the Commercial Film. Reinhold, 1960, 128, illus.

LOCKWOOD, ARTHUR
 Diagrams: A Visual Survey of Graphs, Maps, Charts, and Diagrams for the Graphic Designer. Watson-Guptill, 1969, 144, illus.

LONGSTREET, STEPHEN
 A Treasury of the World's Great Prints: A Collection of the Best-Known Woodcuts, Etchings, Engravings, and Lithographs by Twenty-Three Great Artists, Selected and Presented by Stephen Longstreet. Simon & Schuster, 1961, 333, illus.

LOWRY, BATES
 The Visual Experience. Prentice-Hall and Abrams, 1961, 272.

LUCAS, E. LOUISE
 Art Books: A Basic Bibliography on the Fine Arts. Graphic, 1968, 245.

LUMSDEN, E. S.
 The Art of Etching: A Complete and Fully Illustrated Description of Etching, Drypoint, Soft-Ground Etching, Aquatint and Their Allied Arts, Together with Technical Notes Upon Their Own Work by Many of the Leading Etchers of the Present Time. Dover, 1962, 376, illus.

LYNCH, JOHN
 How to Make Collages. Viking, 1970, 1 vol. (Studio Handbook S7.)

MAGNAN, GEORGE A.
 Using Technical Art: An Industry Guide. Wiley, 1970, 236, illus. (Wiley Series on Human Communication.)

———.
 Visual Art for Industry. Reinhold, 1961, 176, illus.

MARGULIES, WALTER P.
 Package Design. World, 1970, 224, illus.

MARSH, ROGER
 Silk Screen Printing for the Artist. Transatlantic, 1969, 77.

MATES, ROBERT E.
 Photographing Art. Chilton, 1966, 128, illus.

MAURELLO, S. RALPH
 Commercial Art Techniques: A Practical Self-Instruction Course and Reference Handbook. Tudor, 1963, 128, illus.

———.
 How To Do Pasteups and Mechanicals: The Preparation of Art for Reproduction. Tudor, 1960, 160, illus.

MAX, PETER
 The Peter Max Poster Book. Crown, 1970, 1 vol.

MAYER, RALPH
 The Artist's Handbook of Materials and Techniques. 3rd ed. Viking, 1970, 768, illus.

———.
 A Dictionary of Art Terms and Techniques. Crowell, 1969, 447. (Crowell Reference Book.)

McLEAN, RUARI
 Magazine Design. Oxford University Press, 1969, 354, illus.

———.
 Victorian Book Design & Colour Printing. Oxford University Press, 1963, 182.

MEGLIN, NICK
 On-the-Spot Drawing. Watson-Guptill, 1969, 160, illus.

MEILACH, DONA Z.
 Creating Art from Anything: Ideas, Materials Techniques. Reilly & Lee, 1968, 119, illus.

———.
 Printmaking. Pitman, 1965, 47, illus.

MEISSNER, KURT
 Japanese Woodblock Prints in Miniature: The Genre of Surimono. Tuttle, 1970, 143.

MILES, WALTER
 Designs for Craftsmen. Doubleday, 1962, 224, illus.

MILLS, JOHN F.
 Studio and Art-Room Techniques. Pitman, 1965, 112, illus.

MIROW, GREGORY
 Treasury of Design for Artists and Craftsmen. Dover, 1969, 1 vol. (Pictorial Archives Series.)

MUELLER, EARL G.
 The Art of Print. W. C. Brown, 1969, 1 vol. (Art World Series.)

MULLER-BROCKMANN, JOSEF
 ...The Graphic Artist and His Design Problems.... 3rd ed. Hastings House, 1968, 186, illus. (Visual Communication Books.)

MURGATROYD, KEITH
 Modern Graphics. Studio Vista, London, 1969, 159, illus.

MURGIO, MATTHEW P.
 Communications Graphics. Van Nostrand-Reinhold, 1969, 240, illus.

MUSEUM OF GRAPHIC ART
 American Printmaking, the First 150 Years. Museum of Graphic Art, New York, 1969, 180, illus.

MUSOCCHIA, JOHN B., FLUCHERE, HENRI A., and GRAINGER, MELVIN J.
 Airbrush Techniques for Commercial Art. 2nd ed. Reinhold, 1961, 64.

MYERS, BERNARD S., ED.
 McGraw-Hill Dictionary of Art. McGraw-Hill, 1969, 5 vols., illus.

NELSON, ROY P., and FERRIS, BYRON
 Fell's Guide to Commercial Art. F. Fell, New York, 1966, 118, illus.

NEUMANN, ECKHARD
 Functional Graphic Design in the 20's. Reinhold, 1967, 96, illus.

OGURA, RYOZO
 The Lively Art of Ink Painting. Japan Publications, San Francisco, 1968, 127, illus.

PAPP, CHARLES S.
 Scientific Illustration: Theory and Practice. W. C. Brown, 1968, 340.

PAROLA, RENE
 Optical Art: Theory and Practice. Reinhold, 1969, 144, illus.

PASSERON, ROGER
 French Prints of the 20th Century. Praeger, 1970, 181, illus.

PELLEW, JOHN C.
 Painting in Watercolor. Watson-Guptill, 1969, 160, illus.

COMMERCIAL PROGRAMS

PERARD, VICTOR
   The New How to Draw. Pitman, 1963, 144, illus.

PHILIP, JULIA W., ED.
   Who's Who In Commercial Art and Photography: A Guide to Artists, Photographers, Agents and Studios in the Graphics Field. 2nd ed. Art Directors' Institute, New York, 1964, 192, illus.

PINNEY, ROY
   Advertising Photography: A Visual Communication Book. Hastings House, 1962, 160, illus.

PITZ, HENRY C.
   How to Use the Figure in Painting and Illustration. Watson-Guptill, 1965, 144, illus.

———.
   Illustrating Children's Books: History, Technique, Production. Watson-Guptill, 1963, 207.

PLUCKROSE, HENRY A.
   Introducing Crayon Techniques. Watson-Guptill, 1967, 100, illus.

POLLARD, ALFRED W.
   Early Illustrated Books: A History of the Decoration and Illustration of Books in the 15th and 16th Centuries. 2nd ed. Haskell House, 1968, 254, illus. (Books About Books.)

POORE, HENRY R.
   Composition in Art. Sterling, 1967, 96, illus.

POPE, MICHAEL
   Introducing Oil Painting. Van Nostrand-Reinhold, 1969, 88, illus.

POTTER, NORMAN
   What is a Designer: Education and Practice—A Guide for Students and Teachers. Van Nostrand-Reinhold, 1969, 95.

PROBYN, PETER, ED.
   The Complete Drawing Book. Watson-Guptill, 1970, 400, illus.

PROCTOR, RICHARD M.
   The Principles of Pattern for Craftsmen and Designers. Van Nostrand-Reinhold, 1969, 135, illus.

QUICK, JOHN, ED.
   Artists' and Illustrators' Encyclopedia. McGraw-Hill, 1969, 273, illus.

RASMUSEN, HENRY N.
   Printmaking with Monotype. Chilton, 1060, 182, illus.

READ, HERBERT E.
   Art Now. 2nd ed. Pitman, 1960, 336.

———.
   The Meaning of Art. 4th ed. Pitman, 1969, 262, illus.

REED, WALT, COMP., ED.
   The Illustrator in America, 1900-1960's. Reinhold, 1966, 264, illus.

RICKARDS, MAURICE
   Posters of Protest and Revolution. Walker, 1970, 30, illus.

RITTERBUSH, PHILIP
   The Art of Organic Forms. Smithsonian Institution, 1968, 149, illus. (Smithsonian Publication No. 4740.)

ROBB, DAVID M.
   Art in the Western World. 4th ed. Harper, 1963, 782, illus.

RODEWALD, FRED C., and GOTTSCHALL, EDWARD
   Commercial Art as a Business. 2nd ed. Viking, 1970, 1 vol.

ROGER-MARX, CLAUDE
   Graphic Art The 19th Century. McGraw-Hill, 1962, 254, illus.

ROSEN, BEN
   The Corporate Search for Visual Identity: A Study of 15 Outstanding Corporate Design Programs. Van Nostrand-Reinhold, 1970, 259, illus.

ROSENBERG, HAROLD
   Artworks and Packages. Horizon Press, 1969, 232, illus.

ROSS, ROBERT
   Illustration Today. International Textbook, 1963, 292, illus.

ROTH, CLAIRE J., and WEISS, ADELLE
   Art Careers. Walck, 1963, 116, illus.

RUSS, STEPHEN
   Practical Screen Printing. Watson-Guptill, 1969, 96, illus.

RUSSELL, JOHN, and GABLIK, SUZI
   Pop Art Redefined. Praeger, 1969, 240, illus.

SALTER, STEFAN
   From Cover to Cover: The Occasional Papers of a Book Designer. Prentice-Hall, 1969, 270.

SAVAGE, GEORGE
   The Market in Art. Transatlantic, 1969, 1 vol.

SCHWALBACH, MATHILDA V., and SCHWALBACH, JAMES A.
   Screen-Process Printing: For the Serigrapher & Textile Designer. Van Nostrand-Reinhold, 1970, 144, illus.

SCHWARTZ, FRED R.
   Structure and Potential in Art Education. Ginn, 1970, 414, illus.

SEITZ, WILLIAM C.
   The Art of Assemblage. Museum of Modern Art, New York, 1961, 176.

SHAFRAN, ALEXANDER
   Airbrush Photo Retouching Manual: The Techniques of Airbrush Retouching Positive Prints and Negatives. Chilton, 1968, 174, illus.

SORGMAN, MAYO
   Brush and Palette: Painting Techniques for Young Adults. Reinhold, 1965, 168, illus.

STEVENS, HAROLD
   Art in the Round: Elements and Materials of Three-Dimensional Design. Reinhold, 1965, 100, illus.

———.
   Design in Photo-Collage. Reinhold, 1967, 100, illus.

SULLIVAN, MICHAEL
   A Short History of Chinese Art. University of California Press, 1967, 279, illus. (UC Paperback No. 148.)

SUTTER, JEAN, and HERBERT, ROBERT L.
   The Neo-Impressionists. Graphic, 1970, 244, illus.

TAUBES, FREDERIC
   A Guide to Traditional and Modern Painting Methods. Viking, 1963, 135.

TAYLOR, JOHN R.
   The Art Nouveau Book in Britain. MIT Press, 1967, 176.

TOKURIKI, TOMIKICHIRO
   Wood-Block Print Primer. Japan Publications, Tokyo, 1970, 61, illus.

TORCHE, JUDITH
   Acrylic and Other Water-Base Paints for the Artist. Sterling, 1967, 80, illus.

TREVELYAN, JULIAN
   Etching: Modern Methods of Intaglio Printmaking. Watson-Guptill, 1964, 96, illus.

VANCE, LUCILE E., and TRACEY, ESTHER M.
   Illustration Index. 2nd ed. Scarecrow Press, 1966, 527.

WATKINSON, RAYMOND
Pre-Raphaelite Art and Design. Graphic, 1970, 208, illus.

WATSON, DORI
The Techniques of Painting. Van Nostrand-Reinhold, 1970, 160, illus.

WATSON, ERNEST W.
The Art of Pencil Drawing. Watson-Guptill, 1968, 158, illus.

———.
Perspective for Sketchers. Reinhold, 1964, 48, illus.

WEAVER, PETER
Printmaking: A Medium for Basic Design. Reinhold, 1968, 96, illus.

WEIDEMANN, KURT, ED.
Book Jackets and Record Covers. Praeger, 1969, 149.

WHITE, GWEN
Perspective: A Guide for Artists, Architects and Designers. Watson-Guptill, 1968, 80, illus.

WHO'S WHO IN AMERICAN ART
R. R. Bowker, 1936-37- , vol. 1- .

WHO'S WHO IN GRAPHIC ART
Amstutz & Herdeg Graphis Press, Zurich, 1962, 1 vol., illus.

WIGG, PHILIP
Introduction to Figure Drawing. W. C. Brown, 1967, 160.

WILLCOX, DONALD
Wood Design. Watson-Guptill, 1968, 144, illus.

WILSON, JOSÉ, and LEAMAN, ARTHUR
Decorations U.S.A. Macmillan, 1965, 278.

WING, FRANCES S.
The Complete Book of Decoupage. Rev. ed. Coward, 1970, 205, illus.

WINTER, EDWARD
Enamel Painting Techniques. Praeger, 1970, 224, illus.

YOSHIDA, ROSHI, and YUKI, REI
Japanese Print-Making: A Handbook of Traditional and Modern Techniques. Tuttle, 1966, 176.

ZAIDENBERG, ARTHUR
Drawing Self-Taught. Simon & Schuster, 1968, 1 vol., illus.

———.
New Encyclopedia of Drawing, Painting, and the Graphic Arts: A Complete, Fundamental Book of Instruction for Hobbyists, Art Students, and Professional Artists. A. S. Barnes, 1961, 222, illus.

COLOR

BILLMEYER, FRED W., JR., and SALTZMAN, MAX
Principles of Color Technology. Wiley-Interscience, 1966, 181.

BIRREN, FABER
Creative Color. Reinhold, 1961, 128, illus.

———, ED.
The Elements of Color: A Treatise on the Color System of Johannes Itten. Van Nostrand-Reinhold, 1970, 96, illus.

———, ED.
A Grammar of Color: A Basic Treatise on the Color System of Albert H. Munsell. Van Nostrand-Reinhold, 1969, 96, illus.

———.
Principles of Color: A Review of Past Traditions and Modern Theories of Color Harmony. Van Nostrand-Reinhold, 1969, 96, illus.

BURNHAM, ROBERT W., HANES, RANDALL M., and BARTLESON, C. JAMES
Color: A Guide to Basic Facts and Concepts. Wiley, 1963, 249, illus.

DANGER, ERIC P.
How to Use Color to Sell. Cahners, 1969, 237, illus.

FABRI, RALPH
Color: A Complete Guide for Artists. Watson-Guptill, 1967, 175, illus.

GUPTILL, ARTHUR L.
Color Manual for Artists. Reinhold, 1963, 128, illus.

ITTEN, JOHANNES
The Art of Color: The Subjective Experience and Objective Rationale of Color. Reinhold, 1961, 155.

JUDD, DEANE B., and WYSZECKI, GÜNTER
Color in Business, Science and Industry. 2nd ed. Wiley, 1963, 500.

KORNERUP, ANDREAS, and WANSCHER, J. H.
Reinhold Color Atlas. Reinhold, 1962, 224, illus.

MUNSELL, ALBERT H.
A Grammar of Color. Van Nostrand-Reinhold, 1969, 96, illus.

OPTICAL SOCIETY OF AMERICA
The Science of Color. Optical Society of America, Washington, 1963, 385, illus.

OSTWALD, WILHELM
The Color Primer. Van Nostrand-Reinhold, 1969, 96, illus.

RICHMOND, LEONARD
The Technique of Color Mixing. Pitman, 1960, 89, illus.

SALEMME, LUCIA A.
Color Exercises for the Painter. Watson-Guptill, 1970, 160, illus.

SLOANE, PATRICIA
Colour: Basic Principles, New Directions. Reinhold, 1968, 96, illus.

DESIGN

ANDERSON, DONALD M.
Elements of Design. Holt, 1961, 218.

BATES, KENNETH F.
Basic Design: Principles and Practice. World, 1960, 174, illus.

BRADSHAW, CHRISTOPHER
Design. Vista Books, London, 1964, 127, illus. (Facts of Print Series.)

BROCHMANN, ODD
Good or Bad Design? Van Nostrand-Reinhold, 1970, 96, illus.

DE SAUSMAREZ, MAURICE
Basic Design: The Dynamics of Visual Form. Reinhold, 1964, 95.

GARRETT, LILLIAN
Visual Design: A Problem-Solving Approach. Reinhold, 1967, 215, illus.

HURWITZ, ELIZABETH A.
Design: A Search for Essentials. International Textbook, 1964, 221, illus.

INDUSTRIAL DESIGNERS SOCIETY OF AMERICA
Design in America: Selected Work. McGraw-Hill, 1969, 185, illus.

COMMERCIAL PROGRAMS

McILHANY, STERLING
Art As Design, Design As Art: A Contemporary Guide. Van Nostrand-Reinhold, 1970, 155, illus.

NELSON, GEORGE
Problems of Design. 2nd ed. Whitney Publications, New York, 1965, 204.

PROHASKA, RAY
A Basic Course in Design: Introduction to Drawing and Painting. Van Nostrand-Reinhold, 1970, 96, illus.

RANDALL, REINO, and HAINES, EDWARD C.
Design in Three Dimensions. Davis Publications, Worcester, Mass., 1965, 69, illus.

READ, HERBERT E.
Art and Industry: The Principles of Industrial Design. Indiana University Press, 1961, 239, illus.

SCRASE, PAT
Let's Start Designing. Reinhold, 1966, 60, illus.

WILSON, ROBERT C.
An Alphabet of Visual Experience: An Examination of the Basic Principles of Design. International Textbook, 1966, 228, illus.

LETTERING

ANDERSON, CHARLES R.
Lettering. Van Nostrand-Reinhold, 1969, 174, illus.

BALLINGER, RAYMOND A.
Lettering Art in Modern Use. Reinhold, 1965, 96, illus.

BIEGELEISEN, JACOB I.
The ABC of Lettering. 3rd ed. Harper & Row, 1965, 248, illus.

BRINKLEY, JOHN, ED.
Lettering Today. Reinhold, 1965, 143, illus.

DOUGLASS, RALPH
Calligraphic Lettering with Wide Pen and Brush. 3rd ed. Watson-Guptill, 1962, 72.

GATES, DAVID
Lettering for Reproduction. Watson-Guptill, 1969, 191, illus.

GOUDY, FREDERIC W.
The Alphabet: Elements of Lettering. Rev. ed. Dover, 1963, 101, illus.

HAAB, ARMIN, ED.
Lettera: A Standard Book of Fine Lettering.... Hastings House, 1961-1969, 3 vols., illus. (Visual Communication Books.)

LAKER, RUSSELL
Anatomy of Lettering. Rev. ed. Viking, 1966, 96, illus. (Studio Book.)

LAMBERT, FREDERICK
Letter Forms. Hastings House, 1964, 189, illus.

LEACH, MORTIMER
Letter Design in the Graphic Arts. Reinhold, 1960, 192, illus.

LONGYEAR, WILLIAM
Type and Lettering. 4th ed. Watson-Guptill, 1966, 175, illus.

MacDONALD, BYRON J.
The Art of Lettering with the Broad Pen. Reinhold, 1966, 63, illus.

MORISON, STANLEY
Letter Forms: Typographic and Scriptorial. Nattali & Maurice, London, 1968, 167, illus.

MUSEUM OF MODERN ART, NEW YORK
Lettering by Modern Artists. Doubleday, 1964, 1 vol., illus.

OGG, OSCAR
The 26 Letters. 2nd ed. Crowell, 1961, 262.

LITHOGRAPHY

ANTREASIAN, GARO Z., and ADAMS, CLINTON
The Tamarind Lithography Resource Book. Abrams, 1970, 1 vol., illus.

ARNOLD, GRANT
Creative Lithography and How To Do It. Dover, 1964, 214, illus.

CLIFFE, HENRY
Lithography: A Complete Handbook of Modern Techniques of Lithography. Watson-Guptill, 1965, 96, illus.

CUMMING, R. F., and KILLICK, W. E.
Single-Colour Lithographic Machine Operating. Pergamon, 1969, 80, illus. (Industrial and Commercial Education and Training Library.)

HALPERN, GEORGE M., ED.
Self-Study Workbook: Advanced Pressmanship for Offset Lithography...based on three GATF textbooks: Offset Press Operating and Advanced Pressmanship by Charles W. Latham [and] Offset Press Troubles by Robert F. Reed. Graphic Arts Technical Foundation, 1964, 175, illus.
———, ED.
Self-Study Workbook: Chemistry of Lithography...based on the GATF textbook: Chemistry of Lithography by Paul J. Hartsuch. Graphic Arts Technical Foundation, 1965, 207.
———, ED.
Self-Study Workbook: Press Operating For Offset Lithography...based on two GATF textbooks: Offset Press Operating, Textbook 505/6, and Advanced Pressmanship, Textbook 513, by Charles W. Latham. Rev. ed. Graphic Arts Technical Foundation, 1967, 119.

HARTSUCH, PAUL J.
Chemistry of Lithography. Graphic Arts Technical Foundation, 1961, 358, illus. (Textbook 401.)

HIRSCH, S.
Printing From a Stone. Viking, 1968, 1 vol.

HOCH, FRED W.
How to Estimate Offset Lithography. Fred W. Hoch Associates, New York, 1969, 46. (Standard Management Series.)

JAFFE, ERWIN
The Science of Physics in Lithography. Rev. ed. Robert F. Reed, ed. Graphic Arts Technical Foundation, 1964, 147, illus. (Textbook 402.)

JONES, STANLEY
Lithography for Artists. Oxford University Press, 1967, 78, illus. (Handbooks for Artists.)

KNIGIN, MICHAEL, and ZIMILES, MURRAY
The Technique of Fine Art Lithography. Van Nostrand-Reinhold, 1970, 143, illus.

LAWSON, L. E.
Offset Lithography. Vista Books, London, 1963, 184, illus. (Facts of Print Series.)

LITHOGRAPHIC DAMPENING CONFERENCE, CHICAGO, 1967
Papers. Lithographic Dampening Conference, Chicago, 1967, 89, illus.

REED, ROBERT F.
Offset Lithographic Platemaking. Graphic Arts Technical Foundation, 1967, 203, illus. (Textbook 502/4.)
———.
Instruments for Quality Control in Lithography. Lithographic Technical Foundation, 1963, 102, illus.
———.
What the Lithographer Should Know About Ink. Graphic Arts Technical Foundation, 1960, 218, illus. (Textbook 310.)

SHAPIRO, CHARLES, ED.
The Lithographers Manual. 4th ed. Graphic Arts Technical Foundation, 1968, 1 vol., illus.

WEAVER, PETER
The Technique of Lithography. Reinhold, 1965, 176, illus.

WEBER, WILHELM
A History of Lithography. McGraw-Hill, 1966, 259, illus. (Tr. from German.)

WEDDIGE, EMIL
Lithography. International Textbook, 1966, 221, 1 vol.

WOODS, GERALD
Introducing Lithography. Watson-Guptill, 1969, 88, illus.

DATA PROCESSING AND COMPUTER SCIENCE

ABRAMS, PETER, and CORVINE, WALTER
Basic Data Processing. Holt, Rinehart & Winston, 1966, 463, illus.

AMERICAN DATA PROCESSING, INC.
Data Processing Yearbook. American Data Processing, 1952- , annual.

ANTON, HECTOR R., and BOUTELL, WAYNE S.
Fortran and Business Data Processing. McGraw-Hill, 1968, 348, illus. (McGraw-Hill Accounting Series.)

ARNOLD, ROBERT R., et al.
Introduction to Data Processing. Wiley, 1966, 326, illus.

ARNOLD, ROBERT R., HILL, HAROLD C., and NICHOLS, AYLMER V.
Modern Data Processing. Wiley, 1969, 374, illus.

AWAD, ELIAS M.
Business Data Processing. 2nd ed. Prentice-Hall, 1968, 459, illus.
———.
Problems and Exercises in Data Processing. 2nd ed. Prentice-Hall, 1968, 260, illus.

AWAD, ELIAS M., and DATA PROCESSING MANAGEMENT ASSOCIATION
Automatic Data Processing: Principles and Procedures. 2nd ed. Prentice-Hall, 1970, 495, illus.

BENICE, DANIEL D.
Introduction to Computers and Data Processing. Prentice-Hall, 1970, 370. (Applied Mathematics Series.)

BERKOWITZ, NATHAN, and MUNRO, ROBERTSON, JR.
Automatic Data Processing and Management. Dickenson, Belmont, Calif., 1969, 335, illus.

BRANDON, DICK H.
Management Planning for Data Processing. Brandon/Systems Press, Princeton, N.J., 1970, 255, illus.
———.
Management Standards for Data Processing. Van Nostrand, 1963, 404.

BRIGHTMAN, RICHARD W.
Practical Data Processing. Macmillan, 1969, 409, illus.

BRIGHTMAN, RICHARD W., LUSKIN, BERNARD J., and TILTON, THEODORE
Data Processing for Decision-Making: An Introduction to Third-Generation Information Systems. Macmillan, 1968, 468, illus.

BROOKS, FREDERICK P., JR., and IVERSON, KENNETH E.
Automatic Data Processing. Wiley, 1963, 494, illus.
———.
Automatic Data Processing System/360 Edition. Wiley, 1969, 466, illus.

BURGER, ERICH, and SCHUPPE, WOLFGANG
Technical Dictionary of Data Processing, Computers, Office Machines. Pergamon, 1970, 1463.

CARTER, BYRON L.
Data Processing for the Small Business. MacFadden-Bartell, New York, 1966, 190, illus.

CARTER, NORMAN H.
Introduction to Business Data Processing. Dickenson, Belmont, Calif., 1968, 269, illus. (Dickenson Series in Computer and Information Science.)

CASHMAN, THOMAS J., and KEYS, WILLIAM J.
Data Processing: A Text and Project Manual. McGraw-Hill, 1967, 80, illus.

CASHMAN, THOMAS J., et al.
Review Manual for Certificate in Data Processing. Rev. ed. Anaheim Publishing, Anaheim, Calif., 1970, 468.

CLARK, FRANK J.
Information Processing. Goodyear, Pacific Palisades, Calif., 1970, 310, illus.

CLIFTON, HAROLD D.
Systems Analysis for Business Data Processing. Business Books, London, 1969, 250, illus.

COLBERT, DOUGLAS A.
Data Processing Concepts. McGraw-Hill, 1968, 222, illus.

COOK, JOHN E.
What You Should Know About Data Processing. Oceana, 1969, 90. (Business Almanac Series No. 15.)

CRAWFORD, F. ROBERT
Introduction to Data Processing. Prentice-Hall, 1968, 402, illus.

DAVIS, GORDON B.
Computer Data Processing. McGraw-Hill, 1969, 617, illus. (McGraw-Hill Accounting Series.)

DeANGELO, SALVATORE M., and JORGENSEN, PAUL
Mathematics for Data Processing. McGraw-Hill, 1970, 336, illus.

DESMONDE, WILLIAM H.
A Conversational Graphic Data Processing System: The IBM 1130/2250. Prentice-Hall, 1969, 215, illus. (Prentice-Hall Automatic Computation Series.)
———.
Real-Time Data Processing Systems. Prentice-Hall, 1964, 186. (Prentice-Hall Automatic Computation Series.)

EMERY, GLYN
Electronic Data Processing. Elsevier, 1969, 344, illus.

ENGLEBARDT, STANLEY L.
Careers in Data Processing. Lothrop, New York, 1969, 127, illus.

FEINGOLD, CARL
Fundamentals of Punched Card Data Processing. W. C. Brown, 1969, 316.

GIBSON, E. DANA
An Introduction to Automated Data Processing. Business Press, Elmhurst, Ill., 1966, 436, illus.

COMMERCIAL PROGRAMS

GILDERSLEEVE, THOMAS R.
    Computer Data Processing and Programming. Prentice-Hall, 1970, 170.

GREGORY, ROBERT H., and VAN HORN, RICHARD L.
    Automatic Data-Processing Systems: Principles and Procedures. 2nd ed. Wadsworth, Belmont, Calif., 1963, 816. (Wadsworth Accounting and Data Processing Series.)

GROSSMAN, ALVIN, and HOWE, ROBERT L.
    Data Processing for Educators. Educational Methods, Chicago, 1965, 362, illus.

HANSON, PEGGY L.
    Keypunching. 2nd ed. Prentice-Hall, 1970, 144, illus.

HASS, RAY W.
    Data Processing. 3M Education Press, 1966, 4 vols., illus.

HOLMES, JAMES F.
    Data Transmission and Data Processing Dictionary. Rider, 1965, 103.

HONEYWELL ELECTRONIC DATA PROCESSING
    Fundamentals of Electronic Data Processing. Honeywell, 1964, 102.

HORN, JACK
    Computer and Data Processing Dictionary and Guide. Prentice-Hall, 1966, 200, illus.

IBM CORPORATION
    Data Processing Glossary. IBM, 1969, 60.

KEYS, WILLIAM J., and CASHMAN, THOMAS J.
    Basic Principles of Data Processing. McGraw-Hill, 1968, 80, illus.

KRAUSS, LEONARD I.
    Administering and Controlling the Company Data Processing Function. Prentice-Hall, 1969, 282, illus.

LANCASTER, F. W.
    Information Retrieval Systems. Wiley, 1968, 222.

LANGENBACH, ROBERT G.
    Introduction to Automated Data Processing. Prentice-Hall, 1968, 235, illus.

LEVY, JOSEPH
    Punched Card Data Processing. McGraw-Hill, 1967, 243, illus.

―――.
    Punched Card Equipment. McGraw-Hill, 1967, 161.

LIGOMENIDES, PANOS A.
    Information-Processing Machines. Holt, Rinehart & Winston, 1969, 358, illus.

LOTT, RICHARD W.
    Basic Data Processing. Prentice-Hall, 1967, 228. (Prentice-Hall Applied Mathematics Series.)

LUCKY, R. W., SALZ, J., and WELDON, E. J.
    Principles of Data Communication. McGraw-Hill, 1968, 433, illus.

LYTEL, ALLAN
    Fundamentals of Data Processing. Sams, 1964, 319, illus.

MARTIN, EDLEY W.
    Electronic Data Processing: An Introduction. Rev. ed. Irwin, 1965, 561, illus. (Irwin Series in Quantitative Analysis for Business.)

McCARTHY, EDMUND J., and McCARTHY, J. A.
    Integrated Data Processing Systems. Durward Humes, ed. Wiley, 1966, 565, illus.

McGILL, DONALD A. C.
    Punched Cards: Data Processing for Profit Improvement. McGraw-Hill, 1962, 232.

MEETHAM, ROGER
    Information Retrieval: The Essential Technology. Doubleday, 1970, 192, illus. (Doubleday Science Series.)

MORRILL, CHESTER, JR.
    Computers and Data Processing: Information Sources—An Annotated Guide to the Literature Associations and Institutions Concerned with Input, Throughput, and Output of Data. Gale, 1969, 275. (Management Information Guide No. 15.)

O'NEAL, LEELAND R.
    Electronic Data Processing Systems: A Self-Instructional Programmed Manual. Prentice-Hall, 1964, 409.

REICHENBACH, ROBERT R., and TASSO, CHARLES A.
    Organizing for Data Processing. American Management Association, 1968, 159, illus. (AMA Research Study No. 92.)

ROBICHAUD, BERYL
    Understanding Modern Business Data Processing. McGraw-Hill, Gregg Division, 1966, 115, illus.

RODGERS, HAROLD A., JR.
    Funk & Wagnalls Dictionary of Data Processing Terms. Funk & Wagnalls, 1970, 224.

SALTON, GERALD
    Automatic Information Organization and Retrieval. McGraw-Hill, 1968, 514, illus. (McGraw-Hill Computer Science Series.)

SAXON, JAMES A., and STEYER, WESLEY W.
    Basic Principles of Data Processing. 2nd ed. Prentice-Hall, 1970, 332, illus. (Applied Mathematics Series.)

SCHMIDT, RICHARD N., and MEYERS, WILLIAM E.
    Electronic Business Data Processing. Holt, Rinehart & Winston, 1963, 482, illus.

―――.
    Introduction to Computer Science and Data Processing. 2nd ed. Holt, Rinehart & Winston, 1970, 418, illus.

SCHULTZ, LOUISE
    Digital Processing: A System Orientation. Prentice-Hall, 1963, 403, illus. (Prentice-Hall Applied Mathematics Series.)

SHULMAN, ARNOLD R.
    Optical Data Processing. Wiley, 1970, 710, illus. (Wiley Series in Pure and Applied Optics.)

SPERRY RAND CORPORATION
    Fundamentals of Digital Magnetic-Tape Units. 2nd ed. Sams, 1967, 96, illus. (Sams Photofact Publication No. 20,580.)

STERLING, THEODOR D., and POLLACK, SEYMOUR V.
    Introduction to Statistical Data Processing. Prentice-Hall, 1968, 663, illus.

TROLLHANN, LILIAN, and WITTMANN, ALFRED
    Dictionary of Data Processing. Elsevier, 1964, 300.

TURNER, DAVID R.
    Tabulating Machine Operator, Data Processing Machines Operator, Keypunch, Sorter, Reproducer, Interpreter & Collator Operators, Tabulating Machine Trainee (IBM): All Grades Up to Supervising Operator. 2nd ed. Arco, 1969, 320, illus. (Arco Civil Service Test Tutor.)

U.S. BUREAU OF THE BUDGET
    Automatic Data Processing Glossary. USGPO, 1963, 62.

U.S. OFFICE OF EDUCATION, VOCATIONAL AND TECHNICAL EDUCATION DIVISION
    Electronic Data Processing—I: A Suggested Two-Year Post High School Curriculum for Computer Programmers and Business Application Analysts. USOE, 1967, 49. (OE-80024, Technical Education Program Series No. 4.)

―――.
    ...Electronic Data Processing in Engineering, Science, and Business. USOE, 1964, 34. (OE-80030.)

DATA PROCESSING AND COMPUTER SCIENCE

VAN NESS, ROBERT G.
　　Principles of Punched Card Data Processing. Business Press, Elmhurst, Ill., 1967, 321, illus.

WALSH, J. E., et al.
　　Principles of Data Processing. Pitman (Canada), 1968, 279, illus.

WANOUS, SAMUEL J., WANOUS, EDWARD E., and HUGHES, A. E.
　　Introduction to Automated Data Processing. South-Western, 1968, 246, illus.

WENDEL, THOMAS M., and WILLIAMS, WILLIAM H.
　　Introduction to Data Processing and Cobol. McGraw-Hill, 1969, 462, illus.

WHEELER, GERSHON J., and JONES, DONLON F.
　　Business Data Processing: An Introduction. Addison-Wesley, 1966, 152, illus.

COMPUTERS

ALCOSSER, EDWARD, PHILLIPS, JAMES P., and WOLK, ALLEN
　　How to Build a Working Digital Computer. Hayden, 1967, 176, illus.

ALLEN, PAUL
　　Exploring the Computer. Addison-Wesley, 1967, 111, illus.

AMERICAN ASSOCIATION OF JUNIOR COLLEGES
　　The Computer and the Junior College. Roy Sedral and Jim Hill, eds. American Association of Junior Colleges, 1969- , 2 vols.

BARTEE, THOMAS C.
　　Digital Computer Fundamentals. 2nd ed. McGraw-Hill, 1966, 402, illus.

BENREY, RONALD
　　Understanding Digital Computers. Hayden, 1964, 166, illus.

BIBBY, DAUSE L.
　　Your Future in the Electronic Computer Field. R. Rosen Press, 1962, 159. (Careers in Depth.)

BLUM, JOSEPH J.
　　Introduction to Analog Computation. Harcourt, Brace & World, 1969, 175, illus.

BOORE, WILLIAM F., and MURPHY, JERRY R.
　　The Computer Sampler: Management Perspectives on the Computer. McGraw-Hill, 1968, 357.

BURROUGHS CORPORATION (MILITARY FIELD SERVICE DIVISION)
　　Digital Computer Principles. 2nd ed. McGraw-Hill, 1969, 1 vol., illus.

CARROLL, JOHN M.
　　Careers and Opportunities in Computer Science. Dutton, 1967, 191, illus.

CHANDOR, ANTHONY, GRAHAM, JOHN, and WILLIAMSON, ROBIN
　　A Dictionary of Computers. Penguin, 1970, 407, (Penguin Reference Books.)

CLARK, J. O. E.
　　Computers at Work. Hamlyn, London, 1969, 159.

COLE, R. WADE
　　Introduction to Computing. McGraw-Hill, 1969, 336, illus. (McGraw-Hill Computer Science Series.)

COMPUTER INDUSTRY GUIDE, 1969-70.
　　Resource Publications, Princeton, N.J., 1970, 77.

COMPUTER USAGE EDUCATION, INC.
　　Computer Usage/Applications. Eric A. Weiss, ed. McGraw-Hill, 1970, 313, illus. (McGraw-Hill Computer Usage Series.)

―――― .
　　Computer Usage/Fundamentals. Eric A. Weiss, ed. McGraw-Hill, 1969, 411, illus. (McGraw-Hill Computer Usage Series.)

COOPER, M. J.
　　What Computers Can Do: A Guide for the Plain Man. Brandon/Systems Press, Princeton, N.J., 1970, 121, illus.

CROSS, WILBUR
　　A Job with A Future in Computers. Grosset & Dunlap, 1969, 127, illus.

DAVIS, GORDON B.
　　An Introduction to Electronic Computers. McGraw-Hill, 1965, 541, illus.

―――― .
　　An Introduction to the IBM System/360 Computer. McGraw-Hill, 1965, 238, illus.

DESMONDE, WILLIAM H.
　　Computers and Their Uses. Prentice-Hall, 1964, 296, illus.

EADIE, DONALD
　　Introduction to the Basic Computer. Prentice-Hall, 1968, 430, illus. (Prentice-Hall Series in Electronic Technology.)

FARINA, MARIO V.
　　Computers: A Self-Teaching Introduction. Prentice-Hall, 1969, 225, illus.

FAVRET, ANDREW G.
　　Introduction to Digital Computer Applications. Reinhold, 1965, 246, illus.

FISCHER, GEORGE
　　Your Career in Computers. Meredith Press, 1968, 194.

FLORES, IVAN
　　Computer Sorting. Prentice-Hall, 1969, 237, illus.

FORSYTHE, ALEXANDRA I., et al.
　　Computer Science: A First Course. Wiley, 1969, 553, illus.

―――― .
　　Computer Science: Fortran Language. Wiley, 1970, 181.

GALLER, BERNARD A.
　　The Language of Computers. McGraw-Hill, 1962, 244.

GOODLAD, JOHN I., O'TOOLE, JOHN F., JR., and TYLER, LOUISE L.
　　Computer and Information Systems in Education. Harcourt, Brace & World, 1966, 152.

GOULD, I. H., and ELLIS, F. S.
　　Digital Computer Technology: An Introduction to Logic, Design and Practice. Reinhold, 1963, 197, illus.

GREENBERGER, MARTIN, ED.
　　Computers and the World of the Future. MIT Press, 1964, 340, illus.

GRUENBERGER, FRED
　　Computing: An Introduction. Harcourt, Brace & World, 1969, 296, illus.

HALACY, D. S.
　　Computers: The Machines We Think With. Harper & Row, 1962, 279, illus.

HARGREAVES, JOHN
　　Computers and the Changing World: A Theme for the Automation Age. Hutchinson, London, 1967, 163, illus.

COMMERCIAL PROGRAMS

HELLERMAN, HERBERT
    Digital Computer System Principles. McGraw-Hill, 1967, 424.

HEYEL, CARL
    Computers, Office Machines, and the New Information Technology. Macmillan, 1969, 294, illus.

HITCHCOCK, ROBERT, and WILLE, EDGAR
    The Computer and Business Unity. Elsevier, 1969, 229, illus.

HUSKEY, HARRY D., and KORN, GRANINO A., EDS.
    Computer Handbook. McGraw-Hill, 1962, 1288.

JORDAIN, PHILIP B., and BRESLAU, MICHAEL
    Condensed Computer Encyclopedia. McGraw-Hill, 1969, 605, illus.

KARPLUS, WALTER J., ED.
    On-Line Computing: Time-Shared Man-Computer Systems. McGraw-Hill, 1967, 336, illus.

KLERER, MELVIN, and KORN, GRANINO A., EDS.
    Digital Computer User's Handbook. McGraw-Hill, 1967, 1 vol., illus.

LASKOW, ROBERT, and FELDZAMEN, A. N.
    Bright Future Careers with Computers. Chilton, 1969, 217.

LAURIE, EDWARD J.
    Computers and Computer Languages. 2nd ed. South-Western, 1966, 725, illus.

———.
    Computers and How They Work: IBM 1620, IBM 1401, IBM 650, South-Western, 1963, 441, illus.

LEONDES, CORNELIUS T., et al., eds.
    Computer Control Systems Technology. McGraw-Hill, 1961, 649.

LEVIN, HERMAN
    Introduction to Computer Analysis: ECAP for Electronics Technicians and Engineers. Prentice-Hall, 1970, 256, illus.

MAISEL, HERBERT, and WRIGHT, DONALD L.
    Introduction to Electronic Digital Computers: With Emphasis on the System/360, Fortran IV, and PL/1. McGraw-Hill, 1969, 395, illus.

MALEY, GERALD A., and HEILWEIL, MELVIN F.
    Introduction to Digital Computers. Prentice-Hall, 1968, 221, illus. (Prentice-Hall Series in Electronic Technology.)

MANDL, MATTHEW
    Fundamentals of Electronic Computers: Digital and Analog. Prentice-Hall, 1967, 344, illus.

MARTIN, JAMES
    Design of Real-Time Computer Systems. Prentice-Hall, 1967, 629, illus.

MISCHKE, CHARLES R.
    An Introduction to Computer-Aided Design. Prentice-Hall, 1968, 211, illus.

MOURSUND, DAVID G.
    How Computers Do It. Wadsworth, 1969, 124, illus.

MURPHY, JOHN S.
    Basics of Digital Computers. 2nd ed. Hayden, 1970, 3 vols. in 1, illus.

NIKOLAIEFF, GEORGE A., COMP.
    Computers and Society. Wilson, 1970, 226, illus. (Ref. Shelf Vol. 41, No. 6.)

NOLAN, RICHARD L.
    Introduction to Computing Through the Basic Language. Holt, Rinehart & Winston, 1969, 262, illus.

ORLICKY, JOSEPH
    The Successful Computer System: Its Planning, Development, and Management in a Business Enterprise. McGraw-Hill, 1969, 238, illus.

ORR, WILLIAM D.
    Conversational Computers. Wiley, 1968, 227.

PHILLIPS, GEORGE M., and TAYLOR, PETER J.
    Computers. Methuen, London, (Barnes & Noble, dist. 1969, 178, illus.

RESOURCE PUBLICATIONS, INC.
    Index of Opportunity in Computer Science. Resource Publications, Princeton, N.J., 1969, 52. (Career Resource Series.)

RICE, JOHN K., and RICE, JOHN R.
    Introduction to Computer Science: Problems, Algorithms, Languages, Information and Computers. Holt, Rinehart & Winston, 1969, 463, illus.

ROSE, MICHAEL
    Computers, Managers and Society. Penguin, 1969, 267, illus. (Pelican Library of Business & Management.)

RUSCH, RICHARD B.
    Computers: Their History and How They Work. Simon & Schuster, 1969, 126, illus.

SANDERS, DONALD H.
    Computers and Management. McGraw-Hill, 1970, 458.

———.
    Computers in Business: An Introduction. McGraw-Hill, 1968, 396, illus. (McGraw-Hill Accounting Series.)

SCHEID, FRANCIS J.
    Computer Science. McGraw-Hill, 1970, 300. (Schaum's Outline Series.)

SCOTT, NORMAN R.
    Electronic Computer Technology. McGraw-Hill, 1970, 618, illus. (McGraw-Hill Series in Information Processing and Computers.)

SHERR, SOL
    Fundamentals of Display System Design. Wiley, 1970, 484, illus.

SIPPL, CHARLES J.
    Computer Dictionary. Sams, 1966, 766.

SMITH, PAUL T.
    Computers, Systems and Profits. American Management Association, 1969, 200, illus.

SPENCER, DONALD D.
    Fundamentals of Digital Computers. Sams, 1969, 256, illus.

STERLING, THEODOR D., and POLLACK, SEYMOUR V.
    Computers and the Life Sciences. Columbia University Press, 1965, 342, illus.

———.
    Computing and Computer Science: A First Course with Fortran IV. Macmillan, 1970, 398, illus.

TATHAM, LAURA
    The Use of Computers for Profit: A Businessman's Guide. McGraw-Hill, 1969, 291.

TECHNICAL EDUCATION CONSORTIUM, INC.
    Development of a Curriculum to Meet Changing Manpower Needs of the Computer and Business Machine Industries. TEC, Hartford, Conn., 1968, 109.

THOMAS, SHIRLEY
    Computers: Their History, Present Application and Future. Holt, Rinehart & Winston, 1965, 175, illus. (Holt Library of Science Series 2, Vol. 15.)

TOMESKI, EDWARD A.
    The Computer Revolution: The Executive and the New Information Technology. Macmillan, 1970, 276, illus.

DATA PROCESSING AND COMPUTER SCIENCE

U.S. BUREAU OF NAVAL PERSONNEL
    Computer Basics. USBNP, 1964, 2 vols.

———.
    Digital Computer Basics. Dover, 1969, 231, illus.

WEIK, MARTIN H.
    Standard Dictionary of Computers and Information Processing. Hayden, 1969, 336, illus.

WEINSTEIN, SEYMOUR M., and KEIM, ARMAND
    Fundamentals of Digital Computers. Holt, Rinehart & Winston, 1965, 163, illus.

WEISS, ERIC A.
    The PL/1 Converter. McGraw-Hill, 1966, 113.

WEYRICK, ROBERT C.
    Fundamentals of Analog Computers. Prentice-Hall, 1969, 289.

WITHINGTON, FREDERIC G.
    The Real Computer: Its Influence, Uses, and Effects. Addison-Wesley, 1969, 350.

———.
    The Use of Computers in Business Organizations. Addison-Wesley, 1966, 245, illus.

LANGUAGES AND PROGRAMMING

ANDERSEN, CHRISTIAN J.
    An Introduction to ALGOL 60. Addison-Wesley, 1964, 57. (Addison-Wesley Series in Computer Science and Information Processing.)

BARBOUR, EDNA H.
    PL/I: A Self-Instructional Manual. Macmillan, 1970, 301.

BARNETT, LEO, and DAVIS, LOU ELLEN
    Careers in Computer Programming. Walck, 1967, 117, illus. (Careers for Tomorrow.)

BARNETT, MICHAEL P.
    Computer Programming in English. Harcourt, Brace & World, 1969, 259, illus.

BARRON, DAVID W.
    Recursive Techniques in Programming. Elsevier, 1968, 64, illus. (Computer Monograph Series.)

BATES, FRANK, and DOUGLAS, MARY L.
    Programming Language/One. Prentice-Hall, 1967, 375.

BERKELEY, EDMUND C., and BOBROW, DANIEL G., EDS.
    The Programming Language LISP: Its Operation and Applications. MIT Press, 1967, 385.

BERNARD, SOLOMON M.
    System 360 Cobol. Prentice-Hall, 1968, 312, illus.

BLATT, JOHN M.
    Introduction to Fortran IV Programming: Using the Watfor Compiler. Goodyear, Pacific Palisades, Calif., 1968, 313, illus. (Goodyear Computer Series.)

BRADLEY, JOHN H.
    Programmer's Guide to the IBM System/360. McGraw-Hill, 1969, 336, illus.

BREUER, HANS
    Dictionary for Computer Languages. Academic Press, 1966, 332. (APIC Studies in Data Processing No. 6.)

BROWN, GARY D.
    Systems/360 Job Control Language. Wiley, 1970, 292.

CALDERBANK, VALERIE J.
    A Course on Programming in FORTRAN IV. Barnes & Noble, 1969, 88.

CARVER, D. K.
    Introduction to Fortran II and Fortran IV Programming. Wiley, 1969, 224, illus.

CASHMAN, THOMAS J., and SHELLY, GARY B.
    Introduction to Computer Programming IBM System/360 Assembler Language. Anaheim Publishing, Anaheim, Calif., 1969, 1 vol.

CHAPIN, NED
    Programming Computers for Business Applications. McGraw-Hill, 1961, 279, illus.

———.
    360 Programming in Assembly Language. McGraw-Hill, 1968, 532, illus.

COAN, JAMES S.
    Basic Basic: An Introduction to Computer Programming in Basic Language. Hayden, 1970, 256.

COLMAN, HARRY L., and SMALLWOOD, CLARENCE
    Computer Language: An Autoinstructional Introduction to FORTRAN. McGraw-Hill, 1962, 196, illus.

COMPUTER USAGE COMPANY
    Computer Usage: 360 Assembly Programming. Eric A. Weiss, ed. McGraw-Hill, 1970, 420, illus. (Computer Usage Series.)

———.
    Programming the IBM System/360. Wiley, 1966, 316, illus.

COMPUTER USAGE EDUCATION, INC.
    Computer Usage/360 Fortran Programming. Eric A. Weiss, ed. McGraw-Hill, 1969, 400, illus.

COX, DAVID W.
    Computer Programmer. Research, Madison, Wis., 1965, 64. (List of American Occupations Monographs No. 27.)

CUTLER, DONALD I.
    Introduction to Computer Programming. Prentice-Hall, 1964, 216, illus.

DAVIS, SIDNEY
    Your Future in Computer Programming. R. Rosen Press, 1969, 144, illus. (Careers in Depth.)

DODES, IRVING A.
    IBM 1620 Programming for Science and Mathematics. Hayden, 1963, 276, illus.

DUNN, WALTER L.
    Introduction to Digital Computer Problems Using FORTRAN IV: A Self-Instructional Programmed Text. McGraw-Hill, 1969, 384, illus.

FEINGOLD, CARL
    Fundamentals of Cobol Programming. W. C. Brown, 1969, 201, illus.

FICKEN, FREDERICK A.
    The Simplex Method of Linear Programming. Holt, Rinehart & Winston, 1961, 58, illus.

FISCHER, SHANNON R.
    How Computer Programming Works. Cowles, 1970, 264, illus.

FISHER, F. PETER, and SWINDLE, GEORGE F.
    Computer Programming Systems. Holt, Rinehart & Winston, 1964, 643, illus.

FLORES, IVAN
    Computer Programming. Prentice-Hall, 1966, 395, illus. (Prentice-Hall Series in Applied Mathematics.)

GALLER, BERNARD A., and PERLIS, ALAN J.
    A View of Programming Languages. Addison-Wesley, 1970, 1 vol. (Computer Science and Programming Series.)

COMMERCIAL PROGRAMS

GASS, SAUL I.
    Linear Programming. 3rd ed. McGraw-Hill, 1969, 384, illus.

GEAR, CHARLES W.
    Computer Organization and Programming. McGraw-Hill, 1969, 397, illus. (McGraw-Hill Computer Science Series.)

GEORGE, FRANK H.
    An Introduction to Computer Programming. Pergamon, 1968, 1 vol., illus.

GERMAIN, CLARENCE B.
    Programming the IBM 360. Prentice-Hall, 1967, 366, illus.

GOLDEN, JAMES T.
    FORTRAN IV: Programming and Computing. Prentice-Hall, 1965, 270.

GRISWOLD, R. E., POAGE, J. F., and POLONSKY, L. P.
    The SNOBOL 4 Programming Language. Prentice-Hall, 1968, 221, illus.

HAAG, JAMES N.
    Comprehensive Standard Fortran Programming. Hayden, 1969, 312, illus. (Hayden Computer Programming Series.)

HARE, VAN COURT
    Basic Programming. Harcourt, Brace & World, 1970, 246, illus.

———.
    Introduction to Programming: A Basic Approach. Harcourt, Brace & World, 1970, 436, illus.

HARVILL, JOHN
    Basic Fortran Programming. Prentice-Hall, 1968, 1 vol.

HEALY, JEREMIAH J., and DEBRUZZI, D. J.
    Basic Fortran IV Programming: Self-Instructional Manual and Text. Addison-Wesley, 1968, 264.

HELLWIG, JESSICA
    Introduction to Computers and Programming. Columbia University Press, 1969, 215, illus.

HIGMAN, BRYAN
    A Comparative Study of Programming Languages. Elsevier, 1967, 164.

HOLDEN, HERBERT L.
    Introduction to FORTRAN IV. Macmillan, 1970, 134.

HUGHES, JOAN K.
    Programming the IBM 1130. Wiley, 1969, 512, illus.

HUSSON, SAMIR S.
    Microprogramming: Principles and Practices. Prentice-Hall, 1970, 614.

ILLINOIS INSTITUTE OF TECHNOLOGY, RESEARCH INSTITUTE
    APT Part Programming. McGraw-Hill, 1967, 152, illus.

JAMISON, ROBERT V.
    Fortran IV Programming: Based on the IBM System 1130. McGraw-Hill, 1970, 320, illus.

JONES, ROBERT L.
    Fundamental COBOL for IBM System 360. Prentice-Hall, 1969, 245, illus.

KAPUR, GOPAL K.
    IBM 360 Assembly Language Programming. Wiley, 1970, 1 vol.

KATZAN, HARRY, JR.
    APL Programming and Computer Techniques. Van Nostrand-Reinhold, 1970, 1 vol.

KAZMIER, LEONARD J., and PHILIPPAKIS, ANDREAS S.
    Fundamentals of EDP and FORTRAN. McGraw-Hill, 1970, 193, illus.

KEMENY, JOHN G.
    Basic Programming. Wiley, 1967, 1 vol.

KNUTH, DONALD
    The Art of Computer Programming. Addison-Wesley, 1968-69, 2 vols.

LECHT, CHARLES P.
    The Programmer's Algol. McGraw-Hill, 1967, 251.

———.
    The Programmar's Fortran II and IV. McGraw-Hill, 1966, 162.

———.
    The Programmer's PL/1: A Complete Reference. McGraw-Hill, 1968, 427.

LEDLEY, ROBERT S., and WILSON, J. B.
    Fortran IV Programming. McGraw-Hill, 1966, 229.

LEE, R. M.
    A Short Course in FORTRAN IV Programming: Based on the IBM System/360. McGraw-Hill, 1967, 235, illus.

LEEDS, HERBERT D., and WEINBERG, GERALD M.
    Computer Programming Fundamentals. 2nd ed. McGraw-Hill, 1966, 460, illus.

———.
    Computer Programming Fundamentals: "Based on the IBM System 360." McGraw-Hill, 1970, 593, illus.

LEESON, DANIEL N., and DIMITRY, DONALD L.
    Basic Programming Concepts and the IBM 1620 Computer. 2nd ed. Holt, Rinehart & Winston, 1968, 460, illus.

LOSCHETTER, RICHARD F.
    Fundamentals of Machine Language and Autocoder Programming. Rev. ed. Whitehall, Northbrook, Ill., 1969, 190, illus.

LUFTIG, MILTON
    Computer Programmer. Arco, 1965, 192. (Professional Career Exam Series.)

MANN, RICHARD A.
    An IBM 1130 Fortran Primer. International Textbook, 1969, 216, illus.

MANNING, WILLIAM A., and GARNERO, ROBERT S.
    Fortran IV Problem Solver. McGraw-Hill, 1970, 167, illus.

MARKOWITZ, HARRY M., HAUSNER, BERNARD, and KARR HERBERT W.
    Simscript: A Simulation Programming Language. Prentice-Hall, 1963, 138, illus.

McCAMERON, FRITZ A.
    Fortran IV. Irwin-Dorsey, 1970, 215. (Irwin-Dorsey Series in Information Processing.)

———.
    Fortran: Logic and Programming. Irwin, 1968, 246, illus.

McCRACKEN, DANIEL D.
    A Guide to FORTRAN Programming. Wiley, 1961, 88.

———.
    A Guide to IBM 1401 Programming. Wiley, 1961, 199, illus.

McCRACKEN, DANIEL D., and GARBASSI, U.
    A Guide to Cobol Programming. 2nd ed. Wiley, 1970, 1 vol., illus.

MELICHAR, PAUL R.
    COBOL for IBM System/360: Programming Techniques. Science Research Associates, 1968, 208, illus.

MURRAY-SHELLEY, R.
    Teach Yourself Computer Programming. Dover, 1968, 1 vol.

MURRILL, PAUL W., and SMITH, CECIL L.
    An Introduction to Fortran IV Programming: A General Approach. International Textbook, 1970, 276.

NATHAN, ROBERT, and HANES, ELIZABETH
Computer Programming Handbook: A Guide for Beginners. Prentice-Hall, 1962, 214, illus.

NICOL, KEITH
Elementary Programming and Algol. McGraw-Hill, 1965, 147, illus.

NYDEGGER, ADOLPH C.
An Introduction to Computer Programming With an Emphasis on Fortran IV. Addison-Wesley, 1968, 269, illus.

PAYNE, WILLIAM H.
Machine, Assembly, and Systems Programming for the IBM 360. Harper & Row, 1969, 321.

PETERSON, WESLEY W., and HOLZ, JEAN L.
Fortran IV and the IBM 360. McGraw-Hill, 1971, 224.

PLUMB, S. C.
Introduction to FORTRAN: A Program for Self-Instruction. McGraw-Hill, 1964, 203, illus.

POLLACK, SEYMOUR V.
A Guide to Fortran IV. Columbia University Press, 1965, 260, illus.

POLLACK, SEYMOUR V., and STERLING, THEODOR D.
A Guide to PL/I. Holt, 1969, 556, illus.

PRICE, WILSON T.
Elements of Basic Fortran IV Programming, As Implemented on the IBM 1130/1800 Computers. Holt, 1969, 387, illus.

———.
Elements of IBM 1130 Programming. Holt, Rinehart & Winston, 1968, 484.

RAUN, DONALD L.
An Introduction to Cobol Computer Programming for Accounting and Business Analysis. Dickenson, Belmont, Calif., 1966, 254, illus. (Dickenson Series in Computer and Information Science.)

RCA INSTITUTES, INC.
Fundamentals of Electronic Data Processing: An Introduction to Business Computer Programming. Prentice-Hall, 1965, 516, illus.

ROSEN, SAUL
Programming Systems and Languages. McGraw-Hill, 1967, 734. (McGraw-Hill Computer Science Series.)

ROSENBERG, JAMES
Introduction to IBM/360 Assembler Language. Holden-Day, San Francisco, 1970, 127.

RULE, WILFRED P.
Fortran IV Programming. Prindle, Weber & Schmidt, Boston, 1968, 221, illus.

RUMMER, DALE I.
Introduction to Analog Computer Programming. Holt, Rinehart & Winston, 1969, 198, illus.

SAMMET, JEAN E.
Programming Languages: History and Fundamentals. Prentice-Hall, 1969, 785, illus. (Prentice-Hall Series in Automatic Computation.)

SANDERSON, PETER C.
Computer Languages: A Practical Guide to the Chief Programming Languages. Philosophical Library, 1970, 200.

SAXON, JAMES A.
Cobol: A Self-Instructional Manual. Prentice-Hall, 1963, 190, illus.

SAXON, JAMES A., ENGLANDER, HERMAN S., and ENGLANDER, WILLIAM R.
System 360 Programming: A Self-Instructional Manual. Prentice-Hall, 1968, 231.

SCHONBECK, RUDOLPH G.
Fortran IV: For Multi-Programming Systems, With Emphasis on the GE-600 Series Computer. Addison-Wesley, 1968, 243, illus.

SCOTT, THEODORE G.
Basic Computer Programming. Doubleday, 1967, 492. (Tutor Text.)

———.
Computer Programming Techniques. Doubleday, 1964, 664, illus. (Tutor Text.)

SELIGSOHN, I. J.
Your Career in Computer Programming. Messner, 1967, 222, illus.

SHERMAN, PHILIP M.
Techniques in Computer Programming. Prentice-Hall, 1970, 348.

SPENCER, DONALD D.
A Guide to Basic Programming: A Time Sharing Language. Addison-Wesley, 1970, 216, illus.

SPITZBARTH, LAUREL M.
Basic COBOL Programming: Self Instructional Manual and Text. Addison, 1970, 335.

SPROWLS, R. CLAY
Computers: A Programming Problem Approach. Harper & Row, 1966, 388, illus.

———.
Introduction to PL/1 Programming. Harper & Row, 1969, 179.

STABLEY, DON H.
System/360 Assembler Language. Wiley, 1967, 129, illus.

STRUBLE, GEORGE
Assembler Language Programming: The IBM System/360. Addison-Wesley, 1969, 434, illus.

STUART, FREDRIC
Fortran Programming. Wiley, 1969, 353, illus.

———.
Introductory Computer Programming. Wiley, 1966, 155, illus.

SWALLOW, KENNETH P., and PRICE, WILSON T.
Elements of Computer Programming. 2nd ed. Holt, Rinehart & Winston, 1970, 456, illus.

WALNUT, FRANCIS K.
Introduction to Computer Programming and Coding. Prentice-Hall, 1968, 429, illus.

WASHBURN, DALE W.
Computer Programming: A Total Language Approach. Holt, 1970, 490, illus.

WEGNER, PETER
Programming Languages, Information Structures, and Machine Organization. McGraw-Hill, 1968, 401.

WEINBERG, GERALD M.
PL/1 Programming: A Manual of Style. McGraw-Hill, 1970, 288, illus.

———.
PL/1 Programming Primer. McGraw-Hill, 1966, 288, illus.

WEISS, ERIC A.
Programming the IBM 1620: The Hands-On Approach. McGraw-Hill, 1965, 310.

WIMMERT, ROBERT J.
Computer Programming Techniques. Holt, Rinehart & Winston, 1968, 2 vols.

FASHION ARTS

ADAMS, JAMES D.
Naked We Came: A More or Less Lighthearted Look at the Past, Present, and Future of Clothes. Holt, Rinehart & Winston, 1967, 123, illus.

COMMERCIAL PROGRAMS

ADBURGHAM, ALISON
View of Fashion. Allen & Unwin, London, 1966, 285, illus.

ALBERS, ANNI
On Designing. 2nd ed. Wesleyan University Press, 1962, 80, illus.

AMERICAN FASHION PATTERN GRADER
Kogos, 1966, 1 vol.

ANSPACH, KARLYNE
The Why of Fashion. Iowa State University Press, 1967, 378, illus.

ANTOINE-DARIAUX, GENEVIEVE
Elegance: A Complete Guide for Every Woman Who Wants to Be Well and Properly Dressed on All Occasions. Doubleday, 1964, 319, illus.

APPAREL ENGINEERING AND NEEDLE TRADES HANDBOOK
Kogos, 1960, 388, illus.

ARNOLD, JANET
Patterns of Fashion: Englishwomen's Dress and Their Construction. Wace, London, 1966, 2 vols.

ARNOLD, PAULINE, and WHITE, PERCIVAL
Clothes and Cloth: America's Apparel Business. Holiday House, 1961, 355.

BALLARD, BETTINA
In My Fashion. McKay, 1960, 312.

BANCROFT, VIVIAN S.
It's So, Sew Easy: A Guide to Clothing Construction. Burgess, 1962, 157, illus.

BANE, ALLYNE
Creative Clothing Construction. 2nd ed. McGraw-Hill, 1966, 329, illus.

———.
Tailoring. 2nd ed. McGraw-Hill, 1968, 1 vol., illus.

BECK, DORIS M.
Custom Tailoring for Homemakers. Bennett, 1964, 186, illus.

BEITLER, ETHEL J.
Create with Yarn. International Textbook, 1964, 196, illus.

BENDER, MARYLIN
The Beautiful People. Coward-McCann, 1967, 320, illus.

BENNETT-ENGLAND, RODNEY C.
Dress Optional: The Revolution in Menswear. Dufour, 1968, 240, illus.

BETTER HOMES & GARDENS
Sewing Book. Meredith, Des Moines, 1961, 320, illus.

BISHOP, EDNA B., and ARCH, MARJORIE S.
The Bishop Method of Clothing Construction. Rev. ed. Lippincott, 1966, 284.

———.
Fashion Sewing by the Bishop Method. Lippincott, 1962, 233, illus.

BLACK, MARY E.
New Key to Weaving: A Textbook of Hand Weaving for the Beginning Weaver. Rev. ed. Bruce, 1961, 573, illus.

BLACKSHAW, H., and BRIGHTMAN, RAINALD
Dictionary of Dyeing and Textile Printing. Interscience, 1961, 221, illus.

BRENNER, BARBARA
Careers and Opportunities in Fashion. Dutton, 1964, 191, illus.

BROCKMAN, HELEN L.
The Theory of Fashion Design. Wiley, 1965, 332, illus.

BURKE, BETSY
Fashion in Clothes. Pocket Books, 1963, 1 vol. (Emily Post Series.)

BUTLER, ANNE
Embroidery Stitches: An Illustrated Guide. Praeger, 1968, 128, illus.

BUTLER, ANNE, and GREEN, DAVID
Pattern and Embroidery. Branford, Newton Centre, Mass., 1970, 1 vol.

BUTLER, WINIFRED
The Complete Book of Needlework and Embroidery. Putnam, 1967, 196, illus.

BYSTROM, ELLEN
Printing on Fabric: Basic Techniques. Van Nostrand-Reinhold, 1970, 96, illus. (Scandinavian Crafts Series.)

CARLIN, DAVID
Alteration of Men's Clothing. 3rd ed. Fairchild, 1962, 112, illus.

CARLSON, ROSALIN
Creative Knitting and Crocheting. Hearthside Press, 1970, 192, illus.

CARSON, BYRTA
How You Look and Dress. 4th ed. McGraw-Hill, 1969, 310, illus. (American Home and Family Series.)

CHAMBERS, HELEN G., and MOULTON, VERNA
Clothing Selection: Fashions, Figures, Fabrics. 2nd ed. Lippincott, 1969, 1 vol.

COATS & CLARK, INC.
Coats & Clark's Sewing Book: Newest Methods from A to Z. Golden Press, 1967, 192, illus.

COBRIN, HARRY A.
The Men's Clothing Industry: Colonial Through Modern Times. Fairchild, 1970, 381, illus.

COCKETT, SYDNEY R.
Dyeing and Printing. Textile Book Service, Metuchen, N.J., 1964, 113, illus.

COHEN, DAVID V.
A Professional Guide to Men's Clothing in Pattern Construction and Cutting Production. Carlton, New York, 1969, 96, illus. (A Hearthstone Book.)

COHN, WALTER E.
Modern Footwear Materials & Processes: A Topical Guide to Footwear Technology. Fairchild, 1969, 358, illus.

COLICCHIO, ANTOINETTE J.
Patternmaking and Design. Rutgers University, Department of Vocational-Technical Education (Curriculum Laboratory), 1967, 1 vol., illus.

CONTINI, MILA
Fashion: From Ancient Egypt to the Present Day. Odyssey, 1965, 321, illus.

COOPER, GRACE R.
The Invention of the Sewing Machine. Smithsonian Institution, 1968, 158, illus. (Smithsonian Institution Bulletin No. 254.)

CORINTH, KAY
Fashion Showmanship: Everything You Need to Know to Give a Fashion Show. Wiley, 1970, 280, illus.

COX, JANET T.
The Handbook of Piece Goods Merchandising: McCall's Step-by-Step Guide to Buying and Selling Fabrics, Yarn and Notions. McCall Pattern Co., New York, 1970, 318, illus.

CRAIG, HAZEL T.
    Clothing: A Comprehensive Study. Lippincott, 1968, 468, illus.

CRAWFORD, M.D.C.
    One World of Fashion. 3rd ed. Josephine E. Watkins and Beatrice Zelin, eds. Fairchild, 1967, 192.

CRAWFORD, T. S.
    A History of the Umbrella. Taplinger, 1970, 220, illus.

CUNNINGHAM, GLADYS
    Singer Sewing Book. Singer Co., 1969, 428, illus.

CURTIS, IRVING E.
    Fundamental Principles of Pattern Making for Misses' and Women's Garments. 4th ed. The author, South Orange, N.J., 1966, 1 vol.

―――――.
    Intermediate and Technological Problems in Pattern Making for Misses and Ladies Garments. 5th ed. The author, South Orange, N.J., 1964, 1 vol.

D'ASSAILLY, GISÈLE
    Ages of Elegance: Five Thousand Years of Fashion and Frivolity. Graphic, 1968, 251, illus.

DAVES, JESSICA
    Ready-Made Miracle: The American Story of Fashion for the Millions. Putnam, 1967, 256, illus.

DAVIS, MILDRED J.
    The Art of Crewel Embroidery. Crown, 1962, 224, illus.

DELAVAN, BETTY C., ADAMS, AURELIA K., and RICHARDS, LOUISE G.
    Clothing Selection: Application of Theory. 3rd ed. Burgess, 1964, 133, illus.

DILLEY, ROMILDA
    Fundamental Fashion Drawing. Rev. ed. Sterling, 1967, 128, illus.

DINGWALL, E.
    Meet Judy. McGraw-Hill, 1968, 144, illus. (McGraw-Hill Foundation Series.)

DOERR, CATHERINE M.
    Smart Sewing: The Making of Clothing. Macmillan, 1967, 228, illus.

DRESSMAKING MAGAZINE
    Pattern Drafting. Kamakura-Shobo, Tokyo, 1969, 2 vols., illus.

EDOUARD DUBIED et Cie., S.A.
    Dubied Knitting Manual. Dubied, Neuchâtel, Switzerland, 1967, 198, illus.

EAST, MARJORIE, and WINES, MARY E.
    Fashion Your Own: A Guide to Easy Clothing Construction. Houghton, 1964, 216.

ENTHOVEN, JACQUELINE
    The Stitches of Creative Embroidery. Reinhold, 1964, 212, illus.

ERWIN, MABLE D., and KINCHEN, LILA A.
    Clothing for Moderns. 4th ed. Macmillan, 1969, 585, illus.

ESQUIRE
    Esquire Fashion Guide for All Occasions. Rev. ed. Harper & Row, 1962, 204, illus.

―――――.
    Esquire Fashions for Men. Harper & Row, 1966, 253, illus.

FABRE, MAURICE
    History of Fashion. Leisure Arts, London, 1966, 112, illus. (Discovery of Science.)

FAIRCHILD, JOHN
    The Fashionable Savages. Doubleday, 1965, 200, illus.

FASHION GROUP
    Your Future in Fashion Design. R. Rosen Press, 1966, 143, illus. (Careers in Depth.)

―――――.
    Your Future in the Fashion World. R. Rosen Press, 1960, 160. (Careers in Depth.)

FELDMAN, EGAL
    Fit for Men: A Study of New York's Clothing Trade. Public Affairs Press, Washington, 1960, 138.

FELKIN, WILLIAM
    Felkin's History of the Machine-Wrought Hosiery and Lace Manufactures. David & Charles, Newton Abbot, Devon, England, 1967, 596, illus.

FLUGEL, JOHN C.
    The Psychology of Clothes. International Universities Press, 1966, 257, illus.

FRIED, ELEANOR L.
    Is the Fashion Business Your Business? 3rd ed. Fairchild, 1970, 240.

GARLAND, MADGE
    Fashion. Penguin, 1962, 160, illus.

GAWNE, ELEANOR J., and OERKE, BESS V.
    Dress: The Clothing Textbook. 3rd ed. Bennett Books, 1969, 1 vol., illus.

GOLD, ANNALEE
    How to Sell Fashion. Fairchild, 1968, 256, illus.

GREAT BRITAIN, NATIONAL ECONOMIC DEVELOPMENT OFFICE
    Your Future in Clothing: An Economic Development Study of the Future Market for the Clothing Industry. HMSO, London, 1970, 1 vol.

HARD'S YEARBOOK OF THE CLOTHING INDUSTRY
    United Trade Press, London, 1951- , Vol. 1- , annual, illus.

HAYTER, EDITH F.
    Behind the Scenes in Fashion Merchandising. Pageant Press, 1965, 136.

HEAD, EDITH
    How to Dress for Success. Random House, 1967, 211, illus.

HERINGTON, VIOLA B.
    Begin to Sew: Learn the Science Way of Sewing. McKnight & McKnight, 1968, 156, illus.

HILLHOUSE, MARION S.
    Dress Selection and Design. Macmillan, 1963, 216, illus. (Macmillan College Home Economics Series.)

HIRST, IRENE, ED.
    The Complete Book of Needlework. Taplinger, 1963, 320, illus.

HOLLEN, NORMA R.
    Flat Pattern Methods: With Selected Sewing Suggestions. 2nd ed. Burgess, 1965, 167, illus.

HORN, MARILYN J.
    The Second Skin: An Interdisciplinary Study of Clothing. Houghton Mifflin, 1968, 435, illus.

IOWA HOME ECONOMICS ASSOCIATION
    Unit Method of Clothing Construction. 4th ed. Iowa State University Press, 1965, 132, illus.

JAQUE, LINE
    Sew the French Way. Mills & Boon, London, 1961, 254, illus.

COMMERCIAL PROGRAMS

JARNOW, JEANNETTE A., and JUDELLE, BEATRICE, EDS.
Inside the Fashion Business: Text & Readings. Wiley, 1965, 276.

JOHNSON, MARY R.
Mary Johnson's Guide to Altering and Restyling Ready-Made Clothes. Dutton, 1964, 251, illus.

———.
Sew for Your Children. Dutton, 1961, 238, illus.

———.
Sewing the Easy Way. Rev. ed. Dutton, 1966, 256, illus.

JOHNSTON, MEDA P., and KAUFMAN, GLEN
Design on Fabrics. Van Nostrand-Reinhold, 1967, 156, illus.

JONES, FRANCES M.
Tips and Tricks for Tailoring. Interstate, 1966, 156, illus.

JUSTEMA, WILLIAM
The Pleasures of Pattern. Reinhold, 1968, 240, illus.

KINMOND, JEAN
Crochet Patterns. Branford, Newton Centre, Mass., 1969, 128, illus.

KLUPT, HELEN, DONLEY, DOROTHY, and BALENZANO, ROSA
Principles of Fashion Sketching. Fashion Institute of Technology, New York, 1966, 35, illus.

KOGOS, FREDERICK, ED.
Designing and Drafting Shirts for Men and Boys. Kogos, 1962, 55, illus.

KOLODNY, ROSALIE
Fashion Design for Moderns. Fairchild, 1968, 128, illus.

KOPP, ERNESTINE, ROLFO, VITTORINA, and ZELIN, BEATRICE
Designing Apparel Through the Flat Pattern. 3rd ed. Fairchild, 1966, 355.

———.
How to Draft Basic Patterns. Fairchild, 1968, 83, illus. (Textbook of the FIT-Fairchild Series.)

KREVITSKY, NIK
Stitchery Art and Craft. Van Nostrand-Reinhold, 1966, 132, illus.

KUNICK, PHILIP
Sizing, Pattern Construction and Grading for Women's and Children's Garments. Philip Kunick, London, 1967, 168, illus.

KYBALOVÁ, LUDMILA, HERBENOVÁ, OLGA, and LAMAROVÁ, MILENA
The Pictorial Encyclopedia of Fashion. Claudia Rosoux, tr. Crown, 1968, 608, illus.

LAMMER, JUTTA
Print Your Own Fabrics. Watson-Guptill, 1965, 59, illus.

LATZKE, ALPHA
The Wide World of Clothing: Economics, Social Significance, Selection. Ronald, 1968, 312, illus.

LAURY, JEAN R.
Appliqué Stitchery. Van Nostrand-Reinhold, 1966, 136, illus.

LAVER, JAMES
Modesty in Dress: An Inquiry into the Fundamentals of Fashion. Houghton Mifflin, 1969, 186, illus.

LENAHAN, MARIE
Related Art for Dress Design. New Brunswick, N.J., Department of Education (Vocational Division), 1966, 1 vol.

LENZ, BERNIE
The Complete Book of Fashion Modeling. Crown, 1969, 278, illus.

LESCH, ALMA
Vegetable Dyeing: 151 Recipes for Dyeing Yarns and Fabrics with Natural Materials. Watson-Guptill, 1970, 144, illus.

LEVIN, PHYLLIS L.
The Wheels of Fashion. Doubleday, 1965, 244.

LILLOW, IRA
Introducing Machine Embroidery. Watson-Guptill, 1967, 72, illus.

LOCKWOOD, GILLIAN
Making Clothes for Young Children. Watson-Guptill, 1969, 1 vol.

LYLE, DOROTHY S.
The Clothes We Wear. National Education Association, 1966, 32, illus.

LYNCH, MARY, and SARA, DOROTHY
Sewing Made Easy. Doubleday, 1969, 394, illus.

MARGOLIS, ADELE P.
The Complete Book of Tailoring for Women Who Like to Sew. Doubleday, 1964, 439, illus.

———.
The Dressmaking Book: A Simplified Guide for Beginners. Doubleday, 1967, 294, illus.

———.
How to Make Clothes That Fit and Flatter. Doubleday, 1969, 296, illus.

———.
Simplified Tailoring. Theatre Arts Books, 1968, 1 vol.

MASTER DESIGNER
Modern Garment Design and Grading Clothing for Men & Boys. Master Designer, Chicago, 1969, 1 vol.

MAUCK, FRANCES F.
Modern Sewing Techniques. Macmillan, 1963, 307, illus.

McDERMOTT, IRENE E., and NORRIS, JEANNE L.
Opportunities In Clothing: Fashion, Merchandising. Bennett, 1968, 350, illus.

McELWAIN, CHARLOTTE
Knitting with Stop and Go Needles: Basic and Fashion Stitches. Van Nostrand-Reinhold, 1968, 144, illus.

McJIMSEY, HARRIET T.
Art In Clothing Selection. Harper & Row, 1963, 300, illus. (Harper Home Economics Series.)

MEN'S FURNISHINGS.
1969 ed. University of Texas, 1 vol.

MERRIAM, EVE
Figleaf: The Business of Being in Fashion. Lippincott, 1960, 255, illus.

MILLER, IRENE P., and LUBELL, WINIFRED
The Stitchery Book: Embroidery for Beginners. Doubleday, 1965, 96, illus.

MORI, MARIA
Basic Pattern Cutting. Taplinger, 1970, 160, illus.

MOULTON, BERTHA
Garment-Cutting and Tailoring for Students. Theatre Arts Books, 1968, 223, illus.

———.
Simplified Tailoring. Theatre Arts Books, 1969, 111, illus.

MUTOLESE, MICHAEL
Minor and Major Alterations and How to Make Them. H. Daroff & Sons, 1962, 70, illus.

NATIONAL KNITTED OUTERWEAR ASSOCIATION
A Practical Program for Quality Control. NKOA, New York, 1964, 2 pts., 94.

NAYLOR, BRENDA
The Technique of Dress Design. Branford, Newton Centre, Mass., 1967, 154, illus.

NEW YORK (STATE) EDUCATION DEPARTMENT, BUREAU OF CONTINUING EDUCATION (CURRICULUM DEVELOPMENT).
Fashion Merchandising: A Suggested Adult Distributive Education Course Outline. NYSED, Albany, 1969, 64. (VT 009 852.)

NYE, THELMA M., ED.
Cross Stitch Patterns. Van Nostrand-Reinhold, 118, illus.

OERKE, BESS V.
Dress: The Clothing Textbook. Rev. ed. Bennett, 1960, 575, illus.

PALING, D. F.
Warp Knitting Technology. Columbine Press, Manchester, 1965, 389, illus.

PARETI, JOHN, JR.
How to Sell Footwear Profitably. Fairchild, 1967, 170, illus.

J. C. PENNEY COMPANY, INC.
Fashions and Fabrics. J. C. Penney, Fall/Winter 1970, semi-annual, illus.

PETERSEN, GRETE, and SVENNAS, ELSIE
Handbook of Stitches. Van Nostrand-Reinhold, 1970, 64, illus.

PETTIT, FLORENCE H.
America's Printed and Painted Fabrics, 1600-1900. Hastings House, 1970, 256, illus.

PIVNICK, ESTHER B.
Making a Skirt: Including Designs, Patterns, and Adjustments. Hearthside Press, 1967, 126, illus.

POLLARD, L. BELLE
Experiences with Clothing. Ginn, 1965, 403.

POULIN, CLARENCE
Poulin's Garment Altering and Repairing and Tailor Shop Management. Rev. ed. The author, Penacock, N.H., 1967 99, illus.

RAPHEL, MURRY
How to Promote an Infants' and Children's Wear Store. Fairchild, 1960, 58.

REICHMAN, CHARLES
Knitting Dictionary. National Knitted Outerwear Association, New York, 1966, 131, illus.
——, ED.
Advanced Knitting Principles. National Knitted Outerwear Association, New York, 1964, 224, illus. (Knit Goods Technology Manuals.)
——, ED.
Double Knit Fabric Manual. National Knitted Outerwear Association, New York, 1961, 160, illus.
——, ED.
Guide to Manufacture of Sweaters, Knit Shirts and Swimwear. Knitted Outerwear Association, New York, 1963, 203, illus.
——, ED.
Handbook of Knitting Yarns and Knitwear Dyeing Processes. National Knitted Outerwear Association, New York, 1962, 156, illus.
——, ED.
Knitted Stretch Technology. National Knitted Outerwear Association, New York, 1965, 1 vol., illus.
——, ED.
Principles of Knitting Outerwear Fabrics and Garments: A Manual on Basic Stitch Formation and Machine Types. National Knitted Outerwear Association, New York, 1961, 193, illus.

REICHMAN, CHARLES, LANCASHIRE, J. B., and DARLINGTON, K. D.
Knitted Fabric Primer. National Knitted Outerwear Association, 1967, 89, illus.

RHEA, MINI, and LEIGHTON, FRANCES S.
Sew Simply, Sew Right. Fleet, New York, 1969, 215, illus.

RISLEY, CHRISTINE
Machine Embroidery. Branford, Newton Centre, Mass., 1961, 128, illus. (Vista Books.)

ROACH, MARY E., and EICHER, JOANNE B., EDS.
Dress, Adornment, and the Social Order. Wiley, 1965, 429.

ROBINSON, RENEE, and ROBINSON, JULIAN
Streamlined Dressmaking. Crown, 1967, 128, illus.

ROHR, MAYER
Draping: Women's & Misses' Garment Design. Rohr, Waterford, Conn., 1968, 1 vol.
——.
Grading: Women's and Misses' Garment Design, Including Junior, Petite and Teens. Rohr, Waterford, Conn., 1970, 32, illus.
——.
Pattern Drafting and Grading: Women's and Misses' Garment Design. Rev. ed. Rohr, Waterford, Conn., 1968, 1 vol., illus.
——.
Pattern Drafting: Children's Garment Design, Including Grading, Junior Petite, Sub-Teens & Teens. Rohr, Waterford, Conn., 1967, 1 vol., illus.

ROSHCO, BERNARD
The Rag Race: How New York and Paris Run the Breakneck Business of Dressing American Women. Funk & Wagnalls, 1963, 308.

ROWE, PATRICIA L.
Shorthand Fashion Sketching. 5th ed. Fairchild, 1966, 93, illus.

RUSS, STEPHEN
Fabric Printing by Hand. Watson-Guptill, 1965, 112, illus.

RYAN, MARY S.
Clothing: A Study in Human Behavior. Holt, 1966, 341, illus.

THE SALESMAN'S GUIDE, INC.
Men's and Boys' Wear Buyers' Nationwide Directory. Salesman's Guide, 1970, 1 vol.
——.
Women's and Children's Wear and Fashion Accessories Buyers' Nationwide Directory. Salesman's Guide, 1970, 1 vol.

SANDLER, NATHAN
A Basic Understanding of Patternmaking. Sandler, Syosset, N.Y., 1968, 136, illus.

SARA, DOROTHY
The Key to Needlepoint. Tower Publications, New York, 1970, 91, illus.

SCHNEIDER, COLEMAN
Machine Made Embroideries. International Corp., 1968, 238, illus.

SCHWEBKE, PHYLLIS W.
How to Tailor: A Handbook for Home Tailoring. Bruce, 1965, 168, illus.

SCHWEBKE, PHYLLIS W., and KROHN, MARGARET B.
How to Sew: Leather, Suede and Fur. Bruce, 1966, 148, illus.

COMMERCIAL PROGRAMS

SEARLE, VALERIE, and CLAYSON, ROBERTA
    Screen Printing on Fabric. Watson-Guptill, 1968, 104, illus. (Pocket How to Do It Book.)

SEBASTIAN, FANNIE B.
    The Fashion Festival. Christopher Publishing House, Boston, 1962, 86.

SETTLE, ALISON
    Fashion as a Career. Batsford, London, 1963, 128, illus. (Batsford Career Books.)

SLOANE, EUNICE M.
    Illustrating Fashion. Harper & Row, 1968, 319, illus.

SNOOK, BARBARA
    Making Baby Clothes. Taplinger, 1969, 111, illus.

SNYDER, RUTH
    Sewing Made Simple. Doubleday, 1963, 192, illus. (Made Simple Books.)

SOLINGER, JACOB
    Apparel Manufacturing Analysis. Textile Book Publishers, New York, 1961, 796, illus.

SPANIER, GINETTE
    It Isn't All Mink. Random House, 1960, 233, illus.

SPRINGER, JO, and HEDIN, SOLWEIG
    Creative Needlework. Arco, 1969, 128, illus.

STOHLMAN, D. G.
    Sewing Performance & Methods Analysis. 2nd ed. Needle Trades Publishing Corp., Columbia, S.C., 1969, 261, illus.

STUART, JENNIFER
    Make Your Own Hats. Bell, London, 1968, 111, illus.

STURM, MARY M., and GRIESER, EDWINA H.
    Guide to Modern Clothing. 2nd ed. McGraw-Hill, 1968, 590, illus. (American Home and Family Series.)

TANOUS, HELEN N.
    Designing Dress Patterns. Bennett, 1964, 208, illus.

TATE, MILDRED B., and GLISSON, ORIS
    Family Clothing. Wiley, 1961, 412, illus.

TAYLOR, JOHN
    It's a Small, Medium and Outsize World. World, 1967, 132, illus.

TIDBALL, HARRIET
    The Weaver's Book: Fundamentals of Handweaving. Macmillan, 1961, 173.

TOVEY, JOHN
    Weaves and Pattern Drafting. Van Nostrand-Reinhold, 1969, 103, illus.

TYROLER, ELSÉ
    Sewing Pants for Women: A Guide to Perfect Fit. Hearthside Press, 1963, 64, illus.

VANDERHOFF, MARGIL
    Clothes: Part of Your World. Ginn, 1968, 275, illus.

VECCHIO, WALTER
    The Fashion Makers: A Photographic Record. Crown, 1968, 277, illus.

WALCOFF, CHARLES
    Industrial Needle Trades. New Brunswick, N.J., Department of Education (Vocational Division), 1961, 306, illus.

WALKER, BARBARA G.
    A Treasury of Knitting Patterns. Scribner's, 1967, 1 vol.

WARDEN, JESSIE, GOLDING, MARTHA ANN, and STAM, JUDY
    Principles for Creating Clothing: A Visual Approach. Wiley, 1969, 274.

WAUGH, NORAH
    The Cut of Men's Clothes, 1600-1900. Theatre Arts Books, 1964, 160, illus.

———.
    The Cut of Women's Clothes, 1600-1930. Theatre Arts Books, 1968, 336, illus.

WHIFE, ARCHIBALD A.
    The Art of Garment Making. Rev. ed. Tailor & Cutter, London, 1967, 149.

———.
    The Art of Measuring for All Kinds of Tailor-Made Garments. Rev. ed. Tailor & Cutter, London, 1961, 42.

WIGNALL, HARRY
    Hosiery Technology. National Knitted Outerwear Association, New York, 1968, 151.

———.
    Knitting. Pitman, 1964, 132.

WILLIAMS, ELSA S.
    Bargello Embroidery. Van Nostrand-Reinhold, 1967, 64, illus.

———.
    Heritage Embroidery. Van Nostrand-Reinhold, 1967, 112, illus.

WILSON, EUNICE
    A History of Shoe Fashions: A Study of Shoe Design in Relation to Costume for Shoe Designers, Pattern Cutters, Manufacturers, Fashion Students and Dress Designers.... Theatre Arts Books, 1969, 334, illus.

WILSON, JOHN K.
    The Art of Cutting and Fitting. 4th ed. Tailor & Cutter, London, 1966, 90.

WINTERS, ARTHUR W.
    Fashion Sales Promotion Handbook. 3rd ed. Fashion Institute of Technology, 1967, 128.

WOLD, BLANCHE
    A Unit Method of Sewing. Brown, 1960, 142, illus.

COSTUME

BOUCHER, FRANCOIS L. L.
    20,000 Years of Fashion: The History of Costume and Personal Adornment. Abrams, 1967, 441, illus.

BRADFIELD, NANCY M.
    Costume in Detail: Women's Dress 1730-1930. Plays, Boston, 1968, 391, illus.

BRADSHAW, ANGELA
    World Costumes. Macmillan, 1965, 191, illus.

BRAUN-RONSDORF, MARGARETE
    Mirror of Fashion: A History of European Costume, 1789-1929. O. Coburn, tr. McGraw-Hill, 1964, 270.

BROBY-JOHANSEN, RUDOLF
    Body and Clothes: An Illustrated History of Costume. Reinhold, 1968, 235, illus.

BROOKE, IRIS
    Medieval Theater Costume: A Practical Guide to the Construction of Garments. Theatre Arts Books, 1967, 111, illus.

BRUHN, WOLFGANG, and TILKE, MAX
    A Pictorial History of Costume.... Praeger, 1965, 74. (Books That Matter.)

CUNNINGTON, CECIL W., and CUNNINGTON, PHILLIS E.
    Handbook of English Costume in the Nineteenth Century. 2nd ed. Faber & Faber, 1967, 606, illus.

———.
    Handbook of English Mediaeval Costume. Plays, Boston, 1969, 210, illus.

———.
 A Picture History of English Costume. Macmillan, 1960, 160, illus. (Picture Histories Series.)

CUNNINGTON, CECIL W., CUNNINGTON, PHILLIS E., and BEARD, CHARLES
 A Dictionary of English Costume [900-1900]. Dufour, 1960, 281, illus.

CUNNINGTON, PHILLIS E.
 Costume in Pictures. Dutton, 1964, 160, illus. (Dutton Vista Picturebook.)

———.
 Medieval and Tudor Costume. Plays, Boston, 1968, 77, illus.

CUNNINGTON, PHILLIS E., and BUCK, ANNE
 Children's Costume in England: From the Fourteenth to the End of the Nineteenth Century. Barnes & Noble, 1965, 235, illus.

CUNNINGTON, PHILLIS E., and LUCAS, CATHERINE
 Occupational Costume in England: From the Eleventh Century to 1914. Barnes & Noble, 1967, 427, illus.

CUNNINGTON, PHILLIS E., and MANSFIELD, ALAN
 English Costume for Sports and Outdoor Recreation: From the Sixteenth to the Nineteenth Centuries. Barnes & Noble, 1970, 388, illus.

GERNSHEIM, ALISON
 Fashion and Reality, 1840-1914. Faber & Faber, 1963, 104, illus.

GIBBS-SMITH, CHARLES H.
 The Fashionable Lady in the 19th Century. HMSO, London, 1960, 184, illus.

HILL, MARGOT H., and BUCKNELL, PETER A.
 The Evolution of Fashion: Pattern and Cut From 1066 to 1930. Van Nostrand-Reinhold, 1967, 225, illus.

HUENEFELD, IRENE P.
 International Directory of Historical Clothing. Scarecrow Press, 1967, 175.

KELLY, FRANCIS M., and SCHWABE, RANDOLPH
 Historic Costume: A Chronicle of Fashion in Western Europe. B. Blom, 1968, 305, illus.

KÖHLER, KARL
 A History of Costume. Dover, 1963, 463, illus.

LAVER, JAMES
 The Concise History of Costume and Fashion. Abrams, 1970, 288, illus.

———.
 Costume. Hawthorn, 1964, 135, illus.

———.
 Costume in Antiquity. Potter, 1964, 139, illus. (Plates drawn and arranged by Erhard Klepper.)

———.
 Costume in the Theatre. Hill & Wang, 1965, 212, illus.

———.
 Costume Through the Ages. Simon & Schuster, 1963, 144, illus. (Plates drawn and arranged by Erhard Keppler.)

———.
 Women's Dress in the Jazz Age. H. Hamilton, London, 1964, 63, illus. (Hamish Hamilton Monograph.)

LESTER, KATHERINE M., and KERR, ROSE N.
 Historic Costume: A Resume of Style and Fashion from Remote Times to the Nineteen-Sixties. 6th ed. C. A. Bennett, 1967, 287, illus.

LISTER, MARGOT
 Costume: An Illustrated Survey from Ancient Times to the 20th Century. Plays, Boston, 1968, 346, illus.

MORTON, GRACE M., et al.
 The Arts of Costume and Personal Appearance. 3rd ed. Wiley, 1964, 319, illus.

NEVINSON, JOHN L.
 Origin and Early History of the Fashion Plate. Smithsonian Press, Washington, 1967, 92, illus.

OAKES, ALMA, and HAMILTON-HILL, MARGOT
 Rural Costume: Its Origin and Development in Western Europe and the British Isles. Van Nostrand-Reinhold, 1970, 256, illus.

PAYNE, BLANCHE
 History of Costume: From the Ancient Egyptians to the Twentieth Century. Harper & Row, 1965, 607, illus.

PISTOLESE, ROSANA, and HORSTING, RUTH
 The History of Fashions. Wiley, 1970, 336.

STAVRIDI, MARGARET
 History of Costume. Plays, Boston, 1968, 3 vols.

STIBBERT, FREDERIC
 Civil and Military Clothing in Europe: From the First to the Eighteenth Century. B. Blom, 1968, 1 vol., illus.

TRAHEY, JANE, COMP.
 Harper's Bazaar: 100 Years of the American Female. Random House, 1967, 307, illus.

TRUMAN, NEVIL
 Historic Costuming. 2nd ed. Pitman, 1966, 170, illus.

WARWICK, EDWARD, PITZ, HENRY C., and WYCKOFF, ALEXANDER
 Early American Dress: The Colonial and Revolutionary Periods. B. Blom, 1965, 428, illus. (History of American Dress Vol. 2.)

WILCOX, RUTH T.
 The Dictionary of Costume. Scribner's, 1969, 406, illus.

———.
 Five Centuries of American Costume. Scribner's, 1963, 207, illus.

———.
 Folk and Festival Costume of the World. Scribner's, 1965, 1 vol., illus.

WOMEN'S WEAR DAILY
 Sixty Years of Fashion: 1900-1960. Fairchild, 1963, 40, illus.

YARWOOD, DOREEN
 English Costume: From the Second Century B. C. to 1967. 3rd ed. Batsford, London, 1967, 302.

———.
 Outline of English Costume. Plays, Boston, 1968, 48.

JEWELRY

BRYNNER, IRENA
 Modern Jewelry: Design and Technique. Van Nostrand-Reinhold, 1968, 96, illus.

DAVIS, MARY L., and PACK, GRETA
 Mexican Jewelry. University of Texas, 1963, 1 vol.

FRANKE, LOIS E.
 Handwrought Jewelry. McKnight & McKnight, 1962, 222, illus.

GRANDO, MICHAEL D.
 Jewelry: Form and Technique. Van Nostrand-Reinhold, 1970, 80, illus.

HUGHES, GRAHAM
 Modern Jewelry: An International Survey, 1890-1963. Crown, 1963, 256.

LAMMER, JUTTA
 Make Your Own Costume Jewelry. Watson-Guptill, 1965, 56, illus.

COMMERCIAL PROGRAMS

MORTON, PHILIP
    Contemporary Jewelry: A Studio Handbook. Holt, 1970, 308, illus.

PACK, GRETA
    Jewelry Making by the Lost Wax Process. Van Nostrand-Reinhold, 1968, 128, illus.

ROSE, AUGUSTUS F., and CIRINO, ANTONIO
    Jewelry Making and Design: An Illustrated Textbook for Teachers, Students of Design and Craft Workers. 4th ed. Dover, 1967, 306, illus.

SELWYN, ARNOLD
    The Retail Jeweller's Handbook and Merchandise Manual for Sales Personnel. 7th ed. Heywood, London, 1962, 381, illus.

SHOENFELT, JOSEPH F.
    Designing and Making Handwrought Jewelry. McGraw-Hill, 1960, 170, illus.

VON NEUMANN, ROBERT
    The Design and Creation of Jewelry. Chilton, 1961, 228, illus.

WASLEY, RUTH, and HARRIS, EDITH
    Bead Design: A Comprehensive Course for Beginner and Experienced Craftsmen. Crown, 216, illus.

WIENER, LOUIS
    Handmade Jewelry: A Manual of Techniques with A Section on Metal Enameling. 2nd ed. Van Nostrand, 1960, 221, illus.

ZECHLIN, KATHARINA
    Creative Enameling and Jewelry Making. Sterling, 1965, 1 vol.

TEXTILES

ADVANCES IN TEXTILE PROCESSING
    Textile Book Publishing, New York, 1961- , Vol. 1- , illus.

AMERICAN ASSOCIATION OF TEXTILE CHEMISTS AND COLORISTS
    Technical Manual and Yearbook. Howes, New York, 1923- , annual.

AMERICAN FABRICS ENCYCLOPEDIA OF TEXTILES
    Prentice-Hall, 1960, 702, illus.

AMERICAN HOME ECONOMICS ASSOCIATION
    Textile Handbook. 3rd ed. AHEA, 1966, 110.

AMERICAN SOCIETY FOR TESTING MATERIALS
    ASTM Manual on Quality Control of Materials. ASTM, 1933- .

BACKER, STANLEY, and VALKO, EMERY I., EDS.
    Thesaurus of Textile Terms. 2nd ed. MIT Press, 1969, 448.

BARNHARDT, ROBERT A.
    Opportunities in Textile Careers. Universal Publishing & Distributing, 1966, 128. (VGM Career Series V161.)

BOOTH, JOHN E.
    Principles of Textile Testing. 3rd ed. Chemical, 1969, 570.

CARROLL-PORCZYNSKI, CHARLES Z.
    Manual of Man-Made Fibres: Manufacture, Properties, Identification. Chemical, 1960, 304, illus.

CHEETHAM, ROBERT
    Dyeing Fibre Blends: The Processing of Blends, Unions and Mixtures Containing Natural or Man-Made Fibres. Van Nostrand, 1966, 371, illus.

CLARKE, LESLIE J.
    The Craftsman in Textiles. Praeger, 1968, 144, illus.

CONE MILLS CORPORATION, RESEARCH & DEVELOPMENT DIVISION
    Textile Finishing Glossary: 1967 Glossary of Words Commonly Used by the Textile Finishing Industry. 4th ed. Cone, Greensboro, N.C., 1967, 67.

CONE, SYDNEY M., JR.
    Aim for a Job in the Textile Industry. R. Rosen Press, 1969, 155, illus. (Aim High Vocational Guidance Series.)

COWAN, MARY L., and JUNGERMAN, MARTHA E.
    Introduction to Textiles. 2nd ed. Appleton-Century-Crofts, 1969, 326, illus.

DAN RIVER MILLS, INC.
    A Dictionary of Textile Terms. 10th ed. Dan River Mills, Danville, Va., 1967, 127.

DAVISON'S TEXTILE "BLUE BOOK"
    Davison, New York, 1888- , Vol. 1- , illus., annual.

DEMBECK, ADELINE A.
    Guidebook to Man-Made Textile Fibers and Textured Yarns of the World: Film-to Yarn Non-Wovens. Rev. ed. United Piece Dye Works, 1969, 348.

DENNY, GRACE G.
    Fabrics. 8th ed. Lippincott, 1962, 163, illus.

ENGLISH, WALTER
    The Textile Industry: An Account of the Early Inventions of Spinning, Weaving and Knitting Machines. Harlow, Longmans, London, (Humanities, dist.), 1969, 242, illus. (Industrial Archaeology, 4.)

GARNER, WALTER
    Textile Laboratory Manual. 3rd ed. Elsevier, 1966- , Vol. 1- , illus.

GROVER, ELLIOT B., and HAMBY, DAME S.
    Handbook of Textile Testing and Quality Control. Textile Book Publishing, New York, 1960, 614, illus.

HALL, ARCHIBALD J.
    The Standard Handbook of Textiles. 6th ed. Chemical, 1965, 340, illus.

HAMBY, DAME S.
    The American Cotton Handbook. 3rd ed. Interscience, 1965.

HARTUNG, ROLF
    Creative Textile Design: Thread and Fabric. Van Nostrand-Reinhold, 1964, 96, illus.

―――.
    More Creative Textile Design: Color and Texture. Van Nostrand-Reinhold, 1965, 100, illus.

HATHORNE, BERKELEY L.
    Woven Stretch and Textured Fabrics. Interscience, 1964, 359, illus.

HEARLE, J. W. S., and PETERS, RAYMOND H., EDS.
    Fibre Structure. Textile Institute, Manchester, England, 1963, 667, illus.

HOLLEN, NORMA R., and SADDLER, JANE
    Textiles. 3rd ed. Macmillan, 1968, 243, illus.

HOWELL, LEANDER D.
    The American Textile Industry: Competition, Structure, Facilities, Costs. USGPO, 1964, 146, illus. (Agricultural Economic Report No. 58.)

JOSEPH, MARJORY L.
    Introductory Textile Science. Holt, Rinehart & Winston, 1966, 450, illus.

KASWELL, ERNEST R.
    Wellington Sears Handbook of Industrial Textiles. Wellington Sears Co., New York, 1963, 757, illus.

KLAPPER, MARVIN
    Fabric Almanac. Fairchild, 1966, 139, illus.

KOCH, PAUL A.
    Microscopic and Chemical Testing of Textiles. Textile Book Service, New York, 1963, 217, illus.

KOPYCINSKI, JOSEPH V.
    Textile Industry: Information Sources: An Annotated Guide to the Literature of Textile Fibers, Dyes and Dyeing, Design and Decoration Weaving, Machinery, and Other Subjects. Gale, 1964, 194. (Management Information Guide No. 4.)

KORNREICH, E.
    Introduction to Fibres and Fabrics: Their Manufacture and Properties. 2nd ed. Elsevier, 1966, 1 vol.

LABARTHE, JULES
    Textiles: Origins to Usage. Macmillan, 1964, 562, illus.

LINTON, GEORGE E.
    Applied Basic Textiles: Raw Material, Construction, Color, and Finish Fabric Analysis; Chemical and Physical Testing of Textiles; Spot and Stain Removal and Care of Clothing. Duell, 1966, 472, illus.

———.
    Applied Textiles: Raw Materials to Finished Fabrics. 6th ed. Duell, Sloan & Pearce, 1961, 542, illus.

———.
    The Modern Textile Dictionary. 3rd ed. Duell, Sloan & Pearce, 1963, 1077, illus.

———.
    Natural and Man-Made Textile Fibers: Raw Material to Finished Fabric. Duell, 1966, 420, illus.

LYLE, DOROTHY S.
    Focus on Fabrics. National Institute of Drycleaning, Silver Spring, Md., 1964, 571, illus.

MARK, HERMAN F., ATLAS, SHELDON M., and CERNIA, E.
    Man-Made Fibers: Science and Technology. Interscience, 1967- , Vol. 1, illus. (Polymer Engineering and Technology.)

MARSH, JOHN T.
    Crease Resisting Fabrics. Reinhold, 1962, 399, illus.

———.
    An Introduction to Textile Finishing. 2nd ed. Textile Book Service, Metuchen, N.J., 1966, 559, illus.

MILLER, EDWARD
    Textiles: Properties and Behavior. Theatre Arts Books, 1969, 192, illus.

MONCRIEFF, R. W.
    Man-Made Fibres. 4th ed. Wiley, 1966, 742, illus. (Hollywood Books.)

MOSS, ARCHIBALD J. E.
    Textiles and Fabrics: Their Care and Preservation. Chemical, 1961, 560, illus.

NEW YORK (STATE) EDUCATION DEPARTMENT, BUREAU OF CONTINUING EDUCATION (CURRICULUM DEVELOPMENT.)
    Tips for Teaching: Textile and Clothing. New York Education Department, Albany, 1969, 46.

ONIONS, W. J.
    Wool: An Introduction to Its Properties, Varieties, Uses and Production. Interscience, 1962, 278, illus.

PIZZUTO, JOSEPH J.
    Fabric Science: Workbook and Lectures. 4th ed. Textile Press, Pelham, N.Y., 1965, 182, illus.

POTTER, MAURICE D., and CORBMAN, BERNARD P.
    Textiles: Fiber to Fabric. 4th ed. McGraw-Hill, 1967, 495, illus.

PROUD, NORA
    Introducing Textile Printing. Watson-Guptill, 1968, 88, illus.

———.
    Textile Printing and Dyeing. Reinhold, 1965, 118, illus.

RANNEY, MAURICE W.
    Creaseproofing Textiles. Noyes, 1970, 460, illus.

———.
    Flame Retardant Textiles.... Noyes, 1970, 373, illus.

———.
    Soil Resistant Textiles. Noyes, 1970, 216, illus. (Textile Processing Review No. 5.)

———.
    Waterproofing Textiles. Noyes, 1970, 353, illus.

REICHMAN, CHARLES, ED.
    Wool and Synthetic Handbook. National Knitted Outerwear Association, New York, 1967, 192, illus.

ROBINSON, STUART
    A History of Dyed Textiles: Dyes, Fibres, Painted Bark, Batik, Starch-Resist, Discharge, Tie-Dye, Further Sources for Research. MIT Press, 1970, 112, illus.

———.
    A History of Printed Textiles: Block, Roller, Screen Design, Dyes, Fibres, Discharge, Resist, Further Sources for Research. MIT Press, 1970, 152, illus.

ROWAN, RICHARD L.
    The Negro in the Textile Industry. University of Pennsylvania Press, 1970, 1 vol. (Racial Policies of American Industry, Report No. 20.)

RUHM, HERMAN D., JR.
    Marketing Textiles. Fairchild, 1970, 127.

SCHMIDLIN, HANS U.
    Preparation and Dyeing of Synthetic Fibres. Reinhold, 1963, 462, illus.

STOUT, EVELYN E.
    Introduction to Textiles. 3rd ed. Wiley, 1970, 434.

THOMPSON, FRANCIS G.
    Harris Tweed: The Story of a Hebridean Industry. A. M. Kelley, 1969, 191, illus.

TROTMAN, EDWARD R.
    Dyeing and Chemical Technology of Textile Fibers. 3rd ed. Griffin, London, 1964, 639, illus.

UNITED PIECE DYE WORKS
    Guidebook to Man-Made Textile Fibers and Textured Yarns of the World. 3rd ed. United Piece Dye, 1969, 345, illus.

U.S. BUREAU OF LABOR STATISTICS
    Technology and Manpower in the Textile Industry of the 1970's. USGPO, 1968, 87, (Bulletin No. 1578.)

U.S. GENERAL SERVICES ADMINISTRATION
    Textile Test Methods. USGSA, 1968, 1 vol. (Federal Test Method Standard No. 191.)

UNITED STATES OF AMERICA STANDARDS INSTITUTE
    USA Standard Performance Requirements for Textile Fabrics. USASI, 1968, 1 vol.

VON BERGEN, WERNER, ED.
    Wool Handbook: A Text and Reference Book for the Entire Wool Industry. 3rd ed. Wiley, 1963- , illus.

WARD, D. T.
    Tufting: An Introduction. Textile Business Press, Manchester, England, 1969, 135.

WEINER, JACK, ROTH, LILLIAN, and POLLOCK, VERA
    Nonwoven Fabrics. Institute of Paper Chemistry, Appleton, Wis., 1969, 4 vols.

WINGATE, ISABEL B.
    Fairchild's Dictionary of Textiles. 5th ed. Fairchild, 1970, 670.

———.
    Textile Fabrics and Their Selection. 6th ed. Prentice-Hall, 1970, 657, illus.

COMMERCIAL PROGRAMS

WINGATE, ISABEL B., and BURKHOLDER, RALPH
    Laboratory Swatch Book: Textile Fabrics and Their Selection. 6th ed. W. C. Brown, 1970, 1 vol.

FOOD SCIENCE

AAGAARD, ORLENA
    Tasty Cooking for Ulcer Diets. Crown, 1964, 191.

ALD, ROY
    The Complete Soup Cookbook. Prentice-Hall, 1969, 224, illus.

AMENDOLA, JOSEPH
    Ice Carving Made Easy. Rev. ed. Radio City, New York, 1965, 88, illus.

AMERICAN GAS ASSOCIATION, INC.
    Commercial Kitchens. AGA, 1962, 258, illus.

AMERICAN HERITAGE
    The American Heritage Cookbook and Illustrated History of American Eating and Drinking. American Heritage, 1964, 629.

AMERICAN HOSPITAL ASSOCIATION
    Being a Food Service Worker: Student Manual. AHA, Chicago, 1967, 276.

    ———.
    Food Purchasing Guide. AHA, Chicago, 1966, 43.

    ———.
    Food Service Manual for Health Care Institutions. AHA, Chicago, 1966, 332, illus.

    ———.
    Training the Food Service Worker: Instructor's Guide. AHA, Chicago, 1967, 155.

AMERICAN MEAT INSTITUTE FOUNDATION
    The Science of Meat and Meat Products. Reinhold, 1960, 438, illus. (Agricultural Science Series: Animal Science.)

ANDREWS, HELEN H.
    Food Preparation. McGraw-Hill (Canada), 1967, 147, illus. (McGraw-Hill Foundation Series.)

ANGIER, BRADFORD
    Gourmet Cooking for Free. Stackpole, 1970, 190, illus.

ARBUCKLE, WENDELL S.
    Ice Cream. AVI, 1966, 403, illus.

ARCO PUBLISHING COMPANY, INC.
    Dietician. Arco, 1965, 180.

    ———.
    Food Service Supervisor - School Lunch Manager. Arco, 1968, 256.

ARKIN, FRIEDA
    The Cook's Companion: A Dictionary of Culinary Tips and Terms. Doubleday, 1968, 172, illus.

ASSOCIATION OF SCHOOL BUSINESS OFFICIALS OF THE U.S. AND CANADA (RESEARCH COMMITTEE IN SCHOOL FUND SERVICE MANAGEMENT)
    School Food Purchasing Guide: A Special Committee Report. American School Food Service Association, 1968, 144, illus. (Bulletin No. 3.)

AXLER, BRUCE H.
    The Cheese Handbook. Hastings House, 1969, 213.

AYKROYD, WALLACE R.
    The Story of Sugar. Quadrangle Books, 1967, 160, illus.

AYRES, J. C., et al., eds.
    The Safety of Foods: An International Symposium on the Safety and Importance of Foods in the Western Hemisphere Held at the University of Puerto Rico. AVI, 1968, 367, illus.

BARNARD, CAPEL
    The Art of Flambé Cooking. Iliffe Books, London, 1965, 149, illus.

BARROWS, ARTHUR B.
    Profitable Catering. Maclaren, London, 1967, 249, illus.

BEARD, JAMES
    Hors d'Oeuvre and Canapés. Rev. ed. M. Barrows, 1963, 206.

BEAU, FRANK N.
    Quantity Food Processing Guide. Cahners, 1970, 84.

BEILENSON, EDNA
    Festive Seafood Cookery. Peter Pauper, 1969, 60, illus.

BEINERT, FREDERICA L.
    The Art of Making Sauces and Gravies. Doubleday, 1966, 292, illus.

    ———.
    The Art of Making Soufflés. Doubleday, 1967, 264, illus.

BENDER, ARNOLD E.
    Dictionary of Nutrition and Food Technology. 3rd ed. Archon Books, 1968, 143.

    ———.
    Dietetic Foods. Chemical, 1968, 286, illus.

BETTER HOMES & GARDENS
    Better Homes & Gardens New Cook Book. Rev. ed. Meredith Press, 1970, 400, illus.

    ———.
    Famous Foods from Famous Places. Meredith Press, 1964, 224, illus.

    ———.
    Meat Cook Book. Meredith Press, 1969, 160, illus.

    ———.
    Salad Book. Meredith Press, 1969, 160, illus.

BINSTED, RAYMOND, DEVEY, JAMES D., and DAKIN, JOHN C.
    Pickle and Sauce Making. 2nd ed. Food Trade Press, London, 1962, 274, illus.

BLAIR, EULALIA C., and VOLUME FEEDING MANAGEMENT MAGAZINE
    Professional's Recipe Master. Hayden, 1967, 403, illus.

BORGSTRÖM, GEORG
    Fish as Food. Academic Press, 1961, 1 vol., illus.

    ———.
    Principles of Food Science. Macmillan, 2 vols., 1968, illus.

BOWES, ANNA D., and CHURCH, CHARLES F.
    Food Values of Portions Commonly Used. 11th ed. Lippincott, 1970, 180.

BRANDLY, PAUL J., MIGAKI, GEORGE, and TAYLOR, KENNETH E.
    Meat Hygiene. 3rd ed. Lea & Febiger, 1966, 789, illus.

BREITHAUPT, HERMAN A.
    Commercial Cooking: An Instructional Guide for the Hospitality Industry. H. A. Breithaupt, 1970, 117.

BRENNAN, J. G., et al.
    Food Engineering Operations. Elsevier, 1969, 443, illus.

BRENT, CAROL D., ED.
    Blending: The Fine Art of Modern Blending. Rev. ed. Doubleday, 1969, 200, illus.

BRISSEY, GEORGE E.
    Your Future in Food Technology. R. Rosen Press, 1966, 159, illus. (Careers in Depth No. 67.)

FOOD SCIENCE

BRODNER, JOSEPH, CARLSON, HOWARD M., and MASCHAL, HENRY T., EDS.
Profitable Food and Beverage Operation. 4th ed. Ahrens, 1962, 458, illus.

BROTHWELL, DON, and BROTHWELL, PATRICIA
Food in Antiquity: A Survey of the Diet of Early Peoples. Praeger, 1969, 248, illus. (Ancient Peoples and Places Vol. 66.)

BRUNNER, LOUSENE R.
Casserole Treasury. Harper & Row, 1964, 310.

CARRIER, ROBERT
Great Dishes of the World. Random House, 1963, 279, illus.

CARUBA, REBECCA
Cooking with Wine and High Spirits: A Lighthearted Approach to the Art of Gourmet Cooking. Cornerstone, New York, 1970, 155, illus.

CASOLA, MATTEO
Successful Mass Cookery and Volume Feeding. Ahrens, 1969, 308.

CAVANAGH, URSULA M.
Cooking and Catering: The Wholefood Way. Faber & Faber, 1970, 140.

CAVELLERO, GENE
The Colony Cookbook. Bobbs-Merrill, 1970, 212, illus.

CHAMPION, ROMAINE
The Art of Cooking Omelettes. Doubleday, 1963, 165.

CHARLEY, HELEN
Food Study Manual. Ronald, 1961, 1 vol., illus.

CHEMICAL RUBBER COMPANY
Handbook of Food Additives. Chemical Rubber, 1968, 771, illus.

CLAIBORNE, CRAIG
Cooking with Herbs and Spices. Harper & Row, 1970, 1 vol., illus.

———.
An Herb and Spice Cook Book. Harper & Row, 1963, 334, illus.

———.
The New York Times Menu Cook Book. Harper & Row, 1966, 727, illus.

CLARK, MORTON G.
A World of Nut Recipes. Funk & Wagnalls, 1969, 248.

CLARKE, HAROLD C.
Menu Terminology. Pergamon, 1969, 86.

COLLINS, MARY
The McCormick Spices of the World Cookbook. McGraw-Hill, 1964, 330, illus.

CONFERENCE ON FOOD SERVICE INDUSTRY, MANPOWER AND EDUCATION, CHICAGO, 1967
Manpower and Education for the Food Service Industry. National Restaurant Association, Chicago, 1967, 62.

CORNELL UNIVERSITY, SCHOOL OF HOTEL ADMINISTRATION
Tested Quantity Recipes. Cornell University, 1967, 130, illus.

CRANE, WARREN E.
Delectable Desserts. Hayden, 1964, 128, illus.

CROCKER, BETTY
Betty Crocker's Cookbook. Rev. ed. Golden Press, 1969, 1 vol.

CRONAN, MARION L.
The School Lunch. Bennett, 1962, 512, illus.

CROSBY, JUNE, and BATEMAN, RUTH C.
Serve It Cold: A Cookbook of Delicious Cold Dishes. Doubleday, 1969, 224, illus.

CRUM, GERTRUDE
A World of Menus and Recipes. Bobbs-Merrill, 1970, 1 vol.

CRUSE, HELOISE
Heloise's Kitchen Hints. Prentice-Hall, 1963, 186, illus.

CULINARY INSTITUTE OF AMERICA
Introduction to Professional Food Service. Cahners, 1968, 291, illus.

———.
The Professional Chef. 2nd ed. Cahners, 1966, 354, illus.

DALE, MARTIN
How to Read a French Menu. Appleton-Century, 1966, 95, illus.

DALLIN, LYNN
The Pregnant Woman's Low Calorie Cookbook. Doubleday, 1969, 294.

DAY, AVANELLE, and STUCKEY, L.
The Spice Cookbook. David White, 1964, 623.

DE BAUN, STEPHEN
Bountiful Breakfasts: Morning Menu Magic from a Nantucket Inn. Simon & Schuster, 1970, 64.

DeSOLA, RALPH, and DeSOLA, DOROTHY, COMPS.
A Dictionary of Cooking: Approximately Eight Thousand Definitions of Culinary Ingredients, Methods, Terms and Utensils. Meredith Press, 1969, 246.

DESROSIER, NORMAN W.
Attack on Starvation. AVI, 1961, 320.

DICKSON, WILLIAM G., ED.
Quantity Cooking: Basic Skills. Delmar, 1966, 112.

DONALDSON, BEATRICE, and JOHNSON, VIRGINIA K., COMPS.
Standardized Quantity Recipes. College Printing & Typing, Madison, Wis., 1968, 231.

DONOVAN, ANNE C., and IVES, ORVILLE B.
Hospital Dietary Services: A Planning Guide. HEW, 1966, 68, illus. (Hospital and Medical Facilities Series.)

DRURY, JOHN
Rare and Well Done: Some Historical Notes on Meats and Meatmen. Quadrangle Books, 1966, 186, illus.

DYER, CEIL
The Back to Cooking Cookbook. Price, Stern, Sloan, 1970, 157, illus.

ELLIOTT, TRAVIS
Food Service Management. Shoe String, 1970, 212.

EMERY, WILLIAM H.
A Manual of Catering. Baillière, Tindall & Cox, London, 1961, 318, illus.

ERICKSON, CHARLOTTE
The Freezer Cookbook. Chilton, 1968, 411, illus.

ERICSON, MYRTLE H., ED.
Quantity Food Recipes. Cornell Hotel and Restaurant Administration Quarterly, Cornell University, 1970, 1 vol.

FANCE, WILFRED J.
The Student's Technology of Breadmaking and Flour Confectionery. 2nd ed. Routledge & Kegan, Paul, London, 1966, 443, illus.

FARBER, SEYMOUR M., WILSON, NANCY L., and WILSON, ROGER H. L.
Food and Civilization: A Symposium. Thomas, 1966, 341, illus.

COMMERCIAL PROGRAMS

FARM JOURNAL AND COUNTRY GENTLEMAN
    Freezing & Canning Cookbook: Prized Recipes from the Farms of America. Doubleday, 1964, 352, illus.

FARMER, FANNIE M.
    Fannie Farmer Boston Cookbook. 11th ed. Little, 1965, 624, illus.

FIELD, HAZEL E.
    Foods in Health and Disease: A Practical Guide. Macmillan, 214, 1964.

FIELD, MICHAEL
    All Manner of Food. Knopf, 1970, 382, illus.

———.
    Michael Field's Culinary Classics and Improvisations. Knopf, 1967, 223, illus.

FINANCE, CHARLES
    Buffet Catering. Patterson, Chicago, 1970, 256, illus.

FISHER, PATTY, and BENDER, ARNOLD E.
    The Value of Food. Oxford University Press, 1970, 174, illus.

FitzGIBBON, THEODORA
    Game Cooking: A Collection of Recipes with a Dictionary of Rare Game. A. Deutsch, London, 1963, 254.

FOGEL, WALTER A.
    The Negro in the Meat Industry. University of Pennsylvania Press, 1970, 146. (Racial Policies of American Industry, Report No. 12.)

FOLSOM, LEROI A.
    The Instructor's Guide for the Teaching of Professional Cooking. Cahners, 1967, 273. (Prepared for The Culinary Institute of America.)

FONO, PAULETTE, and STACHO, MARIA
    The Crêpe Cookbook: All About the Magic World of Crêpes. Doubleday, 1970, 98, illus. (Little Cookbook Shelf Series.)

FOWLER, SINA F., WEST, BESSIE B., and SHUGART, GRACE S.
    Food for Fifty. 4th ed. Wiley, 1961, 446, illus.

FRANDSEN, J. H., and ARBUCKLE, W. S.
    Ice Cream and Related Products. AVI, 1961, 372, illus.

FRANK, JEANNETTE
    The Modern Meat Cookbook. 2nd ed. Bobbs-Merrill, 1968, 452, illus.

FRAZIER, WILLIAM C.
    Food Microbiology. 2nd ed. McGraw-Hill, 1967, 537, illus.

FREELING, NICOLAS
    The Kitchen: A Delicious Account of the Author's Years as a Grand Hotel Cook. Harper, 1970, 155.

FULLER, JOHN
    Gueridon and Lamp Cookery, Hayden, 1964, 162, illus.

FULLER, JOHN, and RENOLD, EDWARD
    The Chef's Compendium of Professional Recipes. Rev. ed. Heineman, 1966, 340.

FUNK & WAGNALLS COOK'S AND DINER'S DICTIONARY: A LEXICON OF FOOD, WINE, AND CULINARY TERMS.
    Funk & Wagnalls, 1969, 274, illus.

GANCEL, J.
    Gancel's Culinary Encyclopedia of Modern Cooking.... 12th ed. Radio City, New York, 1969, 503.

GEE, A. C.
    Hotel and Institutional Cookery. Barrie & Rockcliff, London, 1969, 1 vol.

GEORGE, NORVIL L., and HECKLER, RUTH D.
    School Food Centers: A Guide to Operating the School Lunch Program. Ronald, 1960, 335, illus.

GIBBONS, EUELL, and GIBBONS, JOE
    Feast on a Diabetic Diet. McKay, 1969, 314.

GOOD HOUSEKEEPING INSTITUTE
    The New Good Housekeeping Cookbook. Dorothy B. Marsh, ed. Harcourt, Brace & World, 1963, 805, illus.

GOOSE, PETER, and BINSTED, RAYMOND
    Tomato Paste, Puree, Juice, and Powder. Food Trade Review, London, 1964, 1 vol., illus.

GORDON, JEAN
    Coffee Recipes: Customs, Facts, Fancies. Red Rose Publications, St. Augustine, Fla., 1963, 96, illus.

GORDON, ROBERT I., and LONDON, ANNE
    Cocktails & Snacks. World, 1965, 256, illus.

GOURMET MAGAZINE
    Gourmet's Menu Cook Book: A Collection of Epicurean Menus and Recipes. Gourmet, 1963, 652, illus.

GREGG, JOSEPH G.
    Cooking for Food Managers: A Laboratory Text—An Introduction to Quantity Food Preparation and Production for Mid-management Food Service Personnel. W. C. Brown, 1967, 148, illus. (Brown Restaurant and Hotel Management Series.)

GRIGSON, JANE
    The Art of Charcuterie. Knopf, 1968, 349, illus.

GRISWOLD, RUTH M.
    The Experimental Study of Foods. Houghton Mifflin, 1962, 577, illus.

GUNDERSON, FRANK L., GUNDERSON, HELEN W., and FERGUSON, EGBERT R., JR.
    Food Standards and Definitions in the United States: A Guidebook. Academic Press, 1963, 269, illus.

HACHTEN, HARVA
    Kitchen Safari. Atheneum, 1970, 256.

HAINES, ROBERT G.
    Food Preparation for Hotels, Restaurants, and Cafeterias. American Technical Society, 1968, 634, illus.

HALE, WILLIAM H.
    The Horizon Cookbook and Illustrated History of Eating and Drinking Through the Ages. American Heritage (Doubleday, dist.), 1968, 768, illus.

HAMM, MARIE R.
    The Second Chafing Dish Cookbook. Prentice-Hall, 1963, 237.

HAWKINS, ARTHUR
    The Complete Seafood Cookbook. Prentice-Hall, 1970, 208, illus.

HEADY, EARL O.
    A Primer on Food, Agriculture, and Public Policy. Random House, 1967, 177.

HEPTINSTALL, WILLIAM
    Gourmet Recipes from a Highland Hotel. Faber & Faber, 1967, 176.

HERSCHDOERFER, SIGISMUND M., ED.
    Quality Control in the Food Industry. Academic Press, 1967– , 3 vols. (Food Science and Technology Series of Monographs.)

HILLMAN, LIBBY
    Lessons In Gourmet Cooking. Hearthside Press, 1963, 318, illus.

HILTON INTERNATIONAL COOKBOOK
    Prentice-Hall, 1960, 206, illus.

HOBBS, BETTY C.
    Food Poisoning and Food Hygiene. 2nd ed. Edward Arnold, London, 1968, 252.

HOKE, ANN
: Restaurant Menu Planning. John Willy, Inc., Evanston, Ill., 1964, 339.

HOLTHAUSEN, HENRIETTE
: Chicken Cookery Round the World. Doubleday, 1966, 360, illus.

HOSPITALITY MAGAZINE
: The Guide to Convenience Foods. Patterson, Chicago, 1968, 320, illus.

HOUSE & GARDEN
: The Art of Carving. Simon & Schuster, 1963, 79, illus.

HUEBENER, PAUL O.
: Gourmet Table Service: A Professional Guide. Ahrens, 1968, 182, illus.

HUGHES, OSEE G.
: Introductory Food. 4th ed. Macmillan, 1962, 502, illus.

INTERNATIONAL FOODSERVICE MANUFACTURERS ASSOCIATION
: Membership Directory.... IFMA, 1970, 36.

IOWA (STATE) DEPARTMENT OF HEALTH (NUTRITION SERVICE)
: Simplified Diet Manual: With Meal Patterns. 3rd ed. Iowa State University Press, 1969, 106.

JACKSON, CHARLES O.
: Food and Drug Legislation in the New Deal. Princeton University Press, 1970, 249.

JAMES, TED, and COLE, ROSALIND
: The Waldorf-Astoria Cookbook. Bobbs-Merrill, 1969, 266, illus.

JAY, JAMES M.
: Modern Food Microbiology. Van Nostrand-Reinhold, 1970, 328, illus.

KAISER, RALPH D.
: The Menu Converter. Kaiser Co., Washington, Vol. 1- , 1968-

KAUFMAN, WILLIAM I.
: Appetizers and Canapes. Doubleday, 1968, 99. (Little Cookbook Shelf Series.)
———.
: The Art of Casserole Cookery. Doubleday, 1967, 122, illus.
———.
: The Chocolate Cookbook. Doubleday, 1968, 168, illus.
———.
: The Fish and Shellfish Cookbook. Doubleday, 1968, 99. (Little Cookbook Shelf Series.)
———.
: The Tea Cookbook. Doubleday, 1966, 188, illus.

KAUFMAN, WILLIAM I., and COOPER, MARY U.
: The Art of Creole Cookery. Doubleday, 1962, 227, illus.

KERR, GRAHAM
: The Graham Kerr Cookbook. Doubleday, 1969, 284, illus.

KINARD, MALVINA C., and BLANCHARD, MARJORIE P.
: The Kitchen Scholar. Citadel Press, 1967, 240, illus.

KINDER, FAYE
: Meal Management. 3rd ed. Macmillan, 1968, 552, illus.

KLAPTHOR, MARGARET
: The First Ladies' Cook Book: Favorite Recipes of All the Presidents of the United States. Home Library Press (for Parents Magazine Press), 1965, 224, illus.

KLEIN, CAMILLE
: The Professional Cook: His Training, Duties and Rewards. 2nd ed. Helios, 1967, 92.

KNOX, ANN
: The Sauce of Life: Sauces, Gravies, Dressings and Garnishes. Arco, 1960, 1 vol.

KOTAS, RICHARD
: An Approach to Food Costing. Barrie & Rockliff, London, 1960, 92. (Practical Press Book.)

KOTSCHEVAR, LENDAL H.
: Quantity Food Purchasing. Wiley, 1961, 619, illus.
———.
: Standards, Principles, and Techniques in Quantity Food Production. 2nd ed. McCutchan, 1966, 708, illus.

KOTSCHEVAR, LENDAL H., and McWILLIAMS, MARGARET
: Understanding Food. Wiley, 1969, 496, illus.

KOTSCHEVAR, LENDAL H., and TERRELL, MARGARET E.
: Food Service Planning: Layout and Equipment. Wiley, 1961, 449, illus.

KRAMER, AMIHUD, and TWIGG, BERNARD A.
: Fundamentals of Quality Control for the Food Industry. 3rd ed. AVI, 1970, 1 vol., illus.

KRANZ, PETER, and KRANZ, NANCY
: The Sauce Cook Book. Stein & Day, 1966, 192, illus.

LACH, ALMA
: Cooking à la Cordon Bleu. Harper & Row, 1970, 416, illus.

LAGER, MILDRED, and JONES, DOROTHEA V. G.
: The Soybean Cookbook. Arco, 1968, 256.

LANDRY, ROBERT
: The Gentle Art of Flavoring. Abelard-Schuman, New York, 1970, 1 vol.

LANGSETH-CHRISTENSEN, LILLIAN, and SMITH, CAROL S.
: The Complete Kitchen Guide: The Cook's Indispensable Book. Grosset & Dunlap, 1968, 292, illus.

LAWRIE, RALSTON A.
: Meat Science. Pergamon, 1966, 368, illus. (Commonwealth and International Library, Food Science and Technology Division, No. 2613.)

LAYTON, THOMAS A.
: The Wine and Food Society's Guide to Cheese and Cheese Cookery. World (with Wine and Food Society, Cleveland), 1967, 254, illus.

LEECH, MILTON, and MASSEY, ROBERT
: The Chicken Cookbook. Doubleday, 1968, 93, illus. (Little Cookbook Shelf Series.)

LEFLER, JANET, RUPP, MILDRED, and CHIAPPERINI, FELICE
: Canapes, Hors d'oeuvres and Buffet Dishes. Hayden, 1963, 169, illus.

LEVIE, ALBERT
: The Meat Handbook. 3rd ed. AVI, 1970, 1 vol., illus.

LEVINSON, LEONARD L.
: The Complete Book of Pickles and Relishes. Hawthorn, New York, 1965, 335.

LIGHT, LUISE
: In Praise of Vegetables. Scribner's, 1966, 265.

LITTLE, BILLIE
: Recipes for Allergies: Including a Primer for Allergies. Rev. ed. Grosset, 1969, 372.

LONGGOOD, WILLIAM F.
: The Poisons in Your Food. Simon & Schuster, 1960, 277.

LONGRÉE, KARLA
: Quantity Food Sanitation. Interscience, 1967, 397, illus.

LOWENBERG, MIRIAM E., et al.
: Food and Man. Wiley, 1968, 341, illus.

COMMERCIAL PROGRAMS

LUCAS, DIONE, and GEIS, DARLENE
 The Gourmet Cooking School Cookbook: Classic Recipes, Menus and Methods as Taught in the Classes of the Gourmet Cooking School. Bernard Geis, 1964, 366, illus.

LUNDBERG, DONALD E., and KOTSCHEVAR, LENDAL H.
 Understanding Cooking. Rev. ed. University of Massachusetts, 1967, 365. (Programed Text.)

MacALLISTER, JOHN J.
 Organizing a Food Training Program. USGPO, 1967, 1 vol. (OE-84033.)

MACKINNEY, GORDON, and LITTLE, ANGELA
 Color of Foods. AVI, 1962, 321.

MALONE, RUTH M.
 Cooking the Holiday Inn Way. Pioneer Press, Little Rock, 1962, 209.

MARQUIS, VIVIENNE, and HASKELL, PATRICIA
 The Cheese Book: A Definitive Guide to the Cheeses of the World.... Simon & Schuster, 1965, 317, illus.

MATZ, SAMUEL A.
 Food Texture. AVI, 1962, 286, illus.

———.
 Water in Foods. AVI, 1965, 275.

MAXIM'S
 Chez Maxim's: Secrets and Recipes from the World's Most Famous Restaurant. McGraw-Hill, 1962, 253, illus.

McCONNELL, MARY, ED.
 Directory of Opportunity in Service World Management [Food Service/Lodging Field]. Reconnaissance, Chicago, 1967, 195, illus.

McCULLY, HELEN, and NODERER, ELEANOR
 Just Desserts. Ivan Obolensky, Inc., 1961, 316.

McLEAN, NEMADJI B.
 Meal Planning and Service. Rev. ed. C. A. Bennett, 1964, 318, illus.

McWILLIAMS, MARGARET
 Food Fundamentals. Wiley, 1966, 379, illus.

MEHTA, K. R.
 Vegetarian Delights: A Cookbook for Health & Happiness. Exposition Press, 1966, 1 vol.

MERRIMAN, BETH
 The Fondue Cookbook. Grosset & Dunlap, 1969, 1 vol.

MEYER, HAZEL
 Hazel Meyer's Freezer Cookbook. Lippincott, 1970, 448.

MIDDLETON, ELSPETH, CARTER, MURIEL R., and VIERIN, ALBERT
 100 to Dinner: Better Cooking for Clubs, Camps and Resorts, Institutions, Industrial Plants, and All Public Dining Places. Rev. ed. University of Toronto Press, 1960, 381, illus.

MONTAGNÉ, PROSPER
 Nouveau Larousse Gastronomique: The Encyclopedia of Food, Wine & Cookery. Larousse, Paris, (Crown), 1967, 1064, illus.

MOONEY, BOOTH
 The Hidden Assassins. Follett, 1966, 230.

MORPHY, COUNTESS
 Mushroom Recipes. Arco, 1966, 128.

MORRIS, MAURICE, and OUTLAND, JOHN G.
 Rotating Seasonal Menus. Ahrens, 1966, 122.

MURPHY, MARGARET D.
 Fondue, Chafing Dish, and Casserole Cookery. Hawthorn, 1969, 290, illus.

NATIONAL ACADEMY OF SCIENCES, NATIONAL RESEARCH COUNCIL (FOOD AND NUTRITION BOARD)
 Prospects of the World Food Supply. NAS, 1966, 84.

NATIONAL ASSOCIATION OF MEAT PURVEYORS
 Meat Buyer's Guide to Portion Control Meat Cuts. NAMP, 1967, 68, illus.

———.
 Meat Buyer's Guide to Standardized Meat Cuts. NAMP, 1968, 84, illus.

NATIONAL LIVESTOCK MEAT BOARD
 Lessons on Meat. NLMB, 1964, 86, illus.

NATIONAL RESTAURANT ASSOCIATION
 Menu Masterpieces. NRA, Chicago, 1965, 208.

———.
 Great American Menus. NRA, Chicago, 1964, 137, illus.

NELSON, JOHN A., and TROUT, G. MALCOLM
 Judging Diary Products. 4th ed. Olsen, 1964, 463, illus.

NEW YORK (STATE) EDUCATION DEPARTMENT
 Quantity Cooking: Basic Skills. Delmar, 1966, 1 vol.

NICHOLS, NELL B.
 America's Best Vegetable Recipes: 666 Ways to Make Vegetables Irresistible. Doubleday, 1970, 336, illus.

O'CONNOR, HYLA N.
 Book of Salads. Arco, 1963, 144, illus.

OLIVER, RAYMOND
 La Cuisine. Tudor, 890, illus.

———.
 The Wine and Food Society's Guide to Classic Sauces and Their Preparation. Wine & Food Society, London, 1968, 197, illus.

OSTRANDER, SHEILA
 Festive Food Decoration for All Occasions. Sterling, 1969, 160, illus.

PARKE, GERTRUDE
 The Big Chocolate Cookbook. Funk & Wagnalls, 1968, 325.

———.
 The Big Coffee Cookbook. Funk & Wagnalls, 1969, 215.

PARKER, MILTON E., and LITCHFIELD, JOHN H.
 Food Plant Sanitation. Reinhold, 1962, 401, illus.

PASLEY, VIRGINIA, and GREEN, JANE
 You Can Do Anything with Crêpes. Simon & Schuster, 1970, 105.

PAYNE, ALMA S., and CALLAHAN, DOROTHY
 The Low Sodium, Fat-Controlled Cookbook. Little, Brown, 1960, 465.

PECKHAM, GLADYS C.
 Foundations of Food Preparation. 2nd ed. Macmillan, 1969, 497, illus.

PERRY-MILLER, MITZI F., et al.
 Clean Plates: Cooking for Young Children. Scribner's, 1964, 159.

PIERCE, ELEANOR B.
 Menu Translator: Pan Am's Guide to Food and Drink Specialties Abroad and at Home. Pan American Airways, 1968, 160, illus.

PILE, ROBERT S.
 Menu Planning for Every Occasion. Doubleday, 1968, 368, illus.

PIRIE, N. W.
 Food Resources: Conventional and Novel. Penguin, 1969, 1 vol. (Pelican A1045.)

POPE, ANTOINETTE
  Antoinette Pope School New Candy Cookbook. 3rd ed. Macmillan, 1967, 180.

POTTER, NORMAN W.
  Food Science. AVI, 1968, 653, illus.

PRICE, FLO, COMP.
  Coffee-Time Desserts: With Dessert Recipes from Some of Her Favorite People. Word Books, Waco, Tex., 1969, 79, illus.

PYKE, MAGNUS
  Food, Science and Technology. 3rd ed. Transatlantic, 1970, 211.

QUICK FROZEN FOODS DIRECTORY OF WHOLESALE DISTRIBUTORS
  Cahners, biennial.

REED, ANN, and PFALTZ, MARILYN
  Your Secret Servant: Fix and Freeze Hors d' Oeuvres for Easy Entertaining. P. & R. Press (Scribner, dist.), 1970, 1 vol.

REITZ, ROSETTA
  Mushroom Cookery. Walker, New York, 1965, 206, illus.

REYNOLDS, PHYLLIS C.
  The Complete Book of Meat. M. Barrows, 1963, 320, illus.

RICHARDS, LENORE
  Quantity Cookery: Menu Planning and Cooking for Large Numbers. 4th ed. Little, Brown, 1966, 660, illus.

RICHARDSON, TREVA M.
  Sanitation for Food Service Workers. Rev. ed. Cahners, 1969, 116, illus.

RICHMOND, SONYA
  International Vegetarian Cookery. Arco, 1965, 192.

RIETZ, CARL A., and WANDERSTOCK, JEREMIAH J.
  A Guide to the Selection, Combination, and Cooking of Foods. AVI, 1965, 2 vols.

ROMBAUER, IRMA, and BECKER, MARION R.
  Joy of Cooking. Rev. ed. Bobbs-Merrill, 1964, 849, illus.

ROSENGARTEN, FREDERIC, JR.
  The Book of Spices. Livingston, Wynnewood, Pa., 1969, 489, illus.

ROSENTHAL, JACOB, and FOLSOM, LE ROI A.
  Opportunities in Food Preparation and Service: The Professional Chef. Universal Publishing & Distributing, Educational Books Division, 1969, 144. (Vocational Guidance Manuals V170.)

ROSS, ANNETTE L.
  Cooking for a Crowd. Doubleday, 1968, 369, illus.

ROSS, JEAN
  Every Customer Is My Guest: A Manual for Food Service in Small Hotels and Restaurants. 4th ed. Nova Scotia Department of Trade & Industry, 1966, 112, illus.

RUBIN, HAROLD
  The Ulcer Diet Cook Book. Lippincott, 1963, 223.

SEBRELL, WILLIAM H., and HAGGERTY, JAMES J.
  Food and Nutrition. Time, Inc., 1967, 200, illus. (Life Science Library.)

SHANNON, ELLEN
  American Dictionary of Culinary Terms: A Comprehensive Guide to the Vocabulary of the Kitchen. Barnes, New York, 1962, 204.

SHERRY, KATE
  Specialty Cuts and How to Cook Them. Tuttle, 1968, 113.

SIAS, BEVERLEE
  The Chicken Cookbook. A. S. Barnes, 1970, 590.

SIMON, ANDRÉ L., and HOWE, ROBIN
  Dictionary of Gastronomy. McGraw-Hill, 1970, 400, illus.

SIMPSON, JEAN I.
  The Frozen Food Cookbook and Guide to Home Freezing. 2nd ed. AVI, 1962, 483, illus.

SMITH, E. EVELYN, CRUSIUS, VERA C., and COLE, JOHN A.
  A Handbook on Quantity Food Management. 2nd ed. Burgess, 1970, 191, illus.

SMITH, FRANCES L.
  Recipes and Menus for Fifty as Used in The School of Domestic Science of the Boston YWCA. Rev. ed. M. Barrows, 1964, 301.

SMITH, GEORGIANA R.
  Table Decoration, Yesterday, Today & Tomorrow. Tuttle, 1968, 288, illus.

SMITH, MARGARET R., and GADEN, EILEEN
  The Blender Cookbook. Doubleday, 1961, 288, illus.

SPRACKLING, HELEN
  The New Setting Your Table: Its Art, Etiquette, and Service. M. Borrows, 1960, 288, illus.

SPUNT, GEORGES
  Memoirs & Menus: The Confessions of A Culinary Snob. Chilton, 1967, 461, illus.

STOCKLI, ALBERT
  Splendid Fare: The Albert Stockli Cookbook. Knopf, 1970, 416, illus.

STOKES, JOHN W.
  Food Service in Industry and Institutions. W. C. Brown, 1960, 261, illus. (Restaurant and Hotel Management Series.)

———.
  How to Manage a Restaurant or Institutional Food Service. W. C. Brown, 1967, 356.

SUNSET
  Sunset Salad Book. 3rd ed. Lane, Menlo Park, Calif., 1966, 96, illus. (Sunset Books.)

TERRELL, MARGARET E.
  Professional Food Preparation: Techniques and Equipment for Large Quantity. Wiley-Interscience, 1970, 1 vol., illus.

THATCHER, FRED S., and CLARK, D. S., EDS.
  Microorganisms in Foods: Their Significance and Methods of Enumeration. University of Toronto Press, 1968, 234.

THORNTON, HORACE
  Textbook of Meat Inspection: Including the Inspection of Rabbits and Poultry. 5th ed. Baillière, Tindall & Gassell, London, 1968, 596, illus.

TOPEL, DAVID G., ED.
  The Pork Industry: Problems and Progress. Iowa State University Press, 1969, 300.

TRACY, MARIAN C.
  The Art of Making Real Soups: A Delicious Collection of Recipes from Round the World. Doubleday, 1967, 249, illus.

———.
  Cooking Fondue. Doubleday, 1970, 99. (Little Cookbook Shelf Series.)

———.
  The Mushroom Cookbook. Doubleday, 1968, 99. (Little Cookbook Shelf Series.)

———.
  New Casserole Cookery. Berkley, New York, 1970, 252.

TREAT, NOLA, and RICHARDS, LENORE
  Quantity Cookery: Menu Planning and Cooking for Large Numbers. 4th ed. Little, Brown, 1966, 660, illus.

COMMERCIAL PROGRAMS

TRUAX, CAROL
   The Art of Salad Making. Doubleday, 1968, 210, illus.

TURNER, DAVID R.
   Dietitian: All Grades up to Head Dietitian, Nutritionist, Home Economist. 5th ed. Arco, 1969, 204, illus. (Arco Civil Service Test Tutor.)

———
   Food Service Supervisor: School Lunch Manager. Arco, 1969, 352, illus. (Arco Civil Service Test Tutor.)

TURNER, JAMES S.
   The Chemical Feast. Grossman, New York, 1970, 273. (Ralph Nader's Study Group Reports.)

U.S. AGRICULTURAL MARKETING SERVICE
   Food Buying Guide for Type A School Lunches. Rev. ed. USGPO, 1964, 75, (U.S. Department of Agriculture No. PA-270.)

U.S. DEPARTMENT OF AGRICULTURE
   The U.S. Government Cook Book. Pocket Books, 1965, 96.

U.S. DEPARTMENT OF AGRICULTURE, AGRICULTURAL RESEARCH SERVICE
   Food Purchasing Guide for Group Feeding. USGPO, 1965, 54. (Agriculture Handbook No. 284.)

U.S. DEPARTMENT OF HEALTH, EDUCATION AND WELFARE
   Training Food Service Personnel for the Hospitality Industry. HEW, 1969, 145.

U.S. DEPARTMENT OF THE INTERIOR, FISH AND WILDLIFE SERVICE
   Let's Cook Fish. USDI, 1967, 55, illus.

U.S. FOOD AND DRUG ADMINISTRATION
   Microscopic-Analytical Methods in Food and Drug Control. USFDA, 1960, 255, illus. (Technical Bulletin No. 1.)

U.S. OFFICE OF EDUCATION
   Quantity Food Preparation: A Suggested Guide. Rev. ed. USGPO, 1967, 39. (OE-82015.)

U.S. OFFICE OF EDUCATION, VOCATIONAL AND TECHNICAL EDUCATION DIVISION
   Food Service Industry: Training Programs and Facilities. USOE, 1961, 183. (Distributive Education Series No. 32.)

———
   Food Processing Technology: A Suggested 2-Year Post High School Curriculum. USOE, 1967, 97. (OE-82016.)

VAIL, GLADYS E., et al.
   Foods: An Introductory College Course. 5th ed. Houghton Mifflin, 1967, 693, illus.

VANDERBILT, AMY
   Complete Cookbook. Doubleday, 1961, 811, illus.

VANDERBILT UNIVERSITY, NASHVILLE
   Hospital Diet Manual. 2nd ed. Vanderbilt University Press, 1969, 158.

VANDIVERT, RITA
   Chicken As You Like It. Rand-McNally, 1968, 159.

VAN ZUYLEN, GUIRNE
   Gourmet Cooking for Everyone. Faber & Faber, 1969, 158.

VARA, ALBERT C., ED.
   Food and Beverage Industries: A Bibliography and Guidebook. Gale, 1970, 215. (Management Information Guide No. 16.)

VILLIARD, PAUL
   The Practical Candymaking Cookbook. Abelard-Schuman, New York, 1970, 1 vol., illus.

VITHALDAS, YOGI, and ROBERTS, SUSAN
   The Yogi Cook Book. Crown, 1968, 137, illus.

VOEGELE, MARGUERITE C., and WOOLLEY, GRACE H.
   Menu Dictionary: Multilingual. Ahrens, 1961, 318, illus.

VOLUME FEEDING MANAGEMENT
   Professional's Recipe Master. Ahrens, 1967, 403.

WALDNER, GEORGE K.
   65 Quality Menus for Quantity Service. Hayden, 1965, 182.

WALDNER, GEORGE K., and MITTERHAUSER, KLAUS
   Professional Chef's Book of Buffets. Cahners, 1968, 232. illus.

WALDO, MYRA
   The Complete Book of Gourmet Cooking for the American Kitchen. Putnam, 1960, 374, illus.

———
   The Complete Round The World Meat Cookbook. Doubleday, 1967, 492, illus.

———
   Cooking for the Freezer. Doubleday, 1960, 236.

———
   Dictionary of International Food & Cooking Terms. Macmillan, 1967, 648, illus.

———
   The International Encyclopedia of Cooking. Macmillan, 1967, 2 vols., illus.

WASON, ELIZABETH
   Cooks, Gluttons & Gourmets: A History of Cookery. Doubleday, 1962, 381, illus.

———
   The Language of Cookery: An Informal Dictionary. World, 1968, 287, illus.

WECHSBERG, JOSEPH
   Dining at the Pavillion. Little, Brown, 1962, 227, illus.

WEISER, HARRY H.
   Practical Food Microbiology and Technology. AVI, 1962, 345, illus.

WENTZ, CARL F.
   Gastronomy: A World Famous Hotel and Restaurant Manager's Guide to Culinary Success. Greenwich Book Publishers, 1960, 101.

WENZEL, GEORGE L.
   Menu Maker. The author, 1966, 1494, illus.

WEST, BESSIE B., WOOD, LeVELLE, and HARGER, VIRGINIA F.
   Food Service in Institutions. 4th ed. Wiley, 1966, 702, illus.

WHEAT FLOUR INSITUTE, CHICAGO
   Eat to Live. Rev. ed. Wheat Flour Institute, 1970, 64, illus.

WILKINSON, JULE, and INSTITUTIONS MAGAZINE
   The Finishing Kitchen. Cahners, 1969, 108. (Success Series.)

———
   The Nautical Way. Cahners, 1968, 92. (Success Series.)

———
   Storage Specifics. Cahners, 1969, 104, illus. (Success Series.)

WILMOT, JENNIE
   Food for the Family: An Elementary College Text. 5th ed. Lippincott, 1960, 735, illus.

WINTER, RUTH
   Poisons in Your Food. Crown, 1969, 248, illus.

WOOD, MARION N.
   Gourmet Food on A Wheat-Free Diet. Thomas, 1967, 128.

ZACHARY, HUGH
   The Beachcomber's Handbook of Seafood Cookery. John F. Blair, Winston-Salem, N.C., 1970, 208, illus.

ZEHR, FARREL J., ED.
   The Pecan Cook Book. Association Press, 1969, 202, illus.

ZIEGLER, PERCIVAL T.
The Meat We Eat. Interstate, 1966, 547, illus.

BAKING AND DECORATING

AMENDOLA, JOSEPH
The Bakers' Manual for Quantity Baking and Pastry Making. 2nd ed. Ahrens, 1960, 206, illus.

AMERICAN CRAFTSMEN'S COUNCIL
Cookies and Breads: The Bakers Art. Van Nostrand-Reinhold, 1967, 92, illus.

BAKING INDUSTRY MAGAZINE
The Cookie Book. Clissold, Chicago, 1968, 106, illus.

BENNION, EDMUND B.
Breadmaking: Its Principles and Practice. 4th ed. Oxford University Press, 1967, 391, illus.

BOWRING, JEAN
New Cake Decorating Book. Arco, 1970, 139, illus.

BRAUÉ, JOHN R.
Uncle John's Original Bread Book: Recipes for Breads, Biscuits, Griddle Cakes, Rolls, Crackers, etc. 2nd ed. Exposition Press, 1965, 198, illus.

CASELLA, DOLORES
A World of Breads. David White, 1966, 310, illus.

CLEM, DELORIS K.
The Cookie Cookbook. A. S. Barnes, 1966, 402, illus.

DANIEL, ALBERT R.
Bakery Materials and Methods: A Book for Every Baker and Confectioner. 4th ed. MacLaren & Sons, London, 1963, 496, illus.

D'ERMO, DOMINIQUE
The Modern Pastry Chef's Guide to Professional Baking. Harper & Row, 1962, 302, illus.

GOOD HOUSEKEEPING
Book of Cake Decorating. Dorothy B. Marsh, ed. M. Barrows, 1961, 192, illus.

GUERTNER, BERYL
Cake Icing and Decorating for all Occasions. Taplinger, 1967, 125, illus.

———.
The Magic of Cake Decorating. Murray, Sydney, (Sportshelf, New Rochelle, N.Y., dist.), 1968, 127, illus.

HECHTLINGER, ADELAIDE
Cooking with Bread. Stephen Greene, Brattleboro, Vt., 1970, 48, illus.

HOPKINS, DENNIS M.
Simple but Effective Cake Decorating. Clissold, Chicago, 1970, 1 vol.

MATZ, SAMUEL A.
Bakery Technology and Engineering. AVI, 1960, 640.

———.
Cookie and Cracker Technology. AVI, 1968, 320, illus.

MØLLER, CARL, MADSEN, LEO, and ROSENTHAL, HELMUT
Danish Cakes. MacLaren & Sons, London, 1965, 236, illus.

MORTON, MARCIA C.
The Art of Viennese Pastry. Doubleday, 1969, 228, illus.

O'CONNELL, DESMOND H.
Aim for a Job in the Bakery Industry. R. Rosen Press, 1967, 158. (Aim High Vocational Series.)

———.
Your Future in the Bakery Industry. Arco, 1970, 158. (Career Guidance Series.)

PATTEN, MARGUERITE
Cake Icing and Decoration. Hamlyn, London, 1965, 1 vol., illus.

PECK, PAULA
The Art of Fine Baking. Simon & Schuster, 1961, 320, illus.

PHILLIPS, BERT J.
The Pastry Chef. A. S. Barnes, 1965, 213, illus.

REICH, LILLY J.
The Viennese Pastry Cookbook: From Vienna with Love. Macmillan, 1970, 320.

RICHARDS, PAUL
Pastry for the Restaurant: Receipts Especially Adapted for Hotels of the European Plan. John Willy, Inc., Evanston, Ill., 1960., 144.

RUSHING, LILITH, and VOSS, RUTH
The Cake Cook Book. Chilton, 1965, 200, illus.

RUSSELL, JOAN
Creative Cake Decoration. 2nd ed. Leonard Hill, London, 1964, 1 vol., illus.

SNYDER, RICHARD V.
65 Buttercream Flowers. 5th ed. Exposition Press, 1965, 240, illus. (Exposition-Banner Book.)

SPENCER, LOUISE
Decorating Cakes and Party Foods: Baking Too! Hearthside Press, 1970, 227.

SULTAN, WILLIAM J.
Elementary Baking. McGraw-Hill, 1969, 268, illus.

———.
Practical Baking. 2nd ed. AVI, 1969, 492, illus.

VERCOE, BERNICE J.
Cake Design and Decoration. Murray, Sydney, 1966, 128, illus.

WILTON, McKINLEY, and WILTON, NORMAN
The Homemaker's Pictorial Encyclopedia of Modern Cake Decorating.... 5th ed. Wilton Enterprises, Chicago, 1968, 228, illus.

———.
Wilton's Wonderland of Cake Decorating. 3rd ed. Wilton Enterprises, Chicago, 1966, 207, illus.

WILTON SCHOOL OF CAKE DECORATION
Modern Cake Decorating. 3rd ed. Wilton Enterprises, Chicago, 1965, 192, illus.

BEVERAGES

ADAM, HANS K.
The Wine and Food Society's Guide to German Cookery. World (with Wine and Food Society, Cleveland), 1967, 215, illus.

ALLEN, HERBERT W.
A History of Wine: Great Vintage Wines from the Homeric Age to the Present Day. Horizon Press, 1962, 304, illus.

———.
The Wines of Portugal. McGraw-Hill, 1964, 192, illus.

AMERINE, MAYNARD A., and CRUESS, WILLIAM V.
The Technology of Wine Making. 2nd ed. AVI, 1967, 1 vol., illus.

AMERINE, MAYNARD A., and JOSLYN, MAYNARD A.
Table Wines: The Technology of Their Production. 2nd ed. University of California Press, 1970, 997, illus.

AMERINE, MAYNARD A., and SINGLETON, VERNON L.
Wine: An Introduction for Americans. University of California Press, 1965, 357, illus.

COMMERCIAL PROGRAMS

ARCO PUBLISHING COMPANY, INC.
Beverage Control Investigator. 2nd ed. Arco, 1961, 224.

AUSTIN, CEDRIC
The Science of Wine. Elsevier, 1968, 216, illus.

BROWN, JOHN H.
Early American Beverages. Tuttle, 1966, 171, illus.

CHURCHILL, CREIGHTON
A Notebook for the Wines of France: A Wine Diary or Cellar Book Listing the Nine Hundred Most Important French Wines and/or Their Vineyards, with Space for the Wine Drinker's Own Records and Notations.... Knopf, 1961, 387, illus.

CROFT-COOKE, RUPERT
Madeira. Putnam, 1961, 224.

HASZONICS, JOSEPH, and BARRATT, STUART
Wine Merchandising. Hayden, 1963, 214, illus.

HORNICKEL, ERNST
The Great Wines of Europe. Putnam, 1965, 229, illus.

HOWE, ROBIN
The Wine and Food Society's Guide to Soups. World, 1967, 198, illus.

JAMES, WALTER
Wine: A Brief Encyclopedia. Knopf, 1960, 208.

JOHNSON, HUGH
Wine. Simon & Schuster, 1966, 264, illus.

KRESSMANN, EDOUARD
The Wonder of Wine. Hastings House, 1968, 227.

LICHINE, ALFRED M.
Wines of France.... 4th ed. Knopf, 1963, 382, illus.

MASSEE, WILLIAM E.
Wines and Spirits: A Complete Buying Guide. McGraw-Hill, 1961, 427, illus.

MENDELSOHN, OSCAR A.
The Dictionary of Drink and Drinking. Hawthorn, 1965, 382.

OZIAS, BLAKE
All About Wine. Crowell, 1967, 144, illus.

PENNING-ROWSELL, EDMUND
The International Wine and Food Society's Guide to the Wines of Bordeaux. Stein & Day, 1970, 320.

RAY, CYRIL
The Wines of Italy. McGraw-Hill, 1966, 192, illus.

ROLLIN, BETTY
The Non-Drinker's Drink Book. Doubleday, 1966, 213, illus.

SCHOONMAKER, FRANK
Encyclopedia of Wine. 4th ed., rev. Hastings House, 1969, 442, illus.

SIMON, ANDRÉ L., COMP.
Wines of the World. McGraw-Hill, 1967, 719.

SLATER, LESLIE G.
The Secrets of Making Wine from Fruits & Berries. Terry, Lilliwaup, Wash., 1965, 90, illus.

THORNER, MARVIN E., and HERZBERG, RONALD J.
Food Beverage Service Handbook. AVI, 1970, 1 vol.

VANDYKE PRICE, PAMELA J.
Winelovers' Handbook. Simon & Schuster, 1969, 80, illus.

VOEGELE, MARGUERITE C., and WOOLLEY, GRACE H.
Drink Dictionary. Ahrens, 1961, 192, illus.

YOXALL, HARRY W.
The International Wine and Food Society's Guide to the Wines of Burgundy. Stein & Day, 1970, 191, illus.

ETHNIC AND GEOGRAPHIC COOKING

AARON, JAN, and SACHS, GEORGINE
The Art of Mexican Cooking. Doubleday, 1965, 309, illus.

AGUILAR, JEANNETTE
The Classic Cooking of Spain. Holt, Rinehart & Winston, 1966, 160, illus.

BAR-DAVID, MOLLY
The Israeli Cook Book. Crown, 1964, 422. (International Cook Book Series.)

BECK, SIMONE, BERTHOLLE, LOUISETTE, and CHILD, JULIA
Mastering the Art of French Cooking. Knopf, 1961, 684, illus.

BENNETT, VICTOR
The South Pacific Cookbook. Prentice-Hall, 1970, 230, illus.

BONI, ADA
Italian Regional Cooking. Dutton, 1969, 1 vol., illus.

BOOTH, GEORGE C.
The Food and Drink of Mexico. Ward Ritchie, Los Angeles, 1964, 190, illus.

BROWN, DALE
The Cooking of Scandinavia. Time-Life Books, 1968, 206, illus. (Foods of the World.)

BROWN, MARION L.
Southern Cook Book. University of North Carolina Press, 1968, 489.

BUDIN, FRANCES M.
Recipes from Ireland: Traditional & Modern. Taplinger, 1966, 79.

CAMERON, SHEILA M.
The Highlander's Cookbook: Recipes from Scotland. Ward Ritchie, Los Angeles, 1966, 113, illus.

CHANG, WONONA W., et al.
An Encyclopedia of Chinese Food and Cooking. Lillian G. Kutscher, ed. Crown, 1970, 512, illus.

CHANTRAINE, CHARLES
La Cuisine Chantraine: The Complete Collection of Original Recipes Created at the Restaurant Chantraine in Brussels. M. Barrows (Morrow, dist.), 1966, 174.

CHAO, PU-WEI (YANG)
How to Cook and Eat in Chinese. 3rd ed. Random House, 1969, 249.

CHILD, JULIA
The French Chef Cookbook. Knopf, 1968, 424, illus.

CHOY, JUNG S.
The Art of Oriental Cooking. Anderson & Ritchie, 1964, 156.

CHU, GRACE
The Pleasures of Chinese Cooking. Simon & Schuster, 1962, 239, illus.

CLARK, MORTON G.
French-American Cooking from New Orleans to Quebec. Funk & Wagnalls, 1967, 238. (Americana Cookery Series.)

CONIL, JEAN
Gastronomic Tour de France. Dutton, 1960, 375, illus.

FOOD SCIENCE

COREY, HELEN
    The Art of Syrian Cookery: A Culinary Trip to the Land of Bible History—Syria and Lebanon. Doubleday, 1962, 186, illus.

CORNFELD, LILIAN
    Israeli Cookery. AVI, 1962, 356, illus.

DeANDRADE, MARGARETTE
    Brazilian Cookery: Traditional and Modern. Tuttle, 1965, 349, illus.

DE KNIGHT, FREDA
    The Ebony Cookbook: A Date with a Dish—A Cookbook of American Negro Recipes. Johnson, 1962, 390, illus.

DEUTSCH, HERMANN B.
    Brennan's New Orleans Cookbook. Crager, New Orleans, 1961, 235, illus.

DIAT, LOUIS
    French Cooking for Americans. Lippincott, 1966, 309.

———.
    Gourmet's Basic French Cookbook: Techniques of French Cuisine. Gourmet, 1961, 654, illus.

DOI, MASARU
    Cook Japanese. Kodansha, Palo Alto, 1969, 129, illus.

———.
    Japanese One-Pot Cookery. 2nd ed. Kodansha, Palo Alto, 1970, 109, illus.

EREN, NESET
    The Art of Turkish Cooking: Delectable Delights of Topkapi. Doubleday, 1969, 308, illus.

FISHER, MARY F.
    The Cooking of Provincial France. Time-Life Books, 1968, 208, illus. (Foods of the World.)

FitzGIBBON, THEODORA
    The Art of British Cooking. Doubleday, 1965, 366.

———.
    A Taste of Ireland: Irish Traditional Food. Houghton Mifflin, 1968, 124, illus.

GARCIA, CLARITA
    Clarita's Cocina: Great Traditional Recipes from a Spanish Kitchen. Doubleday, 1970, 1 vol., illus.

GASKINS, RUTH L.
    A Good Heart and A Light Hand: Ruth L. Gaskins' Collection of Traditional Negro Recipes. Turnpike, Annandale, Va., 1968, 110, illus.

THE GREAT SCANDINAVIAN COOK BOOK: AN ENCYCLOPAEDIA OF DOMESTIC COOKERY
    Crown, 1966, 734, illus.

GUNDEL, KÁROLY
    Hungarian Cookery Book: 140 Hungarian Specialties. 5th ed. Sportshelf, New Rochelle, N.Y., dist., 1964, 103, illus.

HAHN, EMILY
    The Cooking of China. Time-Life Books, 1968, 206, illus. (Foods of the World.)

HAWAII STATE SOCIETY OF WASHINGTON
    Hawaiian Cuisine: A Collection of Recipes from Members of the Society Featuring Hawaiian, Chinese, Japanese, Korean, Filipino, Portuguese, and Cosmopolitan Dishes. Tuttle, 1963, 79, illus.

HAZELTON, NIKA S.
    The Art of Scandinavian Cooking. Macmillan, 1965, 243.

———.
    The Belgian Cookbook. Atheneum, 1970, 256.

———.
    The Best of Italian Cooking. World, 1967, 216, illus.

———.
    The Cooking of Germany. Time-Life Books, 1969, 208, illus. (Foods of the World.)

HEKMAT, FOROUGH-ES-SALTANEH
    The Art of Persian Cooking. Doubleday, 1961, 190, illus.

HELLER, EDNA E.
    The Art of Pennsylvania Dutch Cooking. Doubleday, 1968, 243, illus.

JEFFRIES, BOB
    Soul Food Cookbook. Bobbs-Merrill, 1969, 1 vol.

JOHNSON, ALICE B.
    The Complete Scandinavian Cookbook. Macmillan, 1964, 422.

KAGAWA, AYA
    Japanese Cookbook. Japan Travel Bureau, 1963, 1 vol.

KAISER, INEZ Y.
    Soul Food Cookery. Rev. ed. Pitman, 1969, 104.

KEYS, JOHN D.
    Japanese Cuisine: A Culinary Tour. Tuttle, 1966, 155, illus.

KIMBALL, YEFFE, and ANDERSON, JEAN
    The Art of American Indian Cooking. Doubleday, 1965, 215, illus.

KOPULOS, STELLA, and JONES, DOROTHY P.
    Adventures in Greek Cookery. World, 1966, 283.

KRAUS, BARBARA, ED.
    The Cookbook of the United Nations: 250 Authentic Recipes from 112 Countries. U.N. Association of the U.S.A., 1964- , vols., illus.

KROPOTKIN, ALEXANDRA
    The Best of Russian Cooking. Scribner, 1964, 270.

LAMB, VENICE
    The Home Book of Turkish Cookery. Transatlantic, 1970, 168, illus.

LEE, JIMMY
    Soul Food Cookbook. Award, New York, 1970, 133.

LEONARD, JONATHAN N.
    Latin American Cooking. Time-Life Books, 1968, 206, illus. (Foods of the World.)

LEONE, GENE
    Leone's Italian Cookbook. Harper & Row, 1969, 244.

LIE, SEK-HIANG
    Indonesian Cookery. Crown, 1963, 1 vol.

LIN, HSIANG JU, and TSUIFENG, LIN
    Chinese Gastronomy. Hastings House, 1969, 211, illus.

LOW, EIRENE
    English Cooking in Four Languages. Deutsch, London, 1967, 159.

MA, NANCY C.
    Cook Chinese. 2nd ed. Kodansha, Palo Alto, 1970, 127, illus.

MA, PO-CH'ANG CH'IH
    Mrs. Ma's Chinese Cookbook. Tuttle, 1961, 178.

MAKANOWITZKY, BARBARA N.
    The Russian Cookbook: Recipes from Armenia, Azerbaidzhan, Belorussia, Estonia, Georgia, Latvia, Lithuania, Russia, Turkestan and the Ukraine. Atheneum, 1967, 247.

MILLER, CAREY D., BAZORE, KATHERINE, and BARTOW, MARY
    Fruits of Hawaii: Description, Nutritive Value, and Recipes. 4th ed. University of Hawaii Press, 1965, 229, illus.

COMMERCIAL PROGRAMS

MILLER, JILL N. H.
  Vietnamese Cookery. Tuttle, 1968, 118.

OJAKANGAS, BEATRICE A.
  The Finnish Cookbook. Crown, 1964, 250, illus. (International Cookbook Series.)

OLIVER, RAYMOND
  Gastronomy of France. World (with Wine and Food Society, London), 1967, 335, illus.

OLNEY, RICHARD
  The French Menu Cook Book. Simon & Schuster, 1970, 384, illus.

PELLAPRAT, HENRI P.
  Modern French Culinary Art. World, 1966, 1171, illus.

PERL, LILA
  Rice, Spice, and Bitter Oranges: Mediterranean Foods and Festivals. World, 1967, 272, illus.

ROOT, WAVERLY L.
  The Cooking of Italy. Time-Life Books, 1968, 208, illus. (Foods of the World.)

SAILLAND, MAURICE E.
  Traditional Recipes of the Provinces of France. Doubleday, 1961, 494, illus.

SANDLER, BEATRICE
  African Cookbook. World, 1970, 256, illus.

SARVIS, SHIRLEY
  A Taste of Portugal. Scribner, 1967, 192, illus.

SHERIDAN, MONICA
  The Art of Irish Cooking. Doubleday, 1965, 166.

SIA, MARY L.
  Mary Sia's Chinese Cookbook. 3rd ed. University of Hawaii Press, 1964, 184, illus.

SINGH, BALBIR
  Indian Cookery. Mills & Boon, London, 1967, 207.

SKOURA, SOPHIA
  The Greek Cook Book. Crown, 1967, 230. (International Cook Book Series.)

SPICE ISLANDS COMPANY.
  The Spice Islands Cook Book. Lane, Menlo Park, Calif., 1961, 208, illus.

STAN, ANISOARA
  The Romanian Cook Book. Citadel Press, 1969, 229.

STEINBERG, RAFAEL, et al.
  Pacific and Southeast Asian Cooking. Silver Burdett, 1970, 208, illus. (Foods of the World.)

WALDO, MYRA
  The Complete Book of Oriental Cooking. McKay, 1960, 246.

WASON, ELIZABETH
  The Art of German Cooking. Doubleday, 1967, 256, illus.

WILSON, MARIE M.
  Siamese Cookery. Tuttle, 1965, 109, illus.

WINER, BART, ED.
  Art of French Cooking. Rev. ed. Joseph Faulkner, tr. Golden Press, 1962, 863.

WOLFE, LINDA
  The Cooking of the Caribbean Islands. Time-Life Books, 1970, 208, illus. (Foods of the World.)

WONG, ELLA-MEI
  Chinese Cookery. Arco, 1961, 112.

YARDLEY, MAILI
  Hawaii Cooks. Tuttle, 1970, 112, illus.

YIANILOS, THERESA K.
  The Complete Greek Cookbook: The Best from 3000 Years of Greek Cooking. Funk & Wagnalls, 1970, 1 vol.

NUTRITION

AHRENS, RICHARD A.
  Nutrition for Health. Wadsworth, 1970, 64, illus. (Basic Concepts in Health Science Series.)

BRENNAN, RUTH
  Nutrition. W. C. Brown, 1967, 228.

CHANEY, MARGARET S.
  Nutrition. 6th ed. Houghton, 1960, 534, illus.

COBLE, M. C.
  A Guide to Nutrition and Food Service for Nursing Homes and Homes for the Aged. USGPO, 1965, 87, illus. (Public Health Service Publication No. 1309.)

COOPER, LENNA F., et al.
  Nutrition in Health and Disease. 15th ed. Lippincott, 1968, 685, illus.

FLECK, HENRIETTA, and MUNVES, ELIZABETH A.
  Introduction to Nutrition. Macmillan, 1962, 656, illus. (Macmillan College Home Economic Series.)

FOMON, SAMUEL J.
  Infant Nutrition. Saunders, 1967, 299, illus.

GOLDBLITH, SAMUEL A., and JOSLYN, MAYNARD A., EDS.
  Milestones in Nutrition. AVI, 1964, 1 vol.

GUTHRIE, HELEN A.
  Introductory Nutrition. Mosby, 1967, 464.

HARRIS, ROBERT S., and VON LOESECKE, HARRY W.
  Nutritional Evaluation of Food Processing. Wiley, 1960, 612, illus.

HUTCHISON, SIR ROBERT
  Food and the Principles of Nutrition. 12th ed. Hugh M. Sinclair and Dorothy F. Hollingsworth, eds. Edward Arnold, London, 1969, 644, illus.

KRAUSE, MARIE V.
  Food, Nutrition, and Diet Therapy. 4th ed. Saunders, 1966, 687, illus.

MARKS, HARRIET
  Nutrition and Elementary Food Science. Jacaranda, Brisbane (Tri Ocean, San Francisco, dist.), 1968, 198, illus.

McHENRY, EARLE W.
  Basic Nutrition. Lippincott, 1963, 409.

———.
  Foods Without Fads: A Common Sense Guide to Nutrition. Lippincott, 1960, 159.

NATIONAL ACADEMY OF SCIENCES, NATIONAL RESEARCH COUNCIL (FOOD AND NUTRITION BOARD)
  Recommended Dietary Allowances. 7th ed. NAS, 1968, 101. (Pub. No. 1694.)

PEYTON, ALICE B.
  Practical Nutrition. 2nd ed. Lippincott, 1962, 434, illus.

PROUDFIT, FAIRFAX T., and ROBINSON, CORINNE H.
  Normal and Therapeutic Nutrition. 12th ed. Macmillan, 858, illus.

ROBINSON, CORINNE H.
  Basic Nutrition and Diet Therapy. 2nd ed. Macmillan, 1970, 375, illus.

———.
  Fundamentals of Normal Nutrition. Macmillan, 1968, 669, illus.

FOOD SCIENCE

SIMEONS, ALBERT T.
　Food: Facts, Foibles & Fables—The Origins of Human Nutrition. Funk & Wagnalls, 1968, 150.

STEVENSON, GLADYS T., and MILLER, CORA
　Introduction to Foods and Nutrition. Wiley, 1960, 517, illus.

TANNENBAUM, BEULAH, and STILLMAN, MYRA
　Understanding Food: The Chemistry of Nutrition. McGraw-Hill, 1962, 206, illus.

TAYLOR, CLARA M., and PYE, ORREA F., EDS.
　Foundations of Nutrition. 6th ed. Macmillan, 1966, 564.

WAYLER, THELMA J., and KLEIN, ROSE S.
　Applied Nutrition. Macmillan, 1965, 309, illus.

WILLIAMS, SUE R.
　Nutrition and Diet Therapy. Mosby, 1969, 686, illus.

WILSON, EVA D., et al.
　Principles of Nutrition. 2nd ed. Wiley, 1965, 596.

PROCESSING AND PRESERVATION

BINSTED, RAYMOND, and DEVEY, JAMES D.
　Soup Manufacture: Canning, Dehydration, & Quick-Freezing. 3rd ed. Food Trade Press, London, 1970, 1 vol., illus.

CHARM, STANLEY E.
　The Fundamentals of Food Engineering. AVI, 1963, 592, illus. (AVI Books on Food Processing.)

COPSON, DAVID A.
　Microwave Heating: In Freeze-Drying, Electronic Ovens, and Other Applications. AVI, 1962, 433, illus.

COX, PAT M.
　Deep Freezing: A Comprehensive Guide to Its Theory and Practice. Faber & Faber (Transatlantic, dist.), 1968, 458, illus.

DESROSIER, NORMAN W.
　The Technology of Food Preservation. 3rd ed. AVI, 1970, 488.

GLICKSMAN, MARTIN
　Gum Technology in the Food Industry. Academic, 1969, 590. (Food Science and Technology Monographs.)

GOLDBLITH, SAMUEL A., ED.
　Exploration in Future Food-Processing Techniques. MIT Press, 1963, 92, illus.

GOLDBLITH, SAMUEL A., JOSLYN, MAYNARD A., and NICKERSON, J. T. R.
　Introduction to Thermal Processing of Foods. AVI, 1961, 1128, illus. (Anthology of Food Science Vol. 1.)

GOOWIN, R. W. L.
　Chemical Additives in Food. Little, Brown, 1967, 128.

GRAHAM-RACK, BARRY, and BINSTED, RAYMOND
　Hygiene in Food Manufacturing and Handling. Food Trade Press, London, 1964, 148, illus.

GUTCHO, M.
　Alcoholic Malt Beverages, 1969. Noyes, 1969, 333, illus. (Food Processing Review No. 7.)

GUTTERSON, M.
　Confectionary Products: Manufacturing Processes. Noyes, 1969, 323, illus. (Food Processing Review No. 6.)

HALL, CARL W., and HEDRICK, T. I.
　Drying of Milk and Milk Products. AVI, 1966, 320, illus.

HEID, JOHN L., and JOSLYN, MAYNARD A.
　Fundamentals of Food Processing Operations: Ingredients, Methods, and Packaging. AVI, 1967, 730, illus.

HERSOM, A. C., and HULLAND, E. D.
　Canned Foods: An Introduction to their Microbiology. 5th ed. Chemical, 1964, 291, illus.

JOSLYN, MAYNARD A., and HEID, JOHN L.
　Food Processing Operations: Their Management, Machines, Materials, and Methods. AVI, 1963-64, 3 vols., illus.

JOSLYN, MAYNARD A., ED.
　Methods in Food Analysis: Physical, Chemical, and Instrumental Methods of Analysis. 2nd ed. Academic Press, 1970, 845. (Food Science and Technology Series.)

KARMAS, ENDEL
　Fresh Meat Processing. Noyes, 1970, 236, illus. (Food Processing Review No. 12.)

KEMPF, NORMAN W.
　The Technology of Chocolate. Manufacturing Confectioners, Oak Park, Ill., 1964, 120.

LACHMANN, ALFRED
　Snacks and Fried Products, 1969. Noyes, 1969, 181, illus. (Food Processing Review No. 4.)

LOCK, ARTHUR
　Practical Canning. 2nd ed. Food Trade Press, London, 1960, 299, illus.

MATZ, SAMUEL A.
　Cereal Science. AVI, 1969, 248.

MERORY, JOSEPH
　Food Flavorings: Composition, Manufacture, and Use. 2nd ed. AVI, 1968, 478, illus.

MID-ATLANTIC FOOD PROCESSORS ASSOCIATION, INC.
　... Buyers' Guide and Directory.... Food Processors, annual.

MOUNTNEY, GEORGE J.
　Poultry Products Technology. AVI, 1966, 264, illus.

NATIONAL CANNERS ASSOCIATION
　Laboratory Manual for Food Canners and Processors. AVI, 1968, 2 vols.

NATIONAL FROZEN FOOD ASSOCIATION
　Frozen Food Institutional Encyclopedia. NFFA, New York, n.d., 86.

NATIONAL RESEARCH COUNCIL, FOOD PROTECTION COMMISSION
　Chemicals Used in Food Processing. National Academy of Sciences, NRC, 1967, 294. (NRC Pub. No. 1274.)

———.
　Food Chemical Index. National Academy of Sciences, NRC, 1963- , Vol. 1- , illus. (NRC Pub. No. 1143.)

NOYES, ROBERT
　Dehydration Processes for Convenience Foods, 1969. Noyes, 1969, 367, illus. (Food Processing Review No. 2.)

———.
　Freeze Drying of Foods and Biologicals, 1968. Noyes, 1968, 313, illus. (Food Processing Review No. 1.)

PETERSON, MARTIN S., and TRESSLER, DONALD K.
　Food Technology the World Over. AVI, 1963-65, 2 vols.

PINTAURO, NICHOLAS
　Soluble Coffee Manufacturing Processes. Noyes, 1969, 254, illus.

———.
　Soluble Tea Production Processes. Noyes, 1970, 183, illus.

QUICK FROZEN FOODS PROCESSORS DIRECTORY
　Cahners, annual.

COMMERCIAL PROGRAMS

ROGERS, JOHN L.
    Production of Precooked Frozen Foods. Food Trade Review, London, 1969, 271.

SACHAROW, STANLEY, and GRIFFIN, ROGER C.
    Food Packaging: A Guide for the Supplier, Processor, and Distributor. AVI, 1970, 412, illus.

SCHULTZ, HAROLD W., ED.
    The Chemistry and Physiology of Flavors. AVI, 1967, 552.

SIVETZ, MICHAEL, and FOOTE, H. ELLIOTT
    Coffee Processing Technology. AVI, 1963, 2 vols.

SLADE, FRANK H.
    Food Processing Plant. Vol. 1. Leonard Hill, London, 1967, 381, illus.

SMITH, ORA
    Potatoes: Production, Storing, Processing. AVI, 1968, 642.

STUMBO, CHARLES R.
    Thermobacteriology in Food Processing. Academic Press, 1965, 236, illus. (Food Science and Technology Monographs No. 2.)

TALBURT, WILLIAM F., and SMITH, ORA
    Potato Processing. 2nd ed. AVI, 1967, 588.

TRESSLER, DONALD K., et al.
    The Freezing Preservation of Foods. 4th ed. AVI, 1968- , 4 vols., illus.

TRESSLER, DONALD K., and JOSLYN, MAYNARD A.
    Fruit and Vegetable Juice Processing Technology. AVI, 1961, 1028, illus.

URROWS, GRACE M.
    Food Preservation by Irradiation. U.S. Atomic Energy Commission, Oak Ridge, Tenn., 1968, 58, illus. (Understanding the Atom.)

U.S. BUSINESS AND DEFENSE SERVICES ADMINISTRATION
    Food Irradiation Activities Throughout the World. USGPO, 1968, 91.

VAN ARSDEL, WALLACE B., and COPLEY, MICHAEL J., EDS.
    Food Dehydration. AVI, 1963-64, 2 vols., illus.

VAN ARSDEL, WALLACE B., COPLEY, MICHAEL J., and OLSON, ROBERT L.
    Quality and Stability in Frozen Foods: Time-Temperature Tolerance and Its Significance. Wiley-Interscience, 1969, 384, illus.

WILLIAMS, EDWIN W.
    Frozen Foods: Biography of an Industry. Cahners, 1970, 215, illus.

WOOLRICH, WILLIS R., and HALLOWELL, ELLIOTT R.
    Cold and Freezer Storage Manual. AVI, 1970, 352.

GRAPHIC ARTS

ABEL, OSCAR R., and STRAW, WINDSOR A.
    Mechanism of the Linotype and Intertype. 3rd ed. Lebawarts Press, Brookings, S. Dak., 1961, 322.

ADAMS, JOHN M.
    Optical Measurements in the Printing Industry. Pergamon, 1965, 167, illus.

ALLEN, EDWARD M.
    Harper's Dictionary of the Graphic Arts. Harper & Row, 1963, 295.

ALLEN, LEWIS M.
    Printing with the Handpress. Van Nostrand-Reinhold, 1969, 75, illus.

AMERICAN PHOTOENGRAVERS ASSOCIATION
    The Fundamentals of Photoengraving. American Photoengravers Association, 1966, 48, illus.

ARNOLD, EDMUND C.
    Modern Newspaper Design. Harper & Row, 1969, 500, illus.

BAIN, ERIC K.
    The Theory and Practice of Typographic Design. Hastings House, 1970, 182, illus.

BALLINGER, RAYMOND A.
    Opportunities in Graphic Arts Careers. Vocational Guidance Manuals, 1968, 128, illus. (Career Series Vol. 169.)

BARNETT, MICHAEL P.
    Computer Typesetting: Experiments and Prospects. MIT Press, 1965, 245, illus.

BARROW (W. J.) RESEARCH LABORATORY, RICHMOND, VA.
    Permanence/Durability of the Book: A Two-Year Research Program. Barrow Research, 1963, 2 vols., illus.

BEDELL, EARL L.
    Careers in Graphic Reproduction. Van Nostrand, 1965, 171, illus.

BERRY, WILLIAM T., and POOLE, H. EDMUND
    Annals of Printing: A Chronological Encyclopaedia from the Earliest Times to 1950. University of Toronto Press, 1966, 315, illus.

BERRY, WILLIAM T., JOHNSON, A. F., and JASPERT, W. P.
    The Encyclopaedia of Type Faces. 3rd ed. Pitman, 1962, 420.

BIEGELEISEN, JACOB I.
    The Complete Book of Silk Screen Printing Production. Dover, 1963, 253, illus.

BIEGELEISEN, JACOB I., and COHN, MAX A.
    Silk Screen Techniques. Dover, 1968, 187, illus. (Peter Smith, library rebinding, 1970.)

BIGGS, JOHN R.
    An Approach to Type. 2nd ed. Pitman, 1962, 136, illus.

———.
    Basic Typography. Watson-Guptill, 1968, 176, illus.

BLAND, DAVID
    A History of Book Illustrations: The Illuminated Manuscript and the Printed Book. 2nd ed. University of California Press, Berkeley, 1969, 459.

BRANTLEY, C. OWEN
    How to Sell Printing by Mail. Druillard Press, New York, 1962, 148.

BRUNNER, FELIX
    A Handbook of Graphic Reproduction Processes.... 3rd ed. Hastings House, 1968, 379, illus.

BRUNSDON, JOHN
    The Technique of Etching and Engraving. Reinhold, 1967, 152, illus.

BRUYNINCKX, JOZEF
    Phototypography and Graphic Arts Dimension Control Photography. Ad Compositors, Los Angeles, 1969, 155, illus.

BÜHLER, CURT F.
    William Caxton and His Critics: A Critical Reappraisal of Caxton's Contributions to the Enrichment of the English Language. Syracuse University Press, 1960, 30. (Brewster House Typographical Series No. 3.)

GRAPHIC ARTS

BULINSKI, EUGENE C.
    Anatomy and Mechanics of Layout for Strippers. Graphic Arts, 1968, 48, illus.

———.
    Stripper's Guide to Knowledge. Twin Cities Litho Club, Minneapolis (for National Association of Litho Clubs, New York), 1967, 33.

BURNS, AARON
    Typography. Reinhold, 1961, 111, illus.

BURT, SAMUEL M.
    Technical Education for the Graphic Arts Industry. International Graphic Arts Education Association, Washington, 1963, 47.

CANNON, RUPERT V.
    Graphic Reproduction: Copy Preparation and Processes. Vista Books, London, 1963, 123, illus. (Facts of Print Series.)

CANSLER, RUSSELL N., ED.
    Fundamentals of Offset. A. B. Dick, Chicago, 1966, 76, illus.

CARLSEN, DARVEY E.
    Graphic Arts. Rev ed. C. A. Bennet, 1970, 1 vol., illus.

CARR, FRANCIS
    A Guide to Screen Process Printing. Pitman, 1962, 208, illus. (Facts of Print Series.)

CARROLL, PHIL
    Overhead Cost Control. McGraw-Hill, 1964, 295.

CARTER, HARRY G.
    A View of Early Typography: Up to About 1600. Oxford University Press, 1969, 137, illus. (Lyell Lectures, 1968.)

CARUZZI, RICHARD F., HOCH, FRED W., and HARRIS, CARL B.
    Offset Duplicator Techniques. 4th ed., rev. Fred W. Hoch Associates, New York, 1968, 95, illus.

CAVE, RODERICK
    The Private Press: Five Hundred Years of the Amateur Printer. Watson-Guptill, 1970, 408, illus.

CHAMBERS, ERIC
    Photolitho-Offset. Benn, London, 1967, 282, illus. (Handbooks to Printing.)

CHAMBERS, HARRY T.
    The Management of Small-Offset Print Departments: A Guide to Setting Up and Running Internal and Trade Offset Printing. Business Books, London, 1969, 191, illus.

CHENEY, ORION H.
    Economic Survey of the Book Industry, 1930-1931: As Prepared for the National Association of Book Publishers. R. R. Bowker, 1960, 356, illus.

UNIVERSITY OF CHICAGO PRESS
    A Manual of Style. 12th ed. University of Chicago Press, 1970, 546, illus.

CLAIR, COLIN
    A Chronology of Printing. Praeger, 1969, 228.

CLEAVER, JAMES
    A History of Graphic Art. Greenwood Press, 1969, 282, illus.

CLEETON, GLEN U., PITKIN, CHARLES W., and CORNWELL, RAYMOND L.
    General Printing. 3rd ed. McKnight & McKnight, 1963, 203.

COGOLI, JOHN E.
    Photo-Offset Fundamentals. 2nd ed. McKnight & McKnight, 1967, 384, illus.

THE COMPOSITORS' AND PRINTERS' HANDBOOK
    London Society of Compositors, 1919-

CONNECTICUT CURRICULUM COMMITTEE FOR THE PRINTING TRADES
    Printing Layout and Design. Rev. ed. Delmar, 1968, 201, illus.

COUPE, RAYMOND R.
    Science of Printing Technology. Cassell, London, 1966, 326.

CROY, PETER
    Graphic Design and Reproduction Techniques. G. P. Burden, tr. Hastings House, 1968, 282. (Visual Communication Books.)

CURWEN, HAROLD
    Processes of Graphic Reproduction in Printing. 3rd ed. Faber & Faber, 1963, 171, illus.

DAIR, CARL
    Design with Type. University of Toronto Press, 1967, 162, illus.

DAL, ERIK
    Scandinavian Bookmaking in the Twentieth Century. University of Illinois Press, 1969, 134, illus. (Phineas L. Windsor Series in Librarianship No. 10.)

DAY, KENNETH
    Book Typography, 1815-1965, in Europe and the United States of America. University of Chicago Press, 1966, 401.

DELAFONS, ALLAN
    The Structure of the Printing Industry. Macdonald, 1965, 122.

DENSTMAN, HAROLD, and SCHULTZ, MORTON J.
    Photographic Reproduction, Methods, Techniques, and Applications for Engineering and the Graphic Arts. McGraw-Hill, 1963, 187, illus.

DESSAUER, JOHN H., and CLARK, HAROLD E.
    Xerography and Related Processes. Focal Press, 1965, 520, illus.

DE VINNE, THEO L.
    The Invention of Printing. Gale, 1969, 556, illus. (Original ed., Hart & Co., 1876.)

DIRINGER, DAVID
    The Illuminated Book. Rev. ed. Praeger, 1967, 1 vol.

DOWDING, GEOFFREY
    An Introduction to the History of Printing Types: An Illustrated Summary of the Main Stages in the Development of Type Design from 1440 up to the Present Day [and] An Aid to Type Face Identification. Wace, London, 1961, 277, illus.

EASTMAN KODAK COMPANY
    Graphic Arts Handbook. Kodak, 1968, 1 vol., illus.

ECKMAN, JAMES R.
    The Heritage of the Printer. North American, Philadelphia, 1965- , Vol. 1- , illus.

EDWARDS BROTHERS, INC.
    The Author's Guide to Book Planning and Production. Edwards, Ann Arbor, Mich., 1969, 36, illus.

ELSEVIER'S DICTIONARY OF THE PRINTING AND ALLIED INDUSTRIES IN FOUR LANGUAGES: ENGLISH, FRENCH, GERMAN, DUTCH
    F. J. M. Wijnekus, comp. Elsevier, Amsterdam, New York, 1967, 596.

ENGDAHL, DAVID A.
    Color Printing: Materials, Processes, Color Control. Rev. ed. Amphoto, 1970, 1 vol., illus.

COMMERCIAL PROGRAMS

ENRICK, NORBERT L.
　Quality Control and Reliability: Practice-Tested Methods and Procedures, Based on Scientific Principles and Simplified for Immediate Application in a Variety of Manufacturing Plants. 5th ed. Industrial Press, 1966, 245, illus.

FETTER, ROBERT B.
　The Quality Control System. Irwin, 1967, 141, illus. (Irwin Series in Operations Management.)

FITSGERALD, R. T.
　The Printers of Melbourne. Pitman, Melbourne, 1967, 1 vol.

FRANKLIN, COLIN
　The Private Presses. Dufour, 1969, 240.

FYFFE, CHARLES
　Basic Copy Fitting. Watson-Guptill, 1969, 80, illus.

GARDNER, CHRISTINA
　Typesetting with IBM Executive Typewriters. Gardner Printing, Santa Rosa, Calif., 1967, 180, illus.

GECK, ELISABETH
　Johannes Gutenberg: From Lead Letter to the Computer. Inter Nationes, Bad Godesberg, Germany, 1968, 127, illus.

GENERAL ANILINE & FILM CORPORATION
　Graphic Arts Handbook. GAF, n.d., 50, illus.

GERBER, JACK, COMP.
　A Selected Bibliography of the Graphic Arts. Graphic Arts Technical Foundation, 1967, 84.

GIBSON, PETER
　Modern Trends in Letterpress Printing. Studio Vista, London, 1966, 110, illus. (Facts of Print Series.)

GLAISTER, GEOFFREY A.
　An Encyclopedia of the Book: Terms Used in Paper-Making, Printing, Bookbinding and Publishing. World, 1960, 484, illus.

GRANNIS, CHANDLER B., ED.
　What Happens in Book Publishing. 2nd ed. Columbia University Press, 1967, 467.

GRAPHIC ARTS TECHNICAL FOUNDATION, EDUCATION DEPARTMENT
　Manpower, Recruitment, and Education Programs in Graphic Communications: Addresses Given at the Education Department Sessions, Graphic Arts Technical Foundation Annual Meeting, 1968. GATF, 1968, 90.

GRAPHIC ARTS TYPOGRAPHERS
　Graphic Arts Type Book. Reinhold, 1965, 2 vols.

GROSS, GERALD, ED.
　Publishers on Publishing. R. R. Bowker, 1961, 491.

GRUENBERGER, FRED, ED.
　Computer Graphics: Utility, Production, Art. Thompson Book Co., 1967, 225.

HALPERN, BERNARD R.
　Color Stripping for Offset Lithography. 2nd ed. Graphic Arts Technical Foundation, 1964, 180, illus.

HANDOVER, P. M.
　Printing in London: From 1476 to Modern Times—Competitive Practice and Technical Invention in the Trade of Book and Bible Printing, Periodical Production, Jobbing. Harvard University Press, 1960, 224, illus.

HANSEN, BERTRAND L.
　Quality Control: Theory and Applications. Prentice-Hall, 1963, 498, illus.

HANSON, GLENN
　How to Take the Fits Out of Copyfitting. Mul-T-Rul, Fort Morgan, Colo., 1967, 116, illus.

HARROP, DOROTHY
　Modern Book Production. Bingley, London, 1968, 196, illus.

HATTERY, LOWELL H., and BUSH, GEORGE P.
　Automation and Electronics in Publishing. Spartan Books, Washington, 1965, 206, illus.

HEITNER, LOUIS
　Introduction to Offset. Faculty Press, New York, 1964, 72, illus.

HINWOOD, TONY
　Graphics Ad Library. Business Books, London, 1969, 1 vol.

HOCH, FRED W.
　Handbook for Pressmen. Rev. ed. Fred W. Hoch Associates, New York, 1966, 142, illus.

HOFMANN, ARMIN
　Graphic Design Manual: Principles and Practice. Reinhold, 1965, 172, illus.

HUTCHINGS, REGINALD S.
　A Manual of Decorated Typefaces: A Definitive Guide to Series in Current Use, Including Inline, Outline, Shaded, Three-Dimensional, Stencil, Cameo, Halftone, with Two-Colour and Embellished Designs.... Hastings House, 1965, 96.

―――.
　A Manual of Script Typefaces: A Definitive Guide to Series in Current Use, Selected and Arranged with an Introduction, Commentaries and Appendices. Hastings House, 1965, 92.

―――.
　The Western Heritage of Type Design: A Treasury of Currently Available Typefaces Demonstrating the Historical Development and Diversification of Form of Printed Letters. Cory, Adams & Mackay, London, 1963, 127.

HUTCHINS, MICHAEL
　Typographics: A Designer's Handbook of Printing Techniques. Reinhold, 1969, 96.

HUTT, ALLEN
　Newspaper Design. 2nd ed. Oxford University Press, 1967, 307, illus.

INTERNATIONAL CONFERENCE OF PRINTING RESEARCH INSTITUTES, LONDON, 1963
　Halftone Printing: Proceedings. Pergamon, 1964, 423, illus. (Advances in Printing Science and Technology Vol. 3.)

INTERNATIONAL PAPER COMPANY
　The Pocket Pal: A Graphic Arts Digest for Printers and Advertising Production Managers. 10th ed. IPC, New York, 1970, 181, illus.

INTERNATIONAL PRINTING PRESSMAN AND ASSISTANTS' UNION OF NORTH AMERICA
　A Career As A Printing Pressman. Pressmen's Home, Tenn., n.d., 32.

THE INTERTYPE: ITS FUNCTION, CARE, OPERATION AND ADJUSTMENT
　Intertype Company, Brooklyn, N.Y., 4 vols.

JACOBI, CHARLES T.
　The Printers' Vocabulary: A Collection of some 2500 Technical Terms, Phrases, Abbreviations, and Other Expressions.... Gale, 1969, 158.

JAFFE, ERWIN
　Contact Printing. Graphic Arts Technical Foundation, 1964, 67, illus. (Txn. 518.)

―――.
　Halftone Photography for Offset Lithography. 3rd ed. Graphic Arts Technical Foundation, 1960, 210, illus. (Txb. 508.)

GRAPHIC ARTS

JAYNE, JOHN J.
Small Printing Plant Management. Graphic Arts, 1965, 144.

JENNETT, SEAN
The Making of Books. 4th ed. Praeger, 1967, 512, illus.

JOHNSON, A. F.
Type Designs: Their History and Development. 3rd ed. British Book Centre, 1966, 1 vol., illus.

JOHNSON, ELMER D.
Communication: An Introduction to the History of the Alphabet, Writing, Printing, Books and Libraries. 3rd ed. Scarecrow Press, 1966, 304.

JURAN, JOSEPH M.
Quality Control Handbook. 2nd ed. McGraw-Hill, 1962, 1 vol., illus.

KAGY, FREDERICK D.
Graphic Arts. Rev. ed. Goodheart-Willcox, 1965, 112, illus. (Goodheart-Willcox's Build-a-Course Series.)

KARCH, ROBERT R.
Graphic Arts Procedures. 3rd ed. American Technical Society, 1965, 388, illus.

———.
Printing and the Allied Trades. 5th ed. Pitman, 1962, 669.

KARCH, ROBERT R., and BUBER, EDWARD J.
Graphic Arts Procedures: Offset Processes—Strike On and Film Composition. 3rd ed. American Technical Society, 1967, 570, illus.

KAUFFMANN, DÉSIRÉ
Graphic Arts Crafts. 2nd ed. Van Nostrand, 1962, 261.

KELBER, HARRY, and SCHLESINGER, CARL
Union Printers and Controlled Automation. Free Press, 1967, 318.

KINSEY, ANTHONY
Introducing Screen Printing. Watson-Guptill, 1967, 96, illus.

KNOX, FRANK M.
Knox Standard Guide to Design and Control of Business Forms. McGraw-Hill, 1965, 225.

KOSLOFF, ALBERT
The Art and Craft of Screen Process Printing. Bruce, 1960, 173, illus.

———.
Photographic Screen Process Printing. 3rd ed. Signs of the Times, 1968, 304, illus.

KRONENBERG, SHIRLEY
Cold Type Composition, Equipment and Technique: A Handbook of Typesetting and Layout. The author, Stamford, Conn., 1967, 137, illus.

KUHLER, CHARLES D.
Statistical Quality Control for the Printing Industry. Nonpareil Associates, New Hyde Park, N.Y., 1967, 143.

KUHLER, CHARLES D., and KUHLER, BARBARA L., COMPS.
Quality Control for the Graphic Arts: A Reference Bibliography. Graphic Systems Control, Islip, N.Y., 1968, 1 vol.

LARKEN, HENRY
Compositor's Work in Printing. 2nd ed. Staples Printers, London, 1963, 381.

LASKY, JOSEPH
Proofreading and Copy-Preparation: A Textbook for the Graphic Arts Industry. Mentor Press, 1966, 656, illus.

LATHAM, CHARLES W.
Advanced Pressmanship: Sheet-Fed Presses. Graphic Arts Technical Foundation, 1963, 296, illus. (Txb. 513.)

LATHAM, CHARLES W., and WHITE, JACK W.
Photo Composing: With an Introduction to Punch & Pin Register Systems. Graphic Arts Technical Foundation, 1964, 236, illus. (Txb. 515.)

LAWSON, ALEXANDER S.
A Printer's Almanac. Vol. 2. North American, Philadelphia, 1966, illus. (Heritage of the Printer.)

LEE, MARSHALL
Bookmaking: The Illustrated Guide to Design & Production. R. R. Bowker, 1965, 399, illus. (Balance House Book.)

LEHMANN-HAUPT, HELLMUT
Gutenberg and the Master of the Playing Cards. Yale University Press, 1966, 83, illus.

LEVARIE, NORMA
The Art & History of Books. Heineman, 1968, 315.

LEWIS, JOHN N. C.
The Anatomy of Printing: The Influences of Art and History on Its Design. Watson-Guptill, 1970, 272, illus.

———.
The Twentieth Century Book: Its Illustration and Design. Reinhold, 1967, 272, illus.

———.
Typography: Basic Principles—Influences and Trends Since the 19th Century. Reinhold, 1964, 96, illus. (Studio Paperbacks.)

LEWIS, JOHN N. C., and SMITH, EDWIN
Reproducing Art: The Photography, Graphic Reproduction and Printing of Works of Art. Praeger, 1969, 143, illus.

LIEBERMAN, J. BEN
Types of Typefaces and How to Recognize Them. Sterling, 1967, 132, illus.

LONG, ROBERT P.
Package Printing: The Development and Scope of Package Printing—The Background and Applications in Packaging of the Major and Minor Processes [and] How each Process Works.... Graphic Magazines, 1964, 223, illus.

McGRAW-HILL, INC.
The McGraw-Hill Author's Book. McGraw-Hill, 1968, 74.

McLUHAN, MARSHALL
The Gutenberg Galaxy: The Making of Typographic Man. University of Toronto Press, 1962, 293.

McMURTRIE, DOUGLAS C.
A History of Printing in the United States. Rpt. Burt Franklin, 1969, 2 vols.

MADISON, CHARLES A.
Book Publishing in America. McGraw-Hill, 1966, 628.

MEES, CHARLES E. K.
From Dry Plates to Ektachrome Film: A Story of Photographic Research. Ziff-Davis, 1961, 312, illus.

MELCHER, DANIEL, and LARRICK, NANCY
Printing and Promotion Handbook: How to Plan, Produce, and Use Printing, Advertising, and Direct Mail. 3rd ed. McGraw-Hill, 1966, 451, illus.

MERRIMAN, FRANK
A.T.A. Type Comparison Book. Advertising Typographers Association of America, New York, 1965, 133, illus.

MORISON, STANLEY
Four Centuries of Fine Printing: One Hundred and Ninety-Two Facsimiles of Pages from Books Printed at Presses Established Between 1465 and 1924. 4th ed. Barnes & Noble, 1960, 254.

———.
The Typographic Book, 1450-1935: A Study of Fine Typography Through Five Centuries. University of Chicago Press, 1963, 98.

———.
On Type Designs Past and Present: A Brief Introduction. Rev. ed. Benn, London, 1962, 79, illus.

COMMERCIAL PROGRAMS

MORTON, ALAN
Mechanical Composition. Pergamon, 1969- , vols., illus. (Library of Industrial and Commercial Education and Training, Printing Division)

THE NEW YORK TIMES
Style Book. The New York Times, 1950- , vols.

NEWHALL, BEAUMONT
The Daguerreotype in America. Duell, Sloan & Pearce, 1961, 176.

N. W. AYER & SON'S DIRECTORY: NEWSPAPERS AND PERIODICALS
Ayer, Philadelphia, 1880- , vols., annual.

OSWALD, JOHN C.
Printing in the Americas. Kennikat Press, 1965, 2 vols., illus.

OUDERKIRK, JOHN C.
An Introduction to Printing Plant Layout. Printing Industry of Illinois Association, Chicago, 1966, 94, illus.

THE PENROSE ANNUAL: REVIEW OF THE GRAPHIC ARTS
Hastings House, 1935- , illus.

PHILLIPS, ARTHUR H.
Computer Peripherals and Typesetting: A Study of the Man-Machine Interface Incorporating a Survey of Computer Peripherals and Typographic Composing Equipment. HMSO, London, 1968, 665, illus.

POCKET ENCYCLOPEDIA OF PAPER & GRAPHIC ARTS TERMS
2nd ed. Thomas Printing & Publishing Co., Kaukauna, Wis., 1965, 122.

POLK, RALPH W., and POLK, EDWIN W.
Elementary Platen Presswork. Rev. ed. Bennett, 1965, 148, illus.

———.
The Practice of Printing: Letterpress and Offset. Rev. ed. Bennett, 1964, 328, illus.

PRINTING INDUSTRIES OF METROPOLITAN NEW YORK, INC.
Printers Buying Guide. Printing Industries, New York, 1968-69- , 1 vol.

PRINTING TRADES BLUE BOOK: THE STANDARD DIRECTORY AND REFERENCE BOOK OF THE GRAPHIC ARTS INDUSTRY....
A. F. Lewis, New York, 1916- , vols., illus.

REED, ROBERT F.
Offset Platemaking Deep-Etch. 3rd ed. Lithographic Technical Foundation, 1963, 203, illus.

———.
Offset Press Troubles: Sheet-Fed Presses. Graphic Arts Technical Foundation, 1962, 108, illus. (Txn. 501.)

———, COMP.
Web Offset Press Troubles. 2nd ed. Graphic Arts Technical Foundation, 1968, 1 vol., illus. (Txn. 517.)

REES, HERBERT
Rules of Printed English. Darton, Longman & Todd, 1970, 1 vol.

REINFELD, GEORGE
How To Increase Your Printing Sales. R. Rosen Press, 1967, 153.

———.
Your Future in Printing. R. Rosen Press, 1963, 160. (Careers in Depth No. 34.)

RHODES, DENNIS E.
The Spread of Printing: Eastern Hemisphere—India, Pakistan, Ceylon, Burma, and Thailand. Vangendt, Amsterdam, 1969, 95. (Other titles in the series cover other geographic areas.)

RINHART, FLOYD, and RINHART, MARION
American Daguerreian Art. Crown, 1967, 135, illus.

ROBERTS, RAYMOND
Typographic Design. Benn, London, 1966, 198, illus.

ROBERTSON PHOTO-MECHANIX, INC.
In Focus: A Guideline to the Career Opportunities in Graphic Arts with Special Emphasis on the Process Cameraman, the Techniques and Equipment He Uses. Robertson, Des Plaines, Ill., 1967, 154, illus.

RODRÍGUEZ, CÉSAR
Bilingual Dictionary of the Graphic Arts: English-Spanish, Spanish-English. Rev. ed. G. A. Humphrey, Farmingdale, N.Y., 1966, 448.

ROSEN, BEN
Type and Typography: The Designer's Type Book. Rev. ed. Reinhold, 1967, 406, illus.

ROTHENSTEIN, MICHAEL
Relief Printing. Watson-Guptill, 1970, 224, illus.

RUDER, EMIL
...Typography: A Manual of Design.... Hastings House, 1967, 273. (Visual Communications Books.)

SAYRE, IRENE H.
The Single Color Offset Press. Lithographic Textbook, 1969, 479, illus.

SEYBOLD, JOHN W.
The Market for Computerized Composition. 2nd ed. Printing Industries of America, Computer Section, 1969, 175.

SILVER, GERALD A.
Modern Graphic Arts Paste-up. American Technical Society, 1966, 141, illus. (Graphic Arts Series.)

———.
Printing Estimating. American Technical Society, 1970, 156, illus.

SILVER, ROLLO G.
The American Printer: 1787-1825. University Press of Virginia, 1967, 189, illus.

SIMON, HERBERT
Introduction to Printing: The Craft of Letterpress. Faber & Faber, 1968, 120, illus.

SIMON, IRVING B.
The Story of Printing: From Wood Blocks to Electronics. Harvey House, Irvington, N.Y., 1965, 128, illus.

SIMON, OLIVER
Introduction to Typography. 2nd ed. Faber & Faber, 1963, 164, illus.

SLUCKIN, WLADYSLAW
Imprinting & Early Learning. Aldine, 1965, 147, illus.

SMITH, DATUS C.
Guide to Book-Publishing. R. R. Bowker, 1966, 244, illus.

SPELLMAN, JOHN A.
Printing Works Like This. Roy, 1964, 56, illus.

SPENCER, HERBERT
Pioneers of Modern Typography. Hastings House, 1970, 159, illus. (Visual Communication Books.)

———.
The Visible Word. 2nd ed. Hastings House, 1969, 107, illus. (Visual Communication Books.)

STEVENSON, GEORGE A.
Graphic Arts Encyclopedia. McGraw-Hill, 1968, 492, illus.

STONE, BERNARD, and ECKSTEIN, ARTHUR
Preparing Art for Printing. Reinhold, 1965, 199, illus.

STRAUSS, VICTOR
The Printing Industry: An Introduction to Its Many Branches, Processes, and Products. Printing Industries of America, Washington, 1967, 814, illus.

GRAPHIC ARTS

STUBBE, WOLF
   Graphic Arts in the Twentieth Century. Praeger, 1963, 318, illus.

SUTTON, JAMES, and BARTRAM, ALAN
   An Atlas of Typeforms. Hastings House, 1968, 116, illus.

SWANN, CAL
   Techniques of Typography. Watson-Guptill, 1969, 96, illus.

TEIGEN, KIT
   Graphic Arts: An Introduction—Publishing for Love and Money. Management Development Institute, Wayne, Pa., 1968, 110, illus.

THOMAS, ALAN G.
   Fine Books. Putnam, 1967, 120, illus. (Pleasures and Treasures.)

TINKER, MILES A.
   Legibility of Print. Iowa State University Press, 1963, 329, illus.

TSCHICHOLD, JAN
   Asymmetric Typography. Ruari McLean, tr. Reinhold, 1967, 94, illus.

TUCKER, SPENCER A.
   Cost-Estimating and Pricing with Machine Hour Rates. Prentice-Hall, 1962, 253, illus.

TURNBULL, ARTHUR T., and BAIRD, RUSSELL N.
   The Graphics of Communication: Typography, Layout, Design. 2nd ed. Holt, Rinehart & Winston, 1968, 395, illus.

———.
   Practical Exercises in Typography, Layout, and Design. Holt, Rinehart & Winston, 1968, 291, illus.

TURNER, MARY C., ED.
   Bookman's Glossary. 4th ed. R. R. Bowker, 1961, 212, illus.

TYPE SPECS COMPANY
   Type Specs. Type Specs, New York, 1962, 519.

TYPOMUNDUS 20
   Reinhold, 1964- , 1 vol., triennial.

U.S. CONGRESS, JOINT COMMITTEE ON PRINTING
   Federal Printing Program. USGPO, 1967, 41.

U.S. GOVERNMENT PRINTING OFFICE
   100 GPO Years, 1861-1961: A History of United States Public Printing. USGPO, 1961, 164, illus.

———.
   Specimens of Type Faces in the United States Government Printing Office. USGPO, 1962, 340.

———.
   Style Manual. Rev. ed. USGPO, 1967, 512, illus.

———.
   Typography and Design. Rev. ed. USGPO, 1963, 107, illus. (Training Series.)

UPDIKE, DANIEL B.
   Printing Types, Their History, Forms and Use: A Study in Survivals. 3rd ed. Belknap Press, Cambridge, Mass., 1962, 2 vols., illus.

VAN KRUININGEN, H.
   The Techniques of Graphic Art. Praeger, 1969, 80, illus.

WEINER, JACK, and ROTH, LILLIAN
   Electrostatic Printing. Institute of Paper Chemistry, Appleton, Wis., 1964, 111. (Bibliographic Series No. 212.)

WETHERILL, G. BARRIE
   Sampling Inspection and Quality Control. Methuen, London, 1969, 128, illus.

WHETTON, HARRY, ED.
   Practical Printing and Binding: Odhams Complete Guide to the Printer's Craft. 3rd ed. Odhams, London, 1965, 448, illus.

WILLIAMSON, HUGH A. F.
   Methods of Book Design: The Practice of an Industrial Craft. 2nd ed. Oxford University Press, 1966, 433, illus.

WILSON, ADRIAN
   The Design of Books. Reinhold, 1967, 159, illus.

WOLFE, HERBERT J.
   Printing and Litho Inks. 6th ed. MacNair-Dorland, 1967, 537, illus.

WOLSELEY, ROLAND E.
   Understanding Magazines. 2nd ed. Iowa State University Press, 1969, 458, illus.

YULE, JOHN A. C.
   Principles of Color Reproduction: Applied to Photomechanical Reproduction, Color Photography, and the Ink, Paper, and Other Related Industries. Wiley, 1967, 411, illus. (Wiley Series on Photographic Science and Technology and the Graphic Arts.)

ZAPF, HERMANN
   Manuale Typographicum: 100 Typographical Arrangements with Considerations About Types, Typography and the Art of Printing Selected from Past and Present, Printed in Eighteen Languages. Museum Books, 1968, 1 vol., illus.

ZAPF, HERMANN, and STAUFFACHER, JACK W.
   Hunt Roman: The Birth of a Type. Pittsburgh Bibliophiles, 1965, 1 vol., illus.

BINDING

CORDEROY, J.
   Bookbinding for Beginners. Watson-Guptill, 1967, 104.

DIEHL, EDITH
   Bookbinding, Its Background and Technique. Kennikat Press, 1965, 2 vols., illus.

KLINEFELTER, LEE M.
   Bookbinding Made Easy. Rev. ed. Bruce, 1960, 86, illus.

LEHMANN-HAUPT, HELLMUT
   Bookbinding in America: Three Essays. R. R. Bowker, 1967, 293, illus.

MIDDLETON, BERNARD C. A.
   A History of English Craft Bookbinding Technique. Hafner, 1963, 1 vol.

PERRY, KENNETH F., and BAAB, CLARENCE T.
   The Binding of Books. McKnight & McKnight, 1967, 190, illus.

PLENDERLEITH, HAROLD J.
   The Preservation of Leather Bookbindings. The British Museum, 1967, 32.

ROBINSON, IVOR
   Introducing Bookbinding. Watson-Guptill, 1968, 112, illus.

U.S. GOVERNMENT PRINTING OFFICE
   Theory and Practice of Bookbinding. Rev. ed. USGPO, 1963, 244, illus. (Training Series.)

INK

APPS, ERNEST A.
   Ink Technology for Printers and Students. Chemical, 1964, 3 vols., illus.

ARNOLD, EDMUND C.
   Ink on Paper: A Handbook of the Graphic Arts. Harper, 1963, 323, illus.

COMMERCIAL PROGRAMS

ASKEW, FREDERICK A., ED.
Printing Ink Manual. 2nd ed. Heffer & Sons, London, 1969, 848.

BANKS, WILLIAM H., ED.
Inks, Plates and Print Quality: Proceedings of the Ninth International Conference of Printing Research Institutes held in Rome, 1967. Pergamon, 1969, 333, illus. (Advances in Printing Science and Technology Vol. 5.)

INTERNATIONAL CONFERENCE OF PRINTING RESEARCH INSTITUTES
Printing Inks and Color: Proceedings. W. H. Banks, ed. Pergamon, 1961, 352, illus. (Advances in Printing Science and Technology Vol. 1.)

LARSEN, LOUIS M.
Industrial Printing Inks. Reinhold, 1962, 323, illus.

NATIONAL ASSOCIATION OF PRINTING INK MANUFACTURERS, TECHNICAL COMMITTEE
Printing Ink Handbook. 2nd ed. NAPIM, New York, 1967, 94, illus.

PAPER

AINSWORTH, JOHN H.
Paper: The Fifth Wonder. 3rd ed. Thomas Printing & Publishing Co., Kaukauna, Wis., 1967, 370, illus.

AMERICAN PAPER AND PULP ASSOCIATION
The Dictionary of Paper: Including Pulp, Paperboard, Paper Properties and Related Papermaking Terms. 3rd ed. APPA, 1965, 500.

AMERICAN SOCIETY FOR TESTING MATERIALS, COMMITTEE D-6 ON PAPER AND PAPER PRODUCTS
Paper and Paperboard: Characteristics, Nomenclature, and Significance of Tests. 3rd ed. ASTM, 1963, 129, illus. (ASTM Special Technical Pub. No. 60-B.)

BRITT, KENNETH W., ED.
Handbook of Pulp and Paper Technology. 2nd ed. Reinhold, 1970, 723, illus.

BROWNING, BERTIE L.
Analysis of Paper. Dekker, New York, 1969, 342, illus.

CLAPPERTON, ROBERT H.
The Paper-Making Machine: Its Invention, Evolution and Development. Pergamon, 1967, 365, illus.

DAVIS, DALE S.
Calculations in the Paper Industry. Franklin, Englewood, N.J., 1963, 231, illus.

DE LUCA, JAMES P.
A Manual for Paper Estimating. Nonpareil Associates, New Hyde Park, N.Y., 1967, 113.

HARDMAN, H., and COLE, E. J.
Papermaking Practice. University of Toronto Press, 1960, 334, illus.

———.
Papermaking: Questions and Answers. Lockwood, New York, 1969, 192.

HIGHAM, ROBERT R. A.
A Handbook of Papermaking. Oxford University Press, 1963, 294, illus.

LOCKWOOD'S DIRECTORY OF THE PAPER & ALLIED TRADES
Lockwood Trade Journal, 1873-74- , vols., annual, illus.

MASON, JOHN
Paper Making as an Artistic Craft. Twelve by Eight, Leicester, England, 1963, 95.

MEYER, JEROME S.
Paper. World, 1960, 91, illus.

MOSHER, ROBERT H., and DAVIS, D. S.
Industrial and Specialty Papers: Their Technology, Manufacture and Use. Tudor, 4 vols., 1968- .

NORTHRUP, HERBERT R.
The Negro in the Paper Industry. University of Pennsylvania Press, 1969, 1 vol. (Racial Policies of American Industry Report No. 8.)

THE PAPER CATALOG
Metropolitan New York ed. Walden, Sons & Mott, New York, 1929- , vols., semiannual.

THE PAPER YEAR BOOK...
Ojibway Press, Duluth, 1943- , vols., annual, illus.

PULP AND PAPER MANUFACTURE
McGraw-Hill, 1970, 3 vols., illus.

PULP AND PAPER SCIENCE AND TECHNOLOGY
C. Earl Libby, ed. McGraw-Hill, 1962, 2 vols., illus.

STREIT, FRED
Paper Quality Control. Lockwood, New York, 1968, 129, illus.

SUTERMEISTER, EDWIN
The Story of Papermaking. R. R. Bowker, 1962, 209, illus.

TECHNICAL ASSOCIATION OF THE PULP AND PAPER INDUSTRY, COATING COMMITTEE
Paper Coating Additives. TAPPI, 1963, 155, illus. (TAPPI Monograph Series No. 250.)

———.
Paper Coating Pigments: A Project of the Coating Committee. TAPPI, 1966, 197, illus. (TAPPI Monograph Series No. 30.)

TECHNICAL ASSOCIATION OF THE PULP AND PAPER INDUSTRY, WET STRENGTH AND INTERFIBER BONDING COMMITTEE
Wet Strength in Paper and Paperboard. TAPPI, 1965, 159, illus. (TAPPI Monograph Series No. 29.)

U.S. LIBRARY OF CONGRESS
Papermaking: Art and Craft. Library of Congress, 1968, 96.

WALDEN'S ABC GUIDE & PAPER PRODUCTION YEARBOOK
Walden, Sons & Mott, New York, 1887- , vols., annual.

WEINER, JACK, and BYRNE, JERRY
Drying of Paper and Board. Institute of Paper Chemistry, Appleton, Wis., 1961, 149. (Bibl. Series No. 196.)

WEINER, JACK, and ROTH, LILLIAN
Paper and Its Relation to Printing. 2nd ed. Institute of Paper Chemistry, Appleton, Wis., 1962, 547. (Bibl. Series No. 164.)

———.
Runnability of Printing Paper. Institute of Paper Chemistry, Appleton, Wis., 1965, 135. (Bibl. Series No. 215.)

PHOTOGRAPHY

ADAMS, ANSEL E.
Camera and Lens: The Creative Approach. 2nd ed. Morgan & Morgan, 1970, 304.

———.
Polaroid Land Photography Manual: A Technical Handbook. Morgan & Morgan, 1963, 192, illus.

———.
The Print: Contact Printing and Enlarging. 2nd ed. Morgan & Morgan, 1968, 120, illus.

ASHER, HARRY
Photographic Principles and Practices. Chilton, 1968, 288, illus.

BAINES, HARRY
The Science of Photography. 2nd ed. Wiley, 1967, 318, illus.

BENNETT, EDNA
Nature Photography. 3rd ed. Chilton, 1967, 126, illus.

GRAPHIC ARTS

BOMBACK, EDWARD S.
    Manual of Color Photography. Fountain Press, London, 1965, 412, illus.

BOUCHER, PAUL E.
    Fundamentals of Photography. 4th ed. Van Nostrand, 1963, 535, illus.

CHAMBERS, ERIC
    Camera and Process Work. Benn, London, 1964, 1 vol.

COOTE, JACK H.
    Colour Prints: The Photographic Technique of the Colour Positive. 3rd ed. Chilton, 1968, 252, illus.

CRAEYBECK, A. H. S.
    Gevaert Manual of Photography. 5th ed. Morgan & Morgan, 1962, 458, illus.

CROY, OTTO R.
    Camera Copying and Reproduction. Focal Press, London, (Hastings House), 1964, 256, illus.

———.
    The Complete Art of Printing and Enlarging. 10th ed. Amphoto, 1969, 251, illus.

———.
    Creative Photography. Amphoto, 1970, 1 vol., illus.

EASTMAN KODAK COMPANY
    Kodak Photographic Materials for the Graphic Arts: Films, Glass Plates, Papers. 5th ed. Kodak, 1967, 1 vol., illus. (Kodak Graphic Arts Data Book No. Q2.)

ELISOFON, ELIOT
    Color Photography. Viking, 1961, 153.

ENCYCLOPEDIA OF COLOUR PHOTOGRAPHY
    Fountain Press, London, 1962, 177, illus.

THE ENCYCLOPEDIA OF PHOTOGRAPHY: THE COMPLETE PHOTOGRAPHER—THE COMPREHENSIVE GUIDE AND REFERENCE FOR ALL PHOTOGRAPHERS
    Greystone Press, New York, 1963-64, 20 vols., illus.

FALK, EDWIN A., and ABEL, CHARLES
    Practical Portrait Photography for Home and Studio. 2nd ed. Chilton, 1967, 223, illus.

FEININGER, ANDREAS
    The Color Photo Book. Prentice-Hall, 1969, 408, illus.

———.
    The Complete Photographer. Prentice-Hall, 1965, 344, illus.

———.
    Successful Color Photography. 4th ed. Prentice-Hall, 1966, 271, illus.

THE FOCAL ENCYCLOPEDIA OF PHOTOGRAPHY
    Rev. ed. Focal Press, 1965, 2 vols., illus.

FOLDES, JOSEPH
    Large-Format Camera Practices: Image Control for Professional Photographers. Chilton, 1969, 128, illus.

FOSSETT, R. O.
    Techniques in Photography for the Screen Process Printer. Signs of the Times, 1967, 103, illus.

FRAZIER, WILLIAM
    Printing by Flash. Chilton, 1967, 142, illus.

THE GERMAN PHOTOGRAPHIC ANNUAL
    W. Strache, Stuttgart, 1956- , vols., annual, illus.

GLYCK, ZVONKO
    Photographic Vision. Chilton, 1965, 160, illus.

GOWLAND, PETER
    How to Photograph Women. Rev. ed. Crown, 1967, 128, illus.

HASELGROVE, MAURICE L.
    Photographers' Dictionary. Archer House, 1962, 202, illus.

HERTZBERG, ROBERT E.
    Photo Darkroom Guide. 5th ed. Chilton, 1967, 128, illus.

HUNT, ROBERT W. G.
    The Reproduction of Color in Photography, Printing and Television. 2nd ed. Wiley, 1967, 500, illus.

JACOBSOHN, KURT, and MANNHEIM, LADISLAUS A.
    Enlarging. 19th ed. Focal Press, 1967, 533, illus.

JAFFE, ERWIN, et al.
    Color Separation Photography for Offset Lithography: With an Introduction to Masking. Graphic Arts Technical Foundation, 1965, 229, illus. (GATF No. 509.)

JAMES, THOMAS H., and HIGGINS, GEORGE C.
    Fundamentals of Photographic Theory. 2nd ed. Morgan & Morgan, 1960, 345.

JONAS, PAUL
    Manual of Darkroom Procedures and Techniques. 3rd ed. Chilton, 1967, 128, illus.

KINGSLAKE, RUDOLF
    Lenses in Photography: The Practical Guide to Optics for Photographers. Rev. ed. Barnes, New York, 1963, 278, illus.

KOSAR, JAROMIR
    Light-Sensitive Systems: Chemistry and Application of Nonsilver Halide Photographic Processes. Wiley, 1965, 473, illus. (Photographic Science and Technology and the Graphic Arts Series.)

LACOUR, MARSHALL, and LATHROP, IRVIN T.
    Photo Technology. American Technical Society, 1966, 263, illus.

LANGFORD, MICHAEL
    Basic Photography. Hastings House, 1965, 1 vol.

LARMORE, LEWIS
    Introduction to Photographic Principles. 2nd ed. Dover, 1965, 229, illus.

LINCOLN, MARSHALL
    Electronics for Photographers. Chilton, 1966, 159, illus.

LITZEL, OTTO
    Darkroom Magic. Chilton, 1967, 143, illus.

LOOTENS, JOSEPH G.
    Lootens on Photographic Enlarging and Print Quality. 7th ed. Chilton, 1967, 215, illus.

LURAY, HOWARD L.
    Strobe—The Lively Light: How It Works and How to Use It. 3rd ed. A. S. Barnes, 1963, 170, illus. (Ziff-Davis Book.)

LYONS, NATHAN, ED.
    Photographers on Photography: A Critical Anthology. Prentice-Hall, 1966, 190.

MEES, CHARLES E. K., ED.
    The Theory of the Photographic Process. 3rd ed. Macmillan, 1966, 591, illus.

MERTENS, L. E.
    In-Water Photography: Theory and Practice. Wiley, 1970, 464. (Photographic Science and Technology and the Graphic Arts Series.)

NEBLETTE, CARROLL B.
    Fundamentals of Photography. Van Nostrand-Reinhold, 1970, 351, illus.

———.
    Photography: Its Materials and Processes. 6th ed. Van Nostrand, 1962, 508, illus.

NEBLETTE, CARROLL B., and MURRAY, ALLEN E.
    Photographic Lenses. Rev. ed. Morgan & Morgan, 1970, 1 vol., illus.

COMMERCIAL PROGRAMS

NEWHALL, BEAUMONT
: The History of Photography: From 1839 to the Present Day. Rev. ed. Museum of Modern Art, New York, (Doubleday, dist.), 1964, 215, illus.

———.
: Latent Image: The Discovery of Photography. Doubleday, 1967, 148, illus. (Science Study Series.)

NOEMER, EWALD F.
: The Handbook of Modern Halftone Photography: With Complete Concepts & Practices. 4th ed. Perfect-Graphic-Arts Supply Co., Demarest, N.J., 1970, 1 vol., illus.

NURNBERG, WALTER
: Lighting for Photography: Means and Methods. 16th ed. Chilton, 1968, 209, illus.

PAGE, ANDRÉ
: Photographic Composition. Fountain Press, London, 1961, 94.

PHOTO-LAB INDEX: THE CUMULATIVE FORMULARY OF STANDARD RECOMMENDED PHOTOGRAPHIC PROCEDURES
: Morgan & Morgan, 1939- , vols.

THE PICTORIAL CYCLOPEDIA OF PHOTOGRAPHY
: A. S. Barnes, 1968, 703, illus.

PINNEY, ROY
: Advertising Photography: A Visual Communication Book. Hastings House, 1962, 160, illus.

RHODE, ROBERT B., and McCALL, FLOYD H.
: Introduction to Photography. Macmillan, 1965, 278, illus.

ROBINSON, KARL D., ED.
: Line Photography for the Lithographic Process. Rev. ed. Lithographic Technical Foundation, 1962, 123.

ROTHSCHILD, NORMAN, and KENNEDY, CORA W.
: Filter Guide. 3rd ed. Chilton, 1970, 1 vol., illus.

SAYRE, IRENE H.
: Choosing An Enlarger for the Graphic Arts. Lithographic Textbook, 1966, 144, illus.

———.
: Photography and Platemaking for Photo-Lithography. Rev. ed. Lithographic Textbook, 1969, 461, illus.

SCHARF, AARON
: Creative Photography. Reinhold, 1965, 95, illus.

SNELLING, HENRY H.
: The History and Practice of the Art of Photography. Morgan & Morgan, 1970, 160.

SOBLICK, HERMAN
: Buyers' Guide and Reference Handbook: Photocomposition Methods and Equipment. Quad, Bellmore, N.Y., 1964, 143, illus.

STEVENS, GUY W.
: Microphotography: Photography and Photofabrication at Extreme Resolution. 2nd ed. Wiley, 1968, 510, illus.

STROEBEL, LESLIE D.
: View Camera Techniques. Hastings House, 1967, 311. (Communication Arts Books.)

TIME-LIFE BOOKS
: The Camera. Time-Life Books, 1970, 1 vol., illus. (Life Library of Photography Vol. 1.)

TODD, HOLLIS N., and ZAKIA, RICHARD D.
: Photographic Sensitometry: The Study of Tone Reproduction. Morgan & Morgan, 1969, 312, illus.

U.S. AIR FORCE
: Handbook for Photo Lab Processing. Air Training Command, 1960- , 1 vol., illus. (AF Manual 95-11.)

U.S. BUREAU OF NAVAL PERSONNEL
: Photographer's Mate 3. USGPO, 1961, 447, illus. (Navy Training Course.)

WAKEFIELD, GEORGE L.
: An Introduction to Photography. Chilton, 1969, 191, illus.

ZELIKMAN, VITALIĬ L., and LEVI, S. M.
: Making and Coating Photographic Emulsions. Focal Press, 1965, 312, illus. (Focal Library.)

HOTEL TECHNOLOGY

ADLON, HEDDA
: Hotel Adlon: The Life and Death of a Great Hotel. Horizon Press, 1960, 256, illus.

ALMARODE, RICHARD L.
: Guidelines for Hospitality Education in Junior Colleges. American Association of Junior Colleges, Washington, 1967, 55.

AMERICAN HOTEL ASSOCIATION DIRECTORY CORPORATION
: Hotel & Motel Redbook. AHADC, 1886- , vol. 1- , annual.

AMERICAN HOTEL & MOTEL ASSOCIATION
: ...Directory of Hotel & Motel Systems.... AHMA, 1968- , vols., annual.

———.
: Uniform System of Accounts and Expense Dictionary for Motels-Motor Hotels-Small Hotels. AHMA, 1963, 128, illus.

AMERICAN MOTOR HOTEL ASSOCIATION
: Uniform Classification of Accounts for Motels and Motor Hotels. Tourist Court Journal, Temple, Tex., 1965, 84.

ANDERSON, RONALD A.
: The Hotelman's Basic Law. Insurance Press, Ocean City, N.J., 1965, 493.

ARCHITECTURAL RECORD
: Motels, Hotels, Restaurants and Bars. 2nd ed. McGraw-Hill, 1968, 327.

ARTHUR, R., and GLADWELL, D. C.
: The Hotel Assistant Manager. Barrie & Rockliff, London, 1964, 110.

BATCHELOR, DENZIL
: The English Inn. Batsford, London, 1963, 192, illus.

BATMALE, LOUIS F., and MULLANY GEORGE G., EDS.
: Career Training in Hotel and Restaurant Operation...at City College, San Francisco. San Francisco City College, n.d., 95, illus.

BERKELEY, BERNARD
: Floors and Floor Maintenance. Cornell Hotel & Restaurant Administration Quarterly, Cornell University, School of Hotel Administration, 1967, 107, illus.

———.
: The Selection and Maintenance of Commercial Carpet. Cornell Hotel & Restaurant Administration Quarterly, Cornell University, School of Hotel Administration, 1967, 64, illus.

BERKELEY, BERNARD, and KIMBALL, CYRIL
: The Care, Cleaning and Selection of Floors and Resilient Floor Coverings. Ahrens, 1961, 44.

BRADLEY, LEWIS A.
: Guide for Good Laundry and Linen Service in Hotels and Motor Hotels. Ahrens, 1961, 175, illus.

HOTEL TECHNOLOGY

———.
   The Selection, Care, and Laundering of Institutional Textiles. Cornell Hotel & Restaurant Administration Quarterly, Cornell University, School of Hotel Administration, 1963, 84, illus.

BRANSON, JOAN C., and LENNOX, MARGARET
   Hotel Housekeeping: Principles and Practice. Edward Arnold, London, 1965, 222, illus.

BRIGHAM, GRACE H.
   Housekeeping for Hotels, Motels, Hospitals, Clubs, Schools. Rev. ed. Ahrens, 1962, 158, illus.

CLARK, BILL
   Professional Cleaning and Building Maintenance: How to Organize A Money-Saving Service Business or a Department for Floor and Building Cleaning. Exposition Press, 1960, 344, illus.

COFFMAN, CHARLES D.
   The Full House: A Hotel-Motel Promotion Primer. Cornell University, School of Hotel Administration, 1964, 246, illus.

COMFORT, MILDRED H.
   Conrad N. Hilton, Hotelier: A Biography. T. S. Denison, Minneapolis, 1964, 240. (Men of Achievement Series.)

DALLAS, SANDRA
   No More Than Five In A Bed: Colorado Hotels In the Old Days. University of Oklahoma Press, 1967, 208, illus.

DELDERFIELD, ERIC R.
   Introduction to Inn Signs. Arco, 1969, 176, illus.

DORSEY, LESLIE, and DEVINE, JANICE
   Fare Thee Well: A Backward Look at Two Centuries of Historic American Hostelries, Fashionable Spas & Seaside Resorts. Crown, 1964, 328, illus.

DOSWELL, ROGER
   Towards an Integrated Approach to Hotel Planning. Shoe String, 1970, 302, illus.

DUFFIN, DANIEL J.
   The Essentials of Modern Carpet Installation. 2nd ed. Van Nostrand, 1962, 324, illus.

DUKAS, PETER
   Hotel Front Office Management and Operation. 3rd ed. W. C. Brown, 1970, 174, illus.

DUNSEATH, M.
   The Hotel Bookkeeper-Receptionist. Rev. ed. Barrie & Rockliff, London, 1967, 71, illus.

ECONOMIC DEVELOPMENT COMMISSION FOR HOTELS AND CATERING
   Hotel Accounting: Introduction to a Standard System.... HMSO, London, (British Information Service, dist.), 1969, 45.

END, HENRY
   Interiors Book of Hotels & Motor Hotels. Hill & Wang, 1963, 252, illus. (Whitney Library of Design.)

FEARN, DAVID A.
   Management Systems for the Hotel, Catering and Allied Industries. Business Books, London, (International Publications Service, New York, dist.), 1969, 242, illus.

FELDMAN, EDWIN B.
   Housekeeping Handbook for Institutions, Business, and Industry. F. Fell, New York, 1969, 423.

FRISCHAUER, WILLI
   The Grand Hotels of Europe. Coward-McCann, 1965, 255, illus.

FULLER, JOHN
   Hotel Keeping and Catering as a Career. Batsford, London, 1965, 136, illus. (Batsford Career Books.)

GUNN, CLARE A., and McINTOSH, ROBERT W.
   Motel Planning and Business Management. W. C. Brown, 1964, 248.

HARRIS, KERR, FORSTER & CO.
   Trends in the Hotel-Motel Business. Harris, Kerr, Forster, Atlanta, 1936- , vols., illus., annual.

(W. S.) HATTELL & PARTNERS
   Hotels, Restaurants, Bars. Reinhold, 1962, 146, illus.

HAYNER, NORMAN S.
   Hotel Life. McGrath, College Park, Md., 1969, 195.

HENDERSON, ERNEST
   The World of "Mr. Sheraton." McKay, 1960, 277.

HENKIN, SHEPARD
   Opportunities in the Hotel and Motel Industry. Rev. ed. Universal Publishing & Distributing, 1967, 112. (VGM Career Series V118.)

HICKS, LEONARD, JR., ED.
   Hotel Motel Sales Digest. Hotel Sales Management Association, 1966, 357, illus.

HOROWITZ, MORRIS A.
   The New York Hotel Industry: A Labor Relations Study. Harvard University Press, 1960, 265, illus.

HORWATH & HORWATH, NEW YORK
   Expense and Payroll Dictionary. Rev. ed. American Hotel and Motel Association, 1962, 74.

———.
   Lodging Industry. Horwath & Horwath, New York, 1970- , vols., 56, illus., annual. (Formerly Hotel Operations....)

HORWATH, ERNEST B., TOTH, LOUIS, and LESURE, JOHN D.
   Hotel Accounting. 3rd ed. Ronald, 1963, 513, illus.

HOTEL ASSOCIATION OF NEW YORK CITY, INC.
   Uniform System of Accounts for Hotels. Rev. ed. HANYC, 1963, 102.

HOTEL SALES MANAGEMENT ASSOCIATION
   H.S.M.A. Hotel-Motel Directory and Facilities Guide. HSMA, New York, 1967-68- , vols., annual.

INSTITUTIONS MAGAZINE
   The Components of Communication. Cahners, 1968, 1 vol.

———.
   Purchasing Guide for Institutions Interior Planners. Cahners, 1962, 1 vol., illus.

JACKSON, SAMUEL
   The Savoy: The Romance of a Great Hotel. Dutton, 1964, 317, illus.

KAZARIAN, EDWARD A.
   Work Analysis and Design for Hotels, Restaurants and Institutions. AVI, 1969, 356, illus.

KOTSCHEVAR, LENDAL H.
   How to Select and Care For: Serviceware, Textiles, Cleaning Compounds. Cahners, 1970, 200, illus.

KOZIARA, EDWARD C., and KOZIARA, KAREN S.
   The Negro in the Hotel Industry. University of Pennsylvania Press, 1968, 74. (Racial Policies of American Industry Report No. 4.)

LATTIN, GERALD W.
   Careers in Hotels and Restaurants. Walck, 1967, 107, illus. (Careers for Tomorrow.)

———.
   Modern Hotel and Motel Management. 2nd ed. W. H. Freeman, 1968, 230, illus.

LEFLER, JANET, and CALANESE, SALVATORE
   The Correct Cashier for Hotels and Restaurants. Ahrens, 1960, 59, illus.

COMMERCIAL PROGRAMS

LONG, ROBERT P.
  Castle-Hotels of Europe. 3rd ed. Hastings House, 1969, 127.

LUNDBERG, DONALD E.
  The Hotel and Restaurant Business. Rev. ed. Cahners, 1970, 301.

LUNDBERG, DONALD E., and ARMATAS, JAMES
  The Management of People in Hotels, Restaurants, and Clubs. W. C. Brown, 1964, 231, illus.

McGAVIN, CHARLES T.
  Hotel-Motel Parking Guide, Layouts, Etc. Cornell Hotel & Restaurant Administration Quarterly, Cornell University, School of Hotel Administration, 1969, 40, illus.

MEDLIK, S.
  The British Hotel and Catering Industry: An Economic and Statistical Study. Pitman, 1961, 215, illus.

MILLER, FLOYD
  Statler: America's Extraordinary Hotelman. Statler Foundation, New York, 1968, 240, illus.

PARKS, GEORGE M.
  The Economics of Carpeting and Resilient Flooring: An Evaluation and Comparison. University of Pennsylvania, Wharton School of Finance and Commerce, 1966, 87. (Industrial Research Unit Study No. 41.)

PFEIFFER, WILLIAM B., and VOEGELE, WALTER O.
  The Correct Maid for Hotels and Motels. 2nd ed., rev. Hayden, 1965, 64, illus.

PFEIFFER, WILLIAM B., VOEGELE, MARGUERITE C., and WOOLLEY, GRACE H.
  The Correct Service Department for Hotels, Motor Hotels, Motels and Resorts. Ahrens, 1962, 67, illus.

PODD, GEORGE O., and LESURE, JOHN D.
  Planning and Operating Motels and Motor Hotels. Hayden, 1964, 343, illus.

POMERANTZ, JOEL
  Jennie and the Story of Grossinger's. Grosset, 1970, 325, illus.

PRODUCT NEWS: HOTEL-MOTEL BUYER'S DIRECTORY
  American Hotel & Motel Association, 1960- , vols., illus., semiannual.

FOSTER D. SNELL, INC.
  Carpet Underlays: Performance Characteristics. Institutional Research Council, Inc., 1967, 30.

SONNABEND, ROGER P.
  Your Future in Hotel Management. R. Rosen Press, 1964, 158. (Careers in Depth.)

STEELE, ROBERT V. P.
  Delmonico's: A Century of Splendor. Houghton-Mifflin, 1967, 374, illus.

TAYLOR, DEREK
  Hotel and Catering Sales Promotion. Iliffe Books, London, 1964, 180.

TOURIST COURT JOURNAL
  Modern Motelkeeping. Rev. ed. National Restaurant Association, 1967, 75, illus.

TURNER, ETHEL M.
  A Small Hotel of Your Own: How To Start and Run a Successful Hotel or Guest House. Rev. ed. Arthur Neil, ed. Barrie & Rockliff, London, 1967, 144.

VALLEN, JEROME J.
  The Art and Science of Modern Innkeeping. Ahrens, 1968, 248, illus.

VAN ORMAN, RICHARD A.
  A Room For the Night: Hotels of the Old West. Indiana University Press, 1966, 162, illus.

WATTS, STEPHEN
  The Ritz of Paris. Norton, 1964, 214, illus.

WEISSKAMP, HERBERT
  Hotels: An International Survey. Praeger, 1968, 209, illus.

WHITTINGTON, HAROLD
  Starting and Managing a Small Motel. Small Business Administration, 1963, 70. (Starting and Managing Series Vol. 7.)

WITZKY, HERBERT K.
  Practical Hotel-Motel Cost Reduction Handbook. Ahrens, 1970, 208, illus.

———.
  Modern Hotel-Motel Management Methods. Ahrens, 1964, 278, illus.

ZWARENSTEYN, HENDRIK
  Fundamentals of Hotel Law: The Legal Aspects of the Innkeeper-Guest Relationship. Ronald, 1963, 232.

RESTAURANTS

ATKIN, WILLIAM W., and ADLER, JOAN
  Interiors Book of Restaurants. Hill & Wang, 1960, 215, illus. (Whitney Library of Design.)

BETTS, JIM
  The Restaurant Casebook of Public Relations. J. Betts, 1963, 64, illus.

COMBES, STEVE
  Restaurant French for Hoteliers, Restauranteurs and Catering Students. Barrie & Rockliff, London, 1961, 127.

CORNELL HOTEL & RESTAURANT ADMINISTRATION QUARTERLY
  The Essentials of Good Table Service. Rev. ed. Cornell University, School of Hotel Administration, 1966, 56, illus.

DUKAS, PETER, and LUNDBERG, DONALD E.
  How to Operate a Restaurant. Ahrens, 1960, 276, illus.

FAIRBROOK, PAUL
  Starting and Managing a Small Restaurant. Small Business Administration, 1964, 116, illus. (Starting and Managing Series Vol. 9.)

FULLER, JOHN, and CURRIE, A. J.
  The Waiter. 3rd ed. Barrie & Rockliff, London, 1965, 214, illus.

HARRIS, ELLEN A.
  Professional Restaurant Service. McGraw-Hill (Canada), 1966, 99, illus. (McGraw-Hill Foundation Series.)

HUEBENER, PAUL O.
  Gourmet Table Service: A Professional Guide. Ahrens, 1968, 182, illus.

KENTON, RONALD, and CESERANI, VICTOR
  Theory of Catering. 2nd ed. Edward Arnold, London, 1970, 1 vol.

KLEIN, JEROME E.
  Views to Dine By: The Stories of Panoramic Restaurants Around the World. View Books, 1961, 283, illus.

MILLER, EDMUND, ED.
  Profitable Cafeteria Operation. Ahrens, 1966, 340, illus.

MURPHY, PATRICIA
  Glow of Candlelight: The Story of Patricia Murphy. Prentice-Hall, 1961, 260, illus.

NATIONAL RESTAURANT ASSOCIATION
  A Financial Analysis of the Restaurant Industry, Corporations, Partnerships, and Individually Owned Operations.... NRA, 1963, 94.

———.
 Uniform System of Accounts for Restaurants. NRA, 1968, 150, illus.

NATIONAL RESTAURANT ASSOCIATION and J. WALTER THOMPSON COMPANY
 How to Promote Your Restaurant. NRA, 1965, 141, illus.

NEWELL, MALCOLM
 Mood and Atmosphere in Restaurants. Barrie & Rockliff, London, 1965, 1 vol.

RADIGAN, J. TERRY
 A Financial Analysis of the Restaurant Industry. National Restaurant Association, 1963, 94, illus.

STOKES, JOHN W.
 How to Manage a Restaurant: Or Institutional Food Service. W.C. Brown, 1967, 342, illus. (Restaurant and Hotel Management Series.)

TURNER, ETHEL M.
 A Catering Business of Your Own: How to Start and Run a Successful Restaurant or Café. Rev. ed. Barrie & Rockliff, London, 1967, 224, illus.

U.S. OFFICE OF EDUCATION, MANPOWER DEVELOPMENT AND TRAINING DIVISION
 Waiter-Waitress: A Suggested Guide for a Training Course. USOE, 1969, 56. (VT 010 162.)

WATSON, OLIVE B.
 School and Institutional Lunchroom Management. Parker, West Nyack, N.Y., 1968, 310, illus.

WENZEL, GEORGE L., SR.
 Blueprints for Restaurant Success. Rev. ed. The author, Austin, Tex., 1966, 236, illus.

———.
 Guides to Restaurant Profits. National Restaurant Association, 1966, 576.

———.
 How to Finance a Restaurant. The author, Austin, Tex., 1970, 127, illus.

WESTBROOK, JAMES
 Your Future in Restaurants and Food Service. Arco, 1970, 157.

WHYTE, WILLIAM F.
 Human Relations in the Restaurant Industry. Cornell Hotel & Restaurant Administration Quarterly, Cornell University, School of Hotel Administration, 1963, 44, illus.

INSURANCE

ANGELL, FRANK J.
 Angell's Study Manual of Insurance. New York Insurance Advocate, 1966, 172.

ARCO PUBLISHING COMPANY, INC.
 Insurance Agent and Broker. Rev. ed. Arco, 1970, 352.

ATHEARN, JAMES L.
 Risk and Insurance. Rev. ed. Appleton-Century-Crofts, 1969, 648. (Risk and Insurance Series.)

ATHEARN, JAMES L., and TOOLE, CAMERON S.
 Questions and Answers on Insurance. 2nd ed. Prentice-Hall, 1960, 448.

BICKELHAUPT, DAVID L., and MAGEE, JOHN H.
 General Insurance. 8th ed. Irwin, 1969, 947.

BLACK, KENNETH, KEIR, JACK C., and SURREY, STERLING
 Cases in Life Insurance. Irwin, 1965, 265.

BLUM, ALBERT A.
 Company Organization of Insurance Management. American Management Association, 1961, 80, illus. (AMA Research Study No. 49.)

DAVIDS, LEWIS E.
 Dictionary of Insurance. Littlefield, Adams, 1970, 276.

DENENBERG, HERBERT S., et al.
 Risk and Insurance. Prentice-Hall, 1964, 630, illus. (Prentice-Hall Series in Risk and Insurance.)

EILERS, ROBERT D., and CROWE, ROBERT M., EDS.
 Group Insurance Handbook. Irwin, 1965, 972, illus.

ELLIOTT, CURTIS M.
 Property and Casualty Insurance. McGraw-Hill, 1960, 200. (National Association of Insurance Agents, McGraw-Hill Bookshelf.)

FLETCHER, LINDA P.
 The Negro in the Insurance Industry. University of Pennsylvania Press, 1970, 177. (Racial Policies of American Industry Report No. 11.)

GOSHAY, ROBERT C.
 Information Technology in the Insurance Industry: The Impact of EDP on Managerial Processes and Insurance Functions. Irwin, 1964, 176.

GREENE, MARK R.
 Risk and Insurance. 2nd ed. South-Western, 1968, 854, illus.

GREGG, DAVIS W., ED.
 Life and Health Insurance Handbook. 2nd ed. Irwin, 1964, 1389.

GWERTZMAN, MAX J.
 The Standard Fire Policy. New York Insurance Advocate, 1963, 64. (Legal Analysis Series No. 5.)

HOWARD, WILLIAM M.
 Cases on Risk Management. McGraw-Hill, 1967, 189. (McGraw-Hill Insurance Series.)

HUEBNER, SOLOMON S., BLACK, KENNETH, JR., and CLINE, ROBERT S.
 Property and Liability Insurance. Appleton-Century-Crofts, 1968, 594. (Risk and Insurance Series.)

KULP, CLARENCE A., and HALL, JOHN W.
 Casualty Insurance. 4th ed. Ronald, 1968, 1072.

LEVY, MICHAEL H.
 A Handbook of Personal Insurance Terminology. Farnsworth, 1968, 595.

LONG, JOHN D., and GREGG, DAVIS W., EDS.
 Property and Liability Insurance Handbook. Irwin, 1965, 1301.

MAYERSON, ALLEN L.
 Introduction to Insurance. Macmillan, 1962, 443, illus.

MEHR, ROBERT I., and COMMACK, EMERSON
 Principles of Insurance. 4th ed. Irwin, 1966, 994.

MICHELBACHER, GUSTAV F., and ROOS, NESTER R.
 Multiple-Line Insurers: Their Nature and Operation. 2nd ed. McGraw-Hill, 1970, 320.

MOWBRAY, ALBERT H., BLANCHARD, RALPH H., and WILLIAMS, C. ARTHUR, JR.
 Insurance: Its Theory and Practice in the U.S. 6th ed. McGraw-Hill, 1961, 661.

RIEGEL, ROBERT, and MILLER, JEROME S.
 Insurance Principles and Practices. 5th ed. Prentice-Hall, 1966, 775.

RODDA, WILLIAM H.
 Marine Insurance: Ocean and Inland. Prentice-Hall, 1970, 448.

COMMERCIAL PROGRAMS

———.
    Property and Liability Insurance. Prentice-Hall, 1966, 500. (Prentice-Hall Series in Risk and Insurance.)

RUDY, WILLIAM B.
    How to Sell More Insurance: Fire, Casualty, Surety, and Marine. McGraw-Hill, 1962, 214. (National Association of Insurance Agents, McGraw-Hill Bookshelf.)

SOMMER, ARMAND, and KEDZIE, DANIEL P.
    Your Future in Insurance. R. Rosen Press, 1965, 157. (Careers in Depth.)

STENGEL, CHARLES D., ED.
    Claim Administration: Life and Health Insurance. 2nd ed. International Claim Association, Philadelphia, 1969, 1 vol.

TAYLOR, IRWIN M.
    Law of Insurance. 2nd ed. Oceana, 1968, 116. (Legal Almanac Series No. 37.)

TURNER, DAVID R.
    Insurance Agent and Broker. 5th ed. Arco, 1970, 352, illus. (Arco Self-Tutor for High Test Scores.)

WEBB, GARN H., and BIANCO, THOMAS C.
    Insurance Law: Analysis and Explanation. Holt, Rinehart & Winston, 1970, 103. (Holt/Landmark Law Summaries No. 20.)

WHERRY, RALPH H., and NEWMAN, MONROE
    Insurance and Risk. Holt, Rinehart & Winston, 1964, 300.

WHITE, EDWIN H.
    Business Insurance: Insured Business Continuation Plans for Proprietorships, Partnerships, and Closed Corporations. 3rd ed. Prentice-Hall, 1963, 495.

WILLIAMS, CHESTER A., and HEINS, RICHARD M.
    Risk Management and Insurance. McGraw-Hill, 1964, 619, illus. (McGraw-Hill Insurance Series.)

HEALTH INSURANCE

ARCO PUBLISHING COMPANY, INC.
    Health Insurance Agents' Examination. Rev. ed. Arco, 1970, 256.

DICKERSON, OLIVER D.
    Health Insurance. 3rd ed. Irwin, 1968, 773, illus.

FAULKNER, EDWIN J.
    Health Insurance. McGraw-Hill, 1960, 636, illus.

TURNER, DAVID R.
    Health Insurance Agent: Hospital, Accident, Health, Life. 4th ed. Arco, 1970, 256, illus. (Licensing Exam Series.)

LIFE INSURANCE

ARCO PUBLISHING COMPANY, INC.
    Life Insurance Agents' Examination. Rev. ed. Arco, 1970, 288.

GOLLIN, JAMES
    Pay Now, Die Later: What's Wrong with Life Insurance: A Report on Our Biggest and Most Wasteful Industry. Random House, 1966, 267.

GREIDER, JANICE E., and BEADLES, WILLIAM T.
    Law and the Life Insurance Contract. Rev. ed. Irwin, 1968, 556, illus.

HUEBNER, SOLOMON S., and BLACK, KENNETH, JR.
    Life Insurance. 7th ed. Appleton-Century-Crofts, 1969, 875, illus.

KELSEY, R. WILFRED, and DANIELS, ARTHUR C.
    Handbook of Life Insurance. 4th ed. Institute of Life Insurance, 1969, 88.

LIFE OFFICE MANAGEMENT ASSOCIATION
    Fundamentals of Expense Budgeting in a Life Insurance Company. LOMA, 1969, 1 vol.

MACLEAN, JOSEPH B.
    Life Insurance. 9th ed. McGraw-Hill, 1962, 617, (McGraw-Hill Insurance Series.)

McGILL, DAN M.
    Life Insurance. Rev. ed. Irwin, 1967, 1023, illus.

MEHR, ROBERT I.
    Life Insurance: Theory and Practice. Business Publications, 1970, 1 vol.

MEHR, ROBERT I., and OSLER, ROBERT W.
    Modern Life Insurance: A Textbook of Income Insurance. 3rd ed. Macmillan, 1961, 754, illus.

NOBACK, JOSEPH C.
    Life Insurance Accounting: A Study of the Financial Statements of Life Insurance Companies in the United States and Canada. Irwin, 1969, 440.

REDEKER, HARRY S., and REID, CHARLES K.
    Life Insurance Settlement Options. Rev. ed. Irwin, 1964, 308.

RUSSELL, GEORGE H., and BLACK, KENNETH, JR.
    Human Behavior and Life Insurance. Prentice-Hall, 1963, 267.

INTERIOR DECORATION

AUSTIN, RUTH E., and PARVIS, JEANNETTE O.
    Furnishing Your Home. Ivol Spafford, ed. Houghton Mifflin, 1961, 282, illus.

BARROWS, CLAIRE M., ED.
    Living Walls: How to Appreciate and Install Wallpaper and Wall Coverings. Wallcoverings Council, New York, 1968, 207, illus.

BELL, VICTORIA K.
    The Art of Interior Design: A Text in the Aesthetics of Interior Design. Macmillan, 1960, 343, illus.

———.
    Opportunities in Interior Design and Decoration. Vocational Guidance Manuals, 1963, 126.

BETTER HOMES & GARDENS
    Decorating Book. Meredith Press, 1961, 400, illus.

———.
    Decorating Ideas: New Room-by-Room Decorating Tips. Meredith Press, 1960, 160, illus.

BIRREN, FABER
    Color For Interiors: Historical and Modern. Whitney Publications, New York, 1963, 210, illus.

BRUSHWELL, WILLIAM, ED.
    Painting and Decorating Encyclopedia. Goodheart-Willcox, 1964, 288, illus.

CHESKIN, LOUIS
    How to Color-Tune Your Home. Rev. ed. Quadrangle Books, 1962, 203, illus.

CHLYSTYK, WALTER
    Painting and Decorating. McGraw-Hill, 1965, 104, illus.

COMSTOCK, HELEN, ED.
    The Concise Encyclopedia of American Antiques. Hawthorn, 1965, 848.

INTERIOR DECORATION

DERIEUX, MARY
　Complete Book of Interior Decorating. Rev. ed. Hawthorn, 1964, 466, illus.

DE VAN, DOROTHY S.
　Introduction to Home Furnishings. Macmillan, 1964, 342, illus. (Macmillan College Home Economics Series.)

DOYLE, ROBERT V.
　Your Career in Interior Design. Messner, 1969, 192, illus.

FAULKNER, RAY N., and FAULKNER, SARAH
　Inside Today's Home. 3rd ed. Holt, Rinehart & Winston, 1968, 552, illus.

FLANNERY, NAOMI
　101 Great Window Decorating Ideas. Bantam, 1970, 96, illus.

FLOYD, WAYNE
　Decorating with Photographs. Chilton, 1965, 128, illus.

GREER, MICHAEL
　Your Future in Interior Design. Rev. ed. R. Rosen Press, 1963, 157. (Careers in Depth.)

HATJE, GERD, and HATJE, URSULA
　Design for Modern Living: A Practical Guide to Home Furnishing and Interior Decoration. Abrams, 1962, 318, illus.

HIGHLAND, HAROLD J.
　Audel's Painting and Decorating Manual. Audel, 1961, 592, illus.

HOUSE & GARDEN
　Complete Guide to Interior Decoration.... Simon & Schuster, 1970, 1 vol., illus.

―――――.
　The Modern Interior. Robert Harling, ed. St. Martin's Press, 1965, 304, illus.

HOUSE & GARDEN GUIDE TO INTERIOR DECORATION
　Robert Harling, ed. Condé Nast, London, 1967, 304.

KALINS, DOROTHY G.
　Researching Design in New York: Interiors, Furniture, Decorative Arts. Fairchild, 1967, 127, illus.

KAUFMANN, RUTH
　The New American Tapestry. Van Nostrand-Reinhold, 1967, 104, illus.

KORNFELD, ALBERT
　The Doubleday Book of Interior Decorating. Doubleday, 1965, 216, illus.

KOVEL, RALPH M., and KOVEL, TERRY H.
　Know Your Antiques: How to Recognize and Evaluate any Antique, Large or Small Like an Expert. Crown, 1967, 327, illus.

LEVIN, EVELYN R.
　Let's Decorate Your Home. Cornerstone, New York, 1969, 125, illus.

MAGNANI, FRANCO, and RIVISTA DELL'ARREDAMENTO, EDS.
　Modern Interiors. Jane van Nuis Cahill, tr. Universe, 1970, 161, illus.

MEYERS, GENEVIEVE, ED.
　Decorating Ideas for Every Room. Arco, 1969, 128, illus.

NEWELL, ADNAH C., and HOLTROP, WILLIAM F.
　Coloring, Finishing and Painting Wood. Rev. ed. Bennett, 1961, 478, illus.

OBST, FRANCES M.
　Art and Design in Home Living. Macmillan, 1963, 332, illus.

O'CONNELL, C. B.
　Home Furnishing Self Help. Scarecrow Press, 1968, 181, illus.

L'OEIL
　The Best In European Decoration. Georges and Rosamund Bernier, eds. Reynal, Paris, 1963, 157.

PLIHAL, JANE, and BROWN, MARJORIE
　Evaluation Materials: Physical Home Environment and Psychological and Social Factors. Burgess, 1969, 198, illus.

PLUMB, BARBARA
　Young Designs in Living. Viking, 1969, 160, illus.

POWELL, MYRTIS N.
　Candles in Flower Arrangements. Van Nostrand-Reinhold, 1969, 104, illus.

PRAZ, MARIO
　An Illustrated History of Furnishing: From the Renaissance to the 20th Century. Braziller, 1964, 396.

REED, STANLEY
　Oriental Rugs and Carpets. Putnam, 1967, 120.

REIF, RITA
　Living with Books: 116 Designs for Homes and Offices. The New York Times, 1970, 120.

ROGERS, KATE E.
　The Modern House, U.S.A.: Its Design and Decoration. Harper, 1962, 292.

SEARS, ROEBUCK & COMPANY, CONSUMER INFORMATION SERVICES
　Color in Home Furnishings: Study Guide and Printed Originals. Sears, Skokie, Ill., 1968, 33. (VT 010 126.)

SHULTZ, MORT
　Painting and Wallpapering. Arco, 1969, 128, illus.

SUNSET
　Children's Rooms and Play Yards. Rev. ed. Lane, Menlo Park, Calif., 1970, 1 vol.

TRACY, BERRY
　Nineteenth-Century America: Furniture and Other Decorative Arts. Graphic, 1970, 256, illus.

VAN DOMMELEN, DAVID B.
　Decorative Wall Hangings: Art with Fabric. Funk & Wagnalls, 1962, 178, illus.

―――――.
　Designing and Decorating Interiors. Wiley, 1965, 277, illus.

WAUGH, ALICE
　Interior Design: A Laboratory Manual for House Furnishing. 4th ed. Burgess, 1961, 74, illus.

WEEKS, JEANNE G., and TREGANOWAN, DONALD
　Rugs and Carpets of Europe and the Western World. Chilton, 1969, 251, illus.

WETZLAR, ELISABETH
　Rustic Interiors for Town and Country. Universe, 1970, 130, illus.

WHITON, SHERRILL
　Elements of Interior Design and Decoration. 3rd ed. Lippincott, 1963, 833, illus.

WILKINSON, JULE, and INSTITUTIONS MAGAZINE
　The Three C's of Atmosphere. Cahners, 1968-69, 2 vols., illus. (Success Series.)

FURNITURE

ARONSON, JOSEPH
　The New Encyclopedia of Furniture. Crown, 1967, 484, illus.

COMMERCIAL PROGRAMS

BAST, HERBERT
  Essentials of Modern Upholstery. Bruce, 1963, 172, illus.

BEVIN, ARTHUR
  Upholstery. Arco, 1961, 160, illus.

BICK, ALEXANDER F.
  Contemporary Furniture. Bruce, 1968, 1 vol.

COMSTOCK, HELEN
  American Furniture: A Complete Guide to Seventeenth, Eighteenth, and Early Nineteenth Century Styles. Viking, 1962, 336, illus.

DAL FABBRO, MARIO
  Design and Construction of Upholstered Furniture. McGraw-Hill, 1969, 224.

GLOAG, JOHN
  A Social History of Furniture Design from 1300 B.C. to A.D. 1960. Crown, 1961, 202, illus.

HINCKLEY, F. LEWIS
  A Directory of Antique Furniture: The Authentic Classification of European and American Designs for Professionals & Connoisseurs. Crown, 1967, 214, illus.

HOCHMAN, LOUIE
  How to Refinish Furniture. Arco, 1960, 144, illus.

JOYNER, NINA G.
  Furniture Refinishing at Home. Chilton, 1961, 91, illus.

LUNA, BENJAMIN C.
  Upholstery: Refinishing and Restyling. American Technical Society, 1970, 202, illus.

MENKE, HARDY A.
  Contemporary Wood Furniture: A Book of Distinctive Designs. McKnight & McKnight, 1961, 95, illus.

MILLER, EDGAR G.
  American Antique Furniture: A Book for Amateurs. Dover, 1966, 2 vols., illus.

O'NEILL, JAMES M.
  Early American Furniture. McKnight & McKnight, 1963, 141, illus.

PARKER, PAGE, and FORNIA, JOSEPH G.
  Upholstering at Home. Rev. ed. Chilton, 1970, 1 vol., illus.

TIERNEY, WILLIAM F.
  Modern Upholstering Methods. McKnight & McKnight, 1965, 152, illus.

WANSCHER, OLE
  The Art of Furniture: 5000 Years of Furniture and Interiors. Van Nostrand-Reinhold, 1967, 408, illus.

MARKETING

ALDERSON, WROE, and GREEN, PAUL E.
  Planning and Problem Solving in Marketing. Irwin, 1964, 661, illus.

ALDERSON, WROE, and HALBERT, MICHAEL H.
  Men, Motives, and Markets. Prentice-Hall, 1968, 118, illus. (Prentice-Hall Foundations of Marketing Series.)

ALDERSON, WROE, and SHAPIRO, STANLEY J., EDS.
  Marketing and the Computer. Prentice-Hall, 1963, 443, illus.

ALEXANDER, MILTON, and MAZZE, EDWARD M., EDS.
  Sales Management: Theory and Practice. Pitman, 1965, 550, illus.

ALEXANDER, RALPH S., CROSS, JAMES S., and HILL, RICHARD M.
  Industrial Marketing. 3rd ed. Irwin, 1967, 698, illus.

AMERICAN MANAGEMENT ASSOCIATION
  The Marketing Job: Responsibilities of the Top Man. Elizabeth Marting, ed. AMA, 1961, 448.

AMERICAN MARKETING ASSOCIATION
  Proceedings of the National Conference. AMA, 1920- vols.

ANDERSON, IAN G., ED.
  Marketing & Management: A World Register of Organizations. Institute of Marketing, Beckenham, Kent, England; C.B.D. Research, 1969, 228.

ANDERSON, R. CLIFTON, and CATEORA, PHILIP R., EDS.
  Marketing Insights: Selected Readings. 2nd ed. Appleton-Century-Crofts, 1968, 482, illus.

ARBURY, JAMES N., et al.
  A New Approach to Physical Distribution. American Management Association, 1967, 127, illus.

ASPLEY, JOHN C., et al.
  The Dartnell Sales Promotion Handbook. 11th ed. Dartnell, 1968, 1080, illus.

ATTWOOD, CHARLES
  The Sales Representative's Handbook. Business Books, London, (International Publications Service, dist.), 1969, 209, illus.

BAKER, RICHARD M., and PHIFER, GREGG
  Salesmanship: Communication, Persuasion Perception. Allyn & Bacon, 1966, 422, illus.

BAKER, STEPHEN
  Visual Persuasion: Written and Designed. McGraw-Hill, 1961, 1 vol., illus. (McGraw-Hill Series in Marketing and Advertising.)

BARKSDALE, HIRAM C., ED.
  Marketing in Progress: Patterns and Potentials. Holt, Rinehart & Winston, 1964, 740.

———.
  Marketing: Change and Exchange—Readings from Fortune. Holt, Rinehart & Winston, 1964, 322, illus.

BARNHILL, J. ALLISON, ED.
  Sales Management: Contemporary Perspectives. Scott, Foresman, 1970, 492, illus.

BARTELS, ROBERT, ED.
  Comparative Marketing. Irwin, 1963, 317, illus.

———.
  The Development of Marketing Thought. Irwin, 1962, 284, illus.

———.
  Marketing Theory and Metatheory. Irwin, 1970, 299, illus.

BEARDEN, JAMES H., COMP.
  Personal Selling: Behavioral Science Readings and Cases. Wiley, 1967, 353, illus. (Wiley Marketing Series.)

BECKMAN, THEODORE N., and DAVIDSON, WILLIAM R.
  Marketing. 8th ed. Ronald, 1967, 872, illus.

BELL, MARTIN L.
  Marketing: Concepts and Strategy. Houghton-Mifflin, 1966, 686, illus.

BENDER, JAMES F.
  How to Sell Well: The Art and Science of Professional Salesmanship. McGraw-Hill, 1961, 269.

BERG, THOMAS L.
  Mismarketing: Case Histories of Marketing Misfires. Doubleday, 1970, 253.

BERG, THOMAS L., and SHUCHMAN, ABE, EDS.
  Product Strategy and Management. Holt, Rinehart & Winston, 1963, 610.

MARKETING

BISHOP, JAMES, and HUBBARD, H.
    Let the Seller Beware. National Press, Washington, 1969, 1 vol.

BLACKWELL, ROGER D., ENGEL, JAMES F., and KOLLAT, DAVID T.
    Cases in Consumer Behavior. Holt, Rinehart & Winston, 1969, 431.

BLAKE, ROBERT R., and MOUTON, JANE S.
    The Grid for Sales Excellence: Benchmarks for Effective Salesmanship. McGraw-Hill, 1970, 256.

BLISS, PERRY, ED.
    Marketing and the Behavioral Sciences: Selected Readings. 2nd ed. Allyn & Bacon, 1968, 614.

BODDEWYN, JEAN J.
    Comparative Management and Marketing. Scott, Foresman, 1969, 302, illus.

BOGART, LEO, ED.
    Current Controversies in Marketing Research. Markham, Chicago, 1969, 164.

BOWERSOX, DONALD J., SMYKAY, EDWARD W., and LaLONDE, BERNARD J.
    Physical Distribution Management: Logistics Problems of the Firm. Macmillan, 1968, 469, illus.

BOYD, HARPER W., and CLEWETT, RICHARD M., EDS.
    Contemporary American Marketing: Readings on the Changing Market Structure. Rev. ed. Irwin, 1962, 402, illus.

BOYD, HARPER W., CLEWETT, RICHARD M., and WESTFALL, RALPH
    Cases in Marketing Strategy. Irwin, 1964, 324, illus.

BOYD, HARPER W., and DAVIS, ROBERT T., COMPS.
    Reading in Sales Management. Irwin, 1970, 456.

BOYD, HARPER W., and WESTFALL, RALPH
    Marketing Research: Text and Cases. Rev. ed. Irwin, 1964, 791, illus.

BRITT, STEUART H., and BOYD, HARPER W.
    Marketing Management and Administrative Action. Rev. ed. McGraw-Hill, 1968, 776, illus. (McGraw-Hill Series in Marketing and Advertising.)

BROWN, MILTON P., et al.
    Problems in Marketing. 4th ed. McGraw-Hill, 1968, 898, illus. (McGraw-Hill Series in Marketing and Advertising.)

BUELL, VICTOR P.
    Handbook of Modern Marketing. McGraw-Hill, 1970, 1400.

———.
    Marketing Management in Action. McGraw-Hill, 1966, 340.

BURSK, EDWARD C.
    Text and Cases in Marketing: A Scientific Approach. Prentice-Hall, 1962, 580.

BURSK, EDWARD C., and CHAPMAN, JOHN F.
    Modern Marketing Strategy. Harvard University Press, 1964, 360, illus.

BURSTEIN, MILTON B.
    What You Should Know About Selling and Salesmanship. Oceana, 1969, 85. (Business Almanac Series No. 18.)

BUSINESS INTERNATIONAL
    Winning the Markets of the 1970's. Business International, New York, 1970, 76.

BUSKIRK, RICHARD H.
    Cases and Reading in Marketing. Holt, Rinehart & Winston, 1970, 329, illus.

———.
    Principles of Marketing: The Management View. Rev. ed. Holt, Rinehart & Winston, 1966, 829, illus.

THE BUYER'S MANUAL: A MERCHANDISING HANDBOOK
    Buyer's Manual, New York, 1930- , irregular vols.

BUZZELL, ROBERT D.
    Marketing Research and Information Systems. McGraw-Hill, 1969, 1 vol.

CANFIELD, BERTRAND R.
    Sales Administration: Principles and Problems. 4th ed. Prentice-Hall, 1961, 637, illus.

CATEORA, PHILIP R., and RICHARDSON, LEE, EDS.
    Readings in Marketing: The Qualitative and Quantitative Areas. Appleton, 1967, 462.

CHESKIN, LOUIS
    Secrets of Marketing Success. Trident Press, 1967, 278, illus.

CHRISTENSEN, N. C.
    The Art of Persuasion in Selling. Parker, West Nyack, N.Y., 1970, 224.

CONVERSE, PAUL D., HUEGY, HARVEY W., and MITCHELL, ROBERT V.
    The Elements of Marketing. 7th ed. Prentice-Hall, 1965, 710, illus.

COPULSKY, WILLIAM
    Practical Sales Forecasting. American Management Association, 1970, 109, illus.

COX, KEITH K., and ENIS, BEN M.
    Experimentation for Marketing Decisions. International Textbook, 1969, 122.

COX, REAVIS, ALDERSON, WROE, and SHAPIRO, STANLEY J., EDS.
    Theory in Marketing: Second Series. Irwin, 1964, 414, illus.

COX, REAVIS, GOODMAN, CHARLES S., and FICHANDLER, THOMAS C.
    Distribution in a High-Level Economy. Prentice-Hall, 1965, 331, illus.

CRANE, EDGAR
    Marketing Communications: A Behavioral Approach to Men, Messages, and Media. Wiley, 1965, 569, illus. (Wiley Marketing Series.)

CRISP, RICHARD D.
    Sales Planning and Control. McGraw-Hill, 1961, 402, illus. (McGraw-Hill Series in Marketing and Advertising.)

CRISSY, W. J. E., and KAPLAN, ROBERT M.
    Salesmanship: The Personal Force in Marketing. Wiley, 1969, 366, illus. (Wiley Marketing Series.)

CUNDIFF, EDWARD W., and STILL, RICHARD R.
    Basic Marketing: Concepts, Environment and Decisions. Prentice-Hall, 1964, 576, illus.

D'ANNA, JOHN P.
    Inventory and Profit: The Balance of Power in Buying and Selling. American Management Association, 1966, 123, illus.

DARTNELL CORPORATION
    The Sales Manager's Handbook. Dartnell, 1934- , vols., illus.

DAY, RALPH L., ED.
    Concepts for Modern Marketing. International Textbook, 1968, 324, illus. (International Series in Marketing.)

———.
    Marketing in Action: A Decision Game. Irwin, 1968, 43.

DENING, JAMES, ED.
    Marketing Industrial Goods. Business Books, London, (International Publications Service, New York, dist.), 1968, 223, illus. (Management in Action Series.)

COMMERCIAL PROGRAMS

DeVOE, MERRILL
: The Effective Sales Manager. EMD, Lexington, Ky., 1968, 321, illus.

———.
: How to Tailor Your Sales Organization to Your Markets. Prentice-Hall, 1964, 199.

DICHTER, ERNEST
: Handbook of Consumer Motivations. McGraw-Hill, 1964, 486, illus. (McGraw-Hill Series in Marketing and Advertising.)

DIRKSEN, CHARLES J., KROEGER, ARTHUR, and LOCKLEY, LAWRENCE C., EDS.
: Readings in Marketing. Rev. ed. Irwin, 1968, 673, illus.

DOUGLAS, JOHN, FIELD, GEORGE A., and TARPEY, LAWRENCE X.
: Human Behavior in Marketing. Merrill, 1967, 204, illus.

DOWNING, GEORGE D.
: Sales Management. Wiley, 1969, 392. (Wiley Marketing Series.)

DRAKE, JERRY E., and MILLAR, FRANK I.
: Marketing Research: Intelligence and Management. International Textbook, 1969, 631.

DREW-BEAR, ROBERT
: Mass Merchandising: Revolution & Evolution. Fairchild, 1970, 512, illus.

DUN & BRADSTREET, INC.
: Successful Sales Managing. Apollo Editions, 1969, 204. (Apollo Editions AB-1.)

ELAM, HOUSTON G.
: Marketing. Barrister, 1967, 227. (Bar-Notes College Course Analysis Guide No. 4170-7 Marketing.)

ELDRIDGE, CLARENCE E.
: Marketing for Profit. Macmillan, 1970, 257.

ELLING, KARL A.
: Introduction to Modern Marketing: An Applied Approach. Macmillan, 1969, 431, illus.

ELSBY, FRANK H.
: Marketing and the Sales Manager. Pergamon, 1969, 189, illus. (Commonwealth and International Library, Essentials of Marketing.)

ENGEL, JAMES F., COMP.
: Consumer Behavior: Selected Readings. Irwin, 1968, 233, illus. (American Marketing Association Reprint Series.)

ENGEL, JAMES F., WALES, HUGH G., and WARSHAW, MARTIN R.
: Promotional Strategy. Irwin, 1967, 665, illus.

ENIS, BEN M., and COX, KEITH K.
: Marketing Classics: A Selection of Influential Articles. Allyn & Bacon, 1969, 481, illus.

ENRICK, NORBERT L.
: Market and Sales Forecasting: A Quantitative Approach. International Textbook, 1969, 224.

ERNEST, JOHN W., and DaVALL, GEORGE M.
: Salesmanship Fundamentals: Creative Selling for Today's Market. 3rd ed. McGraw-Hill, 1965, 470, illus.

FISK, GEORGE
: Marketing Systems: An Introductory Analysis. Harper & Row, 1967, 797, illus.

FISK, GEORGE, and DIXON, DONALD F.
: Theories for Marketing Systems Analysis: Selected Readings. Harper & Row, 1967, 195, illus.

FORSTALL, RICHARD, ED.
: Commercial Atlas and Marketing Guide. Rev. ed. Rand McNally, 1970, 658.

FORTUNE
: Markets of the Seventies: The Unwinding U.S. Economy. Viking, 1968, 118, illus.

FRAM, EUGENE H.
: What You Should Know About Small Business Marketing. Oceana, 1968, 1 vol.

FRANK, NATHALIE D.
: Data Sources for Business and Market Analysis. 2nd ed. Scarecrow Press, 1969, 361.

FREY, ALBERT W., and ALBAUM, GERALD, EDS.
: Marketing Handbook. 2nd ed. Ronald, 1965, 1 vol., illus.

GERLACH, JOHN T., and WAINWRIGHT, CHARLES A.
: Successful Management of New Products. Hastings, 1968, 221.

GIBSON, D. PARKE
: The $30 Billion Negro. Macmillan, 1969, 311.

GOLDSTEIN, ALBERT
: Secrets of Overcoming Sales Resistance: 386 Tested Replies to Objections. Parker, West Nyack, N.Y., 1969, 202.

THE GOVERNMENT MARKET
: Haggis Associates, 1966, 3 vols.

GREIF, EDWIN C.
: Basic Problems in Marketing Management. Wadsworth, 1967, 355.

GROSS, ALFRED
: Sales Promotion: Principles and Methods for Intensifying Marketing Effort. 2nd ed. Ronald, 1961, 504, illus.

GROSSMAN, LOUIS H.
: Department Store Merchandising In Changing Environments. Michigan State University, 1970, 229.

GUYTON, WILLIAM J.
: Profitably Marketing Production Teamwork. American Management Association, 1970, 256.

GWINNER, ROBERT F., and SMITH, EDWARD M.
: Sales Strategy: Cases & Readings. Appleton-Century-Crofts, 1969, 558, illus.

HAAS, KENNETH B., and ERNEST, JOHN W.
: Creative Salesmanship: Understanding Essentials.... Glencoe Press, 1969, 322.

HAAS, KENNETH B., and PERRY, ENOS C.
: Sales Horizons. 3rd ed. Prentice-Hall, 401, illus.

HAINES, GEORGE H.
: Consumer Behavior: Learning Models of Purchasing. Free Press, 1969, 216, illus.

HALBERT, MICHAEL H.
: The Meaning and Sources of Marketing Theory. McGraw-Hill, 1965, 330. (McGraw-Hill Marketing Science Institute Series.)

HAMMOND INCORPORATED
: Sales Planning Atlas of the United States and Canada. Hammond, Maplewood, N.J., 1968, 160.

HAMPTON, ROBERT E., and ZABIN, JAMES B.
: College Salesmanship. McGraw-Hill, 1970, 530.

HANSEN, HARRY L.
: Marketing: Text, Cases, and Readings. Rev. ed. Irwin, 1961, 940, illus.

HATTWICK, MELVIN S.
: The New Psychology of Selling. McGraw-Hill, 1960, 276, illus.

HEGARTY, EDWARD J.
: Seven Secrets of Sales Success. McGraw-Hill, 1966, 224, illus.

MARKETING

HEIDINGSFIELD, MYRON S.
Changing Patterns in Marketing: A Study in Strategy. Allyn & Bacon, 1968, 167.

HEIDINGSFIELD, MYRON S., and BLANKENSHIP, ALBERT B.
Marketing. 2nd ed. Barnes & Noble, 1968, 321, illus. (College Outline Series No. 83.)

HILL, RICHARD M.
Wholesaling Management: Text and Cases. Irwin, 1963, 834, illus.

HILTON, PETER
Keeping Old Products New. Prentice-Hall, 1967, 230, illus.

HIRSCH, ALBERT A., and LOVELL, MICHAEL C.
Sales Anticipations and Inventory Behavior. Wiley, 1969, 256.

HOKE, HENRY
What You Should Know about Direct Mail. Oceana, 1966, 91.

HOLLOWAY, ROBERT J.
A Basic Bibliography on Experiments in Marketing. American Marketing Association, 1963, 80.

HOLLOWAY, ROBERT J., and HANCOCK, ROBERT S.
The Environment of Marketing Behavior: Selections from the Literature. 2nd ed. Wiley, 1969, 442. (Wiley Marketing Series.)

———.
Marketing in a Changing Environment. Wiley, 1968, 498, illus. (Wiley Marketing Series.)

HOLMES, PARKER M.
Marketing Research: Principles and Readings. 2nd ed. South-Western, 1966, 662.

HOWARD, JOHN A.
Marketing: Executive and Buyer Behavior. Columbia University Press, 1963, 218, illus.

———.
Marketing Management: Analysis and Planning. Rev. ed. Irwin, 1963, 487.

———.
Marketing Theory. Allyn & Bacon, 1965, 212.

HOWARD, JOHN A., and SHETH, JAGDISH N.
The Theory of Buyer Behavior. Wiley, 1969, 458, illus. (Wiley Marketing Series.)

HUGO, IAN S.
Marketing and the Computer. Pergamon, 1967, 1 vol.

IVEY, PAUL W., and HORVATH, WALTER
Successful Salesmanship. 4th ed. Prentice-Hall, 1961, 454.

JOHNSON, HERBERT W.
Creative Selling. South-Western, 1966, 367.

JONES, FRED M.
Introduction to Marketing Management. Appleton-Century-Crofts, 1964, 1 vol.

JONES, MANLEY H.
The Marketing Process: An Introduction. Harper & Row, 1965, 605.

KELLEY, EUGENE J., et al.
Marketing Management: Annotated Bibliography. American Marketing Association, 1963, 152.

———.
Marketing: Strategy and Functions. Prentice-Hall, 1965, 120. (Prentice-Hall Foundations of Marketing Series.)

KERNAN, JEROME B., and SOMMERS, MONTROSE S., EDS.
Perspectives in Marketing Theory. Appleton-Century-Crofts, 1968, 462, illus.

KERNAN, JEROME B., et al.
Promotion: An Introductory Analysis. McGraw-Hill, 1970, 367.

KLEIN & COMPANY, NEW YORK
Directory of Mailing List Houses. Klein, New York, 1955- , vols., biennial.

KNIGHTS, CHARLES C.
The Technique of Salesmanship: A Textbook of Speciality Selling and Selling for Resale. 4th ed. Pitman (Sportshelf, New Rochelle, N.Y., dist.), 1969, 213.

KONRAD, EVELYN, et al.
Computer Innovations in Marketing. American Management Association, 1970, 387, illus.

LAZO, HECTOR
Marketing. Alexander Hamilton Institute, 1962, 355.

LAZO, HECTOR, and CORBIN, ARNOLD
Management in Marketing: Text and Cases. McGraw-Hill, 1961, 657, illus. (McGraw-Hill Series in Marketing and Advertising.)

LEVITT, THEODORE
Innovation in Marketing: New Perspectives for Profit and Growth. McGraw-Hill, 1962, 253. (McGraw-Hill Series in Marketing and Advertising.)

———.
Marketing Mode. McGraw-Hill, 1969, 1 vol.

LEVY, LEON, FELDMAN, ROBERT, and CORENTHAL, EUGENE J.
Essentials of Merchandise Information: Nontextiles. Pitman, 1968, 320, illus.

LEWIS, EDWIN H.
Marketing Channels: Structure and Strategy. McGraw-Hill, 1968, 174, illus. (Perspectives in Marketing Series.)

LOCKLEY, LAWRENCE C., and DIRKSEN, CHARLES J.
Cases in Marketing. 3rd ed. Allyn & Bacon, 1964, 318.

LOWNDES, DOUGLAS
Marketing: The Uses of Advertising. Pergamon, 1969, 140. (Commonwealth and International Library Essentials of Marketing.)

LUICK, JOHN F., and ZIEGLER, WILLIAM L.
Sales Promotion and Modern Merchandising. McGraw-Hill, 1968, 134, illus. (Perspectives in Marketing Series.)

LYNN, ROBERT A.
Marketing Principles and Market Action. McGraw-Hill, 1969, 290, illus.

MAGEE, JOHN F.
Physical-Distribution Systems. McGraw-Hill, 1967, 189, illus. (Perspectives in Marketing Series.)

MALLEN, BRUCE E., COMP.
The Marketing Channel: A Conceptual Viewpoint. Wiley, 1967, 308, illus. (Wiley Marketing Series.)

MARKET PROFILE 1970
Chain Store Publishing Corp., New York, 1 vol.

MARKS, NORTON E., and TAYLOR, ROBERT M., COMPS.
Marketing Logistics: Perspectives and Viewpoints. Wiley, 1967, 289, illus. (Wiley Marketing Series.)

MASON, RALPH E., and RATH, PATRICIA M.
Marketing and Distribution. McGraw-Hill, Gregg Division, 1968, 566, illus.

MATTHEWS, JOHN B., et al.
Marketing: An Introductory Analysis. McGraw-Hill, 1964, 612, illus.

COMMERCIAL PROGRAMS

MAUSER, FERDINAND F.
  Modern Marketing Management: An Integrated Approach. McGraw-Hill, 1961, 502, illus. (McGraw-Hill Series in Marketing and Advertising.)

MAZZE, EDWARD M., ED.
  Introduction to Marketing: Readings in the Discipline. International Textbook, 1970, 362.

McCARTHY, EDMUND J.
  Basic Marketing: A Managerial Approach. Irwin, 1964, 978, illus.

McCASKILL, WILLIAM L.
  How to Get Through to People in Selling. Parker, West Nyack, N.Y., 1970, 217.

McIVER, COLIN
  Marketing. 3rd ed. Business Books, London, (International Publications Service, New York, dist.), 1968, 195.

McMILLAN, COLIN, and PAULDER, SYDNEY
  Sales Manager's Guide to Selection and Control of Export Agents. Cahners, 1969, 232, illus.

McMURRY, ROBERT N.
  How to Recruit, Select and Place Salesmen. Dartnell, 1964, 181.

McMURRY, ROBERT N., and ARNOLD, J. S.
  How to Build a Dynamics Sales Organization. McGraw-Hill, 1968, 254.

MEGATHLIN, DONALD E., and SHEAFFER, WINIFRED E.
  A Bibliography on New Product Planning. 2nd ed. American Marketing Association, 1966, 1 vol.

MILLER, ERNEST C.
  Marketing Planning: Approaches of Selected Companies. American Management Association, 1967, 101, illus. (Research Study No. 81.)

MONAGHAN, PATRICK
  Writing Letters That Sell: You, Your Ideas, Products & Services. Fairchild, 1968, 208.

MONTGOMERY, DAVID B., and URBAN, GLEN L.
  Management Science in Marketing. Prentice-Hall, 1969, 376, illus.

MORSE, STEPHEN
  The Practical Approach to Marketing Management. McGraw-Hill, 1968, 256.

MOSSMAN, FRANK H., and MORTON, NEWTON
  Logistics of Distribution Systems. Allyn & Bacon, 1965, 396, illus.

MOYER, REED, and HOLLANDER, STANLEY C., EDS.
  Markets and Marketing in Developing Economies. American Marketing Association, 1968, 264, illus.

MYERS, JAMES H., and MEAD, RICHARD R.
  The Management of Marketing Research. International Textbook, 1969, 153.

NATIONAL INDUSTRIAL CONFERENCE BOARD
  Graphic Guide to Consumer Markets. NICB, New York, 1960- , vols., annual.

THE NATIONAL SOCIETY OF SALES TRAINING EXECUTIVES
  The New Handbook of Sales Training. Prentice-Hall, 1967, 556.

NAUHEIM, FERD
  Salesman's Complete Model Letter Handbook. Parker, West Nyack, N.Y., 1967, 203.

NEWMAN, JOSEPH W.
  Marketing Management and Information: A New Case Approach. Irwin, 1967, 390, illus.

———, ED.
  Consumer Behavior Symposium, Stanford University, 1964: On Knowing the Consumer—Proceedings. Wiley, 1966, 247.

NOLAN, CARROLL A., and WARMKE, ROMAN F.
  Marketing, Sales Promotion, and Advertising. 7th ed. South-Western, 1965, 613, illus.

O'DELL, WILLIAM F.
  The Marketing Decision. American Management Association, 1968, 320, illus.

ORENT, NORMAN B.
  Your Future in Marketing. Rev. ed. R. Rosen Press, 1966, 158. (Careers in Depth No. 59.)

OTTESON, SCHUYLER F., PANCHAR, WILLIAM G., and PATTERSON, JAMES M.
  Marketing: The Firm's Viewpoint. Macmillan, 1964, 718, illus. (Macmillan Marketing Series.)

PHELPS, DUDLEY M., and WESTING, JOHN H.
  Marketing Management. 3rd ed. Irwin, 1968, 925, illus.

PHILLIPS, CHARLES F., and DUNCAN, DELBERT J.
  Marketing: Principles and Methods. 6th ed. Irwin, 1968, 925, illus.

PILDITCH, JAMES
  Communication by Design: A Study in Corporate Identity. McGraw-Hill, 1970, 194, illus. (McGraw-Hill European Series in Management and Marketing.)

PRESTON, LEE E.
  Markets and Marketing: An Orientation. Scott, Foresman, 1970, 248, illus.
———, COMP.
  Social Issues in Marketing: Readings for Analysis. Scott, Foresman, 1967, 313, illus.

PRINTERS' INK
  New Products Marketing. Duell, Sloan & Pearce, 1964, 296, illus.

RAND McNALLY & COMPANY
  Commercial Atlas and Marketing Guide. Rand McNally, 1970, 1 vol.

RATH, PATRICIA M., TAPP, GERALD R., and MASON, RALPH E.
  Case Studies in Marketing and Distribution. Interstate, 1965, 180, illus.

RATHMELL, JOHN M.
  A Bibliography on Personal Selling. American Marketing Association, 1966, 1 vol.
———.
  Managing the Marketing Function: Concepts, Analysis, and Application. Wiley, 1969, 636, illus. (Wiley Marketing Series.)
———.
  Salesmanship: Selected Readings. Irwin, 1969, 161, illus. (American Marketing Association Reprint Series.)

RAYMOND, ROBERT S.
  Basic Marketing: Programmed Text and Cases. International Textbook, 1967, 336, illus. (World Series in Marketing.)

REICHARD, ROBERT S.
  Practical Techniques of Sales Forecasting. McGraw-Hill, 1966, 272, illus.

REID, ALLAN L.
  Modern Applied Salesmanship. Goodyear, 1970, 463.

RESOURCE PUBLICATIONS, INC.
  Index Opportunity in Finance, Merchandising and Marketing. Resource Publications, Princeton, N.J., 1969, 68. (Career Resource Series.)

REVZAN, DAVID A.
  Wholesaling in Marketing Organization. Wiley, 1961, 656, illus.

REWOLDT, STEWART H.
  Introduction to Marketing Management. Irwin, 1969, 718, illus.

RICE, CRAIG S.
  How to Plan and Execute the Marketing Campaign: Strategies for Research, Budget, Copy, Media, Merchandising, and Market Testing, Plus an Actual Marketing Campaign Document and 42 Classic Case Histories in Modern Marketing. Dartnell, 1966, 178.

ROBINSON, O. PRESTON, ROBINSON, CHRISTINE H., and ZEISS, GEORGE H.
  Successful Retail Salesmanship: Helping Customers Buy. 3rd ed. Prentice-Hall, 1961, 467, illus. (Prentice-Hall Retailing Series.)

ROBINSON, O. PRESTON, et al.
  Store Salesmanship. 6th ed. Prentice-Hall, 1965, 368.

ROBINSON, PATRICK J., and STIDSEN, BERT.
  Personal Selling in a Modern Perspective. Allyn & Bacon, 1967, 341, illus. (Marketing Science Institute Series.)

ROTH, CHARLES B.
  Lifetime Encyclopedia of Selling Ideas. Prentice-Hall, 1963, 698.

———.
  Secrets of Closing Sales. 4th ed. Prentice-Hall, 1970, 222.

RUSSELL, FREDERIC A., BEACH, FRANK H., and BUSKIRK, RICHARD H.
  Textbook of Salesmanship. 8th ed. McGraw-Hill, 1969, 596, illus.

THE SALESMAN'S GUIDE, INC.
  Directory of Buying Offices & Accounts. Salesman's Guide, 1970, 1 vol.

———.
  Directory of Premium and Incentive Buyers. Salesman's Guide, 1970, 596.

SCHLAIN, BERT H.
  The Professional Approach to Modern Salesmanship. McGraw-Hill, 1966, 278.

SCHORR, JERRY, ALEXANDER, MILTON, and FRANCO, ROBERT J.
  Logistics in Marketing. Pitman, 1969, 403.

SCHWARTZ, GEORGE
  Development of Marketing Theory. South-Western, 1963, 152, illus.

———, ED.
  Science in Marketing. Wiley, 1965, 512, illus. (Wiley Marketing Series.)

SCOTT, RICHARD A., and MARKS, NORTON E., COMPS.
  Marketing and Its Environment: Some Issues and Perspectives. Wadsworth, 1968, 374, illus.

SEARS, ROEBUCK & COMPANY
  1897 Sears, Roebuck Catalogue. Chelsea House, 1968, 786, illus.

SEVIN, CHARLES H.
  Marketing Productivity Analysis. McGraw-Hill, 1965, 137, illus. (Perspectives in Marketing Series.)

SEWELL, J. L.
  Marketing and Market Assessment. Routledge & K. Paul, London, 1966, 188. (British Library of Business.)

SHAPIRO, STANLEY J., and DOODY, ALTON F., COMPS.
  Readings in the History of American Marketing: Settlement to Civil War. Irwin, 1968, 484.

SHAW, STEVEN J., and THOMPSON, JOSEPH W.
  Salesmanship: Modern Viewpoints on Personal Communication. Holt, 1960, 419, illus.

SHEPAROVYCH, ZENON B., ALEXIS, MARCUS, and SIMON, LEONARD S.
  Quantitative Methods in Marketing. American Marketing Association, 1968, 85.

SHULTZ, WILLIAM J.
  American Marketing. Wadsworth, 1961, 655, illus.

SMITH, SAMUEL, BRIEN, RICHARD H., and STAFFORD, JAMES E.
  Readings in Marketing Information Systems: A New Era In Marketing Research. Irwin, 1968, 399, illus.

SMYKAY, EDWARD W., BOWERSOX, DONALD J., and MOSSMAN, FRANK H.
  Physical Distribution Management: Logistics Problems of the Firm. Macmillan, 1961, 283, illus. (Macmillan Marketing Book.)

SOMMERS, MONTROSE S., and KERNAN, JEROME B., COMPS.
  Comparative Marketing Systems: A Cultural Approach. Appleton-Century-Crofts, 1968, 479.

STANTON, WILLIAM J.
  Fundamentals of Marketing. 2nd ed. McGraw-Hill, 1967, 743, illus.

STANTON, WILLIAM J., and BUSKIRK, RICHARD H.
  Management of the Sales Force. 3rd ed. Irwin, 1969, 734, illus.

STEINKAMP, WILBERT H.
  How to Sell and Market Industrial Products. Chilton, 1970, 167, illus.

STERN, MARK E.
  Marketing Planning: A Systems Approach. McGraw-Hill, 1966, 153, illus. (Perspectives in Marketing Series.)

STILL, RICHARD R., and CUNDIFF, EDWARD W.
  Essentials of Marketing. Prentice-Hall, 1966, 186.

———.
  Sales Management: Decisions, Policies and Cases. 2nd ed. Prentice-Hall, 1969, 698.

STRAND, STANLEY
  Marketing Dictionary. Philosophical Library, 1962, 1 vol.

STROH, THOMAS
  Techniques of Practical Selling. Dow Jones-Irwin, 1970, 430.

STURDIVANT, FREDERICK D., ED.
  The Ghetto Marketplace. Free Press, 1969, 316.

TARRANT, JOHN J.
  Tomorrow's Techniques for Today's Salesmen. Hawthorn, 1969, 210.

TAYLOR, THAYER C.
  The Computer in Marketing. Rev. ed. Sales Management, 1970, 120.

TAYLOR, WELDON J., and SHAW, ROY T.
  Marketing: An Integrated, Analytical Approach. 2nd ed. South-Western, 1969, 834.

THOMPSON, JOSEPH W.
  Selling: A Behavioral Science Approach. McGraw-Hill, 1966, 384.

THOMPSON, RALPH B.
  Marketing Theory. Rev. ed. University of Texas, 1970, 79.

THOMPSON, WILLARD M.
  The Basics of Successful Salesmanship: A Self-Teaching Programmed Book. McGraw-Hill, 1968, 292.

COMMERCIAL PROGRAMS

THOMPSON, WILLARD M.
 Salesmanship: Concepts, Management and Strategy. Wiley, 1963, 530, illus.

TILLMAN, ROLLIE, and KIRKPATRICK, C. A.
 Promotion: Persuasive Communication in Marketing. Irwin, 1968, 477, illus.

TOUSLEY, RAYBURN D., CLARK, EUGENE, and CLARK, FRED E.
 Principles of Marketing. Macmillan, 1962, 716, illus.

TROELSTRUP, ARCHIE W.
 The Consumer in American Society: Personal and Family Finance. 4th ed. McGraw-Hill, 1970, 668, illus.

TRUMP, FRED
 Buyer Beware! Abingdon, 1965, 207.

TRUMP, ROSS M.
 Essentials of Marketing Management. Houghton Mifflin, 1966, 1 vol.

UMAN, DAVID B.
 New Product Programs: Their Planning and Control. American Management Association, 1969, 159, illus.

U.S. DEPARTMENT OF COMMERCE, BUSINESS AND DEFENSE SERVICES ADMINISTRATION
 Bibliography on Marketing to Low-Income Consumers. Superintendent of Documents, 1969, 49.

VIGROLIO, TOM, and ZAHLER, JACK
 Marketing and Communications Media Dictionary. NBS Co., Publishing Services Division, Norfolk, Mass., 1969, 425, illus.

VIZZA, ROBERT F., ED.
 New Handbook of Sales Training. Prentice-Hall, 1967, 556.

WALTERS, SHERWOOD G., SNIDER, MAX D., and SWEET, MORRIS L.
 Readings in Marketing. 2nd ed. South-Western, 1970, 1 vol., illus.

WARNER, DANIEL S.
 Marketing and Distribution: An Overview. McGraw-Hill, 1969, 497, illus.

WASSON, CHESTER R., and McCONAUGHY, DAVID H.
 Buying Behavior and Marketing Decisions. Appleton-Century-Crofts, 1968, 547, illus.

WEILBACHER, WILLIAM M.
 Marketing Management Cases. Macmillan, 1970, 358.

WEISS, EDWARD B.
 Management and the Marketing Revolution: Merchandising Strategies for the New Era. McGraw-Hill, 1964, 349.

―――.
 Merchandising for Tomorrow. McGraw-Hill, 1961, 381. (McGraw-Hill Series in Marketing and Advertising.)

―――.
 The Vanishing Salesman. McGraw-Hill, 1962, 282.

WENTZ, WALTER B., and EYRICH, GERALD I.
 Marketing: Theory and Application. Harcourt, Brace & World, 1970, 689, illus. (Harbrace Series in Business & Economics.)

WESTING, JOHN H.
 Modern Marketing Thought. 2nd ed. Macmillan, 1969, 1 vol.

WHITE, BERTHA R.
 The Law of Buying and Selling. Oceana, 1968, 115. (Legal Almanac Series No. 41.)

WHITNEY, ROBERT A., HUBIN, THOMAS, and MURPHY, JOHN D.
 The New Psychology of Persuasion and Motivation in Selling. Prentice-Hall, 1965, 256.

WIGGS, GARLAND D., ED.
 Marketing: Business and Office Specialists. J. G. Ferguson, 1970, 393. (Career Opportunities for Technicians and Specialists Vol. 3.)

WINGATE, JOHN W., and NOLAN, CARROLL A.
 Fundamentals of Selling. 9th ed. South-Western, 1969, 595, illus.

WOOLMAN, LEWIS H.
 Salesmanship: Concepts and Strategies. Wadsworth, 1970, 331, illus.

WOY, JAMES B.
 Business Trends and Forecasting: Information Sources—An Annotated Guide to Theoretical and Technical Publications.... Gale, 1966, 152. (Management Information Guide No. 9.)

YECK, JOHN D., and MAGUIRE, JOHN T.
 Planning and Creating Better Direct Mail. McGraw-Hill, 1961, 387.

ZION, ROGER
 Keys to Human Relations in Selling. Prentice-Hall, 1963, 248.

ZOBER, MARTIN
 Marketing Management. Wiley, 1964, 483. (Wiley Marketing Series.)

FRANCHISING

KURSH, HARRY
 The Franchise Boom. Rev. ed. Prentice-Hall, 1968, 477.

METZ, ROBERT
 Franchising. Hawthorn, 1969, 344, illus.

ROSENBERG, ROBERT, and BEDELL, MADELON
 Profits from Franchising. McGraw-Hill, 1969, 274.

INTERNATIONAL MARKETING

CARSON, DAVID
 International Marketing: A Comparative Systems Approach. Wiley, 1967, 539. (Wiley Marketing Series.)

CONCISE GUIDE TO INTERNATIONAL MARKETS
 International Marketing Association, London, 1968, 1 vol.

DESCHAMPSNEUFS, HENRY
 Selling in Europe: An Introduction to The European Markets. Business Books, London, 1963, 310.

FAYERWEATHER, JOHN
 International Marketing. 2nd ed. Prentice-Hall, 1970, 120, illus.

GLADE, WILLIAM P., et al.
 Marketing in a Developing Nation. D. C. Heath, 1970, 196.

LEIGHTON, DAVID S.
 International Marketing: Text and Cases. McGraw-Hill, 1966, 678, illus.

MAZZE, EDWARD M.
 International Marketing Administration. International Textbook, 1967, 160.

PATTY, C. ROBERT, and VREDENBURG, HARVEY L., EDS.
 Readings in Global Marketing Management. Appleton-Century-Crofts, 1969, 504.

STANLEY, ALEXANDER O.
 Handbook of International Marketing: How to Export, Import, and Invest Overseas. McGraw-Hill, 1963, 680, illus.

MARKETING

WHEELER, LORA J., COMP.
International Business and Foreign Trade Information Sources. Gale, 1968, 221. (Management Information Guide No. 14.)

PACKAGING

CROUWEL, WIM, and WEIDEMANN, KURT, EDS.
Packaging: An International Survey. Praeger, 1968, 188, illus.

JONES, GWENDOLYN, ED.
Packaging Information Sources: An Annotated Guide to the Literature, Associations, and Educational Institutions Concerned with Containers and Packaging. Gale, 1967, 285. (Management Information Guide No. 10.)

MODERN PACKAGING: ENCYCLOPEDIA ISSUE
Packaging Catalog Corp., Bristol, Conn., 1929- , vols., illus., annual.

PACKAGING INSTITUTE
Glossary of Packaging Terms: Standard Definitions of Trade Terms Commonly used in the Packaging Industry. 4th ed. Packaging Inst., New York, 1967, 1 vol.

PILDITCH, JAMES
The Silent Salesman: How to Develop Packaging That Sells. Business Books, London, 1961, 157, illus.

RETAILING

APPLEBAUM, WILLIAM
Store Location Strategy Cases. Addison-Wesley, 1968, 1 vol.

ASSOCIATION OF BETTER BUSINESS BUREAUS
A Guide for Retail Advertising and Selling. ABBB, New York, 1963, 1 vol.

BROOM, H. N., and LONGENECKER, JUSTIN G.
Small Business Management. 2nd ed. South-Western, 1966, 832.

CROWN, PAUL
What You Should Know About Retail Merchandising. Oceana, 1966, 92. (Business Almanac Series No. 3.)

DALRYMPLE, DOUGLAS J., and THOMPSON, DONALD L.
Retailing: An Economic View. Free Press, 1969, 389, illus.

DAVIDSON, WILLIAM R., and DOODY, ALTON F.
Retailing Management. 3rd ed. Ronald, 1966, 905.

DUNCAN, DELBERT J., and PHILLIPS, CHARLES F.
Retailing: Principles and Methods. 7th ed. Irwin, 1967, 808, illus.

EILENBERG, HOWARD
What You Should Know about Research Techniques for Retailers. Oceana, 1968, 91.

FERRY, JOHN W.
A History of the Department Store. Macmillan, 1960, 387.

GARBER, HAROLD, and HELFANT, SEYMOUR
Retail Merchandising and Management with Electronic Data Processing. National Retail Merchants Association, New York, 1966, 1 vol.

GILLESPIE, KAREN R., and HECHT, JOSEPH C.
Retail Business Management. McGraw-Hill, 1970, 596, illus.

GIST, RONALD R.
Retailing: Concepts and Decisions. Wiley, 1968, 534.

HAYETT, WILLIAM
Display and Exhibit Handbook. Reinhold, 1967, 111, illus.

JOHNSTON, JOHN W.
The Department Store Buyer: A View From Inside the Parent-Branch Complexes. University of Texas, 1969, 127. (Studies in Marketing No. 12.)

JONES, FRED M.
Retail Management. Rev. ed. Irwin, 1967, 669, illus.

JUDELLE, BEATRICE
The Branch Manager's Manual. National Retail Merchants Association, New York, 1968, 276, illus.

KILLEEN, LOUIS M.
Techniques of Inventory Management. American Management Association, 1970, 176, illus.

KLEIN, JEROME E., and READER, NORMAN
Great Shops of Europe. National Retail Merchants Association, New York, 1969, 1 vol.

KRIEGER, MURRAY
Decision-Making in Retailing and Marketing. Fairchild, 1969, 352.

LEBHAR, GODFREY M.
Chain Stores in America: 1859-1962. 3rd ed. Chain Store Publishing Corp., New York, 1963, 430.

LOGAN, WILLIAM B., and MOON, H. M.
Facts About Merchandise. 2nd ed. Prentice-Hall, 1967, 372.

MAUGER, EMILY M.
Modern Display Techniques. Fairchild, 1964, 127, illus.

McNAIR, MALCOLM P., and MAY, ELEANOR G.
The American Department Store, 1920-1960: A Performance Analysis Based on the Harvard Reports. Harvard School of Business Administration, 1963, 156.

MINSKY, BETTY J.
Gimmicks Make Money in Retailing. Fairchild, 1963, 88.

MONAGHAN, PATRICK C.
How to Sell Appliances at Retail. Fairchild, 1960, 217.

NATIONAL AUTOMATIC MERCHANDISING ASSOCIATION
Sanitation Regulations Concerning the Vending Industry. 6th ed. NAMA, Chicago, 1968, 27.

NATIONAL RETAIL MERCHANTS ASSOCIATION
The Buyer's Manual. NRMA, New York, 1965, 450.

———.
Housekeeping Manual for Retail Stores. NRMA, New York, 1963, 96.

———.
1969 Manual of Federal Trade Regulations Affecting Retailers. NRMA, New York, 2 vols.

———.
The NRMA Sales Promotion Encyclopedia. NRMA, New York, 1963- , vols.

———.
Merchandising Problems in Opening the New Branch Store. NRMA, New York, 1969, 87.

PAYNE, GEORGE K.
Creative Display. National Retail Merchants Association, New York, 1965, 180, illus.

RACHMAN, DAVID J.
Retail Strategy and Structure: A Management Approach. Prentice-Hall, 1969, 396, illus.

REICH, EDWARD, FELDMAN, ROBERT Q., and LEVY, LEON
Basic Retailing. Pitman, 1960, 334, illus.

RICHERT, G. HENRY, MEYER, WARREN G., and HAINES, PETER G.
Retailing: Principles and Practices. 5th ed. McGraw-Hill, 1968, 581, illus.

COMMERCIAL PROGRAMS

SEGAL, MENDEL
  Sales Management for Small and Medium-Sized Businesses. Parker, West Nyack, N.Y., 1969, 174, illus.

SELTZ, DAVID D.
  Handbook of Retail Promotion Ideas. Hawthorn, 1970, 300.

SLOM, STANLEY
  Profitable Furniture Retailing: For the Home Furnishings Markets. Fairchild, 1967, 240.

STEINBERG, JULES
  Customers Don't Bite: Selling with Confidence. Fairchild, 1970, 182.

STORES OF THE WORLD: BUYERS AND BUYING AGENTS
  6th ed. Newman Books, London, (W. S. Heinman, dist.), 1970, 1 vol.

TELCHIN, CHARLES S., and HELFANT, SEYMOUR
  Plan Your Store for Maximum Sales and Profit. National Retail Merchants Association, New York, 1969, 153, illus.

THOMPSON, DONALD L., and DALRYMPLE, DOUGLAS J., EDS.
  Retail Management Cases. Free Press, 1969, 296.

WEISS, EDWARD B., and WEISS, RICHARD E.
  1010 Tested Ideas That Move Merchandise. McGraw-Hill, 1962, 322.

WILINSKY, HARRIET
  Careers and Opportunities in Retailing. Dutton, 1970, 251, illus.

WINGATE, ISABEL B., et al.
  Know Your Merchandise. 3rd ed. McGraw-Hill, 1964, 672, illus.

WINGATE, JOHN W., and FRIEDLANDER, JOSEPH S.
  The Management of Retail Buying. 3rd ed. Prentice-Hall, 1963, 420, illus.

WINGATE, JOHN W., and SAMSON, HARLAND E.
  Retail Merchandising. 7th ed. South-Western, 1968, 643.

WINGATE, JOHN W., SCHALLER, ELMER O., and GOLDEN-THAL, IRVING
  Problems in Retail Merchandising. 5th ed. Prentice-Hall, 1961, 335.

ZIMMER, ALLEN
  The Strategy of Successful Retail Salesmanship. McGraw-Hill, 1966, 226.

SUPERMARKETS

BRAND, EDWARD A.
  Modern Supermarket Operation. Fairchild, 1963, 259, illus.

BUTT, CLIFFORD, HAILES, WILLIAM D., and HEMENWAY, WESLEY
  Introduction to Supermarket Occupations. Delmar, 1967, 215, illus.

CHARVAT, FRANK J.
  Supermarketing. Macmillan, 1961, 276.

HANDLER, JULIAN H.
  How to Sell the Supermarkets: For Non-Food Manufacturers and Distributors. 3rd ed. Fairchild, 1966, 218, illus.

HAYNES, WILLIAM O.
  Guidelines for Supermarket Management Programs in the Community College. American Association of Junior Colleges, 1968, 32.

KANE, BERNARD J.
  A Systematic Guide to Supermarket Location Analysis. Fairchild, 1966, 171, illus.

REAL ESTATE

AMERICAN APPRAISAL COMPANY
  Boeckh Building Valuation Manual. American Appraisal, Milwaukee, 1967, 3 vols., illus.

AMERICAN INSTITUTE OF REAL ESTATE APPRAISERS
  The Appraisal of Real Estate. 5th ed. AIREA, Chicago, 1967, 474.

ANDERSON, PAUL E.
  Tax Factors in Real Estate Operations. 3rd ed. Prentice-Hall, 1969, 443.

ARCO PUBLISHING COMPANY, INC.
  Quizzer for Real Estate Brokers and Salesmen. Arco, 1966, 104.
  ———.
  Real Estate Assessor-Appraiser. 3rd ed. Arco, 1969, 256.
  ———.
  Real Estate Manager. Arco, 1969, illus.
  ———.
  Real Estate Salesman and Broker. 3rd ed. Arco, 1967, 268.

ATKINSON, HARRY G., and WAGNER, PERCY E.
  Management and Policies of Real Estate Brokerage. Dow Jones-Irwin, 1969, 242.

BABB, JANICE B., and DORDICK, BEVERLY F., EDS.
  Real Estate Information Sources. Gale, 1963, 317. (Management Information Guide No. 1.)

BARROW, SAMUEL W.
  Making Big Money in Real Estate. Prentice-Hall, 1967, 203.

BENENSON, LAWRENCE A.
  Making Money in Real Estate. Grosset & Dunlap, 1963, 96. (Fortune Building Library.)

BENNETT, CHARLES
  How Big Ideas Make Big Money Selling Real Estate. Prentice-Hall, 1961, 274.

BERMAN, DANIEL S.
  How to Organize and Sell a Profitable Real Estate Condominium. Prentice-Hall, 1966, 195.
  ———.
  How to Reap Profits in Local Real Estate Syndicates. Prentice-Hall, 1964, 240.
  ———.
  Urban Renewal: Bonanza of the Real Estate Business. Prentice-Hall, 1969, 220.

BISKIND, ELLIOTT L., and BARASCH, CLARENCE S.
  Law of Real Estate Brokers: A Manual for New York Lawyers, Brokers, Salesmen, and Real Estate Owners and Operators—Licensing, Employment, Litigation Forms. Boardman, 1969, 465.

BOCKL, GEORGE
  How to Use Leverage to Make Money in Local Real Estate. Prentice-Hall, 1965, 224.

BOHON, DAVIS T.
  Complete Guide to Profitable Real Estate Leasing. Prentice-Hall, 1969, 225.

BOWMAN, ARTHUR G.
  Real Estate Law in California. 3rd ed. Prentice-Hall, 1970, 479.

REAL ESTATE

BROWN, ROBERT K.
    Essentials of Real Estate. Prentice-Hall, 1970, 279.

CARTWRIGHT, JOHN M.
    Handbook of Real Estate Law. Prentice-Hall, 1969, 268, illus.

CASE, FREDERICK E.
    Real Estate Brokerage. Prentice-Hall, 1965, 278.

CASEY, WILLIAM J.
    Real Estate Desk Book. 2nd ed. Institute for Business Planning, New York, 287.

CERF, ALAN
    Real Estate and the Federal Income Tax. Prentice-Hall, 1965, 341.

CRAWFORD, CLAN
    Strategy and Tactics in Municipal Zoning. Prentice-Hall, 1969, 205.

DAVEY, HOMER C., and MERCER, H. G.
    Real Estate Principles in California. Prentice-Hall, 1967, 327.

DE BENEDICTIS, DANIEL J.
    The Complete Real Estate Adviser. Trident Press, 1969, 352.

DiPAOLA, EUGENE F.
    How to Multiply Your Real Estate Sales. Prentice-Hall, 1963, 205.

DORIS, LILLIAN
    The Real Estate Office Secretary's Handbook. Rev. ed. Prentice-Hall, 1966, 366.

DOWNS, JAMES C.
    Principles of Real Estate Management. 9th ed. Institute of Real Estate Management, Chicago, 1967, 456.

DURST, SEYMOUR B., and STERN, WALTER H.
    Your Future in Real Estate. Arco, 1970, 159.

EXECUTIVE REPORTS CORPORATION, ENGLEWOOD CLIFFS, N.J.
    Real Estate Man's Tax Desk Manual: Unique Tax Help Specifically for the Real Estate Man. Prentice-Hall, 1969, 1 vol.

FORTNEY, NED J.
    The Successful Practice of Real Estate. Prentice-Hall, 1967, 227.

FRIEDMAN, EDITH J.
    Encyclopedia of Real Estate Appraising. Rev. ed. Prentice-Hall, 1968, 1184.

GARDINER, GEORGE H.
    How I Sold a Million Dollars of Real Estate in One Year. Prentice-Hall, 1969, 237.

GRAY, CHARLES D., and STEINBERG, JOSEPH L.
    Real Estate Sales Contracts: From Preparation Through Closing. Prentice-Hall, 1970, 367.

GROSS, JEROME S.
    Illustrated Encyclopedic Dictionary of Real Estate Terms. Prentice-Hall, 1969, 468, illus.

HELPER, ROSE
    Racial Policies and Practices of Real Estate Brokers. University of Minnesota Press, 1969, 387.

HIMMAH, GAEL C.
    Real Estate Listing Magic. Prentice-Hall, 1965, 210.

HOAGLAND, HENRY E., and STONE, LEO D.
    Real Estate Finance. 3rd ed. Irwin, 1965, 628.

HUSBAND, WILLIAM H., and ANDERSON, FRANK R.
    Real Estate. 3rd ed. Irwin, 1960, 577, illus.

HUSSANDER, MARTIN
    Real Estate Syndicator's Manual and Guide. Prentice-Hall, 1969, 198, illus.

JORGENSEN, ERIK
    Master Forms Guide for Successful Real Estate Sales Agreements. Executive Reports Corp., Englewood Cliffs, N.J., 1970, 1 vol.

KENT, ROBERT
    How to Get Rich in Real Estate. Prentice-Hall, 1969, 224.

KINNARD, WILLIAM N., JR.
    Industrial Real Estate. Society of Industrial Realtors, Washington, 1967, 615, illus.

KIRK, TIM H.
    How to Avoid Beginner's Mistakes in Selling Real Estate. Prentice-Hall, 1963, 253.

KRATOVIL, ROBERT
    Real Estate Law. 5th ed. Prentice-Hall, 1969, 391. (Prentice-Hall Series in Real Estate.)

LUNDBERG, EDNA A.
    Real Estate Practice in California. Prentice-Hall, 1965, 270.

MAIR, GEORGE
    Elementary Real Estate Appraisal. W. C. Brown, 1966, 240.

MAISEL, SHERMAN J.
    Financing Real Estate: Principles and Practices. McGraw-Hill, 1965, 432, illus.

McCALL, CHESTER H.
    How Any Real Estate Salesman Can Turn Himself Into A Selling Giant. Executive Reports Corp., Englewood Cliffs, N.J., (Prentice-Hall, dist.), 1969, 1 vol.

McDONALD, MORTON J. A.
    Master Guide to Successful Real Estate Advertising. Prentice-Hall, 1962, 267, illus.

McMICHAEL, STANLEY L.
    How to Operate a Real Estate Business. Rev. ed. Prentice-Hall, 1967, 351.

McMICHAEL, STANLEY L., and MOSER, LESLIE E.
    How to Make Money in Real Estate. 3rd ed. Prentice-Hall, 1969, 392.

McMICHAEL, STANLEY L., and O'KEEFE, PAUL T.
    How to Finance Real Estate. 3rd ed. Prentice-Hall, 1968, 340, illus.

MORRISSEY, JOHN F.
    Real Estate in a Nutshell: A Simplified Sales Training Manual. Carlton, New York, 1969, 118. (Hearthstone Book.)

MOSER, LESLIE E.
    How to Build a Fortune in Real Estate. Prentice-Hall, 1965, 200.

——.
    How to Find, Qualify, and Induce Real Estate Prospects to Buy. Prentice-Hall, 1967, 224.

——.
    Operating A Successful Real Estate Business. Prentice-Hall, 1970, 301, illus.

NATIONAL ASSOCIATION OF REAL ESTATE BOARDS
    Realtor's Guide to Housing Programs. NAREB, Chicago, 1965, 1 vol.

NATIONAL ASSOCIATION OF REAL ESTATE BOARDS (COMMITTEE ON PROFESSIONAL STANDARDS)
    Interpretations of the Code of Ethics. 2nd ed. NAREB, Chicago, 1964, 221.

COMMERCIAL PROGRAMS

NATIONAL ASSOCIATION OF REAL ESTATE BOARDS and
NATIONAL INSTITUTE OF REAL ESTATE BROKERS
Guide to Commercial Property Leasing. NAREB, Chicago, 1963, 95, illus.

———.
How to Use Taxation and Exchange Techniques in Marketing Investment Real Estate. NAREB, Chicago, 1970, 1 vol.

———.
Marketing Real Estate Successfully. NAREB, Chicago, 1964, 191, illus.

———.
Percentage Leases: The Basis of Equality Between Lessor and Lessee. 11th ed. NAREB, Chicago, 1966, 145, illus.

———.
Real Estate Advertising, Featuring the Broker's Ad Writer. 6th ed. NAREB, Chicago, 1961, 63, illus.

———.
Real Estate Specializations. NAREB, Chicago, 1962, 63, illus.

———.
Real Estate Trader's Handbook. 2nd ed. NAREB, Chicago, 1964, 125, illus.

PEER, DANIEL I.
Real Estate Problems. Greenwich Book, 1960, 59.

PRENTICE-HALL, INC.
Encyclopedic Dictionary of Real Estate Practice. Rev. ed. Prentice-Hall, 1962, 533, illus. (Prentice-Hall Real Estate Series.)

———.
Prentice-Hall Treasury of Money-Making Real Estate Ideas and Practices. Prentice-Hall, 1962, 362.

PUGH, J. W., and HIPPAKA, WILLIAM
California Real Estate Finance. Prentice-Hall, 1966, 428, illus. (Prentice-Hall Series on California Real Estate.)

RENO, RICHARD R.
Profitable Real Estate Exchanging and Counseling. Prentice-Hall, 1965, 301.

RING, ALFRED A.
The Valuation of Real Estate. 2nd ed. Prentice-Hall, 1970, 660, illus. (Prentice-Hall Real Estate Series.)

RING, ALFRED A., and NORTH, NELSON L.
Real Estate Principles and Practices. 6th ed. Prentice-Hall, 1967, 542.

ROBINSON, PETER C.
Real Estate and Insurance As A Career: A Study of the Two Industries Where Combined As One Professional Service Unit. Vantage, 1969, 152, illus.

SCHMUTZ, GEORGE L., and RAMS, EDWIN M.
Condemnation Appraisal Handbook. 2nd ed. Prentice-Hall, 1963, 426.

SCHRAUB, EDGAR D.
Real Estate Investment Course. Prentice-Hall, 1968, 4 vols.

SELDIN, MAURY, and SWESNIK, RICHARD H.
Real Estate Investment Strategy. Wiley, 1970, 256.

SEMENOW, ROBERT W.
Questions and Answers on Real Estate. 6th ed. Prentice-Hall, 1969, 664.

———.
Selected Cases in Real Estate. Prentice-Hall, 1965, 638.

STERNLIEB, GEORGE
The Tenement Landlord. Rutgers University Press, 1969, 269, illus.

STEWART, JAMES I.
Real Estate Appraisal in a Nutshell: A Restatement and Simplification of Theory and Practice. University of Toronto Press, 1967, 255.

STONE, DAVID
How to Operate a Real Estate Trade-In Program. Prentice-Hall, 1962, 221.

———.
Training Manual for Real Estate Salesman. Prentice-Hall, 1965, 333.

TIMONEY, DONALD
How to Boost Your Income to $25,000 a Year in Real Estate. Prentice-Hall, 1968, 224.

TURNER, DAVID R.
Real Estate Salesman & Broker: The National License Guide. 4th ed. Arco, 1969, 352.

UNGER, MAURICE A.
Real Estate, Principles and Practices. 4th ed. South-Western, 1969, 754, illus.

WECHSLER, ABRAHAM S.
Real Estate Law for Salesmen and Brokers: With Questions and Answers for License Examinations. Oceana, 1964, 96.

WEIMER, ARTHUR M., and HOYT, HOMER
Real Estate. 5th ed. Ronald, 1966, 758.

WENDT, PAUL F., and CERF, ALAN R.
Real Estate Investment Analysis and Taxation. McGraw-Hill, 1969, 355, illus.

WINSTEAD, ROBERT W.
Real Estate Appraisal Desk Book. Prentice-Hall, 1968, 242.

SECRETARIAL SCIENCE

AGNEW, PETER L.
Typewriting Office Practice. 4th ed. South-Western, 1968, 1 kit.

AGNEW, PETER L., and CORNELIA, NICHOLAS J.
Office Machines Course of the Full-Keyboard Adding-Listing Machine, Ten-Key Adding-Listing Machine, Rotary Calculator and Key-Driven Calculator. 3rd ed. South-Western, 1962, 124, illus.

AGNEW, PETER L., and PASEWARK, WILLIAM R.
Full-Keyboard Adding-Listing Machine Course for R. C. Allen, Burroughs, Monroe, National, Remington Rand, Smith-Corona and Victor Electric and Manual Machines. 3rd ed. South-Western, 1963, 76, illus.

———.
Key-Driven Calculator Course for the Burroughs, Comptometer, and Plus Calculators. 4th ed. South-Western, 1962, 152, illus.

———.
Rotary Calculator Course for the Friden, Marchant, and Monroe Calculators: Manual, Electric, Semi-Automatic, Fully Automatic. 4th ed. South-Western, 1962, 102, illus.

———.
Ten-Key Adding-Listing Machine and Printing Calculator Course. 3rd ed. South-Western, 1963, 115, illus.

AGNEW, PETER L., et al.
Clerical Office Practice. 4th ed. South-Western, 1967, 630, illus.

———.
Secretarial Office Practice. 7th ed. South-Western, 1966, 616, illus.

AMERICAN RECORDS MANAGEMENT ASSOCIATION
Rules for Alphabetical Filing: As Standardized by the Association. ARMA, 1960, 65.

ANASTASI, THOMAS E., JR.
A Secretary is A Manager. Management Center of Cambridge (Mass.), 1970, 152.

SECRETARIAL SCIENCE

ANDERSON, RUTH I.
    Secretarial Careers. Walck, 1961, 106, illus.

ANDERSON, RUTH I, STRAUB, LURA L., and GIBSON, E. DANA
    Word Finder. 3rd ed. Prentice-Hall, 1969, 250.

ANGUS, MARION, ED.
    Teach Yourself Pitman Shorthand. Pitman, 1967, 287.

ARCHER, FRED C., et al.
    General Office Practice. 3rd ed. McGraw-Hill, 1968, 534, illus.

ARCO PUBLISHING COMPANY, INC.
    Beginning Office Worker. 5th ed. Arco, 1967, 256.

―――.
    ...Clerk-Steno Transcriber. 3rd ed. Arco, 1967, 288, (Civil Service Test Tutor.)

―――.
    ...Stenographer-Typist GS-1 Through GS-7. 5th ed. Arco, 1968, 320. (Civil Service Test Tutor.)

BALSLEY, IROL V., and ROBINSON, JERRY W.
    Integrated Secretarial Studies. Jubilee ed. South-Western, 1964, 375, illus.

BALSLEY, IROL V. W., and WANOUS, SAMUEL J.
    Shorthand Transcription Studies. 4th ed. South-Western, 1968, 244, illus.

BARON, HAROLD, and STEINFELD, SOLOMON C.
    Clerical Record Keeping, Course II. South-Western, 1970, 730, illus.

BASSETT, ERNEST D., AGNEW, PETER L., and GOODMAN, DAVID G.
    Business Filing & Records Control. 3rd ed. South-Western, 1963, 202, illus.

BEAMER, ESTHER K., HANNA, J. MARSHALL, and POPHAM, ESTELLE L.
    Effective Secretarial Practices. 4th ed. South-Western, 1962, 746, illus.

BECKER, ESTHER R., and ANDERS, EVELYN
    The Successful Secretary's Handbook. Harper & Row, 1970, 416, illus.

BECKER, ESTHER R., and ROLLASON, PEGGY N.
    The High Paid Secretary. Prentice-Hall, 1967, 233.

BLEGEN, AUGUST H.
    Records Management Step by Step. Office Publications, Stamford, Conn., 1965, 140, illus.

BOSTICCO, ISABEL L. M.
    Top Secretary. Business Books, London, (International Publications Service, dist.), 1970, 198, illus.

BOWMAN, WALLACE B., and OLIVERIO, MARY E.
    Shorthand Dictation Studies. 3rd Jubilee ed. South-Western, 1966, 674, illus.

BRIGGS, J. ROBERT, and KOSY, EUGENE
    Office Machines, A Collegiate Course: Rotary Calculator, Ten-Key Adding-Listing Machine, Printing Calculator, Full Keyboard Adding-Listing Machine, Key-Driven Calculator. South-Western, 1967, 268, illus.

BUREAU OF BUSINESS PRACTICE, INC.
    The Secretary's Workshop. BBP, Waterford, Conn., 1970, 1 vol.

CARSON, ALBERT B., CARLSON, ARTHUR E., and BOLING, CLEM
    Secretarial Accounting. 8th ed. South-Western, 1967, illus.

CLOKE, MARJANE, and WALLACE, ROBERT
    The Modern Business Letter Writer's Manual. Doubleday, 1969, 215.

COLLISON, ROBERT L.
    Commercial and Industrial Records Storage. de Graff, 1969, 183, illus.

CONTINOLO, GIUSEPPE
    Modern Filing Methods and Equipment. International Publications Service, 1970, 180, illus.

COX, HOMER L.
    How to Write a Letter: Coping with Correspondence. Sterling, 1966, 125, illus.

DARTNELL CORPORATION
    The Dartnell Business-Letter Deskbook. Leslie Llewellyn Lewis, ed. Dartnell, 1969, 288, illus.

DEVLIN, FRANK J.
    Business Communication. Irwin, 1968, 705, illus.

DORIS, LILLIAN, and MILLER, BESSIE M.
    Complete Secretary's Handbook. 3rd ed. Prentice-Hall, 1970, 528.

DUCHAN, SIMON A.
    Basic Dictation. Pitman, 1963, 308.

―――.
    Basic Dictation: Longhand Edition. Pitman, 1963, 226.

EDDINGS, CLAIRE N.
    Secretary's Complete Model Letter Handbook. Prentice-Hall, 1965, 295.

FLYNN, PATRICIA
    The Complete Secretary. Pitman, 1965, 246.

FORKNER, HAMDEN L., et al.
    Correlated Dictation and Transcription-Gregg. Diamond Jubilee ed. Pitman, 1960, 1 vol.

FRAILEY, LESTER E.
    Handbook of Business Letters. 2nd ed. Prentice-Hall, 1965, 918, illus.

FRIEDMAN, SHERWOOD, and GROSSMAN, JACK
    Applied Clerical Practice. 2nd ed. Pitman, 1962, 461, illus.

―――.
    Handbook for Typists. 2nd ed. Pitman, 1962, 72, illus.

―――.
    Modern Clerical Practice. 3rd ed. Pitman, 1968, 441, illus.

―――.
    Secretarial Practice. Pitman, 1960, 504, illus.

FRISCH, VERN A., and SIVINSKI, JOAN
    Applied Office Typewriting. 2nd ed., supp. Gregg, 1961, 1 vol.

GARDINER, A. W.
    Typewriting and Office Duplicating Processes. Hastings, 1968, 205, illus.

GAVIN, RUTH E., and HUTCHINSON, E. L.
    Reference Manual for Stenographers and Typists. 3rd ed. McGraw-Hill, 1961, 188, illus.

GILSON, GOODWIN, and MELLINGER, MORRIS.
    Developing Shorthand Skills: A Graded Program Correlated with New Basic Course in Pitman Shorthand. Pitman, 1965, 265.

GIORDANO, AL
    Basic Business Machine Calculation: A Complete Course. Prentice-Hall, 1970, 384.

GOODMAN, DAVID S.
    President's Letter Book. Prentice-Hall, 1970, 311.

GREENBURG, RAE C.
    Shortrite: A Nu E-Z Shorthand Self-Taught in Hours Speed in Weeks. Pocket Books, 1970, 144, illus.

COMMERCIAL PROGRAMS

GREGG, JOHN R.
　　Applied Secretarial Practice. 6th ed. McGraw-Hill, Gregg Division, 1968, 518, illus.

GREGG, JOHN R., LESLIE, LOUIS A., and ZOUBEK, CHARLES E.
　　Gregg Shorthand Dictionary. McGraw-Hill, 1963, 384. (Diamond Jubilee Series.)

─────.
　　Gregg Shorthand Manual. McGraw-Hill, 1963, 388. (Diamond Jubilee Series.)

─────.
　　Gregg Speed Building. McGraw-Hill, 1964, 511, illus. (Diamond Jubilee Series.)

GREGG, JOHN R., et al.
　　Gregg Speed Building for Colleges. McGraw-Hill, 1966, 512, illus. (Diamond Jubilee Series.)

GRILLO, ELMER V.
　　Control Techniques for Office Efficiency. McGraw-Hill, 1963, 273.

GUTHRIE, MEARL R.
　　Alphabetic Indexing. 3rd ed. South-Western, 1964, 64.

HANNA, J. MARSHALL, et al.
　　Secretarial Procedures and Administration. 5th ed. South-Western, 1968, 776, illus. (Formerly Effective Secretarial Practices.)

HAYDON, DOROTHY F., and GORDON, ELAYNE
　　Practical Dictation and Transcription: Shorthand and Transcription Training for Today's Business. Pitman, 1965, 456.

HORTEN, HANS E.
　　Commercial Correspondence in Four Languages. Hart, 1970, 348.

HOUSE, CLIFFORD R., and KOEBELE, APOLLONIA M.
　　Reference Manual for Office Personnel. 5th ed. South-Western, 1970, 197, illus.

HUFFMAN, HARRY, MULKERNE, DONALD J. D., and RUSSON, ALLIEN
　　Office Procedures and Administration: College Course. McGraw-Hill, 1965, 401, illus.

HUTCHINSON, LOIS I.
　　Standard Handbook for Secretaries. 8th ed. McGraw-Hill, 1969, 638.

ELLENBOGEN, ABRAHAM
　　Effective Business Correspondence. Collier Books, 1963, 128, illus. (Collier Quick and Easy Series.)

JOHNSON, MINA M., and KALLAUS, NORMAN F.
　　Records Management: A Collegiate Course in Filing Systems and Procedures. South-Western, 1967, 362, illus.

KAHN, GILBERT, YERIAN, THEODORE, and STEWART, JEFFREY R.
　　Progressive Filing. 8th ed. McGraw-Hill, Gregg Division, 1969, 118, illus.

KLEIN, ABRAHAM E.
　　New World Secretarial Handbook. World, 1968, 659, illus.

KREY, ISABELLE A., and METZLER, BERNADETTE V.
　　Effective Writing for Business. Harcourt, Brace & World, 1968, 367.

KURTZ, MARGARET A., and PHILLIPS, HELEN L.
　　Technical Typewriting. Addison-Wesley, 1968, 310, illus.

LAMB, MARION M.
　　Your First Year of Teaching Shorthand and Transcription. 2nd ed. South-Western, 1961, 314, illus. (South-Western Publications for Business Teachers No. X95.)

LAURIA, MARIE
　　How To Be A Good Secretary. F. Fell, New York, 1969, 272.

LAWRENCE, NELDA R.
　　Secretary's Business Review: A Professional Handbook. Prentice-Hall, 1960, 514, illus.

LEAHY, EMMETT J., and CAMERON, CHRISTOPHER A.
　　Modern Records Management: A Basic Guide to Records Control, Filing, and Information Retrieval. McGraw-Hill, 1965, 236, illus.

LEE, DOROTHY E.
　　Secretarial Practice for College. 2nd ed. McGraw-Hill, 1965, 170, illus.

LEE, H. I., and BARR, W. N.
　　Practical Secretarial Work. 4th ed. Pitman, 1965, 424.

LESLIE, LOUIS A.
　　20,000 Words. 5th ed. McGraw-Hill, 1965, 256.

LESLIE, LOUIS A., and ZOUBEK, CHARLES E.
　　Gregg Transcription. McGraw-Hill, 1963, 512, illus. (Diamond Jubilee Series.)

LESLIE, LOUIS A., ZOUBEK, CHARLES E., and HOSLER, RUSSELL J.
　　Gregg Shorthand for Colleges. McGraw-Hill, 1965, 2 vols., illus. (Diamond Jubilee Series.)

LESSENBERRY, DAVID D.
　　20th Century Typewriting...: Complete Course. 8th ed. South-Western, 1962, 372, illus.

LESSENBERRY, DAVID D., WANOUS, SAMUEL J., and DUNCAN, CHARLES H.
　　College Typewriting: Basic Course. 8th ed. South-Western, 1969, 141, illus.

LEVINE, NATHAN
　　Typing for Everyone. Arco, 1970, 160, illus.

LIFTON, MARKS, et al.
　　Syllabus and Teaching Suggestions for A Course in Secretarial Practice. New York (State) Education Department, Bureau of Business and Distributive Education, Albany, 1963, 106. (VT 001 087.)

LILES, PARKER, BRENDEL, LEROY A., and KRAUSE, RUTHETTA
　　Typing Mailable Letters, with Facsimile Solutions. 2nd ed. McGraw-Hill, 1969, 158.

LLOYD, ALAN C., ROWE, JOHN L., and WINGER, FRED E.
　　Gregg Typewriting for Colleges: Complete Course. 2nd ed. McGraw-Hill, Gregg Division, 1964, 344, illus.

LOCKE, FLORA M., and DEHR, DOROTHY
　　Office Calculating and Adding Machines. 3rd ed. Wiley, 1969, 520, illus.

MacCLAIN, LENORE F., and DAME, J. FRANK
　　Typewriting Techniques and Short Cuts with 10-Minute Timed Writings. 3rd ed. South-Western, 1961, 106, illus.

MAGER, NATHAN H., and MAGER, S. K.
　　The Office Encyclopedia. Rev. ed. Pocket Books, 1966, 498, illus.

MEEHAN, JAMES R.
　　Using the Rotary Calculator in the Modern Office. McGraw-Hill, Gregg Division, 1965, 116.

MEEHAN, JAMES R., and KAHN, GILBERT
　　How To Use Adding Machines: Ten-Key, Full-Key, Printing Calculator. McGraw-Hill, Gregg Division, 1962, 138, illus.

MENNING, JACK H., and WILKINSON, C. W.
　　Communicating Through Letters and Reports. 4th ed. Irwin, 1963, 686, illus.

MULKERNE, DONALD J., and ANDREWS, M. E.
　　Civil Service Tests for Typists. McGraw-Hill, 1969, 160.

NATIONAL ASSOCIATION OF EDUCATIONAL SECRETARIES
Communications Review: A Handbook on Communications. NAES, Washington, 1963, 80, illus.

———. File It Right and Find It! Rev. ed. NAES, Washington, 1963, 69, illus.

———. A Guide for Planning Inservice Training Programs for Educational Secretaries. NAES, Washington, 1965- , 1 vol.

———. Take A Minute, Save An Hour: A Handbook on Meetings. NAES, Washington, 1961, 27, illus.

NATIONAL BUSINESS EDUCATION ASSOCIATION
Business Education and the Two-Year Community College. NBEA, 1968, 62. (National Business Education Quarterly Vol. 36, No. 2.)

———. Yearbook. NBEA, 1963- , vols., annual.

NATIONAL EDUCATIONAL SECRETARY
Recollections: Reprints of the Best of the National Educational Secretary. National Association of Educational Secretaries, Washington, 1965, 59, illus.

NATIONAL SECRETARIES ASSOCIATION (INTERNATIONAL)
Secretarial Study Guide: Outlines, Procedures, and References for Eleven Secretarial Subjects. NSA, Kansas City, Mo., 1963, 2 vols., illus.

———. Secretaries on the Spot: A Collection of Actual Secretarial Problems and How They Were Solved. 2nd ed. NSA, Kansas City, Mo., 1967, 235, illus.

NOORY, SAMUEL
Shorthand in One Day: With Shorthand Dictionary. A. S. Barnes, 1969, 179.

NOYES, NELL B.
Your Future As A Secretary. R. Rosen Press, 1963, 162.

PACTOR, PAUL, and JOHNSON, MINA M.
Comprehensive Business Machines Course: Full-Keyboard, Ten-Key, Rotary, Key-Driven. Rev. ed. Pitman, 1968, 340, illus.

———. Full-Keyboard Adding Machine Course. 3rd ed. Pitman, 1968, 88, illus.

———. Rotary Calculator Course. Rev. ed. Pitman, 1968, 122, illus.

———. Ten-Key Adding Machine Course. Pitman, 1968, 92, illus.

PARKER PUBLISHING COMPANY
Secretary's Desk Book. Parker, West Nyack, N.Y., 1965, 327.

———. The Successful Secretary. Prentice-Hall, 1964, 312, illus.

PEATE, PATRICIA F.
The Complete Secretary. Pitman, 1965, 246, illus.

PENDERY, JOHN A., and WOODWARD, THEODORE
General Office Practice for Colleges. 5th ed. South-Western, 1965, 282, illus.

———. Secretarial Office Practice for Colleges. 5th ed. South-Western, 1965, 242, illus.

PEPE, PHILLIP S.
Personal Typing in Twenty-Four Hours. 4th ed. McGraw-Hill, 1965, 64, illus.

PITMAN, SIR ISAAC
Pitman's English and Shorthand Dictionary. Pitman, 1964, 834.

PLACE, IRENE M., and HICKS, CHARLES B.
College Secretarial Procedures. 3rd ed. McGraw-Hill, Gregg Division, 1964, 536, illus.

———. Office Management. 2nd ed. Allyn, 1962, 555.

PLACE, IRENE M., and POPHAM, ESTELLE L.
Filing and Records Management. Prentice-Hall, 1966, 290, illus. (Prentice-Hall Professional Business Series.)

POPHAM, ESTELLE L.
Opportunities in Office Occupations. Vocational Guidance Manuals, 1964, 110.

PRENTICE-HALL, INC.
Handbook of Advanced Secretarial Techniques. Prentice-Hall, 1962, 400, illus.

———. Secretary's Factomatic. Prentice-Hall, 1963, 584.

RAHE, HARVES
Shorthand-Secretarial Research Index: A Complete List of Research Studies in the Training and Work of Stenographers and Secretaries, from 1891 to 1965. McGraw-Hill, 1965, 68.

REED, CLINTON A.
Comprehensive Typewriting. Allyn & Bacon, 1964, 496, illus.

REED, JEANNE
Business Writing: A Gregg Text-Kit in Continuing Education. McGraw-Hill, 1970, 256.

ROMEY, KENNETH A., and ANDERSON, YVONNE
A Laboratory Manual in Business Machines: A Complete Course of Study Covering the Training of Operators for All Types of Modern Office and Business Machines. 4th ed. W. C. Brown, 1970, 303, illus.

REIGNER, CHARLES G.
Office Practice for Typists. 2nd ed. Rowe, Baltimore, 1960, 32, illus.

SADAUSKAS, WALLACE B.
Manual of Business Forms. 2nd ed. Office Publications, Stamford, Conn., 1961, 235.

SAVAGE, WILLIAM G., et al.
Business Review for Professional Secretaries. Rev. ed. Pitman, 1963, 1 vol.

SCOTT, WESLEY E., HAMILTON, W. J., and HERTZFELD, A.
Teach Yourself to Type. 2nd ed. Pitman, 1962, 98, illus.

SELDEN, WILLIAM H., STRAUB, LURA L., and PORTER, LEONARD J.
Filing and Finding. Prentice-Hall, 1962, 122, illus.

SHEFF, DONALD A.
Secretarial English. Simon & Schuster, 1968, 1 vol.

SHURTER, ROBERT L., and WILLIAMSON, J. PETER
Written Communication in Business. 2nd ed. McGraw-Hill, 1964, 487, illus.

SISSON, ALBERT F.
Sisson's Word and Expression Locator. Prentice-Hall, 1966, 372.

SKILLIN, MARJORIE E., and GAY, ROBERT
Words into Type. Rev. ed. Appleton-Century-Crofts, 1964, 596, illus.

STANWELL, SHEILA T.
A Typewriting Course in Five Volumes. Pergamon, 1970, 5 vols.

STRAUB, LURA L., and GIBSON, E. DANA
Liquid Duplicating Systems. W. C. Brown, 1960, 130.

———. Stencil Duplicating Systems. W. C. Brown, 1960, 132.

STRONG, EARL P., and WEAVER, ROBERT G.
Writing for Business and Industry: Reports, Letters, Minutes of Meetings, Memos, Dictation. Allyn & Bacon, 1962, 456, illus. (National Office and Management Association Series in Administrative Management.)

COMMERCIAL PROGRAMS

STRONY, MADELINE S.
The Secretary at Work: A Brief Finishing Course in Secretarial Procedures. 3rd ed. McGraw-Hill, Gregg Division, 1966, 186, illus.

STRONY, MADELINE S., GARVEY, M. CLAUDIA, and NEWHOUSE, HOWARD L.
Refresher Course in Gregg Shorthand. McGraw-Hill, 1970, 122. (Diamond Jubilee Series.)

TAINTOR, SARAH A., and MONRO, KATE M.
The Secretary's Handbook: A Manual of Correct Usage. 9th ed. Macmillan, 1969, 530.

THOMAS, DOROTHY P.
Private Secretarial Work. 8th ed. Pitman, 1963, 174.

TURNER, BERNICE C.
The Private Secretary's Manual: A Practical Handbook for Secretaries and Executives. 3rd ed. Prentice-Hall, 1963, 434, illus.

TURNER, EDWARD
...Practice for Clerical, Typing and Stenographic Tests. Arco, 1965, 240.

U.S. OFFICE OF EDUCATION, VOCATIONAL AND TECHNICAL EDUCATION DIVISION
Clerical and Record Keeping Occupations: A Suggested 1-Year Curriculum. USGPO, 1962, 74.

U.S. POST OFFICE
National Zip Code Directory. USGPO, 1965- , Vol. 1- , annual. (POD Pub. No. 65.)

VAN ALLEN, EDWARD J.
Your Future as a Shorthand Reporter. R. Rosen Press, 1969, 140, illus. (Careers in Depth.)

VERMES, JEAN C.
The Secretary's Guide to Dealing With People. Prentice-Hall, 1964, 230.

———.
Secretary's Index to English. Parker, West Nyack, N.Y., 1968, 247.

WALKER, ARTHUR L., ROACH, J. KENNETH, and HANNA, J. MARSHALL
How to Use Adding and Calculating Machines: Ten-Key, Full-Key, Rotary, Key-Driven. 2nd ed. McGraw-Hill, Gregg Division, 1960, 250, illus.

WALKER, CHARLES F., and ROBERTSON, MARY
Practical Business Correspondence for Colleges. 3rd ed. South-Western, 1966, 220.

WANOUS, SAMUEL J.
Personal and Professional Typing. 3rd ed. South-Western, 1967, 179, illus.

WANOUS, SAMUEL J., and WANOUS, EDWARD E.
Automation Office Practice. South-Western, 1964, 103, illus.

WEEKS, BERTHA M.
Filing and Records Management. 3rd ed. Ronald, 1964, 287, illus.

WELLS, WALTER
Communications in Business: A Guide to the Effective Writing of Letters, Reports, and Memoranda. Wadsworth, 1968, 428.

WESLEY, S. M.
Short-Cut Shorthand. Cowles, 1967, 275.

WEST, LEONARD J.
Acquisition of Typewriting Skills, Methods and Research in Teaching Typewriting. Pitman, 1969, 635.

WHALEN, DORIS H.
The Secretary's Handbook. Harcourt, Brace & World, 1968, 229.

WHITCOMB, HELEN, and LANG, ROSALIND
Charm: The Career Girl's Guide to Business and Personal Success. McGraw-Hill, Gregg Division, 1964, 472, illus.

WHITCOMB, HELEN, and WHITCOMB, JOHN
Strictly for Secretaries.... Rev. ed. McGraw-Hill, 1965, 166, illus.

WIENER, SOLOMON
Blue Book of Business Letter Writing. Simon & Schuster, 1969, 191. (Blue Books.)

WINTER, ELMER L.
How To Be An Effective Secretary. Simon & Schuster, 1969, 1 vol.

EXECUTIVE SECRETARY

BECKER, ESTHER R.
How To Be An Effective Executive Secretary. Harper, 1962, 211.

BUREAU OF BUSINESS PRACTICE, INC.
The Executive Secretary's Desk Manual. BBP, Waterford, Conn., 1970, 1 vol.

ENGEL, PAULINE
Executive Secretary's Handbook. Prentice-Hall, 1965, 205.

INGOLDSBY, PATRICIA, and FOCARINO, JOSEPH
The Executive Secretary: Handbook to Success. Doubleday, 1969, 348,

MAYO, LUCY G.
You Can Be an Executive Secretary.... Macmillan, 1965, 278.

MILLER, BESSE M.
Manual and Guide for the Corporate Secretary. Prentice-Hall, 1969, 3 vols., illus.

PRENTICE-HALL, INC.
The Corporate Secretary's Handbook. Prentice-Hall, 1964, 382.

LEGAL SECRETARY

ARCO PUBLISHING COMPANY, INC.
Law and Court Stenographer. 3rd ed. Arco, 1967, 288.

BANDER, EDWARD J.
Law Dictionary of Practical Definitions. Oceana, 1966, 113. (Legal Almanac Series No. 58.)

BANDER, EDWARD J., and WALLACH, JEFFREY J.
Medical Legal Dictionary. Oceana, 1970, 114.

BRADY, PATRICIA S., ED.
Legal Secretary's Handbook. Rev. ed. Parker, West Nyack, N.Y., 1966, 440.

CATALDO, BERNARD F., et al.
Introduction to Law and the Legal Process. Wiley, 1965, 880.

DeMARS, ROSE, and ROSENBERG, HYMAN S.
Legal and Professional Secretary's Lexicon. Central Book, Brooklyn, N.Y., 1966, 345, illus.

FARMER, ROBERT A., et al.
What You Should Know About Contracts. Arco, 1970, 173. (Know Your Law.)

SECRETARIAL SCIENCE

GRAHM, MILTON, CURCHACK, NORMA, and YENGEL, HERBERT
    Legal Typewriting. McGraw-Hill, 1968, 46, illus.

HELLER, MARJORIE K.
    Guide and Compendium for a Lawyer's Secretary. Boardman, 1967, 1 vol.

KLING, SAMUEL G.
    The Complete Guide to Everyday Law. 2nd ed. Follett, 1970, 623.

LESLIE, LOUIS A., and COFFIN, KENNETH B.
    Handbook for the Legal Secretary. McGraw-Hill, 1968, 378, illus.

MILLER, BESSE M.
    Legal Secretary's Complete Handbook. 2nd ed. Prentice-Hall, 1970, 688.

NATIONAL ASSOCIATION OF LEGAL SECRETARIES
    Manual for the Legal Secretarial Profession. West, St. Paul, 1965, 576, illus.

PRENTICE-HALL, INC.
    Legal Secretary's Encyclopedic Dictionary. Prentice-Hall, 1962, 467, illus.

ROSS, MARTIN J.
    Handbook of Everyday Law. Rev. ed. Harper & Row, 1967, 337.

SLETWOLD, EVANGELINE
    Sletwold's Manual of Documents and Forms For The Legal Secretary. Prentice-Hall, 1965, 193.

SCHOEPFER, VIRGINIA
    Desk Companion for Legal Secretaries: Including Word Builder, Latin Words and Phrases, and Medical Terms. W. H. Anderson Co., Cincinnati, 1970, 191.

U.S. DEPARTMENT OF AGRICULTURE, OFFICE OF THE GENERAL COUNSEL
    Glossary of Legal Terms for Secretaries. USFDA, Washington, 1961, 1 vol.

MEDICAL SECRETARY

ALCAZAR, CAROL C., and ALCAZAR, RAFAEL J.
    Medical Typists' Guide for Histories and Physicals. Medical Examination Publishing Co., Flushing, N.Y., 1970, 267.

AMERICAN HOSPITAL ASSOCIATION
    Guide to the Organization of a Hospital Medical Record Department. AHA, Chicago, 1962, 83, illus.

———.
    Medical Record Forms for Hospitals: Guide to Preparation. AHA, Chicago, 1963, 35.

ARTS, ELIZABETH M.
    Medical Office Assistant. Delmar, 1968, 350, illus.

ROBERT J. BRADY COMPANY, EDUCATION AND TRAINING SYSTEMS DIVISION
    Brady's Programmed Orientation to Medical Terminology. Brady Co. (Lippincott, dist.), 1970, 158, illus.

BREDOW, MIRIAM
    Medical Secretarial Procedures. 5th ed. McGraw-Hill, 1966, 378, illus.

BREDOW, MIRIAM, and COOPER, MARIAN G.
    The Medical Assistant: A Guide To Clinical, Secretarial, and Technical Duties. 3rd ed. McGraw-Hill, 1970, 445, illus.

CHERNOK, NORMA B.
    Your Future in Medical Assisting. R. Rosen Press, 1966, 126, illus. (Careers in Depth No. 70.)

DAVIS, PHYLLIS E., and HERSHELMAN, NANCY V.
    Medical Dictation and Transcription. Wiley, 1967, 465.

———.
    Medical Shorthand. Wiley, 1967, 317.

EDMONDSON, FRANCES W.
    Medical Terminology. 4th ed. Putnam, 1965, 306, illus.

———.
    Medical Typing. 3rd ed. Putnam, 1965, 183, illus.

ESHOM, MYRETA
    Medical Secretary's Manual. Appleton-Century-Crofts, 1966, 506, illus.

FREDERICK, PORTIA M., and KINN, MARY E.
    The Office Assistant in Medical Practice. 3rd ed. Saunders, 1967, 461, illus.

FRENAY, SISTER MARY, A. C.
    Understanding Medical Terminology. 4th ed. Catholic Hospital Association, 1969, 286.

GROSS, VERLEE E.
    Ten Study Lessons for Mastering Medical Terminology. Halls of Ivy Press, 1969, 1 vol.

HADLEY, ANNE
    The Medical Secretary As A Word Technician. Lippincott, 1968, 260, illus.

HUFFMAN, EDNA K.
    Medical Records in Nursing Homes. Physicians' Record Co., Berwyn, Ill., 1961, 204, illus.

JeHARNED
    Medical Terminology Made Easy. 2nd ed. Physicians' Record Co., Berwyn, Ill., 1968, 335, illus.

JOHNSON, CARRIE E.
    Medical Spelling Guide: A Reference Aid. Thomas, 1966, 538.

KABBES, ELAINE F.
    Medical Secretary's Guide. Parker, West Nyack, N.Y., 1967, 269, illus.

LAMELA, ALBERTO, and BURNS, JULES P.
    Handbook of Medical and Anatomical Terminology. Charles Mathis, 1967, 240, illus.

LAWTON, M. MURRAY, and FOY, DONALD F.
    A Textbook for Medical Assistants. Mosby, 1967, 465, illus.

MACKICHAN, NEIL D.
    Assisting the General Practitioner: A Manual for the Doctor's Secretary, Receptionist, and Surgery Nurse. Pitman, 1967, 264, illus.

MARKS, JEAN
    Medical Terminology, with Associated Anatomy by Systems: A Handbook for Physicians, Nurses, Medical Secretaries, Attorneys, Insurance Offices, Students. Marks Publishing Service, Albany, 1961, 82, illus.

MILLER, BESSE M.
    Medical Secretary's and Assistant's Handbook. Prentice-Hall, 1960, 236, illus.

ROBERTS, FFRANGCON
    Medical Terms: Their Origin and Construction. 4th ed. Thomas, 1966, 96.

ROOT, KATHLEEN B., and BYERS, EDWARD E.
    The Medical Secretary: Terminology and Transcription with Previews in Gregg Shorthand Simplified. 3rd ed. McGraw-Hill, Gregg Division, 1967, 406, illus.

———.
    Medical Typing Practice. 2nd ed. McGraw-Hill, 1967, 108.

SCHMIDT, JACOB E.
    Structural Units of Medical and Biological Terms: A Convenient Guide, in English. Thomas, 1969, 172.

COMMERCIAL PROGRAMS

SCHWARZROCK, SHIRLEY P., and WARD, DONOVAN F.
　　Effective Medical Assisting. W. C. Brown, 1969, 588, illus.

SIEGFRIED, WALTER R.
　　Typing Medical Forms. McGraw-Hill, 1969, 224, illus.

SKINNER, HENRY A.
　　The Origin of Medical Terms. 2nd ed. Williams & Wilkins, 1961, 438, illus.

SMITH, GENEVIEVE L., and DAVIS, PHYLLIS E.
　　Medical Terminology: A Programed Text. 2nd ed. Wiley, 1967, 289, illus.

SOLTESZ, SHIRLEY E.
　　Selected Medical Terminology. Argyle, 1968, 395, illus. (Argyle Programed Instruction.)

STANTON, ISABEL A.
　　A Dictionary for Medical Secretaries. Thomas, 1960, 175.

STEDMAN, THOMAS L.
　　Medical Dictionary: A Vocabulary of Medicine and Its Allied Sciences, with Pronunciations and Derivations. 21st ed. Williams & Wilkins, 1966, 1836, illus.

STEEN, EDWIN B.
　　Medical Abbreviations. 2nd ed. F. A. Davis, 1967, 102.

STRAND, HELEN R.
　　An Illustrated Guide to Medical Terminology. Williams & Wilkins, 1968, 110, illus.

SZULEC, JEANETTE A.
　　A Syllabus for the Surgeon's Secretary. Medical Arts, Detroit, 1965, 431, illus.

WILLEFORD, GEORGE
　　Medical Word Finder. Parker, West Nyack, N.Y., 1967, 340.

YOUNG, CLARA G., and BARGER, JAMES D.
　　Learning Medical Terminology Step by Step. Mosby, 1967, 327, illus.

SCHOOL SECRETARY

ARCO PUBLISHING COMPANY, INC.
　　School Secretary. Arco, 1966, 232. (Teacher License Test Series.)

SMITH, JOHN A.
　　The School Secretary's Handbook. Prentice-Hall, 1962, 407.

TECHNICAL SECRETARY

ADAMS, DOROTHY, and KURTZ, MARGARET
　　The Technical Secretary: Terminology and Transcription. McGraw-Hill, 1968, 373.

LAIRD, ELEANOR S.
　　Engineering Secretary's Complete Handbook. 2nd ed. Prentice-Hall, 1967, 279, illus.

STAFFORD, ALISON R., and CULPEPPER, BILLIE J.
　　The Science-Engineering Secretary: A Guide to Procedure, Usage, and Style. Prentice-Hall, 1963, 338.

COMMUNITY SERVICE PROGRAMS

AGRICULTURE

AHLGREN, HENRY L., and DELORIT, RICHARD J.
  Crop Production: Principles and Practices. 3rd ed. Prentice-Hall, 1967, 662, illus. (Prentice-Hall Vocational Agriculture Series.)

AKEHURST, B. C.
  Tobacco. Humanities Press, 1968, 551, illus. (Tropical Agriculture Series.)

ALLARD, ROBERT W.
  Principles of Plant Breeding. Wiley, 1960, 485, illus.

AMERICAN ASSOCIATION FOR AGRICULTURAL ENGINEERING AND VOCATIONAL AGRICULTURE
  Building Farm Fences. Rev. ed. AAAEVA, 1969, 36, illus.

———.
  Farm Utility Buildings: Designs, Materials, Plans. Rev. ed. AAAEVA, 1969, 64, illus.

———.
  Planning Farm Fences. Rev. ed. AAAEVA, 1966, 56, illus.

———.
  Planning Water Systems for Farm and Home. Rev. ed. AAAEVA, 1963, 108, illus.

AMERICAN ASSOCIATION OF AGRICULTURAL COLLEGE EDITORS
  Communications Handbook. Interstate, 1967, 152, illus.

AMERICAN SOCIETY OF AGRONOMY
  Pasture and Range Research Techniques. Cornell University Press, 1962, 242, illus.

ANDERSON, JAMES R.
  A Geography of Agriculture. W. C. Brown, 1970, 106, illus. (Brown Foundation of Geography Series.)

ANDREWS, DALE W., and JUERGENSON, ELWOOD M.
  Selected Lessons for Teaching Agricultural Science. 2nd ed. Interstate, 1966, 339, illus.

ARCHER, SELLERS G.
  Soil Conservation. University of Oklahoma Press, 1960, 305, illus.

BEAR, FIRMAN E., ED.
  Chemistry of the Soil. 2nd ed. Reinhold, 1964, 515.

BERGER, KERMIT C.
  Introductory Soils. Macmillan, 1965, 371, illus.

BINKLEY, HAROLD R., and HAMMONDS, CARSIE
  Experience Programs for Learning Vocations in Agriculture. Interstate, 1970, 616

———.
  Farming Programs for Students in Vocational Agriculture. Interstate, 1961, 314, illus.

BISHOP, CHARLES E., ED.
  Farm Labor in the United States. Columbia University Press, 1967, 143, illus.

BLACK, CHARLES A.
  Soil-Plant Relationships. 2nd ed. Wiley, 1968, 792, illus.

BRAKE, JOHN R., ED.
  Farm and Personal Finance. Interstate, 1968, 132.

BREWBAKER, JAMES L.
  Agricultural Genetics. Prentice-Hall, 1964, 156, illus.

BRICKBAUER, ELWOOD A., and MORTENSON, W.
  Approved Practices in Crop Production. Interstate, 1967, 398, illus.

BRITISH CROP PROTECTION COUNCIL
  Insecticide and Fungicide Handbook for Crop Protection. 3rd ed. Hubert Martin, ed. Blackwell Davis, 1969, 387.

BRITISH WEED CONTROL COUNCIL
  Weed Control Handbook. 5th ed. J. D. Fryer and S. A. Evans, eds. Blackwell Davis, 1968, 2 vols., illus.

BUCKMAN, HARRY O., and BRADY, NYLE C.
  The Nature and Properties of Soils: A College Text of Edaphology. 7th ed. Macmillan, 1969, 653, illus.

BUNTING, A. H., ED.
  Change in Agriculture. Praeger, 1970, 828, illus.

BUNTING, BRIAN T.
  The Geography of Soil. Aldine, 1965, 213, illus.

BURNS, JAMES L., et al.
  A Training Program for Vocational Agriculture in Crops, Forestry, and Soil Conservation. Louisiana State Department of Education, Vocational Education Division, Louisiana State University, n.d., 135. (ERIC VT 000 277.)

BURNS, VAN H., et al.
  A Training Program for Vocational Agriculture in Farm Service. Louisiana State Department of Education, Vocational Education Division, Louisiana State University, n.d., 164. (ERIC VT 000 279.)

COMMUNITY SERVICE PROGRAMS

BYRAM, HAROLD M.
    Guidance in Agricultural Education. Interstate, 1966, 298, illus.

CHANCELLOR, RICHARD J.
    The Identification of Weed Seedlings of Farm and Garden. F. A. Davis, 1966, 88, illus.

CHANG, CHING-HU
    Climate and Agriculture: An Ecological Survey. Aldine, 1968, 304, illus.

CHILDERS, NORMAN F.
    Modern Fruit Science: Orchard and Small Fruit Culture. 2nd ed. Rutgers University, Horticultural Publishers, 1961, 893, illus.

CHRISTENSEN, CLYDE M., and KAUFMANN, HENRY H.
    Grain Storage: The Role of Fungi in Quality Loss. University of Minnesota Press, 1969, 153, illus.

CLARK, COLIN
    Starvation or Plenty? Taplinger, 1970, 180.

CLARK, COLIN, and HASWELL, MARGARET
    The Economics of Subsistence Agriculture. 3rd ed. Macmillan, 1967, 245, illus.

CLAWSON, MARION
    Policy Directions for U.S. Agriculture: Long-Range Choices in Farming and Rural Living. Johns Hopkins Press, 1968, 398, illus.

COCANNOUER, JOSEPH A.
    Weeds, Guardians of the Soil. Devin-Adair, 1964, 179, illus.

COOK, RAY L.
    Soil Management for Conservation and Production. Wiley, 1962, 527, illus.

CORN CONGRESS, DELAVAN, WIS., 1964
    Advances in Corn Production: Principles and Practices—Papers. Iowa State University Press, 1966, 476, illus.

DAVIDSON, BRUCE R., and MARTIN, B. R.
    Experimental Research and Farm Production. University of Western Australia Press, 1968, 68. (Agricultural Economic Resources Report No. 7.)

DAVIDSON, RALPH H., and PEAIRS, LEONARD M.
    Insect Pests of Farm, Garden and Orchard. 6th ed. Wiley, 1966, 675, illus.

DONAHUE, ROY L.
    Our Soils and Their Management: Increasing Production Through Soil and Water Conservation. 3rd ed. Interstate, 1970, 683, illus.

    ———.
    Soils: An Introduction to Soils and Plant Growth. 2nd ed. Prentice-Hall, 1965, 363, illus.

DRABLOS, CARROLL J. W., and JONES, BENJAMIN A., JR.
    Highway and Agricultural Drainage Practices. University of Illinois, Engineering Publications Office, 1965, 159, illus. (University of Illinois, Engineering Experiment Station, Bulletin No. 480.)

DUBOV, IRVING, ED.
    Contemporary Agricultural Marketing. University of Tennessee Press, 1968, 270.

DUMONT, RENE
    Types of Rural Economy: Studies in World Agriculture. Barnes & Noble, 1970, 555, illus.

EDWARDS, CLIVE A., and HEATH, GORDON W.
    The Principles of Agricultural Entomology. Thomas, 1964, 418, illus.

ELLIOTT, FRED C., et al.
    Advances in Production and Utilization of Quality Cotton: Principles and Practices. Iowa State University Press, 1968, 532, illus.

ETIENNE, GILBERT
    Studies in Indian Agriculture: The Art of the Possible. University of California Press, 1968, 343.

EVANS, ELFED
    Plant Diseases and Their Chemical Control. Blackwell Davis, 1968, 288, illus.

FARRALL, ARTHUR W., and ALBRECHT, CARL F.
    Agricultural Engineering: A Dictionary and Handbook. Interstate, 1965, 434.

FERTILIZER INSTITUTE
    Analytical Methods. 2nd ed. Fertilizer Institute, 1969, 1 vol.

FITZPATRICK, FREDERICK L.
    Our Plant Resources: Plants and Their Economic Importance. Holt, 1964, 173.

FOSTER, ALBERT B.
    Approved Practices in Soil Conservation. Interstate, 1964, 384, illus.

FOX, KARL A., and JOHNSON, DAVID G.
    Readings in the Economics of Agriculture. Irwin, 1969, 517, illus. (Series of republished articles on economics Vol. 13.)

FOX, RODNEY
    Agricultural and Technical Journalism. Greenwood Press, 1969, 229, illus.

FULLER, GERALD R.
    Education for Agricultural Occupations. Interstate, 1965, 42.

GASPARD, CURREN J., et al.
    A Training Program for Vocational Agriculture in Agricultural Service. Louisiana State Department of Education, Vocational Education Division, Louisiana State University, 1964, 97. (ERIC VT 000 275.)

GIBSON, J. SULLIVAN, and BATTEN, JAMES W.
    Soils: Their Nature, Classes, Distribution, Uses, and Care. University of Alabama Press, 1970, 296, illus.

GREATER DES MOINES CHAMBER OF COMMERCE, AGRICULTURAL COMMITTEE
    Corporate Farming and the Family Farm. Iowa State University Press, 1970, 130.

HADLOW, LEONARD
    Climate, Vegetation & Man. Greenwood Press, 1969, 288, illus.

HADWIGER, DON F.
    Federal Wheat Commodity Programs. Iowa State University Press, 1970, 407, illus.

HAGAN, ROBERT M., HAISE, HOWARD R., and EDMINISTER, TALCOTT W.
    Irrigation of Agricultural Lands. American Society of Agronomy, Madison, Wis., 1967, 1180.

HALL, ISAAC F., and MORTENSON, WILLIAM P.
    The Farm Management Handbook. 4th ed. Interstate, 1963, 437, illus.

HAMILTON, JAMES E., and BRYANT, W. R.
    Profitable Farm Management. 2nd ed. Prentice-Hall, 1963, 394, illus.

HAMLIN, HERBERT M.
    Public School Education in Agriculture. Interstate, 1962, 328.

HARTLEY, GILBERT S., and WEST, TRUSTHAM F.
    Chemicals for Pest Control. Pergamon, 1969, 316, illus. (Commonwealth and International Library, Chemical Industry.)

HARTMANN, HUDSON T., and KESTER, DALE E.
    Plant Propagation: Principles and Practices. 2nd ed. Prentice-Hall, 1968, 702, illus.

HAUVER, WILLIAM E., HAMANN, JOHN A., and KILPATRICK, LESTER
Egg Grading Manual. Rev. ed. USDA, Agricultural Marketing Service, Washington, 1961, 52, illus. (USDA Agriculture Handbook No. 75.)

HEDGES, TRIMBLE R.
Farm Management Decisions. Prentice-Hall, 1963, 628.

HELD, R. BURNELL, and CLAWSON, MARION
Soil Conservation in Perspective. Johns Hopkins Press, 1965, 344.

HELMBERGER, PETER C., and HOOS, SIDNEY S.
Cooperative Bargaining in Agriculture: Grower-Processor Markets for Fruits and Vegetables. University of California, Agricultural Science Division, 1965, 234.

HIGBEE, EDWARD C.
Farms and Farmers in an Urban Age. Twentieth Century Fund, 1963, 183, illus.

HILDRETH, ROLAND J., ED.
Readings in Agricultural Policy. University of Nebraska Press, 1968, 463.

HOOVER, NORMAN K.
Handbook of Agricultural Occupations: Preparation for Technical and Professional Work in Agriculture. Interstate, 1963, 254, illus.

HUGHES, HAROLD D.
Forages: The Science of Grassland Agriculture. 2nd ed. Iowa State University Press, 1962, 707, illus.

HUTCHISON, CHESTER S.
Your Future in Agriculture. R. Rosen Press, 1965, 191, illus. (Careers in Depth.)

INTERNATIONAL ATOMIC ENERGY AGENCY
Value to Agriculture of High-Quality Water From Nuclear Desalination: Report of a 1967 Panel. Unipub, New York, 1969, 278.

INTERNATIONAL RICE RESEARCH INSTITUTE
The Virus Diseases of the Rice Plant. Johns Hopkins Press, 1969, 354.

IOWA STATE UNIVERSITY
Midwest Farm Handbook. 7th ed. Iowa State University Press, 1969, 505, illus.

IOWA STATE UNIVERSITY, CENTER FOR AGRICULTURAL AND ECONOMIC DEVELOPMENT
Food Goals, Future Structural Changes and Agricultural Policy: A National Casebook. Iowa State University Press, 1969, 325.

ISELY, DUANE
Weed Identification and Control in the North Central States. 2nd ed. Iowa State University Press, 1960, 400, illus.

JAMES, SYDNEY C., ED.
Midwest Farm Planning Manual: Input-Output Coefficients, Prices, Paid and Received, Farm Budgets. 2nd ed. Iowa State University Press, 1968, 345, illus.

JANICK, JULES
Horticultural Science. W. H. Freeman, 1963, 472, illus. (Agricultural Science Series.)

JANICK, JULES, et al.
Plant Agriculture. W. H. Freeman, 1970, 246, illus. (Readings from Scientific American.)

———.
Plant Science: An Introduction to World Crops. W. H. Freeman, 1969, 629, illus. (Agricultural Science Series.)

JUERGENSON, ELWOOD M., and BURLINGHAM, H. H.
Selected Lessons for Teaching Off-Farm Agricultural Occupations. Interstate, 1967, 172, illus.

KEARNEY, PHILIP C., and KAUFMAN, DONALD D., EDS.
Degradation of Herbicides. Dekker, 1969, 394, illus.

KIPPS, MICHAEL S.
The Production of Field Crops: A Textbook of Agronomy. McGraw-Hill, 1970, 790, illus.

KLINGMAN, GLENN C.
Weed Control: As A Science. Wiley, 1961, 421, illus.

KNUTI, LEO L., KORPI, MILTON L., and HIDE, J. C.
Profitable Soil Management. Prentice-Hall, 1962, 376, illus. (Prentice-Hall Vocational Agriculture Series.)

KRAMER, PAUL J.
Plant and Soil Water Relationships: A Modern Synthesis. 2nd ed. McGraw-Hill, 1969, 416.

KREBS, ALFRED H.
Agriculture in Our Lives. Interstate, 1964, 700, illus.

KREBS, ALFRED H., and HEMP, PAUL E.
A Study Guide for Placement Employment Programs in Agricultural Business and Industry. Interstate, 1964, 188.

LEONARD, WARREN H.
Cereal Crops. Macmillan, 1963, 824, illus.

LIONBERGER, HERBERT F., and CHANG, H. C.
Farm Information for Modernizing Agriculture: The Taiwan System. Praeger, 1970, 425. (Praeger Special Studies in International Economics and Development.)

LOCKHART, J. A. R., and WISEMAN, A. J. L.
Introduction to Crop Husbandry. Pergamon, 1966, 260, illus. (Commonwealth and International Library, Rural and Environmental Studies Division.)

LÖF, GEORGE O. G., and KNEESE, ALLEN V.
The Economics of Water Utilization in the Beet Sugar Industry. Johns Hopkins Press, 1968, 125, illus.

LOTKOWSKI, WLADYSLAW M.
The Soil. Educational Methods, Chicago, 1966, 123, illus. (EM Self-Instructional Program.)

MARKHAM, JESSE W.
The Fertilizer Industry: Study of an Imperfect Market. Greenwood Press, 1969, 249, illus.

MARTIN, JOHN H., and LEONARD, WARREN H.
Principles of Field Crop Production. 2nd ed. Macmillan, 1967, 1044, illus.

McGINNIES, WILLIAM G., and GOLDMAN, BRAM J., EDS.
Arid Lands in Perspective: Including AAAS Papers on Water Importation into Arid Lands. University of Arizona Press, 1969, 421, illus.

McVICKAR, MALCOLM H.
Using Commercial Fertilizers: Commercial Fertilizers and Crop Production. 3rd ed. Interstate, 1970, 352, illus.

McVICKAR, MALCOLM H., and McVICKAR, JOHN S.
Approved Practices in Pasture Management. 2nd ed. Interstate, 1963, 332, illus.

MELLOR, JOHN W.
The Economics of Agricultural Development. Cornell University Press, 1966, 404, illus.

METCALF, CLELL L.
Destructive and Useful Insects: Their Habits and Control. 4th ed. McGraw-Hill, 1962, 1087, illus.

MILLAR, CHARLES E., TURK, LLOYD D., and FOTH, H. D.
Fundamentals of Soil Science. 4th ed. Wiley, 1965, 491, illus.

MILLER, ROBERT F.
One Hundred Thousand Tractors: The MTS and the Development of Controls in Soviet Agriculture. Harvard University Press, 1970, 423.

MILLER, TEXTON R.
Supervised Practice in Vocational Agriculture: A Student Handbook. Interstate, 1967, 30, illus.

COMMUNITY SERVICE PROGRAMS

MITCHELL, ROGER L.
    Crop Growth and Culture. Iowa State University Press, 1970, 628.

MORTENSON, WILLIAM P.
    Modern Marketing of Farm Products. Interstate, 1968, 364, illus.

MORTENSON, WILLIAM P., and HALL, ISAAC F.
    Approved Practices in Farm Management. 3rd ed. Interstate, 1966, 260, illus.

MURRAY, WILLIAM G.
    Farm Appraisal and Valuation. 5th ed. Iowa State University Press, 1969, 534, illus.

MUZIK, THOMAS J.
    Weed Biology and Control. McGraw-Hill, 1970, 273, illus.

NATIONAL ACADEMY OF SCIENCES, NATIONAL RESEARCH COUNCIL, AGRICULTURAL RESEARCH INSTITUTE
    World Food Needs and Production: Present and Future. NAS, 1966, 231.

NATIONAL ACADEMY OF SCIENCES, NATIONAL RESEARCH COUNCIL, COMMISSION ON EDUCATION IN AGRICULTURE AND NATURAL RESOURCES
    Undergraduate Teaching in the Plant and Soil Sciences. NAS, 1969, 48. (Pub. No. 1704.)

NATIONAL AGRICULTURAL CHEMICALS ASSOCIATION
    Manual of Pesticide Use and Application Laws: A Guide to Laws Affecting the Use and Application of Pesticides. NACA, Washington, 1962, 1 vol.

NATIONAL FARM INSTITUTE
    Bargaining Power for Farmers. Iowa State University Press, 1968, 132.

———.
    Farmers and a Hungry World. Iowa State University Press, 1967, 136, illus.

NATIONAL RESEARCH COUNCIL, COMMITTEE ON REMOTE SENSING FOR AGRICULTURAL PURPOSES
    Remote Sensing with Special Reference to Agriculture and Forestry. National Academy of Sciences, Washington, 1970, 424, illus.

NELSON, AARON G., and MURRAY, WILLIAM G.
    Agricultural Finance. 5th ed. Iowa State University Press, 1967, 561, illus.

OHIO STATE UNIVERSITY, COLUMBUS CENTER FOR VOCATIONAL AND TECHNICAL INSTRUCTION
    Planning and Conducting Cooperative Occupational Experience for Off-Farm Agriculture. Ohio State University, Columbus Center, 1965, 138. (Off-Farm Agricultural Occupations Pub. No. 4.)

OLSEN, H. M.
    Some Principles and Practices of Farmer Cooperatives. Interstate, 1961, 118.

PALAN, RALPH L., and PERSONS, EDGAR A.
    A Course of Study for Adult Farmer Instruction in Farm Management and Farm Business Analysis. 2nd ed. Minnesota University, Agricultural Education Department, 1969, 218. (ERIC VT 010 506.)

PHIPPS, LLOYD J.
    Handbook on Agricultural Education in Public Schools. Interstate, 1965, 774, illus.

———.
    Your Opportunities in Vocational Agriculture. Interstate, 1962, 176.

PRADHAN, SHYAMSUNDERLAL
    Insect Pests of Crops. National Book Trust, New Delhi, 1969, 208, illus.

RASMUSSEN, WAYNE D., ED.
    Readings in the History of American Agriculture. University of Illinois Press, 1960, 340, illus.

REISCHE, DIANA L.
    U. S. Agricultural Policy. Wilson, 1966, 211. (Reference Shelf Vol. 38, No. 3.)

RICHEY, C. B., JACOBSON, PAUL, and HALL, CARL W., EDS.
    Agricultural Engineer's Handbook. McGraw-Hill, 1961, 880, illus.

ROBBINS, WILFRED W., and CRAFTS, ALDEN S.
    Weed Control: A Textbook and Manual. 3rd ed. McGraw-Hill, 1962, 660, illus. (McGraw-Hill Publications in Agricultural Sciences.)

ROY, EWELL P.
    Contract Farming, U.S.A. Interstate, 1963, 572, illus.

———.
    Exploring Agribusiness. Interstate, 1967, 400, illus.

RUSSELL, SIR EDWARD J.
    Soil Conditions and Plant Growth. 9th ed. Wiley, 1961, 688, illus.

RUTGERS UNIVERSITY
    Six Selected Instructional Aids for Teachers of Agriculture. Rutgers University, 1967, 55, illus.

SAUER, CARL O.
    Agricultural Origins and Dispersals: The Domestication of Animals and Foodstuffs. 2nd ed. MIT Press, 1969, 175.

SCARSETH, GEORGE D.
    Man and His Earth. Iowa State University Press, 1962, 199, illus.

SCHEER, ARNOLD H., and JUERGENSON, ELWOOD M.
    Approved Practices in Fruit Production. Interstate, 1964, 504, illus.

SCHILLER, OTTO M.
    Cooperation and Integration in Agricultural Production: Concepts and Practical Application—An International Synopsis. Rev. ed. Asia Publishing, London, 1969, 230, illus.

SCHLEBECKER, JOHN T.
    Bibliography of Books and Pamphlets on the History of Agriculture in the United States, 1607-1967. ABC-Clio, 1969, 183.

SCHNEIDER, GEORGE W., and SCARBOROUGH, CLARENCE C.
    Fruit Growing. Prentice-Hall, 1960, 307, illus. (Prentice-Hall Vocational Agriculture Series.)

SCHULTZ, THEODORE W.
    Transforming Traditional Agriculture. Yale University Press, 1964, 212.

SCOTT, WALTER O., and ALDRICH, SAMUEL R.
    Modern Soybean Production. Farm Quarterly, Cincinnati, 1970, 192, illus.

SHEPHERD, GEOFFREY S., and FUTRELL, GENE A.
    Marketing Farm Products.... 5th ed. Iowa State University Press, 1969, 510, illus.

SIDNEY, HOWARD, ED.
    Agricultural, Forestry and Oceanographic Technicians. J. G. Ferguson, 1970, 344. (Career Opportunities for Technicians and Specialists Vol. 2.)

SIMMS, DENTON H.
    The Soil Conservation Service. Praeger, 1970, 238, illus. (Praeger Library of U.S. Government Departments and Agencies No. 23.)

SLACK, ARCHIE V.
    Defense Against Famine: The Role of the Fertilizer Industry. Doubleday, 1970, 232, illus. (Chemistry in Action Series.)

SLOCUM, WALTER L.
    Agricultural Sociology: A Study of Sociological Aspects of American Farm Life. Harper, 1962, 532, illus. (Harper Social Science Series.)

AGRICULTURE

SMITH, T. LYNN, and ZOPF, PAUL E., JR.
Principles of Inductive Rural Sociology. F. A. Davis, 1970, 558.

SNODGRASS, MILTON M., and WALLACE, LUTHER T.
Agriculture, Economics, and Growth. 2nd ed. Appleton-Century-Crofts, 1970, 489, illus.

SNOWDEN, OBED L., and DONAHOO, ALVIN W.
Profitable Farm Marketing. Prentice-Hall, 1960, 403, illus. (Prentice-Hall Vocational Agriculture Series.)

SOTH, LAUREN K.
Agriculture in an Industrial Society. Holt, Rinehart & Winston, 1966, 64, illus. (American Problems Series.)

SOUTHWORTH, HERMAN M., and JOHNSTON, BRUCE F., EDS.
Agricultural Development and Economic Growth. Cornell University Press, 1967, 608, illus.

SOWERS, GEORGE B., and SOWERS, GEORGE F.
Introductory Soil Mechanics and Foundations. 3rd ed. Macmillan, 1970, 556, illus.

STEPHENSON, WILLIAM A.
Seaweed in Agriculture and Horticulture. Faber & Faber, 1968, 231, illus.

STONE, ARCHIE A.
Careers in Agribusiness and Industry. Interstate, 1965, 292, illus.

SYMONS, LESLIE
Agricultural Geography. Praeger, 1967, 283, illus. (Praeger Surveys in Economic Geography.)

TEUSCHER, HENRY, and ADLER, RUDOLPH
The Soil and Its Fertility. Reinhold, 1960, 446.

TIEDJENS, VICTOR A.
Olena Farm, U.S.A.: An Agricultural Success Story. Exposition Press, 1969, 160, illus. (Exposition-Banner Book.)

TROEH, FREDERICK R., and PALMER, ROBERT G.
Introductory Soil Science: Laboratory Manual. Iowa State University Press, 1966, 95, illus.

TROUGHT, T. E. T.
Farm Pests: An Aid to Their Recognition. F. A. Davis, 1965, 72.

U.S. COMMISSION ON CIVIL RIGHTS
Equal Opportunity in Farm Programs: An Appraisal of Services Rendered by Agencies of the United States Department of Agriculture—A Report. USGPO, 1965, 136, illus.

U.S. DEPARTMENT OF AGRICULTURE
Agricultural Statistics. USGPO, 1936- , vols., annual.

———.
Yearbook of Agriculture. USDA, 1894- , vols., annual.

U.S. DEPARTMENT OF AGRICULTURE, AGRICULTURAL RESEARCH SERVICE.
Soil Dynamics in Tillage and Traction. USDA, 1967, 511, illus.

U.S. DEPARTMENT OF AGRICULTURE, CROPS RESEARCH DIVISION
Suggested Guide for Weed Control 1969. USDA, 1969, 70. (USDA Agriculture Handbook No. 332.)

U.S. OFFICE OF EDUCATION, VOCATIONAL AND TECHNICAL EDUCATION DIVISION
Farm Crop Production Technology: Field and Forage Crop and Fruit and Vine Production Options—A Suggested 2-Year Post High School Curriculum. USOE, 1970, 179, illus. (OE-81016.)

———.
Grain, Feed, Seed, and Farm Supply Technology: A Suggested 2-Year Post High School Curriculum. USOE, 1968, 185, illus. (OE-81014.)

VOISIN, ANDRÉ
Fertilizer Application: Soil, Plant and Animal. Thomas, 1965, 128, illus.

WADLEIGH, CECIL H.
Wastes in Relation to Agriculture and Forestry. USDA, 1970, 112, illus. (USDA Miscellaneous Pub. No. 1065.)

WALL, JOSEPH S., and ROSS, WILLIAM M., EDS.
Sorghum: Production and Utilization. AVI, 1970, 702.

WARE, GEORGE W., and McCOLLUM, JOHN P.
Producing Vegetable Crops. Interstate, 1968, 558, illus.

WARMBROD, JOHN R., and PHIPPS, LLOYD J.
Review and Synthesis of Research in Agricultural Education. Ohio State University, Columbus Center for Vocational and Technical Instruction, 1966, 140.

WEYANT, J. THOMAS, HOOVER, NORMAN K., and McCLAY, DAVID R.
An Introduction to Agricultural Business and Industry. Interstate, 1966, 240, illus.

WILLMAN, HAROLD A.
Handbook and Lesson Guide for Leaders, County Extension Agents and Teachers. 2nd ed. Cornell University Press, 1963, 314, illus.

WILSIE, CARROLL P.
Crop Adaptation and Distribution. W. H. Freeman, 1962, 448, illus. (Agricultural Science Series.)

WILSON, HAROLD K., and RICHER, A. CHESTER
Producing Farm Crops. Interstate, 1960, 336, illus.

WINBURNE, JOHN N., ED.
A Dictionary of Agricultural and Allied Terminology. Michigan State University Press, 1962, 905.

WITTWER, SYLVAN H., and HONMA, SHIGEMI
Greenhouse Tomatoes: Guidelines for Successful Production. Michigan State University Press, 1969, 95, illus.

WOODFORD, EDWIN K., ED.
Crop Production in A Weed-Free Environment. F. A. Davis, 1963, 114, illus.

WRIGLEY, GORDON
Tropical Agriculture: The Development of Production. Praeger, 1969, 376, illus.

EQUIPMENT

AMERICAN ASSOCIATION FOR AGRICULTURAL ENGINEERING AND VOCATIONAL AGRICULTURE.
Farm Electric Motors: Selection, Protection, Drives. Rev. ed. AAAEVA, 1964, 36, illus.

———.
Selecting and Maintaining Field Mowers. AAAEVA, 1966, 128, illus.

———.
Selecting and Storing Tractor Fuels and Lubricants. Rev. ed. AAAEVA, 1970, 55, illus.

———.
Small Engines: Care, Operation, Maintenance and Repair. AAAEVA, 1968, 2 vols., illus.

———.
Tractor Maintenance, Principles and Procedures. Rev. ed. AAAEVA, 1970, 152, illus.

———.
Tractor Operation and Daily Care. Rev. ed. AAAEVA, 1967, 120, illus.

BROWN, ARLEN D., and MORRISON, IVAN G.
Farm Tractor Maintenance. 3rd ed. Interstate, 1962, 256, illus.

ESHELMAN, PHILLIP V.
Tractors and Crawlers. 2nd ed. American Technical Society, 1967, 374, illus.

COMMUNITY SERVICE PROGRAMS

HUNT, DONNELL
Farm Power and Machinery Management: Laboratory Manual & Workbook. 5th ed. Iowa State University Press, 1968, 292, illus.

PHIPPS, LLOYD J.
Mechanics in Agriculture. Interstate, 1967, 820, illus.

PHIPPS, LLOYD J., and JENNE, JEWEL A.
Ideas for Farm Mechanics Projects. Interstate, 1962, 434, illus.

PROMERSBERGER, WILLIAM J., and BISHOP, FRANK E.
Modern Farm Power. Prentice-Hall, 1962, 280, illus. (Prentice-Hall Vocational Agriculture Series.)

SMITH, HARRIS P.
Farm Machinery and Equipment. 5th ed. McGraw-Hill, 1964, 519, illus.

WAKEMAN, TRUMAN J., and McCOY, VERNON L.
The Farm Shop. Macmillan, 1960, 63, illus.

WILSON, LEONARD L., ED.
Farm & Power Equipment Retailer's Handbook. Rev. ed. National Farm and Power Equipment Dealers Association, St. Louis, 1964, 516, illus.

U.S. OFFICE OF EDUCATION, VOCATIONAL AND TECHNICAL EDUCATION DIVISION
Agricultural Equipment Technology: A Suggested 2-Year Post High School Curriculum. USGPO, 1970, 112. (OE-81015.)

LIVESTOCK

ACKER, DUANE
Animal Science and Industry. Prentice-Hall, 1963, 502, illus.

ANDERSON, ARTHUR L., and KISER, JAMES J.
Introductory Animal Science. Macmillan, 1963, 800, illus.

BARRON, NORMAN S.
The Pig Farmer's Veterinary Book. 3rd ed. Thomas, 1962, 182, illus.

BEESON, WILLIAM M., HUNSLEY, ROGER E., and NORDBY, JULIUS E.
Livestock Judging and Evaluation: A Handbook for the Student. Interstate, 1970, 405, illus.

BIDDLE, GEORGE H., and JUERGENSON, ELWOOD M.
Approved Practices in Poultry Production. 3rd ed. Interstate, 1963, 332, illus.

BRIGGS, HILTON M.
Modern Breeds of Livestock. 3rd ed. Macmillan, 1969, 714, illus.

BUNDY, CLARENCE E., and DIGGINS, RONALD V.
Livestock and Poultry Production. 3rd ed. Prentice-Hall, 1968, 723, illus. (Prentice-Hall Vocational Agriculture Series.)

———.
Poultry Production. Prentice-Hall, 1960, 370. (Prentice-Hall Vocational Agriculture Series.)

———.
Swine Production. 2nd ed. Prentice-Hall, 1963, 371, illus. (Prentice-Hall Vocational Agriculture Series.)

CARD, LESLIE E., and NESHEIM, MALDEN C.
Poultry Production. 10th ed. Lea & Febiger, 1966, 400, illus.

CASSARD, DANIEL W., and JUERGENSON, ELWOOD M.
Approved Practices in Feeds and Feeding. Interstate, 1963, 362, illus.

COLE, HAROLD H., ED.
Introduction to Livestock Production, Including Dairy and Poultry. 2nd ed. W. H. Freeman, 1966, 827, illus. (Agricultural Science Series: Animal Science.)

COLETTI, ANTHONY
Handbook for Dairymen. Iowa State University Press, 1963, 307, illus.

COOK, GLEN C., and JUERGENSON, ELWOOD M.
Approved Practices in Swine Production. Interstate, 1962, 329, illus.

CUNHA, TONY J., KOGER, M., and WARNICK, A. C., EDS.
Crossbreeding Beef Cattle. University of Florida Press, 1963, 228, illus.

DAVIS, RICHARD F.
Modern Dairy Cattle Management. Prentice-Hall, 1962, 264, illus.

DIGGINS, RONALD V., and BUNDY, CLARENCE E.
Beef Production. 2nd ed. Prentice-Hall, 1962, 341, illus. (Prentice-Hall Vocational Agriculture Series.)

———.
Dairy Production. 2nd ed. Prentice-Hall, 1961, 341, illus.

DUNNE, HOWARD W., ED.
Diseases of Swine. 3rd ed. Iowa State University Press, 1970, 900.

ENSMINGER, M. EUGENE
Animal Science. 5th ed. Interstate, 1962, 1158, illus. (Animal Agriculture Series.)

———.
Beef Cattle Science. 4th ed. Interstate, 1969, 1020, illus. (Animal Agriculture Series.)

———.
Horses and Horsemanship. 3rd ed. Interstate, 1963, 583, illus. (Animal Agriculture Series.)

———.
Sheep and Wool Science. 4th ed. Interstate, 1970, 900, illus. (Animal Agriculture Series.)

———.
The Stockman's Handbook. 3rd ed. Interstate, 1952, 756, illus. (Animal Agriculture Series.)

———.
Swine Science. 4th ed. Interstate, 1970, 900, illus. (Animal Agriculture Series.)

ESMAY, MERLE L.
Principles of Animal Environment. AVI, 1969, 329.

FAULKNER, LLOYD C., ED.
Abortion Diseases of Livestock. Thomas, 1968, 207.

FISHER, SIR RONALD A.
The Theory of Inbreeding. 2nd ed. Academic Press, 1965, 150, illus.

FOWLER, STEWART H.
Beef Production in the South. Interstate, 1969, 858.

———.
The Marketing of Livestock and Meat. Interstate, 1961, 740, illus.

FRANDSON, ROWEN D.
Anatomy and Physiology of Farm Animals. Lea & Febiger, 1965, 501, illus.

GOODMAN, JOHN W., and TUDOR, DAVID C.
Your Future in Poultry Farming. Prentice-Hall, 1960, 412, illus. (Prentice-Hall Vocational Agriculture Series.)

GUTCHO, M.
Animal Feeds 1970. Noyes, 1970, 353, illus. (Food Processing Review No. 10.)

HAFEZ, E. S. E., ED.
Reproduction in Farm Animals. 2nd ed. Lea & Febiger, 1968, 440, illus.

HANNAH, HAROLD W., and STORM, DONALD F.
Law for the Veterinarian and Livestock Owner. 2nd ed. Interstate, 1965, 212.

JOHANSSON, IVAR
Genetic Aspects of Dairy Cattle Breeding. University of Illinois Press, 1961, 259, illus.

JUERGENSON, ELWOOD M.
Approved Practices in Beef Cattle Production. Interstate, 1964, 353, illus.

———.
Approved Practices in Sheep Production. Interstate, 1963, 360, illus.

JUERGENSON, ELWOOD M., and MORTENSON, WILLIAM P.
Approved Practices in Dairying. 2nd ed. Interstate, 1960, 300, illus.

KEITH, T. B., and BAKER, JOHN P.
Feed Formulation Manual. Interstate, 1967, 100.

LOUISIANA STATE DEPARTMENT OF EDUCATION, VOCATIONAL EDUCATION DIVISION
A Training Program for Vocational Agriculture in Dairy Production. Louisiana State Education Department, 1968, 262. (ERIC VT 010 689.)

MAYNARD, LEONARD A., and LOOSLI, JOHN K.
Animal Nutrition. 6th ed. McGraw-Hill, 1969, 613, illus.

McCULLOUGH, MARSHALL E.
Optimum Feeding of Dairy Animals. University of Georgia Press, 1969, 180, illus.

MORRISON, FRANK B., MORRISON, ELSIE B., and MORRISON, SPENCER H.
Feeds and Feeding: A Handbook for the Student and Stockman. 23rd ed. Moore, Newburgh, N.Y., 1968, 1165, illus.

NATIONAL ACADEMY OF SCIENCES, NATIONAL RESEARCH COUNCIL, AGRICULTURAL RESEARCH INSTITUTE
The Role of Animal Agriculture in Meeting World Food Needs. NAS, 1966, 260.

NATIONAL ACADEMY OF SCIENCES, NATIONAL RESEARCH COUNCIL, COMMISSION ON ANIMAL NUTRITION
Nutrient Requirements of Beef Cattle. 4th ed. NAS, 1970, 58.

———.
Nutrient Requirements of Dairy Cattle. Rev. ed. NAS, 1966, 38. (Pub. No. 1349.)

———.
Nutrient Requirements of Poultry. Rev. ed. NAS, 1966, 28. (Pub. No. 1345.)

NEUMANN, ALVIN L., and SNAPP, ROSCOE R.
Beef Cattle. 6th ed. Wiley, 1969, 767, illus.

NORDBY, JULIUS E., and LATTIG, HERBERT E.
Selecting, Fitting and Showing Beef Cattle. Interstate, 1962, 136, illus.

———.
Selecting, Fitting and Showing Dairy Cattle. Interstate, 1961, 135, illus.

———.
Selecting, Fitting and Showing Horses. Interstate, 1963, 138, illus.

———.
Selecting, Fitting and Showing Poultry. Interstate, 1964, 93, illus.

———.
Selecting, Fitting and Showing Sheep. Interstate, 1962, 119.

———.
Selecting, Fitting and Showing Swine. Interstate, 1961, 95, illus.

PARKER, WILLIAM H.
Health and Disease of Farm Animals for Those Concerned with Animal Husbandry. Pergamon, 1970, 301, illus. (Commonwealth and International Library, Veterinary Science Division.)

PERRY, ENOS J., ED.
The Artificial Insemination of Farm Animals. 4th ed. Rutgers University Press, 1968, 473, illus.

PERRY, TILDEN W.
Feed Formulations Handbook. Interstate, 1966, 233, illus.

PORTER, ARTHUR R., SIMS, J. A., and FOREMAN, C. F.
Dairy Cattle in American Agriculture. Iowa State University Press, 1965, 328, illus.

POULTRY SCIENCE ASSOCIATION
Find Your Career in the Poultry Industry. Interstate, n.d., 44, illus.

RICE, VICTOR A., et al.
Breeding and Improvement of Farm Animals. 6th ed. McGraw-Hill, 1967, 477, illus.

ROUSE, JOHN E.
World Cattle. University of Oklahoma Press, 1970, 2 vols.

SALISBURY, GLENN W., and VANDEMARK, N. L.
Physiology of Reproduction and Artificial Insemination of Cattle. W. H. Freeman, 1961, 639, illus. (Agricultural Science Series.)

SCHAIBLE, PHILIP J.
Poultry: Feeds and Nutrition. AVI, 1970, 636, illus.

TITUS, HARRY W.
The Scientific Feeding of Chickens. Interstate, 1961, 297.

U.S. DEPARTMENT OF AGRICULTURE
Managing Public Rangelands: Effective Livestock Grazing Practices and Systems for National Forests and National Grasslands. USDA, 1967, 30, illus.

WAGNON, KENNETH A., ALBAUGH, REUBEN, and HART, GEORGE H.
Beef Cattle Production. Macmillan, 1960, 537, illus.

WING, JAMES M.
Dairy Cattle Management: Principles and Applications. Reinhold, 1963, 349, illus. (Reinhold Books in Agricultural Science.)

WOOLDRIDGE, WALTER R.
Farm Animals in Health and Disease. 2nd ed. Thomas, 1961, 533, illus.

YOUTZ, H. G., and CARLSON, A. C.
Judging Livestock, Dairy Cattle, Poultry, & Crops. Prentice-Hall, 1962, 195, illus. (Prentice-Hall Vocational Agriculture Series.)

CHILD CARE

ADAIR, THELMA, and ECKSTEIN, ESTHER
Parents and the Day Care Center. Child Welfare League of America, 1969, 36.

ALMY, MILLIE C., CHITTENDEN, EDWARD, and MILLER, PAULA
Young Children's Thinking: Studies of Some Aspects of Piaget's Theory. Teachers College Press, 1966, 153, illus.

AMERICAN ASSOCIATION FOR HEALTH, PHYSICAL EDUCATION AND RECREATION
How We Do It Game Book. Rev. ed. AAHPER, 1964, 352.

———.
...Book of Worldwide Games and Dances. AAHPER, 1967, 160.

COMMUNITY SERVICE PROGRAMS

AMERICAN LIBRARY ASSOCIATION
    Books for Children...: As Selected and Reviewed by The Booklist and Subscription Books Bulletin.... ALA, 1966, 447.

AMES, LOUISE B.
    Child Care and Development. Lippincott, 1970, 426, illus.

ARENA, JAY
    Dangers of Childhood. Moore Publishing Co., Durham, N.C., 1970, 300, illus.

BALDWIN, ALFRED L.
    Theories of Child Development. Wiley, 1967, 618.

BAMMAN, HENRY A., et al.
    Oral Interpretation of Children's Literature. W. C. Brown, 1964, 119, illus. (Brown Education Series.)

BANDURA, ALBERT
    Social Learning and Personality Development. Holt, 1963, 329, illus.

BEADLE, MURIEL
    A Child's Mind: How Children Learn During the Critical Years from Birth to Age Five. Doubleday, 1970, 288, illus.

BENGTSSON, ARVID
    Environmental Planning for Children's Play. Praeger, 1970, 224, illus.

BENNETT, IVY
    Delinquent and Neurotic Children: A Comparative Study. Basic Books, 1960, 532.

BETTELHEIM, BRUNO
    The Children of the Dream. Macmillan, 1969, 363.

BLAND, JANE C.
    Art of the Young Child: Understanding and Encouraging Creative Growth in Children Three to Five. 3rd ed. Museum of Modern Art, New York (New York Graphic Society, dist.), 1968, 57, illus.

BOGUSLAWSKI, DOROTHY B.
    Guide for Establishing and Operating Day Care Centers for Young Children. Child Welfare League of America, 1966, 100.

BOSSARD, JAMES H. S., and BOLL, ELEANOR S.
    The Sociology of Child Development. 4th ed. Harper & Row, 1966, 566, illus.

BRECKENRIDGE, MARIAN E., and MURPHY, MARGARET N.
    Growth and Development of the Young Child. 8th ed. Saunders, 1969, 528, illus.

BRONFENBRENNER, URIE
    Two Worlds of Childhood, U.S. and U.S.S.R. Basic Books, 1970, 190, illus. (Russell Sage Foundation Publisher.)

BUCKLE, D., and LEBOVICI, S.
    Child Guidance Centres. World Health Organization, 1960, 133. (Monograph Series No. 40.)

BUIST, CHARLOTTE A., and SCHULMAN, JEROME L.
    Toys and Games for Educationally Handicapped Children. Thomas, 1969, 240.

BURMEISTER, EVA E.
    Tough Times and Tender Moments in Child Care Work. Columbia University Press, 1967, 274.

RR, D. J.
    Understanding Young Children. McGraw-Hill, 1966, 165, illus. (McGraw-Hill Foundation Series.)

CARMICHAEL, LEONARD
    Manual of Child Psychology. 3rd ed. Paul H. Mussen, ed. Wiley, 1970, 2 vols.

CHAMBERS, DEWEY W.
    Storytelling and Creative Drama. W. C. Brown, 1970, 92, illus.

CHAMPOUX, ELLEN M., and SCHEVE, HELEN
    Child-Care Services: A Tentative Teaching Guide. Kansas State Board for Vocational Education, 1966, 84. (ERIC VT 001 088.)

CHANDLER, CAROLINE A., LOURIE, REGINALD S., and PETERS, ANNE D.
    Early Child Care: The New Perspectives. Laura L. Dittmann, ed. Atherton Press, 1968, 385.

CHILD WELFARE LEAGUE OF AMERICA, INC.
    Day Care: An Expanding Resource for Children. CWLA, 1965, 75.

———.
    National Directory of Child Care Training Courses. CWLA, 1970, 52.

———.
    ...Standards for Child Protective Service. CWLA, 1960, 58.

———.
    ...Standards for Day Care Service. Rev. ed. CWLA, 1969, 123.

———.
    ...Standards for Services of Child Welfare Institutions. CWLA, 1964, 142.

CHILDREN'S BOOKS IN PRINT
    R. R. Bowker, 1969- , vols., annual.

CHOMSKY, CAROL
    The Acquisition of Syntax in Children from 5 to 10. MIT Press, 1969, 126. (Research Monograph No. 57.)

CHUKOVSKY, KORNEI I.
    From Two to Five. Miriam Morton, tr. University of California Press, 1963, 170, illus.

CHURCHILL, EILEEN M.
    Counting and Measuring: An Approach to Number Education in the Infant School. University of Toronto Press, 1961, 220.

CLEMENTS, FREDERICK W., and McCLOSKEY, BERTRAM P., EDS.
    Child Health: Its Origins and Promotion. Edward Arnold, London, 1964, 402, illus.

COHEN, ROSALYN S., ED.
    Optimum Utilization of Community Colleges in the Training of Child Care Workers. Institute for Mental Health, New York, 1969, 1 vol.

CRATTY, BRYANT J., and HUTTON, ROBERT S.
    Experiments in Movement Behavior and Motor Learning. Lea & Febiger, 1969, 217, illus.

DANZIGER, KURT, COMP.
    Readings in Child Socialization. Pergamon, 1970, 337, illus.

DAVIDSON, F., et al.
    Care of Children in Day Centres. World Health Organization, 1964, 189. (Public Health Paper No. 24.)

DEUTSCH, MARTIN, et al.
    The Disadvantaged Child: Selected Papers.... Basic Books, 1967, 400.

DiLEO, JOSEPH H.
    Young Children and Their Drawings. Brunner/Mazel, 1970, 386, illus.

DIMICK, KENNETH M., and HUFF, VAUGHN E.
    Child Counseling. W. C. Brown, 1970, 254.

DINKMEYER, DON C.
    Child Development: The Emerging Self. Prentice-Hall, 1965, 434, illus. (Prentice-Hall Psychology Series.)

DITTMANN, LAURA L., ED.
Early Child Care. Atherton Press, 1968, 385.

DOCKAR-DRYSDALE, BARBARA
Therapy in Child Care: Collected Papers. Harlow, Longmans, London, 1968, 163. (Papers on Residential Work Vol. 3.)

DREW, LOUISE C.
Nursery Manual: A Manual for Administrators in the Church School Nursery Department. Rev. ed. United Church, Boston, 1969, 63, illus.

EDELSON, KENNETH, and OREM, R. C., EDS.
The Children's House Parent-Teacher Guide to Montessori. Putnam, 1970, 259.

ELMER, ELIZABETH
Children in Jeopardy: A Study of Abused Minors and Their Families. University of Pittsburgh Press, 1967, 125, illus. (Contemporary Community Health Series.)

ERIKSON, ERIK H.
Childhood and Society. 2nd ed. W. W. Norton, 1963, 445, illus.

EVANS, ELLIS D., ED.
Children: Readings in Behavior and Development. Holt, Rinehart & Winston, 1968, 571, illus.

FLAPAN, DOROTHY
Children's Understanding of Social Interaction. Teachers College Press, 1968, 86.

FLINT, BETTY M.
The Child and the Institution: A Study of Deprivation and Recovery. University of Toronto Press, 1966, 180.

FORDHAM, MICHAEL
Children As Individuals. Putnam, 1969, 223.

FRADKIN, HELEN, ED.
Organization of Services That Will Best Meet Needs of Children. Child Welfare League of America, 1966, 179.

FROMME, ALLAN
The ABC of Child Care. Simon & Schuster, 1969, 332.

FROST, JOE L.
Early Childhood Education Rediscovered: Readings. Holt, Rinehart & Winston, 1968, 594, illus.

FURMAN, ROBERT A., and KATAN, ANNY, EDS.
The Therapeutic Nursery School: A Contribution to the Study and Treatment of Emotional Disturbances in Young Children. International Universities Press, 1969, 329.

GARDNER, DAVID B.
Development in Early Childhood: The Preschool Years. Harper & Row, 1964, 358, illus.

GEORGIOU, CONSTANTINE
Children and Their Literature. Prentice-Hall, 1969, 501, illus.

GINSBURG, HERBERT, and OPPER, SYLVIA, EDS.
Piaget's Theory of Intellectual Development: An Introduction. Prentice-Hall, 1969, 237, illus. (Prentice-Hall Series in Developmental Psychology.)

GOKULANATHAN, K. S., and VERGHESE, K. P.
Child Care in a Developing Community. 2nd ed. Vantage, 1969, 85, illus.

GOWAN, JOHN C., and DEMOS, GEORGE D., EDS.
The Guidance of Exceptional Children: A Book of Readings. McKay, 1965, 404.

GROW, LUCILLE J.
Requests for Child Welfare Services: A Five-Day Census. Child Welfare League of America, 1969, 64.

GRUENBERG, SIDONIE M., ED.
The New Encyclopedia of Child Care and Guidance. Rev. ed. Doubleday, 1968, 1016, illus.

HADFIELD, JAMES A.
Childhood and Adolescence. Penguin, 1962, 286. (Pelican A531.)

HAWKES, GLENN R., and PEASE, DAMARIS
Behavior and Development from 5 to 12. Harper & Row, 1962, 375, illus.

HURLOCK, ELIZABETH B.
Child Growth and Development. 4th ed. McGraw-Hill, 1970, 374, illus.

HURWITZ, ABRAHAM B., and GODDARD, ARTHUR
Games to Improve Your Child's English. Simon & Schuster, 1969, 352, illus.

HYLTON, LYDIA F.
The Residential Treatment Center: Children, Programs, and Costs. Child Welfare League of America, 1964, 251.

ILLINGWORTH, RONALD S.
The Development of the Infant and Young Child: Normal and Abnormal. 3rd ed. Williams & Wilkins, 1966, 378, illus.

———.
The Normal Child: Some Problems of the First Five Years and Their Treatment. 4th ed. Little, Brown, 1968, 380, illus.

ISAACS, SUSAN S.
Intellectual Growth in Young Children. Schocken Books, 1966, 295.

———.
The Nursery Years: The Mind of the Child From Birth to Six Years. Schocken Books, 1968, 140, illus.

JAMES, HOWARD
Children in Trouble. McKay, 1970, 352.

JOHNSON, RONALD C., and MEDINNUS, GENE R.
Child Psychology, Behavior and Development. 2nd ed. Wiley, 1969, 677, illus.

JOINT COMMISSION ON MENTAL HEALTH OF CHILDREN
Crisis in Child Mental Health: Challenge for the 1970's. Harper & Row, 1970, 578.

KADUSHIN, ALFRED
Child Welfare Services: A Sourcebook. Macmillan, 1970, 544.

KAHN, ALFRED J.
Planning Community Services for Children in Trouble. Columbia, Irvington, N.Y., 1963, 540.

KARL, JEAN
From Childhood to Childhood: Children's Books and Their Creators. John Day, 1970, 175.

KAUFMANN, WILLIAM I., COMP.
UNICEF Book of Children's Songs. Stackpole, 1970, 94, illus.

KEHM, FREDA S., and MINI, JOE L.
Let Children be Children: Questions and Answers About Raising Children from Infancy Through the Pre-Teen Years. Association Press, 1968, 160.

LANDRETH, CATHERINE
Early Childhood: Behavior and Learning. 2nd ed. Knopf, 1967, 388, illus.

LE SHAN, EDA J.
The Conspiracy Against Childhood. Atheneum, 1967, 368.

LEWIS, MARY K.
Acting for Children: A Primer. John Day, 1969, 176, illus.

COMMUNITY SERVICE PROGRAMS

LEWIS, SHARI, and REINACH, JACQUELYN
　The Headstart Book of Be Nimble and Be Quick. McGraw-Hill, 1968, 59, illus.

LIPPMAN, HYMAN S.
　Treatment of The Child in Emotional Conflict. 2nd ed. McGraw-Hill, 1962, 367.

MAIER, HENRY W.
　Three Theories of Child Development: The Contributions of Erik H. Erikson, Jean Piaget, and Robert R. Sears, and Their Applications. Harper & Row, 1965, 314.

MATTERSON, E. M.
　Play and Playthings for the Preschool Child. Rev. ed. Penguin, 1967, 180, illus. (Penguin Handbook PH115.)

McCANDLESS, BOYD R.
　Children: Behavior and Development. 2nd ed. Holt, Rinehart & Winston, 1967, 671, illus.

MENCHAN, WILLIAM M.
　Introduction to Child Development and Parent Education. Rev. ed. Vantage, 1969, 275.

MILLAR, SUSANNA
　The Psychology of Play. Penguin, 1968, 288. (Pelican A974.)

MONTESSORI, MARIA
　The Child in the Family. Nancy Cirillo, tr. Regnery, 1970, 128.

MULLER, PHILIPPE
　The Tasks of Childhood. McGraw-Hill, 1969, 256, illus. (World University Library Series.)

MURPHY, LOIS B., et al.
　The Widening World of Childhood. Basic Books, 1962, 399.

MUSSEN, PAUL H., CONGER, JOHN J., and KAGAN, JEROME
　Readings in Child Development and Personality. 2nd ed. Harper & Row, 1970, 595, illus.

NATIONAL ASSOCIATION FOR THE EDUCATION OF YOUNG CHILDREN
　What Does the Nursery School Teacher Teach? Rev. ed. Elizabeth Doak Tyler, ed. NAEYC, 1965, 56.

NATIONAL FEDERATION OF SETTLEMENTS AND NEIGHBORHOOD CENTERS
　Selected Readings for Trainees for Day Care Aides. NFSNC, 1969, 98.

NEILL, ALEXANDER S.
　Summerhill: A Radical Approach to Child Rearing. Hart, 1960, 392.

NEUBAUER, PETER B.
　Children in Collectives: Child Rearing Aims and Practices in the Kibbutz. Thomas, 1965, 416.

NEWSON, JOHN, and NEWSON, ELIZABETH
　Four Years Old in An Urban Community. Aldine, 1968, 570.

NOBLE, EVA
　Play and the Sick Child. Faber & Faber, 1967, 165.

OPIE, IONA, and OPIE, PETER
　Children's Games in Street and Playground: Chasing, Catching, Seeking, Hunting, Racing, Duelling, Exerting, Daring, Guessing, Acting, Pretending. Clarendon Press, 1969, 371, illus.

OREM, REGINALD C.
　Montessori and the Special Child. Putnam, 1969, 232, illus.

PALMER, MARY W., ED.
　Day Care Aides: A Guide for In-Service Training. National Federation of Settlements and Neighborhood Centers, 1969, 114.

PAVENSTEDT, ELEANOR, ED.
　The Drifters: Children of Disorganized Lower-Class Families. Little, Brown, 1967, 345.

PELLOWSKI, ANNE
　The World of Children's Literature. R. R. Bowker, 1968, 538.

PIAGET, JEAN
　The Language and Thought of the Child. World, 1963, 251, illus.

———.
　The Moral Judgement of the Child. Free Press, 1960, 417. (International Library of Psychology, Philosophy and Scientific Method.)

PITCHER, EVELYN G., and PRELINGER, ERNST
　Children Tell Stories: An Analysis of Fantasy. International Universities Press, 1963, 256.

POWLEDGE, FRED
　To Change A Child: A Report on the Institute for Developmental Studies. Quadrangle Books, 1967, 110, illus.

PROVENCE, SALLY
　Guide for the Care of Infants in Groups. Child Welfare League of America, 1967, 104.

PROVENCE, SALLY, and LIPTON, ROSE C.
　Infants in Institutions. International Universities Press, 1962, 191.

RADLER, DONALD H.
　Success Through Play. Harper & Row, 1960, 140.

RAEBECK, LOIS
　Who am I?: Activity Songs for Young Children. Follett, 1970, 32, illus.

READ, KATHERINE H.
　The Nursery School: A Human Relationships Laboratory. 4th ed. Saunders, 1966, 371, illus.

REBELSKY, FREDA, and DORMAN, LYNN
　Child Development and Behavior: Readings.... Knopf, 1970, 399, illus.

RIDENOUR, NINA, and JOHNSON, ISABEL
　Some Special Problems of Children—Aged Two to Five Years. Rev. ed. Child Study Association of America, 1966, 61.

REISSMAN, FRANK
　The Culturally Deprived Child. Harper & Row, 1962, 140.

RITCHIE, OSCAR W., and KOLLER, MARVIN R.
　Sociology of Childhood. Appleton-Century-Crofts, 1964, 333. (Sociology Series.)

RUBIN, ISADORE, and KIRKENDALL, LESTER A., EDS.
　Sex in the Childhood Years: Expert Guidance for Parents, Counselors and Teachers. Association Press, 1970, 190.

RUDERMAN, FLORENCE A.
　Child Care and Working Mothers: A Study of Arrangements Made for Daytime Care of Children. Child Welfare League of America, 1968, 378, illus.

SCHUBERT, GENEVIEVE W.
　A Sample Wage Earning Training Program for Child Day Care Aides, Designed to Utilize Home Economics Skills and Knowledge and to Meet the Requirements of the Vocational Education Act of 1963. Milwaukee Vocational, Technical and Adult Schools, Home Economics Division, n.d., 62. (ERIC VT 000 892.)

SEIDMAN, JEROME M., ED.
　The Child: A Book of Readings. 2nd ed. Holt, Rinehart & Winston, 1969, 692, illus.

SENN, MILTON J. E., and SOLNIT, ALBERT J.
　Problems in Child Behavior and Development. Lea & Febiger, 1968, 268.

SHEEHY, EMMA D.
Children Discover Music and Dance. Teachers College Press, 1968, 207. (Early Childhood Series.)

SHUEY, REBEKAH M., WOODS, ELIZABETH L., and YOUNG, ESTHER M.
Learning About Children. 3rd ed. Lippincott, 1969, 326, illus.

SIMMONS, HAROLD E.
Protective Services for Children: A Public Social Welfare Responsibility. General Welfare Publications, Sacramento, 1968, 163, illus.

SINGER, ROBERT D., and SINGER, ANNE
Psychological Development in Children. Saunders, 1969, 437, illus. (Saunders Books in Psychology.)

SMART, MOLLIE S., and SMART, RUSSELL C.
Children, Development and Relationships. Macmillan, 1967, 582, illus.

SMILANSKY, SARA
The Effects of Sociodramatic Play on Disadvantaged Preschool Children. Wiley, 1968, 164.

SMITH, CHARLES P.
Child Development. W. C. Brown, 1966, 56. (Psychology Self-Selection Series.)

SMITH, JUDITH M., and SMITH, DONALD E. P.
Child Management: A Program for Parents. Ann Arbor Publishers, 1966, 97.

SMITH, LEONA J.
Guiding the Character Development of the Preschool Child. Association Press, 1968, 127, illus.

SPOCK, BENJAMIN M.
Baby and Child Care. Meredith Press, 1968, 627, illus.

STENDLER, CELIA B.
Readings in Child Behavior and Development. 2nd ed. Harcourt, Brace & World, 1964, 498, illus.

STREAN, HERBERT S.
New Approaches in Child Guidance. Scarecrow Press, 1970, 313.

STUART, HAROLD C., and PRUGH, DANE G., EDS.
The Healthy Child: His Physical, Psychological and Social Development. Harvard University Press, 1960, 507, illus.

SUNSET
Things to Make for Children: Toys, Togs, Party Fun. Lane, Menlo Park, Calif., 1961, 95, illus. (Sunset Book.)

SZUREK, STANISLAUS A., and BERLIN, I. N.
The Antisocial Child: His Family and His Community. Science and Behavior Books, 1969, 224.

THOMAS, ALEXANDER
Behavioral Individuality in Early Childhood. New York University Press, 1963, 135.

TODD, VIVIAN E., and HEFFERNAN, HELEN
The Years Before School: Guiding Preschool Children. 2nd ed. Macmillan, 1970, 671, illus.

TRUBOWITZ, JULIUS
Changing the Racial Attitudes of Children: The Effects of An Activity Group Program in New York City Schools. Praeger, 1969, 228.

U.S. CHILDREN'S BUREAU
Infant Care. Child Care Publications, Bronxville, N.Y., 1962, 245.

U.S. DEPARTMENT OF HEALTH, EDUCATION AND WELFARE
Child Care and Guidance: Suggested Post High School Curriculum. HEW, 1967, 49.

VERVILLE, ELINOR
Behavior Problems of Children. Saunders, 1967, 567.

VINCENT, BEN
Begone Dull Care. HMSO, London, 1968, 102.

VINTON, IRIS
The Folkways Omnibus of Children's Games. Stackpole, 1970, 320, illus.

WAGNER, JOSEPH A.
Children's Literature Through Storytelling. W. C. Brown, 1970, 136.

WATSON, ERNEST H., and LOWREY, GEORGE H.
Growth and Development of Children. 5th ed. Year Book Medical Publishers, Chicago, 1967, 463, illus.

WATSON, ROBERT I.
Psychology of the Child. 2nd ed. Wiley, 1965, 635.

WICKSTROM, RALPH L.
Fundamental Motor Patterns. Lea & Febiger, 1970, 178, illus. (Health Education, Physical Education and Recreation Series.)

WILLIAMS, NORMAN
Child Development. Humanities Press, 1969, 110, illus.

WISHY, BERNARD W.
The Child and the Republic: The Dawn of Modern American Child Nurture. University of Pennsylvania, 1968, 205, illus.

WOLF, KATHERINE M., and AUERBACH, ALINE B.
As Your Child Grows: The First Eighteen Months. Rev. ed. Child Study Association of America, 1962, 30.

WRIGHT, RUTH S.
Report to the Nation on Children and Youth. National Committee for Children and Youth, 1968, 135, illus.

YARROW, MARIAN R., CAMPBELL, JOHN D., and BURTON, ROGER V.
Child Rearing: An Inquiry Into Research and Methods. Jossey-Bass, 1968, 224.

YOUNG, MILTON A.
Buttons Are To Push: Developing Your Child's Creativity. Pitman, 1970, 125.

ZIETZ, DOROTHY
Child Welfare: Services and Perspectives. 2nd ed. Wiley, 1969, 346, illus.

FIRE PROTECTION

AMERICAN INSURANCE ASSOCIATION
Fire Department Pumper Tests and Fire Stream Tables. 7th ed. AIA, 1967, 38, illus.

AMERICAN INSURANCE ASSOCIATION, ENGINEERING AND SAFETY DEPARTMENT
Fire Prevention Code. AIA, 1965, 264.

———.
Fire Resistance Ratings of Beam, Girder and Truss Protections, Ceiling Constructions, Column Protections, Floor and Ceiling Constructions, Roof Construction, Walls and Partitions. AIA, 1964-68, 1 vol., illus.

AMERICAN INSURANCE ASSOCIATION, ENGINEERING AND SAFETY DEPARTMENT, DIVISION OF TECHNICAL SERVICES
Fire, Explosion and Health Hazards of Organic Peroxides: Appendices on Warning and Emergency Placards, Test Methods and Trade Name Index. Rev. ed. AIA, 1966, 90, illus. (Research Report No. 11.)

COMMUNITY SERVICE PROGRAMS

AMERICAN SOCIETY FOR TESTING MATERIALS
    Fire Resistance of Hydraulic Fluids: A Symposium.... ASTM, 1966, 194, illus. (Special Technical Pub. No. 406.)

———. Fire Test Performance. ASTM, 1970, 248.

ARCO PUBLISHING COMPANY, INC.
    Battalion and Deputy Chief, Fire Department. 4th ed. Arco, 1969, 1 vol., illus.

———. Captain, Fire Department: The Complete Study Guide for Scoring High. 3rd ed. Arco, 1968, 384. (Arco Civil Service Test Tutor.)

———. Fire Administration and Technology. 2nd ed. Robert E. McGannon, ed. Arco, 1968, 384.

———. Fireman, F. D. 6th ed. Arco, 1968, 304.

———. Fireman Tests in All States. Robert E. McGannon, ed. Arco, 1965, 1 vol., illus.

———. Stationary Engineer and Fireman: The Complete Study Guide for Scoring High. 5th ed. Arco, 1967, 216, illus. (Arco License Test Tutor.)

BAHME, CHARLES W.
    The Fireman's Law Book. 4th ed. National Fire Protection Association, Boston, 1967, 240.

BATTLE, BRENDAN P., and WESTON, PAUL B.
    Arson. Arco, 1967, 1 vol.

BONADIO, GUSTAVE E.
    Fire Hydraulics. 2nd ed. Arco, 1969, 256.

BUILDING OFFICIALS CONFERENCE OF AMERICA, INC.
    BOCA Basic Fire Prevention Code. BOCA, Chicago, 1966, 95.

BUSH, LOREN S., and McLAUGHLIN, JAMES
    Introduction to Fire Science. Glencoe Press, 1970, 512, illus. (Fire Science Series.)

CASEY, JAMES F.
    The Fire Chief's Handbook. 3rd ed. Reuben Donnelley, 1967, 580, illus.

DA COSTA, PHIL
    One Hundred Years of America's Fire Fighting Apparatus. Floyd Clymer, Los Angeles, 1964, 116, illus.

ERVEN, LAWRENCE W.
    Fire Company Apparatus and Procedures. Glencoe Press, 1969, 338, illus. (Fire Science Series.)

———. First Aid and Emergency Rescue. Harvey Gruber, ed. Glencoe Press, 1970, 408, illus. (Fire Science Series.)

FAVREAU, DONALD F.
    Guidelines for Fire Service Education Programs in Community and Junior Colleges. American Association of Junior Colleges, 1969, 52, illus.

FIRE ENGINEERING
    Fundamentals of Fire Fighting: A Training Guide. Vol. 2. Reuben Donnelley, 1964, 58, illus.

FIRE PROTECTION DIRECTORY, 1970: INCORPORATING FIRE BRIGADES OF THE WORLD
    John L. Eades, ed. Benn, London, 1969, illus.

FIRE PROTECTION HANDBOOK STUDY GUIDE
    Davis, Santa Cruz, Calif., 1969, 2 vols.

FITCH, RICHARD D., and PORTER, EDWARD A.
    Accidental or Incendiary. Thomas, 1968, 214, illus.

GILBERT, KEITH R.
    Fire Engines and Other Firefighting Appliances. HMSO, London, 1966, 48, illus. (Science Museum Illustrated Booklet.)

HAYWOOD, CHARLES F.
    General Alarm: A Dramatic Account of Fires and Fire Fighting in America. Dodd, Mead, 1967, 297, illus.

HUDIBURG, EVERETT
    Fire Fighting: Facilities, Planning, and Procedures. Oklahoma State University, 1962, 103, illus.

HUDIBURG, EVERETT, and SHREVE, JOHN F., COMPS.
    Rescue Practices in Fire Service Training. 3rd ed. Oklahoma State University, 1963, 72, illus.

INTERNATIONAL ASSOCIATION OF FIRE CHIEFS
    Fire Department Pumps, Pumping Equipment, and Pumping: A Reference Manual. IAFC, 1965, 51, illus.

———. A Personnel Manual for Volunteer Fire Companies. IAFC, 1964, 24, illus.

INTERNATIONAL CITY MANAGEMENT ASSOCIATION
    Municipal Fire Administration. ICMA, 1936– , vols., illus.

INTERNATIONAL FIRE ADMINISTRATION INSTITUTE
    Higher Education in the Nation's Fire Service. State University of New York, Albany, Center for Executive Development, 1968, 59. (ERIC ED 020 403.)

INTERNATIONAL FIRE SERVICE TRAINING ASSOCIATION
    Aircraft Fire Protection and Rescue Procedures. Oklahoma State University, 1970, 1 vol.

———. Fire Apparatus Practices. 5th ed. Oklahoma State University, 1970, 1 vol.

———. The Fire Department Officer. 2nd ed. Everett Hudiburg, ed. Oklahoma State University, 1967, 97, illus.

———. Fire Department Support of Automatic Sprinkler Systems: A Course Outline for Instructors. Everett Hudiburg, ed. Oklahoma State University, 1966, 75, illus.

———. Fire Inspection Practices. 3rd ed. Oklahoma State University, 1966, 135, illus.

———. Fire Service First Aid Practices. 4th ed. Oklahoma State University, 1968, 126, illus.

———. Fire Service Instructor Training. 2nd ed. Oklahoma State University, 1966, 81, illus.

———. Fire Service Ladder Practices. 6th ed. Everett Hudiberg and John F. Shreve, comps. Oklahoma State University, 1965, 80, illus.

———. Fire Service Practices for Volunteer Fire Departments. 4th ed. Oklahoma State University, 1965, 131, illus.

———. Fire Stream Practices. 4th ed. Everett Hudiburg, ed. Oklahoma State University, 1966, 131, illus.

———. Fundamental Principles of Science Applied to the Fire Service. 3rd ed. Oklahoma State University, 1967, 125, illus.

———. Leadership in the Fire Service: A Series of Sixteen Lectures by Robert F. Hamm. Oklahoma State University, 1967, 172.

———. Water Supplies for the Fire Service: Supply, Hydrants, Valves, Automatic Sprinkler, and Standpipe Systems. 2nd ed. Oklahoma State University, 1964, 1 vol., illus.

KEIL, ANDREW A.
    Radiation Control: For Fire and Other Emergency Forces. National Fire Protection Association, 1960, 241, illus.

KIMBALL, WARREN Y.
    Effective Streams for Fighting Fires. National Fire Protection Association, 1961, 88, illus.

———. Fire Attack! National Fire Protection Association, 1966-68, 2 vols., illus.

FIRE PROTECTION

——.
Manning for Fire Attack. National Fire Protection Association, 1969, 72.

KIRK, PAUL L.
Fire Investigation: Including Fire-Related Phenomena—Arson, Explosion, Asphyxiation. Wiley, 1969, 255, illus.

KOCH, HARRY W.
Fireman Entrance Examinations: A Study Guide for Civil Service. Ken Books, San Francisco, 1961, 1 vol., illus.

LAYMAN, LLOYD
Attacking and Extinguishing Interior Fires. 4th ed. National Fire Protection Association, 1960, 149, illus.

LITTLE, HUGH
Volunteer Fire Training Manual. 2nd ed. Arco, 1967, 88, illus.

LYONS, JOHN W.
The Chemistry and Uses of Fire Retardants. Wiley, 1970, 500.

MANUAL OF FIREMANSHIP: A SURVEY OF THE SCIENCE OF FIREFIGHTING.
3rd ed. HMSO, London, 1968- , illus.

McGANNON, ROBERT E.
Lieutenant, Fire Department. 4th ed. Arco, 1968, 400. (Civil Service Test Tutor.)

——.
1340 Questions and Answers for Firefighters: Career Training for All Firemen. 2nd ed. Arco, 1965, 248.

MEIDL, JAMES H.
Explosive and Toxic Hazardous Materials. Harvey Gruber, ed. Glencoe Press, 1970, 387, illus. (Fire Science Series.)

——.
Flammable Hazardous Materials. Glencoe Press, 1970, 293, illus. (Fire Science Series.)

NATIONAL ACADEMY OF SCIENCES, NATIONAL RESEARCH COUNCIL, BUILDING RESEARCH ADVISORY BOARD
School Fires: An Approach to Life Safety. NAS, 1960, 58. (Pub. No. 832.)

NATIONAL BOARD OF FIRE UNDERWRITERS
Fire Prevention Code: A Code Prescribing Regulations Governing Conditions Hazardous to Life and Property from Fire, Also a Suggested Ordinance Adopting the Fire Prevention Code and Establishing a Bureau of Fire Prevention. NBFU, 1960, 210.

——.
Fire Resistance Ratings of Beam, Girder and Truss Protections, Ceiling Constructions, Roof Constructions, Walls and Partitions. NBFU, 1964, 1 vol., illus.

——.
Fire Hazards of the Plastics Manufacturing and Fabricating Industries: Evaluation of Fire Properties and Plant Safety Considerations. NBFU, 1963, 119.

NATIONAL FIRE PROTECTION ASSOCIATION
Breathing Apparatus for the Fire Service. NFPA, Boston, 1966, 99, illus.

——.
Code for the Use of Flammable Anesthetics (Recommended Safe Practice for Hospital Operating Rooms). NFPA, Boston, 1962, 56.

——.
Coding System for Fire Reporting. NFPA, Boston, 1969, 144.

——.
Combustible Solids, Dusts, Chemicals and Explosives, 1962-63. NFPA, Boston, 1962, 1 vol., illus.

——.
Fighting Rural Fires. NFPA, Boston, 1961, 129, illus.

——.
Fire Apparatus Maintenance. NFPA, Boston, 1966, 126, illus.

——.
Fire Doors and Windows. NFPA, Boston, 1968, 88.

——.
Fire Hazard Properties of Flammable Liquids, Gases, Volatile Solids. 9th ed. NFPA, Boston, 1965, 133.

——.
Fire Protection Handbook. NFPA, Boston, 1896- , vols., illus.

——.
Fire Service Directory: 1970-71. 3rd ed. NFPA, Boston, 1 vol.

——.
...Fire Terminology. 3rd ed. NFPA, Boston, 1961, 62.

——.
Industrial Fire Brigades Training Manual. NFPA, Boston, 1968, 152.

——.
...Inspection Manual. 3rd ed. NFPA, Boston, 1970, 352.

——.
Management of A Fire Department. NFPA, Boston, 1968, 129.

——.
Manual of Hazardous Chemical Reactions: A Compilation of Chemical Reactions Reported to be Potentially Hazardous. NFPA, Boston, 1964, 102.

——.
National Fire Codes. NFPA, Boston, 1938- , vols., illus.

——.
Operating Fire Department Aerial Ladders. 2nd ed. NFPA, Boston, 1964, 178, illus.

——.
Operating Fire Department Pumpers. 3rd ed. NFPA, Boston, 1965, 180, illus.

——.
Protection of Records. NFPA, Boston, 1963, 107, illus. (NFPA Pub. No. 232.)

——.
Recommended Practice for Protection of Library Collections from Fire. NFPA, Boston, 1969, 32.

——.
Standard for the Protection of Electronic Computer Systems. NFPA, Boston, 1964, 30, illus. (NFPA Pub. No. 75.)

——.
Suggestions for Aircraft Rescue and Fire Fighting Services for Airports and Heliports. NFPA, Boston, 1961, 64, illus. (NFPA Pub. No. 403.)

——.
Year Book: Officers and Committees. NFPA, Boston, 1932-33- , vols.

NATIONAL FIRE PROTECTION ASSOCIATION (INTERNATIONAL)
Code for Safety to Life From Fire in Buildings and Structures. 21st ed. NFPA, 1967, 209. (NFPA Pub. No. 101.)

NATIONAL LEAGUE OF CITIES
The Grading of Municipal Fire Protection Facilities: Its Relationship to Fire Insurance and to the Municipality's Fire Protection Policy. NLC, 1967, 145.

NATIONAL LEARNING CORPORATION
Fire Alarm Dispatcher. National Learning, 1969, 1 vol. (Passbook Series C-256.)

NATIONAL RESEARCH COUNCIL, COMMITTEE ON FIRE RESEARCH
Directory of Fire Research in the United States. 5th ed. NRC, 1970, 374. (Pub. No. 1, 590.)

——.
A Study of Fire Problems... Held at Woods Hole, Mass., July 17 to Aug. 11, 1961.... NRC, 1961, 174.

OHIO STATE DEPARTMENT OF EDUCATION, VOCATIONAL EDUCATION DIVISION
Emergency Victim Care and Rescue: Textbook for Squadmen. 2nd ed. Ohio Trade and Industrial Education Service, 1965, 327, illus.

——.
Fire Service Training. Ohio Trade and Industrial Education Service, 1962, 404, illus.

RUDMAN, JACK
Fireman, Fire Department. National Learning, 1970, 1 vol. (Passbook Series C-259.)

COMMUNITY SERVICE PROGRAMS

RUTTENBERG, STANLEY H., and FRIEDMAN, M.
  Economic Justice: The Needs of Fire Fighters—A Study of Economic Perspectives for the Fire Services. Stanley H. Ruttenberg & Associates, Washington, 1970, 68.

SIMPSON, RICHARD L.
  Basic Firemanship: Training Manual. Grand Island Fire Department, Grand Island, Nebr., 1966, 145, illus.

SYMPOSIUM ON FIRE TESTS, MOISTURE INFLUENCE ON MATERIAL BEHAVIOR, CHICAGO, 1964.
  Moisture in Materials in Relation to Fire Tests. American Society for Testing Materials, 1965, 123, illus. (Special Technical Pub. No. 385.)

SYMPOSIUM ON FIRE TEST METHODS, RESTRAINT AND SMOKE, ATLANTIC CITY, 1966.
  ...A Symposium Presented at the Sixty-Ninth Annual Meeting, American Society for Testing Materials, Atlantic City, N.J., 26 June-1 July, 1966. ASTM, 1967, 225, illus.

SYMPOSIUM ON HIGHER EDUCATION FOR THE FIRE SERVICE, SARATOGA SPRINGS, N.Y.
  Proceedings. New York Executive Department, Office for Local Government, Division of Fire Safety, 1967, 293.

TEXAS A & M UNIVERSITY, COLLEGE STATION, FIREMEN'S TRAINING SCHOOL, TEXAS STATE FIREMEN'S AND MARSHALS' ASSOCIATION.
  Fire Department Pump and Accessories: Principles of Operation. Texas A & M University, 1963, 44.

THOMPSON, NORMAN J.
  Fire Behavior and Sprinklers. NFPA, Boston, 1964, 157, illus.

TILLMAN, ERNEST C.
  "Fire Attack 1 & 2" Study Guide. Davis, Santa Cruz, Calif., 1969, 2 vols.

———.
  "Firefighting Strategy and Leadership" Study Guide. Davis, Santa Cruz, Calif., 1970, 1 vol.

TODD, ALDEN A.
  A Spark Lighted in Portland: The Record of the National Board of Fire Underwriters. McGraw-Hill, 1966, 231.

UNIVERSITY OF MICHIGAN, EXTENSION SERVICE
  The Fire Fighter and Electrical Equipment: A Guide to Self Protection. University of Michigan, 1962, 66, illus. (Bulletin No. 280.)

U.S. BUREAU OF LABOR STATISTICS
  Salary Trends: Firemen and Policemen, 1924-64. USGPO, 1965, 1 vol.

VERVALIN, CHARLES H., ED.
  Fire Protection Manual for Hydrocarbon Processing Plants. Gulf, Houston, Tex., 1964, 386, illus.

WALSH, CHARLES V.
  Firefighting Strategy and Leadership. McGraw-Hill, 1963, 271, illus.

WASHINGTON (STATE) FIRE CHIEFS STANDARDS COMMITTEE
  Design of Fire Stations. University of Washington, 1965, 95, illus.

WOOLLEY, ROI B.
  Home Fire Safety: By Means of Fire Department "In-Service" Company Field Surveys and Inspections. International Association of Fire Chiefs, 1967, 33.

FORESTRY

AGERTER, SHARLENE R., and GLOCK, WALDO S., COMPS.
  An Annotated Bibliography of Tree Growth and Growth Rings, 1950-1962. University of Arizona Press, 1965, 180.

ALLEN, SHIRLEY W.
  An Introduction to American Forestry. 3rd ed. McGraw-Hill, 1960, 466, illus. (American Forestry Series.)

ANDERSON, DAVID A., and SMITH, WILLIAM A.
  Forests and Forestry. Interstate, 1970, 357, illus.

ANDERSON, ROGER F.
  Forest and Shade Tree Entomology. Wiley, 1960, 428, illus.

ARCO PUBLISHING COMPANY, INC.
  U.S. Park Ranger. Arco, 1960, 206.

AVERY, THOMAS E.
  Forester's Guide to Aerial Photo Interpretation. USGPO, 1966, 1 vol.

BARRETT, JOHN W., ED.
  Regional Silviculture of the United States. Ronald, 1962, 610, illus.

BOYCE, JOHN S.
  Forest Pathology. 3rd ed. McGraw-Hill, 1961, 572, illus. (American Forestry Series.)

BROMLEY, WILLARD S., ED.
  Pulpwood Production. Interstate, 1969, 259, illus.

CALIFORNIA REDWOOD ASSOCIATION.
  Redwood File.... CRA, 1970, 1 vol., illus.

———.
  Standard Specifications for Grades of California Redwood Lumber. CRA, 1969, 67.

COOMBS, CHARLES I.
  High Timber: The Story of American Forestry. World, 1960, 223, illus.

CUSHWA, CHARLES T.
  Fire: A Summary of Literature in the United States from the Mid-1920's to 1966. U.S. Southeastern Forest Experiment Station, Asheville, N.C., 1968, 117.

DASMANN, RAYMOND F.
  Wildlife Biology. Wiley, 1964, 231, illus.

DAVIS, KENNETH P.
  Forest Management: Regulation and Valuation. 2nd ed. McGraw-Hill, 1966, 519, illus. (American Forestry Series.)

DEMMON, ELWOOD L.
  Opportunities in a Forestry Career. Rev. ed. Universal Publishing & Distributing, Educational Books Division, 1967, 128. (Vocational Guidance Manuals V114.)

DESCH, HAROLD E.
  Timber: Its Structure & Properties. 4th ed. St. Martin's Press, 1968, 399.

DUERR, WILLIAM A.
  Fundamentals of Forestry Economics. McGraw-Hill, 1960, 579. (American Forestry Series.)

DUERR, WILLIAM A., and CHRISTIANSEN, NEILS B.
  Exercises in the Managerial Economics of Forestry. W. C. Brown, 1964, 325.

EDLIN, HERBERT L.
  What Wood is That? A Manual of Wood Identification. Viking, 1969, 160, illus. (Studio Book.)

EIFERT, VIRGINIA S.
  Tall Trees and Far Horizons. Dodd, Mead, 1965, 301, illus.

ELSEVIER'S WOOD DICTIONARY IN SEVEN LANGUAGES: ENGLISH-AMERICAN, FRENCH, SPANISH, ITALIAN, SWEDISH, DUTCH AND GERMAN
  Elsevier, 1964-69, 3 vols.

ELTON, CHARLES S.
Pattern of Animal Communities. Barnes & Noble, 1966, 432.

ESAU, KATHERINE
Anatomy of Seed Plants. Wiley, 1960, 376, illus.

FARB, PETER, and TIME-LIFE BOOKS
The Forest. Rev. ed. Time-Life Books, 1967, 192, illus. (Life Nature Library.)

FOIL, R. R., ED.
Organization Management in Forestry. Louisiana State University Press, 1970, 112.

FOOD AND AGRICULTURE ORGANIZATION OF THE UNITED NATIONS, FORESTRY AND FOREST PRODUCTS DIVISION.
International Directory of Manufacturers of Forestry Instruments and Hand Tools. FAOUN, 1967, 174.

FORBES, REGINALD D., ED.
Forestry Handbook. Ronald, 1961, 1 vol., illus. (Ronald Handbooks.)

FREEMAN, ORVILLE, and FROME, MICHAEL
The National Forests of America. Putnam, 1968, 194, illus.

FROME, MICHAEL
Whose Woods These Are: The Story of the National Forests. Doubleday, 1962, 360, illus.

GOOR, AMIHUD Y., and BARNEY, CHARLES W.
Forest Tree Planting in Arid Zones. Ronald, 1968, 409, illus.

GRAHAM, SAMUEL A., and KNIGHT, FRED B.
Principles of Forest Entomology. 4th ed. McGraw-Hill, 1965, 417, illus. (American Forestry Series.)

GRIMM, WILLIAM C.
Familiar Trees of America. Harper & Row, 1967, 240, illus.

HANABURGH, DAVID H.
Your Future in Forestry. R. Rosen Press, 1961, 159. (Careers in Depth.)

HARLOW, WILLIAM M., and HARRAR, ELLWOOD S.
Textbook of Dendrology: Covering the Important Forest Trees of the United States and Canada. 5th ed. McGraw-Hill, 1968, 512, illus. (American Forestry Series.)

HARRISON, C. WILLIAM
Forests: Riches of the Earth. Messner, 1969, 191, illus.

HAWLEY, RALPH C.
The Practice of Silviculture. 7th ed. Wiley, 1962, 578, illus.

HUNT, GEORGE M., and GARRAT, GEORGE A.
Wood Preservation. 3rd ed. McGraw-Hill, 1967, 433, illus. (American Forestry Series.)

HUSCH, BERTRAM
Forest Mensuration and Statistics. Ronald, 1963, 474, illus.

INTERNATIONAL LABOR OFFICE, GENEVA
Guide to Safety and Health in Forestry Work. ILO, 1968, 223, illus.

JAMES, N. D. G.
The Forester's Companion. 2nd ed. Blackwell, Oxford, (Transatlantic), 1966, 356, illus.

JEPSEN, STANLEY M.
Trees and Forests. A.S. Barnes, 1969, 155, illus.

KAUFMAN, HERBERT
The Forest Ranger: A Study in Administrative Behavior. Johns Hopkins Press, 1960, 259, illus.

KOLLMANN, FRANZ F. P., and COTE, WILFRED A.
Principles of Wood Science and Technology. Springer-Verlag, New York, 1968, vols., illus.

KRAMER, PAUL J., and KOZLOWSKI, THEODORE T.
Physiology of Trees. McGraw-Hill, 1960, 642, illus.

LINNARTZ, NORWIN E.
The Ecology of Southern Forests. Louisiana State University Press, 1969, 203.

LULL, HOWARD W.
A Forest Atlas of the Northeast. U.S. Forest Service, Northeastern Forest Experiment Station, 1968, 46, illus.

MEYER, HANS A., et al.
Forest Management. 2nd ed. Ronald, 1961, 282, illus.

MILES, ROGER O.
Forestry in the English Landscape: A Study of the Cultivation of Trees.... Faber & Faber, 1967, 303.

MURPHY, RICHARD C., and MEYER, WILLIAM E.
The Care and Feeding of Trees. Crown, 1969, 164, illus.

NATIONAL FIRE PROTECTION ASSOCIATION
Air Operations for Forest, Brush, and Grass Fires: A Report of the NFPA Forest Committee. NFPA, Boston, 1965, 48, illus.

NEW YORK COLLEGE OF FORESTRY, SYRACUSE
Forest Fertilization Research, 1957-1964. NYCF, 1965, 246. (Botanical Review Vol. 3, No. 2.)

NIXON, STUART
Redwood Empire. Dutton, 1967, 256, illus.

NORTH CAROLINA STATE BOARD OF EDUCATION, CURRICULUM LABORATORY
Farm Forestry Laboratory Manual. NCSBE Curriculum Laboratory, Raleigh, 1964, 48. (ERIC VT 000 515.)

OSMASTON, F. C.
The Management of Forests. Hafner, 1968, 384, illus.

PANSHIN, ALEXIS J., and deZEEUW, CARL
Textbook of Wood Technology. Vol. 1, 3rd ed. McGraw-Hill, 1970, 576, illus. (American Forestry Series.)

PANSHIN, ALEXIS J., et al.
Forest Products: Their Sources, Production, and Utilization. 2nd ed. McGraw-Hill, 1962, 538. (American Forestry Series.)

PLATT, RUTHERFORD H.
The Great American Forest. Prentice-Hall, 1965, 271, illus.

PRESTON, RICHARD J.
North American Trees (Exclusive of Mexico and Tropical United States): A Handbook Designed for Field Use, with Plates and Distribution Maps. 2nd ed. Iowa State University Press, 1961, 395, illus.

PRODAN, MICHAIL
Forest Biometrics. Pergamon, 1968, 447, illus.

RENDLE, B. J., COMP.
World Timbers. University of Toronto Press, 1969- , 3 vols., illus.

RICH, STUART U.
Marketing of Forest Products: Text and Cases. McGraw-Hill, 1970, 712. (American Forestry Series.)

RYLE, GEORGE
Forest Service: The First Forty-Five Years of the Forestry Commission of Great Britain. A. M. Kelley, New York, 1969, 340, illus.

SARGENT, CHARLES S.
Manual of the Trees of North America (Exclusive of Mexico).... 2nd ed. Dover, 1965, 2 vols., illus.

COMMUNITY SERVICE PROGRAMS

SARTORIUS, PETER, and HENLE, HANS
  Forestry and Economic Development. Praeger, 1968, 340. (Praeger Special Studies in International Economics and Development.)

SHIRLEY, HARDY L.
  Forest Ownership for Pleasure and Profit. Syracuse University Press, 1967, 214, illus.

———.
  Forestry and Its Career Opportunities. 2nd ed. McGraw-Hill, 1964, 454, illus. (American Forestry Series.)

SISAM, J. W. B.
  Forestry Education at Toronto. University of Toronto Press, 1961, 124.

SKINNEMOEN, K.
  An Outline of Norwegian Forestry. 2nd ed. Det Norske Skogselskap, 1964, 1 vol.

SLOBODKIN, LAWRENCE B.
  Growth and Regulation of Animal Populations. Holt, Rinehart & Winston, 1961, 184, illus. (Biology Studies.)

SOCIETY OF AMERICAN FORESTERS
  American Forestry: Six Decades of Growth. SAF, 1960, 319.

———.
  Forest Cover Types of North America. SAF, 1964, 67.

———.
  Forestry Education in America. SAF, 1963, 402, illus.

STODDARD, CHARLES H.
  Essentials of Forestry Practice. 2nd ed. Ronald, 1968, 362, illus.

———.
  The Small Private Forest in the United States. Resources for the Future, Washington, 1961, 171, illus.

TITMUSS, F. H.
  Commercial Timbers of the World. 3rd ed. Technical Press, London, 1965, 277, illus.

UDELL, GILMAN G., COMP.
  Laws Relating to Forestry Game Conservation, Flood Control and Related Sources. USGPO, 1966, 607.

U.S. DEPARTMENT OF AGRICULTURE, FOREST SERVICE
  National Forest Log Scaling Handbook, Amendment No. 1. USGPO, 1969, 202. (A 13, 36/2: L82/969.)

U.S. FOREST PRODUCTS LABORATORY, MADISON, WIS.
  Lumber and Allied Products. USGPO, 1962, 233, illus. (U.S. Defense Supply Agency, Military Handbook No. MIL-HDBK-7A.)

U.S. FOREST SERVICE
  Handbook on Forest Service Plant Collections. USFS, 1962, 40. (Forest Service Handbook.)

———.
  Law Enforcement: Programmed Instruction. USGPO, 1966, 55.

U.S. OFFICE OF EDUCATION, VOCATIONAL AND TECHNICAL EDUCATION DIVISION
  Forest Technology: A Suggested 2-Year Post High School Curriculum. USGPO, 1968, 151.

VARDAMAN, JAMES M.
  Tree Farm Business Management. Ronald, 1965, 207, illus.

WACKERMAN, ALBERT E., HAGENSTEIN, WILLIAM D., and MICHELL, ARTHUR S.
  Harvesting Timber Crops. 2nd ed. McGraw-Hill, 1966, 540, illus. (American Forest Series.)

WECK, JOHANNES
  Dictionary of Forestry in Five Languages: German, English, French, Spanish, Russian. Elsevier, 1966, 573.

WEST COAST LUMBERMEN'S ASSOCIATION
  Douglas Fir Use Book. WCLA, Seattle, 1930- , vols., illus.

WORRELL, ALBERT C.
  Principles of Forest Policy. McGraw-Hill, 1970, 243. (American Forestry Series.)

YOUNGBERG, CHESTER T., and DAVEY, CHARLES B., EDS.
  Tree Growth and Forest Soils: Proceedings of 3rd North American Forest Soils Conference. Oregon State University Press, 1970, 520, illus.

YOUNGMAN, WILBUR H., and RANDALL, CHARLES E.
  Growing Your Trees. American Forestry Association, Washington, 1966, 72, illus.

LIBRARY TECHNOLOGY

AKERS, SUSAN G.
  Simple Library Cataloging. 5th ed. Scarecrow Press, 1969, 345, illus.

ALDRICH, ELLA V.
  Using Books and Libraries. 5th ed. Prentice-Hall, 1967, 147, illus.

ALEXANDER, CARTER, and BURKE, ARVID J.
  How to Locate Educational Information and Data: An Aid to Quick Utilization of the Literature of Education. 4th ed. Bureau of Publications, Teachers College, Columbia University, 1962, 419, illus.

ALLEN, KENNETH W.
  Use of Community College Libraries. Archon Books, 1970, 161.

AMERICAN ASSOCIATION OF SCHOOL LIBRARIANS, SCHOOL LIBRARY MANPOWER PROJECT.
  School Library Personnel: Task Analysis Survey. American Library Association, 1969, 596.

AMERICAN ASSOCIATION OF SCHOOL LIBRARIANS AND NATIONAL EDUCATION ASSOCIATION, AUDIOVISUAL INSTRUCTION DEPARTMENT
  Standards for School Media Programs. American Library Association, 1969, 66.

AMERICAN LIBRARY ASSOCIATION
  Anglo-American Cataloging Rules. ALA, 1967, 400.

———.
  International Subscription Agents: An Annotated Directory. 2nd ed. ALA, 1969, 87.

———.
  Reference Books for Small and Medium-Sized Public Libraries. ALA, 1969, 185.

———.
  Student Use of Libraries: An Inquiry Into the Needs of Students, Libraries, and the Educational Process. ALA, 1964, 212, illus.

———.
  Young Adult Services in the Public Library. ALA, 1960, 64.

AMERICAN LIBRARY DIRECTORY: A CLASSIFIED LIST OF LIBRARIES, WITH NAMES OF LIBRARIANS AND STATISTICAL DATA.
  R. R. Bowker, 1923- , Vol. 1- .

ARCHER, HORACE R., ED.
  Rare Book Collections: Some Theoretical and Practical Suggestions for Use by Librarians and Students. American Library Association, 1965, 128.

ASH, LEE, ED.
  A Biographical Dictionary of Librarians in the United States and Canada. 5th ed. American Library Association (with Council of National Library Associations), 1970, 1250.

BALLOU, HUBBARD W., ED.
  Guide to Microreproduction Equipment. 2nd ed. National Microfilm Association, 1962, 519, illus.

BENGE, RONALD C.
    Libraries and Cultural Change. Archon Books, 1970, 278.

BENNETT, WILMA
    Occupations Filing Plan and Bibliography: An Alphabetical Fields-of-Work Index for Filing Unbound Occupational Information. Rev. ed. Interstate, 1968, 109.

BOELKE, JOANNE
    Library Technicians: A Survey of Current Developments. 1968, 12. (ERIC 019 530.)

BONK, WALLACE J.
    Use of Basic Reference Sources in Libraries. University of Michigan, Library Science Department, 1963, 236.

BORGWARDT, STEPHANIE
    Library Display. 2nd ed. Witwatersrand University Press, Johannesburg, 1970, 234.

BOWERS, MELVYN K.
    Easy Bulletin Boards for the School Library. Scarecrow Press, 1966, 106, illus.

THE BOWKER ANNUAL OF LIBRARY AND BOOK TRADE INFORMATION.
    R. R. Bowker, 1955-56- , vols., annual.

BOYD, JESSIE E.
    Books, Libraries and You. 3rd ed. Scribner, 1965, 205, illus.

BRADEN, IRENE A.
    The Undergraduate Library. American Library Association, 1970, 158, illus. (ACRL Monograph No. 31.)

BRANSCOMB, HARVIE
    Teaching with Books: A Study of College Libraries. Shoe String Press, 1964, 239.

BREILLAT, PIERRE
    The Rare Books Section in the Library. UNESCO, 1965, 38, illus.

BRIMMER, BRENDA, et al.
    A Guide to the Use of United Nations Documents. Oceana, 1962, 272.

BROGAN, GERALD E., and BUCK, JEANNE T.
    Using Libraries Effectively. Dickenson, Belmont, Calif., 1969, 116. (Effective English Series.)

BROWN, ELEANOR F.
    Bookmobiles and Bookmobile Service. Scarecrow Press, 1967, 471, illus.

———.
    Modern Branch Libraries and Libraries in Systems. Scarecrow Press, 1970, 747, illus.

BUNDY, MARY L., and GOODSTEIN, SYLVIA
    The Library's Public Revisited. University of Maryland, 1967, 84. (Student Contribution Series No. 1.)

BURKE, WILLIAM J., and HOWE, WILL D.
    American Authors and Books: 1640 to the Present Day. Crown, 1962, 834.

BURNSHAW, STANLEY, ED.
    Varieties of Literary Experience: Eighteen Essays in World Literature. New York University Press, 1962, 446.

BURRELL, T. W.
    Learn to Use Books and Libraries: A Programmed Text. Archon Books, 1969, 105.

BURSTEIN, HERMAN
    Getting the Most Out of Your Tape Recorder. Hayden, 1960, 175.

CALIFORNIA STATE DEPARTMENT OF GENERAL SERVICES
    The Library Technical Assistant Program: Guidelines and Course Content for Community College Programs. Mary E. DeNure, ed. Office of the Chancellor, California Community Colleges, 1970, 128.

CANADIAN LIBRARY ASSOCIATION
    The Library Technician at Work: Theory and Practice—Proceedings of a Workshop Held at Thunder Bay, Ontario, May 8-9, 1970. CLA, 1970, 232.

CARROLL, C. EDWARD
    The Professionalization of Education for Librarianship with Special Reference to the Years 1940-1960. Scarecrow Press, 1970, 370.

COCKSHUTT, MARGARET E.
    Basic Filing Rules: For Use in the Course in Library Records. University of Toronto Press, 1961, 28.

CODLIN, ELLEN M., and LAWRIE, ROBERT S., COMPS.
    Handlist of Basic Reference Material for Librarians and Information Officers in Electrical and Electronic Engineering. 5th ed. ASLIB Electronics Group, London, 1969, 50.

COLLISON, ROBERT L.
    Indexes and Indexing: Guide to the Indexing of Books, and Collections of Books, Periodicals, Music, Recordings, Films, and other Material.... 3rd ed. de Graff, 1969, 223.

CONANT, RALPH W., ED.
    The Public Library and the City. MIT Press, 1965, 216.

CONFERENCE ON THE TRAINING OF LIBRARY TECHNOLOGY ASSISTANTS
    Library Technology in California Junior Colleges. Communication Service Corp., 1968, 69.

COOK, MARGARET G.
    The New Library Key. 2nd ed. Wilson, 1963, 184, illus.

COPLAN, KATE
    Poster Ideas and Bulletin Board Techniques: For Libraries and Schools.... Oceana, 1962, 183, illus.

COPLAN, KATE, and CASTAGNA, EDWIN
    The Library Reaches Out: Reports on Library Service and Community Relations by Some Leading American Librarians. Oceana, 1965, 403.

COUNCIL ON LIBRARY TECHNOLOGY
    Directory of Institutions in the United States and Canada Offering or Developing Courses in Library Technology. University of Baltimore, 1968, 48.

COURTNEY, WINIFRED F., ED.
    The Reader's Adviser: A Guide to the Best in Literature. 11th ed. R. R. Bowker, 1968, 1114.

CUNHA, GEORGE D. M.
    Conservation of Library Materials: A Manual and Bibliography on the Care, Repair and Restoration of Library Materials. Scarecrow Press, 1967, 405, illus.

CURRIE, DOROTHY H.
    How to Organize a Children's Library. Oceana, 1965, 184, illus.

CUTTER, CHARLES A.
    Cutter-Sanborn Three-Figure Author Table. Rev. ed. H. R. Huntting Co., Chicopee, Mass., 1969, 34.

DAHL, SVEND
    History of the Book. 2nd ed. Scarecrow Press, 1968, 299.

DAILY, JAY E., and MYERS, MILDRED S.
    Cataloging for Library Technical Assistants. Communications Service Corp., 1969, 110.

DANE, WILLIAM J.
    The Picture Collection Subject Headings. 6th ed. Shoe String Press, 1968, 103.

DAVIDSON, RAYMOND L.
    Audiovisual Machines. International Textbook, 1969, 266.

COMMUNITY SERVICE PROGRAMS

DAVIES, RUTH A.
The School Library—A Force for Educational Excellence. R. R. Bowker, 1969, 386.

DAVINSON, DONALD E.
The Periodicals Collection: Its Purpose and Uses in Libraries. A. Deutsch, London, (British Book Centre, dist.), 1969, 212, illus.

DEZETTEL, LOUIS M.
Record Changers: How They Work. Sams, 1968, 144, illus.

DEWEY, MELVIL
Dewey Decimal Classification and Relative Index. 17th ed. Forest Press, Lake Placid, N.Y., 1965-67, 2 vols.

DOUGLAS, MARY P.
The Primary School Library and its Services. UNESCO, 1961, 104, illus.

DOWNS, ROBERT B.
Books That Changed America. Macmillan, 1970, 280.

———.
Famous Books Since 1492. Barnes & Noble, 1961, 396. (Everyday Handbooks.)

———.
How To Do Library Research. University of Illinois Press, 1966, 179.

———.
Molders of the Modern Mind: 111 Books That Shaped Western Civilization. Barnes & Noble, 1961, 396.

DYKE, FREEMAN H., JR.
How to Manage and Use Technical Information: Getting More Mileage Out of Information and Data by Applying the Systems Approach to Information Handling. Industrial Education Institute, Boston, 1968, 1 vol., illus.

EDUCATIONAL MEDIA COUNCIL
Educational Media Index: A Project of the Educational Media Council. McGraw-Hill, 1964, 14 vols.

FORRESTER, GERTRUDE
Occupational Literature: An Annotated Bibliography. Wilson, 1964, 675.

FOSKETT, ANTONY C.
The Subject Approach to Information. Archon Books, 1969, 310, illus.

FOSKETT, DOUGLAS J.
Information Service in Libraries. 2nd ed. C. Lockwood, London, 1967, 153. (New Librarianship Series.)

GALIN, SAUL, and SPIELBERG, PETER
Reference Books: How to Select and Use Them. Random House, 1969, 312.

GARVEY, MONA
Library Displays: Their Purpose, Construction and Use. Wilson, 1969, 88, illus.

GATES, JEAN K.
Guide to the Use of Books and Libraries. 2nd ed. McGraw-Hill, 1969, 273.

GOULD, GERALDINE N., and WOLFE, ITHMER C.
How to Organize and Maintain the Library Picture/Pamphlet File. Oceana, 1968, 146, illus.

GOVE, PHILIP B., ED.
The Role of the Dictionary. Bobbs-Merrill, 1967, 63.

GREGO, NOEL R., and RUDNIK, M. CHRYSANTHA, EDS.
Job Description and Certification for Library Technical Assistants: Proceedings of the Council on Library Technology Workshop Held January 23-24, 1970. Chicago State College Library, 1970, 68.

GROGAN, DENIS J.
Science and Technology: An Introduction to the Literature. Archon Books, 1970, 231.

GUINAGH, KEVIN
Dictionary of Foreign Phrases and Abbreviations. Wilson, 1965, 303.

HACKETT, ALICE P.
70 Years of Best Sellers, 1895-1965. R. R. Bowker, 1967, 280.

HARRIS, EVELYN J.
Instructional Materials Cataloging Guide. University of Arizona, Bureau of Educational Research and Service, 1968, 27, illus.

HAWKEN, WILLIAM R.
Copying Methods Manual. American Library Association, Library Technology Program, 1966, 375, illus. (LTP Pub. No. 11.)

———.
Enlarged Prints from Library Microforms: A Study of Processes, Equipment, and Materials. American Library Association, 1963, 131.

———.
Photocopying from Bound Volumes: A Study of Machines, Methods and Materials. American Library Association, 1962, 208, illus. (LTP Pub. No. 4.)

HEINTZE, INGEBORG
The Organization of the Small Public Library. UNESCO, 1963, 67.

HENSEL, EVELYN, and VEILLETTE, PETER D.
Purchasing Library Materials in Public and School Libraries: A Study of Purchasing Procedures and the Relationships Between Libraries and Purchasing Agents and Dealers. American Library Association, 1969, 160.

HERNER, SAUL
A Brief Guide to Sources of Scientific and Technical Information. Information Resources Press, Washington, 1970, 102, illus.

HORTON, CAROLYN
Cleaning and Preserving Bindings and Related Materials. 2nd ed. American Library Association, 1969, 87, illus. (LTP Pub. No. 16.)

HOSTROP, RICHARD W.
Teaching and the Community College Library. Shoe String Press, 1968, 170.

HULL, THOMAS G., and JONES, TOM
Scientific Exhibits. Thomas, 1961, 144, illus.

INSTITUTE ON THE USE OF THE LIBRARY OF CONGRESS CLASSIFICATION, NEW YORK, 1966
The Use of the Library of Congress Classification: Proceedings. Richard H. Schimmelpfeng and C. Donald Cook, eds. American Library Association, 1968, 245, illus.

JACKSON, ELLEN
Subject Guide to Major United States Government Publications. American Library Association, 1968, 186.

JENKINS, FRANCES B.
Science Reference Sources. 5th ed. MIT Press, 1969, 231.

JOHNS, ADA W.
Special Libraries: Development of the Concept, Their Organization and Their Services. Scarecrow Press, 1968, 245.

JOHNSON, ELMER D.
A History of Libraries in the Western World. 2nd ed. Scarecrow Press, 1970, 521.

JOHNSON, HERBERT W.
How to Use the Business Library, with Sources of Business Information. 3rd ed. South-Western, 1964, 160, illus.

JOHNSON, ROBERT
Library Skills: A Program for Self-Instruction. McGraw-Hill, 1970, 128.

JONES, HOWARD M., and LUDWIG, RICHARD M.
  Guide to American Literature and Its Backgrounds Since 1890. 3rd ed. Harvard University Press, 1964, 240.

JORDAN, ROBERT T.
  Tomorrow's Library: Direct Access and Delivery. R. R. Bowker, 1970, 200.

KATZ, WILLIAM A.
  Introduction to Reference Work. Vol. 1: Basic Information Sources. Vol. 2: Reference Services. McGraw-Hill, 1969, 376, 254. (McGraw-Hill Series in Library Education.)

KIMBER, RICHARD T.
  Automation in Libraries. Pergamon, 1968, 140, illus. (International Series of Monographs in Library and Information Science Vol. 10.)

KINNEY, MARY R.
  The Abbreviated Citation: A Bibliographical Problem. American Library Association, 1967, 57. (ACRL Monograph No. 28.)

KIRKWOOD, LEILA H.
  Charging Systems. Rutgers University, School of Library Science, 1961, 397.

KISTER, KENNETH F.
  Social Issues and Library Problems: Case Studies in the Social Sciences. R. R. Bowker, 1968, 190.

KNIGHT, DOUGLAS M., and NOURSE, E. SHEPLEY, EDS.
  Libraries at Large: Tradition, Innovation and the National Interest. R. R. Bowker, 1969, 664, illus.

KNIGHT, HATTIE M.
  The 1-2-3 Guide to Libraries. 4th ed. W. C. Brown, 1970, 84, illus.

KNIGHT, GILFRED N., ED.
  Training in Indexing: A Course of the Society of Indexers. MIT Press, 1969, 219.

KRUZAS, ANTHONY T., ED.
  Directory of Special Libraries and Information Centers. 2nd ed. Gale, 1968, 2 vols.

KUJOTH, JEAN S.
  Libraries, Readers and Book Selection. Scarecrow Press, 1969, 470.
  ———, COMP.
  Reading Interests of Children and Young Adults. Scarecrow Press, 1970, 449.
  ———.
  Subject Guide to Periodical Indexes and Review Indexes. Scarecrow Press, 1969, 120.

KURTH, WILLIAM H., and GRIM, RAY W.
  Moving a Library. Scarecrow Press, 1966, 220.

LEIDY, W. PHILIP, ED.
  A Popular Guide to Government Publications. 3rd ed. Columbia University Press, 1968, 365.

LIBRARY TECHNICIANS: A NEW KIND OF NEEDED WORKER— A REPORT OF A CONFERENCE ON LIBRARY TECHNOLOGY SPONSORED BY CATONSVILLE COMMUNITY COLLEGE, HELD IN CHICAGO, ILLINOIS, MAY 26-27, 1967.
  Communication Service Corp., 1967, 28.

LICKLIDER, J. C. R.
  Libraries of the Future. MIT Press, 1965, 219.

LINDEN, RONALD
  Books and Libraries: A Guide for Students. Cassell, London, 1965, 308.

LOIZEAUX, MARIE D.
  Publicity Primer. 4th ed. Wilson, 1967, 122.

LONG, HARRIET G.
  Public Library Service to Children: Foundation and Development. Scarecrow Press, 1969, 162.

LOWRIE, JEAN E.
  Elementary School Libraries. 2nd ed. Scarecrow Press, 1970, 238.

LOWY, GEORGE
  A Searcher's Manual. Shoe String Press, 1965, 104.

MARK, DAVID
  How to Select and Use Your Tape Recorder. 2nd ed. Hayden, 1966, 126, illus.

MARTIN, LOWELL A.
  Library Response to Urban Change: A Study of the Chicago Public Library. American Library Association, 1969, 313, illus.

MARTINSON, JOHN
  Vocational Training for Library Technicians: A Survey of Experience to Date.... Communication Service Corp., 1965, 119.

MERRITT, LeROY C.
  Book Selection and Intellectual Freedom. Wilson, 1970, 100.

MEYER, EDITH P.
  Meet the Future: People and Ideas in the Libraries of Today and Tomorrow. Little, Brown, 1964, 278, illus.

MOORE, EVERETT LeROY, ED.
  Junior College Libraries Development, Needs, and Perspectives. American Library Association, 1969, 104. (ACRL Monograph No. 30.)

MORSE, GRANT W.
  The Concise Guide to Library Research. Washington Square Press, 1966, 214.

MORSE, PHILIP McCORD
  Library Effectiveness. MIT Press, 1968, 214.

NEW YORK (STATE) EDUCATION DEPARTMENT
  Deputy Commissioner of Education's Evaluation Committee on the Experimental Library Technician Program Report. New York State Library, Albany, 1962, 47.

ORNE, JERROLD
  The Language of the Foreign Book Trade: Abbreviations, Terms, Phrases. 2nd ed. American Library Association, 1962, 213.

PENNELL, LOIS G., ED.
  The Bookmobile: A New Look. American Library Association, 1969, 61. (Public Library Reporter No. 14.)

PETERSON, CAROLYN S.
  Reference Books for Elementary and Junior High School Libraries. Scarecrow Press, 1970, 191.

PURDUE UNIVERSITY, SCHOOL OF TECHNOLOGY (OFFICE OF MANPOWER STUDIES)
  The Case for Library Technical Assistants and Library Clerks in Indiana. Purdue University, 1969, 54. (Report No. 69-3.)

RESCOE, STAN A.
  Cataloging Made Easy. 3rd ed. Scarecrow Press, 1962, 210.

RIDDLE, JEAN, LEWIS, SHIRLEY, and MACDONALD, JANET
  Non-Book Materials: The Organization of Integrated Collections. Canadian Library Association, Ottawa, 1970, 58.

ROSSOFF, MARTIN
  Using Your High School Library. 2nd ed. Wilson, 1964, 111, illus.

COMMUNITY SERVICE PROGRAMS

ROTHSCHILD, NORMAN, and WRIGHT, GEORGE B.
Mounting, Projecting & Storing Slides. 2nd ed. Universal Photo Books, 1961, 119, illus. (Universal Photo Guide.)

RUFSVOLD, MARGARET I., and GUSS, CAROLYN
Guides to Newer Educational Media: Films, Filmstrips, Kinescopes, Phonodiscs, Phonotapes, Programmed Instruction Materials, Slides, Transparencies, Videotapes. 2nd ed. American Library Association, 1967, 70.

SAGER, DONALD J.
Reference: A Programmed Instruction. Ohio Library Foundation, Columbus, 1969, 147.

SAHEB-ETTABA, CAROLINE, and McFARLAND, ROGER B.
ANSCR: The Alpha-Numeric System for Classification of Recordings. Bro-Dart, 1969, 212.

SAUNDERS, HELEN E.
The Modern School Library: Its Administration As A Materials Center. Scarecrow Press, 1968, 215.

SAWYER, RUTH
The Way of the Storyteller. Viking, 1965, 1962, 356.

SCHMECKEBIER, LAWRENCE F., and EASTIN, ROY B.
Government Publications and Their Use. 2nd ed. Brookings Institution, 1969, 502.

SCHULTZ, CLAIRE K.
Thesaurus of Information Science Terminology. Rev. ed. Communication Service Corp., 1968, 246.

SEARS, DONALD A.
Harbrace Guide to the Library and the Research Paper. 2nd ed. Harcourt, Brace, 1960, 118, illus.

SEELY, PAULINE A., ED.
ALA Rules for Filing Catalog Cards. 2nd ed., abr. American Library Association, 1968, 100.

———, ED.
ALA Rules for Filing Cards. 2nd ed. American Library Association, 1968, 272.

SHARP, JOHN R.
Some Fundamentals of Information Retrieval. British Book Centre, 1965, 224.

SHEEHAN, SISTER HELEN
The Small College Library. Rev. ed. Corpus Books, Washington, 1969, 232.

SHERA, JESSE H.
Libraries and the Organization of Knowledge. Shoe String Press, 1965, 224.

SHORES, LOUIS, et al.
The Tex-Tec Syllabi: Courses of Study for Library Technical Assistants Prepared for the Texas State Library. Communication Service Corp., 1968, 166.

SLOCUM, ROBERT B., and HACKER, LOIS
Sample Cataloging Forms: Illustrations of Solutions to Problems in Descriptive Cataloging. 2nd ed. Scarecrow Press, 1968, 205.

STOKES, ROY B.
The Function of Bibliography. A. Deutsch, London, 1969, 174. (Grafton Book.)

STROHECKER, EDWIN, ED.
The Library Technical Assistant: A Report of the Orientation Institute on the Library Technician, July 14 to 25, 1969. Spaulding College, Department of Library Science, Louisville, Ky., 1970, 50.

SWAIN, OLIVE, COMP.
Notes Used on Catalog Cards: A List of Examples. 2nd ed. American Library Association, 1963, 82.

SYSTEM DEVELOPMENT CORPORATION
A System Study of Abstracting and Indexing. Management Information Services, Detroit, 1970, 228, illus.

THOMISON, DENNIS
Readings About Adolescent Literature. Scarecrow Press, 1970, 222.

TRINKNER, CHARLES L., ED.
Library Services for Junior Colleges. American Southern, Northport, Ala., 1964, 281.

UNESCO
Microphotography in the Library. UNESCO, 1962, 26.

U.S. LIBRARY OF CONGRESS, SUBJECT CATALOGING DIVISION
Subject Headings Used in the Dictionary Catalogs of the Library of Congress from 1897 through June 1964. 7th ed. Marguerite V. Quattlebaum, ed. Library of Congress, 1966, 1432.

VERRY, HERBERT R.
Microcopying Methods. Rev. ed. Focal Press, 1967, 183, illus. (Focal Library.)

WALL, C. EDWARD, COMP.
Periodical Title Abbreviations. Gale, 1969, 210.

WALLICK, CLAIR H.
Looking for Ideas? A Display Manual for Libraries and Bookstores. Scarecrow Press, 1970, 104, illus.

WALSH, JAMES P.
General Encyclopedias in Print. R. R. Bowker, 1963- , vols., annual.

WETMORE, ROSAMOND B.
A Guide to the Organization of Library Materials in Schools and Small Public Libraries. Rev. ed. Ball State University, 1967, 130, illus.

WHEELER, HELEN R.
The Community College Library: A Plan for Action. Shoe String Press, 1965, 170.

WILLEMIN, SILVENE
Technique of Union Catalogues: A Practical Guide. UNESCO, 1966, 26.

WULFEKOETTER, GERTRUDE
Acquisition Work: Processes Involved in Building Library Collections. University of Washington Press, 1962, 268.

MORTUARY SCIENCE

ALLEN, R. EARL
Memorial Messages. Broadman Press, Nashville, 1964, 96.

ALTMAN, PHILIP
Blood and Other Body Fluids: Analysis and Compilation. Federation of American Societies for Experimental Biology, Washington, 1961, 540, illus. (Biological Handbooks.)

AMERICAN BLUE BOOK OF FUNERAL DIRECTORS
Kate-Boyleston Publishers, New York, 1932- , vols., biennial.

ANDRIST, RALPH K.
The Long Death. Macmillan, 1964, 371.

ARCO PUBLISHING COMPANY, INC.
Mortuary Caretaker. Arco, 1965, 206.

BACHMANN, C. CHARLES
Ministering to the Grief Sufferer. Prentice-Hall, 1964, 144. (Successful Pastoral Counseling Series.)

BAERWALD, REUBEN C., COMP.
Hope in Grief. Concordia Publishing House, 1966, 154.

MORTUARY SCIENCE

BAIRD, WILLIAM R., and BAIRD, JOHN E.
    Funeral Meditations. Abingdon, 1966, 128.

BAYLY, JOSEPH T.
    The View From a Hearse. David C. Cook, 1969, 95.

BENDANN, EFFIE
    Death Customs: An Analytical Study of Burial Rites. Dawson, Farnham, England, 1969, 304.

BERNARD, HUGH Y.
    Law of Death and Disposal of the Dead. Oceana, 1966, 113.

BOOK OF THE DEAD
    University Books, 1960, 704.

BOROS, LADISLAUS
    The Mystery of Death. Herder & Herder, New York, 1965, 201.

BOWERS, MARGARETTA K.
    Counseling the Dying. Nelson, 1964, 133.

THE BROTHERS OF ST. JOSEPH
    To Bury the Dead. BSJ, Bethany, Okla, 1963, 83.

BROTHWELL, DON R.
    Digging Up Bones: The Excavation, Treatment, and Study of Human Skeletal Remains. The British Museum, 1963, 288, illus.

BUDGE, ERNEST A.
    The Mummy: Chapters on Egyptian Funeral Archeology. 2nd ed. Biblo & Tannen, 1964, 404, illus.

CHILES, JOHN R.
    A Treasury of Funeral Messages: Beauty for Ashes. Baker Book House, Grand Rapids, 1960, 161.

CHORON, JACQUES
    Death and Western Thought. Collier Books, 1963, 320.

CHRISTENSEN, JAMES L.
    The Complete Funeral Manual. Revell, 1967, 159.

COMPTON, W. H.
    Funeral Sermon Outlines. Baker Book House, Grand Rapids, 1965, 1 vol.

DAVIES, MAURICE R. R.
    The Law of Burial: Cremation and Exhumation. 2nd ed. Shaw & Sons, London, 1966, 238.

DESROCHES-NOBELCOURT, CHRISTIANE
    Tutankhamen: Life and Death of a Pharoah. Graphic Society, New York, 1963, 312, illus.

DREWES, DONALD W.
    Cemetery Land Planning. James H. Matthews, Pittsburgh, 1964, 91, illus.

DUNNE, JOHN S.
    The City of the Gods: A Study in Myth & Mortality. Macmillan, 1965, 243.

EVANS, WILLIAM E. D.
    The Chemistry of Death. Thomas, 1963, 101. (American Lecture Series Pub. No. 544.)

FORAN, EUGENE F.
    Funeral Service Facts and Figures. National Funeral Directors Association, 1966, 38.

FORD, WILLIAM H.
    Simple Sermons for Funeral Services. Zondervan, Grand Rapids, 1962, 54.

FOSS, MARTIN
    Death, Sacrifice and Tragedy. University of Nebraska Press, 1966, 125.

FREDERICK, L. G., and STRUB, CLARENCE G.
    The Principles and Practice of Embalming. 4th ed. The authors, Dallas, 1967, 712, illus.

FULTON, ROBERT L.
    A Compilation of Studies of Attitudes Toward Death, Funerals and Funeral Directors: Participated in by the Clergy, The Public, Including Critical Segments Thereof, and Funeral Directors. The author, 1967, 47.

———, ED.
    Death and Identity. Wiley, 1965, 415.

GALE, FREDERICK C.
    Mortuary Science, Thomas, 1961, 214, illus.

GATCH, MILTON McC.
    Death: Meaning and Mortality in Christian Thought and Contemporary Culture. Seabury Press, New York, 1969, 216.

GIESEY, RALPH E.
    The Royal Funeral Ceremony in Renaissance France. E. Droz, Geneva, 1960, 233, illus.

GLASER, BARNEY G., and STRAUSS, ANSELM L.
    Awareness of Dying. Aldine, 1965, 305.

———.
    Time for Dying. Aldine, 1968, 270.

GOODRICH, ROBERT E.
    On the Other Side of Sorrow. Abingdon, 1962, 31.

GOODY, JOHN R.
    Death, Property and the Ancestors: A Study of the Mortuary Customs of the Lo Dagoa of West Africa. Stanford University Press, 1962, 452, illus.

GORER, GEOFFREY
    Death, Grief and Mourning. Doubleday, 1965, 205.

GRAHAM, ROSCOE
    Remembered With Love. American Press, New York, 1961, 106.

GROLLMAN, EARL A., COMP.
    Explaining Death to Children. Beacon Press, 1967, 296.

HABENSTEIN, ROBERT W., and LAMERS, WILLIAM M.
    Funeral Customs the World Over. Rev. ed. Bulfin, Milwaukee, 1963, 854, illus.

———.
    The History of American Funeral Directing. Rev. ed. Bulfin, Milwaukee, (for National Funeral Directors Association), 1962, 638, illus.

HARMER, RUTH M.
    The High Cost of Dying. Crowell-Collier & Macmillan, 1963, 256.

HERTZ, ROBERT
    Death, and the Right Hand. Free Press, 1960, 174.

HERZOG, EDGAR
    Psyche and Death. Putnam, 1966, 224. (Studies for C. G. Jung Institute, Zurich.)

HINTON, JOHN
    Dying. Penguin, 1967, 208.

HOFFMAN, FREDERICK J.
    The Mortal No: Death and the Modern Imagination. Princeton University Press, 1964, 507.

HUNNISETT, R. F.
    The Medieval Coroner. Cambridge University Press, 1961, 217.

HUTTON, SAMUEL W.
    Minister's Funeral Manual. Baker Book House, Grand Rapids, 1968, 89.

COMMUNITY SERVICE PROGRAMS

IRION, PAUL E.
    Cremation. Fortress Press, Philadelphia, 1968, 152.
———.
    Funeral: Vestige or Value? Abingdon, 1966, 240.

JACKSON, EDGAR N.
    Christian Funeral: Its Meaning, Its Purpose, and Its Modern Practice. Channel Press, 1966, 184.
———.
    For the Living. Channel Press, 1964, 95.
———.
    Telling A Child About Death. Channel Press, 1965, 91.
———.
    You and Your Grief. Meredith Press, 1961, 64.

JONES, BARBARA M.
    Design for Death. A. Deutsch, London, 1967, 304.

KLUPAR, G. J.
    Modern Cemetery Management. Catholic Cemeteries, Archdiocese of Chicago, 1962, 418, illus.

KREIS, BERNADINE
    Up From Grief. Seabury Press, New York, 1969, 146.

KRIEGER, WILBER M.
    A Complete Guide to Funeral Service Management. Prentice-Hall, 1962, 299, illus.

KÜBLER-ROSS, ELISABETH
    On Death & Dying. Macmillan, 1969, 260.

KURZ, ALBERT L.
    Beyond Discouragement. Vantage, 1969, 124.

KUTSCHER, AUSTIN H.
    But Not to Lose: A Book of Comfort for Those Bereaved. F. Fell, New York, 1969, 288.
———.
    Death and Bereavement. Thomas, 1969, 364.

LAMM, MAURICE
    The Jewish Way in Death and Mourning. Jonathan David, New York, 1969, 265.

LAMONT, CORLISS
    The Illusion of Immortality. 4th ed. F. Ungar, New York, 1965, 303.

LEPP, IGNACE
    Death and Its Mysteries. Macmillan, 1968, 194.

LEWIS, CLIVE S.
    A Grief Observed. Seabury Press, New York, 1961, 60.

LITZINGER, JOHN C.
    Know Your Mortician: An Inside View of the Funeral Profession. Exposition Press, 1963, 50.

LOCKYER, HERBERT
    The Funeral Sourcebook. Zondervan, Grand Rapids, 1967, 187.

MANN, THOMAS C., and GREENE, JANET
    Over Their Dead Bodies: Yankee Epitaphs & History. Greene Press, Brattleboro, Vt., 1962, 103.

MARTIN, EDWARD A.
    Psychology of Funeral Service. 4th ed. Champion, Springfield, Ohio, 1962, 286.

MAYER, JOSEPH S.
    Restorative Art. 4th ed. The author, Bergenfield, N.J., 1961, 398, illus

McLARRY, NEWMAN R.
    When Shadows Fall. Broadman Press, Nashville, 1960, 60.

MILLS, LISTON O., ED.
    Perspectives on Death. Abingdon, 1969, 288.

MITFORD, JESSICA
    The American Way of Death. Simon & Schuster, 1963, 333.

NATIONAL FUNERAL DIRECTORS ASSOCIATION
    Funeral Service as a Profession. NFDA, 1963, 24.

PANOFSKY, ERWIN
    Tomb Sculpture: Four Lectures on Its Changing Aspects From Ancient Egypt to Bernini. Abrams, 1964, 319.

PARROTT, LESLIE
    The Usher's Manual: A Spiritual and Practical Guidebook. Zondervan, Grand Rapids, 1970, 64, illus.

PEALE, NORMAN V.
    The Healing of Sorrow. Doubleday, 1966, 96.

PEARSON, LEONARD
    Death and Dying: Current Issues in the Treatment of the Dying Person. Case Western Reserve University, 1969, 235.

POLSON, CYRIL J., BRITTAIN, R. P., and MARSHALL, T. K.
    The Disposal of the Dead. 2nd ed. Thomas, 1962, 356.

PUCKLE, BERTRAM S.
    Funeral Customs: Their Origin and Development. Singing Tree (Gale, dist.), 1968, 283, illus.

PUGSLEY, CLEMENT H.
    In Sorrow's Lone Hour. Abingdon, 1963, 93.

REIK, THEODOR
    Curiosities of the Self. Farrar, Straus & Giraux, 1965, 211.

REZEK, PHILIPP R.
    Autopsy Pathology.... Thomas, 1963, 845.

RHEINGOLD, JOSEPH C.
    The Mother, Anxiety, and Death. Little, Brown, 1967, 271.

ROSS, JOAN
    Post-Mortem Appearances. 6th ed. Oxford University Press, 1963, 336.

RUITENBEEK, HENDRIK M., ED.
    Death: Interpretations. Delta Books, 1969, 286.

SCOTT, NATHAN A., COMP.
    The Modern Vision of Death. John Knox, 1967, 125.

SNIVELY, WILLIAM D.
    Sea Within: The Story of Our Body Fluid. Lippincott, 1960, 150, illus.

SPRIGGS, A. O.
    The Art and Science of Embalming. Champion, Springfield, Ohio, 1960, 312.
———.
    Champion Restorative Art. Champion, Springfield, Ohio, 1960, 140.

STUEVE, THOMAS F. H.
    Mortuary Law. 3rd ed. Cincinnati College of Embalming, 1963, 101.

SULZBERGER, CYRUS L.
    My Brother Death. Harper, 1961, 225.

SUNDOW, DAVID
    Passing On. Prentice-Hall, 1967, 1 vol.

SWITZER, DAVID K.
    The Dynamics of Grief. Abingdon Press, 1970, 224.

TOURNIER, PAUL
    The Meaning of Grief. John Knox, 1968, 1 vol.

TOYNBEE, ARNOLD, et al.
    Man's Concern with Death. McGraw-Hill, 1969, 280.

WAGNER, JOHANNES, ED.
    Reforming the Rites of Death. Paulis, New York, 1968, 180. (Concilium: Theology in the Age of Renewal—Liturgy Vol. 32.)

WALSH, JOHN E.
　　The Shroud. Random House, 1963, 202.

WESTBERG, GRANGER E.
　　Good Grief: A Constructive Approach to the Problem of Loss. Augustana, Rock Island, Ill., 1962, 57.

WOOD, CHARLES R., COMP.
　　Sermon Outlines for Funeral Services. Kregel, 1970, 64.

ZLOTNICK, DOV, ED., TR.
　　Tractate Mourning (Semahot): Regulations Relating to Death, Burial and Mourning. Yale University Press, 1966, 233.

POLICE SCIENCE

AARON, JAMES E., and SHAFTER, ALBERT J.
　　The Police Officer and Alcoholism. Thomas, 1963, 84.

AARON, THOMAS J.
　　The Control of Police Discretion: The Danish Experience. Thomas, 1966, 107.

ABBOTT, DAVID W., et al.
　　Police, Politics and Race: The New York City Referendum on Civilian Review. American Jewish Committee and Joint Center for Urban Studies of MIT and Harvard University, 1969, 62.

ABBOTT, JOHN R.
　　Footwear Evidence: The Examination, Identification, and Comparison of Footwear Impressions. Thomas, 1964, 100, illus.

ABRAHAMSEN, DAVID
　　Our Violent Society. Funk & Wagnalls, 1970, 298.

―――.
　　The Psychology of Crime. Columbia University Press, 1960, 358.

ADAMS, THOMAS F.
　　Law Enforcement: An Introduction to the Police Role in the Community. Prentice-Hall, 1968, 256, illus.

―――.
　　Training Officers' Handbook. Thomas, 1964, 176.

ALEX, NICHOLAS
　　Black in Blue: A Study of the Negro Policeman. Appleton-Century-Crofts, 1969, 210.

APPLEGATE, REX
　　Crowd and Riot Control, Including Close-Combat Techniques for Military and Police. 6th ed. Stackpole, 1964, 528, illus.

―――.
　　Riot Control: Materiel and Techniques. Stackpole, 1969, 320, illus.

ARCO PUBLISHING COMPANY, INC.
　　Captain, Police Department. 4th ed. Arco, 1967, 416.

―――.
　　Fingerprint Technician. Arco, 1962, 176.

―――.
　　Housing Patrolman. 4th ed. Arco, 1969, 352.

―――.
　　Law Enforcement Positions. 2nd ed. Arco, 1962, 1 vol., illus.

―――.
　　Lieutenant, Police Department: The Arco Text for Job and Test Training. 5th ed. Arco, 1969, 1 vol. (Arco Books for Civil Service Jobs.)

―――.
　　Police Cadet, New York City Police Department. Arco, 1960, 1 vol., illus.

―――.
　　Policewoman. Arco, 1966, 264.

―――.
　　State Trooper. 4th ed. Arco, 1965, 288.

ARM, WALTER
　　The Policeman: An Inside Look at His Role in a Modern Society. Dutton, 1969, 160, illus.

ARONS, HARRY
　　Hypnosis in Criminal Investigation. Thomas, 1967, 240.

ASCH, SIDNEY H.
　　Police Authority and the Rights of the Individual. 2nd ed. Arco, 1968, 136. (Know Your Law.)

ASINOF, ELIOT
　　People vs. Blutcher: Black Men and White Law in Bedford-Stuyvesant. Viking, 1970, 288.

AUBRY, ARTHUR S., JR.
　　The Officer in the Small Department. Thomas, 1961, 416, illus.

THE BANCROFT-WHITNEY COMPANY
　　Drugs and Poisons. William W. Turner, ed. Aqueduct Books, Rochester, N.Y., 1965, 295, illus. (Police Evidence Library.)

BANTON, MICHAEL P.
　　The Policeman in the Community. Basic Books, 1964, 276.

―――.
　　Race Relations. Basic Books, 1967, 434, illus.

BAYLEY, DAVID H., and MENDELSOHN, HAROLD
　　Minorities and the Police: Confrontation in America. Free Press, 1969, 209.

BECKER, HAROLD K.
　　Issues in Police Administration. Scarecrow Press, 1970, 332.

BECKER, HAROLD K., and FELKENES, GEORGE T.
　　Law Enforcement: A Selected Bibliography. Scarecrow Press, 1968, 257.

BECKER, HAROLD K., FELKENES, GEORGE T., and WHISENAND, PAUL M.
　　New Dimensions in Criminal Justice. Scarecrow Press, 1968, 279.

BENSING, ROBERT C., and SCHROEDER, OLIVER, JR.
　　Homicide in an Urban Community. Thomas, 1960, 208, illus.

BERKELEY, GEORGE E.
　　The Democratic Policeman. Beacon Press, 1969, 232.

BLACK, ALGERNON D.
　　The People and the Police. McGraw-Hill, 1968, 246.

BLOCH, HERBERT A., and GEIS, GILBERT
　　Man, Crime and Society: The Forms of Criminal Behavior. Random House, 1962, 642.

BLUM, RICHARD H.
　　Police Selection. Thomas, 1964, 252.

BLUMBERG, ABRAHAM S.
　　Criminal Justice. Quadrangle Books, 1967, 206.

BLUMBERG, ABRAHAM S., and NIEDERHOFFER, ARTHUR, EDS.
　　Ambivalent Force: Perspectives on the Police. Ginn, 1970, 360, illus.

BORDUA, DAVID J., ED.
　　The Police: Six Sociological Essays. Wiley, 1967, 258.

BOSTON POLICE DEPARTMENT
　　Reports, Records and Communications in the Boston Police Department: A System Improvement Study. U.S. Justice Department, Office of Law Enforcement Assistance, 1968, 85, illus.

BOUMA, DONALD H.
　　Kids and Cops: A Study in Mutual Hostility. Eerdmans, 1969, 168.

BRANDSLATTER, ARTHUR F., and RADELET, LOUIS A.
　　Police and Community Relations: A Sourcebook. Glencoe Press, 1968, 480.

COMMUNITY SERVICE PROGRAMS

BRIDGES, BURTIS C.
　　Practical Fingerprinting. Rev. ed. Charles E. O'Hara, ed. Funk & Wagnalls, 1963, 374, illus.

BRISTOW, ALLEN P.
　　Effective Police Manpower Utilization. Thomas, 1969, 116.

─────.
　　Field Interrogation. 2nd ed. Thomas, 1964, 155, illus.

─────.
　　Police Supervision Readings. Thomas, 1970, 1 vol., illus.

BRISTOW, ALLEN P., and GABARD, E. C.
　　Decision-Making in Police Administration. Thomas, 1961, 118, illus. (Police Science Series.)

CAEN, ARTHUR H.
　　Young People and Crime. Day, 1968, 1 vol.

CALDWELL, ROBERT G.
　　Criminology. 2nd ed. Ronald, 1965, 774, illus.

UNIVERSITY OF CALIFORNIA, SCHOOL OF CRIMINOLOGY
　　The Police and the Community: The Dynamics of their Relationship in a Changing Society—A Report Prepared for the President's Commission on Law Enforcement and Administration of Justice. USGPO, 1966, 2 vols. (Field Surveys IV.)

CARNES, ROBERT M., and RYAN, JOHN W.
　　Police Training for Delinquency Prevention and Control, an Appraisal: A Study of the Effectiveness of Juvenile Delinquency Prevention Training Programs Conducted During 1956-59 in Wisconsin and their Impact on local Communities. University of Wisconsin, Madison Bureau of Government Research & Advisory Service, 1961, 45.

CAVAN, RUTH S.
　　Criminology. 3rd ed. Crowell, 1962, 735, illus.

CHAMBLISS, WILLIAM J., COMP.
　　Crime and the Legal Process. McGraw-Hill, 1969, 447, illus. (McGraw-Hill Sociology Series.)

CHAPMAN, SAMUEL G.
　　Dogs in Police Work: A Summary of Experience in Great Britain and the United States. Chicago Public Administration Service, 1960, 101, illus.

─────.
　　Police Patrol Readings. Thomas, 1964, 476, illus.

CHAPPELL, DUNCAN, and WILSON, PAUL R.
　　The Police and the Public in Australia and New Zealand. University of Queensland Press, (International Scholarly Book Service, Zion, Ill., dist.), 1969, 214.

CHEVIGNY, PAUL
　　Police Power: Police Abuses in New York City. Pantheon, 1969, 208.

CIVIL SERVICE PUBLISHING CORPORATION
　　How to Pass Patrolman Examinations, All States: Questions and Answers. Civil Service, Brooklyn, 1964, 1 vol. (Government Career Examination Series 506-S.)

─────.
　　How to Pass Patrolman, Police Department: Past Examinations, Questions and Answers. Jack Rudman, ed. Civil Service, Brooklyn, 1962, 1 vol.

─────.
　　How to Pass Policewoman: Questions and Answers. Civil Service, Brooklyn, 1964, 1 vol.

CIZON, FRANCIS A., and SMITH, WILLIAM H. T.
　　Some Guidelines for Successful Police-Community Relations Training Programs. USGPO, 1970, 45. (Law Enforcement Assistance Administration Contract No. 67-27.)

CLARK, DONALD E., and CHAPMAN, SAMUEL G.
　　A Forward Step: Educational Backgrounds for Police. Thomas, 1966, 97, illus.

CLARK, RAMSEY
　　Crime in America: Observations on its Nature, Cause, Prevention and Control. Simon & Schuster, 1970, 346.

CLEGG, REED K.
　　Probation and Parole: Principles and Practices. Thomas, 1964, 196.

CLEVELAND BUREAU OF GOVERNMENTAL RESEARCH
　　PFI, a Survey: Police-Fire Integration in the United States and Canada. Howard I. Bruce, ed. CBGR, 1961, 77, illus.

CLIFT, RAYMOND E.
　　A Guide to Modern Police Thinking: A Panorama of Policing. 2nd ed. W. H. Anderson Co., Cincinnati, 1965, 362, illus. (Science in Law Enforcement Series.)

─────.
　　Police and Public Safety. W. H. Anderson Co., Cincinnati, 1963, 314, illus. (Science in Law Enforcement Series.)

CLINARD, MARSHALL, and QUINNEY, RICHARD
　　Criminal Behavior Systems: A Typology. Holt, Rinehart & Winston, 1967, 498.

CLOWERS, NORMAN L.
　　Patrolman Patterns, Problems, and Procedures. Thomas, 1962, 280, illus.

COFFEY, ALAN, ELDEFONSO, EDWARD, and HARTINGER, WALTER
　　Human Relations: Law Enforcement in a Changing Community. Prentice-Hall, 1971, 224.

COHEN, BRUCE J., ED.
　　Crime in America: Perspectives on Criminal and Delinquent Behavior. Peacock, Itasca, Ill., 1970, 506, illus.

CONQUEST, ROBERT
　　The Soviet Police System. Praeger, 1968, 103. (Contemporary Soviet Union Series: Institutions and Policies.)

CRAMER, JAMES
　　Uniforms of the World's Police: With Brief Data on Organization, Systems, and Weapons. Thomas, 1968, 199, illus.

CREAMER, J. SHANE
　　The Law of Arrest, Search, and Seizure. Saunders, 1968, 273.

CROCKETT, THOMPSON S., and STINCHCOMB, JAMES D.
　　Guidelines for Law Enforcement Education Programs in Community and Junior Colleges. American Association of Junior Colleges, 1968, 36.

CROWN, DAVID A.
　　The Forensic Examination of Paints and Pigments. Thomas, 1968, 264. (August Vollmer Criminalistic Series.)

CURRY, JESSE E., and KING, GLEN D.
　　Race Tensions and the Police. Thomas, 1962, 137. (Police Science Series.)

DAVIS PUBLISHING COMPANY
　　Municipal Police Administration Tests. Rev. ed. Davis, San Francisco, 1961, 117. (Based on Municipal Police Administration, 1954, 1961.)

─────.
　　Police Promotional Examinations for Sergeants. Davis, San Francisco, 1963, 1 vol.

DAY, FRANK D.
　　Criminal Law and Society. Thomas, 1964, 132.

DIECKMANN, EDWARD A.
　　Practical Homicide Investigation. Thomas, 1961, 96.

DIENSTEIN, WILLIAM
　　How to Write a Narrative Investigation Report. Thomas, 1969, 128. (Police Science Series.)

─────.
　　Technics for the Crime Investigator. Thomas, 1967, 240.

DINITZ, SIMON, and RECKLESS, WALTER C.
　　Critical Issues in the Study of Crime: A Book of Readings. Little, Brown, 1968, 291.

POLICE SCIENCE

DONIGAN, ROBERT L.
    Chemical Tests and the Law. 2nd ed. Northwestern University Traffic Institute, 1966, 343.

DONIGAN, ROBERT L., and FISHER, EDWARD C.
    The Evidence Handbook. Northwestern University Traffic Institute, 1965, 286.

DOUGHERTY, EDWARD E.
    Safety in Police Pursuit Driving. Thomas, 1961, 99, illus. (Police Science Series.)

DRABEK, THOMAS E.
    Laboratory Simulation of a Police Communications System Under Stress. Ohio State University, College of Administrative Science, 1970, 148.

DRZAZGA, JOHN
    Sex Crimes. Thomas, 1960, 250. (Police Science Series.)

———.
    Wheels of Fortune. Thomas, 1963, 376, illus.

DUDYCHA, GEORGE J.
    Psychology for Law Enforcement Officers. Thomas, 1967, 416, illus. (Police Science Series.)

EARLE, HOWARD H.
    Police-Community Relations: Crisis in Our Time. 2nd ed. Thomas, 1970, 205, illus.

EDWARDS, GEORGE C.
    The Police on the Urban Frontier: A Guide to Community Understanding. Institute of Human Relations Press, 1968, 89.

ELDEFONSO, EDWARD
    Law Enforcement and the Youthful Offender: Juvenile Procedures. Wiley, 1967, 346.

ELDEFONSO, EDWARD, COFFEY, ALAN, and GRACE, RICHARD C.
    Principles of Law Enforcement. Wiley, 1968, 284, illus.

EPSTEIN, CHARLOTTE
    Intergroup Relations for Police Officers. Williams & Wilkins, 1962, 194.

EYSENCK, HANS J.
    Crime and Personality. Houghton Mifflin, 1964, 204, illus. (Behavioral Sciences International Series.)

FARMER, DAVID J.
    Civil Disorder Control: A Planning Program of Municipal Coordination and Cooperation. Public Administration Service, Chicago, Ill., 1968, 60.

FLAMMANG, C. J.
    The Police and the Underprotected Child. Thomas, 1970, 310.

FOSDICK, RAYMOND B.
    American Police Systems. Patterson Smith, 1969, 408, illus.

FOX, VERNON
    Guidelines for Corrections Education in Community and Junior Colleges. American Association of Junior Colleges, 1969, 44.

FRAENKEL, JACK R.
    Crime and Criminals: What Should We Do About Them? Prentice-Hall, 1970, 119.

FREEDMAN, ALFRED, and BISKIND, ELLIOTT L.
    The Revised Penal Law Handbook. Clark Boardman, New York, 1967, 109.

FRICKE, CHARLES W.
    Criminal Investigation. 6th ed. Legal Book Store, Los Angeles, 1962, 273, illus.

———.
    5000 Criminal Definitions, Terms and Phrases. 5th ed. Legal Book Store, Los Angeles, 1968, 91.

GAMMAGE, ALLEN Z.
    Basic Police Report Writing. Thomas, 1966, 328, illus.

———.
    Police Training in the United States. Thomas, 1963, 493.

———.
    Your Future in Law Enforcement. R. Rosen Press, 1961, 159. (Careers in Depth.)

GARDNER, ERLE STANLEY
    Cops on Campus and Crime in the Streets. Morrow, 1970, 156.

GEIS, GILBERT, ED.
    The White Collar Criminal: The Offender in Business and the Professions. Atherton Press, 1968, 448.

GERMANN, A. C.
    Police Executive Development. Thomas, 1962, 102, illus.

GERMANN, A. C., DAY, FRANK D., and GALLATI, ROBERT R. J.
    Introduction to Law Enforcement and Criminal Justice. Thomas, 1968, 472, illus.

GIBBONS, DON C.
    Society, Crime and Criminal Careers: An Introduction to Criminology. Prentice-Hall, 1968, 564.

GITCHOFF, G. THOMAS
    Kids, Cops and Kilos. Malter-Westerfield, 1969, 178.

GLUECK, SHELDON, and GLUECK, ELEANOR
    Ventures in Criminology: Selected Recent Papers. Harvard University Press, 1964, 373.

GOCKE, BLYE W.
    Police Sergeants Manual: The Essential Principles of Handling Police Personnel and the Basic Duties of Supervisory Officers, Sergeants.... Legal Book Store, Los Angeles, 1967, 366.

GOURLEY, GERALD D.
    Effective Police Organization and Management: A Report Presented to the Office of Law Enforcement Assistance of the United States Department of Justice for the President's Commission on Law Enforcement and the Administration of Justice. State College at Los Angeles, Department of Police Science and Administration, 1966, 8 vols.

GOURLEY, GERALD D., and BRISTOW, ALLEN P.
    Patrol Administration. Thomas, 1961, 373, illus. (Police Science Series.)

GRIFFIN, JOHN L., WETTEROTH, WILLIAM J., and BOLAND, MARVIN
    Police Training & Performance Study: Project Report Subject to New York City Police Department. New York (City) Police Department, 1969, 569.

GUTTERMAN, MELVIN, ED.
    Arrest, Search and Seizure: Telephone Lecture Series Proceedings. Institute for Community Development and Services, Michigan State University, 1968, 174.

HANNA, DONALD G., and KLEBERG, JOHN R.
    A Police Records System for the Small Department. Thomas, 1969, 95, illus.

HARNEY, MALACHI L., and CROSS, JOHN C.
    The Informer in Law Enforcement. 2nd ed. Thomas, 1968, 160.

HARRIS, RICHARD
    The Fear of Crime. Praeger, 1969, 116.

———.
    Justice: The Crisis of Law, Order, and Freedom in America. Dutton, 1970, 268.

HARRISON, LEONARD H.
    How to Teach Police Subjects: Theory and Practice. Thomas, 1964, 112, illus.

COMMUNITY SERVICE PROGRAMS

HARTUNG, FRANK E.
    Crime, Law and Society. Wayne State University Press, 1965, 320, illus.

HASKELL, MARTIN R., and YABLONSKY, LEWIS
    Crime and Delinquency. Rand McNally, 1970, 517.

HAZELET, JOHN C.
    Police Report Writing. Thomas, 1960, 256, illus. (Police Science Series.)

HEWITT, WILLIAM H.
    A Bibliography of Police Administration, Public Safety, and Criminology to July 1, 1965. Thomas, 1967, 242.

———.
    British Police Administration. Thomas, 1965, 392, illus.

HIGGINS, LOIS L.
    Policewoman's Manual. O. W. Wilson, foreword; Irvin K. Jorgensmeyer, preface; William G. Clark, critique. Thomas, 1961, 169, illus.

HOLCOMB, RICHARD L.
    The Police and the Public. Thomas, 1968, 40, illus.

———.
    Police Patrol. Thomas, 1968, 128, illus.

HOLMAN, MARY
    The Police Officer and the Child. Thomas, 1962, 150, illus.

HOUSTON, L. B.
    Park Police. American Institute of Park Executives, 1963, 1 vol.

IANNONE, N. F.
    Supervision of Police Personnel. Prentice-Hall, 1970, 286, illus.

INBAU, FRED E., and ASPEN, MARVIN E.
    Criminal Law for the Police. Chilton, 1969, 164.

INSTITUTE OF POLICE MANAGEMENT FOR SUPERVISORY AND ADMINISTRATIVE PERSONNEL, DALLAS, 1962.
    Police Management for Supervisory and Administrative Personnel. Thomas, 1963, 117.

INTERNATIONAL ASSOCIATION OF CHIEFS OF POLICE
    Law Enforcement Education Directory. IACP, 1970, 1 vol.

———.
    Proceedings of Police Administrators Conference on Community Relations, Indiana University, Medical Center, Indianapolis, Indiana, June 27-29, 1966. Jeptha S. Rogers, ed. IACP, Chicago, 1966, 112.

THE INTERNATIONAL CITY MANAGEMENT ASSOCIATION
    Municipal Police Administration. 6th ed. ICMA, 1969, 355.

IRWIN, JOHN
    The Felon. Prentice-Hall, 1970, 211, illus.

ISAACSON, IRVING
    Manual for the Arresting Officer. 3rd ed. Legal Publications, Lewiston, Me., 1961, 112. (Manuals and Training Aids.)

JACKSON, BRUCE
    A Thief's Primer. Macmillan, 1969, 243.

JENKINS, HERBERT T.
    Keeping the Peace: A Police Chief Looks at His Job. Harper & Row, 1970, 203.

JOHN JAY COLLEGE OF CRIMINAL JUSTICE, CITY UNIVERSITY OF NEW YORK
    Proceedings of the John Jay College Faculty Seminars. John Jay College, 1969, 73.

JOHNSON, ELMER H.
    Crime, Correction, and Society. Dorsey Press, Homewood, Ill., 1964, 729, illus. (Dorsey Series in Anthropology and Sociology.)

JOINT COMMITTEE ON CONTINUING LEGAL EDUCATION OF THE AMERICAN LAW INSTITUTE AND THE AMERICAN BAR ASSOCIATION
    The Problems of Police Interrogation. ALI, ABA, Philadelphia, 1961, 91.

JOURNAL OF CRIMINAL LAW, CRIMINOLOGY & POLICE SCIENCE
    The Supreme Court & the Police. International Association of Police Chiefs, 1966, 1 vol.

KARLEM, SELMA
    Anglo-American Criminal Justice. Oxford University Press, 1967, 1 vol.

KASSOFF, NORMAN C.
    Organizational Concepts. International Association of Chiefs of Police, Professional Standards Division, 1967, 40, illus.

KATSARIS, W. K.
    Corrections Education: A Survey of Two Year College Programs in the United States and Canada. Tallahassee Junior College, 1969, 62.

KAY, BARBARA A., and VEDDER, CLYDE B.
    Probation and Parole. Thomas, 1963, 228.

KENNEY, JOHN P.
    The California Police. Thomas, 1964, 144.

KENNEY, JOHN P., and WILLIAMS, JOHN B.
    Police Operations: Policies and Procedures. 2nd ed. Thomas, 1968, 211.

KENNEY, JOHN P., and PURSUIT, DAN G.
    Police Work with Juveniles and the Administration of Juvenile Justice. 4th ed. Thomas, 1970, 423, illus.

KING, EVERETT M.
    The Auxiliary Police Unit: Its Formation, Training and Use. Thomas, 1960, 232, illus. (Police Science Series.)

KING, GLEN D., ED.
    First-Line Supervisor's Manual. Thomas, 1970, 160. (Police Science Series.)

KING, RUFUS
    Gambling and Organized Crime. Public Affairs Press, Washington, 1969, 239.

KIRK, PAUL L., and BRADFORD, LOWELL W.
    The Crime Laboratory: Organization and Operation. Thomas, 1965, 132.

KLEIN, HERBERT T.
    The Police: Damned If They Do, and Damned If They Don't. Crown, 1968, 252.

KLOTTER, JOHN C.
    Techniques for Police Instructors. Thomas, 1963, 180.

KLOTTER, JOHN C., and KANOVITZ, JACQUELINE R.
    Constitutional Law for Police. W. H. Anderson, Cincinnati, 1968, 628. (Police Text Series Vol. 1.)

KNUDTEN, RICHARD D.
    Crime in a Complex Society: An Introduction to Criminology. Dorsey Press, Homewood, Ill., 1970, 758, illus. (Dorsey Series in Anthropology and Sociology.)

KOCH, HARRY W.
    Police and Police Type Entrance Examinations. Ken Books, San Francisco, 1960, 1 vol., illus.

KOGA, ROBERT K., and NELSON, JOHN G.
    The Koga Method: Police Baton Techniques. Glencoe Press, 1968, 152, illus. (Glencoe Press Police Science Series.)

KUHN, CHARLES L.
    The Police Officer's Memorandum Book. Thomas, 1964, 80, illus.

LaFAVE, WAYNE R.
Arrest: The Decision to Take a Suspect Into Custody. Little, Brown, 1965, 540. (American Bar Foundation Administration of Criminal Justice Series.)

LANGFORD, BERYL, et al.
Stopping Vehicles and Occupant Control. Thomas, 1960, 104, illus.

LAUER, A. R.
The Psychology of Driving: Factors of Traffic Enforcement. Thomas, 1960, 352, illus.

LENZ, ROBERT R.
Explosives and Bomb Disposal Guide. Thomas, 1965, 320, illus.

LEONARD, CALISTA V.
Understanding and Preventing Suicide. Thomas, 1967, 356.

LEONARD, VIVIAN A.
The Police Communications System. Thomas, 1970, 80.

———.
Police Detective Function. Thomas, 1970, 111.

———.
The Police Enterprise: Its Organization and Management. Thomas, 1969, 94.

———.
Police Organization and Management. 2nd ed. Foundation Press, Mineola, N.Y., 1964, 459, illus. (Police Science Series.)

———.
The Police of the 20th Century. Foundation Press, Mineola, N.Y., 1964, 200, illus. (Police Science Series.)

———.
Police Patrol Organization. Thomas, 1970, 105.

———.
Police Personnel Administration. Thomas, 1970, 132.

———.
The Police Records System. Thomas, 1970, 92.

———.
The Police, The Judiciary and The Criminal. Thomas, 1969, 235.

LEONARD, VIVIAN A., and MORE, HARRY W.
The General Administration of Criminal Justice. Foundation Press, Mineola, N.Y., 1967, 370, illus. (Police Science Series.)

LEWIN, STEPHEN, ED.
Crime and Its Prevention. Wilson, 1968, 244. (Reference Shelf Vol. 40, No. 4.)

LOS ANGELES COUNTY SHERIFF'S OFFICE and GUTHRIE, C. ROBERT
Project Sky Knight: A Demonstration in Aerial Surveillance and Crime Control. U.S. Department of Justice, Office of Law Enforcement Assistance, 1968, 235, illus.

LOTH, DAVID
Crime in the Suburbs. Morrow, 1967, 266.

LOUISELL, DAVID W., KAPLAN, JOHN, and WALTZ, JON R.
Principles of Evidence and Proof. Foundation Press, Mineola, N.Y., 1968, 872.

LUNDEN, WALTER A.
Crimes and Criminals. Iowa State University Press, 1967, 341, illus.

MARDERS, IRVIN E.
How to Use Dogs Effectively in Modern Police Work. Police Science Press, Cocoa Beach, Fla., 1960, 115, illus.

MARX, JERRY
Officer, Tell Your Story: A Guide to Police Public Relations. Thomas, 1967, 173, illus.

MELNICOE, WILLIAM B., and MENNIG, JAN
Elements of Police Supervision. Glencoe Press, 1969, 227. (Glencoe Press Police Science Series.)

MICHIGAN STATE UNIVERSITY, NATIONAL CENTER ON POLICE AND COMMUNITY RELATIONS
A National Survey of Police and Community Relations, Prepared for the President's Commission on Law Enforcement and Administration of Justice. USGPO, 1967, 386. (Field Surveys V.)

MODERN CRIMINAL INVESTIGATION STUDY GUIDE.
Rev. ed. Davis, Santa Cruz, Calif., 1967, 1 vol.

MOENSSENS, ANDRE A.
Fingerprints and the Law. Chilton, 1969, 248.

MOMBOISEE, RAYMOND M.
Community Relations and Riot Prevention. Thomas, 1967, 257.

———.
Industrial Security for Strikes, Riots and Disasters. Thomas, 1968, 516.

———.
Riots, Revolts and Insurrections. Thomas, 1967, 523.

MOSER, ROBERT H.
House Officer Training: A Casual Perspective. Thomas, 1970, 108. (American Lecture Series Pub. No. 768, Monograph in American Lectures in Medical Writing.)

MOYNAHAN, JAMES M.
Police Ju Jitsu. Thomas, 1962, 132, illus.

———.
Police Searching Procedures. Thomas, 1963, 70, illus.

———.
The Yawara Stick and Police Baton. Thomas, 1963, 88, illus.

MURRAY, JOSEPH A.
The Complete Study Guide for Police Administration and Criminal Investigation. 2nd ed. Arco, 1967, 1 vol., various pagings, illus.

———.
Patrolman, Police Department. Arco, 1961, 1 vol., illus.

MYREN, RICHARD A., and SWANSON, LYNN D.
Police Work with Children: Perspectives and Principles. USGPO (for HEW, Social Security Administration, Children's Bureau), 1962, 106.

THE NATIONAL COMMISSION ON THE CAUSES AND PREVENTION OF VIOLENCE.
To Establish Justice, To Insure Domestic Tranquility: The Final Report of the National Commission on the Causes and Prevention of Violence. Praeger, 1970, 277, illus. (New York Times Book.)

NELSON, JOHN G.
Preliminary Investigation and Police Reporting: A Complete Guide to Police Written Communication. Glencoe Press, 1970, 513, illus.

NEWMAN, EDWIN S.
Police, The Law and Personal Freedom. Oceana, 1964, 102. (Legal Almanac Series No. 40.)

NIEDERHOFFER, ARTHUR
Behind the Shield: The Police in Urban Society. Doubleday, 1967, 253.

NORRGARD, DAVID L.
Regional Law Enforcement: A Study of Intergovernmental Cooperation and Coordination. Public Administration Service, Chicago, 1969, 58.

NORTHWESTERN UNIVERSITY, TRAFFIC INSTITUTE
A Bibliography on Police Administration. Northwestern University, 1969, 28.

O'BRIEN, G. M.
The Australian Police Forces. Oxford University Press, 1960, 268, illus.

O'CONNOR, GEORGE W., and VANDERBOSCH, CHARLES G.
The Patrol Operation. International Association of Chiefs of Police, 1967, 232, illus.

COMMUNITY SERVICE PROGRAMS

O'CONNOR, GEORGE W., and WATSON, NELSON A.
Juvenile Delinquency and Youth Crime, the Police Role: An Analysis of Philosophy, Policy and Opinion. International Association of Chiefs of Police, Field Service Division, Research and Development Section, 1964, 135, illus.

ORBAAN, ALBERT
Dogs Against Crime: True Accounts of Canine Training and Exploits in Worldwide Police Work, Past and Present. John Day, 1968, 234, illus.

O'HARA, CHARLES E.
Fundamentals of Criminal Investigation. 2nd ed. Thomas, 1970, 722, illus.

OSTERBURG, JAMES W.
Crime Laboratory: Case Studies of Scientific Criminal Investigation. Indiana University Press, 1968, 330, illus.

PACE, DENNY F., STINCHCOMB, JAMES D., and STYLES, JIMMIE C.
Law Enforcement Training and the Community College: Alternatives for Affiliation. American Association of Junior Colleges, 1970, 60.

PATTERSON, FRANK M., and SMITH, PATRICK D.
A Manual of Police Report Writing. Thomas, 1968, 78.

PAYTON, GEORGE T.
Patrol Procedure. 3rd ed. Legal Book Store, Los Angeles, 1967, 426, illus.

PEEL, JOHN D.
Fundamentals of Training for Security Officers: A Comprehensive Guide to What You Should Be, Know, and Do to Have a Successful Career As a Private Patrolman or Security Officer. Thomas, 1970, 325, illus.

PELL, ARTHUR R.
Police Leadership. Thomas, 1967, 141, illus.

POCK, MAX A.
Consolidating Police Functions in Metropolitan Areas. University of Michigan Law School, 1962, 51.

POLICE AND SHERIFFS ASSOCIATION OF NORTH AMERICA
The Policeman's Handbook of Law: Especially Written for Law Enforcement Officers. PSANA, Milwaukee, 1961, 183.

THE POLICE CHIEF
Police and the Changing Community: Selected Readings. Nelson A. Watson, ed. International Association of Chiefs of Police, 1965, 240, illus.

POLICE SERGEANT'S HANDBOOK.
Davis, Santa Cruz, Calif., 1968, 1 vol.

PREISS, JACK J., and EHRLICH, HOWARD J.
An Examination of Role Theory: The Case of the State Police. University of Nebraska Press, 1966, 286.

PULLING, CHRISTOPHER
The Police. Hale, London, 1962, 127, illus. (Target for Careers.)

QUINNEY, RICHARD
The Social Reality of Crime. Little, Brown, 1970, 339.

RADANO, GENE
Walking the Beat: A New York Policeman Tells What It's Like on His Side of the Law. World, 1968, 192.

RECKLESS, WALTER C.
The Crime Problem. 4th ed. Appleton-Century-Crofts, 1967, 830.

REID, ED.
The Anatomy of Organized Crime in America: The Grim Reapers. Regnery, 1969, 344, illus.

REID, JOHN E., and INBAU, FRED E.
Criminal Interrogation & Confessions. 2nd ed. Williams & Wilkins, 1967, 224, illus.

———.
Truth and Deception: The Polygraph ("Lie Detector") Technique. Williams & Wilkins, 1966, 291, illus.

RICHARDSON, JAMES F.
The New York Police: Colonial Times to 1901. Oxford University Press, 1970, 332. (Urban Life in America Series.)

ROEBUCK, JULIAN B.
Criminal Typology: The Legalistic, Physical-Constitutional-Hereditary, Psychological-Psychiatric and Sociological Approaches. Thomas, 1967, 336.

ROGERS, ARTHUR W., and MAGONE, CLIFFORD R.
Police Officers Manuals, with Forms of Charges and Outlines of Evidence for Criminal Offences. 4th ed. Carswell, Toronto, 1964, 254.

ROSE, THOMAS, COMP.
Violence in America: A Historical and Contemporary Reader. Random House, 1969, 380.

ROUČEK, JOSEPH S.
Sociology of Crime. Greenwood Press, 1961, 551.

ROUSE, O. W., and MELNICOE, W. B.
Beat Patrol and Observation. Rev. ed. Sacramento Department of Education, Bureau of Industrial Education, 1961, 56. (California Peace Officers' Training Pub. No. 65.)

ST. JOHNSTON, T. ERIC, and CHAPMAN, SAMUEL G.
The Police Heritage in England and America. Institute for Community Development Services, Michigan State University, 1962, 45.

SALOTTOLO, LAWRENCE A.
Modern Police Service Encyclopedia: An Up-to-Date, Non-Technical Encyclopedic Handbook, Defining and Describing More Than 2,000 Separate Terms and Subjects From A to Z. Rev. ed. Arco, 1970, 1 vol., illus. (Arco Police Library.)

SAUNDERS, CHARLES B., JR.
Upgrading the American Police Education and Training for Better Law Enforcement. Brookings Institution, Washington, 1970, 182.

SAVITZ, LEONARD D.
Dilemmas in Criminology. McGraw-Hill, 1967, 130. (McGraw-Hill Social Problem Series.)

SCHAFER, STEPHEN
Theories in Criminology: Past and Present Philosophies of the Crime Problem. Random House, 1969, 335.

SCHMIDT, JACOB E.
Police Medical Dictionary. Thomas, 1968, 246.

SCHULTZ, DONALD O., and NORTON, LORAN A.
Police Operational Intelligence. Thomas, 1968, 224.

SCHUR, EDWIN M.
Our Criminal Society: The Social and Legal Sources of Crime in America. Prentice-Hall, 1969, 244. (Spectrum Book.)

SCHWARZ, J. I.
Police Roadblock Operations. Thomas, 1962, 96, illus. (Police Science Series.)

SHORT, JAMES F., COMP.
Modern Criminals. Aldine, 1970, 192, illus. (Transaction Books No. 8.)

SIEGEL, ARTHUR I., FEDERMAN, PHILIP J., and SCHULTZ, DOUGLAS G.
Professional Police-Human Relations Training. Thomas, 1963, 184.

SKOLNICK, JEROME H.
Justice Without Trial: Law Enforcement in Democratic Society. Wiley, 1966, 279.

SMIGEL, ERWIN O., and ROSS, HUGH L.
Crimes Against Bureaucracy. Van Nostrand-Reinhold, 1970, 142.

SMITH, BRUCE
Police Systems in the United States. 2nd ed., rev. Bruce Smith Jr., ed. Harper, 1960, 338, illus.

SMITH, PATRICK D., and JONES, ROBERT E.
Police English: A Manual of Grammar, Punctuation, and Spelling for Police Officers. Thomas, 1969, 77.

SMITH, R. DEAN
Computer Applications in Police Manpower Distribution. International Association of Chiefs of Police, 1964, 1 vol.

SNYDER, LeMOYNE
Homicide Investigation: Practical Information for Coroners, Police Officers, and Other Investigators. 2nd ed. Thomas, 1967, 416, illus.

SODERMAN, HARRY, and O'CONNELL, JOHN J.
Modern Criminal Investigation. 5th ed. Charles E. O'Hara, ed. Funk & Wagnalls, 1962, 559, illus.

SOUTHWESTERN LAW ENFORCEMENT INSTITUTE
Criminal Investigation. Thomas, 1962, 144.

———.
Homicide Investigation Techniques: Personal Experience Accounts of Professionals and Experts. Thomas, 1961, 144, illus.

———.
Law Enforcement and the Juvenile Offender. Thomas, 1963, 120.

———.
Police Management: For Supervisory and Administrative Personnel. Thomas, 1963, 128.

———.
Traffic Law Enforcement: A Guide for Patrolmen. Thomas, 1963, 116, illus.

SPECTER, ARLEN, and KATZ, MARVIN
Police Guide to Search and Seizure, Interrogation and Confession. Chilton, 1967, 64.

SQUIRES, HARRY A.
Guide to Police Report Writing. Thomas, 1964, 104, illus.

STAHL, DAVID, et al., eds.
The Community and Racial Crises. Practising Law Institute, New York, 1966, 364.

STINCHCOMB, JAMES D.
Opportunities in a Law Enforcement Career. Universal Publishing & Distributing, 1970, 1 vol. (VGM Career Series.)

STOREY, ROBERT G.
Our Unalienable Rights. Thomas, 1965, 160.

STUCKEY, GILBERT B.
Evidence for the Law Enforcement Officer. McGraw-Hill, 1968, 344.

STYLES, JIMMIE C., and PACE, DENNY F.
Guidelines for Work Experience Programs in the Criminal Justice System. American Association of Junior Colleges, 1969, 35.

SULLIVAN, JOHN L.
Introduction to Police Science. McGraw-Hill, 1966, 307, illus.

SUPERVISORY TECHNIQUES
Rev. ed. Davis, Santa Cruz, Calif., 1969, 363.

SUTHERLAND, EDWIN H.
Criminology. 8th ed. Lippincott, 1970, 659.

———.
White Collar Crime. Holt, 1961, 272.

SVENSSON, ARNE, and WENDEL, OTTO
Techniques of Crime Scene Investigation. 2nd ed. Joseph D. Nicol, ed. Elsevier, 1965, 540, illus.

SWEARENGEN, THOMAS F.
Tear Gas Munitions: An Analysis of Commercial Riot Gas Guns, Tear Gas Projectiles, Grenades, Small Arms Ammunition and Related Tear Gas Devices. Thomas, 1966, 596, illus.

SYKES, GRESHAM M., and DRABEK, THOMAS E., COMPS.
Law and the Lawless: A Reader in Criminology. Random House, 1969, 437.

TAFT, DONALD R.
Criminology. 4th ed. Macmillan, 1964, 552, illus.

THORWALD, JURGEN
The Century of the Detective. Harcourt, Brace & World, 1965, 500, illus.

———.
Crime and Science: The New Frontier in Criminology. Harcourt, Brace & World, 1967, 494, illus.

TIFFANY, LAWRENCE P., et al.
Detection of Crime: Stopping and Questioning, Search and Seizure, Encouragement and Entrapment. Little, Brown, 1967, 286.

TOWLER, JUBY E.
The Police Role in Racial Conflicts. Thomas, 1964, 132, illus.

———.
Practical Police Knowledge. Thomas, 1960, 216.

TURNER, WILLIAM W., ED.
Case Investigation. Aqueduct Books, Rochester, N.Y., 1965, 2 vols., illus. (Police Evidence Library.)

———, ED.
Criminalistics. Aqueduct Books, Rochester, N.Y., 1965, 518. (Police Evidence Library.)

———.
The Police Establishment. Putnam, 1968, 319.

———.
Traffic Investigation. Aqueduct Books, Rochester, N.Y., 1965, 2 vols. (Police Evidence Library.)

TYLER, GUS
Organized Crime in America: A Book of Readings. University of Michigan Press, 1962, 421. (Ann Arbor Paperbacks AA-127.)

U.S. COMMISSION ON CIVIL RIGHTS
Law Enforcement: A Report on Equal Protection in the South. USGPO, 1965, 188.

U.S. CONGRESS, SENATE COMMITTEE ON GOVERNMENT OPERATIONS (PERMANENT SUBCOMMITTEE ON INVESTIGATIONS)
Riots, Civil and Criminal Disorders. USGPO, 1967- , vols., illus.

U.S. OFFICE OF LAW ENFORCEMENT
The APCO Project: A National Training Manual and Procedure Guide for Police and Public Safety Radio Communications Personnel. USGPO, 1968, 118, illus.

U.S. PRESIDENT'S COMMISSION ON LAW ENFORCEMENT AND ADMINISTRATION OF JUSTICE
The Challenge of Crime in a Free Society: A Report. USGPO, 1967, 340, illus.

———.
Studies in Crime and Law Enforcement in Major Metropolitan Areas. USGPO, 1967, 2 vols. (Field Surveys III.)

U.S. TASK FORCE ON ASSESSMENT OF CRIME
Task Force Report: Crime and Its Impact—An Assessment. U.S. President's Commission on Law Enforcement and Administration of Justice, USGPO, 1967, 1 vol.

U.S. TASK FORCE ON THE POLICE
Task Force Report: The Police. USGPO, 1967, 239, illus.

VALLOW, HERBERT P.
Police Arrest and Search. Thomas, 1962, 119, illus.

COMMUNITY SERVICE PROGRAMS

VANDERBOSCH, CHARLES G.
Criminal Investigation. International Association of Chiefs of Police, Professional Standards Division, 1968, 303, illus.

VEDDER, CLYDE B.
Juvenile Offenders. Thomas, 1967, 264.

VOLLMER, AUGUST
The Police and Modern Society. McGrath, College Park, Md., 1969, 253. (Bureau of Public Administration, University of California Publication.)

VOLLMER, CARL
The Policeman's Manual. 2nd ed. Arco, 1960, 113.

WALKER, DANIEL
Rights in Conflict: Chicago's 7 Brutal Days. Grosset & Dunlap, 1968, 1 vol.

WALL, PATRICK M.
Eye-Witness Identification in Criminal Cases. Thomas, 1965, 248.

WALLS, HENRY
Forensic Science: An Introduction to the Science of Crime Detection. Praeger, 1968, 216, illus.

WATSON, NELSON A., and WALKER, ROBERT N.
Training Police for Work with Juveniles. International Association of Chiefs of Police, 1965, 65. (ERIC VT 009 166.)

WATSON, SAM D.
Dogs for Police Service: Programming and Training. Thomas, 1963, 89, illus.

WEISSMAN, HAROLD H., ED.
Justice and the Law in the Mobilization for Youth Experience. Association Press, 1969, 220.

WESTON, PAUL B.
Combat Shooting for Police. Thomas, 1960, 194, illus. (Police Science Series.)

———.
The Police Traffic Control Function. 2nd ed. Thomas, 1968, 260, illus.

———.
Supervision in the Administration of Justice: Police, Corrections, Courts. Thomas, 1965, 188.

WESTON, PAUL B., and WELLS, KENNETH M.
Criminal Investigation: Basic Perspectives. Prentice-Hall, 1970, 291, illus. (Prentice Series in Law Enforcement.)

WHISENAND, PAUL M.
Police Supervision: Theory and Practice. Prentice-Hall, 1971, 432.

WHISENAND, PAUL M., and CLINE, JAMES
Patrol Operations. Prentice-Hall, 1971, 128.

WHISENAND, PAUL M., and TAMARU, TUG T.
Automated Police Information Systems. Wiley, 1970, 338.

WHITAKER, BENJAMIN C. G.
The Police. Eyre & Spottiswoode, London, 1964, 224.

WHITE, RICHARDSON, and STEIN, JOHN H.
New Careers: The Patrolman Aide—Trainee's Manual. National Institute for New Careers, University Research Corp., Washington, 1968, 154.

WHITTAKER, CHARLES E., and COFFIN, WILLIAM S., JR.
Law, Order and Civil Disobedience. American Enterprise Institute for Public Policy Research, Washington, 1967, 156.

WHITTEMORE, L. H.
Cop! A Closeup of Violence and Tragedy. Holt, Rinehart & Winston, 1969, 305.

WILLIAMS, ED W.
Modern Law Enforcement and Police Science. Thomas, 1967, 392, illus.

WILSON, JAMES Q.
Varieties of Police Behavior: The Management of Law and Order in Eight Communities. Harvard University Press, 1968, 309.

WILSON, ORLANDO W.
Police Administration. 2nd ed. McGraw-Hill, 1963, 528, illus.

———.
Police Planning. 2nd ed. Thomas, 1967, 564, illus.

WOLFGANG, MARVIN E., SAVITZ, LEONARD, and JOHNSTON, NORMAN
The Sociology of Crime and Delinquency. 2nd ed. Wiley, 1970, 676, illus.

WRIGHT, R. GENE, and MARLO, JOHN A.
The Police Officer and Criminal Justice. McGraw-Hill, 1970, 222.

ZARR, MELVYN
The Bill of Rights and the Police. Oceana, 1970, 119. (Legal Almanac Series No. 40.)

RECREATIONAL LEADERSHIP

ARCO PUBLISHING COMPANY, INC.
Playground and Recreation Director's Handbook. 4th ed. Arco, 1967, 166.

———.
Teacher in Community Centers: Physical Education and Recreation. Arco, 1965, 120. (Teacher License Test Series.)

ARTZ, ROBERT M., and BERMONT, HUBERT
The National Recreation and Park Association Guide to New Approaches to Financing Parks and Recreation. Acropolis, 1970, 126, illus.

BUTLER, GEORGE D.
Introduction to Community Recreation. 4th ed. McGraw-Hill, 1967, 612, illus.

CARLSON, BERNICE W., and GINGLEND, DAVID R.
Recreation for Retarded Teenagers and Young Adults. Abingdon, 1968, 316, illus.

CARLSON, REYNOLD E.
Recreation in American Life. Wadsworth, 1963, 530, illus.

CASE, MAURICE
Recreation for Blind Adults: Organized Programs in Specialized Settings. Thomas, 1966, 228, illus.

DOELL, CHARLES E.
Elements of Park & Recreation Administration. 2nd ed. Burgess, 1968, 334, illus.

DOUGLASS, ROBERT W.
Forest Recreation. Pergamon, 1969, 335, illus.

DURAN, DOROTHY B., and DURAN, CLEMENT A.
The New Encyclopedia of Successful Program Ideas. Association Press, 1967, 511.

FITCH, EDWIN M., and SHANKLIN, JOHN E.
The Bureau of Outdoor Recreation. Praeger, 1970, 256, illus. (Library of U.S. Government Departments and Agencies.)

FRIEDBERG, M. PAUL, and BERKELEY, ELLEN P.
Play and Interplay: A Manifesto for New Design in Urban Recreational Environment. Macmillan, 1970, 167, illus.

GUGGENHEIMER, ELINOR C.
　　Planning for Parks and Recreation Needs in Urban Areas. Twayne, 1969, 261, illus.

HALL, J. TILLMAN
　　School Recreation: Its Organization, Supervision and Administration. W. C. Brown, 1966, 164, illus. (Brown Physical Education Series.)

THE INTERNATIONAL CITY MANAGERS' ASSOCIATION
　　Municipal Recreation Administration. 4th ed. ICMA, 1960, 409.

JENSEN, CLAYNE R.
　　Outdoor Recreation in America: Trends, Problems and Opportunities. Burgess, 1970, 285, illus.

KRAUS, RICHARD
　　Recreation Today: Program Planning and Leadership. Appleton-Century-Crofts, 1966, 451, illus.

LABAN, RUDOLF
　　Modern Educational Dance. 2nd ed. Praeger, 1968, 114, illus.

LUCAS, CAROL
　　Recreation in Gerontology. Thomas, 1964, 192, illus.
———.
　　Recreational Activity Development for the Aging in Homes, Hospitals, and Nursing Homes. Thomas, 1962, 68, illus.

MADOW, PAULINE, ED.
　　Recreation in America. Wilson, 1965, 206. (Reference Shelf Vol. 37, No. 2.)

McCALL, VIRGINIA, and McCALL, JOSEPH R.
　　Your Career in Parks and Recreation. Messner, 1970, 190, illus.

MEYER, HAROLD D., BRIGHTBILL, CHARLES K., and SESSOMS, H. DOUGLAS
　　Community Recreation: A Guide to Its Organization. 4th ed. Prentice-Hall, 1969, 456, illus.

NASH, JAY B.
　　Philosophy of Recreation and Leisure. W. C. Brown, 1960, 222.
———.
　　Recreation: Pertinent Readings. W. C. Brown, 1964, 280.

NATHANS, ALAN A.
　　Maintenance for Camps and Other Outdoor Recreation Facilities. Rev. ed. Association Press, 1968, 237, illus.

NATIONAL ACADEMY OF SCIENCES, NATIONAL RESEARCH COUNCIL (EXECUTIVE OFFICES)
　　A Program for Outdoor Recreation Research. NAS, 1969, 90. (Pub. No. 1727.)

RAND McNALLY GUIDEBOOK TO CAMPGROUNDS
　　Rand McNally, New York, 1959- , vols.

RATHBONE, JOSEPHINE L., and LUCAS, CAROL
　　Recreation in Total Rehabilitation. Thomas, 1970, 424.

SHIVERS, JAY S.
　　Leadership in Recreational Service. Macmillan, 1963, 510.
———.
　　Principles and Practices of Recreational Services. Macmillan, 1967, 507.

SMITH, CLODUS R., PARTAIN, LLOYD, and CHAMPLIN, JAMES
　　Rural Recreation for Profit. Interstate, 1968, 304, illus.

U.S. CHILDREN'S BUREAU.
　　Handbook for Recreation. Rev. ed. HEW, Social Security Administration (Children's Bureau), 1960, 148, illus. (Pub. No. 231.)

U.S. FOREST SERVICE
　　Outdoor Recreation in the National Forests. USFS, 1965, 106, illus. (USDA Agricultural Information Bulletin No. 301.)

U.S. OFFICE OF EDUCATION, VOCATIONAL AND TECHNICAL EDUCATION DIVISION
　　Recreation Program Leadership: A Suggested 2-Year Post High School Curriculum. USOE, 1969, 87, illus. (OE-87042.)

WILLIAMS, ARTHUR M.
　　Recreation in the Senior Years. Association Press, 1962, 252.

SOCIAL SERVICE

AMERICAN PUBLIC WELFARE ASSOCIATION
　　Public Welfare Directory.... APWA, Chicago, 1940- , vols., illus., annual.
———.
　　Round Table Reader. Malvin Morton, ed. APWA, Chicago, 1968, 280.

ANTHONY, HELEN
　　Medical Social Work: A Career in Hospital & Community. Educational Explorers, Reading, England, 1968, 119, illus.

ARCO PUBLISHING COMPANY, INC.
　　Social Case Worker. 2nd ed. Arco, 1967, 270.

ARON, RAYMOND
　　Main Currents in Sociological Thought. Basic Books, 1965, 1 vol.

ASBELL, BERNARD
　　Careers in Urban Affairs: Six Young People Talk About Their Professions in the Inner City. Wyden, New York, 1970, 111.

BAGDIKIAN, BEN H.
　　In the Midst of Plenty: The Poor in America. Beacon Press, 1964, 207, illus.

BAIN, READ, ED.
　　Sociology: Introductory Readings. Lippincott, 1962, 483.

BARDILL, DONALD R., and RYAN, FRANCIS J.
　　Family Group Casework. Rev. ed. Catholic University of America Press, 1969, 69.

BECKER, HOWARD S., ED.
　　Social Problems: A Modern Approach. Wiley, 1966, 770.

BELL, EARL H., and SIRJAMAKI, JOHN
　　Social Foundations of Human Behavior: Introduction to the Study of Sociology. 2nd ed. Harper & Row, 1965, 628, illus.

BELL, NORMAN W., and VOGEL, EZRA F., EDS.
　　A Modern Introduction to the Family. Rev. ed. Free Press, 1968, 758.

BELL, WINIFRED
　　Aid to Dependent Children. Columbia University Press, 1965, 248.

BERELSON, BERNARD, and STEINER, GARY A.
　　Human Behavior: Shorter Edition with Teacher's Manual. Harcourt, Brace & World, 1967, 225, illus. (Curriculum-Related Books.)

BIERSTEDT, ROBERT
　　The Social Order. 3rd ed. McGraw-Hill, 1970, 640, illus.

COMMUNITY SERVICE PROGRAMS

BLITSTEN, DOROTHY R.
    The World of the Family: A Comparative Study of Family Organizations in Their Social and Cultural Settings. Random House, 1963, 303.

BORNET, VAUGHN D.
    Welfare in America. University of Oklahoma Press, 1960, 319, illus.

BRADFORD, KIRK A.
    Existentialism and Casework: The Relationship Between Social Casework Theory and the Philosophy and Psychotherapy of Existentialism. Exposition Press, 1969, 82.

BROCK, MARGARET G.
    Social Work in the Hospital Organization. University of Toronto Press, 1969, 117.

CAMPBELL, THOMAS F.
    SASS: Fifty Years of Social Work Education. Case Western Reserve University Press, 1967, 131, illus.

CAVAN, RUTH S.
    The American Family. 4th ed. Crowell, 1969, 556, illus.

CHAMBERS, CLARKE A.
    Seedtime of Reform: American Social Service and Social Action, 1918-1933. University of Minnesota Press, 1963, 326.

CLARK, KENNETH B., and HOPKINS, JEANETTE
    A Relevant War Against Poverty: A Study of Community Action Programs and Observable Social Change. Harper & Row, 1969, 275.

CLEGG, REED K.
    The Welfare World. Thomas, 1968, 128.

COLLINS, ALICE H.
    The Lonely and Afraid: Counseling the Hard to Reach. Odyssey, 1969, 270.

THE COUNCIL ON SOCIAL WORK EDUCATION
    The Community Services Technician: Guide for Associate Degree Programs in the Community and Social Services. CSWE, New York, 1970, 35.

DAVID, GERSON
    Patterns of Social Functioning in Families with Marital and Parent-Child Problems. University of Toronto Press, 1967, 297.

DAVIS, FLOYD J.
    Social Problems: Enduring Major Issues and Social Change. Free Press, 1970, 388.

DAWTRY, FRANK
    Social Problems of Drug Abuse: A Guide for Social Workers. Butterworth, 1968, 115, illus.

DE GRAZIA, ALFRED, and GURR, TED
    American Welfare. New York University Press, 1961, 470.

DIRECTORY OF SOCIAL AND HEALTH AGENCIES OF NEW YORK CITY
    Columbia University Press, 1883- , irregular.

DUHL, LEONARD J., ED.
    The Urban Condition: People and Policy in the Metropolis. Basic Books, 1963, 410.

EDWARDS, DEANE B., ED.
    White Fields for Harvest: Social Welfare in Community Service. Aaron C. Butler Jr., ed. Herald, Independence, Mo., 1970, 442.

EINSTEIN, GERTRUDE, ED.
    Learning to Apply New Concepts to Casework Practice: A Staff Development Seminar. Family Service Association of America, 1968, 135.

EISENSTADT, SHMUEL N., ED.
    Comparative Social Problems. Free Press, 1964, 463.

ELKIN, ROBERT
    A Conceptual Base for Defining Health and Welfare Services.... Family Service Association of America, 1967, 1 vol.

ETZIONI, AMITAI, ED.
    The Semi-Professions and Their Organization: Teachers, Nurses, Social Workers. Free Press, 1969, 328.

FAIRCHILD, HENRY P., ED.
    Dictionary of Sociology and Related Sciences. Littlefield, Adams, Totowa, N.J., 1966, 342.

FAMILY SERVICE ASSOCIATION OF AMERICA.
    Casework Treatment of the Family Unit. FSAA, 1965, 64.

———.
    The Expanding Theoretical Base of Casework. FSAA, 1964, 71.

———.
    Position on Use of Social Work Assistants in Family Service Agencies: Report of the Subcommittee on Use of Social Work Assistants of the FSAA Personnel Committee. FSAA, 1968, 1 vol.

———.
    Range and Emphases of a Family Service Program. FSAA, 1963, 38.

———.
    Trends in Field Work Instruction: Articles Reprinted from Social Casework, 1955-1965. FSAA, 1966, 71.

FARIS, ROBERT E. L., ED.
    Handbook of Modern Sociology. Rand McNally, 1964, 1088, illus. (Rand McNally Sociology Series.)

FELDMAN, FRANCIS L., and SCHERZ, FRANCES H.
    Family Social Welfare: Helping Troubled Families. Atherton Press, 1967, 386.

FERGUSON, ELIZABETH A.
    Social Work: An Introduction. 2nd ed. Lippincott, 1969, 664.

FERMAN, LOUIS A., KORNBLUH, JOYCE L., and HABER, ALAN, EDS.
    Poverty in America: Book of Readings. Rev. ed. University of Michigan Press, 1968, 669, illus.

FINK, ARTHUR E., ANDERSON, C. W., and CONOVER, MERRILL B.
    The Field of Social Work. 5th ed. Holt, Rinehart & Winston, 1968, 534.

FOREN, ROBERT, and BAILEY, ROYSTON
    Authority in Social Casework. Pergamon, 1968, 310.

FRIEDLANDER, WALTER A.
    Introduction to Social Welfare. 3rd ed. Prentice-Hall, 1968, 605.

GARTON, NINA R., and OTTO, HERBERT A.
    The Development of Theory and Practice in Social Casework. Thomas, 1964, 172.

GAY, KATHLYN
    Careers in Social Service. Messner, 1969, 192, illus.

GEISMAR, LUDWIG L.
    Preventive Intervention in Social Work. Scarecrow Press, 1969, 129.

GELL, FRANK
    The Black Badge: Confessions of a Caseworker. Harper & Row, 1969, 226.

GILBERT, NEIL
    Clients or Constituents: Community Action in the War on Poverty. Jossey-Bass, 1970, 208. (Jossey-Bass Behavioral Science Series.)

GIST, NOEL P., and FAVA, SYLVIA F.
    Urban Society. 5th ed. Crowell, 1964, 623, illus.

SOCIAL SERVICE

GLANZ, EDWARD C., and HAYES, ROBERT W.
  Groups in Guidance. 2nd ed. Allyn & Bacon, 1967, 342, illus.

GOLD, HARRY, and SCARPITTI, FRANK R., EDS.
  Combating Social Problems: Techniques of Intervention. Holt, Rinehart & Winston, 1967, 580, illus.

GOLDBERG, GERTRUDE S., et al.
  New Careers: The Social Service Aide, A Manual for Trainees. National Institute for New Careers, University Research Corp., 1968, 182.

GOODE, WILLIAM J.
  The Family. Prentice-Hall, 1964, 120, illus. (Foundations of Modern Sociology Series.)
  ———, ED.
  Readings on the Family and Society. Prentice-Hall, 1964, 242. (Prentice-Hall Readings in Modern Sociology Series.)

GOODRICH, CHARLES H., OLENDZKI, MARGARET C., and READER, GEORGE G.
  Welfare Medical Care: An Experiment. Harvard University Press, 1970, 343.

GOULD, JULIUS, and KOLB, WILLIAM L., EDS.
  A Dictionary of the Social Sciences. Macmillan, 1964, 761.

GOULDNER, ALVIN W., and GOULDNER, HELEN P.
  Modern Sociology: An Introduction to the Study of Human Interaction. Harcourt, Brace & World, 1963, 683.

GROSSER, CHARLES F.
  Helping Youth: A Study of Six Community Organization Programs. HEW, 1968, 72. (JD Pub. No. 1006.)

GROSSER, CHARLES F., HENRY, WILLIAM E., and KELLY, JAMES G., EDS.
  Nonprofessionals in the Human Services. Jossey-Bass, 1969, 263. (Jossey-Bass Behavioral Science Series.)

HALL, PERRY B.
  Family Credit Counseling: An Emerging Community Service. Family Service Association of America, 1968, 127.

HARRINGTON, MICHAEL
  The Other America: Poverty in the United States. Macmillan, 1962, 191.

HASKELL, MARK A.
  The New Careers Concept: Potential for Public Employment of the Poor. Praeger, 1969, 115. (Praeger Special Studies in U.S. Economic and Social Development.)

HERMAN, MELVIN, and MUNK, MICHAEL
  Decision-Making in Poverty Programs: Case Studies from Youth-Work Agencies. Columbia University Press, 1968, 181.

HOLLIS, FLORENCE
  A Typology of Casework Treatment. Family Service Association of America, 1968, 36.

HORTON, PAUL B., and LESLIE, GERALD R.
  The Sociology of Social Problems. 3rd ed. Appleton-Century-Crofts, 1965, 742, illus. (ACC Sociology Series.)

HOSELITZ, BERTHOLD F., ED.
  A Reader's Guide to the Social Sciences. Rev. ed. Free Press, 1970, 425.

INKELES, ALEX
  What is Sociology? An Introduction to the Discipline and Profession. Prentice-Hall, 1964, 120. (Foundations of Modern Sociology Series.)

INTERNATIONAL CONFERENCE ON SOCIAL WELFARE
  Social Welfare and Human Rights. Columbia University Press, 1969, 398.

INTERNATIONAL COUNCIL ON SOCIAL WELFARE.
  Urban Development: Its Implications for Social Welfare.... Columbia University Press, 1967, 462.

JEFFERS, CAMILLE
  Living Poor: A Participant Observer Study of Priorities and Choices. Ann Arbor Publishers, 1967, 123.

KAHN, ALFRED J.
  Theory and Practice of Social Planning. Russell Sage Foundation, New York, 1969, 348.

KING, CLARENCE
  Working with People in Community Action: An International Casebook. Association Press, 1965, 192.

KIRKPATRICK, CLIFFORD
  The Family as Process and Institution. 2nd ed. Ronald, 1963, 705, illus.

KLEIN, PHILIP
  From Philanthropy to Social Welfare. Jossey-Bass, 1968, 328.

KOHS, SAMUEL C.
  The Roots of Social Work. Association Press, 1966, 189.

KONOPKA, GISELA
  Group Work in the Institution: A Modern Challenge. Rev. ed. Association Press, 1970, 304.
  ———.
  Social Group Work: A Helping Process. Prentice-Hall, 1963, 293.

KOSA, JOHN
  Poverty and Health. Harvard University Press, 1969, 449, illus.

KRAMER, RALPH M.
  Participation of the Poor: Comparative Community Case Studies in the War on Poverty. Prentice-Hall, 1969, 273.

KRIESBERG, LOUIS
  Mothers in Poverty: A Study of Fatherless Families. Aldine, 1970, 356.

LANDIS, JUDSON R., ED.
  Current Perspectives on Social Problems. Wadsworth, 1966, 282.

LAZARFIELD, PAUL F., SEWELL, WILLIAM H., and WILENSKY, HAROLD L., EDS.
  The Uses of Sociology. Basic Books, 1967, 902.

LENNARD, HENRY L.
  Patterns in Human Interaction. Jossey-Bass, 1969, 224, illus.

LENSKI, GERHARD E.
  Human Societies: A New Introduction to Sociology. McGraw-Hill, 1970, 450, illus.

LEVINE, MURRAY, and LEVINE, ADELINE
  A Social History of Helping Services: Clinic, Court, School, and Community. Appleton, 1970, 1 vol. (Century Psychology Series.)

LEVITAN, SAR A.
  Programs in Aid of the Poor for the 1970's. Johns Hopkins Press, 1969, 117, illus. (Policy Studies in Employment and Welfare No. 1.)

LIFTON, WALTER M.
  Working with Groups: Group Process and Individual Growth. Rev. ed. Wiley, 1966, 288.

LYNTON, EDITH F.
  The Sub-Professional: From Concepts to Careers. National Committee on Employment of Youth, New York, 1967, 177.

COMMUNITY SERVICE PROGRAMS

MACAROV, DAVID
    Incentives to Work: The Effect of Unearned Income. Jossey-Bass, 1970, 264. (Jossey-Bass Behavioral Science Series.)

MARTINDALE, DON A.
    American Society. Van Nostrand, 1960, 570. (Van Nostrand Sociology Series.)

MARTINSON, FLOYD M.
    Family in Society. Dodd, Mead, 1970, 395, illus.

MAY, EDGAR
    The Wasted Americans: Cost of Our Welfare Dilemma. Harper & Row, 1964, 227, illus.

McCULLOUGH, M. K., and ELY, P. J.
    Social Work with Groups. Routledge & Keegan, Paul, London, (Humanities Press, dist.), 1969, 118. (Library of Social Work.)

McDONAGH, EDWARD C., and SIMPSON, JON E., EDS.
    Social Problems: Persistent Challenges. Holt, Rinehart & Winston, 1965, 604, illus.

MEGGINSON, LEON C.
    Human Resources: Cases and Concepts. Harcourt, Brace & World, 1968, 268.

MERTON, ROBERT K., and NISBET, ROBERT A., EDS.
    Contemporary Social Problems. 2nd ed. Harcourt, Brace & World, 1966, 847, illus.

MEYER, CAROL H.
    Social Work Practice: A Response to the Urban Crisis. Free Press, 1970, 227.

———.
    Staff Development in Public Welfare Agencies. Columbia University Press, 1966, 230.

MIDDLEMAN, RUTH R.
    The Non-Verbal Method in Working with Groups. Association Press, 1968, 285.

MILLER, ROGER R., ED.
    Race, Research and Reason: Social Work Perspectives— Report of the Institute on Research Toward Improving Race Relations, held at Airlie House, Warrenton, Virginia, August 13-16, 1967. National Association of Social Workers, 1969, 190.

MILLER, SEYMOUR M., and RIESSMAN, FRANK
    Social Class and Social Policy. Basic Books, 1968, 302.

MINUCHIN, SALVADOR, et al.
    Families of the Slums: An Exploration of Their Structure and Treatment. Basic Books, 1967, 460, illus.

MITCHELL, GEOFFREY D., ED.
    A Dictionary of Sociology. Aldine, 1968, 224.

———.
    A Hundred Years of Sociology. Aldine, 1968, 310. (Hundred Years Series.)

MONAHAN, FERGUS T.
    A Study of Nonprofessional Personnel in Social Work: The Army Social Work Specialist. Catholic University of America Press, 1960, 201.

MONROE, DONALD, and KEITH, DONALD
    How to Succeed in Community Service. Lippincott, 1962, 283.

MOYNIHAN, DANIEL P., ED.
    On Understanding Poverty: Perspectives From the Social Sciences. Basic Books, 1969, 425. (Perspectives on Poverty No. 1.)

MYRAN, GUNDER A.
    Community Services in the Community College. American Association of Junior Colleges, 1969, 60.

NATIONAL ASSOCIATION OF SOCIAL WORKERS
    Changing Services for Changing Clients. Columbia University Press, 1969, 127.

———.
    Encyclopedia of Social Work. NASW, 1965, 1060.

———.
    Goals of Public Social Policy. Rev. ed. NASW, 1966, 54.

NATIONAL ASSOCIATION OF SOCIAL WORKERS, COMMISSION ON SOCIAL WORK PRACTICE, SUBCOMMITTEE ON UTILIZATION OF PERSONNEL
    Utilization of Personnel in Social Work: Those with Full Professional Education and Those Without—Final Report. NASW, 1962, 40.

NATIONAL CONFERENCE ON SOCIAL WELFARE
    The Social Welfare Forum: Official Proceedings of the Annual Forum. NCSW, New York, 1874- , vols., illus.

———.
    Social Work Practice. Columbia University Press, 1968, 1 vol.

NATIONAL COUNCIL ON ILLEGITIMACY
    Effective Services for Unmarried Parents and Their Children: Innovative Community Approaches. NCI, New York, 1968, 111.

NATIONAL STUDY SERVICE
    Family Credit Counseling: An Emerging Community Service—A Full Report of a Study of Family Credit Counseling Provided Through Nonprofit Community-Based Programs. Family Service Association of America, 1968, 127.

NELSON, LOWRY
    Rural Sociology: Its Origin and Growth in the United States. University of Minnesota Press, 1969, 221.

NICHOLDS, ELIZABETH
    In-Service Casework Training. Columbia University Press, 1966, 308.

———.
    A Primer of Social Casework. Columbia University Press, 1960, 181.

NORTHEN, HELEN
    Social Work with Groups. Columbia University Press, 1969, 270.

O'BRIEN, JOHN A., COMP.
    Family Planning in an Exploding Population. Hawthorn, 1968, 222.

OTTO, HERBERT A., ED.
    Human Potentialities: The Challenge and the Promise. W. H. Green, St. Louis, Mo., 1968, 217.

PANIAGUA, LITA, and JACKSON, VIVIAN C.
    Role-Play in New Careers Training: A Technique for Developing Paraprofessional-Professional Teamwork in Human Service Agencies. New York University, New Careers Training Laboratory, 1968, 50.

PARAD, HOWARD J., ED.
    Crisis Intervention: Selected Readings. Family Service Association of America, 1965, 368.

PARSONS, TALCOTT
    Sociological Theory and Modern Society. Free Press, 1967, 564.

PEARL, ARTHUR, and REISSMAN, FRANK
    New Careers for the Poor: The Nonprofessional in Human Service. Free Press, 1965, 287.

PERLMAN, HELEN H., ED.
    Helping: Charlotte Towle on Social Work and Social Casework. University of Chicago Press, 1969, 307, illus. (Midway Paperback Texts.)

———.
    So You Want to be A Social Worker. Rev. ed. Harper & Row, 1970, 177.

PERLOFF, HARVEY S., ED.
The Quality of the Urban Environment: Essays on "New Resources" in an Urban Age. Johns Hopkins Press, 1969, 332, illus.

PFEIFFER, WILLIAM J., and JONES, JOHN E.
Handbook of Structured Experiences for Human Relations Training. University Associates Press, Iowa City, 1969, 1970, 2 vols.

POMEROY, RICHARD, et al.
Studies in the Use of Health Services by Families on Welfare: Utilization by Publicly-Assisted Families. City University of New York, Center for the Study of Urban Problems, 1969, 192.

PUMPHREY, RALPH E., and PUMPHREY, MURIEL W., EDS.
The Heritage of American Social Work: Readings in Its Philosophical and Institutional Development. Columbia University Press, 1961, 452.

RAAB, EARL, and SELZNICK, GERTRUDE J.
Major Social Problems. 2nd ed. Harper & Row, 1964, 594, illus.

REID, WILLIAM J., and SHYNE, ANN W.
Brief and Extended Casework. Columbia University Press, 1969, 270.

RICHAN, WILLARD C., ED.
Human Services and Social Work Responsibility: 1968 NASW Professional Symposium. National Association of Social Workers, 1969, 382.

RIESSMAN, FRANK, and POPPER, HERMINE I.
Up From Poverty: New Career Ladders for Non Professionals. Harper & Row, 1968, 332.

ROSENBLOOM, RICHARD S., and MARRIS, ROBIN, EDS.
Social Innovation in the City: New Enterprises for Community Development. Harvard University Press, 1969, 200.

SAGER, CLIFFORD J., BRAYBOY, THOMAS L., and WAXENBERG, BARBARA R.
Black Ghetto Family in Therapy: A Laboratory Experience. Grove Press, 1970, 245.

SCHAFFER, ALBERT, et al.
Understanding Social Problems. Merrill, 1970, 358. (Merrill Sociology Series.)

SCOTT, CARL
Ethnic Minorities in Social Work Education. Council on Social Work Education, New York, 1970, 1 vol.

SELIGMAN, BEN B.
Permanent Poverty: An American Syndrome. Quadrangle Books, 1968, 238.

SHATZ, EUNICE, and FISHMAN, JACOB R.
New Careers: Generic Issues in the Human Services, A Sourcebook for Trainees. National Institute for New Careers, University Research Corp., Washington, 1968, 199.

SHERRARD, THOMAS D., ED.
Social Welfare and Urban Problems. Columbia University Press, 1968, 210.

SIMMONS, HAROLD E.
Protective Services for Children: A Public Social Welfare Responsibility. General Welfare Publications, Sacramento, 1968, 163, illus.

SIMPSON, GEORGE
People in Families: Sociology, Psychoanalysis and the American Family. World, 1966, 554. (Meridian Book.)

SIRJAMAKI, JOHN
The Sociology of Cities. Random House, 1964, 328, illus.

SMALLEY, RUTH E.
Theory for Social Work Practice. Columbia University Press, 1967, 327.

SMITH, EDMUND A.
Social Welfare Principles and Concepts. Association Press, 1965, 478.

SMITH, RUSSELL E., and ZIETZ, DOROTHY
American Social Welfare Institutions. Wiley, 1970, 363.

SOCIAL WORK PRACTICE, 1967
Columbia University Press, 1967, 255.

SOONG, ROBERT K., et al.
Social Service Aide Project for the Education and Training of Paraprofessionals: Final Report. YMCA of Metropolitan Chicago, 1969, 149. (ERIC ED 035 062.)

STEIN, HERMAN D., ED.
The Crisis in Welfare in Cleveland: Report of the Mayor's Commission. Case Western Reserve University Press, 1969, 173, illus.
———, ED.
Social Theory and Social Invention. Case Western Reserve University Press, 1968, 187

STINCHCOMB, JAMES D., and DENNARD, CLEVELAND L., EDS.
Community Service and Other New Specialists. J. G. Ferguson, 1970, 292. (Career Opportunities for Technicians and Specialists Vol. 5.)

STREAN, HERBERT S.
The Casework Digest. Scarecrow Press, 1969, 207.

SUEDFELD, PETER
Social Processes. W. C. Brown, 1966, 48. (Psychology Self-Selection Series.)

SULLENGER, THOMAS E., ED.
Neglected Areas in Family Living. Christopher Publishing House, Boston, 1960, 447.

SUNDQUIST, JAMES L., ED.
On Fighting Poverty: Perspectives from Experience. Basic Books, 1969, 256. (Perspectives on Poverty No. 2.)

THEODORSON, GEORGE A., and THEODORSON, ACHILLES G.
A Modern Dictionary of Sociology. Crowell, 1969, 469.

THOMAS, EDWIN J., ED.
Behavioral Science for Social Workers. Free Press, 1967, 512.

THOMAS, ROSE C.
Public Service Careers Program Training Manual for Case Aide Trainees. New York City Department of Social Services, Office of Training, 1968, 49.

TIMMS, NOEL
The Language of Social Casework. Routledge & Keegan, Paul, London, (Humanities Press, dist.), 1968, 116. (Library of Social Work.)

TITMUSS, RICHARD M.
Commitment to Welfare. Pantheon, 1968, 272.

TURNER, JOHN B., ED.
Neighborhood Organization for Community Action. National Association of Social Workers, 1968, 220.

ULMER, MELVILLE J.
The Welfare State, U.S.A.: An Exploration in and Beyond the New Economics. Houghton Mifflin, 1969, 203.

U.S. CHILDREN'S BUREAU.
Social Services for Children and Families in Your State. USGPO, 1969, 1 vol.

U.S. DEPARTMENT OF AGRICULTURE, FEDERAL EXTENSION SERVICE
Training Home Economics Program Assistants to Work

COMMUNITY SERVICE PROGRAMS

with Low Income Families. USGPO, 1965, 112. (ERIC VT 002 571.)

U.S. DEPARTMENT OF HEALTH, EDUCATION AND WELFARE
Toward a Social Report. HEW, 1969, 101.

VINCENT, CLARK E.
Unmarried Mothers. Free Press, 1961, 308.

VOILAND, ALICE L.
Family Casework Diagnosis. Columbia University Press, 1962, 369.

WEISSMAN, HAROLD H., ED.
Community Development in the Mobilization for Youth Experience. Association Press, 1969, 190.

WERNER, HAROLD D.
A Rational Approach to Social Casework. Association Press, 1965, 160.

WHITE, CARL M.
Sources of Information in the Social Sciences: A Guide to the Literature. Bedminister Press, 1964, 498.

WINCH, ROBERT F.
The Modern Family. Rev. ed. Holt, Rinehart & Winston, 1963, 782, illus.

WOODROOFE, KATHLEEN
From Charity to Social Work: In England and the United States. University of Toronto Press, 1968, 247.

YOUNGDAHL, BENJAMIN E.
Social Action and Social Work. Association Press, 1966, 190.

ZALD, MAYER N., ED.
Social Welfare Institutions: A Sociological Reader. Wiley, 1965, 671.

TEACHER AIDE

ADLER, SOL
The Health and Education of the Economically Deprived Child. W. H. Green, St. Louis, Mo., 1968, 172.

AMERICAN ASSOCIATION FOR HEALTH, PHYSICAL EDUCATION AND RECREATION
After-School Games and Sports: Grades 4-5-6. AAHPER, 1964, 60. (Classroom Teacher Series.)

———.
Classroom Activities. Rev. ed. AAHPER, 1963, 64. (Classroom Teacher Series.)

———.
Desirable Athletic Competition for Children of Elementary School Age. AAHPER, 1968, 36.

———.
Health Appraisal of School Children. 4th ed. AAHPER, 1969, 40.

———.
Healthful School Environment. AAHPER, 1969, 296.

———.
Rhythmic Activities: Grades K-6. AAHPER, 1964, 60. (Classroom Teacher Series.)

AMOS, WILLIAM, and OREM, REGINALD C.
Managing Student Behavior. W. H. Green, St. Louis, Mo., 1967, 144.

ARCO PUBLISHING COMPANY, INC.
Early Childhood Education: Teaching Area Exam for the National Teacher Examination. Arco, 1967, 128. (Professional Career Exam Series.)

ASHLOCK, PATRICK, and STEPHEN, ALBERTA
Educational Therapy in the Elementary School: An Educational Approach to the Learning Problems of Children. Thomas, 1967, 120, illus.

ASSOCIATION OF TEACHERS OF MATHEMATICS
Notes on Mathematics in Primary Schools. Cambridge University Press, 1967, 340, illus.

ATWELL, GLADSTONE, ED.
The Manual for Utilization of Auxiliary Personnel. New York City Board of Education, 1970, 96.

AUERBACK, ALINE B.
The Why and How of Discipline. Rev. ed. Child Study Association of America, 1969, 40.

BAIR, MEDILL, and WOODWARD, RICHARD G.
Team Teaching in Action. Houghton Mifflin, 1964, 229, illus.

BANK STREET COLLEGE OF EDUCATION.
Directory of Institutions of Higher Learning Offering Training Programs for Auxiliary Personnel in Education. Bank Street College, New York, 1969, 105.

BARNOUW, ELSA, and SWAN, ARTHUR
Adventures with Children in Nursery School and Kindergarten. Agathon Press, New York, 1970, 276.

BASSETT, GEORGE W.
Innovation in Primary Education: A Study of Recent Developments in Primary Education in England and U.S.A. Wiley-Interscience, 1970, 209.

BECKWITH, MARY
The Effective Elementary School Teacher. Parker, West Nyack, N.Y., 1968, 212, illus.

BELLACK, ARNO A., et al.
The Language of the Classroom. Teachers College Press, 1966, 274, illus.

BENNETT, WILLIAM S., and FALK, R. FRANK
New Careers and Urban Schools: A Sociological Study of Teacher and Teacher Aide Roles. Holt, Rinehart & Winston, 1970, 220.

BEREITER, CARL, and ENGELMANN, SIEGFRIED
Teaching Disadvantaged Children in the Preschool. Prentice-Hall, 1966, 312, illus.

BERKOWITZ, PEARL H., and ROTHMAN, ESTHER P.
The Disturbed Child: Recognition and Psychoeducational Therapy in the Classroom. New York University Press, 1960, 204, illus.

BERNARD, HAROLD W.
Mental Health in the Classroom. McGraw-Hill, 1970, 549.

BEYER, EVELYN
Teaching Young Children. Pegasus, New York, 1968, 235, illus.

BIDDLE, BRUCE J., and ROSSI, PETER H., EDS.
New Media and Education: Their Impact on Society. Aldine, 1966, 417.

BIRCH, HERBERT G., and GUSSOW, JOAN D.
Disadvantaged Children: Health, Nutrition, and School Failure. Harcourt, Brace & World, 1970, 322, illus.

BLACKIE, JOHN H.
Inside the Primary School. HMSO, London, 1967, 146.

BORDAN, SYLVIA D.
Plays as Teaching Tools in the Elementary School. Parker, West Nyack, N.Y., 1970, 249, illus.

BORGER, ROBERT, and SEABORNE, A. E. M.
The Psychology of Learning. Penguin, 1966, 249. (Pelican A829.)

BOTT, R., et al.
The Teaching of Young Children: Some Applications of Piaget's Learning Theory. Schocken Books, 1970, 192, illus.

BOTTOM, RAYMOND
   The Education of Disadvantaged Children. Parker, West Nyack, N.Y., 1970, 225.

BOWER, ELI M.
   Early Identification of Emotionally Handicapped Children in School. 2nd ed. Thomas, 1968, 260, illus.

BOWMAN, GARDA W., and KLOPF, GORDON J.
   New Careers and Roles in the American School. Bank Street College of Education, New York, 1968, 256.

BREMBECK, COLE S.
   Social Foundations of Education: A Cross-Cultural Approach. Wiley, 1966, 540, illus.

BRENNER, MARCELLA, et al.
   Teacher Aides in Action in Elementary and Secondary Schools. Washington School of Psychiatry, 1969, 58.

BRENTON, MYRON
   What's Happened to Teacher? Coward-McCann, 1970, 280.

BROWN, JAMES W.
   A-V Instructional Materials Manual. 2nd ed. McGraw-Hill, 1965, 1 vol.

BROWN, JAMES W., LEWIS, RICHARD B., and HARCLEROAD, FRED F.
   A-V Instruction: Media and Methods. 3rd ed. McGraw-Hill, 1969, 621, illus.

BRUNER, JEROME S.
   The Process of Education. Harvard University Press, 1960, 97.

———.
   Toward a Theory of Instruction. Harvard University Press, 1966, 176.

BURACK, ABRAHAM S., ED.
   One Hundred Plays for Children: An Anthology of Non-Royalty One-Act Plays. Plays, Boston, 1970, 886.

BURTON, WILLIAM H.
   The Guidance of Learning Activities: A Summary of the Principles of Teaching Based on the Growth of the Learner. 3rd ed. Appleton-Century-Crofts, 1962, 581.

BUSH, CLIFFORD L., and HUEBNER, MILDRED H.
   Strategies for Reading in the Elementary School. Macmillan, 1970, 380, illus.

CALDWELL, EDSON
   Group Techniques for the Classroom Teacher. Science Research Associates, 1960, 86.

CARLSON, ELLIOT
   Learning Through Games: A New Approach to Problem Solving. Public Affairs Press, Washington, 1969, 183.

CARR, CONSTANCE, et al.
   A New Careers Guide for Trainers of Education Auxiliaries. New York University, New Careers Training Laboratory, 1968, 190.

CHASNOFF, ROBERT, ED.
   Elementary Curriculum: A Book of Readings. Pitman, 1964, 656.

CHAUNCEY, HENRY, ED.
   Soviet Preschool Education. Holt, Rinehart & Winston, 1969, 2 vols.

CLARK, DONALD H., ED.
   The Psychology of Education. Free Press, 1967, 274.

CLARK, DONALD H., GOLDSMITH, ARLENE, and PUGH, CLEMENTINE
   Those Children: Case Studies from the Inner-City School. Wadsworth, 1970, 334, illus.

COHEN, S. ALAN
   Teach Them All to Read: Theory, Methods and Materials for Teaching the Disadvantaged. Random House, 1969, 329.

CONANT, JAMES B.
   Slums and Suburbs.... McGraw-Hill, 1961, 147.

CORDASCO, FRANCESCO, and BUCCHIONI, EUGENE, EDS.
   Puerto Rican Children in Mainland Schools: A Source Book for Teachers. Scarecrow Press, 1968, 465, illus.

COWLES, MILLY
   Perspectives in the Education of Disadvantaged Children. International Textbook, 1967, 314. (World Series in Educational Psychology and Special Education.)

CRAIG, JENNIE E.
   Creative Art Activities: A Handbook for the Elementary Teacher. International Textbook, 1967, 302.

CRAIG, ROBERT C.
   The Psychology of Learning in the Classroom. Macmillan, 1966, 85. (Psychological Foundations of Education Series.)

CRAM, DAVID
   Explaining "Teaching Machines" and Programming. Fearon, San Francisco, 1961, 86, illus.

CRONBACH, LEE J.
   Educational Psychology. 2nd ed. Harcourt, Brace & World, 1963, 706, illus.

CROW, LESTER DONALD, MURRAY, WALTER I., and SMYTHE, HUGH H.
   Educating the Culturally Disadvantaged Child: Principles and Programs. McKay, 1966, 306, illus.

CRUICKSHANK, WILLIAM M., and JOHNSON, G. ORVILLE, EDS.
   Education of Exceptional Children and Youth. 2nd ed. Prentice-Hall, 1967, 730, illus. (Prentice-Hall Psychology Series.)

CUBAN, LARRY
   To Make A Difference: Teaching in the Inner City. Free Press, 1970, 261, illus.

CULLUM, ALBERT
   Push Back the Desks. Citation Press, 1967, 224, illus.

DADY, MILAN B., ED.
   An In-Service Training Manual for Teacher-Aides. Morehead State University, Research and Development Office, 1969, 220.

DARROW, HELEN F., and VAN ALLEN, R.
   Independent Activities for Creative Learning. Teachers College Press, 1961, 110, illus. (Practical Suggestions for Teaching No. 21.)

DAWSON, HELAINE
   On the Outskirts of Hope: Educating Youth from Poverty Areas. McGraw-Hill, 1968, 329, illus.

DE KIEFFER, R. E., and COCHRAN, LEE W.
   Manual of Audio-Visual Techniques. Prentice-Hall, 1962, 254, illus.

deREGNIERS, BEATRICE S., MOORE, EVA, and WHITE, MARY M., Comps.
   Poems Children Will Sit Still For: A Selection for the Primary Grades. Citation Press, 1969, 128.

DEWEY, JOHN
   The School and Society. University of Chicago Press, 1967, 1 vol.

DE YOUNG, CHRIS A., and WYNN, RICHARD
   American Education. 6th ed. McGraw-Hill, 1968, 550.

DOWDELL, DOROTHY, and DOWDELL, JOSEPH
   Your Career in Teaching. Messner, 1967, 191, illus.

EAKIN, MARY K.
   Subject Index to Books for Intermediate Grades. 3rd ed. American Library Association, 1963, 320.

———.
   Subject Index to Books for Primary Grades. 3rd ed. American Library Association, 1967, 122.

COMMUNITY SERVICE PROGRAMS

EBOCH, SIDNEY C.
    Operating Audio-Visual Equipment. Rev. ed. International Textbook, 1968, 76, illus.

EDUCATORS' GUIDE TO FREE FILMS
    Educators' Progress Service, Randolph, Wis., 1941- , Vol. 1- .

EDUCATORS' GUIDE TO FREE FILMSTRIPS
    Educators' Progress Service, Randolph, Wis., 1949- , Vol. 1- .

ENGELMANN, SIEGFRIED
    Preventing Failure in the Primary Grades. Simon & Schuster, 1969, 396, illus.

ERIKSON, ERIK H., ED.
    Youth: Change and Challenge. Basic Books, 1963, 284.

ESBENSEN, THORWALD
    Working with Individualized Instruction: The Duluth Experience. Fearon, San Francisco, 1968, 122, illus.

FILBIN, ROBERT, and VOGEL, STEFAN
    So You're Going to be A Teacher. Rev. ed. Barron's, Woodbury, N.Y., 1967, 141.

FINE, BENJAMIN
    Underachievers: How They Can Be Helped. Dutton, 1967, 253.

FRANK, JOSETTE
    Your Child's Reading Today. Rev. ed. Doubleday, 1969, 368.

FRASIER, JAMES E.
    An Introduction to the Study of Education. 3rd ed. Harper & Row, 1965, 303, illus. (Exploration Series in Education.)

FREEDMAN, FLORENCE B., and BERG, ESTHER L.
    Classroom Teacher's Guide to Audio-Visual Material. Chilton, 1961, 240, illus.

FROST, JOE L., ED.
    Early Childhood Education Rediscovered: Readings. Holt, Rinehart & Winston, 1968, 594.

GAGNE, ROBERT
    The Conditions of Learning. 2nd ed. Holt, Rinehart & Winston, 1970, 407, illus.

GAITSKELL, CHARLES D., and HURWITZ, AL
    Children and Their Art: Methods for the Elementary School. 2nd ed. Harcourt, Brace & World, 1970, 507, illus.

GATTEGNO, CALEB
    What We Owe Children: The Subordination of Teaching to Learning. Dutton, 1970, 116.

GELFAND, DONNA M.
    Social Learning in Childhood: Readings in Theory and Application. Brooks/Cole, Belmont, Calif., 1969, 1 vol.

GEGA, PETER C.
    Science in Elementary Education. 2nd ed. Wiley, 1970, 640.

GILLESPIE, JOHN T., and LEMBO, DIANA
    Introducing Books: A Guide for the Middle Grades. R. R. Bowker, 1970, 318.

GLASSER, WILLIAM
    Schools Without Failure. Harper & Row, 1969, 235.

GOLDBERG, MIRIAM L., et al.
    The Effects of Ability Grouping. Teachers College Press, 1966, 1 vol.

GOODLAD, JOHN I., and ANDERSON, ROBERT H.
    The Nongraded Elementary School. Rev. ed. Harcourt, Brace & World, 1963, 248.

GOODWIN, ARTHUR B.
    Handbook of Audio-Visual Aids and Techniques for Teaching Elementary School Subjects. Parker, West Nyack, N.Y., 1969, 224, illus.

GRATER, MICHAEL
    One Piece of Paper, for Children and for Teachers. Mills & Boon, London, 1963, 117, illus.

GRAY, SUSAN W., et al.
    Before First Grade: The Early Training Project for Culturally Disadvantaged Children. Teachers College Press, 1966, 120, illus. (Early Childhood Education Series.)

GREEN, EDWARD J.
    The Learning Process and Programmed Instruction. Holt, 1962, 228, illus.

HAMBURG, MORRIS, and HAMBURG, MARION V.
    Health and Social Problems in the School. Lea & Febiger, 1968, 242.

HANEY, JOHN, and ULLMER, ELDON
    Educational Media and the Teacher. W. C. Brown, 1970, 130. (Issues and Innovations in Education Series.)

HANSLOVSKY, GLENDA, MOYER, SUE, and WAGNER, HELEN
    Why Team Teaching? Merrill, 1969, 119.

HARDING, LOWRY W.
    Arithmetic for Child Development. W. C. Brown, 1963, 428.

HASKINS, JIM
    Diary of a Harlem Schoolteacher. Grove Press, 1969, 149.

HATCH, RAYMOND N., and COSTAR, JAMES W.
    Guidance Services in the Elementary School. W. C. Brown, 1961, 202.

HAVIGHURST, ROBERT J.
    Society and Education. 2nd ed. Allyn & Bacon, 1962, 585, illus.

HAYES, ALFRED S.
    Language Laboratory Facilities: Technical Guide for Their Selection, Purchase, Use, and Maintenance. Oxford University Press, 1968, 138, illus. (Language and Language Learning No. 16.)

HENTOFF, NAT
    Our Children Are Dying. Viking, 1967, 141.

HERR, SELMA E.
    Learning Activities for Reading. W. C. Brown, 1961, 168.

HESS, ROBERT D., and BEAR, ROBERTA M., EDS.
    Early Education: Current Theory, Research, and Action. Aldine, 1968, 272, illus.

HEWETT, FRANK M.
    The Emotionally Disturbed Child in the Classroom. Allyn & Bacon, 1968, 1 vol.

HILGARD, ERNEST R., and BOWER, GORDON H.
    Theories of Learning. 3rd ed. Appleton-Century-Crofts, 1966, 661, illus. (Century Psychology Series.)

HILLSON, MAURIE, CORDASCO, FRANCESCO, and PURCELL, FRANCIS P., COMPS.
    Education and the Urban Community: Schools and the Crisis of the Cities. American Book, 1969, 506.

HOLT, JOHN
    How Children Fail. Pitman, 1964, 181.
———.
    How Children Learn. Pitman, 1967, 189.
———.
    The Under-Achieving School. Pitman, 1969, 209.

HOOD, MARGUERITE V.
    Teaching Rhythm and Using Classroom Instruments. Prentice-Hall, 1970, 142, illus.

HOOVER, KENNETH H., and HOLLINGSWORTH, PAUL
    Learning and Teaching in the Elementary School. Allyn & Bacon, 1970, 382.

HORNICK, JOANNE G.
    Elementary Creative Bulletin Boards. Citation Press, 1969, 80.

HUCK, CHARLOTTE S., and KUHN, DORIS Y.
    Children's Literature in the Elementary School. Holt, Rinehart & Winston, 1968, 1 vol.

JACKSON, PHILIP W.
    Life in Classrooms. Holt, Rinehart & Winston, 1968, 177.

JARVIS, OSCAR T., and WOOTTON, LUTIAN R.
    Transitional Elementary School and Its Curriculum. W. C. Brown, 1966, 492.

JOHNSON, LOIS V., and BANY, MARY A.
    Classroom Management: Theory and Skill Training. Macmillan, 1970, 453, illus.

KEMP, JERROLD E., et al.
    Planning and Producing Audiovisual Materials. 2nd ed. Chandler, 1968, 251, illus. (Chandler Publications in Audiovisual Communications.)

KENNEDY, LEONARD M.
    Guiding Children to Mathematical Discovery. Wadsworth, 1970, 429, illus.

KERBER, AUGUST, and BOMMARITO, BARBARA, EDS.
    The Schools and the Urban Crisis: A Book of Readings. Holt, Rinehart & Winston, 1966, 367, illus.

KIRCHNER, GLENN
    Physical Education for Elementary School Children. 2nd ed. W. C. Brown, 1970, 696.

KLOPF, GORDON J., BOWMAN, GARDA W., and JOY, ADENA A.
    A Learning Team: Teacher and Auxiliary. U.S. Office of Education, Bureau of Educational Personnel Development, 1969, 163.

KNIRK, FREDERICK G., and CHILDS, JOHN W.
    Instructional Technology: A Book of Readings. Holt, Rinehart & Winston, 1968, 300.

KOERNER, JAMES D.
    The Miseducation of American Teachers. Houghton Mifflin, 1963, 360, illus.

KOHL, HERBERT R.
    The Open Classroom: A Practical Guide to a New Way of Teaching. The New York Times (Random House, dist.), 1970, 116.

KOPLITZ, EUGENE D.
    Guidance in the Elementary School: Theory, Research and Practice. W. C. Brown, 1968, 392.

KOZOL, JONATHAN
    Death at An Early Age: The Destruction of the Hearts and Minds of Negro Children in the Boston Public Schools. Houghton Mifflin, 1967, 240.

LATCHAW, MARJORIE
    A Pocket Guide of Movement Activities for the Elementary School. 2nd ed. Prentice-Hall, 1970, 346, illus.

LEE, DORRIS M., and ALLEN, R. V.
    Learning to Read Through Experience. 2nd ed. Appleton-Century-Crofts, 1963, 146, illus.

LEEPER, SARAH H., et al.
    Good Schools for Young Children: A Guide for Working with Three-, Four-, and Five-Year-Old Children. 2nd ed. Macmillan, 1968, 465, illus.

LIDDLE, GORDON P., ROCKWELL, ROBERT E., and SACADAT, EVELYN
    Education Improvement for the Disadvantaged Elementary Setting. Thomas, 1967, 128.

LINEBERRY, WILLIAM P., ED.
    New Trends in the Schools. Wilson, 1967, 211. (Reference Shelf Vol. 39, No. 2.)

LOBB, M. DELBERT
    Practical Aspects of Team Teaching. Fearon, San Francisco, 1964, 60.

LONDON, HERBERT, and SPINNER, ARNOLD, EDS.
    Education in the Twenty-First Century. Interstate, 1969, 106.

LUCE, MARNIE
    Counting Systems: The Familiar and the Unusual. Lerner, Minneapolis, 1969, 48, illus. (Math Concept Book.)

LYSAUGHT, JEROME P.
    A Guide to Programmed Instruction. Wiley, 1963, 180, illus.

MARTINSON, JOHN, and GRAHAM, MARTHA D.
    Training Teacher Assistants in Community Colleges: A Survey of Experience to Date. Communication Service Corp., 1968, 123. illus.

MASSIALAS, BYRON G., and ZEVIN, JACK
    Creative Encounters in the Classroom: Teaching and Learning Through Discovery. Wiley, 1967, 274.

MAYER, FREDERICK
    American Ideas and Education. Merrill, 1964, 638, illus.

MAYER, MARTIN
    The Schools. Harper, 1961, 446, illus.

McDONALD, BLANCHE, and NELSON, LESLIE W.
    Methods That Teach. 2nd ed. W. C. Brown, 1965, 360.

MEDINNUS, GENE R., and JOHNSON, RONALD C.
    Child and Adolescent Psychology: Behavior and Development. Wiley, 1969, 787, illus.

MENYUK, PAULA
    Sentences Children Use. MIT Press, 1969, 165. (MIT Research Monograph No. 52.)

MESSER, EUNICE A.
    Children, Psychology and the Teacher. McGraw-Hill, 1967, 207, illus.

MICHAELIS, JOHN U., GROSSMAN, RUTH H., and SCOTT, LLOYD F.
    New Designs for the Elementary School Curriculum. McGraw-Hill, 1967, 428, illus. (McGraw-Hill Series in Education.)

MILES, MATTHEW B., ED.
    Innovation in Education. Teachers College Press, 1964, 689.

MILLER, HARRY L., and SMILEY, MARJORIE B.
    Education in the Metropolis. Free Press, 1967, 304.

MONTESSORI, MARIA
    Spontaneous Activity in Education. Schocken Books, 1965, 355, illus.

MOORE, G. ALEXANDER
    Realities of the Urban Classroom: Observations in Elementary Schools. Praeger, 1967, 188. (Books That Matter.)

MOORE, VARDINE
    Pre-School Story Hour. Scarecrow Press, 1966, 123.

MORGENSTERN, ANNE, ED.
    Grouping in the Elementary School. Pitman, 1966, 128.

COMMUNITY SERVICE PROGRAMS

MORINE, HAROLD, and MORINE, GRETA
　　A Primer for the Inner-City School. McGraw-Hill, 1970, 169, illus.

MORLAN, JOHN E.
　　Preparation of Inexpensive Teaching Materials. Chandler, 1963, 103, illus.

MOWRER, ORVAL H.
　　Learning Theory and Behavior. Wiley, 1960, 555, illus.

MUNSON, HAROLD L.
　　Elementary School Guidance: Concepts, Dimensions, and Practice. Allyn & Bacon, 1970, 348, illus.

NATCHEZ, GLADYS, COMP.
　　Children with Reading Problems: Classic and Contemporary Issues in Reading Disability—Selected Readings. Basic Books, 1968, 445, illus.

NATIONAL AUDIO-VISUAL ASSOCIATION
　　Audio-Visual Equipment Directory.... NAVA, 1953- , vols., illus.

NAYLOR, NAOMI
　　Curriculum Development Program for Preschool Teacher Aides: Final Report. Center for the Study of Crime, Delinquency and Correction, Edwardsville, Ill., 1967, 121. (ERIC ED 013 122.)

NELSON, LESLIE W.
　　Instructional Aids: How to Make and Use Them. 2nd ed. W. C. Brown, 1970, 267.

NELSON, LESLIE W., and LORBEER, GEORGE C.
　　Science Activities for Elementary Children. 4th ed. W. C. Brown, 1967, 192.

NEUBAUER, PETER B.
　　Concepts of Development in Early Childhood Education. Thomas, 1965, 160.

NEW YORK CITY BOARD OF EDUCATION
　　Getting Started in the Elementary School: A Manual for New Teachers. NYCBE, 1967, 202.

NYE, ROBERT E., and NYE, VERNICE T.
　　Music in the Elementary School. 3rd ed. Prentice-Hall, 1970, 660, illus.

OLIVERO, JAMES L., and BUFFIE, EDWARD G., EDS.
　　Educational Manpower: From Aides to Differentiated Staff Patterns—Bold New Venture. Indiana University Press, 1970, 365, illus.

O'QUINN, GARLAND
　　Gymnastics for Elementary School Children. W. C. Brown, 1967, 132.

ORNSTEIN, ALLAN C., and VAIRO, PHILIP D., COMPS.
　　How to Teach Disadvantaged Youth. McKay, 1969, 436.

PASSOW, A. HARRY, ED.
　　Reaching the Disadvantaged Learner. Teachers College Press, 1970, 360.

PASSOW, HARRY, et al., EDS.
　　Education of the Disadvantaged. Holt, Rinehart & Winston, 1967, 503.

PEARSON, NEVILLE P., and BUTLER, LUCIUS, COMPS.
　　Instructional Materials Centers: Selected Readings. Burgess, 1969, 345, illus.

PERKINS, BRYCE, and BECKER, HARVEY A.
　　Getting Better Results from Substitutes, Teacher Aides and Volunteers. Prentice-Hall, 1966, 64. (Successful School Management Series.)

PINES, MAYA
　　Revolution in Learning: The Years from Birth to Six. Harper & Row, 1967, 244.

POLOS, NICHOLAS C.
　　Dynamics of Team Teaching. W. C. Brown, 1965, 160.

POPHAM, W. JAMES, and BAKER, EVA L.
　　Planning an Instructional Sequence. Prentice-Hall, 1970, 138, illus.

PULA, FRED J.
　　Application and Operation of Audiovisual Equipment in Education. Wiley, 1968, 360, illus.

RAFFERTY, MAX L.
　　Max Rafferty on Education. Devin-Adair, 1968, 274.

REGER, ROGER, SCHROEDER, WENDY, and USCHOLD, KATHIE
　　Special Education: Children with Learning Problems. Oxford University Press, 1968, 251.

REISS, ALBERT J., JR., ED.
　　Schools in a Changing Society. Free Press, 1966, 234.

RENFIELD, RICHARD
　　If Teachers Were Free. Acropolis, 1969, 159, illus.

ROBB, MELVIN H.
　　Teacher Assistants. Merrill, 1969, 152, illus. (Coordinated Teacher Preparation Series.)

ROTHSCHILD, NORMAN
　　Making Slide Duplicates, Titles and Filmstrips. 2nd ed. Chilton, 1965, 128, illus.

RUBIN, ELI Z., SIMSON, CLYDE B., and BETWEE, MARCUS C.
　　Emotionally Handicapped Children and the Elementary School. Wayne State University Press, 1966, 286.

RUBINSTEIN, ANNETTE T., ED.
　　Schools Against Children: The Case for Community Control. Monthly Review Press, 1970, 288.

SANDERS, NORRIS M.
　　Classroom Questions: What Kinds? Harper & Row, 1966, 176, illus. (Exploration Series in Education.)

SANDERS, SANDRA
　　Creating Plays with Children. Citation Press, 1970, 96.

SARASON, SEYMOUR B., et al.
　　Anxiety in Elementary School Children: A Report of Research. Wiley, 1960, 351.

SCHERE, RICHARD A., and STARR, BERNARD D., EDS.
　　Learning, Teaching and the New Technologies. Associated Educational Services Corp., Selected Academic Readings Division, 1969, 1 vol.

SCHRAG, PETER
　　Voices in the Classroom: Public Schools and Public Attitudes. Beacon Press, 1965, 292.

SHANK, PAUL C., and McELROY, WAYNE
　　The Paraprofessionals or Teacher Aides: Selection, Preparation, and Assignment. Pendell Publishing Co., 1970, 80, illus.

SHOCKLEY, ROBERT J.
　　Your Future in Elementary School Teaching. R. Rosen Press, 1961, 159. (Careers in Depth.)

SIKS, GERALDINE B.
　　Children's Literature for Dramatization: An Anthology. Harper & Row, 1964, 331.

SKINNER, BURRHUS F.
　　The Technology of Teaching. Appleton-Century-Crofts, 1968, 271, illus. (Century Psychology Series.)

SLAUGHTER, STELLA S.
　　The Educable Mentally Retarded Child and His Teacher. F. A. Davis, 1964, 202.

SMITH, LOUIS M., and GEOFFREY, WILLIAM
　　The Complexities of an Urban Classroom: An Analysis Toward a General Theory of Teaching. Holt, Rinehart & Winston, 1968, 277.

SMITH, WILLIAM I.
　　Guidelines to Classroom Behavior. Book-Lab, Brooklyn, N.Y., 1970, 128, (Guideline Books.)

STAHL, DONA K., and ANZALONE, PATRICIA M.
　　Individualized Teaching in Elementary Schools. Parker, West Nyack, N.Y., 1970, 233, illus.

STEERE, CARYL, et al.
　　Indian Teacher Aide Handbook. Arizona State University, College of Education, 1965, 161.

STEINBERG, SHELDON S., and FISHMAN, JACOB R.
　　New Careers: The Teacher Aide—A Manual for Trainees. National Institute for New Careers, University Research Corp., Washington, 1968, 86.

STEPHENS, THOMAS M.
　　Directive Teaching of Children with Learning and Behavioral Handicaps. Merrill, 1970, 195.

TABA, HILDA, and ELKINS, DEBORAH
　　Teaching Strategies for the Culturally Disadvantaged. Rand McNally, 1966, 295. (Rand McNally Education Series.)

TARBET, DONALD G.
　　Television and Our Schools. Ronald, 1961, 268, illus. (Douglass Series in Education.)

THAYER, VIVIAN T.
　　The Role of the School in American Society. Dodd, Mead, 1960, 530.

THIER, HERBERT D.
　　Teaching Elementary School Science: A Laboratory Approach. D. C. Heath, 1970, 273, illus.

TOFFLER, ALVIN, ED.
　　Schoolhouse in the City. Praeger, 1968, 255, illus.

TORRANCE, ELLIS P.
　　Encouraging Creativity in the Classroom. W. C. Brown, 1970, 133. (Issues and Innovations in Education Series.)

TRAINING TEACHER ASSISTANTS IN COMMUNITY COLLEGES
　　Communication Service Corp., 1968, 123.

TROW, WILLIAM C.
　　Teacher and Technology: New Designs for Learning. Appleton-Century-Crofts, 1963, 198.

TRUBOWITZ, JULIUS
　　Changing the Racial Attitudes of Children: The Effects of an Activity Group Program in New York City Schools. Praeger, 1969, 228. (Special Studies in U.S. Economic and Social Development.)

TRUBOWITZ, SIDNEY
　　A Handbook for Teaching in the Ghetto School. Quadrangle Books, 1968, 175.

VAIL, ESTHER
　　Tools of Teaching: Techniques for Stubborn Cases of Reading, Spelling and Behavior. Thomas, 1967, 176, illus.

VICTOR, EDWARD
　　Science for the Elementary School. 2nd ed. Macmillan, 1970, 785, illus.

WASHINGTON, BENNETTA B.
　　Youth in Conflict: Helping Behavior-Problem Youth in a School Setting. Science Research Associates, 1963, 78.

WASHINGTON SCHOOL OF PSYCHIATRY
　　The Teacher Aide Program. WSP, 1967, 68.

WASKIN, YVONNE, and PARRISH, LOUISE
　　Teacher-Pupil Planning for Better Classroom Learning. Pitman, 1967, 111.

WASSERMAN, MIRIAM
　　The School Fix, NYC, USA. Dutton, 1970, 576.

WEBER, ELMER W.
　　Health and the School Child. Thomas, 1964, 408, illus.

WEBER, EVELYN
　　The Kindergarten: Its Encounter with Educational Thought in America. Teachers College Press, 1969, 282. (Early Childhood Education Series.)

WEBSTER, STATEN W., ED.
　　The Disadvantaged Learner. Chandler, 1966, 3 vols.

WEISZ, VERA C., et al.
　　New Faces in the Classroom: A Junior College's Approach to Training Auxiliary Personnel in Education. Communication Service Corp., n.d., 66.

WESTBY-GIBSON, DOROTHY
　　Grouping Students for Improved Instruction. Prentice-Hall, 1966, 1 vol.

WIDMER, EMMY L.
　　The Critical Years: Early Childhood Education at the Crossroads. International Textbook, 1970, 184, illus.

WIELGAT, JEANNE
　　An Effective Teacher-Aide Program. G. A. Pflaum, Dayton, Ohio, 1969, 55, illus.

WIENER, JACK, and LIDSTONE, JOHN
　　Creative Movement for Children: A Dance Program for the Classroom. Van Nostrand-Reinhold, 1969, 111, illus.

WISE, ARTHUR E.
　　Rich Schools, Poor Schools: The Promise of Equal Educational Opportunity. University of Chicago Press, 1968, 228.

WITTICH, WALTER A., and SCHULLER, CHARLES F.
　　Audio-Visual Materials: Their Nature and Use. 4th ed. Harper & Row, 1967, 554, illus. (Exploration Series in Education.)

WITUCKE, VIRGINIA
　　Literature for Children: Poetry in the Elementary School. W. C. Brown, 1970, 144. (Literature for Children Series.)

WRIGHT, ELIZABETH A.
　　Teacher Aides to the Rescue: Program Guidelines for Better Home-School-Community Partnerships. John Day, 1969, 208.

WYMAN, RAYMOND
　　Mediaware: Selection, Operation and Maintenance. W. C. Brown, 1969, 188, illus.

ENGINEERING PROGRAMS

AERONAUTICAL TECHNOLOGY

ADAMS, CARSBI C., VON BRAUN, WERNER, and ORDWAY, FREDERICK I.
Careers in Astronautics and Rocketry. McGraw-Hill, 1962, 248.

AIR FORCE MATERIALS LABORATORY
Aerospace Structural Metals Handbook. Mechanical Properties Data Center, Traverse City, Mich., 1970, 3 vols., illus.

ALLEN, JOHN E.
Aerodynamics: A Space-Age Survey. Harper & Row, 1963, 128, illus. (Science Today Series.)

ALLEN, RAYMOND C. S.
Theory of Flight for Glider Pilots. 2nd ed. Barnes & Noble, 1969, 110, illus.

AMERICAN HERITAGE
The American Heritage History of Flight. Simon & Schuster, 1962, 416, illus.

ANDRESEN, JACK
Fundamentals of Aircraft Flight and Engine Instruments. Hayden, 1969, 112, illus.

BAIN, DONALD
The Case Against Private Aviation. Cowles, 1969, 208.

BALCHEN, BERNT
The Next Fifty Years of Flight.... Viking, 1960, 214, illus.

BALL, K. J., and OSBORNE, G. F.
Space Vehicle Dynamics. Clarendon Press, 1967, 259.

BARLAY, STEPHEN
The Search for Air Safety: An International Documentary Report On the Investigation of Commercial Aviation Accidents. Morrow, 1970, 376, illus.

BARRY, W. S.
The Language of Aviation. Chatto & Windus, London, 1962, 197, illus.

BEATY, DAVID
The Human Factor in Aircraft Accidents. Stein & Day, 1970, 208, illus.

BERMAN, ARTHUR I.
The Physical Principles of Astronautics: Fundamentals of Dynamical Astronomy and Space Flight. Wiley, 1961, 350, illus.

BERNARDO, JAMES V.
Aviation in the Modern World: The Dramatic Impact Upon Our Lives of Aircraft, Missiles and Space Vehicles. 2nd ed. Dutton, 1968, 382, illus.

BINDER, OTTO O.
Careers in Space. Walker, New York, 1963, 308, illus.

BORDEN, NORMAN E.
Jet-Engine Fundamentals. Hayden, 1967, 179, illus. (Hayden Series in Aeronautical Technology.)

BORDEN, NORMAN E., and CAKE, WALTER
Fundamentals of Aircraft Piston Engines. Hayden, 1970, 192, illus.

BOSE, KEITH W.
Aviation Electronics Handbook. 2nd ed. Sams, 1970, 287, illus. (Sams Photofact Publication AEH-1.)

BOYD, WALDO T.
Your Career in the Aerospace Industry. Messner, 1966, 222, illus.

BRIMM, DANIEL J., and BOGGESS, HARRY E.
Aircraft Maintenance. 4th ed. Pitman, 1962, 475, illus. (Pitman Aeronautical Publications.)

BRYAN, LESLIE A., et al.
Fundamentals of Aviation and Space Technology. University of Illinois, Institute of Aviation, 1966, 162, illus.

BUCK, ROBERT N.
Weather Flying. Macmillan, 1970, 261, illus.

BUNYAN, FREDERICK J.
Your Jet Pilot's Rating. Sports Car Press, 1966, 131, illus. (Modern Aircraft Series.)

CAGLE, M. W., and HALPINE, CHARLES G.
A Pilot's Meteorology. 3rd ed. Van Nostrand-Reinhold, 1970, 416, illus.

CAIDIN, MARTIN
Barnstorming. Duell, Sloan & Pearce, 1965, 304, illus.

———.
Cross-Country Flying. Dutton, 1961, 253.

ENGINEERING PROGRAMS

CAIDIN, MARTIN
 The Man-In-Space Dictionary: A Modern Glossary. Dutton, 1963, 224, illus.

CANBY, COURTLANDT
 A History of Flight. Hawthorn, 1963, 113.

CARGNINO, LAWRENCE T., and KARVINEN, CLIFFORD H.
 Aerospace Propulsion Powerplants. 4th ed. Educational Publishers, Chicago, 1967, 677, illus.

CARROLL, ROBERT L.
 The Aerodynamics of Powered Flight. Wiley, 1960, 275, illus.

CASAMASSA, JACK V., and BENT, RALPH D.
 Jet Aircraft Power Systems. 3rd ed. McGraw-Hill, 1965, 408, illus.

CASWELL, CHARLES H.
 Basic Science for the Aviation Maintenance Technician. McCutchan, 1970, 304, illus.

CAVES, RICHARD E.
 Air Transport and Its Regulators: An Industry Study. Harvard University Press, 1962, 479, illus.

CLARKE, RALPH E.
 A Guide to Aerospace-Defense Contracts. Industrial Press, 1970, 264.

CONROY, CHARLES W.
 The Challenge of Aerospace Power. U.S. Air Force, Civil Air Patrol, 1968, 69, illus.

———. Introduction to Aerospace. U.S. Air Force, Civil Air Patrol, 1963, 56, illus.

———. Navigation and the Weather. U.S. Air Force, Civil Air Patrol, 1966, 124, illus.

CONROY, CHARLES W., and MEHRENS, HAROLD E.
 The Dawning Space Age. U.S. Air Force, Civil Air Patrol, 1963, 248, illus.

COOMBS, CHARLES I.
 Cleared for Takeoff: Behind the Scenes at an Airport. Morrow, 1969, 190, illus.

CORLISS, WILLIAM R.
 Propulsion Systems for Space Flight. McGraw-Hill, 1960, 300, illus.

DAVIES, R. E. G.
 The World's Airlines. Oxford University Press, 1964, 591.

DeGALIANA, THOMAS
 Concise Encyclopedia of Aeronautics. Follett, 1968, 294, illus.

DE LEEUW, HENDRIK
 From Flying Horse to Man in the Moon: A History of Flight From Its Earliest Beginnings to the Conquest of Space. St. Martin's Press, 1963, 310.

DEYARMOND, ALBERT, and ARSLAN, ALBERT
 Fundamentals of Stress Analysis. 2nd ed. Aero, 1960, 256, illus.

DICKINSON, BRIAN
 Aircraft Stability and Control for Pilots and Engineers. Pitman, 1968, 661, illus. (Aeronautical Engineering Series.)

DIXON, PETER L.
 Soaring: An Introduction to Motorless Flight. Ballantine, New York, 1970, 242, illus.

DOMMASCH, DANIEL O., SHERBY, SYDNEY S., and CONNOLLY, THOMAS F.
 Airplane Aerodynamics. 4th ed. Pitman, 1967, 621, illus.

DUCARME, J., GERSTEIN, MELVIN, and LEFEBVRE, A. H., EDS.
 Progress in Combustion Science and Technology. Pergamon, 1960- , vols., illus. (International Series of Monographs in Aeronautics and Astronautics.)

DWIGGINS, DON
 The SST: Here It Comes, Ready or Not—The Story of the Controversial Supersonic Transport. Doubleday, 1968, 294, illus.

EBELING, ALVIN
 Fundamentals of Aircraft Environmental Control. Hayden, 1968, 119, illus. (Hayden Aeronautical Technology Series.)

ELY, LAWRENCE D.
 Your Future in Aerospace Technology. R. Rosen Press, 1962, 153. (Careers in Depth.)

ENCYCLOPEDIA OF AVIATION AND SPACE SCIENCES ABOVE AND BEYOND
 New Horizon, Chicago, 1968, 14 vols.

FAGET, MAXIME A.
 Manned Space Flight. Holt, 1965, 176, illus. (Holt Library of Science.)

FAY, JOHN
 The Helicopter and How it Flies. 2nd ed. Pitman, 1967, 138, illus.

FENTEN, D. X.
 Aviation Careers: Jobs in the Air and on the Ground. Lippincott, 1969, 208, illus.

FRANCIS, MARY
 The Beginner's Guide to Flying. Pelham Books, London, Transatlantic, 1969, 102, illus.

FREDERICK, JOHN H.
 Commercial Air Transportation. 5th ed. Irwin, 1961, 497.

FUCHS, ALICE S.
 Multiengine Flying. Sports Car Press (Crown, dist.), 1969, 116, illus. (Modern Aircraft Series.)

GABLEHOUSE, CHARLES
 Helicopters and Autogiros: A History of Rotating-Wing Aircraft. Lippincott, 1969, 254, illus.

GANTZ, KENNETH F.
 Nuclear Flight: The United States Air Force Programs for Atomic Jets, Missiles and Rockets. Duell, Sloan & Pearce, 1960, 216, illus.

GATLAND, KENNETH W.
 Manned Spacecraft. Macmillan, 1967, 256, illus. (Pocket Encyclopedia of Spaceflight.)

GENTLE, ERNEST J., and CHAPEL, CHARLES E.
 Aviation & Space Dictionary. 4th ed. Aero, 1961, 445, illus.

GIBBS-SMITH, CHARLES H.
 The Aeroplane: An Historical Survey of Its Origins and Development. HMSO, London, 1960, 375.

GODSON, JOHN
 Unsafe at Any Height. Simon & Schuster, 1971, 192.

GOODGER, E. M.
 Principles of Spaceflight Propulsion. Pergamon, 1970, 172, illus. (International Series of Monographs in Aeronautics and Astronautics.)

GROVES, H. W.
 Aeronautical Technical Dictionary: French-English, English-French. Barrie & Rockliff, London, 1966, 286.

AERONAUTICAL TECHNOLOGY

GURNEY, GENE
    Famous Aircraft: The P-38 Lightning. Arco, 1969, 60, illus.

HALDON BOOKS, INC.
    Flight Maneuvers Manual: For Instructors & Students. Haldon Books, Palatine, Ill.,(Aviation Book, dist.), 1968, 1 vol., illus.

HARNSBERGER, CAROLINE T.
    Pilot's Ready Reference: Flying Data Every Pilot Must Know and Use. Aero, 1962, 86, illus.

HARRIS, SHERWOOD
    The First to Fly: Aviation's Pioneer Days. Simon & Schuster, 1970, 316, illus.

HESSE, WALTER J., and MUMFORD, NICHOLAS V. K.
    Jet Propulsion For Aerospace Applications. Pitman, 1964, 617.

HICKS, BETTY
    The Ground School Workbook.... 2nd ed. Iowa State University Press, 1969, 227, illus.

HOLLAND, JOHN H.
    Learning to Fly. Holt, Rinehart & Winston, 1960, 256.

HOOK, THOMAS S.
    Illustrated Flying Basics: First Hour to Private Pilot. Rev. ed. Thomas Hook Associates, Annapolis, 1969, 67, illus.

HORONJEFF, ROBERT
    The Planning and Design of Airports. McGraw-Hill, 1962, 464, illus. (McGraw-Hill Series in Transportation.)

HYMOFF, EDWARD
    Guidance and Control of Spacecraft. Holt, 1966, 176, illus. (Holt Library of Science.)

INTERNATIONAL CORRESPONDENCE SCHOOLS
    Elementary Aerodynamics. 3rd ed. ICS, Scranton, Pa., 1962, 101, illus.

JANE'S ALL THE WORLD'S AIRCRAFT
    Low, Marston, London, McGraw-Hill, 1909- , vols., illus.

KAYTON, MYRON, and FRIED, WALTER R., EDS.
    Avionics Navigations Systems. Wiley, 1969, 666, illus.

KELLY, CHARLES J.
    The Sky's the Limit: The History of the Airlines. Coward-McCann, 1963, 317.

KERSHNER, WILLIAM K.
    The Student Pilot's Flight Manual: Including Emergency Flying by Reference to Instruments. 3rd ed. Iowa State University Press, 1968, 198, illus.

KOLK, W. RICHARD
    Modern Flight Dynamics. Prentice-Hall, 1961, 288, illus. (Prentice-Hall Technology Series.)

LACHNITT, JACQUES
    Aerodynamics. Walker, New York, 1963, 145, illus. (Walker Suns Books SB-16, Physics and Mathematics.)

LEVINE, SOL
    Your Future in NASA. R. Rosen Press, 1969, 185, illus. (Careers in Depth.)

LOWELL, VERNON W.
    Airline Safety is a Myth. Bartholomew House, New York, 1967, 211, illus.

LYON, THOBURN C.
    Practical Air Navigation. 10th ed. Jeppesen, Denver, 1966, 292, illus.

MacDONALD, ALEXANDER F.
    From the Ground Up. 14th ed. Aviation Publishers, Port Credit, Ont., 1963, 176, illus.

MALLAN, LLOYD
    Great Air Disasters. Fawcett, 1962, 144, illus. (Fawcett Book No. 517.)

MANNING, G. E.
    Weather Radar for Pilots: A Handbook. HMSO, London, 1970, 1 vol.

MARKS, ROBERT W., ED.
    The New Dictionary & Handbook of Aerospace with Special Sections on the Moon and Lunar Flight. Praeger, 1969, 531, illus.

MARX, JOSEPH L.
    Crisis in the Skies. McKay, 1970, 274, illus.

MASON, JOHN K.
    Aviation Accident Pathology: A Study of Fatalities. Butterworth, 1962, 358, illus.

McCLEMENT, FRED
    It Doesn't Matter Where You Sit. Holt, Rinehart & Winston, 1969, 238.

McKINLEY, JAMES L., and BENT, RALPH D.
    Basic Science for Aerospace Vehicles. 3rd ed. McGraw-Hill (for Northrop Institute of Technology), 1963, 320, illus.

———.
    Powerplants for Aerospace Vehicles. 3rd ed. McGraw-Hill (for Northrop Institute of Technology), 1965, 480, illus.

McLAUGHLIN, CHARLES
    Space Age Dictionary. 2nd ed. Van Nostrand, 1963, 233, illus.

McMINN, ROBERT E.
    Power for Aircraft. U.S. Air Force, Civil Air Patrol, 1969, 98, illus.

MEHRENS, HAROLD E.
    Aircraft in Flight. U.S. Air Force, Civil Air Patrol, 1970, 58, illus.

MIELE, ANGELO
    Flight Mechanics. Addison-Wesley, 1962, vols., illus. (Addison-Wesley Series in Engineering Sciences: Space Science and Technology.)

MILLER, RONALD E.
    Domestic Airline Efficiency: An Application of Linear Programming. MIT Press, 1963, 174. (Regional Science Studies Series No. 5.)

MILLER, RONALD E., and SAWERS, DAVID
    The Technical Development of Modern Aviation. Praeger, 1970, 351, illus.

MISENHIMER, TED G.
    Aeroscience. Aero Products Research, Culver City, Calif., 1970, 812, illus.

MORGAN, LEN
    Airliners of the World. Arco, 1966, 96, illus.

———.
    Crack Up! Arco, 1968, 64, illus.

MORRISON, RICHARD B., ED.
    Design Data for Aeronautics and Astronautics: A Compilation of Existing Data. Wiley, 1962, 581, illus.

MOSCOW, ALVIN
    Tiger on a Leash. Putnam, 1961, 252, illus.

MUNSON, KENNETH G.
    Aircraft the World Over. I. Allan, London, (Sportshelf, New Rochelle, N.Y., dist.), 1962, 144, illus.

MURCHIE, GUY
    The World Aloft. Houghton Mifflin, 1960, 289, illus.

NATHANSON, FRED E.
 Radar Design Principles: Signal Processing and the Environment. McGraw-Hill, 1969, 626, illus.

NATIONAL AEROSPACE EDUCATION COUNCIL
 Aeronautics and Space Bibliography of Adult Aerospace Books and Materials. 2nd ed. USGPO, 1963, 42.

———.
 Aerospace Highlights: Facts and Figures from the Aerospace World. NAEC, 1962, 54, illus.

———.
 Aviation Education Bibliography. 5th ed. NAEC, 1967, 1 vol.

NAYLER, JOSEPH L.
 Dictionary of Astronautics. Hart, 1964, 320, illus.

NAYLER, JOSEPH L., and OWER, ERNEST
 Aviation: Its Technical Development. Dufour, 1965, 290, illus.

NEW PRIVATE PILOT: YOUR GUIDE TO THE FAA RATING WITH TYPICAL CROSS-COUNTRY WRITTEN EXAMINATIONS
 8th ed. Pan American Navigation Service, North Hollywood, Calif., 1969, 1 vol.

NEWLON, CLARKE
 Aerospace Age Dictionary. Watts, 1965, 282.

NORTHROP INSTITUTE OF TECHNOLOGY
 Electricity and Electronics for Aerospace Vehicles. McGraw-Hill, 1961, 392, illus.

———.
 Maintenance and Repair of Aerospace Vehicles. 3rd ed. McGraw-Hill, 1967, 368, illus.

O'KANE, DICK
 The Making of An Aircraft Mechanic. Westminster, Philadelphia, 1970, 123, illus.

ORDWAY, FREDERICK I.
 Applied Astronautics: An Introduction to Space Flight. Prentice-Hall, 1963, 449, illus.

———.
 Basic Astronautics: An Introduction to Space Science, Engineering, and Medicine. Prentice-Hall, 1962, 587, illus.

PALLETT, EDWIN H. J.
 Aircraft Instrument Manual. Newnes, London, 1964, 198, illus.

PAN AMERICAN NAVIGATION SERVICE
 Ground Instructor Ratings: Basic, Advanced and Instrument—A Guide to the FAA Examinations. 11th ed. PANS, North Hollywood, Calif., 1969, 220, illus.

PAN AMERICAN WORLD AIRWAYS, INC.
 New Horizons U.S.A. Simon & Schuster, 1967, 1 vol.

PARRISH, LEX
 ABC's of Avionics. Sams, 1970, 128, illus.

———.
 Space-Flight Simulation Technology. Sams, 1969, 144, illus.

PIGGOTT, DEREK
 Gliding: A Handbook On Soaring Flight. 2nd ed. Barnes & Noble, 1967, 263.

PURSER, PAUL E., FAGET, MAXIME A., and SMITH, NORMAN F., EDS.
 Manned Spacecraft: Engineering Design and Operation. Fairchild, 1964, 497, illus.

REITHMAIER, LARRY
 Computer Guide for Pilots. Aero, 1970, 1 vol.

———.
 Flight Planning Guide for Pilots. Aero, 1970, 1 vol.

———.
 Radar Guide for Pilots. Aero, 1970, 1 vol.

———.
 Weather Briefing Guide for Pilots. Aero, 1970, 1 vol.

RICHARDS, ELFYN J., and MEAD, D. J., EDS.
 Noise and Acoustic Fatigue in Aeronautics. Wiley, 1968, 512, illus.

RICHMOND, SAMUEL B.
 Regulation and Competition in Air Transportation. Columbia University Press, 1961, 309.

RIVELLO, ROBERT M.
 Theory and Analysis of Flight Structures. McGraw-Hill, 1969, 516, illus.

ROES, NICHOLAS, and KENNEDY, WILLIAM E.
 The Space-Flight Encyclopedia. Follett, 1968, 213, illus.

ROLFE, DOUGLAS, and DAWYDOFF, ALEXIS
 Airplanes of the World, 1490-1969. 3rd ed. Simon & Schuster, 1969, 440, illus.

ROSEBERRY, CECIL R.
 The Challenging Skies: The Colorful Story of Aviation's Most Exciting Years, 1919-1939. Doubleday, 1966, 533, illus.

RUDOLPH, PATRICIA
 Your Future as an Airline Stewardess. R. Rosen Press, 1961, 157. (Careers in Depth.)

SAUNDERS, KEITH
 So You Want to Be An Airline Stewardess. Arco, 1967, 176, illus.

SAVANT, CLEMENT J., et al.
 Principles of Inertial Navigation. McGraw-Hill, 1961, 254.

SCHARFF, ROBERT
 Pilot Your Own Plane. Rev. ed. Sterling, 1967, 156, illus.

SCRIBNER, KIMBALL J.
 Your Future as a Pilot. R. Rosen Press, 1968, 154, illus. (Careers in Depth No. 77.)

SECHLER, ERNEST E., and DUNN, LOUIS G.
 Airplane Structural Analysis and Design. Dover, 1963, 420, illus.

SELLICK, BUD
 Skydiving: The Art and Science of Sport Parachuting. Prentice-Hall, 1961, 248.

SERLING, ROBERT J.
 Loud and Clear: The Full Answer to Aviation's Vital Question—Are the Jets Really Safe? Doubleday, 1969, 327.

———.
 The Probable Cause: The Truth About Air Travel Today. Doubleday, 1960, 287.

SHAPIRO, ASCHER H.
 Shape and Flow: The Fluid Dynamics of Drag. Doubleday, 1961, 186, illus. (Science Study Series S 21.)

SIMONSON, LEROY
 Private Pilot Study Guide. Aviation Book, Glendale, Calif., 1970, 1 vol., illus.

SKOLNIK, MERRILL I.
 Introduction to Radar Systems. McGraw-Hill, 1962, 648, illus.

SMITH, ROBERT T.
 Your FAA Flight Exam: Private and Commercial. Sports Car Press, 1968, 112, illus. (Modern Aircraft Series.)

THE SOCIETY OF AEROSPACE MATERIAL AND PROCESS ENGINEERS
 Aircraft Structures and Materials Application. SAMPE, Azusa, Calif., 1969, 563. (National SAMPE Technical Conference Vol. 1.)

AERONAUTICAL TECHNOLOGY

STAMBLER, IRWIN
Supersonic Transport. Putnam, 1965, 94, illus.

STEVER, H. GUYFORD
Flight. Time-Life Books, 1969, 200, illus. (Life Science Library.)

STEWART, OLIVER
Aviation: The Creative Ideas. Praeger, 1966, 244, illus.

STINTON, DARREL
Anatomy of the Aeroplane. Elsevier, 1966, 321, illus.

STORY, MATTISON L.
Airports, Airways, and Electronics. U.S. Air Force, Civil Air Patrol, 1962, 76, illus.

STRICKLER, MERVIN K., ED.
An Introduction to Aerospace Education. New Horizon, Chicago, 1968, 336, illus.

STRICKLER, MERVIN K., and ZAHAREVITZ, WALTER
Career Opportunities in Aviation. National Aerospace Education Council, 1967, 25.

SWANBOROUGH, F. G.
Vertical Flight Aircraft of the World. Aero, 1964, 120, illus.

TEICHMANN, FREDERICK K.
Fundamentals of Aircraft Structural Analysis. Hayden, 1968, 144, illus.

THOMAS, ROBERT L.
Commercial Pilot's Examination Handbook. Aero, Ft. Worth, 1960, 81, illus.

THOMSON, WILLIAM T.
Introduction to Space Dynamics. Wiley, 1961, 317, illus.

TRANSPORTATION WORKSHOP, WASHINGTON, D.C., AND WARRENTON, VA., 1967
Air Transportation 1975 and Beyond: A Systems Approach—Report. MIT Press, 1968, 516, illus.

TRAYLOR, W. L.
Pilot's Guide to An Airline Career: Including Sample Pre-Employment Tests. 2nd ed. Aviation Book, Glendale, Calif., 1969, 93, illus.

TREAGER, IRWIN E.
Aircraft Gas Turbine Engine Technology. McGraw-Hill, 1970, 463, illus.

U.S. AIR FORCE, CIVIL AIR PATROL
Aerospace Doctrine. USAF, CAP, 1966, 36, illus.

———.
Aircraft Identification: A Programmed Learning Exercise. USAF, CAP, 1965, 87, illus.

———.
Education, Aviation, and the Space Age. USAF, CAP, 1963, 89, illus.

———.
Federal Aviation Regulations: A Programmed Self-Study Guide. USAF, CAP, 1969, 154.

———.
Introduction to Civil Air Patrol. USAF, CAP, 1960, 58, illus.

U.S. BUREAU OF NAVAL PERSONNEL
Aviation Electronics Technician 1 & C. Rev. ed. USBNP, 1961, 557, illus.

———.
Aviation Structural Mechanic, H1 & C. USGPO, 1964, 289, illus. (Navy Training Course.)

U.S. FEDERAL AVIATION ADMINISTRATION, FLIGHT INFORMATION DIVISION
Airman's Information Manual. Aviation Book, Glendale, Calif., 1970, 1 vol., illus.

U.S. FEDERAL AVIATION ADMINISTRATION, AIRPORTS SERVICE
Planning the State Airport System: Prepared by a Joint Committee of the Administration and National Association of State Aviation Officials. FAA, 1968, 60.

U.S. FEDERAL AVIATION AGENCY
Maintenance of Control Lines: An FAA Handbook. FAA, 1963- , 1 vol., illus.

U.S. FEDERAL AVIATION AGENCY, AIR TRAFFIC SERVICE
Contractions. Rev. ed. USGPO, 1963- , 1 vol.

U.S. FEDERAL AVIATION AGENCY FLIGHT STANDARDS SERVICE
Airline Transport Pilot (Airplane) Written Examination Guide. FAA, 1962, 51, illus.

———.
Commercial Pilot Examination Guide. USGPO, 1962, 68, illus.

———.
Ground Instructor Examination Guide: Basic-Advanced. USGPO, 1963, 72, illus.

———.
Private Pilot's Handbook of Aeronautical Knowledge. USGPO, 1963, 161, illus.

U.S. NATIONAL AERONAUTICS AND SPACE ADMINISTRATION, SCIENTIFIC AND TECHNICAL INFORMATION DIVISION
Dictionary of Technical Terms for Aerospace Use. USGPO, 1965, 314, (NASA SP-7.)

U.S. NAVAL AVIATION SAFETY CENTER, NORFOLK, VA.
Handbook for Aircraft Accident Investigators. Rev. ed. USGPO, 1961, 1 vol., illus.

U.S. OFFICE OF NAVAL OPERATIONS
Aviation Medical Safety Training Manual. USONO, 1961, 319, illus.

VAN DEVENTER, C. N.
An Introduction to General Aeronautics. 2nd ed. American Technical Society, 1965, 482, illus.

VAN SICKLE, NEIL D.
Modern Airmanship. 3rd ed. Van Nostrand, 1966, 785, illus.

WAINWRIGHT, LEWIS F.
Aircraft Electrical Practice. Odhams Press, London, 1961, 320, illus.

WALLHAUSER, HENRY T.
Pioneers of Flight. Hammond, 1969, 93, illus.

WEIN, HAROLD H.
Domestic Air Cargo: Its Prospects. Michigan State University, 1962, 96, illus. (Bureau of Business and Economic Research Occasional Paper No. 7.)

WHITNAH, DONALD R.
Safer Skyways: Federal Control of Aviation, 1926-1966. Iowa State University Press, 1967, 417, illus.

WILKINSON, PAUL H.
Aircraft Engines of the World. The author, Washington, 1970, 304, illus.

WILLIAMS, BRAD
The Anatomy of An Airline. Doubleday, 1970, 233.

WILLIAMS, CLIFFORD A.
Aircraft Instrument Control Systems. Odhams Press, London, 1963, 320, illus. (Odhams Books on Aircraft Engineering.)

———.
Aircraft Instruments. Transatlantic, 1961, 240, illus.

WOODS, LESLIE C.
The Theory of Subsonic Plane Flow. Cambridge University Press, 1961, 594, illus. (Cambridge Aeronautical Series No. 3.)

ENGINEERING PROGRAMS

WORLD AIRCRAFT ILLUSTRATED.
Aero, 1961- , vols., illus.

WORLD AVIATION DIRECTORY LISTING COMPANIES AND OFFICIALS
American Aviation Publications, Washington, 1940- , vols.

AIR CONDITIONING, HEATING AND REFRIGERATION

AIRCONDITIONING AND REFRIGERATION INSTITUTE
Bibliography of Training Aids. ARI, Arlington, Va., 1967, 74.

——.
Course Guide for Airconditioning, Heating, and Refrigeration Curriculums. ARI, Arlington, Va., 1968, 180.

ALTHOUSE, ANDREW D., TURNQUIST, CARL H., and BRACCIANO, ALFRED F. F.
Modern Refrigeration and Air Conditioning: Theory, Practice of Refrigeration and Air Conditioning Systems. Goodheart-Willcox, 1968, 1120, illus.

AMBROSE, E. R.
Heat Pumps and Electric Heating: Residential, Commercial, Industrial Year-Round Air Conditioning. Wiley, 1966, 205, illus.

AMERICAN INSURANCE ASSOCIATION
Code for the Installation of Heat Producing Appliances, Heating, Ventilating, Air Conditioning, Blower and Exhaust Systems. AIA, New York, 1967, 95.

AMERICAN SOCIETY OF HEATING, REFRIGERATING AND AIR-CONDITIONING ENGINEERS
ASHRAE Guide and Data Book. ASHRAE, 1961- , vols., illus.

——.
ASHRAE Handbook of Fundamentals. ASHRAE, 1967, 544, illus.

——.
Thermodynamic Properties of Refrigerants. ASHRAE, 1969, 329.

ANDERSON EDWIN P.
Air Conditioning. Audel, 1969, 453, illus.

——.
Audel's Commercial Refrigeration. Audel, 1967, 534, illus.

——.
Audel's Home Gas Heating and Appliance Manual. Audel, 1965, 312, illus.

——.
Audel's Home Refrigeration and Air Conditioning Guide. 2nd ed. Audel, 1966, 566, illus.

——.
Audel's Refrigeration and Air Conditioning Guide for Engineers, Servicemen, Shop Men & Users—A Practical Treatise Covering the Basic Principles, Servicing, Operation and Repair of.... Audel, 1961, 1090, illus. (Audel's Helping Hand Books for Mechanics.)

ANGUS, THOMAS C.
The Control of Indoor Climate. Pergamon, 1968, 110, illus. (International Series of Monographs in Heating, Ventilation and Refrigeration Vol. 4.)

ARCO PUBLISHING COMPANY, INC.
Refrigeration License. 3rd ed. Arco, 1967, 160.

AUSTIN, PHILIP R., and TIMMERMAN, STEWART W.
Design and Operation of Clean Rooms. Business News, Detroit, 1965, 427, illus.

BARTON, JOHN J., ED.
Heating and Ventilating: Principles & Practice. Newnes, London, (Transatlantic), 1964, 504, illus.

BERRY, CHARLES H.
Flow and Fan: Principles of Moving Air Through Ducts.... 2nd ed. Industrial Press, 1963, 232, illus.

BOOTH, K. M.
Dictionary of Refrigeration and Air Conditioning. Elsevier, 1970, 315.

BURKHARDT, CHARLES H.
Domestic and Commercial Oil Burners. 3rd ed. McGraw-Hill, 1969, 538, illus.

CARRIER CORPORATION
Handbook of Air Conditioning System Design. McGraw-Hill, 1965, 1 vol., illus.

COMMITTEE ON INDUSTRIAL VENTILATION
Industrial Ventilation: A Manual of Recommended Practice. 11th ed. CIV, Lansing, Mich., 1970, 300.

CZINKOTA, MICHAEL
How to Select, Install and Service Air Conditioners. Chilton, 1969, 107, illus.

DALY, DONALD F.
Your Future in Air Conditioning and Refrigeration. Arco, 1970, 140. (Career Guidance Series.)

DANIELS, GEORGE
Home Guide to Plumbing, Heating and Air Conditioning. Harper & Row, 1967, 186, illus. (Popular Science Skill Book.)

DOOLIN, JAMES H., ED.
Trouble Shooters Bible: Air Conditioning, Refrigeration, Heat Pumps and Heating. Doolco, Dallas, 1963, 332, illus.

DOSSAT, ROY J.
Principles of Refrigeration. Wiley, 1961, 544, illus.

DWIGGINS, BOYCE H.
Automotive Air Conditioning. Rev. ed. Delmar, 1970, 429.

ELONKA, STEPHEN M., and MINICH, QUAID W.
Standard Refrigeration and Air Conditioning Questions and Answers. McGraw-Hill, 1961, 253, illus.

EMERICK, ROBERT H.
Heating Handbook: A Manual of Standards, Codes, and Methods. McGraw-Hill, 1964, 522, illus.

FABER, OSCAR, and KELL, J. R.
Heating and Air-Conditioning of Buildings. 4th ed. Architectural Press, London, 1966, 567, illus.

FIELD, EDWIN M.
Oil Burners. 2nd ed. Audel (Sams, dist.), 1969, 295, illus.

GATTONE, FELIX
Air Conditioning and Heating Technology—II. Rutgers University, Curriculum Laboratory, 1965, 346. (ERIC VT 010 379.)

GUNTHER, RAYMOND C.
Refrigeration, Air Conditioning and Cold Storage: Principles and Applications. 2nd ed. Chilton, 1969, 1398, illus.

HAINES, JOHN E.
Automatic Control of Heating and Air Conditioning. 2nd ed. McGraw-Hill, 1961, 389, illus.

HEATING, PIPING AND AIR CONDITIONING DIRECTORY: 1969.
Reinhold, 1 vol.

HUTCHINSON, FRANCIS W.
Design of Refrigeration Systems for Air Conditioning. Industrial Press, 1963, 291, illus.

——.
Heating and Humidifying Load Analysis. Ronald, 1962, 494, illus.

INTERNATIONAL DISTRICT HEATING ASSOCIATION
    Principles of Economical Heating Handbook. 4th ed. IDHA, 1970, 1 vol.

INTERNATIONAL FIRE SERVICE TRAINING ASSOCIATION
    Ventilation Practices. 4th ed. Everett Hudiburg and John Shreve, comps. Oklahoma State University, 1965, 51, illus. (Fire Service Training Manuals and Texts.)

INTERNATIONAL INSTITUTE OF REFRIGERATION
    Guide Pratique de L'Entreposage Frigorifique: Practical Guide to Refrigerated Storage. Pergamon, 1966, 239, illus.

KABERLEIN, JOSEPH J.
    Air Conditioning Metal Layout: A Textbook and Working Guide with Practical and Shortened Methods for Laying Out and Forming the Patterns Used in Air Conditioning, Heating and Ventilating—Mathematical Formulas Applied to Sheetmetal Work. Bruce, 1967, 308, illus.

———.
    Short Cuts for Round Layouts. Bruce, 1966, 269, illus.

———.
    Triangulation Short-Cut Layouts: A Textbook and Working Guide with Practical and Modern Methods for Laying Out and Forming Patterns Used for Blower-Exhaust Systems, Heating, and Air Conditioning—Mathematical Formulas Applied to Sheet-Metal Work. Bruce, 1966, 290, illus.

KING, GUY R.
    Basic Air Conditioning: Air Heating, Cooling, Filtration, Circulation. Nickerson & Collins, Chicago, 1965, 374

KUT, DAVID
    Heating and Hot Water Services in Buildings. Pergamon, 1968, 425, illus. (International Series of Monographs in Heating, Ventilation and Refrigeration Vol. 3.)

KUTZ, MYER
    Temperature Control. Wiley, 1968, 212, illus.

LAMERE, BERNARD
    Guide to Home Air Conditioners and Refrigeration Equipment. Hayden, 1963, 125, illus.

LANG, V. PAUL
    Principles of Air Conditioning. Delmar, 1964, 340, illus.

LAUB, JULIAN M.
    Air Conditioning & Heating Practice. Holt, Rinehart & Winston, 1963, 768, illus.

LEMONS, WAYNE, and PRICE, BILL
    How to Repair Home & Auto Air Conditioners. TAB, 1970, 208, illus.

MAGNUS, EDWARD R., and MARLOTT, GRACE D.
    Handbook of Refrigeration and Air Conditioning. Follett, 1966, 784, illus.

MANLY, HAROLD P.
    Drake's Refrigeration Service Manual: An Instruction and Reference Book Covering Maintenance, Trouble Shooting and Repair—Domestic and Commercial Systems. Drake, Chicago, 1962, 370, illus.

MARSH, R. WARREN, and OLIVO, C. THOMAS
    Principles of Refrigeration. Delmar, 1966, 374, illus.

NATIONAL ACADEMY OF SCIENCES, NATIONAL RESEARCH COUNCIL (BUILDING RESEARCH ADVISORY BOARD)
    Heating and Air-Conditioning Ducts Encased in and under Concrete Slabs-on-Ground. NAS, 1961, 41. (Pub. No. 838.)

NATIONAL ACADEMY OF SCIENCES, NATIONAL RESEARCH COUNCIL (BUILDING RESEARCH INSTITUTE)
    New Methods of Heating Buildings. NAS, 1960, 138. (Publ. No. 760.)

PAGE, JOHN S.
    Estimator's Equipment Installation Man-Hour Manual. Gulf, Houston, 1964, 164.

———.
    Heating, Plumbing and Air-Conditioning Man-Hour Manual. Gulf, Houston, 1961, 145.

PRICE, SEYMOUR G.
    Air Conditioning for Building Engineers and Managers: Operation and Maintenance. Industrial Press, 1970, 136, illus.

RAMSEY, MELVIN A.
    Tested Solutions to Design Problems in Air Conditioning and Refrigeration. Industrial Press, 1966, 167, illus.

REED, GEORGE H.
    Refrigeration: A Practical Manual for Apprentices. MacLaren, London, (Hart, New York), 1967, 131, illus.

SHEET METAL AND AIR CONDITIONING CONTRACTORS NATIONAL ASSOCIATION, INC.
    Manual for the Balancing and Adjustment of Air Distribution Systems. SMACCNA, Washington, 1967, 94.

STEPNICK, IVAN C.
    Control Theory and Fundamentals Study Course. Refrigeration Engineers & Technicians Association, 1970, 2 vols.

STOECKER, WILBERT F.
    Principles for Air Conditioning Practice. Industrial Press, 1968, 160.

STROCK, CLIFFORD, and KORAL, RICHARD L., EDS.
    Handbook of Air Conditioning, Heating and Ventilating. 2nd ed. Industrial Press, 1965, 1472, illus.

TRANE AIR CONDITIONING MANUAL
    Rev. ed. Trane, La Crosse, Wis., 1965, 456, illus.

TRICOMI, ERNEST
    ABC's of Air Conditioning. Sams, 1970, 128, illus.

———.
    Air Conditioning Installation and Maintenance. Sams, 1962, 160, illus. (Sams Photofact Pub. No. ACM-1.)

TUDBURY, CHESTER A.
    Basics of Induction Heating. Rider, 1960, 265, illus.

VAN STRAATEN, J. F.
    Thermal Performance of Buildings. Elsevier, 1967, 311, illus. (Elsevier Architectural Science Series.)

VERSAGI, FRANK J.
    Technical Conversations in Air Conditioning & Refrigeration. Business News, Detroit, 1962, 359, illus.

WATT, JOHN R.
    Evaporative Air Conditioning. Industrial Press, 1963, 300, illus.

WOOLRICH, WILLIS R.
    Handbook of Refrigerating Engineering. 4th ed. AVI, 1965-66, 2 vols.

AUTOMOTIVE TECHNOLOGY

ABBEY, STATON
    Chilton's B.M.C. Minicar Repair and Tune-Up Guide. 3rd ed. Chilton, 1966, 142, illus.

ABELL, CARL
    Butane-Propane Power Manual. 2nd ed. Chilton, 1962, 315, illus.

ALLEN, WILLARD A.
    Know Your Car. 2nd ed. American Technical Society, 1967, 184, illus.

ENGINEERING PROGRAMS

ALLEY, WALTER, and BILLIET, WALTER E.
   Disc and Drum Brake Service. American Technical Society, 1970, 188, illus.

ANDERSON, EDWIN P.
   Audel's Domestic Compact Auto Repair Manual. Audel, 1964, 816, illus.

ARCO PUBLISHING COMPANY, INC.
   The Arco Famous Car Series. Arco, 1970- , vols. (Each 80-page volume devoted to a single famous car.)

———. Auto Machinist. 3rd ed. Arco, 1967, 304, illus.

———. Auto Mechanic, Autoserviceman. 4th ed. Arco, 1969, 320, illus. (Arco Civil Service Test Tutor.)

———. Foreman of Auto Mechanics. Arco, 1961, 136.

ASH, DAVID
   Automobile Almanac. Simon & Schuster, 1967, 1 vol.

ATHANSON, WILLIAM J.
   Automobile Body Repair and Paint Guide. 2nd ed. Van Nostrand, 1967, 99, illus.

ATKINSON, HENRY F.
   Mechanics of Small Engines. McGraw-Hill, 1967, 96, illus. (McGraw-Hill Foundation Series.)

ATTEBERRY, PAT H.
   Power Mechanics. Goodheart-Willcox, 1961, 96, illus. (Goodheart-Willcox's Build-a-Course Series.)

AUTO ENGINE TUNE-UP
   2nd ed. Audel, 1970, 416.

AUTOMOBILE MANUFACTURERS ASSOCIATION
   Automobile Facts and Figures. AMA, 1970, 70, illus.

———. Automobiles of America. 2nd ed. Wayne State University Press, 1968, 269, illus. (Savoyard Book.)

———. Community College Guide for Associate Degree Programs in Auto and Truck Service Management. AMA, 1969, 79, illus.

AUTOMOTIVE ELECTRIC ASSOCIATION
   AEA Electrical Specifications Handbook. AEA, Detroit, 1962, 1 vol., illus.

———. AEA Transistor Ignitions Systems Manual. AEA, Detroit, 1964, 76, illus.

———. Air-Cooled Engine Manual. AEA, Detroit, 1968, 158, illus.

———. Course in Automotive Tune-Up. AEA, Detroit, 1968, 144, illus.

AUTOMOTIVE PARTS REBUILDERS ASSOCIATION, INC.
   Counterman's Handbook for Handling of Rebuilt Parts. APRA, 1968, 64, illus.

BARNACLE, HAROLD E.
   Mechanics of Automobiles. Pergamon, 1964, 250, illus.

BARR, RANDOLPH, and FLOCCO, THOMAS
   The Automobile Electrical System. 2nd ed. Chilton, 1968, 628, illus.

BARRIS, GEORGE, and THOMS, WAYNE
   How to Customize Cars and Rods. Arco, 1963, 112, illus.

BASIC CAMS, VALVES, AND EXHAUST SYSTEMS
   Petersen, Los Angeles, 1968, 192, illus. (Hot Rod Magazine Technical Library.)

BASIC CARBURETION AND FUEL SYSTEMS: THE COMPLETE STORY OF THE FUEL SYSTEM FROM TANK TO MANIFOLD
   Petersen, Los Angeles, 1968, 192, illus. (Hot Rod Magazine Technical Library.)

BEELER, SAMUEL C.
   Understanding Your Car. 2nd ed. McKnight & McKnight, 1967, 136, illus.

BEKKER, MIECZYSLAW, G.
   Introduction to Terrain-Vehicle Systems. University of Michigan Press, 1969, 846, illus.

BILLIET, WALTER E., and GOINGS, LESLIE F.
   Automotive Electrical Systems. 3rd ed. American Technical Society, 1970, 393, illus.

BLACK, STEPHEN
   Man and Motor Cars: And Ergonomic Study. W. W. Norton, 1967, 1966, 373, illus.

BLANCHARD, HAROLD, and RITCHEN, RALPH
   Auto Engines and Electrical Systems. 3rd ed. Motor, New York, 1963, 602.

BLOWER, W. E.
   The Complete MG Workshop and Tuning Manual. Bentley, Cambridge, Mass., 1970, 584, illus.

BORGESON, GRIFFITH
   New Hot Rod Handbook. Arco, 1960, 144, illus.

BOTZOW, HERMANN S.
   Auto Fleet Management. Wiley, 1968, 197.

BRADLEY, JAMES J., and TAYLOR, DAWSON
   Your Future in Automotive Service. Arco, 1970, 1 vol.

BRICKER, FREDERICK E.
   Audel's Automobile Guide. Audel, 1966, 735, illus.

BUCKLEY, JOHN R.
   Classic Cars in Color. Batsford, London, 1964, 70, illus.

BUCKWALTER, LEN
   Electronic Gadgets for Your Car. Sams, 1964, 126, illus.

CAMPBELL, COLIN
   Sports Car Engine: Its Tuning & Modification. Bentley, Cambridge, Mass., 1963, 322, illus.

CARROLL, WILLIAM
   Auto Mechanics Basic Engineering Guide. Auto Book, Oceanside, Calif., 1970, 1 vol., illus.

———. Bill Carroll's Automotive Gas Turbines. 2nd ed. Auto Book, Oceanside, Calif., 1969, 129, illus. (Performance Engineering Handbooks.)

CHECK-CHART CORPORATION
   Lubricant Recommendations: Passenger Cars, Trucks and Tractors. Check-Chart, Chicago, 1964, 64.

CHILTON'S AUTO REPAIR MANUAL
   Chilton, 1953- , vols., illus.

CHILTON'S FLAT RATE AND PARTS MANUAL, 1969
   Chilton, 1969, 1504, illus.

CHIRONIS, NICHOLAS P., COMP.
   Gear Design and Application. McGraw-Hill, 1967, 375, illus.

COSTIN, MICHAEL, and PHIPPS, DAVID
   Racing & Sports Car Chassis Design. Bentley, Cambridge, Mass., 1961, 147, illus.

CROUSE, WILLIAM H.
   Automotive Chassis and Body: Construction, Operation, and Maintenance. 3rd ed. McGraw-Hill, 1966, 622, illus. (McGraw-Hill Automotive Mechanics Series.)

———. Automotive Electrical Equipment: Construction, Operation, and Maintenance. 6th ed. McGraw-Hill, 1966, 530, illus.

———. Automotive Engine Design. McGraw-Hill, 1970, 480, illus.

AUTOMOTIVE TECHNOLOGY

———.
Automotive Engines: Construction, Operation, and Maintenance. 3rd ed. McGraw-Hill, 1966, 623, illus. (McGraw-Hill Automotive Mechanics Series.)

———.
Automotive Mechanics. 6th ed. McGraw-Hill, 1970, 550, illus.

———.
Automotive Transmissions and Power Trains: Construction, Operation and Maintenance. 3rd ed. McGraw-Hill, 1967, 626, illus. (McGraw-Hill Automotive Mechanics Series.)

DAVISSON, JACK A.
Design and Application of Commercial Type Tires. Society of Automotive Engineers, New York, 1969, 39, illus.

DE GIORGIO, JOE
Bill Carroll's Dynamometer Tuning Techniques. Auto Book, Oceanside, Calif., 1969, 80, illus. (Performance Engineering Handbooks No. 111.)

DONOVAN, FRANK R.
Wheels for a Nation. Crowell, 1965, 303, illus.

DUMMER, GEOFFREY W. A., and ROBERTSON, J. MACKENZIE
Automobile Electronics Equipment, 1970-71. Pergamon, 1970, 328.

DWIGGINS, BOYCE H.
Automotive Starting and Charging Systems. Delmar, 1970, 280, illus.

———.
Automotive Steering Systems. Delmar, 1968, 248, illus.

EDWARDS, CHARLES E.
Dynamics of the United States Automobile Industry. University of South Carolina Press, 1965, 297.

ESKOW, GERALD W.
Your Future in the Trucking Industry. R. Rosen Press, 1964, 157. (Careers in Depth.)

FISHER, CHARLES H.
Carburetion. 4th ed. Chapman & Hall, London, 1963-1969, 4 vols., illus.

FLINK, JAMES J.
America Adopts the Automobile, 1895-1910. MIT Press, 1970, 304, illus.

FLUID CLUTCHES AND TORQUE CONVERTERS
Chilton, 1968, 166, illus. (Chilton's Automotive Series.)

FREEMAN, PETER
Lubrication and Friction. Pitman, 1962, 82.

GILES, JOHN G.
Gears and Transmissions. Iliffe Books, 1969, 211, illus. (Automotive Technology Series.)

———, ED.
Vehicle Equipment. Iliffe Books, 1969, 236, illus. (Automotive Technology Series Vol. 5.)

———.
Vehicle Operation and Testing. Iliffe Books (Classic Motorbooks, Minneapolis, dist.), 1969, 160, illus. (Automotive Technology Series Vol. 7.)

GLENN, HAROLD T.
Automechanics. 2nd ed. C. A. Bennett, 1969, 544, illus.

———.
Automobile Engine Rebuilding and Maintenance. 2nd ed. Chilton, 1967, 307, illus.

———.
Automotive Smog Control Manual. Cowles, 1968, 147, illus. (Cowles Repair Book.)

———.
Glenn's Auto Repair Manual. Chilton, 1960- , vols., illus., annual.

———.
Glenn's Auto Troubleshooting Guide. Chilton, 1964, 216, illus.

———.
Glenn's Foreign Carburetors and Electrical Systems: Repair and Tune-Up Guide. Chilton, 1965, 188, illus.

———.
Glenn's Foreign Car Repair Manual. Chilton, 1966, 1280, illus.

GLENN, RONALD E., and BLINN, JAMES E.
Mobile Hydraulic Testing. American Technical Society, 1970, 326.

GRAHAM, FRANK D.
Audel's Truck and Tractor Guide for Mechanics and Drivers of Gas & Diesel Motors. Audel, 1960, 1298, illus. (Audel's Helping Handbooks for Mechanics.)

GRAHAM, KENNARD C.
Understanding and Servicing Fractional Horsepower Motors. American Technical Society, 1961, 256, illus.

GREENE, EMMET
Small Foreign Car Guide. Arco, 1967, 112, illus.

GREENLEAF, WILLIAM
Monopoly on Wheels: Henry Ford and the Selden Automobile Patent. Wayne State University Press, Detroit, 1961, 302.

GREENWOOD, DOUGLAS O.
Mechanical Power Transmission: Component Selection and Application. McGraw-Hill, 1962, 372, illus.

GRUSE, WILLIAM A.
Motor Fuels: Performance and Testing. Reinhold, 1967, 280, illus.

———.
Motor Oils: Performance and Evaluation. Reinhold, 1967, 236, illus.

GUNTHER, RAYMOND C.
Lubrication. Chilton, 1970, 1 vol., illus.

HARTFORD, BILL, and DAFFRON, JOE
Car Repairs You Can Make. Arco, 1966, 192, illus.

HEITNER, JOSEPH
Automotive Mechanics: Principles and Practices. 2nd ed. Van Nostrand, 1967, 608, illus.

HOGG, JOHN W.
Auto Body Repair and Refinishing. McGraw-Hill, 1969, 274, illus.

HOT ROD MAGAZINE
Basic Clutches & Transmissions. Petersen, Los Angeles, 1968, 192, illus. (Hot Rod Magazine Technical Library.)

IGNITION MANUFACTURERS INSTITUTE
Automotive Tune-Up Principles and Procedures Textbook. Rev. ed. IMI, 1969, 1 vol.

JAMISON, ANDREW
The Steam-Powered Automobile: An Answer to Air Pollution. Indiana University Press, 1970, 160.

JENNINGS, RALPH E., ED.
The Automotive Dictionary. William Dogan Annual Publications Associates, New York, 1969, 277.

JUDGE, ARTHUR W.
Modern Smaller Diesel Engines: In Theory, Construction, Operation and Maintenance. Bentley, Cambridge, Mass., 1969, 336, illus.

———.
Motor Manuals. Bentley, Cambridge, Mass., 1955- , 8 vols.

KATES, EDGAR J.
Diesel and High-Compression Gas Engines: Fundamentals. 2nd ed. American Technical Society, 1965, 448, illus.

KOSTUR, STANLEY
Automotive Servicing. McGraw-Hill (Canada), 1968, 192, illus. (McGraw-Hill Foundation Series.)

ENGINEERING PROGRAMS

KUNS, RAY F., and DUVALL, J.
    Automotive Essentials. Rev. ed. Bruce, 1966, 489, illus.

LANDY, DICK
    Basic Chassis, Suspension & Brakes: Blue Print for a Trick Chassis. Petersen, Los Angeles, 1969, 192, illus. (Hot Rod Magazine Technical Library.)

LAREW, WALTER B.
    Automatic Transmissions. Chilton, 1966, 209, illus.

———. Carburetors & Carburetion. Chilton, 1967, 167, illus.

———. Ignition Systems. Chilton, 1968, 213, illus. (Chilton's Automotive Series.)

LAWLOR, JOHN
    How to Talk Car. Dodd, Mead, 1965, 123.

LIGHTBAND, D. A., and BICKNELL, D. A.
    Direct Current Traction Motor: Its Design and Characteristics. International Publications Service, 1970, 1 vol.

LIMA, ROBERT F., ED.
    Arco Motor Vehicle Dictionary: Spanish-English, English-Spanish. Arco, 1969, 362.

MARIN, GIANNI
    The Motor Car: An Illustrated History. London House & Maxwell, New York, 1963, 254.

McGRATH, JAMES S.
    The Automobile Transmission and Drive Line. Chilton, 1961, 376, illus. (Chilton's Automobile Mechanics' Series.)

MECHANIX ILLUSTRATED
    Car Care. Arco, 1968, 112, illus.

MOTOR'S AUTO REPAIR MANUAL
    Motor, New York, 1937- , vols., illus.

MOTOR'S TRUCK REPAIR MANUAL
    Motor, New York, 1943- , vols., illus.

NADER, RALPH
    Unsafe at Any Speed: The Designed-in Dangers of the American Automobile. Grossman, 1965, 365, illus.

NASH, FREDERICK C.
    Automotive Fundamentals. McGraw-Hill (Canada), 1969, 199, illus.

NATIONAL AUTOMOBILE DEALERS ASSOCIATION
    Standards of Apprenticeship Recommended by the National Automobile Dealers Association and the Automotive Trade Association Managers for Automobile Mechanics (Automobiles, Trucks, Tractors and other Vehicular Equipment). U.S. Bureau of Apprenticeship and Training, 1966, 26, illus.

NATIONAL AUTOMOTIVE SERVICE
    National Service Data. NAS, Berkeley, Calif., 1934- , vols., illus.

NELSON, WALTER H.
    Small Wonder: The Amazing Story of the Volkswagen. Rev. ed. Little, Brown, 1967, 288, illus.

NEWCOMB, THOMAS P., and SPURR, R. T.
    Automobile Brakes and Braking Systems. Bentley, Cambridge, Mass., 1969, 245, illus. (Motor Manual Series Vol. 8.)

———. Braking of Road Vehicles. Bentley, Cambridge, Mass., 1969, 292, illus.

NEWNES MOTOR REPAIR
    A. J. Coker, ed. Newnes, London, (Arco), 1963, 5 vols., illus.

O'CONNELL, JEFFREY, and MYERS, ARTHUR
    Safety Last: An Indictment of the Auto Industry. Random House, 1966, 226.

O'KANE, DICK
    How to Repair Your Foreign Car. Doubleday, 1968, 178.

PIPE, TED
    Small Gasoline Engines Training Manual. 2nd ed. Sams, 1969, 223, illus.

PURDY, KEN W.
    Wonderful World of the Automobile. Crowell, 1963, 275, illus.

PURVIS, JUDSON A.
    All About Small Gas Engines: How to Fix All Kinds of 2-Cycle and 4-Cycle Engines. Goodheart-Willcox, 1963, 304, illus.

RAYBESTOS MANHATTAN, INC.
    Brake Service Manual for Disc and Drum Brakes. Raybestos, Bridgeport, Conn., 1966, 104.

RICHERT, MELVIN T.
    How to Control Auto Body Sheet Metals. Chilton, 1968, 122, illus.

RITCH, OCEE
    Chilton's Motorcycle Carburetion Systems. Chilton, 1969, 140, illus.

———. Chilton's Motorcycle Electrical Systems. Chilton, 1969, 140, illus.

———. Chilton's Motorcycle Troubleshooting Guide. Chilton, 1966, 94, illus.

HOWARD W. SAMS & COMPANY, INC.
    Small Engines Service Manual. 8th ed. Sams, 1966, 320.

SANDS, LEO G., and RODGERS, LIONEL M.
    Automobile Traffic Signal Control Systems. Chilton, 1969, 200, illus.

SARGENT, ROBERT L.
    Automobile Sheet Metal Repair. 2nd ed. Chilton, 1969, 398, illus.

SERVICE, T. B. D.
    Ford Cars (Anglia, Prefect, Popular, 8 and 10). 4th ed. Arco, 1964, 228, illus.

SMITH, LEROI T., ED.
    Basic Bodywork and Painting. Petersen, Los Angeles, 1969, 192, illus. (Hot Rod Magazine Technical Library.)

———. Complete Book of Engine Swapping, No. 2. Petersen, Los Angeles, 1969, 192, illus. (Petersen Specialty Publication.)

———. How to Fix Up Old Cars. Apollo Editions, 1968, 210, illus.

SMITH, PHILIP H.
    Car Performance and the Choice of Conversion Equipment. Bentley, Cambridge, Mass., 1967, 147, illus.

———. Design and Tuning of Competition Engines. 4th ed. Bentley, Cambridge, Mass., 1967, 464.

———. Tuning for Speed and Tuning for Economy. Bentley, Cambridge, Mass., 1966, 200.

———. Valve Mechanisms for High Speed Engines: Their Design and Development. Bentley, Cambridge, Mass., 1967, 216, illus.

SMITH, PHILIP H., and MORRISON, JOHN C.
    Scientific Design of Exhaust and Intake Systems. 2nd ed. Bentley, Cambridge, Mass., 1968, 246.

STEPHENSON, GEORGE E.
    Small Gasoline Engines. Delmar, 1964, 105, illus.

STOCKEL, MARTIN W.
    Auto Mechanics Fundamentals: How and Why of the Design, Construction and Operation of Automotive Units. Goodheart-Willcox, 1963, 1 vol., illus.

Auto Service and Repair: Servicing, Locating Trouble, Repairing Modern Automobiles—Basic Know-How Applicable to All Makes, All Models. Goodheart-Willcox, 1969, 1 vol.

TAYLOR, DAWSON
Your Future in the Automotive Industry. R. Rosen Press, 1963, 160. (Careers in Depth No. 31.)

TECHNICAL PUBLICATIONS
Motorcycle Service Manual. Bobbs-Merrill, 1966, 240, illus.

TILL, ANTHONY
What You Should Know Before You Have Your Car Repaired. Sherbourne Press, Los Angeles, 1970, 192.

TOBOLDT, WILLIAM K.
Auto Body Repairing and Repainting: Modern, Simplified Methods. Goodheart-Willcox, 1965, 224, illus.

TOBOLDT, WILLIAM K., and JOHNSON, LARRY, EDS.
Motor Service's Automotive Encyclopedia. Goodheart-Willcox, 1970, 768, illus.

TURNER, DAVID R.
Motor Vehicle Operator: Chauffeur, Driver, Auto Engineman. 2nd ed. Arco, 1969, 256, illus. (Arco Civil Service Test Tutor.)

U.S. OFFICE OF EDUCATION, VOCATIONAL AND TECHNICAL EDUCATION DIVISION
Diesel Servicing: (DOT Occupational Code 625.281) A Suggested 2-Year Post High School Curriculum. USOE, 1969, 118, illus. (OE-87045.)

U.S. PANEL ON ELECTRICALLY POWERED VEHICLES
The Automobile and Air Pollution: A Program for Progress—Report to the Commerce Technical Advisory Board. USGPO, 1967- , Vol. 1- , illus.

VENK, ERNEST A., and BILLIET, WALTER E.
Automotive Engines—Maintenance and Repair (Includes Fuel and Ignition Systems). 3rd ed. American Technical Society, 1964, 480, illus. (Automotive Series.)

———.
Automotive Fundamentals. 3rd ed. American Technical Society, 1967, 566, illus.

VENK, ERNEST A., BILLIET, WALTER E., and ALLEY, WALTER V.
Automotive Suspensions, Steering, Alignment and Brakes. 4th ed. American Technical Society, 1970, 417, illus.

VENK, ERNEST A., and SPICER, EDWARD D.
Automotive Collision Work. 3rd ed. American Technical Society, 1964, 390, illus.

———.
Automotive Maintenance and Troubleshooting. 3rd ed. American Technical Society, 1963, 426, illus.

WEIERS, RONALD M.
Licensed to Kill: The Incompetent American Motorist and How He Got That Way. Chilton, 1968, 147, illus.

WEINSTEIN, WILLIAM
The Automobile Engine. Chilton, 1961, 623, illus. (Chilton's Automobile Mechanics Series.)

WENNER, DAVID N.
Basic Ignition and Electrical Systems. Petersen, Los Angeles, 1969, 192, illus. (Hot Rod Magazine Technical Library.)

WETZEL, GUY F.
Automotive Diagnosis and Tune-Up. 4th ed. McKnight & McKnight, 1965, 450, illus.

WHEATLEY, RICHARD C., and MORGAN, B.
Restoration of Antique & Classic Cars. Bentley, Cambridge, Mass., 1964, 199, illus.

WHERRY, JOSEPH H.
Automobiles of the World: The Story of the Development of the Automobile. Chilton, 1968, 713, illus.

CHEMICAL TECHNOLOGY

ALBERT, ADRIEN
Selective Toxicity and Related Topics. 4th ed. Barnes & Noble, 1968, 531, illus.

ALBERT, ADRIEN, and SERJEANT, E. P.
Ionization Constants of Acids and Bases. Methuen, 1962, 179.

ALBERTSON, B.
Photochemical Processes, 1969. Noyes, 1969, 185, illus.

AMERICAN CHEMICAL SOCIETY
Chemical Marketing: The Challenges of the Seventies. ACS, 1968, 199. (Advances in Chemistry Series No. 83.)

———.
Conference on Chemical Technicians Utilization, Education, and Continuing Education. ACS, 1969, 76.

———.
Flavor Chemistry. ACS, 1966, 278. (Advances in Chemistry Series No. 56.)

———.
Literature of Chemical Technology. ACS, 1968, 732. (Advances in Chemistry Series No. 78.)

———.
Natural Pest Control Agents. ACS, 1966, 146. (Advances in Chemistry Series No. 53.)

———.
Organic Pesticides in the Environment. ACS, 1966, 309. (Advances in Chemistry Series No. 60.)

———.
Reagent Chemicals. 4th ed. ACS, 1968, 651.

———.
Searching the Chemical Literature. ACS, 1961, 326. (Advances in Chemistry Series No. 30.)

AMERICAN INSURANCE ASSOCIATION
Hazard Survey of the Chemical and Allied Industries. AIA, 1968, 79. (Technical Survey No. 3.)

ARCO PUBLISHING COMPANY, INC.
Chemist: Assistant Chemist. 4th ed. Arco, 1969, 225. (Civil Service Test Tutor.)

ARIS, RUTHERFORD
Elementary Chemical Reactor Analysis. Prentice-Hall, 1969, 352, illus.

ARNOW, LESLIE E., and LOGAN, MARIE C. D.
Introduction to Laboratory Chemistry. 6th ed. Mosby, 1961, 490, illus.

AYLWARD, G. H., and FINDLAY, T. J. V.
Chemical Data Book. 2nd ed. Wiley, 1966, 88.

BAIN, DONALD M., ED.
The International Chemistry Directory, 1969-70. W. A. Benjamin, 1970, 1111.

BAINES, A., BRADBURY, FRANK R., and SUCKLING, C. W.
Research in the Chemical Industry: The Environment, Objectives and Strategy. Elsevier, 1969, 298, illus.

BANKS, JAMES E.
Chemical Equilibrium and Solutions: A Programmed Introduction. McGraw-Hill, 1967, 172, illus.

BARROW, GORDON M., et al.
Understanding Chemistry. W. A. Benjamin, 1967, 5 vols.

BATES, ROGER G.
Determination of pH: Theory of Practice. Wiley, 1964, 435, illus.

BAUMAN, ROBERT P.
Absorption Spectroscopy. Wiley, 1962, 611, illus.

BEAVEN, G. H., et al.
Molecular Spectroscopy: Methods and Applications in Chemistry. Macmillan, 1961, 336, illus. (Physical Processes in the Chemical Industry Vol. 7.)

BENFEY, OTTO T.
    Introduction to Organic Reaction Mechanisms: An Interface Book of the Advisory Council on College Chemistry and the Commission on Undergraduate Education in the Biological Sciences. McGraw-Hill, 1970, 207, illus. (McGraw Chemistry/Biology Interface Series.)

BENNETT, HARRY
    Chemical Zip Book. Noyes, 1970, 134.

———.
    Concise Chemical and Technical Dictionary. 2nd ed. Tudor, 1962, 1039.

BERG, EUGENE W.
    Physical and Chemical Methods of Separation. McGraw-Hill, 1963, 366, illus.

BLACKBURN, JAMES A., ED.
    Spectral Analysis: Methods and Techniques. Dekker, 1970, 1 vol.

BLACKBURN, THOMAS R.
    Equilibrium: A Chemistry of Solutions. Holt, Rinehart & Winston, 1969, 220

BLANDER, MILTON
    Molten Salt Chemistry. Wiley, 1964, 775.

BOBBITT, JAMES M., et al.
    Introduction to Chromatography. Reinhold, 1968, 160.

BOLTON, EDWARD R., and REVIS, CECIL
    Oils, Fats, and Fatty Foods: Their Practical Examination. 4th ed. Elsevier, 1966, 488, illus.

BOTTLE, R. T., ED.
    The Use of Chemical Literature. 2nd ed. Archon Books, 1969, 294.

BRENNAN, D., and TRIPPER, C. F.
    Laboratory Manual of Experiments in Physical Chemistry. McGraw-Hill, 1967, 256.

BRESCIA, FRANK, et al.
    Fundamentals of Chemistry: A Modern Introduction. Academic Press, 1966, 816, illus.

BRICKER, CLARK E.
    Foundations of Chemistry: A Laboratory Manual. Harcourt, Brace & World, 1966, 207, illus.

BROWN, RUSSELL, and CAMPBELL, G. A.
    How to Find Out About the Chemical Industry. Pergamon, 1969, 218.

BROWN, THEODORE L.
    General Chemistry. 2nd ed. Merrill, 1968, 668.

BROWNING, DAVID R., ED.
    Chromatography. McGraw-Hill, 1970, 151. (Instrumental Methods Series.)

BUTLER, JAMES N.
    Solubility and pH Calculations: The Mathematics of the Simplest Ionic Equilibria. Addison-Wesley, 1964, 104. (Addison-Wesley Series in the Principles of Chemistry.)

CAGLE, CHARLES V.
    Adhesive Bonding: Techniques and Applications. McGraw-Hill, 1968, 351, illus.

CAHN, ROBERT S.
    An Introduction to Chemical Nomenclature. 3rd ed. Plenum Press, 1968, 117.

CAMPBELL, JAMES A.
    Why do Chemical Reactions Occur? Prentice-Hall, 1965, 117, illus. (Foundations of Modern Chemistry Series.)

CARNELL, PAUL H., and REUSCH, ROSETTA N.
    Molecular Equilibrium: A Programmed Course in General Chemistry. Saunders, 1963, 217.

CARTMELL, EDWARD, and FOWLES, GERALD W. A.
    Valency and Molecular Structure. 3rd ed. Van Nostrand, 1966, 315, illus.

CASEY, JAMES P.
    Pulp and Paper: Chemistry and Chemical Technology. 2nd ed. Interscience, 3 vols., 1960-61, illus.

CASTRANTAS, H. M., and BANERJEE, DILAP K.
    Laboratory Handling and Storage of Peroxy Compounds. American Society for Testing Materials, 1970, 27. (ASTM Special Technical Pub. No. 471.)

CHAPMAN, DENNIS
    An Introduction to Lipids. McGraw-Hill, 1969, 141. (European Chemistry Series.)

CHARLOT, GASTON
    Colorimetric Determination of Elements: Principles and Methods. Elsevier, 1964, 449.

CHARLOT, GASTON, and TREMILLON, BERNARD
    Chemical Reactions in Solvents and Melts. P. J. J. Harvey, tr. Pergamon, 1969, 528.

CHAYEN, J., et al.
    A Guide to Practical Histochemistry. Lippincott, 1969, 261, illus.

CHEMICAL BOND APPROACH PROJECT
    Chemical Systems. McGraw-Hill, Webster Division, 1964, 772, illus.

THE CHEMICAL FORMULARY: A COLLECTION OF VALUABLE, TIMELY, PRACTICAL COMMERCIAL FORMULAE AND RECIPES FOR MAKING THOUSANDS OF PRODUCTS IN MANY FIELDS OF INDUSTRY Chemical, 1933- , Vol. 1- .

CHEMICAL MATERIALS CATALOG: THE PROCESS INDUSTRIES' OWN CATALOG OF CHEMICALS AND MATERIALS. Reinhold, 1967- , vols., annual.

CHILTON, THOMAS H.
    Strong Water: Nitric Acid—Sources, Methods of Manufacture, and Uses. MIT, Press, 1968, 170, illus.

CLAPP, LEALLYN B.
    The Chemistry of the OH Group. Prentice-Hall, 1967, 108, illus. (Foundations of Modern Chemistry Series.)

CLARK, GEORGE L., ED.
    The Encyclopedia of Chemistry. 2nd ed. Reinhold, 1966, 1144, illus.

COMPANION, AUDREY L.
    Chemical Bonding. McGraw-Hill, 1964, 155, illus. (McGraw-Hill Series in Undergraduate Chemistry,)

THE CONDENSED CHEMICAL DICTIONARY.
    7th ed. Reinhold, 1966, 1044, illus.

COX, HENRY E., and PEARSON, DAVID
    The Chemical Analysis of Foods. Chemical, 1962, 479, illus.

DAL NOGARE, STEPHEN, and JUVET, RICHARD S., JR.
    Gas-Liquid Chromatography: Theory and Practice. Interscience, 1962, 450.

DEAN, JOHN A.
    Chemical Separation Methods. Van Nostrand-Reinhold, 1969, 398.

de KORÖSY, F. D.
    An Approach to Chemistry. Elsevier, 1969, 500, illus.

DE NAVARRE, MAISON G.
    The Chemistry and Manufacture of Cosmetics. 2nd ed. Van Nostrand, 1962- , Vol. 1- , illus.

DENNY, LYNN C., LUXON, LESTER L., and HALL, BARBARA E.
Handbook: Butane-Propane Gases. 4th ed. Chilton, 1962, 383, illus.

DEWAR, MICHAEL J. S.
An Introduction to Modern Chemistry. Oxford University Press, 1965, 209, illus.

DIAMANT, RUDOLPH M.
The Chemistry of Building Materials. Business Books, London, 1970, 241, illus. (Applied Chemistry Series No. 1.)

DICKEY, GEORGE D.
Filtration. Reinhold, 1961, 353, illus. (Reinhold Chemical Engineering Series.)

DICKSON, THOMAS R.
Computer and Chemistry: An Introduction to Programming & Numerical Methods. Freeman, 1968, 216, illus.

DICTIONARY OF CHEMISTRY AND CHEMICAL TECHNOLOGY
Z. Sobecka, et al., eds. Pergamon, 1962, 724.

DIRECTORIES PUBLISHING COMPANY
Chem Sources. Directories, 1958- , Vol. 1- , annual.

DORIAN, A. F., COMP.
Elsevier's Dictionary of Industrial Chemistry in Six Languages: English/American, French, Spanish, Italian, Dutch and German. Elsevier, Amsterdam, New York, 1964, 2 vols.

DRAGO, RUSSELL S., and MATWIYOFF, NICHOLAS A.
Acids and Bases. D. C. Heath, 1968, 121, illus. (Topics in Modern Chemistry.)

DREISBACH, DALE
Liquids and Solutions. Houghton Mifflin, 1966, 194, illus. (Classic Researches in General Chemistry.)

DURRANS, T. H.
Solvents. 8th ed. Chapman & Hall, London, 1970, 280, illus.

EBLIN, LAWRENCE P.
Chemistry: A Survey of Fundamentals. Harcourt, Brace & World, 1968, 676, illus.

ELIEL, ERNEST L.
Stereochemistry of Carbon Compounds. McGraw-Hill, 1962, 486, illus. (McGraw-Hill Series in Advanced Chemistry.)

EMELÉUS, HARRY J.
The Chemistry of Fluorine and Its Compounds. Academic Press, 1969, 133. (Current Chemical Concepts.)

EUROPEAN CHEMICAL MARKET RESEARCH SOURCES.
Noyes, 1969, 99.

FAITH, WILLIAM L., KEYES, DONALD B., and CLARK, RONALD L.
Industrial Chemicals. 3rd ed. Wiley, 1965, 852, illus.

FARBER, EDUARD
The Evolution of Chemistry: A History of Its Ideas, Methods, and Materials. 2nd ed. Ronald, 1969, 437.

FIESER, LOUIS F., and FIESER, MARY
Style Guide for Chemists. Van Nostrand-Reinhold, 1960, 116, illus.

FINDLAY, ALEXANDER
A Hundred Years of Chemistry. 3rd ed. Humanities, 1965, 335.

FISCHER, ROBERT B., and PETERS, DENIS G.
Chemical Equilibrium. Saunders, 1970, 285, illus.

FLECK, GEORGE M.
Equilibria in Solution. Holt, Rinehart & Winston, 1966, 217, illus.

FLOOD, WALTER E.
The Dictionary of Chemical Names. Littlefield, Adams, 1967, 238. (New Students Outline Series No. 147.)

FOX, ROBERT A.
Fundamentals of Commercial Chemical Development. American Chemical Society, 1970, 120.

FRANTZ, HARPER W., and MALM, LLOYD E.
Chemical Principles in the Laboratory: With Report Forms. W. H. Freeman, 1966, 354, illus. (Books in Chemistry.)
———.
Essentials of Chemistry in the Laboratory. 2nd ed. W. H. Freeman, 1968, 373, illus. (Books in Chemistry.)
———.
Fundamental Experiments for College Chemistry. 2nd ed. W. H. Freeman, 1969, 219.

FREEMAN, MITCHELL
Practical and Industrial Formulary. Chemical, 1962, 297.

GABB, MICHAEL H., and LATCHEM, W. E.
Handbook of Laboratory Solutions. Chemical, 1968, 116.

GALWEY, ANDREW K.
Chemistry of Solids: An Introduction to the Chemistry of Solids and Solid Surfaces. Chapman & Hall, London, 1967, 210. (Science Paperbacks SP42.)

GARARD, IRA D.
Invitation to Chemistry. Doubleday, 1969, 420, illus.

GARDNER, HENRY A., and SWARD, GEORGE G.
Paint Testing Manual: Physical and Chemical Examination of Paints, Varnishes, Lacquers, and Colors. 12th ed. Gardner Laboratory, Bethesda, Md., 1962, 553, illus.

GARDNER, WILLIAM, and COOKE, EDWARD I.
Chemical Synonyms and Trade Names: A Dictionary and Commercial Handbook. 6th ed. CRC Press, 1968, 635. (International Scientific Series.)

GRANT, JULIUS
A Laboratory Handbook of Pulp and Paper Manufacture, Incorporating the 4th Edition of Stevens's "Paper Mill Chemist." 2nd ed. Edward Arnold, London, 1961, 523, illus.
———, ED.
Hackh's Chemical Dictionary. 4th ed. McGraw-Hill, 1969, 738, illus.

GRAY, HARRY B.
Electrons and Chemical Bonding. W. A. Benjamin, 1964, 223, illus.

GREGG, S. J.
The Surface Chemistry of Solids. 2nd ed. Chapman & Hall, London, 1961, 393.

GRISWOLD, ERNEST
Chemical Bonding and Structure. D. C. Heath, 1968, 124, illus. (Topics in Modern Chemistry.)

GRUNWALD, ERNEST
Atoms, Molecules and Chemical Change. 2nd ed. Prentice-Hall, 1965, 354, illus.

GRUSE, WILLIAM A., and STEVENS, DONALD R.
Chemical Technology of Petroleum. 3rd ed. McGraw-Hill, 1960, 675, illus.

GUNSTONE, F. D.
An Introduction to the Chemistry and Biochemistry of Fatty Acids and Their Glycerides. 2nd ed. Chapman & Hall, London, 1968, 209, illus.

ENGINEERING PROGRAMS

GUTCHO, M.
　　Synthetic Perfumery Materials. Noyes, 1970, 273, illus. (Chemistry Process Review No. 45.)

HAHN, ALBERT V., WILLIAMS, ROGER, and ZABEL, HERMAN
　　The Petrochemical Industry: Market and Economics. McGraw-Hill, 1970, 620, illus.

HAHN, PETER A.
　　Chemicals from Fermentation. Doubleday, 1968, 112, illus. (Chemistry in Action Series.)

HAMPEL, CLIFFORD A., ED.
　　The Encyclopedia of the Chemical Elements. Reinhold, 1968, 849, illus.

HANDBOOK OF CHEMISTRY: A REFERENCE VOLUME FOR ALL REQUIRING READY ACCESS TO CHEMICAL AND PHYSICAL DATA USED IN LABORATORY WORK AND MANUFACTURING.
　　Handbook Publishers, Sandusky, Ohio, 1934- , vols.

HANDBOOK OF CHEMISTRY AND PHYSICS: A READY-REFERENCE BOOK OF CHEMICAL AND PHYSICAL DATA
　　Chemical Rubber Co., 1913- , Vol. 1- .

HANOK, ALBERT
　　Manual for Laboratory Clinical Chemistry. Geron-X, Los Altos, Calif., 1969, 406.

HANSON, JAMES R.
　　Introduction to Steroid Chemistry. Pergamon, 1968, 104, illus. (Commonwealth and International Library: A Course in Organic Chemistry.)

HARBERS, EBERHARD
　　Introduction to Nucleic Acids: Chemistry, Biochemistry, and Functions. Reinhold, 1968, 403, illus.

HEFTMANN, ERICH, ED.
　　Chromatography. 2nd ed. Reinhold, 1967, 851, illus. (Reinhold Chemistry Textbook Series.)

HELLMAN, HAROLD
　　Spectroscopy. U.S. Atomic Energy Commission, Technical Information Division, 1968, 60, illus. (Understanding the Atom.)

HENGSTEBECK, ROBERT J.
　　Distillation: Principles and Design Procedures. Reinhold, 1961, 365, illus.

HERCULES, DAVID M., ED.
　　Fluorescence and Phosphorescence Analysis: Principles and Applications. Wiley-Interscience, 1966, 258, illus.

HILDEBRAND, JOEL H., and SCOTT, ROBERT L.
　　Regular Solutions. Prentice-Hall, 1962, 180, illus. (Prentice-Hall International Series in Chemistry.)

HILDITCH, THOMAS P., and WILLIAMS, P. N.
　　The Chemical Constitution of Natural Fats. 4th ed. Wiley, 1964, 745.

HILLS, PETER J.
　　Chemical Equilibria. Edward Arnold, London, 1969, 66. (Studies in Chemistry No. 1.)

HOLMES, JEROME K.
　　Introduction to General Chemistry. 2nd ed. Mosby, 1969, 470, illus.

HOLUM, JOHN R.
　　Elements of General and Biological Chemistry: An Introduction to the Molecular Basis of Life. 2nd ed. Wiley, 1968, 576, illus.

———.
　　Introduction to Principles of Chemistry. Wiley, 1969, 253, illus.

———.
　　Principles of Physical, Organic and Biological Chemistry. Wiley, 1969, 728.

HONEYMAN, JOHN, and GUTHRIE, ROY D.
　　An Introduction to the Chemistry of Carbohydrates. 3rd ed. Clarendon Press, 1968, 144.

HORRIGAN, PHILIP A.
　　The Challenge of Chemistry. McGraw-Hill, 1970, 200, illus.

HOUSE, HERBERT O.
　　Modern Synthetic Reactions. Benjamin, 1965, 309, illus. (Organic Chemistry Monograph Series.)

HUBER, WALTER
　　Titrations in Nonaqueous Solvents. Academic Press, 1967, 252, illus.

HUGHES, D. O., and LATHAM, J. L.
　　Physics for Chemists and Biologists. Chemical, 1970, 377.

INTERNATIONAL ENCYCLOPEDIA OF CHEMICAL SCIENCE
　　Van Nostrand, 1964, 1331, illus.

JAFFE, HANS H., and ORCHIN, MILTON
　　Symmetry in Chemistry. Wiley, 1965, 191, illus.

JOHNSON, MILDRED D.
　　Problem Solving and Chemical Calculations. Harcourt, Brace & World, 1969, 341, illus.

JOHNSON, RONALD C.
　　Introductory Descriptive Chemistry: Selected Non-metals, Their Properties and Behavior. Benjamin, 1966, 144, illus. (General Chemistry Monograph Series.)

JOHNSTONE, SYDNEY J., and JOHNSTONE, MARGERY G.
　　Minerals for the Chemical and Allied Industries. 2nd ed. Wiley, 1961, 788.

JONES, DAVID G.
　　Chemistry and Industry: Applications of Basic Principles in Research and Process Development. Clarendon Press, 1967, 217, illus.

JONES, MARK M.
　　Elementary Coordination Chemistry. Prentice-Hall, 1965, 473, illus.

JONES, W. NORTON
　　Textbook of General Chemistry. Mosby, 1969, 675, illus.

JONES, W. NORTON, and STUBBS, MORRIS F.
　　General Chemistry in the Laboratory: Including Qualitative Analysis. Mosby, 1970, 250, illus.

KASK, UNO
　　Chemistry: Structure and Changes of Matter. Barnes & Noble, 1969, 608. (International Textbook Series.)

KELLER, ROY
　　Basic Tables in Chemistry. McGraw-Hill, 1967, 400, illus.

KIEFFER, WILLIAM F.
　　The Mole Concept in Chemistry. Reinhold, 1962, 118. (Selected Topics in Modern Chemistry.)

KING, EDWARD L.
　　How Chemical Reactions Occur: An Introduction to Chemical Kinetics and Reaction Mechanisms. W. A. Benjamin, 1964, 148, illus. (General Chemistry Monograph Series.)

KINGZETT, CHARLES T.
　　Chemical Encyclopaedia: A Digest of Chemistry and Its Industrial Applications. 9th ed. Van Nostrand-Reinhold, 1967, 1092, illus.

KIRK, RAYMOND E., and OTHMER, DONALD F., EDS.
　　Encyclopedia of Chemical Technology. 2nd ed. Interscience, 1969, 21 vols., illus.

KLOTZ, IRVING M.
　　Chemical Thermodynamics: Basic Theory and Methods. Rev. ed. Benjamin, 1964, 468, illus.

CHEMICAL TECHNOLOGY

KÖRÖSY, FRANCIS D.
    An Approach to Chemistry. Elsevier, 1969, 500.

LAGOWSKI, JOSEPH J.
    The Chemical Bond. Houghton Mifflin, 1966, 200, illus. (Classic Researches in General Chemistry G-2.)

LAIDLER, KEITH J.
    Theories of Chemical Reaction Rates. McGraw-Hill, 1969, 234.

LANDAU, RALPH, and COHAN, ALVIN S., EDS.
    The Chemical Plant from Process Selection to Commercial Operation. Reinhold, 1966, 327, illus.

LANGFORD, COOPER H., and BEEBE, RALPH A.
    The Development of Chemical Principles. Addison-Wesley, 1969, 384.

LEACH, ROYAL B., and EWING, GALEN W.
    Chemistry. Doubleday, 1966, 400. (Tutor Text.)

LEE, GARTH L.
    Principles of Chemistry: A Structural Approach. International Textbook, 1970, 1 vol., illus.

LEE, HENRY, and NEVILLE, KRIS
    Handbook of Epoxy Resins, McGraw-Hill, 1967, 1 vol., illus. (McGraw-Hill Handbooks.)

LEES, R.
    Laboratory Handbook of Methods of Food Analysis. CRC Press, 1968, 181

LEWIS, JACK, and WILKINS, R. G., EDS.
    Modern Coordination Chemistry: Principles and Methods. Wiley-Interscience, 1960, 487, illus.

LITTLEWOOD, ANTHONY B.
    Gas Chromatography. 2nd ed. Academic Press, 1970, 521.

LOBSTEIN, ROBERT
    Guide to Chemical Plant Planning. Noyes, 1969, 524, illus.

MAGEE, R. J., ED.
    Selected Readings in Chromatography. Pergamon, 1970, 144, illus.

MAHAN, BRUCE H.
    Elementary Chemical Thermodynamics. Benjamin, 1963, 155, illus. (General Chemistry Monograph Series.)

MALLINSON, JOHN H.
    Chemical Plant Design with Reinforced Plastics. McGraw-Hill, 1969, 443, illus.

MANUFACTURING CHEMISTS ASSOCIATION
    Case Histories of Accidents in the Chemical Industry. MCA, 1962-66, 2 vols.

———.
    Guide for Safety in the Chemical Laboratory. Van Nostrand, 1966, 234, illus.

MARGOLIS, EMIL J.
    Chemical Principles in Calculations of Ionic Equilibria: Solution Theory for General Chemistry, Qualitative Analysis, and Quantitative Analysis. Macmillan, 1966, 482, illus.

MARSDEN, CYRIL, ED.
    Solvents Guide. 2nd ed. Interscience, 1963, 633.

MARTENS, CHARLES R.
    Emulsion and Water-Soluble Paints and Coatings. Reinhold, 1964, 160, illus.

MASON, BRIAN H.
    Principles of Geochemistry. 3rd ed. Wiley, 1966, 329, illus.

MASTERTON, WILLIAM L., and SLOWINSKI, EMIL J.
    Chemical Principles. 2nd ed. Saunders, 1969, 705, illus.

MATTOCK, G.
    pH Measurement and Titration. Macmillan, 1961, 406, illus. (Physical Processes in the Chemical Industry Vol. 6.)

McCAFFERY, EDWARD L.
    Laboratory Preparation for Macromolecular Chemistry. McGraw-Hill, 1970, 416.

McKELVEY, JAMES M.
    Polymer Processing. Wiley, 1962, 409, illus.

McLELLAN, C. R., DAY, MARION C., and CLARK, ROY W.
    Concepts of General Chemistry. F. A. Davis, 1966, 589, illus.

MEAD, WILLIAM J., ED.
    Encyclopedia of Chemical Process Equipment. Reinhold, 1964, 1065, illus.

MELLAN, IBERT
    Industrial Solvent Handbook. Noyes, 1970, 478, illus.

MELLAN, IBERT, and MELLAN, ELEANOR
    Encyclopedia of Chemical Labeling. Chemical, 1961, 111, illus.

MELLON, MELVIN G.
    Chemical Publications: Their Nature and Use. 4th ed. McGraw, 1965, 324, illus.

MEYER, LEO A.
    Atomic Energy in Industry: A Guide for Tradesmen and Technicians. American Technical Society, 1963, 127, illus.

MEYER, LILLIAN H.
    Food Chemistry. Reinhold, 1960, 385, illus. (Reinhold Organic Chemistry and Biochemistry Textbook Series.)

MIALL, LAURENCE M., ED.
    A New Dictionary of Chemistry. 4th ed. Wiley, 1968, 638, illus.

MIKES, OTAKAR
    Laboratory Handbook of Chromatographic Methods. Van Nostrand, 1966, 434, illus. (Van Nostrand Analytical Chemistry Series.)

MISLOW, KURT
    Introduction to Stereochemistry. W. A. Benjamin, 1966, 1965, 193, illus.

MORTIMER, CHARLES E.
    Chemistry: A Conceptual Approach. Reinhold, 1967, 692, illus. (Reinhold Chemistry Textbook Series.)

MYERS, TERRELL C., and ALLENDER, JEROME S.
    Chemistry of Amino Acids, Peptides, and Proteins: A Programed Text. Harper & Row, 1968, 384.

NASH, LEONARD K.
    Elements of Chemical Thermodynamics. 2nd ed. Addison-Wesley, 1970, 184. (Addison-Wesley Principles of Chemistry Series.)

NATIONAL FIRE PROTECTION ASSOCIATION (INTERNATIONAL)
    Hazardous Chemicals Data 1968. Rev. ed. NFPA, Boston, 1968, 208. (NFPA No. 49-1968.)

NIEDERWIESER, A., and PATAKI, GYÖRGY
    Progress in Thin-Layer Chromatography and Related Methods. Vol. 1. Humphrey, Ann Arbor, 1970, 224.

NOLL, WALTER
    Chemistry and Technology of Silicones. 2nd ed. Academic Press, 1968, 702, illus.

NYMAN, CARL J., and HAMM, RANDALL E.
    Chemical Equilibrium. D. C. Heath, 1968, 117, illus. (Topics in Modern Chemistry.)

ENGINEERING PROGRAMS

OIL AND COLOUR CHEMISTS ASSOCIATION, LONDON
 Paint Technology Manuals. Reinhold, 1961- , vols., illus.

O'MALLEY, ROBERT F.
 Problems in Chemistry. McGraw-Hill, 1968, 288.

OPARIN, ALEXANDER I.
 The Chemical Origin of Life. Thomas, 1964, 152, illus.

ORGANIC SYNTHESES: AN ANNUAL PUBLICATION OF SATISFACTORY METHODS FOR THE PREPARATION OF ORGANIC CHEMICALS.
 Wiley, 1960- , vols., annual.

PADGETT, ROSE
 Textile Chemistry and Testing In the Laboratory. 3rd ed. Burgess, 1962, 153, illus.

PATAI, SAUL
 The Chemistry of Carboxylic Acids and Esters. Interscience, 1969, 1155, illus. (Chemistry of Functional Groups.)

PATAKI, GYÖRGY
 Techniques of Thin-Layer Chromatography in Amino Acid and Peptide Chemistry. Rev. ed. Science Publishers, Ann Arbor, 1968, 218, illus.

PATTI, A. ANNE, and STEIN, ARTHUR A.
 Steroid Analysis by Gas-Liquid Chromatography. Thomas, 1964, 108, illus.

PATTISON, J. B.
 Programmed Introduction to Gas-Liquid Chromatography. Heyden, London, 1969, 283.

PAULING, LINUS C.
 College Chemistry: An Introductory Textbook of General Chemistry. 3rd ed. W. H. Freeman, 1964, 832, illus.

———.
 The Nature of the Chemical Bond and the Structure of Molecules and Crystals: An Introduction to Modern Structural Chemistry. 3rd ed. Cornell University Press, 1960, 644, illus.

PAYNE, CHARLES A., and PAYNE, LAMAR B.
 How to Do An Organic Synthesis. Allyn & Bacon, 1969, 152.

PELLETIER, S. W., ED.
 Chemistry of the Alkaloids. Van Nostrand-Reinhold, 1970, 795, illus.

PERROS, THEODORE P.
 Chemistry. American Book Co., 1967, 676, illus.

PETERSON, SIGFRED S.
 Chemistry in Nuclear Technology. Addison-Wesley, 1963, 374.

PHILLIPS, LESLIE N., and PARKER, D. B. V.
 Polyurethanes: Chemistry, Technology and Properties. Iliffe Books, 1964, 129, illus.

PIMENTEL, GEORGE C., and McCLELLAN, AUBREY L.
 The Hydrogen Bond. Freeman, 1960, 475, illus. (Chemistry Books Series.)

POLLOCK, JAMES R. A., and STEVENS, ROGER, EDS.
 Dictionary of Organic Compounds: The Constitution and Physical, Chemical and Other Properties of the Principal Carbon Compounds and Their Derivatives, Together with Relevant Literature References. 4th ed. Oxford University Press, 5 vols. and supplements, 1965- .

POOLE, J. B., and DOYLE, D.
 Solid-Liquid Separation: A Review and a Bibliography. Chemical, 1968, 1003, illus.

PORTER, GEORGE
 Chemistry for the Modern World. Barnes & Noble, 1963, 116.

QUAY, WILLIAM H., JR.
 The Negro in the Chemical Industry. University of Pennsylvania Press, 1969, 110. (Racial Policies of American Industry Report No. 7.)

REYNOLDS, MOIRA D.
 Clinical Chemistry for the Small Hospital Laboratory. Thomas, 1969, 208, illus.

RICHARDS, J. W.
 Technical Development in the Small Plant. Leonard Hill, London, 1970, 120.

RIEGEL, EMIL R.
 Industrial Chemistry. James A. Kent, ed. Reinhold, 1962, 963, illus.

ROCK, PETER A.
 Chemical Thermodynamics: Principles and Applications. Macmillan, 1969, 508.

RODD, E. H.
 Rodd's Chemistry of Carbon Compounds. 2nd ed. Elsevier, 1964- , 7 parts.

ROYER, DONALD J.
 Bonding Theory. McGraw-Hill, 1968, 275, illus. (McGraw-Hill Undergraduate Chemistry Series.)

SACKHEIM, GEORGE I., and SCHULTZ, RONALD M.
 Chemistry for the Health Sciences. Macmillan, 1969, 471, illus.

SANDERS, PAUL A.
 Principles of Aerosol Technology. Van Nostrand-Reinhold, 1970, 418, illus.

SANDERSON, ROBERT T.
 Chemical Periodicity. Reinhold, 1960, 330, illus. (Reinhold Physical and Inorganic Chemistry Textbook Series.)

SAX, NEWTON I.
 Dangerous Properties of Industrial Materials. 3rd ed. Reinhold, 1968- , 1251, illus.

SCHAUM, DANIEL
 Schaum's Outline of Theory and Problems of College Chemistry. 5th ed. Schaum, 1966, 256, illus. (Schaum's Outline Series.)

SHAW, DUNCAN J.
 Introduction to Colloid and Surface Chemistry. Butterworth, 1966, 186.

SHERMAN, PHILIP
 Industrial Rheology: With Particular Reference to Foods, Pharmaceuticals, and Cosmetics. Academic Press, 1970, 423, illus.

SHREVE, RANDOLPH N.
 Chemical Process Industries. 3rd ed. McGraw-Hill, 1967, 905, illus.

SIENKO, MICHELL J., and PLANE, ROBERT A.
 Chemistry: Principles and Properties. 3rd ed. McGraw-Hill, 1966, 654.

———.
 Experimental Chemistry. 3rd ed. McGraw-Hill, 1966, 306, illus.

SIMPSON, CHARLES H.
 Chemicals from the Atmosphere. Doubleday, 1969, 181. (Chemistry in Action Series.)

SISLER, HARRY H.
 Chemistry in Non-Aqueous Solvents. Reinhold, 1961, 119. (Selected Topics in Modern Chemistry.)

SLACK, R., and NINEHAM, A. W.
 Medical and Veterinary Chemicals. Pergamon, 1968, 2 vols., illus.

SNELL, FOSTER D., and SNELL, CORNELIA T.
Dictionary of Commercial Chemicals. 3rd ed. Van Nostrand, 1962, 714.

SNELL, FOSTER D., and ETTRE, LESLIE S., EDS.
Encyclopedia of Industrial Chemical Analysis. Wiley, 1969, 9 vols.

SNYDER, MILTON K.
Chemistry: Structure and Reactions. Holt, Rinehart & Winston, 1966, 748, illus.

SORENSON, WAYNE R., and CAMPBELL, TOD W.
Preparative Methods of Polymer Chemistry. 2nd ed. Interscience, 1968, 504, illus.

SORUM, CLARENCE H.
Fundamentals of General Chemistry. 2nd ed. Prentice-Hall, 1963, 707, illus. (Prentice-Hall Chemistry Series.)

SPINAR, LEO H.
College Chemistry. Scott, Foresman, 1968, 448, illus.

STEERE, NORMAN V., ED.
Safety in the Chemical Laboratory. American Chemical Society, Chemical Education Division, 1967, 125, illus.

STEPHENSON, RICHARD M.
Introduction to the Chemical Process Industries. Reinhold, 1966, 474, illus.

STERRETT, FRANCES S. K., KENNEDY, SIBILLA E., and SPARBERG, ESTHER B.
A Laboratory Investigation of Concepts in Chemistry. Harper, 1968, 197, illus.

STOCK, RALPH, and RICE, CEDRIC B. F.
Chromatographic Methods. 2nd ed. Barnes & Noble, 1967, 256, illus.

SYNTHETIC ORGANIC CHEMICAL MANUFACTURERS ASSOCIATION, COMP.
SOCMA Handbook: Commercial Organic Chemical Names. American Chemical Society, 1966, 666, illus.

TAYLOR, HARRY F. W., ED.
The Chemistry of Cements. Academic Press, 1964, 2 vols., illus.

THOMAS, CHARLES L.
Catalytic Processes and Proven Catalysts. Academic Press, 1970, 284.

TOON, ERNEST R., ELLIS, GEORGE L., and BRODKIN, JACOB
Foundations of Chemistry. Holt, Rinehart & Winston, 1968, 803, illus.

TREYBAL, R. E.
Liquid Extraction. 2nd ed. McGraw-Hill, 1963, 640, illus. (McGraw-Hill Chemical Engineering Series.)

U. S. OFFICE OF EDUCATION, VOCATIONAL AND TECHNICAL EDUCATION DIVISION
Chemical Technology: A Suggested 2-Year Post High School Curriculum. USOE, 1964, 119. (OE-80031 Technical Education Program Series No. 5.)

VAN THOOR, T. J., ED.
Chemical Technology: An Encyclopedic Treatment—The Economic Application of Modern Technological Developments Based upon a Work Originally Devised by the Late Dr. J. V. Van Oss. Barnes & Noble, 1970, 3 vols., illus.

VANDERWERF, CALVIN A.
Acids, Bases and the Chemistry of the Covalent Bond. Reinhold, 1961, 117, illus. (Selected Topics in Modern Chemistry.)

VAN WINKLE, MATHEW
Distillation. McGraw-Hill, 1967, 684, illus. (McGraw-Hill Chemical Engineering Series.)

WADDAMS, AUSTEN L.
Chemicals from Petroleum: An Introductory Survey. 2nd ed. Chemical (Tudor, dist.), 1969, 244, illus.

WADDINGTON, THOMAS C., ED.
Non-Aqueous Solvent Systems. Academic Press, 1965, 408, illus.

WAHL, ARNOLD C.
Atomic and Molecular Structure: A Pictorial Approach. McGraw-Hill, 1970, 150, illus.

WALL, FREDERICK T.
Chemical Thermodynamics: A Course of Study. 2nd ed. W. H. Freeman, 1965, 451, illus. (Books in Chemistry Series.)

WASER, JURG
Basic Chemical Thermodynamics. W. A. Benjamin, 1966, 278.

WATSON, JAMES D.
The Double Helix: A Personal Account of the Discovery of the Structure of DNA. Atheneum, 1968, 226, illus.

WENDLAND, RAY T.
Petrochemicals: The New World of Synthetics. Doubleday, 1969, 299, illus. (Chemistry in Action Series.)

WHITE, JOHN H.
A. Reference Book of Chemistry. Philosophical Library, 1967, 310.

WHITFIELD, RICHARD C.
Spectroscopy in Chemistry. Longmans, 1969, 91.

WILLIAMS, ARTHUR L., EMBREE, HARLAND D., and DeBEY, HAROLD J.
Introduction to Chemistry. Addison-Wesley, 1968, 712.

ZOLLINGER, HEINRICH
Azo and Diazo Chemistry: Aliphatic and Aromatic Compounds. Interscience, 1961, 444, illus.

ANALYTICAL

ARIS, RUTHERFORD
Introduction to the Analysis of Chemical Reactors. Prentice-Hall, 1965, 337, illus. (Prentice-Hall Physical and Chemical Engineering Sciences International Series.)

BELCHER, RONALD
New Methods in Analytical Chemistry. 2nd ed. Reinhold, 1964, 366, illus.

CHERVENKA, CHARLES H.
A Manual of Methods for the Analytical Ultracentrifuge. Beckman Instruments, Spinco Division, Palo Alto, 1969, 100, illus.

DIXON, JEAN P.
Modern Methods in Organic Microanalysis. Van Nostrand, 1968, 301, illus. (Van Nostrand Analytical Chemistry Series.)

FREISER, HENRY, and FERNANDO, QUINTUS
Ionic Equilibria and Analytical Chemistry. Wiley, 1963, 334, illus.

HAMILTON, LEICESTER F., SIMPSON, STEPHEN G., and ELLIS, DAVIS W.
Calculations of Analytical Chemistry. 7th ed. McGraw-Hill, 1968, 511, illus.

JACOBS, MORRIS B.
The Chemical Analysis of Air Pollutants. Interscience, 1960, 430.

ENGINEERING PROGRAMS

KARCHMER, J. H., ED.
  Analytical Chemistry of Sulfur and Its Compounds. Wiley, 1970- , vols., illus. (Chemical Analysis Vol. 29.)

LAITINEN, HERBERT A.
  Chemical Analysis: An Advanced Text and Reference. McGraw-Hill, 1960, 611, illus. (McGraw-Hill Advanced Chemistry Series.)

McCOY, JAMES
  Chemical Analysis of Industrial Water. Chemical, 1969, 292.

MEITES, LOUIS, ED.
  Handbook of Analytical Chemistry. McGraw-Hill, 1963, 1788. (McGraw-Hill Handbooks.)

PECSOK, ROBERT L., and SHIELDS, L. DONALD
  Modern Methods of Chemical Analysis. Wiley, 1968, 480, illus.

POPOV, ALEXANDER I., and PFLAUM, RONALD T.
  Introductory Analytical Chemistry. Heath-Raytheon, 1966, 310, illus.

SCOTT, RONALD M.
  Clinical Analysis by Thin-Layer Chromatography Techniques. Humphrey, Ann Arbor, 1969, 227.

SIGGIA, SIDNEY
  Survey of Applied Analytical Chemistry. McGraw-Hill, 1968, 288.

SKOOG, DOUGLAS A., and WEST, DONALD M.
  Fundamentals of Analytical Chemistry. 2nd ed. Holt, Rinehart & Winston, 1969, 835, illus.

STANDARD METHODS OF CHEMICAL ANALYSIS
  6th ed. Van Nostrand, 1962-63, 3 vols., illus.

WAKE, WILLIAM C.
  The Analysis of Rubber and Rubber-Like Polymers. Rev. ed. Wiley-Interscience, 1969, 228, illus.

SWIFT, ERNEST H., and SCHAEFER, WILLIAM P.
  Qualitative Elemental Analysis. Freeman, 1962, 469, illus. (Chemistry Books Series.)

QUANTITATIVE

AYRES, GILBERT H.
  Quantitative Chemical Analysis. 2nd ed. Harper & Row, 1968, 710, illus.

BLAEDEL, WALTER J., and MELOCHE, VULLIERS W.
  Elementary Quantitative Analysis: Theory and Practice. 2nd ed. Harper & Row, 1963, 964, illus.

BRUNBLAY, RAY U.
  A First Course in Quantitative Analysis. Addison-Wesley, 1970, 420. (Addison-Wesley Chemistry Series.)

DAY, REUBEN A., JR., and UNDERWOOD, ARTHUR L.
  Quantitative Analysis. 2nd ed. Prentice-Hall, 1967, 482, illus. (Prentice-Hall Chemistry Series.)

FISCHER, ROBERT B., and PETERS, DENNIS G.
  Basic Theory and Practice of Quantitative Chemical Analysis. 3rd ed. Saunders, 1968, 883, illus.

——.
  A Brief Introduction to Quantitative Chemical Analysis. Saunders, 1969, 537, illus.

FLASCHKA, HERMENEGILD A., BARNARD, ALFRED J., JR., and STURROCK, P. E.
  Quantitative Analytical Chemistry. Barnes & Noble, 1969, 2 vols., illus. (International Textbook Series.)

KOLTHOFF, I. M., et al.
  Quantitative Chemical Analysis. 4th ed. Macmillan, 1969, 1199.

VOGEL, ARTHUR I.
  A Text-book of Quantitative Inorganic Analysis: Including Elementary Instrumental Analysis. 3rd ed. Wiley, 1962, 1216, illus.

BIOCHEMISTRY

AWAPARA, JORGE
  Introduction to Biological Chemistry. Prentice-Hall, 1968, 310, illus. (Prentice-Hall Biological Science Series.)

BALDWIN, ERNEST
  Dynamic Aspects of Biochemistry. 5th ed. Cambridge University Press, 1967, 466.

BENNETT, THOMAS P., and FRIEDEN, EARL
  Modern Topics in Biochemistry: Structure and Function of Biological Molecules. Macmillan, 1966, 186.

BRAVERMAN, JOSEPH B.
  Introduction to the Biochemistry of Foods. Elsevier, 1963, 336.

CANTAROW, ABRAHAM, and SCHEPARTZ, BERNARD
  Biochemistry. 4th ed. Saunders, 1967, 898, illus.

DAVIDSON, JAMES N.
  The Biochemistry of the Nucleic Acids. 6th ed. Methuen, London, 1969, 352, illus.

HARRISON, KENNETH
  A Guide-Book to Biochemistry. 2nd ed. Cambridge University Press, 1965, 152, illus.

HARROW, BENJAMIN, and MAZUR, ABRAHAM
  Textbook of Biochemistry. 9th ed. Saunders, 1966, 648, illus.

QUALITATIVE

CHERONIS, NICHOLAS D., ENTRIKIN, JOHN B., and HODNETT, ERNEST M.
  Semimicro Qualitative Organic Analysis: The Systematic Identification of Organic Compounds. 3rd ed. Interscience, 1965, 1060, illus.

CLARK, ROBERT E. D.
  Semi-Micro Inorganic Qualitative Analysis. 4th ed. Pergamon, 1967, 1 vol.

CLIFFORD, ALAN F.
  Inorganic Chemistry of Qualitative Analysis. Prentice-Hall, 1961, 515, illus. (Prentice-Hall Chemistry Series.)

HOGNESS, THORFIN R., JOHNSON, WARREN C., and ARMSTRONG, ALFRED R.
  Qualitative Analysis and Chemical Equilibrium. 5th ed. Holt, Rinehart & Winston, 1966, 590, illus.

NEBERGALL, WILLIAM H., SCHMIDT, FREDERIC C., and HOLTZCLAW, HENRY F., JR.
  College Chemistry with Qualitative Analysis. 3rd ed. Heath-Raytheon, 1968, 760, illus.

SORUM, CLARENCE H.
  Introduction to Semimicro Qualitative Analysis. 4th ed. Prentice-Hall, 1967, 277, illus. (Prentice-Hall Chemistry Series.)

INGRAHAM, LLOYD L.
    Biochemical Mechanisms. Wiley, 1962, 108, illus.

KARLSON, PETER
    Introduction to Modern Biochemistry. 3rd ed. Academic Press, 1968, 483, illus.

KLEINER, ISRAEL S., and ORTEN, JAMES M.
    Biochemistry. 7th ed. Mosby, 1966, 911, illus.

KLOTZ, IRVING M.
    Energy Changes in Biochemical Reactions. Academic Press, 1967, 108, illus.

MAHLER, HENRY R., and CORDES, EUGENE H.
    Biological Chemistry. Harper & Row, 1966, 872, illus.

STEPHENSON, WILLIAM K.
    Concepts in Biochemistry: A Programmed Text. Wiley, 1967, 222.

WILLIAMS, ROGER J., and LANSFORD, EDWIN M., EDS.
    The Encyclopedia of Biochemistry. Reinhold, 1967, 876, illus.

INSTRUMENTATION

BAIR, EDWARD J.
    Introduction to Chemical Instrumentation: Electronic Signals and Operations. McGraw-Hill, 1962, 349, illus.

EWING, GALEN W.
    Instrumental Methods of Chemical Analysis. 3rd ed. McGraw-Hill, 1969, 627.

GUILBAULT, GEORGE G., and HARGIS, LARRY G.
    Instrumental Analysis Manual: Modern Experiments for the Laboratory. Dekker, 1970, 444, illus.

INSTRUMENTATION IN THE CHEMICAL AND PETROLEUM INDUSTRIES
    Plenum Press, 1964, Vol. 1- , illus.

MELOAN, CLIFTON E., and KISER, ROBERT W.
    Problems and Experiments in Instrumental Analysis. Merrill, 1963, 319, illus.

REILLEY, CHARLES N., and SAWYER, DONALD T.
    Experiments for Instrumental Methods: A Laboratory Manual. McGraw-Hill, 1961, 412, illus.

STROBEL, HOWARD A.
    Chemical Instrumentation: A Systematic Approach to Instrumental Analysis. Addison-Wesley, 1960, 653, illus. (Addison-Wesley Chemistry Series.)

WILLARD, HOBART H., MERRITT, LYNNE L., JR., and DEAN, JOHN A.
    Instrumental Methods of Analysis. 4th ed. Van Nostrand, 1965, 784, illus.

INORGANIC

ANGELICI, ROBERT J.
    Synthesis and Technique in Inorganic Chemistry. Saunders, 1969, 203.

BASOLO, FRED, and PEARSON, RALPH G.
    Mechanisms of Inorganic Reactions: A Study of Metal Complexes in Solution. 2nd ed. Wiley, 1967, 701, illus.

CHISWELL, B., and JAMES, D. W.
    Fundamental Aspects of Inorganic Chemistry. Wiley, 1970, 280.

DAY, M. CLYDE, JR., and SELBIN, JOEL
    Theoretical Inorganic Chemistry. 2nd ed. Reinhold, 1969, 590, illus. (Reinhold Chemistry Textbook Series.)

DOUGLAS, BODIE E., and McDANIEL, DARL H.
    Concepts and Models of Inorganic Chemistry. Blaisdell, Waltham, Mass., 1965, 510, illus. (Pure and Applied Sciences Series.)

DRAGO, RUSSELL S.
    Physical Methods in Inorganic Chemistry. Reinhold, 1965, 430, illus. (Reinhold Textbook Series.)

EDWARDS, JOHN O.
    Inorganic Reaction Mechanisms: An Introduction. W. A. Benjamin, 1964, 190, illus. (Physical Inorganic Chemistry Series.)

EMELÉUS, HARRY J., and ANDERSON, JOHN S.
    Modern Aspects of Inorganic Chemistry. 3rd ed. Van Nostrand, 1960, 611, illus.

GOULD, EDWIN S.
    Inorganic Reactions and Structure. Rev. ed. Holt, Rinehart & Winston, 1962, 513, illus.

HARVEY, KENNETH B., and PORTER, GERALD B.
    Introduction to Physical Inorganic Chemistry. Addison-Wesley, 1963, 437, illus. (Addison-Wesley Chemistry Series.)

HUNT, JOHN P.
    Metal Ions in Aqueous Solution. W. A. Benjamin, 1963, 124, illus. (Physical Inorganic Chemistry Series.)

JOLLY, WILLIAM L.
    The Synthesis and Characterization of Inorganic Compounds. Prentice-Hall, 1970, 550. (International Series in Chemistry.)

———.
    Synthetic Inorganic Chemistry. Prentice-Hall, 1960, 196, illus. (Prentice-Hall Chemistry Series.)

JONASSEN, HANS B.
    Technique of Inorganic Chemistry. Wiley, 1963, 6 vols.

KLEINBERG, JACOB, ARGERSINGER, WILLIAM J., JR., and GRISWOLD, ERNEST
    Inorganic Chemistry. Heath-Raytheon, 1960, 680, illus.

KREBS, HEINZ
    Fundamentals of Inorganic Crystal Chemistry. McGraw-Hill, 1968, 405, illus. (European Chemistry Series.)

LEE, JOHN D.
    Concise Inorganic Chemistry. Van Nostrand, 1964, 248, illus.

MACKAY, KENNETH, and MACKAY, ANN
    Introduction to Modern Inorganic Chemistry. International Textbook, 1968, 258.

MELLOR, JOSEPH W., and PARKES, G. D.
    Modern Inorganic Chemistry. 6th ed. Wiley, 1968, 1025.

PASS, GEOFFREY, and SUTCLIFFE, HAYDN
    Practical Inorganic Chemistry: Preparations, Reactions and Instrumental Methods. Chapman & Hall, 1968, 225.

PLANE, ROBERT A., and HESTER, RONALD E.
    Elements of Inorganic Chemistry. W. A. Benjamin, 1965, 188, illus. (Physical Inorganic Chemistry Series.)

SIENKO, MICHELL J., and PLANE, ROBERT A.
    Physical Inorganic Chemistry. W. A. Benjamin, 1963, 166, illus. (Physical Inorganic Chemistry Series.)

WELLS, ALEXANDER F.
    Structural Inorganic Chemistry. 3rd ed. Clarendon Press, 1962, 1055, illus.

ORGANIC

ADAMS, ROGER, JOHNSON, JOHN R., and WILCOX, CHARLES F.
Laboratory Experiments in Organic Chemistry. 6th ed. Macmillan, 1970, 528, illus.

AULT, ADDISON
Problems in Organic Structure Determination. McGraw-Hill, 1967, 250, 184.

BALDWIN, JOHN E.
Experimental Organic Chemistry. 2nd ed. McGraw-Hill, 1970, 197, illus.

BONNER, WILLIAM A., and CASTRO, ALBERT J.
Essentials of Modern Organic Chemistry. Reinhold, 1965, 645, illus.

BRESLOW, RONALD
Organic Reaction Mechanism: An Introduction. 2nd ed. W. A. Benjamin, 1969, 272. (Organic Chemistry Monograph Series.)

BREWSTER, RAY Q.
Organic Chemistry. 3rd ed. Prentice-Hall, 1961, 854, illus.

BREWSTER, RAY Q., VANDERWERF, CALVIN A., and McEWEN, WILLIAM E.
Unitized Experiments in Organic Chemistry. 2nd ed. Van Nostrand, 1964, 271, illus.

BUSBY, REGINALD E., and SHAW, CHARLES J.
Organic Chemistry Problems. Plenum Press, 1967, 300.

CASERIO, MARJORIE C.
Experimental Organic Chemistry. W. A. Benjamin, 1967, 204, illus.

CASON, JAMES, and RAPOPORT, HENRY
Laboratory Text in Organic Chemistry. 2nd ed. Prentice-Hall, 1962, 514, illus. (Prentice-Hall Chemistry Series.)

CHERONIS, NICHOLAS D., and ENTRIKIN, J. B.
Identification of Organic Compounds: A Student's Text Using Semimicro Techniques. Interscience, 1963, 477, illus.

CONROW, KENNETH, and McDONALD, RICHARD N.
Deductive Organic Chemistry: A Short Course. Addison-Wesley, 1966, 405, illus.

CORWIN, ALSOPH H., and BURSEY, MAURICE M.
Elements of Organic Chemistry as Revealed by the Scientific Method. Addison-Wesley, 1966, 746, illus. (Addison-Wesley Series in Chemistry.)

CRESWELL, CLIFFORD J., and RUNQUIST, OLAF
Spectral Analysis of Organic Compounds: An Introductory Programmed Text. Burgess, 1970, 242, illus.

DANIELS, RALPH, and BAUER, LUDWIG
Problems in Organic Chemistry. 2nd ed. F. A. Davis, 1964, 228.

DAUBER, WILLIAM G.
Organic Reactions. Wiley, 1970, 1 vol. (Organic Reactions Series Vol. 18.)

DePUY, CHARLES H., and RINEHART, KENNETH L.
Introduction to Organic Chemistry. Wiley, 1967, 392, illus.

DeWOLFE, ROBERT H.
Carboxylic Ortho Acid Derivatives: Preparation and Synthetic Applications. Academic Press, 1970, 557. (Organic Chemistry Monograph Series Vol. 14.)

FEIGL, FRITZ
Spot Tests in Organic Analysis. 7th ed. Elsevier, 1966, 772, illus.

FERGUSON, LLOYD N.
The Modern Structural Theory of Organic Chemistry. Prentice-Hall 1963, 600, illus. (Prentice-Hall Chemistry Series.)

FIESER, LOUIS F.
Organic Experiments. 2nd ed. Heath-Raytheon, 1968, 342, illus.

FIESER, LOUIS F., and FIESER, MARY
Reagents for Organic Synthesis. Wiley, 1967, 1457, illus.
———.
Topics in Organic Chemistry. Reinhold, 1963, 668.

FINLEY, KAY T., and WILSON, JAMES, JR.
Fundamental Organic Chemistry: An Analytical Approach. Prentice-Hall, 1970, 429, illus.

FOERST, WILHELM, ED.
Newer Methods of Preparative Organic Chemistry. Academic Press, 1963-1968, 5 vols.

FRANKEL, MAX, and PATAI, SAUL
Tables for Identification of Organic Compounds. 2nd ed. Chemical Rubber Co., 1964, 301.

GEISSMAN, THEODORE A.
Principles of Organic Chemistry. 3rd ed. W. H. Freeman, 1968, 883, illus. (Books in Chemistry Series.)

GRIFFIN, RODGER W., JR.
Modern Organic Chemistry. McGraw-Hill, 1969, 513.

HANSCH, CORWIN, and HELMKAMP, GEORGE
Organic Chemistry: An Outline—Problems and Answers. 2nd ed. McGraw-Hill, 1963, 336.

HART, HAROLD, and SCHUETZ, ROBERT D.
Organic Chemistry. 3rd ed. Houghton Mifflin, 1966, 353, illus.

HELMKAMP, GEORGE K., and JOHNSON, HARRY W., JR.
Selected Experiments in Organic Chemistry. 2nd ed. Freeman, 1968, 184.

HENDRICKSON, JAMES B., CRAM, DONALD J., and HAMMOND, GEORGE S.
Organic Chemistry. 3rd ed. McGraw-Hill, 1970, 950, illus.

HINE, JACK S.
Physical Organic Chemistry. 2nd ed. McGraw-Hill, 1962, 552, illus. (McGraw-Hill Advanced Chemistry Series.)

IRELAND, ROBERT E.
Organic Synthesis. Prentice-Hall, 1969, 147. (Foundations of Modern Organic Chemistry No. 10.)

ISAACS, NEIL S.
Experiments in Physical Organic Chemistry. Macmillan, 1969, 323.

KICE, JOHN L., and MARVELL, ELLIOTT N.
Modern Principles of Organic Chemistry: An Introduction. Macmillan, 1966, 449, illus. (Concepts of Chemistry Series.)

KOSOWER, EDWARD M.
An Introduction to Physical Organic Chemistry. Wiley, 1968, 503.

KRAUCH, HELMUT, and KUNZ, WERNER
Organic Name Reactions: A Contribution to the Terminology of Organic Chemistry, Biochemistry and Theoretical Organic Chemistry. 2nd ed. Wiley, 1964, 620.

LINSTROMBERG, WALTER W.
Organic Chemistry: A Brief Course. 2nd ed. D.C. Heath, 1970, 502, illus.

LOWTHER, HAROLD
Organic Chemistry: An Introductory Course. Pergamon, 1964, 197, illus. (Commonwealth and International Li-

brary of Science, Technology, Engineering and Liberal Studies Chemistry Division Vol. 4.)

MARCH, JERRY
Advanced Organic Chemistry: Reactions, Mechanisms and Structure. McGraw-Hill, 1968, 1098, illus. (Advanced Chemistry Series.)

MARMOR, SOLOMON
Laboratory Guide for Organic Chemistry. Heath-Raytheon, 1964, 354, illus.

McFARLAND, JOHN W.
Organic Laboratory Chemistry. Mosby, 1969, 286.

MILLAR, IAN T., and SPRINGALL, H. D.
A Shorter Sidgwick's Organic Chemistry of Nitrogen. Oxford, 1969, 582, illus.

MORRISON, ROBERT T., and BOYD, ROBERT N.
Organic Chemistry. 2nd ed. Allyn & Bacon, 1966, 1204, illus.

NOLLER, CARL R.
Chemistry of Organic Compounds. 3rd ed. Saunders, 1965, 1115, illus.

OKAMOTO, YOSHIYUKI
Organic Semiconductors. Reinhold, 1964, 184, illus.

OWEN, TERENCE C.
Characterization of Organic Compounds by Chemical Methods: An Introductory Laboratory Textbook. Dekker, 1969, 247, illus.

REUTOV, O. A.
Fundamentals of Theoretical Organic Chemistry. 2nd ed. Appleton-Century-Crofts, 1967, 593, illus.

RIDDICK, JOHN A., and BUNGER, WILLIAM B.
Organic Solvents. 3rd ed. Wiley-Interscience, 1970, 487. (Techniques of Chemistry Series Vol. 2.)

ROBERTS, JOHN D., and CASERIO, MARJORIE C.
Basic Principles of Organic Chemistry. W. A. Benjamin, 1964, 1315, illus.

ROBERTSON, GEORGE R., and JACOBS, THOMAS L.
Laboratory Practice of Organic Chemistry. 4th ed. Macmillan, 1962, 383, illus.

SHAPIRO, R. H.
Spectral Exercises in Structural Determination of Organic Compounds. Holt, Rinehart & Winston, 1969, 209.

SHRINER, RALPH L., FUSON, REYNOLD C., and CURTIN, DAVID Y.
Systematic Identification of Organic Compounds: A Laboratory Manual. 5th ed. Wiley, 1964, 458.

SILVERSTEIN, ROBERT M., and BASSLER, G. CLAYTON
Spectrometric Identification of Organic Compounds. 2nd ed. Wiley, 1967, 256, illus.

SITTIG, MARSHALL
Organic Chemical Process Encyclopedia. 2nd ed. Noyes, 1969, 712, illus.

SMITH, L. OLIVER, JR., and CRISTOL, STANLEY J.
Organic Chemistry. Reinhold, 1966, 966, illus. (Reinhold Chemistry Textbook Series.)

SMITH, P. W. G., and TATCHELL, A. R.
Organic Chemistry for General Degree Students. Pergamon, 1969, 2 vols.

STILLE, JOHN K.
Industrial Organic Chemistry. Prentice-Hall, 1968, 128. (Prentice-Hall Foundations of Modern Organic Chemistry Series.)

STULL, DANIEL R., WESTRUM, EDGAR F., JR., and SINKE, GERARD C.
The Chemical Thermodynamics of Organic Compounds. Wiley, 1969, 844, illus.

VAN ORDEN, HARRIS O., and LEE, GARTH L.
Elementary Organic Chemistry: A Brief Course. Saunders, 1969, 329.

WEISS, F. T.
Determination of Organic Compounds: Methods and Procedures. Wiley, 1970, 480. (Chemical Analysis Series Vol. 32.)

WEISS, HOWARD
Guide to Organic Reactions. Burgess, 1969, 247.

WIBERG, KENNETH B.
Laboratory Technique in Organic Chemistry. McGraw-Hill, 1960, 262, illus. (McGraw-Hill Advanced Chemistry Series.)

WOLF, FRANK J.
Separation Methods in Organic Chemistry and Biochemistry. Academic Press, 1969, 237.

YUKAWA, YASUHIDE, ED.
Handbook of Organic Structural Analysis. W. A. Benjamin, 1965, 765, illus.

PHYSICAL

ANDREWS, DONALD H.
Introductory Physical Chemistry. McGraw-Hill, 1970, 640, illus.

DANIELS, FARRINGTON, et al.
Experimental Physical Chemistry. 7th ed. McGraw-Hill, 1970, 669, illus.

GLASSTONE, SAMUEL
The Elements of Physical Chemistry. 2nd ed. Van Nostrand, 1960, 758, illus.

GUCKER, FRANK T., and SEIFERT, RALPH L.
Physical Chemistry. W. W. Norton, 1966, 824, illus.

HANNAY, NORMAN B.
Solid-State Chemistry. Prentice-Hall, 1967, 225, illus. (Fundamental Topics in Physical Chemistry.)

MARON, SAMUEL H., and PRUTTON, CARL F.
Principles of Physical Chemistry. 4th ed. Macmillan, 1965, 886, illus.

MOORE, WALTER J.
Physical Chemistry. 3rd ed. Prentice-Hall, 1962, 844, illus.

OELKE, WILLIAM C.
Laboratory Physical Chemistry. Van Nostrand, 1969, 450, illus.

SALZBERG, HUGH W., et al.
Physical Chemistry: A Modern Laboratory Course. Academic Press, 1969, 528.

SHOEMAKER, DAVID P., and GARLAND, CARL W.
Experiments in Physical Chemistry. 2nd ed. McGraw-Hill, 1967, 490, illus.

TUFFNELL, ROBERT, and LUKE, DUDLEY J.
The Nature of Physical Chemistry. Elsevier, 1970, 322.

WILLIAMS, VIRGINIA R., and WILLIAMS, HULEN B.
Basic Physical Chemistry for the Life Sciences. Freeman, 1967, 382, illus.

ENGINEERING PROGRAMS

CONSTRUCTION TECHNOLOGY

ALUMINUM ASSOCIATION
   Aluminum Construction Manual: Specifications for Aluminum Structures. AA, 1967, 64, illus.

AMBROSE, JAMES E.
   Building Structures Primer. Wiley, 1967, 122, illus.

AMERICAN INSTITUTE OF STEEL CONSTRUCTION
   Manual of Steel Construction. 7th ed. AISC, 1970, 996.
———.
   Structural Steel Detailing. AISC, 1966, 1 vol., illus

AMERICAN INSTITUTE OF TIMBER CONSTRUCTION
   Timber Construction Manual. Wiley, 1966, 1 vol., illus.
———.
   Timber Construction Standards: Recommended Standards, Specifications, and Codes for Use by Architects, Engineers, Fabricators, Contractors, and Others Concerned with Engineered Timber Construction. 5th ed. AITC, Washington, 1969, 1 vol., various pagings, illus.

AMERICAN PUBLIC WORKS ASSOCIATION (SOUTHERN CALIFORNIA CHAPTER) and ASSOCIATED GENERAL CONTRACTORS OF CALIFORNIA (SOUTHERN CALIFORNIA DISTRICT) in JOINT COOPERATIVE COMMITTEE
   Standards Specifications for Public Works Construction. APWA, 1970, 407.

AMERICAN SOCIETY FOR TESTING MATERIALS
   ASTM Standards in Building Codes: Specifications, Methods of Test, Definitions. 6th ed. ASTM, 1968, 1678, illus.

AMERICAN WELDING SOCIETY, INC.
   Code For Welding in Building Construction. AWS, 1969, 1 vol.

ANNETT, FRED A.
   Elevators: Electric and Electrohydraulic Elevators, Escalators, Moving Sidewalks, and Ramps. 3rd ed. McGraw-Hill, 1960, 388, illus.

ANTILL, JAMES M., and WOODHEAD, RONALD W.
   Critical Path Methods in Construction Practice. 2nd ed. Wiley-Interscience, 1970, 414, illus.

ARCHITECTURAL RECORD
   Architectural Engineering: New Structures. McGraw-Hill, 1964, 214, illus.

ARCO PUBLISHING COMPANY, INC.
   Asphalt Worker-Foreman of Asphalt Workers. Arco, 1960, 154.
———.
   Construction Supervisor and Inspector. Arco, 1963, 216.

ASPHALT INSTITUTE
   The Asphalt Handbook. AI, 1966, 500, illus.
———.
   Construction Specifications for Asphalt Concrete and Other Plant-Mix Types. 4th ed. AI, 1969, 1 vol.
———.
   Introduction to Asphalt. 6th ed. AI, 1967, 1 vol.
———.
   Specifications and Construction Methods for Asphalt Concrete and Other Plant-Mix Types. 3rd ed. AI, 1964, 115, illus. (Specification Series No. 1.)

ATKINSON, HENRY F.
   Rough Carpentry and Masonry. McGraw-Hill, 1969, 184, illus. (McGraw Foundation Series.)

BENSON, BEN
   Building Contractor's and Home Builder's Handbook of Bidding, Surveying, and Estimating. Prentice-Hall, 1968, 190, illus.
———.
   Critical Path Methods in Building Construction. Prentice-Hall, 1970, 132, illus.

BENTLEY, HOWARD B., COMP.
   Building Construction: Information Sources. Gale, 1964, 181. (Management Information Guide No. 2.)

BOWLES, JOSEPH E.
   Foundation Analysis and Design. McGraw-Hill, 1968, 659, illus.

BRADY, GEORGE S.
   Materials Handbook: An Encyclopedia for Purchasing Agents, Engineers, Executives, and Foremen. 9th ed. McGraw-Hill, 1963, 968, illus.

BROWNELL, ADON H.
   Builders' Hardware Handbook. 2nd ed. with supplement. Chilton, 1961, 262, illus.

BUILDING OFFICIALS CONFERENCE OF AMERICA, INC.
   BOCA Basic Building Code. 4th ed. BOCA, 1965, 464.

BURBANK, NELSON L., and PFISTER, HERBERT R.
   House Construction Details. 6th ed. Simmons-Boardman, 1968, 473, illus.

CALLENDER, JOHN H., ED.
   Time-Saver Standards: A Handbook of Architectural Design. 4th ed. McGraw-Hill, 1966, 1299, illus.

CARSON, ARTHUR B.
   Foundation Construction. McGraw-Hill, 1965, 424, illus.
———.
   General Excavation Methods. McGraw-Hill, 1961, 392, illus.

CASSIMATIS, PETER J.
   Economics of the Construction Industry. National Industrial Conference Board, New York, 1969, 168, illus. (Conference Board Studies in Business Economics No. 111.)

CHELLIS, ROBERT D.
   Pile Foundations. 2nd ed. McGraw-Hill, 1961, 704, illus.

CLOSE, PAUL D.
   Sound Control and Thermal Insulation of Buildings. Reinhold, 1966, 502, illus.

CLOUGH, RICHARD H.
   Construction Contracting. 2nd ed. Wiley, 1969, 382, illus.

COHEN, HENRY A.
   Public Construction Contracts and the Law. F. W. Dodge, 1961, 400.

COLLINS, FRANK T.
   Manual Critical Path Techniques for Construction. Know How Publications, Berkeley, 1965, 193, illus.
———.
   Manual of Tilt Up Construction. 5th ed. Know How Publications, Berkeley, 1963, 126, illus.

CONDIT, CARL W.
   American Building Art: The Twentieth Century. Oxford University Press, 1961, 427.
———.
   American Building: Materials and Techniques from the First Colonial Settlements to the Present. University of Chicago Press, 1968, 329, illus. (Chicago History of American Civilization.)

COOK, JOHN P.
   Construction Sealants and Adhesives. Wiley, 1970, 269. (Wiley Practical Construction Guides Series.)

CRISPIN, FREDERIC S.
   Dictionary of Technical Terms—Containing Definitions of Commonly Used Expressions in Aeronautics, Architecture, Woodworking and Building Trades.... 11th ed. Bruce, 1970, 455, illus.

DALY, DONALD F.
   Aim for a Job in the Building Trades. R. Rosen Press, 1970, 158, illus. (Aim High Vocational Series.)

CONSTRUCTION TECHNOLOGY

DAVEY, NORMAN
    A History of Building Materials. Phoenix House, London, 1961, 260, illus.

DAVIS, CALVIN V., and SORENSON, KENNETH E., EDS.
    Handbook of Applied Hydraulics. 3rd ed. McGraw-Hill, 1969, 1216.

DAY, B. F., ED.
    Building Acoustics. Elsevier, 1969, 120, illus.

DEATHERAGE, GEORGE E.
    Construction Company Organization and Management. McGraw-Hill, 1964, 300.

―――.
    Construction Estimating and Job Preplanning. McGraw-Hill, 1965, 302, illus.

―――.
    Construction Office Administration. McGraw-Hill, 1964, 311, illus.

―――.
    Construction Scheduling and Control. McGraw-Hill, 1965, 316, illus.

DIETZ, ALBERT G. H.
    Plastics for Architects and Builders. MIT Press, 1969, 129, illus.

DOBROVOLNY, JERRY S.
    Civil Engineering Technology Consultant's Workshop. American Association of Junior Colleges, 1968, 32.

DUBIN, MARTIN D.
    Architectural Supervision of Modern Buildings. Reinhold, 1963, 304.

DUNHAM, CLARENCE W.
    Foundations of Structures. 2nd ed. McGraw-Hill, 1962, 722, illus.

EDWARDS, H. GRIFFITH
    Specifications. 2nd ed. Van Nostrand, 1961, 372, illus. (Technical Series on Building Construction.)

FABER, OSCAR
    Constructional Steelwork Simply Explained. 5th ed., rev. Oxford University Press, 1966, 133, illus.

FELD, JACOB
    Construction Failure. Wiley, 1968, 399.

FLYNN, JOHN E., and SEGIL, ARTHUR W.
    Architectural Interior Systems: Lighting, Air Conditioning, Acoustics. Van Nostrand-Reinhold, 1970, 288, illus.

FOSS, EDWARD W.
    Construction and Maintenance for Farm and Home. Wiley, 1960, 373, illus.

FOSTER, NORMAN
    Construction Estimates from Take-Off to Bid. McGraw-Hill, 1961, 246, illus.

―――.
    Practical Tables for Building Construction. McGraw-Hill, 1963, 248, illus.

GARBER, LEE O., and EDWARDS, NEWTON
    The Law Governing School Property and School-Building Construction. Interstate, 1964, 116.

GATZ, KONRAD, ED.
    Curtain Wall Construction. Praeger, 1967, 174, illus. (Architect and Building News Book.)

GAY, CHARLES M., et al.
    Mechanical and Electrical Equipment for Buildings. 4th ed. Wiley, 1964, 658, illus.

GILL, PAUL
    Systems Management Techniques for Builders and Contractors. McGraw-Hill, 1968, 224.

GRAHAM, FRANK D.
    Audel's Masons' and Builders' Guide: A Practical Illustrated Trade Assistant on Modern Construction.... Audel, 1961- , vols., illus.

―――.
    Audel's Pumps, Hydraulics, Air Compressors: A Practical Guide Covering Theory, Construction and Operation of Modern Pumps, Hydraulic Machinery, Air Compressors, and Blowers.... Audel, 1960, 1 vol., illus.

GRINTER, LINTON E.
    Design of Modern Steel Structures. 2nd ed. Macmillan, 1960, 491, illus.

―――.
    Elementary Structural Analysis and Design. 2nd ed. Macmillan, 1965, 465, illus.

GUTTMANN, WERNER H.
    Concise Guide to Structural Adhesives. Reinhold, 1961, 389, illus.

HALPERIN, DON A.
    Building With Steel: Design Detailing and Erection. 2nd ed. American Technical Society, 1966, 267, illus.

HAMMOND, ROLT
    Modern Foundation Methods. MacLaren, London, 1967, 176, illus.

HARR, MILTON E.
    Foundations of Theoretical Soil Mechanics. McGraw-Hill, 1966, 381.

―――.
    Groundwater and Seepage. McGraw-Hill, 1962, 315.

HENN, WALTER
    Buildings for Industry. Hayden, 1965, 2 vols., illus.

HIGGIN, GURTH, and JESSOP, NEIL
    Communications in the Building Industry: The Report of a Pilot Study. 2nd ed. Tavistock, London, 1965, 125, illus.

HOFFMANN, KURT, and GRIESE, HELGA
    Building with Wood: Form, Structural Design, and Preservation. Praeger, 1966, 169, illus.

HOLZBOCK, WERNER G.
    Hydraulic Power and Equipment. Industrial Press, 1968, 310, illus.

HOPKINSON, RALPH G., and KAY, JOHN D.
    The Lighting of Buildings. Praeger, 1969, 318, illus.

HORNBOSTEL, CALEB
    Materials for Architecture: An Encyclopedic Guide. Reinhold, 1961, 610, illus.

HUNT, WILLIAM D., ED.
    Creative Control of Building Costs. McGraw-Hill, 1967, 239, illus.

HUNTINGTON, WHITNEY C.
    Building Construction: Materials and Types of Construction. 3rd ed. Wiley, 1963, 734, illus.

HUTTON, JOHN
    Building and Construction in Australia. International Publications Service, dist., 1970, 320, illus.

INTERNATIONAL CONFERENCE OF BUILDING OFFICIALS
    A Training Manual in Field Inspection of Buildings and Structures. ICBO, Los Angeles, 1968, 174, illus.

―――.
    Uniform building code. ICBO, Los Angeles, 1927- , vols., illus.

JAMES F. LINCOLN ARC WELDING FOUNDATION
    Modern Welded Structures. JFLAWF, Cleveland, 1963- , vols., illus.

JOHNSON, SIDNEY M.
    Deterioration, Maintenance, and Repair of Structures. McGraw-Hill, 1965, 373, illus.

ENGINEERING PROGRAMS

JOHNSON, SIDNEY M., and KAVANAGH, THOMAS C.
  The Design of Foundations for Buildings. McGraw-Hill, 1968, 393, illus.

JONES, RAYMOND P.
  Construction Estimating: Residential/Commercial. Delmar, 1967, 152, illus.

———.
  Framing, Sheathing & Insulation. Delmar, 1964, 227, illus.

KASPER, SYDNEY H.
  Careers in the Building Trades. Walck, 1964, 128. (Careers for Tomorrow.)

KIDDER, FRANK E., and PARKER, HARRY, EDS.
  Architects' and Builders' Handbook. Wiley, 1931- , vols.

KING, HORACE W., and BRATER, ERNEST F.
  Handbook of Hydraulics. 5th ed. McGraw-Hill, 1963, 571.

KURTZ, EDWIN B.
  The Lineman's and Cableman's Handbook. 4th ed. McGraw-Hill, 1964, 1 vol., illus.

KURTZ, MAX
  Comprehensive Structural Design Guide. McGraw-Hill, 1969, 328, illus.

LAFEVER, MINARD
  The Modern Builder's Guide. Dover, 1969, 146, illus.

LAURSEN, HAROLD I.
  Structural Analysis. McGraw-Hill, 1969, 486.

LEFKOE, M. R.
  The Crisis in Construction: There is an Answer. Bureau of National Affairs, 1970, 189.

LEHIGH UNIVERSITY, DEPARTMENT OF CIVIL ENGINEERING
  Structural Steel Design. Ronald, 1964, 829, illus.

LEWICKI, BOHDAN
  Building with Large Prefabricates. Elsevier, 1966, 460, illus.

LINDSEY, FORREST R.
  Pipefitter's Handbook. 3rd ed. Industrial Press, 1967, 1 vol.

LIPOWSKY, BENJAMIN, and BERSTEN, MURRAY
  A Picture Dictionary and Guide to Building and Construction Terms. Arco, 1960, 27, illus.

LIPSEY, ROBERT E., and PRESTON, DORIS
  Source Book of Statistics Relating to Construction. Columbia University Press, 1966, 307. (National Bureau of Economic Research, General Series No. 82.)

LISACK, J. P.
  A Manpower Report Concerning Occupations, Worker Traits and Qualifications, and Areas of Work in Architectural, Construction, and Related Fields for Jobs Above the Skilled Craftsmen Level. Purdue University, School of Technology (Office of Manpower Studies), 1966, 54. (Manpower Study No. 66-3.)

LOTHERS, JOHN E.
  Advanced Design in Structural Steel. Prentice-Hall, 1960, 583, illus.

LUX, DONALD G., and RAY, WILLIS E.
  The World of Construction. 4th ed. McKnight & McKnight, 1970, 560, illus.

McCORMAC, JACK C.
  Structural Analysis. 2nd ed. International Textbook, 1967, 494.

———.
  Structural Steel Design. International Textbook, 1965, 542.

McGUINNESS, WILLIAM J., and STEIN, B.
  Mechanical and Electrical Equipment for Buildings. 5th ed. Wiley, 1970, 1 vol.

McGUIRE, WILLIAM
  Steel Structures. Prentice-Hall, 1968, 1112, illus. Prentice-Hall Structural Analysis and Design Series.)

McKAIG, THOMAS H.
  Applied Structural Design of Buildings. 3rd ed. McGraw-Hill, 1965, 499.

———.
  Building Failures: Case Studies in Construction and Design. McGraw-Hill, 1962, 261, illus. (Dodge Books.)

McNICKLE, L. S.
  Simplified Hydraulics. McGraw-Hill, 1966, 196, illus.

MEDLYCOTT, ANTHONY
  Applied Building Construction. 2nd ed. Chapman & Hall, London, 1967- , vols.

MERRITT, FREDERICK S., ED.
  Building Code of the City of New York. Van Nostrand-Reinhold, 1970, 836, illus.

———.
  Building Construction Handbook. 2nd ed. McGraw-Hill, 1965, 1 vol., illus. (McGraw-Hill Handbooks.)

MILLER, LAWRENCE C.
  Successful Management for Contractors. McGraw-Hill, 1962, 216.

MODERN PLASTICS.
  Plastics in Building. McGraw-Hill, 1966, 184, illus.

MODULAR BUILDING STANDARDS ASSOCIATION
  Modular Practice: The Schoolhouse and the Building Industry. Wiley, 1962, 198, illus.

MORGAN, WILLIAM
  The Elements of Structure: An Introduction to the Principles of Building and Structural Engineering. Pitman, 1968, 275, illus.

MORRIS, IRVINE E.
  Handbook of Structural Design. Reinhold, 1963, 803.

MUNGER, ELMER L., and DOUGLAS, CLARENCE J.
  Construction Management. Prentice-Hall, 1970, 208. (Engineering Technology Series.)

NATIONAL ACADEMY OF SCIENCES, NATIONAL RESEARCH COUNCIL (BUILDING RESEARCH INSTITUTE)
  Documentation of Building Science Literature. NAS, 1960, 46. (Pub. No. 791.)

———.
  Performance of Plastics in Building. NAS, 1963, 174. (Pub. No. 1004.)

———.
  Preassembled Building Components. NAS, 1961, 180. (Pub. No. 911.)

NATIONAL ASSOCIATION OF HOME BUILDERS
  A Glossary of Building Marketing Terminology. NAHB, Washington, 1965, 54.

NATIONAL ASSOCIATION OF WOMEN IN CONSTRUCTION, PHOENIX CHAPTER
  Construction Dictionary: A Handbook of Construction Terms & Tables. NAWC, Phoenix, 1966, 177.

NATIONAL CONSTRUCTORS ASSOCIATION
  Directory of International Engineering and Construction Services. NCA, Washington, 1968, 75.

NATIONAL PAINT, VARNISH AND LACQUER ASSOCIATION, INC.
  Guide to U.S. Government Paint Specifications. 18th ed. NPVLA, Washington, 1968, 1 vol.

NEWMAN, MORTON
  Standard Structural Details for Building Construction. McGraw-Hill, 1968, 361, illus.

NICHOLS, HERBERT L.
  Moving the Earth: The Workbook of Excavation. 2nd ed. North Castle Books, Greenwich, Conn., 1962, 1 vol., illus.

CONSTRUCTION TECHNOLOGY

NORRIS, CHARLES H., and WILBUR, JOHN B.
  Elementary Structural Analysis. 2nd ed. McGraw-Hill, 1960, 650, illus.

OBERG, FRED R.
  Heavy Timber Construction. 2nd ed. American Technical Society, 1968, 408, illus.

O'BRIEN, JAMES J.
  CPM in Construction Management: Scheduling by the Critical Path Method. McGraw-Hill, 1965, 254.

OHIO STATE UNIVERSITY, INDUSTRIAL ARTS CURRICULUM PROJECT
  The World of Construction. McKnight & McKnight, 1970, 525, illus.

OPPENHEIMER, SAMUEL P.
  Erecting Structural Steel. McGraw-Hill, 1960, 264, illus.

ORAVETZ, JULES A.
  Audel's Practical Guide to Building Maintenance. Audel, 1966, 437, illus.

PAGE, JOHN S.
  Estimator's Construction Man-Hour Manual. Gulf, Houston, 1960, 241.

PALUSCI, LARRY
  Profitable Retailing of Building Supplies. Cahners, 1969, 121, illus.

PARKER, ALBERT D.
  Planning and Estimating Underground Construction. McGraw-Hill, 1970, 300, illus.

———.
  Planning and Estimating Urban Construction. McGraw-Hill, 1970, 350.

PARKER, HARRY
  Simplified Design of Structural Timber. 2nd ed. Wiley, 1963, 265, illus.

———.
  Simplified Engineering for Architects and Builders. 4th ed. Wiley, 1967, 361, illus.

PEURIFOY, ROBERT L.
  Construction Planning, Equipment and Methods. 2nd ed. McGraw-Hill, 1970, 696, illus.

PHILLIPS, B. G.
  Building Law Illustrated: A Guide to Practice. 4th ed. Spon, London, 1967, 249, illus.

PILCHER, ROY
  Principles of Construction Management for Engineers and Managers. McGraw-Hill, 1967, 382.

PRILUCK, HERBERT M., and HOURIHAN, PETER M.
  Practical CPM for Construction. R. S. Means, Duxbury, Mass., 1968, 53, illus.

PULVER, HARRY E.
  Construction Estimates and Costs. 4th ed. McGraw-Hill, 1969, 644, illus.

QUINN, ALONZO DeF.
  Design and Construction of Ports and Marine Structures. McGraw-Hill, 1961, 531, illus.

RADCLIFFE, BYRON M., KAWAL, DONALD E., and STEPHENSON, RALPH J.
  Critical Path Method. Cahners, 1967, 292, illus.

RAMSEY, CHARLES G., and SLEEPER, HAROLD R.
  Architectural Standards. 6th ed. Wiley, 1970, 704, illus.

RANNEY, MAURICE W.
  Fire Retardant Building Products and Coatings. Noyes, 1970, 186, illus.

RAPP, WILLIAM G.
  Construction of Structural Steel Building Frames. Wiley, 1968, 340, illus.

RAY, JESSE E.
  The Art of Bricklaying. 2nd ed. Bennett, 1961, 240, illus.

REINER, LAURENCE E.
  Methods and Materials of Construction: A Guide for Builders, Owners, Architects and Engineers. Prentice-Hall, 1970, 320, illus.

ROARK, RAYMOND J.
  Formulas for Stress and Strain. 4th ed. McGraw-Hill, 1965, 432, illus.

ROSSNAGEL, W. E.
  Handbook of Rigging for Construction and Industrial Operations. 3rd ed. McGraw-Hill, 1964, 383, illus.

ROYER, KING
  Desk Book for Construction Superintendents. Prentice-Hall, 1967, 220, illus.

SANDERSON, RICHARD L.
  Codes and Code Administration: An Introduction to Building Regulations in the United States. Building Officials Conference of America, 1969, 241.

SANDSTROM, GÖSTA E.
  Man the Builder. McGraw-Hill, 1970, 280, illus.

SCHMIDT, JOHN L., LEWIS, WALTER H., and OLIN, HAROLD B.
  Construction Lending Guide: A Handbook of Homebuilding Design and Construction. American Savings & Loan Institute, 1966, 1 vol., illus.

SEAKINS, LESLIE W., and SMITH, SAMUEL
  Practical Brickwork. Chemical, 1965, 199, illus.

SHAFFER, LOUIS R., RITTER, J. B., and MEYER, W. L.
  Critical Path Method. McGraw-Hill, 1965, 212, illus.

SHIELDS, CARL D.
  Boilers: Types, Characteristics, and Functions. F. W. Dodge, 559, illus.

SIMONS, JAMES D., and KOSTER, JOHN C.
  A Complete Insurance Guide for Contractors. Chilton, 1967, 85.

SKEIST, IRVING, ED.
  Plastics in Building. Reinhold, 1966, 466, illus.

SMITH, DENISON L.
  How to Find Out in Architecture and Building: A Guide to Sources of Information. Pergamon, 1967, 232, illus. (Commonwealth and International Library, Library and Technical Information Division.)

SMITH, RONALD C.
  Materials of Construction. McGraw-Hill, 1966, 376, illus.

———.
  Principles and Practices of Heavy Construction. Prentice-Hall, 1967, 343, illus.

———.
  Principles and Practices of Light Construction. 2nd ed. Prentice-Hall, 1970, 354, illus. (Engineering Technology Series.)

SOKOL, ANDREW
  Contractor or Manipulator? A Guide to Construction Financing from Beginning of Construction to Completion. University of Miami Press, 1968, 227, illus.

STEINBERG, JOSEPH, and STEMPEL, MARTIN
  Estimating for the Building Trades. American Technical Society, 1965, 374, illus.

STEINGRESS, FREDERICK M.
  Low Pressure Boilers. American Technical Society, 1970, 170, illus.

STEWART, HARRY L.
  Hydraulic and Pneumatic Power for Production.... 2nd ed. Industrial Press, 1963, 1 vol., illus.

ENGINEERING PROGRAMS

SUNSET MAGAZINE AND SUNSET BOOKS
    How to Build Patio Roofs. Lane, Menlo Park, Calif., 1965, 96, illus.

SYMPOSIUM ON AMERICA'S PRIVATE CONSTRUCTION INDUSTRY AND THE FUTURE AMERICAN CITY
    Proceedings.... American Cement Corp., Los Angeles, 1966, 155.

TAYLOR, ROBERT L., ED.
    Materials & Labor Estimator for the Entire Building Industry. William Dogan Annual Publications Associates, New York, 1967, 366, illus.

THOMAS, PAUL I.
    How to Estimate Building Losses and Construction Costs. Prentice-Hall, 1960, 419.

TOMLINSON, MICHAEL J.
    Foundation Design and Construction. 2nd ed. Wiley, 1969, 785, illus.

TRAXLER, RALPH N.
    Asphalt: Its Composition, Properties, and Uses. Reinhold, 1961, 294, illus.

ULREY, HARRY F.
    Audel's Architects' and Builders' Guide. Audel, 1964, 374, illus.

———.
    Builders' Encyclopedia. Audel, 1970, 480, illus.

———.
    Carpenters' and Builders' Library. 3rd ed. Audel, 1970, 4 vols., illus.

———.
    Carpentry and Building. Audel, 1965, 448.

UNITED NATIONS, ECONOMIC COMMISSION FOR EUROPE
    Directory of Authorities and Principal Organizations Related to the Building Industry. UN, 1968, 77. (Pub. No. E69.)

U.S. ADVISORY COMMISSION ON INTERGOVERNMENTAL RELATIONS
    Building Codes: A Program for Intergovernmental Reform—A Commission Report. USACIR, 1966, 103.

U.S. BUREAU OF RECLAMATION
    Earth Manual: A Guide to the Use of Soils as Foundations and as Construction Materials for Hydraulic Structures. Rev. rpt. USBR, Denver, 1963, 783.

U.S. BUREAU OF YARDS AND DOCKS
    Testing and Licensing of Construction Equipment Operators. USBYD, 1962- , 1 vol., illus.

U.S. DEPARTMENT OF THE ARMY
    Carpentry and Building Construction. USGPO, 1960, 201. (ERIC VT 009 848.)

U.S. OFFICE OF EDUCATION, MANPOWER DEVELOPMENT AND TRAINING DIVISION
    Heavy Construction Equipment Mechanic: A Suggested Guide for a Training Course. USGPO, 1969, 50. (FS5.287.87044.)

U.S. OFFICE OF EDUCATION, VOCATIONAL AND TECHNICAL EDUCATION DIVISION
    Architectural and Building Construction Technology: A Suggested 2-Year Post High School Curriculum. USOE, 1969, 110, illus. (OE-80062, Technical Education Program Series No. 9.)

———.
    Civil Technology—Highway and Structural Options: A Suggested 2-Year Post High School Curriculum. USOE, 1969, 107, illus. (OE-80041, Technical Education Program Series No. 8.)

VAN GAASBEEK, RICHARD M.
    A Practical Course in Roof Framing: The Underlying Principles and Their Application to Practical Work, Especially Written for Foremen, Journeymen and Apprentice Wood-Workers, and as a Textbook for Schools. 4th ed. Drake, Chicago, 1961, 270, illus.

WACHSMANN, KONRAD
    The Turning Point of Building: Structure and Design. Reinhold, 1961, 239, illus.

WALKER, FRANK R.
    The Building Estimator's Reference Book: A Practical and Thoroughly Reliable Reference Book for Contractors and Estimators.... 1915- , vols., illus.

WARD, JACK W.
    Construction Information Source and Reference Guide. Construction Publications, 1970, 134.

WASS, ALONZO
    Building Construction Estimating. 2nd ed. Prentice-Hall, 1970, 324, illus. (Engineering Technology Series.)

———.
    Manual of Structural Details for Building Construction. Prentice-Hall, 1968, 386, illus.

WEAVER, WILLIAM
    Computer Programs for Structural Analysis. Van Nostrand, 1967, 300, illus.

ZUK, WILLIAM
    Concepts of Structure. Reinhold, 1963, 80.

CARPENTRY

DURBAHN, WALTER E., and SUNDBERG, ELMER W.
    Fundamentals of Carpentry. 4th ed. American Technical Society, 1967-69, 2 vols., illus.

EMARY, A. B.
    Building Construction Carpentry. Drake, 1970, 208, illus.

WAGNER, WILLIS H.
    Modern Carpentry: Building Construction Details in Easy-To-Understand Form. Goodheart-Willcox, 1969, 480, illus.

WILSON, JOHN D., and ROGERS, CLELL M.
    Simplified Carpentry Estimating. 6th ed. Simmons-Boardman, 1962, 320, illus.

CONCRETE

ABELES, PAUL W.
    An Introduction to Prestressed Concrete. Concrete Publications, London, 1964- , 1 vol., illus. (Concrete Series.)

AKROYD, T. N. W.
    Concrete: Properties and Manufacture. Pergamon, 1962, 336, illus.

AMERICAN CONCRETE INSTITUTE
    ACI Manual of Concrete Practice. ACI, Detroit, 1968, 3 vols., illus.

———.
    Cement and Concrete Terminology: A Glossary of Terms in the Field of Cement and Concrete Technology. ACI, 1967, 144. (ACI Pub. No. SP-19.)

———.
    Computer Applications in Concrete Design and Technology. ACI, 1967, 143, illus.

BILLINGTON, DAVID P.
    Thin Shell Concrete Structures. McGraw-Hill, 1965, 332, illus.

CERNICA, JOHN N.
    Fundamentals of Reinforced Concrete. Addison-Wesley, 1964, 289, illus.

DAVIES, JOHN D.
    Structural Concrete. Macmillan, 1964, 163, illus. (Commonwealth and International Library of Science, Tech-

nology Engineering and Liberal Studies—Structures and Solid Body Mechanics Division Vol. 1.)

DAY, RICHARD
The Practical Handbook of Concrete and Masonry. Arco, 1969, 128, illus.

DE CRISTOFORO, R. J.
Handy Man's Concrete and Masonry Handbook. Arco, 1960, 144, illus. (Do-It-Yourself Series.)

DUNHAM, CLARENCE W.
The Theory and Practice of Reinforced Concrete. 4th ed. McGraw-Hill, 1966, 629, illus.

EVERARD, NOEL J., and TANNER, JOHN L.
Schaum's Outline of Theory and Problems of Reinforced Concrete Design. Schaum, 1966, 325, illus. (Schaum's Outline Series.)

FABER, OSCAR
Reinforced Concrete. Van Nostrand, 1961, 532, illus.

FELD, JACOB
Lessons from Failures of Concrete Structures. American Concrete Institute, 1964, 179, illus. (ACI Monograph No. 1.)

HUFF, DARRELL
How to Work with Concrete and Masonry. Popular Science, 1968, 179, illus. (Popular Science Skill Book.)

KHACHATURIAN, NARBEV, and GURFINKEL, GERMAN
Prestressed Concrete. McGraw-Hill, 1969, 460, illus.

LARSON, THOMAS D.
Portland Cement and Asphalt Concretes. McGraw-Hill, 1963, 282, illus.

LIBBY, JAMES R.
Prestressed Concrete, Design and Construction. Ronald, 1961, 468, illus.

LIN, T. Y.
Design of Prestressed Concrete Structures. 2nd ed. Wiley, 614, illus.

NATIONAL ACADEMY OF SCIENCES, NATIONAL RESEARCH COUNCIL (BUILDING RESEARCH ADVISORY BOARD)
Crack Control in Concrete Masonry Unit Construction. NAS, 1964, 36. (Pub. No. 1198.)

NEVILLE, ADAM M.
Properties of Concrete. Wiley, 1963, 532, illus.

NEW YORK (STATE) BUREAU OF INDUSTRIAL AND TECHNICAL EDUCATION
Suggested Unit Course in Concrete Form Construction. Delmar, 1962, 106, illus. (Carpentry Series.)

PARKER, HARRY
Simplified Design of Reinforced Concrete. 3rd ed. Wiley, 1968, 310, illus.

PEURIFOY, ROBERT L.
Formwork for Concrete Structures. McGraw-Hill, 1964, 330, illus.

PORTLAND CEMENT ASSOCIATION and NATIONAL READY MIXED CONCRETE ASSOCIATION
Concrete Technology. Delmar, 1965, 144.

POWERS, TREVAL C.
The Properties of Fresh Concrete. Wiley, 1968, 664, illus.

PRESTON, HOWARD K.
Practical Prestressed Concrete. McGraw-Hill, 1960, 340, illus.

———.
Prestressed Concrete for Architects and Engineers. McGraw-Hill, 1964, 196, illus.

PRESTON, HOWARD K., and SOLLENBERGER, NORMAN J.
Modern Prestressed Concrete. McGraw-Hill, 1967, 337, illus.

RAMASWAMY, G. S.
Design and Construction of Concrete Shell Roofs. McGraw-Hill, 1968, 641.

TAYLOR, WALTER H
Concrete Technology and Practice. Elsevier, 1965, 639, illus.

TROXELL, GEORGE E., DAVIS, HARMER E., and KELLY, JOE W.
Composition and Properties of Concrete. 2nd ed. McGraw-Hill, 1968, 480, illus.

U.S. DEPARTMENT OF THE INTERIOR, BUREAU OF RECLAMATION
Concrete Manual: A Manual for the Control of Concrete Construction. USGPO, 1966, 675. (I27.19/2:C74/966.)

WADDELL, JOSEPH J., ED.
Concrete Construction Handbook. McGraw-Hill, 1968, 1 vol., illus

———.
Practical Quality Control for Concrete. McGraw-Hill, 1962, 396, illus.

WANG, CHU-KIA, and SALMON, CHARLES G.
Reinforced Concrete Design. International Textbook, 1965, 754, illus. (International Textbooks in Civil Engineering.)

WINTER, GEORGE, et al.
Design of Concrete Structures. 7th ed. McGraw-Hill, 1964, 660, illus.

WITT, JOSHUA C.
Portland Cement Technology. 2nd ed. Chemical, 1966, 346, illus.

WOODS, HUBERT
Durability of Concrete Construction. American Concrete Institute, 1968, 187, illus. (ACI Monograph No. 4.)

PLUMBING

BABBITT, HAROLD E.
Plumbing. 3rd ed. McGraw-Hill, 1960, 649, illus.

DAVIS, PAUL G.
Plumbing, Heating and Piping Estimator's Guide. McGraw-Hill, 1960, 213.

FRANKLAND, THOMAS W.
Pipe Trades Pocket Manual. Bruce, 1964, 262.

MATTHIAS, ARTHUR J., SMITH, ESLES, SR., and VOLLAND, ROBERT J.
How to Design and Install Plumbing. 4th ed. American Technical Society, 1960, 446, illus.

NATIONAL PLUMBING CODE ILLUSTRATED
Manas Publications, St. Petersburg, Fla., 1968, 1 vol.

ORAVETZ, JULES A.
Audel's Plumbers' and Pipe Fitters' Library. Audel, 1967- , vols., illus.

SURVEYING

BOUCHARD, HARRY
Surveying. 5th ed., rev. Francis H. Moffitt, ed. International Textbook, 1965, 754, illus.

BRINKER, RUSSELL C.
Elementary Surveying. 5th ed. International Textbook, 1969, 620, illus.

DAVIS, RAYMOND E., and KELLY, JOE W.
Elementary Plane Surveying. 4th ed. McGraw-Hill, 1967, 574, illus.

ENGINEERING PROGRAMS

DAVIS, RAYMOND E., FOOTE, FRANCIS S., and KELLY, JOE W.
    Surveying Theory and Practice. 5th ed. McGraw-Hill, 1966, 1096, illus.

HAYWARD, L. M.
    Survey Practice on Construction Sites. Pitman, 1963, 143, illus.

KISSAM, PHILIP
    Surveying Practice. McGraw-Hill, 1966, 416, illus.

PAFFORD, F. William
    Handbook of Survey Notekeeping. Wiley, 1962, 140, illus.

RAYNER, WILLIAM H., and SCHMIDT, MILTON O.
    Elementary Surveying. 4th ed. Van Nostrand, 1963, 485.

———.
    Fundamentals of Surveying. 5th ed. Van Nostrand-Reinhold, 1969, 533, illus.

RIPA, LOUIS C.
    Surveying Manual. McGraw-Hill, 1964, 125.

ROYER, KING
    Applied Field Surveying. Wiley, 1970, 205.

DRAFTING

AMERICAN INSTITUTE FOR DESIGN AND DRAFTING
    Guide for Preparing a Drafting Manual. 2nd ed. 1970.

ARCO PUBLISHING COMPANY, INC.
    Junior Draftsman-Civil Engineering Draftsman. Arco, 1967, 94.

BATHO, ROBERT L.
    A Practical Approach to Technical Illustration. Hart, 1968, 96, illus.

BENNETT, A. E., and SIY, LOUIS J.
    Blueprint Reading for Welders. Delmar, 1960, 145, illus.

BLUM, ROBERT E.
    General Drafting: A Comprehensive Examination. McGraw-Hill, 1969, 32, illus.

BROWN, WALTER C.
    Drafting. Goodheart-Willcox, 1964, 112. (General Shop Series.)

COOVER, SHRIVER L.
    Drawing and Blueprint Reading. 3rd ed. McGraw-Hill, 1966, 368, illus.

———.
    A First Course in Drawing and Blueprint Reading. 3rd ed. McGraw-Hill, 1966, 360, illus. (McGraw-Hill Publications in Industrial Education.)

———.
    Industrial Arts Drawing and Blueprint Reading. 2nd ed. McGraw-Hill, 1961, 312, illus. (McGraw-Hill Publications in Industrial Arts.)

COOVER, SHRIVER L., and HELSEL, JAY D.
    Programmed Blueprint Reading. 2nd ed. McGraw-Hill, 1970, 208, illus.

DIAMOND, THOMAS, and RYAN, ROBERT
    A Primer of Blueprint Reading. Rev. ed. Bruce, 1968, 1 vol.

FEIRER, JOHN L.
    Drawing and Planning for the Industrial Arts. Rev. ed. Bennett, 1963, 376, illus.

FETTER, WILLIAM A.
    Computer Graphics in Communication. McGraw-Hill, 1965, 110, illus. (Engineering Graphics Monograph Series.)

FRENCH, THOMAS E., and VIERCK, CHARLES J.
    Fundamentals of Engineering Drawing. 2nd ed. McGraw-Hill, 1966, 447. (Engineering Drawing Series.)

———.
    Graphic Science: Engineering Drawing, Descriptive Geometry, Graphic Solutions. 3rd ed. McGraw-Hill, 1970, 654, illus.

———.
    A Manual of Engineering Drawing for Student Draftsmen. 10th ed. McGraw-Hill, 1966, 701, illus.

FRYKLUND, VERNE C., and KEPLER, FRANK R.
    General Drafting. 3rd ed. McKnight & McKnight, 1960, 204, illus.

FULLER, DON
    Functional Drafting for Today: How to get the Most from Your Drafting Dollars. Industrial Education Institute, Boston, 1966, 1 vol., illus.

———.
    Getting Top Mileage from Drafting & Design Operations. Cahners, 1965, 400, illus.

GEREVAS, LAWRENCE E.
    Drafting Technology Problems. Sams, 1969, 159, illus.

GIACHINO, JOSEPH W., and BEUKEMA, HENRY J.
    American Technical Society's Drafting. 3rd ed. American Technical Society, 1965, 189, illus.

———.
    Drafting Technology. American Technical Society, 1964, 442, illus.

———.
    Engineering Drafting Problems. American Technical Society, 1965, 200, illus.

———.
    Engineering-Technical Drafting and Graphics. 2nd ed. American Technical Society, 1966, 840, illus.

———.
    Everyday Sketching and Drafting. American Technical Society, 1966, 159, illus.

———.
    Print Reading for Welders. American Technical Society, 1970, 133.

GIBBY, JOSEPH C.
    Technical Illustrations: Procedure and Practice. 3rd ed. American Technical Society, 1970, 352, illus.

GIESECKE, FREDERICK E., et al.
    Engineering Graphics. Macmillan, 1969, 881, illus.

———.
    Technical Drawing. 5th ed. Macmillan, 1967, 882, illus.

GLAZENER, EVERETT R., and CLARK, COLY
    Industrial Arts Drawing: A Text for Introductory Drafting. Steck, Austin, Tex., 1963, 184, illus. (Steck Industrial Arts Series.)

GRANT, HIRAM E.
    Engineering Drawing, Without Problems. McGraw-Hill, 1965, 178.

HALE, E. M., McGINNIS, H., and HILL, C. L.
    Introduction to Applied Drawing. Rev. ed. McKnight & McKnight, 1962, 87.

HAMMOND, ROBERT H.
    Engineering Graphics for Design and Analysis. Ronald, 1964, 534.

HOELSCHER, RANDOLPH P., and SPRINGER, CLIFFORD H.
    Engineering Drawing and Geometry. 2nd ed. Wiley, 1961, 1 vol., illus.

HOELSCHER, RANDOLPH P., SPRINGER, CLIFFORD H., and DOBROVOLNY, JERRY
    Basic Drawing for Engineering Technology. Wiley, 1964, 396, illus.

———.
    Graphics for Engineers: Visualization, Communication, and Design. Wiley, 1968, 917, illus.

HORNUNG, WILLIAM J.
Reinhold Data Sheets for Architects, Engineers, Designers, Draftsmen. Reinhold, 1965, 238, illus.

JENSEN, CECIL H.
Engineering Drawing and Design. McGraw-Hill, 1968, 768, illus.

JENSEN, CECIL H., and MASON, F. H. S.
Drafting Fundamentals. 2nd ed. McGraw-Hill, 1967, 242, illus.

LEVENS, ALEXANDER S.
Graphics: Analysis and Conceptual Design. 2nd ed. Wiley, 1968, 771.

———.
Graphics: With an Introduction to Conceptual Design. Wiley, 1962, 743, illus.

LEVENS, ALEXANDER S., and EDSTROM, A. E.
Problems in Engineering Graphics, Series V1. McGraw-Hill, 1969, 216, illus.

LINCOLN ELECTRIC COMPANY
How to Read Shop Drawings: With Special Reference to Welding and Welding Symbols—Welding Symbols as Standardized by the American Welding Society. Lincoln Electric Co., Cleveland, 1961, 187, illus.

LUZADDER, WARREN J.
Basic Graphics for Design, Analysis, Communications, and the Computer. 2nd ed. Prentice-Hall, 1968, 641, illus.

———.
Basic Graphics for Engineers and Technical Students. Prentice-Hall, 1962, 715, illus.

———.
Fundamentals of Engineering Drawing for Technical Students and Professional Draftsmen. 5th ed. Prentice-Hall, 1965, 726, illus.

MARTIN, C. LESLIE
Design Graphics. 2nd ed. Macmillan, 1968, 307, illus.

McCARTNEY, T. O.
Precision Perspective Drawing. McGraw-Hill, 1963, 239, illus.

PALMQUIST, ROLAND E.
Audel's Answers on Blue Print Reading. 2nd ed. Audel, 1966, 405, illus.

PEARSON, GEORGE
Engineering Drawing. 2nd ed. Oxford University Press, 1965, 164, illus.

RISING, JAMES S., ALMFELDT, MAURICE W., and DeJONG, PAUL S.
Engineering Graphics: Communication, Analysis, Creative Design. 4th ed. W. C. Brown, 1970, 382, illus.

ROSS, STAN
The World of Drafting. McKnight & McKnight, 1970, 348, illus.

ROTMANS, ELMER A., and HORTON, HOMER L.
Drafting Technology. Delmar, 1967, 387, illus.

RULE, JOHN T., and COONS, STEVEN A.
Graphics. McGraw-Hill, 1961, 512, illus.

SCHNEERER, WILLIAM F.
Programmed Graphics. McGraw-Hill, 1967, 520, illus.

SHALKHAUSER, G. W., and COLEMAN, R. M.
Basic Lessons in Technical Drafting: A Step by Step Program. Pruett, Boulder, Colo., 1968, 1 vol., illus.

SOWELA TECHNICAL INSTITUTE
Drafting Technology: A Two Year Post High School Curriculum. Sowela, Lake Charles, La., 1965, 66. (ERIC VT 000 591.)

SPENCER, HENRY C., and DYGDON, JOHN T.
Basic Technical Drawing. 2nd ed. Macmillan, 1968, 484, illus.

STEPHENSON, GEORGE E.
Drawing for Product Planning. Bennett, 1970, 254, illus.

STERN, BENJAMIN J.
Opportunities in a Drafting Career. Universal Publishing & Distributing, 1967, 96, illus. (VGM Career Series No. V162.)

STIRLING, NORMAN
Introduction to the Technical Drawing. St. Martin's Press, 1963, 256.

SVENSEN, CARL L., and STREET, WILLIAM E.
Engineering Graphics. Van Nostrand, 1962, 739, illus.

THOMAS, T. A.
Technical Illustration. 2nd ed. McGraw-Hill, 1968, 203, illus.

U.S. BUREAU OF NAVAL PERSONNEL
Blueprint Reading and Sketching. USGPO, 1968, 1 vol.

———.
Illustrator Draftsman... I. & C. USGPO, 1967, 1 vol. (NAVPERS 10470.)

U.S. DEPARTMENT OF THE ARMY
General Drafting. U.S. Army and U.S. Air Force, 1962, 267. (TM 5-230.)

UTTER, R. F., et al.
Concepts of the True Position Dimensioning System: A Programmed Textbook. Central Scientific, Chicago, 1965, 173, illus.

WALKER, JOHN R., and PLEVYAK, EDWARD J.
Industrial Arts Drafting: Language of Symbols Used in Creative Thinking, Planning. Goodheart-Willcox, 1960, 208, illus.

WALRAVEN, H. DALE
A Handbook of Engineering Graphics. McKnight & McKnight (Taplinger, dist.), 1965, 252, illus.

WRIGHT, LAWRENCE S.
Drafting Technical Communication. McKnight & McKnight, 1968, 435, illus.

ARCHITECTURAL

BELLIS, HERBERT F., and SCHMIDT, WALTER A.
Architectural Drafting. 2nd ed. McGraw-Hill, 1971, 175.

DUNNING, WILLIAM J., and ROBIN, L. P.
Home Planning and Architectural Drawing: An illustrated Guide for the Correlation of Planning Principles and Drafting Techniques. Wiley, 1966, 81.

GOODBAN, WILLIAM T., and HAYSLETT, JACK J.
Architectural Drawing and Planning. McGraw-Hill, 1965, 232, illus. (McGraw-Hill Technical Education Series.)

HEPLER, DONALD E., and WALLACH, PAUL I.
Architecture: Drafting and Design. McGraw-Hill, 1965, 472.

HORNUNG, WILLIAM J.
Architectural Drafting. 4th ed. Prentice-Hall, 1966, 277, illus.

———.
Blueprint Reading: Interpretation of Architectural Working Drawings. Prentice-Hall, 1961, 129, illus.

JACOBY, HELMUT
New Architectural Drawings. Praeger, 1969, 97, illus.

ENGINEERING PROGRAMS

LOCKARD, WILLIAM K.
  Drawing As a Means to Architecture. Reinhold, 1968, 96, illus.

MULLER, EDWARD J.
  Architectural Drawing and Light Construction. Prentice-Hall, 1967, 450, illus.

PATTEN, LAWTON M., and ROGNESS, MILTON L.
  Architectural Drawing. 3rd ed. W. C. Brown, 1968, 1 vol., illus.

RAY, JESSE E.
  Graphic Architectural Drafting. McKnight & McKnight, 1960, 256, illus.

ROGNESS, MILTON L., and DUNCAN, ROBERT I.
  Architectural Drawing Problems. W. C. Brown, 1963, 1 vol.

SPENCE, WILLIAM
  Architecture: Design-Engineering-Drawing. McKnight & McKnight, 1967, 582, illus.

STEGMAN, GEORGE K., and STEGMAN, HARRY J.
  Architectural Drafting: Functional Planning and Creative Design. American Technical Society, 1966, 455, illus.

WAFFLE, HARVEY W.
  Architectural Drawing. Rev. ed. Bruce, 1962, 582.

WYATT, WILLIAM E.
  General Architectural Drawing. Bennett, 1969, 556, illus.

AUTOMOTIVE

JENSEN, LOUIS E.
  Automotive Drawing Interpretation. Delmar, 1962, 159.

WESTON, ERIC B.
  Automobile Engineering Drawing for Technical Students. Chilton, 1966, 107, illus.

ELECTRICAL

BAER, CHARLES J.
  Electrical and Electronics Drawing. 2nd ed. McGraw-Hill, 1966, 402, illus.

COOK, JESSE S.
  Printed Circuit Design and Drafting. Tad Institute, Cambridge, Mass., 1967, 214, illus.

FISHER, HOWARD W.
  Electrical Blueprint Reading & Sketching—Commercial. Delmar, 1967, 162, illus.

KULLER, K. KARL
  Electronics, Drafting. McGraw-Hill, 1962, 286, illus.

MULLIN, RAY C.
  Blueprint Reading and Sketching: Electrical Trades—Residential. Delmar, 1966, 297, illus.

RASKHODOFF, NICHOLAS M.
  Electronic Drafting and Design. Prentice-Hall, 1966, 594, illus. (Prentice-Hall Electronic Technology Series.)
  ———.
  Electronic Drafting Handbook. Macmillan, 1961, 402, illus.

SHIERS, GEORGE
  Electronic Drafting. Prentice-Hall, 1962, 556, illus.

WOLK, ALLEN M.
  Electronics Drafting. Hayden, 1967, 159, illus.

MECHANICAL

ALMON, JOSEPH J.
  Visualized Basic Mechanical Drawing. Bruce, 1961, 160, illus.

AUDEL & COMPANY
  Audel's Mechanical Drawing Guide. Audel, 1960, 158, illus.

BERG, EDWARD, and KRONQUIST, EMIL
  Mechanical Drawing: Instruction Units and Problems. 6th ed. Bruce, 1966, 2 vols., illus.

FRENCH, THOMAS E., and SVENSEN, CARL L.
  Mechanical Drawing. 7th ed. McGraw-Hill, 1966, 570, illus.

FUGLSBY, GLEN O., McGEE, R. A., and STURTEVANT, W. W.
  General Mechanical Drawing. Rev. ed. Bruce, 1963, 210, illus.

HARMAN, EARL W.
  Introduction to Mechanical Drawing. Allyn & Bacon, 1963, 79, illus.

HOOVER, THEODORE W., and SCHUMACHER, HERMAN G.
  Tool & Die Drafting: A Basic Course from Fundamentals Through Simple Layout and Design. 2nd ed. Brakken, Ann Arbor, Mich., 1968, 196, illus.

HORNUNG, WILLIAM J.
  Blueprint Reading: Interpretation of Mechanical Working Drawings. Prentice-Hall, 1969, 166, illus.

IHNE, RUSSEL W., and STREETER, WALTER E.
  Machine Trades Blueprint Reading. 5th ed. American Technical Society, 1966, 194, illus.

LEVENS, ALEXANDER S., and EDSTROM, A. E.
  Problems in Mechanical Drawing—First Course. 3rd ed. McGraw-Hill, 1968, 84, illus.
  ———.
  Problems in Mechanical Drawing—Second Course. 3rd ed. McGraw-Hill, 1967, 176, illus.

McCABE, FRANCIS T., KEITH, CHARLES W., and FARNHAM, WALTER E.
  Mechanical Drafting Essentials. 4th ed. Prentice-Hall, 1967, 1 vol.

YANKEE, HERBERT W.
  Machine Drafting and Related Technology. McGraw-Hill, 1966, 516, illus.

YASLOW, SAMUEL
  Elements of Mechanical Drafting. Industrial Press, 1969, 375, illus.

SHEET METAL

ALMON, JOSEPH J.
  Visualized Basic Sheet Metal Drafting. Bruce, 1963, 176.

BETTERLEY, MELVIN L.
  Sheet Metal Drafting. McGraw-Hill, 1961, 314, illus.

BRETZ, HOWARD
  Sheet Metal Shop Drawing. Industrial Press, 1970, 1 vol.

BUDZIK, RICHARD S.
  Precision Sheet Metal: Blueprint Reading. Sams, 1969, 127, illus.

DAUGHERTY, JAMES S.
  Sheet Metal Pattern Drafting and Shop Problems. Rev. ed. R. E. Powell, ed. Bennett, 1961, 185.

MEYER, LEO A.
Sheet Metal Layout. McGraw-Hill, 1961, 188, illus.

STRUCTURAL

AMERICAN INSTITUTE OF STEEL CONSTRUCTION
The A.I.S.C. Textbook of Structural Shop Drafting. AISC, 1966, 3 vols., illus.

BELLIS, HERBERT F., and SCHMIDT, WALTER A.
Blueprint Reading for the Construction Trades. McGraw-Hill, 1968, 147, illus.

HOOPER, LEE
Introduction to Construction Drafting. Prentice-Hall, 1970, 256.

SHAH, MOTICHAND G., and KALE, C. M.
Principles of Building Drawing. Asia Publishing House, New York, 1966, 111, illus.

SUNDBERG, ELMER W.
Building Trades Blueprint Reading. 4th ed. American Technical Society, 1967- , 1 vol., illus.

ELECTRICAL AND ELECTRONIC TECHNOLOGY

ADAMS, JAMES E.
Electrical Principles and Practices. McGraw-Hill, 1963, 601, illus.

ADAMS, THOMAS M.
Detector and Rectifier Circuits. 2nd ed. Sams, 1966, 128, illus.

ALLIED RADIO CORPORATION
All About High Fidelity & Stereo: Allied's Handbook of High Fidelity and Stereo Fundamentals. Allied, Chicago, 1963, 95, illus.

———.
A Dictionary of Electronic Terms: Concise Definitions of Words Used in Radio, Television, and Electronics. 8th ed. Allied, Chicago, 1968, 112, illus. (Allied Electronics Library.)

———.
Electronics Data Handbook: A Compilation of Formulas and Data Most Commonly Used in the Field of Radio and Electronics. 5th ed. Allied, Chicago, 1966, 112, illus.

ALVAREZ, E. CHARLES, and FLECKLES, DAVID E.
Introduction to Electron Tubes and Semiconductors. McGraw-Hill, 1965, 294, illus.

AMICK, CHARLES L.
Fluorescent Lighting Manual. 3rd ed. McGraw-Hill, 1961, 400, illus.

ANDERSON, CHARLES J., SANTANELLI, ANTHONY, and KULIS, FRED R.
Alternating Current Circuits and Measurements: A Self-Instructional Programed Manual. Prentice-Hall, 1966, 367, illus. (Prentice-Hall Electronic Technology.)

———.
Direct Current: Circuits and Measurements—A Self-Instructional Programed Manual. Prentice-Hall, 1966, 337, illus. (Prentice-Hall Electronic Technology Series.)

ANDERSON, EDWIN P.
Audel's Wiring Diagrams for Light and Power. 2nd ed., rev. Audel, 1964, 312, illus.

ANDERSON, EDWIN P., and PALMQUIST, ROLAND E.
Questions and Answers for Electricians Examinations. 3rd ed. Audel, 1969, 280, illus.

ANDREWS, ALAN
ABC's of Radar. 2nd ed. Sams, 1966, 128, illus. (Sams Photofact Publication ABR-2.)

———.
ABC's of Synchros and Servos: Complete Coverage of How Servomechanisms Operate, and How They are Used in Automatic Control Systems. Sams, 1962, 96, illus. (Sams Photofact Publication ASE-1.)

ANGELO, ERNEST J.
Electronic Circuits. 2nd ed. McGraw-Hill, 1964, 672, illus.

———.
Electronics: BJTs, FETs, and Microcircuits. McGraw-Hill, 1969, 672, illus.

ARCO PUBLISHING COMPANY, INC.
1540 Questions and Answers for Electricians. Arco, 1966, 188.

ARONSON, MILTON H.
Electronic Circuitry for Instruments and Equipment. Rev. ed. Instruments Publishing Co., Pittsburgh, 1961, 312, illus.

ASHLEY, RAY
Electrical Estimating. 3rd ed. McGraw-Hill, 1961, 437, illus.

AZAROFF, LEONID V.
Electronic Processes in Materials. McGraw-Hill, 1963, 462, illus.

BABB, DANIEL S.
Resistive Circuits. International Textbook, 1968, 313, illus. (International Electronics Technology Series.)

BALDWIN, CLIFFORD T.
Fundamentals of Electrical Measurements. Ungar, 1962, 336, illus.

BARDELL, P. R.
Magnetic Materials in the Electrical Industry. 2nd ed. Macdonald, London, 1960, 320, illus.

BARTHOLOMEW, DAVIS
Electrical Measurements and Instrumentation. Allyn & Bacon, 1963, 456, illus.

BASIC ELECTRONIC CIRCUITS.
2nd ed. Chemical Rubber Co., CRC Press Division, 1968, 2 vols. in 1, illus.

BEERENS, A. J. C.
Measuring Methods and Devices in Electronics. Hayden, 1968, 192, illus.

BELL TELEPHONE LABORATORIES
Electronic Communications Systems. Vol. 1, Design Technology; Vol. 2, Materials Technology; Vol. 3, Integrated Device and Connection Technology. Prentice-Hall, 1970, 3 vols.

BENEDICT, REGINALD R., and WEINER, NATHAN
Industrial Electronic Circuits and Applications. Prentice-Hall, 1965, 527, illus. (Prentice-Hall Electronic Technology Series.)

BENNETT, WILLIAM R.
Electrical Noise. McGraw-Hill, 1960, 280.

BENNETT, WILLIAM R., and DAVEY, JAMES R.
Data Transmission. McGraw-Hill, 1965, 356, illus. (Inter-University Electronics Series.)

BERENS, JACK, and BERENS, STEPHEN
Understanding and Troubleshooting Solid-State Electronic Equipment. Chilton, 1969, 176, illus.

BERKLEY, JOSEPH B.
Laboratory Course in Pulse Circuitry. Prentice-Hall, 1969, 206. (Prentice-Series in Electronic Technology.)

ENGINEERING PROGRAMS

BERKOWITZ, BERNARD
Basic Microwaves. Hayden, 1966, 169, illus.

BERNSTEIN, JULIAN L.
Audio Systems. Wiley, 1966, 409, illus. (Wiley Electronic Engineering Technology Series.)

———.
Video Tape Recording. Hayden, 1960, 280, illus.

BISHOP, CALVIN C.
Fundamentals of Electricity. Chilton, 1960, 230, illus.

BLITZER, RICHARD
Basic Pulse Circuits. McGraw-Hill, 1964, 436, illus.

BOHN, ERIK V.
Introduction to Electromagnetic Fields and Waves. Addison-Wesley, 1968, 470.

BOYLESTAD, ROBERT L.
Introductory Circuit Analysis. Merrill, 1968, 575, illus.

BRANSON, LANE K.
Introduction to Electronics. Prentice-Hall, 1967, 594, illus. (Prentice-Hall Electronic Technology Series.)

BRAZEE, JAMES G.
Semiconductor and Tube Electronics: An Introduction. Holt, Rinehart & Winston, 1968, 651, illus.

BREMER, JOHN W.
Superconductive Devices. McGraw-Hill, 1962, 184.

BRITE, ROBERT J., and FIORANELLI, CARLO H.
Synchors and Servos. Sams, 1967, 192, illus.

BROPHY, JAMES J.
Basic Electronics for Scientists. McGraw-Hill, 1966, 471.

BROWN, ROBERT M.
104 Simple One-Tube Projects. TAB, 1969, 192, illus.

BROWN, ROBERT M., and LAWRENCE, PAUL
How to Read Electronic Circuit Diagrams. TAB, 1970, 192, illus.

BROWN, RONALD
Telecommunications: The Booming Technology. Doubleday, 1970, 191, illus.

BUBAN, PETER, and SCHMITT, MARSHALL L.
Understanding Electricity and Electronics. 2nd ed. McGraw-Hill, 1969, 446, illus.

BUKSTEIN, EDWARD J.
ABC's of Transformers and Coils. 2nd ed. Bobbs-Merrill, 1968, 96, illus.

———.
Basic Servomechanisms. Holt, Rinehart & Winston, 1963, 190, illus.

———.
Industrial Electronic Circuits Handbook. Sams, 1962, 127, illus. (Sams Photofact Publication.)

———.
Industrial Electronics Measurement and Control. Sams, 1961, 192, illus.

———.
Understanding Transformers and Coils. Sams, 1962, 96, illus.

BULLIET, L. J.
Servomechanisms. Addison-Wesley, 1967, 276, illus.

BURFORD, WILLIAM B., and VERNER, H. GREY
Semiconductor Junctions and Devices. McGraw-Hill, 1965, 328, illus.

CAMPBELL, JEFF C.
Simplified Industrial Telemetering. Hayden, 1965, 138, illus.

CARLSON, ELMER C.
Ten-Minute Test Techniques for Electronics Servicing. TAB Books, 1967, 176, illus.

CARROLL, GRADY C.
Industrial Instrument Servicing Handbook. McGraw-Hill, 1960, 1 vol., illus.

CARROLL, JOHN M.
Careers and Opportunities in Electronics. Dutton, 1963. 191, illus.

———.
Electron Devices and Circuits. McGraw-Hill, 1962, 344, illus.

———.
Microelectronic Circuits and Applications. McGraw-Hill, 1965, 360, illus.

CARSON, RALPH S.
Principles of Applied Electronics. McGraw-Hill, 1961, 485, illus.

CARTER, HARLEY
Dictionary of Electronics. Hart, 1967, 410, illus.

CARTER, ROBERT C.
Introduction to Electrical Circuit Analysis. Holt, Rinehart & Winston, 1966, 500, illus.

CHERRY, E. M., and HOOPER, DARYL E.
Amplifying Devices & Low-Pass Amplifier Design. Wiley, 1968, 1036,

CHIRLIAN, PAUL M., and ZEMANIAN, ARMEN H.
Electronics. McGraw-Hill, 1961, 335. (McGraw-Hill Electrical and Electronic Engineering Series.)

CHODOROW, MARVIN, and SUSSKIND, CHARLES
Fundamentals of Microwave Electronics. McGraw-Hill, 1964, 297, illus.

CHUTE, GEORGE M.
Electronics in Industry. 3rd ed. McGraw-Hill, 1965, 598, illus.

CLIFFORD, MARTIN
Electronics Data Handbook. Gernsback Library, 1964, 159, illus. (No. 118.)

———.
The Handbook of Electronic Tables. Gernsback Library, 1965, 160, illus.

———.
How to Use Your VOM-VTVM & Oscilloscope. TAB, 1968, 187, illus.

COLLIN, ROBERT E., and ZUCKER, FRANCIS J.
Antenna Theory. McGraw-Hill, 1969- , 1 vol., illus. (Inter-University Electronics Series Vol. 7.)

COMER, DAVID J.
Semiconductor Circuits Lab Manual. Prentice-Hall, 1969, 124.

CONSUMERS POWER COMPANY
Fundamentals of Electricity. Addison-Wesley, 1966, 2 vols.

COOKE, NELSON M., and MARKUS, JOHN
Electronics and Nucleonics Dictionary: An Illustrated Dictionary Giving Up-To-Date Definitions, Abbreviations, and Synonyms for Over 13,000 Terms. 3rd ed. McGraw-Hill, 1966, 743, illus.

COOMBS, CLYDE F., ED.
Printed Circuits Handbook. McGraw-Hill, 1967, 1 vol., illus.

CORCORAN, GEORGE F.
Electronics. 2nd ed. Wiley, 1963, 391, illus.

CORNETET, WENDELL H.
Principles of Electricity and Basic Electronics. 3rd ed. McKnight & McKnight, 1963, 366, illus.

ELECTRICAL AND ELECTRONIC TECHNOLOGY

CROFT, TERRELL W., and CARR, CLIFFORD C., EDS.
Wiring Tables. 8th ed. McGraw-Hill, 1966, 104.

CROFT, TERRELL W., CARR, CLIFFORD C., and WATT, JOHN H., EDS.
American Electricians' Handbook: A Reference Book for Practical Electrical Workers. 9th ed. McGraw-Hill, 1970, 1 vol., illus.

CROW, LEONARD R.
Learning Electricity Fundamentals. 2nd ed. Sams, 1966, 416, illus. (Sams Photofact Publication EFC-2.)

CROWHURST, NORMAN H.
Audio Systems Handbook. TAB, 1969, 189, illus.

———.
Basic Oscillator Handbook. TAB, 1966, 160, illus.

———.
Electronic Design Charts. TAB, 1963, 128, illus.

———.
Electronics Reference Databook. TAB, 1969, 227, illus.

———.
Servicing Modern Hi-Fi Stereo Systems. TAB, 1970, 192, illus.

———, ED.
Understanding Solid-State Circuits. TAB, 1970, 192, illus.

CULLWICK, ERNEST G.
The Fundamentals of Electro-Magnetism. 3rd ed. Cambridge, 1966, 320.

CUTLER, PHILLIP
Electronic Circuit Analysis. McGraw-Hill, 1960, 1967, 2 vols., illus.

———.
Outline for DC Circuit Analysis with Illustrative Problems. McGraw-Hill, 1968, 200, illus.

———.
Semiconductor Circuit Analysis. McGraw-Hill, 1964, 642, illus.

DAHLEN, PHILLIP
Semiconductors From A to Z. TAB, 1968, 265, illus.

DANIELS, A. RICHARD
The Performance of Electrical Machines. McGraw-Hill, 1968, 294, illus.

DARR, JACK
New Ways to Diagnose Electronic Troubles. TAB, 1968, 288, illus.

DAVIDSON, HOMER L.
Servicing the Solid-State Chassis. TAB, 1969, 256, illus.

———.
Troubleshooting the Solid-State Chassis. TAB, 1969, 252, illus.

DAWES, CHESTER L.
Industrial Electricity. 3rd ed. McGraw-Hill, 1960, 2 vols., illus.

DAY, RICHARD
The Practical Handbook of Electrical Repairs. Arco, 1969, 128, illus. (Practical Workshop Library.)

DE FRANCE, JOSEPH J.
Communications Electronics Circuits. Holt, Rinehart & Winston, 1966, 548, illus.

———.
Electrical Fundamentals. Prentice-Hall, 1969, 702, illus.

———.
General Electronics Circuits. Holt, Rinehart & Winston, 1963, 526, illus.

DELPIT, GEORGE H., and JOHNSON, B. STEPHEN
Electronics in Action. 2nd ed. Bennett, 1966, 272, illus.

DESOER, CHARLES A., and KUH, ERNEST S.
Basic Circuit Theory. McGraw-Hill, 1969, 876, illus.

DILLOW, ARTHUR P.
Alternating Current Fundamentals. Sams, 1966, 416, illus. (Sams Photofact Publication ACD-1.)

DOUGHERTY, CHARLES M.
Electronic Technology. American Technical Society, 1967, 268, illus.

DOYLE, JOHN M.
Pulse Fundamentals. Prentice-Hall, 1963, 499, illus.

DUARTE, SALVADOR R., and DUARTE, R. L.
Electronics Assembly Methods. McGraw-Hill, 1964, 242, illus.

DUMMER, GEOFFREY W. A., BRUNETTI, CLEDO, and LEE, LOW K.
Electronic Equipment Design and Construction. McGraw-Hill, 1961, 241, illus.

DUMMER, GEOFFREY W. A., and GRANVILLE, J. W.
Miniature and Microminiature Electronics. Wiley, 1962, 310, illus.

DUMMER, GEOFFREY W. A., and NORDENBERG, HAROLD M.
Fixed and Variable Capacitors. McGraw-Hill, 1960, 288, illus.

DUNSHEATH, PERCY, and TEPPICH, JOHN
Electricity: How It Works. Crowell, 1960, 248, illus.

ECKLUND, E. EUGENE
Repairing Home Audio Systems. McGraw-Hill, 1962, 320.

EDMINISTER, JOSEPH A.
Electric Circuits. McGraw-Hill, 1967, 288, illus. (Schaum's Outline Series.)

EEE MAGAZINE
Electronic Circuit Design Handbook. 3rd ed. TAB, 1970, 383, illus. (T-101.)

EFRON, ALEXANDER
Alternating Current Electricity. Rider, 1961, 96, illus. (Basic Science Series No. 200-10.)

ELECTRONIC TEACHING LABORATORIES, WASHINGTON
Electronic Engineers and Technicians Reference Handbook. Sams, 1963, 224, illus. (Sams Photofact Publication ERH-1.)

ELECTRONIC TECHNICIAN
Useful Electronic Shop Hints. Hayden, 1962, 120.

ELECTRONICS INDUSTRIES ASSOCIATION
Advanced Servicing Techniques. Hayden, 1964, 2 vols., illus.

ELONKA, STEPHEN M., and BERNSTEIN, JULIAN L.
Standard Electronics Questions and Answers. McGraw-Hill, 1964, 2 vols.

ENNES, HAROLD E.
Workshop in Solid State. Sams, 1970, 382, illus.

EVANS, WALTER H.
Introduction to Electronics. Prentice-Hall, 1962, 518, illus.

FABER, RODNEY B., and HEISERMAN, RUSSELL L.
Introduction to Amplifiers. McGraw-Hill, 1968, 208, illus.

———.
Introduction to Electron Devices. McGraw-Hill, 1968, 180, illus.

FANTEL, HANS
ABC's of Hi-Fi & Stereo. Sams, 1963, 96.

FARKAS, LUCIEN L.
Electronic Testing. McGraw-Hill, 1966, 300, illus.

FISKE, KENNETH A., and HARTER, JAMES H.
AC Circuit Analysis Through Experimentation. 2nd ed. Technical Education Press, 1969, 188.

———.
DC Circuit Analysis Through Experimentation. 2nd ed. Technical Education Press, 1968, 368.

ENGINEERING PROGRAMS

FISKE, KENNETH A., and HARTER, JAMES H.
 Solid State Circuit Analysis Through Experimentation. Technical Education Press, 1969, 328.

FOSTER, LEROY E.
 Telemetry Systems. Wiley, 1965, 308, illus.

FRIEDMAN, JACK W., RICE, HARRY G., and McGINTY, GERALD
 Basic Electronics "Autotext": A Programmed Course in Circuits. Prentice-Hall, 1965, 534, illus.

FULLER, A. J. B.
 Microwaves. Pergamon, 1969, 289.

FUNK & WAGNALLS DICTIONARY OF ELECTRONICS
 Funk & Wagnalls, 1969, 230, illus.

GARLAND, D. J., and STAINER, F. W.
 Modern Electronic Maintenance Principles. Pergamon, 1970, 96.

GENERAL ELECTRONIC LABORATORIES
 Experimental Electricity: A Laboratory Manual. McGraw-Hill, 1970, 240, illus.

GERARD, GEOFFREY, ED.
 The Book of Electricity. Warne, 1960, 110, illus.

GERRISH, HOWARD H.
 Electricity and Electronics Teaches Modern Concepts. Goodheart-Willcox, 1968, 336, illus.

———.
 Technical Dictionary: Technical Terms Simplified. Goodheart-Willcox, 1968, 368, illus.

GIBBONS, JAMES F.
 Semiconductor Electronics. McGraw-Hill, 1966, 837, illus.

GILBERT, HORACE D., ED.
 Miniaturization. Reinhold, 1961, 306, illus.

GILES, A. F.
 Electronic Sensing Devices. Newnes, London, 1966, 158, illus. (Newnes International Monographs on Electrical Engineering and Electronics.)

GILLIE, ANGELO C.
 Electrical Principles of Electronics. 2nd ed. McGraw-Hill, 1969, 732.

———.
 Principles of Electron Devices. McGraw-Hill, 1962, 576, illus.

———.
 Pulse and Logic Circuits. McGraw-Hill, 1968, 401, illus.

GLICKSTEIN, CYRUS
 Basic Ultrasonics. Hayden, 1960, 144, illus.

GOODMAN, ROBERT L.
 Advanced Techniques for Troubleshooting with the Oscilloscope. TAB, 1969, 244, illus.

GOTTLIEB, IRVING M.
 Basic Oscillators. Rider, 1963, 202, illus.

GRAF, RUDOLF F.
 Modern Dictionary of Electronics. 3rd ed. Sams, 1968, 593, illus.

GRAHAM, KENNARD C.
 Fundamentals of Electricity. 5th ed. American Technical Society, 1968, 312, illus.

———.
 Industrial and Commercial Wiring. 2nd ed. American Technical Society, 1963, 282, illus.

———.
 Interior Electric Wiring—Residential. 6th ed. American Technical Society, 1961- , 1 vol., illus.

GRAHAM, KENNARD C., and GEBERT, KENNETH L.
 National Electrical Code and Blueprint Reading. 4th ed. American Technical Society, 1968, 155, illus.

GRAY, PAUL E.
 Introduction to Electronics. Wiley, 1967, 331, illus.

GRAZDA, EDWARD E., ED.
 Electronic Design Techniques Selected from Electronic Design. Hayden, 1967, 312, illus.

GREINER, RICHARD A.
 Semiconductor Devices and Applications. McGraw-Hill, 1961, 493.

GRIFFITHS, V. S., and LEE, W. H.
 The Electronics of Laboratory and Process Instruments. Wiley, 1962, 368, illus.

GROB, BERNARD
 Basic Electronics. 2nd ed. McGraw-Hill, 1965, 588.

GROB, BERNARD, and KIVER, MILTON S.
 Applications of Electronics. 2nd ed. McGraw-Hill, 1966, 592, illus.

HAAS, ALFRED
 Basic Industrial Electronics Course. Gernsback Library, 1962, 224, illus. (No. 109.)

HAMILTON, J. ROLAND
 Using Electricity. 2nd ed. Prentice-Hall, 1970, 368.

HARPER, CHARLES A.
 Handbook of Materials and Processes for Electronics. McGraw-Hill, 1970, 1200.

———, ED.
 Handbook of Electronic Packaging. McGraw-Hill, 1969, 1 vol., illus.

HARRIS, L. DALE
 Introduction to Feedback Systems. Wiley, 1961, 363, illus.

HERBST, L. J.
 Discrete and Integrated Semiconductor Circuitry. Chapman & Hall, London, (Barnes & Noble, dist.), 1969, 197, illus.

HERRICK, CLYDE N.
 Electronic Circuits. Merrill, 1968, 721, illus.

———.
 Introduction to Electronic Communications. Merrill, 1969, 688, illus. (International Electrical and Electronics Technology Series.)

———.
 Unified Concepts of Electronics. Prentice-Hall, 1970, 672, illus.

HERRINGTON, DONALD E.
 How to Read Schematic Diagrams. 2nd ed. Sams, 1967, 160, illus.

HEWITT, H., and VAUSE, A. S., EDS.
 Lamps and Lighting: A Manual of Lamps and Electric Lighting. Edward Arnold, London, 1966, 566, illus.

HIBBERD, ROBERT G.
 Integrated Circuits: A Basic Course for Engineers and Technicians. McGraw-Hill, 1969, 177, illus. (Texas Instruments Electronics Series.)

———.
 Solid State Electronics: A Basic Course for Engineers and Technicians. McGraw-Hill, 1968, 170, illus. (Texas Instruments Electronics Series.)

HICKEY, HENRY V., and VILLINES, WILLIAM M., JR.
 Elements of Electronics. 3rd ed. McGraw-Hill, 1970, 768, illus.

HOLT, CHARLES A.
 Introduction to Electro-Magnetic Fields and Waves. Wiley, 1963, 583.

HOWATSON, A. M.
 Principles of Applied Electricity. Chapman & Hall, London, 1969, 371, illus. (Modern Electrical Studies.)

ELECTRICAL AND ELECTRONIC TECHNOLOGY

HUBERT, CHARLES I.
  Operational Electricity: Theory, Characteristics, Applications and Mode of Operation of Circuits and Machines. Wiley, 1961, 530, illus.

———.
  Preventive Maintenance of Electrical Equipment. 2nd ed. McGraw-Hill, 1969, 458, illus.

HUFFSEY, RALPH R., and HUFFSEY, CHARLOTTE A.
  Descriptive Electronics. Holt, Rinehart & Winston, 1970, 365, illus.

HUGHES, LESLIE E., STEPHENS, R. W. B., and BROWN, L. D., EDS.
  Dictionary of Electronics and Nucleonics. Barnes & Noble, 1970, 443, illus.

HUGHES, ROBERT J., and PIPE, PETER
  Introduction to Electronics. Doubleday, 1961, 421, illus. (Tutor Text.)

HUNTER, LLOYD P., ED.
  Handbook of Semi-Conductor Electronics: A Practical Manual Covering the Physics, Technology and Circuit Applications of Transistors, Diodes, and Photocells. 3rd ed. McGraw-Hill, 1970, 1 vol. (McGraw-Hill Handbooks.)

ILLUMINATING ENGINEERING SOCIETY
  IES Lighting Handbook: The Standard Lighting Guide. 4th ed. John E. Kaufman, ed. IES, 1966, 1 vol., illus.

INTERNATIONAL RESISTANCE COMPANY
  The Expanded Glossary of Electronics Terminology. International Resistance Co., Philadelphia, 1965, 28, illus.

ITT EDUCATIONAL SERVICES, INC.
  This is Electronics. Vol. 1, Basic D-C Principles; Vol. 2, Basic A-C Principles; Vol. 3, Circuits; Vol. 4, Applications. Sams, 1969, 4 vols., illus.

JACKSON, HERBERT W.
  Introduction to Electric Circuits. 3rd ed. Prentice-Hall, 1970, 720, illus. (Prentice-Hall Electronic Technology Series.)

JACOBOWITZ, HENRY
  How to Solve Problems in Electricity and Electronics. Hayden, 1962, 185, illus.

JASKI, TOM
  Electronics in Business Machines. A. S. Barnes, 1963, 309, illus.

———.
  Industrial Electronics Made Easy. Gernsback Library, 1961, 288, illus. (Gernsback Book No. 99.)

JOHANNSEN, LAWRENCE A., and JOURNIGAN, RUSSELL P.
  Basic Electronics. Delmar, 1963, 295, illus.

JOHNSON, ERIC R.
  Servomechanisms. Prentice-Hall, 1963, 336, illus. (Electronic Technology Series.)

JOHNSON, J. RICHARD
  Electric Circuits. Holt, Rinehart & Winston, 1970, 2 vols., illus.

———.
  How to Build Electronic Equipment. Hayden, 1962, 290, illus. (Rider Pub. No. 286.)

JOLLEY, E. H.
  Introduction to Telephony and Telegraphy. Hart, 1970, 416, illus.

JONES, ELMER W., and JOHNSTON, JOHN L.
  Adequate Wiring for Home and Farm. Bruce, 1963, 237, illus.

JORGENSEN, FINN
  Handbook of Magnetic Tape Recording: Principles, Applications & Maintenance. TAB, 1970, 256, illus.

JOWETT, CHARLES E.
  Reliability of Electronic Components. Iliffe Books, 1966, 165.

KALISH, ISRAEL H.
  Microminiature Electronics. Sams, 1967, 304, illus.

KEEFE, JOHN E.
  Your Future as an Electronic Technician. Arco, 1970, 160. (Career Guidance Series.)

KELLEJIAN, ROBERT, and JONES, CLIFFORD L.
  Microwave Measurements Manual. McGraw-Hill, 1965, 152, illus.

KENNEDY, GEORGE
  Electronic Communications System. McGraw-Hill, 1970, 736.

KEONJIAN, EDWARD, ED.
  Microelectronics: Theory, Design, and Fabrication. McGraw-Hill, 1963, 383.

KERCHNER, RUSSELL M., and CORCORAN, GEORGE F.
  Alternating-Current Circuits. 4th ed. Wiley, 1960, 602, illus.

KETCHUM, DONALD J., and ALVAREZ, E. CHARLES
  Pulse and Switching Circuits. McGraw-Hill, 1965, 310, illus. (McGraw-Hill Technical Education Series.)

KIDWELL, WALTER M.
  Electrical Instruments and Measurements. McGraw-Hill, 1969, 449, illus.

KINTNER, PAUL M.
  Electronic Digital Techniques. McGraw-Hill, 1968, 315, illus.

KIP, ARTHUR F.
  Fundamentals of Electricity and Magnetism. 2nd ed. McGraw-Hill, 1968, 630.

KLEIN, LARRY, and GILMORE, KEN
  It's Easy to Use Electronic Test Equipment. Rider, 1962, 186, illus. (Rider Pub. No. 308.)

KLOEFFLER, ROYCE G.
  Electron Tubes. Wiley, 1966, 262, illus.

———.
  Industrial Electronics and Control. McGraw-Hill, 1960, 540, illus.

KLOEFFLER, ROYCE G., HORRELL, MAURICE W., and HARGRAVE, LEE E., JR.
  Basic Electronics. 2nd ed. Wiley, 1963, 643, illus.

KOLSTAD, C. KENNETH
  Rapid Electrical Estimating and Pricing: A Handy, Quick Method of Directly Determining the Selling Prices of Electrical Construction Work. McGraw-Hill, 1969, 1 vol., illus.

KORNEFF, THEODORE
  Introduction to Electronics. Academic Press, 1966, 545, illus.

KOSOW, IRVING L.
  Electric Machinery and Control. Prentice-Hall, 1964, 707, illus. (Prentice-Hall Engineering Technology Series.)

KRAUS, ALLAN D.
  Cooling Electronic Equipment. Prentice-Hall, 1965, 390, illus.

KRIEGER, MOSHE
  Basic Switching Circuit Theory. Macmillan, 1967, 256, illus.

KYLE, JAMES
  Servicing Digital Devices. Sams, 1968, 144, illus.

ENGINEERING PROGRAMS

LANCE, ALGIE L.
: Introduction to Microwave Theory and Measurements. McGraw-Hill, 1964, 308, illus. (McGraw-Hill Technical Education Series.)

LANCE, ALGIE L., CONSIDINE, JOSEPH M., and ROSE, DARRELL
: Microwave Experiments. McGraw-Hill, 1966, 180, illus.

LANE, LEONARD C.
: Elementary Industrial Electronics. Hayden, 1962, 2 vols., illus.

LAWRENCE, PAUL
: How to Repair Solid-State Imports. TAB, 1970, 196.

LEACH, DONALD P.
: Basic Electric Circuits. Wiley, 1969, 665, illus.

LEMONS, WAYNE
: Learn Electronics Through Trouble-Shooting. Sams, 1969, 576, illus.

LEMONS, WAYNE, and MONTGOMERY, GLEN
: Small Appliance Repair Guide. TAB, 1970, 224.

LENERT, LOUIS H.
: Semiconductor Physics, Devices, and Circuits. Merrill, 1968, 609, illus. (International Series in Electrical and Electronics Technology.)

LENK, JOHN D.
: Applications Handbook for Electrical Connectors. Sams, 1966, 160, illus. (Sams Photofact Publication ECL-1.)

———.
: Data Book for Electronic Technicians and Engineers. Prentice-Hall, 1968, 185, illus. (Prentice-Hall Electronic Technology Series.)

———.
: Handbook of Electronic Charts, Graphs and Tables. Prentice-Hall, 1970, 224, illus. (Prentice-Hall Electronic Technology Series.)

———, ED.
: Handbook of Electronic Meters: Theory and Application. Prentice-Hall, 1969, 180, illus.

———.
: Handbook of Oscilloscopes: Theory and Application. Prentice-Hall, 1968, 212, illus. (Prentice-Hall Electronic Technology Series.)

———.
: Handbook of Practical Electronic Tests and Measurements. Prentice-Hall, 1969, 302, illus. (Prentice-Hall Electronic Technology Series.)

———.
: How to Use Signal Generators in The Laboratory. Hayden, 1967, 120, illus.

———.
: Practical Semiconductor Data Book for Electronic Engineers and Technicians. Prentice-Hall, 1970, 260, illus. (Prentice-Hall Electronic Technology Series.)

———.
: Understanding Telemetry Circuits. Sams, 1966, 160, illus. (Sams Photofact Publication UTL-1.)

———.
: Understanding UHF Equipment. Sams, 1967, 144, illus. (Sams Photofact Publication 20,557.)

LEWIN, GERHARD S.
: Fundamentals of Vacuum Science and Technology. McGraw-Hill, 1965, 248.

LINDMAYER, JOSEPH, and WRIGLEY, CHARLES Y.
: Fundamentals of Semi-Conductor Devices. Van Nostrand, 1965, 486. (Van Nostrand Electronics and Communications Series.)

LINK, FRED M.
: Portable FM Radiotelephones. Chilton, 1968, 158, illus.

LIPPIN, GERARD
: Circuit Problems and Solutions. Vol. 1, Elementary Methods; Vol. 2, Network Theorems. Hayden, 1967, 1970, 2 vols., illus.

LISTER, EUGENE C.
: Electric Circuits and Machines. 4th ed. McGraw-Hill, 1968, 425, illus.

LITTAUER, RAPHAEL
: Pulse Electronics. McGraw-Hill, 1965, 530, illus.

LITTWIN, SHELDON, ED.
: Pulse Generators in Industrial Electronics. Hayden, 1964, 128, illus.

LIWSCHITZ-GARIK, MICHAEL, and WHIPPLE, CLYDE C.
: Alternating-Current Machines. 2nd ed. Van Nostrand, 1961, 604, illus.

LONG, JAMES D.
: Modern Electronic Circuit Design. McGraw-Hill, 1968, 286, illus.

LONG, WILLIAM E., and MALVINO, ALBERT P.
: Experiments for the Electric Circuits Laboratory. Wiley, 1968, 165.

LOPER, ORLA E.
: Direct Current Fundamentals. Delmar, 1963, 336, illus.

LOPER, ORLA E., and AHR, ARTHUR
: Introduction to Electricity and Electronics. Delmar, 1968, 295, illus.

LURCH, E. NORMAN
: Electric Circuits. Wiley, 1963, 565, illus.

———.
: Fundamentals of Electronics. 2nd ed. Wiley, 1970, 1 vol., illus.

LYTEL, ALLAN H.
: Industrial Electronics. McGraw-Hill, 1962, 456, illus.

MAJMUDAR, HARIT
: Introduction to Electrical Machines. Allyn & Bacon, 1969, 229, illus. (Topics in Electrical Engineering Series.)

MALVINO, ALBERT P.
: Electronic Instrumentation Fundamentals. McGraw-Hill, 1967, 465, illus.

MALVINO, ALBERT P., and LEACH, DONALD P.
: Digital Principles and Applications. McGraw-Hill, 1969, 433, illus.

MANDL, MATTHEW
: Directory of Electronic Circuits: With a Glossary of Terms. Prentice-Hall, 1966, 226, illus.

———.
: Electronic Switching Circuits: Boolean Algebra and Mapping. Prentice-Hall, 1969, 229, illus. (Prentice-Hall Electronic Technology Series.)

———.
: Fundamentals of Electric and Electronic Circuits. Prentice-Hall, 1964, 380, illus.

———.
: Fundamentals of Electronics. 2nd ed. Prentice-Hall, 1965, 674, illus.

———.
: Industrial Control Electronics. Prentice-Hall, 1961, 344, illus.

MARCUS, ABRAHAM
: Basic Electricity. 3rd ed. Prentice-Hall, 1969, 514.

———.
: Basic Electronics. Prentice-Hall, 1964, 622, illus. (Prentice-Hall Industrial Arts Series.)

———.
: Electricity for Technicians. Prentice-Hall, 1968, 490, illus. (Prentice-Hall Electronic Technology Series.)

———.
: Electronics for Technicians. Prentice-Hall, 1969, 496, illus. (Prentice-Hall Electronic Technology Series.)

MARKUS, JOHN
: Sourcebook of Electronic Circuits. McGraw-Hill, 1968, 888, illus.

ELECTRICAL AND ELECTRONIC TECHNOLOGY

MARSHALL, SAMUEL L., COMP.
    Microelectronic Technology: Selected Articles from Semiconductor Products and Solid State Technology. Boston Technical Publishers, 1967, 232, illus.

MASON, SAMUEL J., and ZIMMERMAN, HENRY J.
    Electronic Circuits, Signals and Systems. Wiley, 1960, 616, illus.

MATTSON, ROY H.
    Electronics. Wiley, 1966, 620.

McCLUSKEY, E. J.
    Introduction to the Theory of Switching Circuits. McGraw-Hill, 1965, 318.

McCLUSKEY, E. J., and BARTEE, T. C.
    A Survey of Switching Circuit Theory. McGraw-Hill, 1962, 224.

McDOUGAL, WYNNE L., et al.
    Fundamentals of Electricity. 4th ed. American Technical Society, 1960, 342.

McPARTLAND, JOSEPH F.
    How to Design Electrical Systems: A Complete Manual on Practical Design and Layout of Electrical Systems for Power, Light, Heat, Signals, and Communications in Commercial, Industrial, and Residential Buildings. McGraw-Hill, 1968, 208, illus.

McPARTLAND, JOSEPH F., and NOVAK, WILLIAM J.
    Electrical Design Details. McGraw-Hill, 1960, 231, illus.

———.
    Electrical Equipment Manual. 3rd ed. McGraw-Hill, 1965, 282, illus.

———.
    Practical Electricity. McGraw-Hill, 1964, 90, illus.

MIDDLETON, ROBERT G.
    Electrical & Electronic Signs & Symbols. Sams, 1968, 159, illus.

———.
    Hi-Fi Stereo Servicing Guide. Sams, 1970, 111, illus.

———.
    101 Ways to Use Your Sweep Generator. 2nd ed. Sams, 1966, 160.

———.
    Practical Electricity. 2nd ed. Audel, 1969, 481.

———.
    Troubleshooting with the Oscilloscope. Sams, 1962, 160, illus.

———.
    Using the Oscilloscope in Industrial Electronics. Sams, 1961, 256, illus.

MIDDLETON, ROBERT G., and GOLDSTEIN, MILTON
    Basic Electricity for Electronics. Holt, Rinehart & Winston, 1966, 694, illus.

MILEAF, HARRY, ED.
    Electronics One-Seven. Hayden, 1966, 7 vols. in 1, illus.

MILLER, REX, and CULPEPPER, FRED W., JR.
    Energy, Electricity, and Electronics for Course One of Three Courses in Electricity and Electronics. McKnight & McKnight, 1964, 235, illus.

MILLMAN, JACOB, and HALKIAS, C.
    Electronic Devices and Circuits. McGraw-Hill, 1967, 752.

MITCHELL, BRINTON B.
    Semiconductor Pulse Circuits with Experiments. Holt, Rinehart & Winston, 1970, 379, illus.

MIX, FLOYD
    All About House Wiring. Goodheart-Willcox, 1968, 176, illus.

MORRIS, NOEL M.
    Industrial Electronics: For Engineers and Technicians. McGraw-Hill, 1970, 372.

MORRISON, RALPH
    Grounding and Shielding Techniques in Instrumentation. Wiley, 1967, 144, illus.

MOTOROLA SEMICONDUCTOR PRODUCTS
    Analysis and Design of Integrated Circuits. McGraw-Hill, 1967, 545, illus. (Motorola Solid-State Electronics Series.)

———.
    Integrated Circuits: Design Principles and Fabrication. McGraw-Hill, 1965, 1 vol., illus. (Motorola Solid-State Electronics Series.)

———.
    The Semiconductor Data Book. 3rd ed. Motorola, Phoenix, 1968, 1 vol., illus.

MURPHY, JOHN S.
    Electronics in Industry. Oxford University Press, 1963, 216, illus.

NANAVATI, RAJENDRA P.
    An Introduction to Semiconductor Electronics. McGraw-Hill, 1963, 422, illus.

NATIONAL FIRE PROTECTION ASSOCIATION
    National Electrical Code Handbook. McGraw-Hill, 1932- , vols., illus.

———.
    National Electrical Code, 1965: Tables and Diagrams. National Electrical Contractors Association, Washington, 1965, 53, illus.

NEAL, HARRY E.
    Your Career in Electronics. Messner, 1963, 191.

NEWMAN, BERNARD
    Your Future in the High Fidelity Industry. R. Rosen Press, 1966, 128, illus. (Careers in Depth No. 65.)

NEW YORK INSTITUTE OF TECHNOLOGY
    A Programmed Course in Basic Electricity. 2nd ed. McGraw-Hill, 1970, 336, illus.

———.
    A Programmed Course in Basic Electronics. McGraw-Hill, 1964, 416, illus.

NOLL, EDWARD M.
    Servicing FM-Stereo Receivers. Sams, 1963, 128, illus.

NORDENBERG, HAROLD M.
    Electronic Transformers. Reinhold, 1964, 298, illus.

NORTON, HARRY N.
    Handbook of Transducers for Electronic Measuring Systems. Prentice-Hall, 1969, 704.

NOWAK, JOHN F.
    Practical Residential Wiring. 2nd ed. Van Nostrand, 1960, 511, illus.

O'KELLY, DENIS, and SIMMONS, S.
    An Introduction to Generalized Electrical Machine Theory. McGraw-Hill, 1968, 299.

OLLARD, E. A.
    Elementary Science for Electroplating Students and Foremen. 3rd ed. Draper, Teddington, England, 1969, 128.

OPPENHEIMER, SAMUEL L.
    Semiconductor Logic and Switching Circuits. Merrill, 1966, 185, illus.

OPPENHEIMER, SAMUEL L., and BORCHERS, JEAN P.
    Direct and Alternating Currents. McGraw-Hill, 1963, 392, illus.

OWENS, JAMES B., and SANBORN, PAUL E.
    Electron Tubes at Work. Doubleday, 1964, 557.

———.
    Fundamentals of Electricity. Doubleday, 1963, 533, illus. (Tutor Text.)

PALMQUIST, ROLAND E.
    Guide to the National Electrical Code. Audel, 1968, 439, illus.

ENGINEERING PROGRAMS

PEDERSON, DONALD O., STUDER, JACK J., and WHINNERY, JOHN R.
Introduction to Electronic Systems, Circuits, and Devices. McGraw-Hill, 1966, 457, illus.

PETERS, KEN
Modern Tape Recording and Hi-Fi. 2nd ed. Faber & Faber, 1967, 247, illus.

PHILCO CORPORATION
Electronic and Electrical Fundamentals. Philco, Philadelphia, 1960, 6 vols., illus.

———.
Electronic Precision Measurement Techniques and Experiments. Prentice-Hall, 1964, 336, illus.

———.
Servomechanism Fundamentals and Experiments. Prentice-Hall, 1964, 248, illus.

———.
Electronic Troubleshooting: A Self-Instructional Programed Manual. Prentice-Hall, 1966, 274, illus.

PIERCE, JOHN R.
Electrons and Waves. Doubleday, 1964, 226.

POLLACK, HARVEY
Basic Principles and Applications of Relays. Hayden, 1962, 104, illus. (New York Institute of Technology Industrial Electronics Applications Series No. 250-1.)

———.
Photoelectric Control. Rider, 1962, 136, illus. (New York Institute of Technology, Industrial Electronics Applications Series No. 250-2.)

POLON, DAVID D., ED.
Dictionary of Electronics Abbreviations, Signs, and Symbols. Odyssey, 1965, 747, illus. (Odyssey Scientific Library.)

POWER, T. C.
DC-AC Laboratory Manual. Prentice-Hall, 1968, 145. (Experiments for Electronics Technician Program.)

PRENSKY, SOL D.
Electronic Instrumentation. Prentice-Hall, 1963, 534, illus.

———.
Modern Electronic Voltmeters. Rider, 1964, 224, illus.

PRICE, LESLIE W.
Electronic Laboratory Techniques. Churchill, London, 1969, 265.

PRISE, WALTER J.
Electronic Circuit Packaging. Merrill, 1967, 185, illus. (International Series in Electronics Technology.)

PRITCHARD, D. C.
Lighting. Elsevier, 1970, 96.

PUGH, EMERSON M., and PUGH, EMERSON W.
Principles of Electricity and Magnetism. 2nd ed. Addison-Wesley, 1970, 498, illus.

RAINEY, GILBERT L.
Basic Electricity. Holt, Rinehart & Winston, 1966, 179, illus. (Basic Industrial Electronics Series.)

RAINEY, GRETCHEN R.
Practical Industrial Electronics. Holt, Rinehart & Winston, 1966-67, 5 vols.

RANDLE, GRETCHEN R., ED.
Electronic Industries Information Sources: A Comprehensive Guide to the Literature and Other Data Sources. Gale, 1968, 227. (Management Information Guide No. 13.)

RAYER, FRANCIS G.
Electronics and Computers. A. S. Barnes, 1968, 190, illus.

REED, MYRIL B.
Foundation for Electric Network Theory. Prentice-Hall, 1961, 354.

REID, ROBERT L., and KUBALA, THOMAS S.
Experiments in Alternating Current Circuits. Prentice-Hall, 1968, 120, illus. (Prentice-Hall Electronic Technology Series.)

REITZ, JOHN R., and MILFORD, FREDERICK J.
Foundations of Electromagnetic Theory. Addison-Wesley, 1960, 387.

RICHARDS, RICHARD K.
Electronic Digital Systems. Wiley, 1966, 637, illus.

RICHTER, HERBERT P.
Practical Electrical Wiring, Residential, Farm and Industrial. 8th ed. McGraw-Hill, 1970, 664, illus.

RIDER, JOHN F., and PRENSKY, SOL D.
How to Use Meters. 2nd ed. Rider, 1960, 216, illus. (Pub. No. 144.)

RISSE, JOSEPH A.
Electronic Test Instrument Handbook. Sams, 1962, 288, illus.

———.
Understanding Electronic Test Equipment. Sams, 1968, 192, illus.

RITCHIE, GEORGE L.
Electronics Construction Techniques. Holt, Rinehart & Winston, 1966, 227, illus.

ROHRER, RONALD A.
Circuit Theory: An Introduction to the State Variable Approach. McGraw-Hill, 1970, 314, illus. (McGraw-Hill Electronic Systems Series.)

ROLLIN, BERNARD V.
An Introduction to Electronics. Clarendon Press, 1964, 216, illus.

ROMANOWITZ, HARRY A.
Electrical Fundamentals and Circuit Analysis. Wiley, 1966, 715, illus.

———.
Fundamentals of Semiconductor and Tube Electronics. Wiley, 1962, 620, illus.

———.
Introduction to Electric Circuits. Wiley, 1970, 624, illus.

ROMANOWITZ, HARRY A., and PUCKETT, RUSSELL E.
Introduction to Electronics. Wiley, 1968, 763, illus.

ROSENBERG, MILTON
Audel's Programmed Basic Electricity Course. 2nd ed. Audel, 1966, 264.

ROSENBLATT, JACK, and FRIEDMAN, MORRIS H.
Direct and Alternating Current Machinery. McGraw-Hill, 1963, 420, illus.

ROTH, CHARLES J., JR.
Use of the Oscilloscope: A Programmed Text. Prentice-Hall, 1970, 240, illus.

RUITER, JACOB H., and MURPHY, R. GORDON
Basic Industrial Electronic Controls. Holt, Rinehart & Winston, 1962, 283, illus.

RYDER, JOHN D.
Electronic Fundamentals and Applications. 4th ed. Prentice-Hall, 1970, 618, illus. (Prentice Electrical Engineering Series.)

SAMS & COMPANY, INC.
Basic Electricity and an Introduction to Electronics. 2nd ed. Sams, 1967, 192, illus. (Sams Photofact Publication 20,540.)

———.
Handbook of Electronic Tables and Formulas. 3rd ed. Sams, 1968, 224, illus.

———.
Tube Substitution Handbook. 13th ed. Sams, 1970, 1 vol.

ELECTRICAL AND ELECTRONIC TECHNOLOGY

SANDS, LEO G.
    Electronics Handbook for the Electrician. Chilton, 1968, 220, illus.
——.
    Power Supplies for Electronic Equipment. Rider, 1967, 187, illus.

SAUNDERS, ALBERT C. W.
    Working with the Oscilloscope. 2nd ed. TAB, 1968, 104, illus.
——.
    Working with Semiconductors. TAB, 1969, 221, illus.

SCHAUER, CLARENCE H.
    Appliance Service Technology Programs. Lake Michigan College, Benton Harbor, 1966, 112.

SCHICK, KURT
    Investigating Electrical Theory. McGraw-Hill, 1967, 95, illus.
——.
    Principles of Electrical Theory. McGraw-Hill, 1967, 174, illus.

SCHULTZ, JOHN J.
    Electronic Test and Measurement Handbook. TAB, 1969, 220, illus.

SCHURE, ALEXANDER
    Filters and Attenuators. Rider, 1961, 87, illus. (Rider Pub. No. 166-36, Electronic Technology Series.)
——, ED.
    Industrial Electronics Measurements. Hayden, 1964, 126, illus. (New York Institute of Technology Industrial Electronics Applications Series.)
——.
    Transformers. Rider, 1961, 82, illus. (Electronic Technology Series.)

SCHUSTER, DONALD H.
    Basic Electronic Test Equipment: A Programmed Instruction. McGraw-Hill, 1968, 1 vol., illus.
——.
    Logical Electronic Troubleshooting: A Programmed Book. McGraw-Hill, 1963, 303, illus.

SEELY, SAMUEL
    Electronic Circuits. Holt, Rinehart & Winston, 1968, 752, illus.

SEIDMAN, ARTHUR H., and MARSHALL, SAMUEL L.
    Semiconductor Fundamentals, Devices and Circuits. Wiley, 1963, 278.

SENTZ, ROBERT E.
    Voltage and Power Amplifiers. Holt, Rinehart & Winston, 1968, 282, illus. (Electronics Technology Series.)

SENTZ, ROBERT E., and BARTKOWIAK, ROBERT A.
    Feedback Amplifiers and Oscillators. Holt, Rinehart & Winston, 1968, 218, illus. (Electronics Technology Series.)

SHAW, DENNIS F.
    Introduction to Electronics. Wiley, 1962, 338, illus.

SHEA, RICHARD F., ED.
    Amplifier Handbook. McGraw-Hill, 1968, 1496, illus.

SHIELDS, JOHN P.
    How to Build Electronics Projects. Sams, 1968, 96, illus.

SHIERS, GEORGE.
    Design and Construction of Electronic Equipment. Prentice-Hall, 1966, 362, illus. (Prentice-Hall Electronic Technology Series.)

SHORE, BRUCE H.
    The New Electronics. McGraw-Hill, 1970, 253, illus. (McGraw-Hill Continuing Education for Engineers.)

SHOULTZ, KENNETH G.
    Basic Electricity. St. Martin's Press, 1965, 214.

SHRADER, ROBERT L.
    Electrical Fundamentals for Technicians. McGraw-Hill, 1969, 479, illus. (McGraw-Hill Technical Education Series.)
——.
    Electronic Communication. 2nd ed. McGraw-Hill, 1967, 682, illus.

SHUNAMAN, FRED
    How to Use Test Instruments in Electronics Servicing. TAB, 1970, 256, illus.

SISKIND, CHARLES S.
    Electrical Circuits: Direct and Alternating Current. 2nd ed. McGraw-Hill, 1965, 595, illus.
——.
    Electrical Control Systems in Industry. McGraw-Hill, 1963, 496, illus.

SKINNER, WICKHAM, and ROGERS, DAVID C. D.
    Manufacturing Policy in the Electronics Industry. 3rd ed. Irwin, 1968, 289, illus.

SLURZBERG, MORRIS, and OSTERHELD, WILLIAM
    Essentials of Electricity-Electronics. 3rd ed. McGraw-Hill, 1965, 660, illus.

SMITH, DONALD A.
    ABC's of Vacuum Tubes. Sams, 1967, 128, illus.
——.
    Basic Electronics Problems Solved. TAB, 1970, 190.

SMITH, KENNETH M., and HOLROYD, P.
    Engineering Principles for Electrical Technicians. Pergamon, 1968, 376, illus.

SMYTHE, WILLIAM R.
    Static and Dynamic Electricity. 3rd ed. McGraw-Hill, 1968, 623.

SOISSON, HAROLD E.
    Electronic Measuring Instruments. McGraw-Hill, 1961, 352, illus.

SORKIN, RODNEY B.
    Integrated Electronics. McGraw-Hill, 1970, 211, illus.

SOWA, WALTER A., and TOOLE, JAMES M.
    Special Semiconductor Devices. Holt, Rinehart & Winston, 1968, 190, illus. (Electronics Technology Series.)

SPIELMAN, HAROLD S.
    Electronics Source Book for Teachers. Hayden, 1965, 3 vols., illus.

SQUIRES, TERENCE L.
    Beginner's Guide to Electronics. Newnes, London, 1967, 194, illus. (Newnes Books of Allied Interest.)

STEINBERG, WILLIAM F., and FORD, WALTER B.
    Electricity and Electronics: Basic. 3rd ed. American Technical Society, 1964, 336, illus.

STEPNICK, IVAN C.
    Basic Electricity Study Course. Refrigeration Engineers & Technicians Association, 1969, 191.

STOTT, G. S., and BIRCHALL, G.
    Electrical Engineering Principles for Electrical, Telecommunications, and Installation Technicians. McGraw-Hill, 1969, 236, illus. (Technical Education Series.)

STOUT, MELVILLE B.
    Basic Electrical Measurements. 2nd ed. Prentice-Hall, 1960, 571, illus.

STREATER, JACK W.
    How to Use Integrated-Circuit Logic Elements. Sams, 1969, 136, illus.

SUFFERN, MAURICE G.
    Basic Electrical and Electronic Principles. 3rd ed. McGraw-Hill, 1962, 604, illus.

ENGINEERING PROGRAMS

SUMMER, STEVEN E.
    Electronic Sensing Controls. Chilton, 1969, 192, illus.

SURINA, TUGOMIR, and HERRICK, CLYDE
    Semiconductor Electronics. Holt, Rinehart & Winston, 1964, 429, illus.

SUSSKIND, CHARLES
    The Encyclopedia of Electronics. Reinhold, 1962, 974, illus.

TALLEY, DAVID
    Basic Carrier Telephony. Rev. ed. Hayden, 1966, 208, illus.

TEMES, LLOYD
    Electronic Circuits for Technicians. McGraw-Hill, 1970, 432, illus.

TEXAS INSTRUMENTS, INC.
    Circuit Design for Audio, AM/FM, and T.V. McGraw-Hill, 1967, 352, illus. (Electronics Series.)

THOMAS, HARRY E.
    Handbook for Electronic Engineers and Technicians. Prentice-Hall, 1965, 427, illus.

THOMAS, HARRY E., and CLARKE, CAROLE A.
    Handbook of Electronic Instruments and Measurement Techniques. Prentice-Hall, 1967, 398, illus.

TIMBIE, WILLIAM H.
    Essentials of Electricity. 3rd ed. Wiley, 1963, 302, illus.

TOCCI, RONALD J.
    Fundamentals of Electronic Devices. Merrill, 1970, 497, illus.

TODD, ALVA C., ED.
    Encyclopedia of Electronics Components. Chicago Allied Radio Corp., 1967, 111, illus.

TOMBOULIAN, DIRAN H.
    Electric and Magnetic Fields. Harcourt, Brace & World, 1965, 479.

TRAINING & RETRAINING, INC., NEW YORK
    Basic Electricity/Electronics. Sams, 1964, 5 vols., illus. (Sams Photofact Publication ECY-1-5.)

TRAINING SYSTEMS, INC.
    DC Circuit Principles: A Programed Text. Rider, 1965, 246, illus. (Rider Programodule.)

TREMAINE, HOWARD M.
    Audio Cyclopedia. 2nd ed. Sams, 1969, 1757, illus.

TURNER, DAVID R.
    Electrician and Electrician's Helper: All Grades of Federal, State and City Jobs. 4th ed. Arco, 1969, 320, illus. (Arco Civil Service Test Tutor.)

TURNER, RUFUS P.
    ABC's of Voltage-Dependent Resistors. Sams, 1970, 96, illus.

———.
    Basic Electricity. 2nd ed. Holt, Rinehart & Winston, 1963, 412, illus.

———.
    Basic Electronic Test Instruments. Rev. ed. Holt, Rinehart & Winston, 1963, 297, illus.

———.
    Diode Circuits Handbook. 2nd ed. Sams, 1967, 160, illus.

———.
    How to Use Grid-Dip Oscillators. 2nd ed., rev. Hayden, 1969, 128, illus.

———.
    Practical Oscilloscope Handbook. Hayden, 1964, 2 vols. in 1, illus.

———.
    Semiconductor Devices. Holt, Rinehart & Winston, 1961, 278, illus.

———.
    Waveform Measurements. Hayden, 1968, 86, illus.

TUTHILL, CUYLER A.
    How to Service Tape Recorders. 2nd ed., rev. Hayden, 1966, 165, illus.

U.S. AEROSPACE STUDIES INSTITUTE, COMMUNICATIONS-ELECTRONICS DOCTRINAL OFFICE
    Communications-Electronics Terminology Handbook: A Manual of Definitions, Abbreviations, Acronyms and Designations. Public Affairs Press, Washington, 1965, 547.

U.S. BUREAU OF NAVAL PERSONNEL
    Basic Electricity. Dover, 1962, 448, illus.

———.
    Basic Electronics. Rev. ed. USGPO, 1968, 538, illus. (Navy Training Course.)

———.
    Fundamentals of Electronics. USGPO, 1964, 8 vols., illus.

———.
    Synchro-Servo Fundamentals: Trainee's Guide for Maintenance Training. USGPO, 1963, 282, illus.

U.S. OFFICE OF EDUCATION, VOCATIONAL AND TECHNICAL EDUCATION DIVISION
    Electrical Technology: A Suggested 2-Year Post High School Curriculum. USOE, 1960, 118. (OE80006.)

———.
    Electronic Technology: A Suggested 2-Year Post High School Curriculum. Rev. ed. USOE, 1969, 104. (OE-80009A, Technical Education Program Series No. 2A.)

UPTON, MONROE
    Inside Electronics: The How and Why of Radio, TV, Stereo, and Hi-Fi. Devin-Adair, 1964, 262, illus.

VAN DER ZIEL, ALDERT
    Electronics. Allyn, 1966, 484.

VAN DIJCK, J. G. R.
    The Physical Basis of Electronics. Hayden, 1965, 362, illus.

VAN VALKENBURGH, NOOGER, and NEVILLE, INC.
    Basic Electronic Circuits: A Basic Training Manual.... 2nd ed. Brolet Press, New York, 1965, 1 vol., illus. (Common Core Book.)

———.
    Basic Industrial Electricity. Hayden, 1962, 2 vols., illus.

VAN VELZER, HARRY L.
    Physics and Chemistry of Electronic Technology. McGraw-Hill, 1962, 372.

VERGARA, WILLIAM
    Electronics in Everyday Things. Harper, 1961, 235, illus.

WALSH, JOHN B., and MILLER, KENNETH S.
    Introductory Electric Circuits. McGraw-Hill, 1960, 353, illus.

WANG, SHYH
    Solid-State Electronics. McGraw-Hill, 1966, 778.

WEDLOCK, BRUCE D., and ROBERGE, J. K.
    Electronic Components and Measurements. Prentice-Hall, 1969, 338.

WEICK, CARL B.
    Principles of Electronic Technology. McGraw-Hill, 1969, 388, illus.

WELLARD, CHARLES L.
    Resistance and Resistors. McGraw-Hill, 1960, 264, illus.

WESTCOTT, CHARLES G.
    Tape Recorders: How They Work. 2nd ed. Sams, 1964, 224, illus. (Sams Photofact Publication TRW-2.)

WESTINGHOUSE ELECTRIC CORPORATION
    Westinghouse Electronic Tube Guide: Receiving Tubes, TV Picture Tubes. 7th ed. Westinghouse, Elmira, N.Y., 1967, 182, illus.

ELECTRICAL AND ELECTRONIC TECHNOLOGY

WHEELER, GERSHON J.
　　Introduction to Microwaves. Prentice-Hall, 1963, 242.

WHITE, D. HYWEL
　　Elementary Electronics. Harper & Row, 1966, 172, illus. (Harper's Physics Series.)

WHITFIELD, JOHN F.
　　Electrical Installations Technology. Pergamon, 1968, 354, illus. (Commonwealth and International Library, Electrical Engineering Division.)

WILCOX, GLADE W.
　　Basic Electronics. Holt, Rinehart & Winston, 1960, 402, illus.

WILCOX, GLADE W., and HESSELBERTH, CASSIUS A.
　　Electricity for Engineering Technology. Allyn & Bacon, 1970, 385, illus. (Allyn Electrical Technology Series.)

WINCH, RALPH P.
　　Electricity and Magnetism. 2nd ed. Prentice-Hall, 1963, 606.

WOLFF, EDWARD A.
　　Antenna Analysis. Wiley, 1966, 514, illus.

WOOD, PAUL E.
　　Switching Theory. McGraw-Hill, 1968, 390, illus.

WOOLMAN, MYRON, and VALENTINE, C. GLENN
　　From Electrons to Power: AC & DC—A Programmed Text. Rev. ed. Glencoe Press, 1968, 440, illus.

WRIGHT, RALPH R., and SKUTT, HENRY R.
　　Electronics: Circuits and Devices. Ronald, 1965, 436, illus.

YOUNG, VICTOR
　　Understanding Microwaves. Hayden, 1960, 304, illus.

ZBAR, PAUL B.
　　Basic Electricity. 3rd ed. McGraw-Hill, 1966, 211. (Electronic Industries Association-Voorhees Technical Institute Publication.)

——.
　　Electronic Instruments and Measurements: Laboratory Manual for Electronics Technicians. McGraw-Hill, 1965, 106, illus. (Electronic Industries Association-Voorhees Technical Institute Publication.)

——.
　　Industrial Electronics: Laboratory Manual for Electronics Technicians. McGraw-Hill, 1960, 201, illus.

ZBAR, PAUL B., and ELECTRICAL INDUSTRIES ASSOCIATION-VOORHEES TECHNICAL INSTITUTE
　　Basic Electronics: A Text-Laboratory Manual. 3rd ed. McGraw-Hill, 1967, 261, illus.

——.
　　Electricity-Electronics Fundamentals: A Text-Laboratory Manual. McGraw-Hill, 1969, 272, illus.

ZEINES, BENJAMIN
　　Electronic Communications Systems. Prentice-Hall, 1970, 480, illus. (Prentice-Hall Electronic Technology Series.)

——.
　　Principles of Applied Electronics. Wiley, 1963, 425, illus.

——.
　　Principles of Industrial Electronics. McGraw-Hill, 1966, 378, illus.

ZEPLER, E. E.
　　Electronic Circuit Techniques.... Van Nostrand, 1963, 212, illus.

——.
　　Electronic Devices and Networks.... Van Nostrand, 1963, 217, illus.

ZWICK, GEORGE
　　The Oscilloscope. 3rd ed. Gernsback Library, 1969, 253, illus. (Gernsback Library No. 108.)

ELECTRO-MECHANICAL

BRODSKY, STANLEY M.
　　Report of Electro-Mechanical Technology Curriculum Development Project.... State University of New York, Albany, 1967, 77.

CANFIELD, EUGENE B.
　　Electromechanical Control Systems and Devices. Wiley, 1965, 328, illus.

CHAPMAN, C. R.
　　Electromechanical Energy Conversion. Blaisdell, 1965, 250, illus.

ELLISON, ARTHUR J.
　　Electromechanical Energy Conversion. Reinhold, 1965, 200, illus.

FITZGERALD, ARTHUR E., and KINGSLEY, CHARLES
　　Electric Machinery: The Dynamics and Statics of Electromechanical Energy Conversion. 2nd ed. McGraw-Hill, 1961, 568, illus.

GEHMLICH, DIETRICH K., and HAMMOND, SEYMOUR B.
　　Electromechanical Systems. McGraw-Hill, 1967, 469, illus. (McGraw-Hill Electrical and Electronic Engineering Series.)

GREENWOOD, DOUGLAS C.
　　Manual of Electromechanical Devices, Component Types, Characteristics, and Design Applications. McGraw-Hill, 1965, 337, illus.

KOENIG, HERMAN E.
　　Electromechanical System Theory. McGraw-Hill, 1961, 504, illus.

LESCARBEAU, ROLAND F., et al.
　　A Suggested Curriculum Guide for Electro-Mechanical Technology Oriented Specially to the Computer and Business Machine Fields—Interim Report. Hartford University, War Technical Institute, 1968, 68. (ERIC ED 018 392.)

RONEY, MAURICE W., and PHILLIPS, DONALD S.
　　Electromechanical Technology: A Unified Concepts Approach. American Association of Junior Colleges, 1970, 48.

SALMON, LAWRENCE J.
　　IBM Machine Operation and Wiring. 2nd ed. Wadsworth, 1966, 246, illus.

SKILLING, HUGH H.
　　Electromechanics: A First Course in Electromechanical Energy Conversion. Wiley, 1962, 475, illus.

WOODSON, HERBERT H., and MELCHER, JAMES R.
　　Electromechanical Dynamics. Wiley, 1968, 3 vols., illus.

LASERS AND MASERS

BROTHERTON, MANFRED
　　Masers and Lasers: How They Work, What They Do. McGraw-Hill, 1964, 207, illus.

BROWN, RONALD
　　Lasers: Tools of Modern Technology. Doubleday, 1968, 192, illus. (Doubleday Science Series SD7.)

CARROLL, JOHN M.
　　The Story of the Laser. Dutton, 1964, 181, illus.

LEINWOLL, STANLEY
　　Understanding Lasers and Masers. Hayden, 1965, 96, illus.

ENGINEERING PROGRAMS

LYTEL, ALLAN H.
    ABC'S of Lasers and Masers. 2nd ed. Sams, 1966, 128, illus. (Sams Photofact Publication.)

MARSHALL, SAMUEL L.
    Laser Technology and Applications. McGraw-Hill, 1968, 294, illus.

MELIA, TERENCE P.
    An Introduction to Masers and Lasers. Chapman & Hall, 1967, 162, illus.

PIKE, CHARLES A.
    Lasers and Masers. Sams, 1967, 176, illus.

SIEGMAN, A. E.
    Microwave Solid-State Masers. McGraw-Hill, 1964, 608.

SMITH, WILLIAM V., and SOROKIN, P. P.
    The Laser. McGraw-Hill, 1966, 498.

STEHLING, KURT R.
    Lasers and Their Applications. World, 1966, 201, illus.

TROUP, GORDON
    Masers and Lasers: Molecular Amplification and Oscillation by Stimulated Emission. 2nd ed. Wiley, 1963, 192.

MOTORS

ALERICH, WALTER N.
    Electric Motor Control: Theory and Applications. Delmar, 1965, 236, illus.

ANDERSON, EDWIN P.
    Electric Motors. 2nd ed. Audel, 1968, 422, illus.

BEATER, JACK
    Electric Motor Test and Repair. 2nd ed. TAB, 1966, 160, illus. (T-97.)

DUDLEY, ADOLPHUS M., and HENDERSON, S. F.
    Connecting Induction Motors: Operation and Practice. 4th ed. McGraw-Hill, 1960, 425, illus.

FUCHS, J. DAVID, and GARSTANG, STEPHEN W.
    Electrical Motor Controls and Circuits. Sams, 1966, 288, illus. (Sams Photofact Publication ECW-1.)

HARWOOD, PAISELY B.
    Harwood's Control of Electric Motors. 4th ed. Ralph A. Millermaster, ed. Wiley, 1970, 498, illus.

HELLER, SAMUEL
    Electric Motor Repair Shop Problems and Solutions. TAB, 1960, 186.

HEUMANN, GERHART W.
    Magnetic Control of Industrial Motors. Wiley, 1961- , vols., illus.

IRELAND, JAMES R.
    Permanent Ceramic Magnet Motors: Electrical and Magnetic Design and Application. McGraw-Hill, 1968, 170.

LIBBY, CHARLES C.
    Motor Selection and Application. McGraw-Hill, 1960, 508, illus.

LLOYD, TOM C.
    Electric Motors and Their Applications. Wiley, 1969, 332, illus.

LYTEL, ALLAN H.
    Electronic Motor Control. Sams, 1964, 224.

McINTYRE, ROBERT L.
    AC Motor-Control Fundamentals. McGraw-Hill, 1960, 248, illus.

———.
    Electric Motor Control Fundamentals. 2nd ed. McGraw-Hill, 1966, 378, illus.

ROSENBERG, ROBERT
    Electric Motor Repair: A Practical Book on the Winding, Repair, and Troubleshooting of AC and DC Motors and Controllers. 2nd ed. Holt, Rinehart & Winston, 1970, 2 vols. in 1, illus.

SCHWEITZER, GERALD
    Basics of Fractional Horsepower Motors and Repair. Rider, 1960, 168, illus. (Rider Pub. No. 236.)

SMEATON, ROBERT W., ED.
    Motor Application and Maintenance Handbook. McGraw-Hill, 1969, 1 vol., illus.

VEINOTT, CYRIL G.
    Fractional and Subfractional-Horsepower Electric Motors. 3rd ed. McGraw-Hill, 1970, 475, illus.

RADAR

BOULDING, REGINALD S. H.
    Principles and Practice of Radar. 7th ed. Van Nostrand, 1963, 851.

SKOLNIK, MERRILL I., ED.
    Radar Handbook. McGraw-Hill, 1970, 1536, illus.

TAYLOR, DENIS
    Introduction to Radar and Radar Techniques. Philosophical Library, 1967, 125, illus.

WHEELER, GERSHON J.
    Radar Fundamentals. Prentice-Hall, 1967, 105, illus. (Prentice-Hall Electronic Technology Series.)

RADIO

AMERICAN RADIO RELAY LEAGUE
    Radio Amateur's Handbook. ARRL, 1926- , Vol. 1- , illus.

BERENS, JULIUS, and BERENS, JACK
    Commercial Radio Operator's License Study Guide. Chilton, 1969, 3 vols., illus.

BROWN, ROBERT M., and KNEITEL, THOMAS S.
    Amateur Radio Incentive Licensing Study Guide. Editors & Engineers, 1967, 159, illus.

COOK, ALFRED B., and LIFF, A. A.
    Frequency Modulation Receivers. Prentice-Hall, 1968, 527, illus. (Prentice-Hall Electronic Technology Series.)

FREELAND, R. R.
    Practical CB Radio Servicing. Leo G. Sands, ed. Hayden, 1968, illus.

FRYE, JOHN T.
    Basic Radio Course. Rev. ed. Gernsback Library, 1961, 224, illus.

GHIRARDI, ALFRED A., and DINES, JESS E.
    Radio and Television, Receiver Circuitry and Operation. Rev. ed. Holt, Rinehart & Winston, 1964, 556, illus.

GRAY, LAWRENCE F., and GRAHAM, RICHARD
    Radio Transmitters. McGraw-Hill, 1961, 462.

GRIFFITH, BENJAMIN W.
    Radio-Electronic Transmission Fundamentals. McGraw-Hill, 1962, 612, illus.

HAWKER, JOHN P.
Radio and Television: Principles and Applications. Hart, 1968, 399, illus.

HORNUNG, JULIUS L.
Radio Operating Questions and Answers. 13th ed. McGraw-Hill, 1964, 598, illus.

KING, GORDON J.
Radio and Television Test Instruments. Translantic, 1962, 175, illus.

KIVER, MILTON S.
FM Simplified. 3rd ed. Van Nostrand, 1960, 376, illus.

LENK, JOHN D.
How to Use Signal Generators in Radio/TV/HI-FI Servicing. Hayden, 1967, 128, illus.

MARCUS, ABRAHAM
Radio Servicing: Theory and Practice. 3rd ed. Prentice-Hall, 1960, 649, illus.

MARCUS, ABRAHAM, and MARCUS, WILLIAM
Elements of Radio. 5th ed. Prentice-Hall, 1965, 672, illus. (Prentice-Hall Industrial Arts Series.)

MARCUS, WILLIAM, and LEVY, ALEX
Elements of Radio Servicing. 3rd ed. McGraw-Hill, 1967, 426, illus.

———.
Practical Radio Servicing. 2nd ed. McGraw-Hill, 1963, 624, illus.

NATIONAL RADIO INSTITUTE
Radio-Television-Electronics Dictionary. Rider, 1962, 190, illus.

OLDFIELD, R. L.
Radio-Television and Basic Electronics. 2nd ed., rev. American Technical Society, 1960, 400, illus.

PANNETT, W. E.
Dictionary of Radio and Television. Philosophical Library, 1967, 373, illus.

THE RADIO HANDBOOK.
Editors & Engineers, 1935- , vols., illus.

ROSENTHAL, MURRAY P.
Fundamentals of Radio. Hayden, 1965, 328, illus.

ROWE, FRED D.
How to Locate and Eliminate Radio and TV Interference. 2nd ed. Rider, 1961, 160, illus. (Rider Pub. No. 158.)

SANDS, LEO G.
Easy Way to Service Radio Receivers. TAB, 1968, 173, illus.

———.
Fundamentals of Radio Control. Sams, 1962, 53, illus.

———.
A Guide to Mobile Radio. Chilton, 1967, 210, illus.

SLURZBERG, MORRIS, and OSTERHELD, WILLIAM
Essentials of Radio-Electronics. 3rd ed. McGraw-Hill, 1965, 700, illus.

TEPPER, MARVIN
Basic Radio. Hayden, 1961, 6 vols. in 1, illus.

———.
Basic Radio Repair. Rider, 1963, 2 vols., illus.

WATSON, HERBERT M., et al.
Understanding Radio: A Guide to Practical Operation and Theory. 3rd ed. McGraw-Hill, 1960, 706, illus.

ZBAR, PAUL B.
Basic Radio: Theory and Servicing. 3rd ed. McGraw-Hill, 1969, 208, illus.

ELECTRICAL AND ELECTRONIC TECHNOLOGY

TELEVISION

ANDERSON, EDWIN P.
Television Service Manual. 3rd ed., rev. Robert G. Middleton, ed. Audel, 1969, 535.

ANTHONY, EUGENE
Profitable Television Troubleshooting: A Step-By-Step Guide to Efficient Professional Servicing of Black-and-White Receivers. 2nd ed. McGraw-Hill, 1963, 418, illus. (McGraw-Hill Television, Radio, and Audio Servicing Course.)

BABCOKE, CARL H.
RCA Color TV Service Manual. TAB, 1969, 176, illus.

BELT, FOREST H.
Motorola Color TV Service Manual. TAB, 1969, 160.

———.
Television Servicing/Repair. International Correspondence Schools, 1968, 1 vol., illus.

BUCHSBAUM, WALTER H.
Color TV Servicing. 2nd ed. Prentice-Hall, 1968, 272, illus.

———.
Fundamentals of Television. Rider, 1964, 291, illus.

CANTOR, LEON
How to Select and Install Antennas. Hayden, 1969, 104, illus.

CHESTER, GIRAUD, GARRISON, GARNET R., and WILLIS, EDGAR E.
Television and Radio. 3rd ed. Appleton-Century-Crofts, 1963, 659, illus.

DEUTSCHER, J. NOEL
Your Future in Television. R. Rosen Press, 1963, 158. (Careers in Depth.)

ELECTRONIC TECHNICIAN
Color TV Trouble Factbook. TAB, 1970, 176, illus.

———.
Servicing TV Receiver Circuits: With Special Color Section. TAB, 1967, 224.

———.
TV Troubleshooter's Handbook. 2nd ed. TAB, 1970, 284, illus.

ENNES, HAROLD E.
Television System Maintenance. Sams, 1967, 288, illus. (Sams Photofact Publication.)

———.
Television Tape Fundamentals. Sams, 1966, 256, illus. (Sams Photofact Publication REN-1.)

GOODMAN, ROBERT L.
Practical Color TV Servicing Techniques. TAB, 1968, 295, illus.

GROB, BERNARD
Basic Television: Principles and Servicing. 3rd ed. McGraw-Hill, 1964, 653, illus.

HANSEN, GERALD L.
Introduction to Solid-State Television Systems: Color and Black & White. Prentice-Hall, 1969, 449, illus. (Prentice-Hall Electronic Technology Series.)

JOHNSON, J. RICHARD
How to Troubleshoot a TV Receiver. 2nd ed. Rider, 150, illus.

———.
Practical Television Servicing. 2nd ed. Holt, 1962, 438, illus.

KILLION, WILLIAM D.
Video Transmission Techniques. Dynair Electronics, San Diego, 1968, 51, illus.

ENGINEERING PROGRAMS

KIVER, MILTON S.
    Color Television Fundamentals. 2nd ed. McGraw-Hill, 1964, 335, illus.

———.
    Television Simplified. 6th ed. Van Nostrand, 1962, 637, illus.

KRAVITZ, GEORGE
    Basic TV Course. Gernsback Library, 1962, 224. (Gernsback Library No. 105.)

LENK, JOHN D.
    How to Use Signal Generators in Color TV Servicing Hayden, 1967, 112, illus.

LYTEL, ALLAN H.
    How to Service UHF TV. Rider, 1964, 127, illus.

MARGOLIS, ART
    101 TV Troubles: From Symptom to Repair. TAB, 1970, 218, illus.

———.
    TV Repairs. Arco, 1969, 128, illus.

———.
    TV Servicing Guidebook: Problems and Solutions. TAB, 1968, 192.

MARKUS, JOHN
    Television and Radio Repairing. 2nd ed. McGraw-Hill, 1961, 568, illus.

MARTIN, ALBERT V. J.
    Technical Television. Prentice-Hall, 1962, 557, illus.

MIDDLETON, HERMAN A.
    1970 Tube Caddy—Tube Substitution Guidebook. Hayden, 1970, 128.

MIDDLETON, ROBERT G.
    TV Troubleshooting and Repair. 2nd ed. Hayden, 1963, 216, illus.

OLIPHANT, C. P., and RAY, VERNE M.
    Color TV Training Manual. Rev. ed. Sams, 1965, 223, illus. (Sams Photofact Publication TVC-2.)

RICE, EDWARD F.
    Television Service Training Manual. 2nd ed. Sams, 1968, 240, illus.

SQUIRES, TERRENCE L.
    Beginner's Guide to Colour Television. Transatlantic, 1964, 124, illus.

STREET, R. E.
    Practical Television Circuits. 2nd ed. Transatlantic, 1969, 375, illus.

WHITMER, MELVIN
    Servicing Closed-Circuit Television. Sams, 1967, 192, illus. (Sams Photofact Publication.)

WORTMAN, LEON A.
    Closed-Circuit Television Handbook. 2nd ed. Bobbs-Merrill, 1969, 288, illus.

ZBAR, PAUL B., and SCHILDKRAUT, SID
    Basic Television and Television Receiver Servicing: A Text Laboratory Manual. McGraw-Hill, 1968, 297, illus.

TRANSISTORS

ADAMS, THOMAS M.
    Transistor Circuits. 2nd ed. Sams, 1966, 136, illus. (Electronic Circuit Action Series.)

AMOS, STANLEY W.
    Principles of Transistor Circuits: Introduction to the Design of Amplifiers, Receivers and Other Circuits. 3rd ed. Hayden, 1965, 293, illus.

BARNES, LESLIE
    Transistors for Technical Colleges. Transatlantic, 1965, 194.

BELT, FOREST H., et al.
    1-2-3-4 Servicing Transistor Color TV. Sams, 1970, 224, illus.

CALDWELL, WILLIAM C.
    Practical Transistor Servicing. 2nd ed. Sams, 1965, 191, illus. (Sams Photofact Publication PTC-2.)

CARINGELLA, CHARLES
    Transistorized Amateur Radio Projects. Sams, 1967, 128, illus.

CHISTIAKOV, NIKOLAI I.
    Transistor Electronics in Instrument Technology. Pergamon, 1964, 378, illus.

COBBOLD, RICHARD S.
    Theory and Applications of Field-Effect Transistors. Wiley, 1970, 534, illus.

COOKE-YARBOROUGH, EDMUND H.
    An Introduction to Transistor Circuits. 2nd ed. Interscience, 1960, 158, illus.

CORNING, JOHN J.
    Transistor Circuit Analysis and Design. Prentice-Hall, 1965, 466, illus.

COWLES, LAURENCE G.
    Analysis and Design of Transistor Circuits. Van Nostrand, 1966, 309, illus.

———.
    Transistor Circuits and Applications. Prentice-Hall, 1968, 323, illus. (Prentice-Hall Electronic Technology Series.)

DARR, JACK
    Transistor TV Servicing Made Easy. Sams, 1970, 160, illus.

ELECTRONICS
    Design Manual for Transistor Circuits. John M. Carroll, ed. McGraw-Hill, 1961, 381, illus.

EVANS, JOSEPH
    Fundamental Principles of Transistors. 2nd ed. Van Nostrand, 1962, 332, illus.

FEDERAL ELECTRIC CORPORATION
    Special Purpose Transistors: A Self-Instructional Programed Manual. Prentice-Hall, 1966, 129, illus.

———.
    Transistors: A Self-Instructional Programed Manual. Prentice-Hall, 1963, 430, illus.

FITCHEN, FRANKLIN C.
    Transistor Circuit Analysis and Design. 2nd ed. Van Nostrand, 1966 412, illus. (Van Nostrand Electronics and Communications Series.)

FONTAINE, GUY
    Diodes and Transistors. Hayden, 1963, 480, illus.

———.
    Transistors for Audiofrequency: Audiofrequency Amplification. Hayden, 1967, 384, illus.

GERRISH, HOWARD H.
    Transistor Electronics: Basic Instruction in Electricity and Electronics, with Major Emphasis on Solid State Components. Goodheart-Willcox, 1969, 368, illus.

HAKIM, SAHIR S., and BARRETT, ROBERT
    Transistor Circuits in Electronics: Basic Principles for Amplifier, Oscillator and Switching Applications. Hayden, 1964, 341, illus.

HARRIS, JOHN N., GRAY, PAUL E., and SEARLE, CAMPBELL L.
    Digital Transistor Circuits. Wiley, 1966, 221, illus. (Semiconductor Electronics Education Committee Books Vol. 6.)

ELECTRICAL AND ELECTRONIC TECHNOLOGY

HIBBERD, ROBERT G.
  Transistors: Principles and Applications. Hart, 1965, 304, illus.

HOBERMAN, STUART
  Understanding and Using Unijunction Transistors. Sams, 1969, 95, illus.

HOROWITZ, MANNIE
  Practical Design with Transistors. Sams, 1968, 288, illus.

KENIAN, PAUL R.
  Basic Transistor Course. Gernsback Library, 1962, 224, illus.

KING, GORDON J.
  Servicing Transistor Equipment: A Systematic Guide to the Servicing of Transistor Radio, Television, Tape, and Hi-fi Equipment. Hart, 1968, 151, illus.

KIVER, MILTON S.
  Transistors in Radio, Television, and Electronics. 3rd ed. McGraw-Hill, 1962, 528, illus.

KNEITEL, THOMAS S.
  103 Simple Transistor Projects. Rider, 1964, 120, illus.

LANE, LEONARD C.
  How to Fix Transistor Radios & Printed Circuits. TAB, 1969, 252, illus.

LATHAM, DONALD C.
  Transistors and Integrated Circuits. Lippincott, 1966, 197, illus.

LEACH, DONALD P.
  Transistor Circuit Measurements. McGraw-Hill, 1968, 269, illus.

LIBES, S.
  Repairing Transistor Radios. Hayden, 1960, 159, illus.

LYTEL, ALLAN H.
  Handbook of Transistor Circuits. Sams, 1963, 224, illus. (Sams Photofact Publication.)

———.
  Industrial Transistor Circuits. Sams, 1965, 111, illus.

———.
  Transistor Circuit Manual. Sams, 1961, 255, illus. (Sams Photofact Publication TCM-1.)

MALVINO, ALBERT P.
  Transistor Circuit Approximations. McGraw-Hill, 1968, 404, illus.

MANN, GEORGE B.
  ABC'S of Transistors. 2nd ed. Sams, 1966, 112. (Sams Photofact Publication TRA-2.)

MIDDLETON, ROBERT G.
  Elements of Transistor Technology. Sams, 1963, 288, illus.

NEW YORK INSTITUTE OF TECHNOLOGY
  A Programmed Course in Basic Transistors. McGraw-Hill, 1964, 473, illus.

PRITCHARD, ROBERT L.
  Electrical Characteristics of Transistors. McGraw-Hill, 1967, 715, illus.

RADIO CORPORATION OF AMERICA
  Transistor Manual. RCA, 1966, 480, illus.

RADIO-ELECTRONICS
  Transistors: How to Test Them—How to Build All-Transistor Test Equipment. Gernsback Library, 1961, 96, illus. (Gernsback Library No. 94.)

RCA SERVICE COMPANY, INC.
  Fundamentals of Transistors: A Programmed Text. Prentice-Hall, 1966, 223, illus.

RISTENBLATT, MARLIN P., and RIDDLE, ROBERT L.
  Transistor Physics and Circuits. 2nd ed. Prentice-Hall, 1966, 549, illus.

RODDAM, THOMAS
  Transistor Inverters and Converters. Van Nostrand, 1963, 240, illus.

SAMS & COMPANY, INC.
  Transistor Specifications Manual. 3rd ed. Sams, 1968, 256, illus.

———.
  Transistor Substitution Handbook. Sams, 1961- , Vol. 1- , annual.

SANDS, LEO G., and SHUNAMAN, FRED
  101 Questions & Answers About Transistor Circuits. Sams, 1970, 128.

SCHURE, ALEXANDER
  Basic Transistors. Rider, 1961, 146, illus.

SEARLE, CAMPBELL L.
  Elementary Circuit Properties of Transistors. Wiley, 1964, 306, illus. (Semiconductor Electronics Education Committee Books Vol. 3.)

SEVIN, LEONCE J.
  Field-Effect Transistors. McGraw-Hill 1965, 130, illus. (Texas Instruments Electronics Series.)

SHEA, RICHARD F.
  Transistor Applications. Wiley, 1964, 273.

STANLEY, GEORGE C.
  Transistor Basics: A Short Course. Hayden, 1967, 102, illus.

STONER, DONALD L.
  Transistor Radio Handbook. Bobbs-Merrill, 1963, 178, illus.

TAB
  Popular Tube/Transistor Substitution Guide. TAB, 1969, 157, illus.

TEPPER, MARVIN
  Transistor Ignition Systems. Hayden, 1965, 128, illus.

TEXAS INSTRUMENTS, INC.
  Transistor Circuit Design. McGraw-Hill, 1963, 523, illus.

THOMAS, HARRY E.
  Handbook of Transistors, Semiconductors, Instruments, and Microelectronics. Prentice-Hall, 1968, 453, illus.

THORNTON, RICHARD D.
  Multistage Transistor Circuits. Wiley, 1965, 286, illus. (Semiconductor Electronics Education Committee Books Vol. 5.)

THORNTON, RICHARD D., et al.
  Characteristics and Limitations of Transistors. Wiley, 1966, 180, illus. (Semiconductor Electronics Education Committee Books Vol. 4.)

———.
  Handbook of Basic Transistor Circuits and Measurements. Wiley, 1966, 156, illus. (Semiconductor Electronics Education Committee Books Vol. 7.)

TILLMAN, JOHN R., and ROBERTS, FREDERIC F.
  An Introduction to the Theory and Practice of Transistors. Wiley, 1961, 340, illus.

TRAINING SYSTEMS, INC.
  Simplified Transistor Theory: A Programed Text. Rider, 1965, 228, illus. (Rider Programodule.)

VALDES, LEOPOLDO B.
  The Physical Theory of Transistors. McGraw-Hill, 1961, 370.

ENGINEERING PROGRAMS

VEATCH, HENRY C.
    Transistor Circuit Action. McGraw-Hill, 1968, 310, illus.

WALKER, ROBERT L.
    Introduction to Transistor Electronics. Wadsworth, 1966, 341, illus.

WARD, BRUCE
    Transistor Ignition Systems Handbook. 2nd ed. Sams, 1966, 176, illus.

WELS, BYRON G.
    Transistor Circuit Guidebook. TAB, 1968, 219, illus.

INDUSTRIAL ARTS

ADAMS, JEANNETTE T., and STIERI, EMANUELE
    Complete Woodworking Handbook. Arco, 1960, 576, illus.

ALBERS, VERNON M.
    Amateur Furniture Construction. A. S. Barnes, 1970, 127, illus.

AMERICAN INDUSTRIAL ARTS ASSOCIATION
    ...Conference Proceedings. AIAA, 1964- , Vol. 1- , annual.

ANDERSON, JAMES, and TATRO, EARL E.
    Shop Theory. 5th ed. McGraw-Hill, 1968, 522, illus.

BAKAMIS, WILLIAM A.
    Improving Instruction in Industrial Arts. Bruce, 1966, 269, illus.

BALL, FREDERICK C., and LOVOOS, JANICE
    Making Pottery Without a Wheel: Texture and Form in Clay. Reinhold, 1965, 159, illus.

BARBER, JOHN W., ED.
    Industrial Training Handbook. A. S. Barnes, 1969, 402, illus.

BARLOW, MELVIN L.
    History of Industrial Education in the United States. Bennett, 1967, 512.
    ———.
    Principles of Trade and Industrial Education. University of Texas, Industrial Education Department, 1963, 58.

BEDFORD, JOHN R.
    Metalcraft: Theory and Practice. Transatlantic, 1967, 94, illus.

BILLINGTON, DORA M.
    The Technique of Pottery. Hearthside Press, 1962, 222, illus.

BINNS, CHARLES F.
    The Potter's Craft. 4th ed. Van Nostrand, 1967, 144, illus.

BOYD, T. GARDNER
    Metalworking. Goodheart-Willcox, 1964, 112, illus. (Build-a-Course Series.)

BRENNAN, THOMAS J.
    Ceramics. Goodheart-Willcox, 1964, 96, illus. (General Shop Series.)

BROWN, ROBERT D.
    Industrial Arts Laboratory Planning and Administration. Bruce, 1969, 327, illus.

BRUCE, LEROY F., and MEYER, LEO A.
    Sheet Metal Shop Practice. 3rd ed. American Technical Society, 1965, 296, illus.

BUDZIK, RICHARD S.
    Precision Sheet Metal: Shop Practice. Sams, 1969, 96, illus.
    ———.
    Precision Sheet Metal: Shop Theory. Sams, 1969, 334.

BURT, SAMUEL M.
    Industry and Vocational-Technical Education: A Study of Industry Education-Advisory Committees. McGraw-Hill, 1967, 520.

BUTLER, DAVID F.
    Simplified Furniture Design and Construction. A. S. Barnes, 1970, 118, illus.

CAPRON, J. HUGH
    Wood Laminating. McKnight & McKnight, 1963, 94, illus.

CENCI, LOUIS, and WEAVER, GILBERT G.
    Teaching Occupational Skills. Rev. ed. Pitman, 1968, 274.

CHERRY, RAYMOND
    General Plastics: Projects & Procedures. 4th ed. McKnight & McKnight, 1967, 318, illus.

CHOATE, SHARR
    Creative Casting: Jewelry, Silverware, Sculpture. Crown, 1966, 213, illus.

COCHRAN, LESLIE H.
    Innovative Programs in Industrial Education. McKnight & McKnight, 1970, 114, illus.

COOLEY, R. H.
    Complete Metalworking Manual. Arco, 1967, 288, illus.

COPE, DWIGHT W., and CONAWAY, JOHN O.
    Plastics. Goodheart-Willcox, 1966, 96, illus. (Build-a-Course Series.)

COPE, DWIGHT W., and DICKEY, FLOYD
    Plastics Book. Goodheart-Willcox, 1960, 272, illus.

CRAMLET, ROSS C.
    Woodwork Visualized. Bruce, 1967, 158, illus.

CUNNINGHAM, BERYL M., and HOLTROP, WILLIAM F.
    Woodshop Tool Maintenance. Bennett, 1965, 296, illus.

CURRY, ESTELL H., PARDONNET, ROLLAND H., and SYMES, RUSSELL W.
    General Industrial Arts. Van Nostrand, 1967, 234, illus.

DALE, ALFRED J.
    Modern Ceramic Practice. Transatlantic, 1964, 309, illus.

DeCRISTOFORO, R. J.
    Carpentry. Arco, 1969, 128, illus.
    ———.
    How to Choose and Use Power Tools. Arco, 1960, 142, illus.
    ———.
    Modern Power Tool Woodworking. Magna Publications, Raymond, Miss., 1967, 352, illus.

DICKSON, WILLIAM G.
    Related Information: Machine Technology. Delmar, 1964, 4 vols., illus.

DOUGLASS, JAMES H.
    Woodworking with Machines. McKnight & McKnight, 1960, 181, illus.

DRAGOO, ALVA W., and REED, HOWARD O.
    General Shop Metalwork. 4th ed. McKnight & McKnight, 1964, 144, illus.

EARL, ARTHUR W.
    Experiments with Materials and Products of Industry. McKnight & McKnight, 1960, 351, illus.

EDWARDS, JEANNE
    Creative Crafts. Zondervan, Grand Rapids, 1970, 62, illus.

INDUSTRIAL ARTS

EDWARDS, LAUTON
  Industrial Arts Plastics. Bennett, 1964, 280, illus.

FEIRER, JOHN L.
  Advanced Woodwork and Furniture Making. Rev. ed. Bennett, 1963, 424, illus.

———.
  Cabinetmaking and Millwork. Bennett, 1967, 928, illus.

———.
  General Metals. 3rd ed. McGraw-Hill, 1967, 470, illus. (McGraw-Hill Publications in Industrial Arts.)

———.
  I. A. Bench Woodwork. Bennett, 1965, 208, illus.

———.
  Industrial Arts Education. Center for Applied Research in Education, 1964, 116.

———.
  Industrial Arts Woodworking. 2nd ed. Bennett, 1965, 432, illus.

———.
  Woodworking for Industry: Technology and Practice. Bennett, 1963, 640, illus.

FEIRER, JOHN L., and LINDBECK, JOHN R.
  Metalwork. Rev. ed. Bennett, 1970, 248, illus.

FELKER, CHARLES A.
  Machine-Shop Technology. Rev. ed. Bruce, 1962, 493, illus.

FISHER, BERENICE M.
  Industrial Education: American Ideals and Institutions. University of Wisconsin Press, 1967, 267.

FRASER, ROLAND R., and BEDELL, EARL L.
  General Metal: Principles, Procedures & Projects. 2nd ed. Prentice-Hall, 1962, 260, illus.

FRYKLUND, VERNE C., and LA BERGE, ARMAND J.
  General Shop Woodworking. 6th ed. McKnight & McKnight, 1965, 239, illus.

GIACHINO, JOSEPH W., and GALLINGTON, RALPH O.
  Course Construction in Industrial Arts, Vocational and Technical Education. 3rd ed. American Technical Society, 1967, 314, illus.

GIACHINO, JOSEPH W., and SCHOENHALS, NEIL L.
  General Metals for Technology. Bruce, 1964, 436, illus.

GLAZENER, EVERETT R.
  Basic Metalwork: A Text for the First Year in Metalwork. Steck-Vaughn, 1962, 183, illus.

GLENN, HAROLD T.
  Exploring Power Mechanics. 2nd ed. Bennett, 1967, 200, illus.

GOODMAN, WILLIAM L.
  The History of Woodworking Tools. McKay, 1964, 208, illus.

GOTTSHALL, FRANKLIN H.
  Furniture of Pine, Poplar, and Maple. Bruce, 1966, 111, illus.

GRONEMAN, CHRIS H.
  General Woodworking. 3rd ed. McGraw-Hill, 1965, 353.

———.
  Leathercraft. Rev. ed. Bennett, 1963, 160, illus.

GRONEMAN, CHRIS H., and FEIRER, JOHN L.
  General Shop. 3rd ed. McGraw-Hill, 1963, 470, illus. (McGraw-Hill Publications in Industrial Arts.)

GRONEMAN, CHRIS H., and GLAZENER, EVERETT R.
  Technical Woodworking. McGraw-Hill, 1966, 474, illus. (McGraw-Hill Publications in Industrial Arts.)

GUSTAVSSON, RAGNAR, and OLSON, OLLE
  Creating in Wood with the Lathe. Reinhold, 1968, 92, illus.

HACKETT, DONALD F., and SPIELMAN, PATRICK E.
  Modern Wood Technology. Bruce, 1968, 757, illus.

HALL, CARL
  Elementary Arts and Crafts Projects. W. C. Brown, 1960, 53.

HAMMOND, JAMES J., et al.
  Woodworking Technology. 2nd ed. McKnight & McKnight, 1966, 427, illus.

HAND, JACKSON
  How to Do Your Own Wood Finishing. Popular Science, 1967, 170, illus. (Popular Science Skill Book.)

HARWOOD, JOHN
  Introduction to Mechanics. Arco, 1966, 240, illus.

HAWKINS, LESLIE V.
  Art Metal and Enameling. Bennett, 1967, 234.

HAYWARD, CHARLES H., ED.
  Carpentry for Beginners: How to Use Tools, Basic Joints, Workshop Practice, Designs for Things to Make. Emerson, New York, 1969, 200, illus.

———.
  Furniture Repairs: A Woodworker Handbook. Van Nostrand-Reinhold, 1968, 192, illus.

———.
  Practical Woodwork. Emerson, New York, 1967, 192, illus.

———.
  Staining and Polishing.... Drake, 1969, 214.

HENRY, EDWARD C.
  Electronic Ceramics. Doubleday, 1969, 152, illus.

HJORTH, HERMAN, and FOWLER, EWELL W.
  Basic Woodworking Processes. Rev. ed. Bruce, 1961, 224.

HJORTH, HERMAN, and HOLTROP, WILLIAM F.
  Modern Machine Woodworking. Rev. ed. Bruce, 1960, 280, illus.

HOLTROP, WILLIAM F., and HJORTH, HERMAN
  Principles of Woodworking. Rev. ed. Bruce, 1961, 600, illus.

HORTEN, HANS E. E.
  Woodworking Machines in Four Languages. Hart, 1969, 353, illus.

ICKIS, MARGUERITE, and ESH, REBA S.
  The Book of Arts and Crafts. Dover, 1965, 275, illus.

JOHNSON, HAROLD V.
  General-Industrial Machine Shop. Rev. ed. Bennett, 1970, 413, illus.

———.
  Technical Metals. Bennett, 1967, 462, illus.

JONES, FRANKLIN D.
  Machine Shop Training Course. 5th ed. Industrial Press, 1964, 2 vols., illus.

KENNY, JOHN B.
  Ceramic Design. Chilton, 1963, 321, illus.

KINGERY, WILLIAM D.
  Introduction to Ceramics. Wiley, 1960, 781, illus. (Science and Technology of Materials Series.)

KRAR, STEPHEN F., and ST. AMAND, JOSEPH E.
  Machine Shop Training. 2nd ed. McGraw-Hill (Canada), 1967, 198, illus.

KUHN, W. H.
  Refinishing Furniture. Arco, 1963, 109, illus.

LAPPIN, ALVIN R.
  Plastics Projects and Techniques. McKnight & McKnight, 1965, 136, illus.

ENGINEERING PROGRAMS

LARKMAN, BRIAN
    Metalwork Designs of Today. Transatlantic, 1970, 86, illus.

LEACH, BERNARD H.
    A Potter's Book. Transatlantic, 1962, 294.

LEE, P. WILLIAM
    Ceramics. Reinhold, 1961, 210, illus.

LEIGHBODY, GERALD B., and KIDD, DONALD M.
    Methods of Teaching Shop and Technical Subjects. Delmar, 1966, 201, illus.

LINDBECK, JOHN R., DUENK, LESTER G., and HANSEN, MARK F.
    Basic Crafts. Bennett, 1969, 274, illus.

LINDBECK, JOHN R., and LATHROP, IRVING T.
    General Industry. Bennett, 1969, 332, illus.

LITTRELL, JOSEPH J.
    Guide to Industrial Arts Teaching. Bennett, 1966, 1 vol.

LUDWIG, OSWALD A., and McCARTHY, WILLARD J.
    Metalwork: Technology and Practice. McKnight & McKnight, 1969, 630, illus.

LUNDKVIST-HUSBERG, LIS, and LUNDKVIST, HANS
    Making Ceramics. Reinhold, 1967, 80, illus. (Reinhold Scandinavian Series.)

LUSH, CLIFFORD L., and ENGLE, GLENN E.
    Industrial Arts Electricity. Rev. ed. Bennett, 1965, 160, illus.

MADDEN, IRA C.
    Woodworking for Industrial Arts: Teaches Students to Think and to Plan. Goodheart-Willcox, 1962, 224, illus.

MAGER, ROBERT F.
    Developing Vocational Instruction. Fearon, San Francisco, 1967, 83.

MATTSON, ELMER B.
    Creative Metalworking. Bruce, 1960, 121, illus.
———.
    Creating with Aluminum. Bruce, 1962, 90, illus.

McCARTHY, WILLARD J., and SMITH, ROBERT E.
    Machine Tool Technology. 3rd ed. McKnight & McKnight, 1968, 672, illus.

McDONNELL, LEO P.
    Hand Woodworking Tools. Delmar, 1962, 288, illus.
———.
    Portable Power Tools. Delmar, 1962, 214, illus.

MEILACH, DONA Z.
    Creative Carving: Materials, Techniques, Appreciation. Reilly & Lee, 1969, 120, illus.

MILLER, REX, and SMALLEY, LEE H.
    Selected Readings for Industrial Arts. McKnight & McKnight, 1963, 357, illus.

MILLER, WILBUR R., and BOYD, GARDNER
    Teaching Elementary Industrial Arts: Using Industrial Arts Activities to Help Children Learn More Effectively. Goodheart-Willcox, 1970, 224, illus.

MIX, FLOYD
    Practical Carpentry. Goodheart-Willcox, 1963, 448, illus.

MORRIS, FLOYD
    198 Easy Wood Projects. Goodheart-Willcox, 1970, 96, illus.

NELSON, GLENN C.
    Ceramics: A Potter's Handbook. 2nd ed. Holt, Rinehart & Winston, 1966, 331, illus.

NEUNDORF, WILLIAM, and STEVENS, CLAUDE
    Sheet Metal Practice. McGraw-Hill (Canada), 1962, 1 vol., illus.

NORTON, FREDERICK H.
    Fine Ceramics: Technology and Application. McGraw-Hill, 1970, 507, illus.

OAKLEY, W. R.
    The Arco Workshop Companion. Arco, 1961, 218, illus.

OLSON, DELMAR W.
    Industrial Arts for the General Shop. 3rd ed. Prentice-Hall, 1968, 404, illus.
———.
    Industrial Arts and Technology. Prentice-Hall, 1963, 367, illus.
———.
    Woods & Woodworking for Industrial Arts. 2nd ed. Prentice-Hall, 1965, 260, illus.

PACK, GRETA
    Jewelry and Enameling. 3rd ed. Van Nostrand, 1961, 396.

PARMELEE, C. W.
    Ceramic Glazes. Cahners, 1968, 322, illus.

PELTON, B. W.
    Furniture Making and Cabinet Work. 2nd ed. Van Nostrand, 1961, 536, illus.

PETERS, GEOFF
    Woodturning. Arco, 1961, 160, illus.

PETERSEN, GRETE
    Creative Leathercraft. Sterling, 1960, 92, illus.

PETTERSON, HENRY
    Creating Form in Clay. Reinhold, 1968, 112, illus.

PIEPENBURG, ROBERT E.
    Designs in Wood. Bruce, 1969, 144, illus.

RHODES, DANIEL
    Kilns: Design, Construction and Operation. Chilton, 1968, 240.

ROMERO, A. C.
    Contemporary Designs for Wood. Bruce, 1966, 79, illus.

ROTTGER, ERNST
    Creative Clay Design. Reinhold, 1963, 95, illus.
———.
    Creative Wood Design. Van Nostrand-Reinhold, 1961, 96, illus.

SCHUTZE, ROLF
    Making Modern Furniture. Van Nostrand-Reinhold, 1967, 96, illus.

SHEA, JOHN G.
    Colonial Furniture Making for Everybody. Van Nostrand-Reinhold, 1964, 214, illus.
———.
    Contemporary Furniture Making for Everybody. Van Nostrand-Reinhold, 1965, 192, illus.
———.
    Plywood Working for Everybody. Van Nostrand, 1963, 212, illus.
———.
    Woodworking for Everybody. 4th ed. Van Nostrand-Reinhold, 1970, 224, illus.

SIEGNER, C. VERNON
    Art Metals. Rev. ed. Goodheart-Willcox, 1968, 1 vol., illus. (General Shop Series.)

SILVIUS, GEORGE H., and BOHN, RALPH C.
    Organizing Course Materials for Industrial Education. McKnight & McKnight, 1961, 459, illus.

SILVIUS, GEORGE H., and CURRY, ESTELL H.
    Teaching Successfully in Industrial Education. Rev. ed. McKnight & McKnight, 1967, 645, illus.

SIMPSON, THOMAS
    Fantasy Furniture: Design and Decoration. Van Nostrand-Reinhold, 1968, 92, illus.

SINKANKAS, JOHN
    Gem Cutting: A Lapidary's Manual. 2nd ed. Van Nostrand-Reinhold, 1962, 297, illus.

STEELE, GERALD L.
    Fiberglass: Project & Procedures. McKnight & McKnight, 1962, 159, illus.

STEPHENSON, GEORGE E.
    Power Technology. Delmar, 1968, 296, illus.

STRONG, MERLE E., COMP.
    Curriculum Materials for Trade and Industrial Education, 1963. HEW, U.S. Office of Education, 1964, 88.

SWANSON, ROBERT S.
    Plastics Technology: Basic Materials and Processes. McKnight & McKnight, 1965, 232, illus.

TUSTISON, FRANCIS E., KRANZUSCH, RAY F., and BLIDE, DAN C.
    Metalwork Essentials. Rev. ed. Bruce, 1962, 236, illus.

ULLRICH, HEINZ, and KLANTE, DIETER
    Creative Metal Design. Reinhold, 1967, 119, illus. (Creative Play Series No. 8.)

U.S. BUREAU OF NAVAL PERSONNEL
    Basic Hand Tools. Rev. ed. USBNP, 1963, 227, illus. (Navy Training Course.)

VAN TASSEL, RAYMOND
    Woodworking Crafts. 2nd ed. Van Nostrand, 1960, 196, illus.

VEBLEN, THORSTEIN
    The Instinct of Workmanship: And the State of the Industrial Arts. Norton, 1964, 355.

VERNON, RALPH J.
    Basic Woodwork: A Text for the First Year of Woodwork. Steck-Vaughn, 1963, 144, illus.

VILLIARD, PAUL
    A Manual of Veneering. Van Nostrand-Reinhold, 1968, 208, illus.

WAGNER, WILLIS H.
    Modern Woodworking: Tools, Materials and Procedures. Goodheart-Willcox, 1967, 1 vol., illus.

    Woodworking. Goodheart-Willcox, 1961, 112, illus. (General Shop Series.)

WALKER, JOHN R.
    Machining Fundamentals: Fundamentals Basic to Industry. Goodheart-Willcox, 1969, 512, illus.

    Modern Metalworking: Materials, Tools and Procedures. Goodheart-Willcox, 1968, 1 vol., illus.

WARING, RALPH G.
    Modern Wood Finishing. Bruce, 1969, 206, illus.

WAYE, BASIL E.
    Introduction to Technical Ceramics. McLaren & Sons (Transatlantic, dist.), 1967, 191, illus.

THE WAY THINGS WORK: AN ILLUSTRATED ENCYCLOPEDIA OF TECHNOLOGY.
    Simon & Schuster, 1967, 590.

WILBER, GORDON O., and PENDERED, NORMAN C.
    Industrial Arts in General Education. 3rd ed. International Textbook, 1967, 403, illus.

WILDENHAIN, MARGUERITE
    Pottery: Form and Expression. Van Nostrand-Reinhold, 1962, 157, illus.

WILLE, MILTON
    Art in Wood. Bruce, 1966, 76, illus.

WILLIAMS, WILLIAM A., ED.
    Accident Prevention Manual for Shop Teachers. American Technical Society, 1963, 550, illus.

WOLANSKY, WILLIAM D.
    Woodworking Fundamentals. McGraw-Hill, 1962, 67, illus.

WOODWARD, ROBERT L., and GOLDSMITH, J. LYMAN
    An Introduction to Applied Electricity-Electronics. Prentice-Hall, 1963, 168, illus. (Prentice-Hall Industrial Arts Series.)

WORTHINGTON, ROBERT M., MARGULES, MORTON, and CROUSE, WILLIAM H.
    General Power Mechanics. McGraw-Hill, 1968, 568, illus. (McGraw-Hill Publications in Industrial Education.)

ZIMMERMAN, FRED W.
    Leathercraft. Goodheart-Willcox, 1961, 96, illus. (General Shop Series.)

MECHANICAL TECHNOLOGY

AHRENDT, WILLIAM R., and SAVANT, C. J., JR.
    Servomechanism Practice. 2nd ed. McGraw-Hill, 1960, 566, illus.

AMBROSIUS, EDGAR F., et al.
    Mechanical Measurement and Instrumentation. Ronald, 1966, 572.

AMERICAN FOUNDRYMEN'S SOCIETY
    Basic Principles of Gating. Addison-Wesley, 1967, 78, illus.

    Basic Principles of Risering. Addison-Wesley, 1968, 64, illus.

AMERICAN SOCIETY FOR TESTING MATERIALS
    Book of A. S. T. M. Standards: With Related Material. ASTM, 1939- , vols., illus.

AMERICAN SOCIETY OF TOOL AND MANUFACTURING ENGINEERS
    Gundrilling, Trepanning and Deep Hole Machining. ASTME, 1967, 1 vol.

    Premachining Planning and Tool Presetting. Robert R. Runck, ed. ASTME, 1967, 1 vol.

    Tool Engineers Handbook. McGraw-Hill, 1949- , Vol. 1- , illus.

AMERICAN WELDING SOCIETY
    Thermal Spraying Terms and Definitions. AWS, 1970, 1 vol., illus.

ANSLEY, ARTHUR C.
    Manufacturing Methods and Processes. Rev. ed. Chilton, 1968, 626, illus.

ARCO PUBLISHING COMPANY, INC.
    Apprentice, Mechanical Trades. Arco, 1965, 232.

    Engineering Aide. Arco, 1965, 102.

    Machinist-Machinist's Helper. 2nd ed. Arco, 1968, 320.

ARGES, K. P., and PALMER, AUBREY E.
    Mechanics of Materials. McGraw-Hill, 1963, 448, illus.

ENGINEERING PROGRAMS

BATTINO, RUBIN, and WOOD, SCOTT E.
    Thermodynamics: An Introduction. Academic Press, 1968, 330, illus.

BECKWITH, THOMAS G., and BUCK, N. LEWIS
    Mechanical Measurements. Addison-Wesley, 1961, 559, illus.

BLACK, PERRY O.
    Audel's Machinists Library: Basic Machine Shop Practices. Audel, 1965, 408, illus.

———.
    Audel's Machinists' Library: Machine Shop. Audel, 1965, 504, illus.

———.
    Audel's Machinists' Library: Toolmakers Handy Book. Audel, 1966, 374, illus.

BLACK, PETER
    Mechanical Technology for Higher Engineering Technicians. Pergamon, 1970, 416, illus.

———.
    Mechanics of Machines: A Course for Students. Pergamon, 1967, 536, illus.

BREDIN, HAROLD W., ED.
    Tooling Methods and Ideas. Industrial Press, 1967, 376, illus.

BRENEMAN, JOHN W.
    Mechanics. 3rd ed. McGraw-Hill, 1960, 272, illus.

BRENKERT, KARL
    Elementary Theoretical Fluid Mechanics. Wiley, 1960, 348.

BRIERLEY, ROBERT G., and SIEKMANN, H. J.
    Machining Principles and Cost Control. McGraw-Hill, 1964, 254, illus.

BROOKING, WALTER J., ED.
    Engineering Technicians. J. G. Ferguson, 1970, 386. (Career Opportunities for Technicians and Specialists Vol. 1.)

BURGHARDT, HENRY D., AXELROD, AARON, and ANDERSON, JAMES
    Machine Tool Operation, Part II. 4th ed. McGraw-Hill, 1960, 677, illus.

CHIRONIS, NICHOLAS P., ED.
    Machine Devices and Instrumentation: Mechanical, Electromechanical, Hydraulic, Thermal, Pneumatic, Pyrotechnic, Photoelectric and Optical. McGraw-Hill, 1966, 359, illus.

———.
    Mechanisms, Linkages, and Mechanical Controls. McGraw-Hill, 1965, 368, illus.

CHRISTIE, DAN E.
    Vector Mechanics. 2nd ed. McGraw-Hill, 1964, 622.

CONSIDINE, DOUGLAS M., ED.
    Handbook of Applied Instrumentation. McGraw-Hill, 1964, 1 vol.

DANIELS, HAROLD R., ED.
    Mechanical Press Handbook. 3rd ed. Cahners, 1969, 320, illus.

DATSKO, JOSEPH
    Material Properties and Manufacturing Processes. Wiley, 1966, 543, illus.

DAVIS, HARMER E., et al.
    The Testing and Inspection of Engineering Materials. 3rd ed. McGraw-Hill, 1964, 475, illus.

DEN HARTOG, JACOB P.
    Mechanics. Dover, 1961, 462.

DORN, JOHN E., ED.
    Mechanical Behavior of Materials at Elevated Temperatures. McGraw-Hill, 1961, 529.

EDGAR, CARROLL
    Fundamentals of Manufacturing Processes and Materials. Addison-Wesley, 1965, 515, illus.

EFRON, ALEXANDER
    Exploring Mechanics. Hayden, 1969, 192, illus.

EMERICK, ROBERT H.
    Troubleshooters' Handbook for Mechanical Systems. McGraw-Hill, 1969, 510, illus.

ENGINEERS' COUNCIL FOR PROFESSIONAL DEVELOPMENT, INC.
    Manual of Evaluation Procedure of the Engineering Technology Committee. ECPD, 1969, 36.

ENGINEERS' JOINT COUNCIL
    Demand for Engineers and Technicians. EJC, New York, 1968, 40.

FAIRES, VIRGIL M., and KEOWN, ROBERT M.
    Mechanism. 5th ed. McGraw-Hill, 1960, 332, illus.

FEIRER, JOHN L., and TATRO, EARL E.
    Machine Tool Metalworking: Principles and Practice. McGraw-Hill, 1961, 446, illus.

FOX, EDWARD A.
    Mechanics. Harper & Row, 1967, 431, illus.

FREUDENTHAL, ALFRED M.
    Introduction to the Mechanics of Solids. Rev. ed. Wiley, 1966, 492, illus.

FRIBRANCE, AUSTIN E.
    Industrial Instrumentation Fundamentals. McGraw-Hill, 1962, 776, illus.

GILBRECH, DONALD A.
    Fluid Mechanics. Wadsworth, 1965, 562, illus.

GILES, RONALD V.
    Fluid Mechanics and Hydraulics. McGraw-Hill, 1962, 279, illus. (Schaum's Outline Series.)

GLADSTONE, JOHN
    Mechanical Estimating Guide. 4th ed. McGraw-Hill, 1970, 308.

GRANET, IRVING
    Elementary Applied Thermodynamics. Wiley, 1965, 288, illus.

GRANT, HIRAM E.
    Jigs and Fixtures: Non-Standard Clamping Devices. McGraw-Hill, 1967, 1 vol., illus.

HABICHT, FRANK H.
    Modern Machine Tools. Van Nostrand, 1963, 259, illus.

HATSOPOULOS, GEORGE N., and KEENAN, JOSEPH
    Principles of General Thermodynamics. Wiley, 788, illus.

HENKE, RUSSELL W.
    Introduction to Fluid Mechanics. Addison-Wesley, 1966, 232, illus.

HIGDON, ARCHIE, et al.
    Mechanics of Materials. 2nd ed. Wiley, 1967, 591, illus.

HIRSCHHORN, JEREMY
    Dynamics of Machinery. Barnes & Noble, 1968, 447, illus.

HUDDLESTON, JOHN V.
    Introduction to Engineering Mechanics. Addison-Wesley, 1961, 493, illus.

ILIFFE, J. K.
    Basic Machine Principles. Elsevier, 1968, 86, illus.

INSTRUMENT SOCIETY OF AMERICA
    Standards and Practices for Instrumentation: A Compilation of Complete ISA Recommended Practices, Abstracted

MECHANICAL TECHNOLOGY

Standards for Other Organizations. Herbert S. Kindler and H. Keith Owens, eds. ISA, Pittsburgh, 1963, 1 vol.

JONES, DAVID A., and MULLEN, THOMAS W.
Blow Molding. Reinhold, 1961, 210, illus. (Reinhold Plastics Applications Series.)

JONES, FRANKLIN D., ED.
Engineering Encyclopedia: A Condensed Encyclopedia and Mechanical Dictionary for Engineers, Mechanics, Technical Schools, Industrial Plants.... 3rd ed. Industrial Press, 1963, 1431, illus.

———, ED.
Machine Shop Training Course. 5th ed. Industrial Press, 1969, 2 vols.

JONES, FRANKLIN D., and AMISS, JOHN M.
Use of Handbook Tables & Formulas: Companion Book for Machinery's Handbook. Indiana University Press, 1964, 216.

KALLEN, HOWARD P., ED.
Handbook of Instrumentation and Controls: A Practical Design and Applications Manual for the Mechanical Services. McGraw-Hill, 1961, 1 vol., illus. (McGraw-Hill Handbooks.)

KEMPSTER, MAURICE H. A.
Principles of Jig and Tool Design. Hart, 1968, 296, illus.

KIRK, FRANKLYN W., and RIMBOI, NICHOLAS R.
Instrumentation. 2nd ed. American Technical Society, 1966, 296, illus.

KISSAM, PHILLIP
Optical Tooling for Precise Manufacture and Alignment. McGraw-Hill, 1962, 272, illus.

KOBAYASHI, AKIRA
Machining of Plastics. McGraw-Hill, 1967, 257, illus.

KRAR, STEPHEN F., OSWALD, JAMES W., and ST. AMAND, JOSEPH E.
Technology of Machine Tools. McGraw-Hill, 1969, 516, illus.

KREITH, FRANK
Principles of Heat Transfer. 2nd ed. International Textbook, 1965, 620, illus.

LANGHAAR, HENRY L.
Energy Methods in Applied Mechanics. Wiley, 1962, 350, illus.

LAUER, HENRI, et al.
Servomechanism Fundamentals. 2nd ed. McGraw-Hill, 1960, 491, illus.

LEVINSON, IRVING J.
Introduction to Mechanics. 2nd ed. Prentice-Hall, 1968, 346, illus.

———.
Mechanics of Materials. 2nd ed. Prentice-Hall, 1970, 338, illus.

LINSLEY, HORACE E.
Broaching, Tooling and Practice. Industrial Press, 1961, 1 vol.

LIPSON, CHARLES, and COLWELL, L. V., EDS.
Handbook of Mechanical Wear: Wear, Frettage, Pitting, Cavitation, Corrosion. University of Michigan Press, 1961, 469, illus.

LISTER, J.
Mechanics of Materials. Wiley, 1969, 345.

LLOYD, E. D.
Transfer and Unit Machines. Industrial Press, 1969, 192, illus.

LLOYD, WILLIAM B.
Millwork-Principles and Practices. Cahners, 1966, 426, illus.

MACHINERY
Machinery's Handbook: A Reference Book for the Mechanical Engineer, Draftsman, Toolmaker, and Machinist. Industrial Press, 1914- , vols., illus.

———.
Machinery's Mathematical Tables: A Selection of Most Commonly Used Tables from Machinery's Handbook.... 3rd ed. Industrial Press, 1969, 260, illus.

MECHANICAL ENGINEERS' HANDBOOK
McGraw-Hill, 1916- , vols.

METALWORKING MAGAZINE
Machine Tool Selection Guide. Cahners, 1965, 180, illus.

MICHELL, S. J.
Fluid and Particle Mechanics. Pergamon, 1970, 342.

MOLTRECHT, H. K.
Machine Shop Practice. Industrial Press, 1970, 1 vol.

MORTON, HUDSON T.
Anti-Friction Bearings. 2nd ed. The author, Ann Arbor, 1965, 512, illus.

MOTT-SMITH, MORTON
Principles of Mechanics Simply Explained. Dover, 1963, 171.

NATIONAL TOOL, DIE, AND PRECISION MACHINING ASSOCIATION
Advanced Diemaking. McGraw-Hill, 1967, 166.

———.
Basic Diemaking. McGraw-Hill, 1963, 218, illus.

NAYLER, JOSEPH L., and NAYLER, G. H. F.
Dictionary of Mechanical Engineering. Hart, 1967, 406, illus.

NEVILL, GALE E.
Programmed Principles of Statics. Wiley, 1969, 184, illus.

NORDHOFF, WILLIAM A.
Machine-Shop Estimating. 2nd ed. McGraw-Hill, 1960, 528, illus.

O'HIGGINS, PATRICK
Basic Instrumentation: Industrial Measurement. McGraw-Hill, 1966, 495, illus.

OLSEN, GERNER A.
Elements of Mechanics of Materials. 2nd ed. Prentice-Hall, 1966, 591, illus.

OSTER, JON
Basic Applied Fluid Power: Hydraulics. McGraw-Hill, 1969, 233, illus.

OSTERGAARD, D. EUGENE
Advanced Diemaking. McGraw-Hill, 1967, 166, illus.

———.
Basic Diemaking. McGraw-Hill, 1963, 208, illus.

OWCZAREK, JERZY A.
Introduction to Fluid Mechanics. International Textbook, 1968, 516, illus.

PALMER, FRANK R., and LUERSSEN, GEORGE V.
Tool Steel Simplified: World's Best Selling Handbook of Modern Practice for the Man Who Makes Tools and Dies. 3rd ed. Carpenter Steel Co., Reading, Pa., 1960, 595, illus.

PARKER, JERALD D., BOGGS, JAMES H., and BLICK, EDWARD F.
Introduction to Fluid Mechanics and Heat Transfer. Addison-Wesley, 1969, 612, illus.

PEASE, DUDLEY A.
Basic Fluid Power. Prentice-Hall, 1967, 333, illus.

PESTEL, EDWARD C., and THOMSON, WILLIAM T.
Statics. McGraw-Hill, 1969, 400, illus.

ENGINEERING PROGRAMS

PETERSON, ALDOR C.
Applied Mechanics for Engineers and Technicians: Statics. Allyn & Bacon, 1967, 240, illus.

PHALEN, THOMAS E., JR.
An Introduction to Mechanics. Holt, Rinehart & Winston, 1965, 364, illus.

POLLACK, HERMAN W.
Manufacturing and Machine Tool Operations. Prentice-Hall, 1968, 593, illus.

PORTER, A.
Introduction to Servomechanisms. 2nd ed. Wiley, 1961, 176.

PORTER, HAROLD W., LASCOE, ORVILLE D., and NELSON, CLYDE A.
Machine Shop Operations and Setups. 3rd ed. American Technical Society, 1967, 517, illus.

ROBINSON, J. LISTER
Basic Fluid Mechanics. McGraw-Hill, 1963, 188, illus.

———.
Mechanics of Materials. Wiley, 1969, 345.

ROLT, LIONEL T. C.
A Short History of Machine Tools. MIT Press, 1965, 256, illus.

ROTH, EDWARD S.
Functional Gaging. Society of Manufacturing Engineers, 1970, 135, illus. (Manufacturing Data Series.)

RUNCK, ROBERT R., ED.
Premachining Planning and Tool Presetting. Society of Manufacturing Engineers, 1967, 74. (Manufacturing Data Series.)

SCHUBERT, PAUL B., ED.
Die Methods: Design, Fabrication, Maintenance and Application. Industrial Press, 1966- , vols., illus.

SHARP, JOHN D.
Casting Pit Practice. Iliffe Books, 1968, 141, illus.

SHEPHARD, DENNIS
Elements of Fluid Mechanics. Harcourt, Brace & World, 1965, 498.

SHIGLEY, JOSEPH E.
Dynamic Analysis of Machines. McGraw-Hill, 1961, 645.

SPRINGBORN, R. K., ED.
Non-Traditional Machining Processes. Society of Manufacturing Engineers, 1967, 178. (Manufacturing Data Series.)

STEEL FOUNDERS' SOCIETY OF AMERICA
Steel Castings Handbook. 3rd ed. SFSA, Cleveland, 1960, 670, illus.

STEPHENSON, REGINALD J.
Mechanics and Properties of Matter. 3rd ed. Wiley, 1969, 375, illus.

STERN, BENJAMIN J.
Opportunities in Machine Shop Trades. Rev. ed. Universal Publishing & Distributing, 1965, 112. (VGM Career Series.)

STREETER, VICTOR L.
Fluid Mechanics. 4th ed. McGraw-Hill, 1966, 705, illus.

SWINEHART, HALDON J., ED.
Cutting Tool Material Selection. Society of Manufacturing Engineers, 1968, 155.

TYSON, FORREST C.
Industrial Instrumentation. Prentice-Hall, 1961, 365, illus.

U.S. BUREAU OF NAVAL PERSONNEL
Basic Machines. USGPO, 1965, 161, illus. (Navy Training Course.)

———.
Fluid Power. USBNP, 1966, 234, illus. (Navy Training Course.)

U.S. OFFICE OF EDUCATION, VOCATIONAL AND TECHNICAL EDUCATION DIVISION
Instrumentation Technical: A Suggested 2-Year Post High School Curriculum. USOE, 1966, 119. (OE-80033, Technical Education Program Series No. 61)

———.
Mechanical Technology—Design and Production: A Suggested 2-Year Post High School Curriculum. USOE, 1964, 103. (OE-80019, Technical Education Program Series No. 3.)

VIDOSIC, JOSEPH P.
Metal Machining and Forming Technology. Ronald, 1964, 558, illus.

WAHL, ARTHUR M.
Mechanical Springs. 2nd ed. McGraw-Hill, 1963, 323, illus.

WALKER, WILLIAM F.
Beginner's Guide to Jig and Tool Design. Hart, 1969, 196, illus.

WEEKS, ROBERT P., ED.
Machines and the Man: A Sourcebook on Automation. Appleton, 1961, 338.

WEINGARTNER, C.
Machinists' Ready Reference. Prakken Publications, Ann Arbor, 1962, 176, illus.

WICK, CHARLES H.
Chipless Machining: Methods of Cold Forming Ferrous Metals, Including Heading, Rolling, Spinning, Swaging, Extruding, and High-Energy-Rate Forming. Industrial Press, 1960, 502, illus.

WILKIE BROTHERS FOUNDATION
Fundamentals of Band Machining. Delmar, 1964, 392.

———.
Precision Surface Grinding. Delmar, 1964, 1 vol.

WOODBURY, ROBERT S.
History of the Milling Machine: A Study in Technical Development. MIT Press, 1960, 107, illus. (MIT Technology Monographs, Historical Series No. 3.)

YIH, CHIA-SHUN
Fluid Mechanics: A Concise Introduction to the Theory. McGraw-Hill, 1969, 622, illus.

DESIGN

AMERICAN SOCIETY FOR METALS
Casting Design Handbook. Reinhold, 1962, 326, illus.

AMERICAN SOCIETY OF TOOL AND MANUFACTURING ENGINEERS
Die Design Handbook. 2nd ed. McGraw-Hill, 1965, 788.

———.
Fundamentals of Tool Design. Prentice-Hall, 1962, 492.

———.
Handbook of Fixture Design: A Practical Reference Book of Workholding Principles and Designs for All Classes of Machining, Assembly and Inspection. McGraw-Hill, 1962, 1 vol., illus. (McGraw-Hill Handbooks.)

BLACK, PAUL H., and ADAMS, O. EUGENE, JR.
Machine Design. 3rd ed. McGraw-Hill, 1968, 678, illus.

CARSON, RICHARD F.
Metal Stamping Design: Practical and Economical Design of Stamped Metal Parts. Prentice-Hall, 1961, 199, illus.

CREAMER, ROBERT H.
Machine Design. Addison-Wesley, 1968, 533, illus. (Addison-Wesley Engineering Technology Series.)

DALLAS, DANIEL B.
Progressive Dies: Design and Manufacture. McGraw-Hill, 1962, 301, illus.

DUDLEY, DARLE W., ED.
Gear Handbook: The Design, Manufacture and Application of Gears. McGraw-Hill, 1962, 1 vol., illus. (McGraw-Hill Handbooks.)

FAIRES, VIRGIL M.
Design of Machine Elements. 4th ed. Macmillan, 1965, 624, illus.

HALL, ALLEN S., HOLOWENKO, ALFRED R., and LAUGHLIN, HERMAN G.
Machine Design. McGraw-Hill, 1961, 352, illus. (Schaum's Outline Series.)

HOPKINS, BRUCE R., and DEERE, JOHN
Design Analysis of Shafts and Beams. McGraw-Hill, 1970, 475.

JOHNSON, OLAF A.
Design of Machine Tools. Chilton, 1970, 1 vol.

LINDBECK, JOHN R.
Design Textbook. McKnight & McKnight, 1963, 163, illus.

MYATT, DONALD J.
Machine Design: An Introductory Text. McGraw-Hill, 1962, 294, illus.

NOWOLINSKI, EDMUND A.
Modern Industrial Die Design: A Reference Book Illustrating and Describing the Design of Tools Which Function in Mechanical Presses. Rev. ed. Royalle, Detroit, 1960, 125, illus.

PAQUIN, J. R.
Die Design Fundamentals. Industrial Press, 1962, 1 vol.

PARR, ROBERT E.
Principles of Mechanical Design. McGraw-Hill, 1970, 383, illus.

PHELAN, RICHARD M.
Fundamentals of Mechanical Design. 3rd ed. McGraw-Hill, 1970, 640, illus.

ROTHBART, HAROLD A., ED.
Mechanical Design and System Handbook, McGraw-Hill, 1964, 1 vol.

SIEGEL, MARTIN J., MALEEV, VLADIMIR L., and HARTMAN, JAMES B.
Mechanical Design of Machines. 4th ed. International Textbook, 1965, 576, illus. (International Textbooks in Mechanical Engineering.)

SPOTTS, MERHYLE F.
Design of Machine Elements. 3rd ed. Prentice-Hall, 1961, 583, illus.

———.
Mechanical Design Analysis. Prentice-Hall, 1964, 428, illus.

VALLANCE, ALEX, and DOUGHTIE, VENTON L.
Design of Machine Members. 4th ed. McGraw-Hill, 1964, 520, illus.

WILSON, FRANK W., ED.
Fundamentals of Tool Design. Society of Manufacturing Engineers, 1962, 560.

YATES, EDWIN T.
Guidebook for Mechanical Designers and Draftsmen. Hayden, 1965, 148, illus.

MATERIALS

ANDERSON, J. C., and LEAVER, K. D.
Materials Science. Van Nostrand-Reinhold, 1969, 276.

ARNOLD, LIONEL K.
Introduction to Plastics. Iowa State University Press, 1968, 205, illus.

BENDER, RENE J., ED.
Handbook of Foamed Plastics. Lake, Libertyville, Ill., 1965, 339, illus.

BRISTON, JOHN H., and GOSELIN, C. C.
Introduction to Plastics. Newnes, London, 1968, 147, illus.

COOK, JAMES G.
The Miracle of Plastics. Dial, 1964, 272.

DELMONTE, JOHN
Metal-Filled Plastics. Reinhold, 1961, 240, illus. (Reinhold Plastics Applications Series.)

DiBENNEDETTO, ANTHONY T.
The Structure and Properties of Materials. McGraw-Hill, 1967, 533.

DUBOIS, JOHN H., and JOHN, FREDERICK W.
Plastics. 4th ed. Reinhold, 1967, 342, illus.

FISHLOCK, DAVID
The New Materials. Basic Books, 1967, 240, illus. (Science and Discovery Series.)

GORDON, JAMES E.
The New Science of Strong Materials. Walker, New York, 1968, 269, illus.

HASLAM, JOHN, and WILLIS, H. A.
Identification and Analysis of Plastics. Van Nostrand, 1965, 483, illus.

KAUFMAN, MORRIS
Giant Molecules: The Technology of Plastics, Fibers, and Rubber. Doubleday, 1968, 187, illus. (Doubleday Science Series SD5.)

KRESSER, THEODORE O. J.
Polyolefin Plastics. Van Nostrand-Reinhold, 1969, 179, illus. (Plastics Application Series.)

LAWRENCE, JOHN R.
Polyester Resins. Reinhold, 1960, 251, illus. (Plastics Applications Series.)

LEWIS, THOMAS J., and SECKER, PHILIP E.
Science of Materials. Reinhold, 1965, 256.

MARK, HERMAN F., et al., eds.
Encyclopedia of Polymer Science and Technology: Plastics, Resins, Rubbers, Fibers. Wiley, 1969, 12 vols., illus.

MATERIALS: A SCIENTIFIC AMERICAN BOOK
Freeman, San Francisco, 1967, 210, illus.

McCLINTOCK, FRANK A., and ARGON, ALI S., EDS.
Mechanical Behavior of Materials. Addison-Wesley, 1966, 770, illus. (Metallurgy and Materials Series No. 4545.)

MELLAN, IBERT
Industrial Plasticizers. Macmillan, 1963, 302, illus.

ENGINEERING PROGRAMS

MOFFATT, WILLIAM G., PEARSALL, GEORGE W., and WULFF, JOHN
  Structure and Properties of Materials. Wiley, 1964, 4 vols., illus.

OLEESKY, SAMUEL S., and MOHR, J. GILBERT
  Handbook of Reinforced Plastics of the Society of the Plastics Industry, Inc. Reinhold, 1964, 640, illus.

PARK, WILLIAM R. R., ED.
  Plastics Film Technology. Van Nostrand-Reinhold, 1969, 210.

PASCOE, K. J.
  An Introduction to the Properties of Engineering Materials. Interscience, 1961, 295, illus.

PATTON, W. J.
  Materials in Industry. Prentice-Hall, 1968, 460, illus.

ROSS, ROBERT B.
  Metallic Materials. Chapman & Hall, London, 1968, 936.

SCHLENKER, B. R.
  Introduction to Materials Science. Wiley, 1969, 351.

SHANLEY, FRANCIS R.
  Mechanics of Materials. McGraw-Hill, 1967, 455, illus.

SIMONDS, HERBERT R., ED.
  The Encyclopedia of Plastics Equipment. Reinhold, 1964, 599, illus.

SIMONDS, HERBERT R., and CHURCH, JAMES M.
  A Concise Guide to Plastics. 2nd ed. Reinhold, 1963, 392, illus.
  ———, EDS.
  The Encyclopedia of Basic Materials for Plastics. Reinhold, 1967, 500, illus.

SKEIST, IRVING, ED.
  Handbook of Adhesives. Reinhold, 1962, 683, illus.

SMITH, CHARLES O.
  The Science of Engineering Materials. Prentice-Hall, 1969, 1 vol.

VAN VLACK, LAWRENCE H.
  Elements of Materials Science. 2nd ed. Addison-Wesley, 1964, 445, illus. (Metallurgy and Materials Series.)

WHITTINGTON, LLOYD R.
  Whittington's Dictionary of Plastics. Technomic, Stamford, Conn., 1968, 261.

WINDING, CHARLES C., and HIATT, GORDON D.
  Polymeric Materials. McGraw-Hill, 1961, 406, illus.

WORDINGHAM, J. A., and REBOUL, P.
  Dictionary of Plastics. Philosophical Library, 1964, 211, illus.

METALS AND METALLURGY

ALLEN, DELL K.
  Metallurgy Theory and Practice. American Technical Society, 1969, 663, illus.

ALMEN, JOHN O., and BLACK, PAUL H.
  Residual Stresses and Fatigue in Metals. McGraw-Hill, 1963, 226, illus.

ALUMINUM COMPANY OF AMERICA
  Aluminum: Prepared by Engineers, Scientists, and Metallurgists of Aluminum Company of America. American Society for Metals, 1967, 3 vols., illus.

AMERICAN FOUNDRYMEN'S SOCIETY
  Principles of Production Metallurgy For Ferrous Castings. Addison-Wesley, 1970, 128.

AMERICAN SOCIETY FOR METALS
  Machining Difficult Alloys: A Compendium on the Machining of High-Strength Steels and Heat-Resistant Alloys. Reinhold, 1962, 362, illus.
  ———.
  Metal Progress Materials and Process Engineering Databook. 2nd ed. ASM, 1970, 164.
  ———.
  Metals Handbook. ASM, 1927- , Vol. 1- .

ARMAREGO, E. J., and BROWN, R. H.
  The Machining of Metals. Prentice-Hall, 1969, 437, illus.

AVNER, SIDNEY H.
  Introduction to Physical Metallurgy. McGraw-Hill, 1964, 536, illus.

BEDFORD, JOHN R.
  Basic Course of Practical Metalwork. J. Murray, London, 1960, 96, illus.

BIGGS, WILLIAM D.
  The Brittle Fracture of Steel. Pitman, 1960, 420, illus.

BIRCHON, DONALD
  Dictionary of Metallurgy. Philosophical Library, 1965, 409, illus.

BLACK, PAUL H.
  Theory of Metal Cutting. McGraw-Hill, 1961, 204, illus.

BRANDON, D. G.
  Modern Techniques in Metallography. Van Nostrand, 1966, 266, illus.

BRICK, ROBERT M., GORDON, ROBERT B., and PHILLIPS, ARTHUR
  Structure and Property of Alloys.... 3rd ed. McGraw-Hill, 1965, 503, illus.

BURNS, ROBERT M., and BRADLEY, W. W.
  Protective Coatings for Metals. 3rd ed. Reinhold, 1967, 735, illus. (American Chemical Society Monograph Series No. 163.)

CAHN, ROBERT W., ED.
  Physical Metallurgy. North-Holland, Amsterdam. (Wiley, dist.), 1965, 1100, illus.

COTTRELL, A. H.
  An Introduction to Metallurgy. St. Martin's Press, 1967, 548, illus.

DAVIES, DON E.
  Practical Experimental Metallurgy. Elsevier, 1966, 177, illus.

DENNIS, WILLIAM H.
  A Hundred Years of Metallurgy. Aldine, 1963, 342, illus.
  ———.
  Metallurgy in the Service of Man. Pitman, 1961, 372, illus.
  ———.
  Metallurgy of the Ferrous Metals. Pitman, 1963, 393.

FISHLOCK, DAVID, and HARDS, K. W.
  New Ways of Working Metals. Philosophical Library, 1965, 136, illus.

FLINN, RICHARD A.
  Fundamentals of Metal Casting. Addison-Wesley, 1963, 324, illus. (Metallurgy and Materials Series.)

FORREST, PETER G.
  Fatigue of Metals. Pergamon, 1962, 425.

GREGORY, EDWIN, et al.
  Steel Working Processes: Principles and Practice of Forging, Rolling, Pressing, Squeezing, Drawing and Allied Methods of Metal Forming. Transatlantic, 1964, 240, illus.

GROSSMANN, MARCUS A., and BAIN, EDGAR C.
  Principles of Heat Treatment. 5th ed. American Society for Metals, 1964, 302, illus.

MECHANICAL TECHNOLOGY

HAMPEL, CLIFFORD A., ED.
Rare Metals Handbook. 2nd ed. Reinhold, 1961, 715.

HEINE, RICHARD W., LOPER, CARL R., and ROSENTHAL, PHILIP C.
Principles of Metal Casting. 2nd ed. McGraw-Hill, 1967, 736, illus.

HURD, PAUL S.
Metallic Materials: An Introduction to Metallurgy. Holt, Rinehart & Winston, 1968, 381, illus.

JENNI, CLYDE B.
Basic Metallurgy II: Principles of Production Metallurgy for Ferrous Castings. Addison-Wesley, 1970, 57, illus. (American Foundrymen's Society, Training and Research Institute, Cast Metals Technology Series.)

KONDIC, VOYA
Metallurgical Principles of Founding. Elsevier, 1968, 286, illus.

KURREIN, MAX
Plasticity of Metals: The Mechanical Behaviour and the Changes in Structure of Metals Under Plastic Deformation. Hart, 1969, 270.

LAQUE, FRANCIS L., and COPSON, HARRY R., EDS.
Corrosion Resistance of Metals and Alloys. 2nd ed. Reinhold, 1963, 712.

LIPSETT, CHARLES H.
Metals Reference and Encyclopedia. Atlas, 1968, 379.

McLEAN, DONALD
Mechanical Properties of Metals. Wiley, 1962, 403, illus. (Science and Technology Series.)

MERRIMAN, ARTHUR D.
A Concise Encyclopedia of Metallurgy. Elsevier, 1965, 1178, illus.

NUTT, MERLE C.
Principles of Modern Metallurgy. Merrill, 1968, 512, illus.

O'NEILL, HUGH
Hardness Measurement of Metals and Alloys. 2nd ed. Chapman & Hall, London, (Barnes & Noble, dist.), 1967, 238, illus.

PARKINS, REDVERS N.
Mechanical Treatment of Metals. Elsevier, 1968, 352, illus. (Institution of Metallurgists, Modern Metallurgical Texts No. 5.)

PEARSON, CLAUDE E., and PARKINS, REDVERS N.
The Extrusion of Metals. 2nd ed. Wiley, 1960, 336, illus.

PECKNER, DONALD, ED.
The Strengthening of Metals. Reinhold, 1964, 250, illus.

RICHMAN, MARC H.
An Introduction to the Science of Metals. Blaisdell, Waltham, Mass., 1967, 400, illus. (Blaisdell Book in Pure and Applied Sciences.)

ROBERTS, CORNELIUS S.
Magnesium and Its Alloys. Wiley, 1960, 230, illus. (Science and Technology of Materials Series.)

ROBERTS, GEORGE A., HAMAKER, J. C., JR., and JOHNSON, A. R.
Tool Steels. 3rd ed. American Society for Metals (Reinhold, dist.), 1962, 780, illus.

ROGERS, BRUCE A.
The Nature of Metals. 2nd ed. American Society for Metals, 1964, 324, illus.

ROWE, GEOFFREY W.
An Introduction to the Principles of Metalworking. St. Martin's Press, 1965, 306, illus.

SAVITSKII, EVGENII M.
The Influence of Temperature on the Mechanical Properties of Metals and Alloys. Oleg D. Sherby, ed.; D. Sherby, tr. Stanford University Press, 1961, 303, illus.

SHRAGER, ARTHUR M.
Elementary Metallurgy and Metallography. 2nd ed. Dover, 1961, 390, illus.

SHREIR, L. L., ED.
Corrosion. Wiley, 1963, 2 vols.

SIMONS, ERIC N.
A Dictionary of Alloys. Hart, 1970, 192.

———.
Guide to Uncommon Metals. Hart, 1967, 244.

———.
An Outline of Metallurgy. Hart, 1969, 285, illus.

SLADE, EDWARD
Metals in the Modern World: A Study in Materials Development. Doubleday, 1968, 192, illus. (Doubleday Science Series.)

SMALL, LOUIS
Hardness Theory and Practice. Service Diamond Tool, Ferndale, Mich., 1960, 1 vol., illus.

STANLEY, JAMES K.
Electrical and Magnetic Properties of Metals. American Society for Metals, 1963, 374, illus.

TEGART, WILLIAM J. M.
Elements of Mechanical Metallurgy. Macmillan, 1966, 259, illus. (Macmillan Materials Science Series.)

THOMAS, G. H.
Metalwork: Technology. Transatlantic, 1970, 1 vol.

TWEEDDALE, J. G.
The Mechanical Properties of Metals: Assessment and Significance. Elsevier, 1964, 328, illus. (Institution of Metallurgists, Modern Metallurgical Texts No. 1.)

U.S. OFFICE OF EDUCATION, VOCATIONAL AND TECHNICAL EDUCATION DIVISION
Metallurgical Technology: A Suggested 2-Year Post High School Curriculum. USOE, 1968, 113. (OE-81012, Technical Education Program Series No. 10.)

WEINBERG, FRED
Tools and Techniques in Physical Metallurgy. Dekker, 1970, 2 vols., illus.

WILKINSON, WALTER D.
Properties of Refractory Metals. Gordon & Breach, New York, 1969, 355. (Monograph Series on Metallurgy in Nuclear Technology.)

WOLDMAN, NORMAN E.
Engineering Alloys. 4th ed. Reinhold, 1962, 1354.

AUTOMATIC AND NUMERICAL CONTROL

AMERICAN SOCIETY OF TOOL AND MANUFACTURING ENGINEERS
Numerical Control in Manufacturing. McGraw-Hill, 1963, 504, illus.

BIBBERO, ROBERT J.
Dictionary of Automatic Control. Reinhold, 1960, 282. (Automatic Control Library.)

BRYAN, GEORGE T.
Control Systems for Technicians. Hart, 1969, 328.

CHILDS, JAMES J.
Principles of Numerical Control. 2nd ed. Industrial Press, 1969, 294, illus.

ENGINEERING PROGRAMS

CLARK, ROBERT N.
    Introduction to Automatic Control Systems. Wiley, 1962, 467, illus.

DAVIES, PETER O. A. L.
    An Introduction to Dynamic Analysis and Automatic Control. Wiley, 1966, 299.

DeROY, BENJAMIN E.
    Automatic Control Theory. Wiley, 1966, 274, illus. (Electronic Engineering Technology Series.)

DODES, IRVING A., and GREITZER, SAMUEL L.
    Numerical Analysis. Hayden, 1964, 350, illus.

ERTELL, GLENN G.
    Numerical Control. Wiley, 1969, 149, illus.

HARRISON, HOWARD L., and BOLLINGER, JOHN G.
    Introduction to Automatic Controls. International Textbook, 1963, 349, illus.

HEALEY, MARTIN
    Principles of Automatic Control. Van Nostrand, 1968, 333, illus.

HOWE, RAYMOND E., ED.
    Introduction to Numerical Control in Manufacturing. American Society of Tool and Manufacturing Engineers, 1969, 170, illus.

LESLIE, W. H. P.
    Numerical Control Users' Handbook. McGraw-Hill, 1970, 448.

MARCUS, ABRAHAM
    Automatic Industrial Controls. Prentice-Hall, 1966, 386, illus.

MORSE, HENRY C., and COX, DAVID M.
    Numerically Controlled Machine Tools: The Breakthrough of Autofacture. American Data Processing, Detroit, 183, illus.

MURPHY, GORDON J.
    Basic Automatic Control Theory. 2nd ed. Van Nostrand, 1966, 832.

OLESTEN, NILS O.
    Numerical Control. Wiley, 1970, 646.

ROBERTS, ARTHUR D., and PRENTICE, RICHARD C.
    Programming for Numerical Control Machines. McGraw-Hill, 1968, 265, illus.

THORNHILL, ROBERT B.
    Engineering Graphics and Numerical Control. McGraw-Hill, 1967, 349, illus.

VLAHOS, CHARLES J.
    Fundamentals of Numerical Control. Chilton, 1968, 207, illus.

WARREN, JOHN E.
    Control Instrument Mechanisms. Sams, 1967, 144, illus.

WATKINS, BRUCE O.
    Introduction to Control Systems. Macmillan, 1969, 625, illus. (Macmillan Series In Applied Systems Science.)

STRENGTH OF MATERIALS

BASSIN, MILTON G., BRODSKY, STANLEY M., and WOLKOFF, HAROLD
    Statics and Strength of Materials. 2nd ed. McGraw-Hill, 1969, 463, illus.

BLACK, PETER
    Strength of Materials: A Course for Students. Pergamon, 1966, 454.

BRENEMAN, JOHN W.
    Strength of Materials. 3rd ed. McGraw-Hill, 1965, 192, illus.

CERNICA, JOHN N.
    Strength of Materials. Holt, Rinehart & Winston, 1966, 450, illus.

DenHARTOG, JACOB P.
    Strength of Materials. Dover, 1961, 323.

ECKARDT, OTTMAR W.
    Strength of Materials. Holt, Rinehart & Winston, 1969, 462, illus.

FITZGERALD, ROBERT W.
    Strength of Materials. Addison-Wesley, 1967, 418, illus.

HARRIS, CHARLES O.
    Strength of Materials. 2nd ed. American Technical Society, 1963, 212, illus.

JENSEN, ALFRED, and CHENOWETH, HARRY H.
    Applied Strength of Materials. 2nd ed. McGraw-Hill 1967, 372, illus.

―――.
    Statics and Strength of Materials. 2nd ed. McGraw-Hill, 1967, 374, illus.

PARKER, HARRY
    Simplified Mechanics and Strength of Materials. 2nd ed. Wiley, 1961, 285, illus.

PETERSON, ALDOR C.
    Applied Mechanics: Strength of Materials. Allyn & Bacon, 1969, 294.

PISANI, TORQUATO J.
    Essentials of Strength of Materials. 3rd ed. Van Nostrand, 1964, 283, illus.

PLANTS, HELEN L.
    Programmed Topics in Statics and Strength of Materials. McGraw-Hill, 1966, 178, illus.

SINGER, FERDINAND L.
    Strength of Materials. 2nd ed. Harper, 1962, 590.

SLABY, STEVE M., and TYSON, HERBERT I.
    Statics and Introduction to Strength of Materials. Harcourt, Brace & World, 1969, 370, illus.

TIMOSHENKO, STEPHEN, and YOUNG, DONOVAN H.
    Elements of Strength of Materials. 5th ed. Van Nostrand, 1968, 377, illus.

WELDING

ALTHOUSE, ANDREW D., BOWDITCH, W. A., and TURNQUIST, C.
    Modern Welding. Goodheart-Willcox, 1967, 1 vol., illus.

AMERICAN WELDING SOCIETY
    Brazing Manual. 2nd ed. AWS, 1963, 296, illus.

―――.
    Current Welding Processes. AWS, 1965, 1 vol.

―――.
    Electroslag Welding. 2nd ed. B. E. Paton, ed. AWS, 1962, 1 vol.

―――.
    Index for Welding Standards from 23 Nations. 2nd ed. AWS, 1969, 172, illus.

―――.
    Introductory Welding Metallurgy. AWS, 1968, 1 vol.

―――.
    Modern Joining Processes. AWS, 1966, 139.

―――.
    Recommended Practices for Resistance Welding Coated Low Carbon Steel. AWS, 1970, 1 vol.

―――.
    Standard for Qualification of Welding Procedures and Welders for Piping and Tubing. AWS, 1969, 1 vol.

———. Standard Welding Symbols. AWS, 1968, 1 vol.

———. Terms and Definitions. AWS, 1969, 1 vol.

———. Welding Handbook. 6th ed. AWS, 1968, 5 vols., illus.

ARCO PUBLISHING COMPANY, INC.
Welder. Arco, 1968, 224, illus.

BAKISH, ROBERT A., and WHITE, S. S.
Handbook of Electron Beam Welding. Wiley, 1964, 269, illus. (Science and Technology of Materials Series.)

BERG, L. D. THOMAS
Your Future in Welding. Arco, 1970, 160. (Career Guidance Series.)

GIACHINO, JOSEPH W., WEEKS, WILLIAM R., and BRUNE, ELMER
Welding Skills and Practices. 3rd ed. American Technical Society, 1967, 342, illus.

GIACHINO, JOSEPH W., WEEKS, WILLIAM R., and JOHNSON, G. S.
Welding Technology. American Technical Society, 1968, 474, illus.

GRAHAM, FRANK D.
Audel's Welders' Guide: Questions and Answers. Audel, 1965, 489, illus.

GRIFFIN, IVAN H., and RODEN, EDWARD M.
Basic Arc Welding. Rev. ed. Delmar, 1962, 106, illus.

———. Basic Oxyacetylene Welding. Delmar, 1967, 132, illus.

———. Basic Tig Welding. Delmar, 1962, 101.

———. Welding Processes. Delmar, 1970, 250.

HAIM, GEORGE
Manual for Plastic Welding. Industrial, Cleveland, 1960- vols., illus.

HOLDCROFT, PETER T.
Welding Processes. British Welding Research Association, 1967, 1 vol.

JEFFERSON, THEODORE B., and WOODS, GORHAM
Metals and How to Weld Them. 2nd ed. James F. Lincoln Arc Welding Foundation, Cleveland, 1962, 392, illus.

KOENIGSBERGER, F., and ADAIR, J. R.
Welding Technology. 3rd ed. Hart, 1968, 424, illus.

LANCASTER, JOHN F.
The Metallurgy of Welding, Brazing and Soldering. Elsevier, 1965, 291, illus. (Institution of Metallurgists Modern Metallurgical Texts No. 3.)

LINNERT, G. E.
Welding Metallurgy. 3rd ed. AWS, 1965-67, 2 vols.

MANKO, HOWARD H.
Solders and Soldering: Materials, Design, Production, and Analysis for Reliable Bonding. McGraw-Hill, 1964, 323, illus.

MASSON, FRANK N.
Welding Theory and Practice. St. Martin's Press, 1967, 119.

OLSON, WILLIAM L.
Arc-Welding: A Self-Instructional Guide. Vector Publications, 1966, 1 vol.

PATTON, W. J.
Science and Practice of Welding. Prentice-Hall, 1967, 524, illus.

PENDER, JAMES A.
Welding. McGraw-Hill, 1969, 208, illus.

SACKS, RAYMOND J.
Theory & Practice of Arc Welding. 2nd ed. Van Nostrand, 1960, 478, illus.

SOSNIN, H. A.
Arc Welding Instructions for the Beginner. James F. Lincoln Arc Welding Foundation, Cleveland, 1964, 149, illus.

THOMAS, DONALD W.
Making Better Plastic Welds. Rev. ed. Laramy Products, Cohasset, Mass., 1962, 64, illus.

TUTTLE, CHARLES
Fundamentals of Oxy-Acetylene and Arc Welding. Pitman, 1967, 185, illus.

TWEEDDALE, J. G.
Welding Fabrication. Elsevier, 1969, 3 vols.

THE WELDING ENCYCLOPEDIA
Welding Engineer Publication Co., Chicago, 1921- , vols., illus.

HEALTH SERVICE PROGRAMS

DENTAL CAREERS

ACCEPTED DENTAL REMEDIES: CONTAINING A LIST OF OFFICIAL DRUGS SELECTED TO PROMOTE A RATIONAL DENTAL MATERIAMEDICA, AND DESCRIPTIONS OF ACCEPTABLE NONOFFICIAL ARTICLES
American Dental Association, Council on Dental Therapeutics, Chicago, 1934- , vols.

ADAMS, CHARLES P.
Dental Photography. Wright, Bristol, 1968, 84, illus.

AITKEN, J. T.
Manual of Human Anatomy: Head & Neck. 2nd ed. Williams & Wilkins, 1965-67, 5 vols.

ALLEN, DON L., McFALL, WALTER T., and HUNTER, GROVER C.
Periodontics for the Dental Hygienist. Lea & Febiger, 1968, 211, illus.

AMERICAN ASSOCIATION FOR HEALTH, PHYSICAL EDUCATION AND RECREATION
Teaching Dental Health to Elementary School Children. Rev. ed. AAHPER, 1967, 32. (Classroom Teacher Series.)

AMERICAN ASSOCIATION FOR THE ADVANCEMENT OF SCIENCE
Environmental Variables in Oral Disease. Seymour J. Kreshover and Frank J. McClure, eds. AAAS, 1966, 312, illus. (Pub. No. 81.)

AMERICAN DENTAL ASSISTANTS ASSOCIATION
Dental Terminology: A Continuing Education Course for Dental Assistant. ADAA, 1968, 1 vol.

AMERICAN DENTAL ASSOCIATION
Guide to Dental Materials and Devices. 5th ed. ADA, 1970, 247, illus.

ANDERSON, JOHN N.
Applied Dental Materials. 3rd ed. Blackwell Scientific, 1967, 380, illus.

ANDERSON, PAULINE C.
The Dental Assistant. Delmar, 1965, 321, illus.

BENSON, HAROLD J., and KIPP, KENNETH E.
Dental Science Laboratory Guide. 4th ed. W. C. Brown, 1968, 207, illus.

BERLOVE, IRA J.
Dental-Medical Emergencies and Complications. 2nd ed. Year Book Medical Publishers, Chicago, 1963, 491.

BERNIER, JOSEPH L., and MUHLER, JOSEPH C.
Improving Dental Practice Through Preventive Measures. 2nd ed. Mosby, 1970, 1 vol., illus.

BEVELANDER, GERRIT
Atlas of Oral Histology and Embryology. Lea & Febiger, 1967, 242, illus.

BHASKAR, S. N.
Synopsis of Oral Pathology. 3rd ed. Mosby, 1969, 571, illus.

BLACKMAN, SYDNEY, and POYTON, HERBERT G.
A Manual of Dental and Oral Radiography. Williams & Wilkins, 1963, 192, illus.

BOLDEN, THEODORE E., MOBLEY, EUGENIA L., and CHANDLER, ELZER S.
Dental Hygiene Examination Review Book. 2nd ed. Medical Examination Publishing Co., Flushing, N.Y., 1969- , vols.

BOUCHER, CARL O., ED.
Current Clinical Dental Terminology: A Glossary of Accepted Terms in All Disciplines of Dentistry. Mosby, 1963, 501.
———, ED.
Swenson's Complete Dentures. 6th ed. Mosby, 1970, 650, illus.

BREGSTEIN, SAMUEL J.
Handbook for Dental Assistants, Hygienists, and Secretaries. Prentice-Hall, 1961, 364, illus.

BRERETON, GWENDOLYN
Introduction to Dental Nursing. Mills & Boon, London, 1968, 96, illus.

CAMPBELL, RALPH H.
The Dental Hygienist in Private Practice. W. C. Brown, 1964, 130, illus.

CANNEL, WALTER A.
Medical and Dental Aspects of Fluoridation. M.K. Lewis, 1960, 125.

CIBA FOUNDATION
Caries-Resistant Teeth. Little, Brown, 1965, 338.

CLARK, JAMES W., CHERASKIN, EMANUEL, and RINGSDORF, W. M.
Diet and the Periodontal Patient. Thomas, 1970, 378, illus.

HEALTH SERVICE PROGRAMS

COLLINS, DANIEL A.
  Your Teeth: A Handbook of Dental Care for the Whole Family. Doubleday, 1967, 224, illus.

COWELL, COLIN R., and KANTOROWICZ, GEORGE F.
  Inlays, Crowns & Bridges. Wright, Bristol, 1963, 174, illus.

CUSSLER, MARGARET, and GORDON, EVELYN W.
  Dentists, Patients and Auxiliaries. University of Pittsburgh Press, 1968, 103. (Contemporary Community Health Series.)

THE DENTAL CLINICS OF NORTH AMERICA.
  March 1957- , Vol. 1- , Saunders, illus.

DENTAL MANAGEMENT
  The Business of Dental Practice. Professional Publishing Corp., Stamford, Conn., 1969, 1 vol.

DENTAL SCIENCE HANDBOOK: A MANUAL OF INFORMATION ABOUT DENTAL SCIENCE AND DENTAL PRACTICE PREPARED PRIMARILY FOR THOSE IN VOCATIONS OTHER THAN DENTISTRY
  USGPO, 1970, 1 vol.

DILLON, CHARLES
  Fluorosis and Dental Caries. Carlton, New York, 1969, 170.

DUNNING, JAMES M.
  Principles of Dental Public Health. 2nd ed. Harvard University Press, 1970, 598.

EHRLICH, ANN B., and EHRLICH, STANLEY F.
  Dental Practice Management: The Teamwork Approach. Saunders, 1969, 200, illus.

ENNIS, LEROY M., BERRY, HARRISON M., and PHILLIPS, JAMES E.
  Dental Roentgenology. 6th ed. Lea & Febiger, 1967, 740, illus.

EWEN, SOL J., and GLICKSTEIN, CYRUS
  Ultrasonic Therapy in Periodontics. Thomas, 1968, 1 vol., illus.

FOWLER, JENIFER E. H., COMP.
  Heinemann Modern Dictionary for Dental Students. Heinemann & Cassell, 1962, 364, illus.

FROST, JANE C.
  Your Future in Dental Assisting. R. Rosen Press, 1964, 127. (Careers in Depth.)

FULTON, JOHN T., and HUGHES, JOHN T.
  The Natural History of Dental Diseases. University of North Carolina, 1965, 80, illus.

GALLAGHER, WALTER N.
  Dental Roentgenology Review: A Question and Answer Review of the Technical and Oral Diagnostic Aspects of Dental Radiology for the Practitioner and the Student. William-Frederick Press, New York, 1967, 89.

GARFIELD, SYDNEY
  Teeth, Teeth, Teeth: A Treatise on Teeth. Valiant Books, Beverly Hills, Calif., 1969, 448, illus.

GAUNT, WALTER A.
  Advances in Dental Histology. Williams & Wilkins, 1967, 104, illus.

GOLDMAN, HENRY M.
  An Introduction to Periodontia. 4th ed. Mosby, 1969, 1 vol.

GOLDMAN, HENRY M., and COHEN, D. WALTER
  Periodontal Therapy. 4th ed. Mosby, 1968, 1072, illus.

GOOSE, D. H., and HARTLES, R. L.
  Principles of Preventive Dentistry. Pergamon, 1964, 131, illus. (Pergamon Dentistry Series Vol. 1.)

GREEN, EDWARD J., and KOHN, NATHAN, JR.
  Selection, Hiring and Utilization of Dental Auxiliaries. Saunders, 1970, 487, illus.

GOULDING, ROY
  Handbook of Dental Pharmacology & Therapeutics. Heinemann & Cassell, 1960, 199.

HALL, WALTER A., JR.
  Sear's New Teeth for Old. Mosby, 1969, 101.

HAYES, EDWARD N.
  Hayes' Directory of Dental Supply Houses. Rev. ed. The author, Santa Ana, Calif., 1966-67, 1 vol.

HEARTWELL, C. M., JR.
  Syllabus of Complete Dentures. Lea & Febiger, 1969, 500, illus.

HOLLANDER, LLOYD N.
  Modern Dental Practice: Concepts and Procedures. Saunders, 1967, 197, illus.

HOLLENBACK, G. M.
  Science & Technic of Cast Restoration. Mosby, 1964, 230.

HOLLOWAY, PHILIP J., and SWALLOW, J. N.
  Child Dental Health: A Practical Introduction. Williams & Wilkins, 1969, 212, illus.

INGRAM, FRANK L.
  Radiology of the Teeth and Jaws: Including Dental Radiography. 2nd ed. Williams & Wilkins, 1965, 256, illus.

INTERNATIONAL DENTAL FEDERATION
  A Lexicon of English Dental Terms: With Their Equivalents in Spanish, German, French, Italian. IDF, 1966, 1 vol.

JEFOPOULOS, T.
  Dentifrices. Noyes, 1970, 190, illus.

JENKINS, G. NEIL
  The Physiology of the Mouth. 3rd ed. F. A. Davis, 1965, 512, illus.

JOHNSTON, JOHN F., MUMFORD, GEORGE, and DYKEMA, ROLAND W.
  Modern Practice in Dental Ceramics. Saunders, 1967, 312, illus.

KERR, DONALD A., and ASH, MAJOR M.
  Oral Pathology: An Introduction to General and Oral Pathology for Hygienists. 2nd ed. Lea & Febiger, 1965, 275, illus.

KILPATRICK, HAROLD C.
  Work Simplification in Dental Practice: Applied Time and Motion Studies. Saunders, 1964, 512, illus.

KORNFELD, MAX
  Mouth Rehabilitation: Clinical and Laboratory Procedures. Mosby, 1967, 2 vols., illus.

KUTSCHER, AUSTIN H., et al., EDS.
  Pharmacology for the Dental Hygienist. Lea & Febiger, 1967, 358, illus.

LASKIN, DANIEL M.
  Management of Oral Emergencies. Thomas, 1964, 107, illus.

LAZZARI, EUGENE P., ED.
  Dental Biochemistry. Lea & Febiger, 1968, 222, illus.

LEE, JOHN H.
  Dental Aesthetics: The Pleasing Appearance of Artificial Dentures. Wright, Bristol, 1962, 159, illus.

LEVISON, HENRY
  Textbook for Dental Nurses. 3rd ed. Blackwell Scientific, 1969, 168, illus.

LEVY, SAUL
    Dentist's Handbook of Office and Hospital Procedure. Year Book Medical Publishers, Chicago, 1963, 311.

MARTINELLI, NICHOLAS
    Dental Laboratory Technology. Mosby, 1970, 287, illus.

McCALL, JOHN O.
    Principles of Periodontics. Lippincott, 1964, 83, illus.

McCARTHY, FRANK M., COMP.
    Emergencies in Dental Practice. Saunders, 1967, 452, illus.

McCRACKEN, WILLIAM L.
    Partial Denture Construction: Principles and Techniques. 3rd ed. Davis Henderson and Victor L. Steffel, eds. Mosby, 1969, 476, illus.

MILES, ALBERT E. W., et al.
    Structural and Chemical Organization of Teeth. Academic Press, 1967, 1 vol.

MILLER, CHARLES J.
    Inlays, Crowns, and Bridges: An Atlas of Clinical Procedures. Saunders, 1962, 268, illus.

MONHEIM, LEONARD M.
    General Anesthesia in Dental Practice. 2nd ed. Mosby, 1964, 467, illus.

MUHLER, JOSEPH C.
    Textbook of Biochemistry for Students of Dentistry. 2nd ed. Mosby, 1964, 526, illus.

NEW YORK (STATE) EDUCATION DEPARTMENT
    Dentistry Including Dental Hygiene: Law, Rules, Information. NYSED, Albany, 1968, 80. (Professional Education Handbook No. 10.)

J. M. NEY COMPANY
    The Ney Surveyor Manual. Ney, Bloomfield, Conn., 1965, 99, illus.

NOLTE, WILLIAM A.
    Oral Microbiology. Mosby, 1968, 436, illus.

O'BRIEN, RICHARD C.
    Dental Radiography: An Introduction for Dental Hygienists and Assistants. Saunders, 1966, 171, illus.

O'BRIEN, WILLIAM J., and RYGE, GUNNAR
    Dental Materials: A Programmed Review of Selected Topics. Saunders, 1965, 199, illus.

ORBAN, BALINT J.
    Oral Histology and Embryology. 6th ed. Mosby, 1966, 416, illus.

PAIGE, BARBARA E.
    Your Future As A Dental Hygienist. R. Rosen Press, 1969, 142, illus. (Careers in Depth.)

PANSKY, BEN, and HOUSE, EARL L.
    Review of Gross Anatomy. 2nd ed. Macmillan, 1969, 1 vol.

PARK, VIRGINIA R., and ASHMAN, JOSEPH R.
    A Textbook for Dental Assistants. Saunders, 1966, 509, illus.

PELTON, WALTER J., et al.
    Epidemiology of Oral Health. Harvard University Press, 1969, 167. (Vital and Health Statistics Monographs.)

PENNINGTON, GEORGE W., and CALVEY, T. N.
    Dental Pharmacology. 2nd ed. Blackwell Scientific, F. A. Davis, 1969, 180, illus.

PERMAR, DOROTHY
    Oral Embryology and Microscopic Anatomy: A Textbook for Students in Dental Hygiene. 4th ed. Lea & Febiger, 1967, 168, illus.

PETERSON, SHAILER A.
    Clinical Dental Hygiene. 3rd ed. Mosby, 1968, 429, illus.
———, ED.
    Comprehensive Review for Dental Hygienists. 2nd ed. Mosby, 1969, 312, illus.
———, ED.
    The Dentist and His Assistant. 2nd ed. Mosby, 1967, 445, illus.

PETERSON, SHAILER A., and WINNETT, WADE B.
    Review and Test Manual for the Dental Assistant. Mosby, 1967, 152.

PEYTON, FLOYD A., et al.
    Restorative Dental Materials. 3rd ed. Mosby, 1968, 553, illus.

PHILLIPS, RALPH W., and SKINNER, EUGENE W.
    Elements of Dental Materials for Dental Hygienists and Assistants. Saunders, 1965, 219, illus.
———.
    The Science of Dental Materials. 6th ed. Saunders, 1967, 670, illus.

RAY, GEORGE E.
    Precision Attachments. Williams & Wilkins, 1969, 55, illus. (Dental Practitioner Handbook No. 7.)

REMNICK, HERBERT
    Embryology of the Face and Oral Cavity. Fairleigh Dickinson University Press, 1970, 98, illus.

RICHARDSON, RICHARD E., BARTON, ROGER E., and BRAUER, JOHN C.
    The Dental Assistant. 4th ed. McGraw-Hill, 1970, 672.

ROTHSTEIN, ROBERT J., COMP.
    The Dental Health Team. Lippincott, 1970, 266, illus.

ROYDHOUSE, RICHARD H.
    Materials in Dentistry. Year Book Medical Publishers, Chicago, 1962, 210.

SARNER, HARVEY
    Business Management of Dental Practice. Saunders, 1966, 222.

SCHOUR, ISAAC
    Noyes' Oral Histology and Embryology with Laboratory Directions. 8th ed. Lea & Febiger, 1960, 440, illus.

SCHROETER, CHARLES
    The Dentition of Man: An Atlas of Tooth Morphology. University of Washington Press, 1966, 128, illus.

SCHWARTZ, ARTUR M., and GRATZINGER, MAX
    Removable Orthodontic Appliances. Saunders, 1966, 355, illus.

SCHWARZROCK, LOREN H., and SCHWARZROCK, SHIRLEY P.
    Effective Dental Assisting. 3rd ed. W. C. Brown, 1967, 723, illus.

SCOTT, JAMES H., and SYMONS, NORMAN B. B.
    Introduction to Dental Anatomy. 5th ed. Williams & Wilkins, 1967, 434, illus.

SHAFER, WILLIAM G., HINE, MAYNARD K., and LEVY, BARNET M.
    A Textbook of Oral Pathology. 2nd ed. Saunders, 1963, 768, illus.

SHARRY, JOHN J., ED.
    Complete Denture Prosthodontics. 2nd ed. McGraw-Hill, 1968, 369, illus.

SICHER, HARRY, and DU BRUL, E. LLOYD
    Oral Anatomy. 5th ed. Mosby, 1970, 502, illus.

SILVERMAN, SIDNEY I.
    Oral Physiology. Mosby, 1961, 533, illus.

SOGNNAES, REIDAR F.
    Chemistry and Prevention of Dental Caries. Thomas, 1962, 248, illus.

HEALTH SERVICE PROGRAMS

SOMMER, RALPH F., OSTRANDER, FLOYD D., and CROWLEY, MARY C.
Clinical Endodontics: A Manual of Scientific Endodontics. 3rd ed. Saunders, 1966, 571, illus.

STAFNE, EDWARD C.
Oral Roentgenographic Diagnosis: Including an Appendix on Roentgenographic Technic. 2nd ed. Saunders, 1963, 429, illus.

STEELE, PAULINE F.
Dental Specialities for the Dental Hygienist. Lea & Febiger, 1969, 337, illus.

———, ED.
Dimensions of Dental Hygiene. Lea & Febiger, 1966, 520, illus.

———.
Review of Dental Hygiene: Questions and Answers. Lea & Febiger, 1968, 322, illus.

STOLL, FRANCES A., and CATHERMAN, JOAN L.
Dental Health Education: For Dental Health Educators in School and Community Dental Health Programs.... 3rd ed. Lea & Febiger, 1967, 360, illus.

SWENSON, MERRILL G.
Swenson's Complete Dentures. 5th ed. Mosby, 1964, 798, illus.

TERKLA, LOUIS G., and LANEY, WILLIAM R.
Partial Dentures. 3rd ed. Mosby, 1963, 374, illus.

TYLMAN, STANLEY D.
Theory and Practice of Crown and Fixed Partial Prosthodontics (Bridge). 6th ed. Mosby, 1970, 1023, illus.

U.S. NAVAL DENTAL SCHOOL, BETHESDA, MD.
Dental Technician, General. Rev. ed. U.S. Bureau of Naval Personnel, 1962, 370, illus.

U.S. BUREAU OF NAVAL PERSONNEL
Dental Technician, Prosthetic. 4th ed. USBNP, 1963, 355, illus.

WAINWRIGHT, WILLIAM W.
Dental Radiology: A Complete Illustrated Guide to Short Cone, Long Cone, and Accessory Techniques.... McGraw-Hill, 1965, 585, illus.

WEINBERG, LAWRENCE A.
Atlas of Crown and Bridge Prosthodontics. Mosby, 1965, 283, illus.

WEISS, R. L.
Chairside Psychology in Patient Education: A Self-Instruction Course. USGPO, 1969, 1 vol.

WEST, GERTRUDE I.
The Dental Assistant's Handbook. 3rd ed. Heinemann, 1962, 128, illus.

WHEELER, RUSSELL C.
An Atlas of Tooth Form. 4th ed. Saunders, 1969, 163, illus.

———.
A Textbook of Dental Anatomy and Physiology. 4th ed. Saunders, 1965, 441, illus.

WILKINS, ESTHER M., and McCULLOUGH, PATRICIA
Clinical Practice of the Dental Hygienist. 2nd ed., rev. Lea & Febiger, 1964, 536, illus.

WOODFORDE, JOHN
The Strange Story of False Teeth. Universe, 1968, 137, illus.

WUEHRMANN, ARTHUR H., and MANSON-HING, LINCOLN R.
Dental Radiology. 2nd ed. Mosby, 1969, 455, illus.

YOUNG, WESLEY O., and SHANNON, JEAN H., EDS.
Utilization of Fluorides Applied Topically for the Prevention of Dental Caries. University of Kentucky Press, 1966, 272.

YOUNG, WESLEY O., and STRIFFLER, DAVID F.
The Dentist: His Practice and His Community. 2nd ed. Saunders, 1969, 346, illus.

ENVIRONMENTAL SCIENCE

ADVANCES IN ENVIRONMENTAL SCIENCES....
Wiley-Interscience, 1969- , Vol. 1- , illus.

AMERICAN CHEMICAL SOCIETY
Cleaning Our Environment: The Chemical Basis for Action. ACS, 1969, 1 vol.

AMERICAN CONFERENCE OF GOVERNMENTAL INDUSTRIAL HYGIENISTS
Air Sampling Instruments Manual. 3rd ed. ACGIH, 1967, 433.

AMERICAN FOUNDRYMEN'S SOCIETY
Water Pollution from Foundry Wastes. AFS, 1967, 1 vol.

AMERICAN HOSPITAL ASSOCIATION
Environmental Sanitation. AHA, 1968, 66.

AMERICAN INDUSTRIAL HYGIENE ASSOCIATION
Air Pollution Manual. AIHA, Detroit, 1960- , vols., illus.

AMERICAN PETROLEUM INSTITUTE
Industrial Oily Waste Control Handbook. API, American Society of Lubrication Engineers, 1970, 1 vol.

AMERICAN PUBLIC HEALTH ASSOCIATION
Glossary: Water and Waste-Water Control Engineering. APHA, 1969, 387.

AMERICAN PUBLIC HEALTH ASSOCIATION, PROGRAM AREA COMMITTEE ON AIR POLLUTION
Guide to the Appraisal and Control of Air Pollution. 2nd ed. APHA, 1969, 80.

AMERICAN PUBLIC HEALTH ASSOCIATION, SUBCOMMITTEE ON HEALTH ASPECTS OF AIR POLLUTION
Health Officials' Guide to Air Pollution in Control. APHA, 1962, 52.

AMERICAN PUBLIC WORKS ASSOCIATION, INSTITUTE FOR SOLID WASTES.
Municipal Refuse Disposal: A Basic Manual for Municipal Solid Wastes Management. Rev. ed. Public Administration Service, Chicago, 1970, 535.

ANDERSON, WALT, ED.
Politics and Environment: A Reader in Ecological Crisis. Goodyear, Pacific Palisades, Calif., 1970, 362.

ARTHUR, DONALD R.
Survival: Man and His Environment. English Universities Press, London, 1969, 1 vol.

AYLESWORTH, THOMAS G.
This Vital Air, This Vital Water: Man's Environment Crisis. Rand McNally, 1968, 192, illus.

BARCLAY-SMITH, P., ED.
Oil Pollution of the Sea. British Advisory Committee on Oil Pollution of the Sea, London, 1969, 414.

BATES, MARSTON
The Forest and the Sea: A Book of the Economy of Nature and the Ecology of Man. Random House, 1960, 277.

———.
Man in Nature. 2nd ed. Prentice-Hall, 1964, 116, illus.

BATTAN, LOUIS J.
The Unclean Sky: A Meteorologist Looks at Air Pollution. Anchor Books, 1966, 141, illus. (Science Study Series S46.)

ENVIRONMENTAL SCIENCE

BEHRMAN, ABRAHAM S.
 Water is Everybody's Business: The Chemistry of Water Purification. Doubleday, 1968, 229, illus. (Chemistry in Action Series.)

BESSELIEVRE, EDMUND B.
 The Treatment of Industrial Wastes. McGraw-Hill, 1969, 403, illus.

BLAKE, PETER
 God's Own Junkyard: The Planned Deterioration of America's Landscape. Holt, Rinehart & Winston, 1964, 143, illus.

BLOOM, SANDRA C.
 Pesticides and Pollution. BNA Books, Washington, 1969, 99. (Environmental Management Series.)

BOBY, WILLIAM M. T., and SOLT, GEORGE S.
 Water Treatment Data: A Handbook for Chemists and Engineers in Industry. Hutchinson, London, 1965, 60, illus.

BORGSTROM, GEORG
 Too Many: A Study of Earth's Biological Limitations. Macmillan, 1969, 368, illus.

BOUGHEY, ARTHUR S.
 Ecology of Populations. Macmillan, 1968, 135, illus. (Current Concepts in Biology.)

BRESLER, JACK B.
 Environments of Man. Addison-Wesley, 1968, 289.

BRIGGS, PETER
 Water: The Vital Essence. Harper & Row, 1967, 223, illus.

CALDER, NIGEL
 Eden Was No Garden: An Inquiry Into the Environment of Man. Holt, Rinehart & Winston, 1967, 240.

CALDWELL, LYNTON K.
 Environment: A Challenge for Modern Society. Doubleday, 1970, 312.

CAMP, THOMAS
 Water and Its Impurities. Reinhold, 1963, 355, illus.

CARR, DONALD E.
 The Breath of Life. W. W. Norton, 1965, 175.

―――.
 Death of the Sweet Waters. W. W. Norton, 1966, 257, illus.

CARSON, RACHEL L.
 Silent Spring. Houghton Mifflin, 1962, 368, illus.

CLARK, JOHN W., and VIESSMAN, WARREN, JR.
 Water Supply and Pollution Control. International Textbook, 1965, 575, illus. (Civil Engineering Textbook.)

CLARKE, GEORGE L.
 Elements of Ecology. Wiley, 1965, 560, illus.

COMMONER, BARRY
 Science and Survival. Viking, 1966, 150. (Compass Book C212.)

COOLEY, RICHARD A., and WANDESFORDE-SMITH, GEOFFREY, EDS.
 Congress and the Environment. University of Washington Press, 1970, 277, illus.

COREY, RICHARD C.
 Principles and Practices of Incineration. Wiley, 1969, 336. (Environmental Technology Series.)

COTTAM, WALTER P.
 Our Renewable Wild Lands: A Challenge. University of Utah Press, 1961, 182, illus.

COX, GEORGE W., ED.
 Readings in Conservation Ecology. Appleton-Century-Crofts, 1969, 595, illus.

DANSEREAU, PIERRE, ED.
 Challenge for Survival: Land, Air, and Water for Man in Megalopolis. Columbia University Press, 1970, 235.

DARLING, LOIS
 A Place in the Sun: Ecology and the Living World. Morrow, 1968, 128, illus.

DASMANN, RAYMOND F.
 Destruction of California. Macmillan, 1965, 247, illus.

―――.
 Environmental Conservation. 2nd ed. Wiley, 1968, 375, illus.

DAVIES, J. CLARENCE, III
 The Politics of Pollution. Scribner, 1970, 231. (Studies in Contemporary American Politics.)

DE BELL, GARRETT, COMP.
 The Environmental Handbook. Ballantine, New York, 1970, 365.

DEGLER, STANLEY E., and BLOOM, SANDRA C.
 Federal Pollution Control Programs: Water, Air, and Solid Wastes. BNA Books, Washington, 1969, 111. (Environmental Management Series.)

DEGLER, STANLEY E.
 State Air Pollution Control Laws. BNA Books, Washington, 1969, 86. (Environmental Management Series.)

DEGRÉMONT, S. A.
 Water Treatment Handbook. 3rd ed. H. K. Elliott, London, 1965, 653.

DELAFONS, JOHN
 Land-Use Controls in the United States. 2nd ed. MIT Press, 1969, 203.

DIMMICK, ROBERT L., and AKERS, ANN B., EDS.
 An Introduction to Experimental Aerobiology. Wiley, 1969, 494, illus. (Environmental Science and Technology Series.)

DOUGLAS, WILLIAM O.
 Wilderness Bill of Rights. Little, Brown, 1965, 192, illus.

DUBOS, RENÉ
 So Human An Animal. Scribner, 1968, 267.

ECKENFELDER, W. WESLEY, JR.
 Industrial Water Pollution Control. McGraw-Hill, 1966, 269.

EDELSON, EDWARD, and WARSHOFSKY, FRED
 Poisons in the Air. Pocket Books, 1966, 160. (APB Special.)

EHLERS, VICTOR M., and STEEL, ERNEST W.
 Mechanical and Rural Sanitation. 6th ed. McGraw-Hill, 1965, 663, illus.

EHRENFELD, DAVID W.
 Biological Conservation. Holt, Rinehart & Winston, 1970, 226, illus. (Modern Biology Series.)

EHRLICH, PAUL R.
 The Population Bomb. Ballantine, New York, 1968, 223.

EHRLICH, PAUL R., and EHRLICH, ANNE H.
 Population, Resources, Environment: Issues in Human Ecology. W. H. Freeman, 1970, 383, illus. (Series of Books on Biology.)

EISENBUD, MERRIL
 Environmental Radioactivity. McGraw-Hill, 1963, 430, illus.

ESPOSITO, JOHN C.
 Vanishing Air. Grossman, New York, 1970, 328. (Ralph Nader Study Group Reports.)

HEALTH SERVICE PROGRAMS

EWALD, WILLIAM R., ED.
Environment and Change: The Next Fifty Years. Indiana University Press, 1968, 397.

———.
Environment and Policy: The Next Fifty Years. Indiana University Press, 1968, 459.

———.
Environment for Man: The Next Fifty Years. Indiana University Press, 1967, 308, illus.

FALTERMAYER, EDMUND K.
Redoing America: A Nationwide Report on How to Make Our Cities and Suburbs Livable. Harper & Row, 1968, 242, illus.

FARB, PETER, and TIME-LIFE BOOKS
Ecology. Rev. ed. Time-Life Books, 1969, 192, illus. (Life Nature Library.)

FARBER, SEYMOUR M., and WILSON, ROGER H. L.
The Air We Breathe: A Study of Man and His Environment. Thomas, 1961, 414, illus.

FAUST, RAYMOND J., ED.
Water Quality and Treatment in Public Water Supplies. 3rd ed. McGraw-Hill, 1970, 640.

FLAWN, PETER T.
Environmental Geology: Conservation, Land-Use Planning, and Resource Management. Harper & Row, 1970, 313, illus.

FLYNN, JOHN E.
Interior Environmental Control. Van Nostrand-Reinhold, 1970, 288.

FORTUNE
The Environment: A National Mission for the Seventies. Harper & Row, 1970, 220, illus. (Perennial Library P189.)

GLASS, DAVID C., ED.
Biology and Behavior: Environmental Influences—Proceedings of a Conference Under the Auspices of Russell Sage Foundation and The Rockefeller University. Rockefeller University Press, 1968, 304, illus.

GLOYNA, ERNEST, ED.
Advances in Water Quality Improvement. Austin University Press, 1968, 513.

GOLDMAN, MARSHALL I., ED.
Controlling Pollution: The Economics of a Cleaner America. Prentice-Hall, 1967, 175.

GOLDSTEIN, JEROME
Garbage As You Like It. Rodale Books, Emmaus, Pa., 1969, 243, illus.

GRAHAM, FRANK, JR.
Since Silent Spring. Houghton Mifflin, 1970, 333.

GRAVA, SIGURD
Urban Planning Aspects of Water Pollution Control. Columbia University Press, 1969, 223, illus.

HAGEVIK, GEORGE H.
Decision-Making in Air Pollution Control: A Review of Theory and Practice with Emphasis on Selected Los Angeles and New York City Management Experiences. Praeger, 1970, 217. (Praeger Special Studies in U.S. Economics and Social Development.)

———.
Planning for Environmental Quality. Council of Planning Libraries, Monticello, Ill., 1969, 121. (Exchange Bibliography No. 97.)

HAMER, PHILIP, JACKSON, J., and THURSTON, E. F.
Industrial Water Treatment Practice. Butterworth, 1961, 514, illus.

HARDENBERGH, WILLIAM A., and RODIE, EDWARD B.
Water Supply and Waste Disposal. International Textbook, 1961, 503.

HAVIGHURST, CLARK C., ED.
Air Pollution Control. Oceana, 1969, 230. (Library of Law and Contemporary Problems.)

HEADLEY, JOSEPH C., and LEWIS, JACK N.
The Pesticide Problem: An Economic Approach to Public Policy. Johns Hopkins Press, 1967, 141.

HECHTEL, GEORGE J.
Biological Effects of Thermal Pollution. Marine Sciences Research Center, Northport, N.Y., State University of New York at Stony Brook, 1970, 1 vol.

HELFRICH, HAROLD W., JR.
The Environmental Crisis: Man's Struggle to Live with Himself. Yale University Press, 1970, 187.

HERBER, LEWIS
Crisis in Our Cities. Prentice-Hall, 1965, 239, illus.

———.
Our Synthetic Environment. Knopf, 1962, 285.

HERFINDAHL, ORRIS C.
Quality of the Environment: An Economic Approach to Some Problems in Using Land, Water and Air. Johns Hopkins Press, 1965, 96.

HYNES, H. B. N.
The Biology of Polluted Waters. University of Toronto Press, 1970, 200.

JAMES, GEORGE V.
Water Treatment: A Guide to the Treatment of Water and Effluents Purification. 3rd ed. Technical Press, London, 1965, 307, illus.

JARRETT, HENRY
Resources of the Future: Environmental Quality in a Growing Economy. Johns Hopkins Press, 1966, 173.

JENNINGS, BURGESS H., and MURPHY, JOHN E.
Interactions of Man and His Environment. Plenum Press, 1966, 168, illus.

JONES, JOHN R.
Fish and River Pollution. Butterworth, 1964, 203, illus.

KILBOURNE, EDWIN D., and SMILLIE, WILSON G.
Human Ecology and Public Health. 4th ed. Macmillan, 1969, 462.

KINGSLEY, V. V.
Bacteriology Primer in Air Contamination Control. University of Toronto Press, 1967, 37.

KLEIN, LOUIS
River Pollution. Academic Press, 1966, 3 vols.

LEIGHTON, PHILIP A.
Photochemistry of Air Pollution. Academic Press, 1961, 300, illus. (Physical Chemistry Vol. 9.)

LEINWAND, GERALD, and POPKIN, GERALD
Air and Water Pollution. Washington Square Press, 1969, 160, illus. (Problems of American Society.)

LEITHE, W.
The Analysis of Air Pollutants. Ann Arbor Science, 1970, 304.

LEWIS, ALFRED
Clean the Air! Fighting Smoke, Smog, and Smaze Across the Country. McGraw-Hill, 1965, 96, illus.

LEWIS, HOWARD R.
With Every Breath You Take: The Poisons of Air Pollution, How They Are Injuring Our Health, and What We Must Do About Them. Crown, 1965, 322, illus.

LINTON, RON M.
Terracide: America's Destruction of Her Living Environment. Little, Brown, 1970, 376.

ENVIRONMENTAL SCIENCE

LUND, HERBERT F.
Industrial Pollution Control Handbook. McGraw-Hill, 1970, 1000.

MacAVOY, PAUL W., and PETERSON, DEAN F.
Large-Scale Desalting: A Study in the Engineering Economics of Regional Development. Praeger, 1969, 124, illus.

MAIER, FRANZ J.
Manual of Water Fluoridation Practice. McGraw-Hill, 1963, 234, illus.

MARINE, GENE
America the Raped: The Engineering Mentality and the Devastation of a Continent. Simon & Schuster, 1969, 312.

MARX, WESLEY
The Frail Ocean. Coward-McCann, 1967, 248.

McCLELLAN, GRANT S., COMP.
Protecting Our Environment. Wilson, 1970, 218. (Reference Shelf Vol. 42, No. 1.)

McMILLEN, WHEELER
Bugs or People? Appleton-Century, 1965, 228.

MEETHAM, A. R.
Atmospheric Pollution: Its Origins and Prevention. 3rd ed. Pergamon, 1964, 301, illus.

MELLANBY, KEITH
Pesticides and Pollution. Collins, 1967, 221, illus.

MILNE, LORUS, and MILNE, MARGERY
Water and Life. Atheneum, 1964, 275, illus.

MITCHELL, JOHN G., and STALLINGS, CONSTANCE L., EDS.
Ecotactics: The Sierra Club Handbook for Environment Activists. Pocket Books, 1970, 288.

MOORE, GARY T., ED.
Emerging Methods in Environmental Design and Planning. MIT Press, 1970, 304.

MORGAN, RICHARD F.
Environmental Biology. Pergamon, 1963-66, 4 vols.

MOSS, FRANK E.
The Water Crisis. Praeger, 1967, 305, illus.

MURPHY, EARL F.
Water Purity: A Study in Legal Control of Natural Resources. University of Wisconsin Press, 1961, 212.

NASH, RODERICK
The American Environment: Readings in the History of Conservation. Addison-Wesley, 1968, 236, illus. (Themes and Forces in American History Series.)

NATIONAL ACADEMY OF SCIENCES, NATIONAL RESEARCH COUNCIL, BUILDING RESEARCH INSTITUTE
Cleaning and Purification of Air in Buildings. NAS, 1960, 62. (Pub. No. 797.)

NATIONAL ASSOCIATION OF MANUFACTURERS
Water in Industry. NAM, 1965, 81.

NAVARRA, JOHN G.
Our Noisy World. Doubleday, 1969, 208.

NICHOLSON, MAX
The Environmental Revolution: A Guide for the New Masters of the World. McGraw-Hill, 1970, 366, illus.

NIKOLAIEFF, GEORGE A., ED.
The Water Crisis. Wilson, 1967, 192. (Reference Shelf Vol. 38, No. 6.)

ODUM, EUGENE P.
Ecology. Holt, Rinehart & Winston, 1969, 168, illus.

OVERMAN, MICHAEL
Water: Solutions to a Problem of Supply and Demand. Doubleday, 1969, 192, illus. (Doubleday Science Series.)

PERRY, JOHN
Our Polluted World: Can Man Survive? Watts, 1967, 213.

POLLUTION CONTROL
Cahners, 1969, 2 vols.

POPKIN, ROY
Desalination: Water for the World's Future. Stewart L. Udall, foreword. Praeger, 1968, 235, illus.

POST, ROY G., and SEALE, ROBERT L., EDS.
Water Production Using Nuclear Energy. University of Arizona Press, 1966, 392, illus.

POULTON, E. C.
Environment and Human Efficiency. Thomas, 1970, 328, illus. (American Lecture Series Pub. No. 765, Monograph in the Bannerstone Division of American Lectures in Living Chemistry.)

RANDOLPH, THERON G.
Human Ecology and Susceptibility to the Chemical Environment. Thomas, 1967, 158.

REVELLE, ROGER, and LANDSBERG, HANS H., EDS.
America's Changing Environment. Houghton Mifflin, 1970, 314, illus. (Daedalus Library Vol. 15.)

RIENOW, ROBERT, and RIENOW, LEONA T.
Moment in the Sun: A Report on the Deteriorating Quality of the American Environment. Dial, 1967, 286.

ROCKEFELLER, NELSON A.
Our Environment Can Be Saved. Doubleday, 1970, 176.

ROGERS, EDWARD S.
Human Ecology and Health: An Introduction for Administrators. Macmillan, 1960, 334, illus.

ROOSEVELT, NICHOLAS
Conservation: Now or Never. Dodd, Mead, 1970, 238.

ROSSANO, A. T., JR., ED.
Air Pollution Control: Guidebook for Management. Technomic, Stamford, Conn., 1969, 213.

RUCH, WALTER
Chemical Detection of Gaseous Pollutants. Ann Arbor Science, 1970, 241.

RUDD, ROBERT L.
Pesticides and the Living Landscape. University of Wisconsin Press, 1964, 320. (Conservation Foundation Study.)

SCHIFFERES, JUSTUS J.
Healthier Living: A College Text with Readings in Personal and Environmental Health. 3rd ed. Wiley, 1970, 578, illus.

SCORER, RICHARD
Air Pollution. Pergamon, 1968, 168.

SHEPARD, PAUL, and McKINLEY, DANIEL, EDS.
The Subversive Science: Essays Toward an Ecology of Man. Houghton Mifflin, 1969, 453, illus.

SILVERBERG, ROBERT
The Challenge of Climate: Man and His Environment. Meredith Press, 1969, 326.

SMITH, GUY H.
Conservation of Natural Resources. 3rd ed. Wiley, 1965, 533, illus.

SPIEGLER, K. S., ED.
Principles of Desalination. Academic Press, 1966, 566, illus.

HEALTH SERVICE PROGRAMS

SPROULL, WAYNE T.
　Air Pollution and Its Control. Exposition Press, 1970, 106, illus.

STEEL, ERNEST W.
　Water Supply and Sewerage. 4th ed. McGraw-Hill, 1960, 655, illus.

STERN, ARTHUR C., ED.
　Air Pollution. 2nd ed. Academic Press, 1968- , 3 vols., illus. (Environmental Science, Interdisciplinary Monograph Series.)

STERN, JOHN A., ED.
　Instrumentation for Air Pollution Control: Proceedings of a Symposium.... Instrument Society of America, 1967, 50.

STEWART, GEORGE R.
　Not So Rich as You Think. Houghton Mifflin, 1968, 248, illus.

STILL, HENRY
　The Dirty Animal. Hawthorn, 1967, 298.

UDALL, STEWART L.
　1976: Agenda for Tomorrow. Harcourt, Brace & World, 1968, 173.

ULLMANN, JOHN E., ED.
　Waste Disposal Problems in Selected Industries. Hofstra University, 1969, 284, illus. (Hofstra University Yearbook of Business Series 6, Vol. 1.)

U.S. DEPARTMENT OF HEALTH, EDUCATION AND WELFARE
　Environmental Health Planning Guide. HEW, 1968, 1 vol.

U.S. DEPARTMENT OF HEALTH, EDUCATION AND WELFARE, NATIONAL AIR POLLUTION CONTROL ADMINISTRATION
　Air Pollution Publications: A Selected Bibliography with Abstracts, 1966-1968. USGPO, 1969, 522. (FS 2.24: Ai 7/966-68.)

U.S. FEDERAL WATER POLLUTION CONTROL ADMINISTRATION
　Cost of Clean Water. USGPO, 1968, 4 vols. (I67/2:C82/Vols. 1-4.)

U.S. NATIONAL AIR POLLUTION CONTROL ADMINISTRATION
　Control Techniques for Particulate Air Pollutants. USGPO, 1969, 1 vol. (FS 2.93/3: No. 51.)

U.S. NATIONAL CENTER FOR AIR POLLUTION CONTROL
　Compilation of Selected Air Pollution Control Regulations and Ordinances. Rev. ed. USGPO, 1968, 1 vol. (FS 2: 300:AP.43.)

U.S. OFFICE OF EDUCATION, VOCATIONAL AND TECHNICAL EDUCATION DIVISION
　Water and Wastewater Technology: A Suggested 2-Year Post High School Curriculum. USOE, 1968, 131, illus. (OE-80057, Technical Education Program Series No. 11.)

U.S. WATER RESOURCES COUNCIL
　The Nation's Water Resources: The First National Assessment. USGPO, 1968, 1 vol. (Y3.W29:As 7.)

WALTON, WILLIAM C.
　The World of Water. Taplinger, 1970, 340, illus.

WATER INFORMATION CENTER, INC.
　The Water Encyclopedia. WIC, Port Washington, N.Y., 1970, 1 vol.

WEAVER, ELBERT C., ED.
　Scientific Experiments in Environmental Pollution. Holt, Rinehart & Winston, 1968, 48.

WEINER, JACK, and ROTH, LILLIAN
　Air Pollution in the Pulp and Paper Industry. Institute of Paper Chemistry, Appleton, Wis., 1969, 1 vol. (Bibliographic Series No. 237.)

WHITTEN, JAMIE L.
　That We May Live. Van Nostrand, 1966, 251.

WILBER, CHARLES G.
　The Biological Aspects of Water Pollution. Thomas, 1969, 296, illus.

WOLMAN, ABEL
　Water, Health and Society. Indiana University Press, 1969, 400, illus.

WORLD HEALTH ORGANIZATION
　Air Pollution. WHO, Geneva, 1961, 442, illus. (Monograph Series No. 46.)

――――.
　Environmental Health Aspects of Metropolitan Planning and Development: Report of a W.H.O. Expert Committee (Geneva 1964). WHO, Geneva, 1965, 66. (Technical Report Series No. 297.)

WRIGHT, JAMES C.
　The Coming Water Famine. Coward-McCann, 1966, 255.

INHALATION THERAPY

AMERICAN ASSOCIATION FOR INHALATION THERAPY
　1968 Lecture Outline. AAIT, Riverside, Calif., 1968, 107, illus.

――――.
　1969 Lecture Outline. AAIT, Riverside, Calif., 1969, 171.

BELINKOFF, STANTON
　Introduction to Inhalation Therapy. Little, Brown, 1969, 148.

BROOKS, D. K.
　Resuscitation. Williams & Wilkins, 1967, 320, illus.

CACCAMO, LEONARD P., KESSLER, EDWARD, and AZNEER, J. LEONARD
　Resuscitation: A Programmed Text. F. A. Davis, 1968, 113, illus.

COMMITTEE ON RESPIRATORS, LANSING, MICH.
　Respiratory Protective Devices Manual. CR, 1963, 182.

DEJOURS, PIERRE
　Respiration. Oxford University Press, 1966, 244, illus. (Principles of Physiology Series.)

DeKORNFELD, THOMAS J., and GILBERT, DON E.
　Inhalation Therapy Procedure Manual. Thomas, 1968, 114, illus.

EGAN, DONALD F.
　Fundamentals of Inhalation Therapy. Mosby, 1969, 474.

ELAM, JAMES O., BITTNER, T. J., and STUDLEY, C. L.
　Instruction Manual for Mr. Airway: For Training Classes in All Methods of Rescue Breathing.... Roswell Park Memorial Institute, Anesthesiology Department, Buffalo, N.Y., 1961, 35, illus.

GOTTLIEB, LEON S.
　A History of Respiration. Thomas, 1964, 136, illus.

HEIRONIMUS, TERRING W., III
　Mechanical Artificial Ventilation: A Manual for Students and Practitioners. 2nd ed. Thomas, 1970, 122, illus. (American Lectures in Anesthesiology.)

HOWELL, J. B. L., and CAMPBELL, E. J. M., EDS.
　Breathlessness. F. A. Davis, 1966, 240, illus.

HUNTER, A. R.
　Essentials of Artificial Ventilation of the Lungs. 2nd ed. Little, Brown, 1967, 90.

HURST, JOHN W., ED.
Cardiac Resuscitation. Thomas, 1960, 141, illus.

JUDE, JAMES R., and ELAM, JAMES O.
Fundamentals of Cardio-Pulmonary Resuscitation. F. A. Davis, 1965, 169, illus.

KRACUM, VINCENT D., ED.
Inhalation Therapy Examination Review Book: 1200 Multiple Choice Questions and Referenced Answers. Medical Examination Publishing Co., Flushing, N.Y., 1970- , 1 vol.

LIPPOLD, OLOF
Human Respiration: A Programmed Course. W. H. Freeman, 1968, 128, illus.

LOWRY, THOMAS P., ED.
Hyperventilation and Hysteria: The Physiology and Psychology of Overbreathing and Its Relationship to the Mind-Body Problem. Thomas, 1967, 208, illus.

McHARDY, G. J. R.
Basic Techniques in Human Metabolism and Respiration. F. A. Davis, 1968, 64, illus.

NEW YORK HEART ASSOCIATION
Oxygen. Little, Brown, 1965, 283.

PEARSON, JOHN W.
Historical and Experimental Approaches to Modern Resuscitation. Thomas, 1965, 128, illus.

PETERS, RICHARD M.
The Mechanical Basis of Respiration: An Approach to Respiratory Pathophysiology. Little, Brown, 1969, 393, illus.

PETTY, THOMAS L., and NETT, LOUISE M.
For Those Who Live and Breathe with Emphysema and Chronic Bronchitis. Thomas, 1967, 120.

PILLER, LAURENCE W.
Manual of Cardio-Pulmonary Technology. Thomas, 1964, 300, illus.

ROSENMAN, EUGENE
An Outline of Pulmonary Function and Pulmonary Emphysema. Thomas, 1964, 152, illus.

SAFAR, PETER, ED.
Respiratory Therapy. F. A. Davis, 1965, 434, illus.

SAFAR, PETER, and McMAHON, MARTIN C.
Resuscitation of the Unconscious Victim: A Manual for Rescue Breathing. 2nd ed. Thomas, 1961, 87, illus.

SECOR, JANE
Patient Care in Respiratory Problems. Saunders, 1969, 229. (Monographs in Clinical Nursing No. 1.)

SEEDOR, MARIE M.
Therapy with Oxygen and Other Gases: A Programmed Unit in Fundamentals of Nursing. Teachers College Press, 1966, 172, illus. (Nursing Education Monographs.)

SLONIM, N. BALFOUR, BELL, BETTYE P., and CHRISTENSEN, SHERRYL E.
Cardiopulmonary Laboratory Basic Methods and Calculations: A Manual of Cardiopulmonary Technology. Thomas, 1967, 280, illus.

SYKES, M. K., and CAMPBELL, E. J.
Respiratory Failure. F. A. Davis, 1968, 256, illus.

U.S. COAST GUARD
Cardiopulmonary (Heart-Lung) Resuscitation. USGPO, 1963, Vol. 1- , illus.

WHITTENBERGER, JAMES L., ED.
Artificial Respiration: Theory and Application, by 15 Authors. Harper & Row, 1962, 276, illus.

YACORZYNSKI, G. K., et al.
Investigation of Carbon Dioxide Therapy. Thomas, 1962, 324, illus.

YOUNG, JIMMY A., and CROCKER, DEAN
Principles and Practice of Inhalation Therapy. Year Book Medical Publishers, Chicago, 1970, 363, illus.

MEDICAL LABORATORY TECHNOLOGY

ALLEN, FRANK D.
Essentials of Human Embryology. 2nd ed. Oxford University Press, 1969, 360, illus.

ARCO PUBLISHING COMPANY, INC.
Laboratory Aide. Arco, 1967, 112.

BAKER, FRANCIS J., and BREACH, M. R.
Handbook of Bacteriological Technique. 2nd ed. Butterworth, 1967, 482, illus.

BAKER, FRANCIS J., SILVERTON, R. E., and LUCKCOCK, EVELINE D.
An Introduction to Medical Laboratory Technology. 4th ed. Butterworth, 1966, 655, illus.

BALINSKY, B. I.
Introduction to Embryology. 2nd ed. Saunders, 1965, 273.

BANCROFT, J. D.
An Introduction to Histochemical Technique. Butterworth, 1969, 268.

BERKELEY SCIENTIFIC PUBLICATIONS
National & State Board Examination Questions and Answers for Medical Laboratory Technologists: 2,329 Selected Questions & Answers Covering the Theory and Practice of Clinical Chemistry, Parasitology, Hematology, Bacteriology, Serology & Immunology. Rev. ed. Berkeley Scientific, 275. (Medical Technology Vol. 2.)

BETHKE, EMIL G.
Basic Drawing for Biology Students. Thomas, 1969, 86, illus. (American Lecture Series No. 746.)

BOORMAN, KATHLEEN E., and DODD, BARBARA E.
An Introduction to Blood Group Serology: Theory, Techniques, Practical Applications. 3rd ed. Little, Brown, 1966, 374, illus.

BOYD, WILLIAM C.
Fundamentals of Immunology. 4th ed. Interscience, 1966, 773, illus.

BROWN, B., and GORDON, D., EDS.
Ultrasonic Techniques in Biology and Medicine. Thomas, 1967, 272, illus.

BROWN, GEOFFREY G.
Primer of Histopathologic Technique. Appleton-Century-Crofts, 1969, 224.

BROWN, HAROLD I.
Lectures for Medical Technologists. Thomas, 1964, 718, illus.

BROWN, JACK H. U., and BARKER, SAMUEL B.
Basic Endocrinology for Students of Biology and Medicine. F. A. Davis, 1962, 228, illus.

CARAWAY, WENDELL T.
Microchemical Methods for Blood Analysis. Thomas, 1960, 109, illus.

CHRISTENSEN, HALVOR N.
Body Fluids and the Acid-Base Balance: A Learning Program for Students of the Biological and Medical Sciences. Saunders, 1964, 506, illus.

HEALTH SERVICE PROGRAMS

CHRISTENSEN, HALVOR N.
    pH and Dissociation: A Learning Program for Students of the Biological and Medical Sciences. 2nd ed. Saunders, 1964, 107, illus.

CLARK, GEORGE L., ED.
    The Encyclopedia of Microscopy. Reinhold, 1961, 693, illus.

COLLINS, R. DOUGLAS
    Illustrated Manual of Laboratory Diagnosis: Indications and Interpretations. Lippincott, 1968, 299, illus.

CONN, HAROLD J., DARROW, MARY A., and EMMEL, VICTOR M.
    Staining Procedures. 2nd ed. Williams & Wilkins, 1960, 304.

COWDRY, EDMUND V., and EMMEL, VICTOR M.
    Laboratory Technique in Biology and Medicine. 4th ed. Williams & Wilkins, 1964, 453.

CUNNINGHAM, CHARLES H.
    A Laboratory Guide in Virology. 5th ed. Burgess, 1964, 177, illus.

DALE, SIDNEY L.
    Principles of Steroid Analysis. Lea & Febiger, 1967, 137, illus. (Medical Technology No. 2.)

DAMM, HENRY C., ED.
    Practical Manual for Clinical Laboratory Procedures. Chemical Rubber Co., 1965, 1 vol., illus.

DOLAN, FRANCIS E.
    Comprehensive Review for Medical Technologists. Mosby, 1968, 181.

DORLAND'S ILLUSTRATED MEDICAL DICTIONARY
    Saunders, 1900- , vols., illus.

EARLY, PAUL J., RAZZAK, MUHAMMAD A., and SODEE, D. BRUCE
    Textbook of Nuclear Medicine Technology. Mosby, 1969, 378.

FOGEL, LAWRENCE J.
    Bio-Technology: Concepts and Applications. Prentice-Hall, 1963, 826, illus.

FREDERICK, MOLLY, ED.
    Vision: Readings in Health and Medical Technology Education Programs. American Association of Junior Colleges, 1970, 47, illus.

GALIGHER, ALBERT E., and KOZLOFF, EUGENE N.
    The Essentials of Practical Microtechnique. Lea & Febiger, 1964, 484, illus.

GARB, SOLOMON
    Laboratory Tests in Common Use. 4th ed. Springer, 1966, 192.

GEDDES, L. A., and BAKER, L. E.
    Principles of Applied Biomedical Instrumentation. Wiley, 1968, 479.

GILLIES, ROBERT R., and DODDS, T. C.
    Bacteriology Illustrated. 2nd ed. Williams & Wilkins, 1968, 198, illus.

GOODALE, RAYMOND H., and WIDMANN, FRANCES K.
    Clinical Interpretation of Laboratory Tests. 6th ed. F. A. Davis, 1969, 568, illus.

GRADWOHL, RUTHERFORD B. H.
    Clinical Laboratory Methods and Diagnosis: A Textbook on Laboratory Procedures and Their Interpretation. 6th ed. Sam Frankel and Stanley Reitman, eds. Mosby, 1963, 2 vols., illus.

GRAY, PETER
    Handbook of Basic Microtechnique. 2nd ed. McGraw-Hill, 1964, 302, illus.

———.
    The Use of the Microscope: An Introductory Handbook for Biologists. McGraw-Hill, 1967, 91, illus.

GURR, EDWARD
    Encyclopedia of Microscopic Stains. Williams & Wilkins, 1960, 510.

———.
    The Rational Use of Dyes in Biology and General Staining Methods. Williams & Wilkins, 1965, 434.

GUTFREUND, H.
    An Introduction to Study of Enzymes. Wiley, 1965, 335.

HALL, CECIL E.
    Introduction to Electron Microscopy. 2nd ed. McGraw-Hill, 1966, 397, illus.

HELPER, OPAL E.
    Manual of Clinical Laboratory Methods. 4th ed. Thomas, 1965, 387, illus.

JENSEN, J. TRYGVE
    Introduction to Medical Physics. Lippincott, 1960, 240.

JOHNSON, A. P.
    Organization and Management of Hospital Laboratories. Appleton-Century-Crofts, 1969, 162.

KAHLER, CAROL, ED.
    Guide to Planning: Medical Laboratory Technician. American Association of Junior Colleges, 1969, 48.

KAY, D., ED.
    Techniques for Electron Microscopy. 2nd ed. F. A. Davis, 1965, 574, illus.

KENNEDY, DONALD, COMP.
    From Cell to Organism: Readings from Scientific American. W. H. Freeman, 1967, 256.

LAMELA, ALBERTO
    Handbook of Laboratory Methods for Medical Aides. Charles Mathis, 1966, 277, illus.

LANGLEY, LEROY L.
    Homeostasis. Reinhold, 1965, 114, illus. (Selected Topics in Modern Biology.)

LAWRENCE, CARL A., and BLOCK, SEYMOUR S.
    Disinfection, Sterilization & Preservation. Lea & Febiger, 1968, 808, illus.

LEE, LESLIE W.
    Elementary Principles of Laboratory Instruments. 2nd ed. Mosby, 1970, 215, illus.

LESSING, LAWRENCE P.
    DNA. Macmillan, 1967, 85.

LEUKEMIA SOCIETY
    Closing In: Research on Leukemia. LS, New York, 1967, 128, illus.

LILLIE R. D., and CONN, HAROLD J.
    Conn's Biological Stains: A Handbook on the Nature and Uses of the Dyes Employed in the Biological Laboratory. Williams & Wilkins, 1969, 510, illus.

LINNÉ, JEAN J., and RINGSRUD, KAREN M.
    Basic Laboratory Techniques for the Medical Laboratory Technician. McGraw-Hill, 1970, 399, illus.

LIPPMAN, RICHARD W.
    Urine and the Urinary Sediment: A Practical Manual and Atlas. Thomas, 1967, 152, illus.

LYNCH, MATTHEW J., et al.
    Medical Laboratory Technology and Clinical Pathology. 2nd ed. Saunders, 1969, 1359, illus.

MAHER, DAVID J., ED.
Medical Technology: A Review for Board Examinations. 6th ed. Berkeley Scientific, 1968, 543. (Medical Technology Vol. 1.)

MARK, DONALD D., and ZIMMER, ARTHUR
Atlas of Clinical Laboratory Procedures. McGraw-Hill, Blakiston Division, 1967- , vols., illus.

McALLISTER, RONALD A.
Theory of Chemical Pathology Technique: A Guide for Medical Laboratory Technologists. Butterworth, 1967, 185, illus.

McMANUS, JOSEPH F. A., and MOWRY, ROBERT W.
Staining Methods: Histologic and Histochemical. Hoeber, 1960, 423.

MERCER, E. H., and BIRBECK, M. S. C.
Electron Microscopy: A Handbook for Biologists. 2nd ed. F. A. Davis, 1966, 112, illus.

MORGAN, ROSE M.
Guide Questions for Medical Technology Examinations. Thomas, 1966, 256.

NATIONAL COMMITTEE FOR CAREERS IN MEDICAL TECHNOLOGY
Curriculum Guides for Retraining in Medical Technology. NCCMT, Bethesda, Md., 1968, 312.

———.
A Manual of Cytotechnology. NCCMT, Bethesda, Md., 1962, 1 vol., illus.

NEEDHAM, GEORGE H.
The Microscope: A Practical Guide. Thomas, 1968, 128, illus.

PARKER, RAYMOND C.
Methods of Tissue Culture. 3rd ed. Hoeber, 1961, 358, illus.

PASSOW, H.
Laboratory Techniques in Membrane Biophysics: An Introductory Course. Springer, 1969, 1 vol.

PAUL, GRACE
Your Future in Medical Technology. R. Rosen Press, 1962, 156. (Careers in Depth.)

RHODES, ANDREW J., and VAN ROOYEN, CLENNEL E.
Textbook of Virology: For Students and Practitioners of Medicine and the Other Health Sciences. 5th ed. Williams & Wilkins, 1968, 966, illus.

RICE, EUGENE W.
Principles and Methods of Clinical Chemistry for Medical Technologists. Thomas, 1960, 286, illus.

SANDBORN, EDMUND B.
Cells and Tissues by Light and Electron Microscopy. Academic Press, 1970- , vols., illus.

SIRRIDGE, MARJORIE S.
Medical Technology: Laboratory Evaluation of Hemostasis. Lea & Febiger, 1967, 163. (Medical Technology No. 1.)

SLAYTER, ELIZABETH M.
Optical Methods in Biology. Wiley, 1969, 1 vol.

STEELE, HAROLD C.
The Departmental Laboratory Assistant in Biological Science: A Book of Principles, Methods and Techniques. Dorrance, Philadelphia, 1966, 213.

STEHLI, GEORG J.
The Microscope and How to Use It. Dover, 1970, 157, illus.

TABER, CLARENCE W.
Taber's Cyclopedic Medical Dictionary: A Digest of Medical Subjects—Medicine, Surgery, Nursing, Dietetics, Physical Therapy, Treatment and Drugs. 11th ed. F. A. Davis, 1969, 1 vol., illus.

TAVISS, IRENE, and KIOVUMAKI, JUDITH
Implications of Biomedical Technology. Harvard University Press, 1968, 1 vol. (Research Review Series No. 1.)

TAYLOR, NORMAN B., and TAYLOR, ALLEN E.
The Putnam Medical Dictionary. Putnam, 1961, 933, illus.

U.S. DEPARTMENT OF HEALTH, EDUCATION AND WELFARE, OFFICE OF EDUCATION (NATIONAL COMMITTEE FOR CAREERS IN MEDICAL TECHNOLOGY)
Medical Laboratory Assistant: A Suggested Guide for a Training Program. Manpower Development and Training Program, HEW, 1966, 115, illus.

WEINSTOCK, HAROLD, ED.
Cryogenic Technology. Technical Publishers, Boston, 1969, 199, illus.

WEISER, RUSSELL S.
Fundamentals of Immunology. Lea & Febiger, 1969, 1 vol.

WHITE, WILMA L., et al.
Chemistry for Medical Technologists. 3rd ed. Mosby, 1970, 480, illus.

WILLIER, BENJAMIN, and OPPENHEIMER, J. M.
Foundations of Experimental Embryology. Prentice-Hall, 1964, 225.

WOLF, ARNOLD V., and CROWDER, NORMAN A.
An Introduction to Body Fluid Metabolism. Williams & Wilkins, 1964, 263, illus.

WORLD HEALTH ORGANIZATION
The Training of Health Laboratory Personnel (Technical Staff): Fourth Report of the W.H.O. Expert Committee on Health Laboratory Services (Geneva 1965). WHO, Geneva, 1966, 31. (Technical Report Series No. 345.)

YOUNG, CLARA G., and BARGER, JAMES D.
Introduction to Medical Science. Mosby, 1969, 295, illus.

ANATOMY AND PHYSIOLOGY

ANTHONY, CATHERINE P.
Basic Concepts in Anatomy and Physiology: A Programmed Presentation. 2nd ed. Mosby, 1970, 180, illus.

———.
Textbook of Anatomy and Physiology. 7th ed. Mosby, 1967, 585, illus.

AREY, LESLIE B.
Developmental Anatomy: A Textbook and Laboratory Manual of Embryology. 7th ed. Saunders, 1965, 695, illus.

BASMAJIAN, JOHN V.
Primary Anatomy. 6th ed. Williams & Wilkins, 1970, 404.

BERGER, ANDREW J.
Elementary Human Anatomy. Wiley, 1964, 538, illus.

BEST, CHARLES H.
The Human Body: Its Anatomy and Physiology. 4th ed. Holt, 1963, 754, illus.

CERTIFIED MEDICAL REPRESENTATIVES INSTITUTE, INC.
Human Physiology: A Programmed Text. Wiley, 1969, 227, illus.

CHAFFEE, ELLEN E., and GREISHEIMER, ESTHER M.
Basic Physiology and Anatomy. 2nd ed. Lippincott, 1969, 675, illus.

CROUCH, JAMES E.
Functional Human Anatomy. Lea & Febiger, 1965, 662, illus.

HEALTH SERVICE PROGRAMS

DIENHART, CHARLOTTE M.
  Basic Human Anatomy and Physiology. Saunders, 1967, 247, illus.

DONÁTH, TIBOR
  Anatomical Dictionary with Nomenclatures and Explanatory Notes. Pergamon, 1969, 634.

FRANCIS, CARL C.
  Introduction to Human Anatomy. 5th ed. Mosby, 1968, 464, illus.

FROHSE, FRANZ
  Atlas of Human Anatomy. 6th ed. Barnes & Noble, 1961, 180, illus.

GANS, CARL
  Comparative Anatomy Atlas. Academic Press, 1962, 1 vol.

GRANT, JOHN C. B.
  An Atlas of Anatomy.... 5th ed. Williams & Wilkins, 1962, 1 vol., illus.

GREEN, JOHN H.
  An Introduction to Human Physiology. 2nd ed. Oxford University Press, 1968, 184, illus.

GREISHEIMER, ESTHER M.
  Physiology and Anatomy: With Practical Considerations. 8th ed. Lippincott, 1963, 894, illus.

KIMBER, DIANA C., et al.
  Anatomy and Physiology. 15th ed. Macmillan, 1966, 805.

KING, BARRY G., and SHOWERS, MARY J.
  Human Anatomy and Physiology. 6th ed. Saunders, 1969, 432.

LANGLEY, LEROY L., TELFORD, IRA R., and CHRISTENSEN, JOHN B.
  Dynamic Anatomy and Physiology. 3rd ed. McGraw-Hill, 1969, 817, illus.

LANGLEY, LEROY L., and CHERASKIN, EMMANUEL
  Physiology of Man. 3rd ed. Reinhold, 1965, 658.

LARIMER, JAMES
  Introduction to Animal Physiology. W. C. Brown, 1968, 153, illus. (Concepts of Biology Series.)

LOCKHART, ROBERT D., HAMILTON, G. F., and FYFE, F. W.
  Anatomy of the Human Body. 2nd ed. Lippincott, 1969, 705.

SCHEER, BRADLEY T.
  Comparative Physiology. W. C. Brown, 1968, 248. (Biology Readings Series.)

SINCLAIR, D. C.
  An Introduction to Functional Anatomy. 4th ed. F. A. Davis, 1970, 560.

STARLING, ERNEST H.
  Principles of Human Physiology. 13th ed. Lea & Febiger, 1962, 1579, illus.

TAYLOR, NORMAN B.
  Basic Physiology and Anatomy. Putnam, 1965, 648.

TUTTLE, WAID W., and SCHOTTELIUS, BYRON A.
  Textbook of Physiology. 16th ed. Mosby, 1969, 564, illus.

WARWICK, ROGER
  Introduction to Anatomy. Arco, 1965, 240, illus.

WISCHNITZER, SAUL
  Atlas and Dissection Guide for Comparative Anatomy. W. H. Freeman, 1967, 178, illus.

WOODBURNE, RUSSELL T.
  Essentials of Human Anatomy. 4th ed. Oxford University Press, 1969, 626, illus.

BIO-ELECTRONICS

BOUTKAN, J.
  ABC of the Egg: A Guide to Electrocardiography. Thomas, 1968, 1 vol.

BRADLOW, BERTRAM A.
  How to Produce a Readable Electrocardiogram. Thomas, 1964, 208, illus.

BURCH, GEORGE E., and WINSOR, TRAVIS
  A Primer of Electrocardiography. 4th ed. Lea & Febiger, 1960, 293, illus.

CAMISHION, RUDOLPH C.
  Basic Medical Electronics. Little, Brown, 1964, 204.

DIMOND, E. GREY
  Electrocardiography and Vectorcardiography. 4th ed. Little, Brown, 1967, 152.

———.
  The Exercise Electrocardiogram in Office Practice. Thomas, 1961, 180, illus.

HURST, JOHN W.
  Introduction to Electrocardiography. McGraw-Hill, Blakiston Division, 1968, 1 vol.

SCHAMROTH, L.
  An Introduction to Electrocardiography. 3rd ed. F. A. Davis, 1966, 176, illus.

STACY, RALPH W.
  Biological and Medical Electronics. McGraw-Hill, 1960, 308, illus.

SUPRYNOWICZ, VINCENT A.
  Introduction to Electronics for Students of Biology, Chemistry and Medicine. Addison-Wesley, 1966, 324, illus.

SZENT-GYORGYI, ALBERT
  Bioelectronics. Academic Press, 1968, 1 vol.

YANOF, HOWARD M.
  Textbook of Biomedical Electronics. F. A. Davis, 1965, 361, illus.

ZUCKER, MITCHELL H.
  Electronic Circuits for the Behavioral and Biomedical Sciences: A Reference Book of Useful Solid-State Circuits. W. H. Freeman, 1969, 241.

BIOLOGY

ABERCROMBIE, MICHAEL, HICKMAN, C. J., and JOHNSON, M. L.
  A Dictionary of Biology. Rev. ed. Aldine, 1964, 254, illus.

ABRAMOFF, PETER, and THOMSON, ROBERT G.
  An Experimental Approach to Biology. W. H. Freeman, 1966, 253, illus.

AMERICAN INSTITUTE OF BIOLOGICAL SCIENCES, BIOLOGICAL SCIENCES CURRICULUM STUDY
  Biology Teachers' Handbook. 2nd ed. Wiley, 1970, 692, illus.

BARRY, JOHN M., and BARRY, E. M.
  An Introduction to the Structure of Biological Molecules. Prentice-Hall, 1969, 190, illus. (Biological Science Series.)

BROCK, THOMAS D.
  Biology of Microorganisms. Prentice-Hall, 1970, 737, illus. (Biological Science Series.)

BUFFALOE, NEAL D., and THRONEBERRY, J. B.
  Principles of Biology. 2nd ed. Prentice-Hall, 1967, 402, illus.

COOPER, WILLIAM A.
  A Laboratory Survey of Biology. 2nd ed. Macmillan, 1969, 1 vol.

CURTIS, HELENA
  Biology. Worth Publishers, 1968, 854, illus. (Special edition distributed by Natural History Press for American Museum of Natural History.)

DuPRAW, ERNEST J.
  Cell and Molecular Biology. Academic Press, 1968, 739, illus.

FLICKINGER, REED
  Developmental Biology. W. C. Brown, 1966, 360. (Biology Readings Series.)

FOX, WILLIAM W.
  Careers in the Biological Sciences. Walck, 1963, 114, illus.

GERKING, SHELBY D.
  Biological Systems. Saunders, 1969, 480, illus.

GRAY, PETER
  The Dictionary of the Biological Sciences. Reinhold, 1967, 602, illus.
  ———, ED.
  The Encyclopedia of the Biological Sciences. 2nd ed. Van Nostrand-Reinhold, 1970, 1027, illus. (Reinhold Books in Biological Sciences.)

HANDLER, PHILIP, ED.
  Biology and the Future of Man. Oxford University Press, 1970, 936, illus.

HARDIN, GARRET J., COMP.
  39 Steps to Biology: Readings from Scientific American. W. H. Freeman, 1968, 344, 1 vol.

HENDERSON, I. F., and HENDERSON, W. D.
  A Dictionary of Biological Terms. 8th ed. Van Nostrand-Reinhold, 1963, 64.

JAEGER, EDMUND C.
  The Biologist's Handbook of Pronunciations. Thomas, 1960, 317, illus.
  ———.
  A Source-Book of Biological Names and Terms. 3rd ed. Thomas, 1966, 360, illus.

JOHNSON, CECIL E., ED.
  Human Biology: Contemporary Readings. Van Nostrand-Reinhold, 1970, 240.

KEETON, WILLIAM T.
  Biological Science. W. W. Norton, 1967, 955, illus.
  ———.
  Elements of Biological Science. W. W. Norton, 1969, 1 vol.

KORN, ROBERT W., and KORN, ELLEN J.
  Investigations Into Biology. Wiley, 1965, 402, illus.

LWOFF, ANDRE
  Biological Order. MIT Press, 1962, 101, illus. (Karl Taylor Compton Lectures, 1960.)

MACKEAN, DONALD G.
  The Arco Book of Biology: A Comprehensive Study Guide and Review of Biology for High School and College Students. Arco, 1967, 192, illus.

NASON, ALVIN
  Essentials of Modern Biology. Wiley, 1968, 508.
  ———.
  Textbook of Modern Biology. Wiley, 1965, 796, illus.

NATIONAL ACADEMY OF SCIENCES, NATIONAL RESEARCH COUNCIL (BIOLOGY AND AGRICULTURE DIVISION)
  Systematic Biology. NAS, 1969, 634. (Pub. No. 1692.)

SARNOFF, PAUL
  Careers in Biological Science. Messner, 1968, 192, illus.

SNELL, FRED M., et al.
  Biophysical Principles of Structure and Function. Addison-Wesley, 1965, 390, illus.

TELFER, WILLIAM H., and KENNEDY, D.
  Biology of Organisms. Wiley, 1965, 374.

WADDINGTON, CONRAD H.
  Biology for the Modern World. Barnes & Noble, 1963, 120.

WATSON, JAMES D.
  Molecular Biology of the Gene. W. A. Benjamin, 1965, 1 vol. (Biology Teaching Monograph Series.)

WHITE, EMIL H.
  Chemical Background for the Biological Sciences. Prentice-Hall, 1964, 152, illus. (Foundation of Modern Biology Series.)

WOODGER, JOSEPH H.
  Biological Principles. Humanities Press, 1967, 496.

CYTOLOGY

AFZELIUS, BJORN
  Anatomy of the Cell. University of Chicago Press, 1966, 127.

BAKER, J. R.
  Cytological Technique: The Principles Underlying Routine Methods. 5th ed. Methuen, London, 1966, 149, illus.

BOURNE, GEOFFREY H., ED.
  Cytology and Cell Physiology. 3rd ed. Academic Press, 1964, 780.

BROWN, WALTER V.
  Textbook of Cytology. Mosby, 1969, 1 vol.

GIESE, ARTHUR C.
  Cell Physiology. 3rd ed. Saunders, 1968, 671.

GOLDSTEIN, LESTER
  Cell Biology. W. C. Brown, 1966, 224. (Biology Readings Series.)

GRUNDMANN, E.
  General Cytology. Williams & Wilkins, 1966, 416, illus.

GUTHE, KARL F.
  The Physiology of Cells. Macmillan, 1968, 1 vol. (Current Concepts in Biology Series.)

SPRATT, NELSON T.
  Introduction to Cell Differentiation. Van Nostrand-Reinhold, 1964, 1 vol.

STERN, HERBERT, and NANNEY, DAVID L.
  The Biology of Cells. Wiley, 1965, 548, illus.

SWANSON, CARL P.
  The Cell. 3rd ed. Prentice-Hall, 1969, 150, illus. (Foundation of Modern Biology Series.)

TONER, P. G.
  Cell Structure. Williams & Wilkins, 1968, 1 vol.

UPJOHN COMPANY
  The Cell: A Scope Monograph on Cytology. Upjohn Co., Kalamazoo, Mich., 1965, 1 vol.

WASLEY, G. D., and MAY, J. W.
  Animal Cell Culture Methods. F. A. Davis, 1969, 176, illus.

WHITE, M. J. D.
  The Chromosomes. 5th ed. Methuen, London, 1961, 188.

HEALTH SERVICE PROGRAMS

HEMATOLOGY

ARCHER, R. K.
Hematological Techniques for Use on Animals. F. A. Davis, 1965, 144, illus.

DUNSFORD, IVOR, and BOWLEY, C. CHRISTOPHER
Techniques in Blood Grouping. 2nd ed. Thomas, 1967, 2 vols., illus.

FERGUSON, JOHN H.
Blood and Body Functions. F. A. Davis, 1965, 340.

HAYHOE, F. G. J., and FLEMANS, R. J.
An Atlas of Haematological Cytology. Wiley-Interscience, 1970, 320, illus.

HUHN, DIETER, and STICH, WALTHER
Fine Structure of Blood and Bone Marrow: An Introduction to Electron Microscopic Hematology. Hafner, 1969, 136, illus.

LEWIS, ALVIN E.
Principles of Hematology. Appleton-Century-Crofts, 1970, 388, illus.

LINMAN, JAMES W.
Principles of Hematology. Macmillan, 1966, 621, illus.

MAUER, ALVIN M.
Pediatric Hematology. McGraw-Hill, 1969, 486, illus.

MAUPIN, BERNARD
Blood Platelets in Man and Animals. Pergamon, 1969, 2 vols.

McDONALD, GEORGE A.
Atlas of Haematology. 2nd ed. Williams & Wilkins, 1968, 1 vol.

MIALE, JOHN B.
Laboratory Medicine Hematology. 3rd ed. Mosby, 1967, 1257, illus.

PLATT, WILLIAM R.
Color Atlas and Textbook of Hematology. Lippincott, 1969, 445.

RANGANATHAN, KILNAGER S.
Essentials of Blood Grouping and Clinical Applications. Grune & Stratton, 1967, 178.

ROBERTS, GEORGE F.
An Introduction to Human Blood Groups. Heinemann, London, 1960, 85.

SEIVERD, CHARLES E.
Hematology for Medical Technologists. 3rd ed., rev. Lea & Febiger, 1964, 643, illus.

SIMMONS, ARTHUR
Technical Hematology. Lippincott, 1968, 316, illus.

VROMAN, LEO
Blood. Natural History Press, 1967, 178, illus.

HISTOLOGY

AMERICAN REGISTRY OF PATHOLOGY
Manual of Histologic Staining Methods of the Armed Forces Institute of Pathology. 3rd ed. McGraw-Hill, 1968, 320, illus.

BEVELANDER, GERRIT
Essentials of Histology. 6th ed. Mosby, 1970, 328, illus.

BLOOM, WILLIAM
A Textbook of Histology. 8th ed. Saunders, 1962, 720, illus.

CARPENTER, ANNA-MARY
Human Histology: A Color Atlas. McGraw-Hill, Blakiston Division, 1968, 96, illus.

FALLIS, BRUCE D., and ASHWORTH, ROBERT D.
Textbook of Human Histology. Little, Brown, 1970, 244, illus.

FINERTY, JOHN C., and COWDRY, E. V.
A Textbook of Histology: Functional Significance of Cells and Intercellular Substances. 5th ed. Lea & Febiger, 1960, 573, illus.

FIORE, MARIANO S. H.
An Atlas of Human Histology. 2nd ed. Lea & Febiger, 1963, 224.

GATZ, ARTHUR J.
An Outline Manual for the Study of Histology. 4th ed. Burgess, 1966, 105.

HAM, ARTHUR W.
Histology. 6th ed. Lippincott, 1969, 1 vol.

HERRATH, ERNST VON
Atlas of Histology: Normal Microscopic Anatomy of Man. Hafner, 1966, 184.

LEESON, THOMAS S., and LEESON, C. ROLAND
Histology. 2nd ed. Saunders, 1970, 525.

PREECE, ANN
A Manual for Histologic Technicians. 2nd ed. Little, Brown, 1965, 287, illus.

STILES, KARL A.
Handbook of Histology. 5th ed. McGraw-Hill, Blakiston Division, 1968, 251, illus.

WINDLE, WILLIAM F.
Textbook of Histology. 4th ed. McGraw-Hill, 1969, 551, illus.

WISMAR, BETH L., and ACKERMAN, G. ADOLPH
A Visual Approach to Histology. F. A. Davis, 1970, 71.

LABORATORY ANIMALS

AMERICAN ASSOCIATION FOR LABORATORY ANIMAL SCIENCE
Manual for Laboratory Animal Technicians. AALAS, 1969, 216. (Pub. No. 67-3.)

CHIASSON, ROBERT B.
Laboratory Anatomy of the White Rat. 2nd ed. W. C. Brown, 1969, 1 vol.

GILBERT, STEPHEN G.
Pictorial Anatomy of the Fetal Pig. University of Washington Press, 1963, 45, illus.

MILLS, HARLAN
The Pig Manual: Photographed Dissection of the Fetal Pig. W. C. Brown, 1963, 60.

NATIONAL ACADEMY OF SCIENCES, NATIONAL RESEARCH COUNCIL (INSTITUTE OF LABORATORY ANIMAL RESOURCES)
Nonhuman Primates: Standards and Guidelines for the Breeding, Care, and Management of Laboratory Animals. NAS, 1968, 54. (Pub. No. 1677.)

———.
Rodents: Standards and Guidelines for the Breeding, Care, and Management of Laboratory Animals. NAS, 1969, 52. (SBN 309-01758-0.)

SHORT, DOUGLAS J., and WOODNOTT, DOROTHY P., EDS.
The Institute of Animal Technicians Manual of Laboratory Animal Practice and Techniques. 2nd ed. Thomas, 1969, 462, illus.

SIMMONS, M. L., and BRICK, J. O.
   The Laboratory Mouse: Selection and Management. Prentice-Hall, 1970, 184, illus. (Biological Techniques Series.)

SMITH, ESTHER M., and CALHOUN, MARY
   The Microscopic Anatomy of the White Rat: A Photographic Atlas. Iowa State University Press, 1968, 190, illus.

MICROBIOLOGY

ROBERT J. BRADY COMPANY, EDUCATION AND TRAINING SYSTEMS DIVISION
   Brady's Programmed Introduction to Microbiology. Lippincott, 1969, 174.

BROOKS, STEWART
   A Programmed Introduction to Microbiology. Mosby, 1968, 100, illus.

BURDON, KENNETH L.
   Microbiology. 6th ed. Macmillan, 1968, 818, illus.

BURROW, WILLIAM
   Textbook of Microbiology. 19th ed. Saunders, 1968, 974, illus.

CARPENTER, PHILIP L.
   Microbiology. 2nd ed. Saunders, 1967, 476, illus.

DAVIS, BERNARD D., et al.
   Microbiology: A Text Emphasizing Molecular and Genetic Aspects of Microbiology and Immunology.... Harper & Row, 1967, 1464, illus.

FROBISHER, MARTIN
   Fundamentals of Microbiology: An Introduction to the Microorganisms with Special Reference to the Procaryons. 8th ed. Saunders, 1968, 629, illus.

FROBISHER, MARTIN, SOMMERMEYER, LUCILLE, and FUERST, ROBERT
   Microbiology in Health and Disease. 12th ed. Saunders, 1969, 549, illus.

GEBHARDT, LOUIS P.
   Microbiology. 4th ed. Mosby, 1970, 364, illus.

HARRIGAN, W. F., and McCANCE, MARGARET E.
   Laboratory Methods in Microbiology. Academic Press, 1966, 362, illus.

LYLES, SANDERS T.
   Biology of Microorganisms. Mosby, 1969, 605, illus.

PEPPLER, HENRY J.
   Microbial Technology. Reinhold, 1967, 454, illus.

RUNKLE, ROBERT S., ED.
   Microbial Contamination Control Facilities. Van Nostrand-Reinhold, 1969, 198, illus.

SIROCKIN, G., and CULLIMORE, S.
   Practical Microbiology. McGraw-Hill, 1969, 159, illus.

SISTROM, W. R.
   Microbial Life. 2nd ed. Holt, Rinehart & Winston, 1969, 148.

SMITH, ALICE L.
   Principles of Microbiology. 6th ed. Mosby, 1969, 669, illus.

SWATEK, FRANK E.
   Textbook of Microbiology. Mosby, 1967, 721, illus.

UMBREIT, WAYNE W.
   Modern Microbiology. W. H. Freeman, 1962, 507, illus.

WEDBERG, STANLEY E.
   Introduction to Microbiology. Reinhold, 1966, 426, illus. (Reinhold Books in Biological Sciences.)

———.
   Paramedical Microbiology. Reinhold, 1963, 462, illus.

WHEELER, MARGARET F.
   Basic Microbiology. Lippincott, 1964, 389, illus.

WYSS, ORVILLE, WILLIAMS, O. B., and GARDNER, EARL W., JR.
   Elementary Microbiology. Wiley, 1963, 318.

ZINSSER, HANS, and SMITH, DAVID T.
   Microbiology. 14th ed. Appleton-Century-Crofts, 1968, 1281, illus.

PARASITOLOGY

BLACKLOCK, DONALD B., and SOUTHWELL, THOMAS
   A Guide to Human Parasitology for Medical Practitioners. 7th ed. Williams & Wilkins, 1961, 223, illus.

CHANDLER, ASA C., and READ, CLARK P.
   Introduction to Parasitology: With Special Reference to the Parasites of Man. 10th ed. Wiley, 1961, 822, illus.

JONES, ARTHUR W.
   Introduction to Parasitology. Addison-Wesley, 1967, 458.

NAJARIAN, HAIG H.
   Textbook of Medical Parasitology. Williams & Wilkins, 1967, 155, illus.

NOBLE, ELMER R., and NOBLE, GLENN A.
   Parasitology: The Biology of Animal Parasites. 2nd ed. Lea & Febiger, 1964, 724, illus.

READ, CLARK P.
   Parasitism and Symbiology: An Introductory Text. Ronald, 1970, 316, illus.

SPENCER, FRANCIS M., and MONROE, LEE S.
   The Color Atlas of Intestinal Parasites. Thomas, 1961, 142, illus.

NURSING

ABDELLAH, FAYE G., and LEVINE, EUGENE
   Better Patient Care Through Nursing Research. Macmillan, 1965, 736, illus.

ABDELLAH, FAYE G., et al.
   Patient-Centered Approaches to Nursing. Macmillan, 1960, 205.

ALEXANDER, EDYTHE, et al.
   Nursing Service Administration: Principles and Practice. Mosby, 1962, 270, illus.

ALLGIRE, MILDRED J.
   Nurses Can Give and Teach Rehabilitation: A Manual. 2nd ed. Springer, 1968, 93, illus.

ALTSCHUL, ANNIE
   Psychology for Nurses. 3rd ed. Baillière, Tindall & Cassell, London, 1970, 339, illus. (Nurses' Aid Series.)

AMERICAN ASSOCIATION FOR HEALTH, PHYSICAL EDUCATION, AND RECREATION
   New Dimensions in School Nursing Leadership. AAHPER, 1969, 104.

HEALTH SERVICE PROGRAMS

AMERICAN CANCER SOCIETY
    A Cancer Source Book for Nurses. Rev. ed. ACS, New York, 1963, 120, illus.

———.
    Essentials of Cancer Nursing: A Primer on Cancer for Nurses. ACS, New York, 1963, 125, illus.

AMERICAN NURSES' ASSOCIATION
    Improvement of Nursing Practice. ANA, 1961, 52.

ANDERSON, BERNICE E.
    Nursing Education in Community Junior Colleges. Lippincott, 1966, 319, illus.

ANDERSON, ELLEN
    Workbook of Solutions and Dosage of Drugs. 8th ed. Mosby, 1968, 189.

ANDERSON, MAJA C.
    Basic Nursing Techniques: A Programmed Introduction to Nursing Fundamentals. Saunders, 1968, 305.

———.
    Basic Patient Care: A Programmed Introduction to Nursing Fundamentals. Saunders, 1965, 234, illus.

ANDREOLI, KATHLEEN G., et al.
    Comprehensive Cardiac Care: A Handbook for Nurses and Other Paramedical Personnel. Kimpton, 1968, 153, illus.

ASPERHEIM, MARY K.
    The Pharmacologic Basis of Patient Care. Saunders, 1968, 450.

BARABAS, MARY H.
    Contemporary Head Nursing. Macmillan, 1962, 189, illus.

BARBATA, JEAN C., JENSEN, DEBORAH M., and PATTERSON, WILLIAM G.
    A Textbook of Medical-Surgical Nursing. Putnam, 1964, 1010, illus.

BARNES, ELIZABETH
    Psychosocial Nursing. Tavistock, 1968, 316, illus.

BARRETT, JEAN
    The Head Nurse. Appleton-Century-Crofts, 1962, 397, illus.

BAUER, ANNABEL B.
    An Experimental Inservice Program for Implementing Team Nursing. National League for Nursing, 1966, 69.

BECK, MARY E.
    Nutrition and Dietetics for Nurses. 2nd ed. Livingstone, Edinburgh, 1965, 232, illus.

BELAND, IRENE L.
    Clinical Nursing: Pathophysiological and Psychosocial Approaches. 2nd ed. Macmillan, 1970, 948, illus.

BERGERSEN, BETTY S., KRUG, ELSIE E., and GOTH, ANDRES
    Pharmacology in Nursing. 11th ed. Mosby, 1969, 695, illus.

BERGERSEN, BETTY S., et al., eds.
    Current Concepts in Clinical Nursing. Mosby, 1968-69, 2 vols.

BERMOSK, LORETTA S., and MORDAN, MARY J.
    Interviewing in Nursing. Macmillan, 1964, 187.

BERNARD, JESSIE S., and THOMPSON, LIDA F.
    Sociology Nurses and Their Patients in a Modern Society. 8th ed. Mosby, 1970, 314, illus.

BERNZWEIG, ELI P.
    Nurse's Liability for Malpractice: A Programmed Course. McGraw-Hill, 1969, 266, illus.

BEYERS, VIRGINIA
    Nursing Observation. W. C. Brown, 1968, 128.

BIDDLE, HARRY C., and FLOUTZ, VAUGHN W.
    Chemistry for Nurses: A Combined Text and Laboratory Manual. 6th ed. F. A. Davis, 1963, 371, illus.

BLUMBERG, JEANNE E., and DRUMMOND, ELEANOR E.
    Nursing Care of the Long-Term Patient. Springer, 1963, 134.

BLUME, DOROTHY M.
    Dosage and Solutions. F. A. Davis, 1969, 106, illus.

BOCOCK, E. JOAN
    Microbiology for Nurses. 3rd ed. Baillière, Tindall & Cassell, London, Williams & Wilkins, 1968, 197, illus. (Nurses' Aids Series.)

BOCOCK, E. JOAN, and HAINES, WHEELER R.
    Applied Anatomy for Nurses. 3rd ed. Williams & Wilkins, 1966, 338, illus.

BONNEY, VIRGINIA, and ROTHBERG, JUNE
    Nursing Diagnosis and Therapy. National League for Nursing, 1963, 100.

BORDICKS, KATHERINE J.
    Patterns of Shock: Implications for Nursing Care. Macmillan, 1965, 168, illus.

BOUCHARD, ROSEMARY E.
    Nursing Care of the Cancer Patient. Mosby, 1967, 297, illus.

BOWEN, ELEANOR P.
    Biology of Human Behavior: An Integration of Sciences Applied to Nursing. Appleton-Century-Crofts, 1968, 607, illus.

BRAUN, HAROLD A., and DIETTERT, GERALD A.
    Coronary Care Unit Nursing. 3rd ed. Western Montana Clinic Foundation, Missoula, Mont., 1968, 1 vol.

BROOME, W. E.
    An Introduction to Nursing Bacteriology. Appleton-Century-Crofts, 1969, 131, illus.

BROWN, ESTHER L.
    Newer Dimensions of Patient Care. Russell Sage Foundation, 1961-1965, 3 pts.

———.
    Nursing Reconsidered: A Study of Change. Lippincott, 1970- , vols.

BROWN, MARTHA M., and FOWLER, GRACE R.
    Psychodynamic Nursing: A Biosocial Orientation. 3rd ed. Saunders, 1966, 323.

BRUNNER, LILLIAN S., et al.
    Textbook of Medical-Surgical Nursing. 2nd ed. Lippincott, 1970, 1031, illus.

BULLOUGH, VERN L., and BULLOUGH, BONNIE
    The Emergence of Modern Nursing. 2nd ed. Macmillan, 1969, 277, illus.

BURRELL, ZEB L., and BURRELL, LENETTE O.
    Intensive Nursing Care. Mosby, 1969, 298, illus.

BURTON, GENEVIEVE
    Personal, Impersonal, and Interpersonal Relations: A Guide for Nurses. 2nd ed. Springer, 1964, 260.

BYERS, VIRGINIA E.
    Nursing Observations. W. C. Brown, 1968, 128. (Foundations of Nursing Series.)

CADY, LOUISE L.
    Nursing in Tuberculosis. 2nd ed. Saunders, 1961, 489, illus.

CANADIAN NURSES' ASSOCIATION LIBRARY
    Canadian Nurses' Association Index of Canadian Nursing Studies. CNA, 1969, 55.

CARDEW, EMILY C., ED.
Study Guide for Clinical Nursing: A Co-Ordinated Survey Integrated with Essentials of the Basic Sciences. 2nd ed. Lippincott, 1961, 557, illus.

CARLSON, CAROLYN E.
New Behavioral Concepts & Nursing Intervention. Lippincott, 1970, 341.

COFFIN, MARGARET A.
Nursing Observations of the Young Patient. W. C. Brown, 1970, 112. (Foundations of Nursing Series.)

COHN, HELEN, et al.
A Manual for Nurses in Family and Community Health. Little, Brown, 1969, 77.

COOPER, SIGNE S.
Contemporary Nursing Practice: A Guide for the Returning Nurse. McGraw-Hill, 1970, 348, illus.

COPPLESTONE, JOHN F.
Preventive Aspects of Occupational Health Nursing. Edward Arnold, London, 1967, 120, illus.

CRAYTOR, JOSEPHINE K., and FASS, MARGOT L.
The Nurse and the Cancer Patient. Lippincott, 1970, 260.

CREIGHTON, HELEN
Law Every Nurse Should Know. 2nd ed. Saunders, 1970, 246.

CROW, LESTER D., and CROW, ALICE
Understanding Interrelations in Nursing. Macmillan, 1961, 461, illus.

CRUZE, WENDELL W.
Psychology in Nursing. 2nd ed. McGraw-Hill, Blakiston Division, 1960, 536, illus.

CULVER, VIVIAN M.
Modern Bedside Nursing. 7th ed. Saunders, 1969, 841, illus.

CUMULATIVE INDEX TO NURSING LITERATURE
Glendale Sanitarium & Hospital Publications Service, Glendale, Calif., 1956- , Vol. 1- , annual.

CUNNINGHAM, LYDA S., ED.
Basic Medical-Surgical Nursing: A Book of Readings. W. C. Brown, 1966, 232, illus. (Nursing Readings Series.)

DARWIN, JOAN, and MARKHAM, JOAN
Eye, Nose, Throat and Ear Nursing: An Introduction. Heinemann, 1966, 127, illus.

DAVIS, FRED
The Nursing Profession: Five Sociological Essays. Wiley, 1966, 203, illus.

DEELEY, T. J.
A Guide to Radiotherapy Nursing. Williams & Wilkins, 1970, 104, illus.

DENNIS, LORRAINE
Dennis' Psychology of Human Behavior for Nurses. 3rd ed. Saunders, 1967, 289.

DeYOUNG, LILLIAN
The Foundations of Nursing as Conceived, Learned, and Practiced in Professional Nursing. Mosby, 1966, 279, illus.

DIETZ, LENA D., and LEHOZKY, AURELIA R.
History and Modern Nursing. 2nd ed. F. A. Davis, 1967, 381, illus.

DISON, NORMA G.
An Atlas of Nursing Techniques. Mosby, 1967, 258, illus.

DOLAN, JOSEPHINE A.
Goodnow's History of Nursing. 12th ed. Saunders, 1968, 380.

DOUGLASS, LAURA M., and BEVIS, E. O.
Team Leadership in Action: Principles and Applications to Staff Nursing Situations. Mosby, 1970, 139.

DRYDEN, M. VIRGINIA, COMP.
Nursing Trends: A Book of Readings. W. C. Brown, 1968, 327. (Nursing Readings Series.)

DUNCAN, HELEN A., ED.
Duncan's Dictionary for Nurses. Springer, 1970, 400, illus.

DUNN, HELEN W., and MORGAN, ELIZABETH M.
The Nursing Audit. National League for Nursing, 1968, 44.

EVANS, FRANCES M.
The Role of the Nurse in Community Mental Health. Macmillan, 1968, 227.

FALCONER, MARY W., et al.
The Drug, the Nurse, the Patient. 4th ed. Saunders, 1970, 566, illus.

FIELO, SANDRA B., and EDGE, SYLVIA C.
Technical Nursing of the Adult: Medical Surgical, and Psychiatric Approaches. Macmillan, 1970, 576, illus.

FISCHER, VALENTINA G., and CONNOLLY, ARLENE F.
Promotion of Physical Comfort and Safety. W. C. Brown, 1970, 94, illus. (Foundations of Nursing Series.)

FIVARS, GRACE, and GOSNELL, DORIS
Nursing Evaluation: The Problem and the Process—The Critical Incident Technique. Macmillan, 1966, 228, illus.

FLITTER, HESSEL H.
An Introduction to Physics in Nursing. 5th ed. Mosby, 1967, 239, illus.

FOLTA, JEANNETTE R., and DECK, EDITH S.
A Sociological Framework for Patient Care. Wiley, 1964, 418.

FOREST, BETTY L.
Utilization of Associate Degree Nursing Graduates in General Hospitals. National League for Nursing, 1968, 80.

FOX, DAVID J.
Fundamentals of Research in Nursing. 2nd ed. Appleton-Century-Crofts, 1970, 323, illus.

FRANCIS, GLORIA, and MANJAS, BARBARA
Promoting Psychological Comfort. W. C. Brown, 1968, 105.

FREAM, WILLIAM C.
Applied Human Biology for Nurses. Williams & Wilkins, 1964, 408, illus.

FREEMAN, RUTH B.
Community Health Nursing Practice. Saunders, 1970, 500, illus.

FRENCH, RUTH M.
Nurse's Guide to Diagnostic Procedures. 2nd ed. McGraw-Hill, Blakiston Division, 1967, 313, illus.

FUERST, ELINOR V., and WOLFF, LuVERNE
Fundamentals of Nursing. 4th ed. Lippincott, 1969, 446, illus.

———.
Teaching Fundamentals of Nursing. 4th ed. Lippincott, 1963, 159, illus.

GARLAND, PHYLLIS
Ophthalmic Nursing. 5th ed. Faber & Faber, 1966, 208, illus.

GEITGEY, DORIS A.
A Handbook for Head Nurses. F. A. Davis, 1962, 143.

HEALTH SERVICE PROGRAMS

GEITGEY, DORIS A.
A Study of Some Effects of Sensitivity Training on the Performance of Students in Associate Degree Programs of Nursing Education. National League for Nursing, 1968, 183.

GIBSON, JOHN
The Nurse's Materia Medica. 2nd ed. F. A. Davis, 1970, 1 vol.

———.
Psychiatry for Nurses. 2nd ed. F. A. Davis, 1965, 156.

GILLIES, DEE A., and ALYN, IRENE B.
Saunders' Tests for Self-Evaluation of Nursing Competence. Saunders, 1969, 282.

GOLDMAN, MYER
A Nurse's Guide to the X-Ray Department. Livingstone, Edinburgh, 1967, 82, illus.

GORTON, JOHN V.
Behavioral Components of Patient Care. Macmillan, 1970, 241, illus.

GOVONI, LAURA E., et al.
Drugs and Nursing Implications. Appleton-Century-Crofts, 1965, 313.

GRAGG, SHIRLEY H., and REES, OLIVE M.
Scientific Principles in Nursing. 6th ed. Mosby, 1970, 424, illus.

GRIFFIN, GERALD J., KINSINGER, ROBERT E., and PITMAN, AVIS J.
Clinical Nursing Instruction by Television: A Report on a Two-Year Experiment Using Closed-Circuit Television to Teach Clinical Nursing. Teachers College Press, 1965, 79, illus. (Nursing Education Monographs.)

GUINÉE, KATHLEEN K.
The Aims and Methods of Nursing Education. Macmillan, 1966, 261, illus.

———.
The Professional Nurse: Orientation, Roles and Responsibilities. Macmillan, 1970, 177.

HALSTEAD, HELEN L., et al.
Contemporary Studies in Medical-Surgical Nursing. F. A. Davis, 1967, 312, illus.

HAMMAR, S. L., and EDDY, JO A.
Nursing Care of the Adolescent. Springer, 1966, 232.

HARDMAN, ELIZABETH
An Introduction to Ward Management. Blackwell Scientific (F. A. Davis, dist.), 1970, 195.

HARRIS, CATHERINE F.
Handbook of Dietetics for Nurses. 2nd ed. Baillière, Tindall & Cox, London, 1963, 232, illus. (Baillière's Handbooks for Nurses.)

HAVENER, WILLIAM H., SAUNDERS, WILLIAM H., and BERGERSEN, BETTY S.
Nursing Care in Eye, Ear, Nose and Throat Disorders. 2nd ed. Mosby, 1968, 402, illus.

HAYES, WAYLAND J., and GAZAWAY, RENA
Human Relations in Nursing: A Textbook in Sociology. 3rd ed. Saunders, 1964, 418, illus.

HAYES, EDWARD J., HAYES, PAUL J., and KELLY, DOROTHY E.
Moral Principles of Nursing. Macmillan, 1964, 257, illus.

HAYS, JOYCE S., and LARSON, KENNETH H.
Interacting with Patients. Macmillan, 1963, 282.

HECKEL, ROBERT V., and JORDAN, ROSE M.
Psychology: The Nurse and the Patient. 2nd ed. Mosby, 1967, 344, illus.

HEIDGERKEN, LORETTA E.
Teaching and Learning in Schools of Nursing: Principles and Methods. 3rd ed. Lippincott, 1965, 685, illus.

HENDERSON, VIRGINIA
The Nature of Nursing: A Definition and Its Implications for Practice, Research, and Education. Macmillan, 1966, 84, illus.

HOFFMAN, CLAIRE P., LIPKIN, GLADYS B., and THOMPSON, ELLA M.
Simplified Nursing. 8th ed. Lippincott, 1968, 692, illus.

HOFLING, CHARLES K., LEININGER, MADELEINE M., and BREGG, ELIZABETH
Basic Psychiatric Concepts in Nursing. 2nd ed. Lippincott, 1967, 583, illus.

HOLDSWORTH, VIVIAN E.
Fundamentals of Bedside Nursing. Macmillan, 1968, 110, illus.

HORNEMANN, GRACE V.
Basic Nursing Procedures. Delmar, 1966-68, 2 vols., illus.

HULL, EDGAR, and PERRODIN, CECILIA
Medical Nursing. 6th ed. F. A. Davis, 1960, 798, illus.

INNIS, MARY Q., ED.
Nursing Education in a Changing Society. University of Toronto Press, 1970, 232.

JAMIESON, ELIZABETH M., SEWALL, MARY F., and SUHRIE, ELEANOR B.
Trends in Nursing History: Their Social, International, and Ethical Relationships. 6th ed. Saunders, 1966, 440, illus.

JENSEN, DEBORAH M.
Jensen's History and Trends of Professional Nursing. 6th ed. Mosby, 1969, 339, illus.

JENSEN, DEBORAH M., and TERRY, FLORENCE J.
Principles and Technics of Rehabilitation Nursing. 2nd ed. Mosby, 1961, 344, illus.

JOEL, ALMA L., et al.
Workbook and Study Guide for Medical-Surgical Nursing: A Patient-Centered Approach. 2nd ed. Mosby, 1969, 319.

JOHNSON, MAE M., DAVIS, MARY LOU C., and BILITCH, MARY J.
Problem-Solving in Nursing Practice. W. C. Brown, 1970, 102, illus. (Foundations of Nursing Series.)

JOHNSON, MARGARET A.
Developing the Art of Understanding: A Guide for Nursing Students. Springer, 1967, 230.

JOHNSTON, DOROTHY F.
Essentials of Communicable Disease: With Nursing Principles. Mosby, 1968, 400, illus.

———.
Total Patient Care: Foundations and Practice. 2nd ed. Mosby, 1968, 526, illus.

KEANE, CLAIRE B., and FLETCHER, SYBIL M.
Drugs and Solutions: A Programed Introduction for Nurses. 2nd ed. Saunders, 1970, 180, illus.

KELLY, CORDELIA W.
Dimensions of Professional Nursing. 2nd ed. Macmillan, 1968, 494, illus.

KEMPF, FLORENCE C., and USEEM, RUTH H.
Psychology: Dynamics of Behavior in Nursing. Saunders, 1964, 220.

KERNICKI, JEANETTE, BULLOCK, BARBARA, and MATTHEWS, JOAN
Cardiovascular Nursing. Putnam, 1970, 1 vol.

KOZIER, BARBARA B., and DU GAS, BEVERLY W.
Fundamentals of Patient Care: A Comprehensive Approach to Nursing. Saunders, 1967, 386, illus.

KRIEGEL, JULIA
The Head Nurse: Thoughts and Decisions. Macmillan, 1968, 197, illus.

KRON, THORA
Communication in Nursing. Saunders, 1967, 244.

———.
Nursing Team Leadership. 2nd ed. Saunders, 1966, 172, illus.

KRUEGER, ELIZABETH A.
The Hypodermic Injection: A Programed Unit. Teachers College Press, 1966, 225, illus. (Nursing Education Monographs.)

LEAKE, MARY J.
A Manual of Simple Nursing Procedures. 4th ed. Saunders, 1966, 192, illus.

LESNIK, MILTON J., and ANDERSON, BERNICE E.
Nursing Practice and the Law. 2nd ed. Lippincott, 1962, 400.

LEVINE, MYRA E.
Introduction to Clinical Nursing. F. A. Davis, 1969, 468, illus.

LEWIS, GARLAND K.
Nurse-Patient Communication. W. C. Brown, 1969, 93. (Foundations of Nursing Series.)

LITTLE, DOLORES E., and CARNEVALI, DORIS L.
Nursing Care Planning. Lippincott, 1969, 245.

LOCKERBY, FLORENCE K.
Communication for Nurses. 3rd ed. Mosby, 1968, 120, illus.

MacBRYDE, CYRIL
Signs and Symptoms. Lippincott, 1964, 971.

MacDONALD, GWENDOLINE
Development of Standards and Accreditation in Collegiate Nursing Education. Teachers College Press, 1965, 184. (Nursing Education Monographs.)

MacGREGOR, FRANCES M.
Social Science in Nursing: Applications for the Improvement of Patient Care. Russell Sage Foundation, 1960, 354, illus.

MAEGRAITH, B. G., and GILLES H. M.
Adams and Maegraith: Tropical Medicine for Nurses. 3rd ed. F. A. Davis, 1970, 326.

MAHONEY, ROBERT F.
Emergency and Disaster Nursing. 2nd ed. Macmillan, 1969, 269, illus.

MALONEY, ELIZABETH
Interpersonal Relations. W. C. Brown, 1966, 107. (Nursing Readings Series.)

MASON, MILDRED A.
Basic Medical-Surgical Nursing. 2nd ed. Macmillan, 1967, 508, illus.

MATHENEY, RUTH V., et al.
Fundamentals of Patient-Centered Nursing. 2nd ed. Mosby, 1968, 291, illus.

McDONNELL, VIRGINIA B.
Your Future in Nursing. R. Rosen Press, 1963, 157. (Careers in Depth No. 30.)

McGHIE, ANDREW
Psychology: As Applied to Nursing. 5th ed. Williams & Wilkins, 1970, 344, illus.

McKENNA, FRANCES M.
Thresholds to Professional Nursing Practice. 2nd ed. Saunders 1960, 428, illus.

McNAUGHT, ANN B., and CALLANDER, R.
Nurse's Illustrated Physiology. Williams & Wilkins, 1964, 160.

MEHTA, HIMATLAL R.
Pharmacy for Nurses. 3rd ed. Delta, Boulder, Colo., 1962, 352, illus.

MELTZER, LAWRENCE E., et al.
Concepts and Practices of Intensive Care for Nurse Specialists. Charles Press, Philadelphia, 1969, 469, illus.

MERCER, LIANNE S., and O'CONNOR PATRICIA
Fundamental Skills in the Nurse-Patient Relationship: A Programmed Text. Saunders, 1969, 192, illus.

METHENY, NORMA M., and SNIVELY, WILLIAM D.
Nurses' Handbook of Fluid Balance. Lippincott, 1967, 279, illus.

MILLER, CAROL L.
Nurses and the Law. Interstate, 1970, 232.

MILLER, DULCY B.
The Extended Care Facility: A Guide to Organization and Operation. McGraw-Hill, 1969, 1 vol.

MODELL, WALTER, et al.
Handbook of Cardiology for Nurses: Heart Disease and Its Treatment—The Patient and His Nursing Care. 5th ed. Springer, 1966, 323, illus.

MOOTH, ADELMA E., and RITVO, MIRIAM M.
Developing the Supervisory Skills of the Nurse: A Behavioral Science Approach. Macmillan, 1966, 107.

MORISON, LUELLA J.
Steppingstones to Professional Nursing: Text and Workbook for Student Nurses. 4th ed. Mosby, 1965, 462, illus.

MORISON, LUELLA J., and FARRIS, MARY A.
Approaches for Co-Workers in Professional Nursing. Mosby, 1962, 243, illus.

MOSBY'S COMPREHENSIVE REVIEW OF NURSING
7th ed. Mosby, 1969, 590, illus.

MOWRY, LILLIAN, and WILLIAMS, SUE R.
Basic Nutrition and Diet Therapy for Nurses. 4th ed. Mosby, 1969, 226.

MURCHISON, IRENE A., and NICHOLS, THOMAS S.
Legal Foundations of Nursing Practice. Macmillan, 1970, 529.

NAST, MINNETTE
Simplified Drugs and Solutions for Nurses: Including Arithmetic. 4th ed. Mosby, 1968, 86, illus.

NATIONAL COMMISSION FOR THE STUDY OF NURSING AND NURSING EDUCATION
An Abstract for Action. Jerome P. Lysaught, ed. McGraw-Hill, 1970, 167, illus.

NATIONAL LEAGUE FOR NURSING
Action for Quality: Eleven Papers and a Summary of Presentations at Boston Conference of NLN Council of Associate Degree Programs. NLN, 1968, 68.

———.
A National Survey of Associate Degree Nursing Programs, 1967. NLN, 1969, 140.

———.
Associate Degree Education for Nursing. NLN, 1970, 27. (Pub. No. 23-1309.)

———.
Rehabilitative Aspects of Nursing: A Programmed Instruction Series. NLN, 1966, 2 vols., illus.

HEALTH SERVICE PROGRAMS

NEWCOMB, DOROTHY P.
The Team Plan. 2nd ed. Putnam, 1963, 94.

NORDMARK, MADELYN T., and ROHWEDER, ANNE W.
Scientific Foundations of Nursing. 2nd ed. Lippincott, 1967, 388.

NORRIS, WALTER, and CAMPBELL, DONALD A.
Nurse's Guide to Anesthetics, Resuscitation and Intensive Care. 4th ed. Williams & Wilkins, 1969, 172, illus.

THE NURSING CLINICS OF NORTH AMERICA
Saunders Quarterly. NCNA, 1970- .

NURSING EXAMINATION REVIEW BOOK
Medical Examination Publishing Co., Flushing, N.Y., 1964-66, 7 vols.

O'HARA, FRANK J., and REITH, HERMAN R.
Psychology and the Nurse. 6th ed. Saunders, 1966, 383, illus.

OLSON, LYLA M.
A Nurses' Handbook for Hospital, School and Home. 10th ed. Saunders, 1960, 548, illus.

ORLANDO, IDA J.
The Dynamic Nurse-Patient Relationship: Function, Process, and Principles. Putnam, 1961, 91.

PELLEY, THELMA
Nursing: Its History, Trends, Philosophy, Ethics and Ethos. Saunders, 1964, 238, illus.

PESZNECKER, BETTY L., and HEWITT, HELON E.
Psychiatric Content in the Nursing Curriculum: A Study of Integration Process. University of Washington Press, 1963, 134.

PETERSON, GRACE G.
Working With Others for Patient Care. W. C. Brown, 1968, 148. (Foundations of Nursing Series.)

PHILLIPS, JEANNE S., and THOMPSON, RICHARD F.
Statistics for Nurses: The Evaluation of Quantitative Information. Macmillan, 1967, 550, illus.

PIGORS, PAUL J., PIGORS, FAITH, and TRIBOU, MARITA
Professional Nursing Practice: Cases and Issues. McGraw-Hill, 1967, 537.

PILLEPICH, MARY K.
Development of General Education in Collegiate Nursing Programs: Role of the Administrator. Teachers College Press, 1962, 86, illus. (Nursing Education Monographs No. 2.)

POHL, MARGARET L.
Teaching Functions of the Nursing Practitioner. W. C. Brown, 1968, 136.

PRICE, ALICE L.
The Art, Science, and Spirit of Nursing. 3rd ed. Saunders, 1965, 579, illus.

PRICE, ELMINA M.
Learning Needs of Registered Nurses. Teachers College Press, 1967, 111. (Nursing Education Monographs.)

PSATHAS, GEORGE
The Student Nurse in the Diploma School of Nursing. Springer, 1968, 207, illus.

QUINT, JEANNE C.
The Nurse and the Dying Patient. Macmillan, 1967, 307.

RATNER, MURIEL
Study Guide to Medical and Surgical Nursing. F. A. Davis, 1961, 324.

RAYNER, CLAIRE
Essentials of Outpatient Nursing. Arlington Books, London, 1967, 161, illus.

REDMAN, BARBARA K.
The Process of Patient Teaching in Nursing. Mosby, 1968, 140, illus.

RESOURCE PUBLICATIONS
Index of Opportunity in Nursing. Resource Publications, Princeton, N.J., 1969, 92. (Career Resource Series.)

RIDDLE, JANET T. E.
Elementary Textbook of Anatomy and Physiology: Applied to Nursing. 3rd ed. Williams & Wilkins, 1969, 155, illus.

RIEHL, CARMELLA L.
Emergency Nursing. Bennett, 1970, 286, illus.

RINEHART, ELMA L.
Management of Nursing Care. Macmillan, 1969, 243, illus.

RINES, ALICE R.
Evaluating Student Progress in Learning the Practice of Nursing. Teachers College Press, 1963, 76. (Nursing Education Monographs No. 5.)

ROBINSON, LISA
Psychological Aspects of the Care of Hospitalized Patients. F. A. Davis, 1968, 83.

RODMAN, MORTON J., and SMITH, DOROTHY W.
Pharmacology and Drug Therapy in Nursing. Lippincott, 1968, 738, illus.

ROGERS, MARTHA E.
Educational Revolution in Nursing. Macmillan, 1961, 65.

———.
An Introduction to the Theoretical Basis of Nursing. F. A. Davis, 1970, 144, illus. (Nursing Science Series No. 1.)

———.
Reveille in Nursing. Davis, 1964, 97.

ROSS, AILEEN D.
Becoming a Nurse. Macmillan, 1961, 420.

SACKHEIM, GEORGE I.
Practical Physics for Nurses. 2nd ed. Saunders, 1962, 220.

SANNER, MARGARET C.
Trends and Professional Adjustments in Nursing. Saunders, 1962, 384, illus.

SARNER, HARVEY
The Nurse and the Law. Saunders, 1968, 219.

SAXTON, DOLORES F., and WALTER, JOHN F.
Programmed Instruction in Arithmetic, Dosages, and Solutions. 2nd ed. Mosby, 1970, 60, illus.

SCHMIDT, MILDRED S.
Factors Affecting the Establishment of Associate Degree Nursing Programs in Community Junior Colleges. National League for Nursing, 1966, 120.

SCHOENBERG, BERNARD, PETTIT, HELEN F., and CARR, ARTHUR C., EDS.
Teaching Psychosocial Aspects of Patient Care. Columbia University Press, 1968, 420.

SCHULZ, ESTHER D., and RUDICK, ELEANOR, EDS.
Nursing in Ambulatory Units: A Book of Readings. W. C. Brown, 1966, 100. (Nursing Reading Series.)

SEARS, WILLIAM G.
Anatomy and Physiology for Nurses and Students of Human Biology. 4th ed. Edward Arnold, London, 1965, 373, illus.

———.
Medicine for Nurses. 10th ed. Edward Arnold, London, 1966, 549, illus.

SECOR, JANE
Patient Studies in Medical-Surgical Nursing. Lippincott, 1967, 401.

SEEDOR, MARIE M.
Aids to Diagnosis: A Programmed Unit in Fundamentals of Nursing. Columbia University Press, 1964, 335.

———.
Introduction to Asepsis: A Programmed Unit in Fundamentals of Nursing. 2nd ed. Teachers College Press, 1970, 274, illus. (Nursing Education Monographs No. 3.)

———.
Programed Instruction for Nursing in the Community College. Teachers College Press, 1963, 117, illus. (Nursing Education Monographs No. 4.)

SELLEW, GLADYS
Sociology and Its Use in Nursing Service. 5th ed. Saunders, 1962, 450, illus.

SHAFER, KATHLEEN N., et al.
Medical-Surgical Nursing. 4th ed. Mosby, 1967, 1009, illus.

SHANKS, MARY D., and KENNEDY, DOROTHY A.
The Theory and Practice of Nursing Service Administration. McGraw-Hill, 1965, 303.

SKELLEY, ESTHER G.
Medications for the Nurse. Delmar, 1967, 152, illus.

SKIPPER, JAMES K., and LEONARD, ROBERT C., ED.
Social Interaction and Patient Care. Lippincott, 1965, 399, illus.

SMELTZER, CLARENCE H.
The Interview in Student Nurse Selection. Putnam, 1968, 185, illus.

SMITH, DOROTHY W., and GIPS, CLAUDIA D.
Care of the Adult Patient: Medical-Surgical Nursing. 2nd ed. Lippincott, 1966, 1206, illus.

SMITH, GENEVIEVE W.
Care of the Patient with a Stroke. 2nd ed. Springer, 1967, 160.

SPALDING, EUGENIA K., and NOTTER, LUCILLE E.
Professional Nursing: Foundations, Perspectives and Relationships. 8th ed. Lippincott, 677, illus.

SPRINGER, ERIC W., ED.
Nursing and the Law. Aspen Systems, Pittsburgh, 1970, 188.

SQUIRE, JESSIE E.
Basic Pharmacology for Nurses. 4th ed. Mosby, 1969, 329, illus.

STAUPERS, MABEL K.
No Time for Prejudice: A Story of the Integration of Negroes in Nursing in the United States. Macmillan, 1961, 206, illus.

STEWART, ISABEL M., and AUSTIN, ANNE L., EDS.
History of Nursing. 5th ed. Putnam, 1962, 528.

STORLIE, FRANCES, RAMBOUSEK, ELIZABETH, and SHANNON, EUTHA
Principles of Intensive Nursing Care. Appleton, 1969, 273, illus.

STRAUB, K. MARY, and PARKER, KITTY S., EDS.
Continuity of Patient Care: The Role of Nursing. Catholic University of America Press, 1966, 232, illus.

SUTTON, AUDREY L.
Bedside Nursing Techniques in Medicine and Surgery. 2nd ed. Saunders, 1969, 398, illus.

SWANSBURG, RUSSELL C.
Inservice Education. Putnam, 1968, 340.

———.
Team Nursing: A Programmed Learning Experience. Putnam, 1968, 4 units, illus.

THOMPSON, ELLA M., and MURPHY, CONSTANCE
Textbook of Basic Nursing. 8th ed. Lippincott, 1966, 752, illus.

TOOHEY, MONTY
Medicine for Nurses: With a Chapter on Psychological Medicine. 9th ed. Williams & Wilkins, 1970, 706, illus.

TOWNSEND, CAROLYNN E.
Nutrition and Diet Modifications for the Nurse. Delmar, 1966, 202, illus.

TRAVELBEE, JOYCE
Interpersonal Aspects of Nursing. F. A. Davis, 1966, 235.

TURK, HERMAN, and INGLES, THELMA
Clinic Nursing: Explorations in Role Innovation. F. A. Davis, 1963, 192, illus.

TURNER, DAVID R.
...Nurse: Registered, Practical, Student and Public Health Nurse. 4th ed. Arco, 1970, 384, illus. (Civil Service Test Tutor.)

UJHELY, GERTRUD B.
Determinants of the Nurse-Patient Relationship. Springer, 1968, 271.

———.
The Nurse and Her Problem Patients. Springer, 1963, 180.

U.S. PUBLIC HEALTH SERVICE, NURSING DIVISION
How to Study Nursing Activities in a Patient Unit. Rev. ed. USGPO, 1964, 142, illus. (PHS. Pub. No. 370.)

VAUGHAN, LOUISE M.
Attitudes of Nursing Students Toward Direct Patient Care. Catholic University of America Press, 1964, 196.

WALKER, VIRGINIA H.
Nursing and Ritualistic Practice. Macmillan, 1967, 196.

WENSLEY, EDITH
Nursing Service Without Walls. National League for Nursing, 1963, 64.

WHITE, DOROTHY T.
Abilities Needed by Teachers of Nursing in Community Colleges. National League for Nursing, 1961, 56. (League Exchange No. 56.)

WIEDENBACH, ERNESTINE
Clinical Nursing: A Helping Art. Springer, 1964, 118, illus.

WILLIG, SIDNEY H.
The Nurse's Guide to the Law. McGraw-Hill, 1970, 264, illus.

WILSON, MARION E., and MIZER, HELEN E.
Microbiology in Nursing Practice. Macmillan, 1969, 701, illus.

WINNER, H. I.
Microbiology in Modern Nursing. English Universities Press, London, 1969, 1 vol.

WISTREICH, GEORGE A., and LECHTMAN, MAX D.
Microbiology for Nurses: A Laboratory Manual. McCutchan, 1967, 174, illus.

WOOLRIDGE, POWHATAN J., SKIPPER, JAMES K., and LEONARD, ROBERT C.
Behavioral Science, Social Practice, and the Nursing Profession. Case Western Reserve University Press, 1968, 108.

WORLEY, ELOISE
Pharmacology and Medications for Vocational Nurses. F. A. Davis, 1967, 191, illus.

HEALTH SERVICE PROGRAMS

THE YEARBOOK OF MODERN NURSING: A SOURCE BOOK OF NURSING
Putnam, 1956- , Vol. 1-

YOUNG, HELEN, and LEE, ELEANOR
Lippincott's Quick Reference Book for Nurses. 8th ed. Lippincott, 1962, 800, illus.

ZEITZ, ANN N., et al.
Associate Degree Nursing: A Guide to Program and Curriculum Development. Mosby, 1969, 207, illus.

GERIATRIC

ADAMS, GEORGE F., and McILLWRAITH, P. L.
Geriatric Nursing: A Study of the Work of Geriatric Ward Staff. Oxford University Press, 1963, 77.

HIRSCHBERG, GERALD G., LEWIS, LEON, and THOMAS, DOROTHY
Rehabilitation: A Manual for the Care of the Disabled and Elderly. Lippincott, 1964, 377, illus.

HODKINSON, MARY A.
Nursing the Elderly. Pergamon, 1966, 154, illus. (Commonwealth and International Library, Nursing Studies Division.)

NEWTON, KATHLEEN, and ANDERSON, HELEN C.
Geriatric Nursing. 4th ed. Mosby, 1966, 390, illus.

RUDD, THOMAS N.
The Nursing of the Elderly Sick: A Practical Handbook of Geriatric Nursing. 5th ed. Faber & Faber, 1966, 140.

GYNECOLOGIC

BREWER, JOHN I., MOLBO, DORIS M., and GERBIE, ALBERT B.
Gynecologic Nursing: A Textbook Concerning Nursing Through an Understanding of the Patients Themselves and Their Gynecologic Problems. Mosby, 1966, 171, illus.

FITZPATRICK, GENEVIEVE M.
Gynecologic Nursing. Macmillan, 1965, 242, illus.

MILLER, NORMAN F., and AVERY, HAZEL
Gynecology and Gynecologic Nursing. 5th ed. Saunders, 1965, 440, illus.

NEUROLOGICAL AND NEUROSURGICAL

CARINI, ESTA, and OWENS, GUY
Neurological and Neurosurgical Nursing. 5th ed. Mosby, 1970, 386, illus.

DE GUTIERREZ-MAHONEY, CARLOS G., and CARINI, ESTA
Neurological and Neurosurgical Nursing. 4th ed. Mosby, 1965, 449, illus.

HOOPER, REGINALD
Neurosurgical Nursing. Thomas, 1964, 248, illus.

JACOBS, ERWIN M., and DeNAULT, PHYLLIS M.
Neurology for Nurses: Including Nursing Technics in Neurology. Thomas, 1964, 208, illus.

SCOTT, DONALD F., and DODD, BARBARA
Neurological and Neurosurgical Nursing: An Introduction. Pergamon Press, 1966, 204, illus. (Commonwealth and International Library, Nursing Studies Division.)

NURSES' AIDES

ABDALLAH, MARY C.
Nurse's Aide Study Manual. 2nd ed. Saunders, 1970, 1 vol., illus.

AMERICAN HOSPITAL ASSOCIATION
Being a Nursing Aide: Student Manual. AHA, 1969, 450.

———.
Training the Nursing Aide: Instructor's Guide. AHA, 1969, 256.

CHERESCAVICH, GERTRUDE D.
A Textbook for Nursing Assistants. 2nd ed. Mosby, 1968, 439, illus.

DONOVAN, JOAN E., BELSJOE, EDITH H., and DILLON, DANIEL C.
The Nurse Aide. McGraw-Hill, 1968, 424, illus.

HAUGHTON, MARJORIE, and PARNELL, J. E.
Practical Procedures. Williams & Wilkins, 1969, 149. (Nurses' Aids Series.)

ISLER, CHARLOTTE
The Nurses' Aide in the Hospital. Springer, 1968, 146, illus.

KNOEDLER, EVELYN L.
Manual for the Nurse's Aide. Delmar, 1968, 101, illus.

MICHIGAN LEAGUE FOR NURSING
Guide for Developing a Pre-Employment Training Program for Nurses' Aides. MLN, Detroit, 1968, 40. (ERIC ED 029 102.)

OBSTETRICAL AND MATERNITY

ANDERSON, BARBARA G.
Obstetrics for the Nurse. Delmar, 1966, 167, illus.

BETHEA, DORIS C.
Introductory Maternity Nursing. Lippincott, 1968, 223, illus.

BLEIER, INGE J.
Maternity Nursing: A Textbook for Practical Nurses. 2nd ed. Saunders, 1966, 202, illus.

BOOKMILLER, MAE M., BOWEN, GEORGE L., and CARPENTER, DOLORES
Textbook of Obstetrics and Obstetric Nursing. 5th ed. Saunders, 1967, 574, illus.

BRYANT, RICHARD D., and OVERLAND, ANNA E.
Woodward and Gardner's Obstetric Management and Nursing. 7th ed. F. A. Davis, 1964, 798, illus.

BURNETT, CLIFFORD W.
A Textbook of Obstetric Nursing. Blackwell Scientific, 1964, 257, illus.

DAVIS, MORRIS E., and RUBIN, REVA
De Lee's Obstetrics for Nurses. 18th ed. Saunders, 1966, 535, illus.

FITZPATRICK, ELISE, EASTMAN, NICHOLSON J., and REEDER, SHARON R.
Maternity Nursing. 11th ed. Lippincott, 1966, 638, illus.

GEDDES, AUBREY K.
Premature Babies: Their Nursing Care and Management. Saunders, 1960, 215, illus.

HAMILTON, PERSIS M.
Basic Maternity Nursing. Mosby, 1967, 300, illus.

INGALLS, A. J.
　Maternal and Child Health Nursing. Mosby, 1967, 684, illus.

IORIO, JOSEPHINE
　Principles of Obstetrics and Gynecology for Nurses. Mosby, 1967, 342, illus.

LERCH, CONSTANCE
　Maternity Nursing. Mosby, 1970, 575, illus.

LYTLE, NANCY A.
　Maternal Health Nursing. W. C. Brown, 1967, 220. (Nursing Readings Series.)

McKILLIGIN, HELEN R.
　The First Day of Life: Principles of Neonatal Nursing. Springer, 1970, 117.

SMITH, CHRISTINE S.
　Maternal-Child Nursing. Saunders, 1963, 435, illus.

VAN BLARCOM, CAROLYN C., and ZIEGEL, ERNA, EDS.
　Obstetric Nursing. 5th ed. Macmillan, 1964, 790, illus.

WIEDENBACH, ERNESTINE
　Family-Centered Maternity Nursing. 2nd ed. Putnam, 1967, 429, illus.

ZABRISKIE, LOUISE, et al.
　Maternity Nursing. 11th ed. Lippincott, 1966, 638, illus.

ORTHOPEDIC

BRUNNER, NANCY A.
　Orthopedic Nursing: A Programmed Approach. Mosby, 1970, 181.

KERR, AVICE
　Orthopedic Nursing Procedures. 2nd ed. Springer, 1969, 414, illus.

LARSON, CARROLL B., and GOULD, MARJORIE
　Calderwood's Orthopedic Nursing. 7th ed. Mosby, 1970, 486, illus.

POWELL, MARY
　Orthopaedic Nursing. 6th ed. Livingstone, Edinburgh, 1968, 690, illus.

WIEBE, ANNE M.
　Orthopedics in Nursing. Saunders, 1961, 249, illus.

PEDIATRIC

ANDERSON, NORMA J.
　Workbook for Pediatric Nurses. Mosby, 1970, 159.

BENZ, GLADYS S.
　Pediatric Nursing. 5th ed. Mosby, 1964, 547, illus.

BLAKE, FLORENCE G., and WRIGHT, F. HOWELL
　Essentials of Pediatric Nursing. 7th ed. Lippincott, 1963, 815, illus.

BLAKE, FLORENCE G., WRIGHT, F. HOWELL, and WAECHTER, EUGENIA H.
　Nursing Care of Children. 8th ed. Lippincott, 1970, 588, illus.

BROADRIBB, VIOLET
　Foundations of Pediatric Nursing. Lippincott, 1967, 573, illus.

CLARK, ANN L., et al.
　Patient Studies in Maternal and Child Nursing: A Family-Centered Student Guide. Lippincott, 1966, 305.

HYMOVICH, DEBRA P.
　Nursing of Children: A Guide for Study. Saunders, 1969, 389.

KALAFATICH, AUDREY J.
　Pediatric Nursing. Putnam, 1966, 432, illus.

LATHAM, HELEN C., and HECKEL, ROBERT V.
　Pediatric Nursing. Mosby, 1967, 516, illus.

LEIFER, GLORIA
　Principles and Techniques in Pediatric Nursing. Saunders, 1965, 210, illus.

MARLOW, DOROTHY R.
　Textbook of Pediatric Nursing. 3rd ed. Saunders, 1969, 687, illus.

MEERING, A. B.
　A Handbook for Nursery Nurses. 4th ed. Baillière, Tindall & Cox, London, 1964, 560, illus. (Baillière's Handbooks for Nurses.)

RUDICK, ELEANOR
　Pediatric Nursing. W. C. Brown, 1966, 120. (Nursing Readings Series.)

PRACTICAL

ASPERHEIM, MARY K.
　Pharmacology for Practical Nurses. 2nd ed. Saunders, 1967, 163, illus.

BECKER, BETTY G., and HASSLER, SISTER RUTH ANN
　Vocational and Personal Adjustments in Practical Nursing. Mosby, 1970, 158, illus.

BRIGLEY, CATHERINE M.
　Pediatrics for the Practical Nurse. Rev. ed. Delmar, 1968, 206, illus. (Practical Nursing Series.)

BUSH, CHRISTINE H.
　Personal and Vocational Relationships for Practical Nurses. 2nd ed. Saunders, 1966, 107.

FITCH, GRACE E.
　Arithmetic Review and Drug Therapy of Practical Nurses. Macmillan, 1961, 164, illus.

―――.
　The Role and Responsibilities of the Practical Nurse. Macmillan, 1969, 212.

FITCH, GRACE E., and DUBINY, MARY J., EDS.
　The Macmillan Dictionary for Practical and Vocational Nurses. Macmillan, 1966, 308, illus.

FORREST, JANE
　Practical Nursing and Anatomy for Pupil Nurses. Edward Arnold, London, 1966, 280, illus.

FREEDMAN, MARILYN G., and HANNAN, JUSTINE
　Clinical Workbook for Practical Nurses. 3rd ed. F. A. Davis, 1967, 156.

HASLER, DORIS
　The Practical Nurse and Today's Family. 2nd ed. Macmillan, 1969, 282, illus.

HOWE, PHYLLIS S.
　Nutrition for Practical Nurses. 4th ed. Saunders, 1967, 302, illus.

KEANE, CLAIRE B.
　Essentials of Nursing: A Medical-Surgical Text for Practical Nurses. 2nd ed. Saunders, 1969, 491, illus.

―――.
　Saunders Review for Practical Nurses. Saunders, 1966, 420, illus.

HEALTH SERVICE PROGRAMS

KERSCHNER, VELMA L.
  Simplified Nutrition and Diet Therapy for Practical Nurses. F. A. Davis, 1970, 241, illus.

MOSBY COMPANY
  Mosby's Review of Practical Nursing. 5th ed. Mosby, 1970, 410, illus.

OREM, DOROTHEA E.
  Guides for Developing Curricula for the Education of Practical Nurses. USGPO, 1966, 165.

RAPIER, DOROTHY K., et al., EDS.
  Practical Nursing: A Textbook for Students and Graduates. 4th ed. Mosby, 1970, 640, illus.

ROSS, CARMEN F.
  Personal and Vocational Relationships in Practical Nursing. 3rd ed. Lippincott, 1969, 266, illus.

SCHMIDT, JACOB E.
  Practical Nurses' Medical Dictionary: A Cyclopedic Medical Dictionary for Practical Nurses, Vocational Nurses, and Nurses' Aides. Thomas, 1968, 290.

SHACKELTON, ALBERTA D.
  Practical Nurse Nutrition Education. 2nd ed. Saunders, 1966, 295, illus.

STEVENS, MARION K.
  Geriatric Nursing for Practical Nurses. Saunders, 1965, 271, illus.

THOMPSON, ELEANOR D.
  Pediatrics for Practical Nurses. 2nd ed. Saunders, 1970, 348, illus.

PSYCHIATRIC

BOORER, DAVID, and BOORER, HEATHER
  An Introduction to Psychiatric Nursing. Pergamon, 1966, 175, illus.

BRAY, R. E., and BIRD, T. E.
  The Practice of Psychiatric Nursing. Williams & Wilkins, 1964, 372, illus.

BURD, SHIRLEY F., and MARSHALL, MARGARET A., EDS.
  Some Clinical Approaches to Psychiatric Nursing. Macmillan, 1963, 379, illus.

BURR, JOAN
  Nursing the Psychiatric Patient. Baillière, Tindall & Cassell, London, 1967, 296, illus.

CRAWFORD, ANNIE L., and BUCHANAN, BARBARA B.
  Psychiatric Nursing: A Basic Manual. 3rd ed. F. A. Davis, 1970, 85.

FAGIN, CLAIRE M., ED.
  Family-Centered Nursing in Community Psychiatry: Treatment in the Home. F. A. Davis, 1970, 190.

HOLMES, MARGUERITE J., and WERNER, JEAN A.
  Psychiatric Nursing in a Therapeutic Community. Macmillan, 1966, 166.

HOULISTON, MAY
  The Practice of Mental Nursing. 4th ed. Williams & Wilkins, 1965, 164.

INGRAM, MADELENE E.
  Principles and Techniques of Psychiatric Nursing. 5th ed. Saunders, 1960, 479, illus.

KALKMAN, MARION, et al.
  Psychiatric Nursing. 3rd ed. McGraw-Hill, Blakiston Division, 1967, 310.

LARSON, KENNETH H., et al.
  Direct Care Nursing: A Teaching Program for Psychiatric Nurses. Macmillan, 1968, 271, illus.

LEE, RUTH M.
  Workbook for Nursing in Emotional and Physical Problems. McGraw-Hill, 1967, 415.

LEWIS, GARLAND K., HOLMES, MARGUERITE J., and KATZ, FRED E.
  An Approach to the Education of Psychiatric Nursing Personnel. National League for Nursing, 1961, 124.

MADDISON, DAVID, DAY, PATRICIA, and LEABEATER, BRUCE
  Psychiatric Nursing. 3rd ed. Williams & Wilkins, 1970, 534, illus.

MANFREDA, MARGUERITE L.
  Psychiatric Nursing. 8th ed. F. A. Davis, 1968, 474, illus.

MATHENEY, RUTH V., and TOPALIS, MARY
  Psychiatric Nursing. 5th ed. Mosby, 1970, 346, illus.

MERENESS, DOROTHY, ED.
  Psychiatric Nursing: A Book of Readings. W. C. Brown, 1966, 2 vols. (Nursing Readings Series.)

MERENESS, DOROTHY, and KARNOSH, LOUIS J.
  Essentials of Psychiatric Nursing. 8th ed. Mosby, 1970, 336, illus.

MULLER, THERESA G.
  Fundamentals of Psychiatric Nursing. Littlefield, Adams, 1962, 226. (Nurses' Handbook Series No. 308.)

NATIONAL LEAGUE FOR NURSING
  An Approach to the Teaching of Psychiatric Nursing in Diploma and Associate Degree Programs. NLN, 1967, 65.

NOYES, ARTHUR P., CAMP, WILLIAM P., and VAN SICKEL, MILDRED
  Psychiatric Nursing. 6th ed. Macmillan, 1964, 376.

SIMMONS, JANET A.
  The Nurse-Patient Relationship in Psychiatric Nursing. Saunders, 1969, 189. (Workbook Guides to Understanding & Management.)

TRAIL, IRA D.
  Establishing Relationships in Psychiatric Nursing. Springer, 1966, 61.

TRAVELBEE, JOYCE
  Intervention in Psychiatric Nursing: Process in the One-To-One Relationship. F. A. Davis, 1969, 280.

PUBLIC HEALTH

FREEMAN, RUTH B.
  Public Health Nursing Practice. 3rd ed. Saunders, 1963, 455, illus.

JOHNSON, WALTER L.
  Content and Dynamics of Home Visits of Public Health Nurses. Pt. 2. American Nurses' Foundation, 1969, 134.

KALLINS, ETHEL L.
  Textbook of Public Health Nursing. Mosby, 1967, 480, illus.

LEAHY, KATHLEEN M., and COBB, M. M.
  Fundamentals of Public Health Nursing. McGraw-Hill, 1966, 225, illus.

STEWART, DOROTHY M., and VINCENT, PAULINE A.
  Public Health Nursing: A Book of Readings. W. C. Brown, 1967, 504. (Nursing Readings Series.)

VISITING NURSE SERVICE OF NEW YORK
  Public Health Nursing for the Sick at Home: A Descriptive Study. VNSNY, 1967, 228.

WORLD HEALTH ORGANIZATION
  Aspects of Public Health Nursing. WHO, Geneva, 1961, 185. (Public Health Paper No. 4.)

SURGICAL

ALEXANDER, EDYTHE
  Care of the Patient in Surgery. 4th ed. Mosby, 1967, 898.

ARMSTRONG, KATHARINE F., and JAMIESON, NORNA
  Surgical Nursing. 8th ed. Bailliere, Tindall & Cassell, London, 1969, 373, illus. (Nurses' Aids Series.)

BETSCHMAN, LUCILLE I.
  Handbook of Recovery Room Nursing. F. A. Davis, 1967, 308, illus.

BORDICKS, KATHERINE J.
  Nursing Care of Patients Having Chest Surgery. Macmillan, 1962, 65, illus.

GRAFFAM, SHIRLEY
  Care of the Surgical Patient: A Textbook for Nurses. McGraw-Hill, Blakiston Division, 1960, 311.

HARDMAN, F. G.
  Oral Surgery for Nurses. Williams & Wilkins, 1962, 112.

JUZWIAK, MARIJO
  Nursing Care of the High-Risk Surgery Patient. Mosby, 1970, 1 vol., illus.

LeMAITRE, GEORGE D., and FINNEGAN, JANET A.
  The Patient in Surgery: A Guide for Nurses. 2nd ed. Saunders, 1960, 399, illus.

METHODIST HOSPITAL, HOUSTON, TEX.
  Cardio-Vascular Surgery: A Manual for Nurses, by Members of the Surgical Staff and Members of the Nursing Service Staff. George H. Peddie and Frances E. Brush, eds. Putnam, 1961, 170.

NASH, D. F. ELLISON
  The Principles and Practice of Surgery for Nurses and Allied Professions. 4th ed. Williams & Wilkins, 1969, 1160.

PITORAK, ELIZABETH F., et al.
  Nurses' Guide to Cardiac Surgery and Nursing Care. McGraw-Hill, 1969, 156, illus.

POWERS, MARYANN, and STORLIE, FRANCES
  The Cardiac Surgical Patient: Pathophysiologic Considerations and Nursing Care. Macmillan, 1969, 239, illus.

RAFFENSPERGER, JOHN, and PRIMROSE, ROSELLEN B.
  Pediatric Surgery for Nurses. Little, Brown, 1968, 327.

WILLINGHAM, JACQUELINE
  Logic of Operating Room Nursing. 2nd ed. Springer, 1967, 111.

WILSON, FRANK
  Nursing Care of the Anaesthetized Patient. Blackwell Scientific, 1962, 72, illus.

WOOD-SMITH, DONALD, and POROWSKI, PAULINE C.
  Nursing Care of the Plastic Surgery Patient. Mosby, 1967, 374, illus.

UROLOGIC

KEUHNELIAN, JOHN G., and SANDERS, VIRGINIA E.
  Urologic Nursing. Macmillan, 1970, 407, illus.

MITCHELL, JOHN P.
  Urology for Nurses. 2nd ed. Williams & Wilkins, 1970, 344.

WHITEHEAD, SYLVIA L.
  Nursing Care of the Adult Urology Patient. Appleton-Century-Crofts, 1970, 302, illus.

WINTER, CHESTER C., and ROEHM, MARILYN M.
  Sawyer's Nursing Care of Patients with Urologic Diseases. 2nd ed. Mosby, 1968, 319, illus.

OPTICAL CAREERS

ADLER, FRANCIS H.
  Adler's Physiology of the Eye. 5th ed. Robert A. Moses, ed. Mosby, 1970, 713, illus.

BAKER, JEFFREY
  The Truth About Contact Lenses: Everything the Wearer, or Potential Wearer, Should Know. Putnam, 1970, 256, illus.

BALDWIN, WILLIAM R., and SHICK, CHARLES R.
  Corneal Contact Lenses: Fitting Procedures. Chilton, 1962, 144, illus.

BARSKY, DAVID
  Color Atlas of Pathology of the Eye. McGraw-Hill, Blakiston Division, 1966, 95.

BARTLEY, S. HOWARD
  The Human Organism as a Person. Chilton, 1967, 221, illus. (Principles of Optometry Series.)

BATES, STEVEN S.
  Fundamentals for the Optometric Assistant. Chilton, 1970, 263, illus.

BAUSCH & LOMB
  Ophthalmic Instruments and Professional Furniture. Bausch & Lomb, Rochester, N.Y., 1965, 143.

BECKER, BERNARD, and DREWS, ROBERT C.
  Current Concepts in Ophthalmology. Mosby, 1967, 265, illus.

BEGBIE, G. HUGH
  Seeing and the Eye: An Introduction to Vision. Natural History Press, 1969, 227, illus.

BENNETT, A. G.
  Emsley and Swaine's Ophthalmic Lenses. Hatton Press, London, 1968, illus.

BENTON, CURTIS D., and WELSH, ROBERT C.
  Spectacles for Aphakia. Thomas, 1966, 164, illus.

BIER, NORMAN
  Correction of Subnormal Vision. Butterworth, 1960, 231, illus.

BLAKER, J. WARREN
  Optics I: Lenses, Mirrors and Optical Instruments. Barnes & Noble, 1969, 112, illus. (College Outline Series No. 129.)

———.
  Optics II: Physics and Quantum Optics. Barnes & Noble, 1970, 92, illus. (College Outline Series No. 130.)

BORN, MAX, and WOLF, EMIL
  Principles of Optics: Electromagnetic Theory of Propagation, Interference, and Diffraction of Light. 4th ed. Pergamon, 1970, 808.

BREDEMEYER, HANS G., and BULLOCK, KATHLEEN
  Orthoptics: Theory and Practice. Mosby, 1968, 284, illus.

HEALTH SERVICE PROGRAMS

BROWN, EARLE B.
    Modern Optics. Reinhold, 1965, 645, illus.

COCHET, PAUL, and AMIARD, HUGHES
    Contact Lenses. Little, Brown, 1969, 250.

CONTACT LENS MEDICAL SEMINAR PROCEEDINGS
    Thomas, Vol. 1- , 1968- , biennial.

CORSON, RICHARD
    Fashion in Eyeglasses. Dufour, 1967, 288, illus.

CREIGHTON, CHARLES P.
    Contact Lenses' Fabrication Tables. H. M. Nuwer, Buffalo, N.Y., dist., 1964, 1 vol.

DAVSON, HUGH, ED.
    The Eye. 2nd ed. Academic Press, 1969, 4 vols., illus.
    ———.
    Physiology of the Eye. 2nd ed. Little, Brown, 1963, 492.

DITCHBURN, R. W.
    Light. 2nd ed. Interscience, 1964, 2 vols., illus.

DOWALIBY, MARGARET S.
    The Fundamentals of Cosmetic Dispensing. Professional Press, 1966, 97, illus.

DREW, RALPH
    Professional Ophthalmic Dispensing. Professional Press, 1970, 562, illus.

DUKE-ELDER, WILLIAM S.
    The Practice of Refraction. 8th ed. Mosby, 1969, 329, illus.

ELMSTROM, GEORGE P.
    Optometric Practice Management. Chilton, 1963, 419, illus.

ELMSTROM, GEORGE P., and KOHN, HAROLD
    Synopsis of the Legal Aspects of Contact Lens Practice for Optometrists. Burgess, 1964, 103, illus. (American Academy of Optometry Series Vol. 4.)

EPTING, JOHN B., and MORGRET, FRANK C.
    Ophthalmic Mechanics and Dispensing. Chilton, 1964, 338, illus.

FILDERMAN, IRVING P., and WHITE, PAUL F.
    Contact Lens Practice and Patient Management. Chilton, 1969, 558, illus.

FINCHAM, W. H. A.
    Optics. 7th ed. Chilton, 1965, 412, illus.

FONDA, GERALD
    Management of the Patient with Subnormal Vision. Mosby, 1965, 161, illus.

FOWLES, GRANT R.
    Introduction to Modern Optics. Holt, Rinehart & Winston, 1968, 304, illus.

FRY, GLENN A.
    Geometrical Optics. Chilton, 1969, 290, illus.

GILES, GEORGE H.
    The Principles and Practice of Refraction and Its Allied Subjects. 2nd ed. Chilton, 1965, 554, illus.

GLUCK, IRVIN D.
    Optics: The Nature and Applications of Light. Holt, Rinehart & Winston, 1964, 155, illus. (Holt Library of Science, Series II, No. 18.)

GOLDBERG, JOE B.
    Biomicroscopy for Contact Lens Practice. Professional Press, 1970, 138, illus.

GRAHAM, CLARENCE H., ED.
    Vision & Visual Perception. Wiley, 1965, 637, illus.

GRAHAM-JONES, OLIVER, ED.
    Aspects of Comparative Ophthalmology. Pergamon, 1966, 341, illus.

GRAYMORE, CLIVE N., ED.
    Biochemistry of the Eye. Academic Press, 1970, 783, illus.

GREGG, JAMES R.
    Experiments in Visual Science for Home and School. Ronald, 1966, 158, illus.
    ———.
    How to Communicate in Optometric Practice. Chilton, 1969, 250.
    ———.
    The Story of Optometry. Ronald, 1965, 305, illus.
    ———.
    Your Future in Optometry. R. Rosen Press, 1960, 160, (Careers in Depth Series.)

GREGG, JAMES R., and HEATH, GORDON G.
    The Eye and Sight. D. C. Heath, 1964, 136, illus. (Science Resource Series.)

GREGORY, R. L.
    Eye and Brain: The Psychology of Seeing. McGraw-Hill, 1966, 255.

GROSVENOR, THEODORE P.
    Contact Lens Theory and Practice. Professional Press, 1963, 425, illus.

GUILD OF PRESCRIPTION OPTICIANS OF AMERICA
    Guild Dispensing Manual. GPOA, Newark, N.J., 1962, 130, illus.

HABER, RALPH
    Contemporary Theory and Research in Visual Perception. Holt, Rinehart & Winston, 1968, 814.

HARTSTEIN, JACK
    Questions and Answers on Contact Lens Practice. Mosby, 1968, 199, illus.

HAVENER, WILLIAM H.
    Synopsis of Ophthalmology. 2nd ed. Mosby, 1963, 395, illus.

HELMHOLTZ, HERMAN L. F.
    Helmholtz's Treatise on Physiological Optics. 3rd ed. Dover, 1962, 2 vols., illus.

HERING, EWALD
    Outlines of a Theory of the Light Sense. Harvard University Press, 1964, 317, illus.

HIRSCH, MONROE J., and WICK, RALPH E.
    The Optometric Profession. Chilton, 1968, 359. (Principles of Optometry Series, Vol. 1.)
    ———, eds.
    Vision of the Aging Patient: An Optometric Symposium. Chilton, 1960, 328.
    ———.
    Vision of Children. Chilton, 1963, 434, illus.

HIRSCHHORN, HANS S.
    Your Future As An Optician. R. Rosen Press, 1970, 159, illus. (Careers in Depth Series.)

HOBBS, HENRY E.
    Principles of Ophthalmology. Elsevier, 1965, 240, illus.

I^ARBUS, AL'FRED L.
    Eye Movements and Vision. Plenum Press, 1967, 222, illus.

INTERNATIONAL CONGRESS ON CORNEAL AND SCLERAL CONTACT LENSES, HOUSTON, TEX., 1966
    Corneal and Scleral Contact Lenses: Proceedings. Mosby, 1967, 512, illus.

JESSEN, G.
    Complete Guide to Contact Lenses. Nash, Los Angeles, 1970, 1 vol.

JOHNSON, BENJAMIN K.
  Optics and Optical Instruments: An Introduction with Special Reference to Practical Applications. 2nd ed. Dover, 1960, 224.

JOSEPH, ALEXANDER, and LEAHY, DANIEL J.
  Programmed Physics. Pt. 3: Optics and Waves. Wiley, 1965, 212, illus.

KAPANY, N. S.
  Fiber Optics: Principles and Applications. Academic Press, 1967, 429, illus.

KESTENBAUM, ALFRED
  Applied Anatomy of the Eye. Grune & Stratton, 1963, 292, illus.

KINGSLAKE, RUDOLF, ED.
  Applied Optics and Optical Engineering: A Comprehensive Treatise. Academic Press, 1969, 5 vols.

KITCHELL, FRANK M.
  Opportunities in an Optometry Career. Universal Publishing and Distributing, 1967, 93. (VGM Career Series.)

KLEIN, MILES V.
  Optics. Wiley, 1970, 752.

LARSEN, HANS W.
  Atlas of the Fundus of the Eye. Musksgaard, Copenhagen, 1964, 271, illus. (Scandinavian University Books.)

LEBENSOHN, JAMES E., ED.
  An Anthology of Ophthalmic Classics. Williams & Wilkins, 1969, 407, illus.

LE GRAND, YVES
  Form and Space Vision. Rev. ed. Indiana University Press, 1967, 367, illus.

———.
  Light, Colour and Vision. 2nd ed. Chapman & Hall, London, 1968, 564, illus.

LERMAN, SIDNEY
  Basic Ophthalmology. McGraw-Hill, Blakiston Division, 1966, 499, illus.

LEWISON, LAWRENCE
  You and Your Eyes. Trinity, 1960, 253, illus.

LIPSON, STEPHEN G., and LIPSON, H.
  Optical Physics. Cambridge University Press, 1969, 494, illus.

LONGHURST, RICHARD S.
  Geometrical and Physical Optics. 2nd ed. Wiley, 1967, 592, illus.

LUCKIESH, MATTHEW
  Visual Illusions: Their Causes, Characteristics, and Applications. Dover, 1965, 252, illus.

MACKINNON, LACHLAN
  A Textbook on Light at an Introductory Level. Longmans, 1961, 344.

MANAS, LEO
  Visual Analysis. 3rd ed. Professional Press, 1965, 334, illus.

MANDELL, ROBERT B.
  Contact Lens Practice: Basic and Advanced. Thomas, 1965, 471, illus.

MARTIN-DOYLE, JOHN L. C.
  A Synopsis of Ophthalmology. 3rd ed. J. Wright, Bristol, 1967, 272.

MAY'S MANUAL OF THE DISEASES OF THE EYE FOR STUDENTS AND GENERAL PRACTITIONERS
  Williams & Wilkins, 1900- , vols., illus.

MAZOW, BERNARD
  Synopsis of Corneal Contact Lens Fitting for Optometrists. Burgess, 1969, 87, illus. (American Academy of Optometry Series Vol. 2.)

MONCREIFF, WILLIAM F.
  Refraction: Neurophysiological and Psychological Viewpoints. Thomas, 1968, 112.

MONK, GEORGE S.
  Light: Principles and Experiments. 2nd ed. Dover, 1963, 489, illus.

NEWELL, FRANK W.
  Ophthalmology: Principles and Concepts. 2nd ed. Mosby, 1969, 527, illus.

NEW YORK (STATE) EDUCATION DEPARTMENT
  Registered Optometrists and Registered Ophthalmic Dispensers. NYSED, Albany, 1950-52- , vols., biennial.

NUSSBAUM, ALLEN
  Geometric Optics: An Introduction. Addison-Wesley, 1969, 132.

OGLE, KENNETH N.
  Optics: An Introduction for Ophthalmologists. 2nd ed. Thomas, 1968, 264, illus.

PALMER, CHARLES H.
  Optics: Experiments and Demonstrations. Johns Hopkins Press, 1962, 321, illus.

PAN-AM OPTICAL LABORATORY
  Frames and Rx Lenses. PAOL, Louisville, Ky., 1970, 1 vol.

PATZ, ARNALL, and HOOVER, RICHARD E.
  Protection of Vision in Children. Thomas, 1969, 184, illus.

PIRENNE, MAURICE H. L.
  Vision and the Eye. 2nd ed. Chapman & Hall, London, 1967, 224. (Science Paperbacks SP 47.)

PRITIKIN, ROLAND I.
  Essentials of Ophthalmology. Rev. ed. Moore, 1970, 550, illus.

RICHTER, GÜNTER, COMP.
  Dictionary of Optics, Photography, and Photogrammetry: German-English and English-German. Elsevier, 1966, 502.

RUBIN, MELVIN L., and WALLS, GORDON L.
  Fundamentals of Visual Science. Thomas, 1969, 435.

RUDOLPH, MAE, and MUELLER, CONRAD G.
  Light and Vision. Time-Life Books, 1966, 200, illus. (Life Science Library.)

SALVATORI, PHILIP L.
  The Story of Contact Lenses. Obrig Laboratories, Sarasota, Fla., 1960, 57, illus.

SASIENI, LEWIS S.
  Principles and Practice of Optical Dispensing and Fitting. Chilton, 1962, 384, illus.

SCHAPERO, MAX, CLINE, DAVID, and HOFSTETTER, HENRY, EDS.
  Dictionary of Visual Science. 2nd ed., rev. Chilton, 1968, 804.

SCHEIE, HAROLD G., and ALBERT, DANIEL M.
  Adler's Textbook of Ophthalmology. 8th ed. Saunders, 1969, 509, illus.

SEEMAN, BERNARD
  Your Sight Folklore: Fact and Common Sense. Little, Brown, 1968, 242.

SHURCLIFF, WILLIAM A.
   Polarized Light: Production and Use. Harvard University Press, 1962, 207.

SLOANE, ALBERT E.
   Manual of Refraction. 2nd ed. Little, Brown, 1970, 282, illus.

SNYDER, CHARLES
   Our Ophthalmic Heritage. Little, Brown, 1967, 170, illus.

SOUTHALL, JAMES P. C.
   Mirrors, Prisms and Lenses: A Text-Book of Geometrical Optics. 3rd ed. Peter Smith, 1964, 806.

STEIN, HAROLD A., and SLATT, BERNARD J.
   The Ophthalmic Assistant: Fundamentals and Clinical Practice. Mosby, 1968, 406, illus.

STENSTRÖM, SÖLVE
   Optics of the Eye. Butterworth, 1964, 190.

STIMSON, RUSSELL L.
   The Cosmetic Fitting of Eyewear. Superior Optical Co., Los Angeles, 1961, 1 vol., illus.

———.
   A Lens Pattern Book: Arranged for the Cosmetic Fitting of Eyewear. Superior Optical Co., Los Angeles, 1967, 212, illus.

———.
   Ophthalmic Dispensing. Educational Foundation in Ophthalmic Optics, American Board of Opticianry, Rochester, Minn. (Professional Press, dist.), 1960, 430, illus.

THORNTON, SPENCER P.
   Ophthalmic Eponyms: An Encyclopedia of Named Signs, Syndromes, and Diseases in Ophthalmology. Aesculapius, Birmingham, Ala., 1967, 324.

TOLANSKY, SAMUEL
   Revolution in Optics. Penguin, 1968, 222, illus.

U.S. BUREAU OF NAVAL PERSONNEL
   Basic Optics and Optical Instruments. Dover, 1969, 480, illus.

VAUGHAN, DANIEL, COOK, ROBERT, and ASBURY, TAYLOR
   General Ophthalmology. 4th ed. Lange Medical Publications, Los Altos, Calif., 1965, 358, illus.

WOLFF, EUGENE
   Anatomy of the Eye and Orbit, Including the Central Connections, Development, and Comparative Anatomy of the Visual Apparatus. 6th ed. H. K. Lewis, London, 1968, 529, illus.

WOLKEN, JEROME J.
   Vision: Biophysics and Biochemistry of the Retinal Photoreceptors. Thomas, 1966, 216, illus. (American Lectures in Living Chemistry.)

WRIGHT, HARVEY D.
   Questions and Answers in Ophthalmology. Thomas, 1964, 368. (American Lectures in Living Chemistry.)

———.
   The Rays Are Not Coloured: Essays On the Science of Vision and Colour. Hilger, London, 1967, 154.

WYBAR, KENNETH C.
   Ophthalmology. Williams & Wilkins, 1966, 340, illus.

PHARMACY

ADRIANI, JOHN
   The Pharmacology of Anesthetic Drugs: A Syllabus for Students and Clinicians. 5th ed. Thomas, 1970, 297.

ALBERT, ADRIEN
   Selective Toxicity and Related Topics. 4th ed. Methuen, London, 1968, 531, illus.

AMERICAN DRUG INDEX
   Lippincott, 1956- , vols.

AMERICAN MEDICAL ASSOCIATION, COUNCIL ON DRUGS
   New Drugs. AMA, Chicago, 1965- , vols.

AMERICAN PHARMACEUTICAL ASSOCIATION
   Directory of Pharmacists. APA, Washington, 1964- , vols.

———.
   Handbook of Non-Prescription Drugs. 2nd ed. APA, Washington, 1967, 108, illus.

———.
   Proprietary (trade) Names of Official Drugs: U.S.P. XVII and N.F. XII. APA, 1965, 52.

ANSEL, HOWARD C.
   Introduction to Pharmaceutical Dosage Forms. Lea & Febiger, 1969, 384, illus.

ARNOW, LESLIE E.
   Health in a Bottle: Searching for the Drugs That Help. Lippincott, 1970, 272, illus.

BARLOW, RICHARD B.
   Introduction to Chemical Pharmacology. 2nd ed. Wiley, 1964, 452, illus.

BASLOW, MORRIS H.
   Marine Pharmacology: A Study of Toxins and other Biologically Active Substances of Marine Origin. Williams & Wilkins, 1969, 286, illus.

BECKMAN, HARRY
   Pharmacology: The Nature, Action and Use of Drugs. 2nd ed. Saunders, 1961, 805, illus.

BENTLEY, ARTHUR O.
   Bentley and Driver's Textbook of Pharmaceutical Chemistry. 8th ed. Oxford University Press, 1969, 916, illus.

BERGEL, FRANZ, and DAVIES, D. R.
   All About Drugs. Horizon Press, 1970, 203, illus.

BEVAN, JOHN A.
   Essentials of Pharmacology: A Textbook for Students. Hoeber, 1969, 709.

BOVE, FRANK J.
   The Story of Ergot: For Physicians, Pharmacists, Nurses, Biochemists, Biologists and Others Interested in the Life Sciences. S. Karger, Basel, N.Y., 1970, 297, illus.

BOWMAN, WILLIAM C., RAND, MICHAEL J., and WEST, GEOFFREY B.
   Textbook of Pharmacology. F. A. Davis, 1968, 1031, illus.

BRADLEY, WILLIS T., GUSTAFSON, CARROLL B., and STOKLOSA, MITCHELL J.
   Pharmaceutical Calculations. 5th ed. Lea & Febiger, 1968, 406, illus.

BROOKS, STEWART M.
   Basic Facts of Pharmacology. 2nd ed. Saunders, 1963, 354, illus.

BRUNN, ALICE L.
   How to Find Out in Pharmacy: A Guide to Sources of Pharmaceutical Information. Pergamon, 1969, 130, illus.

BURACK, RICHARD
   The Handbook of Prescription Drugs: Official Names, Prices and Sources for Patient and Doctor. Pantheon, 1967, 181.

BURGEN, A. S. V., and MITCHELL, JAMES F., EDS.
   Gaddum's Pharmacology. 6th ed. Oxford University Press, 1968, 234, illus.

PHARMACY

BURGER, ALFRED.
Selected Pharmacological Testing Methods. Dekker, 1968, 515, illus.

BURN, JOSHUA H.
Lecture Notes on Pharmacology. 8th ed. Blackwell Scientific, 1965, 153.

CHATTEN, LESLIE G.
Pharmaceutical Chemistry. Dekker, 1966- , 1 vol., illus.

CHUTE, AARON H., and HALL, ESTHER J. W.
The Pharmacist in Retail Distribution. 3rd ed. Hemphill, Austin, Tex., 1960, 348, illus.

CLARK, EUSTACE G. C.
Isolation and Identification of Drugs in Pharmaceuticals, Body Fluids, and Post-Mortem Material. Pharmaceutical Press, London, 1969, 870, illus. (Extra Pharmacopoeia Companion Volume.)

CLARK, RALPH W.
Orientation in Pharmacy. 2nd ed. Lea & Febiger, 1961, 182.

CLAUS, EDWARD P., and TYLER, VARRO E.
Pharmacognosy. 6th ed. Lea & Febiger, 1970, 572, illus.

COLEMAN, THOMAS E.
Profitable Drugstore Management. Prentice-Hall, 1970, 221, illus.

CONNORS, KENNETH A.
A Textbook of Pharmaceutical Analysis. Wiley, 1967, 614, illus.

CROSSLAND, JAMES
Lewis's Pharmacology. 4th ed. Williams & Wilkins, 1970, 1376, illus.

CSÁKY, T. Z.
Introduction to General Pharmacology. Appleton-Century-Crofts, 1969, 249, illus.

CURRENT DRUG HANDBOOK
Saunders, 1958- , vols., biennial.

CUTTING, WINDSOR C.
Handbook of Pharmacology: The Actions and Uses of Drugs. 4th ed. Appleton, 1969, 779, illus.

THE DISPENSATORY OF THE UNITED STATES OF AMERICA
Lippincott, 1851- , vols., illus.

DOBBS, EDWARD C.
Pharmacology and Oral Therapeutics For Students and Practitioners. 12th ed. Mosby, 1961, 578, illus.

DOWLING, HARRY F.
Medicines for Man: The Development, Regulation and Use of Prescription Drugs. Knopf, 1970, 347.

DRILL, VICTOR A.
Drill's Pharmacology in Medicine. 3rd ed. Joseph R. Di Palma, ed. McGraw-Hill, 1965, 1488, illus.

DRUGS IN CURRENT USE
Springer, 1955- , vols.

DRUGS OF CHOICE
Mosby, 1958-59- , vols.

ELLIS, PHILIP P., and SMITH, DONN L.
Handbook of Ocular Therapeutics and Pharmacology. 2nd ed. Mosby, 1966, 224.

FERGUSON, FRANK C.
Drug Therapy. Lea & Febiger, 1962, 411.

FERGUSON, FRANK L.
Efficient Drug Store Management. Fairchild, 1969, 252, illus.

GABLE, FRED B.
Opportunities in Pharmacy Careers. Vocational Guidance Manuals, 1964, 144. (VGM Career Series V150.)

GARB, SOLOMON, and CRIM, BETTY J.
Pharmacology and Patient Care. 3rd ed. Springer, 1970, 608, illus.

GARRATT, DONALD C.
The Quantitative Analysis of Drugs. 3rd ed. Thomas, 1964, 940, illus.

GEARIEN, JAMES E., and GRABOWSKI, BERNARD F.
Methods of Drug Analysis. Lea & Febiger, 1969, 281, illus.

GOLDSTEIN, ARNOLD S., and BARMAK, LEONARD
Casebook on Community Pharmacy Management. Lea & Febiger, 1970, 1 vol.

GOODMAN, LOUIS S., and GILMAN, ALFRED Z.
The Pharmacological Basis of Therapeutics. 4th ed. Macmillan, 1970, 1 vol.

GOTH, ANDRES
Medical Pharmacology: Principles and Concepts. 5th ed. Mosby, 1970, 784, illus.

GRAY, CHARLES H., ED.
Laboratory Handbook of Toxic Agents. 2nd ed. Franklin Publishing Co., 1968, 190.

GROLLMAN, ARTHUR, and GROLLMAN, EVELYN F.
Pharmacology and Therapeutics: A Textbook for Students and Practitioners of Medicine and Its Allied Professions. 7th ed. Lea & Febiger, 1970, 1038, illus.

HARRIS, MALCOLM
Pharmaceutical Microbiology. Baillière, Tindall & Cox, London, 1964, 269, illus.

HASSAN, WILLIAM E.
Hospital Pharmacy. 2nd ed. Lea & Febiger, 1967, 384, illus.

HOBLITZELLE, LUCY F., and WINEK, CHARLES L.
Pharmacology Applied to Patient Care. 3rd ed. F. A. Davis, 1969, 250.

HOLLAND, WILLIAM C., KLEIN, RICHARD L., and BRIGGS, ARTHUR H.
Introduction to Molecular Pharmacology. Macmillan, 1964, 250, illus.

HOLMSTEDT, BO, and LILJESTRAND, G., EDS.
Readings in Pharmacology. Macmillan, 1963, 395, illus.

JENKINS, GLENN L., SPERANDIO, GLEN J., and LATIOLAIS, CLIFTON J.
Clinical Pharmacy: A Text for Dispensing Pharmacy. McGraw-Hill, 1966, 379.

JONES, LEO M., and BOOTH, NICHOLAS H.
Veterinary Pharmacology and Therapeutics. 3rd ed. Iowa State University Press, 1965, 1037, illus.

KABAT, HUGH F.
Clinical Pharmacy Handbook. Lea & Febiger, 1969, 1 vol.

KELLER, BERNARD G., and SMITH, MICKEY C., COMPS.
Pharmaceutical Marketing: An Anthology and Bibliography. Williams & Wilkins, 1969, 396, illus.

KOPPÁNYI, THEODORE, and KARCZMAR, ALEXANDER G.
Experimental Pharmacodynamics. 3rd ed. Burgess, 1963, 246, illus.

HEALTH SERVICE PROGRAMS

KRAEMER, JAMES E.
　Your Future in Pharmacy. R. Rosen Press, 1964, 156. (Careers in Depth No. 47.)

KRANTZ, JOHN C., and CARR, C. JELLEFF
　The Pharmacologic Principles of Medical Practice: A Textbook on Pharmacology and Therapeutics for Medical Students, Physicians, and the Members of the Professions Allied to Medicine. 7th ed. Williams & Wilkins, 1969, 1037, illus.

KREIG, MARGARET B.
　Black Market Medicine. Prentice-Hall, 1967, 304, illus.

KREMERS, EDWARD
　History of Pharmacy. 3rd ed. Lippincott, 1963, 464, illus.

LACHMAN, LEON, LIEBERMAN, HERBERT A., and KANIG, JOSEPH L.
　The Theory and Practice of Industrial Pharmacy. Lea & Febiger, 1970, 811, illus.

LAURENCE, DESMOND R.
　Clinical Pharmacology. 3rd ed. Little, Brown, 1966, 678, illus.
　———, ED.
　Evaluation of Drug Activities: Pharmacometrics. Academic Press, 1964, 2 vols., illus.

LEAR, ERWIN
　Chemistry and Applied Pharmacology of Tranquilizers: A Primer for Students and Practitioners. Thomas, 1966, 132, illus.

LEES, BRIAN
　The Medical Background for Successful Drug Detailing. Lees Associates, Lake Bluff, Ill., 1962, 300, illus.

LEONARD, ROBERT M.
　Pharmacology Study Handbook. Andromeda Books, Washington, 1968, 277.

LINGEMAN, RICHARD R.
　Drugs from A to Z: A Dictionary. McGraw-Hill, 1969, 277.

LOOMIS, TED A.
　Essentials of Toxicology. Lea & Febiger, 1968, 162.

LOWENTHAL, WERNER
　Pharmaceutical Calculations: A Self-Instructional Text. Williams & Wilkins, 1969, 419.

MARIEL, SISTER
　Outline of Pharmacology and Therapeutics. Thomas, 1963, 297, illus.

MARKETING SERVICES
　Pharmaceutical Market Research Directory. Metuchen, N.J., 1963, 1962, 146.

MARLER, E. E. J.
　Pharmacological and Chemical Synonyms. 4th ed. Excerpta Medica, New York, 1967, 353.

MARTIN, ALFRED N., SWARBRICK, JAMES, and CAMMARATA, ARTHUR
　Physical Pharmacy: Physical Chemical Principles in the Pharmaceutical Sciences. 2nd ed. Lea & Febiger, 1969, 637, illus.

MARTIN, ERIC W.
　Husa's Pharmaceutical Dispensing: A Textbook and Reference Manual on Drug Development, Pharmaceutical Compounding and Dispensing. 6th ed. Mack, Easton, Pa., 1966, 903, illus.
　———, ED.
　Remington's Pharmaceutical Sciences. Mack, Easton, Pa., 1965, 1 vol.
　———, ED.
　Techniques of Medication: A Manual on the Administration of Drug Products. Lippincott, 1969, 239, illus.

THE MERCK INDEX: AN ENCYCLOPEDIA OF CHEMICALS AND DRUGS
　8th ed. Merck, Rahway, N.J., 1968, 1713, illus.

MEYERS, FREDERICK H., JAWETZ, ERNEST, and GOLDFIEN, ALAN
　Review of Medical Pharmacology. Lange, Los Altos, Calif., 1968, 692.

MIYA, TOM S.
　Laboratory Guide in Pharmacology. 2nd ed. Burgess, 1964, 162.

MODERN DRUG ENCYCLOPEDIA AND THERAPEUTIC INDEX: A COMPENDIUM
　Reuben Donnelley, New York, 1934- , vols.

MOSS, H. G.
　Retail Pharmacist's Handbook. 2nd ed. Newnes, London, 1962, 397, illus.

MUSSER, RUTH D., and O'NEILL, JOHN J.
　Pharmacology and Therapeutics. 4th ed. Macmillan, 1969, 1033.

THE NATIONAL FORMULARY
　American Pharmaceutical Association, Washington, 1888- , vols., illus.

NEWCOMER, JAMES, BUNNELL, KEVIN P., and McGRATH, EARL J.
　Liberal Education and Pharmacy. Teachers College Press, 1960, 125. (Institute of Higher Education Publications.)

OLDHAM, FRANCES K., KELSEY, F. E., and GEILING, E. M. K.
　Essentials of Pharmacology. 4th ed. Lippincott, 1960, 418, illus.

PARROTT, EUGENE L.
　Pharmaceutical Technology: Fundamental Pharmaceutics. Burgess, 1970, 415, illus.

PASZTOR, MAGDA, and HOPKINS, JENNY
　Bibliography of Pharmaceutical Reference Literature. Pharmaceutical Press, London, 1968, 167.

PATON, WILLIAM D., and PAYNE, JAMES P.
　Pharmacological Principles and Practice. Little, Brown, 1968, 417, illus.

PETTIT, WILLIAM
　Manual of Pharmaceutical Law. 3rd ed. Macmillan, 1962, 284.

THE PHARMACEUTICAL ASSOCIATION OF THE PROVINCE OF BRITISH COLUMBIA
　Hospital Pharmacy Manual. Vancouver, B. C., 1964, 1 vol.

PHARMACEUTICAL MANUFACTURERS ASSOCIATION
　Prescription Drug Industry Fact Book. PMA, 1969, 76, illus.

PHARMACEUTICAL SOCIETY OF GREAT BRITAIN
　British Pharmaceutical Codex, 1968. Pharmaceutical Press, London, 1968, 1513.
　———.
　Poisons and T.S.A. Guide for Pharmacists in Retail and Hospital Practice. Pharmaceutical Press, London, 1968, 282.

PHARMACIST'S DICTIONARY OF MEDICAL TERMS
　8th ed. CRC Press, 1967, 290.

THE PHARMACOPEIA OF THE UNITED STATES OF AMERICA
　Mack, Easton, Pa., 1820- , vols., decennial.

PHARMACY EXAMINATION REVIEW BOOK
　Medical Examination Publishing Co., Flushing, N.Y., 1961- , vols.

PLEIN, JOY B., and PLEIN, ELMER M.
Fundamentals of Medications: A Text-Workbook of Dosages, Solutions, Mathematics and Introductory Pharmacology. Lippincott, 1967, 177, illus.

POSER, CHARLES M.
International Dictionary of Drugs Used in Neurology and Psychiatry. Thomas, 1962, 172.

POYNTER, F. N. L.
The Evolution of Pharmacy in Britain. Thomas, 1965, 240, illus.

ROBSON, JOHN M., and STACEY, REGINALD S.
Recent Advances in Pharmacology. 3rd ed. Little, Brown, 1962, 406, illus.

ROUSE, SUE H., and WEBBER, MARION G.
Calculations in Pharmacy. 2nd ed. Lippincott, 1968, 242.

SAPEIKA, N.
Food Pharmacology. Thomas, 1969, 183, illus.

SCHROETER, LOUIS C.
Ingredient X: The Production of Effective Drugs. Pergamon Press, 1969, 157, illus.

SHUSTER, LOUIS
Readings in Pharmacology. Little, Brown, 1962, 294.

SICÉ, JEAN
General Pharmacology. Saunders, 1962, 593, illus.

SMITH, MICKEY C., et al.
Principles of Pharmaceutical Marketing. Lea & Febiger, 1968, 414, illus.

SPROWLS, JOSEPH B., ED.
American Pharmacy: Textbook of Pharmaceutical Principles, Processes, and Preparations. 5th ed. Lippincott, 1960, 493, illus.

———, ED.
Prescription Pharmacy: Dosage Formulation and Pharmaceutical Adjuncts. Lippincott, 1963, 579, illus.

SWARBRICK, JAMES
Current Concepts in the Pharmaceutical Sciences: Biopharmaceutics. Lea & Febiger, 1970, 225.

TEDESCHI, DAVID H., and TEDESCHI, RALPH E.
Importance of Fundamental Principles in Drug Evaluation. Raven Press, New York, 1968, 493, illus.

TREASE, GEORGE E.
Pharmacy in History. Williams & Wilkins, 1965, 272, illus.

———.
A Textbook of Pharmacognosy. 9th ed. Baillière, Tindall & Cassell, London, Williams & Wilkins, 1966, 829, illus.

TURNER, PAUL
Clinical Aspects of Autonomic Pharmacology. Lippincott, 1969, 169, illus.

U.S. FOOD AND DRUG ADMINISTRATION, SCIENCE INFORMATION FACILITY
National Drug Code Directory.... U.S. Consumer Protection and Environmental Health Service, 1969, 1 vol.

U.S. TASK FORCE ON PRESCRIPTION DRUGS
The Drug Prescribers: Background Papers. HEW, USGPO, 1968, 50, illus.

WAISMAN, MORRIS, COMP.
Pharmaceutical Therapeutics in Dermatology. Thomas, 1968, 197, illus.

WARD, C. O.
Experimental Methods in Pharmacology. St. John's University College of Pharmacy, Department of Pharmacology, Pharmacognosy and Allied Sciences, 1969, 1 vol.

WILLIAMS, ALEC
Sustained Release Pharmaceuticals. Noyes, 1969, 273, illus.

WILSON, ANDREW, and SCHILD, HEINZ O.
Applied Pharmacology. 10th ed. Little, Brown, 1968, 721, illus.

WILSON, CHARLES O., et al.
Textbook of Organic Medicinal and Pharmaceutical Chemistry. 4th ed. Lippincott, 1962, 883, illus.

WOODBURY, ROBERT A.
Pharmacology Review: 1350 Multiple Choice Questions and Answers—Completely Referenced. 2nd ed. Medical Examination Publishing Co., Flushing, N.Y., 1966, 174, (Basic Science Review Series.)

WORLD HEALTH ORGANIZATION
Cumulative List of Proposed International Non-Proprietary Names for Pharmaceutical Preparations. WHO, 1962- , vols.

X RAY TECHNOLOGY

AMERICAN COLLEGE OF RADIOLOGY
Planning Guide for Radiologic Installations. 2nd ed. Williams & Wilkins, 1966, 297, illus.

AMERICAN SOCIETY OF RADIOLOGIC TECHNOLOGISTS
Records for Schools of Radiologic Technology. ASRT, Chicago, 1965, 47.

ARCO PUBLISHING COMPANY, INC.
X-Ray Technician. 3rd ed. Arco, 1967, 74.

BASERGA, RENATO, and MALAMUD, D.
Autoradiography: Technics and Applications. Harper & Row, 1969, 1 vol.

BAUER, DONALD D.
A Textbook of Elementary Radiography for Students and Technicians. Thomas, 1965, 242, illus.

BLATZ, HANSON
Introduction to Radiological Health. McGraw-Hill, 1964, 315, illus.

BLEICH, ALAN R.
The Story of X-Rays: From Röntgen to Isotopes. Dover, 1960, 186, illus.

BLEWETT, J. E., and RACKOW, A. M.
Anatomy and Physiology for Radiographers. 2nd ed. Butterworth, 1966, 331, illus.

BLOOM, WILLIAM L., JR., HOLLENBACH, JOHN L., and MORGAN, JAMES A.
Medical Radiographic Technic. 3rd ed. Thomas, 1965, 351, illus.

BRECHER, RUTH, and BRECHER, EDWARD
The Rays: A History of Radiology in the United States and Canada. Williams & Wilkins, 1969, 484, illus.

BRODEUR, ARMAND E.
Radiologic Diagnosis in Infants & Children. Mosby, 1965, 515, illus.

BROWN, JAMES G.
X-Rays and Their Applications. Plenum Press, 1966, 258, illus.

CASARETT, ALISON P.
Radiation Biology. Prentice-Hall, 1968, 368, illus.

CHERNOK, NORMA B., COMP.
Radiology Typists Handbook: A Handy Reference Guide of Medical Terms Used in Radiologic Reports for Typists. Medical Examination Publishing Co., Flushing, N.Y., 1970, 150, illus.

HEALTH SERVICE PROGRAMS

CHESNEY, D. NOREEN, and CHESNEY, MURIEL O.
  Radiographic Photography. 2nd ed. Oxford University Press, 1969, 470, illus.

CLARK, GEORGE L., ED.
  The Encyclopedia of X-Rays and Gamma Rays. Reinhold, 1963, 1149, illus.

CLARK, KATHLEEN C.
  Positioning in Radiography. 8th ed. Intercontinental Medical Book Corp., 1964, 806, illus. (Ilford Manual.)

COATES, RALPH W.
  The Radiographic Position as a Whole. American Society of Radiologic Technicians, Chicago, n.d., 47, illus.

DARLING, DONALD B.
  Radiography of Infants and Children. 2nd ed. Thomas, 1970, 185, illus. (American Lectures in Roentgen Diagnosis Series.)

EASLEY, CHARLES
  Basic Radiation Protection: Principles and Organization. Gordon & Breach, 1969, 132.

EGAN, ROBERT L.
  Technologist Guide to Mammography. Williams & Wilkins, 1968, 123, illus.

EPSTEIN, BERNARD S.
  The Spine: A Radiological Text and Atlas. 3rd ed. Lea & Febiger, 1969, 730, illus.

ETTER, LEWIS E.
  Glossary of Words and Phrases Used in Radiology, Nuclear Medicine and Ultrasound. 2nd ed. Thomas, 1970, 1 vol., illus.
  ———, ED.
  The Science of Ionizing Radiation: Modes of Application. Thomas, 1965, 788, illus.

FRIGERIO, NORMAN A.
  Your Body and Radiation. U.S. Atomic Energy Commission, 1966, 78, illus.

FUCHS, ARTHUR
  Principles of Radiographic Exposure and Processing. 2nd ed. Thomas, 1967, 284, illus.

GILLIAN, REED A.
  Radiography of the Skull. American Society of X-Ray Technicians, Chicago, n.d., 28, illus.

GLOYNA, ERNEST F., and LEDBETTER, JOE O.
  Principles of Radiological Health. Dekker, 1969, 473, illus.

GOODWIN, PAUL N., QUIMBY, EDITH H., and MORGAN, RUSSELL H.
  Physical Foundations of Radiology. 4th ed. Harper & Row, 1970, 397.

GUDE, WILLIAM D.
  Autoradiographic Techniques: Localization of Radioisotopes in Biological Material. Prentice-Hall, 1968, 113, illus. (Prentice-Hall Biological Techniques Series.)

HALACY, DANIEL S., JR.
  X-Rays and Gamma Rays. Holiday House, 1969, 159.

HANHAM, I. W. F.
  Clinical Radiotherapy. F. A. Davis, 1969, 180, illus.

HENRY, HUGH F.
  Fundamentals of Radiation Protection. Wiley-Interscience, 1969, 485, illus.

HOERR, NORMAND L., PYLE, S. IDELL, and FRANCIS, CARL C.
  Radiographic Atlas of Skeletal Development of the Foot and Ankle: A Standard of Reference. Thomas, 1962, 176, illus.

HOLLANDER, MARK B.
  Ultrasoft X-Rays. Williams & Wilkins, 1969, 197.

HOLM, NIELS W., and BERRY, ROGER J., EDS.
  Manual on Radiation Dosimetry. Dekker, 1970, 450, illus.

INTERNATIONAL ATOMIC ENERGY AGENCY
  Atlas of Radiation Dose Distribution. IAEA, 1965-67, Vol. 1- .

INTERNATIONAL COMMISSION ON RADIOLOGICAL PROTECTION
  Radiosensitivity and Spatial Distribution of Dose: Reports of 2 Task Groups of Committee 1. Pergamon, 1969, 118.

JACOBI, CHARLES A.
  Textbook of Anatomy and Physiology in Radiologic Technology. Mosby, 1968, 421, illus.

JACOBI, CHARLES A., and PARIS, DON Q.
  Textbook of Radiologic Technology. 4th ed. Mosby, 1968, 480, illus.
  ———.
  X-Ray Technology. 3rd ed. Mosby, 1964, 452, illus.

JAUNDRELL-THOMPSON, FRED, and ASHWORTH, WILLIAM J.
  X-Ray Physics and Equipment. 2nd ed. Blackwell Scientific, 1970, 1 vol., illus.

JOHN, DAVID H. O.
  Radiographic Processing in Medicine and Industry. Focal Press, 1967, 292. (Focal Library.)

JOHNS, HAROLD
  The Physics of Radiology. Thomas, 1969, 1 vol.

JONES, MALCOLM D.
  Basic Diagnostic Radiology: An Introductory Textbook for Students in the Medical Sciences. Mosby, 1969, 1 vol.

KAELBLE, EMMETT F., ED.
  Handbook of X-Rays: For Diffraction, Emission, Absorption and Microscopy. McGraw-Hill, 1967, 1044, illus.

KEMP, LLOYD A., and OLIVER, RAYMOND
  Basic Physics in Radiology. Blackwell Davis, 1961, 329, illus.

LONGMORE, THOMAS A.
  Medical Photography. 8th ed. Peter Hansell and Robert Ollerenshaw, eds. Chilton, 1969, 538.

LUMSDEN, K., and TRUELOVE, S. C.
  Radiology of the Digestive System. F. A. Davis, 1965, 544, illus.

LUSTED, LEE B., and KEATS, THEODORE E.
  Atlas of Roentgenographic Measurement. 2nd ed. Year Book Medical Publishers, Chicago, 1967, 249, illus.

LYONS, NEIL J., et al.
  Radiographic Positioning. American Society of Radiologic Technologists, Chicago, n.d., 36, illus.

MALLETT, M., COMP.
  A Handbook of Anatomy and Physiology for Student X-Ray Technicians. 4th ed. American Society of Radiologic Technologists, Chicago, 1962, 181, illus.

MARGULIS, ALEXANDER R., and BURHENNE, H. JOACHIM, EDS.
  Alimentary Tract Roentgenology. Mosby, 1967, 2 vols., illus.

McCLENAHAN, JOHN L.
  Radiology As an Art and Other Essays. Thomas, 1967, 89.

MERRILL, VINITA
  Atlas of Roentgenographic Positions. 3rd ed. Mosby, 1967, 3 vols., illus.

MESCHAN, ISADORE
An Atlas of Normal Radiographic Anatomy. 2nd ed. Saunders, 759, illus.

———.
Synopsis of Roentgen Signs. Saunders, 1962, 436, illus.

MESCHAN, ISADORE, and FARRER-MESCHAN, R. M. F.
Radiographic Positioning and Related Anatomy. Saunders, 1968, 388, illus.

MORGAN, JAMES A.
The Art and Science of Medical Radiography. 2nd ed. Catholic Hospital Association, 1966, 145, illus.

MOSS, WILLIAM T., and BRAND, WILLIAM N.
Therapeutic Radiology. 3rd ed. Mosby, 1969, 576, illus.

MURPHY, WALTER T.
Radiation Therapy. 2nd ed. Saunders, 1967, 1020, illus.

NAGY, DÉNES
Radiological Anatomy. Pergamon, 1965, 516, illus.

OHNSTY, JAMES
Aids to Ethics and Professional Conduct For Student Radiologic Technologists. 2nd ed. Thomas, 1968, 160.

OLIPHANT, JOYCE
A Study Guide for Student X-Ray Technicians. Thomas, 1963, 156.

REES, DAVID J.
Health Physics: Principles of Radiation Protection. MIT Press, 1967, 242, illus.

RIDGWAY, ARTHUR, and THUMM, WALTER
The Physics of Medical Radiography. Addison-Wesley, 1968, 494, illus.

ROSS, RAYMOND W., and GALLOWAY, JOHN R.
A Handbook of Radiography. 3rd ed. Lippincott, 1963, 220, illus.

SANTE, LeROY, and FISCHER, HARRY W.
Manual of Roentgenological Technique. Edwards Brothers, 1934- , vols., illus.

SCHWARZ, GERHART S.
Unit-Step Radiography: Simplification of Medical Radiography Through Manual and Automatic Use of an Exposure Value Scale (XVS) System and Standardization. Thomas, 1961, 240, illus.

SEEMAN, HERMAN E.
Physical and Photographic Principles of Medical Radiography. Wiley, 1968, 132, illus. (Wiley Photographic Science and Technology and Graphic Arts Series.)

SELMAN, JOSEPH
The Fundamentals of X-Ray and Radium Physics. 4th ed. Thomas, 1965, 467, illus.

———.
Skull Radiography: A Simplified System. Thomas, 1966, 228, illus.

SHURTLEFF, FORREST E.
Children's Radiographic Technic. 2nd ed. Lea & Febiger, 1962, 92, illus.

SPIRKO, SISTER CHRISTINA
Radiologic Records. Thomas, 1960, 304, illus.

———.
Your Future in Radiologic Technology. R. Rosen Press, 1966, 156. (Careers in Depth.)

SQUIRE, LUCY F.
Fundamentals of Roentgenology. Harvard University Press, 1964, 363, illus.

STEIN, JUSTIN J., and MORGAN, JASPER E.
Basic Principles of Radiation Therapy for X-Ray Technicians and Nurses. University of California Press, Los Angeles, n.d., 117.

STEVENS, MATTHEW, and PHILLIPS, ROBERT I.
Comprehensive Review for the Radiologic Technologist. Mosby, 1968, 181, illus.

TAYLOR, ABRAHAM
X-Ray Metallography. Wiley, 1961, 993, illus.

TILLIER, HENRY
Normal Radiological Anatomy: Radiological Optics and Film Interpretation. Ronan O'Rahily, tr. Thomas, 1968, 382. (Tr. from 2nd French ed.)

UPTON, ARTHUR C.
Radiation Injury: Effects, Principles, and Perspectives. University of Chicago, 1969, 126.

U.S. BUREAU OF RADIOLOGICAL HEALTH, POPULATION EXPOSURE STUDIES SECTION
Population Dose From X-Rays, U.S., 1964: Estimates of Gonad and Genetically Significant Dose from the Public Health Service X-Ray Exposure Study. USGPO, 1969, 1 vol.

U.S. DEPARTMENT OF THE ARMY
Military Roentgenology. U.S. Department of the Army, 1967, 961, illus. (Technical Manual TM 8-280.)

U.S. OFFICE OF EDUCATION, VOCATIONAL AND TECHNICAL EDUCATION DIVISION
Industrial Radiography: Instructor's Guide, and Student Guide and Laboratory Exercises.... USOE, 1968, 3 vols., illus.

U.S. PUBLIC HEALTH SERVICE
Population Exposure to X-Rays: U.S. USGPO, 1964, 218. (PHS Pub. No. 1519.)

WALTER, JOSEPH, and MILLER, H.
A Short Textbook of Radiotherapy for Technicians and Students. 3rd ed. Little, Brown, 1969, 523, illus.

WARRICK, C. K.
Anatomy and Physiology for Radiographers. 3rd ed. Williams & Wilkins, 1970, 1 vol.

WATSON, JOHN C.
Patient Care and Special Procedures in Radiologic Technology. 3rd ed. Mosby, 1969, 234, illus.

WAX, GEROLD J.
Elementary Anatomy and Physiology: For Students in Radiologic and Laboratory Technology. Thomas, 1970, 130, illus.

X-RAY TECHNOLOGY EXAMINATION REVIEW BOOK: 1500 MULTIPLE CHOICE QUESTIONS AND ANSWERS REFERENCED TO TEXTBOOKS
Medical Examination Publishing Co., Flushing, N.Y., 1965- , Vol. 1- .

RELATED MATHEMATICS

ADAMS, LOVINCY J., and JOURNIGAN, RUSSELL
Applied Mathematics for Electronics. Holt, Rinehart & Winston, 1967, 702, illus.

ALVAREZ, E. CHARLES
Using The Slide Rule in Electronic Technology. Hayden, 1962, 108, illus.

ANDREWS, ALAN
Electronics Math Simplified. Sams, 1961, 224, illus. (Sams Photofact Publication MAT-1.)

BARKER, FORREST L.
Mathematics for Electronics. Addison-Wesley, 1968, 742, illus.

HEALTH SERVICE PROGRAMS

BENSON, SIDNEY W.
    Chemical Calculations: An Introduction to the Use of Mathematics in Chemistry. 2nd ed. Wiley, 1963, 254, illus.

BERGTOLD, FRITZ
    Mathematics for Radio and Electronics Technicians. Transatlantic, 1967, 1 vol.

BIDDLE, HARRY C., and SITLER, DISA W.
    Mathematics of Drugs and Solutions. 7th ed. F. A. Davis, 1966, 133.

BLAKELEY, WALTER R.
    Calculus for Engineering Technology. Wiley, 1968, 441, illus.

BRUCKHEIMER, MAXIM, GOWAR, N. W., and SCRATON, R. E.
    Mathematics for Technology: A New Approach. Elsevier, 1968, 558, illus.

BUDZIK, RICHARD S.
    Precision Sheet Metal: Mathematics. Sams, 1969, 349, illus.

CARLO, PATRICK A., and MURPHY, DENNIS H.
    Merchandising Mathematics: A Text-Workbook for the Student of Distribution and Retailing. Delmar, 1967, 127, illus.

CARPER, DON
    Slide Rule in Electronics. Sams, 1967, 160, illus. (Sams Photofact Publication.)

THE CATHOLIC HOSPITAL ASSOCIATION, COMMITTEE ON RADIOLOGIC TECHNOLOGY
    Math Primer for Beginners in Radiologic Technology. CHA, St. Louis, 1966, 131.

CONNECTICUT STATE DEPARTMENT OF EDUCATION, VOCATIONAL EDUCATION DIVISION
    Mathematical Problems for the Fashion Design Course. Connecticut Department of Education, Hartford, 1965, 47. (ERIC VT 008 260.)

COOK, ALICE C., and MACAW, KATHERINE D.
    A Mathematical Guide to Dosage and Solutions. 2nd ed. Saunders, 1962, 237, illus.

COOKE, NELSON M., and ADAMS, HERBERT F. R.
    Arithmetic Review for Electronics. McGraw-Hill, 1968, 176, illus.

―――.
    Basic Mathematics for Electronics. 3rd ed. McGraw-Hill, 1970, 679, illus.

CRAWFORD, HOLLIE W., and McDOWELL, MILTON C.
    Math Workbook for Food Service/Lodging Programs. Institutions Magazine, Chicago, 1970, 228.

CROWDER, NORMAN A.
    The Arithmetic of Computers: An Introduction to Binary and Octal Mathematics. Doubleday, 1960, 472. (Tutor Text.)

CROWHURST, NORMAN H.
    Mathematics for Electronics Engineers & Technicians. Sams, 1964, 256, illus. (Sams Photofact Publication MEA-1.)

EVANS, PAUL L.
    Mathematics for Electronics Technicians. Wiley, 1966, 392, illus.

FERSTER, MARILYN B.
    Arithmetic for Nurses: Programmed for Class Use and Home Study. Springer, 1961, 112, illus.

GRAZDA, EDWARD E., BRENNER, MORRIS, and MINRATH, WILLIAM R., EDS.
    Handbook of Applied Mathematics. 4th ed. Van Nostrand, 1966, 1119, illus.

HART, LAURA K.
    The Arithmetic of Dosages and Solutions: A Programmed Presentation. 2nd ed. Mosby, 1969, 77.

HERRICK, CLYDE N.
    Mathematics for Electronics. Merrill, 1967, 1029, illus. (International Electronics Technology Series.)

HOOD, GEORGE, PARMERLEE, ALBERT S., and BAER, CHARLES J.
    Geometry of Engineering Drawing. 5th ed. McGraw-Hill, 1969, 469, illus.

JACOBOWITZ, HENRY
    Basic Math Course for Electronics. Gernsback, 1962, 160, illus. (Gernsback Library No. 100.)

JESSEE, RUTH W.
    Self-Teaching Tests in Arithmetic for Nurses. 7th ed. Mosby, 1967, 183, illus.

JUSZLI, FRANK L., MAHLER, NORMAN, and REID, JAMES M.
    Basic Mathematics for Electronics. Prentice-Hall, 1967, 450, illus. (Prentice-Hall Technical Mathematics Series.)

KEMP, LLOYD A. W.
    Mathematics for Radiographers. 2nd ed. F. A. Davis, 1964, 240, illus.

LEVINE, SAMUEL
    Vocational and Technical Mathematics in Action. Hayden, 1969, 344, illus. (Hayden Applied Mathematics Series.)

LIPSEY, SALLY I.
    Mathematics for Nursing Science: A Programmed Review. Wiley, 1965, 219.

MALVINO, ALBERT P.
    Calculus for Electronics. Wiley, 1969, 304.

McCLAIN, MARY E.
    Simplified Arithmetic for Nurses. 3rd ed. Saunders, 1966, 108, illus.

NATIONAL RADIO INSTITUTE
    Mathematics for Electronics and Electricity. Rider, 1963, 250, illus.

NUNZ, GREGORY J., and SHAW, WILLIAM L.
    Electronics Mathematics. McGraw-Hill, 1967, 2 vols., illus. (McGraw-Hill Technical Education Series.)

PAULL, STEPHEN
    Topics in Advanced Mathematics for Electronics Technology. Wiley, 1966, 420, illus. (Wiley Electronic Engineering Technology Series.)

PRICE, GERALDINE G.
    Self-Study Guide of Mathematics Used in Nursing. Putnam, 1963, 64.

REYNOLDS, GRAEME C.
    Mathematics and Science for Engineering Technicians' Courses. Butterworth, 1965- , vols., illus.

RIGGENBACH, FRANK
    The Slide Rule with Electronic Applications. Technical Education Press, 1970, 160.

SACKHEIM, GEORGE I., and ROBINS, LEWIS
    Programmed Mathematics for Nurses. 2nd ed. Macmillan, 1969, 262, illus.

SINGER, BERTRAND B.
    Basic Mathematics for Electricity and Electronics. 2nd ed. McGraw-Hill, 1965, 600, illus.

SLADE, SAMUEL, MARGOLIS, LOUIS, and BOYCE, JOHN G.
    Mathematics for Technical and Vocational Schools. 5th ed. Wiley, 1968, 527.

SZABO, N. S., and TANAKA, R. I.
Residue Arithmetic and Its Applications to Computer Technology. McGraw-Hill, 1967, 236.

TINGSTAD, JAMES E.
Mathematics for Pharmacy Students. Wiley, 1964, 106, illus.

TRONAAS, EDWARD M.
Mathematics for Technicians. Prentice-Hall, 1971, 336.

TRUETT, FRED M.
The Arithmetic of Sales Management. American Management Association, 1967, 192.

WEAVER, MABEL E., and KOEHLER, VERA J.
Programmed Mathematics of Drugs and Solutions. Lippincott, 1964, 101.

WESTLAKE, JOHN H., and GORDON, NODEN E.
Applied Mathematics for Electronics. Prentice-Hall, 1968, 608, illus. (Prentice-Hall Technical Mathematics Series.)

RELATED PARAMEDICAL FIELDS

AMERICAN ASSOCIATION OF JUNIOR COLLEGES and NATIONAL HEALTH COUNCIL
A Guide for Health Technology Program Planning. AAJC, 1967, 52.

AMERICAN ASSOCIATION OF MEDICAL RECORD LIBRARIANS
Glossary of Hospital Terms. AAMRL, Chicago, 1969, 95.
―――.
Medical Record Forms for Hospitals: Guide to Preparation. AAMRL, Chicago, 1963.

AMERICAN HOSPITAL ASSOCIATION
Being A Housekeeping Aide: Student Manual. AHA, 1967, 320.
―――.
Being a Ward Clerk: Student Manual. AHA, 1967, 247.
―――.
Housekeeping Manual for Health Care Facilities. Rev. ed. AHA, 1969, 159, illus.
―――.
Report Series No. 3: Hospital Auxiliaries and Volunteers. AHA, 1963, 38.
―――.
Training the Housekeeping Aide: Instructor's Guide. AHA, 1967, 271.
―――.
Training the Ward Clerk: Instructor's Guide. AHA, 1967, 216.
―――.
Horizons Unlimited: A Handbook Describing Rewarding Career Opportunities in Medicine and Allied Fields. AMA, 1966, 134, illus.

AMERICAN MEDICAL ASSOCIATION, ALLIED MEDICAL PROFESSIONS AND SERVICES DEPARTMENT
A Directory of Accredited Allied Medical Educational Programs, 1969-70. AMA, 1970, 1 vol.

ANDERSON, CARL L.
School Health Practice. 4th ed. Mosby, 1968, 468.

ARCO PUBLISHING COMPANY, INC.
Public Health Sanitarian. 3rd ed. Arco, 1966, 244.

BERNSTEIN, LEWIS, and DANA, RICHARD H.
Interviewing and the Health Professions. Appleton, 1970, 170. (Appleton Psychiatry Series.)

BETHLEHEM AREA VOCATIONAL-TECHNICAL SCHOOL, BETHLEHEM, PA.
Health Assistant: A Course of Study. Bethlehem Area Vocational-Technical School, 1967, 42. (ERIC VT 009 774.)

BLYTH, JOHN W., and SOLTESZ, SHIRLEY E.
How to Train Hospital Employees. Argyle, 1967, 1 vol.

CALDWELL, ESTHER, and HEGNER, BARBARA R.
Health Assistant. Delmar, 1969, 221, illus.

CEMBER, HERMAN
Introduction to Health Physics. Pergamon, 1969, 422, illus.

CONFERENCE ON JOB DEVELOPMENT AND TRAINING FOR WORKERS IN HEALTH SERVICES
Training Health Service Workers: The Critical Challenge—Proceedings. USGPO, 1966, 102, illus.

DODGE, BERTHA S.
Hands that Help: Careers for Medical Workers. Little, Brown, 1967, 247, illus.

FINCH, BERNARD
Multilingual Guide for Medical Personnel. Medical Examination Publishing Co., Flushing, N.Y., 1963, 159.

FREIDSON, ELIOT, ED.
The Hospital in Modern Society. Free Press, 1963, 366.

FRENCH, RUTH M.
The Dynamics of Health Care. McGraw-Hill, 1968, 140.

FULLERTON, BILL J., et al.
The Identification of Common Courses in Paramedical Education. Arizona State University, 1966, 158.

GRAD, FRANK P.
Public Health Law Manual: A Handbook on the Legal Aspects of Public Health Administration and Enforcement. American Public Health Association, 1965, 225.

GREENFIELD, HARRY I.
Allied Health Manpower: Trends and Prospects. Columbia University Press, 1969, 195.

HENRY, SARAH T., COMP.
A Preparatory Program for Hospital Housekeeping Aides: Course Description and Teaching Materials. Kentucky University, Instructional Materials Laboratory, 1968, 44.

HEPNER, JAMES O., BOYER, JOHN M., and WESTERHAUS, CARL L.
Personnel Administration and Labor Relations in Health Care Facilities. Mosby, 1969, 391.

HERMAN, HAROLD, and McKAY, MARY E.
Community Health Services. International City Management Association, 1968, 1 vol.

HICKS, FLORENCE
New Careers: The Community/Home Health Aide, Trainee's Manual. National Institute for New Careers, University Research Corp., Washington, 1968, 233.

JODAIS, JANET
Personal Care of Patients—A Text for Health Assistants. Saunders, 1970, 350, illus.

KATZ, ALFRED H., and FELTON, JEAN S.
Health and the Community: Readings in the Philosophy and Sciences of Public Health. Free Press, 1965, 877.

KINSINGER, ROBERT E.
Education for Health Technicians—An Overview. American Association of Junior Colleges, 1965, 35, illus.
―――, ED.
Health Technicians. J. G. Ferguson, 1970, 386. (Career Opportunities for Technicians and Specialists.)

KIRK, WEIR R.
Aim for a Job in a Hospital. R. Rosen Press, 1968, 124, illus. (Aim High Vocational Guidance Series.)
―――.
Your Future in Hospital Administration. R. Rosen Press, 1963, 154. (Careers in Depth No. 37.)

HEALTH SERVICE PROGRAMS

KLANIT, FREDERICK S.
  A Course of Study in Science and Related Technology for the Training of Health Physics Technicians. University Microfilms, Ann Arbor, 1968, 254.

MILLIKEN, MARY E.
  Understanding Human Behavior: A Guide for Health Workers. Delmar, 1969, 174, illus.

NATIONAL COUNCIL FOR HOMEMAKER SERVICES
  Homemaker-Home Health Aides... Training Manual. NCHS, New York, 1967, 181.

NORMAN, JOHN C., ED.
  Medicine in the Ghetto. Appleton-Century-Crofts, 1969, 333.

PERKINS, JOHN J.
  Principles and Methods of Sterilization in Health Sciences. 2nd ed. Thomas, 1969, 560, illus.

PORTERFIELD, JOHN D., ED.
  Community Health: Its Needs and Resources. Basic Books, 1966, 250.

RESOURCE PUBLICATIONS
  Index of Opportunity in Paramedicine. Resource Publications, 1970, 1 Vol.

ROTH, CLAIRE J., and WEINER, LILLIAN
  Hospital Health Services. Walck, 1964, 117, illus. (Careers for Tomorrow.)

SCHMIDT, FRANCES, and WEINER, HAROLD N., EDS.
  Public Relations in Health and Welfare. Columbia University Press, 1966, 278.

SCHMIDT, JACOB E.
  Paramedical Dictionary: A Practical Dictionary for the Semi-Medical and Ancillary Medical Professions. Thomas, 1969, 423.

SMITH, DUNCAN N.
  A Forgotten Sector: The Training of Ancillary Staff in Hospitals. Pergamon, 1969, 178. (Commonwealth and International Library.)

SOBEY, FRANCINE
  The Nonprofessional Revolution in Mental Health. Columbia University Press, 1970, 239.

STRYKER, RUTH P.
  The Hospital Ward Clerk. Mosby, 1970, 179, illus.

TASK FORCE ON HEALTH MANPOWER
  Health Manpower: Action to Meet Community Needs—Report. Public Affairs Press, Washington, 1967, 167, illus.

U.S. DEPARTMENT OF HEALTH, EDUCATION AND WELFARE
  The Allied Health Professions Personnel Training Act of 1966 as Amended. HEW, 1969, 94.

———.
  Training the Auxiliary Health Worker: An Analysis of Functions, Training Content, Training Costs, and Facilities. USGPO, 1968, 36. (PHS Bulletin 1817.)

U.S. NATIONAL ADVISORY COMMISSION ON HEALTH MANPOWER
  Report.... USGPO, 1967, 2 vols.

U.S. NATIONAL INSTITUTE OF HEALTH, RESEARCH GRANTS DIVISION
  Medical and Health Related Sciences Thesaurus. USNIH, Bethesda, Md., 1968, 460. (PHS Bulletin 1031.)

WILBUR, MURIEL B.
  Educational Tools for Health Personnel. Macmillan, 1967, 274, illus.

MEDICAL EMERGENCY

AGUILERA, DONNA C., MESSICK, JANICE M., and FARRELL, MARLENE S.
  Crisis Intervention: Theory and Methodology. Mosby, 1970, 1 vol., illus.

AMERICAN COLLEGE OF SURGEONS, COMMITTEE ON TRAUMA
  Emergency Care of the Sick and Injured: A Manual for Law-Enforcement Officers, Fire-Fighters, Ambulance Personnel, Rescue Squads and Nurses. Saunders, 1966, 128, illus.

AYRES, STEPHEN M., and GIANNELLI, STANLEY
  Care of the Critically Ill. Appleton-Century-Crofts, 1967, 256, illus.

CURRY, GEORGE J., ED.
  Immediate Care and Transport of the Injured. Thomas, 1965, 204, illus.

ECKERT, CHARLES, ED.
  Emergency-Room Care: By 24 Authors. Little, Brown, 1967, 373, illus.

FLINT, THOMAS, and CAIN, HARVEY D.
  Emergency Treatment and Management. 4th ed. Saunders, 1970, 733, illus.

GARB, SOLOMON, and ENG, EVELYN
  Disaster Handbook. 2nd ed. Springer, 1969, 310, illus.

HENDERSON, JOHN
  Emergency Medical Guide. 2nd ed. McGraw-Hill, 1969, 556, illus.

PROCTOR, HENRY, and LONDON, PETER S.
  Principles for First Aid for the Injured. 2nd ed. Butterworth, 1969, 253, illus.

RING, PETER A.
  The Care of the Injured. 2nd ed. Williams & Wilkins, 1969, 166, illus.

SALTER, ROBIN H.
  Common Medical Emergencies: A Guide for Junior Physicians. Wright, Bristol, (Williams & Wilkins, dist.), 1968, 140, illus.

SHARPE, JOHN C., and MARK, FREDRICK W., JR.
  Management of Medical Emergencies. 2nd ed. McGraw-Hill, 1969, 756.

VARGA, CHARLES
  Handbook of Pediatric Medical Emergencies. 4th ed. Mosby, 1968, 694, illus.

YOUNG, CARL B.
  First Aid for Emergency Crews: A Manual on Emergency First Aid Procedures for Ambulance Crews, Law Enforcement Officers, Fire Service Personnel, Wrecker Drivers, Hospital Staffs, Industry, Nurses. Thomas, 1965, 165.

MENTAL HEALTH

FAVAZZA, ARMANDO R., FAVAZZA, BARBARA S., and MARGOLIS, PHILIP M.
  Guide for Mental Health Workers. University of Michigan Press, 1970, 110.

LAMB, H. RICHARD, et al., eds.
  Handbook of Community Mental Health Practice. Jossey-Bass, 1969, 483.

McCLELLAND, LUCILLE H.
Textbook for Psychiatric Technicians. Mosby, 1967, 236, illus.

ROBINSON, ALICE M.
The Psychiatric Aide: A Textbook of Patient Care. 3rd ed. Lippincott, 1964, 226, illus.

OCCUPATIONAL THERAPY

THE AMERICAN OCCUPATIONAL THERAPY ASSOCIATION
Manual on Adapted Equipment for Use in Occupational Therapy. 1962, 1 vol.

CROMWELL, FLORENCE S.
Occupational Therapists' Manual for Basic Skills Assessment of Primary Pre-vocational Evaluation. Fair Oaks, Pasadena, Calif., 1960, 101, illus.

JACKSON, ELINOR, and DUNDON, H. DWYER, EDS.
Occupational Therapy Examination Review. Medical Examination Publishing Co., Flushing, N.Y., 1969, 1 vol.

LEEDY, JACK J., ED.
Poetry Therapy: The Use of Poetry in the Treatment of Emotional Disorders. Lippincott, 1969, 288.

MELDMAN, MONTE J., WELLHAUSEN, MARILYN, and JACOBSON, JOANNE
Occupational Therapy Manual. Thomas, 1969, 78.

O'MORROW, GERALD S., ED.
Administration of Activity Therapy Service. Thomas, 1966, 440, illus.

PETERSEN, GRETE
Creative Leathercraft. Sterling, 1960, 92, illus. (Sterling Craft Books.)

SHUFF, FRANCES L.
Your Future in Occupational Therapy. R. Rosen Press, 1964, 156. (Careers in Depth Series.)

WILLARD, HELEN S., and SPACKMAN, CLARE S., EDS.
Occupational Therapy. 3rd ed. Lippincott, 1963, 473, illus.

WISCONSIN (STATE) BOARD OF HEALTH
Occupational Therapy Assistants Program: Demonstration Project. Wisconsin Board of Health, 1968, 681. (ERIC ED 029 098.)

OPERATING ROOM

ASSOCIATION OF OPERATING ROOM NURSES, TECHNICIAN MANUAL COMMITTEE
Teaching the Operating Room Technician. AORN, 1967, 338.

DAVID HALE FANNING TRADE HIGH SCHOOL, WORCESTER, MASS.
Surgical Technician Procedures. 1963, 46. (ERIC VT 002 114.)

FOSTER, C. A.
Anaesthesia for Operating Theatre Technicians. Lloyd-Luke, London, 1968.

GINSBERG, FRANCES, BRUNNER, LILLIAN S., and CANTLIN, VERNITA L.
A Manual of Operating Room Technology. Lippincott, 1966, 276, illus.

LOUISE, SISTER MARY
The Operating Room Technician. 2nd ed. Mosby, 1968, 282, illus.

REDMOND, JAMES F.
Curriculum Guide for Health Occupations: Surgical Technician. Board of Education, Chicago, 1968, 43. (ERIC VT 009 701.)

PHYSICAL THERAPY

AMERICAN PHYSICAL THERAPY ASSOCIATION and COUNCIL OF PHYSICAL THERAPY SCHOOL DIRECTORS
Physical Therapy Curricula Directory. APTA, 1969- , Vol. 1- .

DOWNER, ANN H.
Physical Therapy Procedures: Selected Techniques. Thomas, 1970, 174, illus.

ETTER, MILDRED F.
Exercise for the Prone Patient. Wayne State University Press, 1968, 161, illus.

HOLLINSHEAD, WILLIAM H.
Functional Anatomy of the Limbs and Back: A Text for Students of Physical Therapy and Others Interested in the Locomotor Apparatus. 3rd ed. Saunders, 1969, 420, illus.

HUDDLESTON, ORA L.
Therapeutic Exercises: Kinesiotherapy. F. A. Davis, 1961, 205, illus.

KRISTY, JEAN, and McDANIEL, LUCY V.
Brain and Nerves of the Human Body: A Programmed Text and Plate Booklet for Physical Therapy Aides. Rancho Los Amigos Hospital, Downey, Calif., 1968, 92. (ERIC ED 033 227.)

McDANIEL, LUCY V.
Programmed Instruction for Aides in Physical Therapy: Final Report. Rancho Los Amigos Hospital, Downey, Calif., 1968, 59. (ERIC VT 007 963.)

McDANIEL, LUCY V., et al.
Bones, Joints, and Muscles of the Human Body: A Programmed Test for Physical Therapy Aides and Plate Booklet. Rancho Los Amigos Hospital, Downey, Calif., 1965, 195. (ERIC VT 009 678.)

INDEX

AD: The International Survey of Advertisements. 5

Aagaard, Orlena, Tasty Cooking for Ulcer Diets. 30

Aaron, James E., The Police Officer and Alcoholism. 95

Aaron, Jan, The Art of Mexican Cooking. 38

Aaron, Thomas J., The Control of Police Discretion: The Danish Experience. 95

Abbey, Staton, Chilton's B.M.C. Minicar Repair and Tune-Up Guide. 121

Abbott, David, Police, Politics and Race: The New York City Referendum on Civilian Review. 95

Abbott, John R., Footwear Evidence. 95

Abdallah, Mary, Nurse's Aide Study Manual. 194

Abdellah, Faye G., Better Patient Care Through Nursing Research. 187; Patient-Centered Approaches to Nursing. 187

Abdy, Jane, The French Poster. 8

Abel, Charles, Practical Portrait Photography for Home and Studio. 49

Abel, Oscar R., Mechanism of the Linotype and Intertype. 42

Abeles, Paul W., An Introduction to Prestressed Concrete. 140

Abell, Carl, Butane-Propane Power Manual. 121

Abercrombie, Michael, A Dictionary of Biology. 184

Abrahamsen, David, The Psychology of Crime. 95; Our Violent Society. 95

Abramoff, Peter, An Experimental Approach to Biology. 184

Abrams, Peter, Basic Data Processing. 15

Acker, Duane, Animal Science and Industry. 78

Ackerman, G. Adolph, A Visual Approach to Histology. 186

Adair, J. R., Welding Technology. 171

Adair, Thelma, Parents and the Day Care Center. 79

Adam, Hans K., The Wine and Food Society's Guide to German Cookery. 37

Adams, Ansel E., Camera and Lens. 48; Polaroid Land Photography Manual. 48; The Print: Contact Printing and Enlarging. 48

Adams, Aurelia K., Clothing Selection. 23

Adams, Carsbi C., Careers in Astronautics and Rocketry. 115

Adams, Charles P., Dental Photography. 173

Adams, Clinton, The Tamarind Lithography Resource Book. 14

Adams, Dorothy, The Technical Secretary. 72

Adams, George, Geriatric Nursing. 194

Adams, Herbert R., Arithmetic Review for Electronics. 206; Basic Mathematics for Electronics. 206

Adams, James D., Naked We Came. 21

Adams, James E., Electrical Principles and Practices. 145

Adams, Jeannette T., Complete Woodworking Handbook. 160

Adams, John M., Optical Measurements in the Printing Industry. 42

Adams, Lovincy J., Applied Mathematics for Electronics. 205

Adams, O. Eugene, Jr., Machine Design. 166

Adams, Roger, Laboratory Experiments in Organic Chemistry. 134

Adams, Thomas F., Law Enforcement. 95; Training Officers' Handbook. 95

Adams, Thomas M., Detector and Rectifier Circuits. 145; Transistor Circuits. 158

Adburgham, Alison, View of Fashion. 22

Adeline, Jules, The Adeline Art Dictionary. 8

Adler, Francis H., Adler's Physiology of the Eye. 197

Adler, Joan, Interiors Book of Restaurants. 52

Adler, Rudolph, The Soil and Its Fertility. 77

Adler, Sol, The Health and Education of the Economically Deprived Child. 108

Adlon, Hedda, Hotel Adlon. 50

Adriani, John, The Pharmacology of Anesthetic Drugs. 200

Advances in Environmental Sciences. 176

Advances in Textile Processing. 28

Afzelius, Bjorn, Anatomy of the Cell. 185

Agerter, Sharlene R., An Annotated Bibliography of Tree Growth and Growth Rings, 1950-1962. 86

Agnew, Peter L., Business Filing & Records Control. 67; Clerical Office Practice. 66; Full-Keyboard Adding-Listing Machine Course. 66; Key-Driven Calculator Course. 66; Office Machines Course. 66; Rotary Calculator Course. 66; Secretarial Office Practice. 66; Ten-Key Adding-Listing Machine and Printing Calculator Course. 66; Typewriting Office Practice. 66

Aguilar, Jeannette, The Classic Cooking of Spain. 38

Aguilera, Donna C., Crisis Intervention. 208

Ahlberg, Gudrun, Block and Silk Screen Printing. 8

Ahlgren, Henry L., Crop Production: Principles and Practices. 73

Ahr, Arthur, Introduction to Electricity and Electronics. 150

Ahrendt, William R., Servomechanism Practice. 163

Ahrens, Richard A., Nutrition for Health. 40

INDEX

Ainsworth, John H., Paper, the Fifth Wonder. 48

Air Force Materials Laboratory, Aerospace Structural Metals Handbook. 115

Airconditioning and Refrigeration Institute, Bibliography of Training Aids. 120; Course Guide for Airconditioning, Heating and Refrigeration Curriculums. 120

Aitken, J., Manual of Human Anatomy: Head and Neck. 173

Akehurst, B., Tobacco. 73

Akers, Ann B., An Introduction to Experimental Aerobiology. 177

Akers, Susan G., Simple Library Cataloging. 88

Akroyd, T., Concrete: Properties and Manufacture. 140

Albaugh, Reuben, Beef Cattle Production. 79

Albaum, Gerald, Marketing Handbook. 58

Albenda, Pauline, Creative Painting with Tempera. 8

Albers, Anni, On Designing. 22

Albers, Vernon M., Amateur Furniture Construction. 160

Albert, Adrien, Ionization Constants of Acids and Bases. 125; Selective Toxicity and Related Topics. 125, 200

Albert, Daniel M., Adler's Textbook of Ophthalmology. 199

Albertson, B., Photochemical Processes, 1969. 125

Albrecht, Carl F., Agricultural Engineering. 74

Albrecht, Val K., Profitable Studio Management. 10

Alcazar, Carol, Medical Typists' Guide for Histories and Physicals. 71

Alcazar, Rafael, Medical Typists' Guide for Histories and Physicals. 71

Alcosser, Edward, How to Build a Working Digital Computer. 17

Ald, Roy, The Complete Soup Cookbook. 30

Alderson, Wroe, Marketing and the Computer. 56; Men, Motives, and Markets. 56; Planning and Problem Solving in Marketing. 56; Theory in Marketing. 57

Aldrich, Ella V., Using Books and Libraries. 88

Aldrich, Samuel R., Modern Soybean Production. 76

Alerich, Walter N., Electric Motor Control. 156

Alex, Nicholas, Black in Blue: A Study of the Negro Policeman. 95

Alexander, Carter, How to Locate Educational Information and Data. 88

Alexander, Edythe, Care of the Patient in Surgery. 197; Nursing Service Administration. 187

Alexander, Milton, Logistics in Marketing. 61; Sales Management. 56

Alexander, Ralph S., Industrial Marketing. 56

Alexis, Marcus, Quantitative Methods in Marketing. 61

Allard, Robert W., Principles of Plant Breeding. 73

Allen, Dell K., Metallurgy Theory and Practice. 168

Allen, Don L., Periodontics for the Dental Hygienist. 173

Allen, Edward M., Harper's Dictionary of the Graphic Arts. 42

Allen, Frank D., Essentials of Human Embryology. 181

Allen, Herbert W., A History of Wine. 37; The Wines of Portugal. 37

Allen, James H., May's Manual of the Diseases of the Eye for Students and General Practitioners. 199

Allen, John E., Aerodynamics; A Space-Age Survey. 115

Allen, Kenneth W., Use of Community College Libraries. 88

Allen, Lewis M., Printing with the Handpress. 42

Allen, Paul, Exploring the Computer. 17

Allen, R. Earl, Memorial Messages. 92

Allen, R. V., Learning to Read Through Experience. 111

Allen, Raymond C. S., Theory of Flight for Glider Pilots. 115

Allen, Shirley W., An Introduction to American Forestry. 86

Allen, Willard A., Know Your Car. 121

Allender, Jerome S., Chemistry of Amino Acids, Peptides, and Proteins. 129

Alley, Walter, Automotive Suspensions, Steering, Alignment and Brakes. 125; Disc and Drum Brake Service. 122

Allgire, Mildred J., Nurses Can Give and Teach Rehabilitation: A Manual. 187

Allied Radio Corporation, All About High Fidelity and Stereo. 145; A Dictionary of Electronic Terms. 145; Electronics Data Handbook. 145

Almarode, Richard L., Guidelines for Hospitality Education in Junior Colleges. 50

Almen, John O., Residual Stresses and Fatigue in Metals. 168

Almfeldt, Maurice W., Engineering Graphics. 143

Almon, Joseph J., Visualized Basic Mechanical Drawing. 144; Visualized Basic Sheet Metal Drafting. 144

Almy, Millie C., Young Children's Thinking. 79

Althouse, Andrew D., Modern Refrigeration and Air Conditioning. 120; Modern Welding. 170

Altman, Philip, Blood and Other Body Fluids. 92

Altschul, Annie, Psychology for Nurses. 187

Aluminum Association, Aluminum Construction Manual. 136

Aluminum Company of America, Aluminum. 168

Alvarez, E. Charles, Introduction to Electron Tubes and Semiconductors. 145; Pulse and Switching Circuits. 149; Using the Slide Rule in Electronic Technology. 205

Alyn, Irene B., Saunders Tests for Self-Evaluation of Nursing Competence. 190

Ambrose, E. R., Heat Pumps and Electric Heating. 120

Ambrose, James E., Building Structures Primer. 136

Ambrosius, Edgar F., Mechanical Measurement and Instrumentation. 163

Amendola, Joseph, The Bakers' Manual for Quantity Baking and Pastry Making. 37; Ice Carving Made Easy. 30

American Accounting Association, A Statement of Basic Accounting Theory. 1

American Appraisal Company, Boeckh Building Valuation Manual. 64

American Association for Agricultural Engineering and Vocational Agriculture, Building Farm Fences. 73; Farm Electric Motors. 77; Farm Utility Buildings. 73; Planning Farm Fences. 73; Planning Water Systems for Farm and Home. 73; Selecting and Maintaining Field Mowers. 77; Selecting and Storing Tractor Fuels and Lubricants. 77; Small Engines. 77; Tractor Maintenance. 77; Tractor Operation and Daily Care. 77

American Association for Health, Physical Education and Recreation, After-School Games and Sports: Grades 4-5-6. 108; Classroom Activities. 108; Desirable Athletic Competition for Children of Elementary School Age. 108; Health Appraisal of School Children. 108; Healthful School Environment. 108; How We Do It Game Book. 79; AAHPER Book of Worldwide Games and Dances. 79; New Dimensions in School Nursing Leadership. 187; Rhythmic Activities: Grades K-6. 108; Teaching Dental Health to Elementary School Children. 173

American Association for Inhalation Therapy, 1968 Lecture Outline. 180; 1969 Lecture Outline. 180

American Association for Laboratory Animal Science, Manual for Laboratory Animal Technicians. 186

American Association for the Advancement of Science, Environmental Variables in Oral Disease. 173

American Association of Agricultural College Editors, Communications Handbook. 73

American Association of Junior Colleges, The Computer and the Junior College, 17; A Guide for Health Technology Program Planning. 207

American Association of Medical Record Librarians, Glossary of Hospital Terms. 207; Medical Record Forms for Hospitals: Guide to Preparation. 207

American Association of School Librarians, School Library Personnel. 88

INDEX

American Association of School Librarians and National Education Association, Department of Audiovisual Instruction, Standards for School Media Programs. 88

American Association of Textile Chemists and Colorists, Technical Manual and Yearbook. 28

American Blue Book of Funeral Directors. 92

American Cancer Society, A Cancer Source Book for Nurses. 188; Essentials of Cancer Nursing. 188

American Chemical Society, Chemical Marketing: The Challenges of the Seventies. 125; Cleaning Our Environment. 176; Flavor Chemistry. 125; Conference on Chemical Technicians Utilization. 125; Literature of Chemical Technology. 125; Natural Pest Control Agents. 125; Organic Pesticides in the Environment. 125; Reagent Chemicals. 125; Searching the Chemical Literature. 125

American College of Radiology, Planning Guide for Radiologic Installations. 203

American College of Surgeons: Emergency Care of the Sick and Injured. 208

American Concrete Institute, ACI Manual of Concrete Practice. 140; Cement and Concrete Terminology. 140; Computer Applications in Concrete Design and Technology. 140

American Conference of Governmental Industrial Hygienists. 176

American Craftsmen's Council, Cookies and Breads. 37

American Data Processing, Inc., Data Processing Yearbook. 15

American Dental Assistants Association, Dental Terminology. 173; Guide to Dental Materials and Devices. 173

American Drug Index. 200

American Fabrics Encyclopedia of Textiles. 28

American Fashion Pattern Grader. 22

American Foundrymen's Society, Basic Principles of Gating. 163; Basic Principles of Risering. 163; Principles of Production Metallurgy for Ferrous Castings. 168; Water Pollution from Foundry Wastes. 176

American Gas Association, Inc., Commercial Kitchens. 30

American Heritage, The American Heritage Cookbook and Illustrated History of American Eating and Drinking. 30; The American Heritage History of Flight. 115

American Home Economics Association, Textile Handbook. 28

American Hospital Association, Being a Food Service Worker. 30; Being a Housekeeping Aide. 207; Being a Nursing Aide. 194; Being a Ward Clerk. 207; Environmental Sanitation. 176; Food Purchasing Guide. 30; Food Service Manual for Health Care Institutions. 30; Guide to the Organization of a Hospital Medical Record Department. 71; Horizons Unlimited. 207; Housekeeping Manual for Health Care Facilities. 207; Medical Record Forms for Hospitals: Guide to Preparation. 71; Report Series No. 3. 207; Training the Food Service Worker. 30; Training the Housekeeping Aide. 207; Training the Nursing Aide. 194; Training the Ward Clerk. 207

American Hotel & Motel Association, ...Directory of Hotel & Motel Systems. 50; Uniform System of Accounts and Expense Dictionary for Motels-Motor Hotels-Small Hotels. 50

American Hotel Association Directory Corporation, Hotel & Motel Redbook. 50

American Industrial Arts Association, ...Conference Proceedings. 160

American Industrial Hygiene Association, Air Pollution Manual. 176

American Institute for Design and Drafting, Guide for Preparing a Drafting Manual. 142

American Institute of Biological Sciences, Biology Teachers' Handbook. 184

American Institute of Certified Public Accountants, Accounting Principles. 1

American Institute of Real Estate Appraisers, The Appraisal of Real Estate. 64

American Institute of Steel Construction, A.I.S.C. Textbook of Structural Shop Drafting. 145; Manual of Steel Construction. 136; Structural Steel Detailing. 136

American Institute of Timber Construction, Timber Construction Standards. 136; Timber Construction Manual. 136

American Insurance Association, Code for the Installation of Heat Producing Appliances, Heating Ventilating, Air Conditioning, Blower and Exhaust Systems. 120; Fire Department Pumper Tests and Fire Stream Tables. 83; Fire, Explosion and Health Hazards of Organic Peroxides. 83; Fire Prevention Code. 83; Fire Resistance Ratings of Beam, Girder and Truss.... 83; Hazard Survey of the Chemical and Allied Industries. 125

American Library Association, Anglo-American Cataloging Rules. 88; Books for Children. 80; International Subscription Agents. 88; Reference Books for Small and Medium-Sized Public Libraries. 88; Student Use of Libraries. 88; Young Adult Services in the Public Library. 88

American Library Directory: A Classified List of Libraries, with Names of Librarians and Statistical Data. 88

American Management Association, The Marketing Job: Responsibilities of the Top Man. 56

American Marketing Association, Proceedings of the National Conference. 56

American Meat Institute Foundation, The Science of Meat and Meat Products. 30

American Medical Association, A Directory of Accredited Allied Medical Education Programs, 1969-1970. 207; New Drugs. 200

American Motor Hotel Association, Uniform Classification of Accounts for Motels and Motor Hotels. 50

American Nurses' Association, Improvement of Nursing Practice. 188

American Occupational Therapy Association, Manual on Adapted Equipment for Use in Occupational Therapy. 209

American Paper and Pulp Association, The Dictionary of Paper. 48

American Perfumer and Cosmetics, ...Cosmetic Formulary. 7

American Petroleum Institute, Industrial Oily Waste Control Handbook. 176

American Pharmaceutical Association, Directory of Pharmacists. 200; Handbook of Non-Prescription Drugs. 200; Proprietary (Trade) Names of Official Drugs. 200

American Photoengravers Association, The Fundamentals of Photoengraving. 42

American Physical Therapy Association and Council of Physical Therapy School Directors, Physical Therapy Curricula Directory. 209

American Public Health Association, Glossary: Water and Waste-Water Control Engineering. 176; Guide to the Appraisal and Control of Air Pollution. 176; Health Officials' Guide to Air Pollution. 176

American Public Welfare Association, Public Welfare Directory. 103; Round Table Reader. 103

American Public Works Association, Standards Specifications for Public Works Construction. 136

American Public Works Association, Institute for Solid Wastes, Municipal Refuse Disposal. 176

American Radio Relay League, The Radio Amateur's Handbook. 156

American Records Management Association, Rules for Alphabetical Filing. 66

American Registry of Pathology, Manual of Histologic Staining Methods of the Armed Forces Institute of Pathology. 186

American Society for Metals, Casting Design Handbook. 166; Machining Difficult Alloys; A Compendium on the Machining of High-Strength Steels and Heat-Resistant Alloys. 168; Metal Progress Materials and Process Engineering Databook. 168; Metals Handbook. 168

American Society for Testing Materials, ASTM Manual on Quality Control of Materials. 28; ASTM Standards in Building Codes. 84, 136; Book of A.S.T.M. Standards, with Related Material. 163; Fire Resistance of

213

INDEX

Hydraulic Fluids. 84; Paper and Paperboard. 48; Fire Test Performance. 84

American Society of Agronomy, Pasture and Range Research Techniques. 73

American Society of Heating, Refrigerating and Air-Conditioning Engineers, A.S.H.R.A.E. Guide and Data Book. 120; A.S.H.R.A.E. Handbook of Fundamentals. 120; Thermodynamic Properties of Refrigerants. 120

American Society of Radiologic Technologists, Records for Schools of Radiologic Technology. 203

American Society of Tool and Manufacturing Engineers, Die Design Handbook. 166; Fundamentals of Tool Design. 166; Gundrilling, Trepanning and Deep Hole Machining. 163; Handbook of Fixture Design. 166; Numerical Control in Manufacturing. 169; Premachining Planning and Tool Presetting. 163; Tool Engineers Handbook. 163

American Welding Society, Brazing Manual. 170; Code for Welding in Building Construction. 136; Current Welding Processes. 170; Electroslag Welding. 170; Index for Welding Standards from 23 Nations. 170; Introductory Welding Metallurgy. 170; Modern Joining Processes. 170; Recommended Practices for Resistance Welding Coated Low Carbon Steel. 170; Standard for Qualification of Welding Procedures and Welders for Piping and Tubing. 170; Standard Welding Symbols. 171; Terms and Definitions. 171; Thermal Spraying Terms and Definitions. 163; Welding Handbook. 171

Amerine, Maynard A., Table Wines: The Technology of Their Production. 37; The Technology of Wine Making. 37; Wine: An Introduction for Americans. 37

Ames, Louise B., Child Care and Development. 80

Amiard, Hughes, Contact Lenses. 198

Amick, Charles L., Fluorescent Lighting Manual. 145

Amiss, John M., Use of Handbook Tables & Formulas. 165

Amos, Stanley W., Principles of Transistor Circuits. 158

Amos, William, Managing Student Behavior. 108

Anastasi, Thomas E., Jr., A Secretary is a Manager. 66

Anders, Evelyn, The Successful Secretary's Handbook. 67

Andersen, Christian J., An Introduction to Algol 60. 19

Anderson, Arthur L., Introductory Animal Science. 78

Anderson, Barbara G., Obstetrics for the Nurse. 194

Anderson, Bernice E., Nursing Education in Community Junior Colleges. 188; Nursing Practice and the Law. 191

Anderson, C. W., The Field of Social Work. 104

Anderson, Carl L., School Health Practice. 207

Anderson, Charles J., Alternating Current. 145; Direct Current. 145

Anderson, Charles R., Lettering. 14

Anderson, David A., Forests and Forestry. 86

Anderson, Donald M., Elements of Design. 13

Anderson, Edwin P., Air Conditioning. 120; Audel's Commercial Refrigeration. 120; Audel's Domestic Compact Auto Repair Manual. 122; Audel's Home Gas and Heating Appliance Manual. 120; Audel's Home Refrigeration and Air Conditioning Guide. 120; Audel's Refrigeration and Air Conditioning Guide for Engineers, Servicemen, Shop Men and Users. 120; Audel's Wiring Diagrams for Light and Power. 145; Questions and Answers for Electricians Examinations. 145; Television Service Manual. 157

Anderson, Edwin P., Electric Motors. 156

Anderson, Ellen, Workbook of Solutions and Dosage of Drugs. 188

Anderson, Frank R., Real Estate. 65

Anderson, Helen C., Geriatric Nursing. 194

Anderson, Ian G., Marketing & Management: A World Register of Organizations. 56

Anderson, J. C., Materials Science. 167

Anderson, James, Machine Tool Operation, Part II. 164; Shop Theory. 160

Anderson, James R., A Geography of Agriculture. 73

Anderson, Jean, The Art of American Indian Cooking. 39

Anderson, John N., Applied Dental Materials. 173

Anderson, John S., Modern Aspects of Inorganic Chemistry. 133

Anderson, John W., Principles of Accounting. 1

Anderson, Maja C., Basic Nursing Techniques. 188; Basic Patient Care. 188

Anderson, Norma J., Workbook for Pediatric Nurses. 195

Anderson, Paul E., Tax Factors in Real Estate Operations. 64

Anderson, Pauline C., The Dental Assistant. 173

Anderson, R. Clifton, Marketing Insights. 56

Anderson, Robert H., The Nongraded Elementary School. 110

Anderson, Roger F., Forest and Shade Tree Entomology. 86

Anderson, Ronald A., The Hotelman's Basic Law. 50

Anderson, Ruth I., Secretarial Careers. 67; Word Finder. 67

Anderson, Walt, Politics and Environment. 176

Anderson, Wilton T., Accounting. 1

Anderson, Yvonne, A Laboratory Manual in Business Machines. 69

Andreoli, Kathleen G., Comprehensive Cardiac Care. 188

Andresen, Jack, Fundamentals of Aircraft Flight and Engine Instruments. 115

Andrews, Alan, ABC's of Radar. 145; ABC's of Synchros and Servos. 145. Electronics Math Simplified. 205

Andrews, Dale W., Selected Lessons for Teaching Agricultural Science. 73

Andrews, Donald H., Introductory Physical Chemistry. 135

Andrews, Helen H., Food Preparation. 30

Andrews, M. E., Civil Service Tests for Typists. 68

Andrist, Ralph K., The Long Death. 92

Angelici, Robert J., Synthesis and Technique in Inorganic Chemistry. 133

Angell, Frank J., Angell's Study Manual of Insurance. 53

Angelo, Ernest J., Electronic Circuits. 145; Electronics: BJTs, FETs, and Microcircuits. 145

Angeloglou, Maggie, A History of Make-Up. 7

Angewandte, Chemie, Newer Methods of Preparative Organic Chemistry. 134

Angier, Bradford, Gourmet Cooking for Free. 30

Angus, Marion, Teach Yourself Pitman Shorthand. 67

Angus, Thomas C., The Control of Indoor Climate. 120

Ankers, Raymond G., Opportunities in an Accounting Career. 1

Annett, Fred A., Elevators. 136

Annual of Advertising, Editorial, Television Art and Design. 5

Ansel, Howard C., Introduction to Pharmaceutical Dosage Forms. 200

Ansley, Arthur C., Manufacturing Methods and Processes. 163

Anspach, Karlyne, The Why of Fashion. 22

Antebi, Michael, The Art of Creative Advertising. 5

Anthony, Catherine, Basic Concepts in Anatomy and Physiology. 183; Textbook of Anatomy and Physiology. 183

Anthony, Eugene, Profitable Television Troubleshooting. 157

Anthony, Helen, Medical Social Work. 103

Anthony, Robert N., Essentials of Accounting. 1; Management Accounting Principles. 1

Antill, James M., Critical Path Methods in Construction Practice. 136

214

INDEX

Antoine-Dariaux, Genevieve, Elegance. 22

Anton, Hector R., Fortran and Business Data Processing. 15

Antreasian, Garo Z., The Tamarind Lithography Resource Book. 14

Anzalone, Patricia M., Individualized Teaching in Elementary Schools. 113

Apparel Engineering and Needle Trades Handbook. 22

Applebaum, William, Store Location Strategy Cases. 63

Applegate, Rex, Crowd and Riot Control: Including Close-Combat Techniques for Military and Police. 95; Riot Control: Material and Techniques. 95

Apps, Ernest A., Ink Technology for Printers and Students. 47

Arbuckle, Wendell S., Ice Cream. 30; Ice Cream and Related Products. 32

Arbury, James N., A New Approach to Physical Distribution. 56

Arch, Marjorie S., The Bishop Method of Clothing Construction. 22; Fashion Sewing by the Bishop Method. 22

Archer, Fred C., College Accounting: Intermediate/Advance. 1; College Accounting: Theory and Practice. 4; Cost Accounting: Theory and Practice. 1; General Office Practice. 66

Archer, Horace R., Rare Book Collections. 88

Archer, R. K., Hematological Techniques for Use on Animals. 186

Archer, Sellers G., Soil Conservation. 73

Architectural Record, Motels, Hotels, Restaurants and Bars. 50; Architectural Engineering: New Structures. 136

Arco Publishing Company, Inc, Accountant Auditor. 1; Apprentice, Mechanical Trades. 163; The Arco Famous Car Series. 122; Asphalt Worker, Foreman of Asphalt Workers. 136; Assistant Accountant, Junior Accountant, Account Clerk. 1; Auto Mechanic, Autoserviceman. 122; Auto Machinist. 122; Battalion and Deputy Chief, Fire Department. 84; Beginning Office Worker. 67; Beverage Control Investigator. 38; Captain, Fire Department. 84; Captain, Police Department. 95; Chemist, Assistant Chemist. 125; Clerk, Steno Transcriber. 67; Construction Supervisor and Inspector. 136; Dietitian. 30; Early Childhood Education. 108; Engineering Aide. 163; Fingerprint Technician. 95; Fire Administration and Technology. 84; Fireman, F. D. 84; Fireman Tests in All States. 84; Food Service Supervisor, School Lunch Manager. 30; Foreman of Auto Mechanics. 122; Health Insurance Agents' Examination. 54; Housing Patrolman. 95; Insurance Agent and Broker. 53; Junior Draftsman, Civil Engineering Draftsman. 142; Laboratory Aide. 181; Law and Court Stenographer. 70; Law Enforcement Positions. 95; Lieutenant, Police Department. 95; Life Insurance Agents' Examination. 54; Machinist, Machinist's Helper. 163; Mortuary Caretaker. 92; 1540 Questions and Answers for Electricians. 145; Playground and Recreation Director's Handbook. 102; Police Cadet, New York City Police Department. 95; Policewoman. 95; Public Health Sanitarian. 207; Quizzer for Real Estate Brokers and Salesmen. 64; Real Estate Assessor, Appraiser. 64; Real Estate Manager. 64; Real Estate Salesman and Broker. 64; Refrigeration License. 120; School Secretary. 72; Social Case Worker. 103; State Trooper. 95; Stationary Engineer & Fireman. 84; ...Stenographer, Typist GS-1 Through GS-7. 67; Teachers in Community Centers. 102; U.S. Park Ranger. 86; Welder. 171; X-Ray Technician. 203

Arena, Jay, Dangers of Childhood. 80

Arey, Leslie B., Developmental Anatomy: A Textbook and Laboratory Manual of Embryology. 183

Argersinger, William J., Inorganic Chemistry. 133

Arges, K. P., Mechanics of Materials. 163

Argon, Ali S., Mechanical Behavior of Materials. 167

Aris, Rutherford, Elementary Chemical Reactor Analysis. 125; Introduction to the Analysis of Chemical Reactors. 131

Arkin, Frieda, The Cook's Companion. 30

Arkin, Herbert, Handbook of Sampling for Auditing and Accounting. 5

Arm, Walter, The Policeman. 95

Armarego, E., The Machining of Metals. 168

Armatas, James, The Management of People in Hotels, Restaurants, and Clubs. 52

Armstrong, Alfred R., Qualitative Analysis and Chemical Equilibrium. 132

Armstrong, Katharine F., Surgical Nursing. 197

Arnheim, Rudolf, Visual Thinking. 8

Arnold, Edmund C., Ink on Paper. 47; Modern Newspaper Design. 42; Profitable Newspaper Advertising. 5

Arnold, Grant, Creative Lithography and How To Do It. 14

Arnold, J. S., How to Build a Dynamics Sales Organization. 60

Arnold, Janet, Patterns of Fashion. 22

Arnold, Lionel K., Introduction to Plastics. 167

Arnold, Pauline, Clothes and Cloth. 22

Arnold, Robert R., Introduction to Data Processing. 15; Modern Data Processing. 15

Arnow, Leslie E., Health in a Bottle. 200; Introduction to Laboratory Chemistry. 125

Aron, Raymond, Main Currents in Sociological Thought. 103

Arons, Harry, Hypnosis in Criminal Investigation. 95

Aronson, Joseph, The New Encyclopedia of Furniture. 55

Aronson, Milton H., Electronic Circuitry for Instruments and Equipment. 145

Arslan, Albert, Fundamentals of Stress Analysis. 116

Arthur, Donald R., Survival: Man and His Environment. 176

Arthur, R., The Hotel Assistant Manager. 50

Arts, Elizabeth M., Medical Office Assistant. 71

Artz, Robert M., The National Recreation and Park Association Guide to New Approaches to Financing Parks and Recreation. 102

Asbell, Bernard, Careers in Urban Affairs. 103

Asbury, Taylor, General Ophthalmology. 200

Asch, Sidney H., Police Authority and the Rights of the Individual. 95

Ash, David, Automobile Almanac. 122

Ash, Lee, A Biographical Dictionary of Librarians in the U.S. and Canada. 88

Ash, Major M., Oral Pathology. 174

Ashburne, Jim G., Financial and Administrative Accounting. 4

Asher, Harry, Photographic Principles and Practices. 48

Ashley, Ray, Electrical Estimating. 145

Ashlock, Patrick, Educational Therapy in the Elementary School. 108

Ashman, Joseph R., A Textbook for Dental Assistants. 175

Ashworth, John, Careers in Accounting. 1

Ashworth, Robert D., Textbook of Human Histology. 186

Ashworth, William J., X-Ray Physics and Equipment. 204

Asinof, Eliot, People vs. Blutcher: Black Men and White Law in Bedford-Stuyvesant. 95

Askew, Frederick A., Printing Ink Manual. 48

Aspen, Marvin E., Criminal Law for the Police. 98

Asperheim, Mary K., The Pharmacologic Basis of Patient Care. 188; Pharmacology for Practical Nurses. 195

Asphalt Institute, The Asphalt Handbook. 136; Construction Specifications for Asphalt Concrete and Other Plant-Mix Types. 136; Introduction to Asphalt. 136; Specifications and Construction Methods for Asphalt Concrete and Other Plant-Mix Types. 136

INDEX

Aspley, John C., The Dartnell Sales Promotion Handbook. 56

Association of Better Business Bureaus, A Guide to Retail Advertising and Selling. 63

Association of National Advertisers, Perspectives in Advertising Management. 5

Association of Operating Room Nurses, Inc., Teaching the Operating Room Technician. 209

Association of School Business Officials of the United States and Canada, School Food Purchasing Guide. 30

Association of Teachers of Mathematics, Notes on Mathematics in Primary Schools. 108

Athanson, William J., Automobile Body Repair and Paint Guide. 122

Athearn, James L., Questions and Answers on Insurance. 53; Risk and Insurance. 53

Atkin, William W., Interiors Book of Restaurants. 52

Atkinson, Harry G., Management and Policies of Real Estate Brokerage. 64

Atkinson, Henry F., Mechanics of Small Engines. 122; Rough Carpentry and Masonry. 136

Atlas, Sheldon M., Man-Made Fibers. 29

Atteberry, Pat H., Power Mechanics. 122

Attwood, Charles, The Sales Representative's Handbook. 56

Atwell, Gladstone, The Manual for Utilization of Auxiliary Personnel. 108

Aubry, Arthur S., Jr., The Officer in the Small Department. 95

Audel and Company, Audel's Mechanical Drawing Guide. 144

Auerbach, Aline B., As Your Child Grows. 83; The Why and How of Discipline. 108

Ault, Addison, Problems in Organic Structure Determination. 134

Austin, Anne L., History of Nursing. 193

Austin, Cedric, The Science of Wine. 38

Austin, Philip R., Design and Operation of Clean Rooms. 120

Austin, Ruth E., Furnishing Your Home. 54

Auto Engine Tune-Up. 122

Automobile Manufacturers Association, Automobile Facts and Figures. 122; Automobiles of America. 122; Community College Guide for Associate Degree Programs in Auto and Truck Service/Management. 122

Automotive Electric Association, Air-Cooled Engine Manual. 122; A.E.A. Electrical Specifications Handbook. 122; A.E.A. Transistor Ignitions Systems Manual. 122; Course in Automotive Tune-Up. 122

Automotive Parts Rebuilders Association, Inc., Counterman's Handbook for Handling of Rebuilt Parts. 122

Auvil, Kenneth W., Serigraphy: Silk Screen Techniques. 8

Avery, Hazel, Gynecology and Gynecologic Nursing. 194

Avery, Thomas E., Forester's Guide to Aerial Photo Interpretation. 86

Avner, Sidney H., Introduction to Physical Metallurgy. 168

Awad, Elias M., Automatic Data Processing. 15; Business Data Processing: 15; Problems and Exercises in Data Processing. 15

Awapara, Jorge, Introduction to Biological Chemistry. 132

Axelrod, Aaron, Machine Tool Operation, Part II. 164

Axler, Bruce H., The Cheese Handbook. 30

Aykroyd, Wallace R., The Story of Sugar. 30

Aylesworth, Thomas G., This Vital Air, This Vital Water. 176

Aylward, G. H., Chemical Data Book. 125

Ayres, Gilbert H., Quantitative Chemical Analysis. 132

Ayres, J. C., The Safety of Foods. 30

Ayres, Stephen M., Care of the Critically Ill. 208

Azaroff, Leonid V., Electronic Processes in Materials. 145

Azneer, J. Leonard, Resuscitation. 180

Baab, Clarence T., The Binding of Books. 47

Babb, Daniel S., Resistive Circuits. 145

Babb, Janice B., Real Estate Information Sources. 64

Babbitt, Harold E., Plumbing. 141

Babcoke, Carl H., RCA Color TV Service Manual. 157

Bachmann, C. Charles, Ministering to the Grief Sufferer. 92

Backer, Morton, Cost Accounting. 5; Modern Accounting. 1

Backer, Stanley, Thesaurus of Textile Terms. 28

Baer, Charles J., Geometry of Engineering Drawing. 206; Electrical and Electronics Drawing. 144

Baerwald, Reuben C., Hope in Grief. 92

Bagdikian, Ben H., In the Midst of Plenty. 103

Bahme, Charles W., The Fireman's Law Book. 84

Bahr, Leonard F., ATA Advertising Production Handbook. 5

Bailey, Royston, Authority in Social Casework. 104

Bain, Donald, The Case Against Private Aviation. 115

Bain, Donald M., The International Chemistry Directory, 1969-70. 125

Bain, Edgar C., Principles of Heat Treatment. 168

Bain, Eric K., The Theory and Practice of Typographic Design. 42

Bain, Read, Sociology: Introductory Readings. 103

Baines, A., Research in the Chemical Industry. 125

Baines, Harry, The Science of Photography. 48

Bair, Edward J., Introduction to Chemical Instrumentation. 133

Bair, Medill, Team Teaching in Action. 108

Baird, John E., Funeral Meditations. 93

Baird, Russell N., The Graphics of Communication. 47; Practical Exercises in Typography, Layout, and Design. 47

Baird, William R., Funeral Meditations. 93

Bakamis, William A., Improving Instruction in Industrial Arts. 160

Baker, Eva L., Planning an Instructional Sequence. 112

Baker, Francis J., Handbook of Bacteriological Technique. 181; An Introduction to Medical Laboratory Technology. 181

Baker, J. R., Cytological Technique. 185

Baker, Jeffrey, The Truth About Contact Lenses. 197

Baker, John P., Feed Formulation Manual. 79

Baker, L. E., Principles of Applied Biomedical Instrumentation. 182

Baker, Richard M., Salesmanship. 56

Baker, Stephen, Visual Persuasion, Written and Designed. 56

Baking Industry, The Cookie Book. 37

Bakish, Robert A., Handbook of Electron Beam Welding. 171

Balchen, Bernt, The Next Fifty Years of Flight. 115

Baldwin, Alfred L., Theories of Child Development. 80

Baldwin, Clifford T., Fundamentals of Electrical Measurements. 145

Baldwin, Ernest, Dynamic Aspects of Biochemistry. 132

Baldwin, John E., Experimental Organic Chemistry. 134

Baldwin, William R., Corneal Contact Lenses. 197

Balenzano, Rosa, Principles of Fashion Sketching. 24

Balinsky, B. I., Introduction to Embryology. 181

Ball, Frederick C., Making Pottery Without a Wheel. 160

Ball, K. J., Space Vehicle Dynamics. 115

Ballard, Bettina, In My Fashion. 22

Ballinger, Raymond A., Direct Mail Design. 8; Layout and Graphic Design. 8; Lettering Art in Modern Use. 14; Opportunities in Graphic Arts Careers. 42

Ballou, Hubbard W., Guide to Microreproduction Equipment. 88

INDEX

Balsley, Irol V., Integrated Secretarial Studies. 67; Shorthand Transcription Studies. 67

Bamman, Henry A., Oral Interpretation of Children's Literature. 80

Bancroft, J. D., An Introduction to Histochemical Technique. 181

Bancroft, Vivian S., It's So, Sew Easy. 22

Bancroft-Whitney Company, Drugs and Poisons. 95

Bander, Edward J., Law Dictionary of Practical Definitions. 70; Medical Legal Dictionary. 70

Bandura, Albert, Social Learning and Personality Development. 80

Bane, Allyne, Creative Clothing Construction. 22; Tailoring. 22

Banerjee, Dilap K., Laboratory Handling and Storage of Peroxy Compounds. 126

Banister, Manly, Etching. 8; Prints. 8

Bank Street College of Education, Directory of Institutions of Higher Learning Offering Training Programs for Auxiliary Personnel in Education. 108

Banks, James E., Chemical Equilibrium and Solutions. 125

Banks, William H., Inks, Plates and Print Quality. 48

Bann, Stephen, Experimental Painting. 8

Banton, Michael P., The Policeman in the Community. 95; Race Relations. 95

Bany, Mary A., Classroom Management. 111

Barabas, Mary H., Contemporary Head Nursing. 188

Barasch, Clarence S., Law of Real Estate Brokers. 64

Barban, Arnold M., Readings in Advertising and Promotion Strategy. 6

Barbata, Jean C., A Textbook of Medical-Surgical Nursing. 188

Barber, John W., Industrial Training Handbook. 160

Barbour, Edna H., PL/I: A Self-Instructional Manual. 19

Barclay-Smith, P., Oil Pollution of the Sea. 176

Bar-David, Molly, The Israeli Cook Book. 38

Bardell, P. R., Magnetic Materials in the Electrical Industry. 145

Bardill, Donald R., Family Group Casework. 103

Barger, James D., Introduction to Medical Science. 183; Learning Medical Terminology Step by Step. 72

Barker, Forrest L., Mathematics for Electronics. 205

Barker, Samuel B., Basic Endocrinology for Students of Biology and Medicine. 181

Barksdale, Hiram C., Marketing in Progress, Patterns and Potentials. 56; Marketing: Change and Exchange—Readings from Fortune. 56

Barlay, Stephen, The Search for Air Safety. 115

Barlow, Melvin L., History of Industrial Education in the United States. 160; Principles of Trade and Industrial Education. 160

Barlow, Richard B., Introduction to Chemical Pharmacology. 200

Barmak, Leonard, Casebook on Community Pharmacy Management. 201

Barnacle, Harold E., Mechanics of Automobiles. 122

Barnard, Alfred J., Jr., Quantitative Analytical Chemistry. 132

Barnard, Capel, The Art of Flambé Cooking. 30

Barnes, Elizabeth, Psychosocial Nursing. 188

Barnes, Leslie, Transistors for Technical Colleges. 158

Barnett, Leo, Careers in Computer Programming. 19

Barnett, Michael P., Computer Programming in English. 19; Computer Typesetting. 42

Barney, Charles W., Forest Tree Planting in Arid Zones. 87

Barnhardt, Robert A., Opportunities in Textile Careers. 28

Barnhill, J. Allison, Sales Management. 56

Barnouw, Elsa, Adventures with Children in Nursery School and Kindergarten. 108

Baron, Harold, Clerical Record Keeping, Course II. 67

Barr, Randolph, The Automobile Electrical System. 122

Barr, W. N., Practical Secretarial Work. 68

Barratt, Stuart, Wine Merchandising. 38

Barrett, Jean, The Head Nurse. 188

Barrett, John W., Regional Silviculture of the United States. 86

Barrett, Robert, Transistor Circuits in Electronics. 158

Barris, George, How to Customize Cars and Rods. 122

Barron, David W., Recursive Techniques in Programming. 19

Barron, Norman S., The Pig Farmer's Veterinary Book. 78

Barrow, Gordon M., Understanding Chemistry III. 125

Barrow, Samuel W., Making Big Money in Real Estate. 64

Barrow (W.J.) Research Laboratory, Permanence/Durability of the Book. 42

Barrows, Arthur B., Profitable Catering. 30

Barrows, Claire M., Living Walls. 54

Barry, E. M., An Introduction to the Structure of Biological Molecules. 184

Barry, John M., An Introduction to the Structure of Biological Molecules. 184

Barry, W. S., The Language of Aviation. 115

Barsky, David, Color Atlas of Pathology of the Eye. 197

Bartee, Thomas C., Digital Computer Fundamentals. 17; A Survey of Switching Circuit Theory. 151

Bartels, Robert, Comparative Marketing. 56; The Development of Marketing Thought. 56; Marketing Theory and Metatheory. 56

Bartholomew, Davis, Electrical Measurements and Instrumentation. 145

Bartkowiak, Robert A., Feedback Amplifiers and Oscillators. 153

Bartleson, C. James, Color: A Guide to Basic Facts and Concepts. 13

Bartley, S. Howard, The Human Organism as a Person. 197

Barton, John J., Heating and Ventilating. 120

Barton, Roger, Handbook of Advertising Management. 6; Media in Advertising. 6

Barton, Roger E., The Dental Assistant. 175

Bartow, Mary, Fruits of Hawaii. 39

Bartram, Alan, An Atlas of Typeforms. 47

Baserga, Renato, Autoradiography. 203

Basic Cams, Valves, and Exhaust Systems. 122

Basic Carburetion and Fuel Systems: The Complete Story of the Fuel System From Tank to Manifold. 122

Basic Electronic Circuits. 145

Baslow, Morris H., Marine Pharmacology. 200

Basmajian, John V., Primary Anatomy. 183

Basolo, Fred, Mechanisms of Inorganic Reactions. 133

Bassett, Ernest D., Business Filing & Records Control. 67

Bassett, George W., Innovation in Primary Education. 108

Bassin, Milton G., Statics and Strength of Materials. 170

Bassler, G. Clayton, Spectrometric Identification of Organic Compounds. 135

Bast, Herbert, Essentials of Modern Upholstery. 56

Batchelor, Denzil, The English Inn. 50

Bateman, Ruth C., Serve It Cold. 31

Bates, Frank, Programming Language/One. 19

Bates, Kenneth F., Basic Design. 13

Bates, Marston, The Forest and The Sea. 176; Man in Nature. 176

Bates, Roger G., Determination of pH. 125

Bates, Steven S., Fundamentals for the Optometric Assistant. 197

217

INDEX

Batho, Robert L., A Practical Approach to Technical Illustration. 142

Batmale, Louis F., Career Training in Hotel and Restaurant Operation. 50

Battan, Louis J., The Unclean Sky. 176

Batten, James W., Soils. 74

Battino, Rubin, Thermodynamics. 164

Battle, Brendon P., Arson. 84

Bauer, Annabel B., An Experimental Inservice Program for Implementing Team Nursing. 188

Bauer, Donald D., A Textbook of Elementary Radiography for Students and Technicians. 203

Bauer, Ludwig, Problems in Organic Chemistry. 134

Bauer, Raymond A., Advertising in America. 6

Bauer, Royal D. M., Auditing. 5

Bauman, Robert P., Absorption Spectroscopy. 125

Bausch & Lomb, Incorporated, Ophthalmic Instruments and Professional Furniture. 197

Bayley, David H., Minorities and the Police. 95

Bayly, Joseph T., The View From a Hearse. 93

Bazore, Katherine, Fruits of Hawaii. 39

Beach, Frank H., Textbook of Salesmanship. 61

Beadle, Muriel, A Child's Mind: How Children Learn from Birth to Age Five. 80

Beadles, William T., Law and the Life Insurance Contract. 54

Beamer, Esther K., Effective Secretarial Practices. 67

Bean, Virginia L., Accounting. 4

Bear, Firman E., Chemistry of the Soil. 73

Bear, Roberta M., Early Education. 110

Beard, Charles, A Dictionary of English Costume. 27

Beard, James, Hors d'Oeuvre and Canapés. 30

Bearden, James H., Personal Selling. 56

Beater, Jack, Electric Motor Test and Repair. 156

Beaty, David, The Human Factor in Aircraft Accidents. 115

Beau, Frank N., Quantity Food Processing Guide. 30

Beaven, G. H., Molecular Spectroscopy. 125

Beck, Doris M., Custom Tailoring for Homemakers. 22

Beck, Mary E., Nutrition and Dietetics for Nurses. 188

Beck, Simone, Mastering the Art of French Cooking. 38

Becker, Bernard, Current Concepts in Ophthalmology. 197

Becker, Betty G., Vocational and Personal Adjustments in Practical Nursing. 195

Becker, E. L., Your Career in Accounting. 1

Becker, Esther R., The High Paid Secretary. 67; How to Be an Effective Executive Secretary. 70; The Successful Secretary's Handbook. 67

Becker, Harold K., Issues in Police Administration. 95; Law Enforcement: A Selected Bibliography. 95; New Dimensions in Criminal Justice. 95

Becker, Harvey A., Getting Better Results from Substitutes, Teacher Aides and Volunteers. 112

Becker, Howard S., Social Problems. 103

Becker, Marion R., Joy of Cooking. 35

Beckman, Harry, Pharmacology. 200

Beckman, Theodore N., Marketing. 56

Beckwith, Mary, The Effective Elementary School Teacher. 108

Beckwith, Thomas G., Mechanical Measurements. 164

Bedell, Earl L., Careers in Graphic Reproduction. 42; General Metal. 161

Bedell, Madelon, Profits from Franchising. 62

Bedford, John R., Basic Course of Practical Metalwork. 168; Metalcraft. 160

Bedford, Norton M., Advanced Accounting. 1; Introduction to Modern Accounting. 1

Beebe, Ralph A., The Development of Chemical Principles. 129

Beeler, Samuel C., Understanding Your Car. 122

Beerens, A. J. C., Measuring Methods and Devices in Electronics. 145

Beeson, William M., Livestock Judging and Evaluation. 78

Begbie, G. Hugh, Seeing and the Eye. 197

Behrman, Abraham S., Water is Everybody's Business. 177

Beilenson, Edna, Festive Seafood Cookery. 30

Beinert, Frederica L., The Art of Making Sauces and Gravies. 30; The Art of Making Souffles. 30

Beitler, Ethel J., Create with Yarn. 22

Bekker, Mieczyslaw G., Introduction to Terrain-Vehicle Systems. 122

Beland, Irene L., Clinical Nursing. 188

Belcher, Ronald, New Methods in Analytical Chemistry. 131

Belinkoff, Stanton, Introduction to Inhalation Therapy. 180

Bell, Bettye P., Cardiopulmonary Laboratory Basic Methods and Calculations. 181

Bell, Earl H., Social Foundations of Human Behavior. 103

Bell, Lawrance F., Basic Accounting and Cost Accounting. 5

Bell, Martin L., Marketing. 56

Bell, Norman W., A Modern Introduction to the Family. 103

Bell, Victoria K., The Art of Interior Design. 54; Opportunities in Interior Design and Decoration. 54

Bell, Winifred, Aid to Dependent Children. 103

Bell Telephone Laboratories, Electronic Communications Systems. 145

Bellack, Arno A., The Language of the Classroom. 108

Bellis, Herbert F., Architectural Drafting. 143; Blueprint Reading for the Construction Trades. 145

Belsjoe, Edith H., The Nurse Aide. 194

Belt, Forest H., Motorola Color TV Service Manual. 157; 1-2-3-4 Servicing Transistor Color TV. 158; Television Servicing/Repair. 157

Bendann, Effie, Death Customs. 93

Bender, Arnold E., Dictionary of Nutrition and Food Technology. 30; Dietetic Foods. 30; The Value of Food. 32

Bender, James F., How to Sell Well. 56

Bender, Marylin, The Beautiful People. 22

Bender, Rene J., Handbook of Foamed Plastics. 167

Benedict, Reginald R., Industrial Electronic Circuits and Applications. 145

Benenson, Lawrence A., Making Money in Real Estate. 64

Benfey, Otto T., Introduction to Organic Reaction Mechanisms. 126

Benge, Ronald C., Libraries and Cultural Change. 89

Bengtsson, Arvid, Environmental Planning for Children's Play. 80

Benice, Daniel D., Introduction to Computers and Data Processing. 15

Bennett, A. E., Blueprint Readings for Welders. 142

Bennett, A. G., Emsley and Swaine's Ophthalmic Lenses. 197

Bennett, Charles, How Big Ideas Make Big Money Selling Real Estate. 64

Bennett, Edna, Nature Photography. 48

Bennett, Harry, Chemical Zip Book. 126; Concise Chemical and Technical Dictionary. 126

Bennett, Ivy, Delinquent and Neurotic Children. 80

Bennett, Thomas P., Modern Topics in Biochemistry. 132

Bennett, Victor, The South Pacific Cookbook. 38

Bennett, William R., Data Transmission, 145; Electrical Noise. 145

Bennett, William S., New Careers and Urban Schools. 108

Bennett, Wilma, Occupations Filing Plan and Bibliography. 89

Bennett-England, Rodney, Dress Optional. 22

Bennion, Edmund B., Breadmaking. 37

INDEX

Benrey, Ronald, Understanding Digital Computers. 17

Bensing, Robert C., Homicide in an Urban Community. 95

Benson, Ben, Building Contractor's and Home Builder's Handbook of Bidding, Surveying, and Estimating. 136; Critical Path Methods In Building Construction. 136

Benson, Harold J., Dental Science Laboratory Guide. 173

Benson, Sidney W., Chemical Calculations. 206

Bent, Ralph D., Basic Science for Aerospace Vehicles. 117; Jet Aircraft Power Systems. 116; Powerplants for Aerospace Vehicles. 117

Bentley, Arthur O., Bentley and Driver's Textbook of Pharmaceutical Chemistry. 200

Bentley, Howard B., Building Construction. 136

Benton, Curtis D., Spectacles for Aphakia. 197

Benz, Gladys S., Pediatric Nursing. 195

Bereiter, Carl, Teaching Disadvantaged Children in the Preschool. 108

Berelson, Bernard, Human Behavior. 103

Berens, Jack, Commercial Radio Operator's License Study Guide. 156; Understanding and Troubleshooting Solid State Electronics Equipment. 145

Berens, Julius, Commercial Radio Operator's License Study Guide. 156

Berens, Stephen, Understanding and Troubleshooting Solid-State Electronic Equipment. 145

Berg, Edward, Mechanical Drawing, 144

Berg, Esther L., Classroom Teacher's Guide to Audio-Visual Material. 110

Berg, Eugene W., Physical and Chemical Methods of Separation. 126

Berg, Kenneth, Readings in International Accounting. 1

Berg, L. Thomas, Your Future in Welding. 171

Berg, Thomas L., Mismarketing: Case Histories. 56; Product Strategy and Management. 56

Bergel, Franz, All About Drugs. 200

Bergen, Polly, The Polly Bergen Book of Beauty, Fashion and Charm. 7

Berger, Andrew J., Elementary Human Anatomy. 183

Berger, Kermit C., Introductory Soils. 73

Bergersen, Betty S., Current Concepts in Clinical Nursing. 188; Nursing Care in Eye, Ear, Nose, and Throat Disorders. 190; Pharmacology in Nursing. 188

Bergtold, Fritz, Mathematics for Radio and Electronics Technicians. 206

Berkeley, Bernard, The Care, Cleaning and Selection of Floors and Resilient Floor Coverings. 50; Floors and Floor Maintenance. 50; Selection and Maintenance of Commercial Carpet. 50

Berkeley, Edmund C., The Programming Language LISP. 19

Berkeley, Ellen P., Play and Interplay. 102

Berkeley, George E., The Democratic Policeman. 95

Berkley, Joseph B., Laboratory Course in Pulse Circuitry. 145

Berkeley Scientific Publications, National & State Board Examination Questions and Answers for Medical Laboratory Technologists. 181

Berkowitz, Bernard, Basic Microwaves. 146

Berkowitz, Nathan, Automatic Data Processing and Management. 15

Berkowitz, Pearl H., The Disturbed Child. 108

Berlin, I. N., The Antisocial Child. 83

Berlove, Ira J., Dental-Medical Emergencies and Complications. 173

Berman, Arthur I., The Physical Principles of Astronautics. 115

Berman, Daniel S., How to Organize and Sell a Profitable Real Estate Condominium. 64; How to Reap Profits in Local Real Estate Syndicates. 64; Urban Renewal. 64

Bermont, Hubert, The National Recreation and Park Association Guide to New Approaches to Financing Parks and Recreation. 102

Bermosk, Loretta S., Interviewing in Nursing. 188

Bernard, Harold W., Mental Health in the Classroom. 108

Bernard, Hugh Y., Law of Death and Disposal of the Dead. 93

Bernard, Jessie S., Sociology Nurses and Their Patients in a Modern Society. 188

Bernard, Solomon M., System 360 Cobol. 19

Bernardo, James V., Aviation in the Modern World. 115

Bernier, Joseph L., Improving Dental Practice Through Preventive Measures. 173

Bernstein, Julian L., Audio Systems. 146; Standard Electronics Questions and Answers. 147; Video Tape Recording. 146

Bernstein, Lewis, Interviewing and the Health Professions. 207

Bernzweig, Eli P., Nurses's Liability for Malpractice. 188

Berry, Charles H., Flow and Fan-Principles of Moving Air Through Ducts. 120

Berry, Harrison M., Dental Roentgenology. 174

Berry, Roger J., Manual on Radiation Dosimetry. 204

Berry, William T., Annals of Printing. 42; The Encyclopaedia of Type Faces. 42

Bersten, Murray, A Picture Dictionary and Guide to Building and Construction Terms. 38

Bertholle, Louisette, Mastering the Art of French Cooking. 38

Besselievre, Edmund B., The Treatment of Industrial Wastes. 177

Best, Charles H., The Human Body. 183

Bethea, Doris C., Introductory Maternity Nursing. 194

Bethers, Ray, Composition in Pictures. 8

Bethke, Emil G., Basic Drawing for Biology Students. 181

Bethlehem Area Vocational-Technical School, Health Assistant. 207

Betschman, Lucille I., Handbook of Recovery Room Nursing. 197

Bettelheim, Bruno, The Children of the Dream. 80

Better Homes and Gardens, Better Homes and Gardens New Cook Book. 30; Decorating Book. 54; Decorating Ideas. 54; Famous Foods from Famous Places. 30; Meat Cook Book. 30; Salad Book. 30; Sewing Book. 22

Betterley, Melvin L., Sheet Metal Drafting. 144

Bettmann, Otto L., Bettman Portable Archive. 8

Betts, Jim, The Restaurant Casebook of Public Relations. 52

Betwee, Marcus G., Emotionally Handicapped Children and the Elementary School. 112

Beukema, Henry J., American Technical Society's Drafting. 142; Drafting Technology. 142; Engineering Drafting Problems. 142; Engineering-Technical Drafting and Graphics. 142; Everyday Sketching and Drafting. 142; Print Reading for Welders. 142

Bevan, John A., Essentials of Pharmacology. 200

Bevelander, Gerrit, Atlas of Oral Histology and Embryology. 173; Essentials of Histology. 186

Bevin, Arthur, Upholstery. 56

Bevis, Em, Team Leadership in Action: Principles and Applications to Staff Nursing Situations. 189

Beyer, Evelyn, Teaching Young Children. 108

Beyers, Virginia, Nursing Observation. 188

Bhaskar, S., Synopsis of Oral Pathology. 173

Bianco, Thomas C., Insurance Law. 54

Bibbero, Robert J., Dictionary of Automatic Control. 169

Bibby, Dause, Your Future in the Electronic Computer Field. 17

Bick, A., Contemporary Furniture. 56

Bickelhaupt, David L., General Insurance. 53

Bicknell, D. A., Direct Current Traction Motor. 124

219

INDEX

Biddle, Bruce J., New Media and Education. 108

Biddle, George H., Approved Practices in Poultry Production. 78

Biddle, Harry C., Chemistry for Nurses. 188; Mathematics of Drugs and Solutions. 206

Biegeleisen, Jacob I., The ABC of Lettering. 14; Art Directors' Book of Type Faces for Artists, Typographers, Letterers, Teachers and Students. 8; The Complete Book of Silk Screen Printing Production. 42; Silk Screen Techniques. 42

Bier, Norman, Correction of Subnormal Vision. 197

Bierman, Harold, Jr., Financial Accounting. 1; Managerial Accounting. 1; Topics in Cost Accounting and Decisions. 5

Bierstedt, Robert, The Social Order. 103

Bigelow, Marybelle S., Alphabets and Design. 8

Biggs, John, Basic Typography. 42

Biggs, John R., An Approach to Type. 42; Craft of Woodcuts. 8

Biggs, William D., The Brittle Fracture of Steel. 168

Bilitch, Mary J., Problem-Solving in Nursing Practice. 190

Billiet, Walter E., Automotive Electrical Systems. 122; Automotive Engines-Maintenance and Repair. 125; Automotive Fundamentals. 125; Automotive Suspensions, Steering, Alignment and Brakes. 125; Disc and Drum Brake Service. 122

Billington, David P., Thin Shell Concrete Structures. 140

Billington, Dora M., The Technique of Pottery. 160

Billmeyer, Fred W., Jr., Principles of Color Technology. 13

Binder, Otto O., Careers in Space. 115

Bing, Samuel, Artistic America, Tiffany Glass and Art Nouveau. 9

Binkley, Harold R., Experience Programs for Learning Vocations in Agriculture. 73; Farming Programs for Students in Vocational Agriculture. 73

Binns, Charles F., The Potter's Craft. 160

Binsted, Raymond, Hygiene in Food Manufacturing and Handling. 41; Pickle and Sauce Making. 30; Soup Manufacture. 41; Tomato Paste, Puree, Juice, and Powder. 32

Birbeck, M., Electron Microscopy. 183

Birch, Herbert G., Disadvantaged Children. 108

Birchall, G., Electrical Engineering Principles for Electrical, Telecommunications, and Installation Technicians. 153

Birchon, Donald, Dictionary of Metallurgy. 168

Bird, T. E., The Practice of Psychiatric Nursing. 196

Birnberg, Jacob, Cost Accounting. 5

Birren, Faber, Color For Interiors: Historical and Modern, 54; Creative Color. 13; The Elements of Color. 13; A Grammar of Color. 13; Principles of Color. 13

Bishop, Calvin C., Fundamentals of Electricity. 146

Bishop, Charles E., Farm Labor in the United States. 73

Bishop, Edna B., The Bishop Method of Clothing Construction. 22; Fashion Sewing by the Bishop Method. 22

Bishop, Frank E., Modern Farm Power. 78

Bishop, James, Let the Seller Beware. 57

Biskind, Elliott L., Law of Real Estate Brokers. 64; The Revised Penal Law Handbook. 97

Bittner, T. J., Instruction Manual for Mr. Airway. 180

Black, Algernon D., The People and the Police. 95

Black, Charles A., Soil-Plant Relationships. 73

Black, Homer A., Accounting in Business Decisions. 1

Black, Kenneth, Jr., Human Behavior and Life Insurance. 54; Life Insurance. 54; Property and Liability Insurance. 53; Cases in Life Insurance. 53

Black, Mary E., New Key to Weaving. 22

Black, Paul H., Machine Design. 166; Residual Stresses and Fatigue in Metals. 168; Theory of Metal Cutting. 168

Black, Perry O., Audel's Machinists Library: Basic Machine Shop Practices. 164; Audel's Machinists Library: Machine Shop. 164; Audel's Machinists Library: Toolmakers Handy Book. 164

Black, Peter, Mechanical Technology for Higher Engineering Technicians. 164; Mechanics of Machines. 164; Strength of Materials. 170

Black, Stephen, Man and Motor Cars. 122

Blackburn, James A., Spectral Analysis. 126

Blackburn, Thomas R., Equilibrium: A Chemistry of Solutions. 126

Blackie, John H., Inside the Primary School. 108

Blacklock, Donald B., A Guide to Human Parasitology for Medical Practitioners. 187

Blackman, Sydney, A Manual of Dental and Oral Radiography. 173

Blackshaw, H., Dictionary of Dyeing and Textile Printing. 22

Blackwell, Roger D., Cases in Consumer Behavior. 57

Blaedel, Walter J., Elementary Quantitative Analysis, Theory and Practice. 132

Blair, Eulalia C., Professional's Recipe Master. 30

Blake, Florence G., Essentials of Pediatric Nursing. 195; Nursing Care of Children. 195

Blake, Peter, God's Own Junkyard. 177

Blake, Robert R., The Grid for Sales Excellence. 57

Blakeley, Walter R., Calculus for Engineering Technology. 206

Blaker, J. Warren, Optics I: Lenses, Mirrors and Optical Instruments. 197; Optics II: Physics and Quantum Optics. 197

Blanchard, Harold, Auto Engines and Electrical Systems. 122

Blanchard, Marjorie P., The Kitchen Scholar. 33

Blanchard, Ralph H., Insurance. 53

Bland, David, A History of Book Illustrations. 42

Bland, Jane C., Art of the Young Child. 80

Blander, Milton, Modern Salt Chemistry. 126

Blankenship, Albert B., Marketing. 59

Blatt, John M., Introduction to Fortran IV Programming. 19

Blatz, Hanson, Introduction to Radiological Health. 203

Blegen, August H., Records Management Step by Step. 67

Bleich, Alan R., The Story of X-Rays, from Röntgen to Isotopes. 203

Bleier, Inge J., Maternity Nursing. 194

Blesh, Rudi, Collage. 10

Blewett, J. E., Anatomy and Physiology for Radiographers. 203

Blick, Edward F., Introduction to Fluid Mechanics and Heat Transfer. 165

Blide, Dan C., Metalwork Essentials. 163

Blinn, James E., Mobile Hydraulic Testing. 123

Bliss, Perry, Marketing and the Behavioral Sciences. 57

Blitsten, Dorothy R., The World of the Family. 104

Blitzer, Richard, Basic Pulse Circuits. 146

Bloch, Herbert A., Man, Crime and Society. 95

Block, Seymour S., Disinfection, Sterilization & Prevention. 182

Bloom, Sandra C., Federal Pollution Control Programs. 177; Pesticides and Pollution. 177

Bloom, William, A Textbook of Histology. 186

Bloom, William L., Jr., Medical Radiographic Technic. 203

Blower, W. E., The Complete MG Workshop and Tuning Manual. 122

Blum, Albert A., Company Organization of Insurance Management. 53

Blum, Joseph J., Introduction to Analog Computation. 17

Blum, Richard H., Police Selection. 95

Blum, Robert E., General Drafting. 142

INDEX

Blumberg, Abraham, Ambivalent Force. 95; Criminal Justice. 95

Blumberg, Jeanne E., Nursing Care of the Long-Term Patient. 188

Blume, Dorothy M., Dosage and Solutions. 188

Blyth, John W., How to Train Hospital Employees. 207

Board of Education, City of New York, Getting Started in the Elementary School. 112

Bobbitt, James M., Introduction to Chromatography. 126

Bobrow, Daniel G., The Programming Language LISP. 19

Boby, William M. T., Water Treatment Data. 177

Bockl, George, How to Use Leverage to Make Money in Local Real Estate. 64

Bockus, H. Williams, Advertising Graphics. 6

Bocock, E. Joan, Microbiology for Nurses. 188; Applied Anatomy for Nurses. 188

Boddewyn, Jean J., Comparative Management and Marketing. 57

Boelke, Joanne, Library Technicians. 89

Bogart, Leo, Current Controversies in Marketing Research. 57; Strategy in Advertising. 6

Boggess, Harry E., Aircraft Maintenance. 115

Boggs, James H., Introduction to Fluid Mechanics and Heat Transfer. 165

Boguslawski, Dorothy B., Guide for Establishing and Operating Day Care Centers for Young Children. 80

Bohn, Erik V., Introduction to Electromagnetic Fields and Waves. 146

Bohn, Ralph C., Organizing Course Materials. 162

Bohon, Davis T., Complete Guide to Profitable Real Estate Leasing. 64

Boland, Charles M., Careers and Opportunities in Advertising. 6

Boland, Marvin, Police Training and Performance Study. 97

Bolden, Theodore E., Dental Hygiene Examination Review Book. 173

Boling, Clem, College Accounting. 2; Secretarial Accounting. 67

Boll, Eleanor S., The Sociology of Child Development. 80

Bollinger, John G., Introduction to Automatic Controls. 170

Bolton, Edward R., Oils, Fats, and Fatty Foods. 126

Bomback, Edward S., Manual of Color Photography. 49

Bommarito, Barbara, The Schools and the Urban Crisis. 111

Bonadio, Gustave E., Fire Hydraulics. 84

Boni, Ada, Italian Regional Cooking. 38

Bonk, Wallace J., Use of Basic Reference Sources in Libraries. 89

Bonner, William A., Essentials of Modern Organic Chemistry. 134

Bonney, Virginia, Nursing Diagnosis and Therapy. 188

Book of the Dead. 93

Bookmiller, Mae M., Textbook of Obstetrics and Obstetric Nursing. 194

Boore, William F., The Computer Sampler. 17

Boorer, David, An Introduction to Psychiatric Nursing. 196

Boorer, Heather, An Introduction to Psychiatric Nursing. 196

Boorman, Kathleen E., An Introduction to Blood Group Serology. 181

Booth, George C., The Food and Drink of Mexico. 38

Booth, John E., Principles of Textile Testing. 28

Booth, K. M., Dictionary of Refrigeration and Air Conditioning. 120

Booth, Nicholas H., Veterinary Pharmacology and Therapeutics. 201

Borchers, Jean P., Direct and Alternating Currents. 151

Bordan, Sylvia D., Plays as Teaching Tools in the Elementary School. 108

Borden, Norman, Fundamentals of Aircraft Piston Engines. 115; Jet-Engine Fundamentals. 115

Bordicks, Katherine J., Nursing Care of Patients Having Chest Surgery. 197; Patterns of Shock. 188

Bordua, David J., The Police: Six Sociological Essays. 95

Borger, Robert, The Psychology of Learning. 108

Borgeson, Griffith, New Hot Rod Handbook. 122

Borgström, Georg, Fish as Food. 30; Principles of Food Science. 30; Too Many. 177

Borgwardt, Stephanie, Library Display. 89

Born, Max, Principles of Optics. 197

Bornet, Vaughn D., Welfare in America. 104

Boros, Ladislaus, The Mystery of Death. 93

Bose, Keith W., Aviation Electronics Handbook. 115

Bossard, James H. S., The Sociology of Child Development. 80

Bosticco, Isabel L. M., Top Secretary. 67

Boston Police Department, Reports, Records, and Communications in the Boston Police Department. 95

Bott, R., The Teaching of Young Children. 108

Bottle, R. T., The Use of Chemical Literature. 126

Bottom, Raymond, The Education of Disadvantaged Children. 109

Botzow, Hermann S., Auto Fleet Management. 122

Bouchard, Harry, Surveying. 141

Bouchard, Rosemary E., Nursing Care of the Cancer Patient. 188

Boucher, Carl O., Current Clinical Dental Terminology. 173; Swenson's Complete Dentures. 173

Boucher, Francois L. L., 20,000 Years of Fashion. 26

Boucher, Paul E., Fundamentals of Photography. 49

Boughey, Arthur S., Ecology of Populations. 177

Boulding, Reginald S. H., Principles and Practice of Radar. 156

Bouma, Donald H., Kids and Cops. 95

Bourne, Geoffrey H., Cytology and Cell Physiology. 185

Boutell, Wayne S., Contemporary Auditing. 5; Fortran and Business Data Processing. 15

Boutkan, J., ABC of the Egg: A Guide to Electrocardiography. 184

Bove, Frank J., The Story of Ergot. 200

Bowditch, W. A., Modern Welding. 170

Bowen, Eleanor P., Biology of Human Behavior: An Integration of Sciences Applied to Nursing. 188

Bowen, George L., Textbook of Obstetrics and Obstetric Nursing. 194

Bower, Eli M., Early Identification of Emotionally Handicapped Children in School. 109

Bower, Gordon H., Theories of Learning. 110

Bowers, Frank, Hair Styles and Beauty Guide. 8

Bowers, Margaretta K., Counseling the Dying. 93

Bowers, Melvyn K., Easy Bulletin Boards for the School Library. 89

Bowersox, Donald J., Physical Distribution Management. 57, 61

Bowes, Anna D., Food Values of Portions Commonly Used. 30

Bowker Annual of Library and Book Trade Information. 89

Bowles, Joseph E., Foundation Analysis and Design. 136

Bowley, C. Christopher, Techniques in Blood Grouping. 186

Bowman, Arthur G., Real Estate Law in California. 64

Bowman, Garda W., A Learning Team: Teacher and Auxiliary. 111; New Careers and Roles in the American School. 109

Bowman, Wallace B., Shorthand Dictation Studies. 67

Bowman, William C., Textbook of Pharmacology. 200

Bowman, William J., Graphic Communication. 9

Bowring, Jean, New Cake Decorating Book. 37

Boyce, John G., Mathematics for Technical and Vocational Schools. 206

Boyce, John S., Forest Pathology. 86

INDEX

Boyd, Gardner, Teaching Elementary Industrial Arts. 162

Boyd, Harper W., Cases in Marketing Strategy. 57; Contemporary American Marketing. 57; Marketing Management and Administrative Action. 57; Marketing Research. 57; Reading in Sales Management. 57

Boyd, Jessie E., Books, Libraries and You. 89

Boyd, Robert N., Organic Chemistry. 135

Boyd, T. Gardner, Metalworking. 160

Boyd, Thomas, Accounting for Management Planning and Decision Making. 3

Boyd, Waldo T., Your Career in the Aerospace Industry. 115

Boyd, William C., Fundamentals of Immunology. 181

Boyer, John M., Personnel Administration and Labor Relations in Health Care Facilities. 207

Boylestad, Robert L., Introductory Circuit Analysis. 146

Boynton, Lewis D., 20th Century Bookkeeping and Accounting. 1

Bracciano, Alfred F., Modern Refrigeration and Air Conditioning. 120

Bradbury, Frank R., Research in the Chemical Industry. 125

Braden, Irene A., The Undergraduate Library. 89

Bradfield, Nancy M., Costume in Detail. 26

Bradford, Kirk A., Existentialism and Casework. 104

Bradford, Lowell W., The Crime Laboratory. 98

Bradley, James J., Your Future in Automotive Service. 122

Bradley, John H., Programmer's Guide to the IBM System/360. 19

Bradley, Lewis A., Guide for Good Laundry and Linen Service in Hotels and Motor Hotels. 50; The Selection, Care, and Laundering of Institutional Textiles. 51

Bradley, W. W., Protective Coatings for Metals. 168

Bradley, Willis T., Pharmaceutical Calculations. 200

Bradlow, Bertram A., How to Produce a Readable Electrocardiogram. 184

Bradshaw, Angela, World Costumes. 26

Bradshaw, Christopher, Design. 13

Brady, George S., Materials Handbook. 136

Brady, Nyle C., The Nature and Properties of Soils. 73

Brady, Patricia S., Legal Secretary's Handbook. 70

Brake, John R., Farm and Personal Finance. 73

Brand, Edward A., Modern Supermarket Operation. 64

Brand, William N., Therapeutic Radiology. 205

Brandly, Paul J., Meat Hygiene. 30

Brandon, D. G., Modern Techniques in Metallography. 168

Brandon, Dick H., Management Planning for Data Processing. 15; Management Standards for Data Processing. 15

Brandslatter, Arthur F., Police and Community Relations. 95

Brandt, Rexford E., Watercolor Techniques. 9

Branscomb, Harvie, Teaching with Books: A Study of College Libraries. 89

Branson, Joan C., Hotel Housekeeping. 51

Branson, Lane K., Introduction to Electronics. 146

Brantley, C. Owen, How to Sell Printing by Mail. 42

Brasseaux, J. Herman, Readings in Auditing. 5

Brater, Ernest F., Handbook of Hydraulics. 138

Braué, John R., Uncle John's Original Bread Book. 37

Brauer, John S., The Dental Assistant. 175

Braun, Harold A., Coronary Care Unit Nursing. 188

Braun-Ronsdorf, Margarete, Mirror of Fashion. 26

Braverman, Joseph B., Introduction to the Biochemistry of Foods. 132

Bray, R. E., The Practice of Psychiatric Nursing. 196

Brayboy, Thomas L., Black Ghetto Family in Therapy. 107

Brazee, James G., Semiconductor and Tube Electronics. 146

Breach, M. R., Handbook of Bacteriological Technique. 181

Brecher, Edward, The Rays: A History of Radiology. 203

Brecher, Ruth, The Rays: A History of Radiology. 203

Breckenridge, Marian E., Growth and Development of the Young Child. 80

Bredemeyer, Hans G., Orthoptics. 197

Bredin, Harold W., Tooling Methods and Ideas. 164

Bredow, Miriam, The Medical Assistant. 71; Medical Secretarial Procedures. 71

Bregg, Elizabeth, Basic Psychiatric Concepts in Nursing. 190

Bregstein, Samuel J., Handbook for Dental Assistants, Hygienists and Secretaries. 173

Breillat, Pierre, The Rare Books Section in the Library. 89

Breithaupt, Herman A., Commercial Cooking. 30

Brembeck, Cole S., Social Foundations of Education. 109

Bremer, John W., Superconductive Devices. 146

Brendel, Leroy A., Typing Mailable Letters, with Facsimile Solutions. 68

Breneman, John W., Mechanics. 164; Strength of Materials. 170

Brenkert, Karl, Elementary Theoretical Fluid Mechanics. 164

Brennan, D., Laboratory Manual of Experiments in Physical Chemistry. 126

Brennan, J. G., Food Engineering Operations. 30

Brennan, Ruth, Nutrition. 40

Brennan, Thomas J., Ceramics. 160

Brenner, Barbara, Careers and Opportunities in Fashion. 22

Brenner, Marcella, Teacher Aides in Action in Elementary and Secondary Schools. 109

Brenner, Morris, Handbook of Applied Mathematics. 206

Brent, Carol D., Blending. 30

Brenton, Myron, What's Happened to Teacher? 109

Brereton, Gwendolyn, Introduction to Dental Nursing. 173

Brescia, Frank, Fundamentals of Chemistry. 126

Breslau, Michael, Condensed Computer Encyclopedia. 18

Bresler, Jack B., Environments of Man. 177

Breslow, Ronald, Organic Reaction Mechanism: An Introduction. 134

Bretz, Howard, Sheet Metal Shop Drawing. 144

Breuer, Hans, Dictionary for Computer Languages. 19

Brewbaker, James L., Agricultural Genetics. 73

Brewer, John T., Gynecologic Nursing. 194

Brewster, Ray Q., Organic Chemistry. 134; Unitized Experiments in Organic Chemistry. 134

Brick, J., The Laboratory Mouse: Selection and Management. 187

Brick, Robert M., Structure and Property of Alloys.... 168

Brickbauer, Elwood A., Approved Practices in Crop Production. 73

Bricker, Clark E., Foundations of Chemistry. 126

Bricker, Frederick E., Audel's Automobile Guide. 122

Bridges, Burtis C., Practical Fingerprinting. 96

Brien, Richard H., Readings in Marketing Information Systems. 61

Brierley, Robert G., Machining Principles and Cost Control. 164

Brigadier, Anne, Collage. 9

Briggs, Arthur H., Introduction to Molecular Pharmacology. 201

Briggs, Hilton M., Modern Breeds of Livestock. 78

Briggs, J. Robert, Office Machines. 67

Briggs, Peter, Water: The Vital Essence. 177

Brigham, Grace H., Housekeeping for Hotels, Motels, Hospitals, Clubs, Schools. 51

Brightbill, Charles K., Community Recreation. 103

Brightman, Rainald, Dictionary of Dyeing and Textile Printing. 22

Brightman, Richard W., Data Processing for Decision-Making. 15; Practical Data Processing. 15

Brigley, Catherine M., Pediatrics for the Practical Nurse. 195

Briloff, Abraham J., The Effectiveness of Accounting Communication. 1

Brimm, Daniel J., Aircraft Maintenance. 115

Brimmer, Brenda, A Guide to the Use of United Nations Documents. 89

Brinker, Russell C., Elementary Surveying. 141

Brinkley, John, Lettering Today. 14

Brion, Marcel, Art Since 1945. 9

Brissey, George E., Your Future in Food Technology. 30

Briston, John H., Introduction to Plastics. 167

Bristow, Allen P., Decision-Making in Police Administration. 96; Effective Police Manpower Utilization. 96; Field Interrogation. 96; Patrol Administration. 97; Police Supervision Readings. 96

Brite, Robert J., Synchros and Servos. 146

British Crop Protection Council, Insecticide and Fungicide Handbook for Crop Protection. 73

British Weed Control Council, Weed Control Handbook. 73

Britt, Kenneth W., Handbook of Pulp and Paper Technology. 48

Britt, Steuart H., Marketing Management and Administrative Action. 57; Measuring Advertising Effectiveness. 6

Brittain, R. P., The Disposal of the Dead. 94

Broadrib, Violet, Foundations of Pediatric Nursing. 195

Broby-Johansen, Rudolf, Body and Clothes. 26

Brochmann, Odd, Good or Bad Design? 13

Brock, Horace R., College Accounting: Intermediate/Advanced. 1; College Accounting. 1

Brock, Margaret G., Social Work in The Hospital Organization. 104

Brock, Thomas D., Biology of Microorganisms. 184

Brockman, Helen L., The Theory of Fashion Design. 22

Brodatz, Phil, The Elements of Landscape. 9; Textures: A Photographic Album for Artists and Designers. 9

Brodeur, Armand E., Radiologic Diagnosis in Infants & Children. 203

Brodkin, Jacob, Foundations of Chemistry. 131

Brodner, Joseph, Profitable Food and Beverage Operation. 31

Brodsky, Stanley M., Report of Electro-Mechanical Technology Curriculum Development Project.... 155; Statics and Strength of Materials. 170

Brogan, Gerald E., Using Libraries Effectively. 89

Bromley, Willard S., Pulpwood Production. 86

Bronfenbrenner, Urie, Two Worlds of Childhood: U.S. and U.S.S.R. 80

Brooke, Iris, Medieval Theater Costume. 26

Brooking, Walter J., Engineering Technicians. 164

Brooks, D. K., Resuscitation. 180

Brooks, Frederick P., Jr., Automatic Data Processing. 15; Automatic Data Processing System/360. 15

Brooks, Leonard, Course in Casein Painting. 9; Course in Wash Drawing. 9

Brooks, Stewart, A Programmed Introduction to Microbiology. 187

Brooks, Stewart M., Basic Facts of Pharmacology. 200

Broom, H. N., Small Business Management. 63

Broome, W. E., An Introduction to Nursing Bacteriology. 188

Brophy, James J., Basic Electronics for Scientists. 146

Brothers of St. Joseph, To Bury the Dead. 93

Brotherton, Manfred, Masers and Lasers: How They Work, What They Do. 155

Brothwell, Don R., Digging Up Bones. 93; Food in Antiquity. 31

Brothwell, Patricia, Food in Antiquity. 31

Brown, Arlen D., Farm Tractor Maintenance. 77

Brown, B., Ultrasonic Techniques in Biology and Medicine. 181

Brown, Dale, The Cooking of Scandinavia. 38

Brown, Earle B., Modern Optics. 198

Brown, Eleanor F., Bookmobiles and Bookmobile Service. 89; Modern Branch Libraries and Libraries in Systems. 89

Brown, Esther L., Newer Dimensions of Patient Care. 188; Nursing Reconsidered: A Study of Change. 188

Brown, Gary D., Systems/360 Job Control Language. 19

Brown, Geoffrey G., Primer of Histopathologic Technique. 181

Brown, Harold I., Lectures for Medical Technologists. 181

Brown, Jack U. U., Basic Endocrinology for Students of Biology and Medicine. 181

Brown, James G., X-Rays and Their Applications. 203

Brown, James W., AV Instructional Materials Manual. 109; AV Instruction: Media and Methods. 109

Brown, John H., Early American Beverages. 38

Brown, L. D., Dictionary of Electronics and Nucleonics. 149

Brown, Marion L., Southern Cook Book. 38

Brown, Marjorie, Evaluation Materials: Physical Home Environment and Psychological and Social Factors. 55

Brown, Martha M., Psychodynamic Nursing: A Biosocial Orientation. 188

Brown, Milton P., Problems in Marketing, 57

Brown, R. H., The Machining of Metals. 168

Brown, Robert D., Industrial Arts Laboratory Planning and Administration. 160

Brown, Robert K., Essentials of Real Estate. 65

Brown, Robert M., Amateur Radio Incentive Licensing Study Guide. 156; How to Read Electronic Circuit Diagrams. 146; 104 Simple One-tube Projects. 146

Brown, Ronald R., Lasers, Tools of Modern Technology. 155; Telecommunications: The Booming Technology. 146

Brown, Russell, How to Find Out About the Chemical Industry. 126

Brown, Theodore L., General Chemistry. 126

Brown, Walter C., Drafting. 142

Brown, Walter V., Textbook of Cytology. 185

Brownell, Adon H., Builders' Hardware Handbook. 136

Browning, Bertie L., Analysis of Paper. 48

Browning, David R., Chromatography. 126

Bruce, Leroy F., Sheet Metal Shop Practice. 160

Bruckheimer, Maxim, Mathematics for Technology. 206

Bruhn, Wolfgang, A Pictorial History of Costume.... 26

Brunblay, Ray U., A First Course in Quantitative Analysis. 132

Brune, Elmer, Welding Skills and Practices. 171

Bruner, Jerome S., The Process of Education. 109; Toward a Theory of Instruction. 109

Brunetti, Cledo, Electronic Equipment Design and Construction. 147

INDEX

Brunn, Alice L., How to Find Out in Pharmacy. 200

Brunner, Felix, A Handbook of Graphic Reproduction Processes.... 42

Brunner, Lillian S., A Manual of Operating Room Technology. 209; Textbook of Medical-Surgical Nursing. 188

Brunner, Lousene R., Casserole Treasury. 31

Brunner, Nancy A., Orthopedic Nursing. 195

Bruns, William J., Accounting and Its Behaviorial Implications. 1; Accounting for Decisions: A Business Game. 1

Brunsdon, John, The Technique of Etching and Engraving. 42

Brushwell, William, Painting and Decorating Encyclopedia. 54

Bruyninckx, Jozef, Phototypography & Graphic Arts Dimension Control Photography. 42

Bryan, George T., Control Systems for Technicians. 169

Bryan, Leslie A., Fundamentals of Aviation and Space Technology. 115

Bryant, Richard D., Woodward and Gardner's Obstetric Management and Nursing. 194

Bryant, W. R., Profitable Farm Management. 74

Brynner, Irena, Modern Jewelry: Design and Technique. 27

Buban, Peter, Understanding Electricity and Electronics. 146

Buber, Edward J., Graphic Arts Procedures: Offset Processes—Strike On and Film Composition. 45

Bucchioni, Eugene, Puerto Rican Children in Mainland Schools. 109

Buchanan, Barbara B., Psychiatric Nursing. 196

Buchsbaum, Walter H., Color T.V. Servicing. 157; Fundamentals of Television. 157

Buck, Anne, Children's Costume in England: From the Fourteenth to the End of the Nineteenth Century. 27

Buck, Jeanne T., Using Libraries Effectively. 89

Buck, N. Lewis, Mechanical Measurements. 164

Buck, Robert N., Weather Flying. 115

Buckle, D., Child Guidance Centres. 80

Buckley, John W., Classic Cars in Color. 122; Contemporary Accounting and Its Environment. 1

Buckman, Harry O., The Nature and Properties of Soils. 73

Bucknell, Peter A., The Evolution of Fashion Pattern and Cut. 27

Buckwalter, Len, Electronic Gadgets and Your Car. 122

Budge, Ernest A., The Mummy. 93

Budin, Frances M., Recipes from Ireland. 38

Budzik, Richard S., Precision Sheet Metal: Blueprint Reading. 144; Precision Sheet Metal: Mathematics. 206; Precision Sheet Metal: Shop Practice. 160; Precision Sheet Metal; Shop Theory. 160

Buell, Victor P., Handbook of Modern Marketing. 57; Marketing Management in Action. 57

Buffaloe, Neal D., Principles of Biology. 184

Buffie, Edward G., Educational Manpower. 112

Buhler, Curt F., William Caxton and His Critics. 42

Building Officials Conference of America, Inc., BOCA Basic Building Code. 136; BOCA Basic Fire Prevention Code. 84

Buist, Charlotte A., Toys and Games for Educationally Handicapped Children. 80

Bukstein, Edward J., ABC's of Transformers and Coils. 146; Basic Servomechanisms. 146; Industrial Electronic Circuits Handbook. 146; Industrial Electronics Measurement and Control. 146; Understanding Transformers and Coils. 146

Bulinski, Eugene C., Anatomy and Mechanics of Layout for Strippers. 43; Stripper's Guide to Knowledge. 43

Bulliet, L. J., Servomechanisms. 146

Bullock, Barbara, Cardiovascular Nursing. 190

Bullock, Kathleen, Orthoptics. 197

Bullough, Bonnie, The Emergence of Modern Nursing. 188

Bullough, Vern L., The Emergence of Modern Nursing. 188

Bundy, Clarence E., Beef Production. 78; Dairy Production. 78; Livestock and Poultry Production. 78; Poultry Production. 78; Swine Production. 78

Bundy, Mary L., The Library's Public Revisited. 89

Bunger, William B., Organic Solvents. 135

Bunnell, Kevin, Liberal Education and Pharmacy. 202

Bunting, A. H., Change in Agriculture. 73

Bunting, Brian T., The Geography of Soil. 73

Bunyan, Frederick J., Your Jet Pilot's Rating. 115

Burack, Abraham S., One Hundred Plays for Children. 109

Burack, Richard, The Handbook of Prescription Drugs. 200

Burbank, Nelson L., House Construction Details. 136

Burch, George E., A Primer of Electrocardiography. 184

Burd, Shirley F., Some Clinical Approaches to Psychiatric Nursing. 196

Burdon, Kenneth L., Microbiology. 187

Bureau of Business Practice, Inc., The Executive Secretary's Desk Manual. 70; The Secretary's Workshop. 67

Burford, William B., Semiconductor Junctions and Devices. 146

Burgen, A. S. V., Gaddum's Pharmacology. 200

Burger, Alfred, Selected Pharmacological Testing Methods. 201

Burger, Erich, Technical Dictionary of Data Processing, Computers, Office Machines. 15

Burghardt, Henry D., Machine Tool Operation, Part II. 164

Burhenne, H. Joachim, Alimentary Tract Roentgenology. 204

Burke, Arvid J., How to Locate Educational Information and Data. 88

Burke, Betsy, Fashion in Clothes. 22

Burke, William J., American Authors and Books: 1640 to the Present Day. 89

Burkhardt, Charles H., Domestic and Commercial Oil Burners. 120

Burkholder, Ralph, Laboratory Swatch Book: Textile Fabrics and Their Selection. 30

Burlingham, H. H., Selected Lessons for Teaching Off-Farm Agricultural Occupations. 75

Burmeister, Eva E., Tough Times and Tender Moments in Child Care Work. 80

Burn, Joshua H., Lecture Notes on Pharmacology. 201

Burnett, Clifford W., A Textbook of Obstetric Nursing. 194

Burnham, Robert W., Color: A Guide to Basic Facts and Concepts. 13

Burns, Aaron, Typography. 43

Burns, James L., A Training Program for Vocational Agriculture in Crops, Forestry, and Soil Conservation. 73

Burns, Jules P., Handbook of Medical and Anatomical Terminology. 71

Burns, Robert M., Protective Coatings for Metals. 168

Burns, Thomas J., The Accounting Sampler. 1

Burns, Van H., A Training Program for Vocational Agriculture in Farm Service. 73

Burnshaw, Stanley, Varieties of Literary Experience. 89

Burr, D. J., Understanding Young Children. 80

Burr, Joan, Nursing the Psychiatric Patient. 196

Burrell, Lenette O., Intensive Nursing Care. 188

Burrell, T. W., Learn to Use Books and Libraries. 89

Burrell, Zeb L., Intensive Nursing Care. 188

Burroughs Corporation, Military Field Service Division, Digital Computer Principles. 17

Burrow, William, Textbook of Microbiology. 187
Bursey, Maurice M., Elements of Organic Chemistry. 134
Bursk, Edward C., Modern Marketing Strategy. 57; Text and Cases in Marketing. 57
Burstein, Herman, Getting the Most Out of Your Tape Recorder. 89
Burstein, Milton B., What You Should Know About Selling and Salesmanship. 57
Burt, Samuel M., Industry and Vocational-Technical Education. 160; Technical Education for the Graphic Arts Industry. 43
Burton, Genevieve, Personal, Impersonal, and Interpersonal Relations: A Guide for Nurses. 188
Burton, Philip W., Advertising Copywriting. 6
Burton, Roger V., Child Rearing: An Inquiry Into Research and Methods. 83
Burton, William H., The Guidance of Learning Activities. 109
Busby, Reginald E., Organic Chemistry Problems. 134
Bush, Christine H., Personal and Vocational Relationships for Practical Nurses. 195
Bush, Clifford L., Strategies for Reading in the Elementary School. 109
Bush, George P., Automation and Electronics in Publishing. 44
Bush, Loren S., Introduction to Fire Science. 84
Business International, Winning the Markets of the 1970's. 57
Buskirk, Richard H., Cases and Readings in Marketing. 57; Management of the Sales Force. 61; Principles of Marketing. 57; Textbook of Salesmanship. 61
Butler, Anne, Embroidery Stitches. 22; Pattern and Embroidery. 22
Butler, David F., Simplified Furniture Design and Construction. 160
Butler, George D., Introduction to Community Recreation. 102
Butler, James N., Solubility and pH Calculations. 126
Butler, Lucius, Instructional Materials Centers. 112
Butler, Winifred, The Complete Book of Needlework and Embroidery. 22
Butt, Clifford, Introduction to Supermarket Occupations. 64
Buzzell, Robert O., Marketing Research and Information Systems. 57
Byers, Edward E., The Medical Secretary. 71; Medical Typing Practice. 71
Byers, Virginia B., Nursing Observations. 188
Byram, Harold M., Guidance in Agricultural Education. 74
Byrne, Jerry, Drying of Paper and Board. 48

Bystrom, Ellen, Printing on Fabric. 22

Caccamo, Leonard P., Resuscitation. 180
Cady, Louise L., Nursing in Tuberculosis. 188
Caen, Arthur H., Young People and Crime. 96
Cagle, Charles V., Adhesive Bonding. 126
Cagle, M. W., A Pilot's Meteorology. 115
Cahn, Robert S., An Introduction to Chemical Nomenclature. 126
Cahn, Robert W., Physical Metallurgy. 168
Caidin, Martin, Barnstorming. 115; Cross-Country Flying. 115; The Man-In-Space Dictionary. 116
Cain, Harvey D., Emergency Treatment and Management. 208
Cake, Walter, Fundamentals of Aircraft Piston Engines. 115
Calanese, Salvatore, The Correct Cashier for Hotels and Restaurants. 51
Calder, Nigel, Eden was No Garden. 177
Calderbank, Valerie J., A Course on Programing in FORTRAN IV. 19
Caldwell, Edson, Group Techniques for the Classroom Teacher. 109
Caldwell, Esther, Health Assistant. 207
Caldwell, Lynton K., Environment: A Challenge for Modern Society. 177
Caldwell, Robert G., Criminology. 96
Caldwell, William C., Practical Transistor Servicing. 158
Calhoun, M. Lois, The Microscopic Anatomy of the White Rat: A Photographic Atlas. 187
California (State) Department of General Services, The Library Technical Assistant Program. 89
California Redwood Association, Redwood File.... 86; Standard Specifications for Grades of California Redwood Lumber. 86
California University, School of Criminology, The Police and the Community. 96
Callahan, Dorothy, The Low Sodium, Fat-Controlled Cookbook. 34
Callander, R., Nurse's Illustrated Physiology. 191
Callender, John H., Time-Saver Standards. 136
Calvey, T. N., Dental Pharmacology. 175
Cameron, Christopher A., Modern Records Management. 68
Cameron, Sheila M., The Highlander's Cookbook. 38
Camishion, Rudolph C., Basic Medical Electronics. 184
Cammarata, Arthur, Physical Pharmacy. 202
Camp, Thomas, Water and Its Impurities. 177
Camp, William P., Psychiatric Nursing. 196

Campbell, Colin, Sports Car Engine: Its Tuning and Modification. 122
Campbell, Donald A., Nurse's Guide to Anesthetics Resuscitation and Intensive Care. 192
Campbell, E. J. M., Breathlessness. 180; Respiratory Failure. 181
Campbell, G. A., How to Find Out About the Chemical Industry. 126
Campbell, James A., Why do Chemical Reactions Occur? 126
Campbell, Jeff C., Simplified Industrial Telemetering. 146
Campbell, John D., Child Rearing: An Inquiry Into Research and Methods. 83
Campbell, Ralph H., The Dental Hygienist in Private Practice. 173
Campbell, Thomas F., SASS: Fifty Years of Social Work Education. 104
Campbell, Tod W., Preparative Methods of Polymer Chemistry. 131
Canadian Library Association, The Library Technician at Work. 89
Canadian Nurses' Association Library, ...Index of Canadian Nursing Studies. 188
Canby, Courtlandt, A History of Flight. 116
Canfield, Bertrand R., Sales Administration: Principles and Problems. 57
Canfield, Eugene B., Electromechanical Control Systems and Devices. 155
Cannel, Walter A., Medical and Dental Aspects of Fluoridation. 173
Cannon, Rupert V., Graphic Reproduction. 43
Cansler, Russell N., Fundamentals of Offset. 43
Cantarow, Abraham, Biochemistry. 132
Cantlin, Vernita L., A Manual of Operating Room Technology. 209
Cantor, Leon, How to Select and Install Antennas. 157
Caples, John, Tested Advertising Methods. 6
Capron, J. Hugh, Wood Laminating. 160
Caraway, Wendell T., Microchemical Methods for Blood Analysis. 181
Card, Leslie E., Poultry Production. 78
Cardamone, Tom, Advertising Agency and Studio Skills. 6
Cardew, Emily C., Study Guide for Clinical Nursing. 189
Carey, John L., The CPA Plans for the Future. 2; Ethical Standards of the Accounting Profession. 2; The Rise of the Accounting Profession. 2
Cargnino, Lawrence T., Aerospace Propulsion Powerplants. 116
Caringella, Charles, Transistorized Amateur Radio Projects. 158
Carini, Esta, Neurological and Neurosurgical Nursing. 194
Carlin, David, Alteration of Men's Clothing. 22

INDEX

Carlis, John, How to Make Your Own Greeting Cards. 9

Carlo, Patrick A., Merchandising Mathematics. 206

Carlsen, Darvey E., Graphic Arts. 43

Carlson, A. C., Judging Livestock, Dairy Cattle, Poultry, and Crops. 79

Carlson, Arthur E., College Accounting. 2; Secretarial Accounting. 67

Carlson, Bernice W., Recreation for Retarded Teenagers and Young Adults. 102

Carlson, Carolyn E., New Behavioral Concepts and Nursing Intervention. 189

Carlson, Elliot, Learning Through Games. 109

Carlson, Elmer C., Ten-Minute Test Techniques for Electronics Servicing. 146

Carlson, Howard M., Profitable Food and Beverage Operation. 31

Carlson, Reynold E., Recreation in American Life. 102

Carlson, Rosalin, Creative Knitting and Crocheting. 22

Carmichael, Leonard, Manual of Child Psychology. 80

Carnell, Paul H., Molecular Equilibrium. 126

Carnes, Robert M., Police Training for Delinquency Prevention and Control, an Appraisal. 96

Carnevali, Doris L., Nursing Care Planning. 191

Carpenter, Anna-Mary, Human Histology: A Color Atlas. 186

Carpenter, Dolores, Textbook of Obstetrics and Obstetric Nursing. 194

Carpenter, Philip L., Microbiology. 187

Carper, Don, Slide Rule in Electronics. 206

Carr, Arthur C., Teaching Psychosocial Aspects of Patient Care. 192

Carr, C. Jelleff, The Pharmacologic Principles of Medical Practice. 202

Carr, Clifford C., American Electricians' Handbook. 147; Wiring Tables. 147

Carr, Constance, A New Careers Guide for Trainers of Education Auxiliaries. 109

Carr, Donald E., The Breath of Life. 177; Death of the Sweet Waters. 177

Carr, Francis, A Guide to Screen Process Printing. 43

Carrier, Robert, Great Dishes of the World. 31

Carrier Corporation, Handbook of Air Conditioning System Design. 120

Carrithers, Wallace M., Business Information and Accounting Systems. 2

Carritt, Edgar F., The Theory of Beauty. 7

Carroll, C. Edward, The Professionalization of Education for Librarianship. 89

Carroll, Grady C., Industrial Instrument Servicing Handbook. 146

Carroll, John M., Careers and Opportunities in Computer Science. 17; Careers and Opportunities in Electronics. 146; Electron Devices and Circuits. 146; Microelectronic Circuits and Applications. 146; The Story of the Laser. 155

Carroll, Phil, Overhead Cost Control. 43

Carroll, Robert L., The Aerodynamics of Powered Flight. 116

Carroll, William, Auto Mechanics Basic Engineering Guide. 122; Bill Carroll's Automotive Gas Turbines. 122

Carroll-Porczynski, Charles Z., Manual of Man-Made Fibres. 28

Carson, Albert B., College Accounting. 2; Secretarial Accounting. 67

Carson, Arthur B., Foundation Construction. 136; General Excavation Methods. 136

Carson, Byrta, How You Look and Dress. 22

Carson, David, International Marketing. 62

Carson, Rachel L., Silent Spring. 177

Carson, Ralph S., Principles of Applied Electronics. 146

Carson, Richard F., Metal Stamping Design. 167

Carter, Byron L., Data Processing for the Small Business. 15

Carter, Harley, Dictionary of Electronics. 146

Carter, Harry, A View of Early Typography. 43

Carter, Muriel R., 100 to Dinner. 34

Carter, Norman H., Introduction to Business Data Processing. 15

Carter, Robert G., Introduction to Electrical Circuit Analysis. 146

Cartmell, Edward, Valency and Molecular Structure. 126

Cartwright, John M., Handbook of Real Estate Law. 65

Caruba, Rebecca, Cooking with Wine and High Spirits. 31

Caruzzi, Richard F., Offset Duplicator Techniques. 43

Carver, D. K., Introduction to Fortran II and Fortran IV Programming. 19

Casamassa, Jack V., Jet Aircraft Power Systems. 116

Casarett, Alison P., Radiation Biology. 203

Case, Frederick E., Real Estate Brokerage. 65

Case, Maurice, Recreation for Blind Adults. 102

Casella, Dolores, A World of Breads. 37

Caserio, Marjorie C., Basic Principles of Organic Chemistry. 135; Experimental Organic Chemistry. 134

Casey, James F., The Fire Chief's Handbook. 84

Casey, James P., Pulp and Paper: Chemistry and Chemical Technology. 126

Casey, William J., Accounting Desk Book. 2; Real Estate Desk Book. 65

Cashin, James A., Careers and Opportunities in Accounting. 2

Cashman, Thomas J., Basic Principles of Data Processing. 16; Data Processing: A Text and Project Manual. 15; Introduction to Computer Programming IBM System/360 Assembler Language. 19; Review Manual for Certificate in Data Processing. 15

Casola, Matteo, Successful Mass Cookery and Volume Feeding. 31

Cason, James, Laboratory Text in Organic Chemistry. 134

Cassard, Daniel W., Approved Practices in Feeds and Feeding. 78

Cassimatis, Peter J., Economics of the Construction Industry. 136

Castagna, Edwin, The Library Reaches Out. 89

Castrantas, H. M., Laboratory Handling and Storage of Peroxy Compounds. 126

Castro, Albert J., Essentials of Modern Organic Chemistry. 134

Caswell, Charles H., Basic Science for the Aviation Maintenance Technician. 116

Cataldo, Bernard F., Introduction to Law and the Legal Process. 70

Cataldo, John W., Graphic Design and Visual Communication. 9

Cateora, Philip R., Marketing Insights. 56; Readings in Marketing. 57

Catherman, J., Dental Health Education. 176

Catholic Hospital Association, Committee on Radiologic Technology, Math Primer for Beginners in Radiologic Technology. 206

Catlett, George R., Accounting for Goodwill. 2

Cavan, Ruth S., The American Family. 104; Criminology. 96

Cavanagh, Ursula M., Cooking and Catering, The Wholefood Way. 31

Cave, Roderick, The Private Press. 43

Cavellero, Gene, The Colony Cookbook. 31

Caves, Richard E., Air Transport and Its Regulators. 116

Cember, Herman, Introduction to Health Physics. 207

Cenci, Louis, Teaching Occupational Skills. 160

Cerepak, John R., Accounting for Business. 2

Cerf, Alan, Real Estate and the Federal Income Tax. 65; Real Estate Investment Analysis and Taxation. 66

Cernia, E., Man-Made Fibers. 29

Cernica, John N., Fundamentals of Reinforced Concrete. 140; Strength of Materials. 170

INDEX

Certified Medical Representatives Institute, Inc., Human Physiology: A Programmed Text. 183

Ceserani, Victor, Theory of Catering. 52

Chace, Franklin T., Principles of Cost Accounting. 5

Chaffee, Ellen E., Basic Physiology and Anatomy. 183

Chamberlain, Betty, The Artist's Guide to His Market. 9

Chambers, Clarke A., Seedtime of Reform: American Social Service and Social Action, 1918-1933. 104

Chambers, Dewey W., Storytelling and Creative Drama. 80

Chambers, Eric, Camera and Process Work. 49; Photolitho-Offset. 43

Chambers, Harry T., The Management of Small-offset Print Departments. 43

Chambers, Helen G., Clothing Selection. 22

Chambers, Raymond J., Accounting, Evaluation, and Economic Behavior. 2

Chambliss, William J., Crime and the Legal Process. 96

Champion, John E., Accounting in Business Decisions. 1

Champion, Romaine, The Art of Cooking Omelettes. 31

Champlin, James, Rural Recreation for Profit. 103

Champoux, Ellen M., Child-Care Services. 80

Chancellor, R. J., The Identification of Weed Seedlings of Farm and Garden. 74

Chandler, Asa C., Introduction to Parasitology. 187

Chandler, Caroline A., Early Child Care. 80

Chandler, Elzer S., Dental Hygiene Examination Review Book. 173

Chandor, Anthony, A Dictionary of Computers. 17

Chaney, Margaret S., Nutrition. 40

Chang, Ching-Hu, Climate and Agriculture. 74

Chang, H. C., Farm Information for Modernizing Agriculture. 75

Chang, Wonona W., An Encyclopedia of Chinese Food and Cooking. 38

Chantraine, Charles, La Cuisine Chantraine. 38

Chao, Pu-wei, How to Cook and Eat in Chinese. 38

Chapel, Charles E., Aviation and Space Dictionary. 116

Chapin, Ned, Programming Computers for Business Applications. 19; 360 Programming in Assembly Language. 19

Chapman, C. R., Electromechanical Energy Conversion. 155

Chapman, Dennis, An Introduction to Lipids. 126

Chapman, John F., Modern Marketing Strategy. 57

Chapman, Samuel G., Dogs in Police Work. 96; A Forward Step: Educational Backgrounds for Police. 96; Police Patrol Readings. 96

Chappell, Duncan, The Police and the Public in Australia and New Zealand. 96

Charley, Helen, Food Study Manual. 31

Charlot, Gaston, Chemical Reactions in Solvents and Melts. 126; Colorimetric Determination of Elements, Principles and Methods. 126

Charm, Stanley E., The Fundamentals of Food Engineering. 41

Charvat, Frank J., Supermarketing. 64

Chasnoff, Robert, Elementary Curriculum. 109

Chatten, Leslie G., Pharmaceutical Chemistry. 201

Chauncey, Henry, Soviet Preschool Education. 109

Chayen, J., A Guide to Practical Histochemistry. 126

Check-Chart Corporation, Lubricant Recommendations: Passenger Cars, Trucks and Tractors. 122

Cheetham, Robert, Dyeing Fibre Blends. 28

Chellis, Robert D., Pile Foundations. 136

Chemical Bond Approach Project, Chemical Systems. 126

Chemical Formulary, A Collection of Valuable, Timely, Practical Commercial Formulae and Recipes for Making Thousands of Products in Many Fields of Industry. 126

Chemical Materials Catalog, The Process Industries' own Catalog of Chemicals and Materials. 126

Chemical Rubber Company, CRC Handbook of Food Additives. 31

Cheney, Orion H., Economic Survey of the Book Industry, 1930-1931. 43

Cheney, Sheldon, A New World History of Art. 9; Primer of Modern Art. 9

Chenoweth, Harry H., Applied Strength of Materials. 170; Statics and Strength of Materials. 170

Cheraskin, Emanuel, Diet and the Peridontal Patient. 173; Physiology of Man. 184

Cherescavich, Gertrude D., A Textbook for Nursing Assistants. 194

Chernok, Norma B., Radiology Typists Handbook. 203; Your Future in Medical Assisting. 71

Cheronis, Nicholas D., Identification of Organic Compounds. 134; Semimicro Qualitative Organic Analysis. 132

Cherry, E. M., Amplifying Devices and Low-Pass Amplifier Design. 146

Cherry, Raymond, General Plastics: Projects and Procedures. 160

Chervenka, Charles H., A Manual of Methods for the Analytical Ultracentrifuge. 131

Cheskin, Louis, How to Color-Tune Your Home. 54; Secrets of Marketing Success. 57

Chesney, D. Noreen, Radiographic Photography. 204

Chesney, Muriel O., Radiographic Photography. 204

Chester, Giraud, Television and Radio. 157

Chevigny, Paul, Police Power. 96

Chiapperini, Felice, Canapes, Hors d'oeuvres and Buffet Dishes. 33

Chiasson, Robert B., Laboratory Anatomy of the White Rat. 186

Chicago University Press, A Manual of Style. 43

Chieffo, Clifford T., Silk-Screen as a Fine Art. 9

Child, Julia, The French Chef Cookbook. 38; Mastering the Art of French Cooking. 38

Child Welfare League of America, Inc., Day Care: An Expanding Resource for Children. 80; National Directory of Child Care Training Sources. 80; ...Standards for Child Protective Service. 80; ...Standards for Day Care Service. 80; ...Standards for Services of Child Welfare Institutions. 80

Childers, Norman F., Modern Fruit Science. 74

Children's Books In Print. 80

Childs, James J., Principles of Numerical Control. 169

Childs, John W., Instructional Technology. 111

Chiles, John R., A Treasury of Funeral Messages. 93

Chilton, Thomas H., Strong Water: Nitric Acid. 126

Chilton's Auto Repair Manual. 122

Chilton's Flat Rate and Parts Manual. 122

Chirlian, Paul M., Electronics. 146

Chironis, Nicholas P., Gear Design and Application. 122; Machine Devices and Instrumentation. 164; Mechanisms, Linkages, and Mechanical Controls. 164

Chistiakov, Nikolai I., Transistor Electronics in Instrument Technology. 158

Chiswell, B., Fundamental Aspects of Inorganic Chemistry. 133

Chittenden, Edward, Young Children's Thinking. 79

Chlystyk, Walter, Painting and Decorating. 54

Choate, Sharr, Creative Casting. 160

Chodorow, Marvin, Fundamentals of Microwave Electronics. 146

Chomsky, Carol, The Acquisition of Syntax in Children from 5 to 10. 80

Choron, Jacques, Death and Western Thought. 93

Choy, Jung S., The Art of Oriental Cooking. 38

227

INDEX

Christensen, Clyde M., Grain Storage: The Role of Fungi in Quality Loss. 74

Christensen, Halvor N., Body Fluids and the Acid-Base Balance. 181; pH and Dissociation. 182

Christensen, James L., The Complete Funeral Manual. 93

Christensen, John B., Dynamic Anatomy and Physiology. 184

Christensen, N. C., The Art of Persuasion in Selling. 57

Christensen, Sherryl E., Cardiopulmonary Laboratory Basic Methods and Calculations. 181

Christiansen, Neils B., Exercises in the Managerial Economics of Forestry. 86

Christie, Dan E., Vector Mechanics. 164

Chu, Grace, The Pleasures of Chinese Cooking. 38

Chukovsky, Kornei, From Two to Five. 80

Church, Charles F., Food Values of Portions Commonly Used. 30

Church, James M., A Concise Guide to Plastics. 168; The Encyclopedia of Basic Materials for Plastics. 168

Churchill, Bonnie, Reba and Bonnie's Guide to Glamour and Personality. 7

Churchill, Creighton, A Notebook for the Wines of France. 38

Churchill, Eileen M., Counting and Measuring. 80

Churchill, Reba, Reba and Bonnie's Guide to Glamour and Personality. 7

Chute, Aaron H., The Pharmacist in Retail Distribution. 201

Chute, George M., Electronics in Industry. 146

Cianciolo, Patricia J., Illustrations in Children's Books. 9

CIBA Foundation, Caries-Resistant Teeth. 173

Cirino, Antonio, Jewelry Making and Design. 28

Civil Service Publishing Corporation, How to Pass Patrolman. 96; How to Pass Patrolman Examinations. 96; How to Pass Policewoman. 96

Cizon, Francis A., Some Guidelines for Successful Police-Community Relations Training Programs. 96

Claiborne, Craig, Cooking with Herbs and Spices. 31; An Herb and Spice Cook Book. 31; The New York Times Menu Cook Book. 31

Clair, Colin, A Chronology of Printing. 43

Clapp, Leallyn B., The Chemistry of the OH Group. 126

Clapperton, Robert H., The Paper-Making Machines. 48

Clark, Ann L., Patient Studies in Maternal and Child Nursing. 195

Clark, Bill, Professional Cleaning and Building Maintenance. 51

Clark, Colin, The Economics of Subsistence Agriculture. 74; Starvation or Plenty? 74

Clark, Coly, Industrial Arts Drawing: A Text for Introductory Drafting. 142

Clark, D. S., Microorganisms in Foods. 35

Clark, Donald E., A Forward Step: Educational Backgrounds for Police. 96

Clark, Donald H., The Psychology of Education. 109; Those Children: Case Studies from the Inner-City School. 109

Clark, Eugene, Principles of Marketing. 62

Clark, Eustace G., Isolation and Identification of Drugs in Pharmaceuticals, Body Fluids, and Post-Mortem Material. 201

Clark, Frank J., Information Processing. 15

Clark, Fred E., Principles of Marketing. 62

Clark, George L., The Encyclopedia of Chemistry. 126; The Encyclopedia of Microscopy. 182; The Encyclopedia of X-rays and Gamma Rays. 204

Clark, Harold E., Xerography and Related Processes. 43

Clark, J. O. E., Computers at Work. 17

Clark, James W., Diet and the Periodontal Patient. 173

Clark, John W., Water Supply and Pollution Control. 177

Clark, Kathleen C., Positioning in Radiography. 204

Clark, Kenneth B., A Relevant War Against Poverty. 104

Clark, Morton G., French-American Cooking from New Orleans to Quebec. 38; A World of Nut Recipes. 31

Clark, Ralph W., Orientation in Pharmacy. 201

Clark, Ramsey, Crime in America. 96

Clark, Robert E., Semi-Micro Inorganic Qualitative Analysis. 132

Clark, Robert N., Introduction to Automatic Control Systems. 170

Clark, Ronald L., Industrial Chemicals. 127

Clark, Roy W., Concepts of General Chemistry. 129

Clarke, Carole A., Handbook of Electronic Instruments and Measurement Techniques. 154

Clarke, George L., Elements of Ecology. 177

Clarke, George T., Opportunities in Advertising Careers. 6

Clarke, Harold C., Menu Terminology. 31

Clarke, Leslie J., The Craftsman in Textiles. 28

Clarke, Ralph E., A Guide to Aerospace-Defense Contracts. 116

Claus, Edward P., Pharmacognosy. 201

Clawson, Marion, Policy Directions for U.S. Agriculture. 74; Soil Conservation in Perspective. 75

Clayson, Roberta, Screen Printing on Fabric. 25

Cleaver, Dale G., Art: An Introduction. 9

Cleaver, James, A History of Graphic Art. 43

Cleeton, Glen U., General Printing. 43

Clegg, Reed K., Probation and Parole. 96; The Welfare World. 104

Clem, Deloris K., The Cookie Cookbook. 37

Clements, Frederick W., Child Health. 80

Cleveland Bureau of Governmental Research, PFI: A Survey—Police-Fire Integration in the United States and Canada. 96

Clewett, Richard M., Cases in Marketing Strategy. 57; Contemporary American Marketing. 57

Cliffe, Henry, Lithography: A Complete Handbook of Modern Techniques of Lithography. 14

Clifford, Alan F., Inorganic Chemistry of Qualitative Analysis. 132

Clifford, Martin, Electronics Data Handbook. 146; Handbook of Electronic Tables. 146; How to Use Your VOM-VTVM and Oscilloscope. 146

Clift, Raymond E., A Guide to Modern Police Thinking. 96; Police and Public Safety. 96

Clifton, Harold D., Systems Analysis for Business Data Processing. 15

Clinard, Marshall, Criminal Behavior Systems. 96

Cline, David, Dictionary of Visual Science, 199

Cline, James, Patrol Operations. 102

Cline, Robert S., Property and Liability Insurance. 53

Cloke, Marjane, The Modern Business Letter Writer's Manual. 67

Close, Paul D., Sound Control and Thermal Insulation of Buildings. 136

Clough, Richard H., Construction Contracting. 136

Clowers, Norman L., Patrolman Patterns, Problems, and Procedures. 96

Coan, James S., Basic Basic: An Introduction to Computer Programming in Basic Language. 19

Coates, Ralph W., The Radiographic Position as a Whole. 204

Coats and Clark, Inc., Coats and Clark's Sewing Book. 22

Cobb, M. M., Fundamentals of Public Health Nursing. 196

Cobbold, Richard S., Theory and Applications of Field-Effect Transistors. 158

Coble, M. C., A Guide to Nutrition and Food Service for Nursing Homes and Homes for the Aged. 40

Cobrin, Harry A., The Men's Clothing Industry. 22

Cocannouer, Joseph A., Weeds, Guardians of the Soil. 74

Cochet, Paul, Contact Lenses. 198

Cochran, Lee W., Manual of Audio-Visual Techniques. 109

Cochran, Leslie H., Innovative Programs in Industrial Education. 160

Cockett, Sydney R., Dyeing and Printing. 22

Cockshutt, Margaret E., Basic Filing Rules. 89

Codlin, Ellen M., Handlist of Basic Reference Material for Librarians and Information Officers in Electrical and Electronic Engineering. 89

Coffey, Alan, Human Relations. 96; Principles of Law Enforcement. 97

Coffin, Kenneth B., Handbook for the Legal Secretary. 71

Coffin, Margaret A., Nursing Observations of the Young Patient. 189

Coffin, William S., Jr., Law, Order and Civil Disobedience. 102

Coffman, Charles D., The Full House: A Hotel/Motel Promotion Primer. 51

Cogoli, John E., Photo-Offset Fundamentals. 43

Cohan, Alvin S., The Chemical Plant From Process Selection to Commercial Operation. 129

Cohen, Bruce J., Crime in America. 96

Cohen, D. Walter, Periodontal Therapy. 174

Cohen, David V., A Professional Guide to Men's Clothing in Pattern Construction and Cutting Production. 22

Cohen, Henry A., Public Construction Contracts and the Law. 136

Cohen, Rosalyn S., Optimum Utilization of Community Colleges in the Training of Child Care Workers. 80

Cohen, S. Alan, Teach Them All to Read: Theory, Methods, and Materials for Teaching the Disadvantaged. 109

Cohn, Helen, A Manual for Nurses in Family and Community Health. 189

Cohn, Max A., Silk Screen Techniques. 42

Cohn, Walter E., Modern Footwear Materials and Processes. 22

Coker, A. J., Newnes Motor Repair. 124

Colbert, Douglas A., Data Processing Concepts. 15

Cole, E. J., Papermaking Practice. 48; Papermaking: Questions and Answers. 48

Cole, Harold H., Introduction to Livestock Production. 78

Cole, John A., A Handbook on Quantity Food Management. 35

Cole, R. Wade, Introduction to Computing. 17

Cole, Rosalind, The Waldorf-Astoria Cookbook. 33

Coleman, Almand R., Financial Accounting. 2

Coleman, R. M., Basic Lessons in Technical Drafting. 143

Coleman, Thomas E., Profitable Drugstore Management. 201

Coletti, Anthony, Handbook for Dairymen. 78

Colicchio, Antoinette J., Patternmaking and Design. 22

Collin, Robert E., Antenna Theory. 146

Collins, Alice H., The Lonely and Afraid: Counseling the Hard to Reach. 104

Collins, Daniel A., Your Teeth. 174

Collins, Frank T., Manual Critical Path Techniques for Construction. 136; Manual of Tilt Up Construction. 136

Collins, Mary, The McCormick Spices of the World Cookbook. 31

Collins, R. Douglas, Illustrated Manual of Laboratory Diagnosis. 182

Collison, Robert L., Commercial and Industrial Records Storage. 67; Indexes and Indexing. 89

Colman, Harry L., Computer Language. 19

Colwell, L. V., Handbook of Mechanical Wear. 165

Combes, Steve, Restaurant French for Hoteliers, Restaurateurs and Catering Students. 52

Comer, David J., Semiconductor Circuits Lab Manual. 146

Comfort, Mildred H., Conrad N. Hilton, Hotelier. 51

Commack, Emerson, Principles of Insurance. 53

Committee on Advertising, Principles of Advertising. 6

Committee on Industrial Ventilation, Industrial Ventilation. 120

Committee on Respirators, Lansing, Michigan, Respiratory Protective Devices Manual. 180

Commoner, Barry, Science and Survival. 177

Communication Service Corporation, Training Teacher Assistants in Community Colleges. 113

Companion, Audrey L., Chemical Bonding. 126

Compton, W. H., Funeral Sermon Outlines. 93

Computer Industry Guide. 17

Computer Usage Company, Computer Usage: 360 Assembly Programming. 19; Programming the IBM System/360. 19

Computer Usage Education, Inc., Computer Usage/Applications. 17; Computer Usage/Fundamentals. 17; Computer Usage/360 Fortran Programming. 19

Computer Yearbook, American Data Processing. 15

Comstock, Helen, American Furniture. 56; The Concise Encyclopedia of American Antiques. 54

Conant, James B., Slums and Suburbs.... 109

Conant, Ralph W., The Public Library and the City. 89

Conaway, John O., Plastics. 160

Condensed Chemical Dictionary. 126

Condit, Carl W., American Building. 136; American Building Art. 136

Cone, Sydney M., Jr., Aim for a Job in the Textile Industry. 28

Cone Mills Corporation, Textile Finishing Glossary. 28

Conference on Food Service Industry Manpower and Education, Chicago, 1967, Manpower and Education for the Food Service Industry. 31

Conference on Job Development and Training for Workers in Health Services, Training Health Service Workers. 207

Conference on the Training of Library Technology Assistants, Library Technology in California Junior Colleges. 89

Conger, John J., Readings in Child Development and Personality. 82

Conil, Jean, Gastronomic Tour de France. 38

Conn, Harold J., Conn's Biological Stains. 182; Staining Procedures. 182

Connecticut Curriculum Committee for the Printing Trades, Printing Layout and Design. 43

Connecticut (State) Department of Education, Mathematical Problems for the Fashion Design Course. 206

Connolly, Arlene F., Promotion of Physical Comfort and Safety. 189

Connolly, Thomas F., Airplane Aerodynamics. 116

Connors, Kenneth A., A Textbook of Pharmaceutical Analysis. 201

Conover, Jessie A., Finishing Touches. 7; Lets Make Faces. 7

Conover, Merrill B., The Field of Social Work. 104

Conquest, Robert, The Soviet Police System. 96

Conrow, Kenneth, Deductive Organic Chemistry. 134

Conroy, Charles W., The Challenge of Aerospace Power. 116; The Dawning Space Age. 116; Introduction to Aerospace. 116; Navigation and the Weather. 116

Considine, Douglas M., Handbook of Applied Instrumentation. 164

Considine, Joseph M., Microwave Experiments. 150

Consumers Power Company, Fundamentals of Electricity. 146

Contact Lens Medical Seminar Proceedings. 198

Contini, Mila, Fashion: From Ancient Egypt to the Present Day. 22

Continolo, Giuseppe, Modern Filing Methods and Equipment. 67

Converse, Paul D., The Elements of Marketing. 57

INDEX

Cook, Alfred B., Frequency Modulation Receivers. 156

Cook, Alice C., A Mathematical Guide to Dosage and Solutions. 206

Cook, Glen C., Approved Practices in Swine Production. 78

Cook, James G., The Miracle of Plastics. 167

Cook, Jesse S., III, Printed Circuit Design and Drafting. 144

Cook, John E., What You Should Know About Data Processing. 15

Cook, John P., Construction Sealants and Adhesives. 136

Cook, Margaret G., The New Library Key. 89

Cook, Ray L., Soil Management for Conservation and Production. 74

Cook, Robert, General Ophthalmology. 200

Cooke, Edward I., Chemical Synonyms and Trade Names. 127

Cooke, Nelson M., Arithmetic Review for Electronics. 206; Basic Mathematics for Electronics. 206; Electronics and Nucleonics Dictionary. 146

Cooke-Yarborough, Edmund H., An Introduction to Transistor Circuits. 158

Cooley, R. H., Complete Metalworking Manual. 160

Cooley, Richard A., Congress and the Environment. 177

Coombs, Charles I., Cleared for Takeoff. 116; High Timber. 86

Coombs, Clyde F., Printed Circuits Handbook. 146

Coons, Steven A., Graphics. 143

Cooper, Grace R., The Invention of the Sewing Machine. 22

Cooper, John H., Mathematics of Accounting. 2

Cooper, Lenna F., Nutrition in Health and Disease. 40

Cooper, M. J., What Computers Can Do. 17

Cooper, Marian G., The Medical Assistant. 71

Cooper, Mary U., The Art of Creole Cookery. 33

Cooper, Signe S., Contemporary Nursing Practice. 189

Cooper, William A., A Laboratory Survey of Biology. 185

Coote, Jack H., Colour Prints. 49

Coover, Shriver L., Drawing and Blueprint Reading. 142; A First Course in Drawing and Blueprint Reading. 142; Industrial Arts Drawing and Blueprint Reading. 142; Programmed Blueprint Reading. 142

Cope, Dwight W., Plastics Book. 160; Plastics. 160

Copeland, Ronald M., Financial Statements. 4

Coplan, Kate, The Library Reaches Out. 89; Poster Ideas and Bulletin Board Techniques. 89

Copley, Michael E., Food Dehydration. 42; Quality and Stability in Frozen Foods. 42

Copplestone, John F., Preventive Aspects of Occupational Health Nursing. 189

Copson, David A., Microwave Heating. 41

Copson, Harry R., Corrosion Resistance of Metals and Alloys. 169

Copulsky, William, Practical Sales Forecasting. 57

Corbin, Arnold, Management in Marketing. 59

Corbman, Bernard P., Textiles: Fiber to Fabric. 29

Corcoran, A. Wayne, Mathematical Applications in Accounting. 2

Corcoran, George F., Alternating-Current Circuits. 149; Electronics. 146

Cordasco, Francesco, Education and the Urban Community. 110; Puerto Rican Children in Mainland Schools. 109

Corderoy, J., Bookbinding for Beginners. 47

Cordes, Eugene H., Biological Chemistry. 133

Cordwell, Miriam, Hair Design and Fashion. 8

Corenthal, Eugene J., Essentials of Merchandise Information: Nontextiles. 59

Corey, Helen, The Art of Syrian Cookery. 39

Corey, Richard C., Principles and Practices of Incineration. 177

Corinth, Kay, Fashion Showmanship. 22

Corliss, William R., Propulsion Systems for Space Flight. 116

Corn Congress, Delavan, Wis., 1964, Advances in Corn Production. 74

Cornelia, Nicholas J., Office Machines Course. 66

Cornell Hotel and Restaurant Administration Quarterly, The Essentials of Good Table Service. 52

Cornell University, School of Hotel Administration, Tested Quantity Recipes. 31

Cornetet, Wendell H., Principles of Electricity and Basic Electronics. 146

Cornfeld, Lilian, Israeli Cookery. 39

Corning, John J., Transistor Circuit Analysis and Design. 158

Cornwell, Raymond L., General Printing. 43

Corson, Richard, Fashion in Eyeglasses. 198; Fashions in Hair. 8

Corvine, Walter, Basic Date Processing. 15

Corwin, Alsoph H., Elements of Organic Chemistry. 134

Costar, James W., Guidance Services in the Elementary School. 110

Costin, Michael, Racing and Sports Car Chassis Design. 122

Cote, Wilfred A., Principles of Wood Science and Technology. 87

Cottam, Walter P., Our Renewable Wild Lands: A Challenge. 177

Cottrell, A. H., An Introduction to Metallurgy. 168

Coughlan, John W., Guide to Contemporary Theory of Accounts. 2

Council on Library Technology, Directory of Institutions in the United States and Canada Offering or Developing Courses in Library Technology. 89

Council on Social Work Education, The Community Services Technician. 104

Country Gentleman, Freezing and Canning Cookbook. 32

Coupe, Raymond R., Science of Printing Technology. 43

Courtney, Winifred F., The Reader's Adviser: A Guide to the Best in Literature. 89

Cowan, Mary L., Introduction to Textiles. 28

Cowdry, E. V., A Textbook of Histology. 186

Cowdry, Edmund V., Laboratory Technique in Biology and Medicine. 182

Cowell, Colin R., Inlays, Crowns and Bridges. 174

Cowles, Laurence G., Analysis and Design of Transistor Circuits. 158; Transistor Circuits and Applications. 158

Cowles, Milly, Perspectives in the Education of Disadvantaged Children. 109

Cox, David M., Numerically Controlled Machine Tools. 170

Cox, David W., Computer Programmer. 19

Cox, George W., Readings in Conservation Ecology. 177

Cox, Henry E., The Chemical Analysis of Foods. 126

Cox, Homer L., How to Write a Letter. 67

Cox, Janet T., The Handbook of Piece Goods Merchandising. 22

Cox, Keith K., Experimentation for Marketing Decisions. 57; Marketing Classics. 58

Cox, Pat M., Deep Freezing. 41

Cox, Reavis, Distribution in a High-Level Economy. 57; Theory in Marketing. 57

Cox, Robert G., Principles of Accounting. 4

Craeybeck, A. H. S., Gevaert Manual of Photography. 49

Crafts, Alden S., Weed Control. 76

Craig, Hazel T., Clothing. 22

Craig, Jennie E., Creative Art Activities: A Handbook for the Elementary Teacher. 109

Craig, Robert C., The Psychology of Learning in the Classroom. 109

Cram, David, Explaining "Teaching Machines" and Programming. 109

Cram, Donald J., Organic Chemistry. 134

Cramer, James, Uniforms of the World's Police. 96

Cramlet, Ross C., Woodwork Visualized. 160

Crane, Edgar, Marketing Communications. 57

Crane, Warren E., Delectable Desserts. 31

Cratty, Bryant J., Experiments in Movement Behavior and Motor Learning. 80

Crawford, Annie L., Psychiatric Nursing. 196

Crawford, Clan, Strategy and Tactics in Municipal Zoning. 65

Crawford, F. Robert, Introduction to Data Processing. 15

Crawford, Hollie W., Math Workbook for Food Service/Lodging Programs. 206

Crawford, John W., Advertising. 6

Crawford, M. D. C., One World of Fashion. 23

Crawford, T. S., A History of the Umbrella. 22

Craytor, Josephine, The Nurse and the Cancer Patient. 189

Creamer, J. Shane, The Law of Arrest, Search, and Seizure. 96

Creamer, Robert H., Machine Design. 167

Creighton, Charles P., Contact Lenses' Fabrication Tables. 198

Creighton, Helen, Law Every Nurse Should Know. 189

Creswell, Clifford J., Spectral Analysis of Organic Compounds. 134

Crim, Betty J., Pharmacology and Patient Care. 201

Crisp, Richard D., Sales Planning and Control. 57

Crispin, Frederic S., Dictionary of Technical Terms.... 136

Crissy, W. J. E., Salesmanship. 57

Cristol, Stanley J., Organic Chemistry. 135

Crocker, Betty, Betty Crocker's Cookbook. 31

Crocker, Dean, Principles and Practice of Inhalation Therapy. 181

Crockett, Thompson S., Guidlines for Law Enforcement Education Programs in Community and Junior Colleges. 96

Croft, Terrell W., American Electricians' Handbook. 147; Wiring Tables. 147

Croft-Cooke, Rupert, Madeira. 38

Cromwell, Florence S., Occupational Therapist's Manual for Basic Skills Assessment of Primary Pre-Vocational Evaluation. 209

Cronan, Marion L., The School Lunch. 31

Cronbach, Lee J., Educational Psychology. 109

Crosby, June, Serve It Cold. 31

Cross, James S., Industrial Marketing. 56

Cross, John C., The Informer in Law Enforcement. 97

Cross, Wilbur, A Job with a Future in Computers. 17

Crossland, James, Lewis's Pharmacology. 201

Crouch, James E., Functional Human Anatomy. 183

Crouse, William H., Automobile Chassis and Body. 122; Automotive Electrical Equipment. 122; Automotive Engine Design. 122; Automotive Engines. 123; Automotive Mechanics. 123; Automotive Transmissions and Power Trains. 123; General Power Mechanics. 163

Crouwel, Wim, Packaging: An International Survey. 63

Crow, Alice, Understanding Interrelations in Nursing. 189

Crow, Leonard R., Learning Electricity Fundamentals. 147

Crow, Lester D., Educating the Culturally Disadvantaged Child. 109

Crow, Lester D., Understanding Interrelations in Nursing. 189

Crowder, Norman A., The Arithmetic of Computers. 206; An Introduction to Body Fluid Metabolism. 183

Crowe, Robert M., Group Insurance Handbook. 53

Crowhurst, Norman H., Audio Systems Handbook. 147; Basic Oscillator Handbook. 147; Electronic Design Charts. 147; Electronics Reference Databook. 147; Mathematics for Electronics Engineers and Technicians. 206; Servicing Modern Hi-Fi Stereo Systems. 147; Understanding Solid-State Circuits. 147

Crowley, Mary C., Clinical Endodontics. 176

Crown, David A., The Forensic Examination of Paints and Pigments. 96

Crown, Paul, What You Should Know About Retail Merchandising. 63

Crowningshield, Gerald R., Cost Accounting. 5

Croy, Otto R., Camera Copying and Reproduction. 49; The Complete Art of Printing and Enlarging. 49; Creative Photography. 49

Croy, Peter, Graphic Design and Reproduction Techniques. 43

Cruess, William V., The Technology of Wine Making. 37

Cruickshank, William M., Education of Exceptional Children and Youth. 109

Crum, Gertrude, A World of Menus and Recipes. 31

Cruse, Heloise, Heloise's Kitchen Hints. 31

Crusius, Vera C., A Handbook on Quantity Food Management. 35

Cruze, Wendell W., Psychology in Nursing. 189

Csáky, T. Z., Introduction to General Pharmacology. 201

Cuban, Larry, To Make a Difference: Teaching in the Inner City. 109

Culinary Institute of America, Introduction to Professional Food Service. 31; The Professional Chef. 31

Cullimore, S., Practical Microbiology. 187

Cullum, Albert, Push Back the Desks. 109

Cullwick, Ernest G., The Fundamentals of Electro-Magnetism. 147

Culpepper, Billie J., The Science-Engineering Secretary. 72

Culpepper, Fred W., Jr., Energy, Electricity and Electronics. 151

Culver, Vivian M., Modern Bedside Nursing. 189

Cumming, R. F., Single-Colour Lithographic Machine Operating. 14

Cumulative Index to Nursing Literature. 189.

Cundiff, Edward W., Basic Marketing. 57; Essentials of Marketing. 61; Sales Management. 61

Cunha, George D., Conservation of Library Materials. 89

Cunha, Tony J., Crossbreeding Beef Cattle. 78

Cunningham, Beryl M., Woodshop Tool Maintenance. 160

Cunningham, Charles H., A Laboratory Guide in Virology. 182

Cunningham, Gladys, Singer Sewing Book. 22

Cunningham, Lyda S., Basic Medical-Surgical Nursing. 189

Cunnington, Cecil W., A Dictionary of English Costume. 27; Handbook of English Costume in the Nineteenth Century. 26; Handbook of English Mediaeval Costume. 26; A Picture History of English Costume. 27

Cunnington, Phillis E., Children's Costume in England.... 27; Costume in Pictures. 27; A Dictionary of English Costume. 27; English Costume for Sports and Outdoor Recreation. 27; Handbook of English Costume in the Nineteenth Century. 26; Handbook of English Mediaeval Costume. 26; Medieval and Tudor Costume. 27; Occupational Costume in England, from the Eleventh Century to 1914. 27; A Picture History of English Costume. 27

Curchack, Norma, Legal Typewriting. 71

Current Drug Handbook. 201

Currie, A. J., The Waiter. 52

Currie, Dorothy H., How to Organize a Children's Library. 89

Curry, Estell H., General Industrial Arts. 160; Teaching Successfully in Industrial Education. 163

Curry, George J., Immediate Care and Transport of the Injured. 208

Curry, Jesse F., Race Tensions and the Police. 96

INDEX

Curry, Othel J., Cost Accounting. 5

Curtin, David Y., Systematic Identification of Organic Compounds. 135

Curtis, Arthur B., Mathematics of Accounting. 2

Curtis, Helena, Biology. 185

Curtis, Irving E., Fundamental Principles of Pattern Making for Misses and Women's Garments. 22; Intermediate and Technological Problems in Pattern Making for Misses and Ladies Garments. 22

Curwen, Harold, Processes of Graphic Reproduction in Printing. 43

Cushwa, Charles T., Fire: A Summary of Literature in the United States from the Mid-1920's to 1966. 86

Cussler, Margaret, Dentists, Patients and Auxiliaries. 174

Cutler, Donald I., Introduction to Computer Programming. 19

Cutler, Merritt, How to Cut Drawings on Scratchboard. 9

Cutler, Phillip, Electronic Circuit Analysis. 147; Outline for DC Circuit Analysis with Illustrative Problems. 147; Semiconductor Circuit Analysis. 147

Cutter, Charles A., Cutter-Sanborn Three-Figure Author Table. 89

Cutting, Windsor C., Handbook of Pharmacology. 201

Czinkota, Michael, How to Select, Install and Service Air Conditioners. 120

Da Costa, Phil, One Hundred Years of America's Fire Fighting Apparatus. 84

Dady, Milan B., An In-Service Training Manual for Teacher-Aides. 109

Daffron, Joe, Car Repairs You Can Make. 123

Dahl, Svend, History of the Book. 89

Dahlen, Phillip, Semiconductors From A to Z. 147

Daily, Jay E., Cataloging for Library Technical Assistants. 89

Dair, Carl, Design with Type. 43

Dakin, John C., Pickle and Sauce Making. 30

Dal, Erik, Scandinavian Bookmaking in the Twentieth Century. 43

Dal Fabbro, Mario, Design and Construction of Upholstered Furniture. 56

Dal Nogare, Stephen, Gas-Liquid Chromatography. 126

Dale, Alfred J., Modern Ceramic Practice. 160

Dale, John D., Managerial Accounting in the Small Company. 2

Dale, Martin, How to Read a French Menu. 31

Dale, Sidney L., Principles of Steroid Analysis. 182

Dallas, Daniel B., Progressive Dies, Design and Manufacture. 167

Dallas, Sandra, No More Than Five In A Bed. 51

Dallin, Lynn, The Pregnant Woman's Low Calorie Cookbook. 31

Dalrymple, Douglas J., Retail Management Cases. 64; Retailing: An Economic View. 63

Daly, Donald F., Aim for a Job in the Building Trades. 136; Your Future in Air Conditioning and Refrigeration. 120

Dame, J. Frank, Typewriting Techniques and Short Cuts. 68

Damm, Henry C., Practical Manual for Clinical Laboratory Procedures. 182

Dan River Mills, Inc., A Dictionary of Textile Terms. 28

Dana, Richard H., Interviewing and the Health Professions. 207

Dane, William J., The Picture Collection Subject Headings. 89

Danger, Eric P., How to Use Color to Sell. 13

Daniel, Albert R., Bakery Materials and Methods. 37

Daniels, A. Richard, The Performance of Electrical Machines. 147

Daniels, Alfred, Painting and Drawing. 9

Daniels, Arthur C., Handbook of Life Insurance. 54

Daniels, Farrington, Experimental Physical Chemistry. 135

Daniels, George, Home Guide to Plumbing, Heating and Air Conditioning. 120

Daniels, Harold R., Mechanical Press Handbook. 164

Daniels, Ralph, Problems in Organic Chemistry. 134

D'Anna, John P., Inventory and Profit. 57

Dansereau, Pierre, Challenge for Survival. 177

Danziger, Kurt, Readings in Child Socialization. 80

D'Arbeloff, Natalie, Creating in Collage. 9

Darling, Donald B., Radiography of Infants and Children. 204

Darling, Lois, A Place in the Sun. 177

Darlington, K. D., Knitted Fabric Primer. 25

Darr, Jack, New Ways to Diagnose Electronic Troubles. 147; Transistor TV Servicing Made Easy. 158

Darrow, Helen F., Independent Activities for Creative Learning. 109

Darrow, Mary A., Staining Procedures. 182

Dartnell Corporation, The Dartnell Business-Letter Deskbook. 67; The Sales Manager's Handbook. 57

Darwin, Joan, Eye, Nose, Throat and Ear Nursing. 189

Dasmann, Raymond F., Destruction of California. 177; Environmental Conservation. 177; Wildlife Biology. 86

D'Assailly, Gisèle, Ages of Elegance. 22

Data Processing Management Association. 15

Datsko, Joseph, Material Properties and Manufacturing Processes. 164

Dauber, William G., Organic Reactions. 134

Daugherty, James S., Sheet Metal Pattern Drafting and Shop Problems. 144

DaVall, George M., Salesmanship Fundamentals. 58

Daves, Jessica, Ready-Made Miracle. 22

Davey, Charles B., Tree Growth and Forest Soils. 88

Davey, Homer C., Real Estate Principles in California. 65

Davey, James R., Data Transmission. 145

Davey, Norman, A History of Building Materials. 137

David, Gerson, Patterns of Social Functioning in Families with Marital and Parent-Child Problems. 104

David Hale Fanning Trade High School, Worcester, Mass., Surgical Technician Procedures. 209

Davids, Lewis E., Dictionary of Insurance. 53

Davidson, Bruce R., Experimental Research and Farm Production. 74

Davidson, F., Care of Children in Day Centres. 80

Davidson, Homer L., Servicing the Solid-State Chassis. 147; Troubleshooting the Solid State Chassis. 147

Davidson, James N., The Biochemistry of the Nucleic Acids. 132

Davidson, Ralph H., Insect Pests of Farm, Garden and Orchard. 74

Davidson, Raymond L., Audiovisual Machines. 89

Davidson, Sidney, Handbook of Modern Accounting. 2; Principles of Accounting. 2

Davidson, William R., Marketing. 56; Retailing Management. 63

Davies, D. R., All About Drugs. 200

Davies, Don E., Practical Experimental Metallurgy. 168

Davies, J. Clarence, III, The Politics of Pollution. 177

Davies, John D., Structural Concrete. 140

Davies, Maurice R., The Law of Burial. 93

Davies, Peter O., An Introduction to Dynamic Analysis and Automatic Control. 170

Davies, R. E., The World's Airlines. 116

Davies, Ruth A., The School Library.... 90

Davinson, Donald E., The Periodicals Collection. 90

Davis, Alec, Package and Print. 9

Davis, Bernard D., Microbiology. 187

INDEX

Davis, Burke, The World of Currier & Ives. 10

Davis, Calvin V., Handbook of Applied Hydraulics. 137

Davis, Dale S., Calculations in the Paper Industry. 48; Industrial and Specialty Papers. 48

Davis, Floyd J., Social Problems. 104

Davis, Fred, The Nursing Profession. 189

Davis, Gordon B., Computer Data Processing. 15; An Introduction to Electronic Computers. 17; An Introduction to the IBM System/360 Computer. 17

Davis, Harmer E., Composition and Properties of Concrete. 141; The Testing and Inspection of Engineering Materials. 164

Davis, Kenneth P., Forest Management. 86

Davis, Lou E., Careers in Computer Programming. 19

Davis, Mary L., Mexican Jewelry. 27

Davis, Mary Lou C., Problem-Solving in Nursing Practice. 190

Davis, Mildred J., The Art of Crewel Embroidery. 22

Davis, Morris E., De Lee's Obstetrics for Nurses. 194

Davis, Paul G., Plumbing, Heating and Piping. 141

Davis, Phyllis E., Medical Dictation and Transcription. 71; Medical Shorthand. 71; Medical Terminology. 72

Davis Publishing Company, Municipal Police Administration Tests. 96; Police Promotional Examinations for Sergeants. 96

Davis, Raymond E., Elementary Plane Surveying. 141; Surveying Theory and Practice. 142

Davis, Richard F., Modern Dairy Cattle Management. 78

Davis, Robert T., Reading in Sales Management. 57

Davis, Sidney, Your Future in Computer Programming. 19

Davison's Textile "Blue Book." 28

Davisson, Jack A., Design and Application of Commercial Type Tires. 123

Davson, Hugh, The Eye. 198; Physiology of the Eye. 198

Dawes, Chester L., Industrial Electricity. 147

Dawson, Helaine, On the Outskirts of Hope: Educating Youth from Poverty Areas. 109

Dawtry, Frank, Social Problems of Drug Abuse. 104

Dawydoff, Alexis, Airplanes of the World, 1490-1969. 118

Day, Avanelle, The Spice Cookbook. 31

Day, B. F., Building Acoustics. 137

Day, Frank D., Criminal Law and Society. 96; Introduction to Law Enforcement and Criminal Justice. 97

Day, Kenneth, Book Typography, 1815-1965. 43

Day, M. Clyde, Theoretical Inorganic Chemistry. 133

Day, Marion C., Concepts of General Chemistry. 129

Day, Patricia, Psychiatric Nursing. 196

Day, Ralph L., Concepts for Modern Marketing. 57; Marketing in Action: A Decision Game. 57

Day, Reuben A., Quantitative Analysis. 132

Day, Richard, The Practical Handbook of Concrete and Masonry. 140; The Practical Handbook of Electrical Repairs. 147

Dean, John A., Chemical Separation Methods. 126; Instrumental Methods of Analysis. 133

DeAndrade, Margarette, Brazilian Cookery. 39

DeAngelo, Salvatore M., Mathematics for Data Processing. 15

Dearden, John, Cost and Budget Analysis. 5; Essentials of Cost Accounting. 5

Deatherage, George E., Construction Company Organization and Management. 137; Construction Estimating and Job Preplanning. 137; Construction Office Administration. 137; Construction Scheduling and Control. 137

DeBaun, Stephen, Bountiful Breakfasts. 31

DeBell, Garrett, The Environmental Handbook. 177

DeBenedictis, Daniel J., The Complete Real Estate Adviser. 65

DeBey, Harold J., Introduction to Chemistry. 131

Debruzzi, D. J., Basic Fortran IV Programming. 20

Deck, Edith S., A Sociological Framework for Patient Care. 189

DeCoster, Don T., Accounting and Its Behavioral Implications. 1

DeCristoforo, R. J., Carpentry. 160; Handy Man's Concrete and Masonry Handbook. 140; How to Choose and Use Power Tools. 160; Modern Power Tool Woodworking. 160

Deeley, T. J., A Guide to Radiotherapy Nursing. 189

Deere, John, Design Analysis of Shafts and Beams. 167

DeFrance, Joseph J., Communications Electronics Circuits. 147; Electrical Fundamentals. 147; General Electronics Circuits. 147

DeGaliana, Thomas, Concise Encyclopedia of Aeronautics. 116

DeGiorgio, Joe, Bill Carroll's Dynamometer Tuning Techniques. 123

Degler, Stanley E., Federal Pollution Control Programs. 177; State Air Pollution Control Laws. 177

DeGrazia, Alfred, American Welfare. 104

Degremont, S. A., Water Treatment Handbook. 177

DeGutierrez-Mahoney, Carlos G., Neurological and Neurosurgical Nursing. 194

Dehr, Dorothy, Office Calculating and Adding Machines. 68

Deinzer, Harvey T., Development of Accounting Thought. 2

DeJong, Paul S., Engineering Graphics. 143

Dejours, Pierre, Respiration. 180

DeKieffer, R. E., Manual of Audio-Visual Techniques. 109

DeKnight, Freda, The Ebony Cookbook. 39

DeKornfeld, Thomas J., Inhalation Therapy Procedure Manual. 180

de Korösy, F. D., An Approach to Chemistry. 126

Delafons, Allan, The Structure of the Printing Industry. 43

Delafons, John, Land-Use Controls in the United States. 177

Delavan, Betty C., Clothing Selection. 23

Delderfield, Eric R., Introduction to Inn Signs. 51

DeLeeuw, Hendrik, From Flying Horse to Man in the Moon: A History of Flight.... 116

Delmonte, John, Metal-Filled Plastics. 167

Delorit, Richard J., Crop Production. 73

Delpit, George H., Electronics in Action. 147

DeLuca, James P., A Manual for Paper Estimating. 48

Demarest, Rosemary, Accounting Information Sources. 2

DeMars, Rose, Legal and Professional Secretary's Lexicon. 70

Dembeck, Adeline A., Guidebook to Man-Made Textile Fibers and Textured Yarns of the World. 28

Demmon, Elwood L., Opportunities in a Forestry Career. 86

Demos, George D., The Guidance of Exceptional Children. 81

Dempsey, Patricia, Best New Hairdos. 8; New Hair Style Ideas. 8

DeNault, Phyllis M., Neurology for Nurses. 194

DeNavarre, Maison G., The Chemistry and Manufacture of Cosmetics. 126

Denenberg, Herbert S., Risk and Insurance. 53

DenHartog, Jacob P., Mechanics. 164; Strength of Materials. 170

Dening, James, Marketing Industrial Goods. 57

Dennard, Cleveland L., Community Service and Other New Specialists. 107

Dennis, Lorraine, Dennis' Psychology of Human Behavior for Nurses. 189

Dennis, William H., A Hundred Years of Metallurgy. 168; Metallurgy of the Ferrous Metals. 168; Metallurgy in the Service of Man. 168

233

INDEX

Denny, Grace G., Fabrics. 28
Denny, Lynn C., Handbook: Butane-Propane Gases. 127
Denstman, Harold, Photographic Reproduction. 43
Dental Clinics of North America. 174
Dental Management, The Business of Dental Practice. 174
Dental Science Handbook. 174
DePuy, Charles H., Introduction to Organic Chemistry. 134
deRegniers, Beatrice S., Poems Children Will Sit Still For. 109
Derieux, Mary, Complete Book of Interior Decorating. 55
D'Ermo, Dominique, The Modern Pastry Chef's Guide to Professional Baking. 37
DeRoy, Benjamin E., Automatic Control Theory. 170
DeSausmarez, Maurice, Basic Design. 13
Desch, Harold E., Timber: Its Structure and Properties. 86
Deschampsneufs, Henry, Selling in Europe. 62
Desmonde, William H., Computers and Their Uses. 17; A Conversational Graphic Data Processing System: The IBM 1130/2250. 15; Real-Time Data Processing Systems. 15
Desoer, Charles A., Basic Circuit Theory. 147
DeSola, Dorothy, A Dictionary of Cooking. 31
DeSola, Ralph, A Dictionary of Cooking. 31
Desroches-Nobelcourt, Christiane, Tutankhamen. 93
Desrosier, Norman W., Attack on Starvation. 31; The Technology of Food Preservation. 41
Dessauer, John H., Xerography and Related Processes. 43
Deutsch, Hermann B., Brennan's New Orleans Cookbook. 39
Deutsch, Martin, The Disadvantaged Child. 80
Deutscher, J. Noel, Your Future in Television. 157
DeVan, Dorothy S., Introduction to Home Furnishings. 55
Devey, James D., Pickle and Sauce Making. 30; Soup Manufacture. 41
Devine, Janice, Fare Thee Well. 51
DeVinne, Theo L., The Invention of Printing. 43
Devlin, Frank J., Business Communication. 67
DeVoe, Merrill, The Effective Sales Manager. 58; How to Tailor Your Sales Organization to Your Markets. 58
Dewar, Michael J., An Introduction to Modern Chemistry. 127
Dewey, John, The School and Society. 109
Dewey, Melvil, Dewey Decimal Classification and Relative Index. 90

DeWolfe, Robert H., Carboxylic Ortho Acid Derivatives. 134
Deyarmond, Albert, Fundamentals of Stress Analysis. 116
DeYoung, Chris A., American Education. 109
DeYoung, Lillian, The Foundations of Nursing as Conceived. 189
deZeeuw, Carl, Textbook of Wood Technology. 87
Dezettel, Louis M., Record Changers: How They Work. 90
Diamant, Rudolph M., The Chemistry of Building Materials. 127
Diamond, Thomas, A Primer of Blueprint Reading. 142
Diat, Louis, French Cooking for Americans. 39; Gourmet's Basic French Cookbook. 39
DiBennedetto, Anthony T., The Structure and Properties of Materials. 167
Dichter, Ernest, Handbook of Consumer Motivations. 58
Dickerson, Oliver D., Health Insurance. 54
Dickey, Floyd, Plastics Book. 160
Dickey, George D., Filtration. 127
Dickey, Robert I., Accountants' Cost Handbook. 2
Dickinson, Brian, Aircraft Stability and Control for Pilots and Engineers. 116
Dickson, Thomas R., Computer and Chemistry. 127
Dickson, William G., Quantity Cooking. 31; Related Information: Machine Technology. 160
Dictionary of Chemistry and Chemical Technology. 127
Dieckmann, Edward A., Practical Homicide Investigation. 96
Diehl, Edith, Bookbinding, Its Background and Technique. 47
Dienhart, Charlotte M., Basic Human Anatomy and Physiology. 184
Dienstein, William, How to Write A Narrative Investigation Report. 96; Technics for the Crime Investigator. 96
Diettert, Gerald A., Coronary Care Unit Nursing. 188
Dietz, Albert G., Plastics for Architects and Builders. 137
Dietz, Lena D., History and Modern Nursing. 189
Diggins, Ronald V., Beef Production, 78; Dairy Production. 78; Livestock and Poultry Production. 78; Poultry Production. 78; Swine Production. 78
DiLeo, Joseph H., Young Children and Their Drawings. 80
Dilley, Romilda, Fundamental Fashion Drawing. 23
Dillon, Charles, Fluorosis and Dental Caries. 174
Dillon, Daniel C., The Nurse Aide. 194

Dillow, Arthur P., Alternating Current Fundamentals. 147
Dimick, Kenneth M., Child Counseling. 80
Dimitry, Donald L., Basic Programming Concepts and the IBM 1620 Computer. 20
Dimmick, Robert L., An Introduction to Experimental Aerobiology. 177
Dimond, E. Grey, Electrocardiography and Vectorcardiography. 184; The Exercise Electrocardiogram in Office Practice. 184
Dines, Jess E., Radio and Television, Receiver Circuitry and Operation. 156
Dingwall, Eric J., Meet Judy. 23
Dinitz, Simon, Critical Issues in the Study of Crime. 96
Dinkmeyer, Don C., Child Development. 80
DiPaola, Eugene F., How to Multiply Your Real Estate Sales. 65
Directories Publishing Company, Chem Sources. 127
Directory of Social and Health Agencies of New York City. Columbia University Press. 104; The Social Welfare Forum, 1967. 106; Social Work Practice. 107
Diringer, David, The Alphabet. 9; The Illuminated Book. 43
Dirksen, Charles J., Advertising Principles and Problems. 6; Cases in Marketing. 59; Readings in Marketing. 58
Dison, Norma G., An Atlas of Nursing Techniques. 189
Dispensatory of the United States of America. 201
Ditchburn, R. W., Light. 198
Dittmann, Laura L., Early Child Care. 81
Dixon, Donald F., Theories for Marketing Systems Analysis. 58
Dixon, Jean P., Modern Methods in Organic Microanalysis. 131
Dixon, Peter L., Soaring: An Introduction to Motorless Flight. 116
Dixon, Robert L., Essentials of Accounting. 2
Dobbs, Edward C., Pharmacology and Oral Therapeutics For Students and Practitioners. 201
Doblin, Jay, One Hundred Great Product Designs. 9
Dobrovolny, Jerry S., Basic Drawing for Engineering Technology. 142; Civil Engineering Technology Consultant's Workshop. 137; Graphics for Engineers. 142
Dockar-Drysdale, Barbara, Therapy in Child Care. 81
Dodd, Barbara E., An Introduction to Blood Group Serology. 181; Neurological and Neurosurgical Nursing. 194
Dodds, T. C., Bacteriology Illustrated. 182

Dodes, Irving A., IBM 1620 Programming for Science and Mathematics. 19; Numerical Analysis. 170

Dodge, Bertha S., Hands that Help: Careers for Medical Workers. 207

Doell, Charles E., Elements of Park and Recreation Administration. 102

Doerr, Catherine M., Smart Sewing. 23

Doherty, William O., Ethical Standards of the Accounting Profession. 2

Doi, Masaru, Cook Japanese. 39; Japanese One-Pot Cookery. 39

Dolan, Francis E., Comprehensive Review for Medical Technologists. 182

Dolan, Josephine A., Goodnow's History of Nursing. 189

Dommasch, Daniel O., Airplane Aerodynamics. 116

Donahoo, Alvin W., Profitable Farm Marketing. 77

Donahue, Roy L., Our Soils and Their Management. 74; Soils. 74

Donaldson, Beatrice, Standardized Quantity Recipes. 31

Donáth, Tibor, Anatomical Dictionary. 184

Donigan, Robert L., Chemical Tests and the Law. 97; The Evidence Handbook. 97

Donley, Dorothy, Principles of Fashion Sketching. 24

Donovan, Anne C., Hospital Dietary Services. 31

Donovan, Frank R., Wheels for a Nation. 123

Donovan, Joan E., The Nurse Aide. 194

Doody, Alton F., Readings in the History of American Marketing. 61; Retailing Management. 63

Doolin, James H., Trouble Shooters Bible: Air Conditioning, Refrigeration, Heat Pumps and Heating. 120

Dopuch, Nicholas, Cost Accounting. 5

Dordick, Beverly F., Real Estate Information Sources. 64

Dorian, A. F., Elsevier's Dictionary of Industrial Chemistry in Six Languages. 127

Doris, Lillian, Complete Secretary's Handbook. 67; The Real Estate Office Secretary's Handbook. 65

Dorland's Illustrated Medical Dictionary. 182

Dorman, Lynn, Child Development and Behavior. 82

Dorn, John E., Mechanical Behavior of Materials at Elevated Temperatures. 164

Dorsey, Leslie, Fare Thee Well. 51

Dossat, Roy J., Principles of Refrigeration. 120

Doswell, Roger, Towards an Integrated Approach to Hotel Planning. 51

Dougherty, Charles M., Electronic Technology. 147

Dougherty, Edward E., Safety in Police Pursuit Driving. 97

Doughtie, Venton L., Design of Machine Members. 167

Douglas, Bodie E., Concepts and Models of Inorganic Chemistry. 133

Douglas, Clarence J., Construction Management. 138

Douglas, John, Human Behavior in Marketing. 58

Douglas, Mary L., Programming Language/One. 19

Douglas, Mary P., The Primary School Library and its Services. 90

Douglas, Ralph, Calligraphic Lettering with Wide Pen and Brush. 14

Douglas, William O., Wilderness Bill of Rights. 177

Douglass, James H., Woodworking with Machines. 160

Douglass, Laura M., Team Leadership in Action: Principles and Applications to Staff Nursing Situations. 189

Douglass, Robert W., Forest Recreation. 102

Dowaliby, Margaret, The Fundamentals of Cosmetic Dispensing. 198

Dowdell, Dorothy, Your Career in Teaching. 109

Dowdell, Joseph, Your Career in Teaching. 109

Dowding, Geoffrey, An Introduction to the History of Printing Types. 43

Dowling, Harry F., Medicines for Man. 201

Downer, Ann H., Physical Therapy Procedures. 209

Downing, George D., Sales Management. 58

Downs, James C., Principles of Real Estate Management. 65

Downs, Robert B., Books That Changed America. 90; Famous Books Since 1492. 90; How to Do Library Research. 90; Molders of the Modern Mind: 111 Books That Shaped Western Civilization. 90

Doyle, D., Solid-Liquid Separation. 130

Doyle, John M., Pulse Fundamentals. 147

Doyle, Robert V., Your Career in Interior Design. 55

Drabek, Thomas E., Laboratory Simulation of a Police Communications System Under Stress. 97; Law and the Lawless. 101

Drablos, Carroll J., Highway and Agricultural Drainage Practices. 74

Drago, Russell S., Acids and Bases. 127; Physical Methods in Inorganic Chemistry. 133

Dragoo, Alva W., General Shop Metalwork. 160

Drake, Jerry E., Marketing Research. 58

Drebin, Allan R., Financial Accounting. 1; Managerial Accounting. 1

Dreisbach, Dale, Liquids and Solutions. 127

Dressmaking, Pattern Drafting. 23

Drew, Louise C., Nursery Manual. 81

Drew, Ralph, Professional Ophthalmic Dispensing. 198

Drew-Bear, Robert, Mass Merchandising. 58

Drewes, Donald W., Cemetery Land Planning. 93

Drews, Robert C., Current Concepts in Ophthalmology. 197

Drill, Victor A., Drill's Pharmacology in Medicine. 201

Drugs In Current Use. 201

Drugs of Choice. 201

Drummond, Eleanor E., Nursing Care of the Long-Term Patient. 188

Drury, John, Rare and Well Done. 31

Dryden, M. Virginia, Nursing Trends. 189

Drzazga, John, Sex Crimes. 97; Wheels of Fortune. 97

Duarte, R. L., Electronics Assembly Methods. 147

Duarte, Salvador R., Electronics Assembly Methods. 147

Dubin, Martin D., Architectural Supervision of Modern Buildings. 137

Dubiny, Mary J., The Macmillan Dictionary for Practical and Vocational Nurses. 195

Dubois, John H., Plastics. 167

Dubos, René, So Human An Animal. 177

Dubov, Irving, Contemporary Agricultural Marketing. 74

DuBrul, E. Lloyd, Oral Anatomy. 175

Ducarme, J., Progress in Combustion Science and Technology. 116

Duchan, Simon A., Basic Dictation. 67; Basic Dictation: Longhand.... 67

Dudley, Adolphus M., Connecting Induction Motors.... 156

Dudley, Darle W., Gear Handbook. 167

Dudycha, George J., Psychology for Law Enforcement Officers. 97

Duenk, Lester G., Basic Crafts. 162

Duerr, William A., Exercises in the Managerial Economics of Forestry. 86; Fundamentals of Forestry Economics. 86

Duffin, Daniel J., The Essentials of Modern Carpet Installation. 51

DuGas, Beverly W., Fundamentals of Patient Care. 191

Duhl, Leonard J., The Urban Condition. 104

Dukas, Peter, Hotel Front Office Management and Operation. 51; How to Operate a Restaurant. 52

Duke-Elder, William S., The Practice of Refraction. 198

Dummer, Geoffrey W., Automobile Electronics Equipment, 1970-71. 123; Electronic Equipment Design and Construction. 147; Fixed and Variable Capacitors. 147; Miniature and Microminiature Electronics. 147

INDEX

Dumont, Rene, Types of Rural Economy. 74

Dun and Bradstreet, Inc., Successful Sales Managing. 58

Duncan, Charles H., College Typewriting: Basic Course, 68

Duncan, Delbert J., Marketing: Principles and Methods. 60; Retailing: Principles and Methods. 63

Duncan, Helen A., Duncan's Dictionary for Nurses. 189

Duncan, Robert I., Architectural Drawing Problems. 144

Dundon, H. Dwyer, Occupational Therapy Examination Review. 209

Dunham, Clarence W., Foundations of Structures. 137; The Theory and Practice of Reinforced Concrete. 140

Dunn, Helen W., The Nursing Audit. 189

Dunn, Louis G., Airplane Structural Analysis and Design. 118

Dunn, Samuel W., Advertising. 6

Dunn, Walter L., Introduction to Digital Computer Problems Using Fortran IV. 19

Dunne, Howard W., Diseases of Swine. 78

Dunne, John S., The City of the Gods. 93

Dunning, James M., Principles of Dental Public Health. 174

Dunning, William J., Home Planning and Architectural Drawing. 143

Dunseath, M., The Hotel Bookkeeper-Receptionist. 51

Dunsford, Ivor, Techniques in Blood Grouping. 186

Dunsheath, Percy, Electricity. 147

DuPraw, Ernest J., Cell and Molecular Biology. 185

Duran, Clement A., The New Encyclopedia of Successful Program Ideas. 102

Duran, Dorothy B., The New Encyclopedia of Successful Program Ideas. 102

Durbahn, Walter E., Fundamentals of Carpentry. 140

Durrans, T. H., Solvents. 127

Durst, Seymour B., Your Future in Real Estate. 65

Duvall, J., Automotive Essentials. 124

Dwiggins, Boyce H., Automotive Air Conditioning. 120; Automotive Starting and Charging Systems. 123; Automotive Steering Systems. 123

Dwiggins, Don, The SST. 116

Dyer, Ceil, The Back to Cooking Cookbook. 31

Dygdon, John T., Basic Technical Drawing. 143

Dyke, Freeman H., Jr., How to Manage and Use Technical Information. 90

Dykema, Roland W., Modern Practice in Dental Ceramics. 174

EEE Magazine, Electronic Circuit Design Handbook. 147

E.I.A. Voorhees Technical Institute, Basic Electronics. 155; Electricity. 155

Eades, John L., Fire Protection Directory, 1970. 84

Eadie, Donald, Introduction to the Basic Computer. 17

Eakin, Mary K., Subject Index to Books for Intermediate Grades. 109; Subject Index to Books for Primary Grades. 109

Earl, Arthur W., Experiments with Materials and Products of Industry. 160

Earle, Howard H., Police-Community Relations. 97

Early, Paul J., Textbook of Nuclear Medicine Technology. 182

Easley, Charles, Basic Radiation Protection. 204

East, Marjorie, Fashion Your Own. 23

Eastin, Roy B., Government Publications and Their Use. 92

Eastman, Nicholson J., Maternity Nursing. 194

Eastman Kodak Company, Graphic Arts Handbook. 43; Kodak Photographic Materials.... 49

Ebeling, Alvin, Fundamentals of Aircraft Environmental Control. 116

Eblin, Lawrence P., Chemistry. 127

Eboch, Sidney C., Operating Audio-Visual Equipment. 110

Eckardt, Ottmar W., Strength of Materials. 170

Eckenfelder, W. Wesley, Jr., Industrial Water Pollution Control. 177

Eckert, Charles, Emergency-Room Care. 208

Ecklund, E. Eugene, Repairing Home Audio Systems. 147

Eckman, James R., The Heritage of the Printer. 43

Eckstein, Arthur, Preparing Art for Printing. 46

Eckstein, Esther, Parents and the Day Care Center. 79

Economic Development Commission for Hotels and Catering, Hotel Accounting. 51

Eddings, Claire N., Secretary's Complete Model Letter Handbook. 67

Eddy, Jo A., Nursing Care of the Adolescent. 190

Edelson, Edward, Poisons in the Air. 177

Edelson, Kenneth, The Children's House Parent-Teacher Guide to Montessori. 81

Edgar, Carroll, Fundamentals of Manufacturing Processes and Materials. 164

Edge, Sylvia C., Technical Nursing of the Adult. 189

Edlin, Herbert L., What Wood is That? 86

Edminister, Joseph A., Electric Circuits. 147

Edminister, Talcott W., Irrigation of Agricultural Lands. 74

Edmondson, Frances W., Medical Terminology. 71; Medical Typing. 71

Edouard Dubied et Cie., S.A., Dubied Knitting Manual. 23

Edstrom, A. E., Problems in Engineering Graphics, Series VI. 143; Problems in Mechanical Drawing: First Course. 144; Problems in Mechanical Drawing: Second Course. 144

Educational Media Council, Educational Media Index. 90

Educators' Guide to Free Films. 110

Educators' Guide to Free Filmstrips. 110

Edwards, Charles E., Dynamics of the United States Automobile Industry. 123

Edwards, Clive A., The Principles of Agricultural Entomology. 74

Edwards, Deane B., White Fields for Harvest: Social Welfare in Community Service. 104

Edwards, George C., The Police on the Urban Frontier. 97

Edwards, H. Griffith, Specifications. 137

Edwards, James D., Accounting. 2

Edwards, Jeanne, Creative Crafts. 160

Edwards, John O., Inorganic Reaction Mechanisms. 133

Edwards, Lauton, Industrial Arts Plastics. 161

Edwards, Newton, The Law Governing School Property and School-Building Construction. 137

Edwards Brothers, Inc., The Author's Guide to Book Planning and Production. 43

Efron, Alexander, Alternating Current Electricity. 147; Exploring Mechanics. 164

Egan, Donald F., Fundamentals of Inhalation Therapy. 180

Egan, Robert L., Technologist Guide to Mammography. 204

Ehlers, Victor M., Mechanical and Rural Sanitation. 177

Ehrenfeld, David W., Biological Conservation. 177

Ehrlich, Ann B., Dental Practice Management. 174

Ehrlich, Anne H., Population, Resources, Environment. 177

Ehrlich, Howard J., An Examination of Role Theory. 100

Ehrlich, Paul R., The Population Bomb. 177; Population, Resources, Environment. 177

Ehrlich, Stanley F., Dental Practice Management: The Teamwork Approach. 174

Eicher, Joanne B., Dress, Adornment, and the Social Order. 25

Eifert, Virginia S., Tall Trees and Far Horizons. 86

Eilenberg, Howard, What You Should Know about Research Techniques for Retailers. 63

Eilers, Robert D., Group Insurance Handbook. 53

Einstein, Gertrude, Learning to Apply New Concepts to Casework Practice. 104

Eisenbud, Merril, Environmental Radioactivity. 177

Eisenstadt, Shmuel N., Comparative Social Problems. 104

Elam, Houston G., Marketing. 58

Elam, James O., Fundamentals of Cardio-Pulmonary Resuscitation. 181; Instruction Manual for Mr. Airway: for Training Classes in All Methods of Rescue Breathing. 180

Elam, Jane, Introducing Linocuts. 9

Eldefonso, Edward, Law Enforcement and the Youthful Offender. 97; Principles of Law Enforcement. 97; Human Relations. 96

Eldridge, Clarence E., Marketing for Profit. 58

Electronic Teaching Laboratories, Washington, Electronic Engineers and Technicians Reference Handbook. 147

Electronic Technician, Color TV Trouble Factbook. 157; Servicing TV Receiver Circuits. 157; TV Troubleshooter's Handbook. 157; Useful Electronic Shop Hints. 147

Electronics, Design Manual for Transistor Circuits. 158

Electronics Industries Association, Advanced Servicing Techniques. 147

Eliel, Ernest L., Sterochemistry of Carbon Compounds. 127

Elisofon, Eliot, Color Photography. 49

Elkin, Robert, A Conceptual Base for Defining Health and Welfare Services.... 104

Elkins, Deborah, Teaching Strategies for the Culturally Disadvantaged. 113

Ellenbogen, Abraham, Effective Business Correspondence. 68

Ellender, Raphael, Basic Drawing. 9

Elling, Karl A., Introduction to Modern Marketing. 58

Ellinger, Richard G., Color Structure and Design. 9

Elliott, Curtis M., Property and Casualty Insurance. 53

Elliott, Fred C., Advances in Production and Utilization of Quality Cotton. 74

Elliott, Travis, Food Service Management. 31

Ellis, Aytoun, The Essence of Beauty:... Perfume and Cosmetics. 7; The Essence of Beauty:... Scent. 7

Ellis, Davis W., Calculations of Analytical Chemistry. 131

Ellis, F. S., Digital Computer Technology. 17

Ellis, George L., Foundations of Chemistry. 131

Ellis, Jessie C., Index to Illustrations. 9

Ellis, Philip P., Handbook of Ocular Therapeutics and Pharmacology. 201

Ellison, Arthur J., Electromechanical Energy Conversion. 155

Elmer, Elizabeth, Children in Jeopardy: A Study of Abused Minors and Their Families. 81

Elmstrom, George P., Optometric Practice Management. 198; Synopsis of the Legal Aspects of Contact Lens Practice for Optometrists. 198

Elonka, Stephen M., Standard Electronics Questions and Answers. 147; Standard Refrigeration and Air Conditioning Questions and Answers. 120

Elsby, Frank H., Marketing and the Sales Manager. 58

Elsen, Albert E., Purposes of Art. 9

Elsevier's Dictionary of the Printing and Allied Industries in Four Languages. 43

Elsevier's Wood Dictionary in Seven Languages: English-American, French, Spanish, Italian, Swedish, Dutch and German. 86

Elton, Charles S., Pattern of Animal Communities. 87

Ely, Lawrence D., Your Future in Aerospace Technology. 116

Ely, P. J., Social Work with Groups. 106

Emary, A. B., Building Construction Carpentry. 140

Embree, Harland D., Introduction to Chemistry. 131

Emeleus, Harry J., The Chemistry of Fluorine and Its Compounds. 127; Modern Aspects of Inorganic Chemistry. 133

Emerick, Robert H., Heating Handbook.... 120; Troubleshooters' Handbook for Mechanical Systems. 164

Emery, Glyn, Electronic Data Processing. 15

Emery, William H., A Manual of Catering. 31

Emmel, Victor M., Laboratory Technique in Biology and Medicine. 182; Staining Procedures. 182

Encyclopedia of Aviation and Space Sciences Above and Beyond. 116

Encyclopedia of Colour Photography. 49

End, Henry, Interiors Book of Hotels and Motor Hotels. 51

Eng, Evelyn, Disaster Handbook. 208

Engdahl, David A., Color Printing. 43

Engel, James F., Cases in Consumer Behavior. 57; Consumer Behavior. 58; Promotional Strategy. 58

Engel, Pauline, Executive Secretary's Handbook. 70

Engelmann, Siegfried, Preventing Failure in the Primary Grades. 110; Teaching Disadvantaged Children in the Preschool. 108

Engineers' Council for Professional Development, Inc., Manual of Evaluation Procedure of the Engineering Technology Committee. 164

Engineers Joint Council, Demand for Engineers and Technicians. 164

Englander, Herman S., System 360 Programming. 21

Englander, William R., System 360 Programming. 21

Engle, Glenn E., Industrial Arts Electricity. 162

Englebardt, Stanley L., Careers in Data Processing. 15

English, Walter, The Textile Industry. 28

Enis, Ben M., Experimentation for Marketing Decisions. 57; Marketing Classics. 58

Ennes, Harold E., Television System Maintenance. 157; Television Tape Fundamentals. 157; Workshop in Solid State. 147

Ennis, LeRoy M., Dental Roentgenology. 174

Enrick, Norbert L., Market and Sales Forecasting. 58; Quality Control and Reliability. 44

Ensminger, M. Eugene, Animal Science. 78; Beef Cattle Science. 78; Horses and Horsemanship. 78; Sheep and Wool Science. 78; The Stockman's Handbook. 78; Swine Science. 78

Enthoven, Jacqueline, The Stitches of Creative Embroidery. 23

Entrikin, John B., Identification of Organic Compounds. 134; Semimicro Qualitative Organic Analysis. 132

Epstein, Bernard S., The Spine: A Radiological Text and Atlas. 204

Epstein, Charlotte, Intergroup Relations for Police Officers. 97

Epting, John B., Ophthalmic Mechanics and Dispensing. 198

Eren, Neset, The Art of Turkish Cooking. 39

Erickson, Charlotte, The Freezer Cookbook. 31

Erickson, Janet D., Print Making Without a Press. 9

Ericson, Myrtle H., Quantity Food Recipes. 31

Erikson, Erik H., Childhood and Society. 81; Youth: Change and Challenge. 110

Ernest, John W., Creative Salesmanship. 58; Salesmanship Fundamentals. 58.

Ertell, Glenn, Numerical Control. 170

Erven, Lawrence W., Fire Company Apparatus and Procedures. 84; First Aid and Emergency Rescue. 84

Erwin, Mable D., Clothing for Moderns. 23

INDEX

Esau, Katherine, Anatomy of Seed Plants. 87

Esbensen, Thorwald, Working with Individualized Instruction. 110

Esh, Reba S., The Book of Arts and Crafts. 161

Eshelman, Phillip V., Tractors and Crawlers. 77

Eshom, Myreta, Medical Secretary's Manual. 71

Eskow, Gerald W., Your Future in the Trucking Industry. 123

Esmay, Merle L., Principles of Animal Environment. 78

Esposito, John C., Vanishing Air. 177

Esquire, Esquire Fashion Guide for All Occasions. 23; Esquire Fashions for Men. 23

Etienne, Gilbert, Studies in Indian Agriculture. 74

Etter, Lewis E., Glossary of Words and Phrases Used in Radiology, Nuclear Medicine and Ultrasound. 204; The Science of Ionizing Radiation. 204

Etter, Mildred F., Exercise for the Prone Patient. 209

Ettre, Leslie S., Encyclopedia of Industrial Chemical Analysis. 131

Etzioni, Amitai, The Semi-Professions and Their Organization. 104

European Chemical Market Research Sources. 127

Evans, Elfed, Plant Diseases and Their Chemical Control. 74

Evans, Ellis D., Children: Readings in Behavior and Development. 81

Evans, Frances M., The Role of the Nurse in Community Mental Health. 189

Evans, Joseph, Fundamental Principles of Transistors. 158

Evans, Paul L., Mathematics for Electronics Technicians. 206

Evans, S. A., Weed Control Handbook. 73

Evans, Walter H., Introduction to Electronics. 147

Evans, William E., The Chemistry of Death. 93

Everard, Noel J., Schaum's Outline of Theory and Problems of Reinforced Concrete Design. 140

Ewald, William R., Environment and Change. 178; Environment and Policy. 178; Environment for Man. 178

Ewen, Sol J., Ultrasonic Therapy. 174

Ewing, Galen W., Chemistry. 129; Instrumental Methods of Chemical Analysis. 133

Executive Reports Corporation, Real Estate Man's Tax Desk Manual. 65

Eyrich, Gerald I., Marketing. 62

Eysenck, Hans J., Crime and Personality. 97

Faber, Oscar, Constructional Steelwork Simply Explained. 137; Heating and Air-Conditioning of Buildings. 120; Reinforced Concrete. 141

Faber, Rodney B., Introduction to Amplifiers. 147; Introduction to Electron Devices. 147

Fabre, Maurice, History of Fashion. 23

Fabri, Ralph, Color. 13

Faget, Maxime A., Manned Spacecraft. 118; Manned Space Flight. 116

Fagin, Claire M., Family-Centered Nursing in Community Psychiatry. 196

Fairbrook, Paul, Starting and Managing a Small Restaurant. 52

Fairchild, Henry P., Dictionary of Sociology and Related Sciences. 104

Fairchild, John, The Fashionable Savages. 23

Faires, Virgil M., Design of Machine Elements. 167; Mechanism. 164

Faith, William L., Industrial Chemicals. 127

Falconer, Mary W., The Drug, the Nurse, the Patient. 189

Falk, Edwin A., Practical Portrait Photography for Home and Studio. 49

Falk, R. Frank, New Careers and Urban Schools. 108

Fallis, Bruce D., Textbook of Human Histology. 186

Faltermayer, Edmund K., Redoing America. 178

Family Service Association of America, Casework Treatment of the Family Unit. 104; The Expanding Theoretical Base of Casework. 104; Position on Use of Social Work Assistants in Family Service Agencies. 104; Range and Emphases of a Family Service Program. 104; Trends in Field Work Instruction. 104

Famous Artists Annual 1: A Treasury of Contemporary Art. 9

Fance, Wilfred J., The Student's Technology of Breadmaking and Flour Confectionery. 31

Fantel, Hans, ABC's of Hi-Fi and Stereo. 147

Farb, Peter, Ecology. 178; The Forest. 87

Farber, Eduard, The Evolution of Chemistry. 127

Farber, Seymour M., The Air We Breathe. 178; Food and Civilization. 31

Farina, Mario V., Computers. 17

Faris, Robert E., Handbook of Modern Sociology. 104

Farkas, Lucien L., Electronic Testing. 147

Farm Journal, Freezing & Canning Cookbook. 32

Farmer, David J., Civil Disorder Control. 97

Farmer, Fannie M., Fannie Farmer Boston Cookbook. 32

Farmer, Robert A., What You Should Know About Contracts. 70

Farnham, Walter E., Mechanical Drafting Essentials. 144

Farrall, Arthur W., Agricultural Engineering. 74

Farrell, Marlene S., Crisis Intervention. 208

Farrer-Meschan, R. M., Radiographic Positioning and Related Anatomy. 205

Farris, Mary A., Approaches for Co-Workers in Professional Nursing. 191

Fashion Group, Your Future in Fashion Design. 23; Your Future in the Beauty Business. 7; Your Future in the Fashion World. 23

Fass, Margot, The Nurse and the Cancer Patient. 189

Faulkner, Edwin J., Health Insurance. 54

Faulkner, Lloyd C., Abortion Diseases of Livestock. 78

Faulkner, Ray N., Art Today. 9; Inside Today's Home. 55

Faulkner, Sarah, Inside Today's Home. 55

Faust, Raymond J., Water Quality and Treatment in Public Water Supplies. 178

Fava, Sylvia F., Urban Society. 104

Favazza, Armando R., Guide for Mental Health Workers. 208

Favazza, Barbara S., Guide for Mental Health Workers. 208

Favreau, Donald, Guidelines for Fire Service Education Programs in Community and Junior Colleges. 84

Favret, Andrew G., Introduction to Digital Computer Applications. 17

Fay, John, The Helicopter and How it Flies. 116

Fayerweather, John, International Marketing. 62

Fearn, David A., Management Systems for the Hotel, Catering and Allied Industries. 51

Federal Electric Corporation, Special Purpose Transistors. 158; Transistors. 158

Federman, Philip J., Professional Police-Human Relations Training. 100

Feigl, Fritz, Spot Tests in Organic Analysis. 134

Feingold, Carl, Fundamentals of Cobol Programming. 19; Fundamentals of Punched Card Data Processing. 15

Feininger, Andreas, The Color Photo Book. 49; The Complete Photographer. 49; Successful Color Photography. 49

Feirer, John L., Advanced Woodwork and Furniture Making. 161; Cabinetmaking and Millwork. 161; Drawing and Planning for Industrial Arts. 142; General Metals. 161; General Shop. 161; I.A. Bench Woodwork. 161; Industrial Arts

Education. 161; Industrial Arts Woodworking. 161; Machine Tool Metalworking. 164; Metalwork. 161; Woodworking for Industry. 161

Feld, Jacob, Construction Failure. 137; Lessons from Failures of Concrete Structures. 141

Feldman, Edmund B., Art as Image and Idea. 9

Feldman, Edwin B., Housekeeping Handbook for Institutions, Business, and Industry. 51

Feldman, Egal, Fit for Men. 23

Feldman, Francis L., Family Social Welfare. 104

Feldman, Robert Q., Basic Retailing. 63; Essentials of Merchandise Information. 59

Feldzamen, A. N., Bright Future Careers with Computers. 18

Felkenes, George T., Law Enforcement. 95; New Dimensions in Criminal Justice. 95

Felker, Charles A., Machine-Shop Technology. 161

Felkin, William, Felkin's History of the Machine-Wrought Hosiery and Lace Manufactures. 23

Felton, Jean S., Health and the Community. 207

Fenten, D. X., Aviation Careers. 116

Ferguson, Egbert R., Jr., Food Standards and Definitions in the United States. 32

Ferguson, Elizabeth A., Social Work. 104

Ferguson, Frank C., Drug Therapy. 201; Efficient Drug Store Management. 201

Ferguson, John H., Blood and Body Functions. 186

Ferguson, Lloyd N., The Modern Structural Theory of Organic Chemistry. 134

Ferman, Louis A., Poverty in America. 104

Fernando, Quintus, Ionic Equilibria and Analytical Chemistry. 131

Ferrara, W., Management Accounting for Profit Control. 3

Ferris, Byron, Fell's Guide to Commercial Art. 11

Ferry, John W., A History of the Department Store. 63

Ferster, Marilyn B., Arithmetic for Nurses. 206

Fertig, Paul E., Using Accounting Information. 2

Fertilizer Institute, Analytical Methods. 74

Fess, Philip E., Accounting Principles. 4

Fetter, Robert B., The Quality Control System. 44

Fetter, William A., Computer Graphics in Communication. 142

Fibrance, Austin E., Industrial Instrumentation Fundamentals. 164

Fichandler, Thomas G., Distribution in a High-Level Economy. 57

Ficken, Frederick A., The Simplex Method of Linear Programming. 19

Field, Edwin M., Oil Burners. 120

Field, George A., Human Behavior in Marketing. 58

Field, Hazel E., Foods in Health and Disease. 32

Field, Michael, All Manner of Food. 32; Michael Field's Culinary Classics and Improvisations. 32

Fielo, Sandra E., Technical Nursing of the Adult. 189

Fieser, Louis F., Organic Experiments. 134; Reagents for Organic Synthesis. 134; Style Guide for Chemists. 127; Topics in Organic Chemistry. 134

Fieser, Mary, Reagents for Organic Synthesis. 134; Style Guide for Chemistry. 127; Topics in Organic Chemistry. 134

Filbin, Robert, So You're Going to be A Teacher. 110

Filderman, Irving P., Contact Lens Practice and Patient Management. 198

Finance, Charles, Buffet Catering. 32

Finch, Bernard, Multilingual Guide for Medical Personnel. 207

Fincham, W. H., Optics. 198

Findlay, Alexander, A Hundred Years of Chemistry. 127

Findlay, T. J., Chemical Data Book. 125

Fine, Benjamin, Underachievers. 109

Finerty, John C., A Textbook of Histology. 186

Fink, Arthur E., The Field of Social Work. 104

Finley, Kay T., Fundamental Organic Chemistry. 134

Finnegan, Janet A., The Patient in Surgery. 197

Finney, Harry A., The Accounting Process. 2; Principles of Accounting, Advanced. 2; Principles of Accounting, Intermediate. 2; Principles of Accounting, Introductory. 2; Principles of Financial Accounting. 2

Fioranelli, Carlo H., Synchors and Servos. 146

Fiore, Mariano S., An Atlas of Human Histology. 186

Fire Engineering, Fundamentals of Fire Fighting. 84

Fire Protection Handbook Study Guide. 84

Fischer, George, Your Career in Computers. 17

Fischer, Harry W., Manual of Roentgenological Technique. 205

Fischer, Robert B., Basic Theory and Practice of Quantitative Chemical Analysis. 132; A Brief Introduction to Quantitative Chemical Analysis. 132; Chemical Equilibrium. 127

Fischer, Shannon R., How Computer Programming Works. 19

Fischer, Valentina G., Promotion of Physical Comfort and Safety. 189

Fisher, Berenice M., Industrial Education. 161

Fisher, Charles H., Carburetion. 123

Fisher, Edward C., The Evidence Handbook. 97

Fisher, F. Peter, Computer Programming Systems. 19

Fisher, H., Electrical Blueprint Reading and Sketching. 144

Fisher, Mary F., The Cooking of Provincial France. 39

Fisher, Patty, The Value of Food. 32

Fisher, Sir Ronald A., The Theory of Inbreeding. 78

Fishlock, David, The New Materials. 167; New Ways of Working Metals. 168

Fishman, Jacob R., New Careers: Generic Issues in the Human Services. 107; New Careers: The Teacher Aide. 113

Fisk, George, Marketing Systems. 58; Theories for Marketing Systems Analysis. 58

Fiske, Kenneth A., AC Circuit Analysis Through Experimentation. 147; DC Circuit Analysis Through Experimentation. 147; Solid State Circuit Analysis Through Experimentation. 147

Fitch, Edwin M., The Bureau of Outdoor Recreation. 102

Fitch, Grace E., Arithmetic Review and Drug Therapy of Practical Nurses. 195; The Macmillan Dictionary for Practical and Vocational Nurses. 195; The Role and Responsibilities of the Practical Nurse. 195

Fitch, Richard D., Accidental or Incendiary. 84

Fitchen, Franklin C., Transistor Circuit Analysis and Design. 158

Fitsgerald, R. T., The Printers of Melbourne. 44

Fitzgerald, Arthur E., Electric Machinery. 155

Fitzgerald, Robert W., Strength of Materials. 170

FitzGibbon, Theodora, The Art of British Cooking. 39; Game Cooking. 32; A Taste of Ireland. 39

Fitzpatrick, Elise, Maternity Nursing. 194

Fitzpatrick, Frederick L., Our Plant Resources. 74

Fitzpatrick, Genevieve M., Gynecologic Nursing. 194

Fivars, Grace, Nursing Evaluation. 189

Flammang, C. J., The Police and the Underprotected Child. 97

Flanagan, George A., Understand and Enjoy Modern Art. 9

Flannery, Naomi, 101 Great Window Decorating Ideas. 55

Flapan, Dorothy, Children's Understanding of Social Interaction. 81

INDEX

Flaschka, Hermenegild A., Quantitative Analytical Chemistry. 132

Flawn, Peter T., Environmental Geology. 178

Fleck, George M., Equilibria in Solution. 127

Fleck, Henrietta, Introduction to Nutrition. 40

Fleckles, David E., Introduction to Electron Tubes and Semiconductors. 145

Flemans, R. J., An Atlas of Haematological Cytology. 186

Fleming, William, Arts and Ideas. 9

Fletcher, Alan, Graphic Design. 9

Fletcher, Linda P., The Negro in the Insurance Industry. 53

Fletcher, Sybil M., Drugs and Solutions. 190

Flickinger, Reed, Developmental Biology. 185

Flink, James J., America Adopts the Automobile, 1895-1910. 123

Flinn, Richard A., Fundamentals of Metal Casting. 168

Flint, Betty M., The Child and the Institution. 81

Flint, Thomas, Emergency Treatment and Management. 208

Flitter, Hessel H., An Introduction to Physics in Nursing. 189

Flocco, Thomas, The Automobile Electrical System. 122

Flood, Walter E., The Dictionary of Chemical Names. 127

Flores, Ivan, Computer Programming. 19; Computer Sorting. 17

Floutz, Vaughn W., Chemistry for Nurses. 18

Floyd, Wayne, Decorating with Photographs. 55

Fluchere, Henri A., Airbrush Techniques for Commercial Art. 11

Flugel, John C., The Psychology of Clothes. 23

Fluid Clutches and Torque Converters. 123

Flynn, John E., Architectural Interior Systems. 137; Interior Environmental Control. 178

Flynn, Patricia, The Complete Secretary. 67

Focarino, Joseph, The Executive Secretary. 70

Foerst, Wilhelm, Newer Methods of Preparative Organic Chemistry. 134

Fogel, Lawrence J., Bio-Technology. 182

Fogel, Walter A., The Negro in the Meat Industry. 32

Foil, R. R., Organization Management in Forestry. 87

Foldes, Joseph, Large-Format Camera Practices. 49

Folsom, Le Roi A., The Instructor's Guide for the Teaching of Professional Cooking. 32; Opportunities in Food Preparation and Service. 35

Folta, Jeannette R., A Sociological Framework for Patient Care. 189

Fomon, Samuel J., Infant Nutrition. 40

Fonda, Gerald, Management of the Patient with Subnormal Vision. 198

Fono, Paulette, The Crepê Cookbook. 32

Fontaine, Guy, Diodes and Transistors. 158; Transistors for Audiofrequency. 158

Food and Agriculture Organization of the United Nations, International Directory of Manufacturers of Forestry Instruments and Hand Tools. 87

Foote, Francis S., Surveying Theory and Practice. 142

Foote, H. Elliott, Coffee Processing Technology. 42

Foran, Eugene F., Funeral Service Facts and Figures. 93

Forbes, Colin, Graphic Design. 9

Forbes, Evelyn, Hairdressing and Beauty As a Career. 8

Forbes, Reginald D., Forestry Handbook. 87

Ford, Walter B., Electricity and Electronics. 153

Ford, William H., Simple Sermons for Funeral Services. 93

Fordham, Michael, Children as Individuals. 81

Foreman, C. F., Dairy Cattle in American Agriculture. 79

Foren, Robert, Authority in Social Casework. 104

Forest, Betty L., Utilization of Associate Degree Nursing Graduates in General Hospitals. 189

Forkner, Hamden L., Correlated Dictation and Transcription: Gregg. 67

Fornia, Joseph G., Upholstering at Home. 56

Forrest, Jane, Practical Nursing and Anatomy for Pupil Nurses. 195

Forrest, Peter G., Fatigue of Metals. 168

Forrester, Gertrude, Occupational Literature. 90

Forstall, Richard, Commercial Atlas and Marketing Guide. 58

Forsythe, Alexandra I., Computer Science: A First Course. 17; Computer Science: Fortran Language. 17

Fortney, Ned J., The Successful Practice of Real Estate. 65

Fortune, Environment. 178; Markets of the Seventies. 58

Fosdick, Raymond B., American Police Systems. 97

Foskett, Antony C., The Subject Approach to Information. 90

Foskett, Douglas J., Information Service in Libraries. 90

Foss, Edward W., Construction and Maintenance for Farm and Home. 137

Foss, Martin, Death, Sacrifice and Tragedy. 93

Fossett, R. O., Techniques in Photography for the Screen Process Printer. 49

Foster, Albert B., Approved Practices in Soil Conservation. 74

Foster, C. A., Anaesthesia for Operating Theatre Technicians. 209

Foster D. Snell, Inc., Carpet Underlays. 52

Foster, Joanna, Illustrators of Children's Books 1957-1966. 10

Foster, Leroy E., Telemetry Systems. 148

Foster, Norman, Construction Estimates from Take-Off to Bids. 137; Practical Tables for Building Construction. 137

Foth, H. D., Fundamentals of Soil Science. 75

Foulke, Roy A., Practical Financial Statement Analysis. 2

Fowler, Ewell W., Basic Woodworking Processes. 161

Fowler, Grace R., Psychodynamic Nursing. 188

Fowler, Jenifer E., Heinemann Modern Dictionary for Dental Students. 174

Fowler, Sina F., Food for Fifty. 32

Fowler, Stewart H., Beef Production in the South. 78; The Marketing of Livestock and Meat. 78

Fowles, Gerald W., Valency and Molecular Structure. 126

Fowles, Grant R., Introduction to Modern Optics. 198

Fox, David J., Fundamentals of Research in Nursing. 189

Fox, Edward A., Mechanics. 164

Fox, Karl A., Readings in the Economics of Agriculture. 74

Fox, Robert A., Fundamentals of Commercial Chemical Development. 127

Fox, Rodney, Agricultural and Technical Journalism. 74

Fox, Vernon, Guidelines for Corrections Education in Community and Junior Colleges. 97

Fox, William W., Careers in the Biological Sciences. 185

Foy, Donald F., A Textbook for Medical Assistants. 71

Fradkin, Helen, Organization of Services That Will Best Meet Needs of Children. 81

Fraenkel, Jack R., Crime and Criminals. 97

Frailey, Lester E., Handbook of Business Letters. 67

Fram, Eugene H., What You Should Know About Small Business Marketing. 58

Francis, Carl C., Introduction to Human Anatomy. 184; Radiographic Atlas of Skeletal Development of the Foot and Ankle. 204

Francis, Gloria, Promoting Psychological Comfort. 189

Francis, Mary, The Beginner's Guide to Flying. 116

Franco, Robert J., Logistics in Marketing. 61

Frandsen, J. H., Ice Cream and Related Products. 32

Frandson, Rowen D., Anatomy and Physiology of Farm Animals. 78

Frank, Elinor, Best Hairdos. 8

Frank, George W., Cost Accounting. 5

Frank, Jeannette, The Modern Meat Cookbook. 32

Frank, Josette, Your Child's Reading Today. 110

Frank, Nathalie D., Data Sources for Business and Market Analysis. 58

Franke, Lois E., Handwrought Jewelry. 27

Frankel, Max, Tables for Identification of Organic Compounds. 134

Frankland, Thomas W., Pipe Trades Pocket Manual. 141

Franklin, Colin, The Private Presses. 44

Frantz, Harper W., Chemical Principles in the Laboratory. 127; Essentials of Chemistry in the Laboratory. 127; Fundamental Experiments for College Chemistry. 127

Fraser, Roland R., General Metal. 161

Frasier, James E., An Introduction to the Study of Education. 110

Frasnay, Daniel, The Artist's World. 9

Frasure, William W., Financial Accounting Concepts. 4; Managerial Accounting. 4

Frazier, William, Printing by Flash. 49

Frazier, William C., Food Microbiology. 32

Fream, William C., Applied Human Biology for Nurses. 189

Frederick, John H., Commercial Air Transportation. 116

Frederick, L., The Principles and Practice of Embalming. 93

Frederick, Molly, Vision: Readings in Health and Medical Technology Education Programs. 182

Frederick, Portia M., The Office Assistant in Medical Practice. 71

Freedman, Alfred, The Revised Penal Law Handbook. 97

Freedman, Florence B., Classroom Teacher's Guide to Audio-Visual Material. 110

Freedman, Marilyn G., Clinical Workbook for Practical Nurses. 195

Freeland, R. R., Practical CB Radio Servicing. 156

Freeling, Nicolas, The Kitchen. 32

Freeman, Larry, Victorian Posters. 9

Freeman, Max H., Accounting 10/12. 2; Gregg Bookkeeping & Accouting. 2

Freeman, Mitchell, Practical and Industrial Formulary. 127

Freeman, Orville, The National Forests of America. 87

Freeman, Peter, Lubrication and Friction. 123

Freeman, Ruth B., Community Health Nursing Practice. 189; Public Health Nursing Practice. 196

Freidson, Eliot, The Hospital in Modern Society. 207

Freiser, Henry, Ionic Equilibria and Analytical Chemistry. 131

Frenay, Sister Mary A., Understanding Medical Terminology. 71

French, Ruth M., The Dynamics of Health Care. 207; Nurse's Guide to Diagnostic Procedures. 189

French, Thomas E., Fundamentals of Engineering Drawing. 142; Graphic Science. 142; A Manual of Engineering Drawing for Student Draftsmen. 142; Mechanical Drawing. 144

Freudenthal, Alfred M., Introduction to the Mechanics of Solids. 164

Frey, Albert W., Advertising. 6; Marketing Handbook. 58

Fricke, Charles W., Criminal Investigation. 97; 5000 Criminal Definitions, Terms, and Phrases. 97

Fried, Eleanor L., Is the Fashion Business Your Business? 23

Fried, Walter R., Avionics Navigation Systems. 117

Friedberg, M. Paul, Play and Interplay. 102

Frieden, Earl, Modern Topics in Biochemistry. 132

Friedlander, Joseph S., The Management of Retail Buying. 64

Friedlander, Walter A., Introduction to Social Welfare. 104

Friedman, Edith J., Encyclopedia of Real Estate Appraising. 65

Friedman, Jack W., Basic Electronics "Autotext." 148

Friedman, M., Economic Justice: The Needs of Fire Fighters. 86

Friedman, Morris H., Direct and Alternating Current Machinery. 152

Friedman, Sherwood, Applied Clerical Practice. 67; Handbook for Typists. 67; Modern Clerical Practice. 67; Secretarial Practice. 67

Frigerio, Norman A., Your Body and Radiation. 204

Frisch, Vern A., Applied Office Typewriting. 67

Frischauer, Willi, The Grand Hotels of Europe. 51

Frobisher, Martin, Fundamentals of Microbiology. 187; Microbiology in Health and Disease. 187

Frohse, Franz, Atlas of Human Anatomy. 184

Frome, Michael, The National Forests of America. 87; Whose Woods These Are. 87

Fromme, Allan, The ABC of Child Care. 81

Frost, Jane C., Your Future in Dental Assisting. 174

Frost, Joe L., Early Childhood Education Rediscovered. 81, 110

Fry, Edmund, Pantographia: Containing Accurate Copies of All the Known Alphabets in the World. 9

Fry, Glenn A., Geometrical Optics. 198

Fryburger, Vernon, Advertising Theory and Practice. 7

Frye, John T., Basic Radio Course. 156

Fryer, J. D., Weed Control Handbook. 73

Fryklund, Verne C., General Drafting. 142; General Shop Woodworking. 161

Fuchs, Alice S., Multiengine Flying. 116

Fuchs, Arthur, Principles of Radiographic Exposure and Processing. 204

Fuchs, J. David, Electrical Motor Controls and Circuits. 156

Fuerst, Elinor V., Fundamentals of Nursing. 189; Teaching Fundamentals of Nursing. 189

Fuerst, Robert, Microbiology in Health and Disease. 187

Fuglsby, Glenn O., General Mechanical Drawing. 144

Fujita, S. Neil, Aim for a Job in Graphic Design/Art. 9

Fuller, A. J., Microwaves. 148

Fuller, Don, Functional Drafting for Today. 142; Getting Top Mileage from Drafting and Design Operations. 142

Fuller, Gerald R., Education for Agricultural Occupations. 74

Fuller, John, The Chef's Compendium of Professional Recipes. 32; Gueridon and Lamp Cookery. 32; Hotel Keeping and Catering as a Career. 51; The Waiter. 52

Fullerton, Bill J., The Identification of Common Courses in Paramedical Education. 207

Fulton, John T., The Natural History of Dental Diseases. 174

Fulton, Paul C., Advertising in the Printed Media. 6

Fulton, Robert L., A Compilation of Studies of Attitudes Towards Death, Funerals and Funeral Directors.... 93; Death and Identity. 93

Funk & Wagnalls Cook's and Diner's Dictionary. 32

Funk & Wagnalls Dictionary of Electronics. 148

Furman, Robert A., The Therapeutic Nursery School. 81

Fuson, Reynold C., Systematic Identification of Organic Compounds. 135

Futrell, Gene A., Marketing Farm Products.... 76

INDEX

Fyfe, F. W., Anatomy of the Human Body. 184

Fyffe, Charles, Basic Copy Fitting. 44

GAF Corporation: Graphic Arts Handbook. 44

Gabard, E. C., Decision-Making in Police Administration. 96

Gabb, Michael H., Handbook of Laboratory Solutions. 127

Gable, Fred B., Opportunities in Pharmacy Careers. 201

Gablehouse, Charles, Helicopters and Autogiros. 116

Gablik, Suzi, Pop Art Redefined. 12

Gaden, Eileen, The Blender Cookbook. 35

Gagne, Robert, The Conditions of Learning. 110

Gaitskell, Charles D., Children and Their Art. 110

Gale, Frederick C., Mortuary Science. 93

Galigher, Albert E., The Essentials of Practical Microtechnique. 182

Galin, Saul, Reference Books. 90

Gallagher, Walter N., Dental Roentgenology Review. 174

Gallati, Robert R., Introduction to Law Enforcement and Criminal Justice. 97

Galler, Bernard A., The Language of Computers. 17; A View of Programming Languages. 19

Gallington, Ralph O., Course Construction in Industrial Arts.... 161

Galloway, John R., A Handbook of Radiography. 205

Galwey, Andrew K., Chemistry of Solids. 127

Gammage, Allen Z., Basic Police Report Writing. 97; Police Training in the United States. 97; Your Future in Law Enforcement. 97

Gancel, J., Gancel's Culinary Encyclopedia of Modern Cooking.... 32

Gans, Carl, Comparative Anatomy Atlas. 184

Gantz, Kenneth F., Nuclear Flight: The United States Air Force Programs.... 116

Garard, Ira D., Invitation to Chemistry. 127

Garb, Solomon, Disaster Handbook. 208; Laboratory Tests in Common Use. 182; Pharmacology & Patient Care, 201

Garbassi, U., A Guide to Cobol Programming. 20

Garber, Harold, Retail Merchandising and Management with Electronic Data Processing. 63

Garber, Lee O., The Law Governing School Property and School-Building Construction. 137

Garcia, Clarita, Clarita's Cocina. 39

Gardiner, A. W., Typewriting and Office Duplicating Processes. 67

Gardiner, George H., How I Sold a Million Dollars of Real Estate in One Year. 65

Gardner, Christina, Typesetting with IBM Executive Typewriters. 44

Gardner, David B., Development in Early Childhood. 81

Gardner, Earl W., Elementary Microbiology. 187

Gardner, Earle S., Cops on Campus and Crime in the Streets. 97

Gardner, Helen, Gardner's Art Through the Ages. 9

Gardner, Henry A., Paint Testing Manual. 127

Gardner, William, Chemical Synonyms and Trade Names. 127

Garfield, Sydney, Teeth, Teeth, Teeth. 174

Garland, Carl W., Experiments in Physical Chemistry. 135

Garland, D. J., Modern Electronic Maintenance Principles. 148

Garland, Madge, Fashion. 23

Garland, Phyllis, Ophthalmic Nursing. 189

Garner, Walter, Textile Laboratory Manual. 28

Garnero, Robert S., Fortran IV Problem Solver. 20

Garrat, George A., Wood Preservation. 87

Garratt, Donald C., The Quantitative Analysis of Drugs. 201

Garrett, Lillian, Visual Design. 13

Garrison, Garnet R., Television and Radio. 157

Garstang, Stephen W., Electrical Motor Controls and Circuits. 156

Garton, Nina R., The Development of Theory and Practice in Social Casework. 104

Garvey, Eleanor M., The Arts of the French Book, 1900-1965. 9

Garvey, M. Claudia, Refresher Course in Gregg Shorthand. 70

Garvey, Mona, Library Displays. 90

Gaskins, Ruth L., A Good Heart and A Light Hand: Ruth L. Gaskins' Collection of Traditional Negro Recipes. 39

Gaspard, Curren J., A Training Program for Vocational Agriculture in Agricultural Service. 74

Gass, Saul I., Linear Programming. 20

Gassner, John, The Nature of Art. 9

Gatch, Milton McC., Death: Meaning and Mortality in Christian Thought and Contemporary Culture. 93

Gates, David, Lettering for Reproduction. 14

Gates, Jean K., Guide to the Use of Books and Libraries. 90

Gatland, Kenneth, Manned Spacecraft. 116; Pocket Encyclopedia of Spaceflight in Color. 116

Gattegno, Caleb, What We Owe Children: The Subordination of Teaching to Learning. 110

Gattone, Felix, Air Conditioning and Heating Technology: II. 120

Gatz, Arthur J., An Outline Manual for the Study of Histology. 186

Gatz, Konrad, Curtain Wall Construction. 137

Gaunt, Walter A., Advances in Dental Histology. 174

Gavin, Ruth E., Reference Manual for Stenographers and Typists. 67

Gawne, Eleanor J., Dress: The Clothing Textbook. 23

Gay, Charles M., Mechanical and Eletrical Equipment for Buildings. 137

Gay, Kathlyn, Careers in Social Service. 104

Gay, Robert, Words into Type. 69

Gazaway, Rena, Human Relations in Nursing. 190

Gear, Charles W., Computer Organization and Programming. 20

Gearien, James E., Methods of Drug Analysis. 201

Gebhardt, Louis P., Microbiology. 187

Geck, Elisabeth, Johannes Gutenberg. 44

Geddes, Aubrey K., Premature Babies. 194

Geddes, L. A., Principles of Applied Biomedical Instrumentation. 182

Gee, A. C., Hotel and Institutional Cookery. 32

Gega, Peter C., Science in Elementary Education. 110

Gehmlich, Dietrich K., Electromechanical Systems. 155

Geier, George J., Accounting for Business. 2

Geiling, E. M., Essentials of Pharmacology. 202

Geis, Darlene, The Gourmet Cooking School Cookbook. 34

Geis, Gilbert, Man, Crime and Society. 95; The White Collar Criminal. 97

Geismar, Ludwig L., Preventive Intervention in Social Work. 104

Geissman, Theodore A., Principles of Organic Chemistry. 134

Geitgey, Doris A., A Handbook for Head Nurses. 189; A Study of Some Effects of Sensitivity Training on the Performance of Students in Associate Degree Programs of Nursing Education. 190

Gelb, Richard L., Your Future in Beauty Culture. 7

Gelfand, Donna M., Social Learning in Childhood. 110

Gell, Frank, The Black Badge: Confessions of a Caseworker. 104

Geller, Louis, Accounting. 2

General Electronic Laboratories, Experimental Electricity. 148

Gentle, Ernest J., Aviation and Space Dictionary. 116

INDEX

Gentry, James A., Finney and Miller's Principles of Accounting, Introductory. 3

Geoffrey, William, The Complexities of an Urban Classroom. 113

George, Frank H., An Introduction to Computer Programming. 20

George, Norvil L., School Food Centers. 32

Georgiou, Constantine, Children and Their Literature. 81

Gerard, Geoffrey, The Book of Electricity. 148

Gerber, Jack, A Selected Bibliography of the Graphic Arts. 44

Gerbie, Albert B., Gynecologic Nursing. 194

Gerevas, Lawrence E., Drafting Technology Problems. 142

Gerhardt, Rodgers, Principles of Cost Accounting. 5

Gerking, Shelby D., Biological Systems. 185

Gerlach, John T., Successful Management of New Products. 58

Germain, Clarence B., Programming the IBM 360. 20

Germann, A. C., Introduction to Law Enforcement and Criminal Justice. 97; Police Executive Development. 97

Gernsheim, Alison, Fashion and Reality, 1840-1914. 27

Gerrish, Howard H., Electricity and Electronics Teaches Modern Concepts. 148; Technical Dictionary. 148; Transistor Electronics. 158

Gerstein, Melvin, Progress in Combustion Science and Technology. 116

Gerstner, Karl, Designing Programs. 9

Gettens, Rutherford J., Painting Materials. 9

Gettings, Fred, Techniques of Drawing. 9

Ghirardi, Alfred A., Radio and Television, Receiver Circuitry and Operation. 156

Giachino, Joseph W., American Technical Society's Drafting. 142; Course Construction in Industrial Arts.... 161; Drafting Technology. 142; Engineering Drafting Problems. 142; Engineering-Technical Drafting and Graphics. 142; Everyday Sketching and Drafting. 142; General Metals for Technology. 161; Print Reading for Welders. 142; Welding Skills and Practices. 171; Welding Technology. 171

Giannelli, Stanley, Care of the Critically Ill. 208

Gibbons, Don C., Society, Crime and Criminal Careers. 97

Gibbons, Euell, Feast on a Diabetic Diet. 32

Gibbons, James F., Semiconductor Electronics. 148

Gibbons, Joe, Feast on a Diabetic Diet. 32

Gibbs, George, Accounting for Management Decisions. 2

Gibbs-Smith, Charles H., The Aeroplane. 116; The Fashionable Lady in the 19th Century. 27

Gibby, Joseph C., Technical Illustrations. 142

Gibson, D. Parke, The $30 Billion Negro. 58

Gibson, E. Dana, An Introduction to Automated Data Processing. 15; Liquid Duplicating Systems. 69; Stencil Duplicating Systems. 69; Word Finder. 67

Gibson, J. Sullivan, Soils. 74

Gibson, John, The Nurse's Materia Medica. 190; Psychiatry for Nurses. 190

Gibson, Peter, Modern Trends in Letterpress Printing. 44

Giese, Arthur C., Cell Physiology. 185

Giesecke, Frederick E., Engineering Graphics. 142; Technical Drawing. 142

Giesey, Ralph E., The Royal Funeral Ceremony in Renaissance France. 93

Gilbert, Don E., Inhalation Therapy Procedure Manual. 180

Gilbert, Horace D., Miniaturization. 148

Gilbert, Keith R., Fire Engines, and other Firefighting Appliances. 84

Gilbert, Neil, Clients or Constituents: Community Action in the War on Poverty. 104

Gilbert, Stephen G., Pictorial Anatomy of the Fetal Pig. 186

Gilbrech, Donald A., Fluid Mechanics. 164

Gildersleeve, Thomas R., Computer Data Processing and Programming. 16

Giles, A. F., Electronic Sensing Devices. 148

Giles, George H., The Principles and Practice of Refraction and Its Allied Subjects. 198

Giles, John G., Gears and Transmissions. 123; Vehicle Equipment. 123; Vehicle Operation and Testing. 123

Giles, Ronald V., Fluid Mechanics and Hydraulics. 164

Gill, Bob, Graphic Design. 9

Gill, Paul, Systems Management Techniques for Builders and Contractors. 137

Gilles, H. M., Adams and Maegraith: Tropical Medicine for Nurses. 191

Gillespie, Cecil M., Accounting Systems. 2

Gillespie, John T., Introducing Books. 110

Gillespie, Karen R., Retail Business Management. 63

Gillian, Reed A., Radiography of the Skull. 204

Gillie, Angelo C., Electrical Principles of Electronics. 148; Principles of Electron Devices. 148; Pulse and Logic Circuits. 148

Gillies, Dee A., Saunders Tests for Self-Evaluation of Nursing Competence. 190

Gillies, Robert R., Bacteriology Illustrated. 182

Gilman, Alfred Z., The Pharmacological Basis of Therapeutics. 201

Gilmore, Ken, It's Easy to Use Electronic Test Equipment. 149

Gilson, Goodwin, Developing Shorthand Skills. 67

Ginglend, David R., Recreation for Retarded Teenagers and Young Adults. 102

Ginsberg, Frances, A Manual of Operating Room Technology. 209

Ginsburg, Herbert, Piaget's Theory of Intellectual Development. 81

Giordano, Al, Basic Business Machine Calculation. 67

Gips, Claudia D., Care of the Adult Patient. 193

Gist, Noel P., Urban Society. 104

Gist, Ronald R., Retailing. 63

Gitchoff, G. Thomas, Kids, Cops and Kilos. 97

Glade, William P., Marketing in a Developing Nation. 62

Gladstone, John, Mechanical Estimating Guide. 164

Gladwell, D. C., The Hotel Assistant Manager. 50

Glaister, Geoffrey A., An Encyclopedia of the Book. 44

Glanz, Edward C., Group in Guidance. 105

Glaser, Barney G., Awareness of Dying. 93; Time for Dying. 93

Glass, David C., Biology and Behavior. 178

Glasser, William, Schools Without Failure. 110

Glasstone, Samuel, The Elements of Physical Chemistry. 135

Glazener, Everett R., Basic Metalwork. 161; Industrial Arts Drawing. 142; Technical Woodworking. 161

Glenn, Harold T., Automechanics. 123; Automobile Engine Rebuilding and Maintenance. 123; Automotive Smog Control Manual. 123; Exploring Power Mechanics. 161; Glenn's Auto Repair Manual. 123; Glenn's Auto Troubleshooting Guide. 123; Glenn's Foreign Car Repair Manual 123; Glenn's Foreign Carburetors and Electrical Systems Guide. 123; Mobile Hydraulic Testing. 123

Glenn, Ronald E., Mobile Hydraulic Testing. 123

Glicksman, Martin, Gum Technology in the Food Industry. 41

Glickstein, Cyrus, Basic Ultrasonics. 148; Ultrasonic Therapy. 174

Glim, Aesop, How Advertising is Written and Why. 6

INDEX

Glisson, Oris, Family Clothing. 26

Gloag, John, A Social History of Furniture Design from B.C. 1300 to A.D. 1960. 56

Glock, Waldo S., An Annotated Bibliography of Tree Growth and Growth Rings, 1950-1962. 86

Gloyna, Ernest F., Advances in Water Quality Improvement. 178; Principles of Radiological Health. 204

Gluck, Felix, Modern Publicity 1969-70. 10; World Graphic Design. 10

Gluck, Irvin D., Optics. 198

Glueck, Eleanor, Ventures in Criminology. 97

Glueck, Sheldon, Ventures in Criminology. 97

Glyck, Zvonko, Photographic Vision. 49

Gocke, Blye W., Police Sergeants' Manual. 97

Goddard, Arthur, Games to Improve Your Child's English. 81

Godson, John, Unsafe at Any Height. 116

Goetz, Billy E., Accounting in Action. 2

Goings, Leslie F., Automotive Electrical Systems. 122

Gokulanathan, K. S., Child Care in a Developing Community. 81

Gold, Annalee, How to Sell Fashion. 23

Gold, Harry, Combatting Social Problems. 105

Goldberg, Gertrude S., New Careers: The Social Service Aide. 105

Goldberg, Joe B., Biomicroscopy for Contact Lens Practice. 198

Goldberg, Louis, The Elements of Accounting. 2

Goldberg, Miriam L., The Effects of Ability Grouping. 110

Goldblith, Samuel A., Exploration in Future Food-Processing Techniques. 41; Introduction to Thermal Processing of Foods. 41; Milestones in Nutrition. 40

Golden, James T., Fortran IV: Programming and Computing. 20

Goldenthal, Irving, Problems in Retail Merchandising. 64

Goldfien, Alan, Review of Medical Pharmacology. 202

Golding, Martha A., Principles for Creating Clothing. 26

Goldman, Bram J., Arid Lands in Perspective. 75

Goldman, Henry M., An Introduction to Periodontia. 174; Periodontal Therapy. 174

Goldman, Marshall I., Controlling Pollution. 178

Goldman, Myer, A Nurse's Guide to the X-Ray Department. 190

Goldsmith, Arlene, Those Children: Case Studies from the Inner-City School. 109

Goldstein, Arnold S., Casebook on Community Pharmacy Management. 201

Goldstein, Albert, Secrets of Overcoming Sales Resistance. 58

Goldstein, Jerome, Garbage As You Like It. 178

Goldstein, Lester, Cell Biology. 185

Goldstein, Milton, Basic Electricity for Electronics. 151

Gollin, James, Pay Now, Die Later. 54

Gombrich, Ernst H., Art and Illusion. 10; The Story of Art. 10

Good Housekeeping, Book of Cake Decorating. 37; The New Good Housekeeping Cookbook. 32

Goodale, Raymond H., Clinical Interpretation of Laboratory Tests. 182

Goodban, William T., Architectural Drawing and Planning. 143

Goode, William J., The Family. 105; Readings on the Family and Society. 105

Goodger, E. M., Principles of Spaceflight Propulsion. 116

Goodlad, John I., Computer and Information Systems in Education. 17; The Nongraded Elementary School. 110

Goodman, Charles S., Distribution in a High-Level Economy. 57

Goodman, David G., Business Filing & Records Control. 67

Goodman, David S., President's Letter Book. 67

Goodman, John W., Your Future in Poultry Farming. 78

Goodman, Louis S., The Pharmacological Basis of Therapeutics. 201

Goodman, Robert L., Advanced Techniques for Troubleshooting with the Oscilloscope. 148; Practical Color TV Servicing Techniques. 157

Goodman, William L., The History of Woodworking Tools. 161

Goodrich, Charles H., Welfare Medical Care. 105

Goodrich, Robert E., On the Other Side of Sorrow. 93

Goodstein, Sylvia, The Library's Public Revisited. 89

Goodwin, Arthur B., Handbook of Audio-Visual Aids and Techniques for Teaching Elementary School Subjects. 110

Goodwin, Paul N., Physical Foundations of Radiology. 204

Goody, John R., Death, Property and the Ancestors. 93

Goor, Amihud Y., Forest Tree Planting in Arid Zones. 87

Goose, D. H., Principles of Preventive Dentistry. 174

Goose, Peter, Tomato Paste, Puree, Juice, and Powder. 32

Goowin, R. W., Chemical Additives in Food. 41

Gordon, D., Ultrasonic Techniques in Biology and Medicine. 181

Gordon, Elayne, Practical Dictation and Transcription. 68

Gordon, Evelyn W., Dentists, Patients and Auxiliaries. 174

Gordon, James E., The New Science of Strong Materials. 167

Gordon, Jean, Coffee Recipes. 32

Gordon, Myron J., Accounting. 2

Gordon, Noden E., Applied Mathematics for Electronics. 207

Gordon, Robert B., Structure and Property of Alloys. 168

Gordon, Robert I., Cocktails & Snacks. 32

Gordon, Stephen F., Making Picture-Books. 10

Gore, Frederick, Painting. 10

Gorer, Geoffrey, Death, Grief and Mourning. 93

Gorton, John V., Behavioral Components of Patient Care. 190

Goselin, C. C., Introduction to Plastics. 167

Goshay, Robert C., Information Technology in the Insurance Industry. 53

Gosnell, Doris, Nursing Evaluation. 189

Goth, Andres, Medical Pharmacology. 201; Pharmacology in Nursing. 188

Gottlieb, Irving M., Basic Oscillators. 148

Gottlieb, Leon S., A History of Respiration. 180

Gottschall, Edward, Commercial Art as a Business. 12

Gottshall, Franklin H., Furniture of Pine, Poplar and Maple. 161

Goudy, Frederic W., The Alphabet. 14

Gould, Edwin S., Inorganic Reactions and Structure. 133

Gould, Geraldine N., How to Organize and Maintain the Library Picture/Pamphlet File. 90

Gould, I. H., Digital Computer Technology. 17

Gould, Julius, A Dictionary of the Social Sciences. 105

Gould, Marjorie, Calderwood's Orthopedic Nursing. 195

Goulding, Roy, Handbook of Dental Pharmacology and Therapeutics. 174

Gouldner, Alvin W., Modern Sociology. 105

Gouldner, Helen P., Modern Sociology. 105

Gourley, Gerald D., Effective Police Organization and Management. 97; Patrol Administration. 97

Gourmet Magazine, Gourmet's Menu Cook Book. 32

Gove, Philip B., The Role of the Dictionary. 90

Govoni, Laura E., Drugs and Nursing Implications. 190

Gowan, John C., The Guidance of Exceptional Children. 81

Gowar, N. W., Mathematics for Technology. 206

Gowland, Peter, How to Photograph Women. 49

Grabowski, Bernard F., Methods of Drug Analysis. 201

Grace, Richard C., Principles of Law Enforcement. 97

Grad, Frank P., Public Health Law Manual. 207

Gradwohl, Rutherford B., Clinical Laboratory Methods and Diagnosis. 182

Grady, Paul, Inventory of Generally Accepted Principles for Business Enterprises. 2

Graf, Rudolf F., Modern Dictionary of Electronics. 148

Graffam, Shirley, Care of the Surgical Patient. 197

Gragg, Shirley H., Scientific Principles in Nursing. 190

Graham, Clarence H., Vision and Visual Perception. 198

Graham, Donald, Composing Pictures. 10

Graham, Frank D., Audel's Masons and Builders Guide. 137; Audel's Pumps, Hydraulics, Air Compressors. 137; Audel's Truck and Tractor Guide for Mechanics and Drivers of Gas and Diesel Motors. 123; Audel's Welders Guide. 171

Graham, Frank, Jr., Since Silent Spring. 178

Graham, Irvin, Encyclopedia of Advertising. 6

Graham, John, A Dictionary of Computers. 17

Graham, Kennard C., Fundamentals of Electricity. 148; Industrial and Commercial Wiring. 148; Interior Electric Wiring—Residential. 148; National Electrical Code and Blueprint Reading. 148; Understanding and Servicing Fractional Horsepower Motors. 123

Graham, Martha D., Training Teacher Assistants in Community Colleges. 111

Graham, Richard, Radio Transmitters. 156

Graham, Roscoe, Remembered With Love. 93

Graham, Samuel A., Principles of Forest Entomology. 87

Graham-Jones, Oliver, Aspects of Comparative Ophthalmology. 198

Graham-Rack, Barry, Hygiene in Food Manufacturing and Handling. 41

Grahm, Milton, Legal Typewriting. 71

Grainger, Melvin J., Airbrush Techniques for Commercial Art. 11

Grando, Michael D., Jewelry. 27

Granet, Irving, Elementary Applied Thermodynamics. 164

Grannis, Chandler B., What Happens in Book Publishing. 44

Grant, Eugene L., Basic Accounting and Cost Accounting. 5

Grant, Florence, The Beautician. 7

Grant, Hiram E., Engineering Drawing. 142; Jigs and Fixtures. 164

Grant, John C., An Atlas of Anatomy. 184

Grant, Julius, A Laboratory Handbook of Pulp and Paper Manufacture. 127; Hackh's Chemical Dictionary. 127

Granville, J. W., Miniature and Microminiature Electronics. 147

Graphic Arts Technical Foundation, Education Department, Manpower, Recruitment, and Education Programs in Graphic Communications. 44

Graphic Arts Typographers, Graphic Arts Type Book. 44

Grater, Michael, One Piece of Paper, for Children and for Teachers. 110

Gratzinger, Max, Removable Orthodontic Appliances. 175

Grava, Sigurd, Urban Planning Aspects of Water Pollution Control. 178

Gray, Charles D., Real Estate Sales Contracts from Preparation Through Closing. 65

Gray, Charles H., Laboratory Handbook of Toxic Agents. 201

Gray, Harry B., Electrons and Chemical Bonding. 127

Gray, Lawrence F., Radio Transmitters. 156

Gray, Paul E., Digital Transistor Circuits. 158; Introduction to Electronics. 148

Gray, Peter, The Dictionary of Biological Sciences. 185; The Encyclopedia of the Biological Sciences. 185; Handbook of Basic Microtechnique. 182; The Use of the Microscope. 182

Gray, Susan W., Before First Grade. 110

Graymore, Clive N., Biochemistry of the Eye. 198

Grazda, Edward E., Electronic Design Techniques Selected from Electronic Design. 148; Handbook of Applied Mathematics. 206

Great Britain Fire Service Department, Manual of Firemanship. 85

Great Britain National Economic Development Office, Your Future in Clothing. 23

Greater Des Moines Chamber of Commerce, Agricultural Committee, Corporate Farming and the Family Farm. 74

Green, David, Pattern and Embroidery. 22

Green, Edward J., The Learning Process and Programmed Instruction. 110; Selection, Hiring and Utilization of Dental Auxiliaries. 174

Green, Emmet, Small Foreign Car Guide. 123

Green, Jane, You Can Do Anything with Crepes. 34

Green, John H., An Introduction to Human Physiology. 184

Green, Paul E., Planning and Problem Solving in Marketing. 56

Green, Peter, Introducing Surface Printing. 10; New Creative Print Making. 10

Greenberger, Martin, Computers and the World of the Future. 17

Greenburg, Rae C., Shortrite: A Nu E-Z Shorthand.... 67

Greene, Janet, Over Their Dead Bodies. 94

Greene, Mark R., Risk and Insurance. 53

Greenfield, Harry I., Allied Health Manpower. 207

Greenfield, Maynard S., Systems and Procedures for Automated Accounting. 4

Greenleaf, William, Monopoly on Wheels: Henry Ford.... 123

Greenwood, Douglas C., Manual of Electromechanical Devices. 149; Mechanical Power Transmission. 123

Greer, Michael, Your Future in Interior Design. 55

Gregg, Davis W., Life and Health Insurance Handbook. 53; Property and Liability Insurance Handbook. 53

Gregg, James R., Experiments in Visual Science for Home and School. 198; The Eye and Sight. 198; How to Communicate in Optometric Practice. 198; The Story of Optometry. 198; Your Future in Optometry. 198

Gregg, John R., Applied Secretarial Practice. 68; Gregg Shorthand Dictionary. 68; Gregg Shorthand Manual. 68; Gregg Speed Building. 68; Gregg Speed Building for Colleges. 68

Gregg, Joseph, Cooking for Food Managers. 32

Gregg, S. J., The Surface Chemistry of Solids. 127

Grego, Noel R., Job Description and Certification for Library Technical Assistants. 90

Gregory, Edwin, Steel Working Processes. 168

Gregory, R. L., Eye and Brain. 198

Gregory, Robert H., Automatic Data-Processing Systems. 16

Greider, Janice E., Law and the Life Insurance Contract. 54

Greif, Edwin C., Basic Problems in Marketing Management. 58

Greiner, Richard A., Semiconductor Devices and Applications. 148

Greisheimer, Esther M., Basic Physiology and Anatomy. 184; Physiology and Anatomy. 183

Greitzer, Samuel L., Numerical Analysis. 170

Greyser, Stephen A., Advertising in America. 6

Griese, Helga, Building with Wood. 137

Grieser, Edwina H., Guide to Modern Clothing. 26

Griffin, Gerald J., Clinical Nursing Instruction by Television. 190

INDEX

Griffin, Ivan H., Basic Arc Welding. 171; Basic Oxyacetylene Welding. 171; Basic Tig Welding. 171; Welding Processes. 171

Griffin, John L., Police Training and Performance Study. 91

Griffin, Rodger W., Modern Organic Chemistry. 134

Griffin, Roger C., Food Packaging. 42

Griffith, Benjamin W., Radio-Electronic Transmission Fundamentals. 156

Griffiths, V. S., The Electronics of Laboratory and Process Instruments. 148

Grigson, Jane, The Art of Charcuterie. 32

Grillo, Elmer V., Control Techniques for Office Efficiency. 68

Grim, Ray W., Moving a Library. 91

Grimm, William C., Familiar Trees of America. 87

Grinter, Linton E., Design of Modern Steel Structures. 137; Elementary Structural Analysis and Design. 137

Griswold, Ernest, Chemical Bonding and Structure. 127; Inorganic Chemistry. 133

Griswold, R. E., The SNOBOL 4 Programming Language. 20

Griswold, Ruth M., The Experimental Study of Foods. 32

Grob, Bernard, Applications of Electronics. 148; Basic Electronics. 148; Basic Television. 157

Grogan, Denis, Science and Technology. 90

Grollman, Arthur, Pharmacology and Therapeutics. 201

Grollman, Earl A., Explaining Death To Children. 93

Grollman, Evelyn F., Pharmacology and Therapeutics. 201

Groneman, Chris H., General Shop. 161; General Woodworking. 161; Leathercraft. 161; Technical Woodworking. 161

Gross, Alfred, Sales Promotion. 58

Gross, Gerald, Publishers on Publishing. 44

Gross, Jerome S., Illustrated Encyclopedic Dictionary of Real Estate Terms. 65

Gross, Verlee E., Ten Study Lessons for Mastering Medical Terminology. 71

Grosser, Charles F., Helping Youth. 105; Nonprofessionals in the Human Services. 105

Grossman, Alvin, Data Processing for Educators. 16

Grossman, Jack, Applied Clerical Practice. 67; Handbook for Typists. 67; Modern Clerical Practice. 67; Secretarial Practice. 67

Grossman, Louis H., Department Store Merchandising In Changing Environments. 58

Grossman, Ruth H., New Designs for the Elementary School Curriculum. 111

Grossmann, Marcus A., Principles of Heat Treatment. 168

Grosvenor, Theodore P., Contact Lens Theory and Practice. 198

Grover, Elliot B., Handbook of Textile Testing and Quality Control. 28

Groves, H. W., Aeronautical Technical Dictionary. 116

Grow, Lucille J., Requests for Child Welfare Services. 81

Gruenberg, Sidonie M., The New Encyclopedia of Child Care and Guidance. 81

Gruenberger, Fred, Computer Graphics. 44; Computing. 17

Grundmann, E., General Cytology. 185

Grunwald, Ernest, Atoms, Molecules and Chemical Change. 127

Gruse, William A., Chemical Technology of Petroleum. 127; Motor Fuels. 123; Motor Oils. 123

Gucker, Frank T., Physical Chemistry. 135

Gude, William D., Autoradiographic Techniques. 204

Guertner, Beryl, Cake Icing and Decorating for all Occasions. 37; The Magic of Cake Decorating. 37

Guggenheimer, Elinor C., Planning for Parks and Recreation Needs in Urban Areas. 103

Guilbault, George G., Instrumental Analysis Manual. 133

Guild of Prescription Opticians of America, Guild Dispensing Manual. 198

Guineé, Kathleen K., The Aims and Methods of Nursing Education. 190; The Professional Nurse. 190

Guinagh, Kevin, Dictionary of Foreign Phrases and Abbreviations. 90

Gundel, Károly, Hungarian Cookery Book. 39

Gunderson, Frank L., Food Standards and Definitions in the United States. 32

Gunderson, Helen W., Food Standards and Definitions in the United States. 32

Gunn, Clare A., Motel Planning and Business Management. 51

Gunstone, F. D., An Introduction to the Chemistry and Biochemisty of Fatty Acids and Their Glycerides. 127

Gunther, Raymond C., Lubrication. 123; Refrigertaion, Air Conditioning and Cold Storage. 120

Guptill, Arthur L., Color Manual for Artists. 13

Gurfinkel, German, Prestressed Concrete. 141

Gurney, Gene, Famous Aircraft. 117

Gurr, Edward, Encyclopedia of Microscopic Stains. 182; The Rational Use of Dyes in Biology. 182

Gurr, Ted, American Welfare. 104

Guss, Carolyn, Guides to Newer Educational Media. 92

Gussow, Joan D., Disadvantaged Children. 108

Gustafson, Carroll B., Pharmaceutical Calculations. 200

Gustavsson, Ragnar, Creating in Wood with the Lathe. 161

Gutcho, M., Alcoholic Malt Beverages, 1969. 41; Animal Feeds 1970. 78; Synthetic Perfumery Materials. 128

Gutenberg, Arthur W., Profitable Studio Management. 10

Gutfreund, H., An Introduction to Study of Enzymes. 182

Guthe, Karl F., The Physiology of Cells. 185

Guthrie, Helen A., Introductory Nutrition. 40

Guthrie, Mearl R., Alphabetic Indexing. 68

Guthrie, Roy D., An Introduction to the Chemistry of Carbohydrates. 128

Gutterman, Melvin, Arrest, Search and Seizure. 97

Gutterson, M., Confectionary Products. 41

Guttmann, Werner H., Concise Guide to Structural Adhesives. 137

Guyton, William J., Profitably Marketing Production Teamwork. 58

Gwertzman, Max J., The Standard Fire Policy. 53

Gwinner, Robert F., Sales Strategy. 58

Haab, Armin, Lettera: A Standard Book of Fine Lettering.... 14

Haag, James, Comprehensive Standard Fortran Programming. 20

Haas, Alfred, Basic Industrial Electronics Course. 148

Haas, Kenneth, Creative Salesmanship. 58; Sales Horizons. 58

Habenstein, Robert, Funeral Customs the World Over. 93; History of American Funeral Directing. 93

Haber, Alan, Poverty in America. 104

Haber, Ralph, Contemporary Theory and Research in Visual Perception. 198

Habicht, Frank, Modern Machine Tools. 164

Hachten, Harva, Kitchen Safari. 32

Hacker, Lois, Sample Cataloging Forms. 92

Hackett, Alice, 70 Years of Best Sellers, 1895-1965. 90

Hackett, Donald, Modern Wood Technology. 161

Hadfield, James, Childhood and Adolescence. 81

Hadley, Anne, The Medical Secretary as a Word Technician. 71

Hadlow, Leonard, Climate, Vegetation and Man. 74

INDEX

Hadwiger, Don, Federal Wheat Commodity Programs. 74

Hafez, E., Reproduction in Farm Animals. 78

Hagan, Robert, Irrigation of Agricultural Lands. 74

Hagenstein, William, Harvesting Timber Crops. 88

Hagevik, George, Decision-Making in Air Pollution Control. 178; Planning for Environmental Quality. 178

Haggerty, James, Food and Nutrition. 35

Hahn, Albert, The Petrochemical Industry. 128

Hahn, Emily, The Cooking of China. 39

Hahn, Peter, Chemicals from Fermentation. 128

Hailes, William D., Introduction to Supermarket Occupations. 64

Haim, George, Manual for Plastic Welding. 171

Haines, Edward, Design in Three Dimensions. 14

Haines, George, Consumer Behavior. 58

Haines, John, Automatic Control of Heating and Air Conditioning. 120

Haines, Peter, Retailing. 63

Haines, Robert, Food Preparation for Hotels, Restaurants, and Cafeterias. 32

Haines, Wheeler, Applied Anatomy for Nurses. 188

Haise, Howard, Irrigation of Agricultural Lands. 74

Hakim, Sahir, Transistor Circuits in Electronics. 158

Halacy, D. S., Computers, the Machines We Think With. 17

Halacy, Daniel, X-Rays and Gamma Rays. 204

Halbert, Michael, The Meaning and Sources of Marketing Theory. 58

Haldon Books, Inc., Flight Maneuvers Manual. 117

Hale, E. M., Introduction to Applied Drawing. 142

Hale, Robert, Drawing Lessons from the Great Masters. 10

Hale, William, The Horizon Cookbook and Illustrated History of Eating and Drinking Through the Ages. 32

Halkias, C., Electronic Devices and Circuits. 151

Hall, Allen, Machine Design. 167

Hall, Archibald, The Standard Handbook of Textiles. 28

Hall, Barbara, Handbook: Butane-Propane Gases. 127

Hall, Carl, Elementary Arts and Crafts Projects. 161

Hall, Carl W., Agricultural Engineer's Handbook. 76; Drying of Milk and Milk Products. 41

Hall, Cecil, Introduction to Electron Microscopy. 182

Hall, Esther, The Pharmacist in Retail Distribution. 201

Hall, Isaac F., Approved Practices in Farm Management. 76; The Farm Management Handbook. 74

Hall, J. Tillman, School Recreation. 103

Hall, John, Casualty Insurance. 53

Hall, Perry, Family Credit Counseling. 105

Hall, Walter, Sear's New Teeth for Old. 174

Hallowell, Elliott, Cold and Freezer Storage Manual. 42

Halperin, Don, Building with Steel. 137

Halpern, Bernard, Color Stripping for Offset Lithography. 44

Halpern, George, Bibliography for Advertising Production. 6; Principles of Advertising. 6; Self-Study Workbook: Advanced Pressmanship for Offset Lithography.... 14; Self-Study Workbook: Chemistry of Lithography.... 14; Self-Study Workbook: Press Operating For Offset Lithography.... 14

Halpine, Charles G., A Pilot's Meteorology. 115

Halstead, Helen L., Contemporary Studies in Medical-Surgical Nursing. 190

Halterman, Jean C., Advertising. 6

Ham, Arthur W., Histology. 186

Hamaker, J. C., Tool Steels. 169

Hamann, John A., Egg Grading Manual. 75

Hamburg, Marion V., Health and Social Problems in the School. 110

Hamburg, Morris, Health and Social Problems in the School. 110

Hamburger, Edward, A Business Dictionary of Representative Terms Used in Accounting. 2

Hamby, Dame S., The American Cotton Handbook. 28; Handbook of Textile Testing and Quality Control. 28

Hamer, Philip, Industrial Water Treatment Practice. 178

Hamilton, G. F., Anatomy of the Human Body. 184

Hamilton, J. Roland, Using Electricity. 148

Hamilton, James E., Profitable Farm Management. 74

Hamilton, Leicester F., Calculations of Analytical Chemistry. 131

Hamilton, Persis M., Basic Maternity Nursing. 194

Hamilton, W., Teach Yourself to Type. 69

Hamilton-Hill, Margot, Rural Costume. 27

Hamlin, Herbert M., Public School Education in Agriculture. 74

Hamm, Marie R., The Second Chafing Dish Cookbook. 32

Hamm, Randall E., Chemical Equilibrium. 129

Hammar, S. L., Nursing Care of the Adolescent. 190

Hammond, George S., Organic Chemistry. 134

Hammond, James J., Woodworking Technology. 161

Hammond, Robert H., Engineering Graphics for Design and Analysis. 142

Hammond, Rolt, Modern Foundation Methods. 137

Hammond, Seymour B., Electromechanical Systems. 155

Hammond, Inc., Sales Planning Atlas of the United States and Canada. 58

Hammonds, Carsie, Experience Programs for Learning Vocations in Agriculture. 73; Farming Programs for Students in Vocational Agriculture. 73

Hampel, Clifford A., The Encyclopedia of the Chemical Elements. 128; Rare Metals Handbook. 169

Hampton, Robert E., College Salesmanship. 58

Hanaburgh, David, Your Future in Forestry. 87

Hancock, Robert S., The Environment of Marketing Behavior. 59; Marketing in a Changing Environment. 59

Hand, Jackson, How to Do Your Own Wood Finishing. 161

Handbook of Chemistry. 128

Handbook of Chemistry and Physics. 128

Handler, Julian H., How to Sell the Supermarkets. 64

Handler, Philip, Biology and the Future of Man. 185

Handover, P. M., Printing in London. 44

Hanes, Elizabeth, Computer Programming Handbook. 21

Hanes, Randall M., Color. 13

Haney, John, Educational Media and the Teacher. 110

Hanham, I. W. F., Clinical Radiotherapy. 204

Hanna, Donald G., A Police Records System for the Small Department. 97

Hanna, J. Marshall, Accounting 10/12. 2; Effective Secretarial Practices. 67; Gregg Bookkeeping & Accounting. 2; How to Use Adding and Calculating Machines. 70; Secretarial Procedures and Administration. 68; Teaching Bookkeeping and Accounting. 4

Hannah, Harold W., Law for the Veterinarian and Livestock Owner. 79

Hannan, Justine, Clinical Workbook for Practical Nurses. 195

Hannay, Norman B., Solid-State Chemistry. 135

INDEX

Hanok, Albert, Manual for Laboratory Clinical Chemistry. 128

Hansch, Corwin, Organic Chemistry. 134

Hansen, Bertrand L., Quality Control. 44

Hansen, Gerald L., Introduction to Solid-State Television. 157

Hansen, Harry L., Marketing. 58

Hansen, Mark F., Basic Crafts. 162

Hanslovsky, Glenda, Why Team Teaching? 110

Hanson, Glenn, How to Take the Fits Out of Copyfitting. 44

Hanson, James R., Introduction to Steroid Chemistry. 128

Hanson, Peggy L., Keypunching. 16

Harbers, Eberhard, Introduction to Nucleic Acids. 128

Harcleroad, Fred F., A-V Instruction. 109

Hardenbergh, William A., Water Supply and Waste Disposal. 178

Hardin, Garret J., 39 Steps to Biology. 185

Harding, Lowry W., Arithmetic for Child Development. 110

Hardman, Elizabeth, An Introduction to Ward Management. 190

Hardman, F. G., Oral Surgery for Nurses. 197

Hardman, H., Papermaking. 48; Papermaking Practice. 48

Hards, K. W., New Ways of Working Metals. 168

Hard's Yearbook of the Clothing Industry. 23

Hare, Van Court, Basic Programming. 20; Introduction to Programming. 20

Harger, Virginia F., Food Service in Institutions. 36

Hargis, Larry G., Instrumental Analysis Manual. 133

Hargrave, Lee E., Jr., Basic Electronics. 149

Hargreaves, John, Computers and the Changing World. 17

Harlan, Calvin, Vision and Invention. 10

Harling, Robert, House and Garden Guide to Interior Decoration. 55

Harlow, William M., Textbook of Dendrology. 87

Harman, Earl W., Introduction to Mechanical Drawing. 144

Harmer, Ruth M., The High Cost of Dying. 93

Harney, Malachi L., The Informer in Law Enforcement. 97

Harnsberger, Caroline T., Pilot's Ready Reference. 117

Harper, Charles A., Handbook of Electronic Packaging. 148; Handbook of Materials and Processes for Electronics. 148

Harr, Milton E., Foundations of Theoretical Soil Mechanics. 137; Groundwater and Seepage. 137

Harrar, Ellwood S., Textbook of Dendrology. 87

Harrigan, W. F., Laboratory Methods in Microbiology. 187

Harrington, Michael, The Other America. 105

Harris, Carl B., Offset Duplicator Techniques. 43

Harris, Catherine F., Handbook of Dietetics for Nurses. 190

Harris, Charles O., Strength of Materials. 170

Harris, Edith, Bead Design. 28

Harris, Ellen A., Professional Restaurant Service. 52

Harris, Evelyn J., Instructional Materials Cataloging Guide. 90

Harris, John N., Digital Transistor Circuits. 158

Harris, Kerr, Forster & Co., Trends in the Hotel-Motel Business. 51

Harris, L. Dale, Introduction to Feedback Systems. 148

Harris, Malcolm, Pharmaceutical Microbiology. 201

Harris, Richard, The Fear of Crime. 97; Justice. 97

Harris, Robert S., Nutritional Evaluation of Food Processing. 40

Harris, Sherwood, The First to Fly. 117

Harrison, C. William, Forests. 87

Harrison, Howard L., Introduction to Automatic Controls. 170

Harrison, Kenneth, A Guidebook to Biochemistry. 132

Harrison, Leonard H., How to Teach Police Subjects. 97

Harrop, Dorothy, Modern Book Production. 44

Harrow, Benjamin, Textbook of Biochemistry. 132

Harry, Ralph G., The Principles and Practice of Modern Cosmetics, Vol. 1. 7; The Principles and Practice of Modern Cosmetic Materials, Vol. 2. 7

Hart, George H., Beef Cattle Production. 79

Hart, Harold, Organic Chemistry. 134

Hart, Laura K., The Arithmetic of Dosages and Solutions. 206

Harter, James H., AC Circuit Analysis Through Experimentation. 147; DC Circuit Analysis Through Experimentation. 147; Solid State Circuit Analysis Through Experimentation. 148

Hartford, Bill, Car Repairs You Can Make. 123

Hartles, R. L., Principles of Preventive Dentistry. 174

Hartley, Gilbert S., Chemicals for Pest Control. 74

Hartman, James B., Mechanical Design of Machines. 167

Hartmann, Hudson T., Plant Propagation. 74

Hartstein, Jack, Questions and Answers on Contact Lens Practice. 198

Hartsuch, Paul J., Chemistry of Lithography. 14

Hartung, Frank E., Crime, Law and Society. 98

Hartung, Rolf, Creative Textile Design. 28; More Creative Textile Design. 28

Harvey, Kenneth B., Introduction to Physical Inorganic Chemistry. 133

Harvill, John, Basic Fortran Programming. 20

Harwood, John, Introduction to Mechanics. 161

Harwood, Paisely B., Harwood's Control of Electric Motors. 156

Haselgrove, Maurice L., Photographers' Dictionary. 49

Haseman, Wilber C., Management Uses of Accounting. 2

Haskell, Mark A., The New Careers Concept: .... Public Employment of the Poor. 105

Haskell, Martin R., Crime and Delinquency. 98

Haskell, Patricia, The Cheese Book. 34

Haskins, Jim, Diary of a Harlem Schoolteacher. 110

Haslam, John, Identification and Analysis of Plastics. 167

Hasler, Doris, The Practical Nurse and Today's Family. 195

Hass, Ray W., Data Processing. 16

Hassan, William E., Hospital Pharmacy. 201

Hassler, Sister Ruth Ann, Vocational and Personal Adjustments in Practical Nursing. 195

Haswell, Margaret, The Economics of Subsistence Agriculture. 74

Haszonics, Joseph, Wine Merchandizing. 38

Hatch, Raymond N., Guidance Services in the Elementary School. 110

Hathorne, Berkeley L., Woven Stretch and Textured Fabrics. 28

Hatje, Gerd, Design for Modern Living. 55

Hatje, Ursula, Design for Modern Living. 55

Hatsopoulos, George N., Principles of General Thermodynamics. 164

Hattell (W. S.) & Partners, Hotels, Restaurants, Bars. 51

Hatterer, Lawrence J., The Artist in Society. 10

Hattery, Lowell H., Automation and Electronics in Publishing. 44

Hattwick, Melvin S., The New Psychology of Selling. 58

INDEX

Haughney, John D., Effective Catalogs. 6

Hauser, Gaylord G., Mirror, Mirror on the Wall. 7

Hausner, Bernard, Simscript: A Simulation Programming Language. 20

Hauver, William E., Egg Grading Manual. 75

Havener, William H., Nursing Care in Eye, Ear, Nose, and Throat Disorders. 190; Synopsis of Ophthalmology. 198

Havighurst, Clark C., Air Pollution Control. 178

Havighurst, Robert J., Society and Education. 110

Hawaii State Society, Hawaiian Cuisine. 39

Hawken, William R., Copying Methods Manual. 90; Enlarged Prints from Library Microforms. 90; Photocopying from Bound Volumes. 90

Hawker, John P., Radio and Television. 157

Hawkes, Glenn R., Behavior and Development from 5 to 12. 81

Hawkins, Arthur, The Complete Seafood Cookbook. 32

Hawkins, Leslie V., Art Metal and Enameling. 161

Hawley, Ralph C., The Practice of Silviculture. 87

Hawthorne, Berkeley F., Woven Stretch and Textured Fabrics. 28

Hay, Leon E., Governmental Accounting. 3

Haydon, Dorothy F., Practical Dictation and Transcription. 68

Hayes, Alfred S., Language Laboratory Facilities. 110

Hayes, Edward J., Moral Principles of Nursing. 190

Hayes, Edward N., Hayes Directory of Dental Supply Houses. 174

Hayes, Paul J., Moral Principles of Nursing. 190

Hayes, Robert W., Groups in Guidance. 105

Hayes, Wayland J., Human Relations in Nursing. 190

Hayett, William, Display and Exhibit Handbook. 63

Hayhoe, F. G. J., An Atlas of Haematological Cytology. 186

Hayner, Norman S., Hotel Life. 51

Haynes, William O., Guidelines for Supermarket Management Programs in the Community College. 64

Hays, Joyce S., Interacting with Patients. 190

Hayslett, Jack J., Architectural Drawing and Planning. 143

Hayter, Edith F., Behind the Scenes in Fashion Merchandising. 23

Hayward, Charles H., Carpentry for Beginners. 161; Furniture Repairs. 161; Practical Woodwork. 161; Staining and Polishing. 161

Hayward, L. M., Survey Practice on Construction Sites. 142

Haywood, Charles F., General Alarm. 84

Hazelet, John C., Police Report Writing. 98

Hazelton, Nika S., The Art of Scandinavian Cooking. 39; The Belgian Cookbook. 39; The Best of Italian Cooking. 39; The Cooking of Germany. 39

Head, Edith, How to Dress for Success. 23

Headley, Joseph C., The Pesticide Problem. 178

Heady, Earl O., A Primer on Food, Agriculture, and Public Policy. 32

Healey, Martin, Principles of Automatic Control. 170

Healy, Jeremiah J., Basic Fortran IV Programming. 20

Hearle, J. W. S., Fibre Structure. 28

Heartwell, C. M., Jr., Syllabus of Complete Dentures. 174

Heath, Gordon G., The Eye and Sight. 198

Heath, Gordon W., The Principles of Agricultural Entomology. 74

Heating, Piping and Air Conditioning Directory. 120

Hecht, Joseph C., Retail Business Management. 63

Hechtel, George J., Biological Effects of Thermal Pollution.... 178

Hechtlinger, Adelaide, Cooking with Bread. 37

Heckel, Robert V., Pediatric Nursing. 195; Psychology. 190

Heckert, Josiah B., Accounting Systems. 2; Controllership. 2

Heckler, Ruth D., School Food Centers. 32

Hedges, Trimble R., Farm Management Decisions. 75

Hedin, Solweig, Creative Needlework. 26

Hedrick, T. I., Drying of Milk and Milk Products. 41

Heffernan, Helen, The Years Before School. 83

Heftmann, Erich, Chromatography. 128

Hegarty, Edward J., Seven Secrets of Sales Success. 58

Hegner, Barbara R., Health Assistant. 207

Heid, John L., Fundamentals of Food Processing Operations. 41

Heidgerken, Loretta E., Teaching and Learning in Schools of Nursing. 190

Heidingsfield, Myron S., Changing Patterns in Marketing. 59; Marketing. 59

Heilweil, Melvin F., Introduction to Digital Computers. 18

Hein, Leonard W., Contemporary Accounting and the Computer. 3

Heine, Richard W., Principles of Metal Casting. 169

Heins, Richard M., Risk Management and Insurance. 54

Heintze, Ingeborg, The Organization of the Small Public Library. 90

Heinz, Jauch, The Computer: An Accounting Tool. 4

Heironimus, Terring W., III, Mechanical Artificial Ventilation. 180

Heiserman, Russell L., Introduction to Amplifiers. 147; Introduction to Electron Devices. 147

Heitner, Joseph, Automotive Mechanics. 123

Heitner, Louis, Introduction to Offset. 44

Hekmat, Forough-es-Saltaneh, The Art of Persian Cooking. 39

Held, R. Burnell, Soil Conservation in Perspective. 75

Helfant, Seymour, Plan Your Store for Maximum Sales and Profit. 64; Retail Merchandising and Management with Electronic Data Processing. 63

Helfrich, Harold W., Jr., The Environmental Crisis. 178

Heller, Edna E., The Art of Pennsylvania Dutch Cooking. 39

Heller, Marjorie K., Guide and Compendium for a Lawyer's Secretary. 71

Heller, Sam, Electric Motor Repair Shop Problems. 156

Hellerman, Herbert, Digital Computer System Principles. 18

Hellman, Harold, Spectroscopy. 128

Hellwig, Jessica, Introduction to Computers and Programming. 20

Helmberger, Peter C., Cooperative Bargaining in Agriculture. 75

Helmholtz, Herman L. F., Helmholtz's Treatise on Physiological Optics. 198

Helmkamp, George K., Organic Chemistry, 134; Selected Experiments in Organic Chemistry. 134

Helper, Opal E., Manual of Clinical Laboratory Methods. 182

Helper, Rose, Racial Policies and Practices of Real Estate Brokers. 65

Helsel, Jay D., Programmed Blueprint Reading. 142

Hemenway, Wesley, Introduction to Supermarket Occupations. 64

Hemp, Paul E., A Study Guide for Placement Employment Programs in Agricultural Business and Industry. 75

Henderson, Ernest, The World of "Mr. Sheraton." 51

INDEX

Henderson, I. F., A Dictionary of Biological Terms. 185

Henderson, John, Emergency Medical Guide. 208

Henderson, S. F., Connecting Induction Motors, Operation and Practice. 156

Henderson, Virginia, The Nature of Nursing. 190

Henderson, W. D., A Dictionary of Biological Terms. 185

Hendrickson, Harvey S., The Accounting Sampler. 1

Hendrickson, James B., Organic Chemistry. 134

Hendriksen, Eldon S., Accounting Theory. 3

Hengstebeck, Robert J., Distillation. 128

Henke, Russell W., Introduction to Fluid Mechanics. 164

Henkin, Shepard, Opportunities in the Hotel and Motel Industry. 51

Henle, Hans, Forestry and Economic Development. 88

Henn, Walter, Buildings for Industry. 137

Henry, Edward C., Electronic Ceramics. 161

Henry, Hugh F., Fundamentals of Radiation Protection. 204

Henry, Sarah T., A Preparatory Program for Hospital Housekeeping Aides. 207

Henry, William E., Nonprofessionals in the Human Services. 105

Hensel, Evelyn, Purchasing Library Materials in Public and School Libraries. 90

Hensley, Millie B., The Art of Make-Up, Skin and Hair Care. 7

Hentoff, Nat, Our Children Are Dying. 110

Hepler, Donald E., Architecture. 143

Hepner, Harry W., Advertising. 6

Hepner, James O., Personnel Administration and Labor Relations in Health Care Facilities. 207

Heptinstall, William, Gourmet Recipes from a Highland Hotel. 32

Hepworth, Samuel R., Essentials of Accounting. 2

Herbenova, Olga, The Pictorial Encyclopedia of Fashion. 24

Herber, Lewis, Crisis in Our Cities. 178; Our Synthetic Environment. 178

Herbert, Robert L., The Neo-Impressionists. 12

Herbst, L. J., Discrete and Integrated Semiconductor Circuity. 148

Hercules, David M., Fluorescence and Phosphorescence Analysis. 128

Herdeg, Walter, Graphis Annual 1965/66. 6; Window Display. 10

Herfindahl, Orris C., Quality of the Environment. 178

Hering, Ewald, Outlines of a Theory of the Light Sense. 198

Herington, Viola B., Begin to Sew. 23

Herman, Harold, Community Health Services. 207

Herman, Melvin, Decision-Making in Poverty Programs. 105

Hermanson, Roger H., Accounting. 2

Herner, Saul, A Brief Guide to Sources of Scientific and Technical Information. 90

Herr, Selma E., Learning Activities for Reading. 110

Herrath, Ernst von, Atlas of Histology. 186

Herrick, Clyde N., Electronic Circuits. 148; Introduction to Electronic Communications. 148; Mathematics for Electronics. 206; Semiconductor Electronics. 154; Unified Concepts of Electronics. 148

Herrington, Donald E., How to Read Schematic Diagrams. 148

Herschdoerfer, Sigismund M., Quality Control in the Food Industry. 32

Hershelman, Nancy V., Medical Dictation and Transcription. 71; Medical Shorthand. 71

Hersom, A. C., Canned Foods. 41

Hertz, Robert, Death and the Right Hand. 93

Hertzberg, Robert E., Photo Darkroom Guide. 49

Hertzfeld, A., Teach Yourself to Type. 69

Herzberg, Ronald J., Food Beverage Service Handbook. 38

Herzog, Edgar, Psyche and Death. 93

Hess, Robert D., Early Education. 110

Hesse, Walter J., Jet Propulsion For Aerospace Applications. 117

Hesselberth, Cassius A., Electricity for Engineering Technology. 155

Hester, Ronald A., Elements of Inorganic Chemistry. 133

Heumann, Gerhart W., Magnetic Control of Industrial Motors. 156

Hewett, Frank M., The Emotionally Disturbed Child in the Classroom. 110

Hewitt, H., Lamps and Lighting. 148

Hewitt, William H., A Bibliography of Police Administration, Public Safety, and Criminology to July 1, 1965. 98; British Police Administration. 98

Heyel, Carl, Computers, Office Machines and the New Information Technology. 18

Hiatt, Gordon D., Polymeric Materials. 168

Hibberd, Robert G., Integrated Circuits. 148; Solid State Electronics. 148; Transistors. 159

Hibbott, H. W., Handbook of Cosmetic Science. 7

Hickey, Henry V., Elements of Electronics. 148

Hickman, C. J., A Dictionary of Biology. 184

Hicks, Betty, The Ground School Workbook.... 117

Hicks, Charles B., College Secretarial Procedures. 69; Office Management. 69

Hicks, Florence, New Careers: The Community/Home Health Aide.... 207

Hicks, Leonard, Jr., Hotel Motel Sales Digest. 51

Hide, J. C., Profitable Soil Management. 75

Higbee, Edward C., Farms and Farmers in an Urban Age. 75

Higdon, Archie, Mechanics of Materials. 164

Higgin, Gurth, Communications in the Building Industry. 137

Higgins, George C., Fundamentals of Photographic Theory. 49

Higgins, Lois L., Policewoman's Manual. 98

Higham, Robert R. A., A Handbook of Papermaking. 48

Highland, Harold J., Audel's Painting and Decorating Manual. 55

Higman, Bryan, A Comparative Study of Programming Languages. 20

Hildebrand, Joel H., Regular Solutions. 128

Hilditch, Thomas P., The Chemical Constitution of Natural Fats. 128

Hildreth, Roland J., Readings in Agricultural Policy. 75

Hiler, Hilaire, Notes on the Technique of Painting. 10

Hilgard, Ernest R., Theories of Learning. 110

Hill, C. L., Introduction to Applied Drawing. 142

Hill, Harold C., Modern Data Processing. 15

Hill, Margot H., The Evolution of Fashion Pattern and Cut. 27

Hill, Richard M., Industrial Marketing. 56; Wholesaling Management. 59

Hill, Vivian R., The Elements of Accounting. 2

Hillhouse, Marion S., Dress Selection and Design. 23

Hillier, Bevis, Posters. 10

Hillman, Libby, Lessons In Gourmet Cooking. 32

Hills, Peter J., Chemical Equilibria. 128

Hillson, Maurie, Education and the Urban Community. 110

Hilton, Peter, Keeping Old Products New. 59

Hilton International Cookbook. 32

250

INDEX

Himmah, Gael, Real Estate Listing Magic. 65

Hinckley, F. Lewis, A Directory of Antique Furniture. 56

Hind, Arthur M., An Introduction to a History of Woodcut. 10

Hine, Jack S., Physical Organic Chemistry. 134

Hines, Maynard K., A Textbook of Oral Pathology. 175

Hinton, John, Dying. 93

Hinwood, Tony, Graphics Ad Lib. 44

Hippaka, William, California Real Estate Finance. 66

Hirsch, Albert A., Sales Anticipations and Inventory Behavior. 58

Hirsch, Monroe J., The Optometric Profession. 198; Vision of the Aging Patient. 198; Vision of Children. 198

Hirsch, S. Carl, Printing from a Stone. 14

Hirschberg, Gerald G., Rehabilitation. 194

Hirschhorn, Hans S., Your Future As An Optician. 198

Hirschhorn, Jeremy, Dynamics of Machinery. 164

Hirst, Irene, The Complete Book of Needlework. 23

Hitchcock, Robert, The Computer and Business Unity. 18

Hjorth, Herman, Basic Woodworking Processes. 161; Modern Machine Woodworking. 161; Principles of Woodworking. 161

Hoagland, Henry E., Real Estate Finance. 65

Hobbs, Betty C., Food Poisoning and Food Hygiene. 32

Hobbs, Henry E., Principles of Ophthalmology. 198

Hoberman, Stuart, Understanding and Using Unijunction Transistors. 159

Hoblitzelle, Lucy F., Pharmacology Applied to Patient Care. 201

Hoch, Fred W., Handbook for Pressmen. 44; How to Estimate Offset Lithography. 14; Offset Duplicator Techniques. 43

Hochman, Louie, How to Refinish Furniture. 56

Hodkinson, Mary A., Nursing the Elderly. 194

Hodnett, Ernest M., Semimicro Qualitative Organic Analysis. 132

Hoelscher, Randolph P., Basic Drawing for Engineering Technology. 142; Engineering Drawing and Geometry. 142; Graphics for Engineers. 142

Hoerr, Normand L., Radiographic Atlas of Skeletal Development of the Foot and Ankle. 204

Hoffman, Claire P., Simplified Nursing. 190

Hoffman, Frederick J., The Mortal No. 93

Hoffmann, Kurt, Building with Wood. 137

Hofling, Charles K., Basic Psychiatric Concepts in Nursing. 190

Hofmann, Armin, Graphic Design Manual. 44

Hofstetter, Henry, Dictionary of Visual Science. 199

Hogarth, Burne, Drawing the Human Head. 10

Hogarth, Paul, Creative Ink Drawing. 10; Creative Pencil Drawing. 10; Drawing People. 10

Hogg, John W., Auto Body Repair and Refinishing. 123

Hogness, Thorfin R., Qualitative Analysis and Chemical Equilibrium. 132

Hoke, Ann, Restaurant Menu Planning. 33

Hoke, Henry, What You Should Know about Direct Mail. 59

Holcomb, Richard L., The Police and the Public. 98; Police Patrol. 98

Holdcroft, Peter T., Welding Processes. 171

Holden, Donald, Art Career Guide. 10

Holden, Herbert L., Introduction to Fortran IV. 20

Holdsworth, Vivian E., Fundamentals of Bedside Nursing. 190

Holland, John H., Learning to Fly. 117

Holland, William C., Introduction to Molecular Pharmacology. 201

Hollander, Lloyd N., Modern Dental Practice. 174

Hollander, Mark B., Ultrasoft X-rays. 204

Hollander, Stanley C., Markets and Marketing in Developing Economies. 60

Hollen, Norma R., Flat Pattern Methods. 23; Textiles. 28

Hollenbach, John L., Medical Radiographic Technic. 203

Hollenback, G. M., Science and Technic of Cast Restoration. 174

Hollingsworth, Paul, Learning and Teaching in the Elementary School. 111

Hollinshead, William H., Functional Anatomy of the Limbs and Back. 209

Hollis, Florence, A Typology of Casework Treatment. 105

Holloway, Philip J., Child Dental Health. 174

Holloway, Robert J., A Basic Bibliography on Experiments in Marketing. 59; The Environment of Marketing Behavior. 59; Marketing in a Changing Environment. 59

Holm, Niels W., Manual on Radiation Dosimetry. 204

Holman, Mary, The Police Officer and the Child. 98

Holmes, Arthur W., Auditing. 5; Elementary Accounting. 3

Holmes, James F., Data Transmission and Data Processing Dictionary. 16

Holmes, Jerome K., Introduction to General Chemistry. 128

Holmes, Marguerite J., An Approach to the Education of Psychiatric Nursing Personnel. 196; Psychiatric Nursing in a Therapeutic Community. 196

Holmes, Parker M., Marketing Research. 59

Holmstedt, Bo, Readings in Pharmacology. 201

Holowenko, Alfred R., Machine Design. 167

Holroyd, P., Engineering Principles for Electrical Technicians. 153

Holt, Charles A., Introduction to Electro-Magnetic Fields and Waves. 148

Holt, John, How Children Fail. 110; How Children Learn. 110; The Under-Achieving School. 110

Holthausen, Henriette, Chicken Cookery Round the World. 33

Holtrop, William F., Coloring, Finishing and Painting Wood. 55; Modern Machine Woodworking. 161; Principles of Woodworking. 161; Woodshop Tool Maintenance. 160

Holtzclaw, Henry F., Jr., College Chemistry with Qualitative Analysis. 128

Holum, J., Elements of General and Biological Chemistry. 128; Introduction to Principles of Chemistry. 128; Principles of Physical, Organic and Biological Chemistry. 128

Holz, Jean L., Fortran IV and the IBM. 21

Holzbock, Werner G., Hydraulic Power and Equipment. 137

Honeyman, John, An Introduction to the Chemistry of Carbohydrates. 128

Honeywell Electronic Data Processing: Fundamentals of Electronic Data Processing. 16

Honma, Shigemi, Greenhouse Tomatoes. 77

Hood, George, Geometry of Engineering Drawing. 206

Hood, Marguerite V., Teaching Rhythm and Using Classroom Instruments. 111

Hook, Thomas S., Illustrated Flying Basics. 117

Hooper, Darryl E., Amplifying Devices and Low-Pass Amplifier Design. 146

Hooper, Lee, Introduction to Construction Drafting 145

Hooper, Reginald, Neurosurgical Nursing. 194

Hoos, Sidney S., Cooperative Bargaining in Agriculture. 75

INDEX

Hoover, Kenneth H., Learning and Teaching in the Elementary School. 111

Hoover, Norman T., Handbook of Agricultural Occupations. 75; An Introduction to Agricultural Business and Industry. 77

Hoover, Richard E., Protection of Vision in Children. 199

Hoover, Theodore W., Tool & Die Drafting. 144

Hopkins, Bruce R., Design Analysis of Shafts and Beams. 167

Hopkins, Claude C., Scientific Advertising. 6

Hopkins, Dennis M., Simple but Effective Cake Decorating. 37

Hopkins, Jeanette, A Relevant War Against Poverty. 104

Hopkins, Jenny, Bibliography of Pharmaceutical Reference Literature. 202

Hopkinson, Ralph G., The Lighting of Buildings. 137

Horn, George F., Posters. 10

Horn, Jack, Computer and Data Processing Dictionary and Guide. 16

Horn, Marilyn J., The Second Skin. 23

Hornbostel, Caleb, Materials for Architecture. 137

Hornemann, Grace V., Basic Nursing Procedures. 190

Horngren, Charles T., Accounting for Management Control. 3; Cost Accounting. 5

Hornick, Joanne G., Elementary Creative Bulletin Boards. 111

Hornickel, Ernst, The Great Wines of Europe. 38

Hornung, Julius L., Radio Operating Questions and Answers. 157

Hornung, William J., Architectural Drafting. 143; Blueprint Reading. 143, 144; Reinhold Data Sheets for Architects, Engineers, Designers, Draftsmen. 143

Horonjeff, Robert, The Planning and Design of Airports. 117

Horowitz, Mannie, Practical Design with Transistors. 159

Horowitz, Morris A., The New York Hotel Industry. 51

Horrell, Maurice W., Basic Electronics. 149

Horrigan, Philip A., The Challenge of Chemistry. 128

Horsting, Ruth, The History of Fashions. 27

Horten, Hans E., Commerical Correspondence in Four Languages. 68; Woodworking Machines in Four Languages. 161

Horton, Carolyn, Cleaning and Preserving Bindings and Related Materials. 90

Horton, Homer L., Drafting Technology. 143

Horton, Paul B., The Sociology of Social Problems. 105

Horvath, Walter, Successful Salesmanship. 59

Horwath, Ernest B., Hotel Accounting. 51

Horwath & Horwath, Expense and Payroll Dictionary. 51; Expense and Payroll Dictionary for Clubs. 3; Lodging Industry. 51

Hoselitz, Berthold F., A Reader's Guide to the Social Sciences. 105

Hosler, Russell J., Gregg Shorthand for Colleges. 68

Hospitality: The Guide to Convenience Foods. 33

Hostrop, Richard W., Teaching and the Community College Library. 90

Hot Rod, Basic Clutches and Transmissions. 123

Hotel Association of New York City, Inc., Uniform System of Accounts for Hotels. 51

Hotel Sales Management Association, H.S.M.A. Hotel-Motel Directory and Facilities Guide. 51

Houck, John W., Outdoor Advertising. 6

Houghton, Marjorie, Practical Procedures. 194

Houliston, May, The Practice of Mental Nursing. 196

Hourihan, Peter M., Practical CPM for Construction. 139

House, Clifford R., Reference Manual for Office Personnel. 68

House, Earl L., Review of Gross Anatomy. 175

House, Herbert O., Modern Synthetic Reactions. 128

House & Garden, The Art of Carving. 33; Complete Guide to Interior Decoration. 55; The Modern Interior. 55

House & Garden Guide to Interior Decoration. 55

Houston, L., Park Police. 98

Howard, John A., Marketing. 59; Marketing Management. 59; Marketing Theory. 59; The Theory of Buyer Behavior. 59

Howard, William M., Cases on Risk Management. 53

Howatson, A. M., Principles of Applied Electricity. 148

Howe, Phyllis S., Nutrition for Practical Nurses. 195

Howe, Raymond E., Introduction to Numerical Control in Manufacturing. 170

Howe, Robert L., Data Processing for Educators. 16

Howe, Robin, Dictionary of Gastronomy. 35; The Wine and Food Society's Guide to Soups. 38

Howe, Warren A., Cost Accounting. 5

Howe, Will D., American Authors and Books. 89

Howell, J. B. L., Breathlessness. 180

Howell, Leander D., The American Textile Industry. 28

Hoyt, Homer, Real Estate. 66

Hubbard, H., Let the Seller Beware. 57

Huber, Walter, Titrations in Nonaqueous Solvents. 128

Hubert, Charles L., Operational Electricity. 149; Preventive Maintenance of Electrical Equipment. 149

Hubin, Thomas, The New Psychology of Persuasion and Motivation in Selling. 62

Huck, Charlotte S., Children's Literature in the Elementary School. 111

Huddleston, John V., Introduction to Engineering Mechanics. 164

Huddleston, Ora L., Therapeutic Exercises. 209

Hudiburg, Everett, Rescue Practices in Fire Service Training. 84

Huebener, Paul O., Gourmet Table Services. 33, 52

Huebner, Mildred H., Strategies for Reading in the Elementary School. 109

Huebner, Solomon S., Life Insurance. 54; Property and Liability Insurance. 53

Huegy, Harvey W., The Elements of Marketing. 57

Huenefeld, Irene P., International Directory of Historical Clothing. 27

Huff, Darrell, How to Work with Concrete and Masonry. 141

Huff, Vaughn E., Child Counseling. 80

Huffman, Edna K., Medical Records in Nursing Homes. 71

Huffman, Harry, Office Procedures and Administration. 68

Huffsey, Charlotte A., Descriptive Electronics. 149

Huffsey, Ralph R., Descriptive Electronics. 149

Hughes, A. E., Introduction to Automated Data Processing. 17

Hughes, D. O., Physics for Chemists and Biologists. 128

Hughes, Graham, Modern Jewelry. 27

Hughes, Harold D., Forages. 75

Hughes, Joan K., Programming the IBM 1130. 20

Hughes, John T., The Natural History of Dental Diseases. 174

Hughes, Leslie E., Dictionary of Electronics and Nucleonics. 149

Hughes, Osee G., Introductory Food. 33

Hughes, Robert J., Introduction to Electronics. 149

Hugo, Ian S., Marketing and the Computer. 59

Huhn, Dieter, Fine Structure of Blood and Bone Marrow. 186

Hull, Edgar, Medical Nursing. 190

Hull, Thomas G., Scientific Exhibits. 90

INDEX

Hulland, E. D., Canned Foods. 41

Hunnisett, R., The Medieval Coroner. 93

Hunsley, Roger E., Livestock Judging and Evaluation. 78

Hunt, Donnell, Farm Power and Machinery Management. 78

Hunt, George M., Wood Preservation. 87

Hunt, John P., Metal Ions in Aqueous Solution. 133

Hunt, Robert W. G., The Reproduction of Color in Photography, Printing and Television. 49

Hunt, William D., Creative Control of Building Costs. 137

Hunter, A. R., Essentials of Artificial Ventilation of the Lungs, 180

Hunter, Grover C., Periodontics for the Dental Hygienist. 173

Hunter, Lloyd P., Handbook of Semi-Conductor Electronics. 149

Huntington, Whitney C., Building Construction. 137

Hurd, Paul S., Metallic Materials. 169

Hurlock, Elizabeth B., Child Growth and Development. 81

Hurst, John W., Cardiac Resuscitation. 181; Introduction to Electrocardiography. 184

Hurwitz, Abraham B., Games To Improve Your Child's English. 81

Hurwitz, Al, Children and Their Art. 110

Hurwitz, Elizabeth A., Design. 13

Husband, William H., Real Estate. 65

Husch, Bertram, Forest Mensuration and Statistics. 87

Huskey, Harry D., Computer Handbook. 18

Hussander, Martin, Real Estate Syndicator's Manual and Guide. 65

Husson, Samir S., Microprogramming. 20

Hutchings, Reginald S., A Manual of Decorated Typefaces. 44; A Manual of Script Typefaces. 44; The Western Heritage of Type Design. 44

Hutchins, Michael, Typographics. 44

Hutchinson, E. L., Reference Manual for Stenographers and Typists. 67

Hutchinson, Francis W., Design of Refrigeration Systems for Air Conditioning. 120; Heating and Humidifying Load Analysis. 120

Hutchinson, Lois I., Standard Handbook for Secretaries. 68

Hutchison, Chester S., Your Future in Agriculture. 75

Hutchison, Sir Robert, Food and the Principles of Nutrition. 40

Hutt, Allen, Newspaper Design. 44

Hutter, Heribert, Drawing. 10

Hutton, Helen, The Technique of Collage. 10

Hutton, John, Building and Construction in Australia. 137

Hutton, Robert S., Experiments in Movement Behavior and Motor Learning. 80

Hutton, Samuel W., Minister's Funeral Manual. 93

Hylton, Delmer P., Principles and Procedures of Modern Accounting Practice. 3

Hylton, Lydia F., The Residential Treatment Center. 81

Hyman, Rebecca, The Complete Guide to Wigs & Hairpieces. 8

Hymoff, Edward, Guidance and Control of Spacecraft. 117

Hymovich, Debra P., Nursing of Children. 195

Hynes, H. B. N., The Biology of Polluted Waters. 178

I.B.M. Corporation, Data Processing Glossary. 16

ITT Educational Services, Inc., This is Electronics. 149

Iannone, N. F., Supervision of Police Personnel. 98

IˆArbus, Al´fred L., Eye Movements and Vision. 198

Ickis, Marguerite, The Book of Arts and Crafts. 161

Ignition Manufacturers Institute, Automotive Tune-up Principles and Procedures Textbook. 123

Ihne, Russel W., Machine Trades Blueprint Reading. 144

Iliffe, J. K., Basic Machine Principles. 164

Illingworth, Ronald S., The Development of the Infant and Young Child. 81; Normal Child. 81

Illinois Institute of Technology, APT Part Programming. 20

Illuminating Engineering Society, IES Lighting Handbook. 149

Inbau, Fred E., Criminal Interrogation & Confessions. 100; Criminal Law for the Police. 98; Truth and Deception. 100

Industrial Designers Society of America, Design in America. 13

Ingalls, A. J., Maternal and Child Health Nursing. 195

Ingles, Thelma, Clinic Nursing. 193

Ingoldsby, Patricia, The Executive Secretary. 70

Ingraham, Lloyd L., Biochemical Mechanisms. 133

Ingram, Frank L., Radiology of the Teeth and Jaws. 174

Ingram, Madelene E., Principles and Techniques of Psychiatric Nursing. 196

Inkeles, Alex, What is Sociology? 105

Innis, Mary Q., Nursing Education in a Changing Society. 190

Institute of Police Management for Supervisory and Administrative Personnel, Police Management for Supervisory and Administrative Personnel. 98

Institute on the Use of the Library of Congress Classification, The Use of the Library of Congress Classification. 90

Institutions, The Components of Communication. 51; The Finishing Kitchen. 36; The Nautical Way. 36; Purchasing Guide for Institutions Interior Planners. 51; Storage Specifics. 36; The Three C's of Atmosphere. 55

Instrument Society of America, Standards and Practices for Instrumentation. 164

Instrumentation in the Chemical & Petroleum Industries. 133

International Association of Chiefs of Police, Law Enforcement Education Directory 1970. 98; Proceedings of Police Administrators Conference on Community Relations. 98

International Association of Fire Chiefs, Fire Department Pumps, Pumping Equipment, and Pumping. 84; A Personnel Manual for Volunteer Fire Companies. 84

International Atomic Energy Agency, Atlas of Radiation Dose Distribution. 204; Value to Agriculture of High-quality Water from Nuclear Desalination. 75

International City Management Association, Municipal Fire Administration. 84; Municipal Police Administration. 98

International City Managers' Association, Municipal Recreation Administration. 103

International Commission on Radiological Protection, Radiosensitivity and Spatial Distribution of Dose. 204

International Conference of Building Officials, A Training Manual in Field Inspection of Buildings and Structures. 137; Uniform Building Code. 137

International Conference of Printing Research Institutes, Halftone Printing. 44; Printing Inks and Color. 48

International Conference on Social Welfare, Social Welfare and Human Rights. 105

International Congress on Corneal and Scleral Contact Lenses, Corneal and Scleral Contact Lenses. 198

International Correspondence Schools, Elementary Aerodynamics. 117

International Council on Social Welfare, Urban Development. 105

INDEX

International Dental Federation, A Lexicon of English Dental Terms. 174

International District Heating Association, Principles of Economical Heating Handbook. 121

International Encyclopedia of Chemical Science. 128

International Fire Administration Institute, Higher Education in the Nation's Fire Service. 84

International Fire Service Training Association, Aircraft Fire Protection and Rescue Procedures. 84; Fire Apparatus Practices. 84; The Fire Department Officer. 84; Fire Department Support of Automatic Sprinkler Systems. 84; Fire Inspection Practices. 84; Fire Service First Aid Practices. 84; Fire Service Instructor Training. 84; Fire Service Ladder Practices. 84; Fire Service Practices for Volunteer Fire Department. 84; Fire Stream Practices. 84; Fundamental Principles of Science Applied to the Fire Service. 84; Leadership in the Fire Service. 84; Ventilation Practices. 121; Water Supplies for the Fire Service. 84

International Foodservice Manufacturers Association, Membership Directory of the International Foodservice Manufacturers Association. 33

International Institute of Refrigeration, ...Practical Guide to Refrigerated Storage. 121

International Labor Office, Geneva, Guide to Safety and Health in Forestry Work. 87

International Marketing Association, Concise Guide to International Markets. 62

International Paper Company, The Pocket Pal. 44

International Poster Annual. 10

International Printing Pressman and Assistants' Union of North America, A Career As A Printing Pressman. 44

International Resistance Company, The Expanded Glossary of Electronics Terminology. 149

International Rice Research Institute, The Virus Diseases of the Rice Plant. 75

The Intertype: Its Function, Care, Operation and Adjustment. 44

Iorio, Josephine, Principles of Obstetrics and Gynecology for Nurses. 195

Iowa Home Economics Association, Unit Method of Clothing Construction. 23

Iowa State Department of Health, Simplified Diet Manual. 33

Iowa State University, Midwest Farm Handbook. 75

Iowa State University Center for Agricultural and Economic Development, Food Goals, Future Structural Changes and Agricultural Policy. 75

Ireland, James R., Permanent Ceramic Magnet Motors. 156

Ireland, Robert E., Organic Synthesis. 134

Irion, Paul E., Cremation. 94; Funeral. 94

Irwin, John, The Felon. 98

Isaacs, Neil S., Experiments in Physical Organic Chemistry. 134

Isaacs, Susan S., Intellectual Growth in Young Children. 81; Nursery Years. 81

Isaacson, Irving, Manual for the Arresting Officer. 98

Iseley, Duane, Weed Identification and Control in the North Central States. 75

Isler, Charlotte, The Nurses' Aide in the Hospital. 194

Itten, Johannes, The Art of Color. 13

Iverson, Kenneth E., Automatic Data Processing. 15; Automatic Data Processing System/360. 15

Ives, Orville B., Hospital Dietary Services. 31

Ivey, Paul W., Successful Salesmanship. 59

Ivins, William M., Jr., Notes on Prints. 10; Prints and Visual Communication. 10

J. C. Penney Co., Inc., Fashions and Fabrics. 25

J. Walter Thompson Company, How to Promote Your Restaurant. 53

Jackson, Bruce, A Thief's Primer. 98

Jackson, Charles O., Food and Drug Legislation in the New Deal. 33

Jackson, Edgar N., Christian Funeral. 94; For the Living. 94; Telling a Child About Death. 194; You and Your Grief. 194

Jackson, Elinor, Occupational Therapy Examination Review. 209

Jackson, Ellen, Subject Guide to Major United States Government Publications. 90

Jackson, Herbert W., Introduction to Electric Circuits. 149

Jackson, J., Industrial Water Treatment Practice. 178

Jackson, Philip W., Life in Classrooms. 111

Jackson, Samuel, The Savoy. 51

Jackson, Vivian C., Role-Play in New Careers Training. 106

Jacobi, Charles A., Textbook of Anatomy and Physiology in Radiologic Technology. 204; Textbook of Radiologic Technology. 204; X-Ray Technology. 204

Jacobi, Charles T., The Printers' Vocabulary. 44

Jacobowitz, Henry, Basic Math Course for Electronics. 206; How to Solve Problems in Electricity and Electronics. 149

Jacobs, Erwin M., Neurology for Nurses. 194

Jacobs, Morris B., The Chemical Analysis of Air Pollutants. 131

Jacobs, Thomas L., Laboratory Practice of Organic Chemistry. 135

Jacobsen, Lyle E., Cost Accounting. 5

Jacobsohn, Kurt, Enlarging. 49

Jacobson, Joanne, Occupational Therapy Manual, 209

Jacobson, Paul, Agricultural Engineer's Handbook. 76

Jacoby, Helmut, New Architectural Drawings. 143

Jaedicke, Robert K., Accounting Flows. 3; Managerial Accounting. 4

Jaeger, Edmund C., The Biologist's Handbook of Pronunciations. 185; A Source-Book of Biological Names and Terms. 185

Jaffe, Erwin, Color Separation Photography for Offset Lithography. 49; Contact Printing. 44; Halftone Photography for Offset Lithography. 44; The Science of Physics in Lithography. 14

Jaffe, Hans H., Symmetry in Chemistry. 128

James, D. W., Fundamental Aspects of Inorganic Chemistry. 133

James F. Lincoln Arc Welding Foundation, Modern Welded Structures. 137

James, George V., Water Treatment. 178

James, Howard, Children in Trouble. 81

James, N. D. G., The Forester's Companion. 87

James, Sydney C., Midwest Farm Planning Manual. 75

James, Ted, The Waldorf-Astoria Cookbook. 33

James, Thomas H., Fundamentals of Photographic Theory. 49

James, Walter, Wine. 38

Jamieson, Elizabeth M., Trends in Nursing History. 190

Jamieson, Norna, Surgical Nursing. 190

Jamison, Andrew, The Steam-Powered Automobile. 123

Jamison, Robert V., Fortran IV Programming. 20

Jane's All The World's Aircraft. 117

Janick, Jules, Horticultural Science. 75; Plant Agriculture. 75; Plant Science. 75

Janis, Arthur, Fundamentals of Modern Bookkeeping. 3

Janis, Harriet, Collage. 10

Jaque, Line, Sew the French Way. 23

Jarneryd, O., Block and Silk Screen Printing. 8

Jarnow, Jeannette A., Inside the Fashion Business. 24

Jarrett, Henry, Resources of the Future. 178

Jarvis, Oscar T., Transitional Elementary School and Its Curriculum. 111

Jaski, Tom, Electronics in Business Machines. 149; Industrial Electronics Made Easy. 149

Jaspert, W. P., The Encyclopaedia of Type Faces. 42

Jauch, Heinz, The Computer: An Accounting Tool. 4

Jaundrell-Thompson, Fred, X-Ray Physics and Equipment. 204

Jawetz, Ernest, Review of Medical Pharmacology. 202

Jay, James M., Modern Food Microbiology. 33

Jayne, John J., Small Printing Plant Management. 45

Jeffers, Camille, Living Poor. 105

Jefferson, Theodore B., Metals and How to Weld Them. 171

Jeffries, Bob, Soul Food Cookbook. 39

Jefopoulos, T., Dentifrices. 174

JeHarned, Medical Terminology Made Easy. 71

Jellinek, J. Stephan, Formulation and Function of Cosmetics. 7

Jenkins, Frances B., Science Reference Sources. 90

Jenkins, G. Neil, The Physiology of the Mouth. 174

Jenkins, Glenn L., Clinical Pharmacy. 201

Jenkins, Herbert T., Keeping the Peace. 98

Jenne, Jewel A., Ideas for Farm Mechanics Projects. 78

Jennett, Sean, The Making of Books. 45

Jenni, Clyde B., Basic Metallurgy II. 169

Jennings, Burgess H., Interactions of Man and His Environment. 178

Jennings, Ralph E., The Automotive Dictionary. 123

Jensen, Alfred E., Applied Strength of Materials. 170; Statics and Strength of Materials. 170

Jensen, Cecil H., Drafting Fundamentals. 143; Engineering Drawing and Design. 143

Jensen, Clayne R., Outdoor Recreation in America. 103

Jensen, Deborah M., Jensen's History and Trends of Professional Nursing. 190; Principles and Technics of Rehabilitation Nursing. 190; A Textbook of Medical-Surgical Nursing. 188

Jensen, Howard G., Accounting. 4

Jensen, J. Trygve, Introduction to Medical Physics. 182

Jensen, Lawrence N., Synthetic Painting Media. 10

Jensen, Louis E., Automotive Drawing Interpretation. 144

Jepsen, Stanley M., Trees and Forests. 87

Jessee, Ruth W., Self-Teaching Tests in Arithmetic for Nurses. 206

Jessen, G., Complete Guide to Contact Lenses. 198

Jessop, Neil, Communications in the Building Industry. 137

Jodais, Janet, Personal Care of Patients. 207

Joel, Alma L., Workbook and Study Guide for Medical-Surgical Nursing. 190

Johannsen, Lawrence A., Basic Electronics. 149

Johansson, Ivar, Genetic Aspects of Dairy Cattle Breeding. 79

John, David H. O., Radiographic Processing in Medicine and Industry. 204

John, Frederick W., Plastics. 167

John Jay College of Criminal Justice, City University of New York, Proceedings of the John Jay College Faculty Seminars. 98

Johns, Ada W., Special Libraries. 90

Johns, Harold, The Physics of Radiology. 204

Johnson, A. F., The Encyclopaedia of Type Faces. 42; Type Designs. 45

Johnson, A. P., Organization and Management of Hospital Laboratories. 182

Johnson, A. R., Tool Steels. 169

Johnson, Alice B., The Complete Scandinavian Cookbook. 39

Johnson, B. Stephen, Electronics in Action. 147

Johnson, Benjamin K., Optics and Optical Instruments. 199

Johnson, Carrie E., Medical Spelling Guide. 71

Johnson, Cecil E., Human Biology. 185

Johnson, Charles E., Accounting. 3; Financial Accounting. 3

Johnson, David G., Readings in the Economics of Agriculture. 74

Johnson, Elmer D., Communication. 45; A History of Libraries in the Western World. 90

Johnson, Elmer H., Crime, Correction, and Society. 98

Johnson, Eric R., Servomechanisms. 149

Johnson, G. Orville, Education of Exceptional Children and Youth. 109

Johnson, G. S., Welding Technology. 171

Johnson, George, Your Career in Advertising. 6

Johnson, Glenn L., Finney and Miller's Principles of Accounting, Introductory. 3

Johnson, Harold V., General-Industrial Machine Shop. 161; Technical Metals. 161

Johnson, Harry W., Jr., Selected Experiments in Organic Chemistry. 134

Johnson, Herbert W., Creative Selling. 59; How to Use the Business Library. 90

Johnson, Hugh, Wine. 38

Johnson, Isabel, Some Special Problems of Children. 82

Johnson, J. Richard, Electric Circuits. 149; How to Build Electronic Equipment. 149; How to Troubleshoot a TV Receiver. 157; Practical Television Servicing. 157

Johnson, James T., Readings in Auditing. 5

Johnson, John R., Laboratory Experiments in Organic Chemistry. 134

Johnson, Larry, Motor Service's Automotive Encyclopedia. 125

Johnson, Lois V., Classroom Management. 111

Johnson, M. L., A Dictionary of Biology. 184

Johnson, Mae M., Problem-Solving in Nursing Practice. 190

Johnson, Margaret A., Developing the Art of Understanding. 190

Johnson, Mary R., Mary Johnson's Guide to Altering and Restyling Ready-Made Clothes. 24; Sew for Your Children. 24; Sewing the Easy Way. 24

Johnson, Mildred D., Problem Solving and Chemical Calculations. 128

Johnson, Mina M., Comprehensive Business Machines Course. 69; Full-Keyboard Adding Machine Course. 69; Records Management. 68; Rotary Calculator Course. 69; Ten-Key Adding Machine Course. 69

Johnson, Olaf A., Design of Machine Tools. 167

Johnson, Robert, Library Skills. 90

Johnson, Ronald Carl, Introductory Descriptive Chemistry. 128

Johnson, Ronald Charles, Child and Adolescent Psychology. 110; Child Psychology, Behavior and Development. 81

Johnson, Sidney M., The Design of Foundations for Buildings. 138; Deterioration, Maintenance, and Repair of Structures. 137

Johnson, Virginia K., Standardized Quantity Recipes. 31

Johnson, Walter L., Content and Dynamics of Home Visits of Public Health Nurses. 196

INDEX

Johnson, Warren C., Qualitative Analysis and Chemical Equilibrium. 132

Johnston, Bruce F., Agricultural Development and Economic Growth. 77

Johnston, Dorothy F., Essentials of Communicable Disease. 190; Total Patient Care. 190

Johnston, John F., Modern Practice in Dental Ceramics. 174

Johnston, John L., Adequate Wiring for Home and Farm. 149

Johnston, John W., The Department Store Buyer. 63

Johnston, Meda P., Design on Fabrics. 24

Johnston, Norman, The Sociology of Crime and Delinquency. 102

Johnstone, Margery G., Minerals for the Chemical and Allied Industries. 128

Johnstone, Sydney J., Minerals for the Chemical and Allied Industries. 128

Joint Commission on Mental Health of Children, Crisis in Child Mental Health. 81

Joint Committee on Continuing Legal Education of American Law Institute and American Bar Association, The Problems of Police Interrogation. 98

Jolley, E. H., Introduction to Telephony and Telegraphy. 149

Jolly, William L., The Synthesis and Characterization of Inorganic Compounds. 133; Synthetic Inorganic Chemistry. 133

Jonas, Paul, Manual of Darkroom Procedures and Techniques. 49

Jonassen, Hans B., Technique of Inorganic Chemistry. 133

Jones, Arthur W., Introduction to Parasitology. 187

Jones, Barbara M., Design for Death. 94

Jones, Benjamin A., Jr., Highway and Agricultural Drainage Practices. 74

Jones, Clifford, Microwave Measurements Manual. 149

Jones, David A., Blow Molding. 165

Jones, David G., Chemistry and Industry. 128

Jones, Donlon F., Business Data Processing. 17

Jones, Dorothea V. G., The Soybean Cookbook. 33

Jones, Dorothy P., Adventures in Greek Cookery. 39

Jones, Elmer W., Adequate Wiring for Home and Farm. 149

Jones, Frances M., Tips and Tricks for Tailoring. 24

Jones, Franklin D., Engineering Encyclopedia. 165; Machine Shop Training Course. 161, 165; Use of Handbook Tables & Formulas. 165

Jones, Fred M., Introduction to Marketing Management. 59; Retail Management. 63

Jones, Gwendolyn, Packaging Information Sources. 63

Jones, Howard M., Guide to American Literature and Its Backgrounds Since 1890. 91

Jones, John E., Handbook of Structured Experiences for Human Relations Training. 107

Jones, John R., Fish and River Pollution. 178

Jones, Leo M., Veterinary Pharmacology and Therapeutics. 201

Jones, Malcolm D., Basic Diagnostic Radiology. 204

Jones, Manley H., The Marketing Process. 59

Jones, Mark M., Elementary Coordination Chemistry. 128

Jones, Raymond P., Construction Estimating. 138; Framing, Sheathing and Insulation. 138

Jones, Robert E., Police English. 101

Jones, Robert L., Fundamental COBOL for IBM System 360. 20

Jones, Stanley, Lithography for Artists. 14

Jones, Tom, Scientific Exhibits. 90

Jones, W. Norton, General Chemistry in the Laboratory. 128; Textbook of General Chemistry. 128

Joplin, Bruce, Effective Accounting Reports. 3

Jordain, Philip B., Condensed Computer Encyclopedia. 18

Jordan, Robert T., Tomorrow's Library. 91

Jordan, Rose M., Psychology. 190

Jorgensen, Erik, Master Forms Guide for Successful Real Estate Sales Agreements. 65

Jorgensen, Finn, Handbook of Magnetic Tape Recording. 149

Jorgensen, Paul, Mathematics for Data Processing. 15

Joseph, Alexander, Programmed Physics. 199

Joseph, Marjory L., Introductory Textile Science. 28

Joslyn, Maynard A., Food Processing Operations. 41; Fruit and Vegetable Juice Processing Technology. 42; Fundamentals of Food Processing Operations. 41; Introduction to Thermal Processing of Foods. 41; Methods in Food Analysis. 41; Milestones in Nutrition. 40; Table Wines. 37

Journal of Criminal Law, Criminology & Police Science, The Supreme Court & the Police. 98

Journigan, Russell P., Basic Electronics. 149

Jowett, Charles E., Reliability of Electronic Components. 149

Joy, Adena A., A Learning Team. 111

Joyner, Nina G., Furniture Refinishing at Home. 56

Judd, Deane B., Color in Business, Science and Industry. 13

Jude, James R., Fundamentals of Cardio-Pulmonary Resuscitation. 181

Judelle, Beatrice, The Branch Manager's Manual. 63; Inside the Fashion Business. 24

Judge, Arthur W., Modern Smaller Diesel Engines. 123; Motor Manuals. 123

Juergenson, Elwood M., Approved Practices in Beef Cattle Production. 79; Approved Practices in Dairying. 79; Approved Practices in Feeds and Feeding. 78; Approved Practices in Fruit Production. 76; Approved Practices in Poultry Production. 78; Approved Practices in Sheep Production. 79; Approved Practices in Swine Production. 78; Selected Lessons for Teaching Agricultural Science. 73; Selected Lessons for Teaching Off-Farm Agricultural Occupations. 75

Jungerman, Martha E., Introduction to Textiles. 28

Juran, Joseph M., Quality Control Handbook. 45

Justema, William, The Pleasures of Pattern. 24

Juszli, Frank L., Basic Mathematics for Electronics. 206

Juvet, Richard S., Jr., Gas-Liquid Chromatography. 126

Juzwiak, Marijo, Nursing Care of the High Risk Surgery Patient. 197

Kabat, Hugh F., Clinical Pharmacy Handbook. 201

Kabbes, Elaine F., Medical Secretary's Guide. 71

Kaberlein, Joseph J., Air Conditioning Metal Layout. 121; Short Cuts for Round Layouts. 121; Triangulation Short-Cut-Layouts. 121

Kadushin, Alfred, Child Welfare Services. 81

Kaelble, Emmett F., Handbook of X-Rays. 204

Kagan, Jerome, Readings in Child Development and Personality. 82

Kagawa, Aya, Japanese Cookbook. 39

Kagy, Frederick D., Graphic Arts. 45

Kahler, Carol, Guide to Planning. 182

Kahn, Alfred J., Planning Community Services for Children in Trouble. 81; Theory and Practice of Social Planning. 105

Kahn, Gilbert, Accounting 10/12. 2; Gregg Bookkeeping & Account-

256

ing. 2; How to Use Adding Machines. 68; Progressive Filing. 68

Kaiser, Inez Y., Soul Food Cookery. 39

Kaiser, Ralph D., The Menu Converter. 33

Kalafatich, Audrey J., Pediatric Nursing. 195

Kale, C. M., Principles of Building Drawing. 145

Kalins, Dorothy, Researching Design in New York. 55

Kalish, Israel H., Microminiature Electronics. 149

Kalkman, Marion, Psychiatric Nursing. 196

Kallaus, Norman F., Records Management. 68

Kallen, Howard P., Handbook of Instrumentation and Controls. 165

Kallins, Ethel L., Textbook of Public Health Nursing. 196

Kamekura, Yusaku, Trademarks and Symbols of the World. 10

Kampmann, Lothar, Creating with Colored Ink. 10; Creating with Printing Material. 10

Kane, Bernard J., A Systematic Guide to Supermarket Location Analysis. 64

Kanig, Joseph L., The Theory and Practice of Industrial Pharmacy. 202

Kanovitz, Jacqueline R., Constitutional Law for Police. 98

Kantorowicz, George F., Inlays, Crowns and Bridges. 174

Kapany, N. S., Fiber Optics. 199

Kaplan, John, Principles of Evidence and Proof. 99

Kaplan, Robert M., Salesmanship. 57

Kapur, Gopal K., IBM 360 Assembly Language Programming. 20

Karch, Robert R., Graphic Arts Procedures. 45; Printing and the Allied Trades. 45

Karchmer, J. H., Analytical Chemistry of Sulfur and Its Compounds. 132

Karczmar, Alexander G., Experimental Pharmacodynamics. 201

Karl, Jean, From Childhood to Childhood. 81

Karlem, Selma, Anglo-American Criminal Justice. 98

Karlson, Peter, Introduction to Modern Biochemistry. 133

Karmas, Edel, Fresh Meat Processing. 41

Karnosh, Louis J., Essentials of Psychiatric Nursing. 196

Karplus, Walter J., On-Line Computing. 18

Karr, Herbert W., Simscript: A Simulation Programming Language. 20

Karrenbrock, Wilbert E., Advanced Accounting. 3; Intermediate Accounting. 3

Karvinen, Clifford H., Aerospace Propulsion Powerplants. 116

Kask, Uno, Chemistry. 128

Kasper, Sydney H., Careers in the Building Trades. 138

Kassoff, Norman C., Organizational Concepts. 98

Kaswell, Ernest R., Wellington Sears Handbook of Industrial Textiles. 28

Katan, Anny, The Therapeutic Nursery School. 81

Kates, Edgar J., Diesel and High Compression Gas Engines. 123

Katsaris, W. K., Corrections Education. 98

Katz, Alfred H., Health and the Community. 207

Katz, Fred E., An Approach to the Education of Psychiatric Nursing Personnel. 196

Katz, Marvin, Police Guide to Search and Seizure, Interrogation and Confession. 101

Katz, William A., Introduction to Reference Work. 91

Katzan, Harry, Jr., APL Programming and Computer Techniques. 20

Kauffmann, Désiré, Graphic Arts Crafts. 45

Kaufman, Donald D., Degradation of Herbicides. 75

Kaufman, Glen, Design on Fabrics. 24

Kaufman, Herbert, The Forest Ranger. 87

Kaufman, Morris, Giant Molecules. 167

Kaufman, William I., Appetizers and Canapes. 33; The Art of Casserole Cookery. 33; The Art of Creole Cookery. 33; The Chocolate Cookbook. 33; The Fish and Shellfish Cookbook. 33; The Tea Cookbook. 33; UNICEF Book of Children's Songs. 81

Kaufmann, Henry H., Grain Storage. 74

Kaufmann, Ruth, The New American Tapestry. 55

Kautsky, Theodore, Ways with Watercolor. 10

Kavanagh, Thomas C., The Design of Foundations for Buildings. 138

Kawal, Donald E., Critical Path Method. 139

Kay, Barbara A., Probation and Parole. 98

Kay, D., Techniques for Electron Microscopy. 182

Kay, John D., The Lighting of Buildings. 137

Kayton, Myron, Avionics Navigation Systems. 117

Kazarian, Edward A., Work Analysis and Design for Hotels, Restaurants and Institutions. 51

Kazmier, Leonard J., Fundamentals of EDP and Fortran. 20

Keane, Claire B., Drugs and Solutions. 190; Essentials of Nursing. 195; Saunders Review for Practical Nurses. 195

Kearney, Philip C., Degradation of Herbicides. 75

Keats, Theodore E., Atlas of Roentgenographic Measurement. 204

Kedzie, Daniel P., Your Future in Insurance. 54

Keefe, John E., Your Future as an Electronics Technician. 149

Keenan, Joseph, Principles of General Thermodynamics. 164

Keeton, William T., Biological Science. 185; Elements of Biological Science. 185

Kehm, Freda S., Let Children be Children. 81

Keil, Andrew A., Radiation Control. 84

Keim, Armand, Fundamentals of Digital Computers. 19

Keir, Jack C., Cases in Life Insurance. 53

Keith, Charles W., Mechanical Drafting Essentials. 144

Keith, Donald, How to Succeed in Community Service. 106

Keith, T. B., Feed Formulation Manual. 79

Kelber, Harry, Union Printers and Controlled Automation. 45

Kell, J. R., Heating and Air-Conditioning of Buildings. 120

Kellejian, Robert, Microwave Measurements Manual. 149

Keller, Bernard G., Pharmaceutical Marketing. 201

Keller, I., Management Accounting for Profit Control. 3

Keller, Roy, Basic Tables in Chemistry. 128

Keller, Thomas F., Financial Accounting Theory. 5; Financial Accounting Theory: Issues and Controversies. 5

Kelley, Eugene J., Marketing. 59; Marketing Management. 59

Kellogg, Rhoda, The Psychology of Children's Art. 10

Kelly, Charles J., The Sky's the Limit. 117

Kelly, Cordelia W., Dimensions of Professional Nursing. 190

Kelly, Dorothy E., Moral Principles of Nursing. 190

Kelly, Francis M., Historic Costume. 27

Kelly, James G., Nonprofessionals in the Human Services. 105

Kelly, Joe W., Composition and Properties of Concrete. 141; Elementary Plane Surveying. 141; Surveying Theory and Practice. 142

Kelly, Richard J., The Advertising Budget. 6

INDEX

Kelly, Rob R., American Wood Type, 1828-1900. 10

Kelsey, F. E., Essentials of Pharmacology. 202

Kelsey, R. Wilfred, Handbook of Life Insurance. 54

Kemeny, John G., Basic Programming. 20

Kemp, Jerrold E., Planning and Producing Audiovisual Materials. 111

Kemp, Lloyd A., Basic Physics in Radiology. 204; Mathematics for Radiographers. 206

Kemp, Patrick S., Accounting for the Manager. 3

Kempf, Florence C., Psychology: Dynamics of Behavior in Nursing. 190

Kempf, Norman W., The Technology of Chocolate. 41

Kempster, Maurice H. A., Principles of Jig and Tool Design. 165

Kenian, Paul R., Basic Transistor Course. 159

Kennedy, Cora W., Filter Guide. 50

Kennedy, D., Biology of Organisms. 185

Kennedy, Donald, From Cell to Organism. 182

Kennedy, Dorothy A., The Theory and Practice of Nursing Service Administration. 193

Kennedy, George, Electronic Communications System. 149

Kennedy, Leonard M., Guiding Children to Mathematical Discovery. 111

Kennedy, Ralph D., Introduction to Financial and Managerial Accounting. 3

Kennedy, Sibilla E., A Laboratory Investigation of Concepts in Chemistry. 131

Kennedy, William E., The Space-Flight Encyclopedia. 118

Kenney, John P., The California Police. 98; Police Operations. 98; Police Work with Juveniles and the Administration of Juvenile Justice. 98

Kenny, John B., Ceramic Design. 161

Kent, Cyril, Starting with Relief Printmaking. 10

Kent, Norman, 100 Watercolor Techniques. 10

Kent, Robert, How to Get Rich in Real Estate. 65

Kenton, Ronald, Theory of Catering. 52

Keonjian, Edward, Microelectronics. 149

Keown, Robert M., Mechanism. 164

Kepler, Frank R., General Drafting. 142

Kerber, August, The Schools and the Urban Crisis. 111

Kerchner, Russell M., Alternating-Current Circuits. 149

Kernan, Jerome B., Comparative Marketing Systems. 61; Perspectives in Marketing Theory. 59; Promotion. 59

Kernicki, Jeanette, Cardiovascular Nursing. 190

Kerr, Avice, Orthopedic Nursing Procedures. 195

Kerr, Donald A., Oral Pathology. 174

Kerr, Graham, The Graham Kerr Cookbook. 33

Kerr, Rose N., Historic Costume. 27

Kerrigan, Harry D., Accounting Systems. 2; Fund Accounting. 3

Kerschner, Velma L., Simplified Nutrition and Diet Therapy for Practical Nurses. 196

Kershner, William K., Student Pilot's Flight Manual. 117

Kessler, Edward, Resuscitation. 180

Kestenbaum, Alfred, Applied Anatomy of the Eye. 199

Kester, Dale E., Plant Propagation. 74

Ketchum, Donald J., Pulse and Switching Circuits. 149

Keuhnelian, John G., Urologic Nursing. 197

Keyes, Donald B., Industrial Chemicals. 127

Keys, John D., Japanese Cuisine. 39

Keys, William J., Basic Principles of Data Processing. 16; Data Processing. 15

Khachaturian, Narbev, Prestressed Concrete. 141

Kice, John L., Modern Principles of Organic Chemistry. 134

Kidd, Donald M., Methods of Teaching Shop and Technical Subjects. 162

Kidder, Frank E., Architects' and Builders' Handbook. 138

Kidwell, Walter M., Electrical Instruments and Measurements. 149

Kieffer, William F., The Mole Concept in Chemistry. 128

Kieso, Donald E., Intermediate Principles of Accounting. 3

Kilbourne, Edwin D., Human Ecology and Public Health. 178

Killeen, Louis M., Techniques of Inventory Management. 63

Killick, W. E., Single-Colour Lithographic Machine Operating. 14

Killion, William D., Video Transmission Techniques. 157

Kilpatrick, Harold C., Work Simplification in Dental Practice. 174

Kilpatrick, Lester, Egg Grading Manual. 75

Kimball, Cyril, The Care, Cleaning and Selection of Floors and Resilient Floor Coverings. 50

Kimball, Warren Y., Effective Streams for Fighting Fires. 84; Fire Attack! 84; Manning for Fire Attack. 85

Kimball, Yeffe, The Art of American Indian Cooking. 39

Kimber, Diana C., Anatomy and Physiology. 184

Kimber, Richard T., Automation in Libraries. 91

Kinard, Malvina C., The Kitchen Scholar. 33

Kinchen, Lila A., Clothing for Moderns. 23

Kinder, Faye, Meal Management. 33

King, Barry G., Human Anatomy and Physiology. 184

King, Clarence, Working with People in Community Action. 105

King, Edward L., How Chemical Reactions Occur. 128

King, Everett M., The Auxiliary Police Unit. 98

King, Glen D., First-Line Supervisor's Manual. 98; Race Tensions and the Police. 96

King, Gordon J., Radio and Television Test Instruments. 157; Servicing Transistor Equipment. 159

King, Guy R., Basic Air Conditioning. 121

King, Horace W., Handbook of Hydraulics. 138

King, Roy, The World of Currier & Ives. 10

King, Rufus, Gambling and Organized Crime. 98

Kingery, William D., Introduction to Ceramics. 161

Kingman, Lee, Illustrators of Children's Books, 1957-1966. 10

Kingslake, Rudolf, Applied Optics and Optical. 199; Lenses in Photography. 49

Kingsley, Charles, Electric Machinery. 155

Kingsley, V. V., Bacteriology Primer in Air Contamination Control. 178

Kingzett, Charles T., Chemical Encyclopaedia. 128

Kinmond, Jean, Crochet Patterns. 24

Kinn, Mary E., The Office Assistant in Medical Practice. 71

Kinnard, William N., Industrial Real Estate. 65

Kinney, Mary R., The Abbreviated Citation: A Bibliographical Problem. 91

Kinsey, Anthony, Introducing Screen Printing. 45

Kinsinger, Robert E., Clinical Nursing Instruction by Television. 190; Education for Health Technicans. 207; Health Technicians. 207

Kintner, Paul M., Electronic Digital Techniques. 149

Kip, Arthur F., Fundamentals of Electricity and Magnetism. 149

Kipp, Kenneth E., Dental Science Laboratory Guide. 173

INDEX

Kipps, Michael S., The Production of Field Crops. 75

Kirchner, Glenn, Physical Education for Elementary School Children. 111

Kirk, Franklyn W., Instrumentation. 165

Kirk, Paul L., The Crime Laboratory. 98; Fire Investigation. 85

Kirk, Raymond E., Encyclopedia of Chemical Technology. 128

Kirk, Tim H., How to Avoid Beginner's Mistakes in Selling Real Estate. 65

Kirk, Weir R., Aim for a Job in a Hospital. 207; Your Future in Hospital Administration. 207

Kirkendall, Lester A., Sex in the Childhood Years. 82

Kirkpatrick, C. A., Promotion. 62

Kirkpatrick, Charles A., Advertising. 6

Kirkpatrick, Clifford, The Family as Process and Institution. 105

Kirkwood, Leila H., Charging Systems. 91

Kiser, James J., Introductory Animal Science. 78

Kiser, Robert W., Problems and Experiments in Instrumental Analysis. 133

Kissam, Philip, Optical Tooling for Precise Manufacture and Alignment. 165; Surveying Practice. 142

Kister, Kenneth F., Social Issues and Library Problems. 91

Kitchell, Frank M., Opportunities in an Optometry Career. 199

Kiver, Milton S., Applications of Electronics. 148; Color Television Fundamentals. 158; F-M Simplified. 157; Television Simplified. 157; Transistors in Radio, Television and Electronics. 159

Klanit, Frederick S., A Couse of Study in Science and Related Technology for the Training of Health Physics Technicians. 208

Klante, Dieter, Creative Metal Design. 163

Klapper, Marvin, Fabric Almanac. 29

Klapthor, Margaret, The First Ladies' Cook Book. 33

Kleberg, John R., A Police Records System for the Small Department. 97

Klein, Abraham E., New World Secretarial Handbook. 68

Klein, Camille, The Professional Cook. 33

Klein, Frederick R., Accounting in Action. 2

Klein, Herbert T., The Police. 98

Klein, Jerome E., Great Shops of Europe. 63; Views to Dine By. 52

Klein, Larry, It's Easy to Use Electronic Test Equipment. 149

Klein, Louis, River Pollution. 178

Klein, Miles V., Optics. 199

Klein, Philip, From Philanthropy to Social Welfare. 105

Klein, Richard L., Introduction to Molecular Pharmacology. 201

Klein, Rose S., Applied Nutrition. 41

Klein & Company, New York, Directory of Mailing List Houses. 59

Kleinberg, Jacob, Inorganic Chemistry. 133

Kleiner, Israel S., Biochemistry. 133

Klemin, Diana, The Illustrated Book. 10

Kleppner, Otto, Advertising Procedure. 6; Exploring Advertising. 6

Klerer, Melvin, Digital Computer User's Handbook. 18

Klinefelter, Lee M., Bookbinding Made Easy, 47

Kling, Samuel G., The Complete Guide to Everyday Law. 71

Klingman, Glenn C., Weed Control. 75

Kloeffler, Royce G., Basic Electronics. 149; Electron Tubes. 149; Industrial Electronics and Control. 149

Klopf, Gordon J., A Learning Team. 111; New Careers and Roles in the American School. 109

Klotter, John C., Constitutional Law for Police. 98; Techniques for Police Instructors. 98

Klotz, Irving M., Chemical Thermodynamics. 128; Energy Changes in Biochemical Reactions. 133

Klupar, G. J., Modern Cemetery Management. 94

Klupt, Helen, Principles of Fashion Sketching. 24

Kneese, Allen V., The Economics of Water Utilization in the Beet Sugar Industry. 75

Kneitel, Thomas S., Amateur Radio Incentive Licensing Study Guide. 156; 103 Simple Transistor Projects. 159

Knight, Douglas M., Libraries at Large. 91

Knight, Fred B., Principles of Forest Entomology. 87

Knight, Gilfred N., Training in Indexing. 91

Knight, Hattie M., The 1-2-3 Guide to Libraries. 91

Knights, Charles C., The Technique of Salesmanship. 59

Knigin, Michael, The Technique of Fine Art Lithography. 14

Knirk, Frederick G., Instructional Technology. 111

Knoedler, Evelyn L., Manual for the Nurse's Aide. 194

Knox, Ann, The Sauce of Life. 33

Knox, Frank M., Knox Standard Guide to Design and Control of Business Forms. 45

Knudten, Richard D., Crime in a Complex Society. 98

Knuth, Donald, The Art of Computer Programming. 20

Knuti, Leo L., Profitable Soil Management. 75

Kobayashi, Akira, Machining of Plastics. 165

Koch, Harry W., Fireman Entrance Examinations. 85; Police and Police Type Entrance Examinations. 98

Koch, Paul A., Microscopic and Chemical Testing of Textiles. 29

Koebele, Apollonia M., Reference Manual for Office Personnel. 68

Koehler, Vera J., Programmed Mathematics of Drugs and Solutions. 207

Koenig, Herman E., Electromechanical System Theory. 155

Koenigsberger, F., Welding Technology. 171

Koerner, James D., The Miseducation of American Teachers. 111

Koga, Robert K., ...Police Baton Techniques. 98

Koger, M., Crossbreeding Beef Cattle. 78

Kogos, Frederick, Designing and Drafting Shirts for Men and Boys. 24

Kohl, Herbert R., The Open Classroom. 111

Kohler, Eric L., A Dictionary for Accountants. 3; Accounting for Management. 3

Köhler, Karl, A History of Costume. 27

Kohn, Harold, Synopsis of the Legal Aspects of Contact Lens Practice for Optometrists. 198

Kohs, Samuel C., The Roots of Social Work. 105

Kolb, William L., A Dictionary of the Social Sciences. 105

Kolk, W. Richard, Modern Flight Dynamics. 117

Kollat, David T., Cases in Consumer Behavior. 57

Koller, Marvin R., Sociology of Childhood. 82

Kollmann, Franz F. P., Principles of Wood Science and Technology. 87

Kolodny, Rosalie, Fashion Design for Moderns. 24

Kolstad, C. Kenneth, Rapid Electrical Estimating and Pricing. 149

Kolthoff, I. M., Quantitative Chemical Analysis. 132

Kondic, Voya, Metallurgical Principles of Founding. 169

Konopka, Gisela, Group Work in the Institution. 105; Social Group Work. 105

Konrad, Evelyn, Computer Innovations in Marketing. 59

Koplitz, Eugene D., Guidance in the Elementary School. 111

259

INDEX

Kopp, Ernestine, Designing Apparel Through the Flat Pattern. 24; How to Draft Basic Patterns. 24

Koppányi, Theodore, Experimental Pharmacodyamics. 201

Kopulos, Stella, Adventures in Greek Cookery. 39

Kopycinski, Joseph V., Textile Industry. 29

Koral, Richard L., Handbook of Air Conditioning, Heating and Ventilating. 121

Korn, Ellen J., Investigations Into Biology. 185

Korn, Granino A., Digital Computer User's Handbook. 18

Korn, Robert W., Investigations Into Biology. 185

Korn, S. Winton, Accounting for Management Planning and Decision Making. 3

Kornbluh, Joyce L., Poverty in America. 104

Korneff, Theodore, Introduction to Electronics. 149

Kornerup, Andreas, Reinhold Color Atlas. 13

Kornfeld, Albert, The Doubleday Book of Interior Decorating. 55

Kornfeld, Max, Mouth Rehabilitation. 174

Kornreich, E., Introduction to Fibres and Fabrics. 29

Körösy, Francis D., An Approach to Chemistry. 129

Korpi, Milton L., Profitable Soil Management. 75

Kosa, John, Poverty and Health. 105

Kosar, Jaromir, Light-Sensitive Systems. 49

Kosloff, Albert, The Art and Craft of Screen Process Printing. 45; Photographic Screen Process Printing. 45

Kosow, Irving L., Electric Machinery and Control. 149

Kosower, Edward M., An Introduction to Physical Organic Chemistry. 134

Koster, John C., A Complete Insurance Guide for Contractors. 139

Kostur, Stanley, Automotive Servicing. 123

Kosy, Eugene, Office Machines. 67

Kotas, Richard, An Approach to Food Costing. 33

Kotschevar, Lendal H., Food Service Planning. 33; How to Select and Care For Serviceware, Textiles, Cleaning Compounds. 51; Quantity Food Purchasing. 33; Standards, Principles and Techniques. 33; Understanding Cooking. 34; Understanding Food. 33

Kovel, Ralph M., Know Your Antiques. 55

Kovel, Terry H., Know Your Antiques. 55

Koziara, Edward S., The Negro in the Hotel Industry. 51

Koziara, Karen S., The Negro in the Hotel Industry. 51

Kozier, Barbara B., Fundamentals of Patient Care. 191

Kozloff, Eugene N., The Essentials of Practical Microtechniques. 182

Kozlowski, Theodore T., Physiology of Trees. 87

Kozol, Jonathan, Death at an Early Age. 111

Kracum, Vincent D., Inhalation Therapy Examination Review Book. 181

Kraemer, James E., Your Future in Pharmacy. 202

Kramer, Amihud, Fundamentals of Quality Control for the Food Industry. 33

Kramer, Paul J., Physiology of Trees. 87; Plant and Soil Water Relationships. 75

Kramer, Ralph M., Participation of the Poor. 105

Krantz, John C., The Pharmacologic Principles of Medical Practice. 202

Kranz, Nancy, The Sauce Cook Book. 33

Kranz, Peter, The Sauce Cook Book. 33

Kranzusch, Ray F., Metalwork Essentials. 163

Krar, Stephen F., Machine Shop Training. 161; Technology of Machine Tools. 165

Kratovil, Robert, Real Estate Law. 65

Krauch, Helmut, Organic Name Reactions. 134

Kraus, Allan D., Cooling Electronic Equipment. 149

Kraus, Barbara, The Cookbook of the United Nations. 39

Kraus, Richard, Recreation Today. 103

Krause, Marie V., Food, Nutrition, and Diet Therapy. 40

Krause, Ruthetta, Typing Mailable Letters. 68

Krauss, Leonard I., Administering and Controlling the Company Data Processing Function. 16

Kravitz, George, Basic TV Course. 158

Krebs, Alfred H., Agriculture in Our Lives. 75; A Study Guide for Placement Employment Programs in Agricultural Business and Industry. 75

Krebs, Heinz, Fundamentals of Inorganic Crystal Chemistry. 133

Kreer, G. Bowman, Advertising Copywriting. 6

Kreig, Margaret B., Black Market Medicine. 202

Kreis, Bernadine, Up From Grief. 94

Kreith, Frank, Principles of Heat Transfer. 165

Kremers, Edward, History of Pharmacy. 202

Kresser, Theodore O. J., Polyolefin Plastics. 167

Kressmann, Edouard, The Wonder of Wine. 38

Krevitsky, Nik, Stitchery Art and Craft. 24

Krey, Isabelle A., Effective Writing for Business. 68

Kriegel, Julia, The Head Nurse. 191

Krieger, Moshe, Basic Switching Circuit Theory. 149

Krieger, Murray, Decision-Making in Retailing and Marketing. 63

Krieger, Wilber M., A Complete Guide to Funeral Service Management. 94

Kriesberg, Louis, Mothers in Poverty. 105

Kristy, Jean, Brain and Nerves of the Human Body. 209

Kroeger, Arthur, Advertising Principles and Problems. 6; Readings in Marketing. 58

Krohn, Margaret B., How to Sew. 25

Kron, Thora, Communication in Nursing. 191; Nursing Team Leadership. 191

Kronenberg, Shirley, Cold Type Composition, Equipment and Technique. 45

Kronquist, Emil, Mechanical Drawing. 144

Kropotkin, Alexandra, The Best of Russian Cooking. 39

Krueger, Elizabeth A., The Hypodermic Injection. 191

Krug, Elsie E., Pharmacology in Nursing. 188

Kruzas, Anthony T., Directory of Special Libraries and Information Centers. 91

Kubala, Thomas S., Experiments in Alternating Current Circuits. 152

Kubler-Ross, Elisabeth, On Death & Dying. 94

Kuh, Ernest S., Basic Circuit Theory. 147

Kuhler, Barbara L., Quality Control for the Graphic Arts. 45

Kuhler, Charles D., Quality Control for the Graphic Arts. 45; Statistical Quality Control for the Printing Industry. 45

Kuhn, Charles L., The Police Officer's Memorandum Book. 98

Kuhn, Doris Y., Children's Literature in the Elementary School. 111

Kuhn, W. H., Refinishing Furniture. 161

Kujoth, Jean S., Libraries, Readers and Book Selection. 91; Reading Interests of Children and Young Adults. 91; Subject Guide to Periodical Indexes and Review Indexes. 91

Kulis, Fred R., Alternating Current. 145; Direct Current. 145

Kuller, K. Karl, Electronics Drafting. 144

Kulp, Clarence A., Casualty Insurance. 53

Kunick, Philip, Sizing, Pattern Construction and Grading for Women's and Children's Garments. 24

Kuns, Ray F., Automotive Essentials. 124

Kunz, Werner, Organic Name Reactions. 134

Kurrein, Max, Plasticity of Metals. 169

Kursh, Harry, The Franchise Boom. 62

Kurth, William H., Moving a Library. 91

Kurtz, Edwin B., The Lineman's and Cableman's Handbook. 138

Kurtz, Frederick C., Introduction to Financial and Managerial Accounting. 3

Kurtz, Margaret, The Technical Secretary. 72; Technical Typewriting. 68

Kurtz, Max, Comprehensive Structural Design Guide. 138

Kurz, Albert L., Beyond Discouragement. 94

Kut, David, Heating and Hot Water Services in Buildings. 121

Kutscher, Austin H., But Not to Lose. 94; Death and Bereavement. 94; Pharmacology for the Dental Hygienist. 174

Kutz, Myer, Temperature Control. 121

Kybalova, Ludmila, The Pictorial Encyclopedia of Fashion. 24

Kyle, James, Servicing Digital Devices. 149

Laban, Rudolf, Modern Educational Dance. 103

Labarthe, Jules, Textiles. 29

La Berge, Armand J., General Shop Woodworking. 161

Lach, Alma, Cooking à la Cordon Bleu. 33

Lachman, Leon, The Theory and Practice of Industrial Pharmacy. 202

Lachmann, Alfred, Snacks and Fried Products, 1969. 41

Lachnitt, Jacques, Aerodynamics. 117

LaCour, Marshall, Photo Technology. 49

LaFave, Wayne R., Arrest. 99

Lafever, Minard, The Modern Builder's Guide. 138

Lager, Mildred, The Soybean Cookbook. 33

Lagowski, Joseph J., The Chemical Bond. 129

Laidler, Keith J., Theories of Chemical Reaction Rates. 129

Laird, Eleanor S., Engineering Secretary's Complete Handbook. 72

Laitinen, Herbert A., Chemical Analysis. 132

Lake, Carlton, Dictionary of Modern Painting. 10

Laker, Russell, Anatomy of Lettering. 14

Laliberte, Norman, Drawing with Ink. 10

LaLonde, Bernard J., Physical Distribution Management. 57

Lamarova, Milena, The Pictorial Encyclopedia of Fashion. 24

Lamb, H. Richard, Handbook of Community Mental Health Practice. 208

Lamb, Lynton, Drawing for Illustration. 10

Lamb, Marion M., Your First Year of Teaching Shorthand and Transcription. 68

Lamb, Venice, The Home Book of Turkish Cookery. 39

Lambert, Frederick, Graphic Design Britain. 11; Letter Forms. 14

Lamela, Alberto, Handbook of Laboratory Methods for Medical Aides. 182; Handbook of Medical and Anatomical Terminology. 71

Lamere, Bernard, Guide to Home Air Conditioners and Refrigeration Equipment. 121

Lamers, William M., Funeral Customs the World Over. 93; History of American Funeral Directing. 93

Lamm, Maurice, The Jewish Way in Death and Mourning. 94

Lammer, Jutta, Make Your Own Costume Jewelry. 27; Print Your Own Fabrics. 24

Lamont, Corliss, The Illusion of Immortality. 94

Lancashire, J. B., Knitted Fabric Primer. 25

Lancaster, F. W., Information Retrieval Systems. 16

Lancaster, John E., The Metallurgy of Welding, Brazing and Soldering. 171

Lance, Algie L., Introduction to Microwave Theory and Measurements. 150; Microwave Experiments. 150

Landau, Ralph, The Chemical Plant from Process Selection to Commercial Operation. 129

Landis, Judson R., Current Perspectives on Social Problems. 105

Landreth, Catherine, Early Childhood. 81

Landry, Robert, The Gentle Art of Flavoring. 33

Landsberg, Hans H., America's Changing Environment. 179

Landy, Dick, Basic Chassis, Suspension & Brakes. 124

Lane, Leonard C., Elementary Industrial Electronics. 150; How to Fix Transistor Radios and Printed Circuits. 159

Laney, William R., Partial Dentures. 176

Lang, Rosalind, Charm. 8, 70

Lang, V. Paul, Principles of Air Conditioning. 121

Langenbach, Robert G., Introduction to Automated Data Processing. 16

Langford, Beryl, Stopping Vehicles and Occupant Control. 99

Langford, Cooper H., The Development of Chemical Principles. 129

Langford, Michael, Basic Photography. 49

Langhaar, Henry L., Energy Methods in Applied Mechanics. 165

Langley, Leroy L., Dynamic Anatomy and Physiology. 184; Homeostasis. 182; Physiology of Man. 184

Langseth-Christensen, Lillian, The Complete Kitchen Guide. 33

Lansford, Edwin M., The Encyclopedia of Biochemistry. 133

Lappin, Alvin R., Plastics Projects and Techniques. 161

Laque, Francis L., Corrosion Resistance of Metals and Alloys. 169

Larew, Walter B., Automatic Transmissions. 124; Carburetors and Carburetion. 124; Ignition Systems. 124

Larimer, James, Introduction to Animal Physiology. 184

Larken, Henry W., Compositor's Work in Printing. 45

Larkman, Brian, Metalwork Designs of Today. 162

Larmore, Lewis, Introduction to Photographic Principles. 49

Larrick, Nancy, Printing and Promotion Handbook. 45

Larsen, E. J., Principles of Auditing. 5

Larsen, Hans W., Atlas of the Fundus of the Eye. 199

Larsen, Louis M., Industrial Printing Inks. 48

Larson, Carroll B., Calderwood's Orthopedic Nursing. 195

Larson, Kenneth H., Direct Care Nursing. 196; Interacting with Patients. 190

Larson, Thomas D., Portland Cement and Asphalt Concretes. 141

Lascoe, Orville D., Machine Shop Operations and Setups. 166

Laskin, Daniel M., Management of Oral Emergencies. 174

Laskow, Robert, Bright Future Careers with Computers. 18

Lasky, Joseph, Proofreading and Copy-Preparation. 45

Lasser, Jacob K., Handbook of Accounting Methods. 3

Latchaw, Majorie, A Pocket Guide of Movement Activities for the Elementary School. 111

Latchem, W. E., Handbook of Laboratory Solutions. 127

Latham, Charles W., Advanced Pressmanship. 45; Photo Composing. 45

Latham, Donald C., Transistors and Integrated Circuits. 159

Latham, Helen C., Pediatric Nursing. 195

INDEX

Latham, J. L., Physics for Chemists and Biologists. 128

Lathrop, Irving T., General Industry. 162; Photo Technology. 49

Latimer, Henry C., Advertising Production Planning and Copy Preparation for Offset Printing. 6

Latiolais, Clifton, Clinical Pharmacy. 201

Lattig, Herbert E., Selecting, Fitting and Showing Beef Cattle. 79; Selecting, Fitting and Showing Dairy Cattle. 79; Selecting, Fitting and Showing Horses. 79; Selecting, Fitting and Showing Poultry. 79; Selecting, Fitting and Showing Sheep. 79; Selecting, Fitting and Showing Swine. 79

Lattin, Gerald W., Careers in Hotels and Restaurants. 51; Modern Hotel and Motel Management. 51

Latzke, Alpha, The Wide World of Clothing. 24

Laub, Julian M., Air Conditioning and Heating Practice. 121

Lauer, A. R., The Psychology of Driving. 99

Lauer, Henri, Servomechanism Fundamentals. 165

Laughlin, Herman G., Machine Design. 167

Laughton, Roy, TV Graphics. 11

Laurence, Desmond R., Clinical Pharmacology. 202; Evaluation of Drug Activities. 202

Lauria, Marie, How to be a Good Secretary. 68

Laurie, Edward J., Computers and Computer Languages. 18; Computers and How They Work. 18

Laursen, Harold I., Structural Analysis. 138

Laury, Jean R., Applique Stitchery. 24

Laver, James, The Concise History of Costume and Fashion. 27; Costume. 27; Costume in Antiquity. 27; Costume in the Theatre. 27; Costume Through the Ages. 27; Modesty in Dress. 24; Women's Dress in the Jazz Age. 27

Lawlor, John, How to Talk Car. 124

Lawrence, Carl A., Disinfection, Sterilization & Preservation. 182

Lawrence, John R., Polyester Resins. 167

Lawrence, Nelda R., Secretary's Business Review. 68

Lawrence, Paul, How to Read Electronic Circuit Diagrams. 146; How to Repair Solid-State Imports. 150

Lawrie, Ralston A., Meat Science. 33

Lawrie, Robert S., Handlist of Basic Reference Material for Librarians and Information Officers in Electrical and Electronic Engineering. 89

Lawson, Alexander S., A Printer's Almanac. 45

Lawson, L. E., Offset Lithography. 14

Lawton, M. Murray, A Textbook for Medical Assistants. 71

Layman, Lloyd, Attacking and Extinguishing Interior Fires. 85

Layton, Thomas A., The Wine and Food Society's Guide to Cheese and Cheese Cookery. 33

Lazarfield, Paul E., The Uses of Sociology. 105

Lazo, Hector, Management in Marketing. 59; Marketing. 59

Lazzari, Eugene P., Dental Biochemistry. 174

Leabeater, Bruce, Psychiatric Nursing. 196

Leach, Bernard H., A Potter's Book. 162

Leach, Donald P., Basic Electric Circuits. 150; Digital Principles and Applications. 150; Transistor Circuit Measurements. 159

Leach, Mortimer, Letter Design in the Graphic Arts. 14

Leach, Royal B., Chemistry. 129

Leahy, Daniel J., Programmed Physics. 199

Leahy, Emmett J., Modern Records Management. 68

Leahy, Kathleen M., Fundamentals of Public Health Nursing. 196

Leake, Mary J., A Manual of Simple Nursing Procedures. 191

Leaman, Arthur, Decorations U.S.A. 13

Lear, Erwin, Chemistry and Applied Pharmacology of Tranquilizers. 202

Leaver, K. D., Materials Science. 167

Lebensohn, James E., An Anthology of Ophthalmic Classics. 199

Lebhar, Godfrey M., Chain Stores in America. 63

Lebovici, S., Child Guidance Centres. 80

Lebowitz, R. B., Accounting Simplified. 3

Lecht, Charles P., The Programmer's Algol. 20; The Programmer's Fortran II and IV. 20; The Programmer's PL/1. 20

Lechtman, Max D., Microbiology for Nurses. 193

Ledbetter, Joe O., Principles of Radiological Health. 204

Ledley, Robert S., Fortran IV Programming. 20

Lee, Dorothy E., Secretarial Practice for College. 68

Lee, Dorris M., Learning to Read Through Experience. 111

Lee, Eleanor, Lippincott's Quick Reference Book for Nurses. 194

Lee, Garth L., Elementary Organic Chemistry. 135; Principles of Chemistry. 129

Lee, H. I., Practical Secretarial Work. 68

Lee, Henry, Handbook of Epoxy Resins. 129

Lee, Jimmy, Soul Food Cookbook. 39

Lee, John D., Concise Inorganic Chemistry. 133

Lee, John H., Dental Aesthetics. 174

Lee, Leslie W., Elementary Principles of Laboratory Instruments. 182

Lee, Low K., Electronic Equipment Design and Construction. 147

Lee, Marshall, Bookmaking. 45

Lee, P. William, Ceramics. 162

Lee, R. M., A Short Course in Fortran IV Programming. 20

Lee, Ruth M., Workbook for Nursing in Emotional and Physical Problems. 196

Lee, W. H., The Electronics of Laboratory and Process Instruments. 148

Leech, Milton, The Chicken Cookbook. 33

Leeds, Herbert D., Computer Programming Fundamentals. 20; Computer Programming Fundamentals. 20

Leedy, Jack J., Poetry Therapy: The Use of Poetry in the Treatment of Emotional Disorders. 209

Leeper, Sarah H., Good Schools for Young Children. 111

Lees, Brian, The Medical Background for Successful Drug Detailing. 202

Lees, R., Laboratory Handbook of Methods of Food Analysis. 129

Leeson, C. Roland, Histology. 186

Leeson, Daniel N., Basic Programming Concepts and the IBM 1620 Computer. 20

Leeson, Thomas S., Histology. 186

Lefebvre, A. H., Progress in Combustion Science and Technology. 116

Lefkoe, M. R., The Crisis in Construction. 138

Lefler, Janet, Canapes, Hors d'oeuvres and Buffet Dishes. 33; The Correct Cashier for Hotels and Restaurants. 51

Le Grand, Yves, Form and Space Vision. 199; Light, Colour and Vision. 199

Lehigh University Civil Engineering Department, Structural Steel Design. 138

Lehmann-Haupt, Hellmut, Bookbinding in America. 47; Gutenberg and the Master of the Playing Cards. 45

Lehner, Ernst, Alphabets and Ornaments. 11

Lehozky, Aurelia R., History and Modern Nursing. 189

Leidy, W. Philip. A Popular Guide to Government Publications. 91

Leifer, Gloria, Principles and Techniques in Pediatric Nursing. 195

Leighbody, Gerald B., Methods of Teaching Shop and Technical Subjects. 162

Leighton, David S., International Marketing. 62

Leighton, Frances S., Sew Simply, Sew Right. 25

Leighton, Philip A., Photochemistry of Air Pollution. 178

INDEX

Leininger, Madeleine M., Basic Psychiatric Concepts in Nursing. 190

Leinwand, Gerald, Air and Water Pollution. 178

Leinwoll, Stanley, Understanding Lasers and Masers. 155

Leithe, W., The Analysis of Air Pollutants. 178

LeMaitre, George D., The Patient in Surgery. 197

Lembo, Diana, Introducing Books. 110

Lemons, Wayne, How to Repair Home and Auto Air Conditioners. 121; Learn Electronics Through Trouble-Shooting. 150; Small Appliance Repair Guide. 150

Lenahan, Marie, Related Art for Dress Design. 24

Lenert, Louis H., Semiconductor Physics, Devices, and Circuits. 150

Lenk, John D., Applications Handbook for Electrical Connectors. 150; Data Book for Electronic Technicians and Engineers. 150; Handbook of Electronic Charts, Graphs and Tables. 150; Handbook of Electronic Meters. 150; Handbook of Oscilloscopes Theory and Application. 150; Handbook of Practical Electronic Tests and Measurements. 150; How to Use Signal Generators in Color TV Servicing. 158; How to Use Signal Generators in the Laboratory. 150; How to Use Signal Generators in Radio/TV/HI-FI Servicing. 157; Practical Semiconductor Databook for Electronic Engineers and Technicians. 150; Understanding Telemetry Circuits. 150; Understanding UHF Equipment. 150

Lennard, Henry L., Patterns in Human Interaction. 105

Lennox, Margaret, Hotel Housekeeping. 51

Lenski, Gerhard E., Human Societies. 105

Lentilhon, Robert W., Principles of Accounting. 1

Lenz, Bernie, The Complete Book of Fashion Modeling. 24

Lenz, Robert R., Explosives and Bomb Disposal Guide. 99

Leonard, Calista V., Understanding and Preventing Suicide. 99

Leonard, Jonathan N., Latin American Cooking. 39

Leonard, Robert C., Behavioral Science, Social Practice, and the Nursing Profession. 193; Social Interaction and Patient Care. 193

Leonard, Robert M., Pharmacology Study Handbook. 202

Leonard, Vivian A., The General Administration of Criminal Justice. 99; The Police Communications Systems. 99; Police Detective Function. 99; The Police Enterprise. 99; The Police, the Judiciary and the Criminal. 99; Police Organization and Management. 99; Police Patrol Organization. 99; Police Personnel Administration. 99; The Police Records System. 99; The Police of the 20th Century. 99

Leonard, Warren H., Cereal Crops. 75; Principles of Field Crop Production. 75

Leondes, Cornelius T., Computer Control Systems Technology. 18

Leone, Gene, Leone's Italian Cookbook. 39

Lepp, Ignace, Death and Its Mysteries. 94

Lerch, Constance, Maternity Nursing. 195

Lerman, Sidney, Basic Ophthalmology. 199

Lescarbeau, Roland F., A Suggested Curriculum Guide for Electro-Mechanical Technology. 155

Lesch, Alma, Vegetable Dyeing. 24

Le Shan, Eda J., The Conspiracy Against Childhood. 81

Leslie, Gerald R., The Sociology of Social Problems. 105

Leslie, Louis A., Gregg Shorthand for Colleges. 68; Gregg Shorthand Dictionary. 68; Gregg Shorthand Manual. 68; Gregg Speed Building. 68; Gregg Transcription. 68; Handbook for the Legal Secretary. 71; 20,000 Words. 68

Leslie, W. H. P., Numerical Control Users' Handbook. 170

Lesnik, Milton J., Nursing Practice and the Law. 191

Lessenberry, David D., College Typewriting: Basic Course. 68; 20th Century Typewriting. 68

Lessing, Lawrence P., DNA. 182

Lester, Katherine M., Historic Costume. 27

Lesure, John D., Hotel Accounting. 51; Planning and Operating Motels and Motor Hotels. 52

Leukemia Society, Closing In. 182

Levarie, Norma, The Art and History of Books. 45

Levens, Alexander S., Graphics. 143; Graphics: Analysis and Conceptual Design. 143; Problems in Engineering Graphics. 143; Problems in Mechanical Drawing: First Course. 144; Problems in Mechanical Drawing: Second Course. 144

Levi, S. M., Making and Coating Photographic Emulsions. 50

Levie, Albert, The Meat Handbook. 33

Levin, Evelyn R., Let's Decorate Your Home. 55

Levin, Herman, Introduction to Computer Analysis. 18

Levin, Phyllis L., The Wheels of Fashion. 24

Levine, Adeline, A Social History of Helping Services. 105

Levine, Eugene, Better Patient Care Through Nursing Research. 187

Levine, Murray, A Social History of Helping Services. 105

Levine, Myra H., Introduction to Clinical Nursing. 191

Levine, Nathan, Typing for Everyone. 68

Levine, Samuel, Vocational and Technical Mathematics in Action. 206

Levine, Sol, Your Future in NASA. 117

Levinson, Irving, Introduction to Mechanics. 165; Mechanics of Materials. 165

Levinson, Leonard L., The Complete Book of Pickles and Relishes. 33

Levison, Henry, Textbook for Dental Nurses. 174

Levitan, Eli L., Animation Art in the Commercial Film. 11

Levitan, Sar A., Programs in Aid of the Poor for the 1970's. 105

Levitt, Theodore, Innovation in Marketing. 59; Marketing Mode. 59

Levy, Alex, Elements of Radio Servicing. 157; Practical Radio Servicing. 157

Levy, Barnett M., A Textbook of Oral Pathology. 175

Levy, Joseph, Punched Card Data Processing. 16; Punched Card Equipment. 16

Levy, Leon, Basic Retailing. 63; Essentials of Merchandise Information. 59

Levy, Michael H., A Handbook of Personal Insurance Terminology. 53

Levy, Saul, Dentist's Handbook of Office and Hospital Procedure. 175

Lewicki, Bohda, Building with Large Prefabricates. 138

Lewin, Gerhard S., Fundamentals of Vacuum Science and Technology. 150

Lewin, Stephen, Crime and Its Prevention. 99

Lewis, Alfred, Clean the Air. 178

Lewis, Alvin E., Principles of Hematology. 186

Lewis, Clive S., A Grief Observed. 94

Lewis, Edwin H., Marketing Channels. 59

Lewis, Garland K., An Approach to the Education of Psychiatric Nursing Personnel. 196; Nurse-Patient Communication. 191

Lewis, Howard R., With Every Breath You Take. 178

Lewis, Jack, Modern Coordination Chemistry. 129

Lewis, Jack N., The Pesticide Problem: An Economic Approach to Public Policy. 178

Lewis, John N. C., The Anatomy of Printing. 45; Reproducing Art. 45; The Twentieth Century Book. 45; Typography. 45

Lewis, Leon, Rehabilitation. 194

Lewis, Mary K., Acting for Children. 81

Lewis, Richard B., A-V Instruction. 109

INDEX

Lewis, Shari, The Headstart Book of Be Nimble and Be Quick. 82

Lewis, Shirley, Non-Book Materials. 91

Lewis, Thomas, Science of Materials. 167

Lewis, Walter H., Construction Lending Guide. 139

Lewison, Lawrence, You and Your Eyes. 199

Li, David H., Accounting, Computers. 3; Cost Accounting for Management Applications. 5

Libby, C. E., Pulp and Paper Science and Technology. 48

Libby, Charles C., Motor Selection and Application. 156

Libby, James R., Prestressed Concrete. 141

Libes, S., Repairing Transistor Radios. 159

Library Technicians: A New Kind of Needed Worker. 91

Lichine, Alfred M., Wines of France. 38

Licklider, J. C. R., Libraries of the Future. 91

Liddle, George P., Education Improvement for the Disadvantaged Elementary Setting. 111

Lidstone, John, Creative Movement for Children. 113

Lie, Sek-Hiang, Indonesian Cookery. 39

Lieberman, Herbert A., The Theory and Practice of Industrial Pharmacy. 202

Lieberman, J. Ben, Types of Typefaces and How to Recognize Them. 45

Life Office Management Association, Fundamentals of Expense Budgeting in a Life Insurance Company. 54

Liff, A. A., Frequency Modulation Receivers. 156

Lifton, Marks, Syllabus and Teaching Suggestions for a Course in Secretarial Practice. 68

Lifton, Walter M., Working with Groups. 105

Light, Luise, In Praise of Vegetables. 33

Lightband, D. A., Direct Current Traction Motor. 124

Ligomenides, Panos A., Information-Processing Machines. 16

Liles, Parker, Typing Mailable Letters. 68

Liljestrand, G., Readings in Pharmacology. 201

Lillie, R. D., Conn's Biological Stains. 182

Lillow, Ira, Introducing Machine Embroidery. 24

Lima, Robert F., Arco Motor Vehicle Dictionary. 124

Lin, Hsiang Ju, Chinese Gastronomy. 39

Lin, T. Y., Design of Prestressed Concrete Structures. 141

Lincoln Electric Company, How To Read Shop Drawings. 143

Lincoln, Marshall, Electronics for Photographers. 49

Lindbeck, John, Design Textbook. 167

Lindbeck, John R., Basic Crafts. 162; General Industry. 162; Metalwork. 161

Linden, Ronald, Books and Libraries. 91

Lindmayer, Joseph, Fundamentals of Semi-Conductor Devices. 150

Lindsey, Forrest R., Pipefitter's Handbook. 138

Lineberry, William P., New Trends in the Schools. 111

Lingeman, Richard R., Drugs from A to Z. 202

Link, Fred M., Portable FM Radiotelephones. 150

Linman, James W., Principles of Hematology. 186

Linnartz, Norwin E., The Ecology of Southern Forests. 87

Linné, Jean J., Basic Techniques for the Medical Laboratory Technician. 182

Linnert, G. E., Welding Metallurgy. 171

Linsley, Horace E., Broaching, Tooling and Practice. 165

Linstromberg, Walter W., Organic Chemistry. 134

Linton, Andrew F., Introduction to Mechanized Accounts and Computers. 3

Linton, George E., Applied Basic Textiles. 29; Applied Textiles. 29; The Modern Textile Dictionary. 29; Natural and Manmade Textile Fibers. 29

Linton, Ron M., Terracide. 178

Lionberger, Herbert F., Farm Information for Modernizing Agriculture. 75

Lipkin, Gladys B., Simplified Nursing. 190

Lipowsky, Benjamin, A Picture Dictionary and Guide to Building and Construction Terms. 138

Lippin, Gerard, Circuit Problems and Solutions. 150

Lippman, Hyman S., Treatment of the Child in Emotional Conflict. 82

Lippman, Richard W., Urine and the Urinary Sediment. 182

Lippold, Olof, Human Respiration. 181

Lipsett, Charles H., Metals Reference and Encyclopedia. 169

Lipsey, Robert E., Source Book of Statistics Relating to Construction. 138

Lipsey, Sally I., Mathematics for Nursing Science. 206

Lipson, Charles, Handbook of Mechanical Wear. 165

Lipson, H., Optical Physics. 199

Lipson, Stephen G., Optical Physics. 199

Lipton, Rose C., Infants in Institutions. 82

Lisack, J. P., A Manpower Report Concerning Occupations. 138

Lister, Eugene C., Electric Circuits and Machines. 150

Lister, Margot, Costume. 27

Litchfield, John H., Food Plant Sanitation. 34

Lithographic Dampening Conference, Papers. 14

Littauer, Raphael, Pulse Electronics. 150

Little, Angela, Color of Foods. 34

Little, Billie, Recipes for Allergies. 33

Little, Dolores, Nursing Care Planning. 191

Little, Hugh, Volunteer Fire Training Manual. 85

Littlefield, James E., Advertising. 6

Littleton, Ananias C., Essays on Accountancy. 3

Littlewood, Anthony B., Gas Chromatography. 129

Littrell, Joseph J., Guide to Industrial Arts Teaching. 162

Littwin, Sheldon, Pulse Generators in Industrial Electronics. 150

Litzel, Otto, Darkroom Magic. 49

Litzinger, John C., Know Your Mortician. 94

Liwschitz-Garik, Michael, Alternating-Current Machines. 150

Lloyd, Alan C., Gregg Typewriting for Colleges. 68

Lloyd, E. D., Transfer and Unit Machines. 165

Lloyd, Tom C., Electric Motors and Their Applications. 156

Lloyd, William B., Millwork-Principles and Practices. 165

Lobb, M. Delbert, Practical Aspects of Team Teaching. 111

Lobstein, Robert, Guide to Chemical Plant Planning. 129

Lock, Arthur, Practical Canning. 41

Lockard, William K., Drawing As a Means to Architecture. 144

Locke, Flora M., Office Calculating and Adding Machines. 68

Lockerby, Florence K., Communication for Nurses. 191

Lockhart, J. A. R., Introduction to Crop Husbandry. 75

Lockhart, Robert D., Anatomy of the Human Body. 184

Locklear, Edmond, Jr., Your Future in Accounting. 3

Lockley, Lawrence C., Cases in Marketing. 59; Readings in Marketing. 58

Lockwood, Arthur, Diagrams: . . . for the Graphic Designer. 11

Lockwood, Gillian, Making Clothes for Young Children. 24

Lockwood's Directory of the Paper and Allied Trades, Lockwood's Trade Journal. 48

INDEX

Lockyer, Herbert, The Funeral Sourcebook. 94

L'Oeil, The Best in European Decoration. 55

Löf, George O., The Economics of Water Utilization in the Beet Sugar Industry. 75

Logan, Marie C. D., Introduction to Laboratory Chemistry. 125

Logan, William B., Facts About Merchandise. 63

Loizeaux, Marie D., Publicity Primer. 91

London, Anne, Cocktails & Snacks. 32

London, Herbert, Education in the Twenty-First Century. 111

London, Peter S., Principles for First Aid for the Injured. 208

Long, Harriet G., Public Library Service to Children. 91

Long, James D., Modern Electronic Circuit Design. 150

Long, John D., Property and Liability Insurance Handbook. 53

Long, Robert P., Castle-Hotels of Europe. 52; Package Printing. 45

Long, Ted, Hair Styles for the Black Woman. 8

Long, William E., Experiments for the Electric Circuits Laboratory. 150

Longenecker, Justin G., Small Business Management. 63

Longgood, William F., The Poisons in Your Food. 33

Longhurst, Richard S., Geometrical and Physical Optics. 199

Longmore, Thomas A., Medical Photography. 204

Longrée, Karla, Quantity Food Sanitation. 33

Longstreet, Stephen, A Treasury of the World's Great Prints. 11

Longyear, William, Advertising Layout. 6; Type and Lettering. 14

Lontoft, Ruth G., Illustrators of Children's Books, 1957-1966. 10

Loomis, Ted A., Essentials of Toxicology. 202

Loosli, John K., Animal Nutrition. 79

Lootens, Joseph G., Lootens on Photographic Enlarging and Print Quality. 49

Loper, Carl R., Principles of Metal Casting. 169

Loper, Orla E., Direct Current Fundamentals. 150; Introduction to Electricity and Electronics. 150

Lorbeer, George C., Science Activities for Elementary Children. 112

Los Angeles County Sheriff's Office, Project Sky Knight. 99

Loschetter, Richard F., Fundamentals of Machine Language and Autocoder Programming. 20

Loth, David, Crime in the Suburbs. 99

Lothers, John E., Advanced Design in Structural Steel. 138

Lotkowski, Wlaydslaw M., The Soil. 75

Lott, Richard W., Basic Data Processing. 16

Louise, Sister Mary, The Operating Room Technician. 209

Louisell, David W., Principles of Evidence and Proof. 99

Louisiana State Department of Education, Vocational Education Division, A Training Program for Vocational Agriculture in Dairy Production. 79

Lourie, Reginald S., Early Child Care. 80

Lovell, Michael C., Sales Anticipations and Inventory Behavior. 59

Lovoos, Janice, Making Pottery Without a Wheel. 160

Low, Eirene, English Cooking in Four Languages. 39

Lowell, Vernon W., Airline Safety is a Myth. 117

Lowenberg, Miriam E., Food and Man. 33

Lowenthal, Werner, Pharmaceutical Calculations. 202

Lowndes, Douglas, Marketing. 59

Lowrey, George H., Growth and Development of Children. 83

Lowrie, Jean E., Elementary School Libraries. 91

Lowry, Bates, The Visual Experience. 11

Lowry, Thomas P., Hyperventilation and Hysteria. 181

Lowther, Harold, Organic Chemistry. 134

Lowy, George, A Searcher's Manual. 91

Lubell, Winifred, The Stitchery Book. 24

Lubowe, Irwin I., Cosmetics and the Skin. 8; New Hope for Your Hair. 8

Lucas, Carol, Recreation in Gerontology. 103; Recreation in Total Rehabilitation. 103; Recreational Activity Development for the Aging in Homes, Hospitals, and Nursing Homes. 103

Lucas, Catherine, Occupational Costume in England. 27

Lucas, Darrell B., Measuring Advertising Effectiveness. 6

Lucas, Dione, The Gourmet Cooking School Cookbook. 34

Lucas, E. Louise, Art Books. 11

Luce, Marnie, Counting Systems. 111

Luckcock, Eveline D., An Introduction to Medical Laboratory Technology. 181

Luckiesh, Matthew, Visual Illusions. 199

Lucky, R. W., Principles of Data Communication. 16

Ludwig, Oswald A., Metalwork. 162

Ludwig, Richard M., Guide to American Literature and its Backgrounds Since 1890. 91

Luerssen, George V., Tool Steel Simplified. 165

Luftig, Milton, Computer Programmer. 20

Luick, John F., Sales Promotion and Modern Merchandising. 59

Luke, Dudley J., The Nature of Physical Chemistry. 135

Lull, Howard W., A Forest Atlas of the Northeast. 87

Lumsden, E. S., The Art of Etching. 11

Lumsden, K., Radiology of the Digestive System. 204

Luna, Benjamin C., Upholstery. 56

Lund, Herbert F., Industrial Pollution Control Handbook. 179

Lundberg, Donald E., The Hotel and Restaurant Business. 52; How to Operate a Restaurant. 52; The Management of People in Hotels, Restaurants, and Clubs. 52; Understanding Cooking. 34

Lundberg, Edna A., Real Estate Practice in California. 65

Lunden, Walter A., Crimes and Criminals. 99

Lundkvist, Hans, Making Ceramics. 162

Lundkvist-Husberg, Lis, Making Ceramics. 162

Luray, Howard L., Strobe. 49

Lurch, E. Norman, Electric Circuits. 150; Fundamentals of Electronics. 150

Lush, Clifford L., Industrial Arts Electricity. 162

Luskin, Bernard J., Data Processing for Decision-Making. 15

Lusted, Lee B., Atlas of Roentgenographic Measurement. 204

Lux, Donald G., The World of Construction. 138

Luxon, Lester L., Handbook: Butane-Propane Gases. 127

Luzadder, Warren J., Basic Graphics for Design, Analysis, Communications, and the Computer. 143; Basic Graphics for Engineers and Technical Students. 143; Fundamentals of Engineering Drawing. 143

Lwoff, Andre, Biological Order. 185

Lyle, Dorothy S., The Clothes We Wear. 24; Focus on Fabrics. 29

Lyles, Sanders T., Biology of Microorganisms. 187

Lynch, John, How to Make Collages. 11

Lynch, Mary, Sewing Made Easy. 24

Lynch, Matthew J., Medical Laboratory Technology and Clinical Pathology. 182

Lynn, Robert A., Marketing Principles and Market Action. 59

Lynton, Edith F., The Sub-Professional. 105

Lyon, Thoburn C., Practical Air Navigation. 117

Lyons, John W., The Chemistry and Uses of Fire. 85

Lyons, Nathan, Photographers on Photography. 49

Lyons, Neil J., Radiographic Positioning. 204

Lysaught, Jerome P., A Guide to Programmed Instruction. 111

265

INDEX

Lytel, Allan H., ABC's of Lasers and Masers. 156; Electronic Motor Control. 156; Fundamentals of Data Processing. 16; Handbook of Transistor Circuits. 159; How to Service UHF TV. 158; Industrial Electronics. 150; Industrial Transistor Circuits. 159; Transistor Circuit Manual. 159

Lytle, Nancy A., Maternal Health Nursing. 195

Ma, Po-Ch'ang (Ch'ih), Cook Chinese. 39; Mrs. Ma's Chinese Cookbook. 39

MacAllister, John J., Organizing a Food Training Program. 34

McAllister, Ronald A., Theory of Chemical Pathology Technique. 183

Macarov, David, Incentives to Work: The Effect of Unearned Income. 106

MacAvoy, Paul W., Large-Scale Desalting. 179

Macaw, Katherine D., A Mathematical Guide to Dosage and Solutions. 206

MacBryde, Cyril, Signs and Symptoms. 191

McCabe, Francis T., Mechanical Drafting Essentials. 144

McCaffery, Edward L., Laboratory Preparation for Macromolecular Chemistry. 129

McCall, Chester H., How Any Real Estate Salesman Can Turn Himself Into A Selling Giant. 65

McCall, Floyd H., Introduction to Photography. 50

McCall, John O., Principles of Periodontics. 175

McCall, Joseph R., Your Career in Parks and Recreation. 103

McCall, Virginia, Your Career in Parks and Recreation. 103

McCameron, Fritz A., Fortran IV. 20; Fortran: Logic and Programming. 20

McCance, Margaret E., Laboratory Methods in Microbiology. 187

McCandless, Boyd R., Children: Behavior and Development. 82

McCarthy, Edmund J., Basic Marketing. 60; Integrated Data Processing Systems. 16

McCarthy, Frank M., Emergencies in Dental Practice. 175

McCarthy, J., Integrated Data Processing Systems. 16

McCarthy, Willard J., Machine Tool Technology. 162; Metalwork. 162

McCartney, T. O., Precision Perspective Drawing. 143

McCaskill, William L., How to Get Through to People in Selling. 60

MacClain, Lenore F., Typewriting Techniques.... 68

McClain, Mary E., Simplified Arithmetic for Nurses. 206

McClay, David R., An Introduction to Agricultural Business and Industry. 77

McClellan, Aubrey L., The Hydrogen Bond. 130

McClellan, Grant S., Protecting Our Environment. 179

McClelland, Lucile H., Textbook for Psychiatric Technicians. 209

McClement, Fred, It Doesn't Matter Where You Sit. 117

McClenahan, John L., Radiology As an Art and Other Essays. 204

McClintock, Frank A., Mechanical Behavior of Materials. 167

McCloskey, Bertram P., Child Health: Its Origins and Promotion. 80

McClure, Frank J., Environmental Variables in Oral Disease. 173

McClure, Leslie W., Advertising in the Printed Media. 6

McCluskey, E. J., Introduction to the Theory of Switching Circuits. 151; A Survey of Switching Circuit Theory. 151

McCollum, John P., Producing Vegetable Crops. 77

McConaughy, David H., Buying Behavior and Marketing Decisions. 62

McConnell, Mary, Directory of Opportunity in Service World Management. 34

McCormac, Jack C., Structural Analysis. 138; Structural Steel Design. 138

McCoy, James, Chemical Analysis of Industrial Water. 132

McCoy, Vernon L., Farm Shop. 78

McCracken, Daniel D., A Guide to Cobol Programming. 20; A Guide to Fortran Programming. 20; A Guide to IBM 1401 Programming. 20

McCracken, William L., Partial Denture Construction. 175

McCullough, M. K., Social Work with Groups. 106

McCullough, Marshall E., Optimum Feeding of Dairy Animals. 79

McCullough, Patricia, Clinical Practice of the Dental Hygienist. 176

McCully, Helen, Just Desserts. 34

McDaniel, Darl H., Concepts and Models of Inorganic Chemistry. 133

McDaniel, Lucy V., Bones, Joints, and Muscles of the Human Body. 209; Brain and Nerves of the Human Body. 209; Programmed Instruction for Aides in Physical Therapy. 209

McDermott, Irene E., Opportunities in Clothing. 24

McDonagh, Edward C., Social Problems. 106

MacDonald, Alexander F., From the Ground Up. 117

McDonald, Blanche, Methods That Teach. 111

MacDonald, Byron J., The Art of Lettering with the Broad Pen. 14

McDonald, George A., Atlas of Haematology. 186

MacDonald, Gwendoline, Development of Standards and Accreditation in Collegiate Nursing Education. 191

Macdonald, Janet, Non-Book Materials: The Organization of Integrated Collections. 91

McDonald, Morton J. A., Master Guide to Successful Real Estate Advertising. 65

McDonald, Richard N., Deductive Organic Chemistry. 134

McDonnell, Leo P., Hand Woodworking Tools. 162; Portable Power Tools. 162

McDonnell, Virginia B., Your Future in Nursing. 191

McDougal, Wynne L., Fundamentals of Electricity. 151

McDowell, Milton C., Math Workbook for Food Service Lodging Programs. 206

McElroy, Wayne, The Paraprofessionals or Teachers' Aides. 112

McElwain, Charlotte, Knitting with Stop and Go Needles. 24

McEwen, William E., Unitized Experiments in Organic Chemistry. 134

McFall, Walter T., Periodontics for the Dental Hygienist. 173

McFarland, John W., Organic Laboratory Chemistry. 135

McFarland, Roger B., ANSCR: The Alpha-Numeric System for Classification of Recordings. 92

McFarland, Walter B., Concepts for Management Accounting. 3

McGannon, Robert E., Lieutenant, Fire Department. 85; 1340 Questions and Answers for Firefighters. 85

McGavin, Charles T., Hotel-Motel Parking Guide, Layouts, Etc. 52

McGee, R. A., General Mechanical Drawing. 144

McGhie, Andrew, Psychology: As Applied to Nursing. 191

McGill, Dan M., Life Insurance. 54

McGill, Donald A. C., Punched Cards. 16

McGinnies, William G., Arid Lands in Perspective. 75

McGinnis, H., Introduction to Applied Drawing. 142

McGinty, Gerald, Basic Electronics "Autotext." 148

McGrath, Earl J., Liberal Education and Pharmacy. 202

McGrath, James S., The Automobile Transmission and Drive Line. 124

McGraw-Hill, Inc., The McGraw-Hill Author's Book. 45

MacGregor, Frances M., Social Science in Nursing. 191

McGuinness, William J., Mechanical and Electrical Equipment for Buildings. 138

McGuire, William, Steel Structures. 138

McHardy, G. J. R., Basic Techniques in Human Metabolism and Respiration. 181

INDEX

McHenry, Earle W., Basic Nutrition. 40; Foods Without Fads. 40

Machinery, Machinery's Handbook. 165; Machinery's Mathematical Tables. 165

McIlhany, Sterling, Art As Design. 14

McIlwraith, P. L., Geriatric Nursing. 194

McIntosh, Robert W., Motel Planning and Business Management. 51

McIntyre, Robert L., AC Motor-Control Fundamentals. 156; Electric Motor Control Fundamentals. 156

McIver, Colin, Marketing. 60

McJimsey, Harriet, Art In Clothing Selection. 24

McKaig, Thomas H., Applied Structural Design of Buildings. 138; Building Failures. 138

MacKay, Ann, Introduction to Modern Inorganic Chemistry. 133

MacKay, Kenneth, Introduction to Modern Inorganic Chemistry. 133

McKay, Mary E., Community Health Services. 207

Mackean, Donald G., The Arco Book of Biology. 185

McKelvey, James M., Polymer Processing. 129

McKenna, Frances M., Thresholds to Professional Nursing Practice. 191

Mackichan, Neil, Assisting the General Practitioner. 71

McKilligin, Helen, The First Day of Life: Principles of Neonatal Nursing. 195

McKinley, Daniel, The Subversive Science. 179

McKinley, James L., Basic Science for Aerospace Vehicles. 117; Powerplants for Aerospace Vehicles. 117

Mackinney, Gordon, Color of Foods. 34

Mackinnon, Lachlan, A Textbook on Light at an Introductory Level. 199

McLarry, Newman R., When Shadows Fall. 94

McLaughlin, Charles, Space Age Dictionary. 117

McLaughlin, James, Introduction to Fire Science. 84

McLean, Donald, Mechanical Properties of Metals. 169

Maclean, Joseph, Life Insurance. 54

McLean, Nemadji B., Meal Planning and Service. 34

McLean, Ruari, Magazine Design. 11; Victorian Book Design and Colour Printing. 11

McLellan, C. R., Concepts of General Chemistry. 129

McLuhan, Marshall, The Gutenberg Galaxy. 45

McMahon, Martin C., Resuscitation of the Unconscious Victim. 181

McManus, Joseph F. A., Staining Methods: Histologic and Histochemical. 183

McMichael, Stanley L., How to Finance Real Estate. 65; How to Make Money in Real Estate. 65; How to Operate a Real Estate Business. 65

McMillan, Colin, Sales Manager's Guide to Selection and Control of Export Agents. 60

McMillen, Wheeler, Bugs or People? 179

McMinn, Robert E., Power for Aircraft. 117

McMurry, Robert N., How to Build a Dynamics Sales Organization. 60; How to Recruit, Select and Place Salesmen. 60

McMurtrie, Douglas C., A History of Printing in the United States. 45

McNair, Malcolm P., The American Department Store, 1920-1960. 63

McNaught, Ann B., Nurse's Illustrated Physiology. 191

MacNeill, James H., Accounting Practice Management Handbook. 3

McNickle, L. S., Simplified Hydraulics. 138

McPartland, Joseph F., Electrical Design Details. 151; Electrical Equipment Manual. 151; How to Design Electrical Systems. 151; Practical Electricity. 151

McRae, Thomas W., The Impact of Computers on Accounting. 3

McVickar, John S., Approved Practices in Pasture Management. 75

McVickar, Malcolm H., Approved Practices in Pasture Management. 75; Using Commercial Fertilizers. 75

McWilliams, Margaret, Food Fundamentals. 34; Understanding Food. 33

Madden, Ira S., Woodworking for Industrial Arts. 162

Maddison, David, Psychiatric Nursing. 196

Madison, Charles A., Book Publishing in America. 45

Madow, Pauline, Recreation in America. 103

Madsen, Leo, Danish Cakes. 37

Maegraith, B., Adams and Maegraith: Tropical Medicine for Nurses. 191

Magee, John F., Physical-Distribution Systems. 59

Magee, John H., General Insurance. 53

Magee, R. J., Selected Readings in Chromatography. 129

Mager, Nathan H., The Office Encyclopedia. 68

Mager, Robert F., Developing Vocational Instruction. 162

Mager, S. K., The Office Encyclopedia. 68

Magnan, George A., Using Technical Art. 11; Visual Art for Industry. 11

Magnani, Franco, Modern Interiors. 55

Magnus, Edward R., Handbook of Refrigeration and Air Conditioning. 121

Magone, Clifford R., Police Officers Manuals. 100

Maguire, John T., Planning and Creating Better Direct Mail. 62

Mahan, Bruce H., Elementary Chemical Thermodynamics. 129

Maher, David J., Medical Technology, a Review for Board Examinations. 183

Mahler, Henry R., Biological Chemistry. 133

Mahler, Norman, Basic Mathematics for Electronics. 206

Mahoney, Robert F., Emergency and Disaster Nursing. 191

Maier, Franz J., Manual of Water Fluoridation Practice. 179

Maier, Henry W., Three Theories of Child Development. 82

Maillard, Robert, Dictionary of Modern Painting. 10

Mair, George, Elementary Real Estate Appraisal. 65

Maisel, Herbert, Introduction to Electronic Digital Computers. 18

Maisel, Sherman J., Financing Real Estate. 65

Majmudar, Harit, Introduction to Electrical Machines. 150

Makanowitzky, Barbara N., The Russian Cookbook. 39

Malamud, D., Autoradiography. 203

Malchman, Lawrence H., Basic Accounting for Managerial and Financial Control. 4

Maleev, Vladimir L., Mechanical Design of Machines. 167

Maley, Gerald A., Introduction to Digital Computers. 18

Mallan, Lloyd, Great Air Disasters. 117

Mallen, Bruce E., The Marketing Channel. 59

Mallett, M., A Handbook of Anatomy and Physiology for Student X-Ray Technicians. 204

Mallinson, John H., Chemical Plant Design with Reinforced Plastics. 129

Malm, Lloyd E., Chemical Principles in the Laboratory. 127; Essentials of Chemistry in the Laboratory. 127; Fundamental Experiments for College Chemistry. 127

Malone, Ruth M., Cooking the Holiday Inn Way. 34

Maloney, Elizabeth, Interpersonal Relations. 191

Malvino, Albert P., Calculus for Electronics. 206; Digital Principles and Applications. 150; Electronic Instrumentation Fundamentals. 150; Experiments for the Electric Circuits Laboratory. 150; Transistor Circuit Approximations. 159

Manas, Leo, Visual Analysis. 199

Mandell, Robert B., Contact Lens Practice. 199

Mandl, Matthew, Directory of Electronic Circuits. 150; Electronic Switching

INDEX

Circuits. 150; Fundamentals of Electric and Electronic Circuits. 150; Fundamentals of Electronic Computers. 18; Fundamentals of Electronics. 150; Industrial Control Electronics. 150

Manfreda, Marguerite L., Psychiatric Nursing. 196

Manjas, Barbara, Promoting Psychological Comfort. 189

Manko, Howard H., Solders and Soldering. 171

Manly, Harold P., Drake's Refrigeration Service Manual. 121

Mann, George B., ABC'S of Transistors. 159

Mann, Richard A., An IBM 1130 Fortran Primer. 20

Mann, Thomas C., Over Their Dead Bodies. 94

Mannheim, Ladislaus A., Enlarging. 49

Manning, G. E., Weather Radar for Pilots, a Handbook. 117

Manning, William, Fortran IV Problem Solver. 20

Mansfield, Alan, English Costume for Sports and Outdoor Recreation. 27

Manson-Hing, Lincoln R., Dental Radiology. 176

Manufacturing Chemists' Association, Case Histories of Accidents in the Chemical Industry. 129; Guide for Safety in the Chemical Laboratory. 129

March, Jerry, Advanced Organic Chemistry. 135

Marcus, Abraham, Automatic Industrial Controls. 170; Basic Electricity. 150; Basic Electronics. 150; Electricity for Technicians. 150; Electronics for Technicians. 150; Elements of Radio. 157; Radio Servicing. 157

Marcus, William, Elements of Radio. 157; Elements of Radio Servicing. 157; Practical Radio Servicing. 157

Marders, Irvin E., How to Use Dogs Effectively in Modern Police Work. 99

Margolis, Adele P., The Complete Book of Tailoring for Women. 24; The Dressmaking Book. 24; How to Make Clothes That Fit and Flatter. 24; Simplified Tailoring. 24

Margolis, Art, 101 TV Troubles. 158; TV Repairs. 158; TV Servicing Guidebook. 158

Margolis, Emil J., Chemical Principles in Calculations of Ionic Equilibria. 129

Margolis, Louis, Mathematics for Technical and Vocational Schools. 206

Margolis, Philip M., Guide for Mental Health Workers. 208

Margules, Morton, General Power Mechanics. 163

Margulies, Walter P., Package Design. 11

Margulis, Alexander, Alimentary Tract Roentgenology. 204

Mariel, Sister, Outline of Pharmacology and Therapeutics. 202

Marin, Gianni, The Motor Car: An Illustrated History. 124

Marine, Gene, America the Raped. 179

Mark, David, How to Select and Use Your Tape Recorder. 91

Mark, Donald D., Atlas of Clinical Laboratory Procedures. 183

Mark, Fredrick W., Jr., Management of Medical Emergencies. 208

Mark, Herman F., Encyclopedia of Polymer Science and Technology. 167; Man-Made Fibers. 29

Market Profile 1970, Chain Store Publishing Corp. 59

Marketing Services Company, Pharmaceutical Market Research Directory, 1963. 202

Markham, Jesse W., The Fertilizer Industry. 75

Markham, Joan, Eye, Nose, Throat and Ear Nursing. 189

Markowitz, Harry M., Simscript: A Simulation Programming Language. 20

Marks, Harriet, Nutrition and Elementary Food Science. 40

Marks, Jean, Medical Terminology. 71

Marks, Norton E., Marketing and Its Environment. 61; Marketing Logistics. 59

Marks, Robert W., The New Dictionary and Handbook of Aerospace.... 117

Markus, John, Electronics and Nucleonics Dictionary. 146; Sourcebook of Electronic Circuits. 150; Television and Radio Repairing. 158

Marler, E. E. J., Pharmacological and Chemical Synonyms. 202

Marlo, John A., The Police Officer and Criminal Justice. 102

Marlott, Grace D., Handbook of Refrigeration and Air Conditioning. 121

Marlow, Dorothy R., Textbook of Pediatric Nursing. 195

Marmor, Solomon, Laboratory Guide for Organic Chemistry. 135

Maron, Samuel H., Principles of Physical Chemistry. 135

Marple, Raymond P., Toward a Basic Accounting Philosophy. 3

Marquis, Vivienne, The Cheese Book. 34

Marris, Robin, Social Innovation in the City. 107

Marsden, Cyril, Solvents Guide. 129

Marsh, John T., An Introduction to Textile Finishing. 29; Crease Resisting Fabrics. 29

Marsh, R. Warren, Principles of Refrigeration. 121

Marsh, Roger, Silk Screen Printing for the Artist. 11

Marshall, Margaret A., Some Clinical Approaches to Psychiatric Nursing. 196

Marshall, Samuel L., Laser Technology and Applications. 156; Microelectric Technology. 151; Semiconductor Fundamentals, Devices and Circuits. 153

Marshall, T. K., The Disposal of the Dead. 94

Martens, Charles R., Emulsions and Water-Soluble Paints and Coatings. 129

Martin, Albert V. J., Technical Television. 158

Martin, Alfred N., Physical Pharmacy. 202

Martin, B. R., Experimental Research and Farm Production. 74

Martin, C. Leslie, Design Graphics. 143

Martin, Edley W., Electronic Data Processing, An Introduction. 16

Martin, Edward A., Psychology of Funeral Service. 94

Martin, Eric W., Husa's Pharmaceutical Dispensing. 202; Remington's Pharmaceutical Sciences. 202; Techniques of Medication. 202

Martin, James, Design of Real-Time Computer Systems. 18

Martin, John H., Principles of Field Crop Production. 75

Martin, Lowell A., Library Response to Urban Change. 91

Martindale, Don A., American Society. 106

Martin-Doyle, John L. C., A Synopsis of Ophthalmology. 199

Martinelli, Nicholas, Dental Laboratory Technology. 175

Martinson, Floyd M., Family in Society. 106

Martinson, John, Training Teacher Assistants in Community Colleges. 111; Vocational Training for Library Technicians. 91

Marvell, Elliott N., Modern Principles of Organic Chemistry. 134

Marx, Jerry, Officer, Tell Your Story. 99

Marx, Joseph L., Crisis in the Skies. 117

Marx, Wesley, The Frail Ocean. 179

Maschal, Henry T., Profitable Food and Beverage Operation. 31

Masheb, Clifford M., Accounting Simplified. 3

Mason, Brian H., Principles of Geochemistry. 129

Mason, F. H. S., Drafting Fundamentals. 143

Mason, John, Paper Making as an Artistic Craft. 48

Mason, John K., Aviation Accident Pathology. 117

Mason, Mildred A., Basic Medical-Surgical Nursing. 191

Mason, Ralph E., Case Studies in Marketing and Distribution. 60; Marketing and Distribution. 59

Mason, Samuel J., Electronic Circuits, Signals and Systems. 151

Massee, William E., Wines and Spirits. 38

Massey, Robert, The Chicken Cookbook. 33

Massialas, Byron C., Creative Encounters in the Classroom. 111

Masson, Frank N., Welding Theory and Practice. 171

Master Designer, Modern Garment Design.... 24

Masterton, William L., Chemical Principles. 129

Materials: A Scientific American Book. 167

Mates, Robert E., Photographing Art. 11

Matheney, Ruth V., Fundamentals of Patient-Centered Nursing. 191; Psychiatric Nursing. 196

Matterson, E. M., Play and Playthings for the Preschool Child. 82

Matthews, Joan, Cardiovascular Nursing. 190

Matthews, John B., Marketing. 59

Matthias, Arthur J., How to Design and Install Plumbing. 141

Mattock, G., pH Measurement and Titration. 129

Mattson, Elmer B., Creating with Aluminum. 162; Creative Metalworking. 162

Mattson, Roy H., Electronics. 151

Matwiyoff, Nicholas A., Acids and Bases. 127

Matz, Adolph, Cost Accounting. 5

Matz, Samuel A., Bakery Technology and Engineering. 37; Cereal Science. 41; Cookie and Cracker Technology. 37; Food Texture. 34; Water in Foods. 34

Mauck, Frances F., Modern Sewing Techniques. 24

Mauer, Alvin M., Pediatric Hematology. 186

Mauger, Emily M., Modern Display Techniques. 63

Maupin, Bernard, Blood Platelets in Man and Animals. 186

Maurello, S. Ralph, Commercial Art Techniques. 11; How to Do Paste-ups and Mechanicals. 11

Mauser, Ferdinand F., Modern Marketing Management. 60

Mautz, Robert K., Intermediate Principles of Accounting. 3

Max, Peter, The Peter Max Poster Book. 11

Maxim's, Chez Maxim's. 34

May, Edgar, The Wasted Americans. 106

May, Eleanor G., The American Department Store: 1920-1960. 63

May, J. W., Animal Cell Culture Methods. 185

Mayer, Frederick, American Ideas and Education. 111

Mayer, Joseph S., Restorative Art. 94

Mayer, Martin, The Schools. 111

Mayer, Ralph, The Artist's Handbook of Materials and Techniques. 11; A Dictionary of Art Terms and Techniques. 11

Mayerson, Allen L., Introduction to Insurance. 53

Maynard, Leonard A., Animal Nutrition. 79

Mayo, Lucy G., You Can Be an Executive Secretary.... 70

May's Manual of the Diseases of the Eye For Students and General Practitioners. 199

Mazow, Bernard, Synopsis of Corneal Contact Lens Fitting for Optometrists. 199

Mazur, Abraham, Textbook of Biochemistry. 132

Mazze, Edward M., International Marketing Administration. 62; Introduction to Marketing. 60; Sales Management. 56

Mead, D. J., Noise and Acoustic Fatigue in Aeronautics. 118

Mead, Richard R., The Management of Marketing Research. 60

Mead, William J., Encyclopedia of Chemical Process Equipment. 129

Mechanical Engineers' Handbook. 165

Mechanix Illustrated, Car Care. 124

Medical Examination Publishing Co., Inc., X-Ray Technology Examination Review Book. 205

Medinnus, Gene R., Child and Adolescent Psychology. 111; Child Psychology, Behavior and Development. 81

Medlik, S., The British Hotel and Catering Industry. 52

Medlycott, Anthony, Applied Building Construction. 138

Meehan, James R., How to Use Adding Machines. 68; Using the Rotary Calculator in the Modern Office. 68

Meering, A. B., A Handbook for Nursery Nurses. 195

Mees, Charles E. K., From Dry Plates to Ektachrome Film. 45; The Theory of the Photographic Process. 49

Meetham, A. R., Atmospheric Pollution. 179

Meetham, Roger, Information Retrieval. 16

Megathlin, Donald E., A Bibliography of New Product Planning. 60

Megginson, Leon C., Human Resources. 106

Meglin, Nick, On-the-Spot Drawing. 11

Mehr, Robert I., Life Insurance. 54; Modern Life Insurance. 54; Principles of Insurance. 53

Mehrens, Harold E., Aircraft in Flight. 117; The Dawning Space Age. 116

Mehta, Himatlal R., Pharmacy for Nurses. 191

Mehta, K. R., Vegetarian Delights. 34

Meidl, James H., Explosive and Toxic Hazardous Materials. 85; Flammable Hazardous Materials. 85

Meigs, Walter B., Accounting. 3; Financial Accounting. 3; Intermediate Accounting. 3; Principles of Auditing. 5

Meilach, Dona Z., Creating Art from Anything. 11; Creative Carving. 162; Printmaking. 11

Meissner, Kurt, Japanese Woodblock Prints in Miniature. 11

Meites, Louis, Handbook of Analytical Chemistry. 132

Melcher, Daniel, Printing and Promotion Handbook. 45

Melcher, James R., Electromechanical Dynamics. 155

Meldman, Monte J., Occupational Therapy Manual. 209

Melia, Terence P., An Introduction to Masers and Lasers. 156

Melichar, Paul R., Cobol for IBM System 360. 20

Mellan, Eleanor, Encyclopedia of Chemical Labeling. 129

Mellan, Ibert, Encyclopedia of Chemical Labeling. 129; Industrial Plasticizers. 167; Industrial Solvent Handbook. 129

Mellanby, Keith, Pesticides and Pollution. 179

Mellinger, Morris, Developing Shorthand Skills. 67

Mellman, Martin, Accounting Theory. 4

Mellon, Melvin Guy, Chemical Publications. 129

Mellor, John W., The Economics of Agricultural Development. 75

Mellor, Joseph W., Modern Inorganic Chemistry. 133

Melnicoe, William B., Beat Patrol and Observation. 100; Elements of Police Supervision. 99

Meloan, Clifton E., Problems and Experiments in Instrumental Analysis. 133

Meloche, Vulliers W., Elementary Quantitative Analysis. 132

Meltzer, Lawrence E., Concepts and Practices of Intensive Care for Nurse Specialists. 191

Menchan, William M., Introduction to Child Development and Parent Education. 82

Mendelsohn, Harold, Minorities and the Police. 95

Mendelsohn, Oscar A., The Dictionary of Drink and Drinking. 38

Menke, Hardy A., Contemporary Wood Furniture. 56

Mennig, Jan, Elements of Police Supervision. 99

Menning, Jack H., Communicating Through Letters and Reports. 68

Men's Furnishings. 24

Menyuk, Paula, Sentences Children Use. 111

INDEX

Mercer, E. H., Electron Microscopy. 183

Mercer, H. G., Real Estate Principles in California. 65

Mercer, Lianne S., Fundamental Skills in the Nurse-Patient Relationship. 191

Merck Index: An Encyclopedia of Chemicals and Drugs. 202

Mereness, Dorothy, Essentials of Psychiatric Nursing. 196; Psychiatric Nursing. 196

Merill, Vinita, Atlas of Roentgenographic Positions. 204

Merory, Joseph, Food Flavorings. 41

Merriam, Eve, Figleaf: The Business of Being in Fashion. 24

Merriman, Arthur D., A Concise Encyclopedia of Metallurgy. 169

Merriman, Beth, The Fondue Cookbook. 34

Merriman, Frank, ATA Type Comparison Book. 45

Merritt, Frederick S., Building Code of the City of New York. 138; Building Construction Handbook. 138

Merritt, LeRoy C., Book Selection and Intellectual Freedom. 91

Merritt, Lynne L., Jr., Instrumental Methods of Analysis. 133

Mertens, L. E., In-Water Photography Theory and Practice. 49

Merton, Robert K., Contemporary Social Problems. 106

Meschan, Isadore, An Atlas of Normal Radiographic Anatomy. 205; Radiographic Positioning and Related Anatomy. 205; Synopsis of Roentgen Signs. 205

Messer, Eunice A., Children, Psychology and the Teacher. 111

Messick, Janice M., Crisis Intervention. 208

Metalworking Magazine, Machine Tool Selection Guide. 165

Metcalf, Clell L., Destructive and Useful Insects. 75

Metheny, Norma, Nurses' Handbook of Fluid Balance. 191

Methodist Hospital, Houston, Texas, Cardio-Vascular Surgery. 197

Metz, Robert, Franchising. 62

Metzler, Bernadette V., Effective Writing for Business. 68

Meyer, Carol H., Social Work Practice. 106; Staff Development in Public Welfare Agencies. 106

Meyer, Edith P., Meet the Future: People and Ideas in the Libraries of Today and Tomorrow. 91

Meyer, Hans A., Forest Management. 87

Meyer, Harold D., Community Recreation. 103

Meyer, Hazel, Hazel Meyer's Freezer Cookbook. 34

Meyer, Jerome S., Paper. 48

Meyer, Leo A., Atomic Energy in Industry. 129; Sheet Metal Layout. 145; Sheet Metal Shop Practice. 160

Meyer, Lillian H., Food Chemistry. 129

Meyer, W. L., Critical Path Method. 139

Meyer, Warren G., Retailing. 63

Meyer, William, The Care and Feeding of Trees. 87

Meyers, Frederick H., Review of Medical Pharmacology. 202

Meyers, Genevieve, Decorating Ideas for Every Room. 55

Meyers, William E., Electronic Business Data Processing. 16; Introduction to Computer Science and Data Processing. 16

Miale, John, Laboratory Medicine Hematology. 186

Miall, Laurence M., A New Dictionary of Chemistry. 129

Micallef, Benjamin A., Electric Accounting Machine Fundamentals. 3

Michaelis, John U., New Designs for the Elementary School Curriculum. 111

Michelbacher, Gustav F., Multiple-Line Insurers. 53

Michell, Arthur S., Harvesting Timber Crops. 88

Michell, S. J., Fluid and Particle Mechanics. 165

Michigan League for Nursing, Guide for Developing a Pre-Employment Training Program for Nurses' Aides. 194

Michigan State University National Center on Police and Community Relations, A National Survey of Police and Community Relations. 99

Mid-Atlantic Food Processors Association, Inc., ...Buyers' Guide and Directory... Food Processors. 41

Middleman, Ruth R., The Non-Verbal Method in Working with Groups. 106

Middleton, Bernard C. A., A History of English Craft Bookbinding Technique. 47

Middleton, Elspeth, 100 to Dinner. 34

Middleton, Herman A., 1970 Tube Caddy—Tube Substitution Guidebook. 158

Middleton, Robert G., Basic Electricity for Electronics. 151; Electrical and Electronic Signs and Symbols. 151; Elements of Transistor Technology. 159; Hi-Fi Stereo Servicing Guide. 151; 101 Ways to Use Your Sweep Generator. 151; Practical Electricity. 151; Troubleshooting with the Oscilloscope. 151; TV Troubleshooting and Repair. 158; Using the Oscilloscope in Industrial Electronics. 151

Midgett, Elwin W., An Accounting Primer. 3

Miele, Angelo, Flight Mechanics. 117

Migaki, George, Meat Hygiene. 30

Mikes, Otakar, Laboratory Handbook of Chromatographic Methods. 129

Mikesell, Rufus M., Governmental Accounting. 3

Milady Publishing Corporation, Standard Textbook of Cosmetology. 7

Mileaf, Harry, Electronics One-Seven. 151

Miles, Albert E., Structural and Chemical Organization of Teeth. 175

Miles, Matthew B., Innovation in Education. 111

Miles, Roger O., Forestry in the English Landscape. 87

Miles, Walter, Design for Craftsmen. 11

Milford, Frederick J., Foundations of Electromagnetic Theory. 152

Millar, Charles E., Fundamentals of Soil Science. 75

Millar, Frank I., Marketing Research. 58

Millar, Ian T., A Shorter Sidgwick's Organic Chemistry of Nitrogen. 135

Millar, Susanna, The Psychology of Play. 82

Miller, Bessie M., Complete Secretary's Handbook. 67; Legal Secretary's Complete Handbook. 71; Manual and Guide for the Corporate Secretary. 70; Medical Secretary's and Assistant's Handbook. 71

Miller, Carol L., Nurses and the Law. 191

Miller, Cary D., Fruits of Hawaii. 39

Miller, Charles J., Inlays, Crowns, and Bridges. 175

Miller, Cora, Introduction to Foods and Nutrition. 41

Miller, Dulcy B., The Extended Care Facility. 191

Miller, Edgar G., American Antique Furniture. 56

Miller, Edmund, Profitable Cafeteria Operation. 52

Miller, Edward, Textiles. 29

Miller, Ernest C., Marketing Planning. 60

Miller, Floyd, Statler: America's Extraordinary Hotelman. 52

Miller, H., A Short Textbook of Radiotherapy for Technicians and Students. 205

Miller, Harry L., Education in the Metropolis. 111

Miller, Herbert E., The Accounting Process. 2; Finney and Miller's Principles of Accounting, Introductory. 3; Principles of Accounting, Advanced. 2; Principles of Accounting, Intermediate. 2; Principles of Accounting, Introductory. 2; Principles of Financial Accounting. 2

Miller, Irene P., The Stitchery Book. 24

Miller, Jerome, Insurance Principles and Practices. 53

Miller, Jill N. H., Vietnamese Cookery. 40

Miller, Kenneth S., Introductory Electric Circuits. 154

INDEX

Miller, Lawrence C., Successful Management for Contractors. 138

Miller, Morris, Fundamentals of Modern Bookkeeping. 3

Miller, Norman F., Gynecology and Gynecologic Nursing. 194

Miller, Paula, Young Children's Thinking. 79

Miller, Rex, Energy, Electricity and Electronics.... 151; Selected Readings for Industrial Arts. 162

Miller, Robert F., One Hundred Thousand Tractors. 75

Miller, Roger R., Race, Research and Reason. 106

Miller, Ronald E., Domestic Airline Efficiency. 117; The Technical Development of Modern Aviation. 117

Miller, Seymour M., Social Class and Social Policy. 106

Miller, Texton R., Supervised Practice in Vocational Agriculture. 75

Miller, Wilbur R., Teaching Elementary Industrial Arts. 162

Millermaster, Ralph A., Harwood's Control of Electric Motors. 156

Milliken, Mary E., Understanding Human Behavior. 208

Millman, Jacob, Electronic Devices and Circuits. 151

Mills, Harlan, The Pig Manual: Photographed Dissection of the Fetal Pig. 186

Mills, John F., Studio and Art-Room Techniques. 11

Mills, Liston O., Perspectives on Death. 94

Milne, Lorus, Water and Life. 179

Milne, Margery, Water and Life. 179

Milo, Mary, Guide to Beauty. 7

Milroy, Robert R., Accounting Theory and Practice: Advanced. 3; Accounting Theory and Practice: Intermediate. 3; Accounting Theory and Practice: Introductory. 3

Milton, Shirley F., What You Should Know About Advertising Copywriting. 6

Mini, Joe L., Let Children be Children. 81

Minich, Quid W., Standard Refrigeration and Air Conditioning Questions and Answers. 120

Minrath, William R., Handbook of Applied Mathematics. 206

Minsky, Betty J., Gimmicks Make Money in Retailing. 63

Minuchin, Salvador, Families of the Slums. 106

Mirow, Gregory, Treasury of Design for Artists and Craftsmen. 11

Mischke, Charles R., An Introduction to Computer-Aided Design. 18

Misenhimer, Ted, Aeroscience. 117

Mislow, Kurt, Introduction to Stereochemistry. 129

Mitchell, Brinton B., Semiconductor Pulse Circuits with Experiments. 151

Mitchell, Geoffrey D., A Dictionary of Sociology. 106; A Hundred Years of Sociology. 106

Mitchell, Herbert S., Manual for School Accounting. 3; School Accounting for Financial Management. 4

Mitchell, James F., Gaddum's Pharmacology. 200

Mitchell, John G., Ecotactics: The Sierra Club Handbook for Environment Activists. 179

Mitchell, John P., Urology for Nurses. 197

Mitchell, Robert V., The Elements of Marketing. 57

Mitchell, Roger L., Crop Growth and Culture. 76

Mitford, Jessica, The American Way of Death. 94

Mitterhauser, Klaus, Professional Chef's Book of Buffets. 36

Mix, Floyd, All About House Wiring. 151; Practical Carpentry. 162

Miya, Tom S., Laboratory Guide in Pharmacology. 202

Mizer, Helen, Microbiology in Nursing Practice. 193

Mobley, Eugenia L., Dental Hygiene Examination Review Book. 173

Modell, Walter, Handbook of Cardiology for Nurses. 191

Modern Criminal Investigation Study Guide. 99

Modern Drug Encyclopedia and Therapeutic Index. 202

Modern Packaging: Encyclopedia Issue, Packaging Catalog Corp., 63

Modern Plastics, Plastics in Building. 138

Modular Building Standards Association, Modular Practice. 138

Moenssens, Andre A., Fingerprints and the Law. 99

Moffatt, William G., Structure and Properties of Materials. 168

Mogelon, Alex, Drawing with Ink. 10

Mohr, J. Gilbert, Handbook of Reinforced Plastics of the Society of the Plastics Industry, Inc. 168

Molbo, Doris, Gynecologic Nursing. 194

Moler, Arthur B., The Moler Manual of Cosmetology. 7

Møller, Carl, Danish Cakes. 37

Moltrecht, H. K., Machine Shop Practice. 165

Momboisee, Raymond, Community Relations and Riot Prevention. 99; Industrial Security for Strikes, Riots and Disasters. 99; Riots, Revolts and Insurrections. 99

Monaghan, Patrick, Writing Letters That Sell. 60

Monaghan, Patrick S., How to Sell Appliances at Retail. 63

Monahan, Fergus T., A Study of Nonprofessional Personnel in Social Work. 106

Moncrieff, R. W., Man-Made Fibers. 29

Moncrieff, William, Refraction: Neurophysiological and Psychological Viewpoints. 199

Monheim, Leonard M., General Anesthesia in Dental Practice. 175

Monk, George S., Light. 199

Monro, Kate M., The Secretary's Handbook. 70

Monroe, Donald, How to Succeed in Community Service. 106

Monroe, Lee S., The Color Atlas of Intestinal Parasites. 187

Montagné, Prosper, Nouveau Larousse Gastronomique. 34

Montessori, Maria, The Child in the Family. 82; Spontaneous Activity in Education. 111

Montgomery, David, Management Science in Marketing. 60

Montgomery, Glen, Small Appliance Repair Guide. 150

Moon, H. M., Facts About Merchandise. 63

Mooney, Booth, The Hidden Assassins. 34

Moonitz, Maurice, The Basic Postulates of Accounting. 4

Moore, Carl L., Managerial Accounting. 4

Moore, Eva, Poems Children Will Sit Still For. 109

Moore, Everett, Junior College Libraries: Development, Needs, and Perspectives. 91

Moore, Francis E., Accounting Systems for Management Control. 4

Moore, G. Alexander, Realities of the Urban Classroom. 111

Moore, Gary T., Emerging Methods in Environmental Design and Planning. 179

Moore, Vardine, Pre-School Story Hour. 111

Moore, Walter J., Physical Chemistry. 135

Mooth, Adelma, Developing the Supervisory Skills of the Nurse. 191

Mordan, Mary J., Interviewing in Nursing. 188

More, Harry W., The General Administration of Criminal Justice. 99

Morgan, B., Restoration of Antique and Classic Cars. 125

Morgan, Elizabeth, The Nursing Audit. 189

Morgan, James A., The Art and Science of Medical Radiography. 205; Medical Radiographic Technic. 203

Morgan, Jasper E., Basic Principles of Radiation Therapy for X-Ray Technicians and Nurses. 205

Morgan, Len, Airliners of the World. 117; Crack Up! 117

INDEX

Morgan, Richard F., Environmental Biology. 179

Morgan, Rose M., Guide Questions for Medical Technology Examinations. 183

Morgan, Russell H., Physical Foundations of Radiology. 204

Morgan, William, The Elements of Structure. 138

Morgenstern, Anne, Grouping in the Elementary School. 111

Morgret, Frank C., Ophthalmic Mechanics and Dispensing. 198

Mori, Maria, Basic Pattern Cutting. 24

Morine, Greta, A Primer for the Inner-City School. 112

Morine, Harold, A Primer for the Inner-City School. 112

Morison, Luella J., Approaches for Co-Workers in Professional Nursing. 191; Steppingstones to Professional Nursing. 191

Morison, Stanley, Four Centuries of Fine Printing. 45; Letter Forms. 14; On Type Designs, Past and Present. 45; The Typographic Book, 1450-1935. 45

Morlan, John, Preparation of Inexpensive Teaching Materials. 112

Moro, Michael D., ...Air Jet Hair Styling for Men. 3

Morphy, Countess, Mushroom Recipes. 34

Morrill, Chester, Jr., Computers and Data Processing. 16

Morris, Floyd, 198 Easy Wood Projects. 162

Morris, Irvine, Handbook of Structural Design. 138

Morris, Maurice, Rotating Seasonal Menus. 34

Morris, Noel, Industrial Electronics. 151

Morrison, Elsie, Feeds and Feeding. 79

Morrison, Frank, Feeds and Feeding. 79

Morrison, Ivan G., Farm Tractor Maintenance. 77

Morrison, John C., Scientific Design of Exhaust and Intake Systems. 124

Morrison, Ralph, Grounding and Shielding Techniques in Instrumentation. 151

Morrison, Richard, Design Data for Aeronautics and Astronautics. 117

Morrison, Robert, Organic Chemistry. 135

Morrison, Spencer H., Feeds and Feeding. 79

Morrissey, John, Real Estate in a Nutshell. 65

Morse, Grant W., The Concise Guide to Library Research. 91

Morse, Henry C., Numerically Controlled Machine Tools. 170

Morse, Philip McCord, Library Effectiveness. 91

Morse, Stephen, The Practical Approach to Marketing Management. 60

Mortenson, William P., Approved Practices in Crop Production. 73; Approved Practices in Dairying. 79; Approved Practices in Farm Management. 76; The Farm Management Handbook. 74; Modern Marketing of Farm Products. 76

Mortimer, Charles E., Chemistry. 129

Morton, Alan, Mechanical Composition. 46

Morton, Grace, The Arts of Costume and Personal Appearance. 27

Morton, Hudson T., Anti-Friction Bearings. 165

Morton, Marcia, The Art of Viennese Pastry. 37

Morton, Newton, Logistics of Distribution Systems. 60

Morton, Philip, Contemporary Jewelry. 28

Mosby Company, Mosby's Review of Practical Nursing. 196; Mosby's Comprehensive Review of Nursing. 191

Moscow, Alvin, Tiger on a Leash. 117

Moser, Leslie E., How to Build a Fortune in Real Estate. 65; How to Find, Qualify, and Induce Real Estate Prospects to Buy. 65; How to Make Money in Real Estate. 65; Operating a Successful Real Estate Business. 65

Moser, Robert H., House Officer Training. 99

Mosher, Robert, Industrial and Specialty Papers. 48

Mosich, A., Financial Accounting. 3

Moss, Archibald, Textiles and Fabrics. 29

Moss, Frank E., The Water Crisis. 179

Moss, H. G., Retail Pharmacist's Handbook. 202

Moss, William, Therapeutic Radiology. 205

Mossman, Frank, Logistics of Distribution Systems. 60; Physical Distribution Management. 61

Motorola Semiconductor Products, Analysis and Design of Integrated Circuits. 151; Integrated Circuits. 151; The Semiconductor Data Book. 151

Motor's Auto Repair Manual, Motor. 124

Motor's Truck Repair Manual, Motor. 124

Mott-Smith, Morton, Principles of Mechanics Simply Explained. 165

Moulton, Bertha, Garment-Cutting and Tailoring for Students. 24; Simplified Tailoring. 24

Moulton, Verna, Clothing Selection. 22

Mountney, George J., Poultry Products Technology. 41

Moursund, David, How Computers Do It. 18

Mouton, Jane S., The Grid for Sales Excellence. 57

Mowbray, Albert H., Insurance. 53

Mowrer, Orval H., Learning Theory and Behavior. 112

Mowry, Lillian, Basic Nutrition and Diet Therapy for Nurses. 191

Mowry, Robert W., Staining Methods. 183

Moyer, Cecil A., Accounting. 1; Intermediate Principles of Accounting. 3

Moyer, Reed, Markets and Marketing in Developing Economies. 60

Moyer, Sue, Why Team Teaching? 110

Moynahan, James, Police Ju Jitsu. 99; Police Searching Procedures. 99; The Yawara Stick and Police Baton. 99

Moynihan, Daniel P., On Understanding Poverty. 106

Mueller, Conrad., Light and Vision. 199

Mueller, Earl G., The Art of Print. 11

Mueller, Gerhard G., International Accounting. 4

Muhler, Joseph C., Improving Dental Practice Through Preventive Measures. 173; Textbook of Biochemistry for Students of Dentistry. 175

Mulkerne, Donald J., Civil Service Tests for Typists. 68; Office Procedures and Administration. 68

Mullany, George G., Career Training in Hotel and Restaurant Operation.... 50

Mullen, Thomas W., Blow Molding. 165

Muller, Edward J., Architectural Drawing and Light Construction. 144

Muller, Phillipe, The Tasks of Childhood. 82

Muller, Theresa G., Fundamentals of Psychiatric Nursing. 196

Muller-Brockmann, Josef, ...The Graphic Artist and His Design Problems.... 11

Mullin, Ray C., Blueprint Reading and Sketching. 144

Mumford, George, Modern Practice in Dental Ceramics. 174

Mumford, Nicholas, Jet Propulsion for Aerospace Applications. 117

Munger, Elmer L., Construction Management. 138

Munk, Michael, Decision-Making in Poverty Programs. 105

Munro, Robertson, Jr., Automatic Data Processing and Management. 15

Munsell, Albert H., A Grammar of Color. 13

Munson, Harold L., Elementary School Guidance. 112

Munson, Kenneth G., Aircraft the World Over. 117

Munves, Elizabeth A., Introduction to Nutrition. 40

Murchie, Guy, The World Aloft. 117

Murchison, Irene A., Legal Foundations of Nursing Practice. 191

Murgatroyd, Keith, Modern Graphics. 11

Murgio, Matthew P., Communications Graphics. 11

Murphy, Constance, Textbook of Basic Nursing. 193
Murphy, Dennis H., Merchandising Mathematics. 206
Murphy, Earl F., Water Purity. 179
Murphy, Gordon J., Basic Automatic Control Theory. 170
Murphy, Jerry R., The Computer Sampler. 17
Murphy, John D., The New Psychology of Persuasion and Motivation in Selling. 62
Murphy, John E., Interactions of Man and His Environment. 178
Murphy, John S., Basics of Digital Computers. 18; Electronics in Industry. 151
Murphy, Lois B., The Widening World of Childhood. 82
Murphy, Margaret D., Fondue, Chafing Dish, and Casserole Cookery. 34
Murphy, Margaret N., Growth and Development of the Young Child. 80
Murphy, Patricia, Glow of Candelight. 52
Murphy, R. Gordon, Basic Industrial Electronic Controls. 152
Murphy, Richard C., The Care and Feeding of Trees. 87
Murphy, Walter T., Radiation Therapy. 205
Murray, Allen E., Photographic Lenses. 50
Murray, Joseph A., The Complete Study Guide for Police Administration and Criminal Investigation. 99; Patrolman, Police Department. 99
Murray, Walter I., Educating the Culturally Disadvantaged Child. 109
Murray, William G., Agricultural Finance. 76; Farm Appraisal and Valuation. 76
Murray-Shelley, R., Teach Yourself Computer Programming. 20
Murrill, Paul W., An Introduction to Fortran IV Programming. 20
Museum of Graphic Art, American Printmaking: The First 150 Years. 11
Museum of Modern Art, New York, Lettering by Modern Artists. 14
Musocchia, John B., Airbrush Techniques for Commercial Art. 11
Musselman, Vernon A., Teaching Bookkeeping and Accounting. 4
Mussen, Paul H., Readings in Child Development and Personality. 82
Musser, Ruth D., Pharmacology and Therapeutics. 202
Mutolese, Michael, Minor and Major Alterations. 24
Muzik, Thomas J., Weed Biology and Control. 76
Myatt, Donald J., Machine Design. 167
Myer, John N., Accounting for Non-Accountants. 4
Myers, Arthur, Safety Last. 124

Myers, Bernard S., McGraw-Hill Dictionary of Art. 11
Myers, James H., The Management of Marketing Research. 60
Myers, Mildred, Cataloging for Library Technical Assistants. 89
Myers, Terrell C., Chemistry of Amino Acids, Peptides, and Proteins. 129
Myers, William E., Introduction to Computer Science and Data Processing. 16
Myran, Gunder A., Community Services in the Community College. 106
Myren, Richard A., Police Work with Children. 99

N. W. Ayer & Son's Directory. 46
Nader, Ralph, Unsafe at Any Speed. 124
Nagy, Dénes, Radiological Anatomy. 205
Najarian, Haig H., Textbook of Medical Parasitology. 187
Nanavati, Rajendra, An Introduction to Semiconductor Electronics. 151
Nanney, David L., The Biology of Cells. 185
Nash, D. F. Ellison, The Principles and Practice of Surgery for Nurses and Allied Professions. 197
Nash, Frederick C., Automotive Fundamentals. 124
Nash, Jay B., Philosophy of Recreation and Leisure. 103; Recreation. 103
Nash, Leonard K., Elements of Chemical Thermodynamics. 129
Nash, Roderick, The American Environment. 179
Nason, Alvin, Essentials of Modern Biology. 185; Textbook of Modern Biology. 185
Nast, Minnette, Simplified Drugs and Solutions for Nurses. 191
Natchez, Gladys, Children with Reading Problems. 112
Nathan, Robert, Computer Programming Handbook. 21
Nathans, Alan A., Maintenance for Camps and Other Outdoor Recreation Facilities. 103
Nathanson, Fred E., Radar Design Principles. 118
National Academy of Sciences, Agriculture Research Institute, The Role of Animal Agriculture in Meeting World Food Needs. 79; World Food Needs and Production. 76
National Academy of Sciences, National Research Council (Animal Nutrition Committee), Nutrient Requirements of Beef Cattle. 79; Nutrient Requirements of Dairy Cattle. 79; Nutrient Requirements of Poultry. 79
National Academy of Sciences, National Research Council (Biology and Agriculture Division), Systematic Biology. 185
National Academy of Sciences, National Research Council (Building Research Advisory Board), Crack Control in Concrete Masonry Unit Construction. 141; Heating and Air-Conditioning Ducts Encased in and under Concrete Slabs-on-Ground. 121; School Fires. 85
National Academy of Sciences, National Research Council (Building Research Institute), Cleaning and Purification of Air in Buildings. 179; Documentation of Building Science Literature. 138; New Methods of Heating Buildings. 121; Performance of Plastics in Building. 138; Preassembled Building Components. 138
National Academy of Sciences, National Research Council (Commission on Education in Agriculture and Natural Resources), Undergraduate Teaching in the Plant and Soil Sciences. 76
National Academy of Sciences, National Research Council (Food and Nutrition Board), Prospects of the World Food Supply. 34; Recommended Dietary Allowances. 40
National Academy of Sciences, National Research Council (Institute of Laboratory Animal Resources), Nonhuman Primates: Standards and Guidelines for the Breeding, Care, and Management of Laboratory Animals. 186; Rodents: Standards and Guidelines for the Breeding, Care, and Management of Laboratory Animals. 186
National Academy of Sciences, National Research Council (National Academy of Sciences Executive Offices), A Program for Outdoor Recreation Research. 103
National Aerospace Education Council, Aeronautics and Space Bibliography of Adult Aerospace Books and Materials. 118; Aerospace Highlights: Facts and Figures.... 118; Aviation Education Bibliography. 118
National Agricultural Chemicals Association, Manual of Pesticide Use and Application Laws. 76
National Association for the Education of Young Children: What Does the Nursery School Teacher Teach? 82
National Association of Educational Secretaries, Communications Revue. 69; File It Right and Find It! 69; A Guide for Planning Inservice Training Programs for Educational Secretaries. 69; Take A Minute, Save An Hour: A Handbook on Meetings. 69
National Association of Home Builders, A Glossary of Building Marketing Terminology. 138
National Association of Legal Secretaries, Manual for the Legal Secretarial Profession. 71
National Association of Manufacturers, Water in Industry. 179
National Association of Meat Purveyors, Meat Buyer's Guide to Portion Control Meat Cuts. 34; Meat Buyer's Guide to Standardized Meat Cuts. 34

INDEX

National Association of Printing Ink Manufacturers, Printing Ink Handbook. 48

National Association of Real Estate Boards, Interpretations of the Code of Ethics. 65; Realtor's Guide to Housing Programs. 65

National Association of Real Estate Boards, National Institute of Real Estate Brokers, Guide to Commercial Property Leasing. 66; How to Use Taxation and Exchange Techniques. 66; Marketing Real Estate Successfully. 66; Percentage Leases. 66; Real Estate Advertising. 66; Real Estate Specializations. 66; Real Estate Trader's Handbook. 66

National Association of Social Workers, Changing Services for Changing Clients. 106; Encyclopedia of Social Work. 106; Goals of Public Social Policy. 106

National Association of Social Workers Social Work Practice Commission, Utilization of Personnel in Social Work. 106

National Association of Women in Construction, Construction Dictionary. 138

National Audio-Visual Association, Audio-Visual Equipment Directory. 112

National Automatic Merchandising Association, Sanitation Regulations Concerning the Vending Industry. 63

National Automobile Dealers Association, Standards of Apprenticeship...for Automobile Mechanics. 124

National Automotive Service, National Service Data. 124

National Board of Fire Underwriters, Fire Prevention Code. 85; Fire Resistance Ratings.... 85

National Board of Fire Underwriters, Engineering Research Division, Fire Hazards of the Plastics Manufacturing and Fabricating Industries. 85

National Business Education Association, Business Education and the Two-Year Community College. 69; Yearbook. 69

National Canners Association, Laboratory Manual for Food Canners and Processors. 41

National Commission for the Study of Nursing and Nursing Education, An Abstract for Action. 191

National Commission on the Causes and Prevention of Violence, To Establish Justice, To Insure Domestic Tranquility.... 99

National Committee for Careers in Medical Technology, Curriculum Guides for Retraining in Medical Technology. 183; A Manual of Cytotechnology. 183

National Conference on Social Welfare, The Social Welfare Forum. 106

National Constructors' Association, Directory of International Engineering and Construction Services. 138

National Council for Homemaker Services, Homemaker-Home Health Aides. 208

National Council on Illegitimacy, Effective Services for Unmarried Parents and Their Children. 106

National Educational Secretary, Recollections: Reprints of the Best of the National Educational Secretary. 69

National Farm Institute, Bargaining Power for Farmers. 76; Farmers and a Hungry World. 76

National Federation of Settlements and Neighborhood Centers, Selected Readings for Trainees for Day Care Aides. 82

National Fire Protection Association, Air Operations for Forest, Brush, and Grass Fires. 87; Breathing Apparatus for the Fire Service. 85; Code for Safety to Life From Fire in Buildings and Structures. 85; Code for the Use of Flammable Anesthetics. 85; Coding System for Fire Reporting. 85; Combustible Solids, Dusts, Chemicals and Explosives. 85; Fighting Rural Fires. 85; Fire Apparatus Maintenance. 85; Fire Doors and Windows. 85; Fire Hazard Properties of Flammable Liquid, Gases, Volatile Solids. 85; Fire Protection Handbook. 85; Fire Service Directory. 85; Fire Terminology. 85; Hazardous Chemicals Data 1968. 129; Industrial Fire Brigades Training Manual. 85; Inspection Manual. 85; Management of a Fire Department. 85; Manual of Hazardous Chemical Reactions. 85; National Electrical Code Handbook. 151; National Electrical Code, 1965 Tables & Diagrams. 151; National Electrical Contractors Association. 151; National Fire Codes, 1969-1970. 85; Operating Fire Department Aerial Ladders. 85; Operating Fire Department Pumpers. 85; Protection of Records, 1963. 85; Recommended Practice for Protection of Library Collections from Fire. 85; Standard for the Protection of Electronic Computer Systems. 85; Suggestions for Aircraft Rescue and Fire Fighting Services for Airports and Heliports. 85; Year Book: Officers and Committees. 85

National Formulary. 202

National Frozen Food Association, Frozen Food Institutional Encyclopedia. 41

National Funeral Directors Association, Funeral Service as a Profession. 94

National Industrial Conference Board, Graphic Guide to Consumer Markets. 60

National Knitted Outerwear Association, A Practical Program for Quality Control. 25

National League for Nursing, Action for Quality. 191; An Approach to the Teaching of Psychiatric Nursing.... 196

National League for Nursing, Department of Associate Degree Programs, A National Survey of Associate Degree Nursing Programs. 191; Associate Degree Education for Nursing. 191

National League for Nursing, Research and Studies Service, Rehabilitative Aspects of Nursing. 191

National League of Cities, The Grading of Municipal Fire Protection Facilities. 85

National Learning Corporation, Fire Alarm Dispatcher. 85

National Live Stock Meat Board, Lessons on Meat. 34

National Paint, Varnish and Lacquer Association, Inc., Guide to U.S. Government Paint Specifications. 138

National Plumbing Code Illustrated. 141

National Radio Institute, Mathematics for Electronics and Electricity. 206; Radio-Television-Electronics Dictionary. 157

National Research Council, Fire Research Committee, Directory of Fire Research in the United States. 85; A Study of Fire Problems. 85

National Research Council, Food Protection Committee, Chemicals Used in Food Processing. 41; Food Chemical Index. 41

National Research Council, Remote Sensing for Agricultural Purposes Committee, Remote Sensing with Special Reference to Agriculture and Forestry. 76

National Restaurant Association, Great American Menus. 34; A Financial Analysis of the Restaurant Industry. 52; How to Promote Your Restaurant. 53; Menu Masterpieces. 34; Uniform System of Accounts for Restaurants. 53

National Retail Merchants Association, The Buyer's Manual. 63; Directory of Art, Mat, Photographic and other Advertising Services. 6; Housekeeping Manual for Retail Stores. 63; Merchandising Problems in Opening the New Branch Store. 63; The NRMA Sales Promotion Encyclopedia. 63; 1969 Manual of Federal Trade Regulations Affecting Retailers. 63

National Secretaries Association, Secretarial Study Guide. 69; Secretaries on the Spot. 69

National Society of Sales Training Executives, The New Handbook of Sales Training. 60

National Study Service, Family Credit Counseling. 106

National Tool, Die, and Precision Machining Association, Advanced Diemaking. 165; Basic Diemaking. 165

Nauheim, Ferd, Salesman's Complete Model Letter Handbook. 60

Navarra, John G., Our Noisy World. 179

Nayler, G. H. F., Dictionary of Mechanical Engineering. 165

Nayler, Joseph L., Aviation: Its Technical Development. 118; Dictionary of Astronautics. 118; Dictionary of Mechanical Engineering. 165

Naylor, Brenda, The Technique of Dress Design. 25

Naylor, Naomi, Curriculum Development Program for Preschool Teacher Aides. 112

Neal, Harry, Your Career in Electronics. 151

Nebergall, William, College Chemistry with Qualitative Analysis. 132

Neblette, Carroll, Fundamentals of Photography. 49; Photographic Lenses. 49; Photography: Its Materials and Processes. 49

Needham, George, The Microscope. 183

Negri, Anna L., Contour Fan Cutting for Professional Hairstyling. 8

Neill, Alexander S., Summerhill: A Radical Approach to Child Rearing. 82

Nelson, Aaron, Agricultural Finance. 76

Nelson, Clyde, Machine Shop Operations and Setups. 166

Nelson, George, Problems of Design. 14

Nelson, Glenn, Ceramics: A Potter's Handbook. 162

Nelson, John A., Judging Dairy Products. 34

Nelson, John G., The Koga Method: Police Baton Techniques. 98; Preliminary Investigation and Police Reporting. 99

Nelson, Leslie W., Instructional Aids. 112; Methods That Teach. 111; Science Activities for Elementary Children. 112

Nelson, Lowry, Rural Sociology. 106

Nelson, Oscar S., Accounting Systems and Data Processing. 4

Nelson, Roy P., The Design of Advertising. 6; Fell's Guide to Commercial Art. 11

Nelson, Walter, Small Wonder: The Amazing Story of the Volkswagen. 124

Nesheim, Malden C., Poultry Production. 78

Nett, Louise M., For Those Who Live and Breathe with Emphysema and Chronic Bronchitis. 181

Neubauer, Peter B., Children in Collectives. 82; Concepts of Development in Early Childhood Education. 112

Neumann, Alvin L., Beef Cattle. 79

Neumann, Eckhard, Functional Graphic Design in the 20's. 11

Neundorf, William, Sheet Metal Practice. 162

Neuner, John J. W., Cost Accounting. 5

Nevill, Gale E., Programmed Principles of Statics. 165

Neville, Adam, Properties of Concrete. 141

Neville, Kris, Handbook of Epoxy Resins. 129

Neville, Inc., Basic Electronic Circuits. 154; Basic Industrial Electricity. 154

Nevinson, John L., Origin and Early History of the Fashion Plate. 27

New Private Pilot, Your Guide to the FAA Rating with Typical Cross-Country Written Examinations. 118

New York (City) Board of Education, Getting Started in the Elementary School: A Manual for New Teachers. 112

New York (State) Bureau of Industrial and Technical Education, Suggested Unit Course in Concrete Form Construction. 141

New York College of Forestry, Forest Fertilization Research, 1957-1964. 87

New York (State) Education Department, Bureau of Continuing Education Curriculum Development, Fashion Merchandising. 25; Tips for Teaching: Textiles and Clothing. 29

New York (State) Education Department, Dentistry. 175; Deputy Commissioner of Education's Evaluation Committee on the Experimental Library Technician Program Report. 91; Quantity Cooking Basic Skills. 34; Registered Optometrists and Registered Ophthalmic Dispensers. 199

New York Heart Association, Oxygen. 181

New York Institute of Technology, A Programmed Course in Basic Electricity. 151; A Programmed Course in Basic Electronics. 151; A Programmed Course in Basic Transistors. 159

New York Times, Style Book. 46

Newcomb, Dorothy P., The Team Plan. 192

Newcomb, Thomas P., Automobile Brakes and Braking Systems. 124; Braking of Road Vehicles. 124

Newcomer, James, Liberal Education and Pharmacy. 202

Newell, Adnah C., Coloring, Finishing and Painting Wood. 55

Newell, Frank W., Ophthalmology. 199

Newell, Malcolm, Mood and Atmosphere in Restaurants. 53

Newhall, Beaumont, The Daguerreotype in America. 46; History of Photography, from 1839 to the Present Day. 50; Latent Image: The Discovery of Photography. 50

Newhouse, Howard L., Refresher Course in Gregg Shorthand. 70

Newlon, Clarke, Aerospace Age Dictionary. 118

Newman, Benjamin, Accounting Theory. 4

Newman, Bernard, Your Future in the High Fidelity Industry. 151

Newman, Edwin S., Police, The Law and Personal Freedom. 99

Newman, Joseph W., Consumer Behavior Symposium. 60; Marketing Management and Information. 60

Newman, Monroe, Insurance and Risk. 54

Newman, Morton, Standard Structural Details for Building Construction. 138

Newnes Motor Repair. 124

Newson, Elizabeth, Four Years Old in An Urban Community. 82

Newson, John, Four Years Old in An Urban Community. 82

Newton, Kathleen, Geriatric Nursing. 194

J. Ney Company, The Ney Surveyor Manual. 175

Nicholds, Elizabeth, In-Service Casework Training. 106; A Primer of Social Casework. 106

Nichols, Aylmer V., Modern Data Processing. 15

Nichols, Herbert L., Jr., Moving the Earth: The Workbook of Excavation. 138

Nichols, Nell B., America's Best Vegetable Recipes. 34

Nichols, Thomas S., Legal Foundations of Nursing Practice. 191

Nicholson, Max, The Environmental Revolution. 179

Nickerson, J. T. R., Introduction to Thermal Processing. 41

Nicol, Keith, Elementary Programming and Algol. 21

Niederhoffer, Arthur, Ambivalent Force. 95; Behind the Shield: The Police in Urban Society. 99

Niederwieser, A., Progress in Thin-layer Chromatography and Related Methods. 129

Nikolaieff, George A., Computers and Society. 18; The Water Crisis. 179

Nineham, A. W., Medical and Veterinary Chemicals. 130

Nisbet, Robert A., Contemporary Social Problems. 106

Niswonger, Clifford R., Accounting Principles. 4

Niven, William, Basic Accounting Procedures. 4

Nixon, Stuart, Redwood Empire. 87

Noback, Joseph C., Life Insurance Accounting. 54

Noble, Elmer R., Parasitology. 187

Noble, Eva, Play and the Sick Child. 82

Noble, Glenn A., Parasitology. 187

Noderer, Eleanor, Just Desserts. 34

Noemer, Ewald, Handbook of Modern Halftone Photography. 50

Nolan, Carroll A., Fundamentals of Selling. 62; Marketing, Sales Promotion, and Advertising. 60

Nolan, Richard L., Introduction to Computing Through the Basic Language. 18

Noll, Edward M., Servicing FM-Stereo Receivers. 151

Noll, Walter, Chemistry and Technology of Silicones. 129

Noller, Carl R., Chemistry of Organic Compounds. 135

INDEX

Nolte, William A., Oral Microbiology. 175

Noory, Samuel, Shorthand in One Day. 69

Nordby, Julius E., Livestock Judging and Evaluation. 78; Selecting, Fitting and Showing Beef Cattle. 79; Selecting, Fitting and Showing Dairy Cattle. 79; Selecting, Fitting and Showing Horses. 79; Selecting, Fitting and Showing Poultry. 79; Selecting, Fitting and Showing Sheep. 79; Selecting, Fitting and Showing Swine. 79

Nordenberg, Harold, Electronic Transformers. 151; Fixed and Variable Capacitors. 147

Nordhoff, William A., Machine-Shop Estimating. 165

Nordmark, Madelyn T., Scientific Foundations of Nursing. 192

Norman, John, Medicine in the Ghetto. 208

Norrgard, David L., Regional Law Enforcement. 99

Norris, Charles H., Elementary Structural Analysis. 139

Norris, Jeanne L., Opportunities in Clothing, Fashion, Merchandising. 24

Norris, Walter, Nurse's Guide to Anesthetics Resuscitation and Intensive Care. 192

North, Nelson L., Real Estate Principles and Practices. 66

North Carolina (State) Board of Education, Farm Forestry Laboratory. 87

Northen, Helen, Social Work with Groups. 106

Northrop Institute of Technology, Electricity and Electronics for Aerospace Vehicles. 118; Maintenance and Repair of Aerospace Vehicles. 118

Northrup, Herbert R., The Negro in the Paper Industry. 48

Northwestern University, Traffic Institute, A Bibliography on Police Administration. 99

Norton, Frederick H., Fine Ceramics. 162

Norton, Harry N., Handbook of Transducers for Electronic Measuring Systems. 151

Norton, Loran A., Police Operational Intelligence. 100

Notter, Lucille E., Professional Nursing. 193

Nourse, E. Shepley, Libraries at Large. 91

Novak, William J., Electrical Design Details. 151; Electrical Equipment Manual. 151; Practical Electricity. 151

Nowak, John F., Practical Residential Wiring. 151

Nowolinski, Edmund A., Modern Industrial Die Design. 167

Noyes, Arthur, Psychiatric Nursing. 196

Noyes, Nell, Your Future As a Secretary. 69

Noyes, Robert, Dehydration Processes for Convenience Foods, 1969. 41; Freeze Drying of Foods and Biologicals, 1968. 41

Noyes Development Corporation, Cosmetics Industry of Europe. 7

Nunz, Gregory J., Electronics Mathematics. 206

Nurnberg, Walter, Lighting for Photography. 50

Nursing Clinics of North America. 192

Nursing Examination Review Book. 192

Nussbaum, Allen, Geometric Optics. 199

Nutt, Merle, Principles of Modern Metallurgy. 169

Nydegger, Adolph C., An Introduction to Computer Programming with an Emphasis on Fortran IV. 21

Nye, Robert E., Music in the Elementary School. 112

Nye, Thelma M., Cross Stitch Patterns. 25

Nye, Vernice T., Music in the Elementary School. 112

Nyman, Carl J., Chemical Equilibrium. 129

Oakes, Alma, Rural Costume. 27

Oakley, W. R., The Arco Workshop Companion. 162

Oberg, Fred R., Heavy Timber Construction. 139

Obermeyer, Ernest, The Myth of Trade Advertising. 6

O'Brien, G. M., The Australian Police Forces. 99

O'Brien, James J., CPM in Construction Management. 139

O'Brien, John A., Family Planning in an Exploding Population. 106

O'Brien, Richard C., Dental Radiography. 175

O'Brien, William, Dental Materials. 175

Obst, Frances M., Art and Design in Home Living. 55

O'Connell, C. B., Home Furnishing Self Help. 55

O'Connell, Desmond H., Aim for a Job in the Bakery Industry. 37; Your Future in the Bakery Industry. 37

O'Connell, Jeffrey, Safety Last: An Indictment of the Auto Industry. 124

O'Connell, John J., Modern Criminal Investigation. 101

O'Connor, George, Juvenile Delinquency and Youth Crime: The Police Role. 100; The Patrol Operation. 99

O'Connor, Hyla, Book of Salads. 34

O'Connor, Patricia, Fundamental Skills in the Nurse-Patient Relationship. 191

O'Dell, Scott, The Psychology of Children's Art. 10

O'Dell, William F., The Marketing Decision. 60

Odum, Eugene P., Ecology. 179

Oelke, William C., Laboratory Physical Chemistry. 135

Oerke, Bess V., Dress: The Clothing Textbook. 23, 25

Ogg, Oscar, The 26 Letters. 14

Ogle, Kenneth, Optics. 199

Ogura, Ryozo, The Lively Art of Ink Painting. 11

O'Hara, Charles, Fundamentals of Criminal Investigation. 100

O'Hara, Frank J., Psychology and the Nurse. 192

O'Higgins, Patrick, Basic Instrumentation: Industrial Measurement. 165

Ohio (State) Department of Education, Vocational Education Division, Emergency Victim Care and Rescue. 85; Fire Service Training. 85

Ohio (State) University, Center for Vocational and Technical Instruction, Planning and Conducting Cooperative Occupational Experience for Off-Farm Agriculture. 76

Ohio (State) University, Industrial Arts Curriculum Project, The World of Construction. 139

Ohman, Anka, Basic Accounting Procedures. 4

Ohnsty, James, Aids To Ethics and Professional Conduct for Student Radiologic Technologists. 205

Oil and Colour Chemists' Association, Paint Technology Manuals. 130

Ojakangas, Beatrice A., The Finnish Cookbook. 40

Okamoto, Yoshiyuki, Organic Semiconductors. 135

O'Kane, Dick, How to Repair Your Foreign Car. 124; The Making of an Aircraft Mechanic. 118

O'Keefe, Paul T., How to Finance Real Estate. 65

O'Kelly, Denis, An Introduction to Generalized Electrical Machine Theory. 151

Oldfield, R. L., Radio-Television and Basic Electronics. 157

Oldham, Frances, Essentials of Pharmacology. 202

Oleesky, Samuel S., Handbook of Reinforced Plastics of the Society of the Plastics Industry, Inc. 168

Olendzki, Margaret, Welfare Medical Care. 105

Olesten, Nils O., Numerical Control. 170

Olin, Harold B., Construction Lending Guide. 139

Oliphant, C. P., Color TV Training Manual. 158

Oliphant, Joyce, A Study Guide for Student X-Ray Technicians. 205

Oliver, Raymond, Gastronomy of France. 40; La Cuisine. 34; The Wine and Food Society's Guide to Classic

Sauces and Their Preparation. 34; Basic Physics in Radiology. 204

Oliver, Robert E., Advertising. 6

Oliverio, Mary, Shorthand Dictation Studies. 67

Olivero, James, Educational Manpower. 112

Olivo, C. Thomas, Principles of Refrigeration. 121

Ollard, E. A., Elementary Science for Electroplating Students and Foremen. 151

Olney, Richard, The French Menu Cook Book. 40

Olsen, Gerner A., Elements of Mechanics of Materials. 165

Olsen, H. M., Some Principles and Practices of Farmer Cooperatives. 76

Olson, Delmar, Industrial Arts and Technology. 162; Industrial Arts for the General Shop. 162; Woods & Woodworking for Industrial Arts. 162

Olson, Lyla, A Nurses' Handbook for Hospital, School and Home. 192

Olson, Norman, Accounting for Goodwill. 2

Olson, Ollie, Creating in Wood with the Lathe. 161

Olson, Robert L., Quality and Stability in Frozen Foods. 42

Olson, William L., Arc-Welding. 171

O'Malley, Robert F., Problems in Chemistry. 130

O'Morrow, Gerald S., Administration of Activity Therapy Service. 209

O'Neal, Leeland, Electronic Data Processing Systems. 16

O'Neill, Hugh, Hardness Measurement of Metals and Alloys. 169

O'Neill, James M., Early American Furniture. 56

O'Neill, John J., Pharmacology and Therapeutics. 202

Onions, W. J., Wool. 29

Oparin, Alexander L., The Chemical Origin of Life. 130

Opie, Iona, Children's Games in Street and Playground. 82

Opie, Peter, Children's Games in Street and Playground. 82

Oppenheimer, J. M., Foundations of Experimental Embryology. 183

Oppenheimer, Samuel, Direct and Alternating Currents. 151; Semiconductor Logic and Switching Circuits. 151

Oppenheimer, Samuel P., Erecting Structural Steel. 139

Opper, Sylvia, Piaget's Theory of Intellectual Development. 81

Optical Society of America, The Science of Color. 13

O'Quinn, Garland, Gymnastics for Elementary School Children. 112

Oravetz, Jules, Audel's Plumbers' and Pipe Fitters' Library. 141; Audel's Practical Guide to Building Maintenance. 139

Orbaan, Albert, Dogs Against Crime. 100

Orban, Balint J., Oral Histology and Embryology. 175

Orchin, Milton, Symmetry in Chemistry. 128

Ordway, Frederick I., Applied Astronautics. 118; Basic Astronautics. 118; Careers in Astronautics and Rocketry. 115

Orem, Dorothea E., Guides for Developing Curricula for the Education of Practical Nurses. 196

Orem, Reginald G., The Children's House Parent-Teacher Guide to Montessori. 81; Managing Student Behavior. 108; Montessori and the Special Child. 82

Orent, Norman, Your Future in Marketing. 60

Organic Syntheses: An Annual Publication of Satisfactory Methods for the Preparation of Organic Chemicals. 130

Orlando, Ida J., The Dynamic Nurse-Patient Relationship. 192

Orlicky, Joseph, The Successful Computer System. 18

Orne, Jerrold, The Language of the Foreign Book Trade. 91

Ornstein, Allan, How to Teach Disadvantaged Youth. 112

Orr, William D., Conversational Computers. 18

Orten, James M., Biochemistry. 133

Osborne, G. F., Space Vehicle Dynamics. 115

Osler, Robert W., Modern Life Insurance. 54

Osmaston, F. C., The Management of Forests. 87

Oster, Jon, Basic Applied Fluid Power. 165

Osterburg, James W., Crime Laboratory. 100

Ostergaard, D. Eugene, Advanced Diemaking. 165; Basic Diemaking. 165

Osterheld, William, Essentials of Electricity-Electronics. 153; Essentials of Radio-Electronics. 157

Ostrander, Floyd D., Clinical Endodontics. 176

Ostrander, Sheila, Festive Food Decoration for All Occasions. 34

Ostwald, Wilhelm, The Color Primer. 13

Oswald, James W., Technology of Machine Tools. 165

Oswald, John C., Printing in the Americas. 46

Othmer, Donald F., Encyclopedia of Chemical Technology. 128

O'Toole, John F., Jr., Computer and Information Systems in Education. 17

Otteson, Schuyler, Marketing. 60

Otto, Herbert A., The Development of Theory and Practice in Social Casework. 104; Human Potentialities. 106

Ouderkirk, John, An Introduction to Printing Plant Layout. 46

Outland, John G., Rotating Seasonal Menus. 34

Overland, Anna, Woodward and Gardner's Obstetric Management and Nursing. 194

Overman, Michael, Water. 179

Owczarek, Jerzy A., Introduction to Fluid Mechanics. 165

Owen, Terence C., Characterization of Organic Compounds by Chemical Methods. 135

Owens, Guy, Neurological and Neurosurgical Nursing. 194

Owens, James B., Electron Tubes at Work. 151; Fundamentals of Electricity. 151

Ower, Ernest, Aviation. 118

Ozias, Blake, All About Wine. 38

Pace, Denny F., Guidelines for Work Experience Programs in the Criminal Justice System. 101; Law Enforcement Training and the Community College. 100

Pack, Greta, Jewelry and Enameling. 162; Jewelry Making by the Lost Wax Process. 28; Mexican Jewelry. 27

Packaging Institute, Glossary of Packaging Terms. 63

Pactor, Paul, Comprehensive Business Machines Course. 69; Full-Keyboard Adding Machine Course. 69; Rotary Calculator Course. 69; Ten-Key Adding Machine Course. 69

Padgett, Rose, Textile Chemistry and Testing in the Laboratory. 130

Pafford, F. William, Handbook of Survey Notekeeping. 142

Page, Andre, Photographic Composition. 50

Page, John S., Estimator's Construction Man-Hour Manual. 139; Estimator's Equipment Installation Man-Hour Manual. 121; Heating, Plumbing and Air-Conditioning Man-Hour Manual. 121

Paige, Barbara, Your Future as a Dental Hygienist. 175

Palan, Ralph L., A Course of Study for Adult Farmer Instruction in Farm Management and Farm Business Analysis. 76

Paling, D. F., Warp Knitting Technology. 25

Pallett, Edwin H. J., Aircraft Instrument Manual. 118

Palmer, Aubrey, Mechanics of Materials. 163

Palmer, Charles E., College Accounting: Intermediate/Advanced. 1; College

INDEX

Accounting: Theory/Practice. 1; College Accounting: Theory and Practice. 4

Palmer, Charles H., Optics. 199

Palmer, Frank, Tool Steel Simplified. 165

Palmer, Mary W., Day Care Aides. 82

Palmer, Robert G., Introductory Soil Science. 77

Palmquist, Roland, Audel's Answers on Blue Print Reading. 143; Guide to the National Electrical Code. 151; Questions and Answers for Electricians Examinations. 145

Palusci, Larry, Profitable Retailing of Building Supplies. 139

Pan-Am Optical Laboratory, Frames and Rx Lenses. 199

Pan American Navigation Service, Ground Instructor Ratings. 118

Pan American World Airways, Inc., New Horizons U.S.A. 118

Panchar, William G., Marketing. 60

Paniagua, Lita, Role-Play in New Careers Training. 106

Pannett, W. E., Dictionary of Radio and Television. 157

Panofsky, Erwin, Tomb Sculpture. 94

Panshin, Alexis J., Forest Products. 87; Textbook of Wood Technology. 87

Pansky, Ben, Review of Gross Anatomy. 175

Paper Catalog. 48

Paper Year Book. 48

Papp, Charles S., Scientific Illustration. 11

Paquin, J. R., Die Design Fundamentals. 167

Parad, Howard J., Crisis Intervention. 106

Pardonnet, Rolland H., General Industrial Arts. 160

Pareti, John J., How to Sell Footwear Profitably. 25

Paris, Don, Textbook of Radiologic Technology. 204; X-Ray Technology. 204

Park, Virginia R., A Textbook for Dental Assistants. 175

Park, William R. R., Plastics Film Technology. 168

Parke, Gertrude, The Big Chocolate Cookbook. 34; The Big Coffee Cookbook. 34

Parker, Albert D., Planning and Estimating Underground Construction. 139; Planning and Estimating Urban Construction. 139

Parker, D. B. V., Polyurethanes. 130

Parker, Harry, Architects' and Builders' Handbook. 138; Simplified Design of Reinforced Concrete. 141; Simplified Design of Structural Timber. 139; Simplified Engineering for Architects and Builders. 139; Simplified Mechanics and Strength of Materials. 170

Parker, Jerald D., Introduction to Fluid Mechanics and Heat Transfer. 165

Parker, Kitty, Continuity of Patient Care. 193

Parker, Milton, Food Plant Sanitation. 34

Parker, Page, Upholstering at Home. 56

Parker, Raymond, Methods of Tissue Culture. 183

Parker, William H., Health and Disease of Farm Animals for Those Concerned with Animal Husbandry. 79

Parker Publishing Company, Secretary's Desk Book. 69; The Successful Secretary. 69

Parkes, G. D., Modern Inorganic Chemistry. 133

Parkins, Redvers, The Extrusion of Metals. 169; Mechanical Treatment of Metals. 169

Parks, George, The Economics of Carpeting and Resilient Flooring. 52

Parmarlee, Albert S., Geometry of Engineering Drawing. 206

Parmelee, C. W., Ceramic Glazes. 162

Parnell, J. E., Practical Procedures. 194

Parola, Rene, Optical Art. 11

Parr, Robert E., Principles of Mechanical Design. 167

Parrish, Lex, ABC's of Avionics. 118; Space-Flight Simulation Technology. 118

Parrish, Louise, Teacher-Pupil Planning for Better Classroom Learning. 113

Parrott, Eugene L., Pharmaceutical Technology. 202

Parrott, Leslie, The Usher's Manual. 94

Parsons, Talcott, Sociological Theory and Modern Society. 106

Partain, Lloyd, Rural Recreation for Profit. 103

Parvis, Jeannette, Furnishing Your Home. 54

Pascoe, K. J., An Introduction to the Properties of Engineering Materials. 168

Pasewark, William R., Full-Keyboard-Adding-Listing Machine Course. 66; Key Driven Calculator Course. 66; Rotary Calculator Course. 66; Ten-Key Adding-Listing Machine and Printing Calculator Course. 66

Pasley, Virginia, You Can Do Anything with Crepes. 34

Pass, Geoffrey, Practical Inorganic Chemistry. 133

Passeron, Roger, French Prints of the 20th Century. 11

Passow, A. Harry, Education of the Disadvantaged. 112; Reaching the Disadvantaged Learner. 112

Passow, H., Laboratory Techniques in Membrane Biophysics. 183

Pasztor, Magda, Bibliography of Pharmaceutical Reference Literature. 202

Patai, Saul, The Chemistry of Carboxylic Acids and Esters. 130; Tables for Identification of Organic Compounds. 134

Pataki, György, Progress in Thin-Layer Chromatography and Related Methods. 129; Techniques of Thin-Layer Chromatography in Amino Acid and Peptide Chemistry. 130

Patillo, James W., The Foundation of Financial Accounting. 4

Paton, William A., Essentials of Accounting. 2

Paton, William D., Pharmacological Principles and Practice. 202

Patrick, A. W., Cost Accounting for Management. 5

Patten, Lawton M., Architectural Drawing. 144

Patten, Marguerite, Cake Icing and Decoration. 37

Patterson, Frank M., A Manual of Police Report Writing. 100

Patterson, James M., Marketing. 60

Patterson, William G., A Textbook of Medical-Surgical Nursing. 188

Patti, A. Anne, Steroid Analysis by Gas Liquid Chromatography. 130

Pattillo, James W., Effective Accounting Reports. 3

Pattison, J. B., Programmed Introduction to Gas-Liquid Chromatography. 130

Patton, W. J., Materials in Industry. 168; Science and Practice of Welding. 171

Patty, C. Robert, Readings in Global Marketing Management. 62

Patz, Arnall, Protection of Vision in Children. 199

Paul, Grace, Your Future in Medical Technology. 183

Paulder, Sydney, Sales Manager's Guide to Selection and Control of Export Agents. 60

Pauling, Linus C., College Chemistry. 130; The Nature of the Chemical Bond and the Structure of Molecules and Crystals. 130

Paull, Stephen, Topics in Advanced Mathematics for Electronics Technology. 206

Pavenstedt, Eleanor, The Drifters. 82

Payne, Alma, The Low Sodium, Fat-Controlled Cookbook. 34

Payne, Blanche, History of Costume. 27

Payne, Charles A., How To Do An Organic Synthesis. 130

Payne, George K., Creative Display. 63

Payne, James, Pharmacological Principles and Practice. 202

Payne, Lamar B., How To Do An Organic Synthesis. 130

Payne, William H., Machine, Assembly, and Systems Programming for the IBM 360. 21

Payton, George T., Patrol Procedure. 100

Peairs, Leonard M., Insect Pests of Farm, Garden and Orchard. 74

Peale, Norman V., The Healing of Sorrow. 94

Pearl, Arthur, New Careers for the Poor. 106

Pearsall, George W., Structure and Properties of Materials. 168

Pearson, Claude E., The Extrusion of Metals. 169

Pearson, David, The Chemical Analysis of Foods. 126

Pearson, George, Engineering Drawing. 143

Pearson, John W., Historical and Experimental Approaches to Modern Resuscitation. 181

Pearson, Leonard, Death and Dying. 94

Pearson, Neville, Instructional Materials Centers. 112

Pearson, Ralph G., Mechanisms of Inorganic Reactions. 133

Pease, Damaris, Behavior and Development from 5 to 12. 81

Pease, Dudley, Basic Fluid Power. 165

Peate, Patricia F., The Complete Secretary. 69

Peck, Paula, The Art of Fine Baking. 37

Peckham, Gladys C., Foundations of Food Preparation. 34

Peckner, Donald, The Strengthening of Metals. 169

Pecsok, Robert L., Modern Methods of Chemical Analysis. 132

Pederson, Donald O., Introduction to Electronic Systems, Circuits, and Devices. 152

Peel, John D., Fundamentals of Training for Security Officers. 100

Peer, Daniel I., Real Estate Problems. 66

Pell, Arthur R., Police Leadership. 100

Pellaprat, Henri P., Modern French Culinary Art. 40

Pelletier, S. W., Chemistry of the Alkaloids. 130

Pellew, John C., Painting in Watercolor. 11

Pelley, Thelma, Nursing. 192

Pellowski, Anne, The World of Children's Literature. 82

Pelton, B. W., Furniture Making and Cabinet Work. 162

Pelton, Walter J., Epidemiology of Oral Health. 175

Pender, James A., Welding. 171

Pendered, Norman, Industrial Arts in General Education. 163

Pendery, John A., General Office Practice for Colleges. 69; Secretarial Office Practice for Colleges. 69

Pennell, Lois G., The Bookmobile. 91

Penning-Rowsell, Edmund, The International Wine and Food Society's Guide to the Wines of Bordeaux. 38

Pennington, George W., Dental Pharmacology. 175

Penrose Annual: Review of the Graphic Arts. 46

Pepe, Phillip, Personal Typing in Twenty-Four Hours. 69

Peppler, Henry J., Microbial Technology. 187

Perard, Victor, The New How to Draw. 12

Perkins, Bryce, Getting Better Results from Substitutes, Teacher Aides and Volunteers. 112

Perkins, John J., Principles and Methods of Sterilization in Health Sciences. 208

Perl, Lila, Rice, Spice, and Bitter Oranges. 40

Perlis, Alan J., A View of Programming Languages. 19

Perlman, Helen, Helping: Charlotte Towle on Social Work.... 106; So You Want to be a Social Worker. 106

Perloff, Harvey S., The Quality of the Urban Environment. 107

Permar, Dorothy, Oral Embryology and Microscopic Anatomy. 175

Perrodin, Cecilia, Medical Nursing. 190

Perros, Theodore P., Chemistry. 130

Perry, Enos C., Sales Horizons. 58

Perry, Enos J., The Artificial Insemination of Farm Animals. 79

Perry, John, Our Polluted World. 179

Perry, Kenneth, The Binding of Books. 47

Perry, Kenneth W., Advanced Accounting. 1

Perry, Tilden W., Feed Formulations Handbook. 79

Perry-Miller, Mitzi F., Clean Plates. 34

Persons, Edgar A., A Course of Study for Adult Farmer Instruction in Farm Management and Farm Business Analysis. 76

Perutz, Kathrin, Beyond the Looking Glass. 7

Pestel, Eduard, Statics. 165

Pesznecker, Betty L., Psychiatric Content in the Nursing Curriculum. 192

Peters, Anne D., Early Child Care. 80

Peters, Dennis G., Basic Theory and Practice of Quantitative Chemical Analysis. 132; A Brief Introduction to Quantitative Chemical Analysis. 132; Chemical Equilibrium. 127

Peters, Geoff, Woodturning. 162

Peters, Ken, Modern Tape Recording and Hi-Fi. 152

Peters, Raymond H., Fibre Structure. 28

Peters, Richard M., The Mechanical Basis of Respiration. 181

Petersen, Eldridge, Who's Who in Advertising. 6

Petersen, Grete, Creative Leathercraft, 162, 209; Handbook of Stitches. 25

Peterson, Aldor, Applied Mechanics for Engineers and Technicians. 166; Applied Mechanics: Strength of Materials. 170

Peterson, Carolyn S., Reference Books for Elementary and Junior High School Libraries. 91

Peterson, Dean F., Large-Scale Desalting. 179

Peterson, Grace G., Working With Others for Patient Care. 192

Peterson, Martin S., Food Technology the World Over. 41

Peterson, Shailer A., Clinical Dental Hygiene. 175; Comprehensive Review for Dental Hygienists. 175; The Dentist and His Assistant. 175; Review and Test Manual for the Dental Assistant. 175

Peterson, Sigfred, Chemistry in Nuclear Technology. 130

Peterson, Wesley W., Fortran IV and the IBM 360. 21

Petterson, Henry, Creating Form in Clay. 162

Pettit, Florence H., America's Printed and Painted Fabrics, 1600-1900. 25

Pettit, Helen F., Teaching Psychosocial Aspects of Patient Care. 192

Pettit, William, Manual of Pharmaceutical Law. 202

Petty, Thomas L., For Those Who Live and Breathe with Emphysema and Chronic Bronchitis. 181

Peurifoy, Robert L., Construction Planning, Equipment and Methods. 139; Formwork for Concrete Structures. 141

Peyton, Alice, Practical Nutrition. 40

Peyton, Floyd A., Restorative Dental Materials. 175

Pfaltz, Marilyn, Your Secret Servant. 35

Pfeiffer, William B., The Correct Maid for Hotels and Motels. 52; The Correct Service Department for Hotels, Motor Hotels, Motels and Resorts. 52

Pfeiffer, William J., Handbook of Structured Experiences for Human Relations Training. 107

Pfister, Herbert R., House Construction Details. 136

Pflaum, Ronald T., Introductory Analytical Chemistry. 132

Phalen, Thomas E., Jr., An Introduction to Mechanics. 166

Pharmaceutical Association of the Province of British Columbia, Hospital Pharmacy Manual. 202

Pharmaceutical Manufacturers Association, Prescription Drug Industry Fact Book. 202

Pharmaceutical Society of Great Britain, British Pharmaceutical Codex, 1968. 202; Poisons and T.S.A. Guide for Pharmacists in Retail and Hospital Practice. 202

INDEX

Pharmacist's Dictionary of Medical Terms. 202

Pharmacopeia of the United States of America. 202

Pharmacy Examination Review Book. 202

Phelan, Richard M., Fundamentals of Mechanical Design. 167

Phelps, Dudley M., Marketing Management. 60

Phifer, Gregg, Salesmanship. 56

Philco Corporation, Electronic and Electrical Fundamentals. 152; Electronic Precision Measurement Techniques and Experiments. 152; Electronic Troubleshooting. 152; Servomechanism Fundamentals and Experiments. 152

Philip, Julia W., Who's Who in Commercial Art and Photography. 12

Philippakis, Andreas S., Fundamentals of EDP and Fortran. 20

Philips, G. Edward, Financial Statements. 4

Phillips, Arthur, Structure and Property of Alloys. 168

Phillips, Arthur H., Computer Peripherals and Typesetting. 46

Phillips, B. G., Building Law Illustrated. 139

Phillips, Bert L., The Pastry Chef. 37

Phillips, Charles, Marketing. 60; Retailing. 63

Phillips, Donald S., Electromechanical Technology. 155

Phillips, George M., Computers. 18

Phillips, Helen L., Technical Typewriting. 68

Phillips, James, Dental Roentgenology. 174

Phillips, James P., How to Build a Working Digital Computer. 17

Phillips, Jeanne, Statistics for Nurses. 192

Phillips, Leslie N., Polyurethanes. 130

Phillips, Ralph W., Elements of Dental Materials for Dental Hygienists and Assistants. 176; The Science of Dental Materials. 175

Phillips, Robert, Comprehensive Review for the Radiologic Technologist. 205

Phipps, David, Racing and Sports Car Chassis Design. 122

Phipps, Lloyd J., Handbook on Agricultural Education in Public Schools. 76; Ideas for Farm Mechanics Projects. 78; Mechanics in Agriculture. 78; Review and Synthesis of Research in Agricultural Education. 77; Your Opportunities in Vocational Agriculture. 76

Photo-Lab Index: The Cumulative Formulary of Standard Recommended Photographic Procedures. 50

Piaget, Jean, The Language and Thought of the Child. 82; The Moral Judgement of the Child. 82

Pictorial Cyclopedia of Photography. 50

Piepenburg, Robert, Designs in Wood. 162

Pierce, Eleanor, Menu Translator. 34

Pierce, John, Electrons and Waves. 152

Piggott, Derek, Gliding. 118

Pigors, Faith, Professional Nursing Practice. 192

Pigors, Paul J., Professional Nursing Practice. 192

Pike, Charles A., Lasers and Masers. 156

Pilcher, Roy, Principles of Construction Management for Engineers and Managers. 139

Pilditch, James, Communication by Design. 60; The Silent Salesman. 63

Pile, Robert S., Menu Planning for Every Occasion. 34

Pillepich, Mary, Development of General Education in Collegiate Nursing Programs. 192

Piller, Laurence W., Manual of Cardio-Pulmonary Technology. 181

Pimentel, George C., The Hydrogen Bond. 130

Pines, Maya, Revolution in Learning. 112

Pinney, Roy, Advertising Photography. 12, 50

Pintauro, Nicholas, Soluble Coffee Manufacturing Processes. 41; Soluble Tea Production Processes. 41

Pipe, Peter, Introduction to Electronics. 149

Pipe, Ted, Small Gasoline Engines Training Manual. 124

Pirenne, Maurice, Vision and the Eye. 199

Pirie, N. W., Food Resources. 34

Pisani, Torquato J., Essentials of Strength of Materials. 170

Pistolese, Rosana, The History of Fashions. 27

Pitcher, Evelyn G., Children Tell Stories. 82

Pitkin, Charles W., General Printing. 43

Pitman, Avis J., Clinical Nursing Instruction by Television. 190

Pitman, Sir Isaac, Pitman's English and Shorthand Dictionary. 69

Pitorak, Elizabeth F., Nurses' Guide to Cardiac Surgery and Nursing Care. 197

Pitz, Henry C., Early American Dress. 27; How to Use the Figure. 12; Illustrating Children's Books. 12

Pivnick, Esther B., Making a Skirt. 25

Pizzuto, Joseph J., Fabric Science. 29

Place, Irene M., College Secretarial Procedures. 69; Filing and Records Management. 69; Office Management. 69

Plane, Robert A., Chemistry. 130; Elements of Inorganic Chemistry. 133; Experimental Chemistry. 130; Physical Inorganic Chemistry. 133

Plants, Helen L., Programmed Topics in Statics and Strength of Materials. 170

Platt, Rutherford H., The Great American Forest. 87

Platt, William R., Color Atlas and Textbook of Hematology. 186

Plein, Elmer M., Fundamentals of Medications. 203

Plein, Joy, Fundamentals of Medications. 203

Plenderleith, Harold J., The Preservation of Leather Bookbindings. 47

Pleuthner, Willard A., 460 Secrets of Advertising Experts. 6

Plevyak, Edward J., Industrial Arts Drafting. 143

Plihal, Jane, Evaluation Materials... Social Factors. 55

Pluckrose, Henry, Introducing Crayon Techniques. 12

Plumb, Barbara, Young Designs in Living. 55

Plumb, S. C., Introduction to Fortran. 21

Poage, J. F., The SNOBOL 4 Programming Language. 20

Pock, Max A., Consolidating Police Functions in Metropolitan Areas. 100

Pocket Encyclopedia of Paper & Graphic Arts Terms. 46

Podd, George O., Planning and Operating Motels and Motor Hotels. 52

Pohl, Margaret L., Teaching Functions of the Nursing Practitioner. 192

Police and Sheriffs Association of North America, The Policeman's Handbook of Law. 100

Police Chief, Police and the Changing Community. 100

Police Sergeant's Handbook, 100

Polk, Edwin W., Elementary Platen Presswork. 46; The Practice of Printing. 46

Polk, Ralph W., Elementary Platen Presswork. 46; The Practice of Printing. 46

Pollack, Harvey, Basic Principles and Applications of Relays. 152; Photoelectric Control. 152

Pollack, Herman, Manufacturing and Machine Tool Operations. 166

Pollack, Seymour, Computers and the Life Sciences. 18; Computing and Computer Science. 18; A Guide to Fortran IV. 21; A Guide to Pl/I. 21; Introduction to Statistical Data Processing. 16

Pollard, Alfred W., Early Illustrated Books. 12

Pollard, L. Belle, Experiences with Clothing. 25

Pollock, James R. A., Dictionary of Organic Compounds. 130

Pollock, Vera, Nonwoven Fabrics. 29

Pollution Control. 179

Polon, David D., Dictionary of Electronics Abbreviations, Signs and Symbols. 152

Polonsky, L. P., The SNOBOL 4 Programming Language. 20
Polos, Nicholas C., Dynamics of Team Teaching. 112
Polson, Cyril J., The Disposal of the Dead. 94
Pomerantz, Joel, Jennie and the Story of Grossinger's. 52
Pomeroy, Richard, Studies in the Use of Health Services by Families on Welfare: Utilization by Publicly-Assisted Families. 107
Poole, H. Edmund, Annals of Printing. 42
Poole, J. B., Solid-Liquid Separation. 130
Poore, Henry R., Composition in Art. 12
Pope, Antoinette, Antoinette Pope School New Candy Cookbook. 35
Pope, Michael, Introducing Oil Painting. 12
Popham, Estelle L., Effective Secretarial Practices. 67; Filing and Records Management. 69; Opportunities in Office Occupations. 69
Popham, W. James, Planning an Instructional Sequence. 112
Popkin, Gerald, Air and Water Pollution. 178
Popkin, Roy, Desalination. 179
Popper, Hermine, Up from Poverty. 107
Popov, Alexander I., Introductory Analytical Chemistry. 132
Porowski, Pauline, Nursing Care of the Plastic Surgery Patient. 197
Porter, A., Introduction to Servomechanisms. 166
Porter, Arthur R., Dairy Cattle in American Agriculture. 79
Porter, Edward A., Accidental or Incendiary. 84
Porter, George, Chemistry for the Modern World. 130
Porter, Gerald, Introduction to Physical Inorganic Chemistry. 133
Porter, Harold W., Machine Shop Operations and Setups. 166
Porter, Leonard J., Filing and Finding. 69
Porterfield, John D., Community Health. 208
Portland Cement Association and National Ready Mixed Concrete Association, Concrete Technology. 141
Poser, Charles M., International Dictionary of Drugs Used in Neurology and Psychiatry. 203
Post, Roy G., Water Production Using Nuclear Energy. 179
Potter, Maurice D., Textiles. 29
Potter, Norman, What is a Designer? 12
Potter, Norman W., Food Science. 35
Poulin, Clarence, Poulin's Garment Altering and Repairing and Tailor Shop Management. 25
Poulton, E. C., Environment and Human Efficiency. 179

Poultry Science Association, Find Your Career in the Poultry Industry. 79
Powell, Mary, Orthopaedic Nursing. 195
Powell, Myrtis N., Candles in Flower Arrangements. 55
Power, T., DC-AC Laboratory Manual. 152
Powers, Maryann, The Cardiac Surgical Patient. 197
Powers, Treval C., The Properties of Fresh Concrete. 141
Powitt, A. H., Lectures in Hair Structure and Chemistry for Cosmetology Teachers. 8
Powledge, Fred, To Change a Child. 82
Poynter, F. N. L., The Evolution of Pharmacy in Britain. 203
Poyton, Herbert G., Manual of Dental and Oral Radiography. 173
Pradhan, Shyamsunderlal, Insect Pests of Crops. 76
Praz, Mario, An Illustrated History of Furnishing. 55
Preece, Ann, A Manual for Histologic Technicians. 186
Preiss, Jack J., An Examination of Role Theory:...the State Police. 100
Prelinger, Ernest, Children Tell Stories. 82
Prensky, Sol D., Electronic Instrumentation. 152; How to Use Meters. 152; Modern Electronic Voltmeters. 152
Prentice, Richard, Programming for Numerical Control Machines. 170
Prentice-Hall, Accountant's Encyclopedia. 4; The Corporate Secretary's Handbook. 70; Encyclopedia of Accounting Forms and Reports. 4; Encyclopedia of Cost Accounting Systems. 5; Encyclopedic Dictionary of Real Estate Practice. 66; Handbook of Advanced Secretarial Techniques. 69; Handbook of Forms for Profitable Accounting Practice. 4; Legal Secretary's Encyclopedic Dictionary. 71; Prentice-Hall Treasury of Money-Making Real Estate Ideas and Practices. 66; Secretary's Factomatic. 69
Preston, Doris, Source Book of Statistics Relating to Construction. 138
Preston, Howard K., Modern Prestressed Concrete. 141; Practical Prestressed Concrete. 141; Prestressed Concrete for Architects and Engineers. 141
Preston, Lee, Markets and Marketing. 60; Social Issues in Marketing. 60
Preston, Richard J., North American Trees. 87
Price, Alice, The Art, Science, and Spirit of Nursing. 192
Price, Bill, How to Repair Home and Auto Air Conditioners. 121
Price, Elmina, Learning Needs of Registered Nurses. 192
Price, Flo, Coffee-Time Desserts. 35

Price, Geraldine G., Self-Study Guide of Mathematics Used in Nursing. 206
Price, Leslie W., Electronic Laboratory Techniques. 152
Price, Seymour, Air Conditioning for Building Engineers and Managers. 121
Price, Wilson T., Elements of Basic Fortran IV Programming. 21; Elements of Computer Programming. 21; Elements of IBM 1130 Programming. 21
Priluck, Herbert M., Practical CPM for Construction. 139
Primrose, Rosellen, Pediatric Surgery for Nurses. 197
Printers' Ink, Advertising. 6; New Products Marketing. 60
Printing Industries of Metropolitan New York, Inc., Printers Buying Guide. 46
Printing Trades Blue Book, The Standard Directory and Reference Book of the Graphic Arts Industry. 46
Prise, Walter J., Electronic Circuit Packaging. 152
Pritchard, D. C., Lighting. 152
Pritchard, Robert L., Electrical Characteristics of Transistors. 159
Pritikin, Roland I., Essentials of Ophthalmology. 199
Probyn, Peter, The Complete Drawing Book. 12
Proctor, Henry, Principles for First Aid for the Injured. 208
Proctor, Richard M., The Principles of Pattern for Craftsmen and Designers. 12
Prodan, Michail, Forest Biometrics. 87
Product News: Hotel-Motel Buyer's Directory. 52
Prohaska, Ray, A Basic Course in Design. 14
Promersberger, William J., Modern Farm Power. 78
Proud, Nora, Introducing Textile Printing. 29; Textile Printing and Dyeing. 29
Proudfit, Fairfax T., Normal and Therapeutic Nutrition. 40
Provence, Sally, Guide for the Care of Infants in Groups. 82; Infants in Institutions. 82
Prugh, Dane G., The Healthy Child. 83
Prutton, Carl F., Principles of Physical Chemistry. 135
Psathas, George, The Student Nurse in the Diploma School of Nursing. 192
Puckett, Russell E., Introduction to Electronics. 152
Puckle, Bertram S., Funeral Customs. 94
Pugh, Clementine, Those Children. 109
Pugh, Emerson M., Principles of Electricity and Magnetism. 152
Pugh, Emerson W., Principles of Electricity and Magnetism. 152

INDEX

Pugh, J. W., California Real Estate Finance. 66

Pugsley, Clement H., On Sorrow's Lone Hour. 94

Pula, Fred, Application and Operation of Audiovisual Equipment in Education. 112

Pulling, Christopher, The Police. 100

Pulp and Paper Manufacture. 48

Pulver, Harry E., Construction Estimates and Costs. 139

Pumphrey, Muriel W., The Heritage of American Social Work. 107

Pumphrey, Ralph, The Heritage of American Social Work. 107

Purcell, Francis P., Education and the Urban Community. 110

Purdue University School of Technology (Office of Manpower Studies), The Case for Library Technical Assistants and Library Clerks in Indiana. 91

Purdy, Ken W., Wonderful World of the Automobile. 124

Purser, Paul, Manned Spacecraft. 118

Pursuit, Dan G., Police Work with Juveniles and the Administration of Juvenile Justice. 98

Purvis, Judson A., All About Small Gas Engines. 124

Pye, Orrea, Foundations of Nutrition. 41

Pyke, Magnus, Food, Science and Technology. 35

Pyle, S. Idell, Radiographic Atlas of Skeletal Development of the Foot and Ankle. 204

Pyle, William, Fundamental Accounting Principles. 4

Quay, William H., Jr., The Negro in the Chemical Industry. 130

Quick, John, Artists' and Illustrators' Encyclopedia. 12

Quick Frozen Foods Directory of Wholesale Distributors. 35

Quick Frozen Foods Processors Directory. 41

Quimby, Edith H., Physical Foundations of Radiology. 204

Quinn, Alonzo, Design and Construction of Ports and Marine Structures. 139

Quinney, Richard, Criminal Behavior Systems. 96; The Social Reality of Crime. 100

Quint, Jeanne, The Nurse and the Dying Patient. 192

Raab, Earl, Major Social Problems. 107

Rachman, David J., Retail Strategy and Structure. 63

Rackow, A. M., Anatomy and Physiology for Radiographers. 203

Radano, Gene, Walking the Beat. 100

Radcliffe, Byron M., Critical Path Method. 139

Radelet, Louis A., Police and Community Relations. 95

Radigan, J. Terry, A Financial Analysis of the Restaurant Industry. 53

Radio Corporation of America, Transistor Manual. 159

Radio-Electronics, Transistors. 159

Radio Handbook. 157

Radler, Donald, Success Through Play. 82

Raebeck, Lois, Who am I? 82

Raffensperger, John, Pediatric Surgery for Nurses. 197

Rafferty, Max J., Max Rafferty On Education. 112

Rahe, Harves, Shorthand-Secretarial Research Index. 69

Rainey, Gilbert, Basic Electricity. 152

Rainey, Gretchen R., Practical Industrial Electronics. 152

Ramaswamy, G. S., Design and Construction of Concrete Shell Roofs. 141

Rambousek, Elizabeth, Principles of Intensive Nursing Care. 193

Rams, Edwin M., Condemnation Appraisal Handbook. 66

Ramsey, Charles G., Architectural Standards. 139

Ramsey, Melvin A., Tested Solutions to Design Problems in Air Conditioning and Refrigeration. 121

Rand, Michael J., Textbook of Pharmacology. 200

Rand McNally & Company, Commercial Atlas and Marketing Guide. 60; Rand McNally Guidebook to Campgrounds. 103

Randall, Charles E., Growing Your Trees. 88

Randall, Clarence B., Systems and Procedures for Automated Accounting. 4

Randall, Reino, Design in Three Dimensions. 14

Randle, Gretchen R., Electronic Industries Information Sources. 152

Randolph, Theron G., Human Ecology and Susceptibility to the Chemical Environment. 179

Randolph, Wis., Educators' Progress Service, Educators' Guide to Free Films. 110; Educators' Guide to Free Filmstrips. 110

Ranganathan, Kilnager, Essentials of Blood Grouping and Clinical Applications. 186

Ranney, Maurice W., Creaseproofing Textiles. 29; Fire Retardant Building Products and Coatings. 139; Flame Retardant Textiles. 29; Soil Resistant Textiles. 29; Waterproofing Textiles. 29

Raphel, Murry, How to Promote an Infants' and Children's Wear Store. 25

Rapier, Dorothy, Practical Nursing. 196

Rapoport, Henry, Laboratory Text in Organic Chemistry. 134

Rapp, William, Construction of Structural Steel Building Frames. 139

Raskhodoff, Nicholas M., Electronic Drafting and Design. 144; Electronic Drafting Handbook. 144

Rasmusen, Henry N., Printmaking with Monotype. 12

Rasmussen, Wayne D., Readings in the History of American Agriculture. 76

Rath, Patricia M., Case Studies in Marketing and Distribution. 60; Marketing and Distribution. 59

Rathbone, Josephine L., Recreation in Total Rehabilitation. 103

Rathmell, John M., A Bibliography on Personal Selling. 60; Managing the Marketing Functions. 60; Salesmanship. 60

Ratner, Muriel, Study Guide to Medical and Surgical Nursing. 192

Raun, Donald L., An Introduction to Cobol Computer Programming for Accounting and Business Analysis. 21

Ray, Cyril, The Wines of Italy. 38

Ray, Delmas D., Accounting and Business Fluctuations. 4

Ray, George, Precision Attachments. 175

Ray, J. C., Independent Auditing Standards. 5

Ray, J. Edgar, Art of Bricklaying. 139

Ray, Jesse, Graphic Architectural Drafting. 144

Ray, Verne M., Color TV Training Manual. 158

Ray, Willis E., The World of Construction. 138

Raybestos Manhattan, Inc., Brake Service Manual for Disc and Drum Brakes. 124

Rayer, Francis G., Electronics and Computers. 152

Raymond, Robert S., Basic Marketing. 60

Rayner, Claire, Essentials of Outpatient Nursing. 192

Rayner, William H., Elementary Surveying. 142; Fundamentals of Surveying. 142

Razzak, Muhammad A., Textbook of Nuclear Medicine Technology. 182

RCA Institutes, Inc., Fundamentals of Electronic Data Processing. 21

RCA Service Company, Inc., Fundamentals of Transistors. 159

Read, Clark, Introduction to Parasitology. 187; Parasitism and Symbiology. 187

Read, Herbert, Art and Industry. 14; Art Now. 12; The Meaning of Art. 12

Read, Katherine H., The Nursery School. 82

Reader, George, Welfare Medical Care. 105

Reader, Norman, Great Shops of Europe. 63

INDEX

Rebelsky, Freda, Child Development and Behavior. 82

Reboul, P., Dictionary of Plastics. 168

Reckless, Walter C., The Crime Problem. 100; Critical Issues in the Study of Crime. 96

Redeker, Harry S., Life Insurance Settlement Options. 54

Redman, Barbara, The Process of Patient Teaching in Nursing. 192

Redmond, James, Curriculum Guide for Health Occupations Surgical Technicians. 209

Reed, Ann, Your Secret Servant. 35

Reed, Clinton, Comprehensive Typewriting. 69

Reed, George, Refrigeration. 121

Reed, Howard O., General Shop Metalwork. 160

Reed, Jeanne, Business Writing. 69

Reed, Myril B., Foundation for Electric Network Theory. 152

Reed, Robert, Instruments for Quality Control in Lithography. 15; Offset Lithographic Platemaking. 15; Offset Platemaking Deep-Etch. 46; Offset Press Troubles. 46; Web Offset Press Troubles. 46; What the Lithographer Should Know About Ink. 15

Reed, Stanley, Oriental Rugs and Carpets. 55

Reed, Walt, The Illustrator in America. 12

Reeder, Sharon, Maternity Nursing. 194

Rees, David J., Health Physics. 205

Rees, Herbert, Rules of Printed English. 46

Rees, Olive M., Scientific Principles in Nursing. 190

Reger, Roger, Special Education. 112

Reich, Edward, Basic Retailing. 63

Reich, Lilly, The Viennese Pastry Cookbook. 37

Reichard, Robert, Practical Techniques of Sales Forecasting. 60

Reichenbach, Robert R., Organizing for Data Processing. 16

Reichman, Charles, Advanced Knitting Principles. 25; Double Knit Fabric Manual. 25; Guide to Manufacture of Sweaters, Knit Shirts. 25; Handbook of Knitting Yarns and Knitwear Dyeing Processes. 25; Knitted Fabric Primer. 25; Knitted Stretch Technology. 25; Knitting Dictionary. 25; Principles of Knitting Outerwear Fabrics and Garments. 25; Wool and Synthetic Handbook. 29

Reid, Allan L., Modern Applied Salesmanship. 60

Reid, Charles, Life Insurance Settlement Options. 54

Reid, Ed, The Anatomy of Organized Crime in America. 100

Reid, James M., Basic Mathematics for Electronics. 206

Reid, John, Criminal Interrogation & Confessions. 100; Truth and Deception. 100

Reid, Robert L., Experiments in Alternating Current Circuits. 152

Reid, William J., Brief and Extended Casework. 107

Reif, Rita, Living with Books. 55

Reigner, Charles, Office Practice for Typists. 69

Reik, Theodor, Curiosities of the Self. 94

Reilley, Charles N., Experiments for Instrumental Methods. 133

Reinach, Jacquelyn, The Headstart Book of Be Nimble and Be Quick. 82

Reiner, Laurence E., Methods and Materials of Construction. 139

Reinfeld, George, How To Increase Your Printing Sales. 46; Your Future in Printing. 46

Reische, Diana L., U.S. Agricultural Policy. 76

Reiss, Albert J., Jr., Schools in a Changing Society. 112

Reissman, Frank, The Culturally Deprived Child. 82; New Careers for the Poor: The Nonprofessional in Human Service. 106

Reith, Herman R., Psychology and the Nurse. 192

Reithmaier, Larry, Computer Guide for Pilots. 118; Flight Planning Guide for Pilots. 118; Radar Guide for Pilots. 118; Weather Briefing Guide for Pilots. 118

Reitz, John R., Foundations of Electromagnetic Theory. 152

Reitz, Rosetta, Mushroom Cookery. 35

Remnick, Herbert, Embryology of the Face and Oral Cavity. 175

Rendle, B. J., World Timbers. 87

Renfield, Richard, If Teachers Were Free. 112

Reno, Richard R., Profitable Real Estate Exchanging and Counseling. 66

Renold, Edward, The Chef's Compendium of Professional Recipes. 32

Rescoe, Stan A., Cataloging Made Easy. 91

Resource Publications, Inc., The Computer Industry Guide. 17; Index of Opportunity in Computer Science. 18; Index of Opportunity in Finance, Merchandising and Marketing. 60; Index of Opportunity in Nursing. 192; Index of Opportunity in Paramedicine. 208

Reuben Donnelley Corporation, Modern Drug Encyclopedia and Therapeutic Index. 202

Reusch, Rosetta N., Molecular Equilibrium. 126

Reutov, O. A., Fundamentals of Theoretical Organic Chemistry. 135

Revelle, Roger, America's Changing Environment. 179

Revis, Cecil, Oils, Fats, and Fatty Foods. 126

Revzan, David A., Wholesaling in Marketing Organization. 61

Rewoldt, Stewart H., Introduction to Marketing Management. 61

Reynolds, Graeme C., Mathematics and Science for Engineering Technicians' Courses. 206

Reynolds, Isaac, Basic Accounting for Managerial and Financial Control. 4

Reynolds, Moira D., Clinical Chemistry for the Small Hospital Laboratory. 130

Reynolds, Phyllis, The Complete Book of Meat. 35

Rezek, Philipp R., Autopsy Pathology. 94

Rhea, Mini, Sew Simply, Sew Right. 25

Rheingold, Joseph C., The Mother, Anxiety, and Death. 94

Rhode, Robert, Introduction to Photography. 50

Rhodes, Ander, Textbook of Virology. 183

Rhodes, Daniel, Kilns. 162

Rhodes, Dennis E., The Spread of Printing. 46

Rice, Cedric, Chromatographic Methods. 131

Rice, Craig, How to Plan and Execute the Marketing Campaign. 61

Rice, Edward F., Television Service Training Manual. 158

Rice, Eugene W., Principles and Methods of Clinical Chemistry for Medical Technologists. 183

Rice, Harry G., Basic Electronics "Autotext." 148

Rice, John K., Introduction to Computer Science. 18

Rice, John R., Introduction to Computer Science. 18

Rice, Victor A., Breeding and Improvement of Farm Animals. 79

Rich, Stuart U., Marketing of Forest Products. 87

Richan, Willard C., Human Services and Social Work Responsibility. 107

Richards, Elfyn J., Noise and Acoustic Fatigue in Aeronautics. 118

Richards, J. W., Technical Development in the Small Plant. 130

Richards, Lenore, Quantity Cookery. 35

Richards, Louise G., Clothing Selection. 23

Richards, Paul, Pastry for the Restaurant. 37

Richards, Richard K., Electronic Digital Systems. 152

Richardson, James, The New York Police. 100

Richardson, Lee, Readings in Marketing. 57

Richardson, Richard, The Dental Assistant. 175

Richardson, Treva M., Sanitation for Food Service Workers. 35

Richer, A. Chester, Producing Farm Crops. 77

INDEX

Richert, G. Henry, Retailing. 63

Richert, Melvin T., How to Control Auto Body Sheet Metals. 124

Richey, C. B., Agricultural Engineer's Handbook. 76

Richman, Marc, An Introduction to the Science of Metals. 169

Richmond, Leonard, The Technique of Color Mixing. 13

Richmond, Samuel B., Regulation and Competition in Air Transportation. 118

Richmond, Sonya, International Vegetarian Cookery. 35

Richter, Günter, Dictionary of Optics, Photography, and Photogrammetry. 199

Richter, Herbert P., Practical Electrical Wiring: Residential, Farm and Industrial. 152

Rickards, Maurice, Posters of Protest and Revolution. 12

Riddick, John A., Organic Solvents. 135

Riddle, Janet, Elementary Textbook of Anatomy and Physiology. 192

Riddle, Jean, Non-Book Materials. 91

Riddle, Robert L., Transistor Physics and Circuits. 159

Ridenour, Nina, Some Special Problems of Children Aged Two to Five Years. 82

Rider, John F., How to Use Meters. 152

Ridgway, Arthur, The Physics of Medical Radiography. 205

Riegel, Emil, Industrial Chemistry. 130

Riegel, Robert, Insurance Principles and Practices. 53

Riehl, Carmella, Emergency Nursing. 192

Rienow, Leona T., Moment in the Sun. 179

Rienow, Robert, Moment in the Sun. 179

Riessman, Frank, The Culturally Deprived Child. 82; New Careers for the Poor. 106; Social Class and Social Policy. 106; Up from Poverty. 107

Rietz, Carl, A Guide to the Selection, Combination, and Cooking of Foods. 35

Riggenbach, Frank, The Slide Rule with Electronic Applications. 206

Rimboi, Nicholas, Instrumentation. 165

Rinehart, Elma, Management of Nursing Care. 192

Rinehart, Kenneth L., Introduction to Organic Chemistry. 134

Rines, Alice, Evaluating Student Progress in Learning the Practice of Nursing. 192

Ring, Alfred A., Real Estate Principles and Practices. 66; The Valuation of Real Estate. 66

Ring, Peter A., The Care of the Injured. 208

Ringsdorf, W. M., Diet and the Periodontal Patient. 173

Ringsrud, Karen M., Basic Techniques for the Medical Laboratory Technician. 182

Rinhart, Floyd, American Daguerreian. 46

Rinhart, Marion, American Daguerreian. 46

Ripa, Louis C., Surveying Manual. 142

Rising, James, Engineering Graphics. 143

Risley, Christine, Machine Embroidery. 25

Risse, Joseph A., Electronic Test Instrument Handbook. 152; Understanding Electronic Test Equipment. 152

Ristenblatt, Marlin, Transistor Physics and Circuits. 159

Ritch, Ocee, Chilton's Motorcycle Carburetion Systems. 124; Chilton's Motorcycle Electrical Systems. 124; Chilton's Motorcycle Troubleshooting Guide. 124

Ritchen, Ralph, Auto Engines and Electrical Systems. 122

Ritchie, George L., Electronics Construction Techniques. 152

Ritchie, Oscar W., Sociology of Childhood. 82

Ritter, J. B., Critical Path Method. 139

Ritterbush, Philip, The Art of Organic Forms. 12

Ritvo, Miriam M., Developing the Supervisory Skills of the Nurse. 191

Rivello, Robert M., Theory and Analysis of Flight Structures. 118

Rivista Dell'Arredamento, Modern Interiors. 55

Roach, J. Kenneth, How to Use Adding and Calculating Machines. 70

Roach, Mary, Dress Adornment. 25

Roark, Raymond J., Formulas for Stress and Strain. 139

Robb, David, Art in the Western World. 12

Robb, Melvin H., Teacher Assistants. 112

Robbins, Wilfred W., Weed Control. 76

Roberge, J. K., Electronic Components and Measurements. 154

Robert J. Brady Company, Brady's Programmed Introduction to Microbiology. 71, 187

Roberts, Arthur, Programming for Numerical Control Machines. 170

Roberts, Cornelius, Magnesium and Its Alloys. 169

Roberts, Ffrangcon, Medical Terms. 71

Roberts, Frederic F., An Introduction to the Theory and Practice of Transistors. 159

Roberts, George, Tool Steels. 169

Roberts, George F., An Introduction to Human Blood Groups. 186

Roberts, John D., Basic Principles of Organic Chemistry. 135

Roberts, Raymond, Typographic Design. 46

Roberts, Susan, The Yogi Cook Book. 36

Robertson, George R., Laboratory Practice of Organic Chemistry. 135

Robertson, J. Mackenzie, Automobile Electronics Equipment, 1970-71. 123

Robertson, Mary, Practical Business Correspondence for Colleges. 70

Robertson Photo-Mechanix, Inc., In Focus. 46

Robichaud, Beryl, Understanding Modern Business Data Processing. 16

Robin, L. P., Home Planning and Architectural Drawing. 143

Robins, Lewis, Programmed Mathematics for Nurses. 206

Robinson, Alice M., The Psychiatric Aide. 209

Robinson, Christine H., Successful Retail Salesmanship. 61

Robinson, Corinne H., Basic Nutrition and Diet Therapy. 40; Fundamentals of Normal Nutrition. 40; Normal and Therapeutic Nutrition. 40

Robinson, Ivor, Introducing Bookbinding. 47

Robinson, J. Lister, Basic Fluid Mechanics. 166; Mechanics of Materials. 166

Robinson, Jerry W., Integrated Secretarial Studies. 67

Robinson, Julian, Streamlined Dressmaking. 25

Robinson, Karl, Line Photography for the Lithographic Process. 50

Robinson, Lisa, Psychological Aspects of the Care of Hospitalized Patients. 192

Robinson, O. Preston, Store Salesmanship. 61; Successful Retail Salesmanship. 61

Robinson, Patrick J., Personal Selling in a Modern Perspective. 61

Robinson, Peter C., Real Estate and Insurance As a Career. 66

Robinson, Renee, Streamlined Dressmaking. 25

Robinson, Stuart, A History of Dyed Textiles. 29; A History of Printed Textiles. 29

Robson, John, Recent Advances in Pharmacology. 203

Rock, Peter A., Chemical Thermodynamics. 130

Rockefeller, Nelson A., Our Environment Can Be Saved. 179

Rockwell, Robert E., Education Improvement for the Disadvantaged Elementary Setting. 111

Rodd, E. H., Rodd's Chemistry of Carbon Compounds. 130

Rodda, William H., Marine Insurance-Ocean and Inland. 53; Property and Liability Insurance. 54

Roddam, Thomas, Transistor Inverters and Converters. 159

Roden, Edward M., Basic Arc Welding. 171; Basic Oxyacetylene Welding.

INDEX

171; Basic Tig Welding. 171; Welding Processes. 171

Rodewald, Fred, Commercial Art as a Business. 12

Rodgers, Harold A., Jr., Funk and Wagnalls Dictionary of Data Processing Terms. 16

Rodgers, Lionel M., Automobile Traffic Signal Control Systems. 124

Rodie, Edward B., Water Supply and Waste Disposal. 178

Rodman, Morton J., Pharmacology and Drug Therapy in Nursing. 192

Rodríguez, César, Bilingual Dictionary of the Graphic Arts. 46

Roebuck, Julian, Criminal Typology. 100

Roehm, Marilyn M., Sawyer's Nursing Care of Patients with Urologic Diseases. 197

Roes, Nicholas, The Space-Flight Encyclopedia. 118

Roger-Marx, Claude, Graphic Art the 19th Century. 12

Rogers, Arthur W., Police Officers Manuals. 100

Rogers, Bruce, The Nature of Metals. 169

Rogers, Clell M., Simplified Carpentry Estimating. 140

Rogers, David C. D., Manufacturing Policy in the Electronics Industry. 153

Rogers, Edward S., Human Ecology and Health. 179

Rogers, John L., Production of Precooked Frozen Foods. 42

Rogers, Kate, The Modern House, U.S.A. 55

Rogers, Martha, Educational Revolution in Nursing. 192; An Introduction to the Theoretical Basis of Nursing. 192; Reveille in Nursing. 192

Rogness, Milton L., Architectural Drawing. 144; Architectural Drawing Problems. 144

Rohn, Fred H., So You Want to Be an Accountant. 4

Rohr, Mayer, Draping. 25; Grading Women's and Misses' Garment Design. 25; Pattern Drafting. 25; Pattern Drafting and Grading. 25

Rohrer, Ronald A., Circuit Theory. 152

Rohweder, Anne, Scientific Foundations of Nursing. 192

Rolfe, Douglas, Airplanes of the World. 118

Rolfo, Vittorina, Designing Apparel Through the Flat Pattern. 24; How to Draft Basic Patterns. 24

Rollason, Peggy N., The High Paid Secretary. 67

Rollin, Bernard V., An Introduction to Electronics. 152

Rollin, Betty, The Non-Drinker's Drink Book. 38

Rolt, Lionel T. C., A Short History of Machine Tools. 166

Romanowitz, Harry A., Electrical Fundamentals and Circuit Analysis. 152; Fundamentals of Semiconductor and Tube Electronics. 152; Introduction to Electric Circuits. 152; Introduction to Electronics. 152

Rombauer, Irma, Joy of Cooking. 35

Romero, A. C., Contemporary Designs for Wood. 162

Romey, Kenneth A., A Laboratory Manual in Business Machines. 69

Roney, Maurice W., Electromechanical Technology. 155

Roos, Nester, Multiple-Line Insurers. 53

Roosevelt, Nicholas, Conservation. 179

Root, Kathleen B., The Medical Secretary. 71; Medical Typing Practice. 71

Root, Waverly L., The Cooking of Italy. 40

Rose, Augustus F., Jewelry Making and Design. 28

Rose, Darrell, Microwave Experiments. 150

Rose, Michael, Computers, Managers and Society. 18

Rose, Thomas, Violence in America. 100

Roseberry, Cecil, The Challenging Skies. 118

Rosen, Ben, The Corporate Search for Visual Identity. 12; Type and Typography. 46

Rosen, Saul, Programming Systems and Languages. 21

Rosenberg, Harold, Artworks and Packages. 12

Rosenberg, Hyman S., Legal and Professional Secretary's Lexicon. 70

Rosenberg, James, Introduction to IBM/360 Assembler Language. 21

Rosenberg, Milton, Audel's Programmed Basic Electricity Course. 152

Rosenberg, Robert, Electric Motor Repair. 156

Rosenberg, Robert, Profits from Franchising. 62

Rosenblatt, Jack, Direct and Alternating Current Machinery. 152

Rosenbloom, Richard S., Social Innovation in the City. 107

Rosengarten, Frederic, Jr., The Book of Spices. 35

Rosenman, Eugene, An Outline of Pulmonary Function and Pulmonary Emphysema. 181

Rosenthal, Helmut, Danish Cakes. 37

Rosenthal, Jacob, Opportunities in Food Preparation and Service. 35

Rosenthal, Murry P., Fundamentals of Radio. 157

Rosenthal, Philip C., Principles of Metal Casting. 169

Roshco, Bernard, The Rag Race. 25

Ross, Aileen, Becoming a Nurse. 192

Ross, Annette, Cooking for a Crowd. 35

Ross, Carmen F., Personal and Vocational Relationships in Practical Nursing. 196

Ross, Hugh L., Crimes Against Bureaucracy. 101

Ross, Jean, Every Customer Is My Guest. 35

Ross, Joan, Post-Mortem Appearances. 94

Ross, Martin J., Handbook of Everyday Law. 71

Ross, Milton S., Skin Health and Beauty. 7

Ross, Raymond W., A Handbook of Radiography. 205

Ross, Robert, Illustration Today. 12

Ross, Robert B., Metallic Materials. 168

Ross, Stan, The World of Drafting. 143

Ross, William, Sorghum. 77

Rossano, A. T., Jr., Air Pollution Control. 179

Rossell, James H., Financial Accounting Concepts. 4; Managerial Accounting. 4

Rossi, Peter H., The New Media and Education. 108

Rossnagel, W. E., Handbook of Rigging. 139

Rossoff, Martin, Using Your High School Library. 91

Roth, Charles, Lifetime Encyclopedia of Selling Ideas. 61; Secrets of Closing Sales. 61

Roth, Charles J., Jr., Use of the Oscilloscope. 152

Roth, Claire J., Art Careers. 12; Hospital Health Services. 208

Roth, Edward, Functional Gaging. 166

Roth, Lillian, Air Pollution in the Pulp and Paper Industry. 180; Electrostatic Printing. 47; Nonwoven Fabrics. 29; Paper and Its Relation to Printing. 48; Runnability of Printing Paper. 48

Rothbart, Harold A., Mechanical Design and System Handbook. 167

Rothberg, June, Nursing Diagnosis and Therapy. 188

Rothenstein, Michael, Relief Printing. 46

Rothman, Esther, The Disturbed Child. 108

Rothschild, Norman, Filter Guide. 50; Making Slide Duplicates. 112; Mounting, Projecting & Storing Slides. 92

Rothstein, Robert J., The Dental Health Team. 175

Rotmans, Elmer A., Drafting Technology. 143

Rottger, Ernst, Creative Clay Design. 162; Creative Wood Design. 162

Roucek, Joseph S., Sociology of Crime. 100

Rouse, John E., World Cattle. 79

Rouse, O. W., Beat Patrol and Observation. 100

INDEX

Rouse, Sue, Calculations in Pharmacy. 203

Rowan, Richard L., The Negro in the Textile Industry. 29

Rowe, Fred D., How to Locate and Eliminate Radio and TV Interference. 157

Rowe, Geoffrey W., An Introduction to the Principles of Metalworking. 169

Rowe, John L., Gregg Typewriting for Colleges. 68

Rowe, Patricia L., Shorthand Fashion Sketching. 25

Roy, Ewell P., Contract Farming, U.S.A. 76; Exploring Agribusiness. 76

Roydhouse, Richard H., Materials in Dentistry. 175

Royer, Donald J., Bonding Theory. 130

Royer, King, Applied Field Surveying. 142; Desk Book for Construction Superintendents. 139

Rubin, Eli, Emotionally Handicapped Children and the Elementary School. 112

Rubin, Harold, The Ulcer Diet Cook Book. 35

Rubin, Isadore, Sex in the Childhood Years. 82

Rubin, Melvin, Fundamentals of Visual Science. 199

Rubin, Reva, De Lee's Obstetrics for Nurses. 194

Rubinstein, Annette T., Schools Against Children. 112

Ruch, Walter, Chemical Detection of Gaseous Pollutants. 179

Rudd, Robert L., Pesticides and the Living Landscape. 179

Rudd, Thomas, The Nursing of the Elderly Sick. 194

Ruder, Emil, . . . Typography. 46

Ruderman, Florence A., Child Care and Working Mothers. 82

Rudick, Eleanor, Nursing in Ambulatory Units. 192; Pediatric Nursing. 195

Rudman, Jack, Fireman, Fire Department. 85

Rudnick, M. Chrysantha, Job Description and Certification for Library Technical Assistants. 90

Rudolph, Mae, Light and Vision. 199

Rudolph, Patricia, Your Future as an Airline Stewardess. 118

Rudoy, Marion, Hair Design and Fashion. 8

Rudy, William, How to Sell More Insurance. 54

Rufsvold, Margaret, Guides to Newer Educational Media. 92

Ruhm, Herman D., Jr., Marketing Textiles. 29

Ruitenbeek, Hendrik M., Death Interpretations. 94

Ruiter, Jacob H., Basic Industrial Electronic Controls. 152

Rule, John, Graphics. 143

Rule, Wilfred, Fortran IV Programming. 21

Rummer, Dale, Introduction to Analog Computer Programming. 21

Runck, Robert R., Premachining Planning and Tool Presetting. 166

Runkle, Robert S., Microbial Contamination Control Facilities. 187

Runquist, Olaf, Spectral Analysis of Organic Compounds. 134

Rupp, Mildred, Canapes, Hors d'Oeuvres and Buffet Dishes. 33

Rusch, Richard B., Computers. 18

Rushing, Lilith, The Cake Cook Book. 37

Russ, Stephen, Fabric Printing by Hand. 25; Practical Screen Printing. 12

Russell, Sir Edward J., Soil Conditions and Plant Growth. 76

Russell, Frederic A., Textbook of Salesmanship. 61

Russell, George H., Human Behavior and Life Insurance. 54

Russell, Joan, Creative Cake Decoration. 37

Russell, John, Pop Art Redefined. 12

Russon, Allien, Office Procedures and Administration. 68

Rutgers University, Beauty Culture, Related Theory. 7; Six Selected Instructional Aids for Teachers of Agriculture. 76

Ruttenberg, Stanley, Economic Justice: The Needs of Fire Fighters. 86

Ryan, Francis J., Family Group Casework. 103

Ryan, John W., Police Training for Delinquency Prevention and Control. 96

Ryan, Mary S., Clothing. 25

Ryan, Robert, A Primer of Blueprint Reading. 142

Ryder, John D., Electronic Fundamentals and Applications. 152

Ryge, Gunnar, Dental Materials. 175

Ryle, George, Forest Service. 87

Sacadat, Evelyn, Education Improvement for the Disadvantaged Elementary Setting. 111

Sacharow, Stanley, Food Packaging. 42

Sachs, Georgine, The Art of Mexican Cooking. 38

Sackheim, George I., Chemistry for the Health Sciences. 130; Practical Physics for Nurses. 192; Programmed Mathematics for Nurses. 206

Sacks, Raymond J., Theory & Practice of Arc Welding. 171

Sadauskas, Wallace B., Manual of Business Forms. 69

Saddler, Jane, Textiles. 28

Safar, Peter, Respiratory Therapy. 181; Resuscitation of the Unconscious Victim. 181

Sager, Clifford J., Black Ghetto Family in Therapy. 107

Sager, Donald J., Reference. 92

Saheb-Ettaba, Caroline, ANSCR: the Alpha-Numeric System for Classification of Recordings. 92

Sailland, Maurice E., Traditional Recipes of the Provinces of France. 40

St. Amand, Joseph E., Machine Shop Training. 161; Technology of Machine Tools. 165

Salemme, Lucia A., Color Exercises for the Painter. 13

Salesman's Guide, Inc., Directory of Buying Offices & Accounts. 61; Directory of Premium and Incentive Buyers. 61; Men and Boys' Wear Buyers Nationwide Directory. 25; Woman's and Children's Wear and Fashion Accessories. 25

Salisbury, Glenn W., Physiology of Reproduction and Artificial Insemination of Cattle. 79

Salmon, Charles G., Reinforced Concrete Design. 141

Salmon, Lawrence J., I.B.M. Machine Operation and Wiring. 155

Salmonson, Roland F., Accounting. 2; Basic Financial Accounting Theory. 4

Salottolo, Lawrence A., Modern Police Service Encyclopedia. 100

Salter, Robin H., Common Medical Emergencies. 208

Salter, Stefan, From Cover to Cover. 12

Salton, Gerald, Automatic Information Organization and Retrieval. 16

Saltzman, Max, Principles of Color Technology. 13

Salvatori, Philip L., The Story of Contact Lenses. 199

Salz, J., Principles of Data Communication. 16

Salzberg, Hugh W., Physical Chemistry. 135

Sammet, Jean E., Programming Languages. 21

Sams & Company, Inc., Basic Electricity and an Introduction to Electronics. 152; Handbook of Electronic Tables and Formulas. 152; Small Engines Service Manual. 124; Transistor Specifications Manual. 159; Transistor Substitution Handbook. 159; Tube Substitution Handbook. 152

Samson, Harland E., Advertising and Displaying Merchandise. 6; Retail Merchandising. 64

Sanborn, Paul E., Electron Tubes at Work. 151; Fundamentals of Electricity. 151

Sandage, Charles H., Advertising Theory and Practice. 7; Readings in Advertising and Promotion Strategy. 6; The Role of Advertising. 7

Sandborn, Edmund B., Cells and Tissues by Light and Electron Microscopy. 183

INDEX

Sanders, Donald H., Computers in Business. 18; Computers and Management. 18

Sanders, Norris M., Classroom Questions. 112

Sanders, Paul A., Principles of Aerosol Technology. 130

Sanders, Sandra, Creating Plays with Children. 112

Sanders, Virginia E., Urologic Nursing. 197

Sanderson, Peter C., Computer Languages. 21

Sanderson, Richard L., Codes and Code Administration. 139

Sanderson, Robert T., Chemical Periodicity. 130

Sandler, Beatrice, African Cookbook. 40

Sandler, Nathan, A Basic Understanding of Patternmaking. 25

Sands, Leo G., Automobile Traffic Signal Control Systems. 124; Easy Way to Service Radio Receivers. 157; Electronics Handbook for the Electrician. 153; Fundamentals of Radio Control. 157; A Guide to Mobile Radio. 157; 101 Questions and Answers About Transistor Circuits. 159; Power Supplies for Electronic Equipment. 153

Sandstrom, Gösta E., Man the Builder. 139

Sanner, Margaret C., Trends and Professional Adjustments in Nursing. 192

Santanelli, Anthony, Alternating Current. 145; Direct Current. 145

Sante, LeRoy, Manual of Roentgenological Technique. 205

Sapeika, N., Food Pharmacology. 203

Sara, Dorothy, The Key to Needlepoint. 25; Sewing Made Easy. 24

Sarason, Seymour B., Anxiety in Elementary School Children. 112

Sargent, Charles S., Manual of the Trees of North America. 87

Sargent, Robert L., Automobile Sheet Metal Repair. 124

Sarner, Harvey, Business Management of Dental Practice. 175; The Nurse and the Law. 192

Sarnoff, Paul, Careers in Biological Science. 185

Sartorius, Peter, Forestry and Economic Development. 88

Sarvis, Shirley, A Taste of Portugal. 40

Sasieni, Lewis S., Principles and Practice of Optical Dispensing and Fitting. 199

Sauer, Carl O., Agricultural Origins and Dispersals. 76

Saunders, Albert C., Working with the Oscilloscope. 153; Working with Semiconductors. 153

Saunders, Charles B., Jr., Upgrading the American Police. 100

Saunders, Helen E., The Modern School Library. 92

Saunders, Keith, So You Want to Be An Airline Stewardess. 118

Saunders, William H., Nursing Care in Eye, Ear, Nose, and Throat Disorders. 190

Savage, George, The Market in Art. 12

Savage, William G., Business Review for Professional Secretaries. 69

Savant, Clement J., Principles of Inertial Navigation. 118; Servomechanism Practice. 163

Savitskii, Evgenii M., The Influence of Temperature on the Mechanical Properties of Metals and Alloys. 169

Savitz, Leonard D., Dilemmas in Criminology. 100; The Sociology of Crime and Delinquency. 102

Sawers, David, The Technical Development of Modern Aviation. 117

Sawyer, Donald T., Experiments for Instrumental Methods. 133

Sawyer, Ruth, The Way of the Storyteller. 92

Sax, Newton I., Dangerous Properties of Industrial Materials. 130

Saxe, Emanuel, Fundamental Accounting. 4

Saxon, James A., Basic Principles of Data Processing. 16; Cobol. 21; System 360 Programming. 21

Saxton, Dolores F., Programmed Instruction in Arithmetic, Dosages, and Solutions. 192

Sayre, Irene, Choosing an Enlarger for the Graphic Arts. 50; Photography and Platemaking for Photo-Lithography. 50; The Single Color Offset Press. 46

Scarborough, Clarence C., Fruit Growing. 76

Scarpitti, Frank R., Combating Social Problems. 105

Scarseth, George D., Man and His Earth. 76

Schaefer, William P., Qualitative Elemental Analysis. 132

Schafer, Stephen, Theories in Criminology. 100

Schaffer, Albert, Understanding Social Problems. 107

Schaible, Philip J., Poultry: Feeds and Nutrition. 79

Schaller, Elmer O., Problems in Retail Merchandising. 64

Schamroth, L., An Introduction to Electrocardiography. 184

Schapero, Max, Dictionary of Visual Science. 199

Scharf, Aaron, Creative Photography. 50

Scharff, Robert, Pilot Your Own Plane. 118

Schattke, Rudolph W., Accounting: Concepts and Uses. 4

Schauer, Clarence H., Appliance Service Technology Programs. 153

Schaum, Daniel, Schaum's Outline of Theory and Problems of College Chemistry. 130

Scheer, Arnold H., Approved Practices in Fruit Production. 76

Scheer, Bradley T., Comparative Physiology. 184

Scheid, Francis, Computer Science. 18

Scheie, Harold G., Adler's Textbook of Ophthalmology. 199

Schepartz, Bernard, Biochemistry. 132

Schere, Richard A., Learning, Teaching and the New Technologies. 112

Scherz, Frances H., Family Social Welfare. 104

Scheve, Helen, Child-Care Services. 80

Schick, Kurt, Investigating Electrical Theory. 153; Principles of Electrical Theory. 153

Schifferes, Justus J., Healthier Living. 179

Schild, Heinz O., Applied Pharmacology. 203

Schildkraut, Sid, Basic Television and Television Receiver Servicing. 160

Schiller, Otto M., Cooperation and Integration in Agricultural Production. 76

Schlain, Bert H., The Professional Approach to Modern Salesmanship. 61

Schlebecker, John T., Bibliography of Books and Pamphlets on the History of Agriculture in the United States, 1607-1967. 76

Schlemmer, Richard M., Handbook of Advertising Art Production. 7

Schlenker, B. R., Introduction to Materials Science. 168

Schlesinger, Carl, Union Printers and Controlled Automation. 45

Schmeckebier, Lawrence F., Government Publications and Their Use. 92

Schmidlin, Hans U., Preparation and Dyeing of Synthetic Fibres. 29

Schmidt, Frances, Public Relations in Health and Welfare. 208

Schmidt, Frederic C., College Chemistry with Qualitative Analysis. 132

Schmidt, Jacob F., Paramedical Dictionary. 208; Police Medical Dictionary. 100; Practical Nurses' Medical Dictionary. 196; Structural Units of Medical and Biological Terms. 71

Schmidt, John L., Construction Lending Guide. 139

Schmidt, Mildred S., Factors Affecting the Establishment of Associate Degree Nursing Programs in Community Junior Colleges. 192

Schmidt, Milton O., Elementary Surveying. 142; Fundamentals of Surveying. 142

Schmidt, Richard N., Electronic Business Data Processing. 16; Introduction to Computer Science and Data Processing. 16

INDEX

Schmidt, Walter A., Architectural Drafting. 143; Blueprint Reading for the Construction Trades. 145

Schmiedicke, Robert E., Principles of Cost Accounting. 5

Schmitt, Marshall L., Understanding Electricity and Electronics. 146

Schmutz, George L., Condemnation Appraisal Handbook. 66

Schneerer, William F., Programmed Graphics. 143

Schneider, Coleman, Machine Made Embroideries. 25

Schneider, George W., Fruit Growing. 76

Schoenberg, Bernard, Teaching Psychosocial Aspects of Patient Care. 192

Schoenhals, Neil L., General Metals for Technology. 161

Schoepfer, Virginia, Desk Companion for Legal Secretaries.... 71

Schonbeck, Rudolph G., Fortran IV: For Multi-Programming Systems. 21

Schoonmaker, Frank, Encyclopedia of Wine. 38

Schorr, Jerry, Logistics in Marketing. 61

Schottelius, Byron A., Textbook of Physiology. 184

Schour, Isaac, Noyes' Oral Histology and Embryology with Laboratory Directions. 175

Schrag, Peter, Voices in the Classroom: Public Schools and Public Attitudes. 112

Schraub, Edgar D., Real Estate Investment Course. 66

Schroeder, Oliver, Jr., Homicide in an Urban Community. 95

Schroeder, Wendy, Special Education: Children with Learning Problems. 112

Schroeter, Charles, The Dentition of Man. 175

Schroeter, Louis C., Ingredient X: the Production of Effective Drugs. 203

Schubert, Genevieve W., A Sample Wage Earning Training Program for Child Day Care Aide.... 82

Schubert, Paul B., Die Methods. 166

Schuetz, Robert D., Organic Chemistry. 134

Schuller, Charles F., Audio-Visual Materials. 113

Schulman, Jerome L., Toys and Games for Educationally Handicapped Children. 80

Schultz, Claire K., Thesaurus of Information Science Terminology. 92

Schultz, Donald O., Police Operational Intelligence. 100

Schultz, Douglas G., Professional Police-Human Relations Training. 100

Schultz, Harold W., The Chemistry and Physiology of Flavors. 42

Schultz, John J., Electronic Test and Measurement Handbook. 153

Schultz, Louise, Digital Processing: A System Orientation. 16

Schultz, Morton J., Photographic Reproduction. 43

Schultz, Ronald M., Chemistry for the Health Sciences. 130

Schultz, Theodore W., Transforming Traditional Agriculture. 76

Schulz, Esther D., Nursing in Ambulatory Units. 192

Schumacher, Herman G., Tool & Die Drafting. 144

Schuppe, Wolfgang, Technical Dictionary of Data Processing, Computers, Office Machines. 15

Schur, Edwin M., Our Criminal Society. 100

Schure, Alexander, Basic Transistors. 159; Filters and Attenuators. 153; Industrial Electronics Measurements. 153; Transformers. 153

Schuster, Donald H., Basic Electronic Test Equipment. 153; Logical Electronic Troubleshooting. 153

Schutze, Rolf, Making Modern Furniture. 162

Schwabe, Randolph, Historic Costume. 27

Schwalbach, James A., Screen-Process Printing. 12

Schwalbach, Mathilda V., Screen-Processing Printing. 12

Schwartz, Artur M., Removable Orthodontic Appliances. 175

Schwartz, Fred R., Structure and Potential in Art Education. 12

Schwartz, George, Development of Marketing Theory. 61; Science in Marketing. 61

Schwarz, Gerhart S., Unit-Step Radiography. 205

Schwarz, J. I., Police Roadblock Operations. 100

Schwarzrock, Loren H., Effective Dental Assisting. 175

Schwarzrock, Shirley P., Effective Dental Assisting. 175; Effective Medical Assisting. 72

Schwebke, Phyllis W., How to Sew: Leather, Suede and Fur. 25; How to Tailor: A Handbook for Home Tailoring. 25

Schweitzer, Gerald, Basics of Fractional Horsepower Motors and Repair. 156

Scorer, Richard, Air Pollution. 179

Scott, Carl, Ethnic Minorities in Social Work Education. 107

Scott, Donald F., Neurological and Neurosurgical Nursing. 194

Scott, James H., Introduction to Dental Anatomy. 175

Scott, Lloyd F., New Designs for the Elementary School Curriculum. 111

Scott, Nathan A., The Modern Vision of Death. 94

Scott, Norman R., Electronic Computer Technology. 18

Scott, Richard A., Marketing and Its Environment. 61

Scott, Robert L., Regular Solutions. 128

Scott, Ronald M., Clinical Analysis by Thin-layer Chromatography Techniques. 132

Scott, Theodore G., Basic Computer Programming. 21; Computer Programming Techniques. 21

Scott, Walter O., Modern Soybean Production. 76

Scott, Wesley E., Teach Yourself to Type. 69

Scrase, Pat, Let's Start Designing. 14

Scraton, R. E., Mathematics for Technology. 206

Scribner, Kimball J., Your Future as a Pilot. 118

Seaborne, A. E.,M., The Psychology of Learning. 108

Seakins, Leslie W., Practical Brickwork. 139

Seale, Robert L., Water Production Using Nuclear Energy. 179

Searle, Campbell L., Digital Transistor Circuits. 158; Elementary Circuit Properties of Transistors. 159

Searle, Valerie, Screen Printing on Fabric. 26

Sears, Donald A., Harbrace Guide to the Library and the Research Paper. 92

Sears, Roebuck & Company, Color in Home Furnishings. 55; 1897 Sears Roebuck Catalogue. 61

Sears, William G., Anatomy and Physiology for Nurses and Students of Human Biology. 192; Medicine for Nurses. 192

Seawell, L. Vann, Accounting Theory and Practice, Advanced. 3; Introductory Accounting. 4

Sebastian, Fannie B., The Fashion Festival. 26

Sebrell, William H., Food and Nutrition. 35

Sechler, Ernest E., Airplane Structural Analysis and Design. 118

Secker, Philip E., Science of Materials. 167

Secor, Jane, Patient Care in Respiratory Problems. 181; Patient Studies in Medical-Surgical Nursing. 192

Seedor, Marie M., Aids to Diagnosis. 193; Introduction to Asepsis. 193; Programmed Instruction for Nursing in the Community College. 193; Therapy with Oxygen and Other Gases. 181

Seeley, Pauline A., ALA Rules for Filing Cards. 92; ALA Rules for Filing Catalog Cards. 92

Seely, Samuel, Electronic Circuits. 153

Seeman, Bernard, Your Sight: Folklore, Fact and Common Sense. 199

Seemann, Herman E., Physical and Photographic Principles of Medical Radiography. 205

Segal, Mendel, Sales Management for Small and Medium-Sized Businesses. 64

Segil, Arthur W., Architectual Interior Systems. 137

Seidman, Arthur H., Semiconductor Fundamentals, Devices and Circuits. 153

Seidman, Jerome M., The Child. 82

Seifert, Ralph L., Physical Chemistry. 135

Seil, Manning D., Advertising Copy and Layout. 7

Seiler, Robert E., Elementary Accounting. 4; Principles of Accounting. 4

Seitz, William C., The Art of Assemblage. 12

Seiverd, Charles E., Hermatology for Medical Technologists. 186

Selbin, Joel, Theoretical Inorganic Chemistry. 133

Selden, William H., Filing and Finding. 69

Seldin, Maury, Real Estate Investment Strategy. 66

Seligman, Ben B., Permanent Poverty: An American Syndrome. 107

Seligsohn, I. J., Your Career in Computer Programming. 21

Sellew, Gladys, Sociology and Its Use in Nursing Service. 193

Sellick, Bud, Skydiving. 118

Selman, Joseph, The Fundamentals of X-Ray and Radium Physics. 205; Skull Radiography. 205

Seltz, David D., Handbook of Retail Promotion Ideas. 64

Selwyn, Arnold, The Retail Jeweller's Handbook and Merchandise Manual. 28

Selznick, Gertrude J., Major Social Problems. 107

Semenow, Robert W., Questions and Answers on Real Estate. 66; Selected Cases in Real Estate. 66

Senger, Frank B., Advertising Copy and Layout. 7

Senn, Milton J., Problems in Child Behavior and Development. 82

Sentz, Robert E., Feedback Amplifiers and Oscillators. 153; Voltage and Power Amplifiers. 153

Serjeant E. P., Ionization Constants of Acids and Bases. 125

Serling, Robert J., Loud and Clear. 118; The Probable Cause: The Truth About Air Travel Today. 118

Service, T. B., Ford Cars. 124

Sessoms, H. Douglas, Community Recreation. 103

Settel, Irving, Exploring Advertising. 6

Settle, Alison, Fashion as a Career. 26

Sevin, Charles H., Marketing Productivity Analysis. 61

Sevin, Leonce J., Field-Effect Transistors. 159

Sewall, Mary F., Trends in Nursing History. 190

Sewell, J. L., Marketing and Market Assessment. 61

Sewell, William H., The Uses of Sociology. 105

Seybold, John W., The Market for Computerized Composition. 46

Shackelton, Alberta D., Practical Nurse Nutrition Education. 196

Shafer, Kathleen N., Medical-Surgical Nursing. 193

Shafer, William G., A Textbook of Oral Pathology. 175

Shaffer, Louis R., Critical Path Method. 139

Shafran, Alexander, Airbrush Photo Retouching Manual. 12

Shafter, Albert J., The Police Officer and Alcoholism. 95

Shah, Motichand G., Principles of Building Drawing. 145

Shalkhauser, G. W., Basic Lessons in Technical Drafting. 143

Shank, Paul C., The Paraprofessionals or Teachers' Aides. 112

Shanklin, John E., The Bureau of Outdoor Recreation. 102

Shanks, Mary D., The Theory and Practice of Nursing Service Administration. 193

Shanley, Francis R., Mechanics of Materials. 168

Shannon, Ellen, American Dictionary of Culinary Terms. 35

Shannon, Eutha, Principles of Intensive Nursing Care. 193

Shannon, Jean H., Utilization of Fluorides. 176

Shapiro, Ascher H., Shape and Flow: the Fluid Dynamics of Drag. 118

Shapiro, Charles, The Lithographers Manual. 15

Shapiro, R. H., Spectral Exercises in Structural Determination of Organic Compounds. 135

Shapiro, Stanley J., Marketing and the Computer. 56; Readings in the History of American Marketing. 61; Theory in Marketing. 57

Sharp, John D., Casting Pit Practice. 166

Sharp, John R., Some Fundamentals of Information Retrieval. 92

Sharpe, John C., Management of Medical Emergencies. 208

Sharry, John J., Complete Denture Prosthodontics. 175

Shatz, Eunice, New Careers. 107

Shaw, Charles J., Organic Chemistry Problems. 134

Shaw, Dennis F., Introduction to Electronics. 153

Shaw, Duncan J., Introduction to Colloid and Surface Chemistry. 130

Shaw, Roy T., Marketing. 61

Shaw, Steven J., Salesmanship. 61

Shaw, William L., Electronics Mathematics. 206

Shea, John G., Colonial Furniture Making for Everybody. 162; Contemporary Furniture Making for Everybody. 162; Plywood Working for Everybody. 162; Woodworking for Everybody. 162

Shea, Richard F., Amplifier Handbook. 153; Transistor Applications. 159

Sheaffer, Winifred E., A Bibliography on New Product Planning. 60

Sheehan, Sister Helen, The Small College Library. 92

Sheehy, Emma D., Children Discover Music. 83

Sheet Metal and Air Conditioning Contractors' National Association, Inc., Manual for the Balancing and Adjustment of Air Distribution Systems. 121

Sheff, Donald A., Secretarial English. 69

Shelly, Gary B., Introduction to Computer Programming: IBM System/360 Assembler Language. 19

Shepard, Paul, The Subversive Science. 179

Sheparovych, Zenon B., Quantitative Methods in Marketing. 61

Shepherd, Geoffrey S., Marketing Farm Products.... 76

Shera, Jesse H., Libraries and the Organization of Knowledge. 92

Sherby, Sydney S., Airplane Aerodynamics. 116

Sheridan, Monica, The Art of Irish Cooking. 40

Sherman, Philip, Industrial Rheology. 130

Sherman, Philip M., Techniques in Computer Programming. 21

Sherr, Sol, Fundamentals of Display System Design. 18

Sherrard, Thomas D., Social Welfare and Urban Problems. 107

Sherry, Kate, Specialty Cuts and How to Cook Them. 35

Sherwood, John F., Principles of Cost Accounting. 5

Sheth, Jagdish N., The Theory of Buyer Behavior. 59

Shick, Charles R., Corneal Contact Lenses, Fitting Procedures. 197

Shields, Carl D., Boilers. 139

Shields, John P., How to Build Electronics Projects. 153

Shields, L. Donald, Modern Methods of Chemical Analysis. 132

Shiers, George, Design and Construction of Electronic Equipment. 153; Electronic Drafting. 144

Shigley, Joseph E., Dynamic Analysis of Machines. 166

Shillinglaw, Gordon, Accounting. 2

Shirley, Hardy L., Forest Ownership for Pleasure and Profit. 88; Forestry and Its Career Opportunities. 88

INDEX

Shivers, Jay S., Leadership in Recreational Service. 103; Principles and Practices of Recreational Services. 103

Shockley, Robert J., Your Future in Elementary School Teaching. 112

Shoemaker, David P., Experiments in Physical Chemistry. 135

Shoenfelt, Joseph F., Designing and Making Handwrought Jewelry. 28

Shore, Bruce H., The New Electronics. 153

Shores, Louis, The Tex-Tec Syllabi. 92

Short, Douglas J., The Institute of Animal Technicians Manual of Laboratory Animal Practice and Techniques. 186

Short, James F., Modern Criminals. 100

Shoultz, Kenneth G., Basic Electricity. 153

Showers, Mary J., Human Anatomy and Physiology. 184

Shrader, Robert L., Electrical Fundamentals for Technicians. 153; Electronic Communication. 153

Shrager, Arthur M., Elementary Metallurgy and Metallography. 169

Shreir, L. L., Corrosion. 169

Shreve, John F., Rescue Practices in Fire Service Training. 84

Shreve, R. Norris, Chemical Process Industries. 130

Shriner, Ralph L., Systematic Identification of Organic Compounds. 135

Shuchman, Abe, Product Strategy and Management. 56

Shuey, Rebekah M., Learning About Children. 83

Shuff, Frances L., Your Future in Occupational Therapy. 209

Shugart, Grace S., Food for Fifty. 32

Shulman, Arnold R., Optical Data Processing. 16

Shultz, Mort, Painting and Wallpapering. 55

Shultz, William J., American Marketing. 61

Shunaman, Fred, How to Use Test Instruments in Electronics Servicing. 153; 101 Questions & Answers About Transistor Circuits. 159

Shurcliff, William A., Polarized Light. 200

Shurter, Robert L., Written Communication in Business. 69

Shurtleff, Forrest E., Children's Radiographic Technic. 205

Shuster, Louis, Readings in Pharmacology. 203

Shyne, Ann W., Brief and Extended Casework. 107

Sia, Mary L., Mary Sia's Chinese Cookbook. 40

Sias, Beverlee, The Chicken Cookbook. 35

Sicé, Jean, General Pharmacology. 203

Sicher, Harry, Oral Anatomy. 175

Sidebotham, Roy, Introduction to the Theory and Context of Accounting. 4

Sidney, Howard, Agricultural, Forestry and Oceanographic Technicians. 76

Siegel, Arthur I., Professional Police-Human Relations Training. 100

Siegel, Martin J., Mechanical Design of Machines. 167

Siegfried, Walter R., Typing Medical Forms. 72

Siegman, A. E., Microwave Solid-State Masers. 156

Siegner, C. Vernon, Art Metals. 162

Siekmann, H. J., Machining Principles and Cost Control. 164

Sienko, Michell J., Chemistry. 130; Experimental Chemistry. 130; Physical Inorganic Chemistry. 133

Siggia, Sidney, Survey of Applied Analytical Chemistry. 132

Siks, Geraldine B., Children's Literature for Dramatization. 112

Silver, Gerald A., Modern Graphic Arts Paste-Up. 46; Printing Estimating. 46

Silver, Rollo G., The American Printer: 1787-1825. 46

Silverberg, Robert, The Challenge of Climate. 179

Silverman, Sidney I., Oral Physiology. 175

Silverstein, Robert N., Spectrometric Identification of Organic Compounds. 135

Silverton, R. E., An Introduction to Medical Laboratory Technology. 181

Silvius, George H., Organizing Course Materials. 162; Teaching Successfully in Industrial Education. 163

Silvoso, Joseph A., Auditing. 5

Simeons, Albert T., Food: Facts, Foibles & Fables. 41

Simmons, Arthur, Technical Hematology. 186

Simmons, Harold E., Protective Services for Children. 83, 107

Simmons, Janet A., The Nurse-Patient Relationship in Psychiatric Nursing. 196

Simmons, M. L., The Laboratory Mouse. 187

Simmons, S., An Introduction to Generalized Electrical Machine Theory. 151

Simms, Denton H., The Soil Conservation Service. 76

Simon, Andre L., Dictionary of Gastronomy. 35; Wines of the World. 38

Simon, Herbert, Introduction to Printing. 46

Simon, Irving B., The Story of Printing. 46

Simon, Leonard S., Quantitative Methods in Marketing. 61

Simon, Oliver, Introduction to Typography. 46

Simonds, Herbert R., A Concise Guide to Plastics. 168; The Encyclopedia of Basic Materials for Plastics. 168; The Encyclopedia of Plastics Equipment. 168

Simons, Eric N., A Dictionary of Alloys. 169; Guide to Uncommon Metals. 169; An Outline of Metallurgy. 169

Simons, Harry, Advanced Accounting. 3; Intermediate Accounting. 3

Simons, James D., A Complete Insurance Guide for Contractors. 139

Simonson, Leroy, Private Pilot Study Guide. 118

Simpson, Charles H., Chemicals from the Atmosphere. 130

Simpson, George, People in Families. 107

Simpson, Jean I., The Frozen Food Cookbook. 35

Simpson, Jon E., Social Problems. 106

Simpson, Richard L., Basic Firemanship. 86

Simpson, Stephen G., Calculations of Analytical Chemistry. 131

Simpson, Thomas, Fantasy Furniture, Design and Decoration. 163

Sims, J. A., Dairy Cattle in American Agriculture. 79

Simson, Clyde B., Emotionally Handicapped Children and the Elementary School. 112

Sinclair, D. C., An Introduction to Functional Anatomy. 184

Singer, Anne, Psychological Development in Children. 83

Singer, Bertrand B., Basic Mathematics for Electricity and Electronics. 206

Singer, Ferdinand L., Strength of Materials. 170

Singer, Jules B., Your Future in Advertising. 7

Singer, Robert D., Psychological Development in Children. 83

Singh, Balbir, Indian Cookery. 40

Singleton, Vernon L., Wine, An Introduction for Americans. 37

Sinkankas, John, Gem Cutting. 163

Sinke, Gerard C., The Chemical Thermodynamics of Organic Compounds. 135

Sippl, Charles J., Computer Dictionary. 18

Sirjamaki, John, Social Foundations of Human Behavior. 103; The Sociology of Cities. 107

Sirockin, G., Practical Microbiology. 187

Sirridge, Marjorie S., Medical Technology: Laboratory Evaluation of Hemostasis. 183

Sisam, J. W. B., Forestry Education at Toronto. 88

Siskind, Charles S., Electrical Circuits. 153; Electrical Control Systems in Industry. 153

INDEX

Sisler, Harry H., Chemistry in Non-Aqueous Solvents. 130

Sisson, Albert F., Sisson's Word and Expression Locator. 69

Sistrom, W. R., Microbial Life. 187

Sitler, Disa W., Mathematics for Drugs and Solutions. 206

Sittig, Marshall, Organic Chemical Process Encyclopedia. 135

Sivetz, Michael, Coffee Processing Technology. 42

Sivinski, Joan, Applied Office Typewriting. 67

Siy, Louis J., Blueprint Reading for Welders. 142

Sizer, John, An Insight into Management Accounting. 4

Skeist, Irving, Handbook of Adhesives. 168; Plastics in Building. 139

Skelley, Esther G., Medications for the Nurse. 193

Skillin, Marjorie E., Words into Type. 69

Skilling, Hugh H., Electromechanics. 155

Skinnemoen, K., An Outline of Norwegian Forestry. 88

Skinner, Burrhus F., The Technology of Teaching. 112

Skinner, Eugene W., Elements of Dental Materials for Dental Hygienists and Assistants. 175; The Science of Dental Materials. 175

Skinner, Henry A., The Origin of Medical Terms. 72

Skinner, Wickham, Manufacturing Policy in the Electronics Industry. 153

Skipper, James K., Behavioral Science, Social Practice, and the Nursing Profession. 193; Social Interaction and Patient Care. 193

Skolnick, Jerome H., Justice Without Trial. 100

Skolnik, Merrill I., Introduction to Radar Systems. 118; Radar Handbook. 156

Skoog, Douglas A., Fundamentals of Analytical Chemistry. 132

Skoura, Sophie, The Greek Cook Book. 40

Skutt, Henry R., Electronics: Circuits and Devices. 155

Slaby, Steve M., Statics and Introduction to Strength of Materials. 170

Slack, Archie V., Defense Against Famine: The Role of the Fertilizer Industry. 76

Slack, R., Medical and Veterinary Chemicals. 130

Slade, Edward, Metals in the Modern World. 169

Slade, Frank H., Food Processing Plant. 42

Slade, Samuel, Mathematics for Technical and Vocational Schools. 206

Slater, Leslie G., The Secrets of Making Wine from Fruits & Berries. 38

Slatt, Bernard J., The Ophthalmic Assistant. 200

Slaughter, Stella S., The Educable Mentally Retarded Child and His Teacher. 112

Slavin, Albert, Basic Accounting for Managerial and Financial Control. 4

Slayter, Elizabeth M., Optical Methods in Biology. 183

Sleeper, Harold R., Architectural Standards. 139

Sletwold, Evangeline, Sletwold's Manual of Documents and Forms For The Legal Secretary. 71

Sloane, Albert E., Manual of Refraction. 200

Sloane, Eunice M., Illustrating Fashion. 26

Sloane, Patricia, Colour. 13

Slobodkin, Lawrence B., Growth and Regulation of Animal Populations. 88

Slocum, Robert B., Sample Cataloging Forms. 92

Slocum, Walter L., Agricultural Sociology. 76

Slom, Stanley, Profitable Furniture Retailing. 64

Slonim, N. Balfour, Cardiopulmonary Laboratory Basic Methods and Calculations. 181

Slowinski, Emil J., Chemical Principles. 129

Sluckin, Wladyslaw, Imprinting & Early Learning. 46

Slurzberg, Morris, Essentials of Electricity-Electronics. 153; Essentials of Radio-Electronics. 157

Small, Louis, Hardness Theory and Practice. 169

Smalley, Lee H., Selected Readings for Industrial Arts. 162

Smalley, Ruth E., Theory for Social Work Practice. 107

Smallwood, Clarence, Computer Language. 19

Smart, Mollie S., Children, Development and Relationships. 83

Smart, Russell C., Children, Development and Relationships. 83

Smeaton, Robert W., Motor Application and Maintenance Handbook. 156

Smeltzer, Clarence H., The Interview in Student Nurse Selection. 193

Smigel, Erwin O., Crimes Against Bureaucracy. 101

Smilansky, Sara, The Effects of Sociodramatic Play on Disadvantaged Preschool Children. 83

Smiley, Marjorie B., Education in the Metropolis. 111

Smillie, Wilson G., Human Ecology and Public Health. 178

Smith, Alice L., Principles of Microbiology. 187

Smith, Bruce, Police Systems in the United States. 101

Smith, Carol S., The Complete Kitchen Guide. 33

Smith, Cecil L., An Introduction to Fortran IV Programming. 20

Smith, Charles A., Financial and Administrative Accounting. 4

Smith, Charles O., The Science of Engineering Materials. 168

Smith, Charles P., Child Development. 83

Smith, Christine S., Maternal-Child Nursing. 195

Smith, Clodus R., Rural Recreation for Profit. 103

Smith, Datus C., Guide to Book Publishing. 46

Smith, David T., Microbiology. 187

Smith, Denison, How to Find Out in Architecture and Building. 139

Smith, Donald A., ABC's of Vacuum Tubes. 153; Basic Electronics Problems Solved. 153

Smith, Donald E., Child Management. 83

Smith, Donn L., Handbook of Ocular Therapeutics and Pharmacology. 201

Smith, Dorothy W., Care of the Adult Patient. 193; Pharmacology and Drug Therapy in Nursing. 192

Smith, Duncan N., A Forgotten Sector. 208

Smith, E. Evelyn, A Handbook on Quantity Food Management. 35

Smith, Edmund A., Social Welfare Principles and Concepts. 107

Smith, Edward M., Sales Strategy. 58

Smith, Edwin, Reproducing Art. 45

Smith, Esles, Sr., How to Design and Install Plumbing. 141

Smith, Esther M., The Microscopic Anatomy of the White Rat: A Photographic Atlas. 187

Smith, Frances L., Recipes and Menus for Fifty. 35

Smith, Genevieve W., Care of the Patient with a Stroke. 193; Medical Terminology. 72

Smith, Georgiana R., Table Decoration, Yesterday, Today & Tomorrow. 35

Smith, Guy H., Conservation of Natural Resources. 179

Smith, Harris P., Farm Machinery and Equipment. 78

Smith, John A., The School Secretary's Handbook. 72

Smith, Judith M., Child Management. 83

Smith, Kenneth M., Engineering Principles for Electrical Technicians. 153

Smith, L. Oliver, Jr., Organic Chemistry. 135

Smith, Leona J., Guiding the Character Development of the Preschool Child. 83

Smith, Leroi T., Basic Bodywork and Painting. 124; Complete Book of

INDEX

Engine Swapping: No. 2. 124; How to Fix Up Old Cars. 124

Smith, Louis M., The Complexities of an Urban Classroom. 113

Smith, Margaret R., The Blender Cookbook. 35

Smith, Mickey C., Pharmaceutical Marketing. 201; Principles of Pharmaceutical Marketing. 203

Smith, Norman F., Manned Spacecraft. 118

Smith, Ora, Potatoes: Production, Storing, Processing. 42; Potato Processing. 42

Smith, P. W., Organic Chemistry for General Degree Students. 135

Smith, Patrick D., A Manual of Police Report Writing. 100; Police English. 101

Smith, Paul T., Computers, Systems and Profits. 18

Smith, Philip H., Car Performance and the Choice of Conversion Equipment. 124; Design and Tuning of Competition Engines. 124; Scientific Design of Exhaust and Intake Systems. 124; Tuning for Speed and Tuning for Economy. 124; Valve Mechanisms for High Speed Engines. 124

Smith, R. Dean, Computer Applications in Police Manpower Distribution. 101

Smith, Richard L., Management Through Accounting. 4

Smith, Robert E., Machine Tool Technology. 162

Smith, Robert T., Your FAA Flight Exam. 118

Smith, Ronald C., Materials of Construction. 139; Principles and Practices of Heavy Construction. 139; Principles and Practices of Light Construction. 139

Smith, Russell E., American Social Welfare Institutions. 107

Smith, Samuel, Practical Brickwork. 139

Smith, Samuel, Readings in Marketing Information Systems. 61

Smith, T. Lynn, Principles of Inductive Rural Sociology. 77

Smith, William A., Forests and Forestry. 86

Smith, William H., Some Guidelines for Successful Police-Community Relations Training Programs. 96

Smith, William I., Guidelines to Classroom Behavior. 113

Smith, William V., The Laser. 156

Smykay, Edward W., Physical Distribution Management. 57, 61

Smythe, Hugh H., Educating the Culturally Disadvantaged Child. 109

Smythe, William R., Static and Dynamic Electricity. 153

Snapp, Roscoe R., Beef Cattle. 79

Snell, Cornelia T., Dictionary of Commercial Chemicals. 131

Snell, Foster D., Carpet Underlays. 52; Dictionary of Commercial Chemicals. 131; Encyclopedia of Industrial Chemical Analysis. 131

Snell, Fred M., Biophysical Principles of Structure and Function. 185

Snelling, Henry H., The History and Practice of the Art of Photography. 50

Snider, Max D., Readings in Marketing. 62

Snively, William D., Nurses' Handbook of Fluid Balance. 191; Sea Within: The Story of Our Body Fluid. 94

Snodgrass, Milton M., Agriculture, Economics and Growth. 77

Snook, Barbara, Making Baby Clothes. 26

Snowden, Obed B., Profitable Farm Marketing. 77

Snyder, Charles, Our Ophthalmic Heritage. 200

Snyder, LeMoyne, Homicide Investigation. 101

Snyder, Milton K., Chemistry: Structure and Reactions. 131

Snyder, Richard V., 65 Buttercream Flowers. 37

Snyder, Ruth, Sewing Made Simple. 26

Sobey, Francine, The Nonprofessional Revolution in Mental Health. 208

Soblick, Herman, Buyers' Guide and Reference Handbook: Photocomposition Methods and Equipment. 50

Social Work Practice. 107

Society of Aerospace Material and Process Engineers: Aircraft Structures and Materials Application. 118

Society of American Foresters, American Forestry. 88; Forest Cover Types of North America. 88; Forestry Education in America. 88

Sodee, D. Bruce, Textbook of Nuclear Medicine Technology. 182

Soderman, Harry, Modern Criminal Investigation. 101

Sognnaes, Reidar F., Chemistry and Prevention of Dental Caries. 175

Soisson, Harold E., Electronic Measuring Instruments. 153

Sokol, Andrew, Contractor or Manipulator? 139

Solinger, Jacob, Apparel Manufacturing Analysis. 26

Sollenberger, Norman J., Modern Prestressed Concrete. 141

Solnit, Albert J., Problems in Child Behavior and Development. 82

Solt, George S., Water Treatment Data. 177

Soltesz, Shirley E., How to Train Hospital Employees. 207; Selected Medical Terminology. 72

Sommer, Armand, Your Future in Insurance. 54

Sommer, Ralph F., Clinical Endodontics. 176

Sommermeyer, Lucille, Microbiology in Health and Disease. 187

Sommers, Montrose S., Comparative Marketing Systems. 61; Perspectives in Marketing Theory. 59

Sonnabend, Roger P., Your Future in Hotel Management. 52

Soong, Robert K., Social Service Aide Project for the Education and Training of Paraprofessionals. 107

Sorenson, Kenneth E., Handbook of Applied Hydraulics. 137

Sorenson, Wayne R., Preparative Methods of Polymer Chemistry. 131

Sorgman, Mayo, Brush and Palette. 12

Sorkin, Rodney B., Integrated Electronics. 153

Sorokin, P. P., The Laser. 156

Sorum, Clarence H., Fundamentals of General Chemistry. 131; Introduction to Semimicro Qualitative Analysis. 132

Sosnin, H. A., Arc Welding Instructions for the Beginner. 171

Soth, Lauren K., Agriculture in an Industrial Society. 77

Southall, James P., Mirrors, Prisms and Lenses. 200

Southwell, Thomas, A Guide to Human Parasitology for Medical Practitioners. 187

Southwestern Law Enforcement Institute, Criminal Investigation. 101; Homicide Investigation Techniques. 101; Law Enforcement and the Juvenile Offender. 101; Police Management. 101; Traffic Law Enforcement. 101

Southworth, Herman M., Agricultural Development and Economic Growth. 77

Sowa, Walter A., Special Semi-Conductor Devices. 153

Sowela Technical Institute, Drafting Technology. 143

Sowers, George B., Introductory Soil Mechanics and Foundations. 77

Sowers, George F., Introductory Soil Mechanics and Foundations. 77

Spackman, Claire S., Occupational Therapy. 209

Spalding, Eugenia K., Professional Nursing. 193

Spanier, Ginette, It Isn't All Mink. 26

Sparberg, Esther B., A Laboratory Investigation of Concepts in Chemistry. 131

Specter, Arlen, Police Guide to Search and Seizure, Interrogation and Confession. 101

Specthrie, Samuel W., Basic Cost Accounting. 5

Spellman, John A., Printing Works Like This. 46

Spence, William, Architecture: Design-Engineering Drawing. 144

Spencer, Donald D., Fundamentals of Digital Computers. 18; A Guide to Basic Programming. 21

Spencer, Francis M., The Color Atlas of Intestinal Parasites. 187

INDEX

Spencer, Henry C., Basic Technical Drawing. 143

Spencer, Herbert, Pioneers of Modern Typography. 46; The Visible Word. 46

Spencer, Louise, Decorating Cakes and Party Foods, Baking Too! 37

Sperandio, Glen J., Clinical Pharmacy. 201

Sperry Rand Corporation, Fundamentals of Digital Magnetic-Tape Units. 16

Spice Islands Company, The Spice Islands Cook Book. 40

Spicer, Edward D., Automotive Collision Work. 125; Automotive Maintenance and Troubleshooting. 125

Spiegler, K. S., Principles of Desalination. 179

Spielberg, Peter, Reference Books: How to Select and Use Them. 90

Spielman, Harold S., Electronics Source Book for Teachers. 153

Spielman, Patrick E., Modern Wood Technology. 161

Spinar, Leo H., College Chemistry. 131

Spinner, Arnold, Education in the Twenty-First Century. 111

Spirko, Sister Christina, Radiologic Records. 205; Your Future in Radiologic Technology. 205

Spitzbarth, Laurel M., Basic COBOL Programming. 21

Spock, Benjamin M., Baby and Child Care. 83

Spotts, Merhyle F., Design of Machine Elements. 167; Mechanical Design Analysis. 167

Sprackling, Helen, The New Setting Your Table. 35

Spratt, Nelson T., Introduction to Cell Differentiation. 185

Spriggs, A. O., The Art and Science of Embalming. 94; Champion Restorative Art. 94

Springall, H. D., A Shorter Sidgwick's Organic Chemistry of Nitrogen. 135

Springborn, R. K., Non-Traditional Machining Processes. 166

Springer, Clifford H., Basic Drawing for Engineering Technology. 142; Engineering Drawing and Geometry. 142; Graphics for Engineers. 142

Springer, Eric W., Nursing and the Law. 193

Springer, Jo, Creative Needlework. 26

Sproul, Adelaide, Print Making Without a Press. 9

Sproull, Wayne T., Air Pollution and Its Control. 180

Sprouse, Robert T., Accounting Flows. 3

Sprowls, Joseph B., American Pharmacy. 203; Prescription Pharmacy. 203

Sprowls, R. Clay, Computers: A Programming Problem Approach. 21; Introduction to PL/I Programming. 21

Spunt, Georges, Memoirs & Menus. 35

Spurr, R. T., Automobile Brakes and Braking Systems. 124; Braking of Road Vehicles. 124

Squire, Jessie E., Basic Pharmacology for Nurses. 193

Squire, Lucy F., Fundamentals of Roentgenology. 205

Squires, Harry A., Guide to Police Report Writing. 101

Squires, Terence L., Beginner's Guide to Color Television. 158; Beginner's Guide to Electronics. 153

Stabile, Toni, Cosmetics. 7

Stabley, Don H., System/360 Assembler Language. 21

Stacey, Reginald S., Recent Advances in Pharmacology. 203

Stacho, Maria, The Crêpe Cookbook. 32

Stacy, Ralph W., Biological and Medical Electronics. 184

Stafford, Alison R., The Science-Engineering Secretary. 72

Stafford, James E., Readings in Marketing Information Systems. 61

Stafne, Edward C., Oral Roentgenographic Diagnosis. 176

Stahl, David, The Community and Racial Crises. 101

Stahl, Dona K., Individualized Teaching in Elementary Schools. 113

Stainer, F. W., Modern Electronic Maintenance Principles. 148

Stallings, Constance L., Ecotactics: The Sierra Club Handbook for Environment Activists. 179

Stam, Judy, Principles for Creating Clothing. 26

Stambler, Irwin, Supersonic Transport. 119

Stan, Anisoara, The Romanian Cook Book. 40

Standard Directory of Advertising Agencies. 7

Standard Methods of Chemical Analysis. 132

Stanley, Alexander O., Handbook of International Marketing. 62

Stanley, Curtis H., Objectivity in Accounting. 4

Stanley, George C., Transistor Basics. 159

Stanley, James K., Electrical and Magnetic Properties of Metals. 169

Stansfield, Richard H., Advertising Manager's Handbook. 7

Stanton, Isabel A., A Dictionary for Medical Secretaries. 72

Stanton, William J., Fundamentals of Marketing. 61; Management of the Sales Force. 61

Stanwell, Sheila T., A Typewriting Course in Five Volumes. 69

Starling, Ernest H., Principles of Human Physiology. 184

Starr, Bernard D., Learning, Teaching and the New Technologies. 112

Stauffacher, Jack W., Hunt Roman: The Birth of a Type. 47

Staupers, Mable K., No Time for Prejudice: A Story of the Integration of Negroes in Nursing in the United States. 193

Stavridi, Margaret, History of Costume. 27

Stedman, Thomas L., Medical Dictionary. 72

Steel, Ernest W., Mechanical and Rural Sanitation. 177; Water Supply and Sewerage. 180

Steel Founders' Society of America, Steel Castings Handbook. 166

Steele, Gerald L., Fiberglass: Project & Procedures. 163

Steele, Harold C., The Departmental Laboratory Assistant in Biological Science. 183

Steele, Pauline F., Dental Specialities for the Dental Hygienist. 176; Dimensions of Dental Hygiene. 176; Review of Dental Hygiene: Questions and Answers. 176

Steele, Robert V., Delmonico's: A Century of Splendor. 52

Steen, Edwin B., Medical Abbreviations. 72

Steere, Caryl, Indian Teacher Aide Handbook. 113

Steere, Norman V., Safety in the Chemical Laboratory. 131

Stegman, George K., Architectural Drafting. 144

Stegman, Harry J., Architectural Drafting. 144

Stehli, Georg J., The Microscope and How to Use It. 183

Stehling, Kurt R., Lasers and Their Applications. 156

Stein, Arthur A., Steroid Analysis by Gas Liquid Chromatography. 130

Stein, B., Mechanical and Electrical Equipment for Buildings. 138

Stein, Harold A., The Ophthalmic Assistant: Fundamentals and Clinical Practice. 200

Stein, Herman D., The Crisis in Welfare in Cleveland. 107; Social Theory and Social Invention. 107

Stein, John H., New Careers: The Patrolman Aide. 102

Stein, Justin J., Basic Principles of Radiation Therapy for X-Ray Technicians and Nurses. 205

Steinberg, Joseph, Estimating for the Building Trades. 139.

Steinberg, Joseph L., Real Estate Sales Contracts. 65

Steinberg, Jules, Customers Don't Bite. 64

Steinberg, Rafael, Pacific and Southeast Asian Cooking. 40

Steinberg, Sheldon S., New Careers: The Teacher Aide. 113

Steinberg, William F., Electricity and Electronics. 153

293

INDEX

Steiner, Gary A., Human Behavior. 103

Steinfeld, Solomon C., Clerical Record Keeping. 67

Steingress, Frederick M., Low Pressure Boilers. 139

Steinkamp, Wilbert H., How to Sell and Market Industrial Products. 61

Stempel, Martin, Estimating for the Building Trades. 139

Stendler, Celia B., Readings in Child Behavior and Development. 83

Stengel, Charles D., Claim Administration. 54

Stenström, Sölve, Optics of the Eye. 200

Stephen, Alberta, Educational Therapy in the Elementary School. 108

Stephens, R. W., Dictionary of Electronics and Nucleonics. 149

Stephens, Thomas M., Directive Teaching of Children with Learning and Behavioral Handicaps. 113

Stephenson, George E., Drawing for Product Planning. 143; Power Technology. 163; Small Gasoline Engines. 124

Stephenson, Ralph J., Critical Path Method. 139

Stephenson, Reginald J., Mechanics and Properties of Matter. 166

Stephenson, Richard M., Introduction to the Chemical Process Industries. 131

Stephenson, William A., Seaweed in Agriculture and Horticulture. 77

Stephenson, William K., Concepts in Biochemistry. 133

Stepnick, Ivan C., Basic Electricity Study Course. 153; Control Theory and Fundamentals Study Course. 121

Sterling, Theodor D., Computers and the Life Sciences. 18; Computing and Computer Science. 18; A Guide to PL/I. 21; Introduction to Statistical Data Processing. 16

Stern, Arthur C., Air Pollution. 180

Stern, Benjamin J., Opportunities in a Drafting Career. 143; Opportunities in Machine Shop Trades. 166

Stern, Herbert, The Biology of Cells. 185

Stern, John A., Instrumentation for Air Pollution Control. 180

Stern, Mark E., Marketing Planning. 61

Stern, Walter H., Your Future in Real Estate. 65

Sternberg, Thomas H., More Than Skin Deep. 7

Sternlieb, George, The Tenement Landlord. 66

Sterrett, Frances S., A Laboratory Investigation of Concepts in Chemistry. 131

Stettler, Howard F., Accounting Systems for Management Control. 4; Auditing Principles. 5; Systems Based Independent Audits. 5

Stevens, Claude, Sheet Metal Practice. 162

Stevens, Donald R., Chemical Technology of Petroleum. 127

Stevens, Guy W., Microphotography. 50

Stevens, Harold, Art in the Round. 12; Design in Photo-Collage. 12

Stevens, Marion K., Geriatric Nursing for Practical Nurses. 196

Stevens, Matthew, Comprehensive Review for the Radiologic Technologist. 205

Stevens, Patricia, How to Set and Style Your Own Wigs. 8

Stevens, Roger, Dictionary of Organic Compounds. 130

Stevenson, George A., Graphic Arts Encyclopedia. 46

Stevenson, Gladys T., Introduction to Foods and Nutrition. 41

Stever, H. Guyford, Flight. 119

Stewart, Dorothy M., Public Health Nursing. 196

Stewart, George R., Not So Rich as You Think. 180

Stewart, Harry L., Hydraulic and Pneumatic Power for Production. 139

Stewart, Isabel M., History of Nursing. 193

Stewart, James I., Real Estate Appraisal in a Nutshell. 66

Stewart, Jeffrey R., Progressive Filing. 68

Stewart, Oliver, Aviation. 119

Steyer, Wesley W., Basic Principles of Data Processing. 16

Stibbert, Frederic, Civil and Military Clothing in Europe. 27

Stich, Walter, Fine Structure of Blood and Bone Marrow. 186

Stickler, Mervin K., An Introduction to Aerospace Education. 119

Stidsen, Bert, Personal Selling in a Modern Perspective. 61

Stieri, Emanuele, Complete Woodworking Handbook. 160

Stiles, Karl A., Handbook of Histology. 186

Still, Henry, The Dirty Animal. 180

Still, Richard R., Basic Marketing. 57; Essentials of Marketing. 61; Sales Management. 61

Stille, John K., Industrial Organic Chemistry. 135

Stillman, Myra, Understanding Food: The Chemistry of Nutrition. 41

Stimson, Russell L., The Cosmetic Fitting of Eyewear. 200; A Lens Pattern Book. 200; Ophthalmic Dispensing. 200

Stinchcomb, James D., Community Service and Other New Specialists. 107; Guidelines for Law Enforcement Education Programs in Community and Junior Colleges. 96; Law Enforcement Training and the Community College. 100; Opportunities in a Law Enforcement Career. 101

Stinton, Darrel, Anatomy of the Aeroplane. 119

Stirling, Norman, Introduction to Technical Drawing. 143

Stock, Ralph, Chromatographic Methods. 131

Stockel, Martin W., Auto Mechanics Fundamentals. 124; Auto Service and Repair. 125

Stockli, Albert, Splendid Fare: The Albert Stockli Cookbook. 35

Stoddard, Charles H., Essentials of Forestry Practice. 88; The Small Private Forest in the United States. 88

Stoecker, Wilbert F., Principles for Air Conditioning Practice. 121

Stohlman, D. G., Sewing Performance & Methods Analysis. 26

Stokes, John W., Food Service in Industry and Institutions. 35; How to Manage a Restaurant. 53, 35

Stokes, Roy B., The Function of Bibliography. 92

Stoklosa, Mitchell J., Pharmaceutical Calculations. 200

Stoll, Frances A., Dental Health Education. 176

Stone, Archie A., Careers in Agribusiness and Industry. 77

Stone, Bernard, Preparing Art for Printing. 46

Stone, David, How to Operate a Real Estate Trade-In Program. 66; Training Manual for Real Estate Salesman. 66

Stone, Leo D., Real Estate Finance. 65

Stoner, Donald L., Transistor Radio Handbook. 159

Stores of The World: Buyers and Buying Agents. 64

Storey, Reed K., The Search for Accounting Principles. 4

Storey, Robert G., Our Unalienable Rights. 101

Storlie, Frances, The Cardiac Surgical Patient. 197; Principles of Intensive Nursing Care. 193

Storm, Donald F., Law for the Veterinarian and Livestock Owner. 79

Story, Mattison L., Airports, Airways, and Electronics. 119

Stott, G. S., Electrical Engineering Principles for Electrical, Telecommunications, and Installation Technicians. 153

Stout, Evelyn E., Introduction to Textiles. 29

Stout, George L., Painting Materials. 9

Stout, Melville B., Basic Electrical Measurements. 153

Strand, Helen R., An Illustrated Guide to Medical Terminology. 72

Strand, Stanley, Marketing Dictionary. 61

Straub, K. Mary, Continuity of Patient Care. 193

Straub, Lura L., Filing and Finding. 69; Liquid Duplicating Systems. 69; Stencil Duplicating Systems. 69; Word Finder. 67

Strauss, Anselm L., Awareness of Dying. 93; Time for Dying. 93

Strauss, Victor, The Printing Industry. 46

Straw, Windsor A., Mechanism of the Linotype and Intertype. 42

Strean, Herbert S., The Casework Digest. 107; New Approaches in Child Guidance. 83

Streater, Jack W., How to Use Integrated-Circuit Logic Elements. 153

Street, R. E., Practical Television Circuits. 158

Street, William E., Engineering Graphics. 143

Streeter, Victor L., Fluid Mechanics. 166

Streeter, Walter E., Machine Trades Blueprint Reading. 144

Streit, Fred, Paper Quality Control. 48

Strickler, Mervin K., An Introduction to Aerospace Education. 119; Career Opportunities in Aviation. 119

Striffler, David F., The Dentist, His Practice and His Community. 176

Strobel, Howard A., Chemical Instrumentation. 133

Strock, Clifford, Handbook of Air Conditioning, Heating and Ventilating. 121

Stroebel, Leslie D., View Camera Techniques. 50

Stroh, Thomas, Techniques of Practical Selling. 61

Strohecker, Edwin, The Library Technical Assistant. 92

Strong, Earl P., Writing for Business and Industry. 69

Strong, Merle E., Curriculum Materials for Trade and Industrial Education, 1963. 163

Strony, Madeline S., Refresher Course in Gregg Shorthand. 70; The Secretary at Work. 70

Strub, Clarence G., The Principles and Practice of Embalming. 93

Struble, George, Assembler Language Programming. 21

Stryker, Ruth, The Hospital Ward Clerk. 208

Stuart, Fredric, Fortran Programming. 21; Introductory Computer Programming. 21

Stuart, Harold C., The Healthy Child. 83

Stuart, Jennifer, Make Your Own Hats. 26

Stubbe, Wolf, Graphic Arts in the Twentieth Century. 47

Stubbs, Morris F., General Chemistry in the Laboratory. 128

Stuckey, Gilbert B., Evidence for the Law Enforcement Officer. 101

Stuckey, L., The Spice Cookbook. 31

Studer, Jack J., Introduction to Electronic Systems, Circuits, and Devices. 152

Studley, C. L., Instruction Manual...in All Methods of Rescue Breathing. 180

Stueve, Thomas F., Mortuary Law. 94

Stull, Daniel R., The Chemical Thermodynamics of Organic Compounds. 135

Stumbo, Charles R., Thermobacteriology in Food Processing. 42

Sturdivant, Frederick D., The Ghetto Marketplace. 61

Sturm, Mary M., Guide to Modern Clothing. 26

Sturrock, P. E., Quantitative Analytical Chemistry. 132

Sturtevant, W. W., General Mechanical Drawing. 144

Styles, Jimmie C., Guidelines for Work Experience Programs in the Criminal Justice System. 101; Law Enforcement Training and the Community College. 100

Suckling, C. W., Research in the Chemical Industry. 125

Suedfeld, Peter, Social Processes. 107

Suffern, Maurice G., Basic Electrical and Electronic Principles. 153

Suhrie, Eleanor B., Trends in Nursing History. 190

Sullenger, Thomas E., Neglected Areas in Family Living. 107

Sullivan, John L., Introduction to Police Science. 101

Sullivan, Michael, A Short History of Chinese Art. 12

Sultan, William J., Elementary Baking. 37; Practical Baking. 37

Sulzberger, Cyrus L., My Brother Death. 94

Summer, Steven E., Electronic Sensing Controls. 154

Sundberg, Elmer W., Building Trades Blueprint Reading. 145; Fundamentals of Carpentry. 140

Sundow, David, Passing On. 94

Sundquist, James L., On Fighting Poverty. 107

Sunset, Children's Rooms and Play Yards. 55; How to Build Patio Roofs. 140; Sunset Salad Book. 35; Things to Make for Children. 83

Supervisory Techniques. 101

Suprynowicz, Vincent A., Introduction to Electronics for Students of Biology, Chemistry and Medicine. 184

Surina, Tugomir, Semiconductor Electronics. 154

Surrey, Sterling, Cases in Life Insurance. 53

Susskind, Charles, The Encyclopedia of Electronics. 154; Fundamentals of Microwave Electronics. 146

Sutcliffe, Haydn, Practical Inorganic Chemistry. 133

Sutermeister, Edwin, The Story of Papermaking. 48

Sutherland, Edwin H., Criminology. 101; White Collar Crime. 101

Sutter, Jean, The Neo-Impressionists. 12

Sutton, Audrey L, Bedside Nursing Techniques in Medicine and Surgery. 193

Sutton, James, An Atlas of Typeforms. 47

Svennas, Elsie, Handbook of Stitches. 25

Svensen, Carl L., Engineering Graphics. 143; Mechanical Drawing. 144

Svensson, Arne, Techniques of Crime Scene Investigation. 101

Swain, Olive, Notes Used on Catalog Cards. 92

Swallow, J. N., Child Dental Health. 174

Swallow, Kenneth P., Elements of Computer Programming. 21

Swan, Arthur, Adventures with Children in Nursery School and Kindergarten. 108

Swanborough, F. G., Vertical Flight Aircraft of the World. 119

Swann, Cal, Techniques of Typography. 47

Swansburg, Russell C., Inservice Education. 193; Team Nursing. 193

Swanson, Carl P., The Cell. 185

Swanson, Lynn D., Police Work with Children. 99

Swanson, Robert S., Plastics Technology. 163

Swarbrick, James, Current Concepts in the Pharmaceutical Sciences: Biopharmaceutics. 203; Physical Pharmacy. 202

Sward, George G., Paint Testing Manual. 127

Swatek, Frank E., Textbook of Microbiology. 187

Swearengen, Thomas F., Tear Gas Munitions. 101

Sweet, Morris L., Readings in Marketing. 62

Swenson, Merrill G., Swenson's Complete Dentures. 176

Swesnik, Richard H., Real Estate Investment Strategy. 66

Swift, Ernest H., Qualitative Elemental Analysis. 132

Swindle, George F., Computer Programming Systems. 19

Swinehart, Haldon J., Cutting Tool Material Selection. 166

Switzer, David K., The Dynamics of Grief. 94

Sykes, Gresham M., Law and the Lawless. 101

Sykes, M. K., Respiratory Failure. 181

Symes, Russell W., General Industrial Arts. 160

Symons, Leslie, Agricultural Geography. 77

INDEX

Symons, Norman B., Introduction to Dental Anatomy. 175

Symposium on America's Private Construction Industry and the Future American City. Proceedings.... 140

Symposium on Fire Test Methods—Restraint & Smoke, Atlantic City, N.J., 1966:...A Symposium Presented at the Sixty-Ninth Annual Meeting, American Society for Testing Materials. 86

Symposium on Fire Tests, Chicago, 1964, Moisture in Materials in Relation to Fire Tests. 86

Symposium on Higher Education for the Fire Service, Saratoga Springs, N.Y., Proceedings. 86

Synthetic Organic Chemical Manufacturers Association, SOCMA Handbook. 131

System Development Corporation, A System Study of Abstracting and Indexing. 92

Szabo, N., Residue Arithmetic and Its Application to Computer Technology. 207

Szent-Gyorgyi, Albert, Bioelectronics. 184

Szulec, Jeanette A., A Syllabus for the Surgeon's Secretary. 72

Szurek, Stanislaus A., The Antisocial Child. 83

TAB, Popular Tube/Transistor Substitution Gude. 159

Taba, Hilda, Teaching Strategies for the Culturally Disadvantaged. 113

Taber, Clarence W., Taber's Cyclopedic Medical Dictionary. 183

Taft, Donald R., Criminology. 101

Taintor, Sarah A., The Secretary's Handbook. 70

Talburt, William F., Potato Processing. 42

Talley, David, Basic Carrier Telephony. 154

Tamaru, Tug T., Automated Police Information Systems. 102

Tanaka, R., Residue Arithmetic and Its Application to Computer Technology. 207

Tannenbaum, Beulah, Understanding Food. 41

Tanner, John L., Schaum's Outline of Theory and Problems of Reinforced Concrete Design. 141

Tanous, Helen N., Designing Dress Patterns. 26

Tapp, Gerald R., Case Studies in Marketing and Distribution. 60

Tarbet, Donald G., Television and Our Schools. 113

Tarpey, Lawrence X., Human Behavior in Marketing. 58

Tarrant, John J., Tomorrow's Techniques for Today's Salesmen. 61

Tasho, Ernest, Hair Styling for Women. 8

Task Force on Health Manpower, Health Manpower. 208

Tasso, Charles A., Organizing for Data Processing. 16

Tatchell, A. R., Organic Chemistry for General Degree Students. 135

Tate, Mildred B., Family Clothing. 26

Tatham, Laura, The Use of Computers for Profit. 18

Tatro, Earl E., Machine Tool Metalworking. 164; Shop Theory. 160

Taubes, Frederic, A Guide to Traditional and Modern Painting Methods. 12

Taussig, Russell, Accounting Principles and Control. 4

Taviss, Irene, Implications of Biomedical Technology. 183

Taylor, Abraham, X-Ray Metallography. 205

Taylor, Allen E., The Putnam Medical Dictionary. 183

Taylor, Clara M., Foundations of Nutrition. 41

Taylor, Dawson, Your Future in Automotive Service. 122

Taylor, Denis, Introduction to Radar and Radar Techniques. 156

Taylor, Derek, Hotel and Catering Sales Promotion. 52

Taylor, Harry F., The Chemistry of Cements. 131

Taylor, Irwin M., Law of Insurance. 54

Taylor, John, It's A Small, Medium and Outsize World. 26

Taylor, John R., The Art Nouveau Book in Britain. 12

Taylor, Kenneth E., Meat Hygiene. 30

Taylor, Norman B., Basic Physiology and Anatomy. 184; The Putnam Medical Dictionary. 183

Taylor, Peter J., Computers. 18

Taylor, Robert L., Materials and Labor Estimator for the Entire Building Industry. 140

Taylor, Robert M., Marketing Logistics. 59

Taylor, Thayer C., The Computer in Marketing. 61

Taylor, Walter H., Concrete Technology and Practice. 141

Taylor, Weldon J., Marketing. 61

Technical Association of the Pulp and Paper Industry, Paper Coating Additives. 48; Paper Coating Pigments. 48; Wet Strength in Paper and Paperboard. 48

Technical Educational Consortium, Inc., Development of a Curriculum to Meet Changing Manpower Needs of the Computer and Business Machine Industries. 18

Technical Publications, Motorcycle Service Manual. 125

Tedeschi, David H., Importance of Fundamental Principles in Drug Evaluation. 203

Tedeschi, Ralph E., Importance of Fundamental Principles in Drug Evaluation. 203

Tegart, William J., Elements of Mechanical Metallurgy. 169

Teichmann, Frederick K., Fundamentals of Aircraft Structural Analysis. 119

Teigen, Kit, Graphic Arts. 47

Telchin, Charles S., Plan Your Store for Maximum Sales and Profit. 64

Telfer, William H., Biology of Organisms. 185

Telford, Ira R., Dynamic Anatomy and Physiology. 184

Temes, Lloyd, Electronic Circuits for Technicians. 154

Tepper, Marvin, Basic Radio. 157; Basic Radio Repair. 157; Transistor Ignition Systems. 159

Teppich, John, Electricity. 147

Terkla, Louis G., Partial Dentures. 176

Terrell, Margaret E., Food Service Planning. 37; Professional Food Preparation. 35

Terrill, William A., Cost Accounting for Management. 5

Terry, Florence J., Principles and Technics of Rehabilitation Nursing. 190

Teuscher, Henry, The Soil and Its Fertility. 77

Texas A & M University, Texas State Firemen's and Fire Marshals' Association, Fire Department Pump and Accessories: Principles of Operation. 86

Texas Instruments, Inc., Circuit Design for Audio, AM/FM, and TV. 154; Transistor Circuit Design. 159

Thatcher, Fred S., Microorganisms in Foods. 35

Thayer, Vivian T., The Role of the School in American Society. 113

Theodorson, Achilles G., A Modern Dictionary of Sociology. 107

Theodorson, George A., A Modern Dictionary of Sociology. 107

Thier, Herbert D., Teaching Elementary School Science. 113

Thomas, Alan G., Fine Books. 47

Thomas, Alexander, Behavioral Individuality in Early Childhood. 83

Thomas, Charles L., Catalytic Processes and Proven Catalysts. 131

Thomas, Donald W., Making Better Plastic Welds. 171

Thomas, Dorothy, Rehabilitation: A Manual for the Care of the Disabled and Elderly. 194

Thomas, Dorothy P., Private Secretarial Work. 70

Thomas, Edwin J., Behavioral Science for Social Workers. 107

Thomas, G. H., Metalwork, Technology. 169

INDEX

Thomas, Harry E., Handbook for Electronic Engineers and Technicians. 154; Handbook of Electronic Instruments and Measurement Techniques. 154; Handbook of Transistors, Semiconductors, Instruments, and Microelectronics. 159

Thomas, J. R., Cosmetology. 7

Thomas, Paul I., How to Estimate Building Losses and Construction Costs. 140

Thomas, Rose C., Public Service Careers Program Training Manual for Case Aide Trainees. 107

Thomas, Shirley, Computers. 18

Thomas, Sidney, The Nature of Art. 9

Thomas, T. A., Technical Illustration. 143

Thomas, William E., Readings in Cost Accounting. 5

Thomison, Dennis, Readings About Adolescent Literature. 92

Thompson, Donald L., Retail Management Cases. 64; Retailing. 63

Thompson, Eleanor D., Pediatrics for Practical Nurses. 196

Thompson, Ella M., Simplified Nursing. 190; Textbook of Basic Nursing. 193

Thompson, Francis G., Harris Tweed. 29

Thompson, Joseph W., Salesmanship. 61; Selling. 61

Thompson, Lida F., Sociology Nurses and Their Patients in a Modern Society. 188

Thompson, Norman J., Fire Behavior and Sprinklers. 86

Thompson, Ralph B., Marketing Theory. 61

Thompson, Richard F., Statistics for Nurses. 192

Thompson, Willard M., The Basics of Successful Salesmanship. 61; Salesmanship. 62

Thoms, Wayne, How to Customize Cars and Rods. 122

Thomson, James C., Healthy Hair. 8

Thomson, Leslie C., Healthy Hair. 8

Thomson, Robert G., An Experimental Approach to Biology. 184

Thomson, William T., Introduction to Space Dynamics. 119; Statics. 165

Thorner, Marvin E., Food Beverage Service Handbook. 38

Thornhill, Robert B., Engineering Graphics and Numerical Control. 170

Thornton, Horace, Textbook of Meat Inspection. 35

Thornton, Richard D., Characteristics and Limitations of Transistors. 159; Handbook of Basic Transistor Circuits and Measurements. 159; Multistage Transistor Circuits. 159

Thornton, Spencer P., Ophthalmic Eponyms. 200

Thorwald, Jurgen, The Century of the Detective. 101; Crime and Science. 101

Throneberry, J. B., Principles of Biology. 184

Thumm, Walter, The Physics of Medical Radiography. 205

Thurston, E. F., Industrial Water Treatment Practice. 178

Tidball, Harriet, The Weaver's Book. 26

Tiedjens, Victor A., Olena Farm, U.S.A. 77

Tierney, William F., Modern Upholstering Methods. 56

Tiffany, Lawrence P., Detection of Crime. 101

Tilke, Max, A Pictorial History of Costume. 26

Till, Anthony, What You Should Know Before You Have Your Car Repaired. 125

Tillier, Henry, Normal Radiological Anatomy. 205

Tillman, Ernest C., Fire Attack. 86; Firefighting Strategy and Leadership Study Guide. 86

Tillman, John R., An Introduction to the Theory and Practice of Transistors. 159

Tillman, Rollie, Promotion. 62

Tilton, Theodore, Data Processing for Decision-Making. 15

Timbie, William H., Essentials of Electricity. 154

Time-Life Books, The Camera. 50; Ecology. 178; The Forest. 87

Timmerman, Stewart W., Design and Operation of Clean Rooms. 120

Timms, Noel, The Language of Social Casework. 107

Timoney, Donald, How to Boost Your Income to $25,000 a Year in Real Estate. 66

Timoshenko, Stephen, Elements of Strength of Materials. 170

Tingstad, James E., Mathematics for Pharmacy Students. 207

Tinker, Miles A., Legibility of Print. 47

Titmuss, F. H., Commercial Timbers of the World. 88

Titmuss, Richard M., Commitment to Welfare. 107

Titus, Harry W., The Scientific Feeding of Chickens. 79

Toboldt, William, Auto Body Repairing and Repainting. 125; Motor Service's Automotive Encyclopedia. 125

Tocci, Ronald J., Fundamentals of Electronic Devices. 154

Todd, Alden A., A Spark Lighted in Portland: The Record of the National Board of Fire Underwriters. 86

Todd, Alva C., Encyclopedia of Electronics Components. 154

Todd, Hollis N., Photographic Sensitometry. 50

Todd, Vivian E., The Years Before School. 83

Toffler, Alvin, Schoolhouse in the City. 113

Tokuriki, Tomikichiro, Wood-Block Print Primer. 12

Tolansky, Samuel, Revolution in Optics. 200

Tolman, Ruth, Guide to Beauty, Charm, Poise. 7

Tomboulian, Diran H., Electric and Magnetic Fields. 154

Tomeski, Edward A., The Computer Revolution. 18

Tomlinson, Michael J., Foundation Design and Construction. 140

Toner, P. G., Cell Structure. 185

Toohey, Monty, Medicine for Nurses. 193

Toole, Cameron S., Questions and Answers on Insurance. 53

Toole, James M., Special Semi-Conductor Devices. 153

Toon, Ernest R., Foundations of Chemistry. 131

Topalis, Mary, Psychiatric Nursing. 196

Topel, David G., The Pork Industry. 35

Torche, Judith, Acrylic and Other Water-Base Paints. 12

Torrance, Ellis P., Encouraging Creativity in the Classroom. 113

Toth, Louis, Hotel Accounting. 51

Toulmin, Harry A., A Treatise on the Law of Foods, Drugs and Cosmetics. 7

Tourist Court Journal, Modern Motelkeeping. 52

Tournier, Paul, The Meaning of Grief. 94

Tousley, Rayburn D., Principles of Marketing. 62

Tovey, John, Weaves and Pattern Drafting. 26

Towler, Juby E., The Police Role in Racial Conflicts. 101; Practical Police Knowledge. 101

Townsend, Carolynn E., Nutrition and Diet Modifications for the Nurse. 193

Toynbee, Arnold, Man's Concern with Death. 94

Tracey, Esther M., Illustration Index. 12

Tracy, Berry, Nineteenth Century America: Furniture and Other Decorative Arts. 55

Tracy, Marian, The Art of Making Real Soups. 35; Cooking Fondue. 35; The Mushroom Cookbook. 35; New Casserole Cookery. 35

Trahey, Jane, Harper's Bazaar: 100 Years of The American Female. 27

Trail, Ira D., Establishing Relationships in Psychiatric Nursing. 196

Training and Retraining, Inc., Basic Electricity/Electronics. 154

INDEX

Training Systems, Inc., DC Circuit Principles. 154; Simplified Transistor Theory. 159

Trane Air Conditioning Manual. 121

Transportation Workshop: Air Transportation 1975 and Beyond. 119

Travelbee, Joyce, Interpersonal Aspects of Nursing. 193; Intervention in Psychiatric Nursing. 196

Traxler, Ralph N., Asphalt. 140

Traylor, W. L., Pilot's Guide to an Airline Career. 119

Treager, Irwin E., Aircraft Gas Turbine Engine Technology. 119

Trease, George E., Pharmacy in History. 203; A Textbook of Pharmacognosy. 203

Treat, Nola, Quantity Cookery. 35

Treganowan, Donald, Rugs and Carpets of Europe and the Western World. 55

Tremaine, Howard M., Audio Cyclopedia. 154

Tremillion, Bernard, Chemical Reactions in Solvents and Melts. 126

Tressler, Donald K., The Freezing Preservation of Foods. 42; Fruit and Vegetable Juice Processing Technology. 42; Food Technology the World Over. 41

Trevelyan, Julian, Etching. 12

Treybal, R., Liquid Extraction. 131

Tribou, Marita, Professional Nursing Practice. 192

Tricomi, Ernest, ABC's of Air Conditioning. 121; Air Conditioning Installation and Maintenance. 121

Trinkner, Charles L., Library Services for Junior Colleges. 92

Tripper, C. F., Laboratory Manual of Experiments in Physical Chemistry. 126

Troeh, Frederick R., Introductory Soil Science. 77

Troelstrup, Archie W., The Consumer in American Society. 62

Trollhann, Lilian, Dictionary of Data Processing. 16

Tronaas, Edward M., Mathematics for Technicians. 207

Trotman, Edward R., Dyeing and Chemical Technology of Textile Fibers. 29

Trought, T. E., Farm Pests. 77

Troup, Gordon, Masers and Lasers. 156

Trout, G. Malcolm, Judging Dairy Products. 34

Trow, William C., Teacher and Technology. 113

Troxell, George E., Composition and Properties of Concrete. 141

Truax, Carol, The Art of Salad Making. 36

Trubowitz, Julius, Changing the Racial Attitudes of Children. 83, 113

Trubowitz, Sidney, A Handbook for Teaching in the Ghetto School. 113.

Truelove, S. C., Radiology of the Digestive System. 204

Truett, Fred M., The Arithmetic of Sales Management. 207

Truman, Nevil, Historic Costuming. 27

Trump, Fred, Buyer Beware! 62

Trump, Ross M., Essentials of Marketing Management. 62

Trusty, L. Sherman, Advanced Men's Hair Styling. 8; Art and Science of Barbering. 8

Tschichold, Jan, Asymmetric Typography. 47

Tsuifeng, Lin, Chinese Gastronomy. 39

Tucker, Spencer A., Cost Estimating and Pricing with Machine Hour Rates. 47

Tudbury, Chester A., Basics of Induction Heating. 121

Tudor, David C., Your Future in Poultry Farming. 78

Tuffnell, Robert, The Nature of Physical Chemistry. 135

Tunick, Stanley B., Fundamental Accounting. 4

Turk, Herman, Clinic Nursing. 193

Turk, Lloyd M., Fundamentals of Soil Science. 75

Turnbull, Arthur T., The Graphics of Communication. 47; Practical Exercises in Typography, Layout, and Design. 47

Turner, Bernice C., The Private Secretary's Manual. 70

Turner, David E., Dietitian. 36; Electrician and Electrician's Helper. 154; Food Service Supervisor. 36; Health Insurance Agent. 54; Insurance Agent and Broker. 54; Motor Vehicle Operator. 125; ...Nurse. 193; Real Estate Salesman & Broker. 66; Tabulating Machine Operator. 16

Turner, Edward, ...Practice for Clerical, Typing and Stenographic Tests. 70

Turner, Ethel M., A Catering Business of Your Own. 53; A Small Hotel of Your Own. 52

Turner, James S., The Chemical Feast. 36

Turner, John B., Neighborhood Organization for Community Action. 107

Turner, Mary C., Bookman's Glossary. 47

Turner, Paul, Clinical Aspects of Autonomic Pharmacology. 203

Turner, Rufus P., ABC's of Voltage-Dependent Resistors. 154; Basic Electricity. 154; Basic Electronic Test Instruments. 154; Diode Circuits Handbook. 154; How to Use Grid-Dip Oscillators. 154; Practical Oscilloscope Handbook. 154; Semiconductor Devices. 154; Waveform Measurements. 154

Turner, William W., Case Investigation. 101; Criminalistics. 101; The Police Establishment. 101; Traffic Investigation. 101

Turnquist, Carl H., Modern Refrigeration and Air Conditioning. 120; Modern Welding. 170

Tustison, Francis E., Metalwork Essentials. 163

Tuthill, Cuyler A., How to Service Tape Recorders. 154

Tuttle, Charles, Fundamentals of Oxy-Acetylene and Arc Welding. 171

Tuttle, Waid W., Textbook of Physiology. 184

Tweeddale, J. G., The Mechanical Properties of Metals, Assessment and Significance. 169; Welding Fabrication. 171

Twigg, Bernard A., Fundamentals of Quality Control for the Food Industry. 33

Tyler, Gus, Organized Crime in America. 101

Tyler, Louise L., Computer and Information Systems in Education. 17

Tyler, Varro E., Pharmacognosy. 201

Tylman, Stanley D., Theory and Practice of Crown and Fixed Partial Prosthodontics. 176

Type Specs Company, Type Specs. 47

Typomundus 20. 47

Tyroler, Else, Sewing Pants for Women. 26

Tyson, Forrest C., Industrial Instrumentation. 166

Tyson, Herbert I., Statics and Introduction to Strength of Materials. 170

Udall, Stewart L., 1976: Agenda for Tomorrow. 180

Udell, Gilman G., Laws Relating to Forestry Game Conservation, Flood Control and Related Sources. 88

Ujhely, Gertrud B., Determinants of the Nurse-Patient Relationship. 193; The Nurse and Her Problem Patients. 193

Ullmann, John E., Waste Disposal Problems in Selected Industries. 180

Ullmer, Eldon, Educational Media and the Teacher. 110

Ullrich, Heinz, Creative Metal Design. 163

Ulmer, Melville J., The Welfare State, U.S.A. 107

Ulrey, Harry F., Audel's Architects and Builders Guide. 140; Builders Encyclopedia. 140; Carpenters' and Builders' Library. 140; Carpentry and Building. 140

Uman, David B., New Product Programs. 62

Umbreit, Wayne W., Modern Microbiology. 187

Underwood, Arthur L., Quantitative Analysis. 132

Unger, Maurice A., Real Estate. 66

United Nations Economic Commission for Europe, Directory of Authorities and Principal Organizations Related to the Building Industry. 140

INDEX

United Nations Educational, Scientific and Cultural Organization, Microphotography in the Library. 92

United Piece Dye Works, Guidebook to Man-Made Textile Fibers and Textured Yarns. 29

U.S. Advisory Commission on Intergovernmental Relations, Building Codes. 140

U.S. Aerospace Studies Institute, Communications-Electronics Terminology Handbook. 154

U.S. Agricultural Marketing Service, Food Buying Guide for Type A School Lunches. 36

U.S. Air Force, Civil Air Patrol, Aerospace Doctrine. 119; Aircraft Identification. 119; Education, Aviation, and the Space Age. 119; Federal Aviation Regulations. 119; Introduction to Civil Air Patrol. 119

U.S. Air Force, Handbook for Photo Lab Processing. 50

U.S. Bureau of Labor Statistics, Salary Trends, Fireman and Policemen. 86; Technology and Manpower in the Textile Industry of the 1970's. 29

U.S. Bureau of Naval Personnel, Aviation Electronics Technician 1 & C. 119; Aviation Structural Mechanic. 119; Basic Electricity. 154; Basic Electronics. 154; Basic Hand Tools. 163; Basic Machines. 166; Basic Optics and Optical Instruments. 200; Blueprint Reading and Sketching. 143; Computer Basics. 19; Dental Technician, Prosthetic. 176; Digital Computer Basics. 19; Fluid Power. 166; Fundamentals of Electronics. 154; Illustrator Draftsman...I & C. 143; Photographer's Mate 3. 50; Synchro-Servo Fundamentals. 154

U.S. Bureau of Radiological Health, Population Exposure Studies Section, Population Dose From X-Rays, U.S., 1964. 205

U.S. Bureau of Reclamation, Earth Manual. 140

U.S. Bureau of the Budget, Automatic Data Processing Glossary. 16

U.S. Bureau of Yards and Docks, Testing and Licensing of Construction Equipment Operators. 140

U.S. Business and Defense Services Administration, Food Irradiation Activities Throughout the World. 42

U.S. Children's Bureau, Handbook for Recreation. 103; Infant Care. 83; Social Services for Children and Families in Your State. 107

U.S. Coast Guard, Cardiopulmonary (Heart-Lung) Resuscitation. 181

U.S. Commission on Civil Rights, Equal Opportunity in Farm Programs. 77; Law Enforcement. 101

U.S. Congress, Joint Committee on Printing, Federal Printing Program. 47

U.S. Congress, Senate Committee on Government Operations (Permanent Sub-Committee on Investigations), Riots, Civil and Criminal Disorders. 101

U.S. Department of Agriculture, Agricultural Research Service, Food Purchasing Guide for Group Feeding. 36; Soil Dynamics in Tillage and Traction. 77

U.S. Department of Agriculture, Agriculture Statistics. 77; Managing Public Rangelands. 79; Suggested Guide for Weed Control, 1969. 77; The U.S. Government Cook Book. 36; Yearbook of Agriculture. 77

U.S. Department of Agriculture, Federal Extension Service, Training Home Economics Program Assistants to Work with Low Income Families. 107

U.S. Department of Agriculture, Forest Service, National Forest Log Scaling Handbook. 88

U.S. Department of Agriculture, Office of the General Counsel, Glossary of Legal Terms for Secretaries. 71

U.S. Department of Commerce, Business and Defense Services Administration, Bibliography on Marketing to Low-Income Consumers. 62

U.S. Department of Health, Education and Welfare, The Allied Health Professions Personnel Training Act of 1966 as Amended. 208; Child Care and Guidance. 83; Environmental Health Planning Guide. 180; Educating Children in Nursery Schools and Kindergarten. Washington, D.C.:...a Social Report. 108; Training Food Service Personnel for the Hospitality Industry. 36

U.S. Department of Health, Education and Welfare, National Air Pollution Control Administration, Air Pollution Publications. 180

U.S. Department of Health, Education and Welfare, Office of Education National Committee for Careers in Medical Technology, Medical Laboratory Assistant. 183

U.S. Department of Health, Education and Welfare, Public Health Service, Training the Auxiliary Health Worker. 208

U.S. Department of Justice and Los Angeles County Sheriff's Department, Project Sky Knight. 99

U.S. Department of the Army, Carpentry and Building Construction. 140; General Drafting. 143

U.S. Department of the Army, Headquarters, Military Roentgenology. 205

U.S. Department of the Interior, Concrete Manual. 141

U.S. Department of the Interior, Fish and Wildlife Service, Let's Cook Fish. 36

U.S. Federal Aviation Administration, Airports Service, Planning the State Airport System. 119

U.S. Federal Aviation Administration, Flight Information Division, Airman's Information Manual. 119

U.S. Federal Aviation Agency, Air Traffic Service, Contractions. 119

U.S. Federal Aviation Agency, Flight Standards Service, Airline Transport Pilot (Airplane) Written Examination Guide. 119; Commercial Pilot Examination Guide. 119; Ground Instructor Examination Guide. 119; Private Pilot's Handbook of Aeronautical Knowledge. 119

U.S. Federal Aviation Agency, Maintenance of Control Lines. 119

U.S. Federal Water Pollution Control Administration, Cost of Clean Water, 180

U.S. Food and Drug Administration, Microscopic-Analytical Methods in Food and Drug Control. 36; National Drug Code Directory. 203

U.S. Forest Products Laboratory, Lumber and Allied Products. 88

U.S. Forest Service, Handbook on Forest Service Plant Collections. 88; Law Enforcement. 88; Outdoor Recreation in the National Forests. 103

U.S. General Services Administration, Textile Test Methods. 29

U.S. Government Printing Office, 100 GPO Years, 1861-1961. 47; Specimens of Type Faces in the United States Government Printing Office. 47; Style Manual. 47; Theory and Practice of Bookbinding. 47; Typography and Design. 47

U.S. Library of Congress, Papermaking. 48

U.S. Library of Congress, Subject Cataloging Division, Subject Headings Used in the Dictionary Catalogs of the Library of Congress from 1897 through June 1964. 92

U.S. National Advisory Commission on Health Manpower, Report.... 208

U.S. National Aeronautics and Space Administration, Scientific and Technical Information Division, Dictionary of Technical Terms for Aerospace Use. 119

U.S. National Air Pollution Control Administration, Control Techniques for Particulate Air Pollutants. 180

U.S. National Center for Air Pollution Control, Compilation of Selected Air Pollution Control Regulations and Ordinances. 180

U.S. National Institute of Health, Research Grants Division, Medical and Health Related Sciences Thesaurus. 208

U.S. Naval Aviation Safety Center, Handbook for Aircraft Accident Investigators. 119

U.S. Naval Dental School, Dental Technician, General. 176

United States of America Standards Institute, USA Standard Performance Requirements for Textile.... 29

U.S. Office of Education, Manpower Development and Training Division, Heavy Construction Equipment Mechanic. 140; Waiter-Waitress. 53

INDEX

U.S. Office of Education, Quantity Food Preparation. 36

U.S. Office of Education, Vocational and Technical Education Division, Agricultural Equipment Technology. 78; Architectural and Building Construction Technology. 140; Chemical Technology. 131; Civil Technology. 140; Clerical and Record Keeping Occupations. 70; Diesel Servicing. 125; Electrical Technology. 154; Electronic Data Processing. 16; ...Electronic Data Processing in Engineering, Science and Business. 16; Electronic Technology. 154; Farm Crop Production Technology. 77; Food Processing Technology. 36; Forest Technology. 88; Grain, Feed, Seed and Farm Supply Technology. 77; Industrial Radiography. 205; Instrumentation Technical. 166; Mechanical Technology. 166; Metallurgical Technology. 169; Recreation Program Leadership. 103; Water and Wastewater Technology. 180

U.S. Office of Education, Vocational Division, Food Service Industry. 36

U.S. Office of Law Enforcement, The APCO Project. 101

U.S. Office of Naval Operations, Aviation Medical Safety Training Manual. 119

U.S. Panel on Electrically Powered Vehicles, The Automobile and Air Pollution. 125

U.S. Post Office Department, National Zip Code Directory. 70

U.S. President's Commission on Law Enforcement and Administration of Justice, The Challenge of Crime in a Free Society. 101; Studies in Crime and Law Enforcement in Major Metropolitan Areas. 101

U.S. Public Health Service Nursing Division, How to Study Nursing Activities in a Patient Unit. 193

U.S. Public Health Service, Population Exposure to X-Rays. 205

U.S. Task Force on Assessment of Crime, Task Force Report. 101

U.S. Task Force on Prescription Drugs, The Drug Prescribers, 203

U.S. Task Force on the Police, Task Force Report. 101

U.S. Water Resources Council, The Nation's Water Resources. 180

University of Michigan Extension Service, The Fire Fighter and Electrical Equipment. 86

Updike, Daniel B., Printing Types. 47

Upjohn Company, The Cell. 185

Upton, Arthur C., Radiation Injury. 205

Upton, Monroe, Inside Electronics. 154

Urban, Glen L., Management Science in Marketing. 60

Urrows, Grace M., Food Preservation by Irradiation. 42

Uschold, Kathie, Special Education. 112

Useem, Ruth N., Psychology. 190

Utter, R. F., Concepts of the True Position Dimensioning System. 143

Vail, Esther, Tools of Teaching. 113

Vail, Gladys E., Foods. 36

Vairo, Philip D., How to Teach Disadvantaged Youth. 112

Valdes, Leopoldo B., The Physical Theory of Transistors. 159

Valentine, C. Glenn, From Electrons to Power. 155

Valko, Emery I., Thesaurus of Textile Terms. 28

Vallance, Alex, Design of Machine Members. 167

Vallen, Jerome J., The Art and Science of Modern Innkeeping. 52

Vallow, Herbert Phillip, Police Arrest and Search. 101

Van Allen, Edward J., Your Future As A Shorthand Reporter. 70

Van Allen, R., Independent Activities for Creative Learning. 109

Van Arsdel, Wallace B., Food Dehydration. 42; Quality and Stability in Frozen Foods. 42

Van Blarcom, Carolyn C., Obstetric Nursing. 195

Vance, Lawrence L., Accounting Principles and Control. 4

Vance, Lucile E., Illustration Index. 12

Van Dean Company, Inc., Van Dean Manual. 8

VanDemark, N. L., Physiology of Reproduction and Artifical Insemination of Cattle. 79

Vanderbilt, Amy, Complete Cookbook. 36

Vanderbilt University, Hospital Diet Manual. 36

Vanderbosch, Charles G., Criminal Investigation. 102; The Patrol Operation. 99

Vanderhoff, Margil, Clothes. 26

Vanderwerf, Calvin A., Acid, Bases and Chemistry of the Covalent Bond. 131; Unitized Experiments in Organic Chemistry. 134

Van Der Ziel, Albert, Electronics. 154

Van Deventer, C. N., An Introduction to General Aeronautics. 119

Van Dijck, J. G. R., The Physical Basic of Electronics. 154

Vandivert, Rita, Chicken As You Like It. 36

Van Dommelen, David B., Decorative Wall Hangings. 55; Designing and Decorating Interiors. 55

Vandyke Price, Pamela J., Winelovers' Handbook. 38

Van Gaasbeek, Richard M., A Practical Course in Roof Framing. 140

Van Horn, Richard L., Automatic Data-Processing Systems. 16

Van Kruiningen, H., The Techniques of Graphic Art. 47

Van Ness, Robert G., Principles of Punched Card Data Processing. 17

Van Orden, Harris O., Elementary Organic Chemistry. 135

Van Orman, Richard A., A Room For the Night. 52

Van Rooyen, Clennel E., Textbook of Virology. 183

Van Sickel, Mildred, Psychiatric Nursing. 196

Van Sickle, Neil D., Modern Airmanship. 119

Van Straaten, J. F., Thermal Performance of Building. 121

Van Tassel, Raymond, Woodworking Crafts. 163

Van Thoor, T. J., Chemical Technology. 131

Van Valkenburgh, Nooger, Basic Electronic Circuits. 154; Basic Industrial Electricity. 154

Van Velzer, Harry L., Physics and Chemistry of Electronic Technology. 154

Van Vlack, Lawrence H., Elements of Materials Science. 168

Van Voorhis, Robert H., College Accounting. 4

Van Winkle, Mathew, Distillation. 131

Van Zuylen, Guirne, Gourmet Cooking for Everyone. 36

Vara, Albert C., Food and Beverage Industries. 36

Vardaman, James W., Tree Farm Business Management. 88

Varga, Charles, Handbook of Pediatric Medical Emergencies. 208

Vaughan, Daniel, General Ophthalmology. 200

Vaughan, Louise M., Attitudes of Nursing Students Toward Direct Patient Care. 193

Vause, A. S., Lamps and Lighting. 148

Veatch, Henry C., Transistor Circuit Action. 160

Veblen, Thorstein, The Instinct of Workmanship. 163

Vecchio, Walter, The Fashion Makers. 26

Vedder, Clyde B., Juvenile Offenders. 102; Probation and Parole. 98

Veillette, Peter D., Purchasing Library Materials in Public and School Libraries. 90

Veinott, Cyril G., Fractional and Subfractional-Horsepower Electric Motors. 156

Venk, Ernest, Automotive Collision Work. 125; Automotive Engines: Maintenance and Repair. 125; Automotive Fundamentals. 125; Automotive Maintenance and Troubleshooting. 125; Automotive Suspensions, Steering, Alignment and Brakes. 125

Vercoe, Bernice J., Cake Design and Decoration. 37

Vergara, William, Electronics in Everyday Things. 154
Verghese, K. P., Child Care in a Developing Community. 81
Vermes, Jean, The Secretary's Guide to Dealing With People. 70; Secretary's Index to English. 70
Verner, H. Crey, Semiconductor Junctions and Devices. 146
Vernon, Ralph J., Basic Woodwork. 163
Verry, Herbert R., Microcopying Methods. 92
Versagi, Frank J., Technical Conversations in Air Conditioning and Refrigeration. 121
Vervalin, Charles H., Fire Protection Manual for Hydrocarbon Processing Plants. 86
Verville, Elinor, Behavior Problems of Children. 83
Victor, Edward, Science for the Elementary School. 113
Vidosic, Joseph P., Metal Machining and Forming Technology. 166
Vierck, Charles J., Fundamentals of Engineering Drawing. 142; Graphic Science. 142; A Manual of Engineering Drawing for Student Draftsmen. 142
Vierin, Albert, 100 to Dinner. 34
Viessman, Warren, Jr., Water Supply and Pollution Control. 177
Vigrolio, Tom, Marketing and Communications Media Dictionary. 62
Villiard, Paul, A Manual of Veneering. 163; The Practical Candymaking Cookbook. 36
Villines, William M., Jr., Elements of Electronics. 148
Vincent, Ben, Begone Dull Care. 83
Vincent, Clark E., Unmarried Mothers. 108
Vincent, Pauline A., Public Health Nursing. 196
Vinton, Iris, The Folkways Omnibus of Children's Games. 83
Visiting Nurse Service of New York, Public Health Nursing for the Sick at Home. 197
Vithaldas, Yogi, The Yogi Cook Book. 36
Vizza, Robert F., New Handbook of Sales Training. 62
Vlahos, Charles J., Fundamentals of Numerical Control. 170
Voege, Ray, Beauty Secrets for the Black Woman. 8
Voegele, Marguerite C., The Correct Service Department for Hotels, Motor Hotels, Motels and Resorts. 52; Drink Dictionary. 38; Menu Dictionary. 36
Voegele, Walter O., The Correct Maid for Hotels and Motels. 52
Vogel, Arthur I., A Textbook of Quantitative Inorganic Analysis. 132
Vogel, Ezra F., A Modern Introduction to the Family. 103

Vogel, Stefan, So You're Going to be A Teacher. 110
Voiland, Alice L., Family Casework Diagnosis. 108
Voisin, André, Fertilizer Application. 77
Volland, Robert J., How to Design and Install Plumbing. 141
Vollmer, August, The Police and Modern Society. 102
Vollmer, Carl, The Policeman's Manual. 102
Volume Feeding Management, Professional's Recipe Master. 30, 36
Von Bergen, Werner, Wool Handbook. 29
Von Braun, Werner, Careers in Astronautics and Rocketry. 115
Von Loesecke, Harry W., Nutritional Evaluation of Food Processing. 40
Von Neumann, Robert, The Design and Creation of Jewelry. 28
Voss, Ruth, The Cake Cook Book. 37
Vredenburg, Harvey L., Readings in Global Marketing Management. 62
Vroman, Leo, Blood. 186

Wachsmann, Konrad, The Turning Point of Building. 140
Wackerman, Albert E., Harvesting Timber Crops. 88
Waddams, Austen L., Chemicals from Petroleum. 131
Waddell, Joseph J., Concrete Construction Handbook. 141; Practical Quality Control for Concrete. 141
Waddington, Conrad H., Biology of the Modern World. 185
Waddington, Thomas C., Non-Aqueous Solvent Systems. 131
Wadleigh, Cecil H., Waste in Relation to Agriculture and Forestry. 77
Waechter, Eugenia H., Nursing Care of Children. 195
Waffle, Harvey W., Architectural Drawing. 144
Wagner, Helen, Why Team Teaching? 110
Wagner, Johannes, Reforming the Rites of Death. 94
Wagner, Joseph A., Children's Literature Through Storytelling. 83
Wagner, Percy E., Management and Policies of Real Estate Brokerage. 64
Wagner, Willis H., Modern Carpentry. 140; Modern Woodworking. 163; Woodworking. 163
Wagnon, Kenneth A., Beef Cattle Production. 79
Wahl, Arnold C., Atomic and Molecular Structure. 131
Wahl, Arthur M., Mechanical Springs. 166

Wainwright, Charles A., Successful Management of New Products. 58
Wainwright, Lewis F., Aircraft Electrical Practice. 119
Wainwright, William W., Dental Radiology. 176
Waisman, Morris, Pharmaceutical Therapeutics in Dermatology. 203
Wake, William C., The Analysis of Rubber and Rubber-Like-Polymers. 132
Wakefield, George L., An Introduction to Photography. 50
Wakeman, Truman J., Farm Shop. 78
Walcoff, Charles, Industrial Needle Trades. 26
Walden, Robert E., Accounting Theory and Practice: Advanced. 3; Accounting Theory and Practice: Intermediate. 3; Accounting Theory and Practice: Introductory. 3; Introductory Accounting. 4
Walden's ABC Guide & Paper Production Yearbook. 48
Waldner, George K., Professional Chef's Book of Buffets. 36; 65 Quality Menus for Quantity Service. 36
Waldo, Myra, The Complete Book of Gourmet Cooking for the American Kitchen. 36; The Complete Book of Oriental Cooking. 40; The Complete Round the World Meat Cookbook. 36; Cooking for the Freezer. 36; Dictionary of International Food & Cooking Terms. 36; The International Encyclopedia of Cooking. 36
Wales, Hugh G., Promotional Strategy. 58
Walker, Arthur L., How to Use Adding and Calculating Machines. 70
Walker, Barbara G., A Treasury of Knitting Patterns. 26
Walker, Charles F., Practical Business Correspondence for Colleges. 70
Walker, Daniel, Rights in Conflict. 102
Walker, Frank R., The Building Estimator's Reference Book. 140
Walker, John R., Industrial Arts Drafting. 143; Machining Fundamentals. 163; Modern Metalworking. 163
Walker, Robert L., Introduction to Transistor Electronics. 160
Walker, Robert N., Training Police for Work with Juveniles. 102
Walker, Virginia H., Nursing and Ritualistic Practice. 193
Walker, William F., Beginner's Guide to Jig and Tool Design. 166
Wall, C. Edward, Periodical Title Abbreviations. 92
Wall, Florence E., The Principles and Practice of Beauty Culture. 8
Wall, Frederick T., Chemical Thermodynamics. 131
Wall, Joseph S., Sorghum. 77

INDEX

Wall, Patrick M., Eye-Witness Identification in Criminal Cases. 102

Wallace, Luther T., Agriculture, Economics and Growth. 77

Wallace, Robert, The Modern Business Letter Writer's Manual. 67

Wallach, Jeffrey J., Medical Legal Dictionary. 70

Wallach, Paul I., Architecture. 143

Wallhauser, Henry T., Pioneers of Flight. 119

Wallick, Clair H., ...A Display Manual for Libraries and Bookstores. 92

Walls, Gordon L., Fundamentals of Visual Science. 199

Walls, Henry J., Forensic Science. 102

Walnut, Francis K., Introduction to Computer Programming and Coding. 21

Walraven, H. Dale, A Handbook of Engineering Graphics. 143

Walsh, Charles V., Firefighting Strategy and Leadership. 86

Walsh, J. E., Principles of Data Processing. 17

Walsh, James P., General Encyclopedias in Print. 92

Walsh, John B., Introductory Electric Circuits. 154

Walsh, John E., The Shroud. 95

Walter, John F., Programmed Instruction in Arithmetic, Dosages, and Solutions. 192

Walter, Joseph, A Short Textbook of Radiotheraphy for Technicians and Students. 205

Walters, Sherwood G., Readings in Marketing. 62

Walton, William C., The World of Water. 180

Waltz, Jon R., Principles of Evidence and Proof. 99

Wanderstock, Jeremiah J., A Guide to the Selection, Combination, and Cooking of Foods. 35

Wandesforde-Smith, Geoffrey, Congress and the Environment. 177

Wang, Chu-kia, Reinforced Concrete Design. 141

Wang, Shyh, Solid-State Electronics. 154

Wanous, Edward E., Automation Office Practices. 70; Introduction to Automated Data Processing. 17

Wanous, Samuel J., Automation Office Practice. 70; College Typewriting; Basic Course. 68; Introduction to Automated Data Processing. 17; Personal and Professional Typing. 70; Shorthand Transcription Studies. 67

Wanscher, J. H., Reinhold Color Atlas. 13

Wanscher, Ole, The Art of Furniture. 56

Ward, Bruce, Transistor Ignition Systems Handbook. 160

Ward, C. O., Experimental Methods in Pharmacology. 203

Ward, D. T., Tufting. 29

Ward, Donovan F., Effective Medical Assisting. 72

Ward, Jack W., Construction Information Source and Reference Guide. 140

Warden, Jessie, Principles for Creating Clothing. 26

Ware, George W., Producing Vegetable Crops. 77

Waring, Ralph G., Modern Wood Finishing. 163

Warmbrod, John R., Review and Synthesis of Research in Agricultural Education. 77

Warmke, Roman F., Marketing, Sales Promotion, and Advertising. 60

Warner, Daniel S., Advertising. 7; Marketing and Distribution. 62

Warnick, A. C., Crossbreeding Beef Cattle. 78

Warren, John E., Control Instrument Mechanisms. 170

Warrick, C. K., Anatomy and Physiology for Radiographers. 205

Warshaw, Martin R., Promotional Strategy. 58

Warshofsky, Fred, Poisons in the Air. 177

Warwick, Edward, Early American Dress. 27

Warwick, Roger, Introduction to Anatomy. 184

Waser, Jurg, Basic Chemical Thermodynamics. 131

Washburn, Dale W., Computer Programming. 21

Washington, Bennetta B., Youth in Conflict. 113

Washington School of Psychiatry, The Teacher Aide Program. 113

Washington (State) Fire Chiefs Standards Committee, Design of Fire Stations. 86

Waskin, Yvonne, Teacher-Pupil Planning for Better Classroom Learning. 113

Wasley, G. D., Animal Cell Culture Methods. 185

Wasley, Ruth, Bead Design. 28

Wason, Elizabeth, The Art of German Cooking. 40; Cooks, Gluttons & Gourmets. 36; The Language of Cookery. 36

Wass, Alonzo, Building Construction Estimating. 140; Manual of Structural Details for Building Construction. 140

Wasserman, Miriam, The School Fix, NYC, USA. 113

Wasson, Chester R., Buying Behavior and Marketing Decisions. 62

Water Information Center, Inc., The Water Encyclopedia. 180

Watkins, Bruce O., Introduction to Control Systems. 170

Watkinson, Raymond, Pre-Raphaelite Art and Design. 13

Watson, Dori, The Elements of Landscape. 9; The Techniques of Painting. 13

Watson, Ernest W., The Art of Pencil Drawing. 13; Growth and Development of Children. 83; Perspective for Sketchers. 13

Watson, Herbert M., Understanding Radio. 157

Watson, James D., The Double Helix, 131; Molecular Biology of the Gene. 185

Watson, John C., Patient Care and Special Procedures in Radiologic Technology. 205

Watson, Nelson A., Juvenile Delinquency and Youth Crime. 100; Training Police for Work with Juveniles. 102

Watson, Olive B., School and Institutional Lunchroom Management. 53

Watson, Robert I., Psychology of the Child. 83

Watson, Sam D., Dogs for Police Service. 102

Watt, John H., American Electricians' Handbook. 146

Watt, John R., Evaporative Air Conditioning. 121

Watts, Stephen, The Ritz of Paris. 52

Waugh, Alice, Interior Design. 55

Waugh, Norah, The Cut of Men's Clothes, 1600-1900. 26; The Cut of Women's Clothes, 1600-1930. 26

Wax, Gerold J., Elementary Anatomy and Physiology. 205

Waxenberg, Barbara R., Black Ghetto Family in Therapy. 107

Way Things Work: An Illustrated Encyclopedia of Technology. 163

Waye, Basil E., Introduction to Technical Ceramics. 163

Wayler, Thelma J., Applied Nutrition. 41

Weaver, Elbert C., Scientific Experiments in Environmental Pollution. 180

Weaver, Gilbert G., Teaching Occupational Skills. 160

Weaver, Mabel E., Programmed Mathematics of Drugs and Solutions. 207

Weaver, Peter, Printmaking. 13; The Technique of Lithography. 15

Weaver, Robert G., Writing for Business and Industry. 69

Weaver, William, Computer Programs for Structural Analysis. 140

Webb, Garn H., Insurance Law. 54

Webber, Marion G., Calculations in Pharmacy. 203

Weber, Elmer W., Health and the School Child. 113

302

Weber, Evelyn, The Kindergarten. 113
Weber, Wilhelm, A History of Lithography. 15
Webster, Staten W., The Disadvantaged Learner. 113
Wechsberg, Joseph, Dining at the Pavillon. 36
Wechsler, Abraham S., Real Estate Law for Salesmen and Brokers. 66
Weck, Johannes, Dictionary of Forestry in Five Languages. 88
Wedberg, Stanley E., Introduction to Microbiology. 187; Paramedical Microbiology. 187
Weddige, Emil, Lithography. 15
Wedlock, Bruce D., Electronic Components and Measurements. 154
Weeks, Bertha M., Filing and Records Management. 70
Weeks, Jeanne G., Rugs and Carpets of Europe and the Western World. 55
Weeks, Robert P., Machines and the Man. 166
Weeks, William R., Welding Skills and Practices. 171; Welding Technology. 171
Wegner, Peter, Programming Languages, Information, Structure and Machine Organization. 21
Weick, Carl B., Principles of Electronic Technology. 154
Weidemann, Kurt, Book Jackets and Record Covers. 13; Packaging. 63
Weiers, Ronald M., Licensed to Kill. 125
Weik, Martin H., Standard Dictionary of Computers and Information Processing. 19
Weilbacher, William M., Marketing Management Cases. 62
Weimer, Arthur M., Real Estate. 66
Weimer, Sally W., Systems and Procedures for Automated Accounting. 4
Weinberg, Fred, Tools and Techniques in Physical Metallurgy. 169
Weinberg, Gerald M., Computer Programming Fundamentals. 20; Computer Programming Fundamentals. 20; PL/1 Programming. 21; PL/1 Programming Primer. 21
Weinberg, Lawrence A., Atlas of Crown and Bridge Prosthodontics. 176
Weiner, Harold N., Public Relations in Health and Welfare. 208
Weiner, Jack, Air Pollution in the Pulp and Paper Industry. 180; Drying of Paper and Board. 48; Electrostatic Printing. 47; Nonwoven Fabrics. 29; Paper and Its Relation to Printing. 48; Runnability of Printing Paper. 48
Weiner, Lillian, Hospital Health Services. 208
Weiner, Nathan, Industrial Electronic Circuits and Applications. 145

Weingartner, C., Machinists' Ready Reference. 166
Weinstein, Seymour M., Fundamentals of Digital Computers. 19
Weinstein, William, The Automobile Engine. 125
Weinstock, Harold, Cryogenic Technology. 183
Weinwurm, Ernest H., Business Information and Accounting Systems. 2
Weir, Walter, Truth in Advertising and Other Heresies. 7
Weiser, Harry H., Practical Food Microbiology and Technology. 36
Weiser, Russell S., Fundamentals of Immunology. 183
Weiss, Adelle, Art Careers. 12
Weiss, Edward B., Management and the Marketing Revolution. 62; Merchandising for Tomorrow. 62; 1010 Tested Ideas That Move Merchandise. 64; The Vanishing Salesman. 62
Weiss, Eric A., Computer Usage/Applications. 17; Computer Usage/Fundamentals. 17; Computer Usage/360 Fortran Programming. 19; The PL/1 Converter. 19; Programming the IBM 1620. 21
Weiss, F. T., Determination of Organic Compounds. 135
Weiss, Howard, Guide to Organic Reactions. 135
Weiss, R. L., Chairside Psychology in Patient Education. 176
Weiss, Richard E., 1010 Tested Ideas That Move Merchandise. 64
Weisskamp, Herbert, Hotels. 52
Weissman, Harold H., Community Development in the Mobilization for Youth Experience. 108; Justice and the Law in the Mobilization for Youth Experience. 102
Weisz, Vera C., New Faces in the Classroom. 113
Welding Engineer Publishing Co., The Welding Encyclopedia. 171
Weldon, E. J., Principles of Data Communication. 16
Wellard, Charles L., Resistance and Resistors. 154
Wellhausen, Marilyn, Occupational Therapy Manual. 209
Wells, Alexander F., Structural Inorganic Chemistry. 133
Wells, Frederick V., Cosmetics and the Skin. 8
Wells, Kenneth M., Criminal Investigation. 102
Wells, Walter, Communications in Business. 70
Wels, Byron G., Transistor Circuit Guidebook. 160
Welsh, Robert C., Spectacles for Aphakia. 197
Wendel, Otto, Techniques of Crime Scene Investigation. 101

Wendel, Thomas M., Introduction to Data Processing and Cobol. 17
Wendland, Ray T., Petrochemicals. 131
Wendt, Paul F., Real Estate Investment Analysis and Taxation. 66
Wenner, David N., Basic Ignition and Electrical Systems. 125
Wensley, Edith, Nursing Service Without Walls. 193
Wentworth, Gerald O., The Accounting Process. 4
Wentz, Carl F., Gastronomy. 36
Wentz, Walter B., Marketing. 62
Wenzel, George L., How to Finance a Restaurant. 53
Wenzel, George L., Sr., Blueprints for Restaurant Success. 53; Guides to Restaurant Profits. 53; Menu Maker. 36
Werner, Harold D., A Rational Approach to Social Casework. 108
Werner, Jean A., Psychiatric Nursing in a Therapeutic Community. 196
Wesley, S. M., Short-Cut Shorthand. 70
West, Bessie B., Food for Fifty. 32; Food Service in Institutions. 36
West, Donald M., Fundamentals of Analytical Chemistry. 132
West, Geoffrey B., Textbook of Pharmacology. 200
West, Gertrude I., The Dental Assistant's Handbook. 176
West, Leonard J., Acquisition of Typewriting Skills. 70
West, Trustham F., Chemicals for Pest Control. 74
West Coast Lumbermen's Association, Douglas Fir Use Book. 88
Westberg, Granger E., Good Grief. 95
Westbrook, James, Your Future in Restaurant and Food Service. 53
Westby-Gibson, Dorothy, Grouping Students for Improved Instruction. 113
Westcott, Charles G., Tape Recorders. 154
Westerhaus, Carl L., Personnel Administration and Labor Relations in Health Care Facilities. 207
Westfall, Ralph, Cases in Marketing Strategy. 57; Marketing Research. 57
Westing, John H., Marketing Management. 60; Modern Marketing Thought. 62
Westinghouse Electric Corporation, Westinghouse Electronic Tube Guide. 154
Westlake, John H., Applied Mathematics for Electronics. 207
Weston, Eric B., Automobile Engineering Drawing for Technical Students. 144
Weston, Paul B., Arson. 84; Combat Shooting for Police. 102; Criminal Investigation. 102;

INDEX

The Police Traffic Control Function. 102; Supervision in the Administration of Justice. 102

Westrum, Edgar F., Jr., The Chemical Thermodynamics of Organic Compounds. 135

Wetherill, G. Barrie, Sampling Inspection and Quality Control. 47

Wetmore, Rosamond B., A Guide to the Organization of Library Materials in Schools and Small Public Libraries. 92

Wetteroth, William J., Police Training and Performance Study. 97

Wetzel, Guy F., Automotive Diagnosis and Tune-Up. 125

Wetzlar, Elisabeth, Rustic Interiors for Town and Country. 55

Weyant, J. Thomas, An Introduction to Agricultural Business and Industry. 77

Weyrick, Robert C., Fundamentals of Analog Computers. 19

Whalen, Doris H., The Secretary's Handbook. 70

Wheat Flour Institute, Eat to Live. 36

Wheatley, Richard C., Restoration of Antique and Classic Cars. 125

Wheeler, Gershon J., Business Data Processing. 17; Introduction to Microwaves. 155; Radar Fundamentals. 156

Wheeler, Helen R., The Community College Library. 92

Wheeler, Lora J., International Business and Foreign Trade Information Sources. 63

Wheeler, Margaret F., Basic Microbiology. 187

Wheeler, Russell C., An Atlas of Tooth Form. 176; A Textbook of Dental Anatomy and Physiology. 176

Wherry, Joseph H., Automobiles of the World. 125

Wherry, Ralph H., Insurance and Risk. 54

Whetton, Harry, Practical Printing and Binding. 47

Whife, Archibald A., The Art of Garment Making. 26; The Art of Measuring for all Kinds of Tailor-Made.... 26

Whinnery, John R., Introduction to Electronic Systems, Circuits, and Devices. 152

Whipple, Clyde C., Alternating-Current Machines. 150

Whisenand, Paul M., Automated Police Information Systems. 102; New Dimensions in Criminal Justice. 95; Patrol Operations. 102; Police Supervision. 102

Whitaker, Benjamin C. G., The Police. 102

Whitcomb, Helen, Charm. 8, 70; Strictly for Secretaries.... 70

Whitcomb, John, Strictly for Secretaries.... 70

White, Bertha R., The Law of Buying and Selling. 62

White, Carl M., Sources of Information in the Social Sciences. 108

White, D. Hywel, Elementary Electronics. 155

White, Dorothy T., Abilities Needed by Teachers of Nursing in Community Colleges. 193

White, Edwin H., Business Insurance. 54

White, Emil H., Chemical Background for the Biological Sciences. 185

White, Gwen, Perspective. 13

White, Jack W., Photo Composing. 45

White, John A., Fundamental Accounting Principles. 4

White, John H., A Reference Book of Chemistry. 131

White, M. J. D., The Chromosomes. 185

White, Mary M., Poems Children Will Sit Still For. 109

White, Paul F., Contact Lens Practice and Patient Management. 198

White, Percival, Clothes and Cloth. 22

White, Richardson, New Careers: The Patrolman Aide. 102

White, S. S., Handbook of Electron Beam Welding. 171

White, Wilma L., Chemistry for Medical Technologists. 183

Whitehead, Sylvia L., Nursing Care of the Adult Urology Patient. 197

Whiteside, Conon D., Accountant's Guide to Profitable Management Advisory Services. 4; Accounting Systems for the Small and Medium-Sized Business. 4

Whitfield, John F., Electrical Installations Technology. 155

Whitfield, Richard C., Spectroscopy in Chemistry. 131

Whitmer, Melvin, Servicing Closed-Circuit Television. 158

Whitnah, Donald R., Safer Skyways: Federal Control of Aviation, 1926-1966. 119

Whitney, Robert A., The New Psychology of Persuasion and Motivation in Selling. 62

Whiton, Sherrill, Elements of Interior Design and Decoration. 55

Whittaker, Charles E., Law, Order and Civil Disobedience. 102

Whittemore, L. H., Cop: A Closeup of Violence and Tragedy. 102

Whitten, Jamie L., That We May Live. 180

Whittenberger, James L., Artificial Respiration. 181

Whittington, Harold, Starting and Managing a Small Motel. 52

Whittington, Lloyd R., Whittington's Dictionary of Plastics. 168

Who's Who In American Art. 13

Who's Who In Graphic Art. 13

Whyte, William F., Human Relations in the Restaurant Industry. 53

Wiberg, Kenneth B., Laboratory Technique in Organic Chemistry. 135

Wick, Charles H., Chipless Machining. 166

Wick, Peter A., The Arts of the French Book, 1900-1965. 9

Wick, Ralph E., The Optometric Profession. 198; Vision of the Aging Patient. 198; Vision of Children. 198

Wickstrom, Ralph L., Fundamental Motor Patterns. 83

Widmann, Frances K., Clinical Interpretation of Laboratory Tests. 182

Widmer, Emmy L., The Critical Years: Early Childhood Education at the Crossroads. 113

Wiebe, Anne M., Orthopedics in Nursing. 195

Wiedenbach, Ernestine, Clinical Nursing. 193; Family-Centered Maternity Nursing. 195

Wielgat, Jeanne, An Effective Teacher-Aide Program. 113

Wiener, Jack, Creative Movement for Children. 113

Wiener, Louis, Handmade Jewelry. 28

Wiener, Solomon, Blue Book of Business Letter Writing. 70

Wigg, Philip, Introduction to Figure Drawing. 13

Wiggs, Garland D., Marketing, Business and Office Specialists. 62

Wignall, Harry, Hosiery Technology. 26; Knitting. 26

Wilber, Charles G., The Biological Aspects of Water Pollution. 180

Wilber, Gordon O., Industrial Arts in General Education. 163

Wilbur, John R., Elementary Structural Analysis. 139

Wilbur, Muriel B., Educational Tools for Health Personnel. 208

Wilcox, Charles F., Laboratory Experiments in Organic Chemistry. 134

Wilcox, Glade W., Basic Electronics. 155; Electricity for Engineering Technology. 155

Wilcox, Ruth T., The Dictionary of Costume. 27; Five Centuries of American Costume. 27; Folk and Festival Costume of the World. 27

Wildenhain, Marguerite, Pottery. 163

Wilensky, Harold L., The Uses of Sociology. 105

Wilinsky, Harriet, Careers and Opportunities in Retailing. 64

Wilkie Bros. Foundation, Fundamentals of Band Machining. 166; Precision Surface Grinding. 166

Wilkins, Esther M., Clinical Practice of the Dental Hygienist. 176

Wilkins, R. G., Modern Coordination Chemistry. 129

Wilkinson, C. W., Communicating Through Letters and Reports. 68

Wilkinson, Jule, The Finishing Kitchen. 36; The Nautical Way. 36; Storage Specifics. 36; The Three C's of Atmosphere. 55

Wilkinson, Paul H., Aircraft Engines of the World. 119

Wilkinson, Walter D., Properties of Refractory Metals. 169

Willard, Helen S., Occupational Therapy. 209

Willard, Hobart H., Instrumental Methods of Analysis. 133

Willcox, Donald, Wood Design. 13

Wille, Edgar, The Computer and Business Unity. 18

Wille, Milton, Art in Wood. 163

Willeford, George, Medical Word Finder. 72

Willemin, Silvène, Technique of Union Catalogues. 92

Williams, Alec, Sustained Release Pharmaceuticals. 203

Williams, Arthur L., Introduction to Chemistry. 131

Williams, Arthur M., Recreation in the Senior Years. 103

Williams, Brad, The Anatomy of An Airline. 119

Williams, Chester A., Jr., Risk Management and Insurance. 54

Williams, Clifford A., Aircraft Instrument Control Systems. 119; Aircraft Instruments. 119

Williams, Ed W., Modern Law Enforcement and Police Science. 102

Williams, Edward W., Frozen Foods. 42

Williams, Elsa S., Bargello Embroidery. 26; Heritage Embroidery. 26

Williams, Hulen B., Basic Physical Chemistry for the Life Sciences. 135

Williams, John B., Police Operations. 98

Williams, Norman, Child Development. 83

Williams, O. B., Elementary Microbiology. 187

Williams, P. N., The Chemical Constitution of Natural Fats. 128

Williams, Roger, The Petrochemical Industry. 128

Williams, Roger J., The Encyclopedia of Biochemistry. 133

Williams, Sue R., Basic Nutrition and Diet Therapy for Nurses. 191; Nutrition and Diet Therapy. 41

Williams, Virginia R., Basic Physical Chemistry for the Life Sciences. 135

Williams, William A., Accident Prevention Manual for Shop Teachers. 163

Williams, William H., Introduction to Data Processing and Cobol. 17

Williamson, Hugh A. F., Methods of Book Design. 47

Williamson, J. Peter, Written Communication in Business. 69

Williamson, Robin, A Dictionary of Computers. 17

Willier, Benjamin, Foundations of Experimental Embryology. 183

Willig, Sidney H., The Nurse's Guide to the Law. 193

Willingham, Jacqueline, Logic of Operating Room Nursing. 197

Willis, Edgar E., Television and Radio. 157

Willis, H. A., Identification and Analysis of Plastics. 167

Willman, Harold A., Handbook and Lesson Guide for Leaders, County Extension Agents and Teachers. 77

Wills, Franz H., Complete Introduction to Fundamentals of Layout for Newspaper and Magazine Advertising. 7

Willson, James D., Controllership. 2

Wilmot, Jennie, Food for the Family. 36

Wilsie, Carroll P., Crop Adaptation and Distribution. 77

Wilson, Adrian, The Design of Books. 47

Wilson, Andrew, Applied Pharmacology. 203

Wilson, Charles O., Textbook of Organic Medicinal and Pharmaceutical Chemistry. 203

Wilson, Eunice, A History of Shoe Fashions. 26

Wilson, Eva D., Principles of Nutrition. 41

Wilson, Frank, Nursing Care of the Anaesthetized Patient. 197

Wilson, Frank W., Fundamentals of Tool Design. 167

Wilson, Harold K., Producing Farm Crops. 77

Wilson, J. B., Fortran IV Programming. 20

Wilson, James, Jr., Fundamental Organic Chemistry. 134

Wilson, James Q., Varieties of Police Behavior. 102

Wilson, John D., Simplified Carpentry Estimating. 140

Wilson, John K., The Art of Cutting and Fitting. 26

Wilson, José, Decorations U.S.A. 13

Wilson, Leonard L., Farm & Power Equipment Retailer's Handbook. 78

Wilson, Marie M., Siamese Cookery. 40

Wilson, Marion E., Microbiology in Nursing Practice. 193

Wilson, Nancy L., Food and Civilization. 31

Wilson, Orlando W., Police Administration. 102; Police Planning. 102

Wilson, Paul R., The Police and the Public in Australia and New Zealand. 96

Wilson, Robert C., An Alphabet of Visual Experience. 14

Wilson, Roger H. L., The Air We Breathe. 178; Food and Civilization. 31

Wilton, McKinley, The Homemaker's Pictorial Encyclopedia of Modern Cake Decorating. 37; Wilton's Wonderland of Cake Decorating. 37

Wilton, Norman, The Homemaker's Pictorial Encyclopedia of Modern Cake Decorating. 37; Wilton's Wonderland of Cake Decorating. 37

Wilton School of Cake Decoration, Modern Cake Decorating. 37

Wimmert, Robert J., Computer Programming Techniques. 21

Winburne, John N., A Dictionary of Agricultural and Allied Terminology. 77

Winch, Ralph P., Electricity and Magnetism. 155

Winch, Robert F., The Modern Family. 108

Winding, Charles C., Polymeric Materials. 168

Windle, William F., Textbook of Histology. 186

Winek, Charles L., Pharmacology Applied to Patient Care. 201

Winer, Bart, Art of French Cooking. 40

Wines, Mary E., Fashion Your Own: A Guide to Easy Clothing Construction. 23

Wing, Frances S., The Complete Book of Decoupage. 13

Wing, James M., Dairy Cattle Management. 79

Wingate, Isabel B., Fairchild's Dictionary of Textiles. 29; Know Your Merchandise. 64; Laboratory Swatch Book. 30; Textile Fabrics and Their Selection. 29

Wingate, John W., Fundamentals of Selling. 62; The Management of Retail Buying. 64; Problems in Retail Merchandising. 64; Retail Merchandising. 64

Winger, Fred E., Gregg Typewriting for Colleges. 68

Winner, H. I., Microbiology in Modern Nursing. 193

Winnett, Wade B., Review and Test Manual for the Dental Assistant. 175

Winsor, Travis, A Primer of Electrocardiography. 184

INDEX

Winstead, Robert W., Real Estate Appraisal Desk Book. 66

Winter, Chester C., Sawyer's Nursing Care of Patients with Urologic Diseases. 197

Winter, Edward, Enamel Painting Techniques. 13

Winter, Elmer L., How to be an Effective Secretary. 70

Winter, George, Design of Concrete Structures. 141

Winter, Ruth, Poisons in Your Food. 36

Winters, Arthur W., Fashion Sales Promotion Handbook. 26

Wischnitzer, Saul, Atlas and Dissection Guide for Comparative Anatomy. 184

Wisconsin (State) Board of Health, Occupational Therapy Assistants Program. 209

Wise, Arthur E., Rich Schools, Poor Schools. 113

Wiseman, A. J. L., Introduction to Crop Husbandry. 75

Wishy, Bernard W., The Child and the Republic. 83

Wismar, Beth L., A Visual Approach to Histology. 186

Wistreich, George A., Microbiology for Nurses. 193

Withington, Frederic G., The Real Computer. 19; The Use of Computers in Business Organizations. 19

Witt, Joshua C., Portland Cement Technology. 141

Wittich, Walter A., Audio-Visual Materials. 113

Wittmann, Alfred, Dictionary of Data Processing. 16

Wittwer, Sylvan H., Greenhouse Tomatoes. 77

Witucke, Virginia, Literature for Children. 113

Witzky, Herbert K., Modern Hotel-Motel Management Methods. 52; Practical Hotel Motel Cost Reduction Handbook. 52

Wixon, Rufus, Principles of Accounting. 4

Wohl, Gerald, The Computer: An Accounting Tool. 4

Wolansky, William D., Woodworking Fundamentals. 163

Wold, Blanche, A Unit Method of Sewing. 26

Woldman, Norman E., Engineering Alloys. 169

Wolf, Arnold V., An Introduction to Body Fluid Metabolism. 183

Wolf, Emil, Principles of Optics. 197

Wolf, Frank J., Separation Methods in Organic Chemistry and Biochemistry. 135

Wolf, Katherine M., As Your Child Grows. 83

Wolfe, Herbert J., Printing and Litho Inks. 47

Wolfe, Ithmer C., How to Organize and Maintain the Library Picture/Pamphlet File. 90

Wolfe, Linda, The Cooking of the Caribbean Islands. 40

Wolff, Edward A., Antenna Analysis. 155

Wolff, Eugene, Anatomy of the Eye and Orbit. 200

Wolff, LuVerne, Fundamentals of Nursing. 189; Teaching Fundamentals of Nursing. 189

Wolfgang, Marvin E., The Sociology of Crime and Delinquency. 102

Wolk, Allen, How to Build a Working Digital Computer. 17

Wolk, Allen M., Electronics Drafting. 144

Wolken, Jerome J., Vision: Biophysics and Biochemistry of the Retinal Photoreceptors. 200

Wolkoff, Harold, Statics and Strength of Materials. 170

Wolman, Abel, Water, Health and Society. 180

Wolpert, Saul, Bookkeeping and Accounting. 4

Wolseley, Roland E., Understanding Magazines. 47

Women's Wear Daily, Sixty Years of Fashion: 1900-1960. 27

Wong, Ella-Mei, Chinese Cookery. 40

Wood, Charles R., Sermon Outlines for Funeral Services. 95

Wood, LeVelle, Food Service in Institutions. 36

Wood, Marion N., Gourmet Food on a Wheat-Free Diet. 36

Wood, Paul E., Switching Theory. 155

Wood, Scott E., Thermodynamics. 164

Woodburne, Russell T., Essentials of Human Anatomy. 184

Woodbury, Robert A., Pharmacology Review. 203

Woodbury, Robert S., History of the Milling Machine. 166

Woodford, Edwin K., Crop Production in a Weed-Free Environment. 77

Woodforde, John, The Strange Story of False Teeth. 176

Woodger, Joseph H., Biological Principles. 185

Woodhead, Ronald, Critical Path Methods in Construction Practice. 136

Woodnott, Dorothy P., The Institute of Animal Technicians Manual of Laboratory Animal Practice Techniques. 186

Woodroofe, Kathleen, From Charity to Social Work. 108

Woods, Elizabeth L., Learning About Children. 83

Woods, Gerald, Introducing Lithography. 15

Woods, Gorham, Metals and How to Weld Them. 171

Woods, Hubert, Durability of Concrete Construction. 141

Woods, Leslie C., The Theory of Subsonic Plane Flow. 119

Woods, Richard S., Accounting Systems and Data Processing. 4

Wood-Smith, Donald, Nursing Care of the Plastic Surgery Patient. 197

Woodson, Herbert H., Electromechanical Dynamics. 155

Woodward, Richard G., Team Teaching in Action. 108

Woodward, Robert L., An Introduction to Applied Electricity-Electronics. 163

Woodward, Theodore, General Office Practice for Colleges. 69; Secretarial Office Practice for Colleges. 69

Wooldridge, Powhatan J., Behavioral Science, Social Practice, and the Nursing Profession. 193

Wooldridge, Walter R., Farm Animals in Health and Disease. 79

Woolley, Grace H., The Correct Service Department for Hotels, Motor Hotels, Motels and Resorts. 52; Drink Dictionary. 38; Menu Dictionary. 36

Woolley, Roi B., Home Fire Safety. 86

Woolman, Lewis H., Salesmanship. 62

Woolman, Myron, From Electrons to Power. 155

Woolrich, Willis R., Cold and Freezer Storage Manual. 42; Handbook of Refrigerating Engineering. 121

Wootton, Lutian R., Transitional Elementary School and Its Curriculum. 111

Wordingham, J. A., Dictionary of Plastics. 168

World Aircraft Illustrated. 120

World Aviation Directory Listing Companies and Officials. 120

World Health Organization, Air Pollution. 180; Aspects of Public Health Nursing. 197; Cumulative List of Proposed International Non-Proprietary Names for Pharmaceutical Preparations. 203; Environmental Health Aspects of Metropolitan Planning and Development. 180; The Training of Health Laboratory Personnel. 183

Worley, Eloise, Pharmacology and Medications for Vocational Nurses. 193

Worrell, Albert C., Principles of Forest Policy. 88

Worthington, Robert M., General Power Mechanics. 163

Wortman, Leon A., Closed-Circuit Television Handbook. 158

Woy, James B., Business Trends and Forecasting. 62

Wright, Donald L., Introduction to Electronic Digital Computers. 18

INDEX

Wright, Elizabeth A., Teacher Aides to the Rescue. 113

Wright, F. Howell, Essentials of Pediatric Nursing. 195; Nursing Care of Children. 195

Wright, George B., Mounting, Projecting & Storing Slides. 92

Wright, Harvey D., Questions and Answers in Ophthalmology. 200; The Rays Are Not Coloured. 200

Wright, James C., The Coming Water Famine. 180

Wright, John S., Advertising. 7

Wright, Lawrence S., Drafting Technical Communication. 143

Wright, R. Gene, The Police Officer and Criminal Justice. 102

Wright, Ralph R., Electronics. 155

Wright, Ruth S., Report to the Nation on Children and Youth. 83

Wrigley, Charles Y., Fundamentals of Semi-Conductor Devices. 150

Wrigley, Gordon, Tropical Agriculture. 77

Wuehrmann, Arthur H., Dental Radiology. 176

Wulfekoetter, Gertrude, Acquisition Work. 92

Wulff, John, Structure and Properties of Materials. 168

Wyatt, Arthur R., Accounting. 1; Advanced Accounting. 1

Wyatt, William E., General Architectural Drawing. 144

Wybar, Kenneth C., Ophthalmology. 200

Wyckoff, Alexander, Early American Dress. 27

Wykes-Joyce, Max, Cosmetics and Adornment. 8

Wyman, Raymond, Mediaware. 113

Wynn, Richard, American Education. 109

Wyss, Orville, Elementary Microbiology. 187

Wyszecki, Günter, Color in Business, Science and Industry. 13

X-Ray Technology Examination Review Book: 1500 Multiple Choice Questions and Answers Referenced to Textbooks. 205

Yablonsky, Lewis, Crime and Delinquency. 98

Yacorzynski, G. K., Investigation of Carbon Dioxide Therapy. 181

Yankee, Herbert W., Machine Drafting and Related Technology. 144

Yanof, Howard M., Textbook of Biomedical Electronics. 184

Yardley, Maili, Hawaii Cooks. 40

Yarrow, Marian R., Child Rearing. 83

Yarwood, Doreen, English Costume. 27; Outline of English Costume. 27

Yaslow, Samuel, Elements of Mechanical Drafting. 144

Yates, Edwin T., Guidebook for Mechanical Designers and Draftsmen. 167

Yearbook of Modern Nursing. 194

Yeck, John D., Planning and Creating Better Direct Mail. 62

Yengel, Herbert, Legal Typewriting. 71

Yerian, Theodore, Progressive Filing. 68

Yianilos, Theresa K., The Complete Greek Cookbook. 40

Yih, Chia-shun, Fluid Mechanics. 166

Yoshida, Roshi, Japanese Print-Making. 13

Young, Carl B., First Aid for Emergency Crews. 208

Young, Clara G., Introduction to Medical Science. 183; Learning Medical Terminology Step by Step. 72

Young, Donovan H., Elements of Strength of Materials. 170

Young, Esther M., Learning About Children. 83

Young, Helen, Lippincott's Quick Reference Book for Nurses. 194

Young, Jimmy A., Principles and Practice of Inhalation Therapy. 181

Young, Milton A., Buttons are to Push: Developing Your Child's Creativity. 83

Young, Victor, Understanding Microwaves. 155

Young, Wesley O., The Dentist, His Practice, and His Community. 176; Utilization of Fluorides. 176

Youngberg, Chester T., Tree Growth and Forest Soils. 88

Youngdahl, Benjamin E., Social Action and Social Work. 108

Youngman, Wilbur H., Growing Your Trees. 88

Youtz, H. G., Judging Livestock, Dairy Cattle, Poultry, and Crops. 79

Yoxall, Harry W., The International Wine and Food Society's Guide to the Wines of Burgundy. 38

Yukawa, Yasuhide, Handbook of Organic Structural Analysis. 135

Yuki, Rei, Japanese Print-Making. 13

Yule, John A. C., Principles of Color Reproduction. 47

Zabel, Herman, The Petrochemical Industry. 128

Zabin, James B., College Salesmanship. 58

Zabriskie, Louise, Maternity Nursing. 195

Zachary, Hugh, The Beachcomber's Handbook of Seafood Cookery. 36

Zaharevitz, Walter, Career Opportunities in Aviation. 119

Zahler, Jack, Marketing and Communications Media Dictionary. 62

Zaidenberg, Arthur, Drawing Self-Taught. 13; New Encyclopedia of Drawing, Painting, and the Graphic Arts. 13

Zakia, Richard D., Photographic Sensitometry. 50

Zald, Mayer N., Social Welfare Institutions. 108

Zapf, Hermann, Hunt Roman: The Birth of a Type. 47; Manuale Typographicum. 47

Zarr, Melvyn, The Bill of Rights and the Police. 102

Zbar, Paul B., Basic Electricity. 155; Basic Electronics. 155; Basic Radio. 157; Basic Television and Television Receiver Servicing. 158; Electricity—Electronics Fundamentals. 155; Electronics Instruments and Measurements. 155; Industrial Electronics. 155

Zechlin, Katharina, Creative Enameling and Jewelry Making. 28

Zeff, Stephen A., Financial Accounting Theory, Issues and Controversies. 5; Uses of Accounting for Small Business. 5

Zehr, Farrel J., The Pecan Cook Book. 36

Zeines, Benjamin, Electronic Communications Systems. 155; Principles of Applied Electronics. 155; Principles of Industrial Electronics. 155

Zeiss, George H., Successful Retail Salesmanship. 61

Zeitz, Ann N., Associate Degree Nursing. 194

Zelikman, Vitalii, Making and Coating Photographic Emulsions. 50

Zelin, Beatrice, Designing Apparel Through the Flat Pattern. 24; How to Draft Basic Patterns. 24

Zemanian, Armen H., Electronics. 146

Zepler, E. E., Electronic Circuit Techniques. 155; Electronic Devices and Networks. 155

Zevin, Jack, Creative Encounters in the Classroom. 111

Ziegel, Erna, Obstetric Nursing. 195

Ziegfeld, Edwin, Art Today. 9

Ziegler, Percival T., The Meat We Eat. 37

Ziegler, William L., Sales Promotion and Modern Merchandising. 59

Zietz, Dorothy, American Social Welfare Institutions. 107; Child Welfare. 83

Zimiles, Murray, The Technique of Fine Art Lithography. 14

Zimmer, Allen, The Strategy of Successful Retail Salesmanship. 64

Zimmer, Arthur, Atlas of Clinical Laboratory Procedures. 183

Zimmerman, Fred W., Leathercraft. 163

INDEX

Zimmerman, Henry J., Electronic Circuits, Signals and Systems. 151

Zinsser, Hans, Microbiology. 187

Zion, Roger, Keys to Human Relations in Selling. 62

Zlotnick, Dov, Tractate Mourning (Semahot). 95

Zober, Martin, Marketing Management. 62

Zollinger, Heinrich, Azo and Diazo Chemistry. 131

Zopf, Paul E., Jr., Principles of Inductive Rural Sociology. 77

Zoubek, Charles E., Gregg Shorthand for Colleges. 68; Gregg Shorthand Dictionary. 68; Gregg Shorthand Manual. 68; Gregg Speed Building. 68; Gregg Transcription. 68

Zucker, Francis J., Antenna Theory. 146

Zucker, Mitchell H., Electronic Circuits for the Behavioral and Biomedical Sciences. 184

Zuk, William, Concepts of Structure. 140

Zwarensteyn, Henrik, Fundamentals of Hotel Law. 52

Zweig, Jeanne, Accountant's Office Manual and Practice Guide. 5

Zwick, George, The Oscilloscope. 155